THE OXFORD HANDBOOK OF

HISTORICAL
PHONOLOGY

OXFORD HANDBOOKS IN LINGUISTICS

Recently published

THE OXFORD HANDBOOK OF JAPANESE LINGUISTICS
Edited by Shigeru Miyagawa and Mamoru Saito

THE OXFORD HANDBOOK OF THE HISTORY OF LINGUISTICS
Edited by Keith Allan

THE OXFORD HANDBOOK OF LINGUISTIC TYPOLOGY
Edited by Jae Jung Song

THE OXFORD HANDBOOK OF CONSTRUCTION GRAMMAR
Edited by Thomas Hoffman and Graeme Trousdale

THE OXFORD HANDBOOK OF LANGUAGE EVOLUTION
Edited by Maggie Tallerman and Kathleen Gibson

THE OXFORD HANDBOOK OF ARABIC LINGUISTICS
Edited by Jonathan Owens

THE OXFORD HANDBOOK OF CORPUS PHONOLOGY
Edited by Jacques Durand, Ulrike Gut, and Gjert Kristoffersen

THE OXFORD HANDBOOK OF LINGUISTIC FIELDWORK
Edited by Nicholas Thieberger

THE OXFORD HANDBOOK OF DERIVATIONAL MORPHOLOGY
Edited by Rochelle Lieber and Pavol Štekauer

THE OXFORD HANDBOOK OF HISTORICAL PHONOLOGY
Edited by Patrick Honeybone and Joseph Salmons

THE OXFORD HANDBOOK OF LINGUISTIC ANALYSIS
Second Edition

Edited by Bernd Heine and Heiko Narrog

THE OXFORD HANDBOOK OF THE WORD
Edited by John R. Taylor

THE OXFORD HANDBOOK OF INFLECTION
Edited by Matthew Baerman

THE OXFORD HANDBOOK OF DEVELOPMENTAL LINGUISTICS
Edited by Jeffrey Lidz, William Snyder, and Joe Pater

THE OXFORD HANDBOOK OF LEXICOGRAPHY
Edited by Philip Durkin

THE OXFORD HANDBOOK OF

HISTORICAL

PHONOLOGY

Edited by

PATRICK HONEYBONE

and

JOSEPH SALMONS

OXFORD

UNIVERSITY PRESS

OXFORD

UNIVERSITY PRESS

Great Clarendon Street, Oxford, OX2 6DP,
United Kingdom

Oxford University Press is a department of the University of Oxford.
It furthers the University's objective of excellence in research, scholarship,
and education by publishing worldwide. Oxford is a registered trade mark of
Oxford University Press in the UK and in certain other countries

First Edition published in 2015

Impression: 1

Published in the United States of America by Oxford University Press
198 Madison Avenue, New York, NY 10016, United States of America

British Library Cataloguing in Publication Data
Data available

Library of Congress Control Number: 2015940246

ISBN 978-0-19-923281-9

Printed and bound by
CPI Group (UK) Ltd, Croydon, CR0 4YY

CONTENTS

PART III TYPES OF PHONOLOGICAL CHANGE

PART IV FUNDAMENTAL CONTROVERSIES IN PHONOLOGICAL CHANGE

PART V THEORETICAL HISTORICAL PHONOLOGY

PART VI SOCIOLINGUISTIC AND EXOGENOUS FACTORS IN HISTORICAL PHONOLOGY

A companion website for this book is available: http://www.historicalphonology.net/

THE CONTRIBUTORS

Ricardo Bermúdez-Otero is Senior Lecturer in Linguistics and English Language at the University of Manchester. His research focuses on the morphosyntax–phonology and phonology–phonetics interfaces, with particular attention to diachronic issues. He works predominantly on Germanic (especially Old, Middle, and Present-Day English) and Romance. His publications on historical phonology include chapters in *Optimality Theory and Language Change* (2003, Kluwer), *The Cambridge Handbook of Phonology* (2007, CUP), and *The Oxford Handbook of the History of English* (2012, OUP).

Juliette Blevins is currently Professor of Linguistics at the CUNY Graduate Center, with research interests in Austronesian, Australian Aboriginal, Native American, and Andamanese languages. Her book *Evolutionary Phonology* (2004, CUP) presents a unique theory synthesizing results in historical linguistics, phonetics, typology and phonological theory. She currently has over 100 publications, most recently in such journals as *Phonology, Oceanic Linguistics*, and *Language and Cognition*.

David Bowie is an Associate Professor at the University of Alaska Anchorage, where he is one of the English Department's linguists. For the past few years he has been conducting research on the sociolinguistic effects of changes in age and religious affiliation, so as to provide insights into the linguistic ramifications of involuntary and voluntary changes in identity. He is also currently laying the groundwork for a planned dialect atlas of Alaskan English.

Joan Bybee is Distinguished Professor Emerita of Linguistics at the University of New Mexico. Her work utilizing large cross-linguistic databases, e.g. *Morphology: A Study of the Relation between Meaning and Form* (1985, Benjamins), *The Evolution of Grammar: Tense, Aspect and Modality in the Languages of the World* (1994, University of Chicago Press, with Revere Perkins and William Pagliuca), provides diachronic explanations for typological phenomena. Her books presenting a usage-based perspective on synchrony and diachrony include *Phonology and Language Use* (2001, CUP), *Frequency of Use and the Organization of Language* (2007, OUP), and *Language, Usage and Cognition* (2010, CUP).

András Cser is Associate Professor at Pázmány Péter Catholic University. He has published on theoretical and historical phonology, specifically on Latin phonology, as well as on the history of linguistics (Hungarian and European). His works include *The Typology and Modelling of Obstruent Lenition and Fortition Processes* (2003, Akadémiai Kiadó).

Alexandra D'Arcy is Associate Professor of Linguistics and Director of the Sociolinguistics Research Lab at the University of Victoria. She is interested in both diachronic and synchronic aspects of language variation and change, and has published in such venues as *Language, Language Variation and Change*, and *Language in Society*.

Patricia J. Donegan is Associate Professor of Linguistics in the University of Hawai'i at Mānoa. With David Stampe, she authored 'The study of natural phonology' (1979) and 'Hypotheses of natural phonology' (2009). In addition to 'The phonetic basis of phonological change' (1993), she has written about vowel systems, phonological acquisition, and the rhythmic basis of typology.

B. Elan Dresher is Professor Emeritus of Linguistics at the University of Toronto. He has published on phonological theory, historical linguistics, learnability, and West Germanic and Biblical Hebrew phonology and prosody. He is the author of *Old English and the Theory of Phonology* (1985, Garland) and *The Contrastive Hierarchy in Phonology* (2009, CUP).

Fred R. Eckman is University of Wisconsin–Milwaukee Distinguished Professor of Linguistics. He has published articles on second-language phonology and second-language syntax in *Language Learning, Applied Linguistics,* and *Studies in Second Language Acquisition (SSLA)*, as well as *Second Language Research*. Most recently he has co-authored with Gregory Iverson 'The role of native language phonology in the acquisition of L2 phonemic contrasts' (2013, *SSLA*).

David Fertig is on the faculty in the Department of Linguistics at the University at Buffalo (SUNY). His most recent book is *Analogy and Morphological Change* (2013, Edinburgh University Press). He is currently working with several colleagues on a new English translation with commentary of major chapters from Hermann Paul's *Prinzipien der Sprachgeschichte*.

Paul Foulkes is Professor in the Department of Language and Linguistic Science at the University of York. He has research interests in phonetics, phonology, sociolinguistics, child language acquisition, and forensic speech science. With Gerry Docherty he is the co-editor of *Urban Voices* (1999, Arnold), and author of over 40 journal articles and book chapters. The latter include state-of-the-science reviews in handbook volumes on phonetics, language and law, English linguistics, and language emergence.

Anthony Fox was, until his retirement in 2003, Head of the Department of Linguistics and Phonetics at the University of Leeds. He has published on phonology, German, historical linguistics, and intonation. His books include *The Structure of German* (1990, OUP), *Linguistic Reconstruction* (1995, OUP), and *Prosodic Features and Prosodic Structure* (2000, OUP).

Matthew J. Gordon is Associate Professor of English at the University of Missouri. His research interests include sociolinguistics and the study of sound change in progress. In addition to publications reporting on this research, he is the author of *Labov: A Guide for the Perplexed* (Bloomsbury, 2013), which profiles the career of one of the leading figures in linguistics.

Mark Hale is on the Linguistics faculty at Concordia University. His research covers topics in phonology, Oceanic, and historical linguistics. He is the author of *Historical Linguistics: Theory and Method* (2007, Blackwell) and co-author of *The Phonological Enterprise* (with C. Reiss) (2008, OUP).

D. Eric Holt is Associate Professor of Spanish and Linguistics at the University of South Carolina. His interests lie in phonological theory, especially as a tool for understanding aspects of the sound structure of Spanish, both modern synchronic and historical diachronic, including dialect variation past and present. In addition to editing and contributing to the volume *Optimality Theory and Language Change* (2003, Kluwer), he also conducts research on the acquisition of connected speech phenomena in Spanish by English-speaking learners, and serves as one of the associate editors of the journal *Studies in Hispanic and Lusophone Linguistics*.

Patrick Honeybone works in the Department of Linguistics and English Language at the University of Edinburgh. He has published on historical and theoretical phonology, has co-edited the volumes *Linguistic Knowledge: Perspectives from Phonology and from Syntax* (2006, *Lingua*) and *Issues in English Phonology* (2007, *Language Sciences*), is an editor of the journal *English Language and Linguistics,* and is the main organizer of the annual Manchester Phonology Meeting.

Gregory K. Iverson is Professor Emeritus of Linguistics. Alongside his work in historical Germanic phonology, much of it with Joseph Salmons, he has authored numerous articles relating to Korean and Japanese phonology and to the acquisition of second-language sound patterns.

Mark J. Jones is a lecturer in Phonetics at City University London. His research interests are the biological and physiological bases of crosslinguistic patterns in phonetics and phonology, speech production, and speaker *vs* listener effects in the evolution of phonetic contrasts and phonological structure.

Brett Kessler is an associate professor at Washington University in St Louis, where he teaches in the Linguistics Program and the Philosophy–Neuroscience–Psychology Program. He works on developing computational techniques for studying language phylogenetics and the psychology of phonemic writing systems, with emphasis on statistical methods for hypothesis testing in linguistics.

Paul Kiparsky is Professor of Linguistics in Stanford University. He has written on phonology, morphology, syntax, metrics, and the Sanskrit grammatical tradition. His interest in the structure of words and the lexicon is reflected in his writings on Lexical Phonology and Stratal OT, on morphosyntactic licensing, and on the principles governing language change.

Madelyn Kissock is on the Linguistics faculty at Concordia University. Her research spans issues in the phonology and syntax of Dravidian languages, particularly Telugu, as well as phonological acquisition. Recent work includes 'Evidence for finiteness in Telugu' (*NLLT*, 2013) and 'Markedness and epenthesis: evidence from Telugu and Polynesia' (in preparation, with Mark Hale).

Martin Kümmel has taken over the chair of Indo-European Linguistics at the University of Jena after having worked at the University of Freiburg for many years. He has published on historical phonology and IE historical grammar, especially Indo-Iranian. He was one of the authors of the *Lexikon der Indogermanischen Verben* (2nd edn 2001, Reichert), and has written two books on the Indo-Iranian verb and one on consonantal sound change (*Konsonantenwandel*, 2007, Reichert). Recently, he has become one of the editors of the *International Journal of Diachronic Linguistics and Linguistic Reconstruction*.

Aditi Lahiri, Fellow of the British Academy and honorary life member of the Linguistic Society of America, is a Professor of Linguistics at the University of Oxford with a research profile and publications in historical and comparative linguistics of Germanic, phonology, phonetics, psycholinguistics, and neurolinguistics.

Roger Lass is Distinguished Professor Emeritus of Linguistics at the University of Cape Town and Honorary Professorial Fellow in Linguistics and English Language at the University of Edinburgh. His main interests are historical linguistics, history of the English language, philosophy of linguistics, and evolutionary biology. Selected publications include *Old English: A Historical Linguistic Companion* (1994, CUP) and *Historical Linguistics and Language Change* (1997, CUP). He was editor of and author of the introduction and the chapter 'Phonology and morphology' in the *Cambridge History of the English Language* volume 3, *1477–1776* (1999, CUP).

Warren Maguire works in the department of Linguistics and English Language at the University of Edinburgh. His research is focused on variation and change in the phonology of regional dialects of English and Scots in Britain and Ireland. He has recently published articles on Pre-R dentalisation in northern England and on Alexander J. Ellis's *The Existing Phonology of English Dialects*. He is co-editor of *Analysing Variation in English* (2011, CUP), and of a special issue of *English Language and Linguistics* on phonological mergers (2013).

Robert Mailhammer works in the School of Humanities and Communication Arts and the MARCS Institute at the University of Western Sydney. His research interests focus on historical linguistics and language documentation, especially on phonology, morphology and semantics. He has published on the history of the Germanic languages, especially on the Germanic strong verbs (*The Germanic Strong Verbs*, 2007, Mouton de Gruyter) and the historical phonology of English, as well as on the Australian Indigenous language Amurdak (*Amurdak Inyman*, 2009, Iwaidja Inyman, with Robert Handelsmann).

Donka Minkova is a Distinguished Professor of English and Associate Dean of Humanities, UCLA. She is the author of *The History of Final Vowels in English* (1991, Mouton de Gruyter), *English Words: History and Structure* (2009, CUP), *Alliteration and Sound Change in Early English* (2003, CUP), and *A Historical Phonology of English* (2014, Edinburgh University Press). She has edited four volumes on the history of English and has published over 70 research articles in the fields of English and Germanic historical phonology, syntax, historical dialectology, and English historical metrics.

Robert W. Murray is Professor of Linguistics at the University of Calgary and an External Senior Fellow at the Freiburg Institute of Advanced Studies. He has also served as Editor and Chair of the Editorial Committee of the *Journal of Germanic Linguistics*, published by Cambridge University Press. He publishes mainly in the areas of historical phonology and the historiography of linguistics, e.g. 'Syllable cut prosody in early Middle English' (2000, *Language*) and 'Language and space: the Neogrammarian tradition' (2010, in *Language and Space: An International Handbook of Linguistic Variation*, ed. Peter Auer and Jürgen Erich Schmidt, Mouton de Gruyter).

Geoffrey S. Nathan is Professor of Linguistics at Wayne State University, located in the English Department. He received a Ph.D. in Linguistics with a specialization in syntax from the University of Hawai'i but has spent most of his career as a phonologist, first at Southern Illinois University Carbondale and then at Wayne State. His primary interests are in Cognitive Phonology, but he has also published on phonetics, the history of linguistics, and recently exploring the relationship between the cognition of language and music. He has written a textbook on phonology within the Cognitive Grammar framework.

Betty S. Phillips works in the Department of Languages, Literatures, and Linguistics at Indiana State University. She has published articles on English historical phonology and is the author of *Word Frequency and Lexical Diffusion* (2006, Palgrave Macmillan).

Thomas Purnell is Associate Professor in the English Department at the University of Wisconsin–Madison. His research and teaching examines the interface between phonetics and phonology with a focus on regional pronunciation. In particular, he is interested in the intersection of ethnically affiliated social groups and sound systems of language.

Eric Raimy is a professor in the Department of English at the University of Wisconsin–Madison. He is the co-editor with Charles Cairns of *The Handbook of the Syllable* (2011, Brill). He is the author of *The Morphology and Phonology of Reduplication* (2000, Mouton de Gruyter). He is a member of the Wisconsin Englishes Project with Thomas Purnell and Joseph Salmons.

Martha Ratliff is Professor of Linguistics at Wayne State University. She writes about Hmong-Mien linguistics, language contact in Southeast Asia, historical linguistics, and tone. Recent publications include *Hmong-Mien Language History* (2010, Pacific Linguistics) and *Meaningful Tone* (reissued 2010, Northern Illinois University Press). She is the co-founder of the Southeast Asian Linguistics Society.

Charles Reiss teaches in the Linguistics Program at Concordia University in Montreal. He is coauthor of *The Phonological Enterprise* (OUP, 2008, with Mark Hale) and *I-language: An Introduction to Linguistics as Cognitive Science* (OUP, 2008/2013, with Daniela Isac). He is currently working on basic logic in phonology.

David Restle works at the University of Munich. He has published on historical phonology, syntax, semantics, and pragmatics, for example *Silbenschnitt–Quantität–Kopplung: zur Geschichte, Charakterisierung und Repräsentation der Anschlußprosodie* (2003, Fink).

Joseph Salmons is the Lester W. J. 'Smoky' Seifert Professor of Germanic Linguistics at the University of Wisconsin–Madison. In addition to articles on phonology and language change, he is most recently the author of *A History of German* (2012, OUP), and serves as executive editor of *Diachronica: International Journal of Historical Linguistics*.

Tobias Scheer is a CNRS researcher working at the laboratory 'Bases, Corpus, Langage' at Nice University. He has worked on the diachronic phonology of German, Slavic, and Romance, and recently published two books on the interface of phonology and morphosyntax (*A Guide to Morphosyntax–Phonology Interface Theories*, 2011, de Gruyter, and *Direct Interface and One-Channel Translation*, 2012, de Gruyter).

Daniel Schreier is Professor of English at the University of Zurich. He has published on varieties of English, contact linguistics, and English historical phonology. His recent publications include *English as Contact Language* (2013, CUP, co-edited with Marianne Hundt) and *The Lesser-Known Varieties of English: An Introduction* (2010, CUP, co-edited with Peter Trudgill, Edgar Schneider, and Jeffrey P. Williams). He is also co-editor of *English World-Wide: A Journal of Varieties of English*.

Laura Catharine Smith is an Associate Professor of Germanic Linguistics in the Department of German and Russian at Brigham Young University. Her research on historical phonology focuses on the role of prosodic templates shaping the Germanic languages. She is also interested in the role of dialect in both language change and second language acquisition, perception, and production.

Christian Uffmann's main research interest is in phonological theory, with a special interest in how it interfaces with sociolinguistic issues, especially language contact. He has published a number of articles on loanword adaptation and creole phonology, and also *Vowel Epenthesis in Loanword Adaptation* (2007, Niemeyer). Within phonological theory, he is particularly interested in phonological representations and their role in a constraint-based model of phonology. He is currently writing a monograph on distinctive feature theory for CUP.

J. Marshall Unger is Professor of Japanese at the Ohio State University. He chaired the Department of East Asian Languages and Literatures 1996–2004, having previously chaired similar departments at the University of Hawaiʻi and the University of Maryland (1988–96). He has published on the history of Japanese, the teaching of Japanese as a second language, and writing systems, script reforms, and impacts of computerization in Japan, China, and Korea.

Adam Ussishkin works in the Department of Linguistics at the University of Arizona, and also has affiliations there with the program in Cognitive Sciences, as well as with the Department of Middle Eastern and North African Studies. He has published articles and book chapters on phonology, morphology, and psycholinguistics, concentrating on Semitic. He serves as a member of the editorial boards for *Journal of Linguistics* and *Ilsienna* (the journal of the International Association of Maltese Linguistics).

Theo Vennemann is Professor Emeritus at the Ludwig-Maximilians-Universität in Munich. He worked as professor of linguistics at UCLA until 1974, then at LMU until 2005. His publications in phonology include *Preference Laws for Syllable Structure* (1988, Mouton de Gruyter) and articles on the history and sound structure of German and Germanic. In addition, he has written on problems of syntax and semantics as well as on the linguistic prehistory of Europe (*Europa Vasconica–Europa Semitica*, 2003, de Gruyter; *Germania Semitica*, 2012, de Gruyter).

Marilyn Vihman is a developmental linguist best known for her book, *Phonological Development* (1996, Blackwell), which appeared in a radically revised second edition in 2014, with updated surveys of research on infant speech perception, segmentation, distributional learning, experimental studies of word learning, and other aspects of phonological development. She is also co-editor, with Tamar Keren-Portnoy, of *The Emergence of Phonology: Whole Word Approaches, Cross-Linguistic Evidence* (2013, CUP), which includes reprints of classics and new empirical studies of phonological development in six languages.

Andrew Wedel works in the Department of Linguistics and Program in Cognitive Science at the University of Arizona. He studies the way that feedback relationships shape language change. His most recent work on the functional load hypothesis has been published in the journals *Language and Speech* and *Cognition*.

Malcah Yaeger-Dror is affiliated with the Cognitive Sciences Program and Department of Linguistics at the University of Arizona, and has been a consultant at Lincoln Laboratories and Linguistics Data Consortium. She has published primarily on sociophonetics, co-editing the introductory text book *Sociophonetics: A Student Guide* (2011, Routledge), as well as books and special issues related to specific problems for analysis of sociophonetic variation and change in progress (most recently, *American Speech* 2010, *Journal of English Linguistics* 2010, *PADS* #94 2010, *Language and Linguistics Compass* 2014, *Language and Communication*, 2014, 2015).

Alan C. L. Yu is Professor of Linguistics and the College at the University of Chicago. He also directs the Phonology Laboratory and the Washo Documentation Project. His research focuses on phonological theory, phonetics, language typology, and language variation and change. He is the author of *A Natural History of Infixation* (2007, OUP) and the editor of *Origins of Sound Change: Approaches to Phonologization* (2013, OUP).

PART I

INTRODUCTION AND CONTEXT

CHAPTER 1

···

INTRODUCTION

Key Questions for Historical Phonology

···

PATRICK HONEYBONE AND JOSEPH SALMONS

HISTORICAL phonology is a broad field, and a deep one. Many perspectives, theories and methods have helped us to understand past phonological states and the ways that they can change, and serious still-consultable work on this has been going on for around two centuries, making historical phonology one of the oldest subfields of linguistics. Can any one volume hope to say something about *all* of this? The chapters gathered here showcase the current richness of our field and show how it is thriving today in remarkable ways. The chapters consider both theory and methodology, and probe both classic problems and entirely new types of data (some of which would have been inconceivable a decade or two ago). We have been truly fortunate in being able to assemble the collection of scholars whose work is included here, from literal founders of modern historical phonology and the thinkers responsible for a number of influential frameworks to a cadre of young colleagues.

Reviewers often focus on the organization of chapters within a collected volume; that is, on the linear surface order. We apologize in advance to any such reviewer or even reader, and urge them to look for more abstract structure. To be sure, taxonomies reified in a table of contents are important, but few will read this volume through cover-to-cover. If you do—and we have, a couple of times, and with different iterations of chapters—we hope you will discern the logic of the organization, but we also fervently hope that it will be obscured by the dark shadow of the dense and spaghetti-like networks of connections across chapters from the first chapter to the last. With this in mind, in this introduction, we draw out some overarching themes of the volume as a series of questions, and show how chapters from across the volume relate to them. We do this in place of the short summaries of chapters that typically make up an introduction in the hope that it will emphasise the interrelatedness of many issues that are discussed in several places in the volume. Chapter 2 provides the critical historical background to the volume and leads into Chapter 3, which extends this a little, and also offers a kind of introduction to the remaining chapters.

The many cross-references across individual chapters should help further to flag up connections and contradictions between chapters, and we encourage readers to consider more than only one chapter on any topic, where possible. Some views expressed in individual chapters are at odds with one another in their assumptions, working principles and analyses—not all chapters can be literally true, as some clearly contradict each other. This is utterly to be desired as it reflects the field, and should encourage readers to consider conflicting opinions on an issue, as described in this chapter or by following the in-chapter cross-references.

One way to approach a handbook like this would have been for us to have determined what views, approaches and theories we take to be right and to commission chapters on them and not commission chapters on views, approaches and theories that we did not think were right. For those who know the field, the foregoing and a glance at the table of contents make plain that we did not adopt that approach. The volume has plenty of representation across generative, broadly 'functionalist', and various psychologically-inspired frameworks, to give perhaps obvious examples. We have certainly implicitly sanctioned some perspectives and not others, based on what we take to be a broad and inclusive sense of what is viable, promising or plausible for moving the enterprise forward. We hope that one role of this volume will be to promote communication and connections across subfields that have often developed too much without connection.

More complex than Gaul, this book is divided into six parts. Part I offers, as well as this overview, a history of our field, focusing mainly on work during the nineteenth and twentieth centuries—as these chapters show, many of the issues discussed in the past connect directly with a range of contemporary concerns. (Likewise, throughout you will see substantive reference made to the historical work of the giants on whose shoulders we stand; the depth of those connections might show that those in the historical sciences may be predisposed to engage with our own disciplinary history.) Part II considers the empirical basis of historical phonology, that is, the sources of evidence for phonological reconstruction and change, and the methodologies that are used to establish this basis and to interpret the evidence. Part III treats the basic types of change that have been recognized in the data which historical phonologists work to interpret, from segmental changes, through analogy, to changes in prosodic domains. Part IV discusses fundamental issues in understanding types of change that historical phonologists consider—issues which are often controversial, and which have implications for any theoretical interpretation of the data. Part V presents a set of theoretical frameworks widely used to analyze and understand phonological change. Every chapter in the volume is informed by particular theories of change, but this part of the book allows proponents of particular theoretical frameworks to explain how and why they believe them to offer insight in understanding what is possible in phonological change, and how change proceeds. Part VI focuses on exogenous and/or social factors in sound change, which are relevant to many chapters in earlier parts of the book but which also deserve a focus of their own. Some of the things covered here (second language acquisition, koineization, loanword adaptation) proceed in rather different ways and have different impacts when compared to endogenous types of change, but they are all clearly relevant to our understanding of how the phonology of languages can change.

The chapters in whole engage with a number of questions which are all central to our understanding of phonological change. We now set out some of these questions—which help to define what historical phonology can and should do—and show how the chapters set about answering them. We refer to the chapters using the authors' surnames in SMALL CAPITALS (and acknowledge that we do not list absolutely *every* connection with every chapter with regard to the points we discuss—a careful reader will discover many more).

1.1 HOW DO WE KNOW THERE HAS BEEN PHONOLOGICAL CHANGE?

This is clearly crucial—how do we know what the data is for historical phonology? It is of fundamental interest both to understand the previous synchronic phonological states of individual languages, and to understand the diachronic changes that have occurred in their histories; and all theoretical work needs to be sure that the data it works with is sound. Many languages have long written histories, and these records can provide vital information on past phonological states, and hence the changes that have occurred between states; LASS, MINKOVA, and UNGER all consider how we can interpret written sources (LASS and MINKOVA for alphabetic systems and UNGER for some non-alphabetic systems). LAHIRI shows how dictionaries and similar resources from past stages of a language's history can provide important evidence, and MINKOVA considers how verse can help, too. Since sound recording became available a century ago, this kind of data can also offer evidence for historical phonologists; MAGUIRE considers this. Contemporary spoken data can also offer crucial evidence for phonological change—especially for the investigation of change in progress, in part thanks to the concept of 'apparent time'—and can also allow us to consider how changes are taken up in communities; GORDON, JONES, D'ARCY and BOWIE & YAEGER-DROR all consider such data, in part how we can collect it, and in part how we can interpret it. YU considers some experimental methodologies which can be used to interpret and elicit data concerning which changes might have occurred in the history of languages. FOX discusses one of the other central sources of information about past phonological states: reconstruction (both comparative and internal), which is vital for languages without written records, and also often important where written records exist, but don't provide enough detail. The study of phonological typology can provide a control on and encouragement for phonological reconstruction; KÜMMEL considers this. Developments in computing have opened up both new methodologies to investigate which changes might be expected, and how they might be expected to pattern; KESSLER considers how computational methods can contribute to our understanding of reconstruction and WEDEL considers the computational simulation of phonological change. This question is complicated by the point that it is not always clear when a *phonological* change has occurred, rather than a phonetic change (if such a distinction is allowed—questions below consider the nature of phonology): is *any* systematic modification of the signal a change that needs to be recognized as phonological, or do we only count as change things that have entered the grammar? One way of answering this is to consider what the smallest quantum of phonological change might be. SCHEER considers the extent to which we should allow for unattested intermediate stages in changes, which is one way of considering how small a change can be; another is to consider when the effects of phonetic biases become phonologized, which is something that BERMÚDEZ-OTERO addresses (see also below on phonologization).

1.2 WHAT MOTIVATES PHONOLOGICAL CHANGE?

A fundamental distinction can be recognized between endogenous (or 'internal') motivations for change and exogenous (or 'external') motivations. Exogenous causes of phonological change seem intuitively to be expected (when speakers of different languages and dialects come into contact, the phonology of the lects that they speak can naturally be affected), but the ways they play out are complex; SCHREIER considers the ways in which new dialects of specific languages can emerge when speakers of 'established' dialects come into contact in large numbers; ECKMAN & IVERSON consider the effect that second language acquisition can have on the phonology of a language; and UFFMANN considers how loanwords are adapted, or not, as they enter a new language (LAHIRI and RATLIFF also consider some effects of loanwords). Endogenous causes for change are, if anything, even more complex, and are probably more controversial. Some argue that the acoustic confusability of sounds is central to such change, as in the Ohalaesque model that YU considers, something which is also assumed in part by BLEVINS and HALE, KISSOCK & REISS (YU considers the possible role of phonetic biases in general). Others, such as BYBEE and PHILLIPS, argue that articulation is the major driver of change; DONEGAN & NATHAN and BLEVINS argue that both articulation and perception are important, and BLEVINS argues for a role for other types of factors, too. Still others give a key role to phonological structure in guiding—'causing' in some sense—phonological change; PURNELL & RAIMY consider how distinctive features (or 'segmental structure') might be implicated in phonological change, as does DRESHER, in part; MAILHAMMER, RESTLE & VENNEMANN argue that universal preference laws guide change, while SMITH & USSISHKIN argue that prosodic templates direct change. Somewhat differently from all this, but still part of endogenous change, analogy can cause changes in the phonology of languages; FERTIG considers some ways in which this can happen; DRESHER argues that reanalysis can follow if other changes have made paradigms ambiguous, and that the learner can be responsible for change (a point further considered in section 1.5, below).

1.3 WHAT KINDS OF PHONOLOGICAL CHANGE ARE POSSIBLE?

What changes have been observed in the histories of languages? What can change into what? There has long been serious work on historical phonology (for two centuries at least, as MURRAY and SALMONS & HONEYBONE describe) and this has led to a good understanding of many possible pathways of phonological change. FERTIG's discussion of analogy shows the kinds of change that this can be related to; CSER offers a comprehensive overview of the basic types of (especially segmental) change that are commonly recognized (other chapters offer more theoretised approaches to the typology of change, e.g. DONEGAN & NATHAN, BLEVINS, MAILHAMMER, RESTLE & VENNEMANN and DRESHER); LAHIRI considers change in stress patterns (and its causes), and RATLIFF discusses change in tonal systems. Tones can emerge through the phonologization of phenomena which are connected to segmental phonology, and this process of phonologization is often, and unsurprisingly, seen as a central type of change in phonology; it is a hotly contested area, discussed here by KIPARSKY and HALE, KISSOCK & REISS; BERMÚDEZ-OTERO describes an articulated model which seeks to predict exactly which stages are possible in the phonologization of phenomena, and what is possible in successive 'rephonologizations' as they change their status within the phonology of a language, eventually becoming lexicalized. SCHEER addresses a related aspect of what types of change are possible, tackling the notions of naturalness in change and the extent to which we can innovate 'crazy' phonological phenomena, which are synchronically real, but which bear little trace of naturalness.

1.4 WHAT IS THE NATURE OF PHONOLOGY?

If we are to say something about how phonology changes, we need an understanding of what phonology *is*. There is vast disagreement about this among phonologists, and that is reflected in this volume, too, as is to be expected—phonologists of all ilks are interested in phonological change, and historical phonology offers different kinds of arguments in favour of different types of phonological models. HALE, KISSOCK, & REISS, for example, assume a radically internal phonology, autonomous from phonetics; BYBEE, for example, argues to the contrary that phonology is directly connected to phonetics and is only emergent from vast numbers of stored exemplars of phonetic episodes. Between these two positions, a large number of views exist. On the formal side, phonology can be conceived of as a derivational entity best modelled using phonological rules, as DRESHER does, or as a constraint-based (Optimality Theoretic) grammar which might be monostratal, eschewing any derivation, as HOLT and UFFMANN consider, or multistratal, retaining some derivationality, as KIPARSKY argues (BERMÚDEZ-OTERO also argues for a stratal model of phonology). Some formal models place considerable weight on the representations employed, as explored by PURNELL & RAIMY at the subsegmental level, and LAHIRI at the suprasegmental level. SCHEER considers both segmental and suprasegmental phonology (that is, everything below and everything above the skeleton), arguing that only the former allows 'unnatural' generalizations. DONEGAN & NATHAN argue that phonology has a natural part (driven by 'processes') and an unnatural part (driven by 'rules'). On the more functionalist, reductionist side, BLEVINS argues that change itself can account for much (if not all) of what we recognize in synchronic grammars as recurrent phonological patterns, meaning that little or no autonomous phonology is necessary, because explanations for these patterns and their distributions are external to the grammar itself. Several other chapters are sympathetic to the exemplar and/or functionalist approach, including MAILHAMMER, RESTLE, & VENNEMANN, MURRAY, PHILLIPS, and WEDEL.

Apart from the above fundamental issues, we could ask many other questions of historical phonologists, and many are addressed in the volume. We consider just two more here, on both of which there is considerable disagreement.

1.5 WHERE DOES CHANGE OCCUR?

There has long been serious debate over the locus of phonological change—*speakers or listeners? children or adults?* In some sense, these two subquestions can be seen as linked: children are listeners in acquisition, and adults are (some of the) speakers. The two are separable, too, however. The first subquestion is relatable to the question of *what motivates phonological change?*, as discussed above. If change is largely driven by acoustics, then we would expect it to mainly occur in the listener, and if articulation drives change, then the speaker has a bigger role. The second subquestion is also hotly contested: HALE, KISSOCK, & REISS assume that all change is inter-generational, due to reanalysis (or simply 'analysis') by children deriving a grammar which is different from that of a previous generation, adopting a position that we might call 'acquisitionism'—(essentially) all change occurs in acquisition. DRESHER and LAHIRI also argue that at least some change must happen in acquisition. FOULKES & VIHMAN, however, argue that what happens in first language acquisition is not like what we see in phonological change, and are thus 'anti-acquistionist' in their argumentation, doubting the role of acquisition in change. BOWIE & YAEGER-DROR consider the evidence for 'lifespan change' which implies that at least some types of change are possible within adults. JONES and YU discuss the role of differences between individuals in terms of the extent to which they participate in the innovation or propagation of change, also in part placing an emphasis on the role of society, something which is central to

D'ARCY's concerns (and D'ARCY also focuses on the notion of 'apparent time', which downplays the role of lifespan change). We could equally wonder whether it is right to consider that a change has occurred until it has spread through a community of speakers, or whether it is fair to consider only a change's structural innovation (WEDEL and D'ARCY, for example, focus on the propagation of change, while YU and PURNELL & RAIMY, for example, focus on understanding innovation.).

1.6 IS PHONOLOGICAL CHANGE EXCEPTIONLESS?

The tenet of exceptionlessness (or 'regularity') in change was famously defended as crucial by the neogrammarians, as MURRAY discusses, but was immediately contested, and is still a subject of impassioned debate. Many argue that exceptionlessness is still a necessary and justified assumption, both in order for us to be able to do reconstruction (see FOX), and in the light of certain theoretical models of phonology. Others argue that it is always a mirage and that all change is lexically gradual. The real debate now, though, is not whether all change is exceptionless, but whether *any* change (or, more importantly, any *type* of change) is, and if so, whether exceptionless changes also show other properties that distinguish them from lexically diffusing change. PHILLIPS argues against exceptionlessness, and others, such as BYBEE and WEDEL argue that frequency effects (of a type that are only possible if change is in principle not exceptionless) give us great insight into phonology; BLEVINS argues that a range of factors can inhibit changes, resulting in patterns that appear irregular. BERMÚDEZ-OTERO, on the other hand, argues that exceptionless, neogrammarian change is well attested, that frequency does not always have an effect, and that, when it does, this need not be taken to indicate the presence of fine phonetic detail in the lexicon. HALE, KISSOCK, & REISS and SCHEER similarly see a clear role for exceptionlessness in our understanding of how change occurs.

1.7 THIS VOLUME

We hope that collecting the range of work found in this volume will encourage debate about these questions (and others) and will lead to answers, or at least progress. Historical phonology touches on a wide range of other areas of linguistics, and we see it as a meeting ground for all of them. Phonological theory, language variation and change, phonetically-oriented research and related laboratory-based work are often more connected in practice than many may realize or even want to acknowledge, and they are deeply tied to traditional concerns of linguistic reconstruction (and thus comparative linguistics) and also to philology. We have striven here, among other things, to help along the acknowledgement of this and to foster better and closer integration of these areas. But above all, we hope that you can feel the stress of progress and excitement in historical phonology that is represented in these pages.

There are doubtless many idiosyncrasies about the volume that could be criticized, and no doubt will be—we have not attempted to normalize authors' transcription or notational conventions, for example, rather choosing to reflect the variation that there is in the discipline; and certain chapters were specifically requested to be short, while others are much longer. There is also a bias toward data from English. In part, this is driven by the field, both in terms of some huge areas of research today—like vocalic chain shifting—and in part by where the laboratory work is being done and where we have large corpora and—quite simply—large numbers of people working on the history of the language. Wherever English is focused on, however, it is always a case study (to exemplify principles or possibilities), and there is also much in these pages on other Indo-European languages, East Asian languages, Semitic, Uralic, and Austronesian, as well as a number of typologically-oriented chapters (where all the world's languages are explicitly relevant). In terms of phonological phenomena, there are also unsurprising biases—the most discussed topic is umlaut, which is considered in detail by KIPARSKY, DONEGAN & NATHAN, and BYBEE, and also features in DRESHER, FOX, BERMÚDEZ-OTERO, and SALMONS & HONEYBONE.

Overall, while the volume is quite comprehensive in important ways, we have not been able to cover certain issues, partly because some authors had to drop out. This, and the fact that we then made efforts to recruit others, so that only a few gaps remain (along with many other bumps along the road—many of which are sadly common in large edited projects) have meant that the volume has taken quite a while from its initial conception to its appearance. We are grateful for everyone's patience; we owe a special debt of gratitude for this and many other things to John Davey of Oxford University Press, a figure of real significance in linguistics. We hope you will all agree that it was worth the wait.

CHAPTER 2

THE EARLY HISTORY OF HISTORICAL PHONOLOGY

ROBERT W. MURRAY

2.1 INTRODUCTION

THIS chapter treats the development of historical phonology during the nineteenth century, from its beginnings to what even today might still be considered its zenith—at least in terms of prestige and impact on the field of linguistics—by the end of the century.[1] Focus is primarily on the two central subfields of the discipline; comparative phonology, with its foundations in 'letter theory', and the investigation of sound change. The chapter is not intended as a survey of the period, but rather treats selected issues that resonate to the present day (parts of Salmons & Honeybone, this volume, pick up the discussion of the development of historical phonology from the twentieth century to the present). Discussion here is limited to particular protagonists, primarily neogrammarians and Hugo Schuchardt.

2.2 FROM *PERMUTATIONES LITTERARUM* TO *BUCHSTABENLEHRE* ('LETTER THEORY')

2.2.1 A Glimpse at the Prehistory of Historical Phonology

General linguistic overviews of the sixteenth and seventeenth centuries often focus on some of the more unusual ideas of the period; for example, that Latin could be derived

[1] This work was completed during my stays as a Senior Research Fellow at the Freiburg Institute of Advanced Studies (May 2009, May/August 2010). I am particularly grateful to the directors of the School of Language and Literature, Peter Auer and Werner Frick, for their invitation to FRIAS.

from Greek and both from Hebrew (Vossius 1664); that Dutch-Flemish was the mother tongue of all languages (Becanus 1569); or that indigenous languages of North America were related to 'Norwegian-Germanic' (Grotius 1552/1884) (see Thomsen 1927: 36–7, Metcalf 1974: 233–44). In fact, however, there was sensible work being done. Indeed, if one were writing a history of synchronic phonology (especially in the sense of 'reducing languages to writing', Pike 1947), it is possible to find shining lights in the sixteenth century; for example, John Hart's insightful and detailed phonological description of his London dialect (see Jespersen 1933: 41, Danielsson 1955, 1963, Lass 1981, this volume, Murray 2002). For historical phonology, however, the situation is different—even incipient notions of anything resembling a modern conception of sound change are difficult to find before the nineteenth century (e.g. Robert 1567, see Lapidge 2002: 53–4).

This is not to say that there was no coherent work being carried out under the general rubric of what would now be considered historical linguistics. One hundred years before William Jones's (1786) famous speech, usually considered to mark the beginning of comparative Indo-European linguistics, Andreas Jäger (1686) delivered a now not-so-famous speech, which is arguably more sophisticated in its conception than Jones's:

> an ancient language, once spoken in the distant past in the area of the Caucasus mountains and spreading by waves of migration throughout Europe and Asia, had itself ceased to be spoken and had left no linguistic monuments behind, but had as a 'mother' generated a host of 'daughter languages', many of which in turn had become 'mothers' to further 'daughters' [...]. Descendants of the ancestral language include Persian, Greek, Italic (whence Latin and in time the modern Romance tongues), the Slavonic languages, Celtic, and finally Gothic and the other Germanic tongues (from Metcalf 1974: 233; see also Campbell 2002: 88)

There can probably be no better instantiation of Wells's (1974: 435) truism that 'concepts, like animals, have a gestation period, but they differ in that they are conceived again and again before they are born'.

It should not be surprising, then, that by the end of the eighteenth century impressive work in comparative linguistics had been carried out, such as Gyarmathi's (1799) treatment of Finno-Ugric (Gulya 1974: 267, Hanzeli 1983). What *is* perhaps surprising is that phonological factors play no role. Thus, whereas today principles of phonological change constitute the cornerstone of the comparative method, the significant successes of early comparative linguistics were based on consideration of non-phonological factors, primarily inflectional morphology. In fact, most historical and etymological work of the time was firmly in the grip of the ancient tradition of letter permutations (*permutationes litterarum*), e.g. in the work of Latin grammarian Varro, 39 BCE (Diderichsen 1974: 280–1, Metcalf 1974: 246–8). While place of articulation was one criterion used to identify cognate letters (*cognatae*)—sets of letters subject to permutation—we are not dealing with a concept of language-specific sound correspondences or change. Indeed, the permutations were often simply conceived of as rewrite rules involving alphabetic symbols. A case is provided by Mayans y Siscar (1737) in his history of Spanish. Typical of work during this period, there are a few short paragraphs on the articulation of sounds (§§4–8), while thirty-six pages list letter permutations according to type (loss, mutation, etc.) and position (word-initial, medial, final). Both the Latin and corresponding Spanish forms are listed; under '*p mudada en b*' there are pairs such as *aperto, abierto* 'open'; *capillo, cabello* 'hair'; etc. In spite of first appearances, we are not dealing with a notion of a phonetically based sound substitution or change, as is apparent in an entry such as '*p mudada en e*'. Here the pair *gypso, yeso* 'gypsum' is provided, and it is proposed—quite literally—that *p* changes into *e* (along with loss of *g*). More generally, as Metcalf (1974: 251) summarizes, the conception of letter permutations was dramatically different from modern approaches:

> the phonetic elements of the language were viewed a-historically, non-genetically, as interchangeable counters (subject, to be sure, to certain restrictions either by nature or by historical evidence); phonetic change was thus not viewed as limited to a specific direction in a specific dialect at a specific period of time. There is therefore no deeper parallel, but only a superficial resemblance to the later concept of the sound laws.

Indeed, only a few glimmers of the new world appear during the eighteenth century, beginning with Lhuyd (1707). Of particular note is Turgot (1756)[1961: 43] who, in his impressive *Etymologie*, recognizes language-specific sound change, the role that systematic correspondences can play as a check in etymology, and even briefly discusses directionality of change; e.g. expected *obtinere > optinere* vs unexpected *optare > obtare* (Diderichsen 1974: 290–4, Hanzeli 1983). Another notable exception was Sajnovics (1770), who in his comparative study of Hungarian and Sami ('Lapp') emphasized the importance of determining sound values and correspondences. In general, however, Malkiel's (1993: 5–6) summary of the working context of the 'pioneering etymologists' is still valid at the end of the eighteenth century: they did not see the need to test proposals 'against any sets of phonetically phrased correspondences, or laws, or rules, precisely because those equations, apart from being very poorly phrased, were not recognized as binding, i.e. endowed with sufficient probatory force to militate for or against acceptance of an etymological conjecture still left pending'. In this context, it is not surprising that the Finno-Ugric sound correspondences already indicated in Sajnovics's (1770) study were subsequently lost in Gyarmathi's (1799) classic work (Hanzeli 1983: xxii–xxiii).

2.2.2 The Early Nineteenth Century: The Beginnings

The emphasis on comparative morphology in historical work continued into the first most influential publication of the nineteenth century, Bopp (1816), which as is often pointed out contained no section dedicated to phonology. Of course phonological factors were not ignored, and already the term 'sound law' (*Lautgesetz*) was used but without general recognition of the systematic nature of sound correspondences and change, and the role that such factors could play in comparative and etymological work (Koerner 1989b: 357–8, Morpurgo Davies 1998: 171). However, our world did change significantly about this time, and Rask (1818) (actually completed in 1814) is a pivotal point. Although influenced by the work of earlier scholars (Diderichsen 1976: 69–77), it was Rask who was able to turn the world on its head by successfully emphasizing the importance of sound correspondences in comparative work, as wonderfully expressed in a famous passage from *An Investigation Concerning the Source of the Old Northern or Icelandic Language*: 'When in such words [that is, 'the most essential, concrete, indispensable, and primary words'] one finds agreement between two languages, and that to such an extent that one can draw up rules for the transition of letters from one to the other, then there is an original relationship between these languages; especially when the similarities in the inflection of languages and its formal organization correspond' (Lehmann 1967: 32, Percival 1974, Pedersen 1983: 36, 51–9, Petersen 1992: 60).

Rask was able to apply his comparative approach to the origins of Old Icelandic with great success (Diderichsen 1976: 33–7). Although his knowledge of phonetics was rudimentary, Rask's work was likely facilitated by the fact that beyond his impressive philological skills he differed from many of his contemporaries in also being an accomplished fieldworker and polyglot who studied many languages with native speakers (Jespersen 1922: 40). Rask also provided a nutshell summary in terms of 'letter transition' rules of the correspondences often referred to as Grimm's Law (Lehmann 1967: 34, Petersen 1992: 77–8), and had other insights that were ahead of his time. For example, he recognized umlaut as an assimilatory change at a distance (a view received initially with scepticism by Grimm; see Benware 1974: 19). Rask (1811) also 'sees the reason of the change in the plural *blöð* as against the singular *blað* in the former having once ended in -*u*, which has since disappeared. This is, so far as I know, the first inference ever drawn to a prehistoric state of language' (Jespersen 1922: 37, also Benware 1974: 20). Here we have an instance of reconstructing a proto form based on a tacit understanding of phonological properties and sound change to account for attested forms. Although Rask could not fully recognize the degree of regularity that letter transitions can display and was still to some extent under the influence of the letter permutation approach, this work, which can reasonably be called comparative 'letter theory' (*Buchstabenlehre*), was instrumental in establishing the modern foundations of historical comparative phonology. Jespersen (1922: 37–8) suggests that if Rask's major work had been published in the year that it was finished (1814) instead of four years later, he might well have been considered 'the founder of the modern science of language' (since it would have preceded such works as Bopp 1816 and Grimm 1819). Still, his work is foundational to comparative phonology, since these ideas were not at all developed in the early work of Bopp and Grimm.

Since the term 'letter theory' is often used with negative connotations, it merits discussion. Although nineteenth-century scholars often used 'letter' to refer to a 'sound', in general this terminological conflation does not imply a state of conceptual confusion. In his thorough study of the period, Kohrt (1985: 1–56) demonstrates that scholars from Bopp to Whitney systematically distinguished the two concepts. Even Grimm (1822: 3), often denigrated for his weak understanding of phonetics, is explicit: 'In representing the sounds in the Germanic languages I normally make use of the present-day letters, whose inadequacy in some cases is readily apparent.' The methodologically careful and phonetically sophisticated Raumer (1837: 25), an early advocate of phonetic accuracy in historical work (see section 2.3.1), could still write: 'Language can be analyzed into individual sounds, forming a sequence in time. When such a sound is written, we call it a letter.' Even as late as 1901 the great phonetician Eduard Sievers writes: 'Current grammatical practice [which he disagrees with, RWM] usually takes letters or sounds as a starting point, and then builds up to consideration of syllables, words, and sentences' (Lehmann 1967: 263), a tradition that resurfaces, for example, in Chomsky (1957b: 13): '... each natural language [in its spoken or written form] has a finite number of phonemes (or letters in its alphabet) and each sentence is representable as a finite number of these phonemes (or letters)' (see Linell 2005: 60).

One significant area of difficulty is the assumed degree of isomorphism between orthography and phonology (a topic of concern for Paul 1920: ch. 21), and it is not to be denied that scholars throughout the nineteenth century varied both in their ability to phonetically interpret the established symbols of a given writing system and in their understanding of the phonetic underpinnings of letters in general (Thomsen 1927: 46, note 1). At the same time, though, letter theory could be so successfully applied precisely because the traditional alphabets being used were, more or less, phonemically based and this type of work does not presuppose a more detailed phonetic analysis (see Lass and Minkova, both this volume). Consequently, the distinction between letter and sound could often be blurred without deleterious effect. Of course, letter theory or, as it evolved, historical comparative phonology (see Fox, this volume), was to become the focal point of nineteenth-century historical linguistics, and below is an outline of its development over the next decades until its high point in the 1870s.

2.2.3 Grimm Letter Theory: A Structuralist Inspiration

Written mostly in Danish, Rask's work did not become as generally well known as it might have. A partial translation of Rask (1818), including the portion on the 'Grimm's Law' correspondences (pp. 12–13), is found in Vater (1822). However, Rask did have major influence on our second important founder of historical phonology, Jacob Grimm. It is often pointed out that while the first edition of Grimm's *Deutsche Grammatik* (1819) had no section on phonology, the second, published only three years later, had a 595-page section entitled 'Von den Buchstaben' ('On the Letters', altered in subsequent editions to *Lautlehre* 'Phonology' without significant change in substance). This second edition was strongly influenced by Rask (who, in turn, wrote a very negative review; Rask 1830).

Grimm's most significant impact for our topic is found in a few pages of the 1822 edition, where he provides a masterful presentation and interpretation of the correspondences that are often referred to as Grimm's Law (pp. 583–92 = Lehmann 1967: 46–60; page numbers below refer to Lehmann, unless otherwise stated).

(1) Grimm's Correspondences

Greek	P	B	F	T	D	TH	K	G	CH
Gothic	F	P	B	TH	T	D	-	K	G
Old High German	B(V)	F	P(V)	D	Z	T	G	CH	K

Presenting the schema in the above table, Grimm states: 'For just as Old High German has sunk one step down from the Gothic in all three grades, Gothic itself had already deviated by one step from the Latin (Greek, Sanskrit)' (p. 51). By grade, Grimm means the three-way division of labial, lingual, and 'guttural', although he attaches no special importance to such factors as place of articulation.

Grimm's analysis is significant in many ways. First, if there needed to be a final nail in the coffin of letter permutation theory, this is it. Grimm specifically states that 'likeness or resemblance of consonants which are in general related is less important than observation of the historical course of gradation, which does not become disturbed or reversed' (p. 55, note 2). For example, the Greek *f*–Gothic *b*–OHG *p* relation cannot be turned into an OHG *f*–Gothic *b*–Greek *p* relation. That would be 'nonsensical, even though in the abstract exactly the same relationships of letters are present ...' (pp. 55–6). Second, even though Grimm believes that some words can resist the general changes ('the stream of innovation has passed them by', p. 57), he is explicit on the degree of regularity of the shifts and their importance for 'the rigor of etymology' (p. 51). He argues that in the case of words having two consonants subject to the rules, the 'correctness' of the etymological relationship is 'unmistakable' (p. 55, note 1). Here there is a strengthening of Rask's position on the importance of sound correspondences relative to morphological ones in identifying etymological and historical relationships. Third, and most important, is the system-based nature of the analysis itself. It is often pointed out that Rask (1818) discovered Grimm's Law before Grimm, and Raumer (1870: 512–13) lists six others who previously had at least discussed subsets of the correspondences. However, one can only concur with Raumer that the earlier treatments are irrelevant over the long term. The significance and innovative aspect of Grimm's analysis lies in its systemic and systematic character.

Accordingly, Lehmann (1999: 2, 6) is well justified in his position that the 'highly structural' aspect of work carried out by Grimm and some of his contemporaries has not been adequately recognized and that the structuralist achievements in the latter part of the nineteenth century, such as Saussure's *Memoire*, are based on a 'view of language' that was already held by Grimm and some contemporaries (also Kohrt 1990: 599–600). This view clearly manifests itself in Grimm's own version of his law. Focusing on the labial grade, Grimm's interpretation can be schematized as in (2) (Grimm believed that the stepwise sinking would continue, forming a *Kreislauf* that would repeat itself).

(2) Grimm's *Kreislauf*

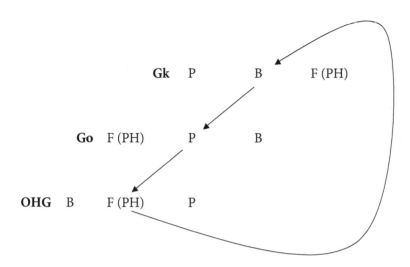

If it is the case that 'structuralism regards language as a relational system of formal (not substantial) elements that can be comprehended precisely and presented in a strictly formal way' (Lehmann 1999: 1, following Bussmann 1983: 509–11), then it can be argued that Grimm's analysis represents a pristine instantiation of structuralist thought (applied albeit in a historical way, *pace* Saussure). A set of elements is identified on the basis of behavioural properties and organized into subsets (grades). Grimm is clear that the behavioural properties of the elements are primary: 'the identity throughout is based on external differences'. This perspective was understood even by Grimm's critics (Rumpelt 1869: 128). The elements maintain their systemic interrelationship as they are governed by a schema of nine rules, where iterative applications of the rule set result in a *Kreislauf* (first, second, etc. sound shifts). The iterative aspect was considered by contemporaries as a particularly innovative characteristic of the analysis (Raumer 1870: 513, who, however, expresses reservations about its validity). Phonetic properties are secondary or even irrelevant.

Of course, the beauty and simplicity of Grimm's analysis is entirely dependent on a high degree of—dare we say, phonological—abstractness and a striking absence of phonetic detail and accuracy. Specifically, the analysis is coherent only assuming a class of 'aspirates' that includes, for example, *ph* [pʰ], *pf* [pᶠ], and *f*, all subsumed under Grimm's F (= PH). There is no doubt that Grimm's variant of letter theory is extremely complex and 'abstruse' (Rask 1830), and we would not want to push a defence of it too far. For example, Grimm (1822: 131) is adamant that *f* is a double sound (that is, *ph*)—the fact that it is written as a single letter is considered irrelevant. He is also consistent in this regard, considering *pf*, for example, to be a triphthong, *pph*. At the same time, though, a simple dismissal of Grimm's general approach as a 'confusion' (*Verwirrung*) of letters and sounds (Rumpelt 1869: 128) is also not appropriate. In this regard, there is no possibility of arguing that Grimm's think-ing was the reflection of a generally underdeveloped science of phonetics. In fact, contem-porary phoneticians were extremely critical. Rapp (1836–41), for example, complained that Grimm's *Buchstabenlehre* left him 'incredibly miserable' (Jespersen 1922: 69) and Raumer (1837: 14, 66)—with the apparent courage of a 22-year-old—ridicules a number of Grimm's claims; for example, he challenges anyone who believes that *f* is not a simple sound (just as *s* is) to divide NHG *f* and provide the analytical proof.

Accordingly, Grimm's 'ignorance' was self-imposed. Indeed, while care must be taken in interpreting Grimm's thinking and his use of terminology, he was explicit in his dislike of phonetics, perhaps linking it to the earlier approach of letter permuta-tions that was not grounded in etymological correspondences: 'When one provides the sounds with purely physiological functions and then sets up an unproven and unprov-able system of pronunciation [...], for me at least the air becomes too thin and I cannot live there' (1840: xv). For Grimm, priority lay on the etymological correspondences as determined by the 'historical course of gradation', and he did not see a way in which phonetics could contribute to the task (Koerner 1989a: 309–11). From this perspec-tive it is understandable why Grimm never revised his 1822 interpretation significantly over the next forty years—as Rumpelt 1869: 128 complains—despite the onslaught of criticism from more phonetically disposed contemporaries. Of course, the topic of 'abstractness' in phonological reconstruction (and phonology in general) plays out in many ways in later structuralist and generative theory (see, e.g., Dresher and Scheer, both this volume). Suffice it to say here that when a linguist such as Foley (1977: 6) states that 'phonological elements are thus properly defined not in terms of their acoustic or articulatory properties, but in terms of the rules they participate in', he stands firmly in the Grimmian tradition.

Much later assessments of Grimm's analysis range from derisive to more charitable—a division that can reflect, in part, the critic's degree of adherence to structuralist princi-ples. For example, Jespersen (1922: 44) states: 'The worst thing is that the whole specious generalization produces the impression of regularity and uniformity only through the highly unscientific use of the word "aspirate."' By contrast, Lehmann (1967: 47) recog-nizes Grimm's weakness in phonetics as a double-edged sword: Grimm was 'fortunate in his ignorance of phonetics, which permitted him to class together consonants which were quite different in articulation, and to produce a statement which passes beyond details to the system.' Regardless of what Grimm himself thought he was doing, there is no doubt that in his analysis 'students caught a glimpse of an entirely new linguistic world' (Pedersen 1931: 38).

2.2.4 Refining Letter Theory (Comparative Phonology): Obstacles, Breakthroughs, Continuity

Even after four decades of intensive application and development in the wake of Grimm's seminal analysis, comparative phonology was unable to reach its full potential in revealing the systematic nature of sound change. A striking fact of Grimm's origi-nal analysis is that the exceptions outnumbered the rule (as dutifully acknowledged by Grimm who presented a well-organized list of exceptional forms). However, even after weeding out onomatopoeic and child language forms, incorrect etymologies, etc. (Lottner 1862), the exceptions were numerous and for the next several decades the posit-ing of ad hoc sound changes remained a more or less acceptable way of going about the business of comparative phonology.

While at first blush one might again suspect that it was an insufficiently developed phonetic foundation that significantly hindered the progress of comparative phonol-ogy, this is not the case. In fact, as discussed above, Grimm's extreme position on pho-netics was not widely shared. Relatively sophisticated phonetic work is already found in Raumer (1837), who makes a strong case for a phonetically informed approach to the study of sound change (section 2.3.1). Influential scholars of the period such as Schleicher (1861–2) and Scherer (1868) were phonetically competent for their pur-poses. Schleicher, who Schuchardt justifiably calls the 'father of the neogrammarians', put phonology/phonetics at the centre of linguistic analysis (Koerner 1989a: 355–7, 361), and Scherer was strongly influenced by Brücke (1856) (Jankowsky 1999a: 247–8). In gen-eral, it is fair to say that practitioners of comparative linguistics had a level of phonetic expertise that was more or less adequate for their purposes, operating as they were at an implicit phonemic or broad phonetic level. As Kiparsky (1974c: 340) puts it: 'I do not see that phonetics played much of a role in the sweeping revision of the comparative method between 1820 and the 1870s' (although see his codicil on p. 342). Indeed, while there was no doubt an ongoing improvement in the general understanding of phonetic issues and sound change, the most formidable obstacles to the progress of comparative phonology were not related to phonetics at all. They were of an entirely different nature, two of which are outlined below.

First, in the attempt to understand the cognate relations of the Indo-European languages there was an overreliance on Sanskrit and Gothic forms based on the intuitively plausible but false assumption that these very early-attested languages will inevitably be the phonologically most conservative and closest to their respec-tive proto-languages. This bias resulted in insurmountable difficulties in the attempt to determine the correspondences and sound changes, particularly in the case of vowel developments, as a simple example shows (following Pedersen 1931: 265). As fate would have it, the original Proto-Indo-European mid vowels had shifted in both Sanskrit and Gothic; thus, the initial vowel in the cognates Sanskrit *ad-mi* 'I eat', Gothic *it-an* 'to eat' were considered original for Proto-Indo-European and Proto-Germanic respectively, in spite of, for example, Latin *ed-o* and Old English *et-an* (whereas now ^{+}e is reconstructed for both Proto-Indo-European and Proto-Germanic). In the earlier work, it was not possible to entertain the possibil-ity that Latin or relatively 'young' languages such as Old English, or for that matter present-day German (*essen*), could be phonologically more conservative in some respects than Gothic or even Sanskrit. Of course, this set of assumptions can only result in a convoluted approach to reconstructed sound changes; for example, in this case, Proto-Indo-European *a* > Proto-Germanic *i* > Old English *e* (as opposed to Proto-Indo-European *e* > Proto-Germanic *e* > Old English *e*). In fact, Grimm's original assumption of a Proto-Germanic three-vowel system survived for forty-two years until Curtius (1864) successfully argued for Proto-Germanic *e*, and correspond-ing *o*. The conclusion that Proto-Indo-European also had a mid-vowel series could not be reached until almost a decade later. In the meantime, a coherent approach to the vowel correspondences and sound change remained elusive (Thomsen 1927: 92–3, Benware 1974, and Morpurgo Davies 1998: 241–4).

Second, early work was not constrained by the uniformitarian hypothesis, the view that prehistoric and ancient languages were subject to the same linguistic, cognitive, and physiological principles as are contemporary languages. A version of uniformitarian-ism was adopted by Whitney (1867: 24, Lass 1997: 24–32) and was to become enshrined in the neogrammarian manifesto (Osthoff & Brugmann 1878 = Lehmann 1967: 200), but in the meantime it was generally assumed that the ancient and later historical lan-guages were of a fundamentally different character and subject to different principles of change. Schleicher's (1861–2) position was extremely influential that the 'life of a lan-guage' (or its history) could be divided into two stages: in the prehistoric period there is 'development' whereas in the historical stage there is 'decline'. The issues are complex, but it was generally assumed that morphological change such as analogy and even some types of sound change did not occur during the development stage (Bynon 1986: 131). Thus, there was strong resistance to the idea, for example, that Sanskrit could show the effects of morphological analogy, since this type of change belongs to the 'decline' cycle. Returning to our simple example, from a Schleicherian perspective not only would the initial vowel of Sanskrit *admi* be incorrectly reconstructed, but also the suffix -*mi* would be considered original (closest to the proto-language), even though it is a blatant conse-quence of analogy; compare Greek *phér-ō, ei-mi*; Sanskrit *bhára-mi, é-mi* 'I bear', 'I go' (Scherer 1868: 71; see Pedersen 1931: 291, 1983: 75–6). Again, significant advancement in the understanding of the degree of regularity of sound change is impossible under such working assumptions.

Many classic articles published in the latter third of the nineteenth century are jus-tifiably considered 'breakthroughs' precisely because their lines of argumentation and conclusions necessitated the rejection of mainstream tenets that were inappropriately constraining comparative phonology. One of the most significant in this regard is Grassmann (1863), proposing his dissimilation law, whereby Proto-Indo-European $D^h \ldots D^h$ dissimilates to $D \ldots D^h$ in Sanskrit, with parallels in Greek (although this was already discussed in Raumer 1837). Beyond explicitly clarifying a set of excep-tions to Grimm's Law, it carries with it two significant implications. First, it must be assumed that Germanic, which did not undergo the dissimilation, is (in some respects) phonologically more conservative and closer to Proto-Indo-European than Sanskrit. Second, it necessitates rejecting the extreme view that sound change does not occur in the early period of development of a language; that is, Sanskrit receives no special status and undergoes sound change just like any other language. In fact, the more 'traditional' grammarians such as Bopp, Pott, and Schleicher resisted making accommodations for Grassmann's Law in their approaches (see Pedersen 1931: 272, Lehmann 1967: 109).

Grassmann's article was important on the road to Hoenigswald's (1978) *annus mirabilis*, 1876, when some of the most remarkable work in the history of linguistics appeared, including Brugmann's Law, the Law of Palatals, and Verner's Law (dated 1877, but already available in the previous year). Brugmann's Law involves the reconstruction of PIE nuclear resonants to account for otherwise opaque correspondences; e.g. Proto-Indo-European +*m̥*, Skt. Gr. -*a(m)*, Lt. -*em*. This particularly brilliant and innovative application of comparative phonology involves the reconstruction of sounds that no longer existed in any of the daughter languages (although, again, this possibility had already been discussed explicitly by Raumer 1837: 13). Following our thread though, Brugmann's contribution is crucial since, like Grassmann's paper, Brugmann challenges Sanskrit's special status and promotes the uniformitarian hypothesis. Similarly, the Law of Palatals (which according to tradition was announced in a Leipzig restaurant in 1876, Collinge 1985: 35) necessitates the reconstruction of a mid-vowel series for Proto-Indo-European, with significant sound changes assumed for Sanskrit.

There is voluminous literature on whether or not the neogrammarian paradigm, which came to dominate linguistics by the end of the nineteenth century, constituted a significant paradigm shift (e.g. Putschke 1969, Koerner 1981). It would seem though that the dramatic shift that historiographers such as Pedersen see between the old and new (= neogrammarian) approaches is better understood in terms of changes in the working assumptions of earlier and later scholars regarding the 'life of a language' and language change. Ultimately, the obstacles relating to the investigation of the Indo-European developments were recognized as such and replaced with modern conceptualizations, resulting in entirely new perspectives. By contrast, letter theory (that is, comparative phonology) itself did not undergo any particularly abrupt transformations. There is no doubt that the work discussed above and others such as Verner's (1877) impressive clarification of the last significant set of exceptions to Grimm's Law are brilliant contributions. However, in terms of the comparative methodology they do not represent dramatic departures from earlier practice, beginning with Rask. Indeed, Verner's own description (Jespersen 1933: ch. 2) of his discovery 'makes it beautifully clear that he was struck in an almost graphic way' by the Sanskrit and Germanic correspondences while looking at a list of cognates in Bopp's grammar; 'phonetic considerations seem to have had nothing to do with it' (Hoenigswald 1974: 353) (nor did the Regularity Hypothesis, another fallacy; see Kiparsky 1974: 340, and section 2.3.4). Historiographies that perpetuate the myth of phonetically based discovery inevitably end up presenting a somewhat incoherent view. For example, Pedersen (1931: 305) states: 'In Verner's hands this method [that is, the 'phonetic point of view' based on Brücke 1856] proved most fruitful, but by a queer trick of fortune the phonetic explanation of his famous law … is hardly tenable in individual details.' Although of course the application of comparative phonology became much more refined and sophisticated over time, Diderichsen (1974: 302) is quite justified in not seeing a neogrammarian 'revolution' but rather only that 'the paradigm was slightly altered in the course of the nineteenth century'. In this respect, the neogrammarian period can be seen as one of 'codification'; even Brugmann (1885: 125) himself considered the neogrammarian tenets to simply constitute *die letzte Consequenz* [the final consequence] (also Delbrück 1885: 6, Thomsen 1927: 82, Wilbur 1972: 101, Koerner 1989b: 90). (Of course, history is to repeat itself about a century later. Generally, the transition from structuralism to generativism in the last half of the twentieth century is no longer viewed as a paradigm shift, but as an extension of structuralist thinking; Koerner 1989b, Goldsmith 2008.)

The continuity itself can be understood in light of the fact that scholars from the time of Grimm to the neogrammarians felt themselves charged with two distinct tasks. On the one hand, as already stated by Grimm's influential contemporary Pott (1833–6, see Pedersen 1931: 304), 'insight into the etymological agreement of sound in related words and forms is the principal matter for us, and we must strive for it zealously', where etymological agreement is the heart of comparative phonology. Pott goes on: 'Insight into the phonetic agreement of sounds is, on the other hand, more incidental.' Even as we approach the end of the century, this separation and dependency relationship is maintained by a neogrammarian of Brugmann's (1880:119, note 1) stature: 'first, on the basis of the phenomena of the history of language, we formulate the so-called sound-laws: the explanation according to the physiology of sounds comes later' (Pedersen 1931: 305). Thus, once 'letter theory' was freed from the fallacies that governed earlier work, it could reach its full potential and reveal the systematic nature of sound change, in terms of sound laws.

Given the impressive success of comparative phonology, it is perhaps not surprising that the neogrammarians proposed a Regularity Hypothesis that is the 'mainstay of our whole science' (Osthoff & Brugmann 1878: 13, from the neogrammarian manifesto):

(3) Regularity Hypothesis: 'Every sound change, inasmuch as it occurs mechanically, takes place according to laws that admit no exception.'

In fact, Schuchardt (1885), a contemporary critic of the neogrammarians not known for his particularly generous assessments, already argued that—in general terms—there is really 'nothing new' in the neogrammarian approach. In hindsight, Schuchardt's view is not particularly provocative or radical in this respect. Interestingly, though, Schuchardt did consider one thing new, the Regularity Hypothesis. At first glance, this seems somewhat surprising since by that time many scholars, not just neogrammarians, were working on the assumption that sound change was, more or less, regular. However, what Schuchardt (1972: 42) saw clearly is that the neogrammarians had transformed Pott's original goal of achieving 'insight into the etymological agreement of sound' into a *principle of sound change*, and here he makes a claim that is without a doubt both provocative and radical: the Regularity Hypothesis—as a principle of sound change (as opposed to a working principle of comparative phonology or etymology)—is wrong (see section 2.3.4).

2.3 SOUND CHANGE

2.3.1 Early Contributions

Focus in this section is on the second prong of nineteenth-century investigation, taking us to the heart of historical phonology—the description and explanation of sound change. Here the century got off to a particularly slow start as reflected in the discussion above. In contrast to comparative phonology's centrality as a research paradigm, historical phonology proper did not become a mainstream endeavour until the latter part of the century. Accordingly, for the early period it suffices to allude to the work of only two scholars, Bredsdorff 1821 (Andersen 1982) and Raumer 1837, 1856 (Lehmann 1967), both of whom were significantly ahead of their times. While Bredsdorff treats various aspects of language change—most notably developing an advanced notion of the role of analogy—much of the discussion is on the motivation of sound change (see Andersen 1982). Indeed, Jespersen (1933: 55, note 1) suggests that Bredsdorff's overall treatment of causality was not superseded until Paul (1880). Raumer is probably best known as an early proponent of the need to determine the sounds of obsolescent and reconstructed languages with phonetic accuracy (in terms of articulatory parameters). He argues already in 1837 that one of the best ways of reconstructing phonetic content is to consider the changes the sound undergoes, under the assumption of expected pathways of change; for example, $t > d > ð$.

2.3.2 The Classification of Sound Changes

Although Pedersen can still say in 1924 that the 'phonetic explanation' of sound change is 'still in its infancy' (he might also say that today, but see Blevins, and Yu, both this volume), the modern foundations of historical phonology are firmly set as the end of the nineteenth century is approached. It is no accident that two of the greatest linguists of the period, Eduard Sievers and Henry Sweet (1877, 1888), were gifted philologists *and* phoneticians (Jankowsky 1999b). The time had come for consolidation and further development of phonetically sophisticated approaches to comparative phonology and the investigation of sound change, and the importance of providing phonetic underpinnings for comparative phonology was emphasized in the neogrammarian manifesto (Osthoff & Brugmann 1878, Lehmann 1967: 202). In this regard, Sievers's *Grundzüge*, the first edition published in 1876, is of utmost importance. Interestingly, Sievers (1881, vi) states that during the preparatory stage of this work he did not consult any literature so as not to be disturbed by the 'influence of foreign ideas'. Perhaps this novel working strategy contributed to the exceptional originality of this work, first published when Sievers was 26 years old. Not only does he manage to set a few stones in the foundation of synchronic phonology, he anticipates structuralist approaches to sound change by fifty years (on Sievers's life and work, see Ganz 1978: 45–55).

One goal of historical phonology is to produce catalogues of sound changes based on various criteria (see Vennemann 1983b, and also Cser, Kümmel, and Blevins, all this volume). Consistent with his view on language-specific phonological systems (§§123–6), Sievers (1901: 273) does not believe a strict systematic classification of sound change having general validity is possible: 'the classificatory factors multiply intersect, and it is not possible to assign primacy once and for all to one particular factor'. Nevertheless, it is important to identify both the specific articulatory factors at play and general types of change. A simplified outline is presented in (4) (Sievers 1901: 273–4).

(4) Sievers's Classification
    Adjustments
        Spatial
        Timing
        Dynamic
        Quantity
    Types
        Spontaneous
        Conditioned
            Combinatorial

Spatial adjustments include changes in place of articulation and degree of constriction (e.g. frication). Timing adjustments relate to the relative sequencing of articulatory movements, but do not involve a change in the movements themselves. Thus, in an assimilation such as *agna* > *aŋna* there is no real change in the actual articulatory gestures, only in the timing of when the velum is lowered. Dynamic adjustments involve a change in the degree of pressure (*Druckstärke*) with concomitant change in the strength of constriction. Sievers distinguishes three subgroups depending on the presence or absence of syllable or word/sentence accent. Dynamic adjustments independent of accent involve segments, e.g. the strengthening of a lenis plosive to fortis. At the syllabic level there can be a distinction between weakly *vs* strongly cut syllables. As a classic example of the effect of word accent he refers to Verner's Law. The final type, quantity adjustments, differs from timing adjustments in that there is no actual change in the articulatory shape of the segment, as in vowel lengthenings.

Under types of changes, Sievers (1901: 275–6) considers the onset of spontaneous changes to be at the free disposal of the speaker. He includes, for example, the Grimm's Law shifting of Proto-Indo-European D > Proto-Germanic T (a set of changes already puzzled over by Raumer 1856). Under conditioned change, he includes the standard 'combinatorial' changes of assimilation, dissimilation, and svarabhakti, but also suprasegmentally induced change such as vowel weakening in unstressed syllables (e.g. reduction of full vowels to schwa).

In general, even a seasoned present-day historical linguist can only be impressed with the wealth of insights that Sievers provides, fully justifying Lehmann's claim that 'by the end of the century Jespersen, Sweet, Sievers and others had gained a control of the subject which has been surpassed only in details' (Lehmann 1967: 257). For example, consistent with his focus on suprasegmental factors, Sievers emphasizes the importance of distinguishing absorption from syncope (p. 296). Absorption is a timing adjustment without change in quantity or syllable count; a vowel is lost but the neighbouring liquid or nasal becomes syllabic, as in Old High German *apful*, German *apfl̩* 'apple'. By contrast, in syncope, quantity is affected and the syllable count is reduced. On another point, the common assumption then (and now) that 'open syllable lengthening' in Germanic languages is due to the effect of the dynamic accent (Prokosch's Law) is rejected. Rather, Sievers attributes vowel lengthening of this type to the phonologization at the segmental level of lengthenings originally occurring within rhythmic groupings (p. 303). For Sievers, the strong dynamic accent does not contribute to vowel lengthening but does the opposite; that is, it gives rise to a 'strongly cut syllable accent' (abrupt cut), which has precisely the effect of preserving vowel shortness (Vennemann 1994a; Becker 1998).

2.3.3 Synchrony, Systems, and Change

The neogrammarians are usually associated with, and often denigrated for, a narrow focus on sound change and sound laws. Regardless of the overall validity of this view, it is certainly the case that Sievers's *Grundzüge* provides no grist for such criticism. Since any diachronic theory presupposes at least a partial synchronic theory (Bartsch & Vennemann 1982), ultimately progress in the development of diachronic theory will be stilted by an impoverished synchronic theory. This was clearly recognized by Sievers, and there is little of the neogrammarian bias toward the historical in his *Grundzüge*. In fact, only section 2.4 consisting of 37 (out of 304) pages is specifically dedicated to diachronic issues (1901 edition). Consistent with the neogrammarian manifesto (Osthoff & Brugmann 1878), Sievers (1901: 6) explicitly states that in the first instance the primary object of study should be the spoken language, and he emphasizes the importance of self-analysis to the training of the historical linguist. 'The linguist's own dialect, spoken since childhood, should be the starting point of all phonetic investigations [...]. Only once all the phonetic phenomena of the native dialect are clearly understood should the linguist gradually move on to the investigation of more distant dialects and languages' (see Lehmann 1967: 262).

Taking the general position that a phonetic analysis should begin at the sentence level and work top-down through rhythmic groups and syllables to the segment (similarly, Paul 1920: 69, and compare Smith & Ussishkin, this volume), it is fair to say that Sievers touches on virtually all topics relevant to modern phonology. Ganz (1978: 49) suggests that in hindsight Sievers's most important contribution is the chapter on 'accent and quantity' in which Sievers distinguishes sentence, word, and syllable accent and treats the interrelationship of accent and vowel/consonant quality/quantity. Ultimately any definition of an individual sound is an abstraction, and Sievers (1901: 8–9) recognizes a phoneme-like abstraction: 'That which finally results as definition of the individual sound is in the end largely an abstraction dependent on arbitrarily selected points of view which is made from the frequently variable forms under which this so-called individual sound can appear in continuous human speech' (see Lehmann 1967: 264).

A remarkable aspect of Sievers's perspective, already in the first edition, is its emphasis on the sound system (strongly influenced by Winteler 1876—on this point, Paul 1920: 53 is decidedly less enthusiastic). Sievers is explicit and his comments require no interpretation. 'Above all, then, one should seek an exact insight into the structure of every phonological system which must be treated. One will do well always to remember that this is determined not so much by the number of sounds themselves which happen to be mixed together in the system as by the relationship of these individual members with one another' (p. 7; Lehmann 1967: 262). This synchronic (structuralist) perspective is usually associated with later work, especially Saussure, who of course studied in Leipzig, the neogrammarian centre. As Bloomfield (1924: 318), also one of the neogrammarians' students, states in his review of Saussure's *Cours*: 'Most of what the author says has long been "in the air" and has been here and there fragmentarily expressed.'

A particularly difficult chapter in Sievers's thinking is his (evolving) view of the relationship between the disciplines of phonetics and linguistics (see Kohler 1981 for discussion of the strengthening of Sievers's 'linguistic phonetics'). Although in the first edition, Sievers portrays phonetics as the necessary foundation for descriptive and historical phonology, already by the third edition (1885 [1901: 46–8]) there is a separation of linguistic phonetics from the natural phonetic sciences (physics and physiology). Indeed, in the second edition Sievers (1881: 36) adds a subsection on 'the infeasibility of general systems.' As Kohler (1981: 162) notes, Sievers 'is convinced that a general descriptive system of speech sounds meeting all the needs [of linguistics and the natural sciences] equally is quite impossible.' In fact, Sievers's position can perhaps best be understood in light of his view of language-specific systems and sound change. He emphasizes that the goals of historical phonetics cannot be achieved simply through a static description of individual sounds and their changes (pp. 6–7). 'One can even say that while for the theoretical phonetician the system and the precise analysis of individual sound classes and sounds which result from it stand in the center of interest, the historical linguist who pursues the historically attested changes and shifts of precisely these formations will derive the most benefit from systematic consideration precisely of the points of contact between the individual subclassifications which the systematizer sets up and tries to keep distinct as best he can' (p. 3, Lehmann 1967: 259).

In this regard, Sievers takes an explicitly system-based approach. 'For in general it is not the individual sound which undergoes change according to certain universally valid laws, but rather there is usually a corresponding development of corresponding series of sounds in corresponding positions' as, for example, in Grimm's Law (p. 7, Lehmann 1967: 262). Then in a view that foreshadows approaches such as Martinet's (1955) functional phonetics, he states: 'Generally specific points of view can also be discovered which help explain the change of one such series of sounds from the

overall constitution of the system as well as of the particular position of that series in
it' (p. 7, Lehmann 1967: 262; see also Gordon, this volume). For example, a change such
as derounding gives insight into the make-up of the entire vowel system (p. 278) (in a
similar vein, see Iverson & Salmons 2003 on voice *vs* spread glottis languages, where
assimilation types inform the posited system). For Sievers, then, it is crucial to precisely
determine a language's sound system and the systemic interrelationships of the individual members. With some oversimplification, it can be stated that in Sievers's view the
primary object of study for the linguist is the language-specific sound system, and that
this task lies outside the domain of phonetics. Here a particular course was set. Already
in 1924 Bloomfield disparages phonetics for its 'endless and aimless listing of the various
sound-articulations of speech' (p. 318), and the separate fields of phonetics and phonology are to become canonized, most notably in the next *Grundzüge* (Trubetzkoy 1939).
Be that as it may, while Sievers did not progress far in his development of 'structuralist'
approaches to sound change, comments such as Jakobson's (1931: 247) criticism of the
neogrammarian 'atomistic-isolating' treatment of sound change (in which no attention
is given to the system within which the change takes place) must be taken with a grain of
salt (see Kohrt 1990). Jakobson's first principle of historical phonology reads as a para-
phrase of Sievers (1876: 4): each change is to be treated in terms of the system within
which it takes place.

A direct continuation of the Sieversian view is found in the Vienna School of dialectology with its rich tradition of *Ortsgrammatiken*, detailed descriptions of German
dialects carried out in the twentieth century (see Wiesinger 1976). On the one hand,
in keeping with Sievers's view of the complexity of synchronic systems, the synchronic
description in an *Ortsgrammatik* is never reduced to a simplified phonemic system. On
the other hand, structuralist-influenced interpretations of sound changes are provided
(see Moulton 1972, Murray 2010: 78–82).

2.3.4 Regularity

There is no doubt that the most difficult chapter of the nineteenth-century investigation
of sound change is still being written. Although the Regularity Hypothesis and sound
laws are often placed at the centre of discussion, it would seem that the real protagonist
lurking in the shadows is the mental lexicon. It is easy to get lost in the voluminous
literature on the sound law controversy (Wilbur 1977), fascinating from both a historio-
graphic and sociological perspective. Restricting discussion to a phonological perspective, focus here is on a few fundamental issues that crystallize in a pristine form at the
end of the century.

The Regularity Hypothesis (or 'Exceptionlessness Hypothesis', see end of section 2.2.4)
is succinctly formulated. Three points require discussion. First, with regards to the
concept of sound change, the neogrammarians crucially distinguish two types:
Lautwandel (phonetic change) *vs* *Lautvertauschung* (sound transposition) (Paul
1920: ch. 3, Kruszewski 1885, 1887, Koerner 1995: xv). Both Paul (1920:§45) and

Sievers (1901: 270, 273) are explicit that only *Lautwandel* is governed by the Regularity Hypothesis—such phonetic change involves a very gradual shifting of sound nuances over time; for example, the vowel *a* gradually moving in the direction of *e* in an *i*-umlaut environment. (Weinreich et al. 1968: 116, reasonably interpret the meaning of the term *Lautwandel* as 'shifts in terms of synchronic process only'.) By contrast, 'abrupt' changes (*Lautvertauschung*) such as dissimilation and metathesis, which do not involve the gradual creation of new phonological material, are explicitly excluded. Such changes only affect individual words and not the language's phonology (*Lautmaterial*) (Sievers 1901: 270). Second, the Regularity Hypothesis only governs 'mechanical' sound changes, those assumed to take place unconsciously. 'It may be considered as generally conceded that sound change is carried out in a fashion that is completely unconscious to the speaker and therefore completely mechanical' (Osthoff 1879: 13). Third, the claim of exceptionlessness refers to the assumption that the sound change is phonetically based, and takes place in all cases where the phonetic conditions are met. Generally today this assumed type of sound change is labelled neogrammarian change.

At this point we come to perhaps the most important point: what changes? Paul (1920: 55) provides an explicit answer: the sound image (*Lautbild*). For Paul, a speaker's perception and production of a language sound depends on a sound image or representation, a mental target that is formed on the basis of what a speaker both produces and hears. However, just as an archer shooting arrows will sometimes miss the mark, a speaker does not precisely hit the sound image target with each production. Here Paul sees endless variation of production around this ideal target, but ultimately it is the sound image that shifts in a particular direction (on variation, see Jones, and D'Arcy, both this volume). Although he would not accept Paul's 'psychologizing', it is fair to say that Bloomfield (1926) continues the line of thinking initiated by his neogrammarian teachers when he states in his 'postulates for the science of language': 'Assumption: Phonemes or classes of phonemes may gradually change. Definition: Such change is *sound change.*' While phrased differently depending on framework, this fundamental assumption stretches from the neogrammarians through Hockett (1965), King (1969), Labov (1994), Blevins (2004), and see also Bermúdez-Otero (this volume). Common to these approaches, given the assumption that it is the abstract 'sound image' that changes (or that is acquired in child language acquisition), is the implication that neogrammarian sound change cannot (or should not) display certain properties in the individual, such as frequency effects or lexical diffusion.

A dramatically different line of thought was developed by Schuchardt (1885/1972) who argued that in proposing the Regularity Hypothesis the neogrammarians were 'mistaking mere observations for causal factors' (Wilbur 1972: 107): 'the theory of the unexceptionability of sound laws is nothing but a hindrance to the further development of the science in the sense of the law of causality. The sound laws are elevated to such heights that the desire for transcending them is far weaker than if they had only the value of great regularities. And yet in any case they are only empirical regularities' (Schuchardt 1972: 63–4). In other words, we are dealing with a 'doctrine that propounded an unconscious and mechanical process of linguistic diffusion which eliminated any need for explanation' (Wilbur 1972: 94).

For Schuchardt all sound changes begin as sporadic changes in individual speakers (where no distinction is made between gradual and abrupt change). A sporadic change can take hold and generalize in three different ways. First, the change can spread from one word to another (lexical diffusion), where often, but not always, frequently used words 'hurry ahead' (Schuchardt 1972: 58). For example, the intervocalic frication of a voiced plosive might first affect frequently used words, and then may (or may not) generalize to less frequently used words. Second, sound changes display phonological generalization (phonetic analogy, see Fertig, this volume); that is, they can generalize from one segment to another of similar type or from one phonological environment to another. For example, frication can begin with velar plosives in intervocalic position and then generalize to other plosives and to other environments. Third, there is a social dimension involving the spread of the change from one individual to another through imitation. Since the social spread of a sound change is based on imitation, a level of consciousness is assumed at all stages (on Schuchardtian thought, see Vennemann 1972: 171–4, theses 1–29).

Of course, Schuchardt's approach is entirely at odds with the mainstream view of neogrammarian sound change as an unconscious gradual shifting of an abstract sound image. The general perspective, however, is compatible with exemplar theoretic models, such as Bybee (2001), with their assumption of rich, phonetically detailed lexical representations, where variant forms of each entry are included in an 'exemplar cloud'. From this type of perspective, a formalization of Schuchardt's theses 24–27 is relatively straightforward:

(5) Schuchardt's Theses 24–27 (from Vennemann 1972: 173–4).
     Sound laws 'exist'. Otherwise they could not generalize. The mode of existence of a sound law is that of a mental representation in the speakers of the language. The mental representation of a sound law is not merely (conscious or unconscious) knowledge of a distribution of sounds but contains directionality (like phonological rules in generative grammar). Sound laws do not necessarily cease to exist when a certain degree of generality has been reached and consolidated. They can continue to exist for generations and be liable to further generalization at any time.

As Vennemann (1972: 171) states: 'Schuchardt's position is that [for example, two variants] can be correlated synchronically by a directional distribution [i.e. a 'sound law']. This position made him a lonely theoretician.' Important is that the directionality that sound change displays through many generations of speakers takes on less of a metaphysical quality. Speakers can at all times make further generalizations based on their exemplar sets, and the 'sound law' (directional distribution) can be reconstructed anew by every generation of children in the acquisition process who will, of course, make their own generalizations by phonetic analogy.

Let us take the liberty here of speculating on what Schuchardt might have expected for the next century or so of historical phonology. Since Schuchardt rejects the conscious–unconscious dichotomy, he would predict the impossibility of distinguishing two types of sound change, (unconscious, gradual) neogrammarian *vs* (conscious, abrupt) lexical diffusion, a prediction that is often seen as borne out (see the difficulties of Labov 1994: 542–3; discussion in Oliveira 1991, Phillips 2006: 1–30, and Phillips, this volume, but compare Bermúdez-Otero, this volume—though the neogrammarian Sievers 1901: 272 made the same prediction). More specifically, Schuchardt would expect evidence of 'neogrammarian' change proceeding by lexical diffusion (see Bybee 2002b, Phillips 2006: 57–95, and also Bybee, and Phillips, both this volume) and evidence of abrupt changes displaying neogrammarian regularity (Blevins 2004a: 268–78, Blevins, this volume—note, however, that this latter possibility is also explicitly accepted by Paul 1920: 73). He might expect psycholinguistic experiments to provide evidence of native speaker sensitivity to subphonemic detail, a prediction also borne out (Miller 1994, Lachs et al. 2003, Yu, this volume). He would also predict that structuralist/generative-based theories, with their 'stripped down abstract lexicons' (without phonetic detail) could face difficulties in attempting to explain why assumed underlying abstractions consistently drift in the same direction through generations of speakers (Kiparsky, this volume). Schuchardt would likely consider the classical generative position that this is not a problem of historical linguistics, but rather a problem of language acquisition (or of sociolinguistics) to be 'dogma' (D'Arcy, Foulkes & Vihman, and Hale et al., all this volume). Compare Schuchardt's position on the imperceptibility hypothesis of the neogrammarians: 'it is in the nature of a dogma that it is impervious to the evidence' (Vennemann 1972: 134). Interestingly, then, although Paul (1886) accused Schuchardt of unscientific behaviour, in hindsight the Schuchardtian view in this respect is relatively coherent. It is the neogrammarian view of a (somewhat mysterious) mechanically operating unconscious (unidirectional) sound change (over many generations) that faces significant empirical and theoretical challenges. (Schuchardt 1972: 64 argues that the neogrammarians were still in the grip of the pre-neogrammarian view, which 'separated speech from human beings'.)

For the Regularity Hypothesis, Schuchardt might accept a version of it as a methodological principle of comparative phonology (e.g. Blust 1996a: 153, Fox, this volume). Even in neogrammarian work itself, there already seemed to be a shift in this respect (which Robins 1978: 13–14 suggests was a response to Schuchardt's criticisms). Thus, Pedersen (1931: 303), a strong advocate of the neogrammarian approach, states: 'Sound-laws are actually laws to us, which we must obey *while we etymologize*.' Similarly, this perspective also seems to be the only appropriate way to interpret such statements as: 'nobody who has pretensions to the scientific can work with exceptions' (Hirt 1939; see Collinge 1978: 76). In other words, exceptions are a given but must be accounted for through whatever means are available; morphological analogy, borrowing, phonetic analogy, partially generalized sound change, competing sound changes, etc. (Schuchardt 1972: 43), and Carl Verner's succinct statement still applies: 'nulla exceptio sine regula' (Pedersen 1983: 76).

2.4 CONCLUSION

Any decent history of historical phonology must end with a twist, and here it is. Although linguists working in exemplar frameworks often make reference to Schuchardt (e.g. Bybee 2002b, Phillips 2006: 3, Phillips, this volume), it was not Schuchardt who most explicitly discussed 'exemplar-theoretic' notions, but rather the neogrammarian Hermann Paul (see Hopper 2009). Indeed, if paraphrased excerpts from Bybee (2001: 6–7) and Paul (1920: 25, 27) are juxtaposed, it is perhaps not immediately obvious which one was written over a century ago:

(a) An individual's mental grammar with its interconnected groups of representations is in a constant state of change. Every act of speaking, hearing, or thinking can add to the grammar, and elements that are not renewed through repeated exposure can gradually lose strength. The networks of the mental grammar are permanently changed through the weakening of old elements and the appearance of new ones.

(b) Language is slowly, gradually, but inexorably mutating under the dynamic forces of language use. The use of forms and patterns affects their representation in memory. High-frequency items have stronger representations. Low-frequency items are more difficult to access and may even become so weak as to be forgotten.

[(a) is loosely, but not inaccurately, translated from Paul 1920; *psychischer Organismus* 'mental grammar', *Vorstellungen* 'representations'; *Assoziationsverhältnisse* 'networks'; see translations in Weinreich et al. 1968: 105–20.]

While Paul failed to produce an entirely coherent theory of sound change (Murray 2010: 76–8), we should not be surprised that a scholar at the end of the nineteenth century was unable to fully reconcile his conception of a rich, ever-changing mental grammar with his goal of accounting for the regularity of sound change. This story is still being written.

CHAPTER 3

....

STRUCTURALIST HISTORICAL PHONOLOGY

Systems in Segmental Change

....

JOSEPH SALMONS AND PATRICK HONEYBONE

3.1 INTRODUCTION

....

ALTHOUGH 'structuralism' is sometimes treated as a finished phase in the historical development of linguistics, the central ideas of structuralist phonology still underlie fundamental thinking in historical phonology to an extent not always recognized;
they also shape ideas in the allied areas of formal phonology and language variation and change. In this spirit, we differentiate here between 'classical structuralism'
(or 'structuralism in a narrow sense'), by which we mean a group of theoretical frameworks
developed in Europe and America, broadly in the first half of the twentieth century, and
'structuralism in a broad sense', which continues in phonology today. Some ideas developed during classical structuralism have been taken into 'basic phonological theory'—
concepts sometimes considered theory-neutral, which all phonologically-informed
work needs to consider. Kiparsky (2014: 81) makes a similar point, calling attention to the
'unexamined structuralist baggage' of historical linguistics, including bottom-up procedures and a focus on mislearning as a, or *the*, source of change.

This chapter focuses on this fundamental and still contemporary substance in structuralist phonology. Section 3.2 considers these ideas in their historical perspective,
taking up where Murray's chapter (this volume) leaves off and finishing at the contemporary period (where this volume's following chapters take off). In some sense, we
provide something of an introduction to those other chapters here (and we thank their
authors for suggestions, particularly Dresher, Kessler, and Scheer), offering a context for
them and a perspective on both how basic structuralist thinking still is to much theorizing about phonological change, and how other work in historical phonology offers some
major challenges and reactions to it.

Before continuing, it is worthwhile to clarify the landscape. 'Structuralism' has a bewildering array of associations with particular ideas, approaches and theories in linguistics and other fields, not all of which will be relevant, or discussed, here (see Dosse 1991, Jackson 1991, and Dresher 1999). Jakobson (1929: 11) was perhaps the first to use the term 'structuralism' in linguistics (Percival 2011), writing: 'Any set of phenomena examined by contemporary science is treated not as a mechanical agglomeration but as a structural whole, and the basic task is to reveal the inner, whether static or developmental, laws of this system'. Jakobson's focus is clearly on the notion of the *system*, which is subject to linguistic 'laws' (what we might call 'principles'). The claim is also that synchronic and diachronic ('static' and 'developmental') analysis can be brought together as a way of understanding the whole.

More recently, Trask's dictionary entry (2000: 326) offers a starting point for the application of such thought to diachrony:

> **Structural explanation of change.** Any proposal to account for language change in terms of the requirements of a linguistic system. Such approaches are most often proposed in connection with phonology; for example, it may be maintained that phoneme systems tend toward symmetry, so that holes in the pattern are filled while phonemes which 'spoil' the symmetry tend to be lost. A standard example is the English fricatives: Old English had only /f θ s ʃ x/, but the acquisition of /v/ and /ʒ/ in loans from French supposedly induced the introduction of /ð/ to partner /θ/, even though the functional load of the contrast is minimal, and /x/ supposedly disappeared because it had no voiced partner.

This highlights central structuralist issues: the role of the *system* itself, *symmetry* within the system (here around a phonological feature), and the fact that the systems involved are systems of *contrasts* (which are *formal* elements). The example illustrates two key mechanisms of change which can create symmetry, split and loss. At the same time, it expressly allows that structural patterns sometimes must be tied to social considerations (although the two are often kept separate), here language contact. Most importantly, as Trask suggests with the repeated use of 'supposedly', careful sifting of the data can show a more nuanced picture: the contrastive voiced fricatives of English, such as /v/, developed from a range of sources, including some with English-internal endogenous origins (see, e.g. Minkova 2011), and Trask's illustration highlights some of the nuance of contrast—that it can develop in highly restricted environments first, and then spread to others.

This chapter considers justifications and challenges for the notions just raised, in both historical and contemporary terms, centered on issues of systems, contrast and symmetry. Section 3.2 links a consideration of the development of structuralist thought on sound change to some of the recent reception of this thinking, section 3.3 then reviews the details of some basic diachronic systemic patterns that have been the core of most structuralist thinking, with an eye toward setting up what they mean for theories of sound change, and section 3.4 concludes.

3.2   A HISTORY OF STRUCTURALIST
HISTORICAL PHONOLOGY

Pace Lass's qualifications (this volume) and Minkova's discussion (this volume), alphabetic writing can be seen as a kind of recognition of the role of contrast in segmental inventories, such that the development of alphabets or similar writing systems were acts of structural phonological analysis in some preliminary sense. This is a far cry from articulated phonology, however, which fully developed as an autonomous discipline only in the twentieth century (Fischer-Jørgensen 1975, Anderson 1985). Before the twentieth century there was mostly a unified 'phonetics-phonology' which at certain times and places was well developed, and certainly involved the consideration of phonological ideas, but largely offered unconnected precursors for structuralist thought.

Some late nineteenth century work by the neogrammarians would now be viewed as sophisticated phonetic description, but other aspects of their work was clearly phonological, considering syllable structure, sonority and some aspects of contrast, for instance. As Murray (this volume) shows, there was also a nascent recognition during that century of the role that phonological systems can play in the organization of language (and in the patterning of change). Fully-fledged 'autonomous' phonology (autonomous, that is, from phonetics) grew out of the context of this nineteenth-century historical work (for which see Murray, this volume, and also especially Morpurgo Davies 1998). The end of this century also saw the earliest signs (in the modern era) of work which focused on synchronic phonological structure, such as Kruszewski (1881) and Baudouin de Courtenay (1895), or which at least recognized the role of contrast in transcription, such as Sweet (1877).

Saussure (1916) emphasized the possibility of a linguistic focus on the synchronic organization of language as well as a diachronic approach (with substantial implications—see Kiparsky, this volume, on 'Saussure's Firewall'). Both he and the two writers typically seen as true founders of autonomous phonology—Trubetzkoy and Jakobson, who in part saw themselves as followers of Saussure—had been trained in neogrammarian ideas. Such early structuralist thinkers were immersed in historical data, but were seeking synchronic linguistic principles. It is thus no surprise that the ideas developed in this period have become central in general historical phonology.

Trubetzkoy (e.g. 1939), Jakobson (e.g. 1931, 1941), and others connected with the Prague Linguistic Circle in the 1920s and 1930s thus maintained and developed ideas on contrast and systematicity which had been implicit or gradually developing in earlier work. While there were continuities, there were also breaks with the past: Anderson (1985: 173) writes that the 'real innovation in structuralist phonemic theory [...] was the notion that the set of phonemes [...] in a given language form a system with an important internal organisation.' These early struturalists were revolutionary in devising a research programme which made these ideas the focus of sustained investigation. This formed the European Structuralism of the first half of the twentieth century, which both influenced and was influenced by those who developed American Structuralism, such as Bloomfield (e.g. 1933). These structuralisms differed, but also shared many similarities: they both worked with an overt distinction between what is now known as underlying and surface phonology ('phonemic' and 'allophonic' levels, along with a recognition of morphophonological analysis), and they both explicitly developed the notion that languages comprised segmental systems. This allowed the classical structuralists to focus explicitly on the extent to which phonological changes affect the number and nature of the contrasts which exist in a phonological system, and to consider the inter-relatedness of both contemporaneous and successive changes, leading to the recognition that segmental changes can (but need not) involve segmental/phonemic splits or mergers. Fox (this volume) and Gordon (this volume) show how important an understanding of splits and mergers can be and Kiparsky (this volume) explores some complications with the notion of split (see also below). A further central point is that phonetic characteristics can become part of the (contrastive) phonology (see below on 'phonologization').

Work from the 1940s until the 1960s elaborated these basic insights in paradigms that can be described as structuralist in both the broad and narrow sense. For example, Martinet (e.g. 1955) was instrumental in recognizing ways in which the maintenance of contrast can be seen to play a role in phonological change in the patterning of chain shifts (see Gordon, this volume, and section 3.3.3, below), Hockett (1955) focused in detail on symmetry and organizational principles in segmental systems, and Hoenigswald (1960) condensed and codified ideas on diachronic merger and split, distinguishing between split with merger (which he called 'primary split') and without ('secondary split'), among other ideas (see section 3.3.2).

European structuralists 'discovered' symmetry as a principle of systemic organization. As Fischer-Jørgensen (1975: 33) notes, there is an implicit assumption of symmetry in Trubetzkoy's (1939) discussion of vowel systems, and the idea is made explicit in later structuralist work, perhaps reaching its zenith in Martinet (1955). Trubetzkoy (1939) argues, for example, that vowel systems tend to have equal numbers of segments at a small number of levels, with equivalent degrees of distance in phonological space between them. Vowel systems are typically either triangular or quadrangular, and 'by far the majority of languages has three-degree vowels systems' (1939: 107), of the type shown in (1). These observations are based on early typological investigations (see Kümmel, this volume for more on the role of typology in phonology). The spacing of symbols is slightly adapted here and the vowel diagrams are inverted to fit in with current practice, retaining Trubetzkoy's symbols (and some of this discussion borrows from Honeybone 2010).

(1) *i*   *u*   *i*   *u*
       e   *o*   *e*   *o*
            a   *ä*   *a*

This means that symmetry is most widespread on the vertical axis in vowels systems—as it exists in both triangular and quadrangular systems—and only quadrangular systems feature symmetry on the horizontal axis. The basic expectation of symmetry in segmental systems thus requires symmetrical units in each phonological slot provided by the language's system (in terms of height and backness for vowels, and laryngeal and place of articulation features for obstruents, for example). Structuralists also worked to explain *why* symmetry should guide the structure of segmental inventories; in part these ideas fit with the notion of markedness, discussed below.

From here it is no real leap to assume that a striving for symmetry in languages is relevant in diachrony as well as synchrony, a basic assumption in the Trask quotation above. Symmetry provided what were argued to be purely phonological descriptions and, even, *explanations* of phonological change. This type of explanation focuses directly on systemic considerations and it is thus 'asocial'—ignoring any social motivation for change—so the ideas considered here are fundamentally directed at understanding endogenously-innovated change, ignoring exogeny. It gives synchronic phonological structure a role in understanding phonological change in a manner described as 'amphichronic' by Kiparsky (2006, and Bermúdez-Otero, this volume).

The period in which these ideas were developed formed the peak of classical, narrow-sense structuralism. These ideas, and the notion that phonological *correlations* can change—not (just) sounds or phonemes—formed the basis of the standard understanding of how phonology worked, linked to a number of other assumptions; for some, these included the notions that phonological units should be understood as elements that were characterized by the *differences* that existed between them and other units in a system, or that the relationship between phonological levels must be one-to-one, forbidding phonemic overlap. The same physical item could have strongly diverging phonological characteristics and behaviour according to the nature of other items present in a phonological system, and modifications of an item could be caused by the segmental environment or by systemic properties. There were differences between European and American structuralisms (Fischer-Jørgensen 1975, Anderson 1985), but the basic thrust—that a focus on phonological contrast and phonological systems is crucial in order to understand phonology—was central to the development of contemporary understandings of phonology, and of phonological change.

It is widely claimed (Anderson 1985, Bromberger & Halle 1989) that the rise of generative phonology, following Halle (1959) and Chomsky & Halle (1968), involved a fundamental paradigm shift. There *were* major breaks with classical structuralism, such as the explicit attention paid to the relationship between morphophonology and low-level/postlexical phonology, the embracing of lengthy derivations, and a major focus on the linear phonological environment in which segments occur, rather than chiefly on their place in a system, but there was also non-negligible continuity (see Goldsmith 2008, Scheer 2011a). The most-often cited fatal flaws of structuralism are typically less aimed directly at its phonological machinery (much of which can still be seen in-use by some today), than at its connection to behaviourist psychology, taxonomic orientation and lack of full engagement with syntax.

While the role of segmental systems in driving phonology was taken out of centre focus, contrast remained crucial (if modified to recognize that surface contrast does not necessarily imply underlying contrast), and analyses of languages in generative materials still made the assumption that a language had defined inventories of segments. Diachronic work of the period, even if influenced by generative ideas, could still consider the effect of changes on segmental systems, such as mergers and splits. Furthermore, the notion that *marked* structures are dispreferred due to deep-rooted phonological machinery has anchored itself in generative theory as part of its structuralist inheritance. For example, Chomsky & Halle (1968: 401–2) argue that a vowel system such as that in (2) is 'more natural, in some significant sense, than one such as' that in (3), which conflicts with markedness expectations (e.g. that no system may have front rounded vowels if it does not also have front unrounded vowels).

(2) i   u
     e   o
        a

(3) ü   ɨ
           ʌ
     œ   a

This connects generative thought with the structuralist expectations of unmarkedness and of order and symmetry in segmental systems. Goldsmith & Laks (to appear) argue against this, quite rightly, that 'new' segments could be lightly assumed in this model without much worry about their consequences for the phonological system, thus Chomsky & Halle could consider proposing /kʷ/ for English in order to account for some morphophonological alternations, without immediately worrying if this also implied a need for /gʷ/. But this did not imply a total rejection of structuralist concerns: on the same page (p. 150) that they consider /kʷ/, Chomsky & Halle also write that '[w]ith the postulation of doubled consonants ... we fill a gap in underlying structures (a 'phonological gap') and extend the symmetry of the system of lexical entries'.

In these senses, we see a continuation of fundamental structuralist ideas after the demise of classical structuralism in the 1960s and 1970s. While narrow-sense structuralism declined, broad-sense structuralism continued, and generative approaches can be seen as structuralist in the broadest sense of the notion.

Dresher (this volume) considers a current rule-based approach to phonological change, of a type fundamentally compatible with classical generative phonology. He shows how such ideas can be overtly mixed with more clearly structuralist ideas—placing considerable explanatory importance on the contrastive hierarchy of phonological features. Features are a clear inheritance from narrow-sense structuralism. Trubetzkoy (1939) considered 'oppositions' between segments, invoking the idea that they are characterized by the relationships that they enter into in languages, tying in with the notion that phonological units should be understood as the set of differences between them and other units in a system. Jakobson developed these ideas (e.g. Jakobson, Fant, & Halle 1952) to provide the basis of contemporary distinctive feature theory, developing a small language-universal set of features which exist independently of the segments that they make up, as segmental 'building blocks'. The use of features and contemporary work in subsegmental phonology can thus also be seen as a continuation of structuralist ideas in a broad sense (see Purnell & Raimy, this volume, on the application of theories of features to the interpretation of phonological change).

There were objections to generative ideas when they were proposed (some are discussed by Scheer, this volume, along with some defence; see also Donegan & Nathan and Mailhammer et al., both this volume), and a new round of anti-generative work in phonological theory arose in the late 1990s and 2000s, often of a radical purely usage-based or exemplar-based type, as in Bybee (2001, this volume) and Phillips (this volume); other such work still allows for the possibility of a formal grammar, as in Blevins (2004a, this volume). Such work discards much of the structural machinery of formal phonology, but need not always reject the broad structuralist importance placed on the role of contrast and system (Sóskuthy 2013, for example, explicitly links exemplar-type modelling with systemic concerns in phonological change). Some such work does make this rejection, however, arguing that complementary distribution does not imply that two phones derive from one underlying segment, and that similar segments occurring in different environments need not count as phonologically the same. A general push-back against phonology, especially formal phonology, has also come from work like Ohala's (see Yu, this volume). While answers vary about how much abstract (phonological) structure and computation actually exists, this tradition eliminates most or potentially all of it. Of all challenges to structuralist principles, this is the most fundamental. Such ideas do represent the end of structuralism in phonology, but are minority positions in the contemporary phonological world.

Less inimical to formal approaches, but still challenging to the idea that purely phonological structure can account for change is the branch of work which can be described as 'dispersion theory'. Dispersion is 'the idea that segments are subject to a pressure to be maximally dispersed in the available phonetic space' (Mielke 2009: 707, and see also Gordon and Holt, both this volume). Vaux & Samuels (2015), themselves critical of the enterprise, describe ways in which this has been developed into 'Dispersion Theory', on the basis that 'consonant inventories tend to evolve so as to achieve maximal perceptual distinctiveness at minimum articulatory cost' (Lindblom & Maddieson 1988), by balancing the impetus to disperse with the impetus to minimize effort. Some work in Optimality Theory (e.g. Flemming 1995/2002, Ní Chiosáin & Padgett 2010) or in frameworks which assume that phonological inventories are subject to the principles of self-organizing systems (e.g. de Boer 2001) argues that such reductionist pressures account for the tendency towards symmetry, and Holt (this volume) considers how dispersion has been integrated into OT. In a sense, this work links to structuralist ideas, aiming to motivate symmetry in systems; it is perhaps the phonetically-based mechanisms adopted to do this that are non-structuralist.

We can also see the influence of broad-sense structuralism in other developments in synchronic and diachronic phonology which have emerged since narrow-sense structuralism faded. In addition to generativism, the other main paradigm has been Labovian variationist sociolinguistic work (see Labov 1972a et seq., and D'Arcy, this volume). This is hardly a challenge to structuralism per se, though see Chambers's (1995: ch. 1) critique of 'categoricity' in formal linguistics. Indeed, Labov's work on chain shifting (most importantly 1994; see Gordon, this volume) is itself classically structuralist. More importantly, Labov's trilogy on language change—almost entirely on SOUND change, in fact—aims to integrate the structural (or 'internal') with the social and the cognitive. Indeed, Labov (1994: ch. 21) posits a set of principles embracing and integrating phonetic, phonological and 'external' factors, and can be seen as broadly structuralist. As laid out in D'Arcy (this volume), patterns of acquisition correlate with patterns of social behaviour and change in response to them, or as she says 'linguistic and social factors are closely interrelated in the development of a change'.

As we have seen, symmetry within systems is one of the most important themes in structuralist historical phonology. Fischer-Jørgensen (1975: 45) explains:

> Trubetzkoy, Jakobson, de Groot and van Wijk all emphasize the tendency towards harmonious systems. Martinet's contribution consists in a reinterpretation of the somewhat vague concept as something more concrete: harmony is a manifestation of economy (a view which was suggested earlier by de Groot (1931)). A system which utilizes a limited number of distinctive features in several pairs is more economical than one with many different distinctive features none of which are put to much work.

Thus, for example, if [±back] is used to make a contrast at one level of vowel height in a system, it is expected that it will be used at other levels, too, so three-level and four-level systems have two vowels at all heights (apart from at the lowest level, which can be central in triangular systems).

The idea that phonological systems are organized symmetrically has been picked up and developed in recent work in formal phonological theory, often with relevance to diachrony. Clements (2003, 2009), for example, argues that the impetus towards symmetry need not be seen as a system-organizing principle in its own right—rather, symmetry is the result of a more fundamental phonological principle. For Clements (picking up the idea that we have just seen discussed in narrow-sense structuralist work), 'the typical 'symmetry' of vowel systems reflects Feature Economy' (2009: 56). Clements (2003) is at pains to explain that the simple requirement for symmetry and the formal expectation of Feature Economy do not make exactly the same predictions: systems can be perfectly symmetrical but not fully economical, for example. This does not mean that an impetus towards economy does not lead towards symmetry, however.

The notion of markedness has also played a major role in formal phonology of various stipes. Theories of markedness asymmetries, such as the fact that if a language has only one set of front vowels, they are always unrounded, developed in narrow-sense structuralism, hand in hand with the development of phonological features, as an attempt to explain patterns in phonology. The notion has been fundamental in Optimality Theory (see Holt, this volume, and the comparative discussion in Kiparsky, this volume) as the basis for many of the constraints assumed in the model. It has also been developed in frameworks which have placed importance on expanded models of segmental structure, working with only privative/unary subsegmental units to account for markedness asymmetries in a theoretical model. Such approaches, often referred to (e.g. in Carr, Durand & Ewen 2005) as the 'Dependency/Government' approach to segmental structure, offer another explanation for the tendencies in vowel systems, deriving the most common patterns in vowel inventories from the set of subsegmental primitives that it allows. The approach is found in Dependency Phonology (e.g. Anderson & Jones 1974, Anderson & Ewen 1987), Particle Phonology (e.g. Schane 1984, 2005) and Government Phonology (e.g. Kaye, Lowenstamm, & Vergnaud 1985, 1990), in part through independent development, and latterly through cross-fertilization (see, e.g. Harris 1994, Botma 2004, Purnell & Raimy, this volume).

These approaches assume that subsegmental phonological representations involve a set of privative primes which are not many in number and which are each used in several ways in the structure of segments. These primes are typically called 'elements' and are fully interpretable in their own right, thus the most common vowels (the only ones found in the smallest triangular system) are composed of one element each, as shown in (4), where the second column represents the most prominent characteristic of the three elements involved.

(4)   vowel   element
       /i/ = palatality = **I**
       /a/ = openness   = **A**
       /u/ = labiality   = **U**

Other vowels are composed of combinations of these elements, thus /y/ is made up of **I** and **U**, as a palatal vowel with labiality (i.e. rounding). In Government Phonology (other approaches differ in the precise implementation) one element is assumed to be the 'head' of an expression (underlined below), which means that any other elements in it are 'dependents'. Thus the three and four-degree triangular systems can be represented as in (5).

(5) Vowel system   Elemental makeup
     i   u   **I̲**   **U̲**
     e   o   **I̲, A**   **U̲, A**
          a   **A̲**
     i   u   **I̲**   **U̲**
     e   o   **I̲, A**   **U̲, A**
     ɛ   ɔ   **I, A̲**   **U, A̲**
          a   **A̲**

This approach builds markedness directly into the set of features assumed, as a front high unrounded vowel has a simple representation, comprising only **I**, whereas a front high rounded vowel is more complex, as it is comprised of **I** and **U** together.

The model fits well with triangular systems, but less obviously with quadrangular systems, as Durand (2005: 83) explains: '[i]f we came across a system like /i e æ, ɑ o u/, it would be modelled as inherently symmetrical in the *SPE* tradition':

(6)   −back   +back

+high, −low   i   u

−high, −low   e   o

−high, +low   æ   ɑ

'By contrast, it would be inherently skewed in a D[ependency] P[honology] approach':

(7)   i   u   **I**   **U**

        e   o   **I**, A   **U**, A

        æ   I, **A**

                 ɑ   **A**

This issue for the Dependency/Government tradition may just be an advantage, in fact, as quadrangular systems are rarer than triangular ones. As the Dependency/Government approach represents such systems as subsegmentally aberrant, it provides a phonological rationale for the observation.

These formal approaches, like dispersion, assume that phonological systems strive to fit a particular form, due to the pressures that they presume (although there is no intention to predict *when* a particular change will occur—surely a fool's errand). All this raises the issue of teleology in sound change. If the structure of a system, including considerations like symmetry in segmental oppositions, is considered a motivation for change, broadly structuralist approaches see language change as language improvement in some sense, e.g. by improving the systematicity of featural contrasts. The idea that language change improves anything, that it is in some sense teleological, is controversial, although teleology is also present in functionalist approaches to change. Luraghi (2010:364-6) reviews key literature on the issue, showing that little common ground exists among the broader community of historical linguists on this point; we note also that symmetrical patterns can often be motivated ateleologically (and, of course, any model needs also to recognize and deal with the fact that not all changes move phonologies in the direction of improved symmetry, or dispersion).

Many structuralist ideas have proven very hardy. While the full (narrow-sense structuralist) frameworks that they emerged from have faded from phonological focus, many of the basic ideas are still important in diachronic phonology, in part because they are still important in (synchronic or amphichronic) phonological theory. To the extent that they are relevant to phonological change, basic structuralist ideas at least provide a taxonomy for describing changes in terms of their impact of systems of contrasts (see below); some argue that they should be expected to intervene in phonological change, determining what is possible in (endogenously innovated) change.

3.3 STRUCTURAL PATTERNS: SOME BASIC SEGMENTAL DIFFERENCES IN DIACHRONY

This section considers selected fundamental concepts of broad-sense structuralist phonology as they play out in diachronic phonology: mergers, splits, chain shifts, and how gaps get or don't get filled. A fuller taxonomy is sketched in Salmons (2010), on which this draws. In each case, we note ways in which current discussion treats the issue. The fundamental issue of phonologization remains actively debated, including by Hale et al., Kiparsky, and Bermúdez-Otero (all this volume) along with related discussion in Fox (this volume). The issues are crucial as they relate to the development of contrasts (often through splits of the sort considered here), and hence of the underlying segments which form systems of the type under consideration here; the debate about when phonologization occurs and how it patterns is so heated and long-lasting that we refer readers to those chapters rather than discussing it here. Our simple goal is to fully (if briefly) introduce a few notions, with exemplification, to foreshadow the substantive discussions of foundational and theoretical issues coming in later chapters. Given the focus on the system, structuralist ideas typically begin with mergers and splits, which change the set of contrasts within a system, and to which we now turn.

3.3.1 Merger

Contrasts between segments can be lost by sound change. This can remove phonemes from a system, as in the currently advancing collapse of /a/ and /ɔ/ in North American English, so that pairs like *cot* and *caught* or *don* and *dawn* are no longer distinguished (see Di Paolo 1988 and much work since). Or it can eliminate contrast positionally, as in final laryngeal neutralization, such as in the disappearance of an earlier contrast between syllable- or word-final /s ~ z, t ~ d/, etc. (Iverson & Salmons 2007, 2011). Classic structuralist work was naturally less concerned with the 'mere alteration in the physical properties of phones' (Hoenigswald 1960: 72) and more in the loss of contrasts. Hoenigswald writes (1960: 72–3, see also Bloomfield on the observation of change, 1933: 346–7):

> in this view, sound change proceeds in small 'imperceptible' steps so long as no contrasts are imperiled or other structural changes are called for. When these things do happen, gradual subphonemic alterations 'become' phonemic. In the almost total absence of large-scale, questionnaire-supported observation of speakers in a community, such a picture can be only guesswork.

Since the rise of quantitative variationist work on sound change, a whole field has been dedicated to answering this challenge, and with tools Hoenigswald may not have imagined when he wrote that. Leaving aside issues of lexical effects (see Phillips, this volume) and frequency effects (see Wedel and Bybee, both this volume), we today have a clearer sense of the fine-grained conditioning involved in changes like mergers (see for example, Maguire, this volume). Even today, for instance, much work treats vowels as single points in a two-dimensional ($F_1 \times F_2$) space, while in fact vowel distinctions may be maintained by vowel dynamics (e.g. Purnell 2008) or phonation differences (Di Paolo & Faber 1990), leading to the rise of the notion of a 'near-merger', which must be further distinguished in terms of production versus perception (see Gordon, this volume). Within consonant systems, questions of synchronic 'incomplete neutralization' rage today for production and perception (Iverson & Salmons 2011: §3), though Kharlamov (2012) demonstrates the challenges involved in rigorous laboratory testing of this question.

3.3.2 Split

In contrast to mergers, splits redistribute some occurrences of a sound to another existing sound (primary split) or increase the number of sounds in the inventory (secondary split), as shown below, when conditioning is lost. (With regard to splits in general, our empirical dataset has grown much richer since classical structuralist times, see Ratliff, this volume, on tonal splits.)

(8)   Primary *vs* secondary split

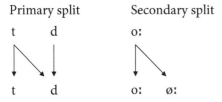

As illustrated, primary split is traditionally seen as rearranging existing distributions rather than changing the overall set of contrasts in a language, though Blust (2012) presents a case for how primary split could reduce an inventory.

A classic secondary split was given in the discussion of Trask at the beginning of this chapter and perhaps the most famous is Germanic *i*-umlaut. As discussed by Kiparsky (this volume) for Old High German, secondary split raises critical problems of how phonologization proceeds, and in particular how it interacts with opacity (see also Iverson & Salmons 2012 on Old Norse *i*-umlaut, and Eckman & Iverson, this volume, on ways in which language contact can cause splits, sometimes modulated by the appearance of lexical strata).

3.3.3 Chain Shifts

Chain shifts involve an interlocking series of changes, where an individual segment takes on some feature or other characteristics of a related one, which in turn interacts in similar fashion with a further segment, famously exemplified by Grimm's Law in obstruent systems and the Great Vowel Shift or the Northern Cities Shift in vowels (see Gordon, this volume). Their treatment goes back to well before structuralism (Sievers 1876, and see Murray, this volume), but was a central phonological concern for Martinet and Hoenigswald, before becoming the focus on phonetic work in variationist circles, where Labov's work stands out for its balance of phonetics and phonology. Building on Sievers, Labov (1994, elsewhere) posited three principles of chain shifting (later refined further), namely that long/tense vowels rise (Principle I), short/lax ones lower (II) and back vowels front (III). That these types of shifts are well attested is laid out in detail by Gordon (this volume), but we note here a couple of difficulties in the mechanisms by which they proceed and in their motivations.

To the first point, chain shifts are widely seen as an alternative to merger (Labov 1994, many others). Yet where low back merger (*cot* ~ *caught*, as above) and the Northern Cities Shift (NCS involving /æ, a, ɔ/ among other vowels, Gordon this volume) meet, Benson et al. (2011) find speakers who show /æ/ raising, the suspected trigger of the NCS, *and* merger. Other 'chains' lack interlocking links, like back vowel fronting (Principle III), which are also called 'solidarity chains'. While /uː/ and /oː/ fronting co-occur closely in American English, nothing about the chronologically earlier fronting of /uː/ forces the movement of /oː/.

Stockwell (1978, see also Labov 1994) identified a potentially more perplexing problem, 'the perseverance problem', or how it is that vocalic chain shifts are so chronic that they appear to be 'a pervasive and persevering characteristic of vowel systems of a certain type' (1978: 337). Simple social motivations seem unlikely to account for this, and some seek structural factors which might prime the pump for these changes, like Salmons et al. (2012) and earlier work which provides evidence that the progress of chain shifts over time follow the patterns of prosodic prominence in the same dialect. The link here is in Child-Directed Speech, where adults appear to use particularly clear realizations of vowels in talking to small children, so that children may systematically acquire slightly different starting points for vowel realizations from those of earlier generations in their own families.

3.3.4 Filling Gaps in Systems

Trubetzkoy's observations on symmetry in phonological systems have largely been confirmed by more recent work. Maddieson (1984: 136), generalizing over the 317 languages that he reviews the sound systems of, writes that '[t]he most prevalent patterns seem to be the so-called "triangular" systems, particularly those of average size, and notably the 5-vowel systems. For example, over a quarter of the 209 languages in the Stanford Phonology Archive have a triangular 5-vowel system consisting of /i, ɛ, a, ɔ, u/, while less than 5 per cent have any of the other 5-vowel configurations; the "square" 4-vowel and 6-vowel systems combined total less than 10 per cent.' And, further, that '[t]he great majority of vowel systems in our sample assume configurations which are predictable from a theory of vowel dispersion ... About 86 per cent of the languages have vowel systems that are built on a basic framework of evenly dispersed peripheral vowels' (Maddieson 1984: 153–4). While by no means *all* languages have symmetrical vowel systems, a large majority do ('dispersion', connects closely with symmetry, as above). This returns us to how and why symmetry exists (or doesn't).

While vowel systems are in a sense 'dispersed', Ohala (1980, also Hall 2011: 36–7) proposes a principle of 'maximum utilization' of features; this links to the work of Clements, discussed above. Not all gaps get filled, for a variety of reasons—some systems simply don't show full symmetry, although no system shows the hypothetical seven-consonant system Ohala (1980: 185, Hall 2011: 36) sketches with seven manner features and five place features:

(9) Hypothetical (unattested) asymmetrical consonant system

	labial	dental	alveolar	retroflex	velar
stop				ɖ	
affricate			ts		
ejective					k'
click		ǀ			
fricative			ɬ		
nasal	m				
liquid			r		

Hall (2011) resolves this apparent conundrum by making a rigorous distinction between contrast and enhancement of contrast, 'representational economy' on the one hand and redundant properties which enhance those contrasts.

In fact, gaps in systems can escape conscious notice to a surprising extent. Iverson & Salmons (2005) call attention to a near-complete phonotactic gap traditionally found in English, namely the absence of tense vowel plus coda /ʃ/. The gap was created by an earlier phonotactic restriction in English (f[ɪ]sk but *f/iː/sk), whereby long vowels didn't occur with coda clusters of the /sk/ type, followed by a change of *sk into [ʃ], leaving the absence of (synchronically expectable) long vowel or diphthong plus the single segment /ʃ/. We leave aside when the shibilant can be considered phonemic, if at all, but the similar phonotactic distribution—viz. a gap with long/tense vowel of diphthong—has figured in the extensive literature about the phonemic status of the velar nasal in languages like English and German. Over the ensuing millennium the gap has been filled by a variety of loanwords from various sources (*gauche* and *quiche* from French, *hashish* from Arabic, etc.). Nonetheless, we can suspect that speakers are aware of the marginal status of this structure given how productive it is in affective or onomatopoeic words like *swoosh* and *sheesh*.

3.3.5 Summary on Structural Patterns

The issues just described—mergers, splits, chain shifts, and the filling of gaps—are key ways of organizing discussions of sound change in classic structuralism and they all remain at the centre of significant debates today, although the ground has shifted. Earlier discussions often focus on the phonology or occasionally on the phonetics. Today, some of the most intriguing work seeks to integrate the phonetics and phonology, such as Hall (2011) from within theoretical phonology and Labov within variation and change.

One further relevant type of diachronic change should be acknowledged. It is implicit in a narrow-sense structuralist viewpoint, although it has not been pursued or even fully recognized until recently. This is 'contrast shift'; that is, a shift in the contrastive structure of an inventory—in the contrastive representation of one or more segments in terms of their featural make-up. Dresher (2009, this volume) traces the idea to Jakobson (1931), and shows that it can fit into contemporary broad-sense structuralist models (see also Purnell & Raimy, this volume). In contrast shift, a shift is recognized in the contrastive status of phonemes, whether or not this is accompanied by mergers, splits, additions or overt shifts in segmental realization.

3.4 CONCLUSION

This chapter introduced and reviewed some history of structuralist historical phonology to contextualize it in two distinct ways: first in terms of some of the central issues that narrow-sense structuralist work on sound change dealt with (and in terms of how those issues are conceived of today) and second in terms of some particularly salient theoretical issues. This brief survey highlights both historical continuities and discontinuities in all this.

The notion of abstract systems of contrasting segments, and a role for such systems in phonological change is a central inheritance from our intellectual forebears. Contemporary work includes much straightforward continuation of those traditions with new tools and frameworks as in the work of Hale et al., Kiparsky, Clements, and Dresher. Others, like Labov (see D'Arcy, this volume) are working to integrate structural considerations into socially informed work on change, while Eckman & Iverson (this volume) argue that L1 structure shapes L2 acquisition and change in contact. Yet others, like Bybee and Ohala, are pushing the boundaries in an effort to minimize the amount of structure and computation that needs to be posited. Whether or not they so actively engage in the battle, almost every chapter in this book builds on or contests the structuralist heritage, and the following discussions will show just how vital structuralist concerns (in the broad and narrow senses) remain to the field.

Structuralist concerns are certainly alive, if still fraught, in contemporary research.

PART II

EVIDENCE AND METHODS IN HISTORICAL PHONOLOGY

....

CHAPTER 4

PHONOLOGICAL RECONSTRUCTION

....

ANTHONY FOX

4.1 INTRODUCTION

THE study of phonological change, as indeed of every other linguistic phenomenon, must be based on an adequate supply of relevant evidence, which may in turn be derived from a number of different sources. Not unnaturally, in the case of phonological change much of the relevant evidence is historical, in the historian's technical sense of being based on written documents of various kinds. Given a suitable methodology for the extraction and interpretation of this evidence (see Minkova, Unger, and Lass, all this volume), we are in principle able to make before-and-after comparisons in real time (see Bowie & Yaeger-Dror, this volume), or even use corpora of recorded speech (see Maguire, this volume), and thus identify the processes of change that have occurred.

But documentary evidence will only take us so far; much of the data we seek lies in preliterate periods and is therefore undocumented; it properly belongs not to *history* but to *prehistory*. This does not mean, however, that it is necessarily irrecoverable, but its recovery requires a different methodology from that which is employed in the interpretation of textual evidence, and the status of the results is also inevitably different. Here we are dealing with the methods of *phonological reconstruction*.

This chapter summarizes the basic procedures of phonological reconstruction (see also Fox 1995). The topic is also considered in most introductions to historical linguistics. Other discussions are included in recent collections, such as Durie & Ross (1996) and Joseph & Janda (2003b).

In the present chapter reconstruction is seen as essentially a practical task which is directed towards the attainment of a specific goal, namely that of determining earlier stages of languages than those that are accessible in documentary sources. But if its results are to command plausibility and credibility it must in some way be answerable to theoretical principles, that is, its procedures should not conflict with theoretical assumptions as to the nature of phonological structure and phonological change. While it is widely acknowledged that reconstruction 'works', in the sense that it delivers plausible results, concerns have been expressed that the theoretical bases on which it rests may nevertheless be in some cases doubtful. One issue here is the status of reconstructions themselves: can they be accepted as real linguistic data, or are they merely quasi-mathematical formulae? Another question relates to the adequacy of the model of linguistic change presupposed by the method: is it compatible with current theoretical views on the nature of linguistic change? Although in this chapter we shall be largely concerned with an exposition of the methodology of phonological reconstruction and an examination of the practical issues involved, we will also look briefly at some of the more theoretical principles which underlie, or perhaps conflict with, this methodology.

Two different methods of reconstruction are generally recognized: the *Comparative Method* and the method of *Internal Reconstruction*. The difference between these two methods does not lie in the ends to which they are directed—both are concerned to reconstruct earlier forms of the languages involved—but in the starting point, and therefore in the procedures required to achieve these ends. As its name indicates, the Comparative Method operates by comparing two or more languages, so that the similarities and differences among the languages provide evidence for their common ancestor; in the case of Internal Reconstruction only a single language is involved, so that the ancestral forms must be established on the basis of those 'internal' characteristics of this single language which point to an earlier state of the language in question. This difference in the starting point means that the two methods are applicable under different circumstances; the Comparative Method requires at least two related languages for its operation, and preferably more (Meillet 1934: 380 proposed a 'three-witness' principle, which requires at least three languages), while Internal Reconstruction is generally applied in the absence of such related languages, as in the case of language isolates or, not infrequently, languages already reconstructed by means of the Comparative Method ('proto-languages'), in order to establish still earlier forms. But since the aims of the two methods are in effect the same, there is inevitably a degree of parallelism in some of the procedures involved, as we shall see below.

Of the two methods, the Comparative Method is more easily reduced to an explicit set of procedures, while Internal Reconstruction is more varied, and a number of different approaches can be recognized within it, which we shall examine below. Hence, although only two methods are generally recognized, Internal Reconstruction subsumes a number of different methods, which have in common only the fact that they are applied to a single language. Furthermore, while the outcomes of the Comparative Method are widely accepted as valid, in some cases those of Internal Reconstruction are regarded as more speculative and therefore less secure, a factor which may account for the much later inclusion of the latter in the accepted repertoire of methods, and the reluctance of some historical linguists to endorse them. However, the more speculative nature of some of the methods of Internal Reconstruction means that it is potentially more powerful, though its results must sometimes be treated with caution.

4.2 THE COMPARATIVE METHOD

The Comparative Method is often taken to be *the* method of reconstruction par excellence, the most reliable and therefore to be preferred. It also has the longer pedigree, though it is not altogether clear when and by whom it was first applied. Language comparison has a long history dating from ancient times; it is implicit in such practical tasks as translation and the learning of foreign languages. It became both more explicit and more significant in the later eighteenth and early nineteenth centuries, when a number of surveys of languages were undertaken, notably those of Pallas in Russia, Hervás in Spain, and Adelung in Germany. However, apart from being largely unsystematic, these surveys have little to do with the later Comparative Method, although they no doubt provided a rich seam of language knowledge that could be mined later. They are basically typological and lack the historical perspective that was to characterize comparative linguistics in the nineteenth century. This historical perspective was provided, in the late eighteenth century, by the 'discovery' of Sanskrit and the realization of its evident historical relationship to the classical languages of Europe. From then on, although typological considerations still continued, language comparison gradually became primarily a historical exercise. (On the early history of historical phonology, see Murray, this volume.)

The development of comparative linguistics in the nineteenth century has been well described in the literature on the history of the discipline (cf. Morpurgo Davies 1998) and does not need to be rehearsed here. But what is worth remarking is that reconstruction itself does not appear to have been the primary aim in the early nineteenth century, and even when it later became so—the best-known example being, perhaps, Schleicher's (1868) reconstruction of a fable in Proto-Indo-European (PIE)—no explicit methodological procedures were presented, though some of the general principles were stated or implied. The reason for this may well lie in the fact that such explicit methodology probably requires a better understanding of the nature and structure of language itself than was available at this time. This understanding had to await the establishment of synchronic linguistics in the early twentieth century and later. The first attempts to formalize the method and provide a linguistic basis for its operation we owe to American structuralist linguists from the 1930s onwards, the culmination of which might legitimately be seen as Henry Hoenigswald's treatise on the subject (Hoenigswald 1960), which serves as the model for all subsequent work. Other contributions were made by members of the Prague School (e.g. Jakobson 1931).

It is also interesting that the term 'comparative method' appears to be of relatively recent origin. The term 'comparative grammar' ('vergleichende Grammatik') was introduced by Bopp in the early nineteenth century (1816), but no use was made of the term 'comparative method' ('vergleichende Methode'). The use of language comparison in order to establish earlier forms of languages was evidently regarded not so much as a *method* in the sense of a set of procedures but more as a general approach. The term 'comparative method' itself was used by Meillet in his book *La méthode comparative en linguistique historique* (1925), but it is uncertain whether he was the first to do so.

It will be evident that—although the Comparative Method evolved and was widely used in the nineteenth century, and this could therefore perhaps be considered its heyday—to understand the methodologies employed we cannot rely on the procedures presented at that time but must interpret the method in terms of more recent conceptions of linguistic structure.

4.2.1 Details of the Method

The application of the Comparative Method can be broken down into a number of discrete steps (see also Kessler, this volume). First, since the Comparative Method operates by comparing forms from related languages, we must establish an appropriate set of forms to be compared. Such a set is called a *correspondence set*. Given such a set, the second step, the establishment of the distinctive phonological entities of the proto-language, can be undertaken. The final step in phonological reconstruction is to interpret these entities in phonetic terms. These steps will be explained and amplified in what follows.

4.2.1.1 *Establishing the Correspondence Sets*

The Comparative Method requires first of all an assumption that the languages to be compared are related, that is, that they are themselves historically derived from the same source; it is, after all, this source that is to be reconstructed. There is inevitably a certain circularity here, since one of the major criteria on which we evaluate the relatedness of the languages is the fact that we can establish correspondences among them, while at the same time we establish correspondences on the assumption of their relatedness. In practice this circularity may not really be vicious, since the two criteria—relatedness and correspondence—are not necessarily sequential but go hand in hand and are mutually supportive. A further requirement is that the forms to be compared are actually 'comparable', though exactly what this means needs to be clarified. To ensure comparability the sounds should be in the same context, and ideally, though not absolutely essentially, this is likely to be obtained by taking 'the same word' in the languages to be compared. But here we encounter a difficulty, since the criteria for establishing 'sameness' among words—essentially semantic and phonetic similarity—are both relative and potentially misleading.

To clarify this, consider the following example. Suppose that we are attempting to reconstruct the consonants of Proto-Romance, the ancestor of the Romance languages. In order to do this we need to establish a set of correspondences in the Romance languages, and we can do this by taking a number of related words in these languages. (1) gives the words for 'dog' in French and Italian:

(1) French: *chien*   [ʃjɛ̃]
     Italian: *cane*   [kaːne]

Since the words have the same meaning and a degree of phonetic similarity we may establish a correspondence between French [ʃ] and Italian [k]. But when we add the Spanish word for 'dog', given in (2), we immediately have a problem:

(2) Spanish: *perro*   [pero]

Should we now include the initial [p] of 'perro' in our correspondence set? Clearly not, although the Spanish word has the same meaning as the French and Italian ones. But it becomes more difficult when we attempt to clarify our criteria for excluding [p]. It cannot be simply that [k] and [p] are phonetically too different; after all, when we compare Latin and Classical Greek we might use the words for 'who' in these languages, which are acknowledged to be comparable, as shown in (3):

(3) Latin: *quis*   [kwis]
     Greek: τις   [tis]

[k] and [t] are surely no less dissimilar than [k] and [p]. But not only is phonetic similarity impossible to quantify, close phonetic similarity is also no guarantee of relatedness. The words for 'god' in Latin and Greek are remarkably similar, with in each case a dental plosive followed by the vowel [e], as in (4):

(4) Latin: *deus*   [deus]
     Greek: θεός   [tʰeos]

Nevertheless, these words are not considered to be related and cannot be used in the Comparative Method.

Neither sameness nor difference of meaning nor phonetic similarity or dissimilarity, though they may play a part, are sufficient criteria for establishing correspondences. The solution here is a methodological one, based on the *regularity of the correspondence*: there is a regular correspondence between French [ʃ] and Italian [k] in certain contexts, and between Latin [kw] and Greek [t], but no such regular correspondence between Spanish [p] and Italian [k] or French [ʃ], nor between Greek [tʰ] and Latin [d] (the regular Latin correspondence with initial Greek [tʰ] is in fact [f]). French [ʃ] and Italian [k] correspond, for example, in the pairs given in (5), among many others:

(5) French: *chèvre, cher, chaîne, cheval*
     Italian: *capra, caro, catena, cavallo*

The regularity of a correspondence is therefore a crucial principle in establishing our set. But there is a further issue. Regularity of correspondences is itself the result of an assumed regularity of phonological change. Such regularity was, of course, a central tenet of late nineteenth-century neogrammarian theory, with the axiom 'sound laws have no exceptions', but it has been the target of considerable criticism since, and ample evidence has been provided that phonological change is not always regular, since changes may be 'diffused' throughout the vocabulary of a language at different rates (compare Murray, Bermúdez-Otero, and Phillips, all this volume; and, on the implications of regularity and irregularity for the Comparative Method, see Durie & Ross 1996.)

The regularity of correspondences may also be disturbed by borrowing, either from related languages or (as has happened on a large scale with the Romance languages) from the earlier source language itself, in this case Latin. French has, for example, borrowed extensively from both Italian and Latin, so that the correspondence between French [ʃ] and Italian [k] does not always hold, even in etymologically related words, e.g. French *canal, capital* corresponding to Italian *canale, capitale*.

These problems do not necessarily invalidate the Comparative Method as such, however, though they do impose some stringent requirements on the selection of terms in the correspondence set, and where these requirements cannot be met—where, for example, we cannot distinguish legitimate from borrowed words—this may limit its accuracy.

There are other obvious requirements for the selection of words on which to base our correspondence set. First, we must clearly exclude loanwords, which, as noted above, can distort the evidence by providing spurious correspondences. Second, we must exclude words whose form may be the result of onomatopoeia, and whose similarity across languages may therefore not reflect a historical relationship.

4.2.1.2 *Establishing the Proto-Phonemes*

The result of the first stage of the phonological reconstruction should be a series of correspondence sets. In comparing some older Indo-European languages (Greek, Sanskrit, Latin, Gothic, and Old Church Slavonic), for example, we are able to establish sets such as those of (6):

(6)	Greek	Sanskrit	Latin	Gothic	O.Ch. Slav.
	t	t	t	θ	t
	d	d	d	t	d

The next step in the reconstruction is to determine the distinctive phonological units of the proto-language of which these sets are reflexes. We must first consider, however, what kind of units these are. Nineteenth-century linguists, who had no explicit phonological theory, assumed that they were reconstructing *sounds*, and the classical reconstructions of Brugmann (Brugmann & Delbrück 1886–1900), which include much phonetic detail, reflect this. But in the light of twentieth-century phonological theory this view has been modified, and the assumption is that we are reconstructing phonological units of some sort. However, in the course of the last century a variety of different units have been postulated in phonological theories. For much of the twentieth century the basic phonological unit was the phoneme (though of course defined in a variety of different ways by different 'schools'), but theoretical phonologists have also proposed other units with different properties, notably distinctive features and the 'systematic' or 'underlying' phonemes of classical generative phonology (largely equivalent to the morphophonemes of structuralist phonology), while phonological structure has been viewed in 'non-linear' terms, and in terms of 'processes' and more recently 'constraints'. It is not yet clear to what extent the methodology of reconstruction can be interpreted in terms of these various different approaches; what seems evident, however, and what will be demonstrated here, is that the procedures are largely dependent on establishing *contrasts* among occurring items, and determining their *distribution*, and they are therefore more compatible with traditional phonemes than with the units of some more recent phonological theories. Therefore, the discussion will be based on this conclusion. Once the reconstruction has been carried out, of course, we are free to reinterpret the results in terms of whatever phonological theory we wish.

In order to understand the operation of the methods of reconstruction we must first identify the processes of phonological change, as seen from a phonemic perspective. In these terms, changes are purely *phonetic*, with no phonological implications, if they do not affect the inventory of phonemes but merely change the realization of the allophones of these phonemes. For example, the glottalization of voiceless plosives or the nasalization of vowels before a nasal consonant in some varieties of English merely result in additional allophones of the phonemes in question and do not, therefore, constitute (underlying) phonological changes. Only if the inventory of phonemes is affected, or if the change results in the reallocation of sounds to a different phoneme, can we legitimately speak of a *phonological* (phonemic) change. In practice, phonological change is of two basic types: *split* and *merger* (see Salmons & Honeybone, this volume); phonetic change is sometimes called *shift*. When, for example, PIE *o became *a in the Germanic languages it *merged* with existing *a, resulting in the loss of a phoneme. The operation of 'i-umlaut' (i-mutation) in the Germanic languages, on the other hand, whereby, for example, Proto-Germanic *muːsi(z) became Old English /myːs/ ('mice'), involved the *split* of earlier *u and *o into two, creating the new front vowels /y/ and /ø/. This kind of split involves the 'phonologization' of an allophonic difference and this can be seen as a two-stage process: (i) the (phonetic) process whereby allophones become different in different contexts—here the fronting of back vowels before *i or *j in the following syllable—and (ii) the loss of the conditioning context, resulting in the change of status of the sounds from allophonic variants to independent phonemes (see Hale, Kissock, & Reiss, Kiparsky, and Bermúdez-Otero, all this volume, for further discussion of phonologization). Stage (i) is purely phonetic, while stage (ii) is the real phonological change. Since the latter is not actually a 'sound change' but the result of a change elsewhere, structuralist phonologists designated this kind of change *secondary split*. The term *primary split* was used for cases which do not result in a new phoneme and which are, in effect, split + merger, since the new sound created by the change merges with an existing phoneme. For example, the change of /s/ to /r/ in Latin ('rhotacism', e.g. *flos* ('flower') but *floris* < *flosis) involves the split of /s/ into /s/ and /r/ and the merger of the /r/ with the existing /r/. Although this process does not create a new phoneme, it results in the change of allegiance of certain allophones from one phoneme to another, and is thus of phonological significance.

These categories of merger, primary split, and secondary split are important for our understanding of the processes of comparative reconstruction since they allow us to distinguish different kinds of phonological change and consequently to recognize a number of different scenarios for comparative reconstruction. Assuming for expository purposes a minimal comparison between two languages, which gives correspondence sets of two items, we find the following scenarios:

Scenario 1: *No change*

Here we have two proto-phonemes *A and *B in the proto-language, and no mergers or splits:

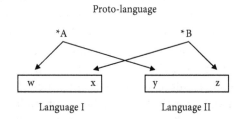

The arrows join the proto-phonemes in the proto-language to their reflexes in the attested languages I and II. Here, w and y represent the reflexes of proto-phoneme *A in Language I and Language II respectively, and x and z the reflexes of proto-phoneme *B. By following the lines we identify the correspondences: this scenario will yield two correspondence sets, w/y and x/z. Reconstruction of the proto-phonemes simply involves equating each correspondence set with a proto-phoneme.

An example of this scenario is the development of PIE *p and *t in Greek and Latin. There is a correspondence between /p/ and /t/ in these languages, for example in πατήρ [patɛːr] and *pater*, 'father', giving the sets p/p and t/t, from which we may reconstruct the proto-phonemes *p and *t. Note, however, that it is unnecessary for the items in the correspondence set to be phonetically the same, as they are here; the scenario is equally applicable to cases where the sounds are different. If, therefore, we add the Germanic reflexes of these sounds, /f/ and /θ/, giving the correspondence sets p/p/f and t/t/θ, we obtain the same result, though here we must make a decision regarding the phonetic properties of the proto-phonemes (see below).

Scenario 2: *Merger in one language*

Here the pattern is similar, except that the proto-phonemes merge in one of the languages:

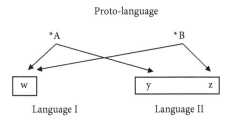

Here, the proto-phonemes *A and *B merge in language I but not in language II. Again, this yields two correspondence sets, w/y and w/z (i.e. w in Language I corresponds to *both* y *and* z in Language II). Note that although there is only one phoneme here in Language I, we still have two correspondence sets, as the phonemes are distinct in Language II, and it is therefore still possible to reconstruct two proto-phonemes in the proto-language by deriving each set from a proto-phoneme.

Consider the merger of *o and *a in Germanic, referred to above. Taking Gothic and Latin we can establish two correspondence sets: a/a (e.g. *akrs/ager* ('field')) and a/o (e.g. *ahtau/octo* ('eight'), yielding two proto-phonemes *a and *o, despite the fact that Gothic has only one phoneme here.

Scenario 3: *Merger in both languages*
Here the merger of the two proto-phonemes takes place in both the languages compared:

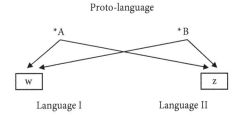

Since there is now only one phoneme in both languages there is only one correspondence set w/z. We are therefore forced (wrongly) to reconstruct only a single proto-phoneme. This scenario therefore does *not* permit us to reconstruct the proto-phonemes of the proto-language. In this scenario the comparative method fails.

The merger of *a and *o in Germanic again provides an example. A similar merger took place in Sanskrit, hence the reflexes of the proto-phonemes *a and *o in both Gothic and Sanskrit are both /a/. Comparison based on these two languages will give only one correspondence set a/a, allowing us to reconstruct only one proto-phoneme instead of two.

Scenario 4: *Primary split*

In this scenario, one of the proto-phonemes (*A) splits in one language, with one of the sounds merging with another phoneme:

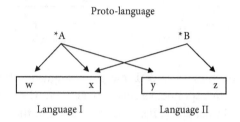

Proto-language

Language I   Language II

Both /w/ and /x/ in language I are reflexes of proto-phoneme *A, which has split; but /x/ has merged with the reflex of proto-phoneme *B. This now produces three correspondence sets, w/y, x/y, and x/z. Three correspondence sets should require us to reconstruct three proto-phonemes, but we only want two. We need a way of distinguishing this case from one where there are three proto-phonemes. Before considering the solution, we shall discuss the case of secondary split.

Scenario 5: *Secondary split*

This scenario is the same as scenario 4 except that the split of proto-phoneme *A in Language I results in a new phoneme:

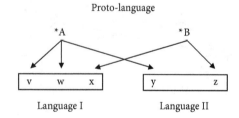

Proto-language

Language I   Language II

This scenario again results in three correspondence sets: v/y, w/y, and x/z, and again this is not what we want. Again, therefore, we need a way of distinguishing this case from one where there are three proto-phonemes.

The solution to both scenarios 4 and 5 depends on the *distribution* of the sets. Split regularly involves the development of an allophone of a phoneme into an independent phoneme, generally as a result of the loss of the context in which it occurs. Provided that this context is preserved in one of the languages compared, it is possible to reconstruct the original proto-phoneme. This is done by examining the contexts in which the correspondence sets are found; where the sets are *in complementary distribution* they will be derived from the same phoneme. This procedure is, of course, exactly the same as the establishment of phonemes in structuralist phonology, though with some differences which will be discussed shortly.

An example of primary split is found in Latin rhotacism. Early Latin *s became /r/ between vowels but remained as /s/ elsewhere. The /r/ merged with existing /r/. When we compare Latin with the related language Oscan we get three correspondence sets: s/s in cases where both languages have /s/ and rhotacism has not occurred, for example Latin *quis* [kwis] and Oscan *pis* ('who'); r/s where rhotacism has occurred in Latin but Oscan retains the /s/, for example Latin *foret* and Oscan *fusít* ('be', imperfect subjunctive); and r/r where both languages have reflexes of the original *r, for example Latin *hortus* and Oscan *húrz* ('garden'). The first two sets are found to be in complementary distribution, since the context in which rhotacism occurs is complementary to contexts where it does not. Hence we can reduce the complementary sets to a single set and reconstruct only two proto-phonemes here (for a recent discussion of primary split see Blust 2012).

Secondary split can be exemplified by i-mutation in the Germanic languages. This takes place in North and West Germanic but not in Gothic, hence Old English often has two phonemes, unmutated and mutated, where Gothic has only one. So, for example, Gothic *bloma* ('flower') corresponds to Old English *bloma*, but Gothic *domjan* ('to judge') corresponds to (early) Old English *døman*. Again the two resulting correspondence sets o/o and o/ø are in complementary distribution (the set o/ø occurs in cases where in Gothic it is followed by -i or -j while o/o occurs elsewhere) and can be reduced to a single proto-phoneme.

The basic procedure for establishing the proto-phonemes using the Comparative Method can therefore be summarized as follows: each correspondence set derives from a proto-phoneme in the proto-language, *unless* the sets are in complementary distribution; complementary sets derive from a single proto-phoneme.

Though this procedure resembles the process of establishing phonemes in structuralist phonology, there are some differences. First, we are, of course, dealing with *sets* rather than with individual sounds. Determining whether these sets are in complementary distribution is therefore not quite the same as examining the distribution of sounds. In particular, the context for the sets is, in fact, itself a *set*. This is evident from the Germanic case cited above; although the distinction between o and ø is found in Old English and not in Gothic, the context which shows them to be complementary is found in Gothic and not in Old English. We therefore need to inspect the set of contexts to determine complementary distribution. As another example consider the reconstruction of Uto-Aztecan plosives (Cowan 1971, from Voegelin). In Tohono O'odham (formerly called Papago) there are two sounds, [tʃ] and [t], which are in complementary distribution in initial position, the former occurring before high vowels, the latter elsewhere. But they contrast word-finally and must therefore be considered distinct phonemes. If we restrict the context to Tohono O'odham, sets containing these sounds will not be in complementary distribution and must therefore be derived from different proto-phonemes. When we bring in the related language Hopi, however, we find that those cases where Tohono O'odham has final [tʃ] are followed in Hopi by a high vowel, but cases where Tohono O'odham has final [t] are followed in Hopi by a non-high vowel.

Thus, the context for the correspondence set is itself a correspondence set, including the contexts of both Tohono O'odham and Hopi.

4.2.1.3 *Assigning Phonetic Properties*

It will be clear from the above that we are dealing with contrast and complementarity of the sets and therefore also of the proto-phonemes themselves. The procedure is not concerned with the phonetic nature of the entities as such. The use of algebraic symbols for the sounds and the proto-phonemes in the above scenarios is intended to emphasize this fact. However, although we clearly cannot know precisely how the proto-phonemes were pronounced, it is nevertheless important that we attempt to assign at least basic phonetic properties if we are to obtain a coherent picture of the phonology of the proto-language and of the phonological changes involved.

A number of points need to be borne in mind in assigning phonetic properties to our proto-phonemes. In the first place, phonological entities such as phonemes are not sounds; classical phoneme theory regarded them either as collections of different sounds (their allophones) or as abstract entities which could be *realized* by sounds. In some cases it may be possible to infer the phonetic properties of allophones of the proto-phonemes from their subsequent developments (e.g. if *k develops into a palatal sound in one context we might conclude that it had a palatal allophone in this context in the proto-language) but in general we are restricted to establishing the general sound type to which the realizations of the phoneme are likely to belong and we cannot provide much detail. The second point to be made, perhaps an obvious one, is that the proto-phonemes must be phonetically *distinct* from one another (this is, of course, implicit in the procedures used in establishing the proto-phonemes in the first place).

To exemplify some of the issues that arise in assigning phonetic properties consider the contrasting correspondence sets of (7):

(7) (i)   t   t   d
     (ii)   d   t   d

Since all the sounds in these sets are dental, we are entitled, in the absence of any further evidence, to conclude that the proto-phonemes are both dental. Since there is a preponderance of [t] in set (i) and of [d] in set (ii), a reasonable assumption is that the proto-phoneme of (i) is *t and of (ii) *d. Underlying this assumption is a principle of 'economy', according to which the solution that requires the smallest number of phonetic changes is to be preferred. Suppose, however, that we add the additional correspondence set of (8):

(8) (iii) d   d   d

Since all the sounds of set (iii) are [d] we would certainly wish to postulate *d as the proto-phoneme here, but although set (i) can still be reconstructed as *t we cannot now reconstruct set (ii) as *d, given that this sound is already pre-empted by set (iii). We must opt for some other sound, related in character to [d], such as, for example, a dental fricative.

This situation is by no means a purely theoretical one. In comparing the sibilants of the Semitic languages Akkadian, Hebrew, Aramaic, Ethiopic, and Arabic, for example, we can establish the correspondence sets of (9) (Cowan 1971, from Bergsträsser), which are not in complementary distribution:

(9) (i)   s   s   s   s   s
    (ii)   ʃ   ʃ   ʃ   s   s

We should evidently take the reconstructed proto-phoneme for (i) to be *s; in (ii) ʃ preponderates and we therefore assume it to be *ʃ. However, a further set, again contrasting with these, is (iii) in 10:

(10) (iii) ʃ   ś   s   ʃ   ʃ

This set presumably has an equal claim to being derived from *ʃ. (The sound transcribed with ś in Hebrew may have been a lateral fricative—Steiner 1998.) The solution in such cases will depend on a number of factors, but it is clear that, contrary to what is sometimes suggested, we cannot merely take the majority sound as our proto-phoneme. Again we must assume a sibilant sound distinct from both [s] and [ʃ].

We may invoke a number of other principles in solving problems of this sort. The first is the phonetic plausibility of the changes which the solution presupposes. Although we cannot rule out unusual changes—some are well attested in the literature—some changes are clearly improbable or at least unlikely due to our knowledge of diachronic typology. A solution which requires a change k > s, for example, is unexceptionable, since such a change is widely attested, whereas one which requires s > k is highly suspect. A related principle is the typology of synchronic phonological systems. Systems tend to have certain properties and to fall into certain types, so that a system of proto-phonemes which has these properties or conforms to a known type is more plausible than one which does not (see Kümmel, this volume, on diachronic and synchronic typology). For example, both vowel and consonant systems tend to be roughly symmetrical, with parallels between front and back vowels and between voiced and voiceless obstruents. Though such parallelism is, of course, not obligatory, and there are numerous exceptions, the tendency is still valid, and can assist in choosing between alternative solutions.

The assignment of phonetic properties to proto-phonemes is not a precise procedure and will very much depend on the particular circumstances. Some recent controversies, such as the so-called 'Glottalic Theory' of Indo-European plosives (Gamkrelidze & Ivanov 1995), depend crucially on the weight given to different principles, such as typological factors, and it is evident that there is not necessarily clear resolution in these cases.

4.2.2 The Comparative Method and Morphological Reconstruction

Our concern in this chapter is with phonological reconstruction but the Comparative Method is not restricted to phonology. In fact most of the earlier reconstructions of Indo-European were based on identifying morphological relationships among languages. However, morphemes are double entities, with both grammatical and phonological properties, and there is reason to believe that most morphological reconstruction is actually primarily concerned with the latter.

Consider, for example, the reconstruction of the case forms of PIE given in (11). These are the forms of the 'dative' case of the word for 'foot' in Sanskrit, Greek, and Latin.

(11) *Sanskrit   Greek   Latin*
       padeː   podi   pediː

Since these forms are grammatically more or less equivalent ('more or less' because the dative case does not have completely identical functions in the three languages) we might seek to reconstruct the PIE dative case on this basis. Such a reconstruction would, however, be entirely spurious. The Sanskrit and Latin forms derive from the original dative form with the suffix *-ei, but the Greek form derives from the original locative form with the suffix *-i. If we want to establish equivalence of inflectional forms this must be done on a phonological basis, as in (12).

(12) *Sanskrit   Greek   Latin*
       padi   podi   pede

These forms are, etymologically speaking, equivalent, since their suffixes all derive from the same source *-i (the PIE locative affix), but morphologically they are completely anomalous: the Sanskrit form is labelled 'locative', the Greek 'dative', and the Latin 'ablative'. Hence it is clear that, in this and many other cases, correspondences among grammatical morphemes can only be determined on a phonological basis and not in terms of their grammatical functions.

4.2.3 The Comparative Method and Phonological Change

One principle on which the process of reconstruction by the Comparative Method depends is, as noted, the assumption that the languages compared are related, deriving from the same source. But by repeating the process, reconstructing further ancestral languages by comparing proto-languages themselves, the method may result in a 'family tree' of related languages, such as that often presented for the Indo-European,

Semitic, or Finno-Ugric languages as a whole. The 'family tree' can therefore be regarded as implicit in the method itself.

The difficulty is that the 'tree' model of language relationships, with its progressive branching, carries with it an implication that discrete splitting is the way that languages actually change. But this is clearly rarely the case; languages change and develop in a variety of ways, including language contact and borrowing and in some cases convergence. We could object to the Comparative Method, therefore, on the grounds that it embodies too narrow a conception of language change, and indeed that it is unable to handle cases of convergence and borrowing.

However, it is also arguable that this is not really the aim of the method; its purpose is to reconstruct only those features of proto-languages which have *continuity* with features of the attested languages which are used in the comparison. It deals, in other words, with linguistic *inheritance* rather than borrowing or mixture. Under this interpretation, the limitations of the tree model may constitute a restriction on the applicability of the method, but they do not invalidate it.

4.3 INTERNAL RECONSTRUCTION

As mentioned earlier, Internal Reconstruction differs from the Comparative Method in being based on the features of one language, and it is therefore appropriately applied to languages without relatives, such as language isolates, for example Basque (cf. Trask 1997), or reconstructed proto-languages. In order to distinguish the results from those of the Comparative Method, languages reconstructed by these means are referred to as 'pre-languages', as opposed to 'proto-languages', and we may also refer to 'pre-phonemes' in preference to 'proto-phonemes'.

The method arose in the late nineteenth century though, as with the Comparative Method, it is difficult to give a precise date or ascribe its development to any specific scholar, especially since arguably it arose as a natural extension of the Comparative Method and was not, therefore, originally considered a distinct method. Further, like the Comparative Method, it was not given an explicit formulation at the time, and had to await later developments in order to receive proper recognition. Nevertheless, both Brugmann (1876) and Saussure (1879) can be credited with early applications of the method, and it was the corroboration of the latter's hypotheses on the Indo-European vowel system, including postulating 'laryngeals', in particular by the decipherment of Hittite, that gave it credibility and respectability.

As already stated, Internal Reconstruction is not a single method, but a group of approaches having in common their reliance on internal features of the language. However, these approaches do have other things in common, as we shall see. Here we shall examine the methods under three headings which are here termed 'Historical morphophonemics', 'Regularization of systems', and 'Universal and typological reconstruction'.

4.3.1 Historical Morphophonemics

Of the methods of Internal Reconstruction, this is the closest in terms of its procedures and underlying assumptions to the Comparative Method. It is also the most circumscribed. But if the Comparative Method lends itself to interpretation in terms of structuralist phonemes, Historical morphophonemics, as the name suggests, is based on the *morphophoneme*, and since this to some extent equates to the 'underlying' phoneme of generative phonology we may consider this approach to be compatible with the latter (for more, see King 1969). The method involves interpreting morphophonemes as reflexes of earlier phonemes, which may thus be reconstructed. As in the case of the Comparative Method, we may consider a number of scenarios and the possibilities that they provide for the reconstruction of pre-phonemes.

Though morphophonemes were not well defined in structuralist phonology, they are best regarded as a set of morphologically related phonemes which occur in alternate forms of morphemes ('allomorphs'). The principle is that different phonological changes occur in different contexts, resulting in different phonemes in different forms of the same morpheme. By reducing these different phonemes to a single invariant form we establish the original pre-phoneme from which they are derived. The procedure is parallel to that employed in the Comparative Method to the extent that we establish a correspondence set (here, the set of alternating phonemes) and establish the pre-phonemes on the basis of contrast and distribution of the sets.

For an example we may turn again to rhotacism in Latin, according to which /s/ became /r/ between vowels, giving alternations such as *flos/flor-*. We examined this process above in terms of the Comparative Method; since it did not take place in Oscan, we were able to compare the Latin and Oscan situations and establish correspondence sets. However, we can also reconstruct the earlier situation on the basis of Latin alone, using Internal Reconstruction. The alternation between /s/ and /r/ constitutes a morphophoneme S and provides us with a correspondence set s/r which is distinct from the set r/r which we could establish in the case of non-alternating phonemes. We assume that the s/r alternation developed from a single phoneme so that the later alternating morphophoneme corresponds to an earlier phoneme which we can reconstruct as *s.

As with the Comparative Method, there is a threefold procedure here: establishing the correspondence sets, determining the pre-phonemes, and assigning phonetic properties. The first stage will generally involve taking allomorphs of morphemes, but again with the proviso that the alternation of phonemes in these allomorphs is *regular*. This proviso excludes the irregular alternations found in cases of *suppletion*, such as *good/bett(er)* or *go/went*, which clearly cannot be used to form correspondence sets.

For the second stage, determining the pre-phonemes, we can again recognize different scenarios.

Scenario 6: *Secondary split*

Pre-language

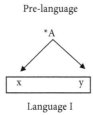

Language I

In this scenario pre-phoneme *A splits into two, creating a new phoneme through the loss of the conditioning context. Since the creation of the new phoneme depends on the loss of the conditioning context, the original pre-phoneme cannot be reconstructed in the absence of comparative evidence (which is not available in the case of Internal Reconstruction) unless there is evidence of an alternating relationship between the phonemes, i.e. they constitute a morphophoneme, in which case we can establish a correspondence set x/y and recover the original pre-phoneme *A.

An example is found in Verner's Law in the Germanic languages, according to which pairs of voiceless and voiced fricatives were produced as reflexes of the Indo-European voiceless plosives, the voicing being dependent on the position of the original Indo-European accent. The accentual context was lost in Germanic but it is still possible to reconstruct a pre-phoneme on the basis of the alternation between the phonemes in the Germanic strong verb paradigms (though it is necessary to use comparative evidence from Sanskrit in order to determine the original context for the alternation). We thus derive the correspondence sets f/v, θ/ð, x/ɣ, and s/r, each of which will correspond to an original pre-phoneme.

Scenario 7: *Primary split*

Pre-language

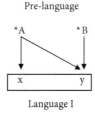

Language I

In this scenario, pre-phoneme *A splits into two alternating phonemes x and y, as in Scenario 1, but y is also the reflex of pre-phoneme *B, so that we have split + merger. This will produce two correspondence sets, since we get the set x/y as the reflex of *A, in which the two phonemes alternate, and the set y/y as the reflex of *B, which does not produce an alternation.

This is the case with Latin rhotacism, as discussed above. Another example is word-final devoicing in German, which results in alternating phonemes in final and non-final positions, e.g. *Bund* ([bunt]) *vs Bund(es)* ([bund-]) ('union'), with the alternating phonemes /t/ and /d/. But there is also a non-alternating phoneme /t/ in *bunt* ([bunt]) *vs bunt(es)* ([bunt-]) ('coloured'). This gives the two correspondence sets t/d and t/t, allowing us to reconstruct two pre-phonemes.

Scenario 8: *Merger*

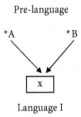

Pre-language

*A   *B

x

Language I

With the Comparative Method, total merger of phonemes can be reconstructed provided that the merger has not taken place in all of the languages compared. With Internal Reconstruction such a merger cannot be reconstructed since there is no evidence of the earlier state of affairs. If the merger is only *partial*, then reconstruction is possible; this has been dealt with under 'primary split', above. There may nevertheless be limited scope for reconstruction, even with total merger, but this requires an extension of the methodology and will be considered under 'universal and typological reconstruction' (section 4.3.3).

Assigning phonetic properties to the pre-phonemes follows exactly the same principles as with the Comparative Method and does not need to be restated here.

4.3.2 System Regularization

Historical morphophonemics works by eliminating alternations, reversing the processes through which these arose and thereby reconstructing the earlier, non-alternating, state. (It is sometimes stated that this is the elimination of irregularities, though this is based on the assumption that phonemic alternations are irregular, which is certainly not always the case.) It is, however, somewhat limited, since it is restricted to specific cases. It is possible to reconstruct on a rather wider scale, however, by means of a process which may be termed 'system regularization'.

System regularization involves extending the principle by which alternations are eliminated to whole classes or categories. This generally involves morphological paradigms but this in turn has implications for phonological features, too. Many languages have different classes of, for example, nouns, verbs, or adjectives, which may have paradigms with the same grammatical categories, such as case, number, or tense, but with different phonological realizations of these categories. The 'declensions' and 'conjugations' of

Latin or Greek, or the different 'ablaut' patterns of Germanic strong verbs, are examples of this. The method works by assuming that such different classes must originally
have had similar forms and that we may reconstruct these forms by eliminating the
differences between them. This is, of course, a bold assumption, and the method must
therefore be used with caution and only in appropriate cases which have adequate phonological justification.

To illustrate the operation of the method we may consider the first three classes of
Germanic strong verbs. In Old English, these have forms such as those of (13).

(13)		Present	Past (Sing.)	Past Participle	
	Class I	*grīpan*	*grāp*	*gripen*	'grasp'
	Class II	*cēosan*	*cēas*	*coren*	'choose'
	Class III	*bindan*	*band*	*bunden*	'bind'
		helpan	*healp*	*holpen*	'help'

Application of the Comparative Method to those forms—drawing on other Germanic
languages such as Gothic and Old High German—allows us to reconstruct the forms of
(14) as the vowels of earlier forms of these verb classes.

(14)		Present	Past	Past Participle
	Class I	*-iː-	*-ai-	*-i-
	Class II	*-iu-	*-au-	*-u-
	Class III	*-i-/*-e-	*-a-	*-u-

We can now proceed to the 'regularization' of these forms. First, we can eliminate the
i/e alternation of Class III, since it can be shown to be dependent on the context: *i is
found before a nasal consonant and *e elsewhere. We can therefore reconstruct an
original pre-phoneme *e here. Further regularization can be achieved if we analyse the
long vowel *iː of Class I as *ii, making it parallel to the pattern of Class II: we now have
-ii-, -ai-, -i- to match -iu-, -au-, -u-, so that both classes have the pattern i + i/u, a + i/u,
Ø + i/u (where Ø = zero vowel). We can now add Class III; having established that the
pre-phoneme of the present stem of this class is *e, with *i as a contextual variant, we
can extend this conclusion to Classes I and II, by considering the *i of this stem as likewise derived from *e when followed by a high vowel, so that this stem has the vowels *ei
(Class I) and *eu (Class II), and the overall pattern is e + i u, a + i/u and Ø + i/u. Class III
conforms to this pattern in the first two stems (without the characteristic vowel), but the
*u of the past participle is apparently irregular. In the case of Classes I and II, the vowel
of this stem is Ø + the characteristic vowel of the class, viz. *i or *u, so that the *i or *u
is left as the sole syllabic element of the stem; Class III does not have such a characteristic vowel, and we find *u here. But verbs of this class have a nasal, /l/ or /r/ following
the vowel, which is the equivalent of the *i and *u of Classes I and II (these, including
the *i and *u, can thus be grouped together as *resonants*). A plausible reconstruction
is therefore to assume that the pre-form of this stem was Ø + resonant, and that the *u
which we reconstruct for this form in Class III by means of the Comparative Method

is a reflex of Ø. We therefore effectively establish a correspondence set u/Ø, where *u appears before a resonant and *Ø elsewhere. The pre-phoneme is *Ø and the syllabic 'slot' in the syllable will have originally been filled by the following resonant, *i and *u in Classes I and II, and a syllabic consonant in Class III. The end result of this process is the regularity of the whole system, which now uniformly contains the series *e, *a, *Ø, each of which is followed by a resonant (N, l, r, i, or u).

We see from this example that this method of Internal Reconstruction involves the elimination of all alternations and therefore the regularization and simplification of whole systems. The implication is that the earlier forms of languages are assumed to lack any such alternations and differences, and that these arose in the course of the language's history. Such an assumption is, of course, highly speculative, and this may be considered a weakness of this particular method. Nevertheless, the method is extremely powerful in yielding earlier forms.

4.3.3 Universal and Typological Reconstruction

The final method of internal reconstruction that we shall consider is the most speculative. To some extent it goes beyond purely internal methods, since it invokes general properties of languages, which may be either universal or typological (see Kümmel, this volume, for some further relevant discussion). In the former case the method relies on language universals, which are regarded as determining the synchronic properties of languages and/or the diachronic processes of change. On the negative side these properties may constrain possible reconstructions, since we are not at liberty to postulate earlier states of languages or processes of change which do not conform to the universals (Comrie 1993).

Thus, in phonology we may assume universal phonetic processes, for example, the palatalization of velar consonants in the neighbourhood of front vowels. A reconstruction which assumes the reverse (palatalization with back vowels, or velarization with front vowels) would be ruled out. Similarly, if all languages must have, say, vowels, then we cannot reconstruct an earlier stage without them. In all such cases our reconstructions will seek to establish earlier forms in compliance with these universal constraints.

There is also a positive side to these constraints, however, in particular with typological properties of languages, since here we may use the constraints not merely to disallow certain reconstructions but also to suggest alternatives. For example, the traditional reconstruction of Indo-European plosives postulates three series: voiceless unaspirated, voiced unaspirated, and voiced aspirated (or 'breathy voiced'). It has been argued, however, that such a system is typologically deviant, since languages should not have voiced aspirates if they do not have voiceless ones (Jakobson 1958). A possible solution is suggested by the typological constraints themselves: either we should postulate an additional series of voiceless aspirates or we should reallocate phonetic properties to all or part of the system (as is done in 'Glottalic Theory'; see Gamkrelidze & Ivanov 1995, and also Kümmel, this volume). This is related to the notion of *markedness*; we opt for 'unmarked' properties, categories, and structures in preference to 'marked' ones in, for example, syllable structures or segment inventories.

A further application of typology is perhaps best illustrated from syntax, though it is also possible in phonology. A commonly accepted syntactic typology (Greenberg 1966) assumes that languages fall into two basic types, VO and OV, according to the order of verb and object, and this is considered also to be reflected in the ordering of other elements, such as adjective (A) and noun (N), and in the use of prepositions or post-positions. The principle here is that these different cases 'harmonize', so that VO languages will tend to have NA and prepositions, while OV languages will have AN and postpositions. In reconstructing syntactic systems, therefore, we will assume such harmony, and restore it where it is not found. English, for example, has VO but AN, so we should reconstruct an earlier stage which had either NA or OV (the latter is the generally accepted solution).

Such cases of harmonizing features appear to be less easy to identify in phonology, and the scope for the application of this particular method may therefore be more limited. However, potential instances may perhaps be found in the case of prosodic features such as accent and quantity. Prague School phonologists (e.g. Trubetzkoy 1939), attempted to establish harmonic relations between accent and quantity types in languages. Such relations could in principle be used to reconstruct earlier characteristics in an analogous manner to syntactic features.

Again it can be seen that such methods are potentially very powerful since they take us well beyond the attested features of the language concerned. However, they rest on assumptions which might be questioned, since they presuppose that the pre-language being reconstructed was typologically consistent and harmonizing, which, to judge from existing languages, is by no means universally true. The method must therefore be used with due circumspection.

4.4 THE STATUS OF RECONSTRUCTIONS

The status of reconstructed forms, whether produced by the Comparative Method or by Internal Reconstruction, is an important theoretical issue that was mentioned at the outset. Since these forms are by definition not attested but are the product of applying the formal procedures of reconstruction methodology, they themselves have often been seen as merely abstract formulae rather than genuine linguistic forms. This 'formalist' (better: 'formulist') view contrasts with the 'realist' view, which regards the reconstructed forms as real languages, which happen not to have been attested (see Fox 1995: 9–14).

The dichotomy is significant, since it affects the whole purpose and rationale of reconstruction, but in a sense it is perhaps unnecessary. On the one hand, a reconstructed language is not actually attested (that is why we must reconstruct it) but is the result of the application of formal methods, as outlined earlier; furthermore, we can never reconstruct all the features of a proto- or pre-language, nor be completely certain as to the phonetic features involved, so it can never be a complete language. On the other hand, there is very little point in reconstructing a formula; if our reconstructed language is to have any value at all we really need to assume that the features we reconstruct are real linguistic features, and indeed in applying our methods we make use of their status as real language in employing, for example, typological or universal factors and in invoking such notions as contrast and distribution, which are properties of real languages.

It is possible to reconcile these positions if we recognize the double nature of reconstruction. On the one hand it is a *formal procedure*, a set of fairly mechanical processes which produce a specific result. In the case of both the Comparative Method and the methods of Internal Reconstruction this result encapsulates the relationships among the forms compared, as asserted by the formulist position. But such a result is in itself rather meaningless if our aim is to recover earlier forms of languages. To be of value to the historical linguist it must clearly be given a *historical interpretation*, and here the realist conception becomes essential: we must regard our reconstructed forms as real language if they are to have any significance at all.

This conclusion implies that there are, logically speaking, two stages in the process of reconstruction (though it must be made clear that these stages are not necessarily sequential but may be simultaneous or interlaced): the application of the methods and the historical interpretation. The former is a formal, mechanical procedure with no historical implications which therefore has some affinity with the formulist view; the latter is an ongoing process of interpretation which gives historical significance to the formal procedure. This point may seem forced, but it is borne out in actual practice. A comparable point is made by Lass (1975) in comparing the procedures involved in generative phonology and Internal Reconstruction. He suggests that these procedures are effectively identical (he is concerned with the method of Internal Reconstruction here termed historical morphophonemics); the difference lies simply in the aims, which are in one case synchronic and in the other historical. He also suggests that the methods by themselves do not always do what they claim, since the result is, in the case of generative phonology, not necessarily psychologically real and in the case of Internal Reconstruction not necessarily historically accurate. The example he gives of the latter is Indo-European ablaut, which would, by consistent application of the methods described above, be eliminated in the pre-language, whereas we know that ablaut alternations were apparently original. Regardless of the validity of this claim, however, the arguments presented by Lass reinforce the view that the methods of reconstruction are logically independent of their historical interpretation.

We may justifiably claim, therefore, that the recognition of a two-stage process of reconstruction largely disposes of the formulist/realist debate, since it recognizes that both aspects are present simultaneously in our procedures.

4.5 CONCLUSION

This chapter has sketched out the basic principles of phonological reconstruction. Inevitably, much background information and theoretical discussion and further exemplification has had to be omitted. However, it is hoped that enough has been done to demonstrate the basic procedures of this essential set of tools in the historical phonologist's workshop and particularly to show that both the Comparative Method and Internal Reconstruction, as applied to phonology, are not vague and ill-defined methods but can be reduced to a series of coherent procedures and well-defined steps. Internal Reconstruction in particular is often regarded as unsystematic and unsound, but if the various procedures which it encompasses are properly differentiated and clarified they can be seen as powerful methods which can yield well-motivated results. Furthermore, both the Comparative Method and Internal Reconstruction can be shown to have sound theoretical underpinnings.

CHAPTER 5

ESTABLISHING PHONEMIC CONTRAST IN WRITTEN SOURCES

DONKA MINKOVA

5.1 THE INDIRECTNESS OF 'DIRECT' WRITTEN EVIDENCE

> History is not an account of facts but of relations that are inferred to have existed between supposed facts. It is not at all easy... to discriminate between facts and inferences. The 'facts' of historical scholarship are often simply useful hypotheses that in turn relate, by rough rules of inference, a variety of secondary 'facts' to each other. The most insightful accounts of historical events turn out to be intricate webs of suppositions and inferences removed at many steps from the citable data on which the conclusions ultimately rest.
>
> (Stockwell 1968: 20)

WITH no direct record of spoken language before sound recording was invented in the nineteenth century, it is axiomatic that the most important 'facts' for any branch of historical linguistics come from written records (see Maguire, this volume, for a consideration of the role of sound recordings). Even methodologies of reconstructing undocumented languages, such as the comparison of cognates ('the comparative method') and argumentation based on language universals and the uniformitarian principle, have to rely on attested forms (see Fox and Kümmel, both this volume). While the primacy of written sources in historical phonology seems self-evident, the interpretation of spelling in relation to the inventory of contrastive entities is riddled with problems. The accessible 'facts' in the history of Western languages are recorded in alphabetic writing systems (see Unger, this volume, for a consideration of evidence from certain nonalphabetic writing systems), yet no written document, at least prior to the IPA, can be taken as a precise record of pronunciation.

This chapter is a counterpoint to Lass (this volume) in looking closer into the limitations of early English written records for the reconstruction of phonological contrast (see also Dresher, this volume, who makes some considerable use of spelling evidence). While focusing on the history of English itself, it provides a model of how, in principle, fundamental issues in interpreting past phonological states can be approached on the basis of both 'direct' evidence from spelling and 'indirect' evidence from poetry. Following a brief historiography of writing in Old English and comments on the relationship between written forms and their phonetic and phonological shapes, section 5.2 turns to a notorious crux in the analysis of Old English: the phonemic or allophonic status of the digraphs <ea>, <eo>, <ie> when they represent monomoraic vowels. Section 5.3 addresses the disjunction between spelling and identity matching of onset <c> and <g> in Old English alliterative verse and examines critically Jakobson's (1966) dictum that rhyme and alliteration must be based on phonemic identity. Both case studies prompt alternative, more probable accounts. The conclusion suggests other ways in which gradient properties can be reconstructed for written languages like Old English and points to the theoretical advantages of a cautiously revisionist approach to full phonemicization.

5.1.1 Writing in Old English

In the British Isles, the earliest indigenous writing was in the *ogham* alphabet used for Old Irish and Latin, in which vowel letters could be assigned different values from one manuscript to the next (Gnanadesikan 2009: 244). There are no extant Old English (OE, c.450–1066) records in the ogham script. Upon arrival in Britain during the fifth century, the Anglo-Saxons introduced runic letters. With over thirty symbols, the Anglo-Saxon runic *futhorc* was much richer than the twenty-four-symbol earlier Germanic *futhark*, or the quite limited sixteen-rune futhark used for Old Norse. The runic inscriptions, especially those found on large, non-portable stones, provide valuable testimony to the earliest forms of Northumbrian OE, e.g. the preservation of runes for distinct <æ> ([-æ-]) and <i> ([-i-]) in unstressed syllables, where later OE uses mostly <-e> (Page 1973).[1] The usefulness of such runic evidence for dating the /æ/ and /i/ merger in that position is bolstered by comparable spellings in eighth-century non-runic manuscripts of the same dialectal provenance: the Northumbrian version of *Cædmon's Hymn* (c.737) has <eci> 'eternal', <dryctin> 'lord', <astelidæ> 'placed', <metudæs> 'of the Creator' *vs* West Saxon (WS) <ece>, <drihten>, <onstealde>, <metodes>.

---

[1] Angled brackets enclose orthographic forms, square brackets enclose IPA sounds without reference to contrastiveness, and slashes enclose contrastive units. I use 'letter' and 'contrastive unit' in the commonly accepted -emic way, though obviously such diachronic categorizations are often inadequate. See Lass (this volume) for a more cautious and fine-grained terminology and coding of the vagaries of medieval spelling.

The bulk of written Old English documentation, however, is outside the futhorc records. Along with their conversion to Christianity, starting in 432, the Irish adopted the Roman alphabet, creating their own version of the letters, known as *Insular Half Uncial* script. It was that script which Irish missionaries passed on to the Anglo-Saxon monks after the establishment of the Christian church and the spread of monastic culture in England during the seventh century. Much early writing was in Latin, but the first documents in OE began to appear by the end of the eighth century. The twenty-three-letter Roman alphabet in its insular form was convenient for Latin, and the letters would have been matched to the nearest sound in OE, but it was inadequate for representing all sounds in the vernacular. Anglo-Saxon consonant letters not found in Latin are *thorn* <þ> and *wynn* <ƿ>, both borrowed from the runic alphabet; another native addition was the letter *eth* <ð>, or *edh*, and the Insular letter form <ȝ>.[2] The letters <q, k, x, z> were used very rarely in OE; they became part of the regular inventory of consonantal letters with the adoption of a later version of the Roman alphabet, the Caroline script, after 1066. In the set of vowel letters: <a, æ, e, i, o, u, y>, only <æ> is specific to Old English, though it, too, is derived from the Latin ligature.

The graphemic-phonemic matching of letters used at any stage in the history of English is rarely, if at all, straightforward. In the last fifteen centuries the actual shape of the letters has changed many times, but whether one finds < d, ꝺ, ꝺ, ð, Ð, Ð, D > or <d>, it is fairly certain that the first and the last letters in the name *David* in any document represent a voiced (or 'lenis') dental or alveolar stop, IPA /d/. One can hardly imagine a simpler case, but even that apparently reliable matching can fail: in early OE documents <d> can be used to represent a fricative, as in <modgidanc> in the Northumbrian version of *Cædmon's Hymn*, 'thought' for later <modgeþanc/modgeðanc>. In Middle English (ME, 1066–*c*.1476), <d> and <th> continued to be problematic: records of the Cumberland township of *Motherby* for the year 1279 show both <Moderbi> and <Motherby>; the <d> (/-d-/) of OE <modor/moder>'mother', also <gader> 'gather', <weder> 'weather' continued to be used for the innovative /-ð-/ in Early Modern English (*c*.1476–1776). In a parallel fashion, OE <byrðen> 'burden', <morðor> 'murder' acquired spellings <burden, borden, bourden> and <morder, mordre, murder, murdre> in ME. Jumping forward to present-day English (PDE), we still find <d> representing regional /ð/ in *adder, bladder, fodder, ladder* (Leicestershire, see Evans 1881: 5), and in American English and Ulster English intervocalic <d> can represent the alveolar tap [ɾ], as in *bedding, ladder, rider*. Indeed, the history of every single consonant could provide a case study of the ambiguities of matching graphemes to sounds.

The situation is even more complicated with vowel letters: not counting <œ> for reconstructed /ø/, not used in West Saxon documents, OE had seven vowel symbols: <a,

---

[2] In edited texts and paleographic transcriptions wynn <ƿ> is commonly replaced by <w> and the Insular letter form <ȝ> is replaced by <g>. The scribes do not keep apart the 'normal' Caroline <g> and the <ȝ> for different sounds. The descendant of the Insular letter form <ȝ>, namely <ȝ> is referred to as *yogh* (Roberts 2005: 8–9).

æ, e, i, o, u, y>, which represent a set of at least sixteen, and possibly as many as twenty contrastive vocalic units in OE.

Like all other early Germanic languages, OE is reconstructed as a language with two sets of vowels, monomoraic (short) and bimoraic (long). However, the OE scribes did not mark vowel length, so that the letter sequence <for> can stand for [fɔr] 'for' or [foːr] 'travelled', <metan> represents both [mɛtən] 'to measure' and [meːtən] 'to meet'. Some diacritics—a superscript curl, a circumflex, and an extra-long macron marking short vowels—do appear in the eleventh century (Hogg 1992: 17), but the credit for the first consistent attempt to represent vowel length in English belongs famously to the monk Orm, who composed almost 19,000 verse lines of biblical narratives found in an auto-graph south-west Lincolnshire manuscript from c.1180. Orm uses double consonant letters to mark short vowels in closed syllables, thus <goddspelless> 'Gospels', <heff-ness lihht> 'heaven's light'. His innovative system is an isolated example, however; there were no followers. Unlike the relatively stable practices of late OE scribes, justifying the assumption of a 'standardized' OE spelling, ME is a time of stunning variety of idiosyn-cratic systems which make interpretation even more difficult, see Lass (this volume).

5.2 DIRECT SPELLING EVIDENCE: THE CONTRASTIVE STATUS OF OE DIGRAPH SPELLINGS

The evaluation of contrast is one of the basic goals of phonological theory. In synchronic studies contrastiveness can be tested experimentally, in acquisition, and in loanword adaptation.[3] Only the latter test is marginally applicable in diachronic phonology, again mediated by the writing system. Nevertheless, positing historical inventories is a neces-sary analytical step, and the study of their properties enriches the empirical base for test-ing current theoretical approaches to contrast. The following sections present two such diachronic test cases.

One of the greatest uncertainties in reconstructing the OE vowel system, repeatedly debated in the last seventy years, surrounds the interpretation of the digraphs <ea>, <eo>, <io>, <ie> representing etymologically monomoraic vowels as in <earm> 'arm', <geolo> 'yellow', <seolh> 'seal', <liornian> 'learn', <hliehhan> 'laugh'.[4] The digraphs appear in environments before coda /-h/, coda liquids, heterosyllabic back vowels, and

---

[3] Each of these evidential sources presents analytical problems, of course: see Maguire (this volume) on the difficulty of matching production to knowledge, or Uffmann (this volume) on loanwords. For an extensive treatment of the production–perception disjunction in acquisition, see McAllister (2009).

[4] The presentation here ignores most of the 'gory' details, amply covered in the literature. The digraphs <io> and <ie> will be taken out of the picture because their use is restricted (Hogg 1992: 21, 24, 189–94). The most comprehensive recent surveys are Hogg (1992), Lass (1994), Lass & Laing (2012), Minkova (2014).

in identifiable palatal contexts. In traditional grammars the digraphs are taken as representing innovative *phonemic* short diphthongs /ĕǎ/, /ĕŏ/, /ĭŏ/, /ĭĕ/, specific to OE. This analysis is perhaps the most glaring example of literal transfer of spelling to phonemic value in the history of English.

The reconstruction of underlyingly contrastive short diphthongs faces a series of objections. The first, and probably the most damaging argument, is the contextual limitation of the 'short' diphthongs, an immediate red flag for any theory of categorical phonemic status (Hayes 2009: 58–64). Second, as argued by Kümmel (this volume), typological parallels are central to the evaluation of competing hypotheses in the reconstruction of past phonological states. The typological argument for contrastive short diphthongs in OE is weak: in addition to the general paucity of languages with contrastive long and short diphthongs, phonemic short diphthongs would make OE unique within its own language family. No other Germanic language, past or present, has contrastive long and short diphthongs that are not circumscribed further, either based on syllable weight as in Icelandic, where there are no short diphthongs in open syllables, or morphologically and phonetically, as in Scots.[5]

A third argument against the phonemic status of these entities comes from subsequent history: in late OE and ME the so-called short diphthongs of OE merged with short monophthongal counterparts: <ea> merges with <æ> and <eo> merges with <eo, e, o, ue>, the latter representing [œ/ø] ~ [e].[6]

Fourth, the number of minimal pairs on which the phonemic distinction can be tested is quite limited and open to alternative accounts, see Stockwell and Barritt (1955, 1961) and Danchev (1975/1976), who offers the most detailed critique of the minimal pairs' test. To illustrate with some of the most frequently cited minimal pairs: the orthographic distinction between *bearn* 'child' *vs bær* 'bore', p.t. sg., is far from conclusive because the form *bær* could be influenced by the past plural form *bæron*, which has the long vowel, and by the related form *-bære*, as in *leohtbære* 'light-bearing, luminous', *lustbære* 'joy-bearing, desirable'. We also find <barn>, <bærn> for 'child'. Another 'last resort' pair, *ærn* 'house' *vs earn* 'eagle' (Jeremy Smith 2009: 56–7) is also dubious because the spellings <earn> for 'house' and <ærn> for 'eagle' are firmly in evidence. The pair <wæl> 'slaughter' ~ <weall> 'wall' may be kept apart on the basis of the geminate /-ll/ in <weall>, which is also well attested as <wall>. Not least, as Lass argues for Middle English (this volume),

---

[5] Schrijver (2009) observes that Old Irish has a 'marginal but real contrast' between /iu/ and /iŭ/, where, however, the quantitative difference is accompanied by a difference in the sonority peak—the <u> in the long diphthongs is the peak, implying that <i> stands for an on-glide, while in /iŭ/ the <i> is the peak. The relevance of the contrast for the reconstruction of the OE inventory is doubtful: <iu> for /iŭ/ is not part of the digraph controversy (Hogg 1992: 21); the spelling is interpreted as representing a glide + vowel sequence irrespective of vowel length (Campbell 1959: section 172). More relevantly, a Celtic parallel runs into the problem of non-existent <ea> in Old Irish, while <ea> is central to the OE debate.

[6] The argument that *lengthened* /ĕǎ/ ([æː]) merged with the true diphthongal /ea/ (/ɛə/) in late OE and ME (Hogg 1992: 17–18) does not help the position that /ĕŏ/ was an independent phoneme; allophones can jump ship and merge with pre-existing phonemes.

speakers, scribes, and readers have contextual expectations which limit the value of the classical minimal pairs test.

The strongest defence of the phonemic status of /ēa/, /ēo/ is consistency of spelling. The argument is valid if we stay within very narrow geographical and chronological confines, yet it is fragile if we take a broader view of the Old English 'language'. The digraphs alternate with <a>, <æ>, <e> commonly: West Saxon (WS) <healdan> 'hold', <eall> 'all', Anglian <haldan>, <all>, early WS <forgietan> 'forget', late WS <forgitan>, Anglian <forgetan>, WS <feohtan> 'to fight', Anglian <fehtan>. Admittedly the digraph spellings are fairly uniform in the 'focused' variety of late WS OE. However, the coherence of the practices brings this variety closer to a supra-regional 'prestige' text language; the orthographic homogeneity can be attributed to the strong normative tendencies characteristic of the Winchester school and the stability of the Ælfrician texts. Scribal codification notwithstanding, it appears that since the diphthongal spellings occur in well-defined environments, it makes good phonetic sense to treat them as representing allophones of the respective non-diphthongal vowels with which they later merge. Nevertheless, the phonemic interpretation is deeply ensconced even in the most recent authoritative phonological accounts of OE (Hogg 1992, Lass 1994).[7]

The 'digraph controversy', one of the most 'complex and acrimonious debates in the history of OE scholarship' (Lass 1994: 45), was conducted in terms of a theory of phonology that separates phonemes from allophones categorically. In an original attempt to break away from that strict dichotomy, Danchev (1975/1976) proposes an interpretation of the 'short diphthongs' as 'weak phonemes', forming a syntagmatic unit with the adjacent palatal or velar consonant, where the whole group functions as a 'strong' phoneme with high functional load. His study, which provides the first large database and the clearest presentation of the arguments for and against a traditional phonemic contrast for the controversial digraphs, anticipates subsequent recognition of gradience in the production and perception of contrast.

Current phonological theory recognizes that segmental inventories are comprised of units that can range from fully contrastive to less clearly so, including the possibility of free variation (Goldsmith 1995, 12, Hayes 2009: 58–61).[8] In principle, the OE situation parallels the gradience illustrated by the tensing of [æ] to [eːə] in American English. The process is gradual in some northern dialect areas, categorical in the Mid-Atlantic cities, and lexically idiosyncratic before /d/ in Philadelphia; see Harris (1990b), Bermúdez-Otero (2007), Gordon (this volume).

The point of the comparison to testable current phonological events is that even apparently thoroughly studied correspondences between spelling and phonological structure require fresh interpretations. Projecting back from the present, we can say that the OE short digraphs never stood for stable and fully contrastive entities.

---

[7] White (2004) resurrects an argument by Daunt (1939) that the digraph spellings represent consonantal properties and not diphthongs. For a reaction, see Jeremy Smith (2009: 55–8).

[8] Good overviews of speakers' reactions to phonemic *vs* allophonic distinctions, and the ontological status of the phoneme, are found in Derwing, Nearey, & Dow (1986) and Lotto & Holt (2000).

The realizations [ēa], [ēo] are best analysed as 'not-yet-integrated semi-contrasts', a status halfway between a phoneme and an allophone (Goldsmith 1995: 12). The perceptibility of the semi-contrast is determined by the local phonotactic context. Treating phonemic contrastiveness in scalar terms renders vacuous the objections to both the phonemic and the allophonic interpretations for the diverse and fluid dialects covered by the umbrella term 'Old English'. Evidently, the whole issue deserves a reappraisal based on an exhaustive survey of the relevant forms in the *Dictionary of Old English* (*DOE*);[9] new quantitative data will allow a more precise mapping of the allophone–phoneme continuum posited here. Moreover, the 'diagraph controversy' reappraised can now be applied to more general theoretical inquiries: why do monomoraic diphthongs provide unstable phonological contrasts unless bolstered by additional syntagmatic cues, what features in these contour segments are contrastive, and how the hierarchy of features in this case compares to other featural hierarchies in English and elsewhere.

5.3 INDIRECT HISTORICAL SOURCES: IDENTITY IN VERSE AND SEGMENTAL CATEGORIZATION

'Written evidence' in the case of OE is the umbrella term for *all* surviving texts, ranging from literary masterpieces of lasting aesthetic value to legal and administrative documents, charters, glosses, occasional writs and letters. Here belongs also the information from non-manuscript spelling evidence, the writing on coins, usefully gleaned and analysed in Colman (1992).[10] All extant OE texts can be mined for attestations of particular scribal forms; such data are at the more direct end of the continuum of indirectness that written evidence presents. At the other end is evidence from verse. Some of the oldest surviving texts in the history of English are verse compositions; poetry was a and primary vehicle of religious and secular instruction, the creation of historical records, and entertainment. Verse was the leading form of verbal art in Anglo-Saxon England and throughout the Middle Ages. Examining the poetic records for linguistic reconstruction is a time-honoured method in historical linguistics (Penzl 1957). It is the closest we can come to 'metalinguistic' evidence for the phonology of the poet or scribe. The philological backbone of English historical phonology, to take Luick (1914–40) as an example, draws extensively on evidence from rhymes. The next section addresses specific instances of the treatment of identity in OE verse that warrant a revision of the canon and bear on larger issues of phonological markedness and contrast.

---

[9] See <http://www.doe.utoronto.ca/tools/tools.html>.

[10] Among the best examples of different interpretations of OE orthographic data depending on one's theoretical bias are King (1992) and Lass (1994).

Hayes (1988) divides the metrical rules internalized by poets into *correspondence* rules and *identity* rules. Correspondence or alignment rules refer to the proper matching of linguistic units to the abstract metrical template or its parts, e.g. stressed syllables are placed in ictic/strong positions, the edges of words are matched to the edges of verse constituents, the number of syllables in speech corresponds to the number of verse positions in the template. Identity rules, also known as parametrical rules, refer to the sameness of the linguistic material in rhyme, alliteration (initial rhyme), and assonance. These aesthetically and mnemonically cohesive schemas are both universal and specific to a particular verse tradition. The specificity of the Germanic alliterative tradition is that the recurrence can be located only in the onset of stressed or stressable syllables, that the clusters /sp-, st-, sk-/ allow only self-alliteration, other clusters alliterate on the leftmost consonant, and that all vowels cross-alliterate.

The common denominator for all identity rules is that recurrent units in verse correspond to categories at a more abstract level of linguistic representation. That general principle was first formulated by Baudouin de Courtenay (1913/1917). With respect to segmental identity rules in rhyme, Jakobson's specific statement that 'The PHONEMIC equivalence of rhyming words is compulsory' (1966: 426–7) still defines the most widely practised approach to linking verse patterns to speech.[11] In English, identity of the syllable onset in alliteration, and of the stressed syllable peak and coda in masculine rhyme,[12] is therefore arguably a firm basis for the reconstruction of segmental histories. The applicability of the principle is testable in periodic rhyming and alliterative verse in other modern languages, and it has been confirmed repeatedly in psycholinguistic studies of pre-literate perception of alliteration and rhyme (Carroll and Snowling 2001).

Within the Germanic tradition of alliterative verse the cohesiveness of the lines rests on identity of the onsets of syllables bearing, or capable of bearing, stress. The *Beowulf* epic, whose 6240 verses make it the longest alliterative composition in any Germanic language, shows only fourteen otherwise 'regular' lines without alliteration. Another twenty-three lines show both non-alliteration and other metrical deficiencies (Fulk 1997: 46). In the OE poetic corpus overall, alliteration is by far the most reliable single feature: in 26,088 verses of OE poetry, only thirty-six, or .001 percent, lack alliteration (Hutcheson 1995: 169).

Such numbers argue strongly in favour of the inherent, rather than scribally imposed, requirement of alliterative identity. The overwhelming regularity makes irrelevant the issue of how 'literate' the OE verse tradition was; both the poets, or *scops*, composing orally, and the later scribes and copyists, to whom we owe the written records of the oral compositions, must have relied on the systematic patterns of identity in their language.

---

[11] Jakobson's maxim obviously refers to pure rhymes, not assonances or slant rhymes. Manaster Ramer (1994) offers a critique of attempts to match verse structure to representations at levels deeper than the traditional phonemic level.

[12] Other rhyme schemas in English include post-tonic syllables: feminine rhyme, as in *perish:cherish*, or triple rhyme as in *clarity:rarity*. On the non-equivalence of phonological rhyme and verse rhyme see Aroui (2009: 18–28).

To draw a parallel with modern spelling, the poet could say '[This truth came] *borne with bier and pall*', the scribe could write <came born with beer and Paul>,[13] yet the message to the listener would be the same. In modern elicitation experiments with literate adults orthography may be a confounding factor in decisions on identity (see Perin 1983 and the discussion in Derwing, Nearey, & Dow 1986: 58–64). While it can be a challenge to separate knowledge of the visual form of the letter from the speaker's 'naïve' phonological categorization, the systematic nature of alliteration and the oral tradition of composing verse make it highly unlikely that the OE scribes were influenced by orthography in a period preceding silent reading. Although the spelling in the OE poetic corpus does not offer many examples, we can still find clear instances of discrepancy between spelling and intended *sound* in alliteration: <ch-> in <**Ch**annaneum> alliterates with <c> in <**c**yninges> in *Andreas* 778, <**Christus**>:<**c**læne> in *Summons* l.11, evidently /k-/ alliterations, while in *Genesis* A we find <**ch**us> alliterating on <h->:<**h**atene> (l.1617) and <**h**eafodwisa> (l.1619). Similarly, <**Ph**araon, **Ph**ilipus> alliterate on /f-/ (*Paris Psalter, Menologium* etc.), initial <þ> or <ð> are used interchangeably for alliterating /θ/, as in: <**ð**rittiges>:<**þ**reohund> (*Genesis* 1308), and orthographic <h> is ignored in vowel alliteration, as in <**H**abrahame>:<**ea**forum> (*Andreas* 779). Note also the possibility of using non-alphabetical representations, as if the scribe was 'texting' in e.g. *siomode in sorgum / VII nihta first* (*Eelne* 694), *þa se ðeoden / ymb XIII gear* (*Genesis* 2304).[14]

The extent to which evidence from verse is incorporated into the historical accounts varies. Hogg (1992: 8) sets aside the evidence from verse: 'The characteristics of this variety [poetic texts] are not considered in this work except where individual forms are of more general relevance'. The rationale is that the 'common poetic dialect' of the extant OE verse obscures some aspects of linguistic structure. As we saw in section 5.2, uniformity of spelling is characteristic of West Saxon, but two considerations make discarding the testimony of verse data unwarranted. First, there is consensus regarding the oral basis of the compositions; without explicit instruction, for which there is no evidence, the scops must have drawn on their competence regarding the categorical identity of the segments that they were matching in alliteration. Second, the OE poetic corpus material is far from homogeneous. Fulk (1992), a milestone in the revival of using linguistic criteria for the dating of OE poems, has shown convincingly that the convergence of different linguistic properties yields a composition timeline, on which the texts can be positioned with a high degree of probability. Once the chronology of the texts is established independently, different alliterative practices in the early and the late verse can become the cornerstone for inquiry into the status of various phonological features.

A revealing illustrative case for the perception of identity is presented by the use of the letters <c> and <g> in the OE alliterative corpus. Here the alliterative matching maps

---

[13] Alfred Lord Tennyson *In Memoriam*, LXXXV, cited in Bradley (1919).

[14] The OE word for 7 is *seofon*; 13 is *þreotiene*. The letters thorn (<þ>) and edh (<ð>) represent a voiceless dental fricative [θ] word-initially.

out persistence or change in categorical identity of the velars in the absence of corresponding scribal evidence.[15] In the poetic corpus stressed onsets spelled <c> alliterate
freely from the earliest to the latest datable poems:

oððe þone **c**ynedom / **c**iosan wolde

'or that **k**ingdom / **ch**oose would   (*Beowulf*: 2376, c.725–825)

cyning a**c**endest, / þa þu þæt **c**ild to us

'**k**ing brought forth /when you the **ch**ild to us'   (*Descent into Hell*: 85, c.960)

clene **C**udberte / on **c**ildhade

'**c**lean **C**uthbert / in **ch**ildhood'   (*Durham*: 16, c.1100)

On the other hand, words with initial <g> for early OE **/ɣ/ and inherited Germanic
/j/ alliterate freely only in the early poems and are kept apart in verse composed after the
middle of the tenth century:

geongum ond ealdum, / swylc him **g**od sealde

'to young and old / such as him God gave'   (*Beowulf*: 72, c. 725–825)

gearo and **g**eornful, / **g**ylpwordum spræc

'yare and yearning / yelping words spoke'   (*Battle of Maldon*: 274, 991)

and ðær **G**addes mæg / **g**rund **g**esohte

'and there Gadd's relative / ground sought'   (*Battle of Maldon*: 287, 991)

In the later examples, the initial palatal approximant /j/ and the initial velar stop /g/
alliterate only within their own categories (see Fulk 1992: 258–9; Minkova 2003: ch. 3).
The consistency of treating all <c-> onsets as identical, but keeping the <g-> onsets separate in the late verse, challenges the dating of the velar changes in some authoritative
accounts of OE and opens up a new window into the effect that different phonological
features have on the way in which categorical distinctions are internalized.

To elucidate the argument, consider more background on OE velars: The palatalization and affrication of the OE voiceless velar stop /k/: **[k] > [c] > [tʃ] when adjacent to
etymologically front vowels, as in OE *cinn* 'chin', *cīld* 'child', *līc* 'body', is assumed to have
been parallel to the change of **/ɣ/ > **[g] > [ɟ] > [dʒ], as in OE *ecg* 'edge', *hrycg* 'ridge',
sengean 'singe' in historical geminates and after nasals. The phonemicization of the new
affricates /tʃ/ and /dʒ/ is dated to the ninth century (Hogg 1992: 272) or even earlier,
during 'the transition [from Germanic] to Old English' (Lass 1994: 53–9). On a separate
track, the OE voiced velar fricative **/ɣ/ was palatalized to [j] before front vowels as in

---

[15] The letter <c> can alternate occasionally with <k> in OE; the latter was not fully adopted until after
the Conquest when it was popularized by Anglo-Norman scribes. OE <c> is never used for [s]. The letter
<g> is a typographical/editorial convenience, see note 2 above.

giefan 'to give', *giernan* 'to yearn', or it became [g] elsewhere, as in *gamen* 'game', *growan* 'to grow'. The [j] allophone of /ɣ/ merged with the inherited Germanic /j/, as in *geong* 'young' and *gear* 'year'.

The assumption that poets have recourse to distinctive categories makes a ninth-century or earlier date of the phonemicization of [tʃ] < [c] most unlikely. Similarly, an early, even 'pre-historic', dating of the fortition of */ɣ/ to [g] by some authorities, runs into the problem of across-the-board <g-> matching in the early verse.[16] As argued in Minkova (2003), alliteration of all <c>-initial words in the entire OE corpus was based on a unified underlying abstract representation of /k/, with surface forms realized in conformity with the palatal or non-palatal context. Affrication was a gradual process, much obscured by paradigmatic analogy, yet the verse usage indicates that a full integration of a new contrastive element /tʃ/ into the underlying system has to be dated between *c.* 1000–1100. In this instance, Jakobson's dictum of the phonemic nature of identity in rhyme is sufficient to make the case for late phonemicization, though, as pointed out in Bermúdez-Otero (2005), it may not be necessary.[17]

Applied to the practice of alliterating all <g>-initial words in the early verse, allowing e.g. <geong> 'young' (with Germanic /j-/) to be paired with /ɣ/ in <god> 'God' (*Beowulf*.72), on the other hand, does present a problem for a blanket assumption that the rules of identity in rhyme and alliteration *must* refer to phonemes. Hayes (1988: 227) recognizes that 'Taken in the strictest sense, this [Jakobson's claim] cannot be true' and supports his reservation with an example from French and Latin metres which involve contrastive stress, while stress is predictable in those languages. Along these lines, we can propose that the conundrum of early <g-> alliteration in OE is another example of the projection of finer featural distinctions into the rules of identity used by the poets. Minkova (2003: 113–21) justified the unexpected bundling together of /j/ and /ɣ/ on the basis of their shared continuancy and dorsality, and the unusual phonetic closeness of the palatal approximant /j/ and the palatal fricative allophone [ʝ] from /ɣ/. Of note is also the complex phonological nature of [ʝ], involving both dorsal and coronal articulations suggesting that the identity of <g-> onsets rests on the violability of a 'weakly present' place feature [coronal] in the approximant. Addressing the same problem, Bermúdez-Otero (2005: 443) takes the weakness of the secondary place contrast one step further and makes a more targeted proposal, identifying the contrast [dorsal] *vs* [coronal] in /ɣ/:/j/ as insufficiently salient, observing that that contrast is not phonemic anywhere else in the system. Moreover, /ɣ/ and /j/ are neutralized in palatal environments, as in *geong* 'young' < /j/ *vs gieldan* 'yield' < */ɣ/.

The example of /ɣ/:/j/ alliteration in early OE thus provides indirect evidence for the gradience of what constitutes linguistic sameness in the system. Verse analysis shows

[16] See Minkova (2003: 118) for the research history and Hogg (1992: 31, 288–9) for non-verse-based arguments in favour of late, *c.*1000, fortition of /ɣ/ to /g/.

[17] Note, however, that abandoning the hypothesis of late phonemicization of /tʃ/ in favour of violability of coronality, parallel to the account of /ɣ/:/j/ below, would weaken the claim that the opposition of [dorsal] *vs* [coronal] in the system is isolated and therefore non-salient in verse.

that the scops' practice refers to a hierarchy of feature discreteness, in which an isolated secondary place contrast can be ignored for the purpose of identity. The fact that the place feature for the dorsal continuants is neutralizable, and that it applies to a limited range of phonemes, characterizes the feature as phonologically inactive, in line with the diagnostics for feature-ordering discussed in Dresher (2009: 71–4).

On the other hand, when we find that the boundary /j/–/g/ is not crossed in the late OE verse, we can posit a different type of contrast. The fortition of /ɣ/ > /g/ leads to the more robust contrast /j/:/g/ which rests on a manner feature that is distinctive across the system. More generally, the different practice before and after fortition of /ɣ/ lends diachronic support to the reality of the featural make-up and the existence of phonetically based markedness principles. Further, a hypothesis that the /ɣ/:/j/ opposition in early OE is perceptually marked and therefore treated differently from other contrasts, supports the view that perceptual markedness is a property of the entire system of contrasts and not a property of individual sounds, as argued in Flemming (2004).

An alternative pathway, also referring to the weak contrastiveness of [dorsal] vs [coronal] in early OE, but without assuming contrastiveness of the higher-level place feature, is also plausible:

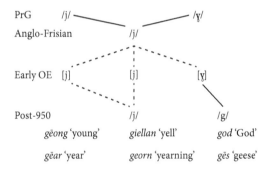

PrG   /j/ ——————————— /ɣ/
Anglo-Frisian   /j/

Early OE   [j]   [j]   [ɣ]

Post-950   /j/   /g/
        gēong 'young'   giellan 'yell'   god 'God'
        gēar 'year'   georn 'yearning' gēs 'geese'

A new element in this reconstruction is the chronology of phonemic /ɣ/. Minkova (2003) assumed continued contrastiveness of the Proto Germanic velar fricative in early OE, following the standard accounts in the literature. There is a simpler, philologically defensible scenario: the palatalization of the velar fricative before WG *e, i, a, eu, au, io*, an Ingwaeonic development, definitely shared with Old Frisian (Nielsen 1981: 142), undermined the status of */ɣ/, which became allophonic. Pre-existing /j/ absorbed the 'new' Anglo-Frisian [j] < */ɣ/, represented in the futhark by an old rune X. The velar fricative realization, for which the Anglo-Saxon futhorc devised a different rune, survived as a positional allophone of /j/. This is the stage at which *God, yell,* and *young* alliterated freely.

Allophonic occlusion of the PrG velar fricative to [g] was under way in the earliest documents word-medially; the stop appeared in gemination (*frogga* 'frog') and after nasals (PrG *straŋgiþō* > OE *strengðu* 'strength'), providing the landing site for the post-900 fortition of initial [ɣ] before back vowels. The decisive factor in the phonemicization of /g/ was the appearance of post i-umlaut velars followed by derived front vowels in words such as *gild, geese, giddy*; these newly created strings solidified the continuancy contrast between /j/ and /g/.

Associating the loss of the /j/ - /ɣ/ contrast with Anglo-Frisian salvages Jakobson's generalization for the alliterative practice the earliest poems. Note that the observation that the coronal-dorsal contrast is low-ranked and easily ignored still holds, but in this revised reconstruction it refers to positional allophones rather than to contrastive entities. No phonemic violations are incurred in post-950 compositions in which the robust /j/ - /g/ manner contrast is respected by poets and scribes.

Ultimately, the data from alliteration of velars in OE verse highlight both the usefulness and the challenges of the notion of the phoneme for establishing inventories of contrastive sounds in any language. Indeed, if we take the position that the OE poets are our best witnesses of which entities were phonologically contrastive, we would be justified in revising our account of OE prior to *c*.950 by positing only a single fully distinctive voiced continuant with surface realizations [ɣ] and [j].[18]

5.4 CONCLUDING REMARKS

This chapter covers only a small subset of the ways in which the analysis of written records can throw light on current issues of phonological structure. The two case studies highlight the problematic nature of positing finite and invariable phonemic inventories based on written sources and call for a re-examination of historical reconstructions assuming such inventories. The focus on the instability of the contrast between monophthongs and diphthongs in some positions, and the changing identity criteria for velar onsets in Old English, extend the empirical and methodological basis for the analysis of contrastiveness.

A related area of inquiry where Old English data can be used would be the analysis of contour segments. The existence of medial affricates [tʃ] and [dʒ] from geminated [k] and [g] in in earlier Germanic, as in <þeccean> from **þacjan* 'to cover' and <bycg(e)an>, Gothic *bugjan* 'to buy' is universally accepted, yet their analysis as single entities or composite units has not been worked out. In PDE /t͡ʃ/ and /d͡ʒ/ are treated as singletons, yet we don't know whether they were similarly perceived in OE.[19] Hogg (1992: 37) posits a contrast between a singleton /dʒ/ and geminate /ddʒ/ for OE, but acknowledges that

---

[18] Neither Minkova (2003), nor Bermúdez-Otero (2005) consider that possibility. Lass (1994: 57) is aware of the tenuousness of the /ɣ/:/j/ contrast, but he accepts it as phonemic, 'even if there is not a huge number of contrasting items, and few minimal pairs'. His anxiety is justified: the single minimal pair he cites, *geoc* 'yoke' vs *gyldan* 'to gild', can be accounted for on the same basis as the non-merger of /k/ before i-umlauted vowels, as in *cēlan* 'to cool' with /k/ before etymologically front vowels as in *cēowan* 'to chew'; for the latter, see Minkova (2003: 97–9).

[19] Cruttenden (2008: 182–4) provides a full survey of the arguments in favour of and against the analysis of /tʃ/ and /dʒ/ as single phonemes in present-day English.

the contrast lacks distributional justification. Further research on the spellings and the behaviour of <-cc-> and <cg> in metre is therefore promising, especially with respect to the contribution of these segments to syllable weight in a tradition where syllable quantity is assumed to be relevant and onset-maximal syllabification is posited after short stressed vowels. Fresh empirically driven analyses of spelling would be both descriptively illuminating and would provide a useful testing ground for current phonological theories. The electronic research tools, available from the *DOE*, cover the entire corpus of OE texts and make available exact counts of variant word and phrase spellings.[20] The proliferation of large and searchable electronic databases for other historically attested and currently spoken languages provides a strongly positive angle on the 'indirectness' of direct written evidence and allows statistical modelling to be part of the argumentation about the architecture of the phonological system. Ultimately, studies of that type enrich the scope and the gamut of test cases for evaluating the various probabilistic models of phonological change as surveyed in Zuraw (2003).

---

[20] The *DOE* Web Corpus database consists of at least one copy of every surviving Old English text. The website states that 'The total size is not quite five times the collected works of Shakespeare'.

CHAPTER 6

....

INTERPRETING DIFFUSE ORTHOGRAPHIES AND ORTHOGRAPHIC CHANGE

....

J. MARSHALL UNGER

6.1 INTRODUCTION

....

WHETHER based on abjads, abugidas, syllabaries, or alphabets in the strict sense (Daniels & Bright 1996: 4), all writing systems like the ones treated in Minkova and Lass (both this volume) are COMPACT in that the principal letter forms and auxiliary diacritics they employ almost never number more than a few dozen.[1] The only full writing systems[2] that regularly use hundreds of letter-like symbols involve Chinese characters. These DIFFUSE writing systems were or are used in and around China—the Sino-Xenic sphere.[3] Despite the widespread misconception that Chinese characters in these writing systems represent whole words or even abstract meanings—why else bother with such an enormous inventory of symbols?—they are in fact the counterparts of ORTHOGRAPHIC WORDS in compact

---

[1] The syllabary of the Yi minority of southern China, which involves about 800 distinct letter-like symbols, is extraordinarily large, but is used primarily for ritual purposes, not as an ordinary means of written communication. See Daniels & Bright (1996: 239–43).

[2] Partial writing systems, such as ad hoc pictographies incapable of transcribing all the well-formed utterances of a natural language, also exist, but are seldom more than indirectly helpful to the historical linguist.

[3] Though inspired by graphic features of Chinese texts, the diffuse writing systems of Tangut and Jurchin (Daniels & Bright 1996: 189, 228–38) were not derived directly from the Chinese writing system. Work continues on their decipherments, which will shed light on the history of Tibeto-Burman and Tungusic languages, respectively, but our pictures of these two short-lived languages are mere sketches compared with the detailed view of the 'big three' Sino-Xenic languages still spoken by millions. I believe the term Sino-Xenic was coined by Samuel E. Martin and first used by him in Martin (1953: 4).

writing systems. Like them, they function, to varying degrees and depending on context, both logographically and phonographically.[4]

In the principal Sino-Xenic lands—Vietnam, Korea, and Japan—literary Chinese (Vietnamese *hán văn*, Korean *hanmun*, Japanese *kanbun*) was long the prestige language of the ruling elites. Local literati augmented texts received from China with new compositions, and each of the local languages absorbed countless loanwords directly from literary Chinese. New combinations of characters and their loan readings were formed as needed. In Meiji period Japan, such innovations proliferated as erudite translations of Western terms, some of which were later borrowed into Korean or Chinese. In this sense, literary Chinese of the Sino-Xenic sphere was comparable to Latin, Greek, Arabic, and Sanskrit in other parts of the world (described in Ostler 2005). But whereas each of these came with a compact orthography, Chinese writing was diffuse and adapting it to the transcription of each of the vernacular languages required considerable effort and ingenuity.[5]

By combining the rich lode of information implicit in the vast inventory of characters and their myriad usages throughout East Asia with the findings of the comparative method and internal reconstruction, one can recover a large amount of linguistic history from early texts despite their superficial opacity.

6.2 CHINESE

Compared with contemporary Indians, ancient Chinese were remarkably incurious about the workings of language, but starting in the first millennium BC, helpful lexical materials begin to appear. For historical phonology, the most important is no doubt the *Qie yun* of 601 AD, a rhyme table whose authors strove to create a matrix of syllables with a slot for every type of syllable phonemically distinct in some dialect of the time. Chinese poetry makes use of rhymes that involve all the parts of syllables other than initial consonants, which may be zero, including tone.

Also important was the development in the sixth century of a technique called *fanqie* for specifying the pronunciation of a character (say A) in terms of the initial of another character (B) and non-initial remainder, or final (including tone), of a third (C).

---

[4] Indeed, texts that virtually abandon the logographic strategy for the sake of phonographic precision, such as IPA transcriptions, are too exacting for ordinary use; systems that abandon the phonographic strategy, as do cryptographic codes for the sake of secrecy, are unlearnable. Apart from these extreme cases, no full writing system adheres to just a single transcriptive strategy—*pace* Sampson (1985); see Unger (2005a). The impression that some do arises from the false assumption that the smallest graphic elements of a particular system (e.g. Chinese characters, alphabetic letters) represent the same kinds of linguistic units (e.g. words, phonemes) on all occasions.

[5] This was surely a major reason for the much slower and later rise of vernacular writing within the Sino-Xenic sphere. Pollock (2006) does not emphasize this point because he sees the history of vernacular writing in Japan as more exceptional than it was.

By compiling transitive lists of such equations ($A = BC$, $B = DE$, $C = FG$,..., $F = AH$, $G = CI$, ...), one can obtain sets of characters that stand for rhyming syllables (e.g. {A, C, E, G, I, ...}) or share the same initial sounds (e.g. {A, B, D, F,...}). Word lists in which Chinese words were written in Tibetan alphabetic script, and analysis of the Chinese characters chosen to transcribe Sanskrit words in Buddhist texts provide a third point of entry into Middle Chinese of the first millennium. Many studies (e.g. Hashimoto 1978) discuss the analysis of these materials in detail.

By combining all these written sources of information with results obtained by applying the comparative method to extant Chinese dialects, a long line of scholars has developed a highly detailed picture of Middle Chinese phonology. Though a single authoritative Middle Chinese reconstruction does not yet exist, there is general agreement on the main points of its phonological structure, and scholarly attention has tended to shift toward exploration of specific stages.[6] Perhaps the most interesting general finding is that comparison of dialects does not lead one to reconstruct a system more complex than the matrix implicit in *Qie yun*.

Nevertheless, Middle Chinese is not the historical counterpart of proto-Chinese; distinct dialects had existed for centuries before. Thanks to the internal graphic structure of individual characters, it is possible to push the horizon back many centuries earlier, into the Han dynasty and even earlier periods.[7] Though some characters (such as 十) are graphically unanalysable or, like 明, appear to be purely logographic compounds, most were formed by combining a common character, taken as a phonogram for a particular syllable, with all or part of another, which gives a thesaurus-like hint of the semantic range of a morpheme with the same or similar syllabic value.[8] Under the assumption that, in the oldest stages of the language, identical 'phonetic' elements in such 'phonetic-signific' graphic compound characters represented identical syllables at the relevant stage, one can construct networks of equivalences that, when informed by data from known dialects, make it possible to deduce the phonological structure of pre-Middle Chinese morphemes. Although work in reconstructing Old Chinese and

---

[6] Full documentation of the vast scholarly literature in English and other languages, especially Chinese and Japanese, is not feasible within the scope of this chapter. An early phonemic treatment of the pioneering work of Bernhard Karlgren is Samuel E. Martin (1953). Pulleyblank (1991) and Schuessler (2009) are two other well-known reconstructions, though because of methodological disagreements, some scholars hesitate to use the word 'reconstruction' for these results.

[7] Identifiable ancient foreign names transcribed with Chinese characters are also helpful but rare. Borrowings from Chinese into languages of the Sino-Xenic sphere can be used to advance reconstructions of Chinese, but become problematic when used in studies of the historical phonology of Sino-Xenic languages since they create opportunities for circular reasoning. The traditional idea that character shapes developed along a single path from oracle bone and bronze inscriptions to texts of the Qin and Han dynasties has been challenged by Galambos (2006). This critique, if sustained, could have a significant impact on our understanding of the earliest stages of Chinese.

[8] The character 十 corresponds to modern Mandarin *shi* 'ten'; 明 to *ming* 'bright' (cf. 日 *ri* 'sun', 月 *yue* 'moon'). In the character 問 *wen* 'ask', 門 *men* 'gate' is the phonetic element (the w- ≠ m- reflecting later sound changes) and 口 *kou* 'mouth' is the signific. Compare the similar-looking 間 *jian* 'interval'. Since the early forms of the syllables associated with 日 and 門 do not resemble any reconstructable antecedent of *jian* 'interval', 間 may have been a logographic compound of some kind.

proto-Chinese is far from complete, it is now widely acknowledged, for instance, that Middle Chinese tones developed compensatorily when certain syllable-final consonants (e.g. *-s) were lost, and that in the oldest stages of Chinese, syllables could be augmented with prefixes and suffixes.[9] Clues to how this morphology worked can be gleaned from comparisons of Sinitic and Tibeto-Burman languages, all of which are believed to be related, though there are competing theories about the phylogeny and chronology of the family.

Because Chinese characters transcribe entire syllables, it is perilously easy to draw the conclusion that every word of Chinese, at least at some ancient time, was monosyllabic, which is not the case.[10] Nevertheless, the seemingly logographic nature of Chinese characters, combined with the cultural prestige of Chinese texts, made it exceedingly difficult to adapt the Chinese writing system to the phonology or morphology of the unrelated languages of the cultures of the Sino-Xenic sphere. What happened instead was that new methods were devised—sometimes but not always with Chinese graphics as a point of departure—to transcribe the non-Chinese languages.

6.3 JAPANESE

Apart from early Chinese ethnological writing with transcriptions of names we presume were in some early form of Japanese, the writing of Japanese began after the introduction of Chinese characters from the Korean peninsula. They were soon used in several different ways. Apart from their appearance in Chinese loanwords, in which they were read with loan pronunciations now called *on* readings, they were also employed to transcribe all or part of various Japanese words. Sometimes this involved standard glosses (*kun*) on individual characters or short character strings, in which case the characters can be regarded as logograms. But a character might also be pressed into service as a phonogram representing the Old Japanese syllable (or, rarely, first two syllables) with which one of its *on* or *kun* readings began. Readers and writers were expected to know the rules for this evolving, complex system, and be able to apply them fluently. As the number of phonographically used characters increased and new readings (of both kinds) accumulated over time, this grew more difficult, and the practice of graphically deforming characters used phonographically became common, giving rise to *kana*, first clearly seen in texts dating from the early tenth century.

The use of *kana* and their graphically undeformed precursors, called *man'yōgana* after the large eighth-century poetry anthology *Man'yōshū*, can be analysed to reveal a great deal of information about Japanese historical phonology.

---

[9] For more on tonogensis, see Ratliff (this volume).
[10] This myth has been thoroughly debunked in such works as DeFrancis (1984) and Unger (2005a).

6.3.1 Kana

Table 6.1 shows the basic shapes of modern *hiragana* and *katakana* and their historical sources.[11] Changes in the *kana* spellings of various words in Middle Japanese (roughly 900–1600) reveal phonemic changes in the literary language; these are summarized in Table 6.2 which lists syllables that had two or more historical spellings.[12] Martin (1987) describes at length how orthographic variations (including Korean and Portuguese transcriptions of Middle Japanese) and internal reconstruction dovetail. There are four kinds of anachronistic spellings of general importance.

6.3.1.1 *Labial Glide Loss*

The morae /wi we wo/ have merged, respectively, with /i e o/. The *kana* for /wi we/ are not used in current orthography; those for /wo/ are retained only for the so-called accusative particle *o* < *wo* (still sometimes so romanized). The morae /kwa gwa/, still heard in a few dialects, have generally merged into /ka ga/, respectively. We can date changes of this kind by noting when (assuming faithful copying of manuscripts) writers begin to use the *kana* for /wo/ and /o/, /ha/ and /wa/, etc. in a confused way.

6.3.1.2 *Labial Stop Lenition*

Likewise, the postpositions *e* 'to, toward' and *wa* '(subdued focus)' are written with the *kana* for /ha he/, respectively. Modern /h/ goes back to *p, as shown by the parallel distributions of the morphophonemic alternations /h ~ b/, /t ~ d/, /s ~ z/, and /k ~ g/. In (word or phrase) medial position, *p merged with /w/, which was non-distinctive before /u/, vanished before /i/ and /e/, and much later, before /o/.[13] In this case, the philological evidence is less clear, and there is some controversy as to the dates of the changes and whether medial *p proceeded to [w] by way of [β] or [ɸ].

6.3.1.3 *Coronal Mergers*

In the modern standard language, the distinctions /di du/ ≠ /zi zu/ have collapsed—one hears only [dʒi (d)zi]—but the distinctive *kana* (e.g. /di/ ぢ ≠ /zi/ じ, /du/ づ ≠ /zu/ ず) are still available. *Hiragana* for /di/ and /du/ are still used when the morphophonemic source is transparently /ti/ or /tu/ (i.e. [tʃi] or [tsɨ]); a few dialects maintain the

---

[11]   The modern assignment of one *hiragana* and one *katakana* to each mora of the language was not completed until the twentieth century. Obsolete alternative *hiragana* forms are referred to as *hentaigana*; obsolete alternative *katakana* forms are called *itaigana*, though sometimes they are also called *hentaigana*.

[12]   We leave aside here a discussion of the graphic differences among *hiragana* and *katakana* and the historical reasons for them, as these developments proceeded independently of historical developments in phonology.

[13]   In initial position, *p- lenited to /h/ = [ç] before /i/ or /y/, [ɸ] before /u/, else [h]. Modern /p/ survives in mimetic expressions and loanwords, more often in two-mora clusters (e.g. *syuppatu* 'departure') than not (e.g. *perapera* 'fluently'). Remarkably, though in native and Sino-Japanese words /w/ now occurs only before /a/, it unquestionably remains a phoneme.

Table 6.1 Modern Japanese *kana* and their *kanji* sources

	w-	r-	y-	m-	h-	n-	t-	s-	k-	Ø-	
kana	わ ワ	ら ラ	や ヤ	ま マ	は ハ	な ナ	た タ	さ サ	か カ	あ ア	-a
kanji	和	良	也	末	波 八	奈	太 多	左 散	加	安 阿	
kana	ゐ ヰ	り リ		み ミ	ひ ヒ	に ニ	ち チ	し シ	き キ	い イ	-i
kanji	爲 井	利		美 三	比	仁	知 千	之	幾	以 伊	
kana		る ル	ゆ ユ	む ム	ふ フ	ぬ ヌ	つ ツ	す ス	く ク	う ウ	-u
kanji		留 流	由	武 牟	不	努 奴	川	寸 須	久	宇	
kana	ゑ ヱ	れ レ		め メ	へ ヘ	ね ネ	て テ	せ セ	け ケ	え エ	-e
kanji	惠 慧	礼		女	部	祢	天	世	計 介	衣 江	
kana	を ヲ	ろ ロ	よ ヨ	も モ	ほ ホ	の ノ	と ト	そ ソ	こ コ	お オ	-o
kanji	遠 乎	呂	與	毛	保	乃	止	會	己	於	

Notes: a. *Katakana* are shown to the right of the corresponding *hiragana* (unshaded cells). The *kanji* from which the *kana* is/are believed to have arisen are shown beneath (shaded cells). NB /si/ = [ʃi], /ti/ = [tʃi], /tu/ = [tsi], /hi/ = [çi], /hu/ = [ɸɯ] in the standard language.

b. Morae of the form CyV are written by combining *kana* for Ci with a small version of the *kana* for yV, e.g. /kya/ きゃ キャ; /syu/ = [ʃɯ] しゅ シュ; /tyo/ = [tʃo] ちょ チョ. This kind of digraphic notation has been extended to innovative morae such as /kwo/ クォ, /ye/ イェ, etc., which in the standard language occur only in new loanwords.

c. A diacritic called *dakuten* indicates the voicing of an obstruent initial; e.g. /gi/ ぎ ギ; /zu/ ず ズ; /de/ で デ; /bo/ ぼ ボ. Modern /p/ is marked with another diacritic, called *handakuten*; e.g. /pa/ ぱ パ.

d. The mora nasal /N/ (usually romanized as syllable-final *n*) is written with *hiragana* ん and *katakana* ン. The mora obstruent /Q/ is notated with *hiragana* っ, *katakana* ッ —small versions of the *kana* for /tu/.

e. Because the morae /we/, /wi/, and /wo/ have merged with /e/, /i/, and /o/, respectively, their *kana* are obsolete, but を ヲ have been retained for the postposition *o* < *wo*.

f. Symbols with shapes similar to those of *katakana* ム マ フ ク were used in musical notation in China during the Song dynasty (Pian 1967: 59), but it is unclear to what extent such continental precedents were known by or influenced the Japanese who created *kana* shapes.

Source: Unger (2005b: 96)

Table 6.2 Pre-1945 *kana* spellings of syllables with more than one historical source

i	いゐひ		
u	うふ		
e	えゑへ		
o	おをほふ		
ka	かくわ	ga	がぐわ
zi	じぢ		
zu	ずづ		
wa	わは		
yū	ゆうゆふいういふ		
ō	おうおほわうあうはう		
kō	こうこふかうかふくわう	gō	ごうごふがうがふぐわう
sō	そうさうさふ	zō	ぞうざうざふ
tō	とうたうたふ	dō	どうだうだふ
nō	のうのふなうなふ		
hō	ほうほふはうはふ	bō	ぼうぼふばうばふ	pō ぽうぽふぱうぱふ
mō	もうまう		
yō	ようやうえうえふ		
rō	ろうろふらうらふ		
kyū	きゅうきうきふ	gyū	ぎゅうぎう
syū	しゅうしうしふ	zyū	じゅうじうじふぢゆう
tyū	ちゅうちう		

Table 6.2 Continued

nyū	**にゅう** にう にふ					
hyū	**ひゅう** ひう	byū	**びゅう** びう			
ryū	**りゅう** りう りふ					
kyō	**きょう** きやう けう けふ	gyō	**ぎょう** ぎやう げう げふ			
syō	**しょう** しやう せう せふ	zyō	**じょう** じやう ぜう **ぢゃう** でう でふ			
tyō	**ちょう** ちやう てう てふ					
nyō	**にょう** ねう					
hyō	**ひょう** ひやう へう	byō	**びょう** びやう べう	pyō	**ぴょう** ぴやう ぺう	
myō	**みょう** めう					
ryō	**りょう** りやう れう れふ					

Note: The spelling of each syllable now regarded as normative is given in boldface.

Source: Unger (2005b: 100).

distinctions phonemically. Phonemically, /dyV/ ≠ /zyV/ (V = /a u o/) morae pattern like /di/ ≠ /zi/.

6.3.1.4 *Vowel Sequence Reductions*

Modern native and Sino-Japanese words contain morae of the shapes /Cya Cyu Cyo/, and a few dialects still retain /kwa gwa/ ≠ /ka ga/. In current orthography, morae with intrasyllabic glides are written by combining the appropriate high-vowel and glide-initial *kana* (now slightly reduced in size); e.g. ジ ヨ /zyo/, く わ /kwa/. But older spellings, especially of Sino-Japanese words, show that /CyV/ morae arose from multiple sources as illustrated in Table 6.2.

6.3.2 Man'yōgana

Although there is now just one *hiragana* and one *katakana* letter for each mora (ignoring voiced obstruents, /CyV/ morae, /N/, and /Q/), most morae could, in earlier times, be written with a number of different *kana*, each derived from a different Chinese

Table 6.3 *Man'yōgana* syllable inventory

	a	ka, ga	sa, za	ta, da	na	pa, ba	ma	ya	ra	wa
	a	ka, ga	sa, za	ta, da	na	pa, ba	ma	ya	ra	wa
1		ki, gi				pi, bi	mi			
i			si, zi	ti, di	ni			(yi)	ri	wi
2		kwi, gwi				pwi, bwi	mwi			
u	u	ku, gu	su, zu	tu, du	nu	pu, bu	mu	yu	ru	(wu)
1		kye, gye				pye, bye	mye			
e			se, ze	te, de	ne			ye	re	we
2		ke, ge				pe, be	me			
1		kwo, gwo			nwo					
o			so, zo	to, do		po	mo	yo	ro	wo
2		ko, go			no					

Note: Many references distinguish *Cwo ≠ Co* for C = *s, z, t, d, m, y*, and *r* in the eighth century before *Man'yōshū*, but in that work there are enough interchanges among *man'yōgana* in the two allegedly different sets of *man'yōgana* for each initial to conclude that the phonemic distinctions had already collapsed (Lange 1973).

character. Before the graphic deformations that gave rise to *kana* proper, an even wider variety of characters functioned in this way. For instance, in fragmentary writings from before the eighth century, the syllable /ta/[14] could be represented by 多, 侈, or 陁; in *Man'yōshū*, 他, 丹, 駄, 當, 手, 田, and other characters were also so used; in *Nihon shoki*, we also find 塔, 淡, 哆, 大, 柁, 黨, and 託 (Igarashi 1969: 161). In this list, 手 and 田 are *kungana* (/ta/ is a Japanese gloss on the Chinese morpheme corresponding to each character); all the rest are *ongana* (/ta/ was (part of) an *on*, or loan pronunciation, of the corresponding Middle Chinese syllable).[15]

When we find these characters in the spellings of certain words, we deduce that they stood for /ta/ on the basis of later evidence, including modern reflexes of the words and/or early annotations telling us how they were traditionally read. Most important, we can find double writings in which a syllable believed to be /ta/ in different instances of a particular word is written indifferently with two different characters in the list. The interlocking set of such pairs for all words proves that the characters on the list could be used interchangeably for the same phonemic syllable (Table 6.3).

It has long been known, however, that the *man'yōgana* lists for certain Old Japanese (OJ) syllables do not share this last vital property. For example, the antecedent

---

[14] In Old Japanese, with just three exceptions, vowel-only morae occurred only word-initially in native words; hence, there is no need to distinguish mora from syllable at this stage of the language.

[15] Some early *ongana* values do not coincide with Sino-Japanese character readings, and were presumably introduced 'second-hand' from sources on the Korean peninsula. See Case (2000), Unger (2012).

of modern /hi/ could be written with such characters as either (1) 比, 必, 卑, 賓, 嬪, 臂 (all *ongana*), 日, 氷, 負, 飯, and 檜 (all *kungana*) or (2) 非, 悲, 斐, 肥, 飛 (*ongana*), 火, 干, 乾, and 樋 (*kungana*). The characters in EACH set are found to be used interchangeably for one another, as in the case of /ta/, but overlapping distribution of members of (1) for members of (2) is NOT found until late in the Old Japanese period (which ended around 900). Consequently, we are forced to conclude that members of (1) and (2) represented phonemically distinct syllables in the eighth century and earlier. The distinction may be written /pi/ (1) ≠ /pwi/ (2), in light of Middle Chinese reconstructions of the syllables corresponding to the *ongana*, Japanese internal reconstruction of the morphemes that gave rise to the *kungana*, and other evidence, most importantly the distribution of the syllables with respect to inflectional endings of verbs and adjectives.[16]

6.4 KOREAN

Prior to the invention of the Korean alphabet (*hunmin cheng-ŭm* or *han'gŭl*), literary Chinese was the dominant written language of the peninsula. Pre-alphabetic methods for writing Korean itself are described below. In addition, special mention should be made of certain place-names written with Chinese characters between the fourth and eighth centuries AD. The principal source for these names, which were replaced by new Sino-Korean names under the Silla kingdom of the eighth century, are gazetteers in *Samguk sagi*, a history compiled in 1145. (A few old place-names are found in earlier Chinese and Japanese sources.) Kim Pusik, who compiled *Samguk sagi*, lists these names under the rubrics Koguryŏ and Paekche, the two kingdoms that vied with Silla for domination of the peninsula, but the linguistic identity of these old names is in dispute (compare Beckwith 2007 with Unger 2009, 2014).

A typical example involves a place once named 難隱別, a sequence of characters abnormal for literary Chinese, that was renamed 七重縣 'sevenfold county'. The string 難隱別 was evidently meant to be phonographic, and may be reconstructed as Middle Chinese *nan-in-bet, Old Korean *nanipel, or something similar. This does not resemble any word of Korean that means or might have been used to indicate 'sevenfold', but it does bring to mind Old Japanese *nana* 'seven' and *pye* 'layer, -fold', which would naturally have formed the compound *nana-pye*. Insofar as the name is listed in the gazetteer for Koguryŏ, one might assign it to the Koguryŏan language, which one might then theorize was related in some way to Japanese. There exists, however, evidence suggesting that the rulers of the kingdom of Koguryŏ were culturally and linguistically related to the rulers of Paekche and Silla; that they controlled the area where the place is

---

[16] It is often said that eighth-century Japanese had eight vowels, but whether or not the vocalic nuclei of certain syllables can be decomposed into a diphthong or a vowel with an onset or offset is a secondary issue; even though some OJ syllables (e.g. /Cwo/ ≠ /Co/) turn out to have been in nearly complementary distributions, there is no serious doubt that they were phonemically distinct.

located only briefly; and that speakers of pre-Japanese anciently lived on the peninsula before migrating to the islands. The name may therefore merely reflect an early stage of Japanese.

6.5 Vietnamese

As in Korea, literary Chinese was the dominant mode of written communication. But a system for writing Vietnamese called *chữ nôm* began to rival the use of literary Chinese during the early fifteenth century. *Chữ nôm* 'southern script' combined the use of native glosses on certain common Chinese characters (contrastively called *chữ hán* 'Chinese script' or *chữ nho* 'scholars' script') with invented ones that represented monosyllabic native morphemes. Vietnamese literati generally formed these by combining two existing Chinese characters much as the Chinese themselves combined 'phonetic' and 'signific' graphic elements to form the vast majority of individual characters. The word *chữ nôm* itself was, for example, written 字喃, in which 字, a graphic reduplication of 字 'character', was created in Vietnam, and 喃, which stood for a Chinese verb meaning 'chatter' or 'mumble'; this was because, viewed as a signific-phonetic compound, it was appropriate for the syllable *nôm* in this word.

   Chữ nôm, never a popular form of writing, died out in the first half of the twentieth century as the alphabetic *quốc ngữ* system gained ascendancy.[17]

6.6 Innovations in the Korean and Japanese Systems

Innovations in the inventory of characters were not confined to Vietnam. In Korea, a few novel characters, called *kukja*, somewhat like the graphic compounds of *chữ nôm*, were created from time to time, but they played an insignificant role in the adaptation of Chinese characters to the writing of Korean. Prior to the invention of the Korean alphabet in the fifteenth century, three methods were employed to varying extents: *hyangch'al*, *kugyŏl*, and *idu* (see Lee & Ramsey 2000: 46–55). *Hyangch'al* was an attempt to reflect Korean word order with Chinese characters, some of which were to be glossed while others provided phonetic cues to intervening syllables; very few *hyangch'al* texts survive—the system flourished in the eighth century but died out soon thereafter—and there are many uncertainties concerning the functions of particular characters in the texts. In *kugyŏl*, characters were interpolated into *hanmun* texts to indicate Korean

---

[17] As DeFrancis (1977) explains, the need to educate and recruit the general population in resistance to French and Japanese imperialism was a compelling reason to adopt an alphabetic writing system.

postpositions and auxiliary verb inflections phonographically. Some of the interpolated characters were graphically reduced in the manner of Japanese *katakana*. In *idu* (the practice of which varied over time), certain Sino-Korean collocations were maintained but permuted, with phonographic characters interpolated to produce a text somewhat like the mixed used of Chinese characters and *kana* in medieval and modern Japanese, but with no graphic differentiation of characters used in different functions. *Idu* continued in use after the introduction of the alphabet.

In Japan, novel characters, called *kokuji*, were a slightly more prominent feature of the writing system than the *kukja* of Korean, but still played a minor role. The mixed-modality writing system of Old Japanese must have been inspired by, if not directly borrowed from, peninsular writing practices, but developed in different directions. The way in which some of the earliest *kanbun* texts deviate from normative literary Chinese syntax makes it clear that their authors intended them to be read as Japanese. This involved assigning glosses to certain characters, permuting their order as needed, and adding grammatical elements (postpositions and auxiliary predicates) for which there were no graphic counterparts in the Chinese texts. The method developed over centuries, culminating in a system during the Muromachi Period (*c*.1333–1467) in which each individual character was glossed, producing a conspicuously non-colloquial but intelligible rendering (*yomikudashi*). Interlinear notations were sometimes added to assist readers. Text was composed of top-to-bottom lines spanning the page from right to left; glosses in *kana* were placed to the right of each line; subscript-like codes were placed on the left to indicate the required order of reading characters. Information of use in historical phonology is contained in the glosses.[18]

6.6.1 Diacritical Notations

Syllables of Middle Chinese were traditionally analysed as having four tones (the development of which into the four tones of the modern standard language and the tones of other so-called dialects is quite complicated). When it was necessary to indicate them, it was customary to place a dot in one of the four corners of the imaginary square within which the character for the syllable in question was written. This practice was adapted in Korea and Japan in different ways.

In Korea, dots were placed to the left of syllables constructed from letters of the alphabet in Middle Korean documents. It is now widely believed that the absence of a dot indicated low pitch, a single dot indicated high pitch, and a pair of dots indicated a rising pitch contour. In such Japanese lexicographical works as *Ruiju myōgishō* (?1083), dots were used in similar fashion, but the interpretation of which indicated high and which low pitch remains unsettled.[19]

---

[18] Reference works in English on the *kanbun* notational system include Crawcour (1965), Komai and Rohlich (1988), and Frellesvig (2010).

[19] On the history and adaptation of such markings for the indication of pitch accent distinctions in Middle Japanese, see de Boer (2010). On early Japanese lexicography, see Bailey (1960).

Dots in the corners or at the midpoints of the sides of the imaginary writing square were also used in Japan for a time to encode Japanese particles and inflectional terminations required for the translation-like reading of *kanbun* texts. This system, called *wokototen*, was believed to be unique to Japan, but now appears to have developed in conjunction with stylus-impressed notations that were also used in Korea. It is to be distinguished from the use of *kana* and other marks to facilitate the reading of *kanbun* texts mentioned at the end of the previous section.

6.6.2 Stylus-Impressed Notations

Although inkless notations are mentioned in such early texts as *Kagerō nikki* 蜻蛉日記 (where they are called *mono no saki*), *Genji monogatari* 源氏物語 (*tsumajirushi*), and *Takamura monogatari* 篁物語 (*kakuhichi*), actual examples of them were not known until September 1961 when Kobayashi Yoshinori noticed stylus-impressed markings on a manuscript dating from the mid tenth century in an exhibit of treasures from Mt Kōya (Kobayashi 1987). By March 2003, Kobayashi could report 3265 examples of *kakuhitsu* found throughout Japan. Although examples are found in Buddhist and non-Buddhist *kanbun* texts as well as in Japanese texts, *kakuhitsu* are generally based on contemporary *onna-de* 'woman's hand', i.e. *hiragana*, and appear to reflect vernacular language. Since July 2000, evidence of the use of inkless notations in Korea starting in the seventh century has come to light; they have been found in texts from Dunhuang dating from the early fifth century (Kobayashi 2003).

6.7 CONCLUSION

The foregoing summarizes the most important facts about diffuse writing relevant to the topic of historical phonology. It is perhaps worth adding two points of more general intellectual interest that emerge from an accurate understanding of diffuse writing systems.

First, the long history and richness of the Chinese writing system are by no means insurmountable obstacles to phonological reconstruction. There is nothing in the history of diffuse writing systems that justifies doubting that speech is the primary modality of language. Postmodernist insistence on the Otherness of diffuse writing systems and those who use them is poorly supported by empirical facts.

Second, the cultural cohesion of the so-called Sino-Xenic sphere, to the extent it exists, is evidently the result of ideas shared through and common practices used in the reading and writing of literary Chinese poetry and prose, not the mere use or adaptation of the Chinese writing system. The interpretation of experimental results in psycholinguistics as indicative of fundamental cognitive differences between people living within and without the Sino-Xenic sphere should therefore be viewed with great scepticism.

CHAPTER 7

....

INTERPRETING ALPHABETIC ORTHOGRAPHIES

Early Middle English Spelling

....

ROGER LASS

Every script is a cultural implement subject to human ingenuity and error, created under certain circumstances for certain purposes and a certain language. To be sure, there are common traits, and economy of effort clearly is one of the guiding principles of human behaviour. Yet there is plenty of room for waste, extravagance and manifestations of the human mind defying bare utility. Cultural inertia [...] and normativism [...] are strong forces at work in every literate community. They have little to do with writing systems as such or with their efficiency, yet they exercise a strong influence on their formation.

Florian Coulmas, *Writing Systems: An Introduction to their Linguistic Analysis* (2003)

7.1 PRELIMINARIES[1]

....

HISTORICAL linguistics was solely the study of written language until August 1877. Then Thomas Edison began The New Age: audible speech entered our database with his cylinder recording of 'Mary had a little lamb' (see Maguire, this volume, for a consideration of the role of sound recordings in historical phonology).

Written language is not merely parasitic on spoken language, and whatever it is it is not 'transcription'. It is not strictly 'language' either, though it may approximate it and

---

[1] For further rather different discussion of the topic of this chapter, see Lass (1997: ch. 2).

give us important information about it. Unlike natural languages orthographies are at least in the first instance *designed*; we don't know how natural languages arose, but it was surely not through deliberate human agency.[2] Over time designed orthographies tend to lose autonomy, and are subject to continual redesign leading to often radical change, typically at the instigation of individual writers in writing communities that have not undergone 'standardization' (or 'homogenization': Coulmas 2003). Many languages (perhaps most older ones) come down to us as the outputs of such communities manifested in 'text languages' (Fleischman 2000), where 'the language' is equivalent to 'the set of attested non-identical idiolects', and each idiolect can properly be called 'a language'. Orthographies may also be institutionally or socially manipulated, as in standardization or spelling reform; but they are always subject to arbitrary interference in a way that language is not.

This chapter is limited in two important respects. First, almost all of it, both empirical and theoretical, will concern English at various periods, and most of that early Middle English, particularly of the Southwest Midlands. Second, there will be virtually no consideration of 'phonology' in the theoretical sense, but primarily of mapping between some kind of systemic elements and surface phonetics, and the protocols for establishing phonetic values in dead languages. In particular, issues of underlying theoretical stance (in the sense of where these analyses are in the arena of modern theoretical linguistics) and problems of distinctiveness will be ignored. The two main concerns will be the structure of orthographic systems in relation to what they purport to represent (which are almost certainly in these cases not 'phonemes' or any other modern theoretical units), and the protocols for assigning rough phonetic values to orthographical output.

I restrict myself to this limited material because it is what I know best at first hand, in the sense of having worked for over a decade on details of scribal practice. This enables me to deal in perhaps excruciating detail with the real orthographic behaviour of single humans (as representatives of writing traditions) and avoid reifying 'languages'. It also provides a counterpoint to Minkova (this volume), who treats related matters in terms of the representation of contrast in the history of English (see also Dresher, this volume, who makes some considerable use of spelling evidence, and Unger, this volume, who considers evidence from certain nonalphabetic writing systems). But what I have to say about English will probably be generally projectable, at least in principle, both to other varieties of early English and to other alphabetic systems. Though whether the kinds of praxis I analyse here appear in medieval Slavic or Romance or other systems I do not know, as I have not worked with texts in those traditions. The work discussed here is the result of working from diplomatic transcriptions with no modern editorial intervention. It may differ in detail from most or all other alphabetic systems, but it will furnish examples of analytical praxis applicable to any alphabetic

---

[2] I exclude of course artificial languages like Esperanto from this discussion.

tradition. Whether all the phenomena appear in some given case is an empirical matter.

Writing is a mnemonic for speakers who know the language being written, but not entirely what it might at first appear to be, a means for preserving phonology. (It is better at preserving morphosyntax.) Many of the properties of written language may be indexical rather than linguistically informative: spelling differences between dialects may have no phonological reference, but be important geographical markers (McIntosh 1956), and we often find complex orthographical dialect continua with no or very little phonological reference in the variation (see Laing & Lass 2003). Some spelling features may just be personally indexical. So we must understand both linguistic and indexical functions. We must also realize, as we will see, that the tasks many early writers assigned to spelling were not always the same as current ones, even at times apparently opposed.

7.2 ALPHABETS

7.2.1 Fundamentals

A spelling system or orthography is a (usually fuzzy) mapping between some selected set of linguistic units and a set of graphic characters (possibly also fuzzy) so as to 'represent a language' visually.[3] Prototypically, the mapping in an alphabet (as opposed to a syllabary or a 'morphographic' system like Chinese) is between segments[4] and written characters. Alphabetic scripts produce linear strings of graphs that are rough icons of strings of segment-size units, but rarely 'classical' phonemes—the sort one could arrive at by commutation.[5] But very often, except in the unhistorical fantasies that appear as normalized edited texts (see Lass 2004), and not always even in these, 'emic' characterizations are inappropriate or clumsy, and we do better following the apparent praxis of the writer rather than our own anachronistic prescriptions. At least in the early western orthographies I am most familiar with we avoid anachronism and gain in descriptive power by taking as our point of departure a version of the classical/medieval *littera* and its associated terminology (see section 7.4, and Murray, this volume, on the not-unrelated matter

---

[3] What one means by 'a language' is less simple than it seems. This topic tends to be so slippery that there will be a lot of scare quotes in this chapter. The notion 'represent a language' is not clear either, since orthographies obviously represent only a proper subset of what there is to be represented, and sometimes leave out huge amounts that we as linguists would rather like to see.

[4] Let us assume we know what segments are, and that they really 'exist'. There is no space here to get into the morass of argument on this topic. For discussion see Coulmas (2003: ch. 5).

[5] Though minimal-pair commutation as an analytic device and a desideratum for system construction had already been developed in the twelfth century, in the work of the Icelandic First Grammarian (Benediktsson 1972). But this is not general praxis in pre-modern—or even modern—times.

of 'letter theory').[6] We also do better taking a primarily historical rather than synchronic stance in analysing the mappings in pre-modern systems (see section 7.4). The analysis of standardized systems is often conceptually simpler than that of non-standardized ones, but even familiar standard orthographies like that of Classical Latin do not typically yield to full analysis in terms of contrastive segments.

Even patently non-distinctive segments may be represented (e.g. the velar nasal in Greek and Gothic, which occurs only before velars). Mapping does not have to be from the single segment: clusters may be represented as single graphs, e.g. Greek ξ /ks/ or Hebrew צ /ts/. Such single graphs can have different structures: Greek ξ has no syntactic parse in initial position (ξένος /ksen-o-s/ GUEST, STRANGER), but usually does finally (φάλαγξ /phalank-s/ PHALANX, where the /s/-portion = 'nom sg'), i.e. ξ can mean /ks/ or /k+s/. On the other hand digraphs or even trigraphs may represent single segments, as in English 'sh', German 'sch' for /ʃ/. Mapping does not even have to correspond to segmental order (cf. English initial 'wh' in dialects that retain the *which/witch* contrast).[7] It can occasionally even apparently be 'prosodic' in the Firthian sense (e.g. Firth 1948).[8] Alphabetic characters may also be purely diacritic, e.g. the variable use of double consonant graphs in West Germanic to show that the preceding vowel is short, or doubling of vowel graphs in German and Dutch to show length. And graphs can also indicate zero, as in English 'silent -e'. An alphabet then is an inventory of symbol shapes that tend more often than not to have segmental reference and to be mapped in one way or another—often not directly or unambiguously—to phonetic substance. (Just look at the six examples of 'o'[9] in the last eleven words of the preceding sentence.) And finally many linguistic elements may not be mapped at all (sections 7.3–7.4), or there may be overlaps or multiple shapes for single segments or sequences (section 7.4).

'Ideal' biunique spelling systems—one character per segment and vice versa—are vanishingly rare. Most orthographies carry the idiosyncratic preferences of their designers or users. And those of any decent age bear historical baggage: e.g. English 'gh' in

---

[6] Bybee (2001, this volume) mounts a strong challenge to the traditional phoneme/unit notion. She argues for a theoretical framework in which the segmental inventories of languages are neither exhaustive nor composed of discrete 'units', but are rather constantly shifting networks of variables, responsive to usage and type and token frequency. Language 'systems' under this interpretation are always *in posse*, never *in esse* except as the result of linguists' methodologically forced choices. This, rather than the emic approach, which was rather 'exotic' at least before the twentieth century, may be one of the factors driving the design of many earlier orthographies. 'A language' as input to writing may be considered in most cases to be an abstraction from this kind of fuzzy system.

[7] There is no doubt that the items written 'hw' in Old English and 'hw' or 'wh' in Middle English are historically clusters: their origin is Germanic *xw-. There is no agreement as to what they represent in Middle English (if indeed only one thing), and there are both voiceless [w] and [hw] types in different Modern English dialects. I have chosen to interpret these as clusters, which seems to me the simplest account.

[8] In one thirteenth-century English MS, London Dulwich College MS XXII (*Le Estorie del Euangelie*), spellings like *waht* WHAT, *wehn* WHEN, *wehr* WHERE, *wihlc* WHICH occur alongside forms in initial *wh*-. It is reasonable to suppose that the scribe heard voiceless friction but was not precisely sure where it was; the variable placements suggest he took it as a property of the syllable as a whole (see Lass & Laing 2009: 115).

[9] For conventions of representation, see section 7.4.

eight, night, through, which represent a long-vanished /x/. They also tend to have considerable non-biunique representation (English /ʃ/ in *shoe, vicious, ocean, nation, passion, chic, schist*...). This may be exacerbated by intensive contact with other orthographies, as in the case of English borrowing 'qu' from Latin and French to indicate /kw/, replacing the original OE 'cw',[10] both in native words (*quick* < OE *cwicu*) and loans (*question* < Anglo-French *questiun*).

The mapping does not have to be just from low-level units either. We also find:

(i) *Logography.* Non-biunique category/symbol relations allow a form of logographic writing: the spelling indicates not only a phonological string, but typically one member of a set of homophones: English *right, wright, rite.* These distinctions often reflect historical origin: *right* < OE *riht, wright* < *wyrhta, rite* < OF *rite*; but sometimes not: English *deer, dear* < OE *dēor, dēore.*[11]

(ii) *Morphophonemic writing* ('morphography'). While alphabetic praxis generally represents at a 'surface segment' level (even in the case of logographs), some languages represent morphophonemically as well. German has final obstruent devoicing, but does not systematically indicate this in spelling, thus the famous German *Bund* LEAGUE, pl *Bünde* /bʊnt, bʏndə/, but *bunt* COLOURFUL, inflected *bunte* /bʊnt, bʊntə/, etc. The 'd' in *Bund* (according to surface phonotactics 'unpronounceable') signals that /d/ will appear stem-finally if a vowel-initial suffix follows. It is structurally indexical: it marks both morpheme identity and the existence of an alternation, not simply phoneme composition 'at the surface'.

7.2.2 Diacritics

Diacritics are shapes that may or may not be 'full' members of the alphabet but rather 'modifiers' of proper or primary ones. They may be letters in special uses, fragments of letters, or arbitrary signs like accents, diereses, etc. The Icelandic First Grammarian (12th c.) gives the most explicit early analysis of the principle, which he uses in his description of the new letters he wants to introduce into Icelandic, so that every representation can be *réttrædir,* CORRECTLY PRONOUNCEABLE. Note particularly his discrimination between 'basic' entire *stafir* (STAVES, *litterae*) and fragments used for diacritic purposes (§84, modified from Haugen's 1950b translation).

In addition to the five vowel-letters, which already were in the Latin alphabet: *a, e, i, o, u,* I have added the four letters that are now written here: *ǫ, ę, ø, y. Ǫ* has its loop from *a,* and its circle from *o,* because it is a blending of their two sounds, spoken with a

---

[10] Actually OE uses the runic letter wynn 'ƿ' to represent /w/; I use the standard but anachronistic transliteration 'w' here as in the handbooks and dictionaries.

[11] I do not use 'logographic' the way 'ideographic' was used in older descriptions of Chinese (see Unger, this volume): 1, 2, @, & are not logographs but might be ideographs in the sense of 'writing ideas'.

less open mouth than *a*, but more than for *o*. Ę is written with the loop of *a*, but with the whole shape of *e*, since it is a blend of the two, spoken with a less open mouth than *a*, but more than *e*.[12] Ø is made from the sounds of *e* and *o* together, and therefore written with the (cross) stroke of *e* and the circle of *o*. *Y* is the sounds of *i* and *u* made into one sound, spoken with a less open mouth than *i* but more than *u*, so it shall have the first branch of the capital letter *u*.[13]

The direction of diacritic 'instruction' does not have to be the same as that of reading. It can be perpendicular, as in the First Grammarian's 'ę'; or contrary, as in English final 'silent -*e*', which is read backwards to its left, e.g. causing a vowel to be read long: the instruction is read right-to-left ('regressively') during a reading process that goes left-to-right. Germanic, unlike Goidelic Celtic, rarely uses 'progressive' diacritics, i.e. ones that give instructions about what follows (e.g. in Irish 'i' before a consonant graph is a diacritic for palatalization). The First Grammarian suggests other possibilities, such as angled linear diacritics in the middle of a character which do not have a 'direction' of reading but modify the letter shape as a whole non-directionally.

Most Germanic and many other orthographies show a number of properties that seem to make little synchronic sense, but have relatively clear historical explanations. One is a general tendency for -VCC(V)- sequences in writing (where the first V is stressed) to be interpreted as having short vowels, and for -VC(V)- to indicate long vowels (in English only -VCV-). So German *gut* /guːt/ GOOD, inflected *gute*, *Gott* /gɔt/ GOD. These conventions arise primarily from early lengthening in open syllables and shortening before geminates. A V:C sequence may be written with a double vowel graph, as in German *Aal* /aːl/ EEL; this is usual for all vowels in Netherlandic and for some mid vowels in English; it is only one of a number of devices in German, which also uses 'h' as a length diacritic equivalent to a second vowel graph, e.g. *zehn* TEN /tseːn/.[14]

---

[12]   Some interpretation is needed: *minnr opnum munni* 'with less open mouth' must mean 'opener, with lower tongue/jaw' when it refers to the diacritic function of the 'loop of *a*' with respect to <o, e>, but 'rounded' when it refers to the diacritic functions described for distinguishing <ø, y>. This is a descriptive problem until well into the seventeenth century: John Hart (1569) makes the same conflation, so that both 'lower than x' and 'more rounded than x' are described as involving less opening of the mouth. The post-classical Latin terminology is partly at fault, since it does not mesh with observation: the position of the tongue on the front/back axis is notoriously hard to observe, and in effect vowels are classified on a single dimension with rounding and height conflated under 'aperture'. Wallis (1653) is still unaware of the anatomy, but he does classify rounded vowels as *labiales* (see Lass 1999: 61–3). This does not make early phoneticians useless for discovering the values to be attached to letters: it just makes our conclusions less certain and our work harder.

[13]   '*?and the straight branch of I'. This is a guess, in line with editorial tradition; there is material missing but no gap in the MS. The description of 'y', even filled out, is a little difficult. I suspect that by 'the first branch of the capital letter U' (though the scribe writes lower-case) he must mean the *figura* <V> with one of the other sides extended into an angled descender (i.e. the structure of his <ø> figura). See also Lass & Laing (2012: §6).

[14]   Another use of 'h' in German is as a hiatus marker which must not be a glottal stop, as in *gehen*, *ziehen*. This may lead to spelling pronunciations, which violate the former phonotactic constraint that /h/ only appears morpheme-initially. The same thing happens in many English (especially US)

7.3 'DEFECTS' AND FUNCTIONALITY

There appear to be no general rules for how much of a language's system actually has to be represented, or how clearly interpretable it has to be. The Cypriot syllabary failed to represent half the vowels and two-thirds of the consonants (Lass 1997: 51–2); and a 'consonantal' script like Hebrew does not represent vowels at all; in effect it writes not words but roots and the skeletons of affixes.[15] Most tone languages do not write their tones.[16]

But such 'problems' are expectable. The processing of spoken and written utterances is not the same, but there are fundamental commonalities. As Gillian Brown remarks (1977: 11):

> [...] listeners are not simply passive processors who undertake automatic signal recognition exercises as acoustic signals are fed into them and so construct 'a meaning' [...] the signals they receive [...] are frequently so debased that a signal-recognition processor simply does not have adequate data to work on, and cannot even get started.

How then do receivers manage to recognize what they receive? Brown again:

> The answer is that humans are active searchers for meaning. As soon as someone begins to speak, the co-operative human listener is actively trying to work out what he is saying, what he is likely to say next and what he is likely to mean by what he says [...] Armed with all this activated knowledge the listener monitors the incoming acoustic signal, which will simultaneously shape and confirm his expectations.

That is, texts are encoded objects that are supposed to mean something, and the decoder's task is to find some meaning. This has consequences also for the producers of written utterances: since they too are recipients with their other hats on, and know (if not explicitly) what the task is, there is nothing to stop them engaging in further signal degradation (for whatever reason)—under the assumption that as both producers and recipients they know what will work and what will not.

We can profitably use this strategic similarity in visual and auditory language processing in analysing the spelling systems of older writers.[17] There are two mottoes that ought to be engraved on the armorial bearings of all historical linguists:

dialects where word-internal (but still syllable-initial) 'h' comes to be pronounced in words like *vehicle*. Spelling not only takes phonology as its primary input, it can also map into it, in so-called 'spelling pronunciation'.

[15] Vowel signs are written in certain genres, e.g. pedagogical and liturgical texts.

[16] For a marvellous analytical survey of the world's major writing systems, alphabets and all other types, see Coulmas (1989).

[17] There will be differences in the complexity of this task, depending on the type of language. Standard written languages are (ideally, in intention) minimally variable; their conventions tend to be

- Writing is not transcription.
- Spellings are mnemonics for native speakers (in the first instance).

Unpacked (cf. Laing & Lass 2003: §1, Lass & Laing 2005):

- A textual heritage is the product of native or near-native speaking profes-sionals[18] writing for audiences with whom they shared a corpus of linguistic knowledge.
- The apparent 'disorder' or 'defectiveness' of many past orthographic systems is an artefact of our own lack of understanding and our habits of reading and analysis. The mutual expectations of early scribes and their readers could be very different from ours—particularly in the aesthetics and logic of orthographic design.
- Many scribes were capable of sophisticated and subtle linguistic analysis—though often in terms of distinctly non-'structuralist' criteria.
- The 'natural state' for a language is to manifest variation at every descriptive level.

But if spelling is for the speaker, none of this really matters. Pretty much any kind of 'defective' spelling will do, as long as the reader can be assumed to have some idea in advance of what a word is likely to be, or what the range of choices is. In the present context, no reader who knows English would have any trouble reconstituting the defective representation *spllng*, and we could decide if we wished to use 'x' or 'q' for /ʃ/. There is also no reason to assume that maximal clarity and speed of recovery are what either systems or their users are always (or even mostly) after. There can be an element of 'secrecy', especially if literacy is restricted in a society. This can shade off into sheer love of complexity, playfulness, and puzzle-making (see Laing & Lass 2003: §3).

The privileged status of the speaker (and therefore his cultural norms) means that we have no right to expect systems that cohere with our modern ideas of 'good' ortho-graphic praxis. Contrariwise, we have a duty to assume that the spellers are doing some-thing that they assume is interpretable, and our job is to develop a hermeneutic that non-anachronistically provides techniques for anything we are likely to come across in past writing, whether the work of scribes or early typesetters, or of 'naive' (untrained) writers.

---

more transparent to the decoders, or at least easier to learn, because the whole literate population has been inducted into the code. Non-standard variable written languages are more complex: many are characterized by obscure and text-specific conventions, so that the negotiation between encoder and decoder is more elaborate than we are accustomed to.

[18] They at least are the main contributors to what historians study. A less accessible part of the heritage is that of amateurs (e.g. correspondence, journals, other 'naive' output). But the principles of interpretation are pretty much the same, since these systems represent the use of the professional ones by the untrained, perhaps under less constraint because of the lack of familiarity with models. See Lass (1987).

7.4 WHY PHONEMES AND GRAPHEMES ARE USUALLY UNHELPFUL

7.4.1 Introduction

The notion that orthography constitutes an 'emic' level like structuralist versions of phonology is a non-starter with most historical alphabetic systems (as well as modern ones: a notable exception is Finnish, which is as phonemic as it gets). Most historical orthographies simply do not represent what we *know* (on other grounds) must have been the 'underlying' phonemic systems. We know this only indirectly, and it is usually impossible to unravel orthographical/phonological mappings except by appealing to the past, often quite distant, and the future as well, as well as to metalinguistic commentary if available.

For instance, most Middle English varieties from the thirteenth century on almost certainly had two pairs of long mid vowels, an opener and a closer, one front and one back. Except for suggestions in the orthographies of certain text languages,[19] this distinction is not indicated in general and never more than partially. The only way we know about it is by looking at their etymologies: what seems to have been the case in Old English, when they were at least partly written differently,[20] and how the identically written categories developed in later periods (mainly from the sixteenth and seventeenth centuries; see Lass 1999: §3.4.2). As a more familiar example, except for the good luck of there being a native if difficult tradition of metrics, we only really know that Latin had long and short vowels, and which words had which, on the basis of IE reconstructions and comparative method, and the history of the later Romance languages. None of the evidence is orthographic. So paradoxically doing apparently 'synchronic' analyses of the import of older orthographies is virtually always etymology. What appears to be 'interpretation' turns out largely to be reconstruction. The IE properties that inform our judgement of length in Latin and earlier Romance are themselves reconstructed. So is everything before 1877, except—used with care because of problems of metalanguage and/or anatomical knowledge—the writings of contemporary phoneticians.

In orthography we are in a partly different world from where we are in linguistics proper. So I base a central portion of my exposition not on any modern theory of orthography/phonology mapping, but on a modified version of a classical and medieval framework, plus standard philological procedures.

---

[19] Scribes often used 'a' as a diacritic for openness, so 'ee' and 'ea' would stand for something like [eː] and [ɛː] respectively. See Lass & Laing (2012). These categories largely merged in most dialects outside of Ireland, hence *meet, meat* are now homophones.

[20] Open [ɛː] usually represents OE *ǣ* or *e* lengthened in open syllables, close [eː] represents OE *ē*.

7.4.2 Economy, Prodigality, *Littera*, and Substitution[21]

So far I have talked loosely of 'phonemes', and otherwise been cagey about terminology, avoiding 'grapheme' because of its bundling with 'phoneme' and the various 'structuralist' traditions and their emphasis on distinctiveness and redundancy; instead I have used 'graph', 'symbol', 'character' indifferently, representing graphic categories in inverted commas and phonetic/phonological ones in various brackets. Now I can say what I mean. I depart from modern frameworks because they do not always seem to provide the best analyses for early writers or reflect accurately what they appear to be doing. Older writers are frequently not 'structuralist', and it seems better to use a theoretical framework and notation that also are not and are closer to what scribes would have learned in school—though I will take considerable liberties in exposition.

To limit myself to the post-classical West, one major schoolbook would have been the *Ars maior* of Aelius Donatus (fl. 5th century AD). In book I is a canonical statement:

> Littera est pars minima vocis articulatae ... littera est vox, quae scribi potest individua ... accidunt cuique littera tria, nomen figura potestas, quaeritur enim, quid vocatur littera, qua figura sit, qua possit.

In a slightly exegetical translation:

> *Littera* is the smallest unit of articulated sound ... *littera* is (a) sound which is capable of being written alone ... *littera* has three properties: name, shape, power [= sound value]. For one must ask what the *littera* is called, what its shape is, and what its power is.

The *littera* is an abstract object, under the classical interpretation a member of a universal phonetic alphabet. Each *littera* has only one possible *potestas*. But post-classical scribes generally did not construe *littera* in quite this sense: indeed our interpretive task would be much easier if they had. Much of the doctrine however does remain implicitly, and an idea of what were the canonical interpretations of particular *litterae* may help us in figuring out what later writers intend. They often had a much more complex vision, which I will use as the basis for some of the exegesis here. At the very least the notion of *littera* and its accompanying terminology carry no modern theoretical baggage, which leaves my field of discourse freer.[22]

I follow the conventions developed by Michael Benskin (1997: 1 n.1, 2001: 194 n. 4) and used by Margaret Laing and myself in a number of places (Laing & Lass 2003, Lass & Laing 2005, 2012, *LAEME* and elsewhere). *Litterae* are in inverted commas, the *figurae*

---

[21] Some of the material in section 7.4 is borrowed with modification from *LAEME*, introduction, ch. 2, and Lass & Laing (2012: §6).

[22] For general background on *littera*, see Abercrombie (1949); on the Middle Ages in particular Benediktsson (1972); on Middle English *LAEME*, introduction, ch. 2.

occurring in particular manuscript systems are in angled brackets (not to be interpreted as 'graphemes'), and *potestates* are in square brackets. Glosses and the names of lexical items are in small capitals. Standard citation forms, manuscript forms without specific litteral reference, etymological categories and reconstructions are in 'uninformative' italics.

The stream of *litterae* in writing is represented by a sequence of *figurae*. Except where the concepts *littera* and *figura* overlap (e.g. where in some Middle English systems the *litterae* thorn 'þ' = [θ ~ ð] and 'y' are realized by identical *figurae*) at the system level we therefore talk about a *littera* as the superordinate for all the different possible *figurae* that different scribes, or any one scribe, may adopt for it.

7.4.3 Substitution Sets[23]

Spelling systems can be loosely classified as 'economical' or 'prodigal' (Laing 1999, Laing & Lass 2003). An economical system makes some approach towards the ideal[24] of one *littera* one *potestas*; a prodigal one allows considerable multivocal relationship. These notions of course are relative: all systems are somewhere on a cline between the two. And even the most prodigal systems may be economical in some particulars. For instance, I know of no system that uses 'p' multivocally; but there are many Middle English ones that use 'eo' for a very large number of *potestates* (Lass & Laing 2005, and see section 7.4.4). Similarly I know no Middle English (or any other) systems with multiple representations for [p], but many with large substitution sets for [x] (see below).

To illustrate the two system types consider the spellings of OE *-ht*[25] (as in NIGHT < *niht*, BOUGHT < *bōhte*, etc.) in four hands in the same manuscript: Cambridge, Trinity College B.14.39 (323) (hereafter Trinity: SW Midlands, second half of the thirteenth century). Here are the patterns for the four main hands that contribute text in English, with frequencies of different spellings:

Scribe A: 'st' 89, 't' 55, 'tt' 4, 'cst' 3, 'ct' 2, 'th' 2, 'chit' 1, 'cht' 1, 'cðth' 1, 'sþ' 1, 'th' 1, 'thth' 1, 'tth' 1

Scribe B: 'st' 90, 't' 21, 'tt' 3, 'd' 1

Scribe C: 't' 19, 'tt' 3

Scribe D: 't' 11, 'st' 10, 'cht' 8, 'ch' 4, 'ct' 3, 'd' 2, 'th' 2, 'tht' 2, '3t' 2, 'dt' 1, 'tf' 1, 'tt' 1

---

[23] All early Middle English material is cited from *LAEME*, the *Linguistic Atlas of Early Middle English*. This is a particularly good source because the transcriptions are diplomatic: there is no emendation, and all spelling variation and idiosyncrasy are registered. Furthermore the corpus consists of lexicogrammatically tagged texts, and its enabling software is such that an orthographic dictionary for any individual text can be extracted, enabling us to study spelling with more precision than otherwise, not allowing us to reify 'the language' but restricting us to individual text languages.

[24] For us anyhow. There is no universal reason why it should be, as is clear from much scribal praxis.

[25] As I noted in section 7.4.1, it is typically necessary (or at least useful, highly convenient, and traditional) to interpret early orthographic representations first in terms of etymology, not synchronic phonology, as that is often available if at all only via the etymological categories being represented.

Scribes B and C are (at least relatively) economical in their approach to words containing this historical sequence; A and D are profligate.

A set of *litterae* in variation for the same *potestas* or etymological category is a *Litteral Substitution Set* (LSS: cf. Laing 1999; Laing & Lass 2003). Thus Scribe C has for OE -*ht* the LSS {'t', 'tt'}, B has the LSS {'st', 't', 'tt', 'd'}, D {'t', 'st', 'cht', 'ch', 'ct', 'd', 'th', 'tht', 'ʒt', 'dt', 'tf', 'tt'}, and A {'st', 't', 'tt', 'cst', 'ct', 'th', 'chit', 'cht', 'cðth', 'sþ', 'th', 'thth', 'tth'}.

The inverse of an LSS is a *Potestatic Substitution Set* (PSS: Laing & Lass 2003: 262–3). So for Scribe D the *littera* 'ʒ' ('yogh') maps to the PSS {[h], [x], [j], [w], [ɣ]}. For instance [h]: *ʒu* HOW < OE *hū*; [x] *driʒten* LORD < OE *dryhten*; [j]: *ʒe* YE < OE *gē*; [w]: *roʒen* TO ROW < OE *rōwan*; [ɣ]: *daʒes* DAYS < OE *dagas*. A system prodigal in one direction is likely to be so in the other—prodigality is a fundamental design style.

This substitutive praxis is revisionist. According to Donatus's definition, each *littera* has a *potestas*, as inseparable from it as its name and shape ('accidunt cuique littera tria'). Just as the *potestas* is a local property ('accident') of the *littera*, so each *littera* would seem to be appropriately connected with just one *potestas*; at least nothing in the text appears to grant a licence for multiple representation. But as far as I know there was never any period in the early history of any written language when there was not some spelling variation, so the principle was breached from the outset. The general classical definition does not prevent the use of the doctrine of *littera* as a hermeneutic device; it merely suggests that the medieval notion is different in major ways from the late antique one.

I use this terminological framework to avoid confusion with concepts like 'phoneme' and 'grapheme', which for the most part are not intended, and also deliberately to set the occasionally somewhat unorthodox discussion in an unfamiliar metalanguage.

7.4.4 Knowing What a Word is in Order to Read it: 's' in Trinity Scribe B

The (relatively) 'structuralist' orthography, with its essentially contrastive logic, is familiar to the non-specialist; but there are orthographies, as the data above suggests, that operate at least partly on quite different design principles. These are unlikely to be familiar to most readers, and therefore deserve some discussion. They are typical of languages with no supraregional prestige variety, where the usual case is that writers write their own regional dialects, or since these generally are not standardized, in essence their own idiolects, or versions of the variable language current in a particular text community. They may appear at first sight 'alphabetic' and transcriptional, but are also both strongly lexigraphic and litteral-substitutive, sometimes to the extent of appearing to constitute a different 'natural kind' from any familiar modern ones. The principles they operate on are quite distinct from 'structuralist' ones, but no less transparent in the end—with some work.

Any reader of a text brings background knowledge to it; ours is different from that of the original audience, but we can use it analogously to make sense of texts. The criteria are in the end the same: written representations are ultimately badges of word identity,[26] and the reader has to know in advance, or be able to work out, which word is likely meant.

Some writers design orthographies that in part appear deliberately to do quite the opposite of 'transcribing'. Consider a case where the contemporary reader and the scholar seven centuries later both have equally good reasons to believe in the existence of a certain contrast, but the writer chooses a representative style that deliberately obscures it. In outline, we and the original audience 'know' that there are two distinctive units /X/ and /Y/ 'in the language', but the scribe quite uniformly represents both with the *littera* that we think is appropriate only for /Y/:

Expected	Actual
/X/ → 'X', /Y/ → 'Y'	/X/, /Y/ → 'Y'

Here is a small database: all non-affixal V + 'st' sequences in a sample from Trinity Scribe B. The items are given with simplified versions of the *LAEME* tags, just sufficient to identify them lexically and grammatically.[27] The tags are in two parts: a 'Lexel' (lexical element) between $ and /, and a 'Grammel' (grammatical element) to the right of /. The Lexels are either the ModE congeners of the ME words, or quasi-etymological identifiers.[28]

$ae:ht/n eiste 1x	$buy/vpt13 boust 1x
$apostle/n (a)postel(s) 3x	$catch/vpp icaist 1x
$aright/av arist 1x irist 1x	$christian/aj cʳistine 5x
$best/aj best 5x	$fight/vi fiste 1x
$betae:can/vpt13x be-taiste 1x	$fo:stor/n foster 1x
$bright/aj brist(e) 9x	$ghost/n gost 8x
$bright/aj-cpv bristore 1x	$ha:tan/vpt13 heiste 4x
$bring/vpp (i)broust 3x	$knight/npl cnistes 2x
$bring/vpt13 brouste 2x brovste 1x	$last/vi lasten 1x
$bring/vpt23 brousten 1x	$last/vps13 last 1x lest 1x
$burst/vSpp iborsten 1x	$light/n list 2x
$burst/vi bersten 1x	$light/vi listen 1x
$burst/vpt13 barst 1x	$light/vpt13 list(e) 3x
$buy/vpp <(i)boust> 2x aboust 1x	$may/vpt11 miste 1x

---

[26] This is the case even for systems that do not mark word division, like Sanskrit or archaic Greek.

[27] The tags have been minimized to show only essential grammatical information; details such as argument function (subject, direct or indirect object, prepositional object), certain semantic differentia of polysemous words and other details like occurrence in rhyme position have been omitted.

[28] Grammatical abbreviations: aj = adjective, -cpv = comparative, G = genitive, n = noun, pl = plural, pp = past participle, ps = present tense, pt = past tense, S = strong (verb), sj = subjunctive, v = verb, vi = infinitive. Number and person are indicated by integers in that order: e.g. /vpt13/ = 'verb, past tense, singular, 3rd person', /vpt23/ = 'plural, 3rd person'. In the Lexels etymological length is marked with a colon.

$may/vpt13 miste 3x

$may/vpt23 misten 2x mistin 1x

$may/vsjpt11 miste 1x

$might/n mist(e)(n) 10x

$mo:t/vps12 most 1x

$naught/n noust 4x

$night/n nist 5x naist(e) 2x

$pouste/n pouste 4x

$priest/nG *prestes* 1x

$rest/n rest 1x

$right/aj rist(e) 6x

$righteous/aj rist(e)-wis(e) 2x

$seek/vpp isoust 1x

$sehtan/vpp-pl saiste 1x

$sister/n soster 2x

$steadfast/aj studeuast 1x

$teach/vpt13 taiste 1x

$thought/n þoust(es) 5x

$þy:strig/aj þest ⁱi 1x

$weccan/vpt13 awaste 1x

$witan/vps12 wost 1x

$witan/vpt11 wiste 1x

$witan/vpt13 wiste 1x

$witan/vpt23 wisten 1x

$witan/vsjpt13 wiste 1x

$witan/vpt13 wiste 6x

$witan/vpt23 wisten 1x

$work/vpp-pl (i)wroust 5x

We cannot escape at the outset, as the tagging shows, that we already pretty much know what the words are, because we originally met them in context, and can read Middle English too. Regardless of prior expectations about deployment of 's', normally the context gives us both part of speech and lexical identity. E.g. *list* cannot be the word for CUNNING, ART (OE *list*) or BORDER, EDGE (OE *līst*) in:

> on þe holi meidan he sende list ant glem (f 21v) ON THE HOLY MAIDEN HE SENT *LIST* AND GLEAM

It can only be LIGHT (OE *liht*); if we had any doubt *glem*, which must be GLEAM, would tell us. So this 's' (representationally) 'is not an [s]'.[29] Contrariwise, we have to read 's' as [s] in *gost* since there is no word where *gost* could represent *[goxt], nor (on syntactic and collocational grounds) can it mean the present 2 sg of GO but only GHOST in:

> þe holi gost from heuene to hire com (f 22r) THE HOLY *GOST* FROM HEAVEN TO HER CAME

These are easy cases, but they make the point. It does not really matter too much (within certain limits defined by each text) how words are spelled. As long as there is something where you expect something, and you know as a competent reader what the utterance is supposed to be, almost anything would be quite acceptable. How this is done is simple: the writing of OE -*ht* as 'st' does not represent an English 'sound change', but is an inverse spelling based on a French change [st] > [xt ~ ht] (Pope 1952: §§1178(ii), 1216). This usage is unsurprising in the work of scribes virtually all of whom wrote French as well as English.

---

[29] The representation [x] does not mean specifically a velar fricative, but simply some non-anterior fricative which derives from what in OE is usually written 'h'.

But sometimes nothing can be as good as something. In the category we would interpret as 'OE -*ht*- words', Scribe B uses mainly 'st'; but there are eleven instances of zero
instead of expected 's':

$bring/vpp ibrout 1x
$bring/vpt22 broutest 1x
$naught/n nout 3x
$not/neg nout 1x
$thought/n þout 3x
$work/vpp wrout 1x
$work/vpt23 wrouten 1x

How should we treat these? First, if we insert an 's'-as-[s] in the 'empty' position, we
get non-words like *BROUST, *NOUST. And the other likely reading for 'ou', i.e. [uː] as
in *out* OUT or *hous* HOUSE, is ruled out the same way: there appear to be no likely ME
words *[nuːt] or *[wruːt]. These then are not [uː] words, just as the particular example quoted above of *list* is not an [s] word, and *broust* is not either. They are clearly
interpretable as 's'-as-zero words. And which 's' it would have been had it been present, 's'-as-[s] or 's'-as-[x] we determine from our linguistic knowledge (e.g. *ibrout*
would have to be BROUGHT < *ge-brōhte*). And on another level, these eleven forms
suggest strongly that phonetically [x] in this cluster has been variably lost (as it clearly
has in the language of Scribe C, whose LSS for this category is {'t', 'tt'}). Thus the LSS
for -*ht* will include zero. And the level of capture will be largely lexical: each word can
have its own LSS.

So each word has a set of representations (including a potential one-member set), in
which a range of graphic items or shapes can substitute:

Element (*potestas*) Sequence	LSS
[-st]	{'st'}
[-xt]	{'st', 'Øt'}[30]

Given this kind of organization, 'st' is a member of two LSSs, each of which defines a different etymological class and presumably a different phonological unit.

7.4.5 Where 'emes' Fail: Trinity Scribe A

The writing system of Trinity Scribe B is similar to many other text languages recorded in
the *LAEME* corpus in an important respect: it displays two distinctly non-'structuralist'
properties:

---

[30] The justification for zero *litterae* is given in *LAEME*, introduction, §2.3.5.

- the designer is often not particularly concerned with biunique or even close to biunique grapheme/phoneme mapping;
- the orthography (and frequently the language it represents) may be highly variable.

Here is one example of the impossibility of 'classical' grapheme/phoneme mappings in another variable and prodigal language from the same MS, that of Scribe A. Consider these forms:

$/P13F³¹: hoe, ho, heo, he
$be/v: boe-, beo-, be-
$boar/n: boer-
$heart/n: hoerte, herte, horte
$knee/n: cnoe
$kneel/v: cnel-
$to/im: toe, to

There is no way we can make either historical or synchronic sense at any level but the orthographic from 'inside' the data. We have a number of LSSs for the nuclear vowels of particular lexemes, and only that:

SHE: {'oe', 'o', 'eo', 'e'}
BE: {'oe', 'eo', 'e'}
HEART: {'oe', 'e', 'o'}
TO: {'oe', 'o'}
BOAR, KNEE: {'oe'}
KNEEL: {'e'}

In ModE the items group as follows:

[iː]: SHE, BE, KNEE, KNEEL
[ɑː]: HEART
[ɔː]: BOAR
[uː]: TO

If we project back, on the basis of our knowledge of Old English and the supporting argumentation that allows us to interpret that language, we find:

ēo: SHE, BE, KNEE, KNEEL
eo: HEART
ā: BOAR
ō: TO

---

³¹ 'Pronoun, sg, 3rd person, feminine', i.e. 'she'. Where the Grammel is sufficient to identify an item, the tag does not include a Lexel.

So there are two four-way groupings that happen to coincide. And neither of these is suggested by the actual data, which even ('perversely', from the structural viewpoint) separates two forms with the same root, KNEE and KNEEL (OE *cnēow, cnēowlian*).

If we look at other examples from the same hand, we find that 'e' and 'o' are used for the following historical categories:[32]

'e': OE *e, ē, æ, ǣ, eo, ēo,*
'o': OE *o, ō, a, ā, eo, ēo, ū, u*

And each of these categories will yield multiple LSSs, not unlike the picture we got above. Such orthographies are not based primarily on 'structural' analyses of a lect. Rather they are complex systems whose designer has interests other than those he apparently 'ought to have', and manages to write a language that, with some effort and a bit of historical knowledge both prior and subsequent, we can make perfectly good sense of. But it is not clear on orthographic evidence, which is our primary data, what the internal structure of the sound system is,[33] or how many of the LSSs conceal potential phonetic (or phonemic) variation, or how much inverse spelling there is that might make us believe in the non-existence of contrasts that history suggests ought to have been there. We are concerned in interpreting these texts with forms, not 'systems'. The notion 'phonological system' is not necessarily directly relevant to the task of providing a useful surface representation of forms, which is what the historical interpretation of spelling is.

The possibility of spelling by LSS rather than 'transcriptionally' has important implications for historians. Most of all, it means that a characteristic and familiar way of speaking is no longer generally viable, but has to be justified for each individual case. We cannot assume that spelling differences represent phonological differences, or distinguish the '(merely) graphic' from the 'phonetic'. The more highly substitutive an orthography is, the less information it may furnish for the study of phonological structure or change. For this we require the orthography to be more directly 'representational'. But in certain prodigal systems, the choice of the members of LSSs may indeed tell us something about phonological changes that are going on or have recently occurred. This was indeed the case with the use of zero for 's' discussed above.

---

[32] For similar, even more complex overlaps, see the discussion of other SWML texts in Laing & Lass (2003), Lass & Laing (2005).

[33] This can hold even if there is only one system in question. Highly variable lects can be seen as special kinds of 'Mischsprachen', with layers of different ages and degrees of innovativeness in shifting coexistence. And in our data this problem is superadded to the purely scribal question of what kind of copying is being done, the nature of the exemplar(s), shifts in attention or strategy by the scribe. For a survey of these problems, see Benskin & Laing (1981).

7.5 Phonetic Interpretation

7.5.1 How Can we Know about *Potestates?*

We seem to know the values of the *litterae* in many ancient systems, and if we are uncertain we look them up in handbooks. I have made a number of assumptions about *potestates* in past orthographies.

What kind of evidence can possibly provide these values, and what degree of delicacy can we or ought we to be allowed to claim? These are crucial issues, and rarely if ever unpacked. At the risk of some tedium I want to show roughly how such values are arrived at. We assume most characters in orthographic strings represent phonetic categories.[34] I use the term 'phonetic' to cover, loosely, both modern 'phonetic' and 'phonological': one often cannot tell in older texts, for which conventional, exhaustive phonological systems are unavailable or not intended by scribes, what level of 'sound substance' one is dealing with. So let us just say that we want to pair *litterae* with 'broad' phonetic categories. Where do we get the information to do this?

If an orthography derives, entirely or partly, from a well-known 'classical' system that has a native metalinguistic tradition (like Latin, Greek or Sanskrit, post-fifteenth-century English) we have a starting point. Subsequent and prior history gives us an extended information base. For instance, with very little reflection, when we look at a text in a roman-based spelling we know little about, we feel safe in saying that *e* will not represent a consonant and *k* will not represent a labial. And further, though this is a bit dodgier, that *e* will be a mid-vowel, not high or low.

How might we assign a reasonable phonetic value to a pre-modern orthographic string? This procedure is generally taken as unproblematical, but there are both difficulties and principles of some importance, which deserve to be made explicit. We are so used to 'canonical' phonetic values and total lack of justifying argument that it is difficult to find an exposition of interpretive principle. What I present here is more painfully detailed than anything one is likely to find in any handbook; but to make the enterprise rational we need such usually unmentioned detail. My example is a token spelled *niht* and clearly meaning NIGHT in an early ME text. What are our sources of information?

(i) Comparative evidence from more archaic IE: Latin *noct-*, Greek *nukt-*, Lithuanian *nakt-*, etc. imply (given our background knowledge of IE comparative linguistics, so this like everything else is indirect) a distant reconstruction **nokt-*. This already suggests that the shape is CVCC. We can also use phonetic descriptive evidence from those ancient languages that have such a tradition, e.g. Greek and Latin (cf. Allen 1965: 14–16). There is comparative evidence from modern

---

[34] For a typical example of one that does not, consider the obligatory final 'e' that must follow word-final 'v' in English, even after short vowels (*love, dove*).

Germanic as well: German *Nacht*, Dutch *nacht* fit with the suggested ancient IE forms having undergone spirantization, but Swedish *natt* [nat:], Modern English *night* [naɪt] suggest further major changes: here deletion of the segment represented as [k] in Latin and [x] in German, and compensatory lengthening of the final consonant in Swedish and lengthening and diphthongization of the root vowel in English. This is a common lenition trajectory, stop > fricative > zero.[35] Our attempts to interpret also create history (cf. Lass 1997: ch. 1). That is, 'history', in the sense that we can perceive it, is to a large extent the output of our praxis. It 'exists' in an abstract sense, but often it comes into being (and phonic value is a classic example) only through our operations on data.

(ii)   The history of forms within Old English. We find among others *naeht, neaht,* and *niht*; further exploration of OE sound changes suggests that the original Germanic vowel was **a*, with later changes involving fronting to **æ*, 'breaking' to *ea*, and raising eventually to *i*, giving a high vowel in English whereas all other Germanic dialects have a low vowel. At least these italic 'philological' values are what are suggested by the *litterae* employed, given the traditions of their usage in Latin-derived scripts. There is no evidence suggesting that 'n' ever had any *potestas* but [n], so we can take it for granted, as we can probably take [t] for 't'.

(iii) Later developments in English. Spelling, rhyme practice, and phonetic description from the sixteenth to seventeenth century suggest coexistence of types with medial [x], [ç], or [h] (generally preceded by short vowels), and forms with a diphthong but no consonant before the final [t]: see Lass (1999: §3.5.1) for details. The lenition hierarchy eventually gets repeated where a segment has remained. The evidence from both history and phonetic description starting from the sixteenth century suggests that the ME vowel was [i] (on why the early descriptions suggest [i], not [ɪ], see Lass 1989, 1999: §3.1.2.1).

(iv)   Verse evidence. This is useful for 'gh' only in this case. If a poet (assuming he is accurate, which is a big if) rhymes OE -*ht* words with words that cannot have had the coda fricative, then this shows that he does not have it either. So if such a poet rhymes *night* with *quite, sprite* this shows that the fricative has vanished, since the latter two are French loans in historical -*īt*. And knowing the history we can claim that this text language (that of the 1596 edition of Spenser's *Faërie Queene*) has lost whatever the 'h' in OE -*ht* represented.[36]

(v)   Modern dialect evidence. Forms of 'night' with a non-anterior fricative exist in Scots, e.g. [nɪxt]; unless we want to propose something as odd as late [x] epenthesis, which the historical evidence in any case does not support, we must interpret this as a survival, and once again the notion that the *potestas* of medial 'h' is some kind of non-anterior fricative is supported.

---

[35] The expected intermediate stage [h] appears as well, but the evidence is from the sixteenth century and later. See below.

[36] It is even clearer in this text, as the inverse spellings *quight, spright* appear, where 'gh' can have no phonetic import.

(vi) The argument for the nuclear vowel is exceedingly complex, but one of the strongest strands in it is not later material (the 'Great Vowel Shift' intervened after loss of whatever 'h' was),[37] and our strongest evidence is probably the Latin-based orthographic tradition. But putting all the evidence together we could probably conclude that our ME *niht* was something very like [nixt], (or [niçt] if you prefer palatalization).[38]

Note the type of argument: from ancient forms, subsequent forms, the period under investigation and metalinguistic commentary over the whole temporal range. Historical argumentation is typically not 'linear' but 'reticulate': our claims are based on convergence or 'consilience' of many different arguments from different temporal strata and data sets and theoretical positions. This argument has actually been a particularly simple one: those for vowels for instance are more complex, involving detailed comparative reconstruction, judgements on the range of likely *potestates* of Latin and Greek *litterae*, poorer early phonetics, the behaviour of Latin and Greek loans in languages of all periods, studies of sixteenth- to seventeenth-century orthoepic testimony, etc. I will not go into any further examples, but we can be reasonably happy with such judgements, which are based on general consideration of the available evidence and the long tradition of scholarship that has led to something of a consensus.

7.5.2 Level of Resolution

We have already seen how we can get a rough idea of what a given *littera* or litteral sequence stands for. But how far can we (or should we) get beyond this kind of rough specification? What do we really mean by a *potestas* for a *littera* in a historical text?

We could of course cop out, as many scholars have, and be content with a 'formulaic' structuralism (the Saussurean legacy) in which we do not worry about phonetic values but are 'abstract' enough to be seriously concerned with nothing but 'oppositions': /i/ vs /y/ could as easily be Fred *vs* Mary or ɛ *vs* ɛ.[39] But since the output of our work is supposed to be some version of a natural language we require phonetic specification, in which case /i/ must mean (at least) something that if heard would be likely to be transcribed by a responsible phonetician (if shakily) as [i], and not as anything else.

Assuming that we need some kind of phonetic representation to do any linguistics at all, the Hard Question remains: how fine should our resolution be? In representing historical categories and *potestates* above I used conventional italicized 'philological'

---

[37] On the Great Vowel Shift and why I use scare quotes for it see the discussion in Lass (2006:§2.7.2).

[38] Palatalization had to have occurred at some point, since only 'h' that could not have represented palatalized segments can descend with [f] as *potestas* (ROUGH < OE *rūh* but FIGHT < *fehtan*). But it is not necessarily early. Some Germanic dialects do not palatalize their 'velar fricative', e.g. most forms of Dutch and Yiddish, which have a uvular [χ] or velar [x] after front vowels as the reflex of Gmc *x.

[39] Cf. Jakobson & Halle (1956:11): 'all phonemes denote nothing but mere otherness'.

symbols and IPA symbols quite loosely, without saying what I meant by them. The best they could be in historical interpretation, where we have no live informants, is signs for 'ranges' of phonetic quality. We could of course adopt a strongly realist view that would have our outputs be something close to 'pronunciations'; this would be lovely but foolish because unattainable.

Somewhere between [Fred] and [i] (= 'precisely the value of Cardinal Vowel 1') lies the range we can operate in safely. The solution to the problem is in effect a matter of tact. In practice we limit both the number of phonetic parameters and the number of points on each parameter to a kind of 'safe' minimum, which allows for naturalistic specification at a fineness of detail adequate for our purposes and historically insightful, which is in keeping with what we know of both historical input and present development—as well as with what we know of language history in general (much of which we know circularly through making choices about values).

The further back in time we go, the harder it is to specify phonetic values with any precision. All our symbols are 'broad', but some are broader than others. The level we choose might best be called 'poorly resolved broad transcription' (Laing & Lass 2003), which is in general, I think, the right way to represent historical sound substance. That is, we hope that our reconstructions are well enough supported so that if a responsible phonetician equipped with a time machine were able to hear the items represented, the symbol in question would not be too outlandish a transcriptional response. This is partly standard wishful thinking, and partly our assessment of the results of work in comparative and historical linguistics over the past two centuries.

For instance, we would be very much surprised if Latin *amor* LOVE were to have anything other than a low vowel in first position followed by a labial nasal, a rounded mid back vowel, and some kind of 'rhotic'. How much further we could get than this is open to question: we do not have any good evidence as to whether the first vowel was front, central, or back or whether the second was high or low mid. But we can be pretty sure that the rhotic was a trill in Classical Latin: the contemporary phoneticians tell us rather precisely that it is tremulous and vibrates (Allen 1965: 32). Of course there are many kinds of trills, different numbers of taps, retroflexion or lack of it, etc. But we can use a coarse term like 'voiced coronal trill' and get away with it, and indeed this is as far as we get and is not bad at all.

So each segmental representation is equivalent to a 'range' or 'smear' of values with roughly the coordinates that the symbol in question would occupy in a modern phonetic transcription. Therefore the use of [ ] in our discourse is allowed, though it should be borne in mind that because we lack precise knowledge its use in etymologies, transcriptions, and statements of changes is essentially 'typological' rather than 'phonetic' in any more highly resolved sense. It is a representation of 'sound substance' at an unspecified but undoubtedly very coarse level. This may not be where we would want to get to but it's not a bad place to be. To be able to tell that some segment was probably a low vowel is better than knowing only that it was a vowel, and far better than having no idea at all of what it was.

CHAPTER 8

··

THE ROLE OF TYPOLOGY
IN HISTORICAL PHONOLOGY

··

MARTIN KÜMMEL

8.1 INTRODUCTION

HISTORICAL phonology has to deal with the problem that historical data normally do not provide all the information we need to understand the phonology or phonological history of a given language (see Lass, Minkova and Unger, all this volume, on the limits and possibilities of interpretation of historical data from written sources for past stages of languages).[1] Therefore, parts of historical linguistic 'reality' have to be reconstructed, which means that we must produce a hypothesis which sets up probable or at least possible synchronic stages and possible or preferably probable changes (see Fox, this volume). To evaluate the probability of such assumed states and changes, typological considerations can be used, among others. Linguistic typology mostly involves comparing languages around the world (or across a given area) synchronically. This contrasts with the 'comparative method' of historical reconstruction, i.e. the comparison of genetically related languages aiming at the reconstruction of their ancestor (see Fox, this volume). Typology can, however, be both synchronic and diachronic—we can compare reconstructions with what can be found synchronically (for discussions of which, see Maddieson 1984 and Maddieson & Precoda 1989, both often referred to as 'USPID'—the 'UCLA Phonological Segment Inventory Database'—, and Mielke 2008), and we can also compare the changes which would be needed to map a reconstruction onto attested stages of a language with what is thought to be diachronically common (see Cser, this volume, on basic types of change, and Blevins, this volume, and also Mailhammer et al., this volume, for a more

[1] The present chapter builds on the first part of my contribution to the proceedings of 'The Sound of Indo-European' conference, held in Copenhagen 2009, published as Kümmel (2012), and extensively reworked for this volume. I profited much from discussion with the editors, but of course all remaining faults are my own. This work would not have been possible without a Heisenberg Fellowship from the Deutsche Forschungsgemeinschaft (DFG).

theorized approach). Typological comparison aims at finding linguistic patterns that result from general or even universal factors rather than language-specific developments, especially 'types', i.e. bundles of features typically patterning together. Typological data represent an empirical background for judging the probability of proposed historical reconstructions: if a phenomenon or a change is cross-linguistically well attested, it can be considered as generally more probable than a less well-supported alternative. Typological considerations thus cannot be decisive on their own, but they may tip the balance in favour of one or the other solution in reconstruction.

Sound change and synchronic phonological typology may also be related in the opposite way, since sound change can be used to explain attested sound patterns as having emerged by change; cf. the arguments in Hansson (2008) or Mielke (2008)—based on a typological investigation—that distinctive features are not innate but emergent from phonological patterns, one important source of which may be sound change (cf. Bybee, this volume). These approaches will, however, not be the focus of this chapter.

In this chapter I exemplify some relevant theoretical principles and their application to historical phonology in connection with one of the most famous cases where typological data have been explicitly applied to historical phonology, namely the 'Glottalic Theory' of the Proto-Indo-European (PIE) stop system.

8.2 THE RECONSTRUCTION OF PIE STOP SERIES

The stop system of the parent language of the IE family was originally reconstructed as the system of Old Indo-Aryan (Sanskrit), with voiceless and voiced unaspirated as well as voiceless and voiced aspirated stops. However, with the acceptance of the so-called laryngeal theory the traditionally reconstructed voiceless aspirated stops were widely interpreted as secondary and therefore disappeared from the reconstructed PIE phonemic inventory. The resulting reconstruction now consisted of voiceless unaspirated stops (tenues), voiced unaspirated stops (mediae), as well as voiced aspirates (mediae aspiratae, MA). This new reconstruction was immediately challenged as typologically problematic, mainly because the traditional mediae aspiratae no longer had support from voiceless aspirates (see section 8.2.1).

A reinterpretation of the traditional system was also supported by some peculiar distributional facts: it has been observed that mediae are suspiciously absent from endings and suffixes (cf. Hopper 1973: 156–7, Dunkel 2001: 3–4, 9), while aspirates can occur (if not in the most basic layers) and tenues seem to be the norm. This points to a marked status of the mediae *vs* the tenues and aspirates. These obviously form a class, as is shown by some root structure constraints: stops in one root (if not preceded by *s* or a nasal, cf. de Vaan 1999) must be either both tenues or aspirates, while mediae may co-occur with each other type but not with another media. These constraints for mediae are

Table 8.1 Different reconstructions of PIE stop series

T	H	G	K	V
*t	*t	*tʰ~t	*t	*tʰ
*dꜰ	*dꜰ/d	*dꜰ~d	*dʰ	*ḍ
*d	*t'/ṭ	*t'	*ḍ['ḍ]	*t'

(T = 'neo-traditional'; H = Hopper 1973/1977; G = Gamkrelidze & Ivanov 1973; K = Andreev 1957; Kortlandt 1978, 1985; V = Normier 1977, Vennemann 1984)

similar to constraints found for glottalic stops (ejectives) in some languages, giving rise to the idea that the traditional mediae should be reinterpreted as 'glottalic' stops (Gamkrelidze & Ivanov 1973, Hopper 1973), and the mediae aspiratae might have been non-glottalic voiced stops. This is the core of the so-called 'glottalic theory' of PIE stops.

Table 8.1 gives an overview of four different 'glottalic' models compared with the neo-traditional 'non-glottalic' model of PIE stops. Table 8.2 gives an overview of the basic reflexes of PIE stop series (as traditionally reconstructed) in the (proto-languages of the) main branches of IE; in both tables phonologically conditioned variants are marked by a tilde (~), and dialectal variants or alternative reconstructions are marked by a slash (/). In both tables, dental stops serve as examples for the whole series.

Kortlandt's 'pre-glottalized lenis' may be interpreted as 'creaky voiced' (Ladefoged & Maddieson 1996: 53 ff.), 'voiced laryngealized' (Maddieson 1984: 111 ff.), or 'voiceless implosive' (Ladefoged & Maddieson 1996: 87–90), all of which may represent one phonological class (cf. Clements & Osu 2002: 313); on the relics of voicing and aspiration in Tocharian, cf. Ringe (1996a: 47 ff., 64 ff.); for Italic, cf. Stuart-Smith (2004). For a general survey of the glottalic theory, see Salmons (1993), critical discussions are also found in Mayrhofer (1986); Barrack (2002, 2003) and Kümmel (2007: 299–310).

Now, what is the basis for reconstructing the PIE stops series? Three main types of stop correspondences between the individual IE branches can be observed in the material (cf. Table 8.2). In one case, the main reflexes are plain voiceless or (less often) voiceless aspirated, traditionally reconstructed as plain voiceless stops (*tenues*). In the second case, we mostly find voicing and/or aspiration, and therefore voiced aspirates (*mediae aspiratae*) were traditionally reconstructed. To be sure, these sounds in attested IE languages are phonetically neither voiced nor aspirated, but articulated with 'breathy voice' (or 'murmured'; cf. Ladefoged & Maddieson 1996: 57 ff.), placed between voicelessness and modal voice on the continuum of vocal-fold configurations. Phonologically, however, this may still be interpreted as a combination of voicing and aspiration, exhibiting both features (and thus 'doubly marked').[2] In the third case, the reflex is never aspirated and normally voiced, but it may be voiceless in languages where the tenues are (or had been) distinctly aspirated, and

---

[2] Independent of their phonological status, these sounds will be marked by ꜰ rather than subscript .. in the present chapter.

Table 8.2 Main reflexes of PIE stop types in the different branches (simplified)

IE (non-glottalic)	*t	*dʰ	*d
Anatolian	t/t:	d/ḍ	d/ḍ
Tocharian	t	t~ts < *dʰ	ts/Ø/t < *d
Indo-Iranian	t~tʰ	dʰ~d	d
Armenian	tʰ~t	d/dʰ	t/t'
Greek	t	tʰ~t	d
Italic	t	f-<*θ-~ð~d	d
Celtic	t/tʰ	d~-ð-	d~-ð-
Germanic	θ~t	d~-ð-	t
Balto-Slavic	t	d	:d (ˀd?)
Albanian	t	d	d

this series was traditionally reconstructed as plain voiced (*mediae*). Thus we arrive at a system with one plain voiceless series, but two contrasting 'voiced' series that must have been distinguished by an additional feature. One major uncertainty in all this is the definition of the kind of opposition traditionally described by the term 'voice/voicing': while the feature of voicing ([±slack vocal folds]) is certainly unproblematic for many languages (including large parts of IE), there are also many cases where this is quite problematic, and the opposition seems to be mainly based on different features. In such cases linguists often use the (sometimes deliberately) imprecise terms 'fortis' *vs* 'lenis' which can variably refer to either aspiration ([±spread glottis]) or differences in duration or articulatory strength ('tense' *vs* 'lax').[3] The description of laryngeal phonology in such languages is still not fully agreed and needs further clarification. Within IE, especially Anatolian, Germanic, Celtic, Armenian, and at least some Iranian languages warrant mention. Bear in mind in the following that terms like 'voiced', etc. may refer to something (potentially very) different phonologically.

8.2.1 Synchronic Typology

Against the reconstructed system with voiced aspirates the following typological objections have been raised:

1. Voiced aspirates never occur without contrasting voiceless aspirates (and an *h*-sound) according to Jakobson (1958: 22–3). However, this is not entirely true: There is at least one language that exhibits 'voiced aspirates' without possessing voiceless aspirates, namely Kelabit in Northern Borneo (cf. Blust 1974, 2006). In fact, the voiced aspirates there are even more correctly called 'voiced aspirates' than

---

[3] On the problem of voiced *vs* lenis and related matters, see Iverson & Salmons (1995) and related literature.

the sounds attested in IE languages, since the latter are breathy voiced [dʰ], while the Kelabit aspirates are not really murmured, but rather described as beginning voiced and ending with voiceless aspiration, [dtʰ] (Blust 1974:50; cf. Ladefoged & Maddieson 1996: 62–3). But still these different phones might be considered to belong to one phonological class combining 'voicing' and 'aspiration' (or [+slack voice], [+spread glottis]).

2. According to Hopper (1973: 141) 'a typologically plausible triple stop system should have only one voiced series'. But this is not really true either if we consider the variation found in the world's languages. Even if most attested system types with two voiced series are quite rare, one such type is rather frequent: about 16 percent of the three series languages counted by Maddieson (1984: 28–9) exhibit a system of voiceless stops opposed to plain voiced explosives and voiced implosive stops. In this sample (as in Greenberg 1970), implosives were not distinguished from laryngealized voiced stops (cf. Clements & Rialland 2008: 55–6, Hamann & Fuchs 2008:104–5). However, recent research has provided evidence that 'implosives' should rather be defined as 'nonexplosive' or 'nonobstruent' stops—ingressive airstream being only a secondary feature (see Stewart 1989: 231 ff., Clements & Osu 2002, 2005, Clements & Rialland 2008: 56–7)—and that 'laryngealized voiced stops' are 'nonexplosive' stops with distinctive glottalization and less voicing, something like [ʔd̥] (Clements & Rialland 2008: 56–7). But even if that distinction is made, the type remains rather frequent (mainly in Africa). The parallel to PIE is not perfect, since this type does not show two voiced *explosive* series, as traditional Indo-European is assumed to do. But as changes from nonexplosives to explosives seem to be rather common (cf. Stewart 1989: 236 ff.; Clements & Rialland 2008: 59), the PIE system might easily be derived from such a type.

All this means that the (neo-)traditionally reconstructed system of PIE is probably not impossible—and we should be cautious not to normalize data without a compelling reason (see Kortlandt 1985: 185, following Dunkel 1981: 566; cf. Haider 1983: 81). But of course such a system is still improbable, so different models of PIE should be tested: which of them are better attested and therefore more probable?

In what follows I give an overview of three-stop series systems and their frequency in languages of the world, mainly based on the UPSID database as given in Maddieson (1984), but also including later additions to that database and other languages as well that I happen to know about. Parallels to systems reconstructed for PIE are indicated by the abbreviations used in Table 8.1 above.

There is much uncertainty in the data of this very broad sample as it is based on descriptions of very different quality and phonetic-phonological precision. This is especially problematic in the case of VOT distinctions, since 'voiced' and 'voiceless' may often be rough labels covering real voicing distinctions as well as other features like aspiration or duration (as already mentioned). For a rough statistical generalization these uncertainties cannot be avoided at our present state of knowledge, but it should not be forgotten that, e.g. phonological voicing might be less frequent than normally assumed.

8.2.1.1 *Three-Stop System Types Cross-Linguistically*

I illustrate the stops by the respective dental-alveolar stops: the stops series are divided by a tilde (~), ordered from the widest opening of the vocal cords to the narrowest: tʰ > t > dʱ > d > ɗ > t'; after a description of the system type, the names of languages are given that (seem to) belong to this type. The number of languages in Maddieson (1984) is given as (UPSID X) after the type schema.

(a) Frequent types
   (1) The 'Caucasian' type (= H',V), i.e. two non-glottalic stops (with some kind of VOT distinction) and one ejective. Maddieson (1984) distinguished three different types, namely tʰ ~ t ~ t' (UPSID 12) or tʰ ~ d ~ t' (UPSID 5) or t ~ d ~ t' (UPSID 13). But since descriptions of the same languages often differ depending on whether voicing or aspiration is taken to be the decisive feature distinguishing the two non-ejective stop series, it seems better to lump them together: Ossetic, Artvin Armenian (IE); Kabardian; Georgian (Kartvelian); South Arabian, Ethiopic (Semitic); Dizi, Kefa (Omotic); Tlingit, Navaho, Chipewa, Hupa, Tolowa (Na-Dené); Haida; Klamath (Plateau Penutian); Chontal, Tzeltal (Mayan); Kwakw'ala (Wakash); Quileute (Chemaku); Puget Sound (Salish); Pomo, Yana (Hoka); Acoma (Tarascan); Wichita (Sioux); Quechua, Jaqaru (Quechumaran); Gununa-Kena (Chon), etc.
   (2) The 'Greek' type, i.e. aspirated, voiceless, voiced (three different VOT settings): tʰ ~ t ~ d (UPSID 19): Romani, Panjabi, Kashmiri, Shina, Kalam Kohistani, Wotapuri, Tirahi, Khowar, Shumashti, Dameli, Northern Pashai; Khotanese, Northern Zazaki, Kurmanji Kurdish; Agulis/Sasun Armenian; Ancient Greek (IE); Thai (Tai-Kadai); Burmese (Tibeto-Burmese); Burushaski (?), etc.
   (3) The 'implosive' type (= K'), i.e. two explosives and one implosive: t ~ d ~ ɗ (UPSID 12): Katcha, Kadugli, Dan, Ogbia, Tarok, Doayo, Mbatto (Niger-Kordofanian); Tama, Mursi, Daju (Nilosaharan); Angas, Margi, Dangaleat; Laal (Afro-Asiatic); *Proto-Mon-Khmer, Proto-Monic/Old Mon (Austro-Asiatic); Gorontalo, Bima, Hawu, Ngad'a (Austronesian); *Proto-Tai? (Tai-Kadai); with ɓ only: Aizi, Bete, Kpelle, Gwari; Mumuye (Niger-Kordofanian).
(b) Rare types
   All other combinations seem to be significantly rarer.
   (1) A type that combines implosives and ejectives in one 'glottalic' series (cf. also Salmons 1993: 53–4): t ~ d ~ t'/ɗ (UPSID 3): Ik (Nilosaharan); Iraqw, Hausa (Afro-Asiatic); ?Hamer (Omotic); Mam, Tzutujil (Mayan).
   (2) A variant of (a3) with aspiration instead of voicing for the non-implosive series: tʰ ~ t ~ ɗ (UPSID 3): Swahili (N-K); Vietnamese, Khmer, Khmu? (Austro-Asiatic); Karen, Phlong (Sino-Tibetan).

(3) Variant of (a3) with laryngealized stops rather than implosives (= K'): t ~ d ~ ḍ (UPSID 2): Lugbara (Nilosaharan); Kera, Lame?, Kanakuru? (Afro-Asiatic); *Proto-Tai? (Tai-Kadai).

(4) The same type with aspiration rather than voicing: t^h ~ t ~ ḍ (UPSID 2): Lakkia, Lungchow (Tai-Kadai); Cham (Austronesian); t^h ~ d ~ ḍ (UPSID 2): ?Somali (Afro-Asiatic); Wapishana (Arawakan).

(5) A type similar to (a1) but with laryngealized voiceless stops instead of ejectives: t^h ~ t ~ ṭ (UPSID 1): Korean (?); Tol (Hoka).

(6) Pre-nasalization combined with a VOT opposition: t^h ~ t ~ ^{n}d (UPSID 2): Hakka (Sinitic); Nambakaengo (Central Melanesian); similarly t ~ d ~ ^{n}d (UPSID 1): Sinhalese, Divehi (closely related, IE).

(7) A VOT opposition combined with breathy voice: t^h ~ t ~ $d^ɦ$ (not in UPSID): Erevan Armenian (IE); Xhosa (N-K); *Old Chinese (Sinitic); similarly t^h ~ $d^ɦ$ ~ d (not in UPSID): Sivas Armenian (IE).

(8) A variant of (a1) with implosives instead of voiced explosives: t^h ~ ɗ ~ t' (UPSID 1): Maidu (Maiduan).

(9) 'Aspiration' only in (partly) voiced stops (= T): t ~ dt^h ~ d (not in UPSID): Kelabit (Austronesian).

(c) Systems not (yet) attested

(1) Ejectives and allophonic aspiration both for voiceless and voiced stops (= G): t^h/t ~ $d^ɦ$/d ~ t'.

(2) Ejectives and breathy voiced stops (= H): t ~ $d^ɦ$ ~ t'.

(3) Laryngealized stops with aspirated 'lenis' stops (= K): t ~ $d^ɦ$/$d̥^h$ ~ ḍ.

This overview shows that some proposed 'glottalic' systems are not attested at all if all phonetic specifications are taken into account: there is no system with breathy voice and ejectives, as in the two earliest 'glottalic' proposals, nor is there a system with laryngealized lenes and lenis aspirates, as Kortlandt originally proposed. But variants of these proposals do very much better: If breathy voice (or aspiration) was post-PIE, all 'glottalic' systems correspond to system types attested by significantly more than one known language—while 'non-glottalic' PIE does not. We have to conclude that 'glottalic' reconstructions of PIE do indeed provide a more probable synchronic system. But is this synchronic plausibility matched by a corresponding diachronic plausibility?

8.2.2 Diachronic Typology

We do not yet possess a worldwide database of sound changes corresponding to the large synchronic sample of Maddieson (1984), and therefore, we still have to work with more limited data. Even smaller comprehensive collections on sound change from a typological perspective are rare, because historical linguists normally concentrate on individual language families, and much typological work has been synchronic. Most statements in the literature therefore rely on data accidentally known to linguists but not on systematic observation. A worldwide collection of sound correspondences has been done by Brown, Holman, & Wichmann (2013) using data from the ASJP project (MPA Leipzig) in a lexical list of forty items. However, this method is not really diachronic and cannot indicate the direction of change lying behind a particular correspondence. Furthermore, their classification of sounds is too phonetically coarse with regard to obstruent articulation. A more comprehensive database of sound changes is being constructed by the UniDia project, <www.diadm.ish-lyon.cnrs.fr/unidia/index.php>, but so far the data are limited in terms of families covered. Consonantal changes from the history of a rather large sample of some 200 languages have been collected and classified by the present author (Kümmel 2007), but this sample is genetically and areally biased, including only IE, Uralic, and Semitic languages. However, in the absence of more exhaustive data, this investigation may be used as a provisional basis for testing the probability of changes presupposed by different reconstructions of PIE. It does at least cover most of the areas where the older IE languages were spoken, and their neighbours. In the following, I compare the basic values of the ten main branches of IE, as given in Table 8.2, with respect to their derivation from the competing proposals for the reconstruction of earlier stages.

1. The traditional tenues are represented as follows: voiceless aspirates (t^h) in three branches (although this is somewhat dubious for Celtic, and in Germanic they underwent further developments); plain voiceless stops (t) in the remaining seven. In terms of features this means that all branches point to [−voice], and three have [+asp] *vs* seven with [−asp].

   The most probable alternatives would be to reconstruct voiceless unaspirated stops or voiceless aspirated stops. In the first case, we would have to assume secondary aspiration (partially followed by secondary fricativization) in a minority of branches—changes that are quite frequent and assured for younger stages of IE languages from different branches (see Kümmel 2007: 168 ff.). Alternatively, we would have to assume secondary de-aspiration in most branches—this is certainly possible, but not so well attested (Job 1989: 128–9, Kümmel 2007: 93–4) and should thus be judged less probable. To sum up: a system with unaspirated voiceless stops as predecessors of the tenues is most probable from a diachronic viewpoint. This means that Hopper's and Kortlandt's models are as good as the traditional model, but Vennemann's and Gamkrelidze's are less likely.

2. The traditional aspiratae show a more complicated picture: eight of ten branches have [+voice] segments, while aspiration ([+asp]) is attested or presupposed in half of the branches.

   The majority of languages exhibits voiced plosives. Aspiration is directly attested in two branches (Indo-Iranian d^h and Greek t^h), and at least two further branches show some traces of it. In Italic, we find voiceless fricatives in initial position but voiced ones in internal position, but since internal voicing might be secondary, voiceless fricatives could have been the primary reflex (at least initially, cf. Stuart-Smith 2004: 202–3), and these might go back to voiceless aspirates as in Greek; in any case, devoicing is more probable for voiced aspirates rather than fricatives. In Tocharian, the respective dental stop merged with the distinct reflex of a simple voiced stop only before a following original aspirate which suggests the dissimilation of aspiration like in Sanskrit, pointing to aspiration as well as voicing as original features (cf. Ringe 1996b: 47–8). In Modern Armenian we find plain voiced stops, breathy voiced stops, voiceless ('lenis' or 'fortis') stops, and voiceless aspirated stops. Therefore, breathy voiced stops ($d^{ɦ}$) have to be reconstructed for previous stages of quite a few modern dialects and probably for Proto-Armenian.[4] In Germanic, most dialects show voiced fricatives in postvocalic position but stops in initial and postnasal positions (a typologically frequent pattern of allophony), corresponding to voiced or voiceless stops in High German.

All these reflexes can easily be derived from the 'voiced aspirates' of the traditional model and the identical 'murmured' stops of Hopper's model or the 'allophonically aspirated' voiced stops of Gamkrelidze's model, but what would the other models presuppose? If a plain voiced stop had been original, we would have to assume a secondary development to breathy voice for five branches—and such a change does not seem well attested (at least for languages that do not already exhibit an aspiration opposition; cf. Kümmel 2007: 171–2). If we start from original voiceless lenis stops, we would have to assume unconditioned voicing for most branches, and typological evidence for such a kind of change seems to be meagre (Kümmel 2007: 47 ff.). Models with voiceless aspirates would not do better, since it is not probable for (voiceless) aspirated stops to become unconditionally voiced or breathy voiced (for conditioned voicing; cf. Kümmel 2007: 53). To sum up, the non-glottalic model is as probable diachronically as all glottalic models with 'voiced aspirates' (viz. K, H, G), but clearly better than the others. However, it should not be forgotten that on the basis of the sample, statements on the probability of changes to breathy voice may not be too reliable, as most languages in the sample only have inherited breathy voice. The inclusion of data from other language families might thus provide more insights (see section 8.3).

3. Last but not least, the traditional mediae show the following reflexes: voicing (with [+voice]) is present in eight branches; aspiration does not really occur; one or maybe two branches can show glottalization, but at least eight branches do not. In Armenian the dialectal reflexes include ejectives, voiceless lenis stops, and fortis stops (with rather long duration). In Germanic, dialectal reflexes include aspirated stops, pre-aspirated stops, pre-glottalized stops, and affricates, but plain voiceless stops are attested in some regions of almost all sub-branches, and their distribution rather looks like that of an archaism (cf. Kümmel 2007: 295). For these two subfamilies the traditional model requires the assumption of a 'Lautverschiebung' from voiced to voiceless stops, and evidence from loanwords seems to corroborate this (cf. Rasmussen 1987: 9–12 = 1999: 224–7). Since changes of that kind are clearly

---

[4] See Garrett (1998) against the assumption of Pisowicz (1976) and Vaux (1998: 238–41) that the development of breathy voicing was a post-Old-Armenian innovation from simple voiced stops.

attested in the later history of IE languages and others (cf. Kümmel 2007: 138 ff.), they cannot be considered problematic—but of course, the preservation of voiceless stops as per most 'glottalic' models would not be a problem either. Although the appearance of glottalic or laryngealized articulation in some dialects would be accounted for most easily by the 'glottalic' models, it might also be secondary. But for the majority of branches, most 'glottalic' models have to posit a change from voiceless glottalized stops to plain voiced ones. Such a change is not easy to support typologically and therefore rather unlikely (cf. Job 1989, Kümmel 2007: 47–8, 189–90). Since it is much more probable for pre-glottalized lenis stops (= laryngealized plosives) than for ejectives, we can conclude again that the phonetic details of Hopper's, Gamkrelidze's, and Vennemann's models are not favoured by diachronic typology, the details of Kortlandt's are clearly better, but the traditional model is the most probable.

I conclude that the diachronic typology of systemic developments clearly favours the traditional reconstruction of the plosives as against all 'glottalic' models, but the best of the latter seems to be Kortlandt's. Note that Kortlandt has argued for direct reflexes of glottalized PIE mediae in more IE branches than is normally assumed (see the summary in Kortlandt 1985, but also 1978, 1981, 1988, 1997). However, his arguments are not based on typology (for critical discussion cf. Kümmel 2007: 303–9, 2012: 299–301).

8.2.3 Typological Conclusion

To sum up the findings of the typological investigation into this case study: synchronic typology favours 'glottalic' models, but diachronic typology rather contradicts this. Typology alone does not resolve the issue. To put it differently: the internal structure of the PIE system as well as synchronic typology plead for a revision of the traditional reconstruction, while diachronic typology rather favours the traditional approach.

Therefore, a model based on Pedersen's old (1951) assumption might be best (even if positing additional changes): pre-PIE could have had a different system that shifted to the traditionally reconstructed one already in PIE (cf. Miller 1977a, 1977b, Haider 1983). The most probable source of the PIE 'mediae' would have been 'voiced' as was the source of the 'aspirates': PIE *t ~ $\d{d}$ ~ d < **t ~ d ~ D[+voiced]. If the later aspirates had originally been ordinary voiced stops, what might have characterized the later 'mediae'?

8.3 A 'NONOBSTRUENT' SOLUTION

From the perspective of system typology, the most promising solution to this last question above will be an implosive—or rather a 'nonexplosive' stop. As already mentioned, recent work shows that (voiced) implosives are distinguished from normal stops mainly by the fact that there is no pulmonic air pressure behind the closure and thus no puff with release; even if there is an obstruction, there is simply no air that 'wants to get through'. In this respect, implosives are not obstruents—although in other respects they clearly are. In this sense implosives are 'nonobstruent' stops rather than glottalic stops.

Such a reconstruction might also help to explain why PIE stops were neutralized to 'mediae' in final position (cf. Kümmel 2007: 301 ff.): probably stops were not released in this position, and unreleased stops were more similar to nonexplosive stops than to explosives. Haider (1983: 84 ff.) had proposed reconstructing pre-PIE implosives as the source of the 'mediae', but with the assumption that such sounds must be classified as glottalic; in a similar fashion, Salmons (1993: 42–3, 53–4) pointed out advantages of positing (glottalic) implosives coexisting with ejectives within one glottalic series (as in languages like Hausa, above). A very similar scenario has now also been argued for independently by Weiss (2009) and supported by a possible diachronic parallel: in Cao Bang, a northern Thai language, an older opposition of implosives and voiced explosives was changed into an opposition of simple voiced stops and breathy voiced stops. In fact, a similar intermediate stage is most probable for other Tai or Mon-Khmer languages where original voiced stops have turned into voiceless aspirates, while contrasting implosives became voiced explosives and the original voiceless stops remained unaspirated, as, e.g. Old Mon > Nyah Kur (Diffloth 1984); Proto-Tai > Thai, Lao, and Saek (cf. Li 1977, Pittayawat 2009)—in contrast to cognate languages where the old implosives were preserved and the plain voiced stops were devoiced without aspiration. Also, in Madurese, original plain voiced stops became voiceless aspirates, while new plain voiced stops arose from different sources (mainly borrowing, Stevens 1966: 152–5). Thus, a shift from plain voiced stops to breathy voiced stops seems to be better attested than concluded above on the basis of more limited data.

A similar opposition is found in West African Kwa systems like Mbatto with 'lenis' implosives = nonexplosive stops *vs* 'voiced fortes' with possibly redundant murmur, as argued by Stewart (1989: 236–7). In their neighbourhood a system shift parallel to Grimm's Law seems to be attested in cognate Tano languages (Stewart 1989: 237 ff., 1993): *t > *tʰ > θ; *d > *dʱ > ð; *ɗ > t, which might provide a parallel for Germanic and Armenian.

If we thus assume original implosives, we have to consider the chronology of their shift to simple voiced stops that triggered the development of phonemic breathy voice in the original voiced stops. Was it already PIE, or did it only apply to dialectal IE? It should be borne in mind that there is no evidence for breathy voice in Anatolian, Celtic, and Balto-Slavic, and, seemingly, the languages from Messapian to Phrygian—i.e. in some languages of the western, southern, and northeastern periphery. This might point to a central IE innovation that spread to most but not all dialects.

Typological considerations from both synchronic and diachronic perspectives may thus point to the IE stop system reconstructed in Table 8.3 (for the dorsal series cf. Kümmel 2007: 310–27), but there remain many points to be clarified.

Table 8.3 Early and late (P)IE stops

	labial	coronal	'palatal' = velar	labiovelar	'velar' = uvular?
voiceless	*p	*t	*k	*kʷ	(*q?)
voiced > breathy	*b>bʱ	*d>dʱ	*g>ǵʱ	*gʷ>ǵʷʱ	(*ɢ>ɢʱ?)
implosive > voiced	*ɓ>b	*ɗ>d	*ɠ>g	*ɠʷ>gʷ	(*ɢ>ɢ?)

8.4 CONCLUSION: TYPOLOGY
AND SOUND CHANGE

As the example discussed here has shown, typological evidence can be (and has in fact always been[5]) used as a tool for deciding between competing accounts of diachronic phonology. Even if typological data normally allow us to make statements about probabilities rather than universals, this does not affect their value too much. Within the field of phonological typology the distinction between synchronic and diachronic typology is important. Synchronic typology can help to evaluate proposals about synchronic language systems of historical languages—not only those reconstructed as a whole but also those phonological aspects of attested historical languages that are not directly observable: proposed synchronic stages are more plausible if they can be supported by typological probability. Diachronic typology contributes crucially to the evaluation of proposed sound changes: the plausibility of changes is in fact an important criterion for judging alternative accounts of diachronic phonology, be it the reconstruction of proto-languages or smaller aspects for unattested periods of attested language histories; and to be plausible, proposed changes should be possible or even probable from a typological perspective. However, as the discussion shows, our knowledge of diachronic typological tendencies is certainly underdeveloped and we badly need better and broader collections of reliable data even more than in synchronic typology. To make typological arguments stronger, a better basis is needed.

---

[5] Even the comparative method partly builds on judgements about the probability of changes which were always based on a kind of comparative evidence that is typological rather than anything else; cf. Salmons (1993: 68–9) on the relation of 'naturalness' to diachronic typology.

CHAPTER 9

··

COMPUTATIONAL AND QUANTITATIVE APPROACHES TO HISTORICAL PHONOLOGY

··

BRETT KESSLER

9.1 INTRODUCTION

COMPUTATIONAL historical phonology is a difficult field to delineate. In fact, it can be argued that there is no such discipline. There are no core methodologies that are taught in every linguistics department and routinely employed by all historical linguists; indeed, there might not be any computational methods that the majority of historical linguists even consider valid. Difficult as it is to define the state of the art in computational historical phonology, this chapter seeks to provide a general overview of threads of computer-assisted research that have been pursued by several researchers for several years. It focuses primarily on computerized methods that use phonological criteria such as sound correspondences and sound similarity to investigate genetic relations between languages. A secondary focus is on phonetic comparisons between language varieties without regard to their genetic relationships.

A glaring omission is any discussion of the computer simulation of linguistic change, because Wedel (this volume) is dedicated to that important field, which would be almost inconceivable without computer models. For some other areas of research for which computers are often vital, see Yu (this volume) on experimental methods and Maguire (this volume) on corpus phonology.

9.2 COMPARATIVE METHOD

The comparative method as described in textbooks sounds straightforwardly algorithmic. The following recipe is a synthesis of several descriptions; see for example Fox (this volume) for more detail, and the papers in Durie & Ross (1996).

- Data collection: the linguist collects words that express the same or related concepts in two or more languages. These words are potential cognates.
- Alignment: for each concept, the potential cognate words are aligned phone-by-phone, forming a list of potential sound correspondences.
- Evaluating correspondences: correspondences that occur in several words and help to exhaustively account for entire pairs of cognates are retained; words that cannot be explained by retained correspondences are rejected as non-cognate.
- Reconstruction of sounds: for each sound correspondence, the most likely proto-sound is hypothesized.
- Reconstruction of lexicon: reconstructed sounds are used to hypothesize how the sources of the cognate words were pronounced in the protolanguage.
- Subgrouping: correspondences are accounted for as the result of sound changes that split the protolanguage into a tree of intermediate protolanguages.
- Evaluation: tests are run to make sure all the posited rules work, ideally on new data as well as old.

Stated as a sequence of simple steps, the comparative method looks like a natural candidate for computer implementation, and work toward that goal began as early as 1964 (Kay). As practicing linguists would attest, the problem is actually much more complex than this sketch suggests, and even today there exists no program into which linguists can pour their field notes and get back a full historical analysis of a language family. Instead, development has been proceeding along two tracks. One line of work set as its goal the development of aids for the historical linguist: the computer would do what it could do best, and its human assistant would do the rest. The other line of research concentrated on addressing the more complex problems, typically as an academic exercise in computational linguistics.

An early example of a tool that did a small part of the work well was the COMPASS program of Frantz (1970). Its main contribution was to tabulate the alignments hypothesized by a human linguist. The Electronic Neogrammarian of Hewson (1974) and the Reconstruction Engine of Lowe and Mazaudon (1994) did such things as generating reconstructions from attested words. Hewson (1993) found this helpful in finding cognates across Algonquian languages that had undergone semantic shift.

Another set of programs concentrated on helping with the evaluation phase of the work. Smith (1969) wrote a program to apply 21 rules, in sequence, to derive Russian words from Proto-Indo-European reconstructions. Similarly, Eastlack (1977) implemented the sound changes between Proto-Romance and Old Spanish as a suite of 42 ordered rules; given the Proto-Ibero-Romance reconstruction, the program would apply the rules and verify that the output matched the attested Old Spanish form. The Phono program of Hartman (1993) expressed the reconstructed segments by feature representations, allowing the researcher to write sound change rules at the featural level.

Most of the early programmers found that the stumbling block to fully implementing the comparative method lay very early in the procedure, in the alignment step. Kay (1964) wrote that the ideal procedure was to try all possible alignments and then solve for the ideal set of correspondences across the entire list of words. He then demonstrated that that procedure took several hours when used on just four pairs of CVC words. Kessler (1995) introduced the less ideal but much faster Levenshtein, or string-edit, criterion (Levenshtein 1965, Kruskal 1999). This criterion finds the cost of converting Word 1 into Word 2. The operations permitted are deleting a phoneme from Word 1, inserting into Word 2 a phoneme not found in Word 1, and substituting in Word 2 a phoneme different from that in Word 1. All of these operations have costs associated with them, typically fixed at 1 unit; matching identical phonemes in the two words has a cost of 0. The Levenshtein distance is defined to be the cheapest possible transformation. For example, when comparing [aḷːi] and [bʲehi], two words for 'cattle', a lowest-cost transformation would be to insert a [bʲ] (cost 1), substitute [e] for [a] (cost 1), substitute [h] for [ḷː] (cost 1), and match up [i] with [i] (cost 0), for a total cost of 3. Sounds associated by a substitution operation or by an identity match are considered a correspondence. When used on cognates, Levenshtein tends to give reasonable alignments, because on average, cognate sounds are more likely to be identical than are randomly matched sounds.

(1)   a ḷ i
        | | |
    bʲ e h i

Many researchers have made modifications to the basic Levenshtein algorithm in order to more closely conform to intuitions about what sorts of sounds are most likely to correspond to each other. The earliest modification was to assign smaller costs to substitutions that are phonetically close to each other, which would seem advisable because cognate sounds tend to be phonetically closer to each other than to randomly selected sounds (Paul 1880). Adapting a technique introduced by Grimes & Agard (1959), Kessler (1995) described each phone as a bundle of 12 phonetic features, each of which took on numeric values. The difference between two phones, and thus the cost of aligning the one with the other, was the average of the corresponding values of each of the 12 features. Kondrak (2000) reported good alignment of cognates in a model that incorporated properties such as the ability to ignore potential affixes; weighting features differentially such that some, perhaps place of articulation, are treated as more important than others; and incorporating one-to-many alignments, so as to better model breaking and fusion. Kondrak (2005) addressed the problem that Levenshtein does not take phonetic context into account by showing how it can treat sequences of segments as the basic units. Wieling, Prokić, & Nerbonne (2009) evaluated several variants, including one that permits crossing association lines, modelling metathesis. They reported especially good success with a version that adapts its substitution costs to favour the sound correspondences that are more frequent in the data.

The Levenshtein technique has been enormously popular in computational linguistics and many other fields that need to compare strings of symbols. Despite two decades of research, though, it is still not clear which variant works best for which problems. Indeed, researchers in several domains have reported that adding sophisticated phonetic information to the basic Levenshtein algorithm had little or no effect on accuracy in several domains (Kessler 1995 for dialectometry; Heeringa 2004, and Heeringa et al. 2006, for perceptual differences between words; Holman, Brown et al. 2011 for language cladistics). There are also other contenders for alignment procedures, including pair hidden Markov models (Mackay & Kondrak 2005), which take a long time to construct—they must be trained on large amounts of data—but perform very well once trained.

Subgrouping has been another aspect of the comparative method that has received a lot of attention from computational researchers, though not particularly often purely from the standpoint of phonology (see below under Cladistics for a brief discussion).

9.3 LANGUAGE RELATEDNESS

One important problem in historical linguistics is determining whether languages are related to each other. The comparative method is an excellent way of adducing evidence for relatedness. Unfortunately, almost any investigation that uses the comparative method turns up some evidence of language relatedness, even among unrelated languages, because of the factor of chance. Languages have large vocabularies but small phonological inventories, which means that some sound correspondences are likely to turn up if one looks hard enough. The upshot is that the results of most research, such as Vajda's (2010) fascinating proposal linking the Yeniseian languages of Asia and the Na-Dené languages of North America, are very difficult to evaluate, because opinions differ on how much evidence is enough (see, e.g. the critical review Campbell 2011). It would be useful if some statistical techniques could tell how to interpret the probativeness of a set of evidence. In most social sciences, researchers ask how likely it is that the data gathered in an experiment could be due to chance. If that probability is 0.05 or lower, most social scientists say it is statistically significant. Is such a thing possible in a historical social science, where experimentation is much more severely constrained?

9.3.1 The Significance of an Observation

The first mathematical technique developed to address this problem was probabilistic reasoning. Collinder (1947) decided that there must be a Uralic-Altaic family, because he found a set of 13 similarities shared by many of those languages. He reasoned that the odds of 13 similarities occurring by chance were vanishingly small. Hymes (1956) was more specific: Tlingit has a series of verb prefixes which come in the same order (aligned by function) as those typical of Athapaskan languages; the odds of that happening by chance are 12,168,189,440,000 to 1, therefore Tlingit is related to that family. Nichols (1996) calculated that any language for which the word for 'widow' has the consonants /w/, /j/, /dʰ/, /w/, in that order, must be Indo-European, because the probability is 0.00000625, which, even when multiplied by the number of languages in the world, is less than 0.05.

Such demonstrations can be indicative, but not fully probative, for several reasons. First, linguists do not know enough to reliably calculate the probability that a particular event would occur in a language. This would either require uncannily precise knowledge of how languages are structured, or accurate counts based on surveying large numbers of languages that are known not to be related or to have influenced each other, not even indirectly. Second, even if the probabilities adduced were completely believable and accurate, it is very unclear how to interpret them. The reasoning behind such demonstrations is that the lower the probability of an observation, the less likely it could occur by chance. This is true enough, but in a very complicated system, as the world of language is, there will be many coincidences of very low probability. It is unclear how unexpected a single coincidence must be in order to definitively refute the idea that it is truly a coincidence; certainly that number is much, much smaller than 0.05.

In practice, science rarely proceeds by looking for amazing coincidences. If psychologists or shoe salesmen were looking to prove a relationship between IQ and shoe size, they wouldn't scour the world for an individual with an extremely high IQ who wears extremely big shoes, and demonstrate how unlikely that individual is. The ideal situation is to have many observations, drawn in a way that is unbiased with respect to one's research hypothesis. They might try to draw a random sample of a reasonably large number of people, at least several dozen, and measure their IQ and their shoes. With a large unbiased sample one can reasonably hope to compute statistical significance: how likely any correlation found is due to chance.

9.3.2 The Significance of Recurrent Sound Correspondences

Historical linguists search for recurrent sound correspondences between words of the same meaning because they believe that the association between sounds and meaning is arbitrary (Saussure 1916). If the same pair of segments repeatedly correspond when words of the same meaning are matched up, either a massive coincidence has happened or there is a historical connection between the languages.

Ross (1950) stated this conceptualization more precisely. Take two languages, say English and Latin. For a given concept, say 'thin', find the word that expresses it in English (*thin*) and note its initial phoneme, /θ/. Do the same for Latin *tenuis*, /t/. In a table whose rows are headed by English phonemes and whose columns are headed by

Latin phonemes, add a tally mark for the /θ/≙/t/ cell (read: /θ/ corresponds to /t/). Pick another concept and repeat. After having sampled a large number of words, sum up the rows and columns. Now, in any cell, such as that for /θ/≙/t/, the number one expects to see, if the languages are not historically connected, would depend on those marginal counts. If out of 1000 words one had found 200 words beginning /θ/ in English and 150 words beginning /t/ in Latin, one would expect to find, by chance alone, (200 × 150) / 1000 = 30 tally marks in that /θ/≙/t/ cell. By the degree to which the actually observed tally exceeds the expectation, one would lean toward accepting that English and Latin may be historically connected, i.e. descended from the same parent language in a way such that the same proto-sound became /θ/ in English and /t/ in Latin. Ross reasoned that if one selects the concepts in an unbiased way—crucially one would not toss out the word *think* just because one knows in advance that *cogito* does not begin with a /t/—the cells of the table constitute a fairly large number of observations over which one can evaluate the null hypothesis. Over the table as a whole, are the tallies in the cells skewed so much from their expected counts that one can feel comfortable rejecting the default assumption of chance?

Unfortunately, reformulating the question in this way did not immediately lead to an answer. The ordinary test for association in a contingency table is a chi-squared test, which typically requires quite a bit more data than one is likely to have. Ross's procedure ends up with many cells whose expected counts would be very small, which would result in many false negatives if a standard chi-squared test is used. The ideal solution is a cumulative application of the hypergeometric distribution, but that takes so long to compute that even in the computer age researchers look for ways to avoid it (Wu 1993). Ringe (1992, 1993) used binomial approximations to the hypergeometric, a tack not uncommon among statisticians (Wu 1993), but Baxter & Manaster Ramer (1996) showed that there are realistic scenarios under which such approximations can lead to false positives.

Other workarounds look at ways of making the table less sparse so that easy statistics such as chi-squared can be used. Villemin (1983) reasoned that one can determine whether any particular sound correspondence such as /θ/≙/t/ recurs significantly more often than expected by reducing the entire table to a 2 × 2 table, so that the rows might be /θ/ and not-/θ/ and the columns might be /t/ and not-/t/. That would have worked if Villemin had stuck with that one test, but he independently tested each cell in the same way. As Ringe (1992) pointed out, if a table has 400 cells, that would mean running 400 separate tests. But if one asks 400 times whether correspondence counts have less than a 5 percent probability of occurring by chance, it stands to reason that about 5 percent of those tests will yield a positive result by chance. That is, such an approach is almost guaranteed to conclude that any two languages are historically connected.

A statistically more valid approach to making the values in tables less sparse is to ignore certain phonetic contrasts. One tack is to have a single row and column for all vowels (Ringe 1992). This makes the table smaller and therefore the tallies in the cells bigger, making a chi-squared test more valid. Ignoring phonetic differences within a certain class of segments could be especially beneficial if one believes the distinctions within the segment type are particularly prone to loss or irregular changes, as vowels are in many languages. Other types of detail that might be worth ignoring in this way include phonation or manner of articulation. Kessler (2001) reported reasonable results when lumping together all consonants with the same place of articulation.

Ross's original (1950) idea was to make tables denser by using a thousand pairs of words. It may seem surprising then that linguists rarely use more than one or two hundred words (Villemin 1983 used 215 words; Ringe 1992 preferred 100), but there are several reasons for limiting the size of the word list. The most crucial reason is that each pair of words must be independent with respect to the arbitrariness hypothesis on which the test is founded. Consider what would happen if one used an entire English–Finnish bilingual dictionary: one would find, among others, a massively recurring correspondence between word-initial /ʌ/ and /e/. That sounds very impressive, but once one realized that almost all of those correspondences occurred in words that started with *un-* in English and *epä-* in Finnish, it would be clear that one is mostly dealing with a single morpheme, whose derivatives should be counted collectively as a single instance of /ʌ/≙/e/. Thus it is clear that word lists must be trimmed so as to include no two words that start with the same morpheme. Furthermore, vocabulary that is exempt from Saussurian arbitrariness, such as onomatopoeia and sound-symbolic words, should also be excluded from the test. And it is also important to exclude loanwords from most studies. If one were trying to discover whether Turkish shared a common parent with Urdu, one would not want to include on the list the many loanwords from Persian into each language. Thus there are many exclusions that need to be made just to satisfy the logic of the test (Kessler 2001); feeding in entire dictionaries would not only invalidate the test, but would probably end up biasing most analyses toward concluding that languages are related.

A less obvious problem with including hundreds of words is that not all words are equally probative. After many centuries, related languages are more likely to still share reflexes of the same word for 'eye' than for 'river' (Oswalt 1975). A test should ideally use only concepts that share the same low lexical replacement rate across the languages of the world. Quite a few studies have investigated which concepts have the lowest replacement rates (Swadesh 1955, Dyen, James, & Cole 1967, Oswalt 1970, 1975, Kruskal, Dyen, & Black 1973, Lohr 1999, Holman, Wichmann, Brown, Velupillai, Müller, & Bakker 2008, Tadmor, Haspelmath, & Taylor 2010). Swadesh himself started with 225 concepts in 1950 and was down to 100 in 1955; more recently several linguists have used lists of only two or three dozen concepts (e.g. Dolgopolsky 1986, Starostin 1991, Baxter & Manaster Ramer 2000, Holman et al. 2008). Although what constitutes the perfect universal concept list, if there is such a thing, is not yet settled, it is clear that only a fraction of the concepts from the Swadesh lists have the stability to be useful in even moderately deep linguistic relationships. At best, adding less stable concepts to the test waters down the evidence for language relatedness because the words for those concepts are more likely to be unrelated; this makes the data in the sound-correspondence table look overall closer to chance than it otherwise would be. At worst, less stable concepts are more likely to be loanwords, which can do real damage if they slip past the tester. Indeed, McMahon & McMahon (2003) actually used some words from the Swadesh lists, which were once considered the gold standard for stable, basic vocabulary, to look for patterns contraindicative of common descent. In light of all these issues, it now appears inadvisable to fill out sound-correspondence tables by adding more concepts. If anything, the concept list should probably be radically reduced from the hundred or more concepts that have been used in the past (Damerau 1975, Villemin 1983, Ringe 1992, Kessler 2001).

One promising technique for assessing the statistical significance of sound-correspondence tables uses rearrangement techniques to estimate what chance levels of correspondence would be (Kessler 2001). By definition, a significance level p in a statistical test is the probability that the observed evidence, or even more evidence, would occur by chance. There are many possible ways to construe *evidence* in sound-correspondence tables. Perhaps the approach that best captures the spirit of the comparative method is R^2, the sum of the square of the number of recurrences in each cell. There are also different ways of construing what *by chance* means: How can one decide what R^2 would be if the two languages definitely were not related? The most straightforward way to operationalize that idea is to note that if the languages were not related, then, by the arbitrariness principle, any word (sound sequence) in either language could have any meaning; or, to put it another way, any word in the one language could in principle have the same meaning—pair up with—any word in the second language. For example, when comparing French with German, the attested data would show:

(2) 'tooth'   dent   Zahn
    'stone'   pierre   Stein
    'ten'   dix   zehn

and one of six ways of rearranging that data fragment without regard to meaning would be

(3) dent   zehn
    pierre   Zahn
    dix   Stein

Following through with this toy example, the observed data would yield an R^2 of 1 (2 instances, therefore 1 recurrence, of /d/$\hat{=}$/t͡s/, squared), whereas this chance configuration would yield an R^2 of 0 (no recurrences). Of course, this is only one possible way to rearrange the data. Ideally one would try all possible arrangements and see what proportion of them has an R^2 at least as high as the observed R^2. In this case one would get $2/6 = 0.33$, which would be the p value. With larger word lists, where it would take too long to do all possible rearrangements, one can get a very good approximation of p by

Monte Carlo techniques: computing R^2 over at least a thousand random rearrangements (Good 1994).

This first application, seeing whether the number of recurrent sound correspondences suffices to prove that two languages are related, has been described in some detail not just because it is a particularly long-lived topic of research, but also because it brings to the fore many techniques and questions that are good to keep in mind when considering many other types of computational historical phonology problems.

- The use of word lists is common in quantificational techniques. Many historical linguists have a reflexive aversion to them because they have been used as such mostly in glottochronology, which is widely discredited because its practitioners more often than not made naïve assumptions about lexical replacement rates. But it would be a mistake to equate all uses of word lists. In this specific case, it would be especially strange to be suspicious of the use of word lists inasmuch as the traditional comparative method has as its core the compilation of recurrent sound correspondences across words (Rankin 2005).
- The Swadesh concept lists are not sacrosanct. It often makes sense to use smaller lists selected primarily on the basis of their expected retention rates. However, this need must be balanced against the fact that a reasonable number of words is required to afford some statistical stability in the results.
- Any usefully sophisticated computational technique does not yield 'the answer'. Instead of saying that Japanese is related to Korean, the computer estimates the probability that the evidence is due to chance.
- Reliable estimates of statistical significance entail feeding in data that is not preselected by whether it supports the researcher's hypothesis.
- Lots of data is good, but uninformative data is bad. Computational methods need to find ways to privilege the most informative data. This was shown here of concepts that tend to have low retention rates across languages. Another example is that the initial phoneme of a word tends to be the most stable through time; throwing additional phonemes into the test just tends to water things down and make it harder to show that languages are related (Kessler 2001). This neglect of available data may seem undesirable, but statistical techniques are, after all, intended as an additional tool to supplement, not overthrow, other types of analyses.

Computers can automate many things, and indeed the rearrangement test described here relies crucially on delegating a lot of work to the computer. But linguists still have to work as hard as before to prepare their data for processing, such as by discarding words that violate the arbitrariness hypothesis. A recurring problem in quantitative linguistics is that people do not do this sort of preprocessing. They rarely say why, but a common belief seems to be that inaccuracy doesn't matter: the law of big numbers means that all errors will cancel each other out. In reality, of course, only randomly distributed errors cancel each other out. Researchers who fail to preprocess their data often conclude that languages are related. Villemin (1983), for example, concluded that Japanese and Korean were related to each other, but regrettably had neglected to exclude from the data set words that both languages had borrowed from Chinese.

9.3.3 The Significance of Sound Similarity

Tabulating recurrent sound correspondences across word lists is essentially a phonological methodology, in that the point is to find how many sounds survive from a putative parent language. Nevertheless the technique described in the previous subsection does not really ask linguists to apply a lot of phonological knowledge, unless they choose the option of collapsing sets of phonologically similar sounds into one row or column. But Oswalt (1970) introduced a new way of testing whether languages are related: languages whose words for the same concept sound more similar than one would expect are diagnosed as being genetically related.

The very idea of using phonetic similarity sounds heretical, because historical linguists have always had to spend no small amount of time patiently explaining that Basque and Mayan are not necessarily related even though an enthusiast has found dozens of words with somewhat similar meaning that have somewhat similar sounds. The community is only just beginning to settle down from the furore (e.g. Campbell 1988, Matisoff 1990, Salmons 1992c, Ringe 1996a) over claims made by a highly respected linguist that eyeballing words for similarities across languages is a satisfactory way to prove that large numbers of languages are related (Greenberg 1971, 1987, 2002). But, notwithstanding the fact that many people have applied phonetic similarity in ways that can most charitably be described as irreproducible, the core of the theory is sound. As languages diverge, an original sound will either remain the same in all descendants or it will begin to split into two sounds, which usually remain rather similar in the first instance (Paul 1880). Thus the words for concepts in two daughter languages will be more similar than those in two unrelated languages, with the measurable similarity decreasing gradually over time.

The main issues are whether one can objectively measure phonetic similarity and figure out whether the amount measured is greater than chance levels. This latter problem can easily be handled in the same way it was handled above for sound-recurrency tables: rearrangement significance tests. The general notion of rearrangement statistics for phonetic similarity measures was introduced by Oswalt (1970), who compared the observed similarity statistic with the statistic he got when words were shifted 100 times by a constant factor. Baxter & Manaster Ramer (2000) recast this test as a Monte Carlo rearrangement test, using enough rearrangements to make the test truly informative.

Rearrangement tests give linguists a great deal of flexibility in designing tests for measuring the phonetic similarity or difference between words in two different languages. A useful convention, though, is to conceptualize the tests as metrics, or distance functions. That is, if two words are identical in all important ways, the measurement would be 0; words that are not identical would get a positive measurement; the more different they are, the more that measurement would differ from 0; and the number should be the same whether A is compared to B or vice versa. Oswalt (1970) used the simplest possible metric. For him, two words were either similar (0) or not (1). It is also possible to have multivalued or continuous metrics that express just how different the words are (Kessler & Lehtonen 2006, Kessler 2007).

An important question is what parts of the words should be compared. It is tempting to devise a metric that takes all the information in the two words into account—one hates to be wasteful with hard-won data—but significance tests have more power when they are fed only high-quality data. Some small-scale experiments (Kessler 2007) suggest that it is best to consider only the first phoneme of each root, comparing the two only with respect to place of articulation. This finding matches the rule of thumb that as words change over time, the place of articulation of the initial phoneme tends to be the most stable feature, and indeed most researchers simply worked with this feature without further ado. Oswalt (1970), for example, experimented with different metrics, but their one constant was that words that begin with different places of articulation had to be considered dissimilar (distance 1). Baxter & Manaster Ramer (2000) got at the same thing by classifying words as similar if and only if their initial phonemes fell in the same Dolgopolsky class. Dolgopolsky (1986) had set up 10 mutually exclusive equivalence classes for sounds, grouping together those sounds that are more likely to correspond in cognates in the Eurasian languages he investigated. For the most part these classes were characterized by place of articulation. Turchin, Peiros, and Gell-Mann (2010) also used Dolgopolsky classes and rearrangement significance tests (the bootstrap method) in their testing of the Altaic hypothesis.

Currently, there is little evidence that one metric is significantly better than another. The obvious way to calibrate and evaluate such metrics would be to take a large random sample of languages and show that one metric is better than another at giving positive results for languages known to be related and negative results for languages known to be unrelated. An inconvenient fact standing in the way of doing that is that no pair of natural languages is known a priori to be unrelated—indeed the monogenesis of all languages is a viable theory. If one metric reveals a weak connection between Indo-European and Uralic, and another does not, there is no gold standard for deciding which is correct (Kessler 2007). Computational techniques are subject to the same epistemological asymmetry as the traditional comparative method: it is possible to give a convincing demonstration that two languages are related to each other, but it is not possible to demonstrate that they are not related to each other.

Databases are now available with substantial lexical information on a great many of the languages of the world. It is tempting to process them all in order to find as many relatives as possible. But caution is in order. The data must be carefully processed to omit onomatopoeia, loanwords, and redundant morphemes, a task that may prove difficult for thousands of ill-attested languages. Even more importantly, one expects to get lots of false positives when lots of tests are run: approximately at the same proportion as the chosen significance cut off, which is typically 5 percent. Massive searches for significant data require techniques such as false discovery rate analysis (Benjamini & Hochberg 1995) to help limit the reporting of false positives.

9.4 PHONETIC PHENETICS

In phenetics, the goal is to classify objects on the basis of their synchronic similarity. A phenetic analysis is often the first step in a historical analysis. Because phenetics tends to be simpler than a full-scale historical analysis, it can provide a quick lay of the land, helping the linguist generate hypotheses. Similar languages are more likely to be in the same family or branch than dissimilar languages; similar dialects are more likely to have shared more history than dissimilar ones. There can also be an advantage in the relative theory-neutrality of phenetics. Purely historical analyses, especially if they are driven by a very specific model of language change, may yield incomplete or confusing results that a linguist might be able to better interpret with the aid of good analyses and visualizations of the phenetic landscape.

One of the first applications of a truly quantitative phenetics in linguistics was dialectometry (Séguy 1971), which produced rich visualizations of the similarities between dialects of the same language. The earliest studies emphasized lexical variation, but later studies incorporated some phonological issues; for example, Babitch and Lebrun (1989) classified Acadian French dialects by their realization of /r/. Kessler (1995) introduced a purely phonetic phenetic procedure, comparing the full pronunciations of words that share the same gloss in different Gaelic dialects (Wagner 1958). The phonetic distance between each pair of dialects was taken by summing the distance between the words for each of 51 concepts. The distance between two matching words was defined in terms of the Levenshtein distance between them.

Of course, there are many different linguistically informed ways to compare phones, and several researchers have come up with different schemes (for a fuller review, see Kessler 2005). One improvement has been to give greater weight to some features than others (Juola 1996, Kondrak 2002). Another approach has been to back off from features entirely, on the theory that the important differences between sounds is not simply a linear function of their individual features taken independently (but cf. Nerbonne & Heeringa 1997, who found features advantageous). Oakes (2000) gave substitutions one of two different weights, based on whether they are an example of a well-known type of sound change. Heeringa (2004) tried using acoustic features, including a comparison between the spectrograms of the sounds in question.

In order to better conceptualize the patterns between what may be thousands of pairs of dialects or languages, it is convenient to group them by how similar they are. Babitch and Lebrun (1989) used UPGMA (unweighted pair group method with arithmetic mean: Michener & Sokal 1957), a simple agglomerative clustering technique that is often effective in phenetic studies. They went through the entire distance matrix and found the dialects that have the smallest phenetic distance between them. Those dialects were proclaimed to be a dialect group, which then replaced its two members in the distance matrix; the distance between that group and all the other dialects were treated as the average of the distance from each of its members. This process then continued iteratively until there was only one big dialect left. The chain of dialects within dialects can be expressed as a binary tree or as a box diagram in the manner of Dyen, Kruskal, and Black (1992). Kessler (1995) tried UPGMA clustering for Gaelic in order to verify that the groups that emerged were the same as those found by dialectologists, and they were.

There are many alternatives to UPGMA clustering as a final step, such as neighbour joining (Saitou & Nei 1987), cluster analysis, and multidimensional scaling (Kruskal & Wish 1978, Heeringa 2004). As for many other techniques in computational linguistics, these new methods in phenetic analysis are often borrowed from other disciplines. Felsenstein (2008) described three programs for evaluating distance matrices in biology—Fitch, Kitsch, and Neighbor—which were developed as part of the PHYLIP package for phylogenetic research in biology (Felsenstein 2009). SplitsTree (Huson 1998, Huson & Bryant 2006) incorporates many different algorithms for processing distance matrices, including those allowing them to be visualized as networks. Networks are much like trees, except that inconsistencies in the data are explicitly represented by branches that connect ordinary splitting branches. McMahon & McMahon (2005) present a good introduction to the use of these techniques for historical linguistics.

McMahon, Heggarty, McMahon, & Maguire (2007) used SplitsTree to study phonetic similarity between English dialects. Instead of a concept list, they began with a list of 60 reconstructed Proto-Germanic words and compared the reflexes in 19 descendant language varieties, mostly accents of English. Thus German *Hund* was compared with its English cognate *hound*, not with the synonymous *dog*. Instead of using the automatic Levenshtein procedure, the sounds of each word were hand-aligned to their Proto-Germanic ancestor, so that the programs could compute the distances between sounds known to be cognate. Distances between pairs of sounds were performed primarily on the basis of phonetic features. The distance information was fed into SplitsTree, using two algorithms: Neighbor-Joining, which draws trees, and NeighborNet, which draws networks. For both algorithms, fairly reasonable representations emerged, with much reticulation in the latter case. Interesting results were explored by plotting the distance between three localities on each of the 60 cognate sets. For instance, General American English was shown to be closer to Scottish and Irish English than to the dialects of England it derives from historically. By plotting the distances each Glasgow pronunciation is from both General American and English Received Pronunciation, the researchers found the words where the Glasgow pronunciation was closer to the former than to the latter: most were words like *year, four, fire,* and *horn,* revealing that General American clusters with Scottish because of their shared retention of the rhotic gesture in syllable codas.

A good deal of research is continuing into phonetic phenetics. One of the more difficult outstanding problems is that it is unclear how to measure precisely how successful any specific methodology is: is there a gold standard that says how similar two languages or lects are? Heeringa and colleagues (2006) may have come the closest to this ideal, when they correlated their various distance scoring methods with scores obtained by asking humans to rate how similar utterances were. But phenetic analysis may be used not just when researchers are directly interested in similarity between language varieties, but also when they are preparing the groundwork for a historical analysis. In such cases, it may make sense to fine-tune the methodology so that the distances it yields correlate with known linguistic connections rather than perceptual judgements.

9.5 CLADISTICS

Cladistics is the evolutionary development of a language family. Cladistics can be thought of as classical subgrouping, at least as the latter is most rigorously defined. The definition excludes groups that are defined solely along phenetic, geographic, or cultural lines.

Despite the strict distinction between cladistics and phenetics, it is common in both biology and linguistics to use a phenetic analysis as an approximation to a cladistic analysis. Phenetic analyses tend to take only seconds of computer time; full cladistic analyses may take days or weeks. A significant problem, though, is that there are plenty of well known, commonly occurring diachronic situations that lead to conflicts between cladistics and phenetics. The most serious issue is illustrated by the aforementioned McMahon et al. (2007) results that suggested grouping General American with the other rhotic accents. It may well be true that to some ears, at least, General American sounds more Scottish than English on account of its many /r/ sounds. However, in this case the rhotic accents share a retention (symplesiomorphy) from early Modern English, not an innovation (synapomorphy), and so grouping them together on that basis would be cladistically incorrect. Another problem is that individual historical events can yield massively different distance measures. A single apocope event in one language could make all of its words substantially different from the words in another branch; whereas a series of conditioned changes affecting only a few features in a few words may result in negligible effects on overall vocabulary distance. Or a change affecting a frequent phone like /r/ would have a more profound effect on the distance matrices than multiple changes affecting an infrequent phone like /v/. To this must be added the usual diachronic bugaboos: consider the effect on distance matrices of a sound change followed by its reversal ([t] > [θ] > [t]), identical sound changes occurring independently, and, of course, borrowings. Users of phenetic models must constantly keep in mind the fact that they are doing something that is fundamentally different from classical phylogenetic reasoning.

Is it possible that computer programs can be turned loose on large databases and tasked with producing a cladogram for all the languages of the world? The Automated Similarity Judgment Program project is doing something very much like that, classifying thousands of languages and dialects by their lexical similarity to each other (Brown, Holman, Wichmann, & Velupillai 2008, Müller et al. 2010). As the ASJP researchers make clear, however, several cautions are in order if one is looking specifically for a phylogenetic analysis. All of the warnings given earlier still apply, including the need to preprocess data and the general caution that phenetic analyses may correlate strongly with phylogenetics, but they may also diverge spectacularly in some cases. In addition, it needs to be noted that finding a measurable amount of similarity between languages is not the same as proving they are related, until one demonstrates that the similarity exceeds chance levels. The fact that phenetic trees give reasonable results for languages known to be related invites the inference that the nodes they draw at higher levels are equally reliable, when it fact they may be based largely on similarities due to chance.

There also exist computer programs for performing cladistic analyses in ways close to traditional manual subgrouping. Programs that have been used by linguists include MrBayes (Ronquist, Huelsenbeck, & van der Mark 2005) and PAUP* (Swofford 2007). The linguist identifies phylogenetic characters; for historical phonologists, these might be sound correspondences. A character matrix is set up, showing which reflex each language has. The computer program then attempts to find the tree or trees that can account for that character matrix while optimizing certain conditions. For example, the program may try to set up branching so as to minimize the number of sound changes.

I will not go into much detail about cladistic programs here, mostly because their use in phonology is still highly experimental. Most of the best known cladistic analyses in linguistics have used few if any phonological characters. Of the 376 phylogenetic characters used by Ringe, Warnow, and Taylor in their Indo-European classification (2002), only 22 were phonological. More commonly, linguists use only lexical data (e.g. Gray & Atkinson 2003) or typological data (e.g. Dunn, Levinson, Lindstrom, Reesink, & Terrill 2008), or both (e.g. Wichmann & Saunders 2007). There is no real state of the art for phonology-based cladistics, so the reader is directed to more general treatments of linguistic cladistics. McMahon & McMahon (2005) have given a gentle introduction to the field, and Nichols & Warnow (2008) have supplied a thorough tutorial and review of the literature, including some methods I am here characterizing as phenetic.

Using computers for cladistics is clearly the wave of the future, but the present is still unsettled. Experiments such as those of Nakhleh, Warnow, Ringe, & Evans (2005) and reviews such as Nichols & Warnow (2008) have demonstrated that varying the methodologies very often leads to incompatible results. Another difficulty is that coming up with the best tree to fit the data is ridiculously time-consuming, because the number of possible trees that can be drawn increases superexponentially with the number of languages. Even the heuristics designed to make a best guess without actually inspecting all the alternatives may take days or weeks to run, and it is never quite clear when they are finished. In addition to these problems, there remain, as always, all the familiar problems from traditional subgrouping, such as deciding on the probability that sound change may repeat independently. Nevertheless, computational cladistics holds great promise for linguistics, and has been perhaps the most fervent area of computational linguistic research of recent years.

CHAPTER 10

....

SIMULATION AS
AN INVESTIGATIVE TOOL
IN HISTORICAL PHONOLOGY

....

ANDREW WEDEL

COMPLEX pathways of change are common in systems where system elements interact repeatedly and where future interactions are influenced by the outcomes of previous interactions. Language is such a system at many timescales and levels of organization. For example, the classic S-shaped curve of the spread of a change through a lexicon or a population has been argued to arise in part through feedback interactions, as an initially tentative change begins to cohere into a new model for learning and imitation and then snowballs into a new norm (see e.g. Bybee 2001, Blythe & Croft 2012). In this chapter, I review the use of computational simulation as a tool for exploring and testing hypotheses generated from models of change that include roles for cyclic interactions (see Kessler, this volume, for a discussion of other ways in which computational methods have been used in historical phonology). Work in linguistics making use of computational simulation is often associated with arguments against domain-specific innateness, but this is not a necessary feature of such work. Simulation is simply a tool for exploring cyclic interactions between factors over time and is agnostic about the sources of those factors. Under the assumption that language change is not fully deterministic, that is, that a current language pattern constrains but does not fully predict the trajectory of future language change, computational simulation is a useful tool for exploring models of diachronic change. In the first section, I describe the properties of complex systems that make simulation a valuable tool in their study, and in the following sections I review three case studies from the literature on language change that illustrate the use of simulation to test and expand hypotheses.

10.1 Cycling, Feedback,
and Language Change

Systems with many repeatedly interacting, similar parts frequently exhibit *feedback*, in which the occurrence of a given event influences the likelihood or nature of a similar event in the future. A primary requirement for feedback is that the effects of a particular interaction persist in the system long enough to impact future interactions. When this is the case, the effects of interactions can compound on one another, creating qualitatively and quantitatively different change over time than could be caused by any single interaction. Positive feedback arises when a given event makes a similar event more likely in the future, while negative feedback makes a future similar event less likely. A familiar example of positive feedback is the population growth that occurs when individuals have offspring at greater than the replacement rate. In this case, the birth of each additional individual makes a subsequent birth more likely. In the social domain, positive feedback can result in 'self-fulfilling prophecies': a belief can influence behaviour in a way that provides further evidence for that belief, which then influences more people to share that belief, and so on. Additional classic social examples include the relationship between consumer confidence and economic activity, and the celebrity feedback cycle in which celebrity attracts media attention which begets yet greater celebrity. Positive feedback promotes change and can result in runaway processes. Within phonology, analogy-driven positive feedback has been proposed to play a role in the development of categorical sound patterns (e.g. Wedel 2007, 2012; see also Hare & Elman 1995).

Negative feedback arises when an event makes a similar event less likely in the future, as when a growing population outstrips its supply of resources. In this case, each additional birth lowers the probability of a subsequent birth through increased competition. Negative feedback often promotes stability, and can limit or shape systemic changes driven by positive feedback. Examples of this sort include population growth checked by parasite load, thunderstorm structure in which an updraft that creates precipitation is quashed by the resulting downdraft, and economic overextension reversed by the collapse of credit. In language, anti-homophony effects that inhibit sound change from going to completion may represent a kind of negative feedback (Blevins & Wedel 2009, Wedel 2012).

Both kinds of feedback represent instances of *circular causality*, in which a cause-and-effect chain loops back on itself. Systems exhibiting circular causality often spontaneously develop higher-order, emergent structures in a general process referred to as *self-organization*. Familiar examples of self-organization include the formation and movement of sand dunes, storms, traffic jams, trading patterns in stock markets, and so forth.[1] Language as well, at many levels and timescales, has been argued to provide

---

[1] Beyond resources available on the web on self-organization and related concepts, excellent published resources include *At Home in the Universe: The Search for the Laws of Self-Organization and Complexity* (Kauffman 1995), *A Self-Made Tapestry* (Ball 1999), and *Self-Organization in Biological Systems* (Camazine et al. 2001).

the necessary conditions for self-organizational pathways of change (e.g. Lindblom et al. 1984, Ohala 1989, Lindblom 1992, Keller 1994, Hare & Elman 1995, Steels 2000, Bybee 2001, Blevins 2004a, MacWhinney 2006, Pisoni & Levi 2007, Wedel 2007, Beckner et al. 2009, Wedel 2012). As a consequence, tools for studying this type of complex system could be increasingly useful for linguists concerned with patterns of language change.

10.2 STUDYING SYSTEMS CHARACTERIZED BY FEEDBACK CYCLING

Strongly reductionist approaches often prove inadequate to study systems that include complex feedback loops and circular causality. In these types of systems, significant system behaviours arise through the interaction of system elements over time, and as a result, an approach that attempts to understand large-scale structures by studying their pieces in isolation simply cannot identify any of these types of structure-formation pathways. In turn, however, the properties of feedback-influenced systems provide their own difficulties in model description and testing. To start with, a verbal description of a model including interacting feedback loops is often difficult to assess critically. In part, the difficulty in assessing verbal descriptions of models including feedback arises because change does not arise through a linear chain of cause and effect.[2] Instead, change emerges incrementally through countless, individually inconsequential nudges between distinct system elements over time, making it impossible to precisely pinpoint any particularly significant locus of causation. Rather, in these systems causation is *distributed* across multiple dimensions of the system, including time.

Secondly, feedback-driven systems often display tipping points or *phase transitions*. As a system slowly evolves over time under some set of interacting feedback pathways, accumulated change can create the conditions for a qualitatively new positive feedback pathway, which can then rapidly pull the system in a new direction (see Cooper 1999 for linguistic examples). As a result, an event that would be nearly inconsequential when the system is far from a tipping point can have a dramatic effect when a system is poised at the cusp of one.

As a consequence of these complex properties of feedback-influenced systems, it can be difficult to critically assess a model including feedback that is described verbally. In fact, systems involving interacting feedback loops are notorious for producing unanticipated and even counter-intuitive results.[3] This is one of the ways that computational simulation

---

[2] It may be this lack of easily identified causation that has given rise to the somewhat misleading term *self-organization*.

[3] For example, see the 'Traffic' model in the NetLogo model library, <http://ccl.northwestern. edu/netlogo/models/TrafficBasic>, which investigates features of traffic flow that can influence the development and dissolution of traffic jams. In this model, it is shown that when a driver anticipates changes in the speed of the car in front in order to smooth out accelerations and decelerations, the probability of a traffic jam *increases*. In contrast, sudden acceleration and braking make a jam less likely.

can make a significant contribution. Simulation represents a tool in a reductionist experimental paradigm, but one that preserves and focuses on larger-scale interactions between system elements rather than isolating and studying elements themselves. A model involving interacting feedback loops must specify or otherwise predict the properties of system elements that create feedback, as well as the conditions under which these interactions take place. These specifications can then be built into a simplified model system and tested computationally. If the simplified model system reproduces the phenomenon under study to a satisfactory degree of accuracy, the larger model is not contradicted. In the following section, I describe a case study of this sort that assesses a model of morphophonological change using the Old English past-tense system as a test case.

In addition to serving as a performance test, experiments can be carried out with simulations that would not be possible in the real world, for example, by successively removing particular feedback pathways of the model. Experiments of this sort can confirm to the researcher that a particular feedback pathway is contributing as expected to the model behaviour, and perhaps as importantly, can serve as illustrations of the model's workings to a reader (Peck 2004). In a subsequent section, I review a more abstract case study examining factors influencing the propagation of a change through a speech community, in which an important tool is the structured removal and addition of particular factors.

10.3 TESTING A MODEL WITH DATA: CHANGE THROUGH LEARNING

A major pathway for change in language arises through the cyclic transformations between E- and I-language over generations of learners (Chomsky 1986). I(nternal) language is 'language-in-the-mind', the set of neural structures that correspond to the grammatical and lexical system of a speaker. E(xternal) language roughly corresponds to the set of utterances produced in a speech community from which I-language is acquired and modified through usage. These different forms are in constant interplay as successive generations learn and use language (Figure 10.1).

The role the E–I language chain may play in language change is illustrated in miniature in the familiar Telephone Game. In this party game, the first in a line of people whispers a sentence into their neighbour's ear, who whispers what they understood to the next person, and so on down the line. Whispering degrades the signal sufficiently that errors arise as listeners reconstruct a sentence from the signal under the influence of contextual, semantic, and grammatical factors. Because each listener has no way of distinguishing which parts of what they hear accurately reflect the original sentence and which do not, errors in reconstruction become part of the new lexical and grammatical context that influences subsequent reconstruction errors. It is this property that makes the Telephone Game so entertaining: the result is different from the original utterance in a way that is hard to predict, and furthermore could not plausibly have arisen through

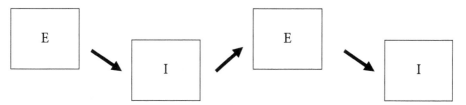

FIG. 10.1 The E-language–I-language transmission chain.

one single transfer no matter how poorly articulated the original utterance. This is because each reconstructed error brings new features to the sentence that cannot be distinguished by the hearer from the original 'correct' features. In contrast, in the absence of iteration, all that can be modulated is the intelligibility of the initial set of words, with the result that a smaller potential range of plausible interpretations is available. In general, whenever transmission of a pattern proceeds via repeated reconstructions from error-prone data—as in both the Telephone Game and language—patterns arise that are difficult to account for solely by reference to the starting point (Nicolas & Prigogine 1977, Kirby 1999, 2000, Kirby & Hurford 2002).

In cyclic systems like the Telephone Game, the directions of change are largely determined by the factors that underlie patterns of reconstruction. In the domain of language change, analogy (in the simple sense of a bias toward some existing pattern) has been proposed to be a major factor influencing the acquisition of patterns from primary input data (reviewed in Hock 2003); see Dresher (this volume) for a contrasting view of analogy, and Fertig (this volume) for a general consideration of the concept. When the patterns in a linguistic system are both highly salient and coherent, we expect most learners to abstract the same basic grammatical system from the input data around them. However, tension arises when analogical systems contain multiple possible generalizations that cannot all be satisfied simultaneously. Hare & Elman's seminal simulation study 'Learning and morphological change' (1995) provides an example of how this tension and its partial resolution over generational reconstructions of grammar may account for the evolution of morphophonological patterns.

Within the domain of morphophonology, local similarity bias in the form of analogical extension has been argued to influence the course of change over time (e.g. Hock 2003, Garrett 2008). Likewise, pockets of formally similar irregulars ('gangs') have been shown to be more likely to recruit new members than formally isolated irregulars (Bybee & Moder 1983, Stemberger & MacWhinney 1988). Under this general model, coherent generalizations over forms act as attractors[4] in diachronic change. These patterns of similarity-based extension and, plausibly, resistance to extension are consistent with a model in which local similarity effects play a significant role in the formation of larger-scale morphophonological regularities. In an excellent example of using simulation to explore this kind of model, Hare & Elman (1995) used iterated, error-prone

[4] An *attractor* is a system state toward which other nearby states tend to evolve.

learning by a sequence of neural networks to model the evolution of the English past tense from Late Old English to the modern system.

In Early Old English, there were at least ten different forms of past-tense markings on verbs, split among four weak subclasses taking a t/d suffix, and at least six strong classes marking the past tense through ablaut. (See also Fertig, this volume.) Over the last millennium the system has simplified considerably to the current state in which the t/d suffix applies to the vast majority of verbs. Hare and Elman begin with the proposal that sound changes in Early Old English made the existing system of multiple past-tense classes more difficult to learn by obscuring cues to class membership—and that the corresponding increased probability of errors set into motion the course of events resulting in the system we see today. Specifically, their model proposes that analogically biased learning and production error is sufficient to account for the types of change that have occurred, whether in weak or regular forms, or strong, irregular forms.

Hare and Elman used a connectionist neural network learning architecture as the backbone of their simulation of this process. However, it is important to note from the outset that their model is not inherently dependent on a specifically connectionist system. They use a connectionist architecture because it naturally exhibits two particular features that are central to their model: that learning is supported both by frequency of presentation on the one hand, and by pattern generality on the other—any other computational implementation that has these general properties would provide qualitatively similar results. This can be thought of as an influence of frequency at two levels of abstraction: the frequency of individual forms matters, but also the frequency of a pattern shared over individual forms. The influence of frequency and generality on learning and production error phenomena is supported by a wide range of theoretical and experimental work; for representative examples, see Bybee (1985), Hock (1991), Lindblom (2000), Long & Almor (2000), Albright & Hayes (2002), Ernestus & Baayen (2003), and Mielke (2008).

Within their model, the neural network has the ability, in principle, to acquire all present–past-tense pairs by rote. However, the probability of learning a given present–past-tense mapping adequately is greater if that present–past-tense pair is frequent in the learning input, and is also greater to the extent that the mapping pattern is shared by other phonologically similar verbs. Conversely, the network is least likely to adequately learn present–past-tense pairs correctly when they are infrequent and/ or when they contradict larger patterns within the input data. Finally, when a network has *not* acquired a present–past-tense pair adequately, it may produce an incorrect past-tense form. The probability of any particular error is biased both by frequency and similarity: an error is more probable if it reproduces a frequent pattern, but it is also more probable if it reproduces the pattern of other phonologically similar verbs. As a result, idiosyncratic, infrequent past-tense forms are the least likely to be learned well, and if they are mislearned, they are most likely to be regularized either toward a highly general, frequent pattern, and/or to a pattern exhibited by very similar verbs.

This simulation architecture is in fact a sophisticated version of the Telephone Game. To start, recall that a number of sound changes occurred in Early Old English that obscured phonological cues to verb class membership (see Hare & Elman 1995: 61). In this simulation, a connectionist neural net with limited computational resources was given the task of learning the correct present–past-tense pairings of a large set of Old English verb forms as they existed in the period just after these sound changes had occurred. These verb forms were presented to the network for learning in frequencies that correspond to their predicted actual frequencies. These differences in presentation frequencies, in conjunction with imposed limitations in computational resources, deprived the network of the ability to always to learn all forms by rote with 100% accuracy. As a consequence, if a given verb's correct present–past mapping was parallel to other similar verbs' mappings, it would have a greater chance of being reproduced accurately because the neural net could rely on generalization to guess a correct past-tense form if rote memorization failed. On the other hand, if a given verb's present–past mapping was idiosyncratic, it would have a lower probability of being reproduced accurately.

As a consequence, although the network learned the correct past tenses for nearly all the verbs, those that it learned incorrectly tended to be those verbs that were highly irregular given the sound changes that had occurred, especially if they were also infrequent such that the network had fewer opportunities to learn their mappings. Verbs were usually mislearned through inferring a more broadly represented past-tense pattern rather than the pattern that was presented for learning. As predicted, however, the network occasionally also mislearned a regular verb if it was sufficiently similar to a very frequent irregular verb, or to a well-represented group of less frequent irregular verbs. The number of errors produced by any single trained network was quite small, however, as is generally true for any individual acquiring a language.

To model the evolution of English over many generations, Hare and Elman presented the output of one network, complete with its small number of incorrectly learned present–past mappings, to a new network. The output of this second network was then passed on to a third, and so on. This process of repeated transfer of knowledge has been termed *iterated learning* (Kirby 2000, Smith, Kirby, & Brighton 2003). Each network learned the pattern of the previous network nearly 100% correctly, but because the errors of each network were passed on to the next, errors were able to accumulate such that after a number of generations, the pattern of regularity and irregularity had shifted significantly from its starting point. Supporting Hare & Elman's contention that iterated learning under analogical pressure can account for attested patterns in morphophonological change, the shifts that did occur in each run of the simulation, though different each time in their details, paralleled the historical changes that occurred in Old English. More than just showing how changes can gradually accumulate over time, however, this kind of model exhibits competing structural attractors of the sort that are hypothesized to influence language change (e.g. Cooper 1999, Blust 2007, Chitoran & Hualde 2007, Wedel 2007, 2009). In this case, for example, the four original English weak verb classes differed in their phonological coherence and in their class size, and as in reality, within this simulation those classes that were least coherent and smallest tended to be absorbed by the others—at first slowly, but then with increasing speed

(Hare & Elman 1995: 77–8). This acceleration occurs because of the feedback between class coherence and size, and the ability of a class to attract new members. The process snowballs as a class gathers new members and thereby becomes a yet more powerful attractor. This kind of positive feedback is a general feature of models that include analogy as a pathway for change.

10.4 SIMULATION AS A TOOL TO CARRY OUT 'IMPOSSIBLE' EXPERIMENTS

Simulations are useful whenever an object of study is a product of compounding interactions, since they allow us to observe trajectories of change with much greater control of relevant variables (Cangelosi & Parisi 2002). Moreover, we can add and remove factors in a way that is not possible in the real world. This strategy provides a powerful additional tool to explore the ramifications of models of this type. In a foundational paper, Nettle (1999) uses this strategy to explore factors that are required to allow randomly occurring variants to spread and become established within a reasonably large speech community.[5]

A long-standing question in historical linguistics is how an initially isolated change can survive and propagate throughout a community, given that language learners tend to converge on a common form. In real languages, rare variants are occasionally adopted and spread in a rising S-shaped curve (D'Arcy, this volume). But how can this happen, assuming that learners converge on a local norm rather than acquiring language through imitating just one person? To the extent that learners acquire language on the basis of a wide sample of speakers, rare variants should never be able gain a foothold in a speech community (see Keller 1994: 99 and Nettle 1999). Is it possible that high levels of variation through imperfect learning are occasionally sufficient to overcome this threshold? Alternatively, can biases toward learning particular kinds of variants be sufficient to allow a new variant to survive and propagate?

In Nettle's simulation a community of speakers is modelled as a population of 400 individuals arranged in a 20 × 20 grid, where distance within the grid represents social proximity. Individuals are born, live for five rounds, and then die after which a new individual is born in their place. There are two linguistic variants p and q that are in competition within the community, and within two rounds each new individual acquires one of the two variants from neighbouring individuals with a probability related to four different factors:

- Social proximity. The influence of nearby individuals is greater than that of individuals further away in the grid.

---

[5] I omit details of the simulation here; see Nettle (1999) for full discussion.

- Frequency. A variant held by many other individuals is more likely to be acquired than a variant held by few.
- Inherent bias. Acquisition may be inherently biased toward one or the other variant.
- Status. Individuals with greater 'prestige' exert greater relative influence.

The influence of these general factors is taken from Social Impact Theory (Latane 1981, see also Boyd & Richerson 1985), in which the probability of learning some cultural variant is hypothesized to be related to the overall 'social impact' of individuals expressing that variant on a learner. Given a formula specifying the relationship of these factors, the probability that any new individual will acquire p vs q can be calculated. Finally, because this model is not concerned with the processes underlying actuation of change, the simulation includes a pre-set 5% chance that the alternative variant will spontaneously arise ('actuate') in any new individual. This provides a steady supply of a minority variant which may or may not propagate depending on these other factors.

All simulations begin with a population in which variant p is the norm, and no inherent bias toward or away from p or q. Under these conditions, the 5% probability that an individual may acquire q rather than p results in a stable pattern in which a few dispersed individuals happen to have variant q, but the community standard remains p. Variant q cannot spread, because there are always an excess of p variants in the learning set for new individuals. However, a few things might aid the spread of q. For example, one could simply increase the probability that the alternative variant will spontaneously arise in a given individual. Alternatively, one could reduce the influence of more socially distant individuals in order to give rare q variants more relative influence on acquisition by neighbouring individuals. Neither of these is helpful under the conditions of the simulation, however. As the probability of variation increases, the mix of p and q just approaches 50:50, and decreasing the range of social influence just produces a patchwork quilt of p and q-using subcommunities.

What about inherent bias? If the bias in acquisition is set sufficiently toward q and away from p, an eventual community-wide switch from $p > q$ can in fact occur, but as Nettle notes, in order for this to occur the bias toward q must be so strong that it would be unlikely for p to ever become established in the first place. Finally, within Social Impact Theory individuals can have differential influence on the spread of a variant on the basis of status. To explore this factor, Nettle varies the distribution of status across the set of individuals and finds that when rare members of the community have very high relative status, if one of those individuals happens to acquire variant q it can in fact spread through the entire population in an S-type curve.

Nettle's contribution exemplifies the use of simulation to explore competing hypotheses in ways that would be otherwise difficult or impossible. Recall that the impetus for Nettle's exploration is the assumption that learners acquire language based on a sample over a large set of speakers. If this is the case, rare variants should never be able to gain a foothold from which to spread. Nettle uses simulation to isolate and test the influence of actuation probability, social proximity, and inherent bias and finds that none of these alone can explain the rare spread of a variant through a simulated community to become the new norm. In contrast, if learners tend to acquire language from a narrower set of high-status models, rare variants can occasionally arise and spread. Interestingly, this suggests that the original assumption may simply be incorrect, and that language variants can in fact be acquired from a very narrow range of influential speakers rather than from the larger set of speakers in contact with the learner.

When a small number of individuals exert strongly disproportionate influence, the effective population size is small which allows events such as the rare actuation of a sound change a greater chance of influencing the trajectory of the population.[6] However, it is clear that functional articulatory and perceptual factors influence the course of change as well; otherwise, we should observe as many diachronic changes that are phonetically unnatural as natural. Recall though that when Nettle explored the possibility that functional biases are solely responsible for propagation of change, he found that functional biases have to be sufficiently strong that anti-functional patterns should never occur. Since this is not the case, Nettle argues that the probability of actuation of particular changes may be influenced by functional biases, but that social factors are the critical engine of propagation. Further explorations can easily be envisaged: for example, can rare variants spread when only a subset of the population is biased toward learning from particular high-status individuals?

10.5 EXPLORING THE ROLES OF NEGATIVE VERSUS POSITIVE FEEDBACK

Our third case study illustrates the interaction of proposed positive and negative feedback mechanisms within a model of sound change. Since Baudouin de Courtenay (1895), a recurring theme in some strands of phonological research has been that biases in production, perception, and learning operate continually to influence the range of variants that arise and propagate through a speech community, and that the synchronic properties of a given phonological system cannot be understood independently from these processes (e.g. Ohala 1989, Labov 1994, 2001, Bybee 2001, Blevins 2004a). A corresponding current in my own work has been understanding how the feedback among particular types of biases can induce the self-organization of higher-order patterns within a lexicon over time. In particular, evidence for the storage and reproduction of experienced variation predicts that given a highly networked lexicon structure, biases on the production and perception of individual words in usage can influence the long-term trajectory of change in the broader sublexical system (Bybee 2002b, Wedel 2007, Hay & Maclagan 2012).

---

[6] For more on this point, see the literature on genetic drift in biological populations (e.g. Masel 2011).

I have argued (2004, 2007) that a general cognitive bias toward variants that are similar to previous experience can account for the emergence of conventionalized phonological behaviour, given storage of phonetic detail in memory and a similarity-based feedback loop between perception and production. A central prediction of this model is that similarity is self-reinforcing: the more items that exhibit a pattern, the greater the resulting bias in variation toward that pattern (cf. the discussion of Hare & Elman's 1995 study above). This positive feedback loop provides a way to think about the development and spread of a range of phonological phenomena (Wedel 2007), but it also suggests that in the absence of countervailing support for contrast, all distinctions in a lexicon should inevitably collapse. And phoneme contrasts do sometimes merge, such as the merger between the vowels /ɔ/ (as in the word *caught*) and /ɑ/ (as in the word *cot*) in many North American dialects of English. If a bias promoting phoneme category merger were allowed to proceed unchecked, all phonemic contrast would eventually collapse, and with it all linguistic contrast. At the same time however, several lines of evidence suggest that there may be a bias toward maintenance of *lexical* contrast in usage. A measure of direct evidence for a lexical contrast maintenance effect in usage comes from laboratory studies (Baese-Berk & Goldrick 2009, Peramunage et al. 2011) showing that the voice onset time distinction for word-initial stops is enhanced in the production of words that have a minimal pair distinguished by initial stop voicing, such as *pat* versus *bat*. Further, at the level of language change a study of diachronically recent phoneme contrast mergers in eight languages showed that merger probability was strongly, inversely predicted by the number of minimal pairs distinguished by that phoneme contrast (Wedel et al. 2013). This finding is consistent with the nearly century-old functional load hypothesis, which states in general that phonemic contrasts are less likely to be lost if they do more 'work' expressing meaning contrast in a language (e.g. Trubetzkoy 1939, Martinet 1952, Hockett 1967, Surendran & Niyogi 2006, Blevins & Wedel 2009, Silverman 2010, Kaplan 2011).

But how might enhancement of contrast between words lead to the maintenance of contrast between phonemes in general? Many tokens of a phoneme in usage, after all, do not define a minimal pair for the lexical items they appear in. One possibility lies in the diverse observations that for a sound change in progress, patterns often appear to spread from word to word (Wang 1969, Bybee 2002b, Phillips 2006, this volume, Hay & Maclagan 2012). Evolutionary models incorporate these observations by proposing that the lexicon operates as a densely interconnected network of representations at different levels of organization (reviewed in Wedel 2012; cf. the connectionist system employed by Hare & Elman 1995). In this case, a general bias towards similarity should promote the spread of patterns both from word to word and from sound to sound (Kraljic & Samuel 2005, Mielke 2008).

This possibility was explored in a computational system modelling an exemplar-based information storage and transmission loop between two agents in communication (Figure 10.2; Wedel 2012). This computational system illustrates the emergence and shift of groupings of tokens at two nested levels of organization, corresponding abstractly to a lexical system and a sublexical system respectively. The important pieces of the simulation architecture are (i) a similarity bias in production, creating a positive feedback

Production:
(i) An exemplar is randomly chosen from a word category as a production target
(ii) Target is biased toward previously heard exemplars at the word and sound levels (black boxes, respectively)

Perception:
(i) Percept is compared to all exemplars in all categories.
(ii) Percept stored as a new exemplar in the best fitting category, with a probability matching its relative fit.

FIG. 10.2 Computational simulation architecture.

loop promoting collapse of distinctions at the segment level, and (ii) a negative selection against ambiguity between words.

Each agent begins a run of the program with a lexicon of four word categories, each seeded with a set of exemplars of previously encountered tokens of that word. Each word exemplar consists of an ordered series of two segment exemplars. The available space for segment exemplars is pre-divided into two labelled dimensions, which for heuristic purposes we can think of as phonetically-based dimensions such as voice onset time (VOT) or tongue height (Lindblom et al. 1984). Segment dimensions are represented as arbitrary scales from 0–100, where individual segment exemplars map to a single point on the scale. Each segment exemplar therefore references two kinds of information: a dimensional category label (e.g. tongue height), and a point on that dimension (e.g. a target tongue height position). Word exemplars correspondingly map to points in a two-dimensional space defined by their sequence of segment exemplars, e.g. [12, 20]. This multilevel exemplar structure (Wedel 2009, Walsh et al. 2010) allows the computational system to record and respond to the distribution of exemplar values of a particular segment both within word categories and also across all words.

The agents take turns producing and categorizing tokens of word categories for each other. In production, a random word exemplar is chosen by the speaking agent, which is then biased stochastically toward other existing exemplars in the lexicon in proportion to similarity. In categorization, the listening agent compares the produced token to all exemplars in memory, and then stores it as a new exemplar in the best-fitting category. If a selection against ambiguity is included in the simulation, the probability of storage of a token as a new exemplar in the listener's memory is lower if the token is substantially ambiguous between word categories.

To set a baseline, runs of the computational simulation can be done without any negative selection against word ambiguity (cf. 'impossible experiments' discussed above). Figure 10.3a shows the initial state of one agent's lexicon. The four clusters of sublexical tokens are purposely positioned at the start within the available space such that no word category contains a distribution of segment tokens that overlaps significantly with that of any other word category. This corresponds to a situation in which there are no segment categories shared between words. After 4000 rounds of the simulation (Figure 10.3b), the distributions of segment tokens for each word category have collapsed due to the similarity bias in production, such that all words are now 'homophonous'.

Figure 10.3c shows the end point of a different run of the system starting with the same distribution of word tokens as in Figure 10.3a, but with the negative selection against

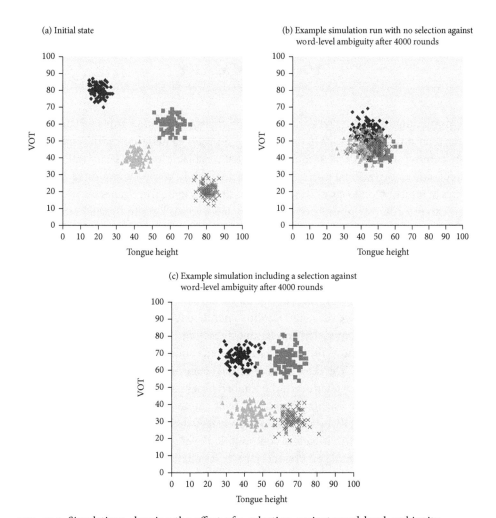

FIG. 10.3 Simulations showing the effect of a selection against word-level ambiguity.

word ambiguity in place. In this case, the system settles into a stable state in which word tokens remain contrastive, but in which segment distributions come to be shared across word categories, as can be seen in the vertical and horizontal arrangement of word token distributions in the graph. This system illustrates how a similarity bias at a lower level of organization can interact with a contrast bias at a higher level to produce an analogue of a lexical system exhibiting duality of patterning. Note that segments remain contrastive in this system even though there is no selection for contrast between tokens at the segment level. The behaviour of this model is parallel to the hypothesized behaviour of real linguistic systems, in which selection for a particular phonetic form of a sub-lexical category in *some* words should promote that phonetic form in *all* words in which the category appears. This is entirely analogous to the biological case in which selection for a particular genetic variant in a subset of individuals in a population will promote the spread of that variant to the entire population over time. More generally, this system illustrates the ability of a *local* similarity bias on variation to create coherent *global* behaviour using a simple computational model.

10.6 SUMMARY

Diachronic linguistics involves trajectories of change that often run over timescales longer than a researcher's lifespan, involving multiple generations within entire language communities. As a consequence, the data available is necessarily fragmentary, indirect, and observational rather than experimental. In response, we integrate many sources of information to constrain and test models, ranging from generation-spanning historical records, to laboratory studies of error biases in individual utterances. Computational simulation is an additional method that offers complementary strengths to this endeavour. The weakness of simulation is that it is abstractly related to human language, but it offers the great strength of allowing fully manipulable and transparent experiments to be run on the abstract logical relationships within a model of language change. These experiments can serve both to test whether a model can accommodate a finding from real language data, and also to generate new hypotheses by exploring the boundary behaviour of a model in 'impossible' situations.

I have summarized above three different computational simulations that exemplify these different strengths. The Hare & Elman (1995) experiment hypothesized that a historically established set of changes in the English past-tense system could be modelled via sequential imperfect learning, modelled by a connectionist network set up in an iterated-learning chain (Kirby 1999). Through errors deriving from analogical extension in the connectionist architecture compounded over generations of networks, Hare and Elman found that simulated present–past-tense relationships evolved in a way parallel to that which is historically recorded. Because a simulation can be run arbitrarily many times, this model of a period in English language history could be repeated to build a statistical distribution of outcomes in order to show that this general result was not unusual. The results obtained by Hare and Elman's model are consistent with the larger model that 'regular' and 'irregular' verb forms can be all learned and processed within the same analogical framework.

Nettle's (1999) simulation created a more abstract simulation of a speech community with several concurrent generations, asking what factors could allow rare variants to propagate across the community and become to the new norm. This simulation used no 'real-world' data at all, but instead built-in factors that have been variously hypothesized to underlie propagation of change. By systematically varying the conditions of the simulation, he showed that only the factor of social status was able to produce the desired S-shaped propagation pattern. This generates a larger hypothesis about the conditions that are necessary for the propagation of initially rare linguistic variants within a population.

Finally, the simulations described in Wedel (2012) use a toy system with a logical structure parallel to that proposed by general exemplar-based, evolutionary models of change. This computational system illustrates that within a lexicon in which detail is stored at multiple networked levels, a bias toward contrast at the lexical level can interact with a bias toward similarity at the sublexical level to produce a constrained phoneme inventory. This set of simulations illustrates how simulation can be used to simplify a model, and to carry out 'impossible' experiments with that model in order to gain a better understanding of its boundary conditions.

In sum, computational simulation serves as an important tool for model-building and testing when studying feedback-influenced systems. Frequently, a simulation can serve as a direct result itself, as when it provides an existence proof that a given pattern can arise through a defined set of interactions. It also can serve as an efficient way to communicate results to an audience: because feedback interactions are often difficult to visualize, simulations provide very effective supporting illustrations for verbal or analytic arguments. But simulations are often at their most useful when they help us test models in greater detail than would be possible otherwise. Just as with a theoretical model, one can always build in enough machinery to make a simulation do what one wants it to do. As we saw, however, a particularly valuable contribution of a simulation lies in asking what conditions, assumptions, and pathways *must* be included to achieve some desired behaviour.

CHAPTER 11

USING CORPORA OF RECORDED SPEECH FOR HISTORICAL PHONOLOGY

WARREN MAGUIRE

11.1 INTRODUCTION

How were the Proto-Indo-European stops (never mind the laryngeals) really pronounced? What was the nature of Old English ‹æ›, ‹ea›, and ‹ēa›, and how were they distinguished? What was 'so scharp, slytting and frotyng and unschape' about northern Middle English dialects? Was there a difference between the vowels in the MEAT and MATE lexical sets in sixteenth-century London English and, if so, what was it? How did Ben Jonson pronounce /r/, 'the dog's letter', and what was the nature of the allophonic variation he seems to describe? These questions (for background to some of the questions, see the contributions by Kümmel, Minkova, and Gordon in this volume) and many others like them from the history of English and other languages could easily be answered if we had audio recordings of speakers from those periods of history.

But of course audio recordings only began to be produced in the second half of the nineteenth century (Morton 2004: 2–7), and recordings of speech didn't become common until the early twentieth century (the British Library's online archive of *Early Spoken Word Recordings* in English contains samples going back as far as 1905). Even so, they have transformed the way we think about language and how we analyse phonology, synchronic and diachronic. This chapter discusses not only the (obvious) advantages of using corpora of recorded speech for historical phonological analysis but also some of the problems we encounter when we attempt to do so. Its focus is on English, but the same issues apply to any language. For the purposes of this chapter, a corpus of audio recordings of speech may be defined as 'a body of language data which can serve as a basis for linguistic analysis and description' (Bauer 2002: 98) made up of audio recordings, analogue or digital (see Bauer 2002 and D'Arcy 2011 for further discussion of the meaning of the term 'corpus' and for excellent overviews of different types, examples, and uses of linguistic corpora).

11.2 ADVANTAGES

Although audio recordings are only available for the last few generations of speakers, it is still possible to investigate language change in real time (see Bowie and Yaeger-Dror, this volume) using them. Thomas (2001) is an excellent illustration of what we can learn by comparing audio recordings from the early twentieth century (of North American speakers born in the second half of the nineteenth century) with recordings of speakers from the same localities at the end of the twentieth century. The changes he identifies in vowel systems are often striking, and Thomas's study shows that the history of recorded speech is already long enough for us to study language change in real time. Other instructive examples of such research include Purnell, Salmons, & Tepeli (2005) and Purnell, Salmons, Tepeli, & Mercer (2005), who analyse fortition of word-final stops in Wisconsin English in real time, and Wagener (1997), who analyses changes in German in the United States using recordings from two different time periods. Another striking example of this is the examination of change in the pronunciation of /r/ in Montreal French, using trend and panel studies, reported in Sankoff & Blondeau (2007). It is only through the use of recorded corpora that we can see change, or lack of change, during the lifespan in such detail, and investigate such crucial questions in historical phonology at all.

Given the short history of recording technology, and the difficulty of finding comparable recordings from different time periods (see Section 11.4), real-time studies are often not possible. But corpora of recorded speech are ideal for studying language change in 'apparent time' (see Bailey 2002). By analysing the speech of comparable speakers from different age cohorts, we can, with some reservations, gain insights into language change even when we have no other evidence. Thus, for example, a number of apparent time studies of a corpus of Tyneside English from the 1990s (the *Phonological Variation and Change in Contemporary British English* [PVC] corpus) have revealed that the variety has been subject to a range of exogenous changes such as glottal replacement, change in the realization of /r/, and levelling of localized vowel pronunciations (see, e.g. Milroy et al. 1994, Watt & Milroy 1999, and Foulkes & Docherty 2000). Highly localized patterns are most characteristic of the speech of older working-class males, whilst patterns which are known to be spreading through varieties of British English are most characteristic of young female speech.

Even with only an hour-long recording of someone's speech, we can, to a reasonable extent, identify the likely phonemic distinctions they have, the typical realizations of these phonemes, their major allophones (including cross word-boundary phenomena), and get a good indication of the lexical distribution of these phonemes. When we analyse samples of the speech of a group of speakers who have roughly the same linguistic system, we can add even more detail to the picture, since what we may be lacking for one speaker might be present for another, giving us a wider indication of the parameters of variation in the speech community (even if we cannot assume that all of this variation is present in the speech of every individual).

This information can be correlated with geographic, social, and historical factors which help us to explain why these individuals' phonologies are the way they are. Two areas in historical phonology which have benefitted enormously from the study of audio recordings are chain shifts and mergers (see Gordon, this volume, for a detailed overview). Relying as we must on written evidence, it is almost impossible to see the English Great Vowel Shift in action—no matter how good the evidence from spelling, rhymes, puns, and metalinguistic comment, it can never give us an up-close view of how a chain shift actually happens (but see the chapters by Lass, Minkova, and Unger in this volume for how far we can push orthographic evidence in this kind of analysis). With audio recordings, we can see in minute detail how each phoneme is pronounced, the degree of variation in their pronunciation, how close they are in phonetic space, what phonetic factors are involved in maintaining distinctions between them, and the social distribution of the change. Labov (1994: 113–291) is a groundbreaking study of what we can learn about chain shifts from examining corpora of recorded speech. So although we will never be able to investigate the Great Vowel Shift in the same way, we can learn from changes such as the Northern Cities Shift about the forces and principles that were likely to have been in operation in earlier stages of the history of the phonology of English and other languages. Likewise, the availability of audio recordings has revolutionized the study of phonemic mergers (see Labov 1994: 295–418 for detailed discussion). Take the example of the 'NURSE–NORTH Merger' in Tyneside and Northumberland English (see Wells 1982: 374–5, Watt 1998a, 1998b, and particularly Maguire 2008). This reported merger, under an [ɔ:]-type vowel, is amply attested (for what that is worth) in written representations of the dialect and in phonetic transcriptions in traditional dialect studies. But nowadays it is very much restricted to the speech of older working-class males, and is only variable even there, suggesting that it is disappearing from the speech community. How did this apparent reversal of the merger come about, and might it be the case that this was never a merger in the first place? Fortunately we have several corpora of recorded speech from the northeast of England in the twentieth century which allow us to explore this phenomenon in detail. In particular, the recordings produced by the *Tyneside Linguistic Survey* (TLS; Pellowe et al. 1972, Allen et al. 2006[1]) in the early 1970s are a rich source of information on vernacular Tyneside speech. A detailed phonetic analysis of these recordings (Maguire 2008) reveals a complex picture of variation, with some speakers having no merger of the NURSE and NORTH lexical sets, others having complete merger (in production at least—see Section 11.3), and still others having some degree of overlap in the phonetic realizations of the two vowels (from slight overlap to almost, but

---

[1] The PVC and TLS recordings are available online: <http://research.ncl.ac.uk/necte/>.

not quite, complete phonetic identity). The picture which emerges is much more complex than that available from other sources—the existence of the merger is confirmed, but only for some speakers, and the existence of substantial overlap but statistical non-identity of the two vowels suggests that the merger may never have been complete for many speakers, or may be being reversed in a rather subtle fashion in the speech community. Figures 11.1 and 11.2 reveal the kinds of complex patterns that are still retrievable from these legacy recordings, which were made at a time when acoustic analysis was difficult and not commonly done, and which have degraded quite considerably since they were made. The speaker in Figure 11.1 (working-class male, born 1930s) has a merger in production of the NURSE and NORTH vowels on both the F1 and F2 dimensions (i.e. there is no statistical difference between the distributions of the two vowels), but retains a significant distinction between these and the SERVE subset of NURSE (i.e. those words which had late Middle English /er/). This is exactly the pattern we would expect in the area from traditional dialect studies such as the *Survey of English Dialects* (SED; Orton & Dieth 1962–71), and it is reassuring to see an acoustic analysis of this TLS recording confirm the pattern identified by the impressionistic traditional dialect analyses. The speaker in Figure 11.2 (a working-class male, born 1920s), on the other hand, does not distinguish SERVE from the rest of NURSE but does have statistically distinct NURSE and NORTH lexical sets (on both F1 and F2 dimensions). However, the two lexical sets overlap to a large extent and are in a situation of near merger.

It is noteworthy that it is really only through phonetic analysis of recorded speech that the important phenomenon of near merger (Gordon, this volume) can be identified, and the existence of the substantial TLS corpus allows us to identify another example of this in Tyneside English.

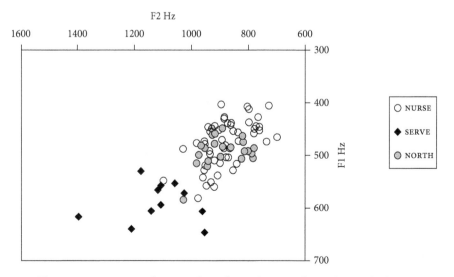

FIG. 11.1 The NURSE, SERVE, and NORTH lexical sets for a working-class male, born 1930s.

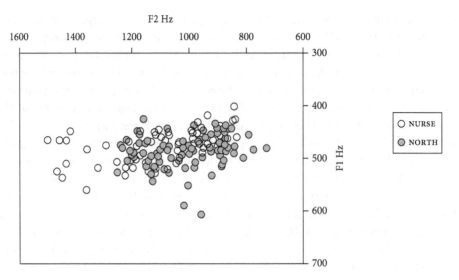

FIG. 11.2 The NURSE and NORTH lexical sets for a working-class male from Tyneside, born 1920s.

11.3 LIMITATIONS

It is clear, then, that corpora of recorded speech are an enormous boon for anyone working on historical phonology, and where they are available historical phonologists can hardly fail to take them into account. Despite the obvious benefits of corpora of recorded speech, however, I wish to highlight some rather important problems here, too.

Most importantly, and something which the richness of data available to us in corpora may almost make us forget, is the fact that speech is not phonology. Whether we envisage phonology as an abstract system rather indirectly related to speech (e.g. Hale & Reiss 2008 and Hale et al., this volume) or as a malleable cognitive state which is in a constant feedback loop with what we say and hear (e.g. Bybee 2001, Bybee, this volume), speech is an articulatory and acoustic phenomenon whilst phonology is mental representation. Even if we lose the ability to hear or speak (e.g. through deafness, expressive aphasia, or dysarthria), we do not lose our knowledge of our native language's sound patterns. So what we capture in corpora is not phonology either—but rather electronic or magnetic encodings of speech sound waves. Although speech is our main body of *evidence* for phonology, we must always remember that there are radical differences between the two (see Ritt 2004: 3–7), and some of these come sharply into focus when we attempt phonological analysis on the basis of audio recordings.

One problem is that a recording of a person's speech can only ever be a snapshot of their linguistic behaviour, no matter how long the recording. Assuming that you live for seventy years (and many people in the Western world are living much longer), you'll have been alive for about 613,600 hours. Even if the time you spend speaking (and listening) is only a fraction of this, and even if our speech is endlessly repetitive (at the phonetic and phonological levels at least), it is obvious that an hour-long recording of your speech represents only a tiny fragment of your linguistic repertoire.

Even so, corpora of (relatively) short recordings have proven to be extremely useful for analysing a wide range of phonetic and phonological features, as the vast body of sociophonetic work illustrates, for example. But recorded corpora are less useful when we want to understand the nature of complex phonological phenomena. Good examples of this are T-to-R (Buchstaller et al. 2013), found especially in northern English Englishes, and the Scottish Vowel Length Rule (Aitken 1981). T-to-R involves alternation between /t/ and /r/ in word-final, typically foot-internal position, as in *hit* [hɪt], *hit it* [ˈhɪɹɪt], and *lot* [lɒt], *lot of* [ˈlɒɹə]. This phenomenon is readily apparent in recordings of speakers from northern England (see Docherty et al. 1997), but the precise conditions for the alternation are very difficult to define, involving as they do the nature of the preceding vowel, metrical position, word frequency, and lexicalization. Although recordings will reveal that some words in some environments will be subject to T-to-R, they will not tell us all of the words that can be affected, how often they are affected, all of the metrical constraints on the phenomenon, and, least of all, which words cannot be affected (since absence of evidence is not evidence of absence, certainly not in a relatively small sample). Even hundreds of hours of recordings of a range of speakers might not reveal the full picture, and it is no wonder that other techniques have been explored for investigating T-to-R in these dialects (Buchstaller et al. 2013). Similarly, the Scottish Vowel Length Rule (SVLR) involves alternations in vowel length and quality dependent upon following phonemes, morpheme boundaries, and, in all likelihood, metrical position and lexical or frequency affects. Capturing a substantial part of this in an audio recording is unlikely (not to mention the difficulty of determining vowel length rules in short samples of speech where other factors, such as speech rate, obscure the picture even further). Just to give a concrete example, Table 11.1 summarizes the numbers of words and tokens in the PRICE lexical set for two older working-class male speakers (J34 and F35) of Tyneside English from the PVC corpus. This rich corpus of

Table 11.1 Numbers of PRICE words and tokens for two speakers in the PVC corpus

Environment	J34		F35		Total	
	Words	Tokens	Words	Tokens	Words	Tokens
+ voiceless C	18	39	18	90	27	128
+ voiced fricative	4	8	5	9	7	17
+ other voiced C	14	38	16	26	23	65
+ schwa	5	9	2	3	7	12
+ morpheme boundary	15 (14)	75 (22)	5 (4)	198 (6)	16 (15)	273 (28)
Total	56 (55)	169 (116)	46 (45)	326 (134)	80 (79)	495 (234)

vernacular Tyneside speech from the mid 1990s reveals that the PRICE vowel is subject to SVLR conditioning in Tyneside English (Milroy 1995), such that [aɪ]-type allophones are found before voiced fricatives, schwa (including [ə] derived from earlier /r/ in this non-rhotic variety) and morpheme boundaries, and an [ɛi]-type diphthong is found elsewhere. In approximately 45 minutes of conversation with each other, J34 and F35 produced over 4000 words each, and 169 (56 words) and 326 (46 words) PRICE tokens respectively. This looks like a good number of tokens for analysis, although there are very few tokens for some environments (e.g. before voiced fricatives and before schwa). But when we divide the tokens up into individual speakers, lexical items, historical lexical sets, and phonological environments, things look less promising. Thus, the word *aye* ('yes'), which may well be phonologically atypical, is overwhelmingly common. If we remove it from the analysis (resulting in the bracketed figures in Table 11.1), the number of tokens is substantially reduced (116 and 134), and data for the pre-morpheme boundary environment is suddenly very sparse. This is especially the case for words where the vowel is morpheme-final but followed by past tense/past participle *-(e)d* (i.e. four items in total, *died, terrified, tied, tried*) which are crucial for understanding the role of morphology in SVLR conditioning (since they reveal whether or not it is morpheme boundaries rather than word boundaries which condition the vowel alternation). Additionally, some of the words where the vowel is followed by a morpheme boundary belong to a different historical lexical set (e.g. *die, fly, high*) which may pattern differently (with final [ɛi] rather than [aɪ]) in modern Tyneside English (see Milroy 1995), further complicating the picture. All of this means that it may be impossible to draw any significant conclusions about the pronunciation of the PRICE vowel in morpheme-final position in the speech of these two individuals, who constitute exactly half of the older working-class male cohort in the corpus, even assuming that the tokens involved are of sufficient quality to allow meaningful phonetic analysis.

These data raise another issue which is problematic for anyone using recorded audio corpora for historical phonological analysis. In addition to words such as *die, fly*, and *high* belonging to a different historical lexical set, other PRICE words belong to different historical sets again. Words spelt *-ight* typically derive from Middle English /ixt/, and are still sometimes pronounced with an [iː]-type vowel in Tyneside English, whilst words spelt with *-ind* typically derive from Middle English /ind/, and may still occasionally be heard with [ɪ]. These pronunciations are so deeply embedded in the vernacular that they rarely occur in recorded speech, but are often known even when they are not used. This means that there is a significant disjunction between production and knowledge that cannot be bridged by relying on recorded corpora alone.

For instance, you might talk to (and record) me for hours without realizing that I have, as part of my phonology, a variable distinction between MEET [i] and MEAT [i]~[e] (which may in turn, depending upon phonological environment and probabilistic factors, be different than MATE [ɪə]; see Milroy & Harris 1980). Unless I'm talking to someone with a similar accent and social background to myself in a very informal situation, I'm unlikely to use the lower variant of MEAT at all (which I only use some of the time even then), and it would take many hours of recordings of such speech to gain an appreciation of the lexical, phonological, and phonetic characteristics of it. Conversely, acoustic analysis of the recordings from the TLS (Maguire 2008) suggests that some speakers have a very localized merger of the NURSE and NORTH lexical sets. But we have no idea what was going on inside these speakers' heads—did they know there was a possible (more standard) distinction, and could they have produced it if put on the spot (e.g. in a reading task)? One suspects that some might have been able to do so, which puts a question mark over the whole idea that these speakers have a merger at all (since a merger in production but not in perception can hardly be described as a phonological merger). So what we hear is, in all likelihood, a representation of only a fragment of what the speakers know, and this is crucial for understanding things such as splits, mergers, and lexical distributions of phonemes.

11.4 METHODOLOGICAL CONSIDERATIONS

These problems relate to a number of methodological issues which affect our understanding of the speech that we analyse, and it is clear that using recorded corpora for historical phonology is far from straightforward (even assuming the recordings we have are of sufficient quality to make analysis worthwhile, which may not be the case for old legacy corpora). The 'Observer's Paradox' (Labov 1966: 86) is a well-known effect which can influence the kind of speech we record in the first place, so that the material we are working with may not be wholly representative of the vernacular we hope to study. Furthermore, the speakers and styles of speech we have recorded may not be strictly comparable with other corpora of recordings or with other kinds of data. Thus, the PVC (mid 1990s) consists of a stratified sample of speakers from the West End of Newcastle upon Tyne in naturalistic dyadic conversations, the TLS (early 1970s) is a collection of one-to-one semi-formal interviews with a fairly random sample of residents from Gateshead (including some non-natives), the SED audio recordings (mid 1950s) from the area are one-to-one interviews with older male manual labourers from villages surrounding Tyneside who were chosen on the basis that their speech was particularly old-fashioned and divergent from Standard English, and the SED phonetic transcriptions represent the interpretations of the fieldworker attempting to record only the most localized forms of speech used by these same individuals. Beyond that, we have a substantial body of nineteenth-century dialect literature from the Tyneside area which represents the attempts of a diverse range of writers to capture the essence of the dialect orthographically. We shouldn't expect these bodies of data to have recorded the same kinds of speech, with the result that differences between them may be attributable to a range of factors other than language change.

It is not surprising, then, that researchers analysing phonology using corpora of recorded speech often use additional techniques to supplement the information they get from them. These approaches include targeted elicitation tasks such as word-lists and reading passages (e.g. Trudgill 1974), probing of speakers' knowledge of phonological patterns through direct questioning (e.g. Maguire et al. 2010, Buchstaller et al. 2013), judgement tasks such as minimal pair and commutation tests (see Labov 1994: 353–7), and perception experiments such as the Coach Test (Labov 1994: 403–6).

But the importance of recorded corpora of speech cannot be overstated. Without them our insights into synchronic and diachronic phonology are severely limited. We can't discover everything about a person's phonology or about the shared properties of the phonologies of groups of speakers, but corpora are a very good place to start and give us much that we might want to know. Furthermore, they introduce a strong element of objectivity and accountability to the data which is not possible with intuitions and general observations. Their importance for historical phonology is only going to increase as the history of recorded corpora lengthens.

....

CHAPTER 12

EXPLORING CHAIN SHIFTS, MERGERS, AND NEAR-MERGERS AS CHANGES IN PROGRESS

....

MATTHEW J. GORDON

12.1 INTRODUCTION

....

THIS chapter addresses two categories of change, chain shifts and mergers, that have long been a part of the discussion in historical phonology and another, near-merger, that represents a more recent addition to this conversation. Fundamentally, both chain shifts and mergers entail changes to the relationship between two sounds. We can appreciate why they are treated together if we see them as alternative outcomes of a change situation. Both may involve the encroachment of one sound into the phonological space of another. If the second sound changes so that the phonemic contrast between the two is maintained, then the result is a chain shift. If the second phoneme does not change, the distinction between the sounds is lost with the result being a merger.[1] Behind this general description lie important distinctions within each category of change including differences of conditioned versus unconditioned merger and of push versus drag chains discussed below (see Salmons & Honeybone, this volume, for a consideration of the structuralist background to views on the role of contrasts and systems in change).

Chain shifts and mergers, like other types of sound change, have traditionally been studied as historical events. My focus in this chapter, however, is on research that

---

[1] Framed in terms of a language's phonemic inventory, another type of change, a split, is also relevant. Indeed, since splits can result in the addition of a phoneme, they represent the opposite of a merger. Nevertheless, this type of change has not figured prominently in the research tradition reviewed here; on the concept of phonemic split, see Salmons & Honeybone, Fox and Cser (all this volume).

attempts to investigate such changes while they are still active. The modern study of language change in progress was pioneered by William Labov in his landmark Martha's Vineyard study (1963) and advanced greatly in later work especially Labov et al. (1972) and Labov (1994). In his investigations into language change, Labov has positioned his work as building on foundations laid by earlier generations of scholars.[2] We find evidence of this in the questions he explores and in his efforts to bring historical patterns and active changes under the same explanatory rubric (see D'Arcy, this volume, Gordon 2013). By any measure, the research agenda begun by Labov has been tremendously productive. While not without its problems, it has opened new windows on the mechanisms and principles at work in language change. Indeed, much of the value of this paradigm lies in the perspective gained by considering changes while they are active. A researcher investigating an ongoing change has access to a more fine-grained picture of the social and linguistic embedding of that change than would be available in the study of almost any historical change. The challenge lies in trying to make sense of this rich detail, in seeking patterns amidst the often chaotic variation.

Variationist sociolinguistics, as Labov's approach has come to be called, takes up this challenge and has brought fresh insights into the study of traditional concepts like chain shifts and mergers. In this chapter I consider how changes of these types have been examined in variationist studies. My discussion is intended to highlight many of the central questions at issue though I generally keep a methodological focus. My goal is not to argue for any particular view of the mechanisms driving chain shifts and mergers, but rather to point out fruitful directions for pursuing answers to the key theoretical questions. The examples I consider deal exclusively with vocalic changes. This bias reflects a disparity in the variationist literature on mergers and chain shifts where most work has dealt with vowel changes. Many of the core issues raised and the analytic techniques described are equally applicable to the study of consonantal changes, though this is certainly truer for mergers than for chain shifts.

12.2 CHAIN SHIFTS

The concept of chain shifting touches on a range of fundamental issues in historical phonology. Unlike, say, *merger* or *split*, the label *chain shift* implies not just a description of what happened but an explanation of why the observed changes happened: a change in one sound caused a reactive change in another. Indeed it is the motivations and mechanisms implied in a chain shift that have made the very concept so controversial (see, e.g. Hock 1991, Stockwell & Minkova 1997, and Bermúdez-Otero and Salmons & Honeybone, both this volume).

---

[2] For example, Labov's (1994) formulation of general patterns of chain shifting draws heavily on insights from Sweet (1888) and Sievers (1876).

We can get a sense of what is at issue in debates about chain shifting by considering the case of parallel or solidarity shifts. A prototypical vocalic chain shift involves one vowel entering the space of a neighbouring vowel and that neighbour moving out of its home space. The process may start with either vowel. When one vowel flees the encroachment of its neighbour, it is called a push chain. When one vowel shifts to fill space recently vacated by its neighbour, it is called a pull or drag chain. In a parallel shift, by contrast, the changes do not bring one vowel into another's territory, rather the vowels take similar trajectories away from their original locations. For example, in many dialects of English the back vowels /uw/ and /ow/ (or the GOOSE and GOAT classes in Wells's 1982 system)[3] undergo fronting. As they shift forward they generally maintain their difference in height with neither moving into the other's path. The changes that constitute a parallel shift are often interpreted as related through a process of phonological analogy: the movement of one vowel establishes a pattern that becomes generalized to other vowels (see Durian & Joseph 2011). This process might be framed in terms of phonological features so that, e.g. vowels marked as [+back] change to [-back]. The connectedness of the elements leads some authors (e.g. Hock 1991) to treat parallel shifts as a type of chain shift. After all, many cases of drag and push chains are just as amenable to an interpretation that they stem from generalization of some phonological rule. For example, the shifting of the Middle English vowels /ɛ:/ and /e:/ to /e:/ and /i:/, respectively, as part of the Great Vowel Shift can be seen as the product of a generalized raising process.

On the other hand, some examples of chain shifting are not readily interpretable in terms of phonological analogy (see Fertig, this volume, for a consideration of analogy in phonological change). The American English pattern known as the Southern Shift, for example, involves a putative link between the monophthongization of /aj/ (PRICE) and the lowering of the nucleus of /ej/ (FACE). These changes entail distinct phonetic and phonological processes that cannot be described by a single rule. Instead their relatedness makes sense only in terms of the dynamics of vowel space: the loss of the glide in PRICE makes it possible for FACE to lower without risking perceptual confusion with the PRICE class (e.g. *raid* can fall to *ride* once *ride* is smoothed to something like *rod*).

Variationist researchers have investigated cases of parallel shifting as well as cases of the drag and push variety. These investigations have generally sought to proceed with a minimum of abstraction, and thus have tended to situate chain shifting in the realm of phonetics, treating connections between shifting elements as adjustments made in a continuous phonetic space (e.g. Labov 1991: 8). This framing is generally consistent with phonetic theories of 'adaptive dispersion' (e.g. Lindblom 1986, Johnson 2000, Hall 2011, and see also Holt, this volume), which posit that the processes shaping vowel systems

---

[3] To aid in cross-dialect comparison, I refer to vowel phonemes using the key words from Wells (1982) though I take some shortcuts with the labels from that system, which is designed to accommodate phonological variation across all dialects of English. For example, the /æ/ phoneme, discussed below in relation to the Northern Cities Shift in American English, covers not only Wells's TRAP class but also his BATH class, and /ɑ/ in most American dialects includes Wells's LOT and PALM classes.

work to maximize perceptual contrast. Still, sociolinguists do not often make such connections explicit. Indeed, questions related to the motivations underlying adjustments in vowel space have not received much attention in the variationist literature. For this reason, a definitional issue such as whether a parallel shift represents a type of chain shift or a distinct phenomenon remains an open question (but see Labov 2010: 91–3).

Most researchers studying active shifts seem to accept the general principle of chain shifting (i.e. that movement of one sound can trigger movement of a neighbouring sound) while remaining agnostic or, more commonly, silent on the nature of the causation implied. Nevertheless, the focus of variationist investigations in this area has been on shifts of the push or drag variety, and in this way such changes serve as prototypes. It is, after all, these types of shifts that dominate Labov's extensive discussions of chain shifting (1994, 2010), and the model he outlines for how shifting operates, a non-teleological account drawing on mechanical processes inherent in auditory perception, describes push- and drag-chain movements.[4] For these reasons, my discussion concentrates on this conception of chain-shifting as movements of vowels toward or away from their neighbours.[5]

12.2.1 Preserving Distinctions

A fundamental component of any definition of chain shifting is the preservation of phonemic contrasts; while the phonetic values of affected phonemes are altered in a chain shift, no distinctions are lost. This observation has led to the interpretation that the avoidance of merger is a driving force in the process (e.g. Martinet 1952), but one need not accept such a teleological interpretation to acknowledge the basic principle that chain shifts result, by whatever means, in a preservation of contrast. In this way the question becomes an empirical one: how can we observe the maintenance of phonemic distinctions in an ongoing chain shift?

One might address this question rather straightforwardly by simply comparing the number and distributions of phonemes pre- and post-shift (as seen in the speech of conservative and innovative speakers respectively). The absence of merger would constitute proof of the preservation of distinction. Tests described below for the study of merger could be used to demonstrate empirically that the shifting sounds have not led to any loss of contrast. Still, we might be inclined to expect more of a chain shift if we consider the preservation of contrast to be fundamental to its definition. In this view, the maintenance of distinctions is not an inadvertent consequence of chain shifting, but rather an integral dimension of the process. Whether we believe that chain shifting is driven

---

[4] Interesting parallels can be found between Labov's (1994) account of change due to probability matching and the tenets of Exemplar Theory which has been developed and tested empirically in a number of studies (see Pierrehumbert 2002).

[5] I am grateful to Thomas Purnell, Malcah Yaeger-Dror, and the editors whose comments on a draft of this chapter prompted me to clarify my descriptions of how variationists understand chain shifting.

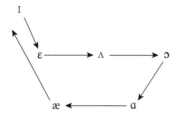

FIG. 12.1 One view of the Northern Cities Shift (based on Labov 1994: 191[6]).

by functional principles (Martinet 1952) or mechanical processes (Labov 1994, 2010), we might expect to find evidence that the principle of contrast preservation is somehow shaping the operations of a putative chain shift.

One place to search for this evidence in the case of vocalic changes is in the position-ing of shifting elements in vowel space. Chain shifting involves one vowel shifting in space, and another vowel adjusting. If preservation of contrast is playing a role, it might be apparent in that adjustment. The issue is most obviously applicable, in the case of a push chain, where the adjustment is a movement away from the encroaching vowel. In this way, some margin of security between the vowels is maintained. Such reactions are testable, and I review some studies that have explored these issues empirically below in considering questions of relatedness. Throughout this discussion it is useful to recall that positioning in vowel space is just one factor contributing to vocalic distinction. A broad range of phonetic differences (e.g. duration, diphthongization, nasality) are rel-evant to the question of contrast between vowels (see Section 12.3.3).

As an overview of the challenge inherent in demonstrating that the preservation of distinctions is fundamental to the chain shift process we can consider the case of the Northern Cities Shift (NCS), a series of changes active in the Great Lakes region of the US. Scholars stressing an interpretation of the changes as a chain shift might repre-sent the shift as in Figure 12.1. When the NCS is portrayed in this way, the principle of contrast preservation seems clearly to be at work. The individual changes appear to be joined in a loop with each vowel shifting to maintain its distance from its neighbours. Nevertheless, on the ground, that is, amid the variable pronunciations used in a given speech community, the tidiness of this image is harder to discern.

Acoustic analysis offers one perspective on inter- and intra-speaker variation. Instrumental measurement of various components of the speech signal has become a critical tool in the study of chain shifts and other phonological variables.[7] In the study of vowels, the frequencies of the first and second formants (F1 and F2) are commonly used as acoustic correlates of height and backness respectively, and plotting the measured

---

[6] In more recent representations of the Northern Cities Shift, Labov includes an alternative path of shifting for /ɛ/, which is sometimes lowered (see Labov et al. 2006: 190 and Labov & Baranowski 2006).

[7] Foulkes and Docherty (2006) review the literature in this area as does Thomas (2011), who also offers a comprehensive description of many of the techniques employed in the growing subfield of sociophonetics.

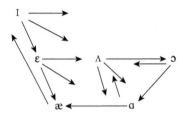

FIG. 12.2 An alternative view of the Northern Cities Shift (based on Gordon 2001).

F1 and F2 frequencies in two-dimensional charts is a common way of representing the positions of vowels. For the NCS case, the acoustic evidence tends to show a much messier picture than Figure 12.1 implies. Formant frequency plots (F1 x F2) such as those presented by Labov et al. (2006: 208–11) suggest that the shifting vowels follow many more trajectories than indicated above, with the result that they not only approach each other but in many cases come to occupy overlapping ranges in vowel space.[8] Similar findings based primarily on auditory analysis of several NCS speakers from Michigan led me to an alternative representation of the shift as in Figure 12.2.

From a portrait like this, it is harder to make a case that contrast preservation operates as a guiding principle in the NCS. Certainly these observations raise questions about the particular case of the NCS and whether it is properly interpreted as a chain shift (see Gordon 2001), but they highlight a broader question of how we can determine whether contrast preservation plays a role in any suspected case of chain shifting. Is it even fair to expect vowels involved in a chain shift to keep their distance (in articulatory or acoustic space) from each other throughout the shift?

As an alternative approach to contrast preservation we might step back from spatial relations among vowels and focus on phonological conditioning. If we think about maintenance of contrast as a problem of homophony avoidance, we see the potential significance of context-sensitive effects. In many chain shifts the vowels show a kind of allophonic patterning, with some phonological environments favouring the shift and others disfavouring it. If similar conditioning effects apply to neighbouring vowels, phonemes can have overlapping allophonic ranges without necessarily endangering the contrast between them. By the same token, conflicting responses to phonological conditioning could put a contrast between neighbouring vowels in a shift at risk.

---

[8] F1 and F2 measurements offer a very limited picture, representing just one slice of the speech signal. It would be premature to interpret overlapping distributions in F1 x F2 space as indications of vowel merger or even necessarily as compromises of the distinctions. Vowels that occupy the same acoustic space may differ in length. In fact, Labov and Baranowski (2006) demonstrate that a very small difference in duration (c. 50 msec) can serve to preserve a perceptual distinction between overlapping vowels. Vowels may also differ dynamically, showing significant spectral changes over the course of their articulations. Diphthongs may differ in the direction and length of their gliding, and even with monophthongs we often discover substantial changes rather than steady states (see, e.g. Jacewicz et al. 2006, Purnell 2008).

Some studies of active chain shifts have explored contrast preservation in these terms. I examined the question in my study of the NCS in Michigan (2001) and found mixed results. In some cases neighbouring vowels seemed to respond in consistent ways to certain phonological contexts, and in other cases the conditioning seemed to increase the likelihood of homophonic confusion. Labov et al. (2006: 253) tested for consistent conditioning effects between the monophthongization of PRICE (/aj/) and lowering of FACE (/ej/), which, as noted above, are elements of a pattern labelled the Southern Shift (also Labov 2010: 295–300). Their statistical analysis finds no such correlations leading them to conclude that, 'the unit of chain shifting is not the allophone but the phoneme' (2006: 254). Still, a study of vowel shifting in New Zealand (Langstrof 2006) suggests that conclusion does not apply in all cases. Langstrof examines a shift in the front vowels whereby the vowels of DRESS and TRAP are raised and the vowel of KIT is centralized. Using acoustic data (measurements of F1 and F2) he compares the positions of these vowels, and his statistical analysis tests for the effects of phonological environment. The results reveal a consistent effect: shifting of each of the three vowels is more extreme in the context of a preceding alveolar consonant. In this way Langstrof's study supports a view that contrast preservation in the process of chain shifting may be sensitive to phonological conditioning.

12.2.2 Relatedness of Shifting Elements

As outlined above, the model of chain shifting implies some kind of causation even though scholars differ in their conceptions of the nature of the causal connections between elements of a shift. There is general agreement that if we are to suggest that two changes constitute a chain shift, one has to be a reaction to the other. In other words, the occurrence of the second change is not a coincidence but rather a result of the first. In this section I consider various dimensions of this question of relatedness with a focus on how researchers might explore links among putatively connected changes.

12.2.2.1 *Chronological Connections*

How changes participating in a chain shift are connected in time is one aspect of the question of relatedness. Obviously, in order to posit that change A is the cause of change B we must determine that A occurred prior to B. Matters of chronology are also fundamental to distinguishing push chains from drag chains. The methods for exploring these relations are largely those used in attempts to date any language change. In addition to 'real-time' historical evidence, researchers examining active changes commonly incorporate 'apparent-time' data by sampling the speech of subjects from a broad age range (see Bailey 2002, and also D'Arcy, and Bowie & Yaeger-Dror, both this volume).

Determining the chronological order of changes in a chain shift might seem to be a fairly straightforward matter, and certainly the right kinds of data can help make it so. Consider, for example, the front vowel shift in New Zealand English. As noted above, this shift involves raising of the DRESS and TRAP vowels and centralization of the KIT vowel. As reviewed by Langstrof (2006: 142) and Maclagan & Hay (2007: 2), some scholars have interpreted the situation as a drag chain spurred by the shifting of KIT, while others posited a push-chain scenario begun by the raising of TRAP. The historical picture of these changes is exceptionally rich due to the available material in the Origins of New Zealand English corpus which includes recordings from speakers born in the middle of the 19th century (i.e. the first generation of English-speaking settlers). What these data show is that TRAP (and DRESS) were already relatively high in the speech of the earliest English immigrants and continued to raise with succeeding generations, while centralization of KIT is not heard among the oldest groups and only appears with those born in the twentieth century. Thus, the real-time and apparent-time evidence supports the interpretation of the shift as a push chain (see Langstrof 2006).

In cases where the historical evidence is sparser, chronological relationships between shifting elements can be harder to discern. As I have argued elsewhere (Gordon 2001, 2002), this is the case with the Northern Cities Shift. Labov has proposed a chronology that has the shift initiated by the raising of TRAP (Labov 1994: 195, Labov et al. 2006: 190), but the evidence for this scenario is largely circumstantial.[9] The problem boils down to this: the real-time picture (e.g. dialectological research in the linguistic atlas tradition) gives no clear indications that the NCS was active in the mid-twentieth century (see Boberg 2001, Gordon 2001), but sociolinguistic research in the late 1960s finds the shift well established across a wide geographic range with many of the individual vowel pieces already showing substantial movement. It seems as if the NCS appeared suddenly and spread rapidly, and thus, it is very difficult to establish the relative ordering of the individual changes.

12.2.2.2 *Testing Relatedness*

Clarifying the temporal ordering of changes in a chain shift is an essential piece in the puzzle, but chronological evidence alone will not suffice as proof of a causal connection. Other types of evidence are useful to building a case for relatedness.

Many of the issues raised above in discussing the preservation of phonemic contrast are also relevant here. Examining the relative positions of the shifting elements in vowel space, especially from a diachronic perspective attained through real- or apparent-time data, may contribute valuable support for a chain-shift interpretation if a case for coordinated movements can be made. Similarly, evidence of shared allophonic patterns across putatively related changes would also strengthen a chain-shift argument.

We might also think about phonemic contrasts from a paradigmatic perspective and consider the potential relevance of vowel types or subclasses. For example, the vowel inventory of English contains a set of long (or tense) vowels which contrast with the short (or lax) vowels. These classes differ phonetically (e.g. long vowels often show

---

[9] Labov (2010) argues that the shift was precipitated by the migration of people from various regions to upstate New York with the building of the Erie Canal in the early nineteenth century. The sociolinguistic ecology inherent in Labov's proposal offers a plausible mechanism for the initiation and spread of these changes, but I find Labov's dating of the NCS to the 1820s problematic (see Gordon 2012).

upglides) and distributionally (e.g. long vowels may appear word-finally). These classificational differences are relevant to contrast maintenance and thus to claims of relatedness. The threat to phonemic contrast is highest when a vowel encroaches on another vowel of the same subclass since these vowels have more in common (phonetically and phonologically) than do vowels of different subclasses.

Preliminary to the search for causal connections between sound changes is the question of where to look; that is, at what level of organization should we expect to see such connections? The matter is of great theoretical significance as it gets to the heart of chain shifting. Does this process operate at the level of the language system or at the level of the individual user? Does chain shifting shape each affected speaker's phonology or do the patterns emerge only from generalizing across a dialect or a community? Labov is quite explicit on this question:

> An individual does not carry out a chain shift, or maximize a distribution. The [chain-shift] rule is a generalization describing the behavior of a speech community over time, and it seeks to unify a number of distinct stages or phenomena that may take as long as three generations. [1994: 264-5]

In this view chain shifting is guided by a kind of invisible hand shaping the vowel system over the long term,[10] and we should not expect to see its operation at any particular point in time or in any individual speaker's phonology. Nevertheless, standard accounts of chain shifting often imply that individuals do play some role in the process. Such a role is evident in Martinet's conception of the process as motivated by 'the basic necessity of securing mutual understanding' (1952: 126). Even the antifunctionalist account proposed by Labov himself (1994, 2010) seems to rely on interactions between individual speaker-hearers. Regardless of one's theoretical stance, there is room for an empirical exploration of this question. Even if we do not consider evidence of causal connections at the level of the individual speaker necessary to establish that a given set of changes constitutes a chain shift, it must be admitted that this evidence certainly would strengthen such a claim.

Langstrof (2006) offers a model for examining chain-shift effects at the level of the individual.[11] As noted, Langstrof tracked the movements of the TRAP, DRESS, and KIT vowels in New Zealanders born between the 1890s and the 1930s. Relying on acoustic data (F1 and F2 measurements) he compares groups of speakers by age to demonstrate the overall pattern of push-chaining in apparent time. He also tests for chain-shifting effects at the level of individual speakers using correlational statistics. This analysis produced several significant results consistent with the view that chain-shift connections

---

[10]   This conception of the dynamics of vowel space is certainly consistent with influential accounts of the long-term evolution of phonological systems such as Lindblom's adaptive dispersion theory (e.g. 1986).

[11]   In Gordon (2001) I examine this issue with regard to the Northern Cities Shift using very different (and less statistically sophisticated) methods.

do shape an individual's vowel space. For example, Langstrof found that speakers with high TRAP vowels tend also to have high DRESS vowels (as measured in F1), and those with high DRESS vowels tend to have centralized KIT vowels (as measured in F2). This suggests that the mechanisms at work in a chain shift, whatever their nature, operate on individual vowel systems.

12.2.3 Has a Sharper Picture of Chain Shifting Emerged?

The guiding assumption of the research described here is that the study of active changes in progress opens new perspectives on the process of linguistic innovation. How has the process of chain shifting been illuminated by investigating changes in progress?

The key components of my answer to this question have been outlined above. By way of summary I review a valuable study that offers insights into how chain shifts may fruitfully be investigated and what researchers might expect to find: Maclagan & Hay's (2007) examination of recent developments in the New Zealand front vowel shift. They examine the speech of New Zealanders born between 1930 and 1984, focusing on the continuing impact of DRESS raising. Their sample of 80 speakers is stratified to facilitate comparisons across the parameters of age, gender, and social class. They use group data to establish the overall pattern of change: DRESS is raising and coming very close to the range of the high FLEECE vowel. Their analysis of the social variables shows that DRESS and FLEECE are increasingly overlapping in vowel space as measured by F1 and F2 and that this trend is more advanced among younger speakers, women, and members of the non-professional classes—a social profile common to many changes in progress. From a structuralist perspective, this situation seems an unlikely site for chain-shift effects given that vowels of different subclasses are involved. DRESS is traditionally a member of the short (lax) vowels and FLEECE is traditionally a long (tense) vowel, and for reasons noted above, chain shifts are more common between vowels of the same subclass. Nevertheless, Maclagan & Hay make a strong case for a chain shift, arguing that raising of DRESS leads FLEECE to react, not by changing its position as KIT did, but by diphthongizing. In this way the study raises new possibilities about the kinds of reactions we might find in a chain shift. The study also shines light on the key issue of contrast preservation. Maclagan & Hay explored contextual effects in their data comparing the behaviour of the vowels in voiceless and voiced contexts. By examining vowel duration as well as positioning in acoustic space, they found that the perceptual contrast between DRESS and FLEECE was most at risk in the environment of a following voiceless consonant, and their statistical analysis demonstrated that it was in this environment that diphthongization of FLEECE was most prevalent. They also examined this relationship at the level of the individual speaker and found a statistically significant correlation such that the closer DRESS and FLEECE are in one's vowel space, the greater that person's tendency to diphthongize FLEECE in voiceless contexts.

We might draw several lessons from Maclagan & Hay's work. First, the connection established between raising of DRESS and diphthongization of FLEECE suggests that researchers should approach potential chain shifts with an open mind in terms of the kinds of changes they may involve. Second, the finding that diphthongization was strongest in the environment of greatest phonetic similarity for the vowels suggests that the effects of contrast preservation can be detected in the chain-shift process. And, finally, the statistical analysis suggests that those effects and/or other mechanisms driving chain shifting can be seen at the level of the individual speaker. Of course, just because Maclagan & Hay found such correlations does not mean that we should expect them of any study of chain shifting. Such findings support an argument for a causal connection between changes, but given the limitations in our knowledge of how chain shifting works, it is unclear whether we should expect to find such evidence in every case.

12.3 MERGERS

The core concept of merger is simple enough: a distinction between two or more sounds is lost. The student of language history identifies a merger by comparing two points in time and noting that contexts occupied by different sounds at the earlier point come to be occupied by a single sound at the later point. For researchers examining mergers in progress this same basic principle obtains though certain complications arise. In fact the structural possibilities are more complicated even for the study of completed mergers. Several patterns of merger are described by Hoenigswald (1960; see also Fox and Salmons & Honeybone, both this volume). From the traditional typologies of merger, two patterns are especially relevant in studies of active changes: (a) unconditioned merger, in which a phonemic contrast is lost in all phonological contexts, and (b) conditioned merger, in which the phonemic contrast is lost only in certain environments. In the former case, the language's phonemic inventory is reduced as a single phoneme takes over the distribution formerly occupied by two or more phonemes. With conditioned merger, on the other hand, the language retains all its phonemes but the distinction between two of them is neutralized in certain contexts.

Treatments of merger in historical phonology often represent the process abstractly as seen, for example, in the mathematical grid diagrams presented by Hoenigswald (1960). Such representations indicate the connections between different stages in history, but they say little about the transition from one stage to the other. Studying mergers as changes in progress brings new perspectives on the intermediate stages in the process and, ideally, new insights into the processes at work.

12.3.1 What is Lost?

Fundamental to the definition of merger is the loss of a phonemic distinction. In structuralist terms this is in theory straightforward. Examining the distributions of sounds over time one can establish that a prior contrast has been eliminated. From the perspective of the language system, where there were two phonemes there is now one. When, however, we examine the change from the perspective of a broader communicative context, we see that possibilities are more varied.

Language users are ordinarily both speakers and hearers, and both roles are relevant to how mergers operate. Losing a distinction between sounds involves losing the ability to produce that distinction as well as the ability to perceive it. We expect these two abilities to go together, and in most cases they do. Thus, a person who has a given phonemic contrast will consistently pronounce the sounds distinctly and will reliably hear the difference between the sounds. Conversely, a person who has merged the given sounds will not produce a consistent difference between them and will not be able to distinguish the sounds even when spoken by someone who has a contrast. With training, merged speakers may be able to learn to hear a distinction, but it is not one they would normally attend to.

12.3.2 Testing for Mergers

Researchers examining mergers in progress have developed a variety of methods to investigate both production and perception of contrasts (see further Labov 1994, Thomas 2011). The most common technique is one adapted from structuralist approaches: the minimal-pair test. The procedure is relatively simple. A list of potential minimal pairs involving the relevant sounds is constructed, and pronunciations of these target words are elicited by having subjects read aloud the written list. Alternatively the words can be elicited using pictures or some other technique designed to reduce the potential complications of spelling. After each pair of words is pronounced, the investigator asks the subject whether the words sound the same or different. In this way, the test captures both production and perception evidence for each subject; it records how the sounds are pronounced and whether the speaker perceives a contrast between them.

While minimal pair testing provides a useful and convenient means of examining the status of a merger, it is a rather blunt instrument, and caution is advised in applying it and interpreting its results. It is not an appropriate instrument for all speech communities nor for all cases of merger. One set of issues stems from the fact that the elicitation part of the task draws maximal attention to the features under study. Subjects are aware that their pronunciation is at issue and are therefore likely to produce their most careful style, which may differ significantly from their speech in less-monitored contexts. On the other hand, because it is the ability to produce and perceive a contrast that is fundamentally what this procedure tests, it is appropriate to examine usage in a context most favourable to the appearance of that contrast. Still, a fuller picture of the change will emerge if the minimal pair data are compared to usage in relatively unguarded situations.

Similar caveats pertain to the perception part of the minimal pair test. The task calls for subjects' metalinguistic judgements. On the surface the test is asking subjects to rely on their auditory perception of their own speech. It is clear, however, that other factors may intervene. One potential influence when dealing with literate subjects is spelling.

There appears to be a widely held principle at least among English speakers that orthography reflects, or should reflect, pronunciation or vice versa (for some discussion of this, see Lass and Minkova, both this volume). Thus, when presented with two words spelled differently, some people will report a difference in pronunciation even when they fail to produce such a difference.[12]

One conclusion to be drawn from this discussion is that minimal pair testing provides a conservative estimate of the extent of a merger in progress. We have considered three possible outcomes of the test. A subject might (a) distinguish the sounds in production and in perception, (b) merge the sounds in production and perception, or (c) merge the sounds in production but report a distinction in perception. Some in this last category may in fact be merged speakers, but would not be counted as such without some additional evidence.

Some problems inherent in the perception component of the minimal pair test can be addressed by examining perceptual responses to actual speech signals using some form of what is called a 'commutation test' in the structuralist tradition. The basic technique has the subject listen to recordings of words illustrating the phonological contrast under study and then identify which word is spoken (see, e.g. Labov 1994: 356-7, Labov et al. 1972, Di Paolo & Faber 1990). Researchers today commonly use various discrimination tasks developed in laboratory phonetics. These tests may present listeners with recordings of two words and ask them to judge whether they sound the same, or they may hear three words and be asked to determine which two sound more alike (see Thomas 2011: 68-9).

These commutation tests offer a useful complement to the minimal pair test. Because they measure the perception of a phonemic contrast through a listening task, the kinds of metalinguistic judgements about whether there should be a distinction (informed by spelling, sociolinguistic norms, etc.), which are a concern with minimal pair testing, are less likely to shape the outcomes here.[13] By the same token, however, research in this area has highlighted problems in assuming that speech perception is ever free of 'extralinguistic' influences. An excellent example is Hay, Warren, & Drager's (2006) work on the 'NEAR/SQUARE diphthong merger' in New Zealand English. They examined perceptions of this active merger using an innovative style of a commutation test. In

---

[12] To gain a sense of the magnitude of the potential confounding influence of spelling on minimal pair judgements I have used 'control' items on written questionnaires. For example among the minimal pairs I include *caught* ~ *coat*, a pair for which all speakers of American English should have a contrast, and *whole* ~ *hole*, a pair for which no speaker should have a contrast. However, the results reveal an interesting discrepancy in the reactions to these pairs. Consistent with expectations, very few respondents judged *caught* and *coat* to sound the same. Out of 3,654 respondents, less than 1 percent (n = 26) counted *caught* and *coat* as the same. For *whole* ~ *hole*, by contrast, 19 percent of the 3,654 respondents reported hearing some difference. Johnson (2010) reports similar findings from a comparable written survey using the pairs *born* ~ *barn* and *paws* ~ *pause*.

[13] For an example of an approach to testing perception of contrast in a more naturalistic setting, see Labov's discussion of the 'coach' test (1994: 403-6), which involves having subjects discuss the content of a recorded narrative. This approach virtually eliminates the potential bias of metalinguistic judgements because the subjects are not aware that speech differences are even at issue.

their experiment, participants heard a series of words which they were asked to identify. The voices were paired with different photos meant to represent the speakers heard. By manipulating the pairings of visual and auditory stimuli, the researchers were able to illustrate how perceptions of the vowels involved in this on-going merger were affected by perceived social differences including age and class. Among other things, this project underscores the fact that there is much more to the perception of a phonemic contrast than a simple minimal pair test can reveal.

12.3.3 Methods of Analysing Mergers

As with the study of chain shifts (and other phonological variables), researchers have relied both on auditory (impressionistic) judgements and on acoustic measurements in their analyses of mergers in progress. The former involves carefully and repeatedly listening to recorded samples of speech and transcribing the sounds heard. When analysing minimal pair data, the investigator may simply make a judgement of whether the words are pronounced the same or differently.

Technological advances have made acoustic analysis more widely available over the last two decades, and researchers have increasingly come to rely on this approach. Ideally instrumental techniques provide a richer picture of the phonetic situation though this has not always been the result. Some, mainly early, studies began (and some also ended) their examination of merger by plotting frequency data measured at a single point in a vowel's trajectory in an F1 by F2 grid. Overlapping distributions in this two-dimensional vowel space were taken as evidence of merger. The limitations of this approach are obvious. While we expect merged vowels to overlap in vowel space, F1 and F2 measurements at a single point in the vowel's duration cannot tell the whole story. There is a wealth of other information in the speech signal that might be contributing to a phonetic difference between the vowels.

For example, work by Irons (2007) and Majors (2005) demonstrates the value of taking acoustic measurements at multiple points in a vowel's trajectory. In separate studies these researchers examined the merger of /ɑ/ (LOT) and /ɔ/ (THOUGHT), an active change in many varieties of American English, and found that the improved picture of spectral change gained by taking multiple measurements of each vowel across its duration was crucial to understanding the sociolinguistic variation observed.[14] Quantitative differences are also known to play a role in distinguishing sounds, and thus vowel length is another factor to explore in studies of active merger, and both Irons (2007) and Majors (2005) did so. Phonation type (e.g. creaky *vs* breathy voice) offers another candidate feature to consider. As described in more detail below, Di Paolo & Faber (1990) found distinct phonation patterns serving to preserve vocalic contrasts in their work on conditioned mergers in Utah.

---

[14] Purnell (2008) illustrates the benefits of similar techniques in the study of a vowel shift.

12.3.4 Has a Sharper Picture of Merger Emerged?

As noted, guiding the discussion here is the premise that the study of active changes opens new perspectives on the process. How has the process of merger been illuminated by investigating mergers in progress?

Certainly it must be acknowledged that this line of research has documented the merger process in much more detail than had been available from the study of completed changes. In some cases this additional detail reveals aspects of the process that might not be visible in the study of a completed change. Consider, for example, Gordon & Maclagan's (2001) study of the NEAR/SQUARE merger in New Zealand. In keeping with the assumption that adolescents represent the cutting edge of active sound changes, the researchers gathered speech samples from over 100 teenagers to examine their status on the merger of the /iə/ (NEAR) and /eə/ (SQUARE) vowels. The project began in 1983 and they repeated the sample every five years until 1998. This longitudinal design allows Gordon and Maclagan to track the progress of this change in real time. Their results document the steady progress of the merger from just 51 percent of the subjects merged in the first sample (1983) to 72 percent merged fifteen years later. The study also reveals some interesting phonetic variability. In the earliest sample there was a tendency for the merged vowel to be realized as [eə], but over time the merger seems to have settled on [iə] as its realization. This change in direction certainly has implications for the understanding of this particular merger, but it serves here as an illustration of the kind of detail about the change process that does not often emerge from studies of historical changes.

Studies of merger in progress also provide insights to questions at the heart of any study of language change. One such question is the 'transition problem', which represents the challenge of explaining how a language moved from one state to a later state (Weinreich, Labov, & Herzog 1968). One dimension of this problem involves the question of how change operates across generations. Johnson's (2010) study of competing mergers in New England explores this issue by investigating changes in apparent time at the regional, community, and even family levels. With regard to the latter, he documents various patterns within several households as a way of exploring the relative influences of families and peers on children's phonologies.

Language-internal dimensions of the transition problem have also been central to studies of mergers in progress. Research on how mergers proceed has led to a typology of mechanisms. Trudgill & Foxcroft (1978) first proposed a distinction between 'merger by approximation,' which involves the gradual coming together of phonemes in phonetic space,[15] and 'merger by transfer,' in which words are recategorized from

---

[15] Irons (2007) noted a valuable twist to the usual scenario of vowels converging in acoustic space with his 'merger by glide loss'. In Kentucky, the LOT and THOUGHT vowels occupy the same corner of vowel space, but the distinction between the classes was traditionally maintained by pronouncing the latter vowel as an upgliding diphthong. Irons's analysis shows that the smoothing of this diphthong results in a merger for many younger speakers.

one phoneme class to another. Most mergers studied by historical linguists are of the approximation type, representing a phonetically gradual process in keeping with neogrammarian conception of sound change (see Murray, and Bermúdez-Otero, both this volume, for a discussion of 'neogrammarian' change). Mergers by transfer, by contrast, result from contact between dialects and operate at a fairly conscious level as the pronunciations of individual words are changed as a result of social prestige or stigma attached to the forms. Herold (1990) added to this typology a third category, merger by expansion, which operates below the level of consciousness but happens more abruptly than merger by approximation. Rather than converging in phonetic space, the phonemes involved in merger by expansion maintain their original ranges as the lexical distributions that separate them collapse. The phonemic contrast is lost, but the phonetic range of the new phoneme is roughly equivalent to the union of the range of the two phonemes that merged (Labov 1994: 322). In Herold's study, this process was connected to particular sociohistorical events involving an influx of non-native speakers to the region she studied, but the basic mechanism may be applicable in other situations (e.g. Johnson 2010).

12.3.5 Near-Merger

Among the most significant discoveries to emerge from studies of active mergers is the phenomenon of near-merger. The ordinary expectation in situations of merger, as noted, is for production and perception to pattern together. Someone who preserves the phonemic contrast will consistently produce and perceive the sounds as different while someone who has merged the sounds will do neither. Minimal pair testing may locate some subjects who report that words are distinct even though their pronunciation belies this claim (as can be shown by applying a listening test), but we might dismiss these cases as the consequences of spelling bias or similar ideological factors. A much greater challenge to our understanding of the process is posed by the reverse situation; that is, by subjects who consistently distinguish sounds in their production but do not perceive a contrast between them. Indeed this strikes many linguists as impossible, and the suggestion has met with substantial resistance, as Labov (1994: ch. 12) describes. Still, evidence of such cases, labeled 'near-' or 'apparent-mergers', continues to accumulate.

The first reports of this phenomenon came from Labov et al. (1972: 236–46; see also Labov 1994: ch. 12), who describe the case of a teenager from New Mexico where a conditioned merger of /uw/ (GOOSE) and /ʊ/ (FOOT) before /l/ was active. Acoustic analysis and commutation tests established that this speaker produced a consistent vocalic distinction between words like *fool* and *full* that he did not hear. Nevertheless, it is difficult to assess this concept of near-merger based on reports of isolated cases. From the early descriptions, the phenomenon seems to be almost an idiosyncrasy of a few speakers. We are left to wonder how common near-mergers are and what role they may play in the process of change.

Fortunately, since then, a number of broader community surveys have explored it in more detail. Labov's extensive study of Philadelphia speech has examined a potential case of near-merger involving /ɛɹ/ and /ʌɹ/ (e.g. *ferry ~ furry*) with a variety of experimental techniques (see Labov 1994: 397–418). Research in Utah has shown that the pattern found in New Mexico operates across the broader region and involves a conditioned loss of several tense/lax vowel distinctions before /l/, creating apparent homophones of pairs such as *feel ~ fill* and *fail ~ fell* as well as *fool ~ full* (Di Paolo 1988, Di Paolo & Faber 1990). The Intermountain Language Survey investigated this trend by sampling dozens of speakers across three generations (Di Paolo 1988). Self-reported judgements from the subjects as well as impressionistic transcriptions from the investigators suggested mergers were in progress for these vowel pairs. Acoustic analysis, however, indicated the situation was more complicated than it appeared. Di Paolo & Faber (1990) examined the phonetic details in terms of formant structures (e.g. F1 and F2) as well as phonation types. The latter involves differences of voice quality such as breathiness or creaky voice. Contradicting the earlier impressions of merger, they found that speakers maintain a distinction at the phonetic level. Interestingly the same kind of distinction was not necessarily found with every speaker. Some kept the vowels separate in acoustic space through consistent differences in formant frequencies while others, who showed no contrast in $F_1 \times F_2$ space, used different phonation types to distinguish the tense and lax vowels. A listening experiment confirmed the persistence of the distinctions.

Demonstrating that near-merger can be widespread in a speech community lends credence to the concept and expands its explanatory value. One important application of the near-merger concept has been to cases of apparent reversals of mergers. It is widely held that mergers cannot be undone. Labov attributes this position to Paul Garde and frames 'Garde's Principle' as 'mergers are irreversible by linguistic means' (Labov 1994: 311). Nevertheless, there are instances of reported mergers seemingly having come undone at a later time. Maguire (this volume) discusses a case from the northeast of England where a previously lost distinction between the NORTH and NURSE vowels appears to have been found. The well-known '*meat/mate* problem' in Early Modern English seems to stand as another case challenging Garde's Principle (Milroy & Harris 1980, Labov 1994). Various strands of evidence suggest that the vowel class of *meat* (from Middle English /ɛː/) merged with the class of *mate* (from Middle English /aː/) in the sixteenth century. The problem stems from the fact that the *meat* class appears to have later separated from *mate* and today has merged with the class of *meet* (from Middle English /eː/). According to Garde's principle, once merged, *meat* and *mate* could not have separated, but of course they are separate which must mean that they were never merged. This is the solution that Labov (1994) adopts, and he offers the concept of near-merger as a way of understanding the apparently contradictory accounts of a *meat/mate* merger. Accordingly, those reports reflect the perception of a merger that had not actually gone to completion (i.e. a near-merger). Some phonetic distinction must have been maintained so that the classes could later separate as *meat* rose to merge with *meet*.

To be sure, Labov's proposal is not the only solution to problems like the apparent *meat/mate* merger. Milroy & Harris (1980), for example, examine the situation in Hiberno-English where these vowels are still reportedly merged. Their solution to the historical problem relies on the coexistence of two phonological systems within a single community. In this case, the local vernacular system merges *meat* and *mate*, but speakers also have access to a more standard system in which *meat* merges with *meet*. The implication of this synchronic situation for the historical problem is that the merger of *meat* and *mate* need not have been reversed, rather the system in which it existed may simply have been supplanted by an alternative one in which the vowels were distinct (see also Milroy 1992b).

These contrasting solutions to the *meat/mate* problem highlight the fundamental challenge of interpreting historical evidence. The concept of near-merger opens up some new possibilities, but also raises new questions. Certainly the discovery of near-mergers complicates our understanding of perception. It appears that speakers can hear subtle phonetic differences well enough to reproduce them but without enough conscious attention to recognize that they are actually hearing them.

12.4 CONCLUSION

The decades since Labov pioneered new methods for studying language change have seen an explosion in scholarship in variationist sociolinguistics, and nowhere has the fruitfulness of this approach been more evident than in explorations of chain shifts and mergers. Traditional questions have been reexamined from fresh perspectives, and new avenues of inquiry have been opened. Investigating sound change in progress, a hallmark of research in this vein, certainly brings many advantages but also presents new challenges. Exploring active changes allows investigators access to a wealth of evidence unimaginable in the case of historical changes. This evidence not only illuminates the facts of a particular situation but may also bring to light new possibilities for understanding the processes in general. As some of the discussion here has highlighted, however, the rich perspective enabled by in-depth study of ongoing changes does not always point clearly in a single interpretative direction. Nevertheless, on balance, it is clear that variationist research has opened new avenues of investigation and, in doing so, has brought fresh insights into the study of chain shifting and mergers and thus into the forces shaping language structure more generally.

PART III

TYPES OF PHONOLOGICAL CHANGE

CHAPTER 13

BASIC TYPES OF PHONOLOGICAL CHANGE

ANDRÁS CSER

13.1 INTRODUCTION

THIS chapter gives a conspectus of the classical types of sound change, that is, those types that were not described in terms specific to either structuralist or post-structuralist theories, but are in this sense common to all strands of historical phonology. In other words, I present a classification or taxonomy of sound changes.

Taxonomies tend to serve three purposes. First, they provide a field of research with a descriptive framework which gives a primary orientation to practitioners for their more refined enquiries and a system in which to organize their disparate findings. Second, they provide a more or less standardized terminology which greatly facilitates scientific communication. Third, a good taxonomy that is not founded on accidental properties may lead to insights not envisaged by its originators. The classical taxonomy of sound changes certainly fulfills the first two functions in that it represents a shared asset known to all historical linguists. As for the third, doubt may justifiably arise. It is well known, for instance, that the apparent symmetries suggested by the terminology (weakening *vs* strengthening, deletion *vs* insertion, assimilation *vs* dissimilation) conceal cross-linguistically highly asymmetrical types, and a large part of actual research on sound changes and phonological processes is concerned with demonstrating that some established types are in fact epiphenomenal or marginal. It is not my purpose to defend, in any sense, these claims or the taxonomy presented. Discussions of controversial issues and theory-specific arguments are found throughout this volume, key ones referenced here.

The bulk of this chapter falls into two parts. In one I discuss general classificatory labels prevalent in the literature. This is a cursory presentation of what I consider the fundamental notions underlying virtually any discussion in historical phonology (conditioning of changes, the phonological levels affected, basic structural consequences, persistent rules as distinct from change proper). In the other part the major types of sound change are presented under nine headings (assimilation, dissimilation, deletion, insertion, lenition, fortition, metathesis, lengthening, shortening). My intention is to be as theory-neutral as possible and not anchor discussion in any framework—and thus make it useful for readers of any theoretical allegiance.

13.2 GENERAL CATEGORIES

13.2.1 Conditioned—Unconditioned—Sporadic Change

Conditioned (or context-dependent) changes affect phonological units in a part of the vocabulary that is characterized by a specific phonological environment. For instance, [k] > [tʃ] / _ V[–back], as in Late Latin or several other languages. Unconditioned (spontaneous or context-free) changes, by contrast, take place in all words that include the affected segment or feature with no regard to its phonological environment. The Old French deaffrications [tʃ] > [ʃ] and [dʒ] > [ʒ] (as in *cher* 'dear', *jour* 'day') took place across the board and ultimately the language was left without a single affricate at that stage. Similarly, Proto-Semitic [g] > Classical Arabic [dʒ] (or [ɟ]) and Proto-Semitic [p] > Classical Arabic [f] (as in **glp* > *jalafa* 'to carve, skin', see Moscati 1980: 24 ff.)[1] were unconditioned changes. Many unconditioned changes may have originated in specific environments, i.e. as conditioned changes, and may then have generalized to other environments, such as the Old English [sk] > [ʃ] change, which probably began before palatal vowels.[2]

Sporadic changes are unsystematic in the sense that they take place only in a small number of words which are not phonologically distinguishable from the rest of the relevant forms. For instance, Middle English [r] was lost before coronal consonants in certain words, cf. *cuss ~ curse*, *bust ~ burst*, but the change did not become systematic (though it may be seen as an early precursor of the general coda r-loss of the non-rhotic dialects). To take a different example, while the change Proto-Finno-Ugric [p] > Hungarian [f] / #_ (Sammallahti 1988: 515) is systematic in that it affected the vast majority of **[p]*-initial words, in a handful of forms the [p] remains unchanged—a case of sporadic retention (e.g. **peljä* > *fül* 'ear', **porV* > *por* 'dust', respectively). Negative conditioning is seen in cases in which the non-triggering environment is significantly more specific than the triggering environment, as in Grimm's Law, where [p t k kʷ] > [f θ x xʷ] except after obstruents (as in Proto-Indo-European [PIE] **stə-* > English *stand* or **oktō*

---

[1] I use orthographic forms (including conventional transliterations and reconstructions) rather than phonetic transcriptions when the former are sufficient to highlight the relevant detail.

[2] Apparent exceptions are later borrowings, e.g. *skulk*, or result from metathesis, e.g. *ask* (Old English *ascian ~ acsian*).

> Old English *eaht* > Modern English *eight*); in other words, negative conditioning is conditioned retention rather than conditioned change.[3]

While the distinctions just described are immensely useful and therefore universally used, they are not as self-explanatory as they seem at first sight. If we take the example of conditioned change above ([k] > [tʃ] / _ V[–back]), we realize immediately that it captures two endpoints of a change which is likely to have been gradual, something along the lines of [k] > [kʲ] > [c] > [tʃ]. Given that [k] was palatalized before palatal vowels, the change from the [kʲ] stage on was unconditioned because it affected all instances of this particular segment. This leaves us with only the first stage ([k] > [kʲ]) as a conditioned change. But is this really a change? Is it not much more likely that [k] had always been palatalized before palatal vowels, that is, that we are dealing here with a persistent rule (see section 13.2.4), a more or less universal fact of coarticulation? Without hair-splitting, I want to show that the distinction between conditioned *vs* spontaneous changes is inherently structural and relates to changes in phonemes *vs* changes in allophones at least as much as to facts of sound shape and phonological environment.

13.2.2 Featural—Segmental—Prosodic Change

Phonological changes may also be classified in terms of which level of the phonological representation they affect. Many changes only affect one feature (or some features), as in most of my examples so far (palatalizations, fricativizations, etc.). Some affect segments in their entirety, e.g. total assimilations (see section 13.3.1.1). Such (featural and segmental) changes are generally distinguished from prosodic changes, which take place on higher levels of phonological organization. Prosodic changes include lengthenings and shortenings, rearrangements of syllable structure, changes in tone and stress patterns, and for some linguists also epenthesis.[4] For example, the Latin change [j] > [i] / C_ (as in PIE **kapjō* > Latin *capiō* 'I get') involves no change at the segmental or featural level since, under many analyses, the melodic content of [i] and [j] is the same;

---

[3] Obviously this traditional distinction between sporadic *vs* non-sporadic (systematic or regular) changes is ultimately based on the neogrammarian idea that the default case is for sound changes not to be sporadic. This is not the place to disentangle the complicated issue of regularity, neogrammarian-type change and lexical diffusion; see Murray (this volume) for a historical survey focused on the nineteenth century, Phillips (this volume) for arguments in favour of the existence of lexical diffusion, and Bermúdez-Otero (this volume) for arguments in favour of the existence of neogrammarian-type change. I intentionally avoid the term *diffusional* because the traditional classification as presented here depends less on the details of the actual processes than on the (perceived) outcome.

[4] Since ideas of phonological representation differ greatly from theory to theory, various phonologists draw the line between prosodic and other types of changes at different places. The most inclusive on the prosodic side is Natural Phonology; for its typology of changes, see Kiparsky (1988b: 376–84) and Donegan & Nathan (this volume). Only lengthening and shortening are described here in some detail as prosodic changes (section 13.3.2). On other types of prosodic change, see Ratliff, Lahiri, and Smith & Ussishkin (all this volume).

what changes is only the syllabification of the segments (phonologically *[kap.io:] > [ka.pi.o:]). Other well-known changes include the general shift of Proto-Germanic stress to the stem-initial syllable[5] or the lengthening of stressed vowels in open syllables in a number of languages (e.g. Late Latin *pater* > *pāter* 'father') or compensatory lengthening, which by definition follows upon the loss of another segment in the same word, as in Latin *nisdos* > *nīdus* 'nest'.

13.2.3 Phonologization—Morphologization—Lexicalization

These terms refer to stages in what is often called the life cycle of phonological change (see Bermúdez-Otero and Kiparsky, both this volume). Phonologization means, under one interpretation, the stage when the low-level physiological variation that ultimately gives rise to the majority of sound changes becomes a 'cognitively controlled pattern of phonetic implementation' (Bermúdez-Otero 2007: 503), i.e. it enters the phonic domain of language in the broad sense. The narrower structuralist interpretation of the term was established by Jakobson (1990 [1931]) and refers specifically to the emergence of a contrast, where there was previously only allophony, through the loss or subsequent change of the conditioning environment. A case in point is the phonologization of the voicing distinction between fricatives in Middle English through the loss of final short vowels, degemination and the borrowing of voiced-fricative-initial French words, e.g. Old English *baðian* -[ð]- > Early Middle English *bathen* -[ð]- > Late Middle English *bathe* [baːð] (> Modern English *bathe*) *vs* Old English *bæð* -[θ] > Middle English *bath* [baθ] (> Modern English *bath*), where voiced fricatives had been originally intervocalic allophones of the voiceless fricatives.[6] Segments resulting from persistent rules (see section 13.2.4) rather than sound change can also be phonologized, e.g. English [ŋ] after the loss of morpheme-final [g] as in *sing*.[7]

Morphologization refers to the stage at which an alternation introduced by a sound change becomes restricted to some morphological category and begins to function as its exponent. Morphologized patterns can no longer be captured in phonological terms. The West and North Germanic sound change known as i-umlaut, in which V → [−back] /_ (CC) [i j], has been heavily morphologized in German, where it now systematically appears in the comparative and superlative of adjectives (*klug* 'clever' ~ *klüger, klügste; alt* 'old' ~ *älter, älteste*) as well as in the plural of many nouns (*Bruder* ~ *Brüder* 'brother', *Wort* ~ *Wörter* 'word') and in the subjunctive of many verbs (*ich wäre* 'I would be' *vs ich war* 'I was').

---

[5] Prior to the shift, stress could fall on various syllables depending on a combination of phonological, morphological and lexical factors, in accordance with the patterns inherited from PIE.

[6] According to Laker (2009) the phonologization of voiced fricatives took place earlier and was also due to Brittonic language contact and language shift.

[7] For more on phonologization, see Hale et al. and Kiparsky (both this volume).

The same change may be said to have undergone lexicalization in English, where it left only erratic residue (*foot ~ feet, mouse ~ mice, old ~ elder*) in the long run. Lexicalization means that the results of a change manifest themselves as ossified lexical idiosyncracies without any systematic (phonological or grammatical) aspect to them. To take another example, the Latin verb *īre* 'to go' has a different stem vowel in the 1SG *vs* 2SG: *e-ō vs ī-s*. This results from the systematically different reflexes of the original sequence *[ej] in prevocalic *vs* preconsonantal position, namely [j] > Ø / V_V, hence **ej-ō > eō*, but [ej] > [iː] / _C, hence **ej-s > īs*. While these were systematic sound changes in the pre-history of Latin, the resulting alternations were levelled out everywhere except in the paradigm of *īre*, which preserves this as an isolated irregularity.

13.2.4 Sound Change *vs* Persistent Rule

It is important to distinguish between sound changes proper, which operate within a limited time span, and persistent rules, which 'remain in effect over a long period of time during the history of a language, and … exert [their] influence whenever, through the operation of other changes, [their] structural description comes to be fulfilled' (Chafe 1968: 131).[8] Typical cases of the latter include contact voice assimilation of obstruents (not a sound change *sensu stricto* in most languages), many harmony phenomena or constraints on syllable structure. To illustrate this, consider two superficially similar phonological phenomena from two unrelated languages. In Late Latin, a prothetic vowel [i] appeared in the environment #_[s]C, cf. epigraphic ISCRIPTA for *scripta* 'written', also French *écrit* etc. In Classical Arabic, a similar prothetic vowel (strictly speaking a [ʔ]V sequence) appears whenever morphological operations result in an (utterance-)initial CC sequence, e.g. *salima* 'to be safe' → *istalama* 'to obtain' after *t*-infixation. The difference is that the Latin change is a real sound change: it had not operated before the Late Latin period, and ceased to operate after it (at least in the majority of Romance languages, cf. French *scruter* 'to scan', *squale* 'shark'; it has remained stable in Spanish), whereas in Arabic there had been a general ban on initial clusters since Proto-Semitic, which operates to this day (although its domain may vary, cf. Watson 2002:61 ff.).

Persistent rules play an important role in loanword adaptation as well. The Italian word *tulipano* 'tulip' comes from Turkish *tülbend,* but the extra word-final vowel does not result from sound change, it merely reflects a phonotactic fact of the borrowing language (with very few exceptions no Italian lexical word ends in a consonant).[9]

---

[8] Chafe's interpretation in its original context is not purely diachronic, though it clearly subsumes what is meant here. The term persistent rule has been used by other phonologists with a different, more strictly synchronic meaning (most notably Myers 1991).

[9] On loanword adaptation in general, see Uffmann (this volume).

13.3 MAJOR TYPES OF SOUND CHANGE

13.3.1 Featural and Segmental Changes

13.3.1.1 *Assimilation*

Assimilation refers to changes in which a segment acquires a property specifically in an environment characterized by that property. Assimilations can be of several kinds and three major parameters are useful in their description.

First, they can be total or partial. In total assimilation, a segment is replaced by a copy of another segment that conditions the change, as in Latin [d]C > CC (except if the consonant is [j] or [w]), e.g. *adligare* > *alligare* 'to tie', *adferre* > *afferre* 'to carry'. In partial assimilation, only some features are transferred from the conditioning environment to the affected segment, as in Latin [−cont] > [+nas] / _ [+nas], e.g. **swepnos* > *somnus* 'dream, sleep' or **deknos* > *di*[ŋ]*nus* 'worthy' (Sihler 1995: 206–8). In some cases, if the conditioning segment and the affected input segment happen to differ only in the relevant feature, the outcome of partial assimilation may look like the outcome of a total assimilation even though it is not, e.g. Latin **supmos* > *summus* 'topmost', an instance of the latter (partial assimilation).

Second, assimilations can be dependent upon strict linear adjacency, in which case they are called contact assimilation (both in the preceding paragraph are of this kind), or they can involve non-adjacent segments in which case they are called distant assimilation, e.g. Karakand [b] > [m] /_VN, e.g. **baŋa* > *maŋa* 'to me'[10] or the well-known (West and North) Germanic change called i-umlaut (see Donegan & Nathan, Kiparsky, Bybee, Fox, Bermúdez-Otero, and Salmons & Honeybone, all this volume), in which V > [−back] /_ (CC) [ij], e.g. **mūsiz* > **mÿsiz* (> *mice*). A subtype of such assimilatory changes between non-adjacent vowels is also called metaphony, especially in Romance linguistics.

Third, based on directionality we distinguish between regressive (or anticipatory) and progressive (or perseverative) assimilation, depending on whether the conditioning segment follows or precedes the affected segment, respectively. I-umlaut, for instance, is regressive because [i] and [j] only palatalize vowels that precede them, and so are the Latin and Karakand nasal assimilations above. By contrast, the West Hungarian change [j] > [c] / [p k f]_ , e.g. *apja* > *ap*[c]*a* 'his father' is progressive: voiceless obstruents turn [j] into a voiceless stop only if it follows them.

13.3.1.2 *Dissimilation*

Dissimilation, significantly rarer than assimilations, refers to changes in which a segment loses a property specifically in an environment characterized by that property. Dissimilations can be contact *vs* distant and progressive *vs* regressive.[11]

---

[10] See Mansuroğlu (1959: 94). The same change is attested in certain other Turkic languages as well.

[11] In theory, one could also distinguish between total *vs* partial dissimilations, but it would be difficult to say what the former actually means. It could refer to haplological loss, as in Classical Arabic

Contact dissimilation is found, for instance, in Middle Greek, where stops turn into fricatives before stops, e.g. Classical Greek *hepta* '7', *oktō* '8' > Modern Greek *efta, oxto*. Distant dissimilation can be exemplified from a much earlier period of Greek, where Grassmann's Law deaspirated stops if they were followed in the next syllable by another aspirate, e.g. PIE *$b^hejd^h\bar{o}$* > Classical Greek *peit$^h\bar{o}$* 'I suggest, convince'.[12]

Both of the above dissimilations are regressive. Progressive dissimilations are also attested, e.g. Thurneysen's Law in Gothic (Collinge 1985: 183–91), which voices certain fricatives after unstressed vowels that are preceded by voiceless consonants and, conversely, devoices fricatives after unstressed vowels that are preceded by voiced consonants (*weitwo*[ð]*-iþa* 'witness' but *wairþ-i*[ð]*a* 'worth', with etymologically the same suffix). Another well-known example of progressive manner dissimilation is the *mn* > *mr* change in Spanish, e.g. Latin *homine(m)* > **omne* > **omre* > *hombre* 'man' (Penny 2002: 89); for place dissimilation cf. PIE *rd^h* > Latin *rb*, as in **werd^h-* > *verbum*, cf. English *word*.

13.3.1.3 *Deletion*

The different kinds of deletion that sounds undergo have been given a variety of appellations depending on whether the change affects vowels or consonants, and also on their position within the word (initial *vs* internal *vs* final). It is not always clear whether these, especially the latter, are useful criteria, since sounds are often deleted in intersecting environments, e.g. preconsonantally both in initial and medial position, or in medial preconsonantal and in final position. This is a reason why the cover term deletion is replacing time-honoured terms such as aphaeresis (initial vowel), syncope (internal vowel), apocope (final vowel). A further source of confusion is that the gradual weakening (see section 13.3.1.5) of sounds that may lead to loss in the long run (such as that of coda [r] in the non-rhotic dialects of English) is not always distinguished terminologically from the more abrupt and categorical kinds of loss often encountered in clusters, e.g. in French *mettre le ballon* [metləbalõ] 'put the ball' with dropping of the [r] in the [t]_[l] environment, or Middle Indic, where all initial consonant clusters lost one consonant (e.g. Sanskrit *prajvalati* > Prakrit *pajjalati* 'ignites', Masica 1991:175).

Examples of deletion include the following. Pre-Latin [s] was deleted before all voiced consonants (except [r]), as in PIE **slewbrikos* > *lūbricus* 'slippery' or **nisdos* > *nīdus*, cf. English *nest*; as the latter example shows, word-internally it triggered compensatory lengthening (cf. section 13.3.2). Final short vowels as well as short vowels in medial open syllables were deleted in Old Hungarian, e.g. *hodu* > *had* 'clan', *uruszág* > *ország* 'land,

---

tatanazzalu > *tanazzalu* 'you lower yourself', but the term is rarely used in such a way. A case in point is Kortlandt (1985: 194), who describes the loss of the initial consonant in PIE **dwidkṃti* > (**widkṃti* >) dialectal Greek *wīkati* '20' as total dissimilation. Paul (1995[1880]: 65) also classifies changes like the loss of the second nasal in Old High German *cuning* > German *König* 'king' as dissimilation along with haplology.

[12] The devoicing of aspirates is probably independent of Grassmann's Law, though the relation between the two is not unproblematic, see Collinge (1985: 47–61).

country', also in early loanwords, e.g. Slavonic *malina* > Hungarian *málna* 'raspberry'. In Gallo-Romance–Old French, nearly all coda consonants (internally as well as finally) were deleted, e.g. Latin *rupta* > French *route* 'road, way', *ultra* > *outre* 'beyond', *costa* 'rib' > *côte* 'coast, rib', *est* > [e] 'is'. Initial unstressed vowels were deleted in Middle Greek, thus Classical Greek *opsárion* > Modern Greek *psári* 'fish' or *egráp^hete* 'you.PL wrote' > *gráfate* (but *égrap^hes* > *égrafes* 'you.SG wrote').

13.3.1.4 *Insertion (Epenthesis)*

These changes, like deletions, are also known by a variety of names depending on the position and the type of the inserted segment, but are most frequently just referred to as insertion or epenthesis. Initial epenthesis (also known as prothesis) is found e.g. in Bohemian Czech, where #[o] > #[vo] regularly (*on* > *von* 'he', *okno* > *vokno* 'window', Short 2002: 529). The Late Latin epenthesis #[s]C > #[is]C (*schola* > Spanish *escuela* 'school') was mentioned above (section 13.2.4). Word-medial epenthesis is known as excrescence if it is the epenthesis of a consonant between other consonants, anaptyxis if it is the epenthesis of a vowel (practically always between two consonants); anaptyctic vowels are sometimes referred to as svarabhakti vowels. Excrescent consonants appear in many languages in the middle of consonant clusters including a liquid or a nasal, cf. Classical Greek *anēr* 'man' but genitive *andros* (<*anr-os*) much like Latin *ponere* 'put' > French *pondre* 'lay eggs', *similare* 'resemble' > *sembler* 'seem' or Old English *þunor* (noun), genitive *þunres*, *þunrian* (verb) etc. > Modern English *thunder*. Anaptyctic vowels break up consonant clusters as in the Russian reflexes of Proto-Slavonic liquid + consonant clusters, e.g. Proto-Slavonic **berg-* > Russian *béreg* 'bank', **melko* > *molokó* 'milk', and vowels are inserted in a variety of languages to resolve syllabic sonorants, e.g. PIE **tn̥-* 'hold, stretch' > Proto-Germanic **þun-* (> English *thin*, German *dünn*), Classical Greek *tanuō* 'to stretch', Proto-Slavonic **tĭn-* (> Czech *tenký* 'thin, fine' etc.). Final epenthesis (paragoge) is very rare; paragogic consonants appear e.g. in Middle English *soun* > Modern English *sound*, *ageines* > *against* or in the German pronouns *jemand* 'somebody', *niemand* 'nobody', both compounds of *man* 'one, man'.

13.3.1.5 *Lenition (Weakening)*

Lenitions are encountered in the history of a wide variety of languages. This class is rather heterogeneous and is generally seen as involving the movement of conso-nants towards a more vowel-like articulation (i.e. voiceless > voiced, stop > fricative, obstruent > liquid/glide, oral constriction > purely glottal articulation). It is crucially dependent on a concept of consonant strength or some scalar quality (like sonority or complexity) with a similar function, and is thought to be typical of what are referred to as weak positions (primarily intervocalic and coda position and unstressed syllables); furthermore, for some linguists, shortening, assimilation as well as deletion are subcases of lenition (or, in the case of deletion, even its summation).[13] On the one hand, lenitions

---

[13] See Hyman (1975: 165), Lass (1984: 177 ff.), Hock (1986: 82), Kiparsky (1988b: 377), Harris-Northall (1990: 127). For typological aspects, see Kümmel (2007, this volume).

perhaps more than any other of the processes discussed in this chapter have been in the focus of phonological research and theorizing for the past quarter century;[14] on the other hand, the somewhat diffuse nature of the concept of lenition has given rise to various, often conflicting, attempts at describing its properties and classifying the relevant changes.[15] Also note that weakening (though not normally lenition) is a term often used for the reduction of unstressed vowels, as in English.

Let us look at a handful of examples that are relatively uncontroversial. In Proto-Brittonic and Proto-Gaelic, [b d g m] > [v ð ɣ ṽ] / V_V, e.g. Proto-Celtic *sodjo- > Old Irish [suðʲe] 'seat', *tegesos > [tiɣʲe] 'house', Latin probo > Welsh pro[v]i 'test, prove', Latin similis > Old Irish [saṽalʲ] 'similar' (Russell 1995:30, 236 ff.). In Pali, [d] > [l] / V_V, as in Sanskrit pīḍā > Pali pīlā 'pain'.[16] In Middle English, fricatives were voiced word-finally if the last syllable of the word was unstressed, cf. misse[z], wi[ð], i[z].

13.3.1.6 *Fortition (Strengthening)*

The presumed mirror-image of lenition, though much rarer, fortition involves a change of consonants towards less vowel-like qualities (devoicing, occlusion, loss of sonorancy). In Pre-Classical Greek, for instance, [j] > [c] > [t] / [p pʰ]_, as in *tupjō > tuptō 'hit' (cf. Sihler 1995: 194–5); in (Old or Middle) Spanish the voiced coronal fricatives were devoiced in all environments ([ʐ z ʒ] > [ʂ s ʃ]), as in dezir 'say', casa 'house' and fijo 'son', respectively (later [ʃ] > [x]; Penny 2002: 98 ff.); in High German, [w j] > [b g] / [r l]_, e.g. Middle High German swalwe > Modern German Schwalbe 'swallow', verje > Ferge 'ferryman'. Fortitions are usually thought to be typical of initial and onset positions, though cross-linguistic evidence on this point is controversial, and in general the environments of fortition are much less typical than those of lenition (Cser 2003: 81–3). Word-final devoicing, a cross-linguistically very frequent change, tends to appear as a problem in the literature because in final position lenition is presumed to be more typical (it being a weak position), but phonologists are more prone to classify devoicing as fortition since it involves loss of voice, a vowel-like quality (see e.g. Hyman 1975: 168, Lavoie 2001: 7, and Szigetvári 2008).

13.3.1.7 *Metathesis*

The term *metathesis* refers to changes in which the linear order of segments is rearranged. For a long time, such changes were regarded as marginal phenomena *vis-à-vis* sound changes in a purportedly stricter sense of the word basically because in most cases they could not be described as resulting from gradual articulatory displacement and because many of the examples known were sporadic and isolated.[17] More recently, however, metathesis has emerged as an important and interesting topic for phonetics and

---

[14] See Honeybone (2008) for the history of research on lenition.

[15] For this latter point, see Szigetvári's recent discussion (2008) as well as Cser (2003: 15–27).

[16] See Masica (1991: 170). The other voiced stops turned into fricatives and later disappeared completely.

[17] For the classical exposition of this neogrammarian tenet, see Paul (1995[1880]: 63–6).

phonology as well as historical linguistics, and many cases have been found in a variety of languages where metathesis operates as systematically as sound changes with a more respectable pedigree.[18]

Metathesis may involve adjacent consonants, as in Classical Greek, where C[son][j] > [j]C[son], e.g. *$k^harjō$ > $k^hairō$ 'I am happy', *$p^hanjō$ > $p^hainō$ 'I show' (for the data with a different interpretation see Sihler 1995: 195), cf. also the Old English variations of the type *ascian ~ acsian* (> *ask*). It may involve a consonant and an adjacent vowel, as in Old English [r]VC[cor] sequences, which variably appeared as V[r]C[cor]: *hors ~ hros* (> *horse*), *rinnan ~ irnan* (> *run*), or in South and West Slavonic, where V[l] and V[r] sequences regularly metathesize, e.g. Proto-Slavonic **berg-* > Czech *břeh* 'riverbank', **melko* > *mléko* 'milk' (Schenker 2002: 74–6, cf. section 13.3.1.4). It may also involve non-adjacent consonants, as in Latin *parabola* 'comparison' > Spanish *palabra* 'word' or Hungarian *malo[ʒ]a* > *ma[ʒ]ola* 'type of wine/grape/raisin'. Finally, it may manifest itself in the repositioning of a single consonant, as in South Italian Greek, e.g. Classical Greek *gambrós* 'son-in-law' > South Italian Greek *grambó, $k^hondrós$* 'thick, rough' > *xrondó* and *pikrós* 'bitter' > *prikó* (Blevins and Garrett 2004: 130). It is noteworthy that many of these examples involve [r]: it has long been known that liquids are overrepresented in metathesis phenomena by a wide margin.

13.3.1.8 *Further Terms*

Since phonological changes are often named after their output, an array of terms derive from basic terminology for places and manners of articulation, thus we speak of labialization, retroflexion, palatalization, velarization, pharyngealization, glottalization, voicing (also called sonorization), affrication, fricativization, assibilation, nasalization, rhotacism, lambdacism, lengthening, shortening, diphthongization (with breaking as a subtype), monophthongization, raising, lowering, centralization, rounding; corresponding and similarly self-explanatory terms that refer to the input or, in other words (but not in a theoretical sense), to the loss rather than the acquisition of a property are devoicing, delabialization, denasalization, debuccalization, unrounding and so on. Note that these changes cross-classify the major types in sections 13.3.1.1, 13.3.1.2, 13.3.1.5, 13.3.1.6; for instance, a particular nasalization or palatalization can be an assimilation (in most cases it is), and voicing can be assimilation, dissimilation or lenition.

13.3.2 Prosodic Changes

13.3.2.1 *Lengthening and Gemination*

Traditionally the term lengthening is reserved for vowels, while the lengthening of consonants is referred to as gemination. Whether this practice is justified is not at issue here;

---

[18] The most relevant discussions include Hume (2001, 2004) and Blevins & Garrett (1998, 2004).

I refer to all changes that make any kind of segment perceptibly longer as lengthening. Virtually all known lengthenings are conditioned. Vowels frequently get lengthened under stress and, conversely, shortened in unstressed syllables. The relation between syllable structure and length is an interesting question. In many languages vowels in open syllables are lengthened, and thereby light syllables are eliminated, as in Late Latin, where this happened in stressed syllables: *pater* > *pāter* 'father'. At the same time, in several languages closed syllables can also trigger lengthening if they end in a sonorant. In Late Old English, short vowels were lengthened before sonorant-initial clusters such as [mb nd ld rd], e.g. Old English *cild* > Middle English *chīld, climban* > *clīmben, feld* > *feeld*.[19] In Colloquial Hungarian short vowels are lengthened when followed by a tautosyllabic [r], e.g. [boːr] 'wine', dative [boːrnɒk], but [borom] 'my wine'. A similar change is reported in the Mayan language Q'eqchi', in which vowels were lengthened before clusters beginning with a sonorant (e.g. *kenq'* > *kēnq'* 'bean', Campbell 2004: 45).

Sometimes the lengthening of one segment appears causally connected to the loss of another, adjacent or non-adjacent, segment. Such cases are referred to as compensatory lengthening. The Latin change exemplified by **nisdos* > *nīdus* 'nest' has been mentioned earlier; there, lengthening is intimately connected to the loss of [s] before voiced consonants. The Pre-Classical Greek lengthening exemplified by **eperansa* > *eperāna* 'I finished' shows that for compensatory lengthening to take place the triggering segment—which is lost—does not need to be adjacent to the segment undergoing the lengthening. When there is adjacency, it is clear that the line between segment deletion with compensatory lengthening on the one hand and total assimilation on the other is difficult to draw on a formal basis, and so is the line between compensatory lengthening and certain kinds of lenitions/vocalizations (e.g. Standard Hungarian *föld* [føld] *vs* Dialectal Hungarian [føːd] or [fø͡yd] 'land').[20]

The adjacency of sonorants sometimes triggers the lengthening of consonants. The West Germanic Gemination is a change of this kind. In this process, consonants except [r] were lengthened when followed by [j], e.g. Proto-Germanic **framjan* > Old English *fremman* 'perform' (Hogg 1992: 73). This change only took place after short stems (cf. **sandjan* > *sendan* 'send' or *dōmjan* > *dēman* 'deem'), which exemplifies the general tendency for such changes to be sensitive to the overall prosodic properties of the word.

13.3.2.2 *Shortening and Degemination*

Shortenings of consonants (also called degemination) as well as of vowels are usually conditioned changes, though unconditioned shortenings are also found. English is a case in point for the latter: during the Late Old English and Early Middle English periods all long consonants were shortened and no geminates are found in the language to this

---

[19] See Hogg (1992: 213–14) and Ritt (1994: 81 ff.). Length changes are analysed differently in a syllable cut framework, see Murray (2000) and Mailhammer (2007).

[20] For the most recent comprehensive treatment of compensatory lengthening, see Gess (2011). See further Kavitskaya (2002), Kiparsky (2011), and Wetzels & Sezer's (1985) collection, along with Hayes (1989), a classic discussion.

day (apart from some that straddle transparent morpheme boundaries, e.g. *unnatural*). Perhaps more typically, shortenings—like many instances of lengthening—can be sensitive to the general prosodic contours of phonological words. Vowels are often shortened in unstressed syllables (as in Late Latin or in Late Old English), which may be seen as a form of reduction. In Early Latin, long vowels were shortened in disyllables that were iambic in terms of syllable weight (*modō* > *modŏ* 'only'), and long consonants were shortened in word final position (*as* 'unit of money' but genitive *ass-is*) and sporadically when followed by a heavy syllable (*ob+mittere* > *ommittere* > *omittere* 'omit').

13.4 CONCLUSION

As stated at the outset, my purpose was to present compactly the general categories and terms in which discussions of particular changes or of theoretical issues are traditionally couched. Practically all of the notions briefly introduced here are in the focus of interesting debates, a fact I indicated at various points. On that account this chapter not only serves as an introduction to the types of sound change as such; it also serves as an introduction to many other chapters in this volume in which these theoretical debates are presented in much more detail.

CHAPTER 14

··

ANALOGY AND MORPHOPHONOLOGICAL CHANGE

··

DAVID FERTIG

14.1 INTRODUCTION

··

SAYING that a linguistic form has changed over time can either mean that there have been changes in some properties of what we nevertheless consider to be the same form before and after, or that one form has been replaced by another that has the same meaning/function but is otherwise completely independent of the earlier form. According to Paul's influential idealization (1880), change motivated by phonetic factors ('sound change') is entirely of the former type, change that depends on grammatical patterns ('analogical change') is entirely of the latter, and the development of the forms of a language is largely a story of the interaction between these two non-overlapping types of change (Fertig 2013). For example, analogical change frequently has the effect of eliminating or extending morphophonological patterns of alternation that arose through sound change,[1] as when the alternation between long vowels in the present tense and short vowels in the past of a number of English weak verbs, e.g. *keep-kept; mean-meant*, which arose through regular shortening of long vowels before double consonants, was later eliminated in several verbs through regularization, e.g. *believed* (< earlier *beleft*), *deemed* (< *dempt*), or when the umlaut alternation between the singular and plural forms of German nouns was extended to many items where it had not

---

[1] Linguists differ in how they define morphophonology (≈ morphology ≈ morphophonemics). Some understand it broadly to include all types of phonemic differences among what are regarded as realizations of the same morpheme. Others exclude either suppletive or purely phonologically conditioned alternations or both (cf. Dressler 1985, Donegan & Nathan, this volume). I assume here a definition that includes all non-suppletive alternations.

arisen phonologically: Middle High German *boum-boume* 'tree(s)' > Modern Standard German *Baum-Bäume*. In addition to such interactions, this chapter explores changes that depend on both phonetic (perceptual) motivations and grammatical patterns (sections 14.2 and 14.3), as well as different views on what counts as a grammatical pattern (section 14.7).

14.2 DEFINING ANALOGY

The notion of analogy as a major factor in language history whose effects interact with, are often confused with, but in principle can be clearly distinguished from those of sound change was developed by the neogrammarians in the 1870s and 1880s (see Murray, this volume, for a discussion of neogrammarian ideas). Paul (1877, 1880), the preeminent neogrammarian theoretician, understood analogy as a general theory of the acquisition, representation, and productive use of morphosyntactic and morphophonological categories and relations. Within this framework, he defined an analogical formation (*Analogiebildung*) from the perspective of an individual speaker in terms of the distinction between (analogical) production and (non-analogical) reproduction. Whereas the latter involves speakers recalling and using forms that they have previously heard from others, the former occurs when speakers produce meaningful forms that they may have never encountered based on patterns that they have discerned across the forms that they have learned. Many regularly inflected forms that speakers produce are undoubtedly analogical formations. English speakers, for example, presumably do not memorize and may have never heard the plurals of many low-frequency nouns such as *tapestries, fedoras, guillotines*. In the relatively rare cases where production does not yield the same form as reproduction, we have the possibility of an analogical innovation (*analogische Neubildung/ Neuschöpfung*), i.e. an analogical formation that deviates from established usage.

Paul characterized analogical formations as the solving of proportional equations, where a minimal equation consists of four terms: A : B = C : x, e.g. *walk* : *walked* :: *flip* : x (with the solution: x = *flipped*). Later historical linguists have come to treat the proportional equation as a convenient, theory-neutral way to represent analogical innovations. For Paul, the whole point of the model lay in the crucial stipulation that the terms of the proportion can only be whole word forms belonging to the same grammatical system. This makes proportional equations anything but theory neutral. The model reflects Paul's staunch advocacy of a word-and-paradigm approach to morphology wherein the mental grammar contains no representations of abstract elements smaller than whole words (i.e. stems or affixes) (cf. James Blevins 2004).

To understand Paul's model and the later distinction between 'proportional' and 'non-proportional' analogy, it is important not to conflate his word-and-paradigm ('proportional') theory with the relatively theory-neutral stipulation that (proportional) analogical change involves production, as opposed to reproduction, i.e. that the products of analogical innovation are completely independent of the traditional forms that they replace. English speakers would presumably be most likely to produce analogical *clinged* if they had never even encountered the traditional form *clung*. There is no sense in which *clung* 'becomes' *clinged*. The two forms are related only through their identical meaning/function.

This raises two important, closely related questions: (1) What is the status of certain types of change such as folk etymology (e.g. *hangnail* < OE *angnægl*, where the *h*- must be attributed to an etymologically unjustified association with *hang*) and contamination (e.g. *nauther* > *neither* due to the influence of *either*)? These are analogy-like in that they involve (perceived) morphological or semantic relations between words but the innovative form is clearly not independent of the older form (section 14.3). (2) Are all analogical innovations (in Paul's narrow sense) truly the result of pure production, or do they sometimes involve an interaction of production and reproduction? This question frequently comes up in connection with paradigm levelling (section 14.4) but is equally relevant to other types of change. Is it possible, for example, that the early Middle English speakers who first produced innovative past tense forms of *leap* with the weak -*t* suffix (*leept*) had actually heard the traditional strong form *leep* (< Old English *hléop*) many times and were 'reproducing' the form that they believed other speakers had intended to produce? The influence of the more common weak pattern could have biased their phonological analysis and convinced them that perceived tokens of *leep* were actually intended *leept* with simplification of the final consonant cluster. This development would then bear a strong resemblance to folk etymology, even though it can be modelled as a strictly 'proportional' innovation.

A minority of later scholars have adopted something close to Paul's narrow definition of analogical innovation (Jeffers & Lehiste 1979, cf. Hock 2003:444), but broader definitions have become the norm, necessitating the proportional *vs* non-proportional distinction (see section 14.3). These broader conceptions have been criticized as a 'wastebasket' (Campbell 2004:104, cf. King 1969:127, Kiparsky 1992:56), and the conceptual distinction between sound change and analogy is certainly much clearer under a narrow definition, but the validity of the neogrammarian claim that all change in forms can be attributed to sound change, analogy, or borrowing depends on a broad definition of analogy. Paul did not manage to resolve this dilemma; he repeats the sound-change-analogy-borrowing mantra while explicitly acknowledging the existence of processes such as folk etymology and contamination that are, by his own account, neither sound change, analogy, nor borrowing.

Some scholars argue that 'everything in language is analogical' (Anttila 1977:12, cf. Anttila 2003, Itkonen 2005). We must be careful not to confuse this general sense of 'analogical' with its use as a technical term in historical linguistics. Analogy, in a general sense, clearly plays a major role in all cognition and in many aspects of language change. In a technical sense, however, most historical linguists reserve the label 'analogical' for overt changes in the phonetic/phonological make-up of forms (section 14.2.2) that depend on grammatical patterns and relations. Remaining disagreements over the scope of analogical change are then largely a matter of different conceptions of grammar (section 14.7; Hock 2003, Blevins, this volume).

14.2.1 Analogy *vs* Rules

Historical linguists of all theoretical persuasions use the terms 'analogy' and 'analogical' in reference to certain types of change, and in the neogrammarian tradition, 'rule' is often used in a non-technical sense to refer to any regularity or valid generalization (cf. MacWhinney 1975: 66). In current morphological theory, however, it is common to draw a clear distinction between rules and analogy and between rule-based and analogy-based frameworks. Rules are usually defined as explicit and abstract, in the sense of being dissociated from any words that instantiate them, whereas analogy is based on direct relations among mental representations of words in an associative network (Skousen 1989, Becker 1990, Moder 1992, Booij 2010: 88–93). A rule-based model of English inflection, for example, might include an operation of adding -*ed* to a verb to form the past tense. This operation would be represented in the grammar separately from any actual verbs. An analogy-based account, by contrast, might posit that exemplars of present and past tense verb forms are stored in memory, allowing users to produce new past tense forms based on the patterns they discern across the stored forms, without necessarily abstracting out any explicit rules. The learner's primary task in a rule-based model is thus one of abstraction; once the rules and underlying lexical representations are in place, the morphologically complex forms on which they were based can be discarded from memory. This contrasts sharply with the learner's task in an analogy-based model, which is largely a matter of organizing forms into some kind of mental network that captures the lexical, morphosyntactic, and phonetic relations among them (Bybee 1988).

There is increasingly widespread acceptance among linguists that some kind of associative network plays an important role in morpho(phono)logy, perhaps alongside abstract rules. Dual-mechanism models, for example, hold that regular inflection, such as the English past tense in -*ed*, involves explicit rules, while irregular inflection (e.g. *sing-sang-sung; hide-hid-hidden*) is handled by analogy (Pinker & Prince 1988, Clahsen 1999). Some scholars maintain that all morphology—and perhaps syntax as well—is based entirely on an associative network (e.g. Rumelhart & McClelland 1986, Skousen 1989, Becker 1990, for applications to sound change, see Bybee, this volume, and on the modeling of grammatical change, see Hare & Elman 1995, Wanner 2006, Wedel, this volume).

14.2.2 Analogy and Reanalysis

Following Paul, most historical linguists restrict the definition of analogical change to overt developments, i.e. observable changes in surface forms (e.g. Saussure 1995[1916]:221). The relative importance of covert reanalysis versus overt analogical innovation to the larger story of grammatical change is a topic of ongoing debate (Haspelmath 1998, Bybee 2009), but a long tradition regards underlying reanalyses as the more significant—and more interesting—side of the story. Paul devoted just a few pages of the *Prinzipien* to the solving of proportional equations, followed by several entire chapters on various kinds of covert reanalysis. Saussure labeled analogical innovations 'un fait insignifiant' (227) in contrast with the covert 'changements d'interprétation' (232) that precede them (cf. Andersen 1980, Hopper & Traugott 2003).

Especially relevant to morphophonology is the type of reanalysis known as 'morphologization' (Joseph & Janda 1988, Cser, this volume, Bermúdez-Otero, this volume) or 'morphophonologization' (Garrett & Blevins 2009), whereby an alternation that was previously purely phonologically conditioned acquires morphological conditioning or even becomes associated with a morphosyntatic function. A classic example is umlaut in German, and to a lesser extent in English (see Kiparsky, Fox, and Bybee, all this volume). Umlaut arose as a phonetic assimilation conditioned by a high front vowel or glide in an unstressed syllable following the affected segment. The phonological conditioning factors were lost long ago, but umlaut alternations in some paradigms found a morphological function, e.g. as the sole marker of the plural in nouns such as *tooth-teeth, mouse-mice*; or as a supplemental marker of tense in *tell-told, sell-sold*. In derivation, umlaut distinguishes a number of denominal verbs from the corresponding nouns or adjectives, e.g. *blood-bleed, food-feed, gold-gild, full-fill*.

The opposite development, 'demorphologization', appears to be much rarer (Joseph & Janda 1988). One possible example involves the alternation in the past tense of some Dutch strong verbs between short vowels in the singular and long vowels in the plural, e.g. /nɑm/ (sg.) - /naːmen/ (pl.) 'took'. In present-day Dutch, this alternation looks exactly parallel to that which occurs in some nouns, such as /bɑt/ (sg.) - /baːden/ (pl.) 'bath(s)'. Booij (2002a: 59) attributes the alternation in both the nouns and the verbs to the sound change known as open-syllable lengthening. This is undoubtedly correct for the nouns, but most classes of Germanic strong verbs inherited an ancient ablaut alternation between the singular and the plural in the preterite indicative (cf. Lass 1990), and in the predecessors of the Dutch verbs in question, the alternation was between Indo-European *o*-grade in the singular and lengthened *ē*-grade in the plural. After *o* > *a* in Germanic and then *ē* > *ā* in West Germanic, this came to look like a purely quantitative alternation. The singular-plural ablaut alternations in the past tense were levelled in all other strong verb classes in the later Middle Ages. The /ɑ/-/aː/ alternation seems to owe its survival to the fact that it could be 'demorphologized', i.e. reanalysed as a purely phonologically conditioned alternation between short vowels in closed syllables and long vowels in open syllables (Fertig 2005).

14.2.3 Analogical Change as Imperfect Learning

Certain key aspects of the generative conception of analogical change follow from a rule-based model of the mental grammar that is largely static, in the sense that once acquisition is complete, the grammar can be used to produce and comprehend utterances without this use having any impact on the grammar, much as a conventional computer program can be run any number of times without affecting the program (see, for example, Hale et al., and Dresher, both this volume). The neogrammarians conceived of the (analogy-based) mental grammar as dynamic, in constant flux, as many researchers also see it today (e.g. Bybee 2006, this volume). Bolinger (1968: 88) sums up the essence of this view succinctly: 'Never a word spoken but language becomes a bit different from what it was, however microscopically. What we say displaces what we might have said and strengthens those words at the expense of others'. Under a static model, analogical change has its primary locus in the transmission of the language to new learners. The actual production of new forms does not itself constitute change; it is merely a manifestation of underlying changes in the mental grammar that result from 'imperfect learning' (Kiparsky 1965, and compare Foulkes & Vihman, this volume, and Hale et al., this volume). If the mental grammar is dynamic, however, and contains representations of word forms, some of which are created as a consequence of overt innovations and all of which can be reinforced through repetition, then the production of innovative forms is not a mere symptom of change; it is constitutive of grammatical change. While the neogrammarians saw transmission to new learners as the main locus of covert reanalysis, they regarded analogical innovation as a drama played out at the moment of speaking: the traditional form competes with one or more potential innovations generated by the grammar. Imperfect learning is just one of a number of factors that might increase the odds of an analogical innovation winning out over a traditional form. Others would include momentary memory lapses and the priming effects of recently encountered forms. A new mental representation is created the first time an innovative form is uttered and then gets reinforced on each subsequent use, increasing its odds of winning again the next time (Jespersen 1922).

Generativists argue that this neogrammarian conception of analogical innovation may work well enough for the familiar textbook examples of word-by-word changes, but that many important kinds of analogical change involve 'sweeping' extensions of patterns to entire classes of candidate forms. It is an empirical question whether a change that ultimately comes to affect all candidate forms truly applied to them all simultaneously. Hock (1986: 268-9) argues, for example, that this was not the case with the elimination of the final-devoicing alternation in Yiddish, a favourite early-generative example of 'rule loss', e.g. Middle High German *liet* 'song' (gen. sg. *liedes*) > Yid. *lid* (pl. *lider*).

Since Kiparsky's early work, it has been common to associate 'across-the-board analogy' with phonological as opposed to morphological rules (Kiparsky 1973b: 12, 1974a: 262, Hock 1986, 2003, Hale & Reiss 2008, Dresher, this volume). In fact, however, morphological changes that involve the extension of particular affixes to new (sub)paradigms, rather than the movement of lexical items between classes, often seem to display across-the-board behaviour, e.g. the extension of the 3rd plural ending -*en* from the preterite and subjunctive to the present indicative in German, replacing earlier -*ent*.

One type of phonological change that does seem to show consistent across-the-board behaviour is the simplification of the conditions on the input to which, or the phonological contexts in which, a rule applies, resulting in an extension or generalization of the rule's effects, as when final devoicing is extended from fricatives to all obstruents or when the German rule that changes pre-consonantal *s* to *ʃ* is extended to apply before stops, a development whose progress is partly reflected in the orthography of the modern standard, where the <sch> spelling is only used before liquids and nasals, e.g. *schlecht* 'bad', *schmal* 'narrow' *vs* <s> in *Stein* 'stone', *springen* 'jump', even though the pronunciation is now ʃ in all these cases (King 1969: 58–62, Benware 1996). Some argue that such developments constitute sound change, rather than analogy, in that they do not involve morphological, syntactic, or semantic relations among forms (McMahon 1994: 82). Critics of the neogrammarian framework, going back to Schuchardt (1885), have always regarded such changes as 'phonetic analogy', but the important distinction that they draw between phonetic and 'conceptual' analogy is missing from the generative approach (cf. section 14.7; Hermann 1931, Vennemann 1972b).

14.3 Proportional *vs* Non-proportional Analogy

As suggested in section 14.1, the fundamental distinction between proportional and non-proportional analogy is not really primarily about proportions per se. It might be less confusing to adopt Oertel's (1901: 154–5) terminology and distinguish between 'analogical creation' and 'associative interference'. The former involves speakers' productive use of their mental grammars (which Paul modelled with proportional equations); the latter involves the influence of one form on another, either in perception (folk etymology) or production (contamination). Whereas the products of analogical creation can be completely independent of any forms that they replace, associative interference is more like sound change in that the new form is an altered continuation of an existing form, or in some cases might be best characterized as a coalescence of two existing forms.

The primary question in traditional work has always been: how do the very first tokens of an innovative form arise in the speech of individuals who never heard that form from others (cf. Jones, this volume)? For analogical creation, the productive capacity of innovators' mental grammars provides an obvious answer that presents no problems for neogrammarian orthodoxy. For associative interference, on the other hand, the answer to this question is much less straightforward. How does it happen that innovators learn the existing form well enough to use it, yet wind up altering its phonological makeup? Paul suggested three good answers: 1) intended tokens of the old form may be misheard (or, we might add, be phonologically reanalysed) by learners, with related forms biasing their perceptions (1880: 183; all page numbers are from the 2nd edition of 1886); 2) simultaneous neural activation of semantically related items (1880: 132–9), or of an existing form and a competing analogical creation (1880: 166–7), may result in a blending of the two; or 3) speakers may deliberately deviate from prevailing usage (1880: 182).

Many cases of folk etymology can be accounted for either by the kind of mishearing described by Paul—and labelled CHANGE by Juliette Blevins (2004a, this volume)—or by a reanalysis similar to the kinds of hypo- and hypercorrection described by Ohala

(1993; cf. Blevins's CHANCE and CHOICE, Yu, this volume). In folk etymology, the mis-hearing or reanalysis can be specifically attributed to an association with a form that is taken to be morphologically or lexically related. The ending -*most* in words such as *foremost* and *utmost*, for example, is etymologically distinct from the word *most*. Old English -*mest* would have wound up with a reduced schwa by normal sound change. The reanalysis of -*mest* as a reduced form of *most* gave rise to the etymologically unjusti-fied ('hypercorrective') pronunciation with *o*. Non-standard *upmost* for *utmost* could be analyzed as 'hypocorrective' folk etymology.

Paul attributes contamination to the simultaneous neural activation in production of semantically related items. The semantic link must be much tighter here than is required for folk etymology, but there need be no phonetic similarity between the items at all. Most accounts point out that the items involved frequently occur in close proximity in utterances, so that they are related both paradigmatically (i.e. semantically) and syntag-matically. The most frequently cited examples involve adjacent numerals: e.g. English *eleven* < Proto-Gmc. **ainlif* under the influence of *ten*; Latin *novem* 'nine' instead of expected **noven* under the influence of *decem* 'ten' (Osthoff 1878b, Hock & Joseph 2009: 163). Contamination and folk etymology probably work in concert in cases where a tight semantic bond is matched by coincidental phonetic similarity, as in English *femelle* > *female* under the influence of *male*.

14.4 THE STATUS OF PARADIGM LEVELLING

Although the neogrammarians used the term levelling (*Ausgleichung*) for all types of (pro-portional) analogical change, '(analogical) levelling' is now usually understood to refer to the elimination or reduction of stem alternations. Quite a few linguists classify regulariza-tions that include but are not limited to the elimination of a stem alternation as 'levellings'. Blevins & Blevins (2009: 6) offer *cleave-clove* > *cleave-cleaved* as an example of levelling (cf. Bybee 2001: 116, Campbell 2004: 106, Garrett 2008: 129). This contrasts with the more com-mon practice of restricting 'levelling' to changes that consist only of the (partial or com-plete) elimination of a stem alternation (e.g. Jeffers & Lehiste 1979: 55–7, Andersen 1980, Hock 1986: 168–82, Dresher 2000). Thus *knife-knives* > *knife-knifes* would be an instance of both levelling and regularization, but *cleave-clove* > *cleave-cleaved* would not be levelling because the new past tense form also shows the extension of the regular -*ed* suffix.

These definitional issues are important for substantive questions such as whether par-adigm levelling is 'proportional', i.e. whether it amounts to the extension of a pattern that happens to be non-alternating, or whether it must instead be attributed to some kind of general bias that favours non-alternating stems independently of any model. Garrett (2008) and Hill (2007) argue unequivocally that levelling is proportional. Paul also ultimately came to this conclusion (1920: 116 n.1, cf. Hock 2003: 444, 458n.9, 459n.11). Kiparsky (1992: 58) gives a concise statement of the opposing position: 'LEVELING [...] is 'non-proportional' because it does not require a non-alternating model paradigm' (see also Jeffers & Lehiste 1979). Most are more cautious, arguing that levelling is partially or probably proportional (Osthoff 1879: 42–4, Bybee 1980, Hock 1986: 179–82, Fertig 1999, 2000, Reiss 2006).

Since everyone would agree that regularization, even where it coincides with levelling, as in the *knives > knifes* example, is always amenable to a proportional account, any empirical case for either position must focus on non-regularizing levelling. Partial levelling can refer either to the elimination of a stem alternation between some forms in a paradigm but not across the entire paradigm (e.g. *speak-spake-spoken > speak-spoke-spoken*) or to cases where stem alternants become more similar to each other without becoming identical. Elimination of consonant alternations in Germanic strong verbs are partial levellings because the vocalic ablaut alternation is retained. An English example occurs in the verbs *swear* and *swell*, where the regular loss of *w* between a consonant and a back vowel (compare *sword* and *two*) must have resulted in past/participle forms such as *sore/sorn* and *sol/soln* in Middle English. The *w* was then restored in these forms after the *wo* sequence became phonologically possible again.

You can usually find a proportional model for a partial levelling if you look hard enough, but many scholars are not convinced that this can be the whole story of levelling, partial or otherwise. Those who take this position often assume that it can only mean that some kind of universal preference for non-alternation is at work. Some relate this preference to a general 'one-form-one-function' principle (Vennemann 1972a, 1993, Anttila 1977, Mayerthaler 1981). Others propose a more specific constraint favouring stem-uniformity within paradigms (Kiparsky 1971, McCarthy 2005, Holt, this volume). Recent work makes clear, however, that the bias in favour of non-alternation could be entirely system-dependent (Wurzel 1984: 169–72, Albright 2005: 39–41). Speakers/learners draw higher-order generalizations about the morphophonological patterns of their language, so rather than assuming that human beings are predisposed from the outset to prefer non-alternating stems, one could postulate that learners just figure out at some point that non-alternation is the norm in their language, and this awareness then biases their perception and production in ways that lead to leveling, even where there are few if any non-alternating models for the particular pattern in question. The strong tendency for non-alternation to be the norm across many of the world's languages can then be accounted for in terms of how stem alternations—in contrast to affixal marking of morphological distinctions—develop historically (Bybee & Newman 1995).

14.5 THE DIRECTION(S) OF ANALOGICAL CHANGE

There are two dimensions of directionality in analogical change. The directional tendency on the interparadigmatic axis has long been attributed largely to type frequency, e.g. inflectional classes with more members tend to attract new items at the expense of smaller classes (e.g. Paul 1877: 329, Osthoff 1879: 33, Bloomfield 1933: 409, Wurzel 1984). Kuryłowicz is perhaps the most prominent critic of this view (cf. also Marcus et al. 1995, Garrett 2008, and see Wedel, this volume, for related discussion).

As for the intraparadigmatic axis, many start with the claim that analogical innovations follow a basic→derived direction (Kuryłowicz 1964, 1966[1945-59], Andersen 1980), i.e. basic forms function as unchanging 'pivots' (Hock 1986: 215) around which derived forms are replaced. There are differing views on what constitutes basicness, especially in inflectional morphology. Many define it in terms of morphosyntactic unmarkedness (e.g. Mayerthaler 1981), others in purely formal terms, e.g. the basic form is the one from which the shape of others in the paradigm is predictable (Vennemann 1972a, 1972c, Albright 2005, 2008); and some see it as simply a matter of relative frequency. The mechanics of directionality are most straightforward in frequency-based accounts: learners are most likely to acquire the highest-frequency forms first, know them best, and guess at others on that basis (Wedel, this volume). A number of researchers have argued, however, that learners do not just base their paradigms on whichever forms they happen to encounter first, that universal principles and/or what learners have already figured out about their inflectional system guide them to base their guesses only on certain forms: those that are morphosyntactically unmarked (Lahiri 2000b, cf. Andersen 2001) and/or those that they have discovered to be generally most reliable for predicting the rest of the paradigm (Albright 2005, 2008). Others argue that we need to take the function of an alternation into account in order to determine, case by case, the extent to which the basic→derived relation is a morphosyntactic or a (morpho)phonological matter (Andersen 1980:30-6).

Finally, the levelling of some alternations seems to occur essentially simultaneously with the demise of their phonological motivation, suggesting that learners may simply be unable to make any sense of the alternations and just interpret them as noise, choosing one alternant or the other, perhaps at random, to use throughout the paradigm (Dresher 2000, Kiparsky, this volume).

14.6 OTHER TYPES OF MORPHOPHONOLOGICAL ANALOGICAL CHANGE

Beyond straightforward levellings and extensions of alternations, there are a number of other types of change affecting morphophonological patterns that are uncontroversially analogical in nature.

Cases where reanalysis and extension make an alternation predictable in the originally unpredictable direction are sometimes labelled 'rule inversion' (Vennemann 1972c, Hock 1986: 253, cf. Paul 1880: 97). This often involves sentence sandhi, the best-known example being the r-Ø alternation in some varieties of English (*the idea-r is*).

Moulton (1967) identified a type of 'morphophonemic analogy' that produces new phonemes by combining distinctive features already in use in the system. His example was the creation in eastern Swiss German dialects of a new front rounded vowel phoneme /œ/ that corresponds to an existing back vowel /ɔ/ in a way that parallels the other umlaut alternations in these dialects, e.g. /o/-/ø/. Hock (2003: 454) endorses Moulton's view that such developments are 'phonologically motivated as making the vowel system more symmetrical', but the fact that the changes had this effect does not mean that it played any role in their motivation. It is not clear why the morphological parallelism across paradigms would not be an entirely sufficient motivation for the creation of the new phoneme (cf. Vennemann 1972a: 193).

Garrett & Blevins (2009) discuss several cases of 'analogical morphophonology' where the phonological conditions for the analogical extension of a 'fortuitous pattern' are completely unrelated to the motivation for the original alternation (cf. Andersen 1980: 28).

Finally, Bloomfield (1933: 365-6) argued that allophonic alternations can sometimes be levelled or extended analogically (cf. Hock 1986: 206-9). For some linguists, these developments amount to proof that the alternations are no longer allophonic; for others, they raise fundamental questions about the relationship between phonetics and phonology (cf. Steriade 2000).

14.7 Who Needs Morphology?

Whereas the changes discussed above all crucially involve alternations among morphologically related forms, a number of linguists (e.g. Sturtevant 1917: 80–1, Hock 1986: 162–4, Kiparsky 1992: 58, cf. Hermann 1931: 24) have maintained that purely distributional phonotactic patterns can also give rise to a type of (necessarily non-proportional) analogical change. An important recent example is Kiparsky's (1995) argument that so-called lexical diffusion is a type of non-proportional analogy. A primary example involves English words that had long /uː/ following the Great Vowel Shift: e.g. *food, roof, hood, book*. The vowel in a subset of these words has since undergone shortening, which has been spreading through the set. Kiparsky accounts for the lexical diffusion of this shortening as follows: the phonological rule assigning a single mora to stressed /u/ is first generalized beyond its original environment to become the default wherever the vowel is followed by a velar. This extension has no immediate overt consequences, however, because all of the words with initial coronals are specified in the lexicon as having long vowels, i.e. as exceptions to the default rule. These exceptions are then subject to being 'regularized' through 'item-by-item simplification of the lexicon' (648). Kiparsky's claim that 'the mechanism is analogical in just the sense in which, for example, the regularization of *kine* to *cows* is analogical' (641) is misleading, as Hale (2003) points out, because morphological regularization is typically proportional, whereas Kiparsky's phonological 'regularization' is, as he notes, non-proportional (cf. Phillips, this volume). Kiparsky argues that 'the learner [...] selectively intervenes in the data, favoring those variants which best conform to the language's system. Variants which contravene language-specific structural principles will be hard to learn [...]' (655), but this begs the basic—and for non-proportional analogy always thorny—question discussed in section 14.3: how do the very first short-vowel variants of a word arise in the speech of individuals who have heard only long-vowel tokens from others? You could plausibly hypothesize that speakers with underlying long vowels sometimes produce ambiguous surface tokens, which the default rule predisposes learners to perceive as short. This makes the parallels with certain recognized kinds of non-proportional analogy clear (see section 14.3).

These parallels may help us understand lexical diffusion, but note that calling this analogy while maintaining that regular, phonetically motivated sound change is not analogy simply reflects one particular view of the nature of grammar. If we understand the distinction between sound change and analogy to be essentially one between phonetically and grammatically motivated change, then where—and whether—we draw the line between the two obviously depends entirely on our conception of grammar (cf. Phillips, Blevins, both this volume). For the neogrammarians, the mental grammar included morphological, morphophonological, and syntactic patterns and relations, but Paul, in particular, explicitly rejected the notion that a 'sound system' (1880: 50) could have any kind of cognitive reality (cf. Murray, this volume). Saussure, who fully endorsed a neogrammarian conception of analogy, may have believed in a synchronic phonological system but insisted that it was utterly irrelevant to language change (Kiparsky, this volume). If you believe, however, that purely phonotactic generalizations are represented in the mental grammar and sometimes motivate changes in word forms, it is hard to see any legitimate reason for regarding such changes as less 'analogical' than, for example, folk etymology.

Alternatively, if 'language users store clouds of exemplars that reflect the tokens they have actually experienced rather than abstract phonological units', such that there is 'no distinction between phenomena that are 'in' the grammar *vs* those that are not' (Bybee, this volume), then 'phonetic analogy' (Schuchardt 1885, Vennemann 1972a) based on relations among individual exemplars could play a much more pervasive role in sound change.

14.8 THE INTERPLAY OF SOUND CHANGE AND ANALOGY

Language change is often portrayed as a perpetual battle between 'blind' sound change, which disrupts the system, and analogical change, which restores some order, either by tidying up the mess or by improvising new structures out of the raw material provided by sound change. This narrative is a relic of older conceptions of grammar in which only morphology is fully recognized as a system; it can be generalized to cover the interaction of changes with various grammatical and extra-grammatical motivations.

Both Brugmann (1876: 319 n.33) and Paul (e.g. 1877: 395-6) initially assumed that analogy could sometimes block an otherwise regular sound change from affecting certain (classes of) words. Paul, for example, accounted for the final -*s* in the gen. sg. of several feminine nouns in Old Saxon, e.g. *burges* 'town', *nahtes* 'night', by positing that in these words the -*s* of the Proto-Germanic gen. sg. ending *-ais/-aiz*, which was normally lost in West Germanic, exceptionally 'remained intact' (*unversehrt geblieben wäre*) because the analogical influence of the *a*-stem nouns, where the -*s* of the proto-Gmc. ending *-esa/-asa* was regularly retained, resulted in a 'prevention' (*Verhinderung*) of the regular loss of the final consonant in *-ais/-aiz*. Osthoff (1878a: 325-7) pointed out that this kind of account makes no sense in light of the neogrammarian understanding of (proportional) analogical change as a replacement of one form with another. It may sometimes happen as a result of analogy that a regular sound change winds up never manifesting itself in some forms, but analogy does not 'protect' (Osthoff 1878a: 327) the older forms from the sound change. Rather, it may replace those forms with others that are not subject to the sound change. In the example above, gen. sg. forms with reflexes of the *-ais/-aiz* ending could have been replaced by analogical forms with reflexes of the *-esa/-asa* ending at any time, after which point the fate of the final consonant in the *-ais/-aiz* ending would have become irrelevant for those words. Any resemblance between the new analogical forms and those that they replaced would be purely coincidental (cf. Paul 1886a: 62-3, Esper 1973: 42).

The notion of 'preventive analogy' (Hock 1986: 46-7) continues to be debated. Not all suggested examples are fully comparable to those addressed by Osthoff (cf. Trask 1996: 107), and Osthoff's points need to be reconsidered in light of the non-proportional aspects of analogical change discussed in sections 14.2-14.3 above.

A related claim is that analogical reactions to sound change are triggered primarily when the mess produced by the latter has become intolerable or unlearnable (Paul 1877: 328, Dresher 2000). This notion has been generalized to other domains (Lightfoot 1979).

14.9 SUMMARY AND CONCLUSIONS

The historical development of linguistic forms has traditionally been portrayed as a story of the interactions of phonetically-motivated sound changes and analogical changes that depend on morphological, syntactic, or semantic relations among forms (see sections 14.1 and 14.8). Morphophonological patterns of alternation that arise through sound change, for example, are frequently eliminated or extended through analogical change (see sections 14.1, 14.4, 14.5, and 14.6). The idealization according to which every change can be unambiguously assigned to one of these two types, with the distinction between the two corresponding to that between production and reproduction, starts to break down when we consider 'non-proportional' processes such as folk ety-mology (see section 14.3). Ultimately, it becomes clear that even many instances of ostensibly straightforward analogical change have an element of phonetic (perceptual) motivation (see section 14.2). Conceptions of the mental grammar that differ from that of the neogrammarians raise even more fundamental questions about the rationale for traditional definitions of analogical change (see section 14.7).

Lass's (1997: 386) pessimistic assessment that 'we understand as much (or as little) about analogy as the neogrammarians did' is a valuable reminder not only of the slow and inconsistent pace of progress but also of the extraordinary achievement of the neogrammarians, especially Paul (1877, 1880), who sketched out a theory of the role of analogy in language change that is as important for current debates as anything that has been written since. Nevertheless, we must acknowledge genuine advances in a number of areas, especially in our understanding of many important types of covert reanalysis (e.g. Andersen 1973, 1980, 2006, Timberlake 1977, Lass 1990, Ohala 1993) and in experimental investigations and explicit modelling of morphological acquisition, representation, and processing (e.g. Bybee & Moder 1983, Rumelhart & McClelland 1986, Hare & Elman 1995, Clahsen 1999, Albright 2009, Gerken et al. 2009, Wedel, this volume).

CHAPTER 15

CHANGE IN WORD PROSODY
Stress and Quantity

ADITI LAHIRI

15.1 INTRODUCTION

DIACHRONIC data has become consistently more relevant to models of linguistic structure. However, segmental developments dominate phonological discussions compared to word prominence and stress, and stress systems are generally less meticulously described and discussed. Textbooks rarely index changes in stress or metrical systems, although related phenomena like quantity and weight may be discussed at length. In this chapter, we address change in stress systems under the broader perspective of *prosody*, meaning all aspects of phonological grammar that relate to phonological quantity, syllable structure, foot structure and stress.[1] While prosodic changes are principally phonological, they can be affected by morphological structure as well. Phonological properties of affixes and phonological domains that result from root-cum-affixes affect prosodic organization. For instance, an affix may provide a domain which would trigger shortening, deletion or gemination and have serious prosodic consequences (cf. English suffix {-ity} triggers Trisyllabic Shortening as in *sane~sanity*, or OE causative suffix /j/ which causes gemination *tem-j-an > temman* 'to tame'). Alternatively, a difference in stress organization may express differences in morphological categories, as in *tormént*$_{\text{VERB}}$ ~ *tórment*$_{\text{NOUN}}$.

Analyses of synchronic phonological systems make a case for assuming that assignment of stress is part of a complex system of metrical organization rather than the realization of emphasis on a particular vowel. Metrical organization includes foot construction, assembling syllables into feet, and edge prominence. An alteration in any one part may lead to a change in the entire system. A major difficulty in understanding

---

[1] For a different approach to the prosodic issue of syllable structure in diachrony, see Mailhammer et al., this volume.

prosodic change is that even if the outward realization of stress has not changed, the underlying prosodic organization may have changed. A trisyllabic word, with a sequence of three light syllables, bearing main stress on the middle syllable, could be analysed as a trochaic or an iambic pattern, with an initial or final unfooted syllable. The ambiguity is due to the fact that this prominence could be obtained depending on whether the foot is aligned to the right or the left edge of the word, as in (1). Only a larger data set can determine the real organization.

(1) Ambiguity in a [ŏ ő ŏ] word

Trochee (right edge)	Iamb (left edge)
X	X
(x .)	(. x)
[ŏ ő ŏ]$_\omega$	[ŏ ő ŏ]$_\omega$

Motives for sound change are diverse, as explored in many chapters of this volume, especially articulatory, acoustic and/or auditory ones (see especially Donegan & Nathan, Bybee, and Blevins, all this volume) and phonological ones (see especially Dresher, Purnell, & Raimy, and Kiparsky, all this volume). For word prominence, however, uncertainties of articulatory and acoustic correlates of stress make it more difficult to directly relate stress change to phonetic causes alone. It is equally difficult to reliably compare the phonetic correlates of stress differences between dialects. Nevertheless, native listeners are aware of prosodic differences across dialects, and orthoepists, then and now, have recorded certain fixed patterns of what (they think) they heard.

This chapter highlights the consequences of normal language transmission through generations, interacting with language contact and the nativization of loans leading to prosodic reorganization. For any change of stress pattern to become part of the phonological grammar, the underlying prosodic system must reorganize, or else the shift will be unstable. Lahiri (2002) and Dresher & Lahiri (2005) drew attention to a characteristic of grammars called *pertinacity*. A rule or pattern may persist over time, though its realization may change. This type of pertinacity can be summed up as *same pattern, different output realization*. A converse kind of pertinacity exists where output forms persist despite changes in the grammar, which involve a reanalysis of the output form, triggered by changes elsewhere in the system. This type of pertinacity can be summed up as *different pattern, same output realization*. Since learners acquire their grammars guided by the output forms they are exposed to, we do not expect these forms—especially those that make up the 'core' or 'primary' data—to change in the course of acquisition.[2] Reanalysis of grammar that does not involve an immediate change in output forms is thus a significant type of language change. Changes in stress systems are prime examples of both types of pertinacity.

---

[2] Foulkes and Vihman's chapter on first language acquisition suggests that change in acquisition is not as common as some have argued. This is not incompatible to our point of view because, to a large extent, they are concerned about change in observable outputs.

Word stress is not merely a matter of locating the syllable which carries maximum prominence. Word prosody implies metrical organization composed of independent, but interrelated parameters. A description of the parameters that provide underlying metrical organization enables us to provide a typology of possible types of word-prosodic change. In section 15.4, we draw data specifically from Old English (OE) to Middle English (ME), drawing attention to the overarching principle of *pertinacity* which constrains language learners from making abrupt changes.

15.2 STRESS PARAMETERS

In languages where word stress is significant, every word has one main stress, typically aligned with one edge of a word. Stress contrasts predictably require more than one syllable to be discernible. The term 'phonemic' stress usually implies that minimal pairs exist which contrast only in stress, e.g. *pérmit*$_{NOUN}$ ~ *permít*$_{VERB}$ or German *Áugust* ~ *Augúst* 'proper name ~ month'. Languages with 'fixed' stress allow a specific syllable at one edge of a word to bear main stress; for example, in Bengali and Finnish main stress falls always on the initial syllable, while word-final stress is typical for French or Turkish. However, even in languages where stress can occur more 'freely', main prominence is restricted within a three-syllable window at a word edge. Main stress in the middle of a word would be fortuitous in the sense that this may happen only when the centre of a word converges with an edge. In a five-syllable word like *univérsity*, stress falls on the middle syllable, the third-syllable from either edge (cf. Hayes 1995). As we shall see, the preference in English happens to be the right edge of a word.

Although stress prominence appears on a syllable, the organization of stress patterns involves a larger constituent, the *foot*. Metrical feet group syllables together based on organized principles and are the best means of characterizing stress patterns. Complex stress patterns are difficult to account for without metrical organization, particularly when words carry secondary stresses. For instance, *còriánder* and *aspáragus* have four syllables each, but main stress falls on different parts of the word and only the former has secondary stress. The pattern can be accounted for by assuming that *(còri)(án)der* has two feet, with main stress on the right foot while *a(spára)gus* has only one.

Thus, we need to distinguish factors such as syllable quantity and weight, a typology of feet, and principles for grouping syllables into feet. The correlation between a syllable's internal structure and its weight is language dependent, but in languages where syllable weight plays a significant role, syllables with long vowels and closed syllables usually count as heavy.[3] Headedness (which edge of the foot is strong) allows for two

---

[3] This may not always be the case (Hayes 1995) and not even geminates are always heavy. In Malayalam, it has been claimed that syllables closed by geminate consonants are light while other closed syllables are heavy (Mohanan & Mohanan 1984). Controversy also exists with ambisyllabic consonants which were historically geminates as in German and Dutch; some claim that these contribute to weight while others do not.

types of feet, left-headed trochees and right-headed iambs (2a).[4] Two further considerations are necessary in grouping syllables into feet, direction of parsing (2b) and the
word-edge which is most prominent (2c). An additional factor necessary in some languages is the potential inertia of a final prosodic constituent (2d).[5] These are summarized in (2).

(2) Stress parameters
    (a) Foot type: Trochee/Iamb
    (b) Foot direction: Right-to-Left / Left-to-Right
    (c) Main Stress: Right/Left
    (d) Extrametricality: Yes/No

In what follows, we show that a change in any of these parameters need not necessarily produce a difference in surface prominence. Only a subset of words in a language
provides the critical evidence for setting the parameters. For instance, on the basis of
a word such as *húrricàne* one cannot determine whether the foot type in English is an
iamb or a trochee, since there are two feet each of which is a heavy syllable. After reviewing proposed foot types, we show how differences in parameter settings may or may not
reveal surface differences and how identical surface stress patterns may be analysed by
different parameters. We argue that these are precisely the type of situations which may
lead to a change in metrical organization.

In quantity-sensitive systems, ideally feet are asymmetric such that the head of a foot
is always aligned to a heavy syllable. However, if only light syllables are available, then
these would be grouped into feet as well.

(3) Quantity sensitive Trochees and Iambs
   (x   .)   (x   .)   (.   x)   (.   x)
   [σ̄ σ]$_\omega$ [σ̆ σ̄]$_\omega$ [σ σ̄]$_\omega$ [σ̆ σ̄]$_\omega$
          Trochees   Iambs

Other than the basic foot types in (3), evidence supports some variation in the above
claims.[6] A moraic trochee as suggested in Hayes (1995) is not asymmetric; i.e. if the head
of the foot is bimoraic, then the foot itself must consist only of one syllable.

    [4] Feet are assumed to be binary and unparsed syllables remain unfooted.
    [5] The reverse of extrametricality is catalexis where a prosodic constituent is added rather
than subtracted from the foot structure. Thus, a catelectic mora or syllable would be a syllable
without any segmental information which could be added to the edge of a word to construct a
well-formed foot.
    [6] The metrical approach to stress was pioneered by Liberman & Prince (1977 et seq.), and other
approaches include Kager, Hayes, Halle, & Vergnaud, Halle & Idsardi. We take Hayes (1995) as a reference
point for ease of exposition. A valuable compendium of research material on word prosody of European
languages is van der Hulst (1999). For modern Germanic stress patterns, see the following: English
(Chomsky & Halle 1968, Kager 1989); German (Wiese 1996); Dutch (Kager 1989, Booij 1995, Trommelen &
Zonneveld 1999).

(4) Moraic Trochee

    X   X

    (x   .)   (x)

    [σ σ]$_\omega$ [ō]$_\omega$

    Disyllabic   Monosyllabic

The difference between an asymmetric trochee and a moraic trochee can be seen by grouping sequences of light (L) and heavy (H) syllables into feet as in (5). The first three words from the left are parsed identically, but the last two show marked differences. (d) has two feet under the moraic trochee analysis but one foot in the asymmetric grouping. As for (e), both allow two feet with identical prominence patterns, but in the moraic trochee analysis the medial light syllable remains unfooted, which may have different consequences if such syllables are reduced or deleted.

(5) Variations in trochees

    (i) Asymmetric Trochee (as in 3)

       (a)   (b)   (c)   (d)   (e)

       (x .)   (x)   (x .)   (x .)   (x .) (x)

       [L L]$_\omega$ [H]$_\omega$ [L   L L]$_\omega$ [H L L]$_\omega$ [H L H]$_\omega$

    (ii) Moraic Trochee

       (x .)   (x)   (x .)   (x) (x .)   (x)   (x)

       [L L]$_\omega$ [H]$_\omega$ [L   L L]$_\omega$ [H L L]$_\omega$ [H L H]$_\omega$

With identical feet, the direction of parsing can lead to crucial differences in grouping. (6) illustrates a series of parsing possibilities with the aid of moraic trochees and iambs. A word with a [HLL] sequence shows identical grouping for both moraic trochee and iamb irrespective of the direction of parsing. However, for the other words, we find major differences.

(6) Direction of parsing

    (i) Moraic Trochee - Right to Left

        (x .) (x)   (x) (x .)   (x)   (x .)

        [L L L   H L]$_\omega$ [H L L]$_\omega$ [H L L L]$_\omega$

    (ii) Moraic Trochee - Left to Right

        (x .)   (x)   (x) (x .)   (x) (x .)

        [L L L   H L]$_\omega$ [H L L]$_\omega$ [H L L L]$_\omega$

    (iii) Iamb - Right to Left

        (.   x) (.   x)   (x) (.   x)   (x)   (.   x)

        [L L L   H L]$_\omega$ [H L L]$_\omega$ [H L L L]$_\omega$

    (iv) Iamb - Left to Right

        (.   x) (.   x)   (x) (.   x)   (x) (. x)

        [L L L   H L]$_\omega$ [H L L]$_\omega$ [H L L L]$_\omega$

Consequently, identical sequences of heavy and light syllable words may reveal different foot structures following a change in the direction of parsing, but not always. Sequences like [LLLHL] or [HLL] are insufficient to determine accurately the direction of parsing for an iamb. These are just the sorts of circumstances where the language learner will have different options for parsing a subset of the data. If the crucial piece of data is not available, the learner can opt for a different analysis than the previous generation, leading to change. For instance, when faced with two stresses on a word with a sequence of [HLL], the learner could deduce an iambic foot where the direction of parsing could be from either direction. If the learner opts for left-to-right (6iv) even if the correct analysis was right-to-left (6iii), and continues to generalize the pattern on a [HLLL] word, she would incorrectly fail to assign a stressed foot on the final syllable.

The third parameter is more straightforward in the sense that it is limited to assigning main stress, either on the right or left word-edge. If we consider the parsing data with an iamb as in (6iv), we can see how the choice of edges will contribute to different main stress.

(7) Choice of word edge for main stress
Iamb - Left to Right: Main Stress Right

```
         X                    X               X
(.   x) (.   x)        (x) (.   x)       (x) (.   x)
[L  L  L  H  L]ω       [H  L   L]ω       [H  L  L  L]ω
```

Iamb - Left to Right: Main Stress Left

```
   X           X              X               X
(.   x) (.   x)        (x) (.   x)       (x) (.   x)
[L  L  L  H  L]ω       [H  L   L]ω       [H  L  L  L]ω
```

If a consonant, syllable or even foot is not included in the parsing, this invokes extrametricality. In Latin, it is essential to assume an extrametrical final syllable, since stress assignment entirely ignores the structure or weight of this syllable, as in (8). We also add the basic pattern for English nouns where again an extrametrical syllable is apparent.

(8) Extrametricality in Latin and English
Latin: Moraic Trochee, Right to Left, Main Stress Right, Final syllable extrametrical

```
X                  X                  X               X
(x    .)           (x)                (x)             (x) (x)
[L   L <H>]ω       [H  L <H>]ω        [L  H <H>]ω      [H  H <H>]ω
mí   ni <mus>      múr mu  <ris>       re  féc <tus>    in  cǔ <dis>
```

English nouns: Moraic Trochee, Right to Left, Main Stress Right, Final syllable extrametrical

```
X                  X                  X               X
(x    .)           (x)                (x)             (x) (x)
[L   L <L>]ω       [H  L <H>]ω        [L  H <H>]ω      [H  H <H>]ω
mí   ni <mum>      cón so  <nant>      e  líp <sis>    ar thrí <tis>
    minimum           consonant         ellipsis        arthritis
```

The stress parameters not only provide the means of describing metrical patterns in languages, but allow us to determine expected types of changes. As we have seen, a single parameter is insufficient to provide the range of patterns that may exist in a language. The interaction of several parameters allows us to determine the actual patterns. Even then, only a subset of words point to the correct set of parameters for a given language. A pattern such as [ŏ́ŏŏ] is not enough to tell us whether the foot is a trochee or an iamb. Thus, a change in a single parameter will not affect all words, only a subset. The next section lays out the types of opacity of stress patterns, which may lead to a change in the metrical organization of a language. Since stress changes are closely related to weight, we examine possible modifications in syllable quantity and weight. We focus on two conflicting ways systems may or may not change: different metrical patterns, same output realization *versus* different output realizations but with similar metrical patterns.

15.3 OPACITY IN STRESS SYSTEMS

Opacity can occur in stress systems in two ways; many words can have ambiguous metrical interpretations, or the same underlying pattern persists, but due to other interacting processes, surface variation arises. We discuss each in turn.

Same output, different grammars: a typical example where numerous words maintain the same prominence pattern for generations, which is eventually reinterpreted as a different rule, occurred in Latin.[7] Pre-Classical Latin is assumed to have had stress on the *left* edge, while Classical Latin as we have seen above, clearly prefers stress on the *right* edge. The opposite happened in Bengali, where Old Bengali preferred stress on the *right* edge, while Modern Bengali stress is reminiscent of Proto-Germanic with stress strictly assigned to the *left* edge. With the available parameters one might argue that these are clear instances of a change in where the main stress falls. If we consider the Latin examples in (8) and only change *Main Stress Left* to *Main Stress Right* keeping all other parameters constant, what would be the outcome?

(9) Hypothetical early Latin parameters with *Main Stress Left*
     Other parameters: Moraic Trochee, Right to Left, Final syllable extrametrical

(i)	(ii)	(iii)	(iv)
X	X	X	X
(x .)	(x)	(x)	(x) (x)
[L L <H>]$_\omega$	[H L <H>]$_\omega$	[L H <H>]$_\omega$	[H H <H>]$_\omega$
mí ni <mus>	múr mu <ris>	re féc <tus>	†in cŭ́ <dis>

⁷ Jacobs (2000) proposed an asymmetric (rather than moraic) trochee for Latin stress.

Comparing (8) and (9), only in one example is the main stress different when the *Main Stress* parameter changed; main stress in *incŭdis* shifted from the leftmost foot (9iv) to the right in Classical Latin, but the other words are stressed exactly as before since they only have one foot. This makes sense in a scenario with two feet and two stresses, possibly adjacent. The native speaker has difficulty in deciding which is the main prominence, particularly if stress clash occurs within phrases triggering variation. For example, main stress on *thirtéen* can shift to the first syllable in the phrase *thírtèen mén* due to a clash in stress. Such alternations may lead to a shift in the main-stress alignment, which could have happened in Latin.

The same surface patterns can be produced by two different underlying metrical systems. The surface evidence of the *Main Stress* parameter is restricted to certain types of words, namely those that have more than one foot, and when the change occurred, it must have resulted from ambiguity in words with two feet. In fact, the change is quite minor involving a decision as to which foot to give more prominence to when a word has more than one.

An alteration in any of these parameters may lead to a stress shift in only a few words and not others; Latin would be an example where many words maintain exactly the same surface forms although the underlying pattern has changed. Consequently, to deduce the stress parameters correctly, the language learner requires sets of unambiguous words. This is difficult since many words in our lexicons could be accounted for by various stress parameters. Consider the words in (10). A learner faced with these stress patterns could easily opt for any of the four sets of parameters given below.

(10) Different parameters eliciting identical stress patterns

	'L L L	L 'H L	'H H	'H L H
	prósody	*agénda*	*bándage*	*cónsonant*
	(i)	(ii)	(ii)	(iv)
Extrametricality	Final syllable	Final syllable	None	Final syllable
Foot Type	Moraic Trochee	Moraic Trochee	Moraic Trochee	Moraic Trochee
Direction of Parsing	Right to Left	Left to Right	Left to Right	Right to Left
Main Stress	Left	Right	Left	Right

All four options give the correct stress patterns in these words. The disambiguating example we need is a word like *América*, with the pattern [L'LLL]. The only option that covers the full range of data is (10iv). Thus, the possibilities of change are many. If three groups of learners came up with a separate option based on the first set of words, and if they resisted changing the pattern despite the newer data, or if they never come across the new data, then their dialects will differ from their parents, giving the same outputs with different underlying grammars.

Same grammar, different outputs: a different problem arises when the same underlying system persists, but different surface realizations can occur. This occurs particularly when other word prosodic changes (such as changes in syllable quantity) intervene. Metrical structure governing stress is sensitive to the number and weight of syllables. The latter is sensitive to vowel and consonant length and the internal structure of syllables. All may change independently of stress, which in turn influences a change in foot structure.

More languages contrast vowel than consonant length, but the older Germanic languages show both vowel and consonant quantity contrast. For example, OE nominal stems were of the following types: CVC, CV̄C, CVC_aC_a, CVC_aC_b.

(11) Syllable structure of OE monosyllabic nominal stems

dæg	mūs	webb	word
'day'	'mouse'	'web'	'word'

Interestingly, the contexts in which vowels and consonants are lengthened or shortened appear to differ. The most frequent context for vowel lengthening or shortening is prosodic: *closed syllable shortening, open syllable lengthening,* and variations therein. In contrast, consonantal lengthening or gemination is often due to some process of assimilation.

A frequent type of gemination occurs when a consonant is followed by a sonorant, leading to complete regressive assimilation, as in the Latin data in (12). In West Germanic, the suffix or stem extension /j/ triggered gemination if the preceding syllable was light, as in the West Germanic data in (12).

(12) Gemination contexts

Latin	/n/ + /l,r/ > /lː, rː/		
	in-legal > *illegal,* in-regular > *irregular*		
West Germanic (approximation)	V̆jCV̆	> V̆CːV̆	(C≠r)
OE	cyn j es	> cynnes	kin-GEN
OHG	kun j es	> kunnes	

Our interest is in the effect of gemination on foot structure. After gemination, the medial long consonant invariably closes the preceding syllable, and if a closed syllable counts as heavy, the foot structure changes among other effects. Compare the nouns with original H H stems in OE, which belong to two different stem classes, *a*-stem and *ja*-stem respectively; only *wēsten* is subject to gemination because it has a stem extension /j/.[8] As a result of gemination, the second syllable in *wēstenne* becomes heavy, ending with a long consonant, with immediate consequences for foot structure (Dresher & Lahiri 1991).[9]

---

[8] The textbook context is that light syllable followed by /j/ would geminate the coda consonant: cyn+j+e > cynne. However, OE gemination is more complex and is constrained by foot structure (cf. Lahiri 1982, Fikkert et al. 1994). If a light syllable is part of the head of the foot, it does not geminate: æþel+j+e > æþele and not *æþelle. The lengthening syllable need not bear main stress, as we see in wēsten+j+e > wēstenne.

[9] A variant on the trochee proposed for Germanic by Dresher & Lahiri (1991, 2005 Lahiri & Dresher 1999) is a resolved trochee, where the head must dominate *at least* two morae. Consequently, it behaves

(13)

OE nouns with two heavy syllables and gemination

(i)	cīcen			H H	'chicken.NOM.SG.'
(ii)	wēsten(n)			H H	'desert.NOM.SG.'
(iii)	cīcen - e	>	cīcene	H L L	'chicken.DAT.SG.'
(iv)	wēsten -j - e	>	wēstenne	H H L	'desert.DAT.SG.'

OE foot structure (cf. fn 9) with destressing of the final non-branching foot (underlined H̲)

(a)	(b)	(c)	(d)
X	X x	X	X
([x] .)	([x])([x] .])	([x]) ([x])	([x])([x])
[H L L]_ω	[H H L]_ω	[H H̲]_ω	[H H̲]_ω
cī ce ne	wē sten ne	cī cen	wē sten
cíccene	wéstènne	cícen	wésten

In OE, secondary stress is blocked on non-branching feet (13c,d). The critical result of gemination in (13iv) leads to an HHL sequence, while (13iii) maintains an HLL sequence. Demoting the final non-branching foot has equal effect on the nominative singular forms (13c,d), but the dative singular forms suddenly differ. The word *wéstènne* (13b) keeps its secondary stress on the second syllable while (13a) carries only main stress. Consequently, gemination had a direct consequence on the surface stress pattern distinguishing two classes of nouns, which were exactly parallel before gemination. Thus, the underlying foot structure remains, but surface realizations have changed.

The other side of the coin is degemination, which converts a geminate into a singleton. An obvious context for degemination is when another consonant follows, as in OE: *fyll-an* 'to fill-INF', *fyll-d-e* > *fylde* 'to fill-PAST-INDICATIVE.1P,3P'; *cyss-an* 'to

like the usual quantity sensitive trochee, but if the first syllable is light, the second will be included in the head. Such a foot is only possible when parsing *must* begin from the initial syllable. (A) compares parsing possibilities grouping syllables from the left edge of a word.

(A) Resolved Moraic Trochee: the head of the foot is indicated within square brackets

([x])	([x])	([x] .)	([x] .)	([x] .)	([x] .) ([x])
[L L]_ω	[H]_ω	[L H L]_ω	[L L L]_ω	[H L]_ω	[H L H]_ω

Other than stress, evidence for the variations in prosodic structure come from segmental rules sensitive to metrical feet, like foot-based vowel deletion or epenthesis. Our goal is not to defend our analysis against others, but to point out that if a particular foot type can be motivated for an earlier period, any change in its formation will be reflected in the metrical organization in a later period. Different analyses have been proposed by Idsardi (1994) to these facts; although technicalities differ, the essential pattern remains the same, namely that resolution leads to LX=H. Dresher & Lahiri propose the same foot for Gothic to account for Sievers' Law, claiming a different syllabification pattern for Cj clusters than Murray & Vennemann (1983), which affects foot structure. Kiparsky (2000b) also has a different analysis when accounting for Sievers' Law. Crucially it is impossible to determine how the proposed constraints in Kiparsky (2000b) can lead to initial stress, high vowel deletion or secondary stress in Old English. Thus, even if the Sievers' Law analysis works, it does not account for the OE data.

kiss-INF', *cyss-d-e* > *cyste* 'to kiss-PAST-INDICATIVE.1P,3P' (Lahiri 2009). Degemination can, however, occur without any obvious syllabic context; most modern Germanic languages have lost original geminates: *cyss* is still written with two fricatives but pronounced as [kɪs]. Although degemination led to the loss of quantity, the metrical structure was not affected. A German example shows this: the word *Küsse* 'kiss-PL' now consists of two light syllables (LL) rather than an HL sequence when gemination was present, but main stress has remained on the initial for centuries.

Shortening and lengthening a stressed vowel can have similar consequences. Perhaps the best example of shortening and the effect on the overall stress pattern comes from Trisyllabic shortening (TSS). In (14), the OE words have the structures HHL and HLL, where the first word has two feet while the second has only one. TSS has the effect of shortening the first stressed vowel (Lahiri & Fikkert 1999).

(14) Trisyllabic Shortening (TSS) and Metrical shortening from Old to Middle English (in TSS, a stressed long vowel is shortened when preceding two unstressed syllables)

Old English	(i) láverke	(ii) cícene
Foot structure	([H])([H]L)	([H] L) L
TSS	([L H] L)	([L L] L)
Middle English	láverke	cícene
	lark	*chicken*

Although OE words already tended to be short, they could have more than one foot and carry two stresses as in *ōpèrne*. After shortenings such as TSS, native English words with two feet tended to be no longer than a single foot, like *láverke* and *cícene*. Again the metrical structure itself has not changed, but surface realizations have.

The opposite of TSS was open syllable lengthening (OSL) which applied to most West Germanic languages (Lahiri & Dresher 1999). However, interacting with TSS, OSL had no substantial effect on trisyllabic words: *láverke* > OSL *láverke* > TSS *láverke*. But disyllabic words did show a lasting effect as in the long initial vowel in words like *naked, beadle, beacon*, such that an original LH word would become HL after OSL and final consonant extrametricality. Again, lengthening did not have an immediate effect on stress, but moved words towards a much preferred trochaic foot.

Consequently, any change in consonant and vowel quantity directly influences syllable structure, which in turn may affect the number of feet in a word.[10] Nevertheless, as in these instances where surface realizations of words have changed, the underlying metrical pattern can remain consistent despite the increase or decrease in the number of feet.

---

[10] The reverse also holds, in the sense that constraints on syllable structure can lead to a change in vowel and consonant quantity. An example is the OE nominalizing suffix *-þ* which formed nouns from adjectives: *streng-þ* 'strength', *fȳl-þ* 'filth', *þīef-þ* 'theft'. Later, English developed a constraint of closed syllable shortening, which affected all superheavy stem syllables and words with suffixes which were closely attached to the stem leading to vowel shortening: *filth, theft*. This also affected some verbs with original long vowels whose regular past tense suffix was then reinterpreted as a *-t*, leading to a vowel alternation: *cēpan* 'keep', *cēp-te; keep, kept*.

Thus, many forces are at play within a given language without any outside interference, which may trigger changes only in a part of the system while the rest of the grammar remains constant. There are, however, outside influences as well which may play a role in initiating change and we turn to these next.

15.3.1 Interpretation of Surface Opacity and Language Contact

As we have seen, individual stress patterns of words do not always lead to an unambiguous answer as to which parameters are crucial for determining the metrical system of a language. The surface stress patterns of the words in (10) could be accounted for with different parameters, and only an addition of a fifth word with a particular sequence of syllables, allowed us to choose between the options. The surface opacity makes it quite clear that the data relevant for setting parameters from generation to generation is vulnerable to change. Yet rarely do native speakers change their prosodic patterns and we are very sensitive to non-native stress patterns.

There is, however, the additional issue of language contact.[11] A significant change in most Germanic languages is the shift of main stress to the right edge of a word from earlier left-edge prominence, and the general claim is that contact with Romance languages is to blame. How does this happen? If adult native speakers are so sensitive to non-native patterns, how do foreign patterns not only become absorbed, but actually trigger substantial changes? Recall that the Germanic shift is the reverse of the change from pre-Classical Latin to Latin where left-edge prominence moved to the right edge (cf. (9)). As noted, monopedal words remained ambiguous to the setting of the edge parameter; main stress on the rightmost or leftmost foot gave the same results. The shift must have occurred in words with two feet, and some of which could be adjacent.

Consider two scenarios that may lead to prosodic change—reanalysis of the system due to opacity *vs* influence from a different metrical system. Recall that metrical change involves a change in one or more parameters and occurs when native speakers encounter data which are ambiguous in terms of certain parameters (i.e. same surface pattern, different metrical systems). But speakers are conservative and pertinacious in maintaining underlying systems. Loans or internal prosodic changes in quantity can lead to changes in surface realizations, but without changing the system. Thus there is always a conflict between *surface change, but same grammar* versus *surface same, but different grammar*. To examine how these conflicting scenarios actually interact, we take English as a case study to trace how and why the shifts occurred, in section 15.4. We propose the sequence of events in (15) (see footnote 9 for the Resolved Moraic Trochee).

---

[11] Similar issues are discussed in Eckman & Iverson (this volume), with reference to Second Language Acquisition and Uffmann (this volume) with reference to Loanword Adaptation (including a discussion of the adaptation or maintenance of stress in loanwords), and see also Ratliff (this volume) for a consideration of the role of contact in tonogenesis.

(15) Approximate dates of change in metrical structure from Old English till 1660

Foot: Resolved moraic trochee throughout
Extrametricality: OE none, from late OE final syllable
c. 1400: Foot direction *left*, Main stress *left*
c. 1530: Foot direction *right*, Main stress *left*
c. 1660: Foot direction *right*, Main stress *right*

15.4 CASE STUDY: CHANGE IN THE STRESS SYSTEM OF ENGLISH

Three aspects of modern English stress are rather different from early English patterns and require explanation: (i) the shift of stress from word-initial position in some loans while maintaining the stress pattern of native words; (ii) absorbing stress-affecting affixes, and (iii) the introduction of noun-verb doublets alternating in stress. As we will see, Romance loans did not come in carrying the stress of the donor language. We will argue that the shift occurred in stages; neither French nor Latin patterns were absorbed without alteration.

15.4.1 Stress in Old English

While there is complete consensus that Proto-Germanic stress fell on the left edge, with some modifications, most synchronic accounts of modern Germanic (Icelandic being the exception) would agree that word prominence tends to be on the right edge. This represents a radical change in some words, but not others as shown in (16).

(16) Proto-Germanic to Modern Germanic

  (i) PGmc stress pattern: main stress on leftmost syllable irrespective of syllable weight

    Ĺ L   H̀ L   Ĺ H L   Ĺ L L   Ĺ H H   H́ L L

  (ii) Modern Germanic languages (approximation): main stress on penultimate syllable if heavy

    L̀ L   H́ L   L H́ L   Ĺ L L   L H́ H   H́ L L

The diachronic scenario given above was described by Lahiri, Riad, & Jacobs (1999) as a change from the *Resolved Moraic Trochee, Left-to-Right, Main Stress Left* to the modern languages with *Moraic Trochee, Right-to-Left, Main Stress Right*. Scholars differ on details, but the overall sequence remains the same. In this section, we sketch the story for English, relying on Dresher & Lahiri (2005) and Fikkert, Dresher, & Lahiri (2006). Although undoubtedly Latin and Old French loans did have an effect on English stress, the change in the parameters did not happen all at once. Parameter changes went step-wise, the foot direction changing first, followed by main stress prominence shifting to the right.

15.4.2 Old English to Early Middle English

The OE foot, or *Germanic Foot*, is an expanded (resolved) moraic trochee (cf. foot-note 9) where the head must contain at least two moras and the dependent at most one. The two moras of the head need not come from the same syllable. As we have seen that not all surface forms provide evidence for metrical structure, examples are given in (17), varying in syllable structure and weight (Dresher & Lahiri 1991).

(17)

Old English: Resolved Moraic Trochee (the head of the foot is indicated by [])

```
([x    ])        ([ x ])      ([x      ]  .)   ([x  ]  .)    ([x]  .)
[L   L]ω         [H]ω         [L   H   L]ω     [L L   L]ω    [H   L]ω
lo  fu           word         fæ  rel  du      we ru da      wor du

(a) lofu         (b) word     (c) færeld       (d) weruda    (e) word


([x   ]  .) ([x])     ([x ])([x ]  .)   ([x ].)        ([x ])([x ])
[H   L    H]ω         [H    H   L]ω     [H L L]ω       [H    H]ω
héa fu    des         ó    þèr ne       ní te nu       ó     þer

(f) héafdes           (g) óþèrne        (h) nítenu     (i) óþer
```

In (17e), the initial heavy syllable has two moras and occupies the head of the foot; the second syllable is light (one mora), and occupies the dependent branch. In (17d), the initial syllable is light, and so the second light syllable joins it (a process called *resolution*) to make up the head position of the foot. The third syllable occupies the dependent position. (17c) is similar, except resolution is with a heavy syllable. Two light syllables may form a foot, but it is non-branching as in (17a).

Evidence for the resolved foot also comes from syncope processes like *High Vowel Deletion*, which deletes high vowels in the weak branch of the foot. In the examples above, only the double underlined [u] are deleted. Thus, since the word-final [u] in *nítenu* is not in the dependent branch of the foot, it survives, while the [u]s in *héafudes* and *wordu* are deleted, yielding *héafdes* and *word*. The final high vowel in the non-branching foot of *lofu* is not deleted.

What concerns us here are the stress patterns. In Old English, main stress falls on the leftmost foot. However, not all subsequent feet bear secondary stress;

only *branching feet* can bear secondary stress. This is indicated by an underlined H-syllable, which marks non-branching non-initial feet. Thus, *héafdes* and *óþer* have only one stress, while *óþèrne* bears secondary stress. The lack of secondary stress on a word-final non-branching foot, is in effect, defooting and has the consequence of making the final closed syllable light. This is a significant change because, in effect, the final consonant is now being interpreted as extrametrical, as shown in (18).

(18) Interpretation of de-footing as final consonant extrametricality

([x] .)	([x]) ([x] .)	([x] .)	([x] .)
[H L L]_ω	[H H L]_ω	[H L L]_ω	[H L]_ω
hếa f<u>u</u> de<s>	ố þèr ne	nî te nu	ố þe<r>
(a) *héafdes*	(b) *óþèrne*	(c) *nîtenu*	(d) *óþer*

We have seen before that another process which affected quantity, during the transition from Old to Middle English, is Trisyllabic Shortening (TSS), already applicable in OE. As in (14), the interaction of these rules led to a metrical shortening such that OE words that had more than one foot were reduced to a single foot in ME: OE *lávèrke*, ME *láverke*.

(19) Metrical shortening with TSS

	OE	(i) *héringes	(ii) *láverke	(iii) cícenes	(iv) clávere
Defooting		([H])([H])([H̲])	([H])([H]L)	([H]L)([H̲])	([H]L)L
Extrametricality		([H])([H] L)	—	([H]L) L	—
TSS		([L H] L)	([L H] L)	([L L] L)	([L L] L)
ME		héringes	láverke	cícenes	clávere

The changes sketched above had no effect on the position of main stress, and the stress system in early ME remained essentially as in OE. However, TSS did metrically 'shorten' words and with the addition of final consonant extrametricality, many words that had more than one foot in OE were reduced to a single foot in ME (Lahiri & Dresher 1999: 709). Although OE words already tended to be short, they could have more than one foot and carry two stresses as noted already for *óþèrne*. Following defooting and further metrical shortenings, native English words tended to be no longer than a single foot, like *láverke* and *cícenes*.

OE suffixes were, as their descendants still are today, 'stress neutral', suggesting that they did not participate in the stress domain and main stress always fell on the first syllable, indicative of compound stress: *fréondscipe*. Nothing until now suggests that there was data to prompt a shift in directionality or position of main stress. In the eleventh to twelfth century, the phonological system faced an onslaught of French borrowing after the Norman Conquest. French loans poured in, and one could imagine that the ground was fertile for a change in stress, as claimed in early generative accounts like Halle & Keyser (1971).[12]

15.4.3 Stress in Chaucer c.1400—Language Contact

According to Halle & Keyser (1971), in addition to a Germanic stress rule, a Romance stress rule was added to English around Chaucer's period.[13] The new rule incorporated two different patterns in Chaucer:

(20) Stress patterns that should be covered by the Romance Stress Rule
    (a) French pattern responsible for Chaucer's final stress in words with final tense vowels like *honóur* and *citée*
    (b) Latin pattern responsible for stress on the penultimate syllable if heavy (*engéndred*), otherwise on the antepenult (*Zépherus*)

Their storyline is that this rule originally competed against the dominant OE stress rule, and was gradually extended over subsequent centuries. The relatively few early borrowings from Latin were secured by a much larger number of French words with the French stress pattern. This is possible under such an analysis, since the French and Latin stress rules are united. The later (*c.*1650) onslaught of Latin borrowings provided further evidence for a pattern that had already gained a foothold in English.

This appears to be flawed in several respects. First, under any analysis, Latin and French stress rules are dissimilar enough to yield quite different patterns. Second, the French pattern has no lasting effect on English prosody. Third, the Latin stress pattern, as distinct from the French pattern, is hardly attested in Chaucer. We consider each in turn and argue that Romance loans had little effect during Chaucer's period.

The stress rules of Latin and French are indeed rather different and should yield different stress patterns.

(21) The French stress rule
    (a) Final vowel (tense or lax) is stressed unless it is schwa: *abbót, seculér, sectíon, opportún, honóur;*
    (b) Otherwise, the penultimate vowel is stressed: *opposíte, divíne, Egípte, exíled, govérne, servíce, baréyne*

---

[12] The next section develops and expands the analysis in Dresher & Lahiri (2005).

[13] Halle & Keyser's (1971) rule for OE was essentially initial stress, combined with a *Stress Retraction Rule,* which retracted the stress from the final syllable to the initial syllable for prefixed nouns like *ándgiet* (pp. 89-91). The latter was justified under the assumption of a derivational pattern like: {and+gíet}$_{VERB}$ > {ánd+giet}$_{NOUN}$.

(22) The Latin stress rule
   (a) A tense (<u>not</u> lax) final vowel is stressed: *chanóun, degrée, honóur, vertú;*
   (b) Otherwise, the penultimate syllable is stressed iff it is heavy (i.e. either it
        has a tense vowel or is closed by a consonant): *Caríbdis, divíne, govérne,*
        Neptúnus;
   (c) Otherwise, the antepenult is stressed: *Cappáneus, Týdeus, Zépherus.*

One major difference is the treatment of final syllables. Latin does not permit word-
final stress unless the word ends with a tense vowel while French prefers final stress
unless there is a word-final schwa. Consequently, for the words in (23) French and
Latin stress rules would give different patterns. The words in (23a) have to be marked as
exceptions to the unified Romance stress rule.

(23) Disylllabic words with different French and Latin stress patterns
   (a) French: *abbót, Jhesús, Judíth, Oréb, tempést*
   (b) Latin: *ábbot, Jhésus, Júdith, Óreb, témpest*

Another inconsistency occurs in words with more than two syllables, where the final
vowel is schwa and the penultimate syllable is light. Here, the French rule would give
penultimate stress, while Latin has antepenultimate stress. Halle & Keyser claim that
Old French words all had heavy penults, thus avoiding a conflict in words borrowed
from that source, but many words borrowed into English from Latin had light penults
and followed the Latin, not the French rule, undermining a unified approach to Old
French and Latin stress patterns.
    A second difficulty is that the French stress pattern has had no lasting effect on English
prosody. Words with French stress in Chaucer could have been stressed according to the
native English pattern, as required by the meter.

(24) Chaucer's metrical doublets (Halle & Keyser 19971: 103)
   (a) *Fúl wél shĕ sóong the* sérvĭcĕ *dyvyne*   (A.Prol.122)
   (b) *Lóo, hów thĭs théef koude hĭs* sĕrvícĕ *béedĕ*   (G.C.Y. 1065)

A word like *service* could receive word-initial or penultimate stress. The final *e* must
have been pronounced, else the lines would lack the requisite number of syllables. In
(24a), it must have three syllables and bear initial stress. No other stress assignment is
possible in this word since an odd position can be occupied by a stressed syllable only
when it is not adjacent to unstressed syllables on both sides. In contrast, in (b) stress
must fall on the penultimate syllable. Hence we find doublets in Chaucer such as *citée ~*
cítee, comfórt ~ cómfort, divérs ~ díverse, Plató ~ Pláto, presént ~ présent, etc. With few
exceptions, the present day English reflexes of Romance words with French stress in
Chaucer have initial stress consistent with Germanic stressing, such as *ábbot, bárren,*
cíty, cómfort, Égypt, fórtune, gíant, góvern, hónour, Pláto, sérvant, sólemn, témpest,
tórment (noun), *vírtue, sérvice, sécular, séction.*

Furthermore, in many modern English words stress has been retracted from the final syllable as in Chaucer: *ascéndant* (cf. *ascénd*, Chaucer *ascendént*), *cánon* (Chaucer *chanóun*), and *purvéyance* (cf. *purvéy*, Chaucer *purveyáunce*; the more usual ME form was *púrvey-*). The few exceptions to the generalization are *degrée*, *divíne*, and *rewárd* with final stress (see below).

Thus, in general, Romance loans borrowed before the fifteenth century have initial stress in Modern English irrespective of the weight of the initial syllable (Svensson & Hering 2003), as shown in (25).

(25) Romance loans with initial stress before 15th century
    (a) Stem vowel is short in Modern English (from Dresher & Lahiri 2005)
        alcove, talent (893), *baron* (1200), *senate* (1205), *jealous* (1250), *palace* (1290), *channel* (1300), *gallon* (1300), *panel* (1300), *coral* (1305), *profit* (1325), *metal* (1340), *satin* (1366), *moral* (1380), *volume* (1380), *second* (1391), *Latin* (1391)
    (b) Stem vowel is long in Modern English
        basin (1220), *moment* (1240), *vacant* (1290), *odour* (1300), *process* (1330), *paper* (1374), *raisin* (1382), *patent* (1387), *famous* (1400).

Today, many early and late trisyllabic loans bear initial stress. These words may once have been longer. Examples include *báttery* (c 1500), *cápital* (1290), *ópera* (1648), *énemy* (c 1340), *crócodile* (c 1300), *érudite* (c 1425), etc.[14] In contrast, disyllabic Romance loans with final stress in English, which went entirely against any OE stress pattern, tend to have been borrowed much later: *canal* (1449), *bourgeois* (1564), *gazelle* (1582/1700), *moustache* (1585), *gazette* (1605), *hotel* (1644), *champagne* (1664), *salon* (1715), *bouquet* (1716), *brochure* (1765), *beret* (1850), *taboo* (1777), *mirage* (1800). There are, however, dialectal differences and some of these words are pronounced with initial stress in British English: *bourgeois, salon, brochure, beret, mirage*. Indeed, certain words which have final stress nowadays had initial stress earlier as *cement* (1300) where ME *síment* had initial stress until the nineteenth century, or *antique* which was identical in pronunciation to *ántic* until the eighteenth century. For the month *July*, final stress can be traced back to Johnson's period.

A third problem is that the Latin stress pattern, as distinct from the Old French one, is hardly attested in Chaucer. If, as argued, the Latin stress pattern is distinct from that of Old French, evidence for the introduction of a Latin-type stress rule into English in Chaucer's time must rest on words that exemplify this pattern. However, such words are rather rare in Chaucer, and tend to be Latin names. Halle & Keyser cite the following instances (p. 99).

(26) Latin-type stress in Chaucer
    Antepenultimate if penultimate is light: *Căppánĕŭs, Týdĕŭs, Zéphĕrŭs*
    Else penultimate: *Căríbdĭs, Sătúrnĕs*

---

[14] The dates are from the *OEED* (*Oxford English Etymological Dictionary*).

We conclude that there is no clear evidence that either the Old French or the Latin stress rule gained a foothold in English at the time of Chaucer (see also Minkova 1997, Redford 2003, and compare Ratliff, this volume, on the care that needs to be taken when invoking contact as a cause for change in a prosodic system). Our hypothesis is that early loans were originally borrowed as morphologically simplex (we follow Lahiri & Fikkert 1999, also Minkova & Stockwell 1996). Thus, *reverence* was not initially derived from *revere*, nor *austerity* from *austere*. This accounts for the stress patterns of these words, and provides evidence that direction of parsing and placement of main stress had not changed before 1530. Further evidence comes from words that exhibit so-called 'Medial Laxing' where the stressed vowel in the verb is unstressed and short in the noun.[15] In these medial-laxing pairs, the 'derived' forms have stress consistent with the OE pattern, firmly secure in the initial syllable, and moreover are often borrowed earlier than the base form.

(27) Medial Laxing ('underived' ~ 'derived')
      abstain (1380) ~ *abstinence* (1300); *confide* (1455) ~ *confidence* (1430); *reside* (1460) ~ *resident* (adj.) (1382); *finite* (1493/1597) ~ *infinite* (1385); *potent* (1500) ~ *impotent* (1390): *preside* (1611) ~ *president* (1375); *revere* (1661) ~ *reverence* (1290).

If these pairs were not really morphologically related when they were borrowed, why do the 'underived' forms (typically verbs) bear stress on the second syllable? Recall that this pattern is consistent with the native model of unstressed prefixed verbs. The only non-initial stress in OE was found in prefixed verbs: *forbēodan* 'to forbid', *becú-man* 'to become', *fullfýllan* 'to fulfill'. Furthermore, as Halle & Keyser point out, pairs like *bígang*$_{NOUN}$ ~ *begángen*$_{VERB}$ 'practice ~ to practice' are very much part of the OE system (also see footnote 13). In all probability, loans such as *revére* could be treated as if they had unstressed prefixes.

Thus, most 'derived' words that came into the language during Chaucer's period and earlier were borrowed as indivisible wholes. Only later was the derivational relationship established. For the fifteenth-century native speaker the underlying stressed vowels in *reverence* or *president* were short, and the first syllable of the 'derived' forms (typically nouns) in (27) were part of the stem and not treated as affixes. Thus, despite loans and variable surface realizations, the stress parameters in early ME remained largely the same.

(28) Stress parameters around 1400

Foot	Resolved moraic trochee
Extrametricality	Consonant
Foot direction:	Left to Right
Main stress	Left

---

[15] These words are problematic and treated as exceptions in all current analyses, including Liberman and Prince 1977 (morphological shortening), Kiparsky 1979 (sonorant destressing), Myers 1987 (medial laxing), and Kager 1989 and Gussenhoven 1994 (lexical exceptions).

15.4.4 Change in Direction of Parsing (c 1570)

Old English words tended to be short and suffixes were, as their descendants still are today, stress neutral. With metrical shortening, native words tended to be no longer than a single foot. Therefore, evidence for setting the parameters of directionality and main stress was in short supply. The loans in the preceding section show that it was not sufficient to borrow Latin words to provoke a change in directionality. What led to this change?

Following Danielsson (1948), Poldauf (1981), and others, we associate this change with the introduction of words with Latin suffixes such as *-able/-ible,-ation,-ic(al),-ity,-ator,* etc., each of which could be a foot on their own and behaved like original compounds where the second element would bear stress: *brȳdgùma* 'bridegroom', *dǽgsèage* 'daisy'. However, the absorption of these words was still not straightforward as we can see from the sixteenth and seventeenth century literature. Peter Levins's *Manipulus Vocabulorum,* printed in 1570, is perhaps most important for the study of change in stress patterns in English. It is a reverse (rhyming) dictionary, indicating the location of stress. Although Levins lists many words that appear to have stress on the right edge, a fairly large number do not conform to a straightforward Latin stress rule.

(29) Levins's stress patterns

non-initial			initial		
FINAL	PENULT	ANTEPENULT	4σ	4,5σ	3σ
quarrél	oriéntal	antíquitie	hóspitable	dívisible	túrpentine
lamént	advénture	infírmitie	prósperity	délectable	défective
debáte	recógnise	memórial	ádolescencie	nóminative	cánonise
flagón	conféssour	agréeable	précipitate	téstamentary	mármalad

Levins's remarkable list leaves little doubt that initial stress was very much present even in this period. To account for these patterns, Halle & Keyser evoke a stress retraction rule since their Romance stress rule would normally always provide stress on the right edge; thus, the Romance stress rule would predict *canoníse*, requiring stress retraction to give the main stress at the left edge, *cánonise*. As we have seen, little evidence suggests that the earlier loans had any effect on the stress parameters of English and no Romance rule was in evidence in the mid 1400s. A century later, when many more words had come into the language, the stress parameters seem to require some adjustment.

What appears to be happening is that native speakers of English continue their Germanic nominal/verbal distinction, where initial light syllables of verbs are treated as prefixes. We can deduce four notable facts from Levins's dictionary. First, when disyllabic verbs are marked with final stress, the first syllable continues to function like a prefix: *depúte, recórd, contráct, rebél, quarrél, rewárd*. Four corresponding nouns have initial stress, suggesting that this analysis is on the right track: *députe, rébel, quárrel, récord*. Second, suffixes like *-ity, -ible/-able, -ate* were not following 'normal' Romance stress rules. Indeed, there are no words in *-ory* which do not have word-initial stress. Third, in comparison to verbs, very few disyllabic nouns bear final stress: *flagón*. Fourth, there has been a substantial increase in longer verbs ending in non-schwa vowels due to the suffixed loans: *-ory, -ate, -ity*.

Which parameters changed during Levins's period? During the earlier period, morphologically complex words were always coming in as simplex forms, as is typical for borrowing crosslinguistically. This appears to have continued in the sixteenth century, during the early Shakespearean period. Consequently, suffixed words with *-ible/-able*, *-ity* were treated as monomorphemic. Nevertheless, unlike the earlier period where all words like *admirable* and *residence* bore initial stress, there are some exceptions and one begins to find surface alternations like *húmidity* versus *antíquity*. Without doubt there is still a very strong main stress parameter associated with the left edge. However, during the mid sixteenth century we begin to see three interacting reanalyses taking place.

First, and most important, we perceive the onset of morphologically governed stress alternating doublets in the synchronic grammar: nouns *rébel, quárrel*; verbs *rebél, quarrél*. This was a consequence of borrowed verbs being stressed on the root (parallel to *forgíve*), thereby strengthening the number of unstressed prefixes. The pattern is, however, not novel. Old English did have doublets, where the noun was derived from the verb, but with clear quantity distinction in the related prefixes: $b\bar{i} \sim be, \acute{a}nd \sim on$. Prefixed disyllabic noun and verb pairs occurred, where the verb was derived from the noun: *ándswaru* 'answer' ~ *ándswarian* 'to answer', but these would always carry stress on the same syllable. What was new in Levins were doublets with stress differences as *tórment*$_{NOUN}$ ~ *tormént*$_{VERB}$. Thus, the existing OE prefix-extrametricality for verbs increased.

(30) Noun~verb pairs in Levins
    (a)   X   (b)   X
           (x   .)   (x   .)
           ([μμ])   ([μ μ]
        \<re> bel $_{VERB}$ re be\<l> $_{NOUN}$

The second factor is that although it is highly likely that as before most suffixed nouns came in underived, we do not systematically find word-initial stress as in Chaucer's *réverence*. Words with initial stress like *précipitate, bárbarity* need to be contrasted with *fratérnity, infírmity*. A careful look at the data suggests that despite a preference for the left edge, the parameter that has changed is the direction of parsing, which now begins from the right edge.

(31) Levins's parameters: Germanic Foot, Direction *right*, Main stress *left*; non branching secondary feet are defooted

(a) X
    (x   .)
    (μ μ μ)
    se ve ri ty
    L L L L

(b) X   x
    (x) (x) (x .)
    [μμ] [μμ] μ μ
    ad ver sa ry
    H H L L

(c) X   x
    (x) (x) (x)
    [μ μ] [μμ] μ μ
    an ni ver sa ry
    L L H L L

(d) X   x
    (x) (x) (x .)
    [μ μμ] [μμ] μ μ
    sa tis fac to ry
    L H H L L

In (32) we can directly compare the parameters around 1400 with those proposed for Levins. Main stress is aligned to the left of a word.

(32) Main and secondary stress with foot direction left (OE) versus foot direction right (Levins)

	(a)	(b)	(c)	(d)	(e)
OE	(Ĺ L L) L	(Ĺ L) (Ḧ L)	(Ĺ H) (Ḧ L) L	(Ĺ H L)	(Ḧ L) (L L)
Levins	Ĺ (L L L)	(Ĺ L) (Ḧ L)	(Ĺ H) (Ḧ) (L L)	Ĺ (H L)	(Ḧ) (L̇ L L)

The two sequences which differ in main stress are (32a,d). The pattern in (32d) is largely found in verbs such as *recognize, fraternize,* or in affixed words beginning with light syllables which have a prefix-like structure such as *agreeable, fraternal,* etc. To establish the foot direction, however, the pattern in (32a) is critical. A further point is that additional support for the continuing existence of resolution, i.e. LX=H, comes from the lack of secondary stress on final feet in (32c,e), neither of which can bear stress since the feet are not branching.

Final superheavy syllables increase slightly, including ones with final long vowels. English ears would have been unfamiliar with these words and consequently the option was either to use straightforward Germanic stress (word-initial) or lexicalize them with final stress, which happened during Shakespeare's time (*flagón, turmóil, survéy*), but they reverted to initial stress as the native system prevailed. A few instances of final long vowels are becoming acceptable.

15.4.5 After Levins: the 'Countertonic Principle' and Syllable Extrametricality (*c.*1790)

It was not sufficient to borrow Latin words to provoke a change in main stress although the directionality parameter changed. The noun-verb alternations continued to stabilize, marking the prefix as extrametrical. As Cooper (1768: 113) notes, 'some nouns by translating the Accent are changed into verbs', continuing with pairs like *refúse ~ refúse, tórment ~ tormént*.

Nevertheless, initial stress remains rather stable. According to Lowe's *Critical Spelling Book* (1755), stress was prescribed on initial syllables in words like *ácademy, cónfessor, délectable* rather than *acádemy, cónfessor, deléctable*, which shows a strong mid-eighteenth century preference for the left edge. Danielsson (1948) attributes to Walker (1791) the observation that classical words were pronounced in English with alternating secondary stresses (e.g. Latin *àcadémia*). When 'Englished', the tonic and countertonic changed places to conform to English 'speech habits' (e.g. *ácadèmy*). The *Countertonic Principle* shows that the main stress parameter remained set to *left* for some time after the change of directionality to *right*. The addition of words stressed according to the Countertonic Principle would have *increased* evidence for main stress *left*. Thus, a word like *ácadèmy* clearly shows two feet, of which the left has main stress.

What was the next parameter change? Halle & Keyser point to the differences between Levins's period and that of John Walker (1791), who also wrote a pronunciation dictionary:

(33) Four syllable word-stress (based on Halle & Keyser)

	c.1570	*c*.1791
Levins/Walker	Levins	Walker
ádversary	*réfractory*	*refráctory*
sédantary	*ánniversary*	*annivérsary*
cónsistory	*péremptory*	*perémptory*

Words like *ádversary* were stressed in the same way while others like *refráctory* had shifted to the antepenultimate syllable. Levins, as noted above, had only initial stress in words with *-ory/-ary*. Halle & Keyser argue that the words in the first column are derived by the early stress retraction rule, pulling the stress to the first syllable, but that those in column 3 are lexically stored.

We should consider some other examples before coming to any conclusion about changes in parameters. Consider the words in (34).

(34) Further words from Walker - two, three and four syllable words

    cástigate   *invéstigate*   *confíscate*   *vácate*

Halle & Keyser also drew attention to words like *confíscate*, stressed on the penultimate in Shakespeare (born six years before Levins's book was published), but not in Levins. Walker, in contrast to Levins, has a much larger number of words where stress falls on the penultimate in trisyllabics. Furthermore, in four syllable words, we see consistently different patterns between Levins and Walker. This variation between three and four syllable words sets the stage for a reanalysis in the treatment of the final syllable. Unlike Levins, where the left edge was clear except for prefix-like words, it is not clear how to differentiate *cónsistory* (4σ) and *confíscate* (3σ) in terms of an unstressed prefix analysis.

Nevertheless, main stress left remains strong, given that words like *ádversary* and *cónsistory* still bear stress on the left edge.

This was the onset of final syllable extrametricality. First, many of the words in (33) could also be accounted for by assuming the final syllable to be extrametrical, and hence would have had no surface change. Recall that secondary stress did not appear on the third foot of words like *ádvèrsary* and hence the final syllable played little role in stress assignment. Second, the deviations between Walker and Levins largely depend on the internal structure of disyllablic suffixes. The head of the foot on the suffixes *-ory* or *-ary*, bore no stress, and so the initial vowel of the suffixes *-o* or *-a* would very easily have been reduced to schwa. If so, syllable extrametricality was almost inevitable for the next generation. Compare the Levins-Walker words in (35).

(35) Foot direction *right*, Main stress *left*, (Levins)

(a)	X				(b)	X	
	(x)	(x .)				(x)	(x .)
	[μ μμ]	[μ μ]				[μμ]	[μμ] μ μ
	re frac	to ry				ad	ver sa ry

Foot direction *right*, Main stress *left*, *final syllable extrametrical* (Walker)

(c)	X			(d)	X	
	(x)				(x)	(x .)
	μ [μ μ μ]	μ			[μμ]	[μμ] μ μ
	re frac to	<ry>			ad	ver sa <ry>

Walker and Levins also differed as to the main stress in *anniversary*: Levins had main stress on the initial syllable while Walker stressed the antepenultimate syllable. Note that with the stress parameters that Walker had, he would have obtained two feet, and as he was a proponent of making the words 'English', he would have used his countertonic principle and obtained *ánnivèrsary*.

A further ambiguity now arises for the foot type which was still a resolved trochee during Levins's period; otherwise *réfractory* and *sátisfactory* would not have borne main stress. During the end of the eighteenth century with the onset of extrametricality, the foot type also becomes opaque and a moraic trochee analysis would also work for Walker. Clearly, however, the main stress still appears to be on the left edge, as words like *ádversary* suggest. In such cases, the same words that provoked a change of directionality to *right* reinforced the evidence for main stress *left*.

15.4.6 Main Stress Right

The turning point must have been right after the onset of syllable extrametricality when the resolved trochee also became opaque. Probably as in the shift from the left edge to the right edge in Classical Latin, words with two feet were ambiguous for main stress.

Words like *ádvèrsary* and *sátisfàctory* had two feet and therefore two stresses. In running speech, if stress clash occurs, main stress would shift to the right rather than the left edge. Second, some trisyllabic loans lost their final vowel and ended up with final stress, like *bazaar* from earlier *bazaroo*. Third, suffixes such as *-ade, -ee, -eer, -esque, -ette, -oon*, became more established, adding to sets of words with two feet. Though words like *càscáde, cànnonér* may have entered the language earlier, they may not have systematically had final stress until a later date. In (36) compare Walker's pattern using a regular moraic trochee with main stress on the right edge where it is invariably the words with two feet that diverge.

(36) Main stress left versus right
      Walker: Foot direction *right*, Main stress *left, final syllable extrametrical*

    (a)   X   (b) X

        (x)   (x)   (x)

        μ [μμ] μ μ   [μμ] [μμ] μ μ

        re frac to \<ry>   ad   ver sa \<ry >

    Foot direction *right*, Main stress *right, final syllable extrametrical*

        X   X

        (x)   (x)   (x)

        μ [μ μ] μ μ   [μμ] [μμ] μ μ

        re frac to \<ry>   ad   ver sa \<ry >

Despite hundreds of years of loans, the urge to keep a foot at the leftmost edge remains as we see in many new loans such as *Ticonderóga* (Hayes 1981). The changes in the parameters were step-wise and it is off the mark to suggest that English moved abruptly from a 'Germanic' to a 'Romance' stress system.

15.5 CONCLUSION

Although changes in stress systems are not as well described or widely discussed as other aspects of phonology, we can still trace their history. Historical data for metrical organization include verse, as well as records of orthoepists, and for reconstruction we rely on comparative evidence. The lacunae within historical linguistics, where changes in metrical systems remain unreported, are probably related to the fact that stress changes are rarer than segmental modifications. Native speakers are very sensitive to 'non-native accent' and incorrect stress placement. Thus, any change in word stress from one generation to another must be subtle and discrete, since speakers are pertinacious in maintaining their grammar. The question remains: how do such systems change?

Word stress is not merely prominence on a single syllable or vowel; rather, it emerges as a combination of several parameters, such as foot type, quantity sensitivity, direction of foot parsing and word edge preference for main stress. Moreover, extrametricality determines whether any particular prosodic constituent at word edge plays an active role in setting the parameters. Change in any one parameter may lead to an alteration of stress patterns but it may affect only small portion of words. The reverse also holds; the same surface stress pattern may be the result of different parameter settings. Consequently, any change in stress systems is rather complex and, indeed, stress patterns are surprisingly pertinacious, and universal metrical preferences and constraints govern possible and impossible prosodic shifts. Even under external influence, acquisition and learnability appear to be necessary factors.

Again, how does a parameter change? We drew attention to a characteristic of grammars called *pertinacity*. A rule or pattern may persist over time though its realization changes. An example is the persistence of a particular metrical pattern in a language, though it may apply to new forms and no longer apply to forms that it used to apply to. As a case study we argued that the Germanic Foot continued over a long period. This type of pertinacity can be summed up as *same pattern, different output realization*. There is a converse kind of pertinacity where output forms persist despite changes in the grammar. Such changes involve a reanalysis of the output form, provoked by changes elsewhere in the system. This type of pertinacity can be summed up as *different pattern, same output realization*. Since learners acquire their grammars guided by the output forms they are exposed to, we do not expect these forms—especially those that make up the 'core' or 'primary' data—to change in the course of acquisition. Reanalysis of grammar that does not involve an immediate change in output forms is thus a significant type of language change. Changes in stress systems are prime examples of both types of pertinacity.

CHAPTER 16

···

TONOEXODUS, TONOGENESIS, AND TONE CHANGE

···

MARTHA RATLIFF

16.1 INTRODUCTION

···

IN this chapter, I define a 'tone language' narrowly as a language in which individual words in the lexicon must include a specification for tone, such tones being drawn from a paradigmatic set of two or more contrastive level or contour pitches. Unlike accent (realized primarily by pitch) or stress (realized by a complex set of features, of which pitch is only one), tone is not limited to prominent syllables, but is realized on most 'tone-bearing units' in a way that does not privilege one or two syllables over the others in a word. I subscribe to Hyman's (2006) view that tone languages and stress languages define two prototypes, and that 'pitch-accent' languages, which many have taken pains to distinguish from tone languages, do not represent a coherent type, but rather take elements from both. In discussing the origin of tone, the loss of tone, and change in tone, I therefore leave quasi-tonal languages such as Japanese, Swedish, and Ancient Greek out of the account.

Roughly half the world's languages are characterized by tone used to distinguish words from one another (Yip 2002, Maddieson 2008a).[1] Tone contrasts are also commonly used for grammatical purposes in tone languages of the African type (Ratliff 1992). Tone languages are concentrated in three geographical areas: East and Southeast Asia, Sub-Saharan Africa, and Mesoamerica. Outside of these areas, tone is found in the Athabaskan language family and appears to have developed independently in a number

---

[1] These are usually associated with the syllable or mora, but also common are African languages in which lexical 'tone melodies' do not require that these melodies be consistently realized on particular syllables or morae.

of other languages in the Americas. The first question that arises in a cross-linguistic account of 'tonogenesis', the origin of distinctive tone in tone languages, is why such an account is more important or more natural than its inverse, a cross-linguistic account of 'tonoexodus', or the historical loss of tone in atonal languages.[2] Although traditional historical methods can only show the rise and fall of tone across time as a cyclic process (Matisoff 1973, 1999), there is work from independent quarters to suggest that tone may have been a component of early human language:[3] (1) Studies of acquisition of tone by children show that lexical tone is acquired before segmental phonology (e.g. Hua & Dodd 2000), and thus may be basic to the nature of human language. (2) Certain theories on the evolution of human language hold that early language and early music co-evolved, and that semantically significant tone was an important connection between the two (Brown 2000, Mithen 2005). (3) Furthermore, recent genetic studies of two new alleles (haplogroups) of the genes *ASPM* and *Microcephalin* show a correlation between the development of these haplogroups (dated 5,800 and 37,000 years ago, respectively), and the *absence* of tone, leading the investigators to propose that these genes created a small bias against the acquisition of tone, which, over time, could have led speakers to favour atonal languages (Dediu & Ladd 2007, Ladd, Dediu, & Kinsella 2008).

This chapter accordingly sketches a few cases of tonoexodus first. The subsequent discussion of tonogenesis will be organized by the location of those segmental features that give rise to distinctive tone, whether in the syllable coda, the syllable onset, or the syllable nucleus. A review of how tones, once born, can change in both phonetic realization and in number will follow. The chapter closes with discussion of the role of language contact in the acquisition and modification of tones and tone systems.

16.2 TONOEXODUS

The best attested pathway for tone loss is through reinterpretation of a prominent tone, or a tone in proximity to toneless syllables, as an accent (see Salmons 1992a, and 1992b for a summary). A case study of this type of reanalysis is given by Shih (1985) for the Min Chinese variety spoken in Fuzhou, Fujian Province, China. It has also been reported that some tone languages such as Swahili (Schadeberg 2009: 90) and the Northwest Mandarin Chinese variety spoken in Wutun, Qinghai Province, China (Janhunen

---

[2] The term 'tonogenesis' was coined by James A. Matisoff (1970). It has been so successful that its source is now rarely mentioned.

[3] In sub-Saharan Africa, the place where human language presumably arose, there is no evidence to suggest the origin of tone (Childs 2003: 86). The simplest explanation is that the ancestors of the Niger-Congo, Nilo-Saharan, and Khoisan languages spoke tone languages themselves. However, traditional methods cannot help us determine whether or not tone languages were spoken in Africa at a time predating these protolanguages, so we cannot assume on this basis that early human language was tonal.

et al. 2008) have lost their tones as a result of contact with speakers of atonal languages. Finally, it is possible that a language may lose tone through radical tone mergers.

Two clusters of atonal languages—within the Bantu group and the Atlantic group—occur in the otherwise tonal Niger-Congo family. A very similar internal account for the loss of tones in these two groups has been proposed by Clements & Goldsmith (1984) for Bantu, and by Childs (1995) for Atlantic.

Bantu and Atlantic languages exhibit a wide range of prosodic systems, from lexical tone to stress-accent, with languages characterized by various 'mixed' systems, involving both tone and accent, in-between. For Bantu, Clements & Goldsmith first note that there is agreement on the likelihood that both the older Proto-Niger-Congo and the younger Proto-Bantu languages were tone languages with two distinctive tones (p. 3). They dismiss a contact explanation for tone loss in some Bantu languages, claiming that it is impossible to identify a contact language or group that could have had such an effect. They claim that the reanalysis of tone as accent was primarily dependent on language-internal factors, and happened independently in different languages. The structural prerequisite for reanalysis of a tone system as an accent system is the morphological complexity of the Bantu verb, combined with the propensity of tone to spread in these languages (pp. 4–5). The Bantu verbal complex involves both prefixes (agreement and tense morphemes) and suffixes (derivational 'extensions'). The verbal extensions are typically toneless, and take their tone from the root. The domain of tone spreading is the whole complex word, much as the domain for accent is the word, rather than the syllable. The relationship between root tone and its toneless suffixes thus mirrors the relationship between accented and unaccented syllables in an accent language, and provides the structural 'bridge' for the reanalysis. They also make the interesting connection between the widely-attested tone change which lowers a high tone after another high tone ('Meeussen's Rule', a particular manifestation of the Obligatory Contour Principle) and the reanalysis of a tone language as an accent language, since in a two-tone language it reduces the potential for a four-way contrast in disyllabic nominals from HH, HL, LH, and LL to a three-way contrast: HL, LH, and LL. The latter set of contrasts could then easily be reinterpreted as 'initial-accented, final-accented and unaccented' (p. 7). They speculate that the motivation for such a 'drift toward accentual reanalysis in Bantu languages' is that it is a simpler system for children to learn; the rules need make reference to only one element, the accent, and the grammar needs only make reference to a single linear representation (pp. 15–17; see also Lahiri, this volume, on the role of learnability in the reanalysis of prosodic systems, and Foulkes & Vihman, this volume, for a further consideration of the role of acquisition in change).

Childs (1995) reviews the complexity of prosodic systems in the Atlantic branch of Niger-Congo, represented by tone languages in the south (Temne, Kisi) and either tone (Basari, Bedik) or accent languages (Fula, Serer, Wolof) in the north. There are also languages in this group that show complex interactions of tone and accent, such as Balanta, which has an accent on the first syllable of the root, lexical tone on nouns, and grammatical tone on verbs (p. 8). Although he writes that the case is less clear in Atlantic than in Bantu, he finds evidence that the loss of tone in the languages of this group is also linked to the morphologically complex verb: 'Verb extensions cause the verb root to be analyzed as accented since the extensions are without tone (cf. Clements & Goldsmith 1984). Since these extensions are suffixed, it is on the left that accent appears, particularly as verbs are mono- or disyllabic. Lexical tones on verbs are overridden and this leads to the loss of all lexical tone' (p. 10).

There are also cases where tone languages appear to be losing tone through radical tone merger in the present day, a trend which, if it continues, could lead to complete tone loss. A preliminary study of the Central Vietnamese dialect of Nghe An province by Pham (2005) is one such case. The reflexes of the six historical tone categories (see section 16.3.1 below) are remarkably similar in pitch and in contour—all are slightly falling—whereas tones in the same historical categories in Northern and Southern Vietnamese have distinct contours which make full use of the speaker's pitch range. Mergers to sets of as few as three tonemes have taken place, and the remaining tones for those individuals studied are differentiated on the basis of a very slight F_0 difference and a phonation contrast between modal voice and breathy voice. The author refers to these dialects as 'the most conservative dialects of Vietnamese' (p. 183), which suggests that this state of affairs could reflect an early stage of tonogenesis rather than one of tonoexodus, but given the lack of glottalization as a perceptual cue for tone (widespread elsewhere in Vietnamese, and taken as the first manifestation of Vietnamese tone in historical accounts), coupled with the date of Vietnamese tonogenesis (c. sixth century CE), these mergers more likely signal an early stage of tonoexodus.

16.3 TONOGENESIS

The reason greater attention has been given to tonogenesis than tonoexodus is that we understand more about tonogenetic processes than tone loss. A number of import-ant cases (Vietnamese, Chinese, Athabaskan) have occurred within reach of historical study; several other cases have occurred more recently, or are occurring now (Khmu). The following cross-linguistic consideration of tonogenetic processes will be organized according to the locus of the feature(s) that phonologized into a tone contrast: the syl-labic coda, the syllabic onset, or the syllabic nucleus (see also Hale et al., this volume, for some consideration of the phonologization of tone).

16.3.1 Tone from Coda Consonant Features

The account of Vietnamese tonogenesis from coda consonant features proposed by André G. Haudricourt in 1954 confirmed Przyluski's 1924 claim that Vietnamese was a Mon-Khmer language and that its tones, although similar to those of Thai and Chinese in structure and function, had developed internally. Haudricourt's article has been cited

Table 16.1 Tonogenesis in White Hmong

1. Atonal stage	CV		CV?		CVH		CVC$_{vl}$	
2. Tonogenesis	CV(level)		CV(rising)		CV(falling)		CVC$_{vl}$(atonal)	
3. Tone split	*t-	*d-	*t-	*d-	*t-	*d-	*t-	*d-
	upper	lower	upper	lower	upper	lower	upper	lower
4. White Hmong	[tɔ⁵⁵]	[tɔ⁵³]	[tɔ²⁴]	[tɔ²²]	[tɔ³³]	[tɔ³¹]	—	[tɔ²¹ʔ]
	'deep'	'hill'	'mix'	'wait'	'pierced'	'sink'		'there'

repeatedly in the decades since it first appeared with good reason; it is the single most important contribution to our understanding of the historical development of tone in Asian languages. It has been extended to explain the first wave of tonogenesis in almost all of the major tone language families of China and Southeast Asia: Chinese (see Unger, this volume), Tai-Kadai, and Hmong-Mien.[4]

Haudricourt's view of tonogenesis can be exemplified using the 'minimal septet' of White Hmong words presented in Table 16.1. In atonal Stage 1, syllables are categorized into four types: open syllables, syllables ending with a final -ʔ, syllables ending with a final -h, and syllables with final voiceless stop consonants. The loss of the two final laryngeal consonants led to a three-way tone contrast as represented in Stage 2: level (from *-ø), rising (from *-ʔ), and falling (from *-h). Syllables with final voiceless stop consonants retained these consonants through the initial phase of tonogenesis, and thus remained distinctive (and atonal). In Stage 3, voiceless and voiced onsets merged to voiceless, giving rise to an upper register (< *C$_{vl}$-) and lower register (< *C$_{vd}$-) version of each original tone,[5] thereby doubling the set of distinctive tones from three to six. 'Deep' and 'hill', for example, derive from the same open syllable type, but have different tones in the modern language since 'deep' < *t- and 'hill' < *d-. The loss of final stop consonants added a fourth major tone category, subject to the same split triggered by the merger of voiceless and voiced onsets.

It is clear that the phonetic values of the modern-day words (where '5' is the highest pitch and '1' is the lowest) do not retain the reconstructed values: although 'deep' is high level, as expected, 'hill' is not low level, but is rather high falling. Although 'mix' is rising, it is mid-rising rather than high rising, and 'wait' is low level rather than low rising. And although 'sink' is low falling, 'pierced' is not high falling, but is rather mid level. Once generated, tones in Asian languages tend to change rapidly and in unexpected ways, as discussed in section 16.4.

---

[4] Many Tibeto-Burman languages are tonal as well, but Tibeto-Burman tones in cognate words do not correspond to one another in such a way that the Vietnamese model can be extended to cover them (Matisoff 1999).

[5] It is confusing that within the domain of prosody, the term 'register' has been used both as a label for the two sets of tones ('upper' and 'lower') that follow from the merger of voiceless and voiced obstruents and as an alternate term for phonation type.

This account of tonogenesis has been complicated by the observation that laryngeal contrasts in coda and onset consonants do not transfer directly to the adjacent vowel as a pitch contrast, but first go through an intermediate phase of contrastive phonation (Thurgood 2002). The role of phonation explains exceptions to the Vietnamese story, cases where cognates with a particular syllable shape in related Mon-Khmer languages do not acquire the Vietnamese tones that Haudricourt's model predicts (Gage 1985, Diffloth 1990). The problem is that the first tone category, derived from open syllables, does not contain all words reconstructed with open syllables—a good number of these words fall into the second category, which should have had a final glottal stop. But if the Viet-Muong precursor to tonal Vietnamese had had phonation contrasts (and there is comparative evidence that it did), syllables with creaky voice would have fallen together with CV? syllables into the second tone category. Intermediate phonation contrasts from coda and onset consonants can also help explain the development of tone in Hmong-Mien where breathiness or creakiness may still be attested as a component of tone, and the development of tone from voiced onsets in Khmu (Mon-Khmer) and Punjabi (on these, see section 16.3.2).

Another case of tonogenesis from loss of final laryngeals is reported for tone languages in the Athabaskan family (Kingston 2005). Almost all of the tonal Athabaskan languages (northern and eastern Canada, northern and eastern Alaska, and the Apachean languages of the southwest United States) have lost final glottalized consonants and thus the plain/glottalized contrast in the coda, whereas almost all of the atonal Athabaskan languages (southern and western Alaska, Western British Columbia, and the Pacific Coast) have retained glottalized consonants in the coda (p. 140). The development of tone can thus be correlated with, and, on the basis of the Asian model, linked to the loss of final glottalized consonants.

A related kind of tonogenesis from coda consonant features has been described for the Uto-Aztecan language Hopi (Manaster-Ramer 1986). In different varieties of Hopi, a low tone corresponds to a 'voiceless syllable final' (p. 154) in a related language: -h, -s ($< *-^hs$), preaspiration on the following syllable onset (which presumably re-syllabified with the preceding syllable), or a voiceless semivowel or sonorant. Since the resultant low tone is realized on the second mora of a long vowel, yielding a falling tone rather than a low-level tone, the effect of tonogenesis here is analogous to that proposed by Haudricourt for the development of the falling tone in Vietnamese following the loss of inherited *-h ($< *-s$). A similar source for a low tone (from a following preaspirated consonant or a voiceless fricative) is reported for the Austronesian language Cem of New Caledonia (Rivierre 1993: 162).

16.3.2 Tone from Onset Consonant Features

Perhaps the most geographically widespread tonogenetic trigger is the transfer of a contrast in onset consonant voicing to the following vowel (Hombert 1978: 78, Yu, this volume, Hale, Kissock, & Reiss, this volume). As described above, the widespread tone split that followed the initial development of tone from final consonants in East and Southeast Asia is of this type. But tone may also come from a transfer of features from the onset to the vowel in the first instance.

Those Mon-Khmer languages other than Vietnamese that have developed tone have usually done so by transferring the onset voicing contrast to the following vowel (Svantesson 1991: 67). The effect of voicing on pitch can also be seen in the well-known effect of 'depressor' consonants that cause a tone lowering on the following vowel in some African languages, and is hypothesized to be the source of tones in the Chadic subfamily of Afroasiatic (Wolff 1987). Even languages that have not developed tone in the strict sense of the word show the pitch-lowering effect of voiced aspirated (or 'murmured') consonants; the best-known case is that of the Indo-European language Punjabi (Ohala 1973, Purcell et al. 1978, Bhaskararao 1999). More examples of this type of tonogenesis from Tibeto-Burman could be added to the list.

Although the majority of Mon-Khmer languages of Southeast Asia (with the notable exception of Vietnamese) are atonal, some Mon-Khmer languages that are developing tone do so in this manner. For example, Premsrirat (1999) describes the stages of tone development in seven different dialects of Khmu. Dialects spoken in the eastern area (northwestern Vietnam and northeastern Laos) do not have tone, but have many more onset consonants than those in the west, including four as opposed to two voiced stops and a contrast between voiced and voiceless sonorants. Dialects spoken in the western area (northwestern Laos, northern Thailand, and the Sipsongpanna region in China) have developed either a register (phonation) system or a tone system, representing different stages of tonogenesis. As seen below, in a dialect spoken in Udomsaj Province, Laos (West Khmu 1), a breathy/clear register contrast correlated with original onset consonant voicing has developed. In another dialect spoken in Thailand (West Khmu 2), these same syllables appear as voiceless aspirated stops with clear voice and a lowered tone. In yet another dialect spoken in Luang Namtha Province, Laos (West Khmu 3), these syllables are pronounced with voiceless unaspirated stops and a lowered tone.

	East Khmu	West Khmu 1	West Khmu 2	West Khmu 3
'rice wine'	buːc	pṳːc	phùːc	pùːc

In South Asia, tonogenesis has also been traced to a contrast in onset voicing, although in this case, distinctive voiced aspirated consonants played a role. A contrastive low tone developed in Punjabi from original word-initial voiced aspirated consonants (bh-, dh-, gh-) in the onset, which subsequently devoiced (Gill & Gleason 1972). Bhaskararao (1999: 340–344) reports that there are languages in northern India in the Himalayan region that display different stages of development along this line: *bhV > bhV̀ (Mandeali), *bhV > bV̀ (Northern Haryanvi), *bhV > bV̀ > pV̀ (Punjabi, Kangri, Dogri).

In the Khmu and Punjabi cases, an originally voiced onset consonant did not give a lowered tone on the following vowel immediately; as in tonogenesis from loss of coda consonants described in section 16.3.1, the first step was the development of a breathy vowel, yielding a phonation contrast (breathy/clear), rather than a tone contrast (low/high). If phonation contrasts may arise from either the end or the beginning of the syllable, then the possibility exists that in some Asian languages with two stages of tonogenesis, phonation contrasts from the end of the syllable might not have changed to pure tone contrasts before the second wave of tonogenesis from the front of the syllable began. This is exactly the situation I have reconstructed for Hmong-Mien, which has left traces of different phonation types meeting in the middle of the syllable (Ratliff 2010: 193–197). These traces are of four types: (1) The reflexes of syllables with voiced onsets in the protolanguage still show phonetically lower tones than their voiceless onset counterparts in words belonging to tone categories that can be traced back to syllables with a final -ʔ or -h. These lowered reflexes can be explained if we assume that the breathiness from the original voiced initial, supported by the non-modal quality of the rest of the syllable, whether breathy or creaky, kept the pitch of these syllables depressed. In open clear voice syllables, however, initial-induced breathiness was not as easily sustained; we thus often find the pitch of the 'lower register' tone in this category to be higher than the corresponding upper register tone. (2) There are vestiges of breathiness and creakiness within the modern languages exactly where we would expect them to be if a phonation contrast from the back of the syllable had met a phonation contrast from the front of the syllable. For example, the proto-syllables that began with voiced consonants (and so contributed breathiness from the front) and ended in -h (and so contributed breathiness from the back) are the most reliably breathy syllables in Hmong-Mien languages today. (3) It is well-known that vowel raising is one effect of lax or breathy voice (Thurgood 2002: 349ff.). There are vowel quality splits in the Zongdi language only in those tone categories that would have had breathy phonation type from both the front and a marked phonation type from the back of the syllable; in these categories, the vowels are /e, əa, o, u, u, ɯ, ei/ instead of the expected /æ, a, ɔ, o, ou, ə, æi/, respectively. (4) Complex contour tones (rising-falling or falling-rising) only exist in those tone categories that would have been *clear-creaky or *breathy-creaky originally. Syllables of mixed phonation type may seem odd, but they are well-attested in modern Mon-Khmer languages of the area (for example, see Luang-Thongkum 1991 on Chong).

Another account of tonogenesis from onset consonant features comes from Africa. The Chadic language subfamily of Afroasiatic is characterized by the presence of tone, but since not all Afroasiatic subfamilies contain tone languages, it is assumed that Chadic languages acquired tone after having split from Proto-Afroasiatic. Wolff (1987) explains that most specialists have assumed that Chadic (and some languages of the other southernmost subfamilies, Cushitic and Omotic) acquired tone through contact with people speaking tone languages; in the case of Chadic, the best candidates are speakers of Niger-Congo languages. However, Wolff argues that the familiar tonogenetic process of pitch-lowering after voiced consonants caused tonogenesis in Chadic languages, citing evidence from the central Chadic-speaking area where lowered tones are still associated with voiced onsets in several different languages. Chadic thus differs slightly from the tonogenetic development sketched above: the voicing of initial obstruents assigned pitch to the following vowels, but it was not a trade-off; the voicing contrast was not lost in the process (p. 199).[6]

A minor type of tonogenesis that involves onset consonant features is one triggered by the aspiration of a voiceless aspirated stop. It is the cause of sporadic tertiary tone splits (following the first two waves of tonogenesis caused by loss of coda consonants and merger of voiced and voiceless onsets) in the Asian tone language area, and has been described as the source of the high tone in the Austronesian languages Cem and Pac in New Caledonia (Rivierre 1993: 160).

16.3.3 Tone from Syllable-Internal Features

Less frequently, tone can arise from features of the syllabic nucleus or from whole-syllable features. Three such cases are the development of tone from vowel length, from vowel quality, and from the voice quality of the whole syllable. The last type of tonogenesis (from voice quality, or 'register',[7] to tone) is clearly the same as the last part of a process that originates in coda or onset consonants. But a register contrast can also be taken as the starting point for tonogenesis, as in the Mon-Khmer case cited below.

The development of tone has been attributed to vowel length in three languages from different atonal families: the Mon-Khmer language Hu (Svantesson 1991), the Austronesian language Cem of New Caledonia (Rivierre 1993, 2001) and the Finno-Ugric language Estonian (Lehiste 2004). Of these three cases, only Hu shows a robust connection between vowel length and the significant use of tone; in the latter two cases the tones that developed from long vowels play only a marginal role. The Hu languages show a low-high tone contrast that reflects a long-short vowel contrast in Proto-Palaungic (< Proto-Mon-Khmer), which has been verified both by comparative evidence and instrumental measurement (Svantesson 1991). The Austronesian language Cem has developed a low tone in a number of ways, one of which is from long / aa/ (Rivierre 1993: 162–163). Estonian is characterized by an unusual three-way length contrast. Lehiste (1978, 2004) has shown through experiments involving synthetically manipulated tokens of a minimal triplet that the cue speakers use to identify the 'overlong' vowel is not greater length, but a distinctive rise-fall pitch contour on the vowel. This is the result of the re-association of a pitch contour formerly realized over two syllables to the long vowel of the first syllable in the wake of syncope/apocope, in conjunction with the compensatory lengthening of the long vowel to overlong.

Since high vowels tend to have slightly higher F_o, a vowel quality contrast might be expected to generate a phonological pitch contrast in some languages, but Hombert, Ohala, & Ewan (1979) observe that this is not a common type of tonogenesis, perhaps

---

[6] This has happened in Asia as well. The Hmongic language A-Hmao has undergone the areal tone split on the basis of onset voicing, but has nonetheless retained the voicing contrast in onset obstruents (Wang & Mao 1995: 7).

[7] See footnote 5.

because the higher F_o is a property of the whole vowel, not just the first portion of the vowel to which hearers may be more sensitive. Nonetheless, tonogenesis in the Omotic language Gimira (Tesfaye & Wedekind 1994) is claimed to be a case of this sort: based on measurements that indicate that high vowels /i/, /y/, and /u/ show 'extra-high' allotones of the high tone in the related language Shinasha, vowel height is proposed as at least part of the reason for a greater number of tone contrasts in Gimira.

Luang-Thongkum (1990) has described a register system in the Mon (Mon-Khmer) language of Thailand in which the registers are now developing pitch as a significant cue. In this language, the tense vowels have an F_o that is significantly higher than that of the lax vowels. She also examines the contribution of pre-vocalic consonants to the development of pitch contrasts, and comes to the following conclusion: '... tones or lexically contrastive pitches have developed primarily from voice register governing the whole syllable. The phonation types of the consonants, voiced and voiceless, play a less important role. Their contribution is to add more tones to the tonal system (high vs low) which already exists' (p. 13). That not all Mon-Khmer register contrasts come from consonants in the first place has been shown by Diffloth (1982) for the Katuic language Pacoh, which is why it is important to differentiate this process from the onset consonant > register > tone process described for Khmu in section 16.3.2. In the Pacoh case, Diffloth traces the origin of tense voice ('pharyngealization') in three long mid vowels to a redistribution of vowels in a very crowded vowel space. Original long mid vowels /ee/ and /oo/ lowered and tensed (to /ɛɛ/ and /ɔɔ/) in a move to accommodate two new long mid vowels: /ee/ (from *ɯʌ) and /oo/ (from *əə) (pp. 56-59).

16.4 Changes in Tones and Tone Inventories

16.4.1 Phonetic Changes

Once born, a tone is not necessarily stable. Although the most salient phonetic cue of a tone is relative pitch, tone may be signalled by other phonetic cues as well: voice quality, vowel duration, pitch movement, and even vowel quality may also help hearers identify particular tokens as representative of a particular tone (Andruski & Ratliff 2000). The complex composition of a tone, as much as its phonological environment, gives ample opportunity for tones to change as one component of the abstract toneme comes to the fore while another recedes. For example, in Hmong-Mien, as in Vietnamese, the tones of original open syllables with voiceless onsets are hypothesized to have been level and high, and the tones of original open syllables with voiced onsets are hypothesized to have been level and low, but the phonetic values of the modern-day reflexes of these two original tones at 23 different sampling sites are quite diverse (Wang & Mao 1995). Just as many contour tones as level tones are attested, and in half the locations the low register tone (from an original voiced onset) has a higher tone than the corresponding high register tone (from an original voiceless onset). It is thus impossible to predict the phonetic value of any modern tone in this tone category on the basis of its historical origin.

Another obvious phonetic change that has occurred as phonation systems born in the East and Southeast Asian area evolved into tone systems is that the inherently lower pitch of breathy voiced syllables became the dominant cue for the category, at the expense of the breathiness, which in many, but not all, cases subsequently disappeared (Thurgood 2002).

16.4.2 Mergers and Splits

Tones not only change within themselves; like segmental splits and mergers (Gordon, Cser, and Salmons & Honeybone, all this volume), tone distinctions may also either multiply or disappear. A fruitful approach to the historical study of tone in wide use by linguists studying Asian languages with large tone inventories has been the mapping of tone splits and mergers across closely related languages. Haudricourt's tonogenetic model yields eight basic tone categories: four contrasts from the end of the syllable times two contrasts from the front of the syllable (see section 16.3.1). These eight tone categories may split further in the Southeast Asian area on the basis of one or more of the following additional contrasts: aspiration, prenasalization, preglottalization in the onset, and vowel length in closed syllables. Given the high number of potential tone contrasts in these languages, it is not surprising to find complex and highly specific patterns of tone split and merger that prove useful in defining dialect areas and reconstructing low-level subgroups. Tone splits and mergers have been studied especially closely in the Tai family using William Gedney's 'tone box', presented in abbreviated form in Table 16.2 below, that allows the fieldworker to record data in a way that will elucidate tone splits and mergers for any Tai language variety encountered (Gedney 1972, Hudak 2004).

The columns of the box indicate the absence or presence of a specific type of syllable-final consonant in the protolanguage that gave rise to four potential tone

Table 16.2 Gedney's 'tone box'

	A	B	C	D-short	D-long
*s-,*hm-,	eat	egg	rice	flea	broken
*ph- ...	leg	split	shirt	ripe	gums
*p- ...	year	forest	aunt	frog	lungs
	eye	chicken	boil	liver	wing
*ʔ-, *ʔb- ...	fly	shoulder	crazy	fishhook	sunshine
	red	scold	village	raw	bathe
*b-, *m-, *l - ...	hand	father	water	bird	knife
	rice field	dry field	wood	tie up	child

contrasts; the last column is split in two to indicate the first possible type of tertiary split, one according to vowel length in syllables closed by a stop consonant. The four rows of the tone box correspond to four different onset classes: voiceless fricatives, sonorants, and aspirated stops; voiceless unaspirated stops; glottalized consonants; and voiced consonants. Each of the 20 cells so determined contains three or four Proto-Tai words of the shape defined by the intersection of each row and column; the fieldworker can thus efficiently determine through elicitation of just a few words which tone splits and mergers have taken place in a particular language.

Tone inventories expand (and contract) in African languages as well, of course. Clements & Rialland (2008: 70–74) have mapped the number of tone levels attested in Africa, and have reported that Wedekind's (1985) account of the source of five level tones in Bench Gimira (Omotic) can serve to explain other 'tonally loaded' languages of Africa as well. A split of three level tones into four or five level tones is a result of monosyllabicization in these languages. They illustrate the development with two closely-related Gur languages, Gulmancema of Burkina Faso (three levels) and Moba of Togo (four levels):

Gulmancema	Moba	
ò kándì [káⁿdì]	ù kǎnt	"s/he stepped over ..."
ò kándí	ù kánt	"s/he steps over ..."

What is phonetically a non-distinctive higher high tone in Gulmancema preceding a low tone becomes an overhigh toneme in Moba upon loss of the final syllable.

16.4.3 Flip-Flops

A challenge to historical phonologists is presented by those cases in which the high and low tones in a two-tone language are reversed in a sister language, so that cognate words consistently have a high tone in one language and a low tone in the other. The most satisfying type of account for unexpected patterns of this sort focuses on the phonetic details of the sounds that triggered tonogenesis at the time of the feature transfer (Hombert 1984, Kingston 2003). Kingston gives a persuasive explanation of two different types of high tone to low tone correspondences in Athabaskan languages at two different historical periods that depend on an understanding of low-level phonetic facts (Kingston 2003, 2005). The first took place within Athabaskan languages that developed tones from final glottal and glottalized consonants. Two paths were taken: in one 'low' group of languages (e.g. Gwich'in) the constricted voice preceding stem-final glottalic consonants involved slack vocal folds leading to creaky voice quality, but in another 'high' group of languages (e.g. Chipewyan) it involved stiff vocal folds leading to tense voice quality. 'The final stage is a shift from speakers' producing one or the other constricted voice quality with its characteristic F_0 value, low in creaky voice and high in tense voice, to producing the F_0 value alone, in modal voice' (Kingston 2005: 163). The result is a regular correspondence between low tone in one group of Athabaskan languages and high tone in another.

Kingston uses his explanation of the second variety of Athabaskan 'flip-flop' to account for high tone to low tone correspondences in some Bantu languages as well. These cases of tone reversal all follow from the syntagmatic nature of tone realization. According to Kingston, these flip-flops are due to perceptual mistakes—either (1) the late realization of a tone that leads listeners to assign the tone of the preceding syllable to the following syllable, an effect made more likely when the second syllable is shortened, or (2) the exaggeration of one tone value before a tone of the opposite value. In the latter case, the *unexaggerated* tones are liable to be mistaken for tones of the opposite value (Kingston 2003: 85–108).

In Africa, Wolff (1987: 211) reports that Kanakuru has the opposite values from those predicted for (and found in) other Chadic languages: a low tone (a L-H pattern) follows voiceless and glottalized stops and a high tone (a H-L pattern) follows voiced stops (Newman 1974: 14). Wolff accounts for this by positing a simple tone dissimilation rule. However, this unexpected pattern could be more satisfactorily explained if we consider the range of phonetic detail that could have led to such an unusual outcome, following Hombert and Kingston. For example, higher tones develop following voiced implosives (Ohala 1973); the voiced stops of Kanukuru may have been pronounced in this way at the time of tonogenesis. Hombert also points out that some hearers attend more closely to the initial portion of the vowel and generalize to the whole syllable, whereas others attend more closely to the direction of the pitch change, and would thus hear a rising tone following a voiced stop onset as high, and a falling tone following a voiceless stop onset as low. It is conceivable that different communities of speaker/hearers phonologized different portions of the same pitch contour, giving rise to opposite values for the same historical tone category.

16.5 LANGUAGE CONTACT AND TONE CHANGE

16.5.1 Broad Invocation of a Contact Explanation

The prosodic aspects of language—not only tone, but also word structure, metrical structure, and vowel length—are highly diffusible through contact, as has often been pointed out (e.g. Salmons 1992a, Donegan 1993b, Donegan & Stampe 2002, Matisoff 2006, Ratliff 2007, Lahiri, this volume). It is not accidental that languages of the South China/Southeast Asian sprachbund not only all have tone, but are all tone languages of the same type, with large tone inventories, unitary contour tones as well as level tones, non-modal phonation working within the tone system as a perceptual cue, and primarily lexical rather than grammatical tone function. Furthermore, as explained above, historical research has shown that these languages developed their tone systems in the same way. The distribution of tone languages within the Tibeto-Burman and Afroasiatic families, families half of whose languages are tonal and half atonal, also show the effect of contact. The tone languages in these families are in geographic proximity to other tone languages: Tibeto-Burman tone languages are in the east near Chinese, Tai-Kadai and Hmong-Mien languages rather than in the west, and Afroasiatic tone languages are in the south near Niger-Congo languages rather than in the north. The case of Vietnamese is even more striking, since the vast majority of Mon-Khmer (and Austroasiatic) languages are atonal, and the emergence of tone in Vietnamese occurred in the middle of the period of Chinese presence in the area, roughly between 100 BC and 900 AD.

One can find appeal to a broad contact explanation for the presence of tone in languages one would expect to be atonal. For example, '... within Afroasiatic, all Chadic languages are tonal; since Proto-Afroasiatic was probably not tonal, the most likely source of tone in Chadic is early and continued contact with non-Afroasiatic tone languages' (Schuh 2003, quoted in Clements & Rialland 2008: 72). Furthermore, it has been claimed that not just tones but the entire Asian system of tonal contrasts (four tone categories times two registers) was originally Chinese & was borrowed by Hmong-Mien, Tai, and Vietnamese, all of which were originally atonal: '... Vietnamese, under direct Chinese domination lost the... initial syllables of MK [Mon-Khmer] while directly borrowing the tonal system...' (Benedict 1997: 4).

Yet such a broad use of contact as an explanation for the presence of tone ultimately fails to satisfy, because it does not explain exactly *how* tones were either transferred to—or stimulated to develop in—previously atonal languages under contact with neighbouring (or dominating) tone languages (see also Lahiri, this volume, on the care that needs to be exercised when invoking contact as cause for change in a prosodic system). A more refined understanding of the nature of the interaction that leads to tone development in atonal languages will come from studies of tonogenesis and tone change under contact in specific multilingual communities, and the application of these findings to an account of tone diffusion across languages under contact in the distant past.

16.5.2 Studies of Language Contact and Tone Change

The two focused studies summarized briefly below involve contact between genetically unrelated languages and the tonal outcomes.

In the first, Luang-Thongkum (1997) presents a case study of language change in progress among younger speakers of Mien, a Hmong-Mien tone language, in a village near Chiangmai, Thailand. Standard Thai, also a tone language, is used as the medium of instruction in the local school, and both Northern Thai and Standard Thai are spoken widely. In this dialect of Mien, speakers are in the process of reducing their number of tones from six to five, bringing Mien in line with Standard Thai, and are also adjusting the phonetic values of the tones themselves to be more in accord with the phonetic values of Thai tones.

In the second case, Tsat, an originally atonal Austronesian language of Hainan Island, developed a complex system of tones under the influence of neighbouring

Table 16.3 Tsat tonogenesis

	Tsat	Chinese (Tanchou)	Li (Tongshi)	Li (Yuanmen)
high level	55	55	55	55
falling	42	—	43	42
mid level	33	22	33	44
rising	24	35	13	13
low level	11	11	11	11

tone languages (see Thurgood 1999 for a full account and further references). Tones developed in Tsat under the influence of the local (Min) varieties of Chinese and the Tai-Kadai language Li. The tone system that developed in Tsat is similar in nature to the Thai-influenced Mien described by Luang-Thongkum: the number of tones and the tone values are almost the same as those of these two neighbouring languages which Tsat speakers know well, a case of surface convergence, as can be seen in Table 16.3.

The key difference between this situation and the early Sinospheric contact situation that gave rise to tones in the classic fashion described by Haudricourt is that Tsat developed tones in its own way, in a two-by-three system, where the initials started the tonogenetic process and the later split was conditioned by the finals. Chinese borrowings in Tsat are pronounced with whatever tone is phonetically most similar (Thurgood, p.c. 2002): 'it is not being argued that the Tsat tonal *system* is borrowed from one of these languages' (Thurgood 1999: 231).

16.5.3 Tone Diffusion under Contact in the Past

Elsewhere I have categorized modern-day or recent studies of the type described above according to the nature of the donor and the nature of the borrower in an effort to understand the type of contact situation that could have led to a transfer of tone from Chinese to Proto-Hmong-Mien between 1,500 and 2,000 years ago (Ratliff 2005, 2010; for a somewhat different categorization of outcomes given the same set of contact situations involving tone and loanwords, see Uffmann, this volume). My findings should also help clarify the contact situation between Chinese and Vietnamese and the contact situation between Chinese and Proto-Tai that led to the development of identical tone systems across these languages. The most puzzling problem is how one language could have borrowed not only individual tones (which is itself problematic), but an entire tone system: the perfect tone category correspondences in Chinese loanwords from the Early Middle Chinese period—where a Chinese word occupies exactly the same cell in a Chinese tone chart defined by final laryngeal and onset voicing as does the Hmong-Mien loanword in an analogous Hmong-Mien tone chart—has been attributed to the fact that Hmong-Mien borrowed the entire four-by-two tone system from

Chinese (Ying 1972, Benedict 1997, Matisoff 1999). In Table 16.4 below, following the convention in work on Asian tone languages, the letters 'A, B, C, D' refer to primary tone category as determined by the syllable-final consonant and the numbers '1, 2' refer to secondary tone category as determined by the voicing of the syllable-initial consonant, as given in the last column (cf. Table 16.1 in section 16.3.1).

But how do speakers hear and borrow tone categories or tone systems? It has long been assumed that Chinese was tonal before its neighbours were, but a close study of contact situations where the donor was tonal and the borrower atonal has shown that this was probably not the case.

Of the four possible contact scenarios involving a donor, a borrower, and the features [+tone] and [−tone], three can be ruled out for the situation at the time the borrowings in Table 16.4 took place. Simplifying the picture to the most common outcomes under these three contact scenarios: (1) if Chinese had been atonal and Hmong-Mien had been tonal at the time of these borrowings, a prominent stress in Chinese loanwords might have been interpreted as either a common tone or a special 'loan tone' (see cases of English loanwords in Thai and Cantonese, and Thai loanwords in Malay); (2) if Chinese and Hmong-Mien had both been tonal at the time of these borrowings, we would expect Hmong-Mien speakers to have mapped each Chinese tone to its closest equivalent in Hmong-Mien, regardless of historical tone category (see modern loans from Chinese to the other tonal languages of the area and the Mien/Thai contact situation presented above); and (3) if Chinese had been tonal and Hmong-Mien had been atonal at the time of these borrowings—the most widely-held assumption concerning language contact and change in this case—we would expect loanwords either to have been borrowed without tone, had they been few in number (see cases of loanwords from Chinese and other tone languages in English), or, in a case of close and prolonged contact, such as that described for Tsat in the context of tone languages on Hainan Island, we might expect first monosyllabization followed by a novel kind of tonogenesis within the atonal borrower. None of these contact situations would have yielded a pattern similar to this one: identically structured systems,

Table 16.4 Chinese/Hmong-Mien tone category correspondences

	Mandarin	Middle Chinese	White Hmong	Hmong-Mien	Syllable type in both families
金	jīn 'metal'	kim A1	kub [ku⁵⁵] 'gold'	*kjeəm A1	$C_{vl}V(N)$
銀	yín 'silver'	ngin A2	nyiaj [njia⁵²]	*ɲʷjən A2	$C_{vd}V(N)$
桶	tǒng 'bucket'	thuwng-ʔ B1	thoob [thɔŋ⁵⁵]	*thɔŋ-ʔ B1	$C_{vl}V(N)$-ʔ
瓦	wǎ 'tile'	ngwæ-ʔ B2	vuas [vua²²]	*ŋʷæ-ʔ B2	$C_{vd}V(N)$-ʔ
炭	tàn 'charcoal'	than-h C1	thee [thɛŋ³³]	*than-h C1	$C_{vl}V(N)$-h
箸	zhù 'chopsticks'	drjo-h C2	rawg [rau³¹]	*drou-h C2	$C_{vd}V(N)$-h
百	bǎi 'hundred'	pæk D1	pua [pua³³]	*pæk D1	$C_{vl}VC$
十	shí 'ten'	dzyip D2	kaum [kau²¹]	*gjuɛp D2	$C_{vd}VC$

and borrowed words which occupy analogous places in the systems of both donor and borrower language.

But if neither Hmong-Mien *nor* Chinese had tones at the time these early loans were made, it is possible to imagine how the striking cross-family correspondence of tone categories in loanwords could have arisen. Hmong-Mien could have borrowed the Chinese words along with the segmental material which eventually gave rise to tones intact. Then if both had developed tones in exactly the same way, out of the laryngeal features of word-final consonants as tonogenesis swept across the area—started by an unknown trigger language, not necessarily by Chinese—then these regular correspondences would have appeared. Although Chinese contact is probably to be credited with making Hmong-Mien and other languages of the south monosyllabic-word languages and thus 'tone prone' (Matisoff 1973: 89), it is not clear that Chinese acquired tones before other languages in the area. Since the later merger of initials and compensatory tone split are understood as happening in a wave across the whole area, it is plausible that the initial wave of tonogenesis was an areal phenomenon as well. If we accept the proposal that Hmong-Mien borrowed its earliest Chinese loanwords before tones developed, it is no longer necessary to answer the ill-conceived question of how these languages might have borrowed a tone system and historical tone categories. The question then gets 'pushed backward' to how these languages became predominantly monosyllabic-word languages, with the same onset contrast (voiced/voiceless) and the same coda consonants (nasals, voiceless stops, -h, -ʔ).

In the case of the proliferation of tone levels in African languages (see section 16.4.2), Clements & Rialland (2008) have come to a similar conclusion. The tones themselves were not borrowed in the 'tonally loaded' languages of East and West Africa that contrast four or five tone levels,[8] but there was diffusion of the prosodic preconditions for the development of additional tone levels: 'While systems with multiple tone levels usually arise from internal factors, the fact that such systems cluster together suggest areal diffusion, if not of multiple tonal levels directly, then of the phonological factors (loss of syllables, etc.) that underlie them' (p. 74).

---

[8] Most of these languages lie within a band across equatorial Africa, with one Khoisan outlier in Botswana. Most interesting for the question of contact and change are those three areas where the languages are not closely related: the Ivorian zone (Kru, Mande, Kwa), the Nigerian-Cameroon zone (Adamawa-Ubangi, Idomoid, Cross River, Jukunoid Northern Bantoid), and the CAR-DRC border zone (Adamawa-Ubangi and Bantu) (Clements & Rialland 2008: 73).

CHAPTER 17

··

THE ROLE OF PROSODIC TEMPLATES IN DIACHRONY

··

LAURA CATHARINE SMITH AND ADAM USSISHKIN

17.1 INTRODUCTION

IT has been widely observed among the world's languages that prosodic templates can shape lexical classes by determining canonical forms of words (e.g. McCarthy & Prince 1986, 1995, Holsinger 2000, Wiese 1996, 2001, Booij 1998). While templatic well-formedness shapes small sets of items in some languages, it defines most vocabulary in others. We argue that when viewed diachronically, prosodic templates provide a grounded explanation for otherwise divergent sound patterns across languages. We draw evidence from Mixtec, Semitic, and Germanic and show how each language or language family provides evidence for distinct roles for prosodic templates in change.

We provide a brief background in section 17.2 on templates in sound change and turn in section 17.3 to patterns best accounted for using prosodic templates. In section 17.4 we explore why forms may fail to conform to prescribed templates, highlighting the tension between prosody and other phonological and morphological forces. Lastly, dialect data in section 17.5 illustrate the resilience of templates across time in languages, where sometimes templatic effects have been expanded, while in other cases they have been lost or obscured. This section brings our discussion full circle before we close in section 17.6.

17.2 BACKGROUND TO PROSODIC TEMPLATES AND SOUND CHANGE

Until the early 1980s, theories of sound change focused overwhelmingly on the segmental or featural levels with little attention paid to structures above the segment.

With Murray & Vennemann's (1983) seminal article on the Preference Laws for syllable structure and Vennemann's (1988) book elaborating on those laws, researchers began searching for motivations for sound change above the segment at the syllabic level (see Mailhammer, Restle, & Vennemann, this volume, for a contemporary consideration of such work). Drawing on Vennemann's earlier synchronic work on Syllabic Phonology (e.g. Vennemann 1972b, 1974b, 1978), Murray & Vennemann's new Preference Laws demonstrated that sound change can result from preferences for syllables to conform to the ideal CV shape. Seeking explanations for sound change up the prosodic hierarchy emerged on the heels of work in synchronic phonology (e.g. Vennemann 1972b, 1978), providing researchers with a means of connecting seemingly divergent sound patterns across unrelated language families. Many historical phonologists adopted these developments from synchronic phonology as has been done with other theoretical advances before and since, e.g. feature geometry.

Another key development likewise offers historical linguists a further set of tools to explain sound change and patterns across the lexicon, namely prosodic templates. Templates generally require reference to specific prosodic structures, moving our focus up yet another level in the prosodic hierarchy from the syllable to the foot. Many phonologists, starting in the late 1970s, focused on this area, with one of the best known phonological approaches to use prosodic templates being the programme initiated by McCarthy & Prince (1986, *et seq.*). To account for a range of synchronic patterns, including reduplication, truncation, language games, and other nonconcatenative processes, McCarthy & Prince proposed the Prosodic Morphology Hypothesis (PMH), which simply states that all such processes manipulate and refer only to 'authentic units of prosody'. These units are defined as the hierarchical components of the prosodic hierarchy (e.g. Selkirk 1980a,b) illustrated in (1):

(1) The Prosodic Hierarchy

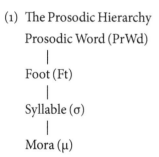

Prosodic Word (PrWd)
|
Foot (Ft)
|
Syllable (σ)
|
Mora (μ)

So what are these templates in practical terms and how do we view them here for the purposes of this chapter? We use the term 'template' in a broad sense, following Macken & Salmons (1997) who state that 'a prosodic template is a conventionalized unit—a single unit—that imposes constraints on the surface form of words and, in so doing, encodes a particular relationship between words thus related' (p. 37). In this broader sense, templates can account for divergent phenomena ranging from the required surface structure of Semitic verbs or nouns, to the choice of plural suffix in Dutch or German so that the plural form matches a specified prosodic shape, to even the licensing of features or segments that surface or not based on their position relative to the template (see below). By taking a more general approach to the term template, we see that predetermined prosodic patterns play a role in determining what segments or features can and will surface in the phonology and morphology of a language. Such an approach to templates has been taken elsewhere in phonology, including by adherents of Government Phonology who have made substantial use of templates in their work (e.g. Caha & Scheer 2008). Moreover, Harris (2004), Wiese (2001), and others have argued for the important role of the foot in shaping the phonology and morphology of various languages, an assumption we likewise make in our discussions of prosodic templates in this chapter. We nevertheless remain somewhat agnostic with regard to specific theoretical frameworks, to help introduce a broader audience to the benefits of appealing to prosodic templates in explaining language change.

Recent work proposes in fact that while many patterns robustly support the Prosodic Morphology Hypothesis, others show that it may be better viewed as a strong tendency rather than an absolute. Blevins (2010a) states that 'phonological form classes... may best be modeled as statistical positive generalizations over the lexicon'. For instance, in Proto-Austronesian over 90 percent of lexical bases were bisyllabic.[1] While this prevalence for bisyllabicity is certainly reflected in modern-day Austronesian languages, it is not an exception-free generalization.

Another important theme currently being explored by various researchers (Bybee 2001, Pierrehumbert 2001, Blevins 2004a, 2010a, Chitoran & Hualde 2007, Wedel 2007), and one we apply here, is that strong statistical generalizations could exert an effect on language change without being exceptionless. That is, it should not be surprising to uncover patterns that while robust are nonetheless not exhaustively followed within a particular language. Given the impressive number of cues and features language learners can attend to (e.g. Newport & Aslin 2004), we expect to find noisiness in the data, in other words exceptions to the expected patterns. Thanks to research most recently by Blevins (2004 *et seq.*, this volume), historical linguistics is seen by some as playing a larger role in our understanding of synchronic patterns. Blevins argues that common sound patterns evidenced both synchronically and diachronically stem from the fact that languages at any point in time are simply the result of earlier language change. In other words, synchronic patterns are the result of diachronic developments. Consequently, understanding the role of prosodic templates in the history of a language helps us better account for the patterns we see synchronically. Moreover, these templates could be viewed as an additional means of automation of repeated behaviours, namely matching words to specified shapes and patterns that take hold in the language, which automation Bybee (this volume) notes plays a key role in language change and they serve as patterns that speakers use to perceive and produce language (cf. Fertig, this volume).

---

[1] We acknowledge that reconstructions are not attested, and that comparative reconstruction often introduces biases, including shaping a proto-lexicon into something more uniform in some ways than the actual language might have been (see Fox, this volume for a discussion of issues related to reconstruction).

We begin here with an overview of foot types found cross-linguistically. One of the most comprehensive surveys of foot typology is found in Hayes (1995), which contains not only a wealth of data on prosodic and metrical structures in language but also examines attested patterns, discovering an unexpected asymmetry (see also Lahiri, this volume, for a discussion of foot typology, and of the role of feet in phonological change). Of four logical possibilities, just three foot types appear to be prevalent cross-linguistically: the moraic trochee, the syllabic trochee, and the moraic iamb. Interestingly, the syllabic iamb is missing. Again, while robust patterns exist, further study frequently reveals that 'universals' are less universal than originally thought. We advocate a similar view here for templates in general: templatic effects can predominate in a language even if they are not absolute. Moreover, while templatically-driven changes can in principle apply throughout an entire language, they tend to apply within a given set of lexical classes (Smith 2004, 2007b, 2009, Ussishkin 2005, Blevins 2010a).

Of relevance here are the syllabic and moraic trochee. The syllabic trochee consists of a stressed-unstressed syllable sequence as in (2a). Foot boundaries are indicated by '[ ]':

(2) (a) Syllabic trochee
     [σ́ σ]
     wín.ter
  (b) Moraic trochee
    (i) Old High German *gasti* 'guest'
      [H] L   Syllabic level (H=heavy σ (2 or more morae); L=light σ (1 mora))
      μμ μ   Moraic level (μ=mora)
      [gas] ti Segmental level
    (ii) Old Saxon *stedi* 'town, place'
      [L L] Syllabic level
      μ μ   Moraic level
      [ste.di] Segmental level

The moraic trochee, on the other hand, is based on the amount of segmental material found within a syllable's rhyme, material referred to as morae (μ). When rhymes consist of VC, e.g. [gas], or a single long vowel, V̄, e.g. [thrā], they are considered minimally bimoraic and form a heavy syllable (H). These heavy syllables are capable of forming their own foot (cf. 2bi). A monomoraic syllable containing just a short vowel is considered light, unable to form a foot on its own, e.g. the final syllable *ti* in *gasti* above in (2bi). However, a sequence of two light syllables (LL), e.g. *ste+di* with their two morae combined can form a foot equal to that of a single heavy syllable (cf. 2bii) (cf. Hayes 1995).[2] Foot structure provides one means speakers use to perceive and segment sounds and words, starting already in the first year of life (Jusczyk et al. 1999).

---

[2] In Germanic, the prosodic equivalence of LL with H is known as resolution (Dresher & Lahiri 1991; cf. also Lahiri, this volume).

Previous research has demonstrated repeatedly that phonetic considerations, combined with potential misperceptions (Ohala 1981, 1989, Blevins 2004a, this volume, Blevins & Wedel 2009; see also Yu, this volume) may play a major role in language change. One of our goals is to complement this work with arguments that language change can also be shaped by prosodic considerations that can be captured with a template.

17.3 ROLE OF PROSODIC TEMPLATES IN (MORPHO-)PHONOLOGICAL CHANGE

Drawing on evidence from three unrelated language families, we illustrate the range of language changes and structures for which prosodic templates can account. While not all language families or languages exhibit prosodically-driven changes, some languages do; the evidence below thus shows the breadth of languages and structures that are templatically-shaped, underscoring the fact that these templates are neither accidental nor coincidental. We start with morphological and phonological evidence from Semitic, before turning to lenition, onset licensing and harmony in Highlands Mixtec. We then conclude with historical and dialect examples from West Germanic.

17.3.1 Well-known Templatic Properties: Semitic

We begin with the Semitic sub-group of the Afro-Asiatic language family. Semitic languages are well-known for what has become known in the literature as 'root-and-pattern morphology', a sub-type of nonconcatenative morphology, a more general label for morphological processes requiring an interface between morphology and phonology. This interface is manifested via the persistent and pervasive template patterns found across the Semitic languages. Much evidence has accumulated in the synchronic literature concerning templatic effects in Semitic (e.g. McCarthy 1979, 1981, Ussishkin 2005, Bat-El 2011). Perhaps the best-known examples from Semitic concern verbal classes (known in the Semitic literature as *binyanim*), which are defined by templates holding consistently throughout various categories. In general, the template tends to correlate with syntactic properties, though not always (Laks 2010, 2011). Well-known verbal templatic structures are found in a diverse array of languages, including the Semitic stratum of verbs in Maltese, all verbs in Arabic and Hebrew, and verbs in Ethio-Semitic languages (which are templatic despite failing to conform to the binyan system in Arabic and Hebrew). Other morphological categories are likewise marked by templates; nouns also exhibit numerous templatic properties, though across Semitic nouns seem to not be limited to as strict a set of templates as verbs.

One question in diachronic approaches concerns how these templates arose. Furthermore, it is important to examine what tendencies exist across Semitic languages and dialects. Recent evidence from dialectal study reveals some robust patterns. Simpson (2009) presents a vast array of dialectal data from numerous Semitic dialects showing that a single type of change (vowel deletion and reduction) results in modification of templates from previous stages of the language but reinforces different templates, affecting verbal systems in particular. The result is that where the change has taken place, the inflected verbs that are affected lose a syllable of the stem template, resulting in CCVC-stems. To begin, consider the Classical Arabic inflected perfective verbal paradigm in (3):

(3) Classical Arabic verbal inflection for the perfective verb 'to write':

	Singular	Plural
1st person	katab-tu	katab-na:
2nd person masc.	katab-ta	katab-tum
2nd person fem	katab-ti	katab-tunna
3rd person masc	katab-a	katab-u:
3rd fem	katab-at	katab-na

Note that in Classical Arabic, the verbal stem (*katab*) conforms consistently to a bisyllabic template. However, across numerous dialects of Arabic descended from Classical Arabic, vowel reduction is a common occurrence. According to Simpson (2009), such reduction usually targets either the final stem vowel under vowel-initial suffixation (e.g. Classical Arabic *kátab-at* > Jewish Tunisian *kə́tb-ət* 'to write fem.sg.perf.') or the first stem vowel under specific prosodic conditions (when the final vowel attracts stress; see data in (4)):

(4) Pretonic reduction in Al-Mahabšeh dialect of Yemen (data from Simpson 2009; originally from Diem 1973: 72)

	SG	PL
1	ktab-t	ktab-na
2M	ktab-t	ktab-tu
2F	ktab-ti	ktab-tinna
3M	ktab	ktab-u
3F	ktab-an	ktab-na

In (4), the stem consistently surfaces as monosyllabic, so the typical bisyllabic Classical Arabic template does not hold for this dialect. Rather than a trochee consisting of [CV.CV] (the final C in CVCVC is extrametrical; see McCarthy & Prince 1995), in this dialect the stem becomes a monosyllabic moraic trochee of the shape CVCC. Similar changes are found in numerous related forms of Arabic described in detail by Simpson (2009), including, the Al-Mahabšeh dialect of Yemen, Cairene, Upper Egyptian, and Khartoum Arabic, the Levantine dialects of Palmyra and Baksinta, Meccan Arabic, Yemeni southern plateau Arabic, Baghdad Christian and Jewish Arabic, Eastern Libyan Arabic, and Kuwaiti Arabic. In addition, Simpson documents such changes in Babylonian and Palestinian Jewish Aramaic, other Aramaic dialects, Biblical Hebrew, Geʿez, and Tigre.

These phonologically induced changes result in a system that maintains consonantal melodies consistently across paradigms of related words as well as a consistent prosodic pattern. As Simpson (2009) argues, these outcomes result from reinterpretation over time of segmentally-conditioned alternations and prosodically-conditioned alternations. Templatic behaviour thus emerges as the result of these alternations over time.

It is well-known that Arabic makes use of the foot in its templatic structure. McCarthy & Prince (1990) and Hayes (1995), among others, have observed before that moraic trochees explain metrical and stress facts in Classical Arabic and in many spoken varieties. This observation forms the core of Ussishkin's (2000) prosodic account of Classical Arabic verb structure, where the productive verbal classes are seen to involve a single moraic trochee in uninflected stems.

17.3.2 Prosodic Templates in Highlands Mixtec

In one of the first diachronic analyses to incorporate a prosodic template, Macken & Salmons (1997) demonstrated that a series of sound changes and patterns found in Highlands Mixtec could not be explained solely based on syllables. Instead, these changes could be accounted for using a bisyllabic template. An Otomanguean language spoken in southern Mexico, Highland Mixtec displays templatic effects in the behaviour of glides, *sC* clusters, lenition of medial consonants, vowel harmony and tonal melodies. As they argue, 'the distinction between the foot template and other syllable sequences in the grammar is crucial for all [these] phonological processes [...], because non-template syllables fail to participate in those processes which should otherwise be available to monosyllabic morphemes' (p. 42). Their template is provided in (5).

(5) Mixtec template (Macken & Salmons 1997)
   ω minimum = σσ

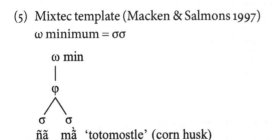

   We highlight a few trends that can be related to this template.

17.3.2.1 *Loss of Template-medial Consonants*

In both the San Miguel and Chalcatongo dialects, medial consonants in *ivɨ* sequences are lost but to differing degrees. In the examples in (6), Chalcatongo is more innovative, eliminating medial /b/, i.e. [v], from sequences that surface as Cɨvɨ in San Miguel (Macken & Salmons 1997: 456):

(6) Medial /b/ loss in Chalcatongo

San Miguel		*Chalcatongo*	*Gloss*
(a) Cɨvɨ	>	Cɨu	
ndívɨ̀		ndiù	'egg'
kɨvɨ̀		kɨù	'day'
andívɨ́		andíú	'sky'
kɨ̀vɨ		kɨu	'enter'
(b) Cɨʔvɨ	>	Cɨʔu	
síʔvɨ́		síʔu	'name'
tɨʔvi		tɨʔu	'to suck'
lɨʔvɨ́		lɨʔú	'slick'
sɨ̀ʔvɨ		tesɨ̀ʔu	'spit~to spit'

According to Macken & Salmons, Chalcatongo Mixtec lost labial obstruents in template-medial position. As the examples in (6a) show, this loss would have resulted in dispreferred syllable structure CVCV → CVV à la Murray & Vennemann (1983) with the loss of the consonant in syllable onset position. This runs counter to Vennemann's (1988: 13–21) Head Law which states that the syllable onset is a position of strengthening since the greater the consonantal strength of an onset, the more preferred it will be (cf. Mailhammer et al., this volume). Although the labial glides have indeed strengthened to /b/ in word-initial syllable onsets, they have conversely undergone deletion in syllable onsets word-medially. In sum, syllable structure cannot account for these data. If the syllable alone were responsible, then we would expect strengthening and retention of /b/ in syllable onsets regardless of whether these onsets were in word-initial or medial-position. When viewed from a templatic perspective, however, the explanation is more straightforward. Simply put, [v] is retained in template-initial position, but lost in template-medial position. Macken & Salmons (1997: 51) explain this as follows: 'Synchronically, the tendency is for the first syllable of the template to carry substantially more phonological material than the second [...] just as the tendency toward CVV roots reflects the second-position weakening tendencies'.

17.3.2.2 *sC-clusters*

Syllable structure also fails to account for the distribution of *sC*-clusters. While many have attributed (s)(C)V sequences as part of the syllable canon, this approach misses a critical generalization, namely that *sC*-clusters are not found in all syllable onsets. These clusters are restricted to template-initial position.[3] Arising from *sV* sequences prefixed onto roots and still evidenced in the alternation between *s-* and *sa*-causatives, the loss of the prefix vowel worsens syllable structure, e.g. **sVCVCV** > **sCVCV**. This change, however, prosodically reshapes the words such that the preferred disyllabic structure at the very heart of the template in Mixtec is reestablished. Indeed adherence to the foot template trumps syllabic preferences. But perhaps most notably, vowel loss creates these new clusters in the grammar in precisely the strongest prosodic position where the most contrasts and phonological material are licensed, namely in template-initial position, the same position where glides were strengthened to [b], rather than lost.

17.3.2.3 *Vowel Harmony*

A number of other developments and patterns can also be explained using the same template already proposed above for Chalcatongo. One such pattern among innovative speakers in Chalcatongo is vowel harmony that typically eliminates the contrast between /i/ and /ɨ/ found in San Miguel in favour of /ɨ/:

(7) Chalcatongo vowel harmony: i~ɨ
     San Miguel   *Chalcatongo*
     (a) CɨCi   >   CɨCɨ
         niñi   niñɨ́   'corncob'
         sándɨžɨ   sá-ndɨžɨ   'to play tricks on'
         kɨ́ži   kɨži   'jug'
     (b) CiCɨ   >   CɨCɨ
         čiŋgɨ   čɨ́ŋgɨ́   'to curl'
         žitɨ   žitɨ   'candle'

While /ɨ/ can co-occur with the so-called 'outer vowels' /i, a, u/ in San Miguel as illustrated by (7a) and (b), evidence from Chalcatongo Mixtec demonstrates the 'increasingly restrictive limits on the amount and type of phonological material the prosodic template can carry' (p. 52). An autosegmental account of vowel harmony can be applied across the template, where '/i/ assimilates to the backness of the /ɨ/' (p. 55) regardless of which syllable the /i/ is initially found in. In other words, within the template, just one single value is licensed for the feature [back].

Despite superficial differences between these seemingly divergent phonological changes, the Mixtec analysis illustrates how one common structure, namely the prosodic template, can shape a language. While syllabic analyses encounter difficulties accounting for the individual changes, peering up the prosodic hierarchy to the foot level not only helps account for individual problems such as *sC*-clusters and glide strengthening

---

[3] Although Macken & Salmons (1997) provide a detailed explanation of *sC*-clusters, there are unfortunately no explicit examples provided in their article. It is for that reason that no examples are provided in this section.

and loss, but it helps unify a broader set of sound patterns and developments, including vowel harmony.

17.3.3 Prosodic Templates in Germanic

Germanic has been the focus of many analyses employing the prosodic template in recent years both synchronically, e.g. German and Dutch plurals (Booij 1995, 1998, Wiese 1996, 2001), and diachronically, e.g. lenition, vowel loss and reduction (Holsinger 2000, 2009, Smith 2004, 2007a,b, 2009, etc.). Perhaps most striking is the resilience of the foot-based template to shape entire classes of words or sequences of sounds across the history of the West Germanic languages despite the fact that the trochee at the heart of the template has changed from moraic in the earliest Germanic languages to the syllabic trochee of the modern languages (on our analysis; compare Lahiri, this volume). Data below illustrate this resilience with a few examples.

17.3.3.1 *Vowel Loss and Reduction: Old Saxon i-Stem Nouns*

For more than a thousand years, West Germanic vowels in unstressed syllables have been subject to reduction and loss, particularly word-finally, as described in the *Auslautgesetze* or Laws of Finals (cf. Prokosch 1939, Boutkan 1995) resulting in the loss of inflectional endings and ultimately the collapse of entire verb and noun classes. While all vowels were subject to the *Auslautgesetze, i* and *u* were initially more resilient to loss and reduction than others. Prokosch (1939: 134) noted that these vowels were first lost 'after a long syllable, or after two syllables (which phonetically, or metrically, amounts to the same thing)' before they disappeared after short syllables. Prosody's critical role in loss and retention is perhaps best illustrated by Old Saxon (OS) *i*-stem nouns. Germanic nouns were historically formed from three parts, namely a root+thematic vowel+inflectional ending (number and case), e.g. OS *ferd+i+o* 'journey, pl. gen.' With the loss of many inflectional endings, the thematic vowels, especially in the nominative and accusative singular forms, became exposed word-finally and subject to additional loss.[4] As illustrated in (8), the short final *i* was lost after heavy stems (or so-called long syllables), i.e. those ending in either VCC (e.g. *fard* 'journey') or V̄C (*quān* 'woman'), but retained after light stems, i.e. stressed short syllables, i.e. stems ending in VC, e.g. *uuini* 'friend' and *stedi* 'city'.[5]

---

[4] The consonants *z* and *n* forming the singular nominative and accusative inflectional endings respectively were prone to loss (cf. Bammesberger 1990), e.g. +stadiz > OS stedi 'place, town'.

[5] Long *i*, e.g. *i* formed by coalescence of *i* with a following *j*, was not subject to loss like its short counterpart. It could be argued that the long vowel was able to form a foot on its own thus protecting it longer. Additionally, long vowels typically underwent reduction to a short vowel over time while short vowels often underwent loss. Moreover, short vowels followed by additional endings, e.g. OS *enstim* 'honour, dat. pl.' were protected within the trochaic ending.

(8) *i*-loss and retention after Old Saxon heavy versus light stems

Heavy Stems = Long syllables		Light Stems = Stressed short syllable
VCC	V̄C	VC
fard (f.) 'journey'	quān (f.) 'woman'	uuini (m.) 'friend'
gast (m.) 'guest'	thrād (m.) 'thread'	stedi (f.) 'city'
burg (f.) 'town,city'	wāg (m.) 'wave'	seli (m.) 'room'
uurm (m.) 'worm'	brūd (f.) 'woman'	friundskepi (m.) 'friendship'

By appealing to a template based on the moraic foot rather than solely on the shape of the preceding stem syllable, a simple generalisation emerges regardless of whether the word is monosyllabic, e.g. [+]*wurmi*[6] >*wurm* 'worm', or polysyllabic, e.g. *friundskepi* 'friendship'.

(9) *i*-loss and retention in Old Saxon (Smith 2007b; cf. also Vennemann 1995)

Heavy Stems						Light Stems		
[H]	L		[H]	L		[L	L]	
[μμ]	μ		[μμ]	μ		[μ	μ]	
C₀VC.	Ci		C₀V̄#.	Ci		C₀V.	Ci	
far	di	> fard	tī	di	> tīd	se	li	> seli
gas	ti	> gast	brū	di	> brūd	ste	di	> stedi

In the case of the heavy stem nouns in (9), the heavy syllable of the root formed its own foot leaving the light syllable containing the thematic vowel *i* unfooted. This unfooted *i* was consequently lost. Conversely, for the light stem nouns, the syllable containing the *i* was footed with the preceding light syllable thereby forming a LL foot via resolution.[7] By eliminating the unfooted vowels, the noun stems fit the trochaic foot template shaping this lexical class:

(10)   [H]L > [H]
        [L L] > [L L]

Indeed the preservation and loss of *i* was driven by the need to fit the words of this noun class to the trochaic template. Words were not all shortened alike; only

---

[6] A raised "+" signifies a reconstructed form.

[7] See Lahiri (this volume), for a discussion of foot structure and resolution in Germanic. Although Lahiri's Germanic foot differs somewhat from that used here, the principle of resolution at work in the West Germanic languages is nevertheless highlighted.

the [H]L > [H] change was necessary to eliminate prosodically extraneous material. Since the [LL] sequence already satisfied the template, the footed thematic vowel was preserved in these words for a longer time. The template was thus the means of reshaping words: vowels which were not mapped to the template were unlicenced and thus lost.[8] This analysis situates this sound change within the broader context, providing a more unified approach to understanding prosodically-driven changes in Germanic.

17.3.3.2 *Consonants: Lenition of Medial Stops in German Dialects*

Holsinger (2000, 2009) has demonstrated that lenition processes in West Germanic as divergent as elision, flapping, and spirantization as well as fortition processes can be unified in terms of a prosodic template based on the trochaic foot. Consider the lenition data in (11):

(11) Medial simplification, final retention: Buttelstedt (Thuringian—East Central German, Kürsten & Bremer 1910: 46)
  (a) Inflection

Dialect	Standard German	
wind ~ winə	*Wind, Winde*	'wind, winds'
khind ~ kinr̩	*Kind, Kinder*	'child, children'
blind ~ blinr̩	*blind, blinder*	'blind, blind [masc.sg. strong adj.]'

  (b) Derivation

wind ~ winɪχ	*Wind, windig*	'wind, windy'
hund ~ hunəχn̩	*Hund, Hündchen*	'dog, doggy'
rind ~ rinr̩	*Rind, geil sein*	'cow, randy (←cow)'

In these examples, [d] is retained word-finally in nasal+obstruent clusters, e.g. *blind*, but lost medially although the stop is in syllable-onset position, typically a position of strengthening (Vennemann 1988). Holsinger (2000, 2009) argues that the full range of phonemic contrasts, e.g. /t/ versus /d/, in templatically-driven dialects are exhibited primarily in template-initial position. Template-medially, on the other hand, these contrasts are neutralized or the obstruent is lost even if in syllable-onset position. Just as for Mixtec above, medial onsets are considered the weak branch of the template and are consequently the target site for lenition processes (cf. (12)). Holsinger refers to these types of patterns as 'weak position constraints' where phonological features like [spread glottis], are fully expressed in some prosodic positions, such as foot-initially, but weakly expressed if not lost entirely in others, e.g. foot-medially as seen in (12).

---

[8] Cf. Smith (2007a) for a similar approach to account for Old Frisian Vowel Balance.

(12) Template-medial lenition in West Germanic

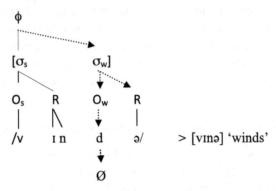

> [vɪnə] 'winds'

As with Mixtec, analyses based on syllable structure alone cannot account for loss of obstruents in syllable onsets in word-medial position. Within the prosodic template, however, the onset of the strong branch is the sole position in which the full range of features and contrasts is retained. Consequently, a templatic analysis provides the most straightforward account of these lenition processes akin to those found in Mixtec above.

17.4 TEMPLATE BLOCKING

Although templates can appear to be imposed across all forms, documented cases exist in which a template fails to apply as expected. In each instance clear morphological or phonological factors prevent the template's application. In this section, we outline examples from both the Semitic and West Germanic languages.

17.4.1 Template Blocking in Semitic

In Hebrew and Arabic, data which fail to conform to the prescribed template fall into two categories. The first category includes morphologically-based template blocking: in Hebrew, verbal stems are overwhelmingly bisyllabic, conforming to the optimal prosodic word (Ussishkin 2000, 2005, Bat-El 2003). However, of the seven verbal categories of binyanim found in the language, one of them has a trisyllabic stem: the *hitpaʿel* binyan. All verbs in this class have three syllables, rather than two. As Ussishkin (2005) explains, the reason for this over-large word is morphologically-based. Namely, the affixal material for the *hitpaʿel* class contains three vowels, each of which becomes a syllable nucleus, and the presence of this material overrides the bisyllabic template observed in the remaining verbal categories.

The second category of template blocking is phonologically-based. Laks (2010) documents cases of unattested verbs in the verbal systems of Hebrew and Palestinian Arabic.

These gaps are unexpected, and have no sensible morphosyntactic basis; rather, Laks (2010) argues that these gaps are the result of what would otherwise be phonologically ill-formed words. The following examples from Laks (2010: 6) illustrate a case of otherwise productive decausativization of a *pi'el* verb to a *hitpa'el* verb being blocked; compare well-formed *hitlaxlex* with questionable **hittanef*.

(13) MH Decausativization (pi'el → hitpa'el):
    (a) dan lixlex et ha-xeder
        'Dan made the room dirty'
    (b) ha-xeder hitlaxlex
        'The room became dirty'
    (c) dan tinef et ha-xeder
        'Dan made the room filthy'
    (d) (?) ha-xeder hittanef
        'The room became filthy'

In fact, such blocking occurs consistently when the verbal stem is *t*- or *d*-initial, and when such forms are morphologically needed, other verbal categories must be called upon to fill the gap. For example, the verb *diber* 'speak' has a derived reciprocal form in the *nif'al* binyan, since a *hitpa'el* form would violate phonotactic restrictions against two adjacent coronal stops, resulting instead in the less common *nif'al* form *nidbar* 'talk to one another'. As Laks (2010) observes, a *pi'el-nif'al* pair is highly unusual and in fact is always the result of a blocked form in another binyan.

Turning to the examples in (14) from the Maltese dialect of Marsaxlokk, on the southeast coast of the island of Malta, inflected forms conform to a bisyllabic template, even when this template is achieved by two medial adjacent consonants.[9]

(14a) Imperfective paradigm for 'do'

	SG	PL
1	nạmæl	nạmlæw
2	tạmæl	tạmlæw
3m	yạmæl	yạmlæw
3f	tạmæl	

However, a clearly non-etymological vowel is usually epenthesized to break up triconsonantal clusters arising as a reflex of affixation. This results in some trisyllabic forms, as seen in the dialect data documented by Schabert (1976):

---

[9] Many thanks to Andrew Simpson for providing the Maltese data cited here.

(14b) Imperfective paradigm for 'spread (out)': paradigm with epenthesis (Schabert 1976)

	SG	PL
1	nifræš	nifiršæw
2	yifræš	tifiršæw
3m	yifræš	yifiršæw
3f	tifræš	

Similar phonotactically-based blocking occurs in Palestinian Arabic, as also documented by Laks (2010). Palestinian Arabic disallows *nn* and *nm* clusters, and when such clusters might otherwise result from the application of a productive derivational process, the derived verb occurs in a different binyan. This manifests in the seventh binyan, usually used for passive verbs. To illustrate, consider the active form *nafa* 'deny'; as an *n*-initial form, the otherwise expected passive form **innafa* is disallowed. As in Hebrew, occasionally some forms find a way to surface, but always in a different binyan, one otherwise not used for expressing passives. In this way, *nisi* 'forget' has a related passive form *intasa* 'be forgotten', rather than the otherwise expected **innasa*.

17.4.2 Old High German *jan*-Verbs

Data from Old High German (OHG) *jan*-verbs likewise reveal that the template can be overridden by phonotactics and morphological transparency. In Germanic the weak verbs formed their preterite by adding a dental preterite ending, e.g. *-ta* or *-da*,[10] to the verb root + connecting vowel. For the *jan*-verbs the connecting vowel was *i*, e.g. *den+i+ta* 'lengthened', *hoor+i+ta* 'heard'. In many if not most West Germanic languages this connecting vowel was lost when unfooted after a heavy stem, but retained when footed after a light stem as in (15):

(15) (a) Retention of *i* after light (LL) *jan*-verbs in OHG

Light (LL)
F
[L L]   +ta
μ μ
CV CV   +ta
Light [*ne ri*]   + ta \<nerita\>

---

[10] Cf. Hill (2010) on the origin of the Germanic weak preterite ending.

(b) Loss of *i* after heavy (H) and polysyllabic *jan*-verbs in OHG

Heavy (HL>H)				Polysyllabic (LLL>LH)			
F				F			
[H	]	L	+ta	[L	L]		+ta
μμ		μ		μ	μ		
C$_0$VC		Ci	+ta	CV	CV		+ta
C$_0$VV		Ci	+ta				
Heavy [*tran*]		*ki*	+ta <trancta>	**Poly.** [*ni*	*da*]	*ri* +ta	<nidarta>
[*hō*]		*ri*	+ta <hōrta>				

In short, the dental preterite ending was affixed to the right edge of the foot-based template. Any connecting vowel left unfooted, i.e. unmapped to the template would be lost permitting the preterite ending to affix directly to the foot edge. While a number of exceptions can be found, these exceptions systematically prevent phonotactic violations and difficult sound combinations or they help to maintain morphological transparency.[11] Consider the following examples:

(16) Avoidance and repair of complex clusters

	Infinitive and Expected Preterite	a. *i*-loss blocked	b. Epenthesis
i.	*ga-bauhnen* → *ga-bauhnta*	*bauhnida* *gabauhnita*	*pauhhanta* *pouchenta*
ii.	*irtruosanen* → *irtruosanta*[12]	*erdruasnita*	--------

The expected preterite forms would have been subject to *i*-loss following the heavy verb stems. However, as the asterisk indicates, these forms are unattested.[13] Simply, if syncope occurred, it would lead to strongly dispreferred clusters, e.g. *-hnt-* and *-snt-* violating West Germanic phonotactics. Speakers had two processes available to avoid these clusters. First, *i*-syncope could be blocked altogether (16a) or an anaptyctic vowel, typically *a*, could be inserted to break up the cluster. Interestingly, the infinitive

---

[11] While Smith & Pulsipher (2008) have shown that geminates found in the present tense did under certain circumstances lead light stem verbs to be treated as heavy, this is beyond the scope of the chapter.

[12] Graff (1834–1842) lists this verb under ⁺*ardrōsnjan* and Lehmann (1986) lists ⁺*ufar-trusnjan* 'sprinkle over' as a potential cognate.

[13] The superscript "⁺" indicates a reconstructed form, while "*" suggests an impossible unattested form that should not be reconstructed.

irtruosanen already had an *a* before the stem final *n* akin to the output of epenthesis for *pauhhanta*. With the expected loss of *i* following this stem, the *a* already found in the infinitive form could have served to avoid any dispreferred cluster from arising in the first place. Yet when this vowel did not appear in the preterite, the alternative process, namely the blocking of *i*-loss, had the similar result of avoiding the dispreferred cluster -*snt*-.

In another set of apparent exceptions, *i* is retained following heavy or polysyllabic stems ending in *d* or *t*. These exceptions, however, are more restricted in their occurrence and typically limited to a specific set of manuscripts:

(17) Retention of *i* after heavy or polysyllabic stems ending in *t* or *d* (Smith 2004)

Exception	OHG Manuscript
chundita	Frg. 51. 53
cunditun, cunditi	Tatian
ahtitun	Tatian
zundeta	Mcp.
baldita	F

The failure of *i* to undergo syncope may be the result of the Obligatory Contour Principle (OCP) which 'prohibit[s] adjacent identical elements on the gestural tier' (Broselow 1995: 179; cf. also McCarthy 1986). Assuming voicing assimilation of -*dt*- or -*td*- to either -*dd*- or -*tt*-, the resulting gestures would be identical. To avoid the adjacency of two such identical segments, syncope of *i* could be blocked as the examples above illustrate. The result would be stems which violate the prosodic template since the unsyncopated *i* would be in an unfooted syllable:

(18) Foot structure of *baldita*

[H] L + ta
bal di ta

In these dialects the avoidance of OCP violations has a clear priority over strict adherence to the prosodic template. The failure to syncopate *i* helps maintain morphological transparency between the stems and preterite endings, since the *t* or *d* of the stem is kept distinct from the dental of the preterite suffix.

The examples from Semitic and Germanic thus illustrate the conflict between different levels of the prosodic hierarchy and the ability of lower level phonotactic requirements or morphological transparency to override the prosodic template.

17.5 Resilience, Expansion, Loss of Templates: The Importance of Dialect Data

One crucial area of study that helps elucidate how templates behave when viewed from a diachronic perspective is the realm of non-standard or dialectal language varieties. These varieties provide scholars with a rich array of data that provide key insights into the nature of structural properties in language. With respect to prosodic templates, data of this type can help us figure out whether templatic restrictions are in a stable state at a given time within a language. In this section, we examine templates from this perspective for Semitic and Germanic.

17.5.1 Template Resilience and Productivity in Semitic

Examples from the Semitic family illustrate just how pervasive templatic structure is in these languages. The clearest cases come from the Semitic verbal systems, in which all verbs must conform to a template.

In Hebrew, templatic requirements on verbs are stronger than on nouns. All Hebrew verbs that trace their source to a borrowed word are actually denominal, having been formed on the basis of a borrowed noun in the language. Such nouns are borrowed with no templatic modification, nor any prosodic modification for that matter, such that even the stress tends to correlate with the stress in the source language. Bat-El (1994) provides numerous data illustrating this phenomenon, including those given in (19):

(19) *English noun*   *Hebrew noun*
     nostalgia   nostalgia
     transfer   transfer
     striptease   streptiz

When such Hebrew nouns become verbs, they are required by the grammar to conform to the rigid templatic system which includes seven binyans or verbal categories, resulting in rigid application of prosodic structure:

(20) *Hebrew verb*   *Gloss*
     nistelg   'he was nostalgic'
     trinsfer   'he transferred'
     striptez   'to perform a striptease'

More recently, Laks (2010) has documented additional English to Hebrew loans that again illustrate the resilience of the verbal template system:

(21)

Base		Derived verb	
esemes	'sms'	simes	'send an sms message'
rifer	'refer'	rifrer	'refer'
model	'model'	midel	'make a model'
deliver	'deliver'	dilver	'deliver a set up'
pančer	'puncture'	pinčer	'puncture'

Template resilience can also be seen in Maltese, where heavy lexical borrowing has occurred. In Maltese, Italian verbs that were borrowed relatively long ago conform to the binyan system of Maltese, unlike recent borrowings which undergo circumfixation of *i- -ja*. For instance, consider the following pairs of forms:

(22) baččaċ   'he made chubby'   tbaččaċ   'he became chubby'
     pitter   'he painted'   tpitter   'he was painted'
     serp   'snake'   serrep   'he zigzagged'

Most telling is the third example, which shows the noun-verb pair *serp* 'snake'/*serrep* 'he zigzagged'. Mifsud (1995) notes that only verbs borrowed relatively long ago behave this way; the more typical pattern for borrowed verbs in Maltese is to ignore the Semitic-based templatic requirements and simply append a concatenative circumfix, as in the form *ittowja* 'he thawed'.

Additional data can be found in Palestinian Arabic, which as documented by Laks (2008, forthcoming) shows verb innovations that always conform to the existing verbal templates. Laks has documented such cases as attested in Elihay (2005), and as the data below illustrate, such forms tend to occur productively in the second verbal binyan of the language, with the template CVCCVC:

(23)

Base		Derived Verb	
sayn	'sign'	sayyan	'sign'
formæt	'format'	farmat	'format'
breyk	'brake'	barrak	apply brakes'
iks	'X'	akkas	'put an X on somebody'
haši:š	'hashish'	haššaš	'smoke hashish'
umma	'nation'	ammam	'nationalise'
milħ	'salt'	mallaħ	'add salt'

Other examples can be found in verbal binyan 5, with the template tCVCCVC, the result of not only templatic resilience but also morpho-syntactic considerations (this binyan tends to host verbs derived by thematic operations such as decausativization, reflexivization, and reciprocalization):

(24)

Base		Derived Verb	
a. Decausatives			
nərvəs	'nervous'	tnarvas	'become nervous'
amrika	'America'	t'amrak	'become Americanized'
markaz	'center'	tmarkaz	'become centralized'
armala	'widow'	trammel	'be widowed'
kahrabe	'electricity'	tkahrab	get electrocuted'
hawa	'air'	thawwa	get aired out'
dəprəs	'depression'	(t)dabras	'become depressed'
azme	'crisis'	t'azzam	'reach a crisis'
'irq	'root'	t'arwaq	'become rooted'
b. Reflexives			
ħija:b	'veil'	tħaja:b	'put on a veil'
kundara	'shoe'	tkandar	'put on a shoe'
badle	'suit'	tbaddal	'put on a suit'
juzda:n	'wallet/purse'	tjazdan	'use a wallet/purse'
kæjuəl	'casual'	tkajwal	'put on casual cloths'
ħinna	'henna'	tħanna	'henna one's hair'
hištaxlel	'become upgraded'	tšaxlal	'upgrade oneself'
c. Reciprocals			
biznəs	'business'	tbaznas	'do business together'

17.5.2 Expansion and Loss of the Prosodic Template: Dutch Diminutives

As the examples from Old Saxon and Old High German illustrate, the trochee played a key role in shaping both nouns and verbs historically. Although the type of trochee changed from moraic to syllabic, and the lexical classes impacted 500–1000 years ago no

longer exist, e.g. *i*-stems in Germanic are long gone and no longer exist in their previous form, the trochee nevertheless continues to play a role shaping lexical classes in the
modern daughter languages. Notably data from the dialects provide clearer insights into
the role of the prosodic templates in the actual dialects.

In Dutch, the diminutive ending -*(T)je*[14] is attached to the end of nouns. However,
nouns ending in sonorants have one additional stipulation: an additional schwa appears
after light noun stems, e.g. *ball-e-tje* 'little ball', i.e. those ending in VC, but no schwa
occurs after heavy noun stems, e.g. *laan-tje* 'little lane', i.e. those ending in $\bar{V}$C or VCC,
or disyllables, e.g. *bakker-tje* 'little baker'.

Bisyllabic (σσ) and heavy (H) stems pattern together in taking the -*Tje* diminutive
ending, while light stems have both schwa and -*Tje*:

(25) Prosodic shapes of stems pre- and post-diminutive formation[15]

Original stem		Diminutive Formation		Prosodic Shape of Stem Output
[H]	laan	[H] + Tje	laantje	[H] + Tje
[σ́σ]	bezem	[σ́σ] + Tje	bezempje	[σ́σ] + Tje
L	bal	[L+e] + tje	balletje	[σ́σ] + tje[16]

Recall from above that [σ́ σ] (where σ_1 is typically L, σ_2=L or H) was equivalent to [H]
in early Germanic, forming a trochee via resolution, although in that case, [H] referred
to a heavy syllable rather than a heavy stem comprised of superheavy syllable as argued
for here for Dutch.[17] L. C. Smith (2009) thus argues that -*Tje* is simply affixed to the
right edge of the prosodic template requiring the noun to end either in a heavy stem,
i.e. superheavy syllable (*laan+tje*) or a bisyllabic stem (*bezemp+je*). However, when the
noun stem is L, e.g. *bal*, unable to form a foot on its own, schwa expands the stem so
that it fits the prosodic template allowing the diminutive suffix to attach to σ́σ, i.e. *balle-*.
Although a L stem ending in *VC* could arguably form its own foot, it undergoes epenthesis to conform to the specific shape of the prosodic templates [H], i.e. *VCC* or *V:C*, or

---

[14] *T* represents a voiceless stop that matches the place of articulation of the preceding consonant, or
appears as *t* after a vowel.
[15] For more details to this limited description of Dutch diminutives, the reader is directed to
L. C. Smith (2009) and Booij (1995).
[16] In this environment, the dental-initial suffix -*tje* is affixed without additional assimilation as
suggested by -*Tje*.
[17] The reader should note that light and heavy refer to stem types not syllable types. Light stems end in
either light or heavy syllables, whereas heavy stems end in superheavy syllables. Superheavy syllables play
an important role in Dutch prosody in that they can attract stress which would typically be assigned via
the syllabic trochee. In this way, these superheavy syllables do exist on par elsewhere in the language with
the syllabic trochee (cf. Booij 1995 and van Oostendorp 2002 for details regarding Dutch stress placement
and superheavy syllables).

[σ́ σ] required for suffixation. In sum, schwa epenthesis lengthens light stems to fit the prosodic template necessary for diminutivization.

This template is akin to that used for OS *i*-stem nouns over a thousand years ago, where the prosodic equivalence between H and σ́σ motivated the modification of noun stems. This is notable since the foot of Modern Dutch is generally considered to be syllabic. Yet these heavy stems, in this case resulting from superheavy syllables, continue to play a role in Dutch prosody today. While the role of these superheavy syllables is known in the accent system, they also play a role in the dialects in diminutive formation. Here, light noun stems are expanded not by the use of schwa, but rather by lengthening the stem vowel to create a [H] stem:[18]

(26) Extension of light noun stems to one foot by vowel lengthening

Dialect	Base noun	Diminutive
Bolsward	stal 'stall'	staaltsje
Nij Beets	stof 'material'	staafke
Eelde	bom 'tree'	boohmpii[19]

Indeed, in some dialects two competing forms may co-exist as the example for *bal* 'ball' from the Drentish dialect of Hoogeveen illustrates (p.c. Geert Booij):

(27) Possible diminutive forms for *bal* in Hoogeveen

[L L] + chien	[H] + chien
ba le chien	baal chien

In these dialects speakers can either lengthen the stem vowel or add schwa to ensure the noun stem fits the prescribed template for diminutive formation.

In other dialects, the role of the template itself is changing. It has either been extended beyond those stems ending in sonorants, e.g. Huizen, or it is falling out of use altogether, e.g. in Formerum. Compare light stem nouns from these two dialects in (28). Forms differing from Standard Dutch diminutives are highlighted.

---

[18] Dutch dialect data come from the Goeman-Taeldeman-Van Reenen project supported by the Meertens Institute and published as *Morfologische atlas van de Nederlandse dialecten* (MAND).This project recorded speakers from 613 dialects in the Netherlands, Belgium, and Friesland from 1980 to 1995.
   [19] *h* in this example represents a lengthened vowel.

(28) Diminutive forms of light noun stems in Huizen and Formerum dialects of Dutch

	Standard Dutch		Huizen Data	Formerum data
	Base noun	Diminutive	Diminutive	Diminutive
No schwa expected	bed 'bed'	bedje	bɛdətçən	bɛ̞ːtsə
	pad 'path'	padje	padətçən	pɔtsə
	rib 'rib'	ribje	rɪbətçən	rɪpkə
Schwa expected	kar 'car'	karretje	kʰarətçən	karəkə
	kam 'comb'	kammetje	kamətçən	kiˑmkə
	kom 'bowl'	kommetje	kɔmətçən	kumkə
	man 'man'	mannetje	mánətçən	mantsə
	ring 'ring'	ringetje	rɪŋətçən	rɪŋkjə
	stal 'stall'	stalletje	stalətçən	staɬtsə
	tang 'tongs'	tangetje	taŋətçən	taŋkjə
	zon 'sun'	zonnetje	zɔnətçən	sɔntsə

As the Huizen examples illustrate, schwa epenthesis occurs not only as expected with stems ending in sonorants, but it has also been extended to apply to other light nouns ending in obstruents. Conversely, the Formerum data reveals that other than for *karretje* [karəkə], schwa epenthesis does not regularly occur where it would be expected after light stems ending in sonorants. Whereas the use of the diminutive template has been extended in Huizen, just 100km away in Formerum, the template has all but fallen out of use in the latter location. Moreover, despite the shift to a syllabic trochee from the moraic trochee of West Germanic elsewhere in Dutch, we still see the use of a quantity sensitive stem at work in the language shaping diminutive formation.

17.6 CONCLUSION

We have examined the role played by prosodic templates (and thus by the foot) in language change. Data from numerous languages in three unrelated language families show pervasive effects of foot-based prosodic templates in shaping the outcome of language change over time. One of the most important results is to demonstrate that no matter how different the genesis of the respective templates investigated in the individual languages and language families, the templates that ultimately emerge are a crucial factor in shaping a variety of morphological classes and licensing features and segments in various template positions. These templates provide a unified approach to divergent language patterns not only within languages but cross-linguistically. Indeed what has been well known to guide our understanding of the Semitic languages can provide insights that help us comprehend patterns in Germanic and elsewhere.

In the end, we stand firmly with Blevins (2010a) in calling for additional research on prosodic templates, and importantly, we have justified why such research should draw on data centering on language change, as well as on data from numerous varieties of spoken language, including dialectal data. Like much current work in linguistic theory, our research here validates approaches that value data from previously understudied language varieties.

PART IV

FUNDAMENTAL CONTROVERSIES IN PHONOLOGICAL CHANGE

CHAPTER 18

··

FIRST LANGUAGE ACQUISITION AND PHONOLOGICAL CHANGE

··

PAUL FOULKES AND MARILYN VIHMAN

OVERVIEW

IN this chapter we summarize discussions of the role of acquisition in (especially segmental) phonological change, from the neogrammarians to twenty-first-century textbooks (section 18.1), before considering varying definitions of 'acquisition', 'phonology' and 'change' (section 18.2). We then review more closely the few previous studies based on systematic empirical analysis (section 18.3). In section 18.4 we present new empirical data from our own research in developmental phonology and sociophonetics. We believe this is the largest dataset yet assembled to address the issue. The analyses both lead to the conclusion that patterns of child phonology differ in several respects from patterns typically found in change, and thus that developmental errors are not a prime influence on change (compare the approach in Lahiri and Dresher, both this volume, especially, and also those in Bermúdez-Otero, D'Arcy, Hale et al., Ratliff, and Wedel, all also this volume).

18.1 INTRODUCTION

One of the longest-standing maxims of linguistic thought is that children's language provides a source for language change. In a very early discussion, Schleicher (1861 [1971: 19]) notes parallels between children's errors and diachronic change in a range of languages. For example, his 3-year-old son Ernst:

> sometimes changed gutturals into labials, e.g. in *schnapen* for *Schnaken* ['crane fly'], *schimpen* for *Schinken* ['ham']. The same sound changes of the gutturals in individual Indo-European languages are well known.

Similar generalizations are made by Grammont (1902: 61), who concludes:

> [t]outes les modifications fonétiques, morfologiques ou sintaxiques qui caractérisent la vie des langues apparaissent dans le parler des enfants. ['[a]ll the phonetic, morphological and syntactic changes that characterize the life of languages are found in the speech of children.']

Grammont discusses changes in French, citing examples of similar patterns in the speech of one child. For example, vowel dissimilation in *néni* for *fini* ['finished'] parallels historical developments such as Latin *finire* > Old French *fenir* ['to finish'].

While Schleicher and Grammont stop short of imputing direct causality, explicit comments on the role of children in effecting change date back at least to Paul (1886a: 34; translation from Weinreich et al. 1968: 108). He argues:

> the processes of learning language are of supreme importance for the explanation of changes ... they represent the most important cause of these changes.

Various explanations have been offered for the apparent role of acquisition in change. Sweet (1888) and Sully (1896) suggest that change results from imperfect learning. Sweet blames this on organic differences in children's vocal tracts relative to adult ones, as well as laziness and carelessness in children's speech. For morphological change, Müller (1890) ascribes the loss of irregular paradigmatic forms to children's natural tendency to simplify. Similarly, Meillet (1951: 74) claims that each child creates the language anew, also highlighting the role of linguistic exposure in the child's environment:

> Pour chaque individu, le langage est ... une recréation totale faite sous l'influence du milieu qui l'entoure. ['For every individual, language is ... a total recreation effected under the influence of the surrounding environment.']

The lines of reasoning that characterized discussion of acquisition and change in those days echo in more recent work. Generative linguists readily adopted the view that imperfect learning is a cause of change. For example, following Meillet, Halle (1962: 66) hypothesizes that the child 'constructs his own optimal grammar by induction from the utterances to which he has been exposed'. The child may arrive at a different grammar from that of adults, since a set of utterances may be generated by more than one grammar. Kiparsky (1965: 4) continues this reasoning:

> Imperfect learning is due to the fact that the child does not learn a grammar directly but must recreate it for himself on the basis of a necessarily limited and fragmentary experience with speech. It is in no way surprising that the grammar should change in the process of transmission across generations of speakers.

Similar comments continue to be expounded in contemporary textbooks. For instance, Fromkin, Rodman, & Hyams (2011: 528) state:

> A basic cause of change is the way children acquire the language. No one teaches a child the rules of grammar. Each child constructs the rules of her language alone, generalizing rules from the linguistic input she receives.

While the logic of such comments may appear sound, others have signalled scepticism about children's role in change. Saussure (1916 [1974: 149]), for example, reflects on similarities between changes and children's errors, but considers the problem of change 'undented' by a simple comparative approach. He continues:

> what prompts a generation to retain certain mistakes to the exclusion of others that are just as natural is not clear. From all appearances the choice of faulty pronunciations is completely arbitrary, and there is no obvious reason for it. Besides, why did the phenomenon break through at one time rather than another?

Bloomfield (1933: 386), like Saussure, highlights unresolved questions of 'why here?' and 'why now?', arguing: 'no permanent factor ... can account for specific changes which occur at one time and place and not at another'. Drachman (1978) likewise concludes: '[t]he role of primary acquisition in language change seems to have been exaggerated'. Whereas Andersen (1973, 1978) took as given that the source of diachronic change or innovation was the child learner, Kiparsky (1988) found the arguments of Drachman (1978) and Vihman (1980; see section 18.1.3) sufficiently persuasive to take issue with Andersen (although not with his own earlier claims). He states that 'empirical study of child phonology gives little support for [the notion of a pervasive role for acquisition in sound change] ... The class of typical or potential sound changes does not match the class of typical or potential child language processes' (Kiparsky 1988: 390). Other commentators go even further, completely dismissing the potential role of children. For example, Aitchison (2003: 739) states bluntly that 'babies do not initiate changes'.

Debate on the relationship between acquisition and change, then, has persisted for 150 years—in effect, the lifetime of modern linguistics. However, perhaps surprisingly, it seems that no consensus has emerged. The principal reason for the lack of agreement, in our view, is the scarcity of attempts to assess the validity of the claim empirically (as noted by Jespersen 1922, though little has changed). Although some authors provide examples to illustrate similarities between patterns in child speech and language change, few do so systematically. Instead, most marshal anecdotal or cherry-picked examples, often from a single child. More egregiously, some writers lay out arguments without reference to data. Remarkably few systematic empirical studies have been conducted to explore whether children's 'errors' are genuinely universal, whether these errors do indeed emerge as changes, or whether there are other types of change that do *not* appear in children's speech. Particularly lacking is cross-linguistic evidence to support the assumption that children everywhere make the same mistakes. The few exceptions are reviewed in section 18.3 (also Baron 1977 and Hooper 1980 on syntactic and morphological change).

A further problem is the lack of unity on what is meant by the actual terms 'acquisition' and 'change'. Few scholars offer any formal definition of their use of these terms. The problem is further compounded by more general debates over the delimitation of 'phonology', especially with respect to its relationship with phonetics (see also Scheer, and Hale et al., both this volume).

Before presenting our own empirical data, we first turn in more detail to definitions of terms, as this enables us to draw out various important methodological and theoretical issues that underpin the debate.

18.2 TERMS OF REFERENCE

18.2.1 Acquisition and Children

Although few if any commentators explicitly define 'acquisition' (or 'children'), we infer that most refer solely to first language acquisition, and to developmental processes manifested prior to the end of an assumed critical period (Lenneberg 1967). This is therefore the frame of reference we adopt when presenting our data in section 18.4.

However, it is difficult to evaluate or compare studies without consideration of what the authors consider to be their objects of study. First, we should not treat children as if they form a homogeneous speech community. 'Child' is a very broad demographic category (Aitchison 2003: 738). The linguistic patterns of 2-year-olds differ from those of 3-, 6-, or 12-year-olds. Social influences, motor skills and cognitive capacities vary across the age range. Moreover, variability within and across children must be considered. Children do not learn a language at the same rate or in the same sequence. It also goes without saying that generations of speakers do not arrive in well organized, discrete groups like coach parties of tourists arriving at their destination (Manly 1930). Cross-generational comparison must therefore take account of the fact that any differences will be manifested gradually and perhaps over a long timescale.

Second, we must ask the question: when does acquisition begin and end? We could ask specifically at what age the critical period ends, and even whether it is necessary to assume a critical period (Johnson & Newport 1989, Bialystok & Hakuta 1999, Birdsong 2005). It is certainly clear that language may change over the lifespan (Harrington 2006, Bowie & Yaeger-Dror, this volume). To that extent it can be argued that acquisition is not solely restricted to childhood. Might adult language development also shed light on change (compare D'Arcy, this volume)? To address the question of timescale also demands consideration of *what* is being acquired, which in the case of phonology is not straightforward (see section 18.2.2).

Third, in many societies acquisition of second and further languages is the norm rather than the exception, a process that may well extend into adulthood. For some individuals there may be learning of second dialects of the initial language. To what extent do L2 or D2 acquisition shed light on change (compare Iverson & Eckman, this volume)?

Consideration of such issues is essential to gather appropriate evidence to fully assess the role of acquisition in change. However, we set such issues aside and concentrate on evidence from infants and young children.

18.2.2 Phonology and Phonological

In discussions of acquisition and change, as in linguistics generally, the terms 'phonology' and 'phonological' are used with fluid meanings. For some writers the terms clearly refer to the abstract system of processes and the inventory of contrasts, distinct from phonetic realization (e.g. Blevins 2004a: 91, this volume). Naturally there is also variability in the specific issues investigated and terms used, reflecting the theoretical position adopted. In the generative tradition, for instance, Halle (1962) and Kiparsky (1965, 1968) discuss acquisition of transformational rules (see also Dresher, this volume). Stampe (1969, 1979) sought evidence to support the hypothesis of innateness (see also Donegan & Nathan, this volume), while in Optimality Theory discussion of change focuses on reorganizing the constraint hierarchy (Holt, this volume).

For other researchers, however, the principal focus may instead be phonetic realization. In his detailed consideration of chain shifts in vowel systems, for example, Labov (2001) discusses phonemic mergers and splits. These are examples where the system of phonological contrasts undergoes reduction or expansion (see further Gordon, this volume). However, Labov also discusses changes in which there is no effect on the *number* of elements in the system, but rather in the orientation and coordination of their associated phonetic patterns (fronting, raising, etc.), sometimes in coordinated patterns that maintain the overall system of contrasts. In such cases the issue of change is arguably phonetic rather than phonological, in a strict sense. Also worthy of comment is the fact that discussions of acquisition and change invariably focus on matters of segmental contrast or realization. Studies of variation and change in suprasegmental features are rare (but see Local 1982, and compare Lahiri, and Ratliff, both this volume) and we are not aware of any comments linking developmental patterns to variation or change in suprasegmental phonology.

We do not highlight these differences in definition or approach in order to align ourselves with any particular position. In addressing the potential influence of acquisition on phonological change, though, it is imperative to delimit appropriate objects of study. Are we to claim that children are responsible for changes at the phonetic level, for those that affect abstract elements and processes, or for both?

18.2.3 Change

What is a sound change? The answer to this question of course depends in part on one's conception of phonology. But what counts as change rather than variation? Again, answers differ through the literature. Many nineteenth-century commentaries on acquisition and change were delivered in the context of discussions of the comparative reconstruction of Proto-Indo-European (PIE). The focus was therefore on differences between states of languages over centuries or even millennia. For example, Schleicher considers parallels between children's errors and the relationship between PIE and modern Germanic, with reference to processes such as Grimm's Law. The changes involved are extreme enough for us to categorize the end points as different, mutually unintelligible languages, in which the change is complete.

By contrast, more recent discussions often refer to ongoing or incomplete processes. Recognizing synchronic variation as an essential stage in the development of change was the first major contribution to historical issues from quantitative sociolinguistics (Weinreich et al. 1968). It is hypothesized that any historically complete change must have progressed through a period of synchronic variation where the old and new forms coexisted (in the speech community if not necessarily in the minds and mouths of individuals).

This conception allows us to consider change from rather different perspectives than did Schleicher and his contemporaries. It is possible to distinguish the linguistic constraints on a given form from the social constraints on its usage. We can identify change not in absolute terms but as statistical shifts whereby an old form reduces in currency relative to an incoming form. We can examine contexts of use to assess whether a form is spreading through the lexicon or grammar. We can also consider differences in usage within subsections of a speech community rather than its entirety. Change may thus be conceptualized as the first adoption of a linguistic form by a subgroup within a community (defined, for example, by social class or age), or as a form appearing in new (socio-) linguistic domains (for example, when a traditionally stigmatized form becomes acceptable in formal styles).

It is furthermore important to distinguish *actuation* (or *initiation, innovation*) from *transmission* (or *promulgation, spread, restructuring, propagation*) through both the speech community and the grammar. *Actuation* refers to the initial appearance of a new form, for example, a phonetic variant previously unrecorded in the language. Efforts to explain actuation have generally been experimental (e.g. Ohala 1989, Foulkes 1997), grounded on the principle that vocal tracts and perceptual systems are essentially universal. Observing consistent patterns of variation in pronunciation and perception can therefore shed light on how such variations may emerge and eventually become phonologized (see further Yu, and also Hale et al., Bermúdez-Otero, and Kiparsky, all this volume).

Most commentaries on the role of acquisition in change limit discussion to actuation: children's forms that differ from those of adults are cited as variants that may, in time, crystallize as long-term change. But in order to explain change fully we must also address the issue of *transmission*: how, when and why is an innovation adopted by other speakers such that it gains a permanent foothold in the language? It is therefore not enough simply to list new forms used by particular children: we also need to establish how and why other speakers might adopt them. Furthermore, it may take a long time for historical changes to reach completion. For example, Labov (2001: 419) estimates that the current stable variation of English (ing) has taken over a thousand years to emerge and settle (also Keller 1994: 159). Therefore, we must ask not only how phonological patterns for one generation differ from those of the previous generation, but also how successive generations transmit the change in the same direction. Sociolinguistic studies, in particular, offer insights into transmission processes (Tagliamonte & D'Arcy 2009, D'Arcy, this volume).

18.2.4 Summary

In consideration of the issues raised in section 18.2, it is clear that drawing conclusions from previous commentaries is problematic. Studies may, explicitly or implicitly, have quite different conceptions of the key issues and adopt different methods to explore links between acquisition and change. We now turn to previous empirical approaches.

18.3 EMPIRICAL STUDIES OF ACQUISITION AND PHONOLOGICAL CHANGE

18.3.1 Developmental Studies

A systematic comparison of developmental patterns and regular sound changes has been carried out in three studies, which we summarize briefly.

18.3.1.1 *Greenlee & Ohala (1980)*

Greenlee & Ohala (1980) adapt Ohala's well-known approach to adult speakers, focusing on the physical constraints imposed by the perceptual system and vocal tract. They identify patterns in child language that may be explained with reference to natural dynamic properties of the vocal tract, aerodynamics, or varying perceptual responses to ambiguous signals. Such patterns are shown in some cases to parallel patterns found in change, and thus could constitute innovations that ultimately lead to change. For example, [n] and [l] show close acoustic similarity, and children do confuse them. Synchronic alternations and historical changes between /n/ and /l/ are also fairly common.

   Greenlee & Ohala refrain from identifying children as a cause of change, arguing that the underlying physical causes are effectively the same as those of adults, who therefore might themselves be responsible for innovations. It should be noted, however, that this line of reasoning is flawed in one crucial respect: the vocal anatomy and physiology of a child are not scale models of those of adults (Lieberman, Crelin, & Klatt 1972). For example, the child's tongue is large in relation to the size of the oral cavity (Stark 1980; Kent 1981), making palatal contact in the articulation of dentals or alveolars a more likely outcome for the young child than for the adult. Greenlee & Ohala also leave unanswered (as does Blevins 2004a) the question of asymmetric sound changes, where two sounds are perceptually similar yet change invariably involves developments in one direction. For instance, cross-linguistic patterns almost always show /θ/ developing into /f/ and not vice versa (see also Foulkes 1997 on /f/ > /h/).

18.3.1.2 *Locke (1983)*

Locke (1983) is primarily interested in establishing similarities between child pro-duction and adult phonology, supported by some quantitative analyses but also by selected examples of similarities and differences between developmental processes and cross-linguistic patterns of change and allophony (including final devoicing, final dele-tion, and cluster reduction). Locke notes the temptation to ascribe the origins of change to children, but declines to take an interpretable position on the matter:

> It is clear that sound change ultimately involves both children and adults, and that many of the historically confirmed cases of phonological change are remarkably like the transient developmental changes of childhood. But ... relatively little is known about the relative contributions to sound change of children and adults ... My own view is that the child is both an agent of sound change and a victim of sound change. (1983: 116)

Locke also notes a number of cases where child data are not mirrored by sound change (fronting of consonants) or vice versa (lenition of stop to fricative, where children are more likely to do the reverse).

18.3.1.3 *Vihman (1980)*

Vihman (1980) focuses on three common developmental processes, especially in the first year of word use: consonant harmony, long word reduction, and consonant clus-ter reduction, comparing them to possible parallel cases among well-established sound changes. Prefiguring her conclusions, she asserts at the outset that

> though many disparate parallels may be found, some of the most common or typical child language processes are either virtually non-existent or totally different in detail in adult synchronic processes and in sound change. (1980: 305)

Vihman provides a quantitative analysis of word forms from 11 children learning English, Spanish, Czech, Slovenian, or Estonian. The sample is based on the availability of a full word-list for the child, whether from a diarist parent (including Vihman her-self for two children acquiring Estonian), or from transcribed data based on recordings undertaken as part of a research project. The children's ages ranged from about 1 year, for first word use, to 2;6.

Consonant harmony, although not a universal of child language as sometimes claimed (Smith 1973), affected an average of 14% of the words produced by 13 children included in an earlier study (Vihman 1978, based only on target words presenting the challenge of a C_1 ... C_2 sequence) and as much as one-third of those words for some children. The process is rarely found in adult grammars, however, and must therefore be rare as a diachronic process (Drachman 1978).

Long-word reduction occurred in the word production of all 11 children included in Vihman's 1980 sample (see further Echols & Newport 1992, Vihman 1996: 201ff.). The analysis applied only to words of more than two syllables—a challenge for the child that is relatively rare in English but frequent in Spanish, for example. Omission of syllables is common in child speech (affecting a mean of 56% of the long words attempted in Vihman's sample, with a range from 26% to 90%) and is also widely reported in sound change. The details differ in acquisition compared with the historical record, however. In the case of the children, although the number of long words attempted was relatively small, the overall tendencies are clear (where percentages are used to compare stressed and unstressed syllables across languages of differing accentual patterns). First, the stressed syllable was very rarely omitted. Second, the final syllable was typically retained even when unstressed (78% of all 3- and 4-syllable words)—a fact that can now be safely ascribed to the final-syllable lengthening that is characteristic of both adult and child production (Snow 1998, Vihman, DePaolis, & Davis 1998). Third, the children's data show that in the case of long-word reduction it is the full syllable, not only the vowel, that is generally lost (e.g. Estonian *muusika* 'music'> [muːsi]).

Since the loss, especially of unstressed syllables, is well documented in the history of languages, we can consider how these patterns compare with those reported as sound changes. For this purpose Vihman (1980) consulted historical grammars for Germanic (Prokosch 1939), Slavic (Shevelov 1964) and Spanish (Menéndez-Pidal 1949), and a personal collection of Western Finnic cognates. Some factors affecting historical syllable loss are relative distance from the stressed syllable (possibly based on alternating stresses), syllable weight and vowel quality: none of these were features of the process of long-word reduction seen in the 11 children. On the other hand, final vowels are highly likely to be lost, at least in initial-stress languages like the Germanic languages and Estonian, again in contrast with the child data, regardless of stress pattern. Finally, in virtually every case in the historical record it is not full syllables that are lost but only the vowel (Latin *septimana* 'week' > Old Spanish *sedmana* > Modern Spanish *semana*).

Cluster reduction is again a prominent feature of child word production, typically until age 3 or later (Grunwell 1982). The children in Vihman's sample reduced 52–100% of the clusters present in words they attempted (mean 80%). A few patterns are again readily identifiable within the observed cases of cluster reduction. Where a cluster comprises stop+liquid (in either order), the stop—a sound type produced in children's first words, cross-linguistically, while liquids are rarely seen in those words (Menn & Vihman 2011)—was far more likely to be retained. Similarly, in cluster reduction fricatives or nasals were likely to be retained when followed by a liquid, while stops were more likely to be retained from target stop+fricative clusters and even more so from fricative+stop clusters.

The only clusters more likely to be preserved as a whole than reduced are combinations of nasal+stop. Voicing is crucial here: a voiceless obstruent is likely to be retained in the face of cluster reduction while a voiced obstruent is likely to be lost, leaving the nasal (Braine 1974 discusses the perceptual reasons for this asymmetry in child production). The strength hierarchy that emerges from these data conforms closely to the well-established facts of overall order of production for children (mainly based on motor control issues), with stops and nasals—prominent in babble and first words—being followed by fricatives, then liquids (Yeni-Komshian et al. 1980).

As for the historical record, consider the trends observed in the sources mentioned above. For Slavic, where cluster reduction is prominent, patterns of change are quite different from the child data: consonant+liquid tended to be preserved in Common Slavic, although /t,d+l/ was later reduced to /l/ in several Slavic languages; clusters of stop+fricative or nasal were reduced by loss of the stop in Common Slavic. In the history of Spanish, Latin stop+/r/ tended to be preserved initially; voiceless stop+/l/ was palatalized in central dialects and reduced to /ʎ/, while /bl/ was preserved but /gl/ was reduced to /l/. Medially, liquid+stop clusters were preserved while voiced stop+liquid clusters were sometimes reduced to liquid only. Clusters of medial nasal+stop were sometimes reduced to the nasal in Castilian, sometimes with palatalization of the nasal.

In Western Finnic the few examples of cluster reduction are all medial. Loss of /n/ before /s/, with or without compensatory vowel lengthening, occurs here as in many other languages. Older loan words in Finnish and Estonian from Russian or German consistently show loss of the first consonant of any word-initial cluster, regardless of consonantal type (e.g. Russian *gramota* 'reading and writing' > Estonian *raamat* 'book', Finnish *raamattu* 'bible'; German *Spiegel*, Estonian *peegel* 'mirror', German *Frau* 'wife, woman', Finnish *rouva* 'Mrs.', etc.).

Finally, in Germanic, though cluster reduction is uncommon, liquids tend to be retained in cases of fricative+liquid or liquid+nasal while the nasal tends to be lost in cases of nasal+fricative (as in Finnic) or stop+nasal. Summarizing, then, liquids appear highly favoured in all four families, fricatives are retained more frequently than nasals, and position in the cluster is sometimes relevant, especially initially. Each of these tendencies contradicts the observed child patterns.

Vihman (1980) disregarded many processes reported in adult languages, such as vowel harmony, but this process is rare in child data, most likely because vowel production and planning are less problematic for the developing child than are consonant production and planning (Stoel-Gammon 1992). Similarly, interactions between consonant and vowel (e.g. nasalization, palatalization) play a large role in language change but are rarely reported for child language.

In conclusion, although two of the three processes examined do play a role in both developmental and historical contexts, once we have considered the details of each subtype we find it considerably less tempting to ascribe causality for change to the developing child, at least where the early stages of word production are concerned.

A final point made in Vihman (1980) is worth repeating: whereas contrast is a key principle in adult language, and is therefore often evoked as playing a role in change or resistance to change diachronically, for children the situation is very different. The child speaks largely of the here and now, to familiar interlocutors, whether at home or at nursery; where communication breaks down (from an adult point of view), the child often shifts topics without missing a beat (Vihman 1981), a good indication of their relative indifference to precise lexical (and so phonological) choice. Thus omission of a segment or syllable is unlikely to cause problems. At the same time, if clarity is not an issue for the child, recall certainly is:

> What does pose a problem for the child is the burden placed on his capacities for storage and retrieval of units of information as his vocabulary increases exponentially (by literally hundreds of words a month, in some cases). [Vihman 1980: 315]

Here consonant harmony, for example, plays a useful role in limiting the bits of information per word that the child must retain (Vihman 1978, Menn 1983). The need for such constraints fades as the child's familiarity with phonotactics increases (Storkel 2001, Edwards, Beckman, & Munson 2004). Although aspects of morphophonemics may take several more years to master, the error types analysed here are typically no longer part of productive phonology after age 3 or 4.

18.3.2 Sociolinguistic Studies

Sociolinguistic studies of acquisition are scarce (see Roberts 2002). However, several important issues emerge from these studies, in particular concerning the nature and type of input, and the social context in which learning unfolds.

18.3.2.1 *Input and Influence*

Weinreich et al. (1968: 145) criticize the simple model of acquisition and change described by Halle (1962) and others (discussed in section 18.1), because of its reliance on the 'unexamined assumption that the children's grammars are formed upon the data provided by their parents' speech'. The primary input for language learning need not be a sample of the language used between adults. Thus it may be methodologically inappropriate to focus on comparisons between children's speech patterns and those of adults. Children also learn from other children, especially once they begin to interact with peers on a regular basis. Several studies show that children's phonetic and phonological patterns are closely aligned with those of their caregivers early on, but diverge later as the peer group becomes more important (Foulkes et al. 2005, Smith et al. 2007). Young children are also often diverse as a group. A clear example is provided by studies in the new town of Milton Keynes (Kerswill 1995, Kerswill & Williams 2005). A large number of in-migrants to the town created a complex dialect contact situation. Kerswill & Williams tracked the linguistic development of three groups of children and their parents: 4-year-olds, who were still cared for at home, and schoolchildren aged 8 and 12. Analysis of several phonological variables revealed that the 4-year-olds' production patterns closely resembled those of their parents, and reflected the mix of dialects in the community. Older children, however, showed a more homogeneous, levelled dialect, with little influence of minority home dialects. Kerswill (1995) considers whether developmental patterns might lead to change, noting that Milton Keynes children displayed several processes that are also ongoing sound changes in British English. These include vocalization of /-l/, labiodental /r/, and [f, v] for /θ, ð/. Kerswill found that some developmental patterns were common in the youngest children, then gradually disappeared as their speech matured—but re-emerged as dialectal features in pre-adolescents. These studies show that peer influence during adolescence exerts an especially strong effect on linguistic patterns, with non-standard forms transmitted most readily at this stage in life (Weinreich et al. 1968, Labov 2001, Hazen 2002, D'Arcy, this volume). Such findings suggest that differences between generations are more likely to be seen during later development than at the earliest stages of acquisition.

More recent studies shed further light on the nature of input, showing that it varies between children and according to social factors such as age and gender (of both child and adult). Hazen (2002) reviews studies of children whose parents speak different dialects, and for whom phonological learning may therefore involve multiple targets. Foulkes et al. (2005) examined consonantal realizations in child-directed speech (CDS) by a group of women from Newcastle, north-east England (see section 18.4.2). The main focus was on forms of intervocalic /p t k/, which are realized locally as voiced, glottalized/laryngealized and lenited stops (typically transcribed [b̥d̥g̃]). Local variants occurred in around 90% of tokens in speech between adults, but only 36% of tokens in CDS. Mothers instead preferred plain oral stops, as in standard English. Individual mothers varied in their use of the local variants (occupying the full range: 0–100%). Moreover, variation was observed within CDS as a function of child age. Standard variants decreased across the age range, and were statistically more frequent in CDS to girls. Input also varies according to style of speech. Labov (2001: 420) argues that style variation is crucial for the transmission of sociolinguistic variation. Speech to children varies in formality, with more formal language associated with teaching and discipline, and characterized by greater usage of standard forms. Smith et al. (2007) examined CDS patterns in Buckie, Scotland, and indeed found that mothers used standard forms more in formal interactions, and local variants in less formal ones (play, intimacy).

18.3.2.2 *Social Variation in Transmission of Change*

Sociolinguistic studies regularly show that changes are adopted by some subgroups in a society earlier than others. Gender-based differences, for example, are found in almost all societies that have been investigated. Typically, females lead the transmission of changes, and are sometimes a generation ahead of males in their community (Labov 2001: 306). If acquisition were the primary cause of change it would be impossible to explain why this should be. Given essentially the same vocal tracts and general developmental abilities, there is no reason why girls should create or adopt new forms earlier than boys. Similarly, Labov (2001) provides extensive documentation that changes generally originate in the middle of the socioeconomic hierarchy. Milroy (1987) shows that changes are more likely to be transmitted in open social networks, where individuals enjoy physical and social mobility. She further suggests that different social structures may be conducive to transmission of different types of change (Milroy 2007). These facts, too, are inexplicable if we seek causes of change in development. Clearly, social context affects what is learned and when.

Finally, transmission requires interaction in structured social groups, with influence typically flowing from the more socially influential individuals, or groups, to the less so. Aitchison (2003: 739), in dismissing the role of children in promoting change, points out that babies do not form influential social groups. Their speech patterns are thus unlikely to be adopted by other speakers.

18.3.3 Summary

These studies show that there may be significant differences between the features of the target language being acquired and the raw materials upon which acquisition is based. Simple comparison of adult and child forms may therefore not be appropriate for assessing learning or variation in developmental forms as a route to change. Leaving such matters aside, however, we turn now to some new empirical data.

18.4 DATA

We present two datasets, from a developmental study and a sociolinguistic investigation. Both are drawn from monolingual children learning British English. Our aim in both cases is to establish a systematic and accountable corpus of child speech. We have gathered our data from transcripts prepared for other purposes, as part of larger projects. Patterns from the corpora have been identified independently of prior expectation about: (i) the sorts of developmental forms that we might find, and (ii) potential parallels with phonological change.

The two datasets differ in several respects. The recordings were collected and analysed using frameworks and methods from different traditions, with different assumptions concerning the phonological targets to be acquired. The developmental data were collected in a longitudinal study comparing late talkers to typically developing children, with no specific attention to either the community or the phonetics of the parents' speech; they reflect a single developmentally based 'moment' for the entire group. The sociolinguistic data were collected to assess the nature and time-course of learning detailed phonetic and phonological patterns, based on previous sociophonetic studies of the adult community (Docherty et al. 1997, Docherty & Foulkes 1999).

Ideally we would like to compare our child data against an inventory of sound changes reported cross-linguistically in a balanced sample of languages (akin to the phoneme inventory information provided by Maddieson 1984). However, no such inventory exists (a fact noted by Ferguson 1990, and the intervening years have not fundamentally changed the situation; see further Kümmel, this volume). We draw on Blevins's (2004a) summary of common changes from 99 languages where appropriate. In addition, we note changes commonly reported in the historical phonology literature. We acknowledge that such evidence is not ideal. It may not be based on empirically robust data collection, many of the same examples may have been borrowed across different texts, and data are often pre-selected to illustrate theoretical claims.

18.4.1 Data from a Developmental Study[1]

The data summarized above from Vihman (1980) covered only the first year or so of word production and focused on three common processes. To complement this, we now review data from the transcribed recordings of a much larger sample of typically developing monolingual English-learners from North Wales (TDs; N = 11, 6 boys) and late talkers (LTs: children who had few words and no word combinations at 24 months; N = 21, 14 boys) from both North Wales and York (Vihman, Keren-Portnoy, Whitaker, Bidgood & McGillion 2013). The children range in age from 2;4 to 4;2, with most between 3 and 4 years. The 30-minute recording sessions (one for each child, at home, with a familiar adult interlocutor) took place 14 months (±2) after each child had been transcribed as using about 25 words in a 30-minute session, a developmental point corresponding roughly to the end of the single-word period. All these children are regularly producing longer utterances (mean length of utterance: 2.7 words).

We consider the full range of error types seen in these children. We do not attempt to relate these data in any systematic way to historical data, since, as noted above, no convenient inventory of historical processes is available. Instead, we report all of the error types made by these children, expanding the age range covered by Vihman (1980) while restricting ourselves to English and offering some general comments on similarities to, and differences from, well-attested historical processes.

Whereas the children described in Vihman (1980) were all typically developing, some of the children in the present corpus began to talk late. Since LTs tend to make more phonological errors at a later age, while producing longer sentences and conversing more frequently with interlocutors outside their immediate family, the influence, if any, of 'imperfect learning' is at least as likely to be traceable to them as to the very young children analysed in Vihman (1980).

Whereas Vihman (1980) calculated proportions of errors over words produced for her sample of children within the single-word period, this would be inappropriate for these more advanced children. To establish overall frequency of occurrence, however, one can assume that each instance of an error type occurred in a different utterance (although this is not strictly true). Accordingly, for example, the 108 instances of stopping of /ð/

---

[1] Our thanks to Amy Bidgood, who carried out much of the error analysis reported in section 18.4.1.

by TDs can be taken to have occurred (at most) in 108/1100 (11*100-utterance samples), or 9.82% of the utterances produced by TDs. The next most frequent error, consonant deletion (in any position) occurred, in the two samples combined, in 302 utterances, or 9.44% of all utterances produced. About half of the error types occurred in no more than 2% of all utterances produced in either sample.

Table 18.1 lists the 43 error types identified in the 100-utterance sample of two or more of the 32 children. Error types that occurred no more than once only for any one child are taken to be speech errors and are disregarded, as are error types that occurred more than once yet only sporadically and in the speech of only one child.

It is apparent that in the spontaneous running speech of these children very few error types account for more than a small proportion of the errors—and some of the more common ones may reflect parental usage (e.g. stopping of /ð/), although an attempt was made to take dialect differences into account. The LT sample is not quite twice as large but accounts for well over twice the errors. Nevertheless, each error type accounts for only a small proportion of the total, and the ordering of error-type use for the LTs is only marginally different from that of the TDs.

Consonant deletion is the second most common process, evidenced in some form by all but one child; this includes both initial and final positions. In Table 18.2 we provide examples of the error types that we discuss, drawing, in each case, on the TD child who made the error most frequently.

Final consonant deletion (1) occurs for several children, but the incidence is low. Initial consonant deletion (2) affects function words far more than content words, which may reflect adult casual speech usage (but could also be ascribed to misperception of non-salient syllables). No other error type accounts for as much as 10% of the errors identified for the TDs; many, such as consonant insertion, appear to be one-off careless productions: e.g. Martin: *zip* [snɪp] (possibly a lexical error).

Palatalization, which, as noted above, might be expected as a natural consequence of the specific characteristics of the child vocal tract, accounts for 4% of TD errors, and 6% of LT errors. In most cases it is the alveolar sibilants /s, z/ that are palatalized (3). 'Palatal fronting' (i.e. /ʃ/ → [s]), which is more commonly mentioned in the child phonology literature, here accounts for only 1% of the errors in either group (4).

Of the processes detailed for younger children in Vihman (1980), weak syllable deletion is the most common, accounting for 3% of TD errors and 4% of LT errors, occurring in the speech of 21 children (5). The most common occurrence is word-final unstressed syllable omission in words—or any position in phrases. The process is thus different from what we see in first words, but the occurrences are rare.

Consonant harmony, however, is expected only rarely in children of this age (Grunwell 1982), and indeed accounts for just 1% of the errors for the TDs and 2% for the LTs (6). Note that it is difficult, in running speech, to distinguish consonant harmony as a process from speech errors of the kind found in adults (see Jaeger 2005). Virtually all of the errors are single occurrences, rather than the stable lexical use we see in younger children.

Finally, cluster reduction is divided here into a number of distinct processes (7–11). All of these error types combined account for 9% of TD and 10% of LT errors. The type of

Table 18.1 Error types identified in 100-utterance samples for each of 32 children aged 2;4–4;2, ordered by typically developing children's errors. 'Instances' refers to the raw occurrences of each error; '%' refers to the proportion of each error type observed in relation to all errors identified in the sample; 'children' refers to the number of children who exhibited each error type. C = consonant

Error types	Typically developing (N = 11)			Late talkers (N = 21)		
	instances	%	children	instances	%	children
stopping of /ð/	108	11.46	10	280	12.13	19
/C/ deletion	91	9.66	11	211	9.14	20
velar fronting	82	8.70	5	125	5.41	10
gliding of /r, l/	67	7.11	9	168	7.28	17
'lisping' or /θ/ for /s/ substitution	58	6.16	7	115	4.98	14
palatalization	41	4.35	7	128	5.54	11
gliding (other)	37	3.93	7	48	2.08	7
/C/ insertion	32	3.40	8	81	3.51	16
/l/ vocalization	32	3.40	6	36	1.56	5
glottal stopping	30	3.18	5	35	1.52	8
weak syll. deletion	26	2.76	6	84	3.64	15
/Cr/ reduction	25	2.65	6	61	2.64	8
/sC/ reduction	23	2.44	5	58	2.51	10
/ð/ substitution	20	2.12	5	26	1.13	5
fricativization	20	2.12	6	71	3.07	14
velarization	20	2.12	4	71	3.07	10
affricate reduction	16	1.70	5	64	2.77	11
/CC/ reduction (other)	15	1.59	5	53	2.30	15
nasalization	15	1.59	2	48	2.08	8
affricativization	14	1.49	3	54	2.34	9
/Cl/ reduction	14	1.49	3	39	1.69	8
nasal-/l/ alternation	14	1.49	3	21	0.91	5
lateralization	13	1.38	3	15	0.65	1
syllable insertion	12	1.27	2	27	1.17	8
/C/ harmony	11	1.17	3	39	1.69	10
blending	11	1.17	3	19	0.82	4
/v/ substitution	11	1.17	4	9	0.39	1
/CC/ deletion	9	0.96	2	11	0.48	2
metathesis	9	0.96	3	16	0.69	5
palatal fronting	9	0.96	2	13	0.56	2
contiguous assimilation	8	0.85	1	18	0.78	3
glide stopping	8	0.85	3	9	0.39	3
/l/ stopping	7	0.74	2	7	0.30	2
stopping of /s/	7	0.74	2	39	1.69	6
/θ/ substitution	7	0.74	1	26	1.13	6
labialization	5	0.53	0	56	2.43	11
glottalization	4	0.42	1	13	0.56	2
stopping of /z/	4	0.42	0	17	0.74	3

Table 18.1 Continued

Error types	Typically developing (N = 11)			Late talkers (N = 21)		
	instances	%	children	instances	%	children
nasal stopping	2	0.21	0	26	1.13	7
stopping of /f/	2	0.21	1	46	1.99	5
stopping of /ʃ/	2	0.21	1	3	0.13	1
degliding	1	0.11	0	9	0.39	2
stopping of /v/	0	0.00	0	14	0.61	4
TOTAL	942	99.98		2,309	100.02	

Table 18.2 Examples of errors (child age in year;months.days)

Example	Child	Age	Target	Production
(1) final /C/ deletion	Owen	3;0.5	*like*	[laɪ]
(2) initial /C/ deletion	Owen	3;0.5	*yellow*	[ɛləʊ]
(3) palatalization	Ali	3;1.10	*that is beans*	[daçɪçbiːç]
(4) palatal fronting	Andy	3;0.11	*paintbrush*	[peɪʔbɒs]
(5) weak syllable deletion	Jude	2;6.10	*Barcelona*	[baθəʊn] (said twice in this form)
(6) consonant harmony	Ali	3;1.10	*more*	[mɔːm] (/C/ insertion + harmony)
(7) /Cr/ reduction	Owen	3;0.5	*fried*	[faid]
(8) /sC/ reduction	Tomos	3;1.5	*strawberry*	[dɔːbiː]
(9) /Cl/ reduction	Tomos	3;1.5	*plate*	[pʰeɪʔtʰ]
(10) cluster blending	Owen	3;0.5	*play*	[feɪ]
(11) other cluster reduction	Ali	3;1.10	*milk*	[mɪk]
			stand	[tad]

reduction is the same as that described by Vihman (1980): retention of the non-liquid—and, in the case of 'other' cluster reduction, which generally involves nasals, retention of the nasal in most cases.

In summary, taking exhaustive account of all the mispronunciations made by children who are well beyond the single-word stage, we find a wide range of different errors, none used consistently or with great frequency by any of the children. What were pervasive errors for some children at the younger age (consonant harmony, syllable deletion) are now sporadic, with a suggestion of lexical rather than phonological errors in some cases. Where errors are still fairly common at this developmental point (cluster reduction), they agree with the analysis of earlier child errors in being quite different in detail from those found in sound change. None of this appears to offer much support for the hypothesis that change has its roots in mislearning by children.

18.4.2 Data from a Sociophonetic Study

Data are drawn from the *Emergence of Structured Variation* (*ESV*) corpus, comprising recordings from first-born children from Newcastle (Docherty et al. 2002). The main aim of *ESV* was to track acquisition of sociolinguistic variants. Forty children (20 boys) were recorded in a cross-sectional design at ages 2;0, 2;6, 3;0, 3;6 and 4;0. Ten children were followed longitudinally over the same age range (yielding a further 52 recordings). Recordings ranged from 15 to 45 minutes, involving free play and picture-book tasks with the mother. The original transcriptions focused on words containing /t/ in several phonological and prosodic contexts (Table 18.3). Auditory transcriptions were supported by acoustic analysis.

The original transcriptions were reanalysed for this chapter, in order to identify common deviations from adult target forms which might constitute innovations. We also assessed the children's role in transmission, comparing their use of variants known to be participating in ongoing changes.

Since the *ESV* project was interested in variation, we took a sociolinguistically and phonetically informed view of phonological targets and considered all variants of /t/ that are found in normal adult speech. Thus we did not consider the target necessarily to be [t]. Previous work had revealed a range of variants associated with particular contexts, varying in voicing, pre-aspiration, glottaling/laryngealization, and place and manner of articulation (Docherty et al. 1997, Foulkes & Docherty 2006). Table 18.4 summarizes the most frequently encountered phonetic forms in the child corpus.

A search of sources on sound change revealed a number of common processes that affect /t/ or all voiceless stops. These are summarized in Table 18.5, and form a set of predicted potential changes to be tested via the dataset.

The first five changes listed in Table 18.5 were investigated as potential innovations. Glottaling and pre-aspiration are already present in the Newcastle dialect, and participate in ongoing change. They were therefore examined as transmission changes. Consonant harmony was not analysed as it is virtually unknown in change, despite being common in child language.

Examination of transcriptions was quantitative and fully accountable, that is, all tokens of target /t/ were considered (N = 3,804) in the contexts listed in Table 18.4. 'Accuracy' was judged relative to documented adult variants, again as shown in

Table 18.3 Phonological contexts included in /t/ analysis

Context	Definition	Examples
Initial	word-initial pre-vowel	*teddy, top, table*
Medial	V__(#)V, foot-internal	*water, it is*
	__l	*little, bottle*
	T-to-R contexts	*put a, get on*
Final	turn final; excludes consonant clusters	*cat, boat, what?*

Table 18.4 Variants of /t/ found in child corpus

Context		Accurate	Inaccurate (examples)
Initial		t tʰ tˢ	tʃ t̪ ɬ tθ θ s c cʰ k x q h
Medial	V__(#)V foot-internal	t tʰ tˢ ɾ d d̪ʔ	deletion
	__l	t tʰ tˢ ɾ d d̪ʔ	consonant harmony
	T-to-R contexts	t tʰ tˢ ɾ d d̪ʔ ɹ ʋ	
turn-final		t tʰ tˢ ʔ ʰt t̚	

Table 18.5 Common sound changes affecting /t/

Type	Source	Language(s)	Notes
1. voicing/deaspiration	Lavoie (2001)	Urubu-Kapoor	
2. place change,	Scheer (this volume)	Hawai'ian	rare; mainly occurs
e.g. /t/ > /k/	Blevins (2004a: 123)	Austronesian	where /k/ is lacking in
	Fox (1995: 82)		inventory
3. frication/affrication	Ohala (2005)	Mvumbo	mainly occurs pre-close
	Lavoie (2001)	West Greenlandic	vowel or intervocalically
4. /t/ > /h/	Gillies (2009: 251)	Scottish Gaelic	synchronic mutation
5. deletion	Blevins (2004a: 165)	50 Australian	rare in initial position,
		aboriginal lgs	more common
			elsewhere
6. glottaling	Fabricius (2000), etc.	English	context sensitive
7. pre-aspiration	Silverman (2003)	Icelandic	mostly in final contexts
8. consonant harmony	Blevins (2004a: 230)	?	rare in sound change

Table 18.4. In all cases phonological context was taken into account, since some variants are conditioned by context, and context-free sound changes appear to be unusual in adult languages (Blevins 2004a). For example, voicing was not considered for medial /t/, as statistically most adult variants are voiced. Frication/affrication of /t/ is also found for adults, so only certain fricative/affricate forms were considered inaccurate (e.g. [s, x]). Errors defined as 'release type' had [t] produced accurately but the fricative release occurred at a different place of articulation from those used by adults (usually [tʃ]). We concentrate on data from the children in the cross-sectional study. Longitudinal data showed similar patterns.

18.4.2.1 *Potential Innovations*

Data are shown in Figures 18.1–18.3 (initial, medial and final /t/, respectively; medial contexts are combined for simplicity). In each figure overall accuracy is shown via a dotted line oriented to the right-hand axis. Error types are aligned to the left-hand axis. Data are pooled from eight children at each age.

Figures 18.1–18.3 all show a clear rising trend for accuracy by age. Error types are more frequent for younger children, gradually diminishing to low rates for the oldest children (mostly under 2% per context for the 4;0 group).

In each context we also see peaks in the distribution of some error types (voicing in initial context, affrication and stop place medially, and [h] finally). These peaks are all due to one or two children showing high use of the process. For instance, the peak in final [h] is generated by one boy who contributes 40 of the 56 tokens to the 3;0 group. Moreover, [h] is also lexically restricted for him, with 37 tokens occurring on *what?* Interestingly, patterns for the children in the longitudinal study also showed numerous peaks. We interpret peaks as an indication that the children were experimenting with articulatory strategies at certain points in their development, eventually dispensing with phonetic forms that are not sufficiently good matches to adult usage.

The apparent rising trend in medial deletion can also be ascribed to two high scoring individuals, one each aged 3;6 and 4;0. Both children mostly show deletion in a small set of common words: *get, got, getting, what, not, it*. Although not previously reported for adults in Newcastle, deletion of /t/ in connected speech has been noted for other English dialects, especially with frequent words (e.g. Fabricius 2000: 85), and we have also since observed both this and final [h] in the speech of Newcastle adults. Deletion may therefore in fact reflect advanced articulatory skills, emerging as the children develop rapid and fluent speech. Turn-final deletion, by contrast, is rare (as in the developmental data, section 18.4.1) and decreases with age.

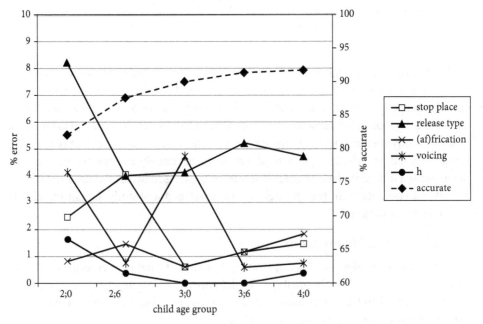

FIG. 18.1 Accuracy and error types (%) by age group, initial /t/. Accuracy is plotted against the right axis, error types against the left axis.

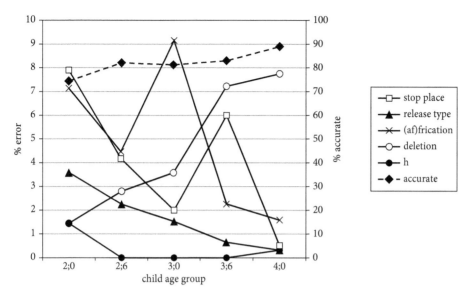

FIG. 18.2 Accuracy and error types (%) by age group, medial /t/. Accuracy is plotted against the right axis, error types against the left axis.

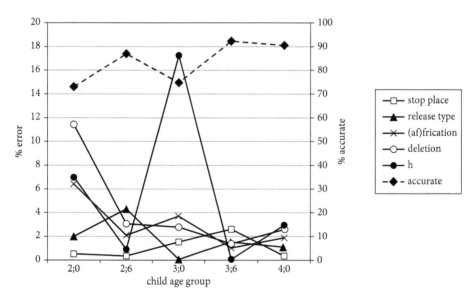

FIG. 18.3 Accuracy and error types (%) by age group, final /t/. Accuracy is plotted against the right axis, error types against the left axis.

For initial /t/ the most frequent error is release type. This mainly comprises realizations transcribed as [tʃ], with 33 of 37 such tokens preceding a close or close-mid vowel /iː eː uː oː ɪ ʊ/. This pattern is indeed predicted as a conditioned sound change. Ohala (2005), for example, hypothesizes that alveolar stops are likely to affricate adjacent to close front vowels. The narrow channel created by the stop closure yields a higher volume velocity of airflow at the stop release, which may generate frication in the post-alveolar region. The release type error is also less frequent in medial and final contexts. This might be explained by the high incidence of initial stress in English words, resulting in greater airflow at word onset and thus a greater likelihood of generating turbulent airflow at stop release. Initial release type errors remain relatively stable across the age range, but are still low in overall frequency (4–5% from 2;6 onwards).

Stop place errors in initial context are generally palatal (16/21 tokens), such as *tiger* [cʰ-]. This pattern appears at odds with what is expected for change: in sound change palatals usually arise via fronting of velars, not retraction of alveolars (Fox 1995: 82, Ohala 2005). However, differences in the shape and size of children's vocal tracts relative to adult ones predict a high incidence of [c] for /t/ (see section 18.3.1.1). /t-/ → [k-] is vanishingly rare (2 tokens in 1016), as predicted in change. In medial context, by contrast, stop place errors are mostly [k] (38/49 errors, with five more transcribed as uvular, all by the same child). All [k/q] tokens occur in the words *little* or *bottle*. This lexically restricted error is common for British children and might reflect lexical variants used in CDS. (We do not attribute the retraction of /t/ to the final /l/, since in Newcastle coda /l/ is not velarized and no other /-l/ words are affected.)

In summary, these data, like those considered in section 18.4.1, offer little support for the hypothesis that child errors are a likely source of innovations. The observation of peaks is difficult to reconcile as an indication of new forms emerging that might eventually pervade the whole dialect. They seem far too restricted, with respect to both individuals and time windows, to have much chance of being adopted and transmitted. Lexically restricted patterns such as [k] in *little*, *bottle* might in principle indicate a lexical diffusion change, but in this case such forms are common for British English-speaking children and are not usually acceptable adult forms. Finally, with the exception of initial [tʃ-], error patterns in the data appear to be counter to known patterns of change.

18.4.2.2 *Transmission Changes*

Both turn-final glottaling and pre-aspiration are sound changes in progress in Newcastle, both statistically more common for females. Pre-aspiration is reported in detail in Foulkes & Docherty (2006). Overall there is considerable variability in the frequency of pre-aspiration for both children and mothers. Usage by younger children shows a statistically significant correlation with that of their mothers. Older children, however, produce pre-aspiration at high rates, whether or not their mothers do so. Moreover, girls produce more pre-aspiration than boys at 3;6 and 4;0.

A comparable pattern is found for glottaling. Final glottal stops are rare in Newcastle, and are especially attracted to tag questions (Docherty et al. 1997). It was not possible to assess systematically whether tags affected the child data, but since tags are discourse features we would only expect to see them in the speech of older children. In the cross-sectional data 13.5% of all turn-final /t/ were realized as glottals, with considerable variation between children (0–85% if we include children in the longitudinal sample). When examined by age group (Figure 18.4), the rate of glottaling increases significantly in line with age (Pearson's $r = 0.354$, df $= 38$, $p = 0.025$, 2-tailed), although much of this effect

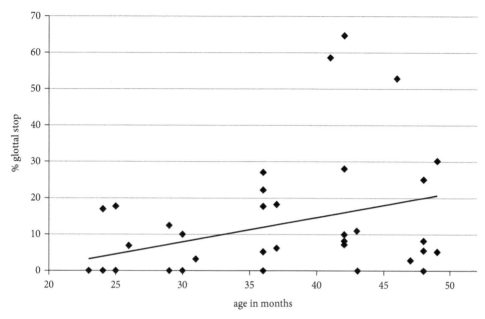

FIG. 18.4 Glottal stop usage (%) by age group, final /t/. 8 speakers per age group. (Note that some data points are wholly overlapped.)

is due to the three high-scoring older children (all boys). Longitudinal data also show an overall rising trend, however. The gender pattern is not the same as that found for adults. Boys used more glottals than girls (18.9% vs 7.7% overall), and in all age groups except at 2;6.

In sum, for both pre-aspiration and glottaling the children appear to be accelerating ongoing changes (compare the 'incrementation' pattern as considered by D'Arcy, this volume). Note that the higher usage by older children, and for pre-aspiration the emerging gender differentiation, indicate that the forms have been acquired as learned sociolinguistic variants, not as the result of error by immature speakers.

18.4.2.3 *Summary*

As was the case with the data presented in section 18.4.1, we see little evidence for errors as the source of change. We do see, however, that older children are participating in changes in progress.

18.5 CONCLUSION

We have reviewed previous commentaries on child language as a source of (segmental) change, highlighting the fact that there has been little consensus and remarkably few systematic attempts to address the issue empirically. We therefore assembled two large datasets to assess impartially whether error data are suggestive of change. We acknowledge that these datasets do not settle the debate definitively, being limited to a small set of phonological units and processes in one language. We also concur with Bloomfield (1933): no single explanation is likely to satisfy all nuances of what is a very complex question.

However, our conclusion is that early errors are highly unlikely to lead to change. Errors diminish with time, and some early processes disappear by around age 3. Others appear and disappear sporadically, and are limited to particular individuals. Initiation changes, if ascribed to vocal tract dynamics or perceptual factors, are no more likely to be the responsibility of children than of adults. It is also imperative to acknowledge the extent of variation between individuals learning the same language, especially at younger ages, a fact largely ignored by previous commentators. For a new generation to recast a grammar would appear unlikely when members of that generation take so many different paths to acquire it (see further Vihman et al. 1994).

Children's role in transmitting changes in progress is more readily demonstrable. But it is to the performance of older rather than younger children that we must look, and it is more profitable to conceptualize child patterns as learned features than as errors. Understanding the social context in which learning takes place is crucial, to explain why certain individuals influence others linguistically, and why linguistic variants confer some sort of social or communicative advantage to language users.

The answers to many other questions about change remain partial. To what extent are innovations the product of vocal tract dynamics, and to what extent the product of forces internal to the grammar (cf. Jones, this volume)? In transmission, what factors are necessary for, or conducive to, new forms being transmitted? Finally, for both innovation and transmission, we can only echo Saussure and Bloomfield: 'why here?, why now?'

....

CHAPTER 19

HOW DIACHRONIC IS SYNCHRONIC GRAMMAR? CRAZY RULES, REGULARITY, AND NATURALNESS

....

TOBIAS SCHEER

19.1 INTRODUCTION

....

REGULARITY in linguistic patterning is the result of grammatical computation: it is due to the fact that lexically stored pieces are run through a computational system (made of rules or constraints) before they reach the surface. What we see, then, are the traces that grammar leaves on the lexical ingredients, and these traces are regular.

This view is held in generative quarters at least for synchronic patterning. Another classical tenet which is intuitive and widespread among linguists is the idea that phonological processes are natural. This may mean a variety of things (Postal's 1968: 53 ff. Natural Condition is an influential early reference), but essentially has two requirements: (1) there are constraints on which segment any other segment can alternate with (i.e. the relationship between A and B in A → B / C is not arbitrary), and (2) there is a non-arbitrary causal relationship between the triggering context (C in our example) and the structural change observed (A → B).

This chapter tackles the question of naturalness in generative phonology: what is an innocent rule[1] (k → t͡s / __i,e), what is a suspicious rule (k → s / __i), and what is a crazy rule (k → m / __ŋ)? Crazy rules are rules that make no (phonetic or phonological) sense (Bach & Harms 1972). It also enquires into the sources of computation-created regularity. In both cases, diachrony underlies synchronic patterns (see Blevins, this volume, for

---

[1] I talk about rules throughout, rather than about constraints, when referring to phonological computation. All statements could be translated into constraints.

a related position). The real issue at stake in the chapter, then, is the relationship between synchronic computation and diachronic evolution in sound patterns. How much diachrony, if any, is in synchronic grammar? How does it get there? How is diachronic information represented in the synchronic computational system? Can computation itself age, and if so, what does the diachronic evolution of a phonological rule look like? Of course there is no cognitive computation over time: the human brain cannot compute a twenty-first-century output form based on an input form from, say, the nineteenth century (see the opening dilemma in Hale et al., this volume). Given this, what might it mean for a phonological process to be diachronic: aren't all rules necessarily synchronic?

The classical generative position sees sound change as the result of a modification of the rule system through rule addition, rule suppression, or rule reordering (e.g. Halle 1962, Kiparsky 1968: 174–5, King 1969: 39 ff., Dresher, this volume).[2] Generativists thus implicitly claim that synchronic alternations and diachronic innovations are the same thing: they are the product of grammatical computation, and this computation is only synchronic. Strictly speaking, then, there is no such thing as diachronic innovation: diachronic patterns are simply 'old' synchronic computation which may have aged and is looked at with hindsight. Today's synchronic processes are tomorrow's diachronic patterns, and what we identify as diachronic processes today were synchronically active processes at some earlier stage. In sum, diachrony in sound patterns is a matter of computation and of nothing else.

An alternative scenario is Bach & Harms's (1972) idea that grammar need not evolve by modifying its rule inventory, but rather by modifying existing rules. Hence A → B / C may age by substituting, say, B with Z. This is how crazy rules are born, i.e. rules which 'make no sense', phonetically or phonologically. This chapter discusses crazy rules and presents one in detail: the alternation between l and ʁ that is found in external sandhi in certain varieties of Sardinian (section 19.5). My aim is to evaluate the consequences of crazy rules for phonological theory: are these patterns really the result of synchronic phonological computation? Which (ideally theory-neutral) criteria allow us to decide whether an alternation derives from distinct lexical items or is the result of computation? In the latter case, how do we know whether this computation is (1) phonological, (2) morphophonological (in the structuralist sense), (3) allomorphic, or (4) analogical?

I consider the response of a number of phonological frameworks to crazy rules; they fall into two major categories, either claiming that 'small is beautiful' (such that phonology is shrunk: only a small subset of what Chomsky & Halle 1968 (henceforth *SPE*) managed is due to phonological computation) or that 'big is beautiful' (*SPE* was right: anything can turn into anything in any context). The former approach defines and upholds a notion of naturalness, the latter does not (sections 19.3 and 19.6). (Non-generative approaches to change are considered elsewhere in this handbook, for example in Phillips, this volume, and Bybee, this volume.)

---

[2] See the critique of this position in Hale et al. (this volume). Of course, this position also allows for the restructuring of underlying forms. This is not spontaneous, but the result of pressure from the computational system. Innovation, generativists say, is only due to the modification of the rule system.

Finally, the chapter shows that crazy rules are only ever *melodically* crazy: there is no craziness reported from syllable structure or stress assignment (section 19.7). This provides further evidence that the areas above and below the skeleton are fundamentally different in kind.

19.2 DIACHRONIC AND SYNCHRONIC PHONOLOGY: THE SAME OR DIFFERENT?

19.2.1 Processes: a large Overlap, also in What is Unattested

Let us begin by asking whether synchronic and diachronic regularity are the same: is phonology one, or are there two distinct phonologies, one diachronic, the other synchronic? If there are two, we might expect that the two computational systems produce different patterns because they may be inherently different (compare Kiparsky, this volume, on 'Saussure's Firewall').

Even a cursory consideration shows that synchronic and diachronic patterns by and large overlap. We do not need here to review pattern after pattern in order to see whether there is a synchronic and a diachronic match (e.g. Ohala 1992: 310 ff., 1993: 239 ff.). Rather, let us take a global look at the processes that exist on both sides.

I distinguish here between *processes* and *patterns*. Palatalization is a process, while k → t͡ʃ /__i,e is a pattern. The same processes are known from synchronic alternations and diachronic evolution. Closed syllable shortening, open syllable lengthening, and compensatory lengthening for example are found both in diachronic and synchronic phonology. On the other hand, closed syllable lengthening, open syllable shortening, and compensatory shortening are as outlandish on the synchronic side as they are in diachronic evolution.[3]

What is interesting is that the list of processes that are absent from the record also seem to coincide. This is true for closed syllable lengthening, open syllable shortening, and compensatory shortening, but also for a very broad and deeply rooted asymmetry in phonology such as the absence of velarization, as opposed to the plethora of palatalizations that occur. The general trend is fairly consensual: there is a great overlap between the phonological processes found in synchronic and diachronic phonology, both in terms of occurring and non-occurring items.

---

[3] The notions 'closed syllable lengthening' and 'open syllable shortening' are frequently misunderstood. Cases where vowel lengthening in closed syllables is observed in isolated forms or for melodic reasons (e.g. before voiced consonants) *do not* count as closed syllable lengthening. What would count is the existence of a *causal relationship* between the syllabic environment and the modification of length. Hence a closed syllable shortening is a shortening that is *specifically* triggered by closed syllables. It therefore occurs in *all* closed syllables and only in this environment. The same goes for putative closed syllable lengthening, which would be a process whereby short vowels lengthen *specifically* in closed syllables and *nowhere else*.

Are there *any* phonological processes that occur synchronically, but are absent from the diachronic record, or vice versa? Candidates that exhale a distinctly diachronic flavour include metathesis and rhotacism. The former was already suspicious to the neogrammarians, who excluded from sound change all processes that do not substitute one segment with another, as well as those that cannot be gradient in the substitution of the old by the new form (e.g. Hock 1991: 630–1, Murray, this volume). Metathesis meets both criteria: there is no way of having a consonant jump over another segment just a little bit. On top (or because) of its disqualification from the class of sound changes, metathesis was held to be 'inherently sporadic', rather than systematic and regular (Lass 1997: 134). Together with analogy, haplology, and dissimilation, metathesis was thus classified as a 'psychological' change (i.e. one which is partly under the spell of conscious control, as opposed to sound change, which is a natural event).

The presence of metathesis in the synchronic computation of certain languages is certainly beyond any doubt. Sardinian for instance has a metathesis in external sandhi, i.e. that applies across word boundaries, which therefore guarantees synchronic activity.[4] In the dialects of Genoni and Sestu Campidanese (see map under example (4)), the R of vowel-initial words of the shape VRTV such as ['ɛrba] 'grass' appears to the left of the initial vowel if preceded by a consonant-final word: /sa ɛrba/ 'the (sg.) grass' and /papaat ɛrba/ 'he eats grass' come out as ['srɛβa] and [papaa'ðrɛβa], respectively (data from Molinu 1998: 142, Bolognesi 1998: 54–5, 419, see Lai 2014).

I leave open the question whether similar evidence (with a guarantee of online activity) can be found for other processes such as rhotacism. In any event, all 'diachronic' processes must have been innovated by speakers: there must have been a point when some synchronic event occurred. It is therefore not clear how the distinction between diachronic and synchronic metatheses makes sense, anyway.

19.2.2 Patterns: Regular and Suspicious

Let us now consider the match between synchronic and diachronic *patterns* that instantiate phonological processes. Both synchronic and diachronic practitioners are confronted with outlandish-looking patterns like English velar softening, whereby the velars k,g seem to be turned into s, d͡ʒ before i (*electri*[k] - *electri*[s]-*ity, analo*[g]*ue* - *analo*[d͡ʒ]-*y*). The question as to whether velar softening is a synchronically active process whereby the surface variation is derived from a common underlying form of the root was a matter

---

[4] On my view, words are not stored together in the lexicon, except for certain constructions such as idioms and the like. The idea that more constructions are stored than is traditionally believed is developed by Construction Grammar (see e.g. Bybee 2001: 167 ff. on the phonological side, and also Bybee, this volume). Whatever the amount of constructions stored (and unless the existence of an online computational system that concatenates items is denied), the argument based on external sandhi remains unaffected: the alternations at hand do not selectively occur in some constructions. They are observed whenever the intervocalic context is met.

of quarrel for decades and still is today,[5] namely with regard to the abstractness debate of the 1970s (Kiparsky 1968–73 *et passim*, on which more below). The lexicalist alternative considers *electricity* and *analogy* as single, i.e. morphologically non-complex, lexical entries whose pronunciation requires no concatenation and no phonological activity.

While phonologists will probably agree that English velar softening is a suspicious pattern, it is not exactly trivial to define what 'outlandish-looking' really means: cross-linguistic (and also diachronic) experience leads us to mistrust k → s, since typical results of palatalization are t͡s and t͡ʃ, or possibly [c]. Velar softening also is riddled with restrictive phonological and morphological conditions (as is common in suspicious synchronic alternations). Unlike typical palatalizations, it occurs only before i, rather than before all front vowels, and is restricted to a number of suffixes, such as *-y*, *-ity*, and *-ism*, which Kiparsky (1982b: 40–1) identifies as belonging to class 1: velar softening does not occur morpheme-internally (*king* is not pronounced *[s]ing) or before i-initial class 2 suffixes (*hik-ing* is not *hi[s]-ing, etc.). But there are also exceptions to this pattern: *monar*[k] - *monar*[k]-*ism, patriar*[k] - *patriar*[k]-*y*.

Finally, while the alternation may be productive with recent loans, it fails the productivity test with words like *Iraq*: native speakers seem unable to even parse *Ira*[s]*ity* ('the property of being typically like Iraq'), but are able to make sense of *Ira*[k]*ity*.

In addition to what intuition, experience, and the cross-linguistic typology of palatalizations might tell us, velar softening thus bears a number of characteristics that arouse suspicion: limited regularity, limited productivity, morphological conditioning, and questionable phonetic/phonological plausibility.

19.2.3 Unattested Intermediate Stages in Diachronic and Synchronic Analysis

My aim is not to argue for a specific synchronic treatment of velar softening: much ink has been spilled on that, and a consensus may still be far off. My point is that those patterns which are suspicious in synchronic phonology raise exactly the same reservations on the diachronic side. Historical phonologists will not accept that a k could change directly into s. The reaction on the diachronic side is broadly agreed on, unlike the uncertainty in synchronic treatments: there must have been an unattested intermediate stage, t͡s in our case. What the synchronic picture thus offers traces of is k > *t͡s > s, where the original velar was affected by two entirely independent processes, a perfectly regular and unsuspicious palatalization to t͡s, followed by context-free deaffrication.

For English velar softening, we can show that this scenario is correct: velar softening entered the language through extensive borrowing of French vocabulary from the eleventh century on. Modern French has the same alternation (*électrique* [k] - *électric-ité* [s]),

---

[5] Among much else, relevant literature includes Halle (2005) and McMahon (2007). Green (2007: 175 ff.) provides an overview.

and we know that Latin k was pronounced t͡s before i,e in Old French and Norman (e.g. Bourciez & Bourciez 1967: 128 ff.), which was exported to Britain after the battle of Hastings. Consistent with this scenario is also the fact that only class 1 suffixes effect velar softening: it is well known that affix classes typically arise through language contact that mixes vocabulary strata of different origins (e.g. Mohanan 1982): class 1 affixes are of Romance origin, while class 2 affixes represent the Germanic heritage.

Encouraged by numerous cases of this kind, it is established practice since at least neogrammarian times to make sense of suspicious diachronic evolutions by postulating unattested intermediate stages. There is a broad consensus among diachronicians that there are no 'crazy' diachronic processes, only incomplete data. Labov (1972b: 100) formulates it thus: '[t]he great art of the historical linguist is to make the best of [...] bad data—'bad' in the sense that it may be fragmentary, corrupted, or many times removed from the actual production of native speakers.'[6]

SPE's rule ordering allowed phonologists to adopt the same strategy, to make suspicious synchronic alternations look like perfectly regular phonological derivations. The only thing that needed to be done was to make the intermediate stages synchronic: instead of relating two forms that are diachronically distant, they were understood as intermediate derivational stages that relate an underlying and a surface form. Hence in our example, instead of k > * t͡s > s, the synchronic derivation transforms //k// into /t͡s/ by a regular palatalization rule, which is followed by a context-free deaffrication rule that derives [s] (Chomsky & Halle 1968: 224).

The effect of this kind of abstract analysis is that synchronic grammar mimics recent diachronic evolution. On the basic perspective of early generative phonology (phonological change is rule addition, subtraction, reordering), the diachronic evolution of English velar softening involves the addition of context-free t͡s → s, ordered after the original palatalization rule k → t͡s. Synchronic grammar may thus recapitulate historical events and literally memorizes them through the piling up of rules.

19.3 BUILDING ON THE RUINS OF THE ABSTRACTNESS DEBATE: THE QUEST FOR THE HOLY GRAIL

The abstractness debate was never decided: despite much effort, nobody was or is able to provide a set of formal criteria (called the 'evaluation measure' or 'evaluation metrics' in the

---

[6] Blust (2005) takes exception to this view: he discusses a host of sound changes in the Austronesian family (e.g. *y > p, *dr > kʰ, *b > k) and concludes that unattested intermediate stages should only be assumed if there is relevant dialectal or historical evidence. Crazy-looking sound changes of the kind he discusses are to be interpreted as one-step modifications of the diachronically primitive form. In this sense Blust represents the big-is-beautiful position (on which more in section 19.3.2) in sound change.

1970s, e.g. Kiparsky 1974b) that allows us to decide whether an item that seems morphologically complex is really considered as such by the grammatical system, and if so, whether or not its computation is phonological in nature. Competing computational mechanisms are a distinct morphophonological device (present in structuralism), allomorphy, and analogy.

Ricardo Bermúdez-Otero (p.c.) has described this as the Holy Grail of phonology: phonologists need to decide whether an alternation falls into the realm of phonological computation *before* they propose a phonological analysis for it. Syntacticians do not face the same issue: sentences are not stored (except for idioms and the like; see note 4 and Scheer 2004b). I consider below two extreme positions on this quest, represented by four theories. Optimality Theory is not among them because the issue is not high on its agenda: the debate is typical of the 1970s, where it was the central line of division between orthodox *SPE* on the one hand and revolutionary Natural Generative Phonology (inside the generative realm) as well as Natural Phonology on the other.

Much like *SPE*, much OT literature jumps into a phonological analysis without considering whether the alternation at hand is phonological. Unlike the four theories discussed, OT has not established a set of properties that define what counts as a possible phonological process. This is not unrelated to a strong tendency in OT to scramble everything: deciding whether an alternation is phonological or not presupposes that phonology and non-phonology are distinct. This, however, is far from obvious in OT, where phonetics and morphology are often held to be mixed with phonology (in the same constraint ranking or even in the same constraint): the computational power of OT feeds a natural inclination to blur or abandon modular contours (Kingston 2007: 432; Scheer 2010: 208 ff., 2011b: §523).[7]

19.3.1 Small is Beautiful

Natural Phonology, Natural Generative Phonology,[8] and Government Phonology minimize synchronic phonological computation ('small is beautiful'). By contrast, Hale & Reiss (2008 among other references) maximize phonological computation, which is granted the ability to transform any segment into any other segment in whatever context. Both points of view are considered in this volume, the former by Donegan & Nathan, the latter by Hale et al.

---

[7] There is individual work in OT that has clear modular demarcation lines, and this is also typically where the Holy Grail is considered: cases in point include Bermúdez-Otero 2012: 44 ff., 2013), Bermúdez-Otero & McMahon (2006: 383 ff.), Green (2003, 2004).

[8] Natural Phonology originates in David Stampe's (1972) PhD and directly inspired Natural Generative Phonology, although the theories took quite different directions in the 1970s. Natural Phonology is explored in Donegan & Nathan (this volume), and references for Natural Generative Phonology include Vennemann (1974a,b) and Hooper (1976a), with some echoes found in the ideas in Mailhammer et al. (this volume). Despite their differences, both share the idea that much of what *SPE* thought of as phonological computation belongs in the lexicon or morphophonology, and this is the point to be made here.

In the two 'Natural' Phonologies, the mechanism that takes over the function of those alternations that do not qualify for synchronic phonological computation is morphophonology: following structuralist thinking, morphophonology is an independent computational system where the structural change of a rule A → B / C may be phonological, while the conditioning context C is morphological. In this perspective, velar softening is expressed as k → s / __-ity/-ism, etc. Note that this mechanism is different from allomorphy which manages cases such as *good-better* and would need to assume two distinct lexical forms of the same morpheme (electri/k/ and electri/s/ in our case): the rule k → s / __-ity/-ism transforms roots that have only one single underlying form.

The criteria in (1) are used to decide whether a given alternation is the result of phonological computation or not. If not, alternatives are the lexicon, morphophonology, allomorphy, and analogy.[9]

(1) an alternation cannot be phonological
   a. if it is not 100% regular, i.e. surface-true OR
      [Natural Generative Phonology, Government Phonology]
   b. if it has conditioning factors that are morphological (i.e. non-phonetic) OR
      [Natural Phonology, Natural Generative Phonology, Government Phonology]
   c. if there is no plausible causal relationship between the change observed and the triggering context
      [Natural Phonology, Government Phonology]

Usually (1a) and (1b) go hand in hand. Following Baudouin de Courtenay (1895), Natural Generative Phonology proposes a diachronic perspective on regularity (e.g. Vennemann 1972b): alternations are born as phonetic regularities, then move into grammar where they are first phonological but at some point start to add morphological conditions, followed by lexical factors, and finally are levelled out or eliminated from the language by some other means. During this life cycle, alternations become less and less regular: they apply to 100 percent of those items that satisfy the triggering conditions in their initial stage, but adding morphological and/or lexical conditions subtract more and more items from their influence (this notion of a 'life cycle' can be contrasted with that discussed by Bermúdez-Otero, this volume).

The question as to how much of what we see is controlled by phonology is thus, if not identical, at least concomitant with the question of how much diachrony there is in synchronic sound patterns. A recurrent observation is that what we see in synchronic patterning are more or less fossilized processes that once ruled over larger parts or all of the language.

---

[9] See Singh (1994) on morphophonology. Donegan & Stampe (1979: 143 ff.) consider the criteria that set apart phonological from non-phonological computation in Natural Phonology: the former produce processes (natural, innate, either obligatory or optional, style- and tempo-dependent, apply involuntarily and unconsciously, also to slips of the tongue, are not markers of any grammatical value), the latter rules (conventionalized, learned, style- and tempo-independent, always obligatory, do not apply to slips of the tongue, serve grammatical functions).

Natural Generative Phonology requires a phonetic interpretation of (1b): phonological processes must be phonetically transparent and hence surface-true (the True Generalization Condition, Hooper 1976a: 13 ff.). Government Phonology and Natural Phonology do not share this view. In Natural Phonology, phonetic factors also include intention, which may not be realized: a vowel may be nasalized before nasals that are deleted on the surface. Also, phonetic factors include tempo, style, effort, and attentiveness to speech. In Government Phonology, conditioning factors are *never* phonetic: they are only phonological. The GP version of (1b) thus, rather, assumes that an alternation cannot be phonological if it has conditioning factors that are non-phonological (i.e. morphological).

(1c) is an explicit condition on phonological processes in Government Phonology: 'non-arbitrariness: There is a direct relation between a phonological process and the context in which it occurs' (Kaye et al. 1990: 194; see also Gussmann 2007 and Pöchtrager 2006: 19 ff.). In NP, the causality between the triggering context and change appears in the opening sentence in Stampe's (1972: 1) dissertation: '[a] phonological process is a mental operation that applies in speech to substitute, for a class of sounds or sound sequences presenting a specific common difficulty to the speech capacity of the individual, an alternative class identical but lacking the difficult property.'

The small-is-beautiful option thus shrinks phonology: most of what *SPE* thought is due to phonological computation (say, 90 percent), is in fact something else (lexicalized alternations, morphophonology, allomorphy, possibly analogy).

19.3.2 Big is Beautiful

Hale & Reiss (2000a,b, 2008) take exactly the opposite position: 'big is beautiful'. Their work most clearly expresses the 'abstract' tradition which holds that phonological processes are phonetically arbitrary, arguing that phonological computation does not care for the objects that are manipulated, or for the causal relationship between the triggering context and the change observed: anything can become anything in any context. That is, X, Y, and C are interchangeable in X → Y / C: n → ŋ/ __k,g is as good a phonological process as n → ŋ/ __p,b and n → m / __k,g, or n → p / __n.

On this perspective, substance is entirely divorced from phonological computation. Substance (or melody) is everything that occurs below the skeleton, i.e. depending on the theory, binary or monovalent features, or unary primes. The substantive/melodic world works as Ohala assumes, Hale & Reiss (2000a: 162 f., 2008: 169 f.) argue: phonetics already accounts for the alternations of this type. Allowing the phonology to do this work again would be what they call 'substance abuse'. The restrictions that phonology, a purely cognitive system, imposes on phonological computation are of a different kind: they concern everything that substance, i.e. phonetics, is not responsible for. Syllable structure is an example: there is no phonetic rationale for syllabic conditioning. Syllable-related processes are thus truly phonological in kind, and the occurring and non-occurring patterns must follow from genuinely phonological restrictions on the computational system. The same holds true for the absence of outlandish logical possibilities such as 'stress every prime-numbered syllable'.

Given that nothing objects against melodically outlandish rules such as n → ŋ/ __p,b, Hale & Reiss need a reason why there are substance-related universals at all: many logically possible patterns do not occur in natural language. The answer, Hale & Reiss (2000a, 2008: 158 f.) argue, lies outside of phonology, and also outside of synchronic computation: substance is phonetics, and non-occurring patterns are due to the fact that phonetics does not produce them. They endorse the widespread idea (which is dubious, see Foulkes & Vihman, this volume) that sound change is due to misperception in the course of first-language acquisition. A rule such as n → ŋ/ __p,b could thus perfectly well exist in phonological computation, but it does not occur because phonetics/misperception does not produce the relevant pattern. In other words, substance-related universals are accidental, rather than systematic gaps at the phonological level: they are due to the fact that children's misperception is based on universal properties of the phonetic signal and universal properties of the human system of sound perception.

19.4 EVIDENCE AGAINST SMALL IS BEAUTIFUL: CRAZY RULES

Evidence that supports the big-is-beautiful perspective comes from so-called crazy rules. Bach & Harms (1972) use this term for rules that make no phonetic sense. A number of cases have been reported in the literature: see Buckley (2000, 2003) on Southern Pomoan (i → u / d__), Vennemann (1972a) on Sanskrit (palatalization before a), and Hyman (2001: 147 ff.) on Ndebele (where labials palatalize before w).

The goal of Bach & Harms (1972) is to understand how crazy rules come into being. They assume that crazy rules are not crazy at birth: they are perfectly plausible at first (in the sense that the trigger and the effect are plausibly related phonetically), but then a diachronic substitution occurs (of X, Y, and/or C in X → Y / C) that creates craziness without the language reacting against this departure from (phonetic) transparency. That is, craziness is a property of rule *change*, rather than of rules: 'some rather strong plausibility conditions seem to play a crucial part in determining what rules a language can initiate, these same conditions do not seem to bear any relation to changes that take place in rules' (Bach & Harms 1972: 6).

The literature often makes a parallel with fashion, where an originally functional piece of clothing may lose its function but continues to exist because it now represents the social status or group identity of the bearers (e.g. Postal 1968: 283, Lass 1997: 326, Calabrese 2005: 46 f.).

Bach & Harms (1972: 16 ff.) discuss a crazy rule in the Oboyan dialect of Russian: like in Russian and other Eastern Slavic languages, the vowel inventory is restricted in pre-tonic position. But the specific pattern in Oboyan is strange: after palatal consonants, pre-tonic non-high vowels appear as [i] if the following stressed vowel is [ɛ,ɔ,a], while they are [a] in case the following stressed vowel is [e,o,i,u]. If anything, the reverse is expected. Bach & Harms argue that the key to the problem is the fact that [ɛ,ɔ] were high vowels in Common Slavic, so-called yers which today alternate with zero, and which are also said to have been lax: [ɪ,ʊ]. Hence the original rule would produce [i] before high lax vowels (i.e. some kind of schwas), and [a] before all other vowels. This is significantly more plausible: the colour of the vowel that is weakened because of its pre-tonic position is entirely determined by the preceding palatal if there is no influence through vowel harmony from the following vowel, i.e. when this vowel is a colourless schwa itself. Otherwise [a] is encountered.

In further diachronic evolution, a context-free rule has changed all high lax vowels of the language into [ɛ,ɔ] (so-called yer vocalization). Bach & Harms argue that facing this situation, speakers have adapted the rule according to the phonetic properties of the new triggers: [ɛ,ɔ] are [+low]. Under this reanalysis, [+low] vowels are triggers, and this extends to independent [a] which was never a trigger diachronically speaking. Speakers do not care for these considerations though, and happily use the modified rule, which has become crazy and is now triggered by [ɛ,ɔ,a].

Bach & Harms (1972: 9) explicitly blame spontaneous sound shifts for making plausible rules implausible: '[w]here we have documentary evidence we find that this further shift [i.e. which causes craziness] occurs later, and rather significantly, it generally occurs by context-free rule.' That is, individual vocabulary items (X, Y, and/or C in X → Y / C) are arbitrarily replaced by diachronic evolution without this changing anything in the operational character of the rule.

Typical discussions of crazy rules do not provide information regarding regularity, productivity, and possible morphological conditioning. The Sardinian case presented in the following section clearly displays all the characteristics of a synchronically active, productive, and morphologically unconditioned rule. In addition, the dialectal continuum allows us to control for diachronically intermediate stages, which faithfully reproduce Bach & Harms's scenario of how crazy rules come into being.

19.5 SARDINIAN L → ʁ IN EXTERNAL SANDHI

19.5.1 Context

The sardinian dialects constitute a well-studied body of evidence: dialectologists have produced descriptions since Wagner (1941); Contini (1987) offers a particularly detailed picture. All data are oral, gained through elicitation. Also, sociological factors and language contact are typically controlled for.[10]

---

[10] The discussion below closely follows Molinu (2009), where more detailed material and literature can be found. Lucia Molinu, to whom I am indebted, has confirmed data beyond that considered here.

The Sardinian evidence is particularly apt for our purpose since it offers an unques-
tionable guarantee for the synchronic character of the alternation observed: external
sandhi. Phonological rules that apply across word boundaries (which are thus treated
as if they were not there) is an areal feature that Sardinian shares with Middle Italian
dialects (Giannelli & Savoia 1978, Contini 1986, Dalbera-Stefanaggi 2001, Marotta
2008). Processes that apply in external sandhi cannot be due to lexicalization since word
sequences are not stored in the lexicon (except for idioms and the like, see note 4). That
is, were English velar softening to apply across word boundaries (e.g. /I like it/ → [aj
lajs ɪt]), there would be no way to escape the conclusion that it is a synchronically
active rule.

19.5.2 The Alternation in Genoni

The Genoni dialect of Sardinian has a crazy rule that applies in external sandhi, and may
also be observed morpheme-internally in diachronic evolution (i.e. through comparison with Latin): l → ʁ / V__V.[11] (2) provides illustration (# represents a word boundary,
an utterance boundary).

(2) Genoni Sardinian l → ʁ / V__V

  a. in external sandhi after C-final words

##__	C#__V	gloss
'lampaðaza	in 'lampaðaza	June, in June
'lettu	i 'llɛttuzu	bed, the beds
'longu	'vu 'llongu	long, it was long

  b.

##__	C#V	gloss
o'riɣaza	iz o'riɣaza	ear, the ears
aʃu'ɣau	'kaɳɖu 'vuð aʃu'ɣau 'bẽi	dried, when (the wheat) had well dried

  c. in external sandhi after V-final words

##__	V##__V	gloss
'laðru	su 'ʁaðru	bacon, the bacon
'liŋgwa	sa 'ʁiŋgwa	tongue, the tongue

[11] Descriptions do not agree on whether the result is a uvular [ʁ] or a pharyngeal [ʕ] fricative.
Bottiglioni (1922: 37), Pellis (1934: 68), Wagner (1941: §188), Bolognesi (1998: 465), and Molinu
(2009) report [ʁ], while Contini (1987) and Cossu (2000) transcribe [ʕ]. Contini (1987 I: 355 note 2,
2006: 192) admits variation between [ʁ] and [ʕ] based on the vocalic context and speech rate (Molinu
2009: 133, note 7 describes this variation). I assume [ʁ] here; the variation is irrelevant for the argument: a
pharyngeal would only make the rule crazier.

'littɛra	ũa 'ʁittɛra	letter, a letter
'lɔŋga	'braβa 'ʁɔŋga	long, long beard
li'mɔ̃i	'binti ʁi'mɔ̃izi	lemon, twenty lemons
'lampaðaza	ɛ kkomin'tsau	June, June has just
	'ʁampaðaza	begun

d. word-internally in intervocalic position V__V

Genoni	Northern Sardinian	Latin	gloss
'piʁu	'pilu	pilu(s)	hair
'tʃeʁu	'kelu	caelu(m)	sky
da'ʁori	dɔ'lɔrɛ	dolore(m)	pain
'oʁia	'olia	oliva	olive

(2a) shows that word-initial l appears as such after consonant-final words, while it surfaces as ʁ after vowel-final words under (2c). Under (2a) the word [in] 'in' is overtly consonant-final; the presence of a word-final consonant in the words [i] 'definite article, plural' and ['vu] '(it) was', however, is not overt. It is established under (2b) where the two items are followed by vowel-initial words. In classical autosegmental terms, the word-final consonant of *is* and '*fut* would be said to be floating: it is elided when the following word is sonorant-initial. Its position is preserved, though, and targeted by the following consonant, which spreads and appears as a geminate (note that word-initial consonants do not geminate after word-final stable consonants as in [in 'lampaðaza]).

The word-internal evidence in (2d) does not allow us to conclude anything regarding a synchronically active process l → ʁ / V__V: since there are no alternations, we may have underlying forms that bear the lateral (e.g. /pilu/ 'hair') or the uvular fricative (/piʁu/ 'hair').[12] The former abstract analysis would allow the rule to take a free ride on /pilu/, whose lateral would be absolutely neutralized. There is no evidence from other word-internal positions: the lateral has undergone unrelated changes in branching onsets (where it appears as r: Lat. *plenu(m)* > 'prẽu 'full', flore(m) > 'frɔri 'flower') and internal coda position (where it has also become r, but in addition was subject to metathesis, with subsequent gemination of the following consonant: Lat. *culpa* > 'kruppa 'mistake'). Finally, there is no evidence for final codas since there are no l-final words in Sardinian.

This said, (2d) shows that a diachronic evolution produced ʁ on the basis of the Latin lateral. The end point of this evolution is identical with the result of the synchronically active process under (2a–c).

---

[12] Relevant to this discussion may be that Genoni has no opposition between [ʁ] and [l]: the former is always a contextual variant of the latter (rather than the reverse, at least diachronically). Contini (1987: 551, 559), however, argues for underlying /ʁ/ in word-internal contexts (Molinu 2009: 149).

19.5.3 Diatopic Variation of the Alternation

Let us now consider the dialectal variation on the island regarding the result of the external sandhi rule in (3).[13]

(3) diatopic variation in Sardinia:
     word-initial l in external sandhi after V-final words

	dialect	result	utterance-initial	V#__V	Gloss
a.	North (Budduso)	l	'luna	sa 'luna	moon, the moon
b.	Genoni	ʁ	'latti	su 'ʁatti	milk, the milk
	Sestu Campidanese	ʁ	'luʒi	sa 'ʁuʒi	light, the light
c.	San Vito	ʔ	'lũʔã	sa 'ʔũʔã	moon, the moon
d.	Nurachi	zero	'limba	sa 'imba	tongue, the tongue
e.	Sanluri	w	'linna	sa 'winna	wood, the wood
f.	Cruccuris	β	'longu	ũu gu'teɖɖu 'βongu	long, a long knife
g.	Gesturi	gʷ	'leppuri	su 'gweppuri	hare, the hare

The north of the island does not show any alternation of l in external sandhi. The table is further divided into those varieties where the absolute regularity of the alternation in external sandhi is confirmed in the fieldwork of the authors: l ~ ʁ in Genoni (Molinu 1998, 2009) and Sestu Campidanese (Bolognesi 1998: 43–4), l ~ ʔ in San Vito (Contini 1987 I: 486, note 48). By contrast, the regularity across the lexicon of the alternations under (3d–g) for any given variety is not warranted: existing descriptions (Contini 1987; Virdis 1978) report cross-lexical variation (also across individual utterances) whereby the most frequent realization in … V#__V … is the lateral; the resulting segments mentioned are less frequently observed.

The map in (4) shows the distribution of the varieties.[14]

---

[13] Data are from Contini (1987 I: 485–6, Budduso, Nurachi, Gesturi, San Vito, but Contini does not represent the latter in his map that is shown here in (4)), Wagner (1941: §194, Sanluri, Cruccuris), Bolognesi (1998: 43–4, Sestu Campidanese), Molinu (2009, Genoni) (see also Virdis 1978: 55 ff.). Very similar variation is found in Occitan dialects of the Massif Central (France) where Latin [l] appears as [ɫ], [w], [gʷ], [g], [ɣ], and [ʁ] in intervocalic position (Dauzat 1938: 63).

[14] Numbers are points of inquiry (villages) where Contini conducted fieldwork. The map only shows word-internal intervocalic l, and systematically distinguishes between l before u (witness word: *filu* 'thread') and before other vowels (witness word: *mela* 'apple'). In the former context *w* and related reflexes are often missing altogether. Also note that 'ρ' which Contini uses for the transcription in the Genoni area stands for ʕ.

(4) Latin l in Sardinian according to Contini (1987 II: map 68)

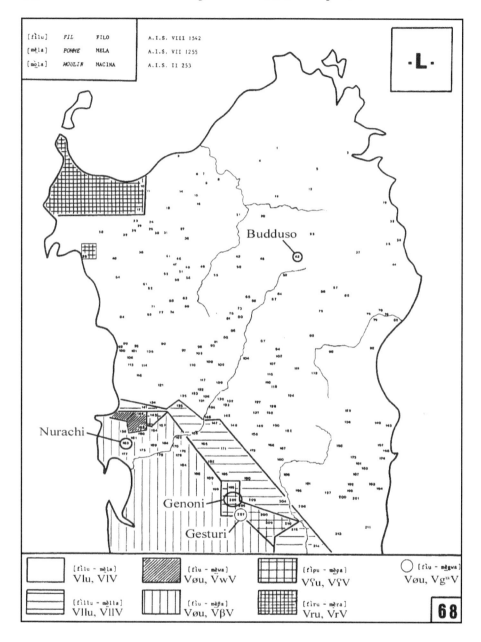

Based on this evidence, a number of diachronic scenarios have been established in the dialectological literature, following the classical idea that the diatopic variation provides a trace of the diachronic evolution. That is, realizations of a common diachronically primitive item that appear in the neighbourhood of 'extreme' outputs, i.e. those that are the most 'distant' from the original segment, are intermediate stages that the 'extreme' reflex went through.

The pieces of the puzzle offered by the diatopic variation are thus [w], [β], [g^w], [ʁ] and [ʔ]. Wagner (1941: §196–7) introduced the idea that the first development of the Latin lateral was a velarization that produced [ɫ]. All reflexes attested in dialects are then the result of further evolution based on this velar lateral (attested by Wagner 1941: §187).

19.5.4 Diachronic Scenarios

On these grounds, the basic diachronic scenario is a chain of successive lenitions in intervocalic position: l > ɫ > w > ø. The literature proposes a number of secondary paths in order to accommodate other reflexes: β may be a strengthening based on w (Wagner 1941: §§196–7) or a development of g^w which is parallel to the evolution k^w > bb that is attested in Sardinian (Lat. *aqua* > *ábba*) (Virdis 1978: 57). Contini (1987: 355) and Molinu (2009: 131 ff.) interpret g^w as a strengthening based on w, and ʁ as a development of g^w (via *ɣ^w). Finally, Molinu (2009: 147) argues that the glottal stop is a case of hiatus resolution in a subset of dialects where lenition of the lateral produced zero. The overall picture is as in (5).

(5) Diachronic scenario

$$g^w \;\rightarrow\; {}^*\gamma^w \rightarrow\; ʁ$$

$$l \;\rightarrow\; {}^*ɫ \;\rightarrow\; w \;{\overset{\nearrow}{\underset{\searrow}{\rightarrow}}}\; ø \;\rightarrow\; ʔ$$

$$β$$

This diachronic analysis is based on the insight that variation in space reflects diachronic evolution. It also assumes that each step has a phonetic or phonological motivation (although it is not obvious why the intervocalic context should promote fortitions). Bolognesi (1998: 464 ff.) on the other hand abandons any phonetic or phonological plausibility as well as any diachronic or diatopic reasoning altogether: for him the present-day picture is the result of Labovian change whereby arbitrary variation in the phonetic signal is promoted to grammatical value in order to serve as a vector for social differentiation. That is, the alternations at hand are unnatural and arbitrary: anything can turn into anything without going through any 'plausible' intermediate stage. The question, then, is whether inherent variation in the signal is able to produce ʁ when l or ɫ are the phonetic target.

19.5.5 Tests for the Grammatical Status of the Alternation

Tests for the status of the alternation could include (1) recent loans, (2) slips of the tongue, (3) performance of natives when speaking a foreign language, and (4) language games. Especially the latter three are critical for Natural Phonology, where alternations are divided into processes (which are natural) and rules (which are conventional). Both are produced by computation, but by different computational systems; only that responsible for natural processes is phonological in kind. According to NP, tests (2) through (4) are yardsticks that divide processes and rules: the former are carried over into slips of the tongue, L2, and language games, the latter are not (see note 9). Unfortunately I could not come by any secure information regarding the behaviour of the l-ʁ alternation in relevant Sardinian dialects.

There is, however, evidence regarding loanwords. In Genoni, *libru* 'book' is borrowed from Italian: were it native, the *b* would be lenited, either to *v* (*livru*) or to zero (*liru*). Molinu reports from her own fieldwork that 'the book' instantiates the alternation: *su 'ʁibru*. Bolognesi (1998) mentions analogous cases from Sestu: *lɛpurɛ - ssu ʁɛpurɛ* 'hare, the hare' (pp. 464–5), *lũa - ssa ʁũa* 'moon, the moon' (pp. 169, 464), *luʒi - 'kussa 'ʁuʒi* 'light, that light' (p. 169). Bolognesi (1998: 18) also reports word-internal cases from Sestu: *tɛʁevi'ziɔɔi* 'television', *tɛ'ʁeffɔɔu* 'telephone', *pisi'kkɔʁɔyu* 'psychologist'.

In some dialects, l in loans appears as a geminate, in which case it does not participate in the alternation. Molinu reports both word-internal and word-initial cases from Genoni: *tɛllevi'ziɔɔi* 'television', *tɛ'lleffɔɔu* 'telephone', *pisi'kkɔllɔyu* 'psychologist', *'lɔttu - su 'llɔtu* 'lotto, the lotto', *'lira - sa 'llira* 'lira, the lira (former currency of Italy)'. There is no apparent reason for the gemination, which is absent from the donor language. Also, the lateral is the only segment that is 'spontaneously' geminated in loans. A possible interpretation, then, is to consider the gemination as 'preventive': speakers 'do not want' the lateral to undergo the l-ʁ alternation and therefore protect the lateral by geminating it. Interestingly, Lucia Molinu reports the same unmotivated and selective gemination of the lateral when Genoni natives speak Italian.

19.6 CONSEQUENCES
FOR PHONOLOGICAL THEORY

19.6.1 Big-is-Beautiful Enforced for NGP
and GP, but not for NP

Let us now see how the three small-is-beautiful theories from section 19.3.1 fare in the face of the Sardinian evidence: are they forced to admit that the l-ʁ alternation is the result of online phonological computation?

I first identify those mechanisms that cannot be held responsible. The occurrence of the alternation in external sandhi guarantees its synchronic (rather than diachronic) character. Together with the fact that it is 100 percent regular in relevant dialects,[15] it also leaves no room for a lexicalization-based solution (sequences of words are not stored in the lexicon).

Remaining non-phonological candidate mechanisms are (1) a morphophonological computational system (MP rules in NGP), (2) allomorphy, and (3) analogy. The alternation does not show the hallmarks of analogy: all relevant items are concerned (rather than a subset), and there is no impact of type- or token frequency. Allomorphy is not an option either: morphemes (and possibly phonological conditions) select allomorphs, but words do not select 'allo-words'. A selection of the root alone by the preceding word is not workable since affixes are merged before independent words become visible to the derivation. Also, alternations that are the result of morphophonological or allomorphic computation require some morphological condition. Since the Sardinian l-ʁ does not have any, it cannot be the result of these devices.

The successive elimination of candidate mechanisms leaves us with just phonological computation. This is true for NGP and GP, but not quite for NP. As was mentioned earlier, in NP the computational system that manages alternations which in NGP and GP are morphophonological is not defined by the fact that these alternations have morphological conditions. Processes (phonological computation) are natural, while rules (non-phonological computation) are conventional. Patricia Donegan (p.c.) *expects* conventionalized alternations to bear morphological conditions, but this is not a necessary property of rules. NP can thus interpret Sardinian l-ʁ as a conventionalized rule. Note that it could not be a natural process since these, on NP standards, always have a plausible causality (see (1c)).

The same result arises from NGP's and GP's requirement that phonological computation is 100 percent regular (see (1a)): since this is the case for Sardinian l-ʁ, the two theories must consider it phonological. NP, on the other hand, allows the results of phonological computation to be non-surface-true. As regularity is no criterion for NP to decide whether an alternation is natural or conventionalized, Sardinian l-ʁ may be either.

It thus appears that NGP and GP are forced to recognize Sardinian l-ʁ as a truly phonological alternation. In other words, they will have to acknowledge that Hale and Reiss's 'big-is-beautiful' position is correct. NP has an escape hatch. In NP, the only evidence that allows us to decide whether alternations are natural or conventional are slips of the tongue, language games, and L2. Because only alternations with a plausible causality qualify as natural processes, NP predicts that Sardinian l-ʁ will not be carried over into these three areas.

---

[15] Authors are explicit on this. Contini (1987 I: 485–6 notes 47–8) for example claims absolute regularity for Nureci (point of inquiry 195), Nuragus (205), Isili (208), Nurri (210), and Orroli (212) (all l ~ ʁ), as well as for San Vito (l ~ ?).

19.6.2 OT

It was mentioned in section 19.3 that (a few initiatives aside) OT is not really concerned with the question of how to identify possible phonological processes. Parallel to *SPE*, OT simply analyses all alternations in terms of phonological constraint interaction. Hence it seems that OT is on the big-is-beautiful side by the simple absence of reflection, and therefore receives support from crazy rules in general and Sardinian l-ʁ in particular. Appearances are deceptive, though: the consequences for OT may turn out to be more dramatic than for other theories because two cornerstones of the theory, universal markedness and the finite character of the constraint set, are impacted.

If crazy rules exist in phonological computation, they need to be managed by constraints. The set of constraints, however, is supposed to be finite and universal: if anything can be a crazy constraint, there must be as many constraints as there are crazy rules, which makes the constraint set potentially infinite. One way out would be to go along with *SPE* and mimic the diachronic evolution (which is not crazy) in the synchronic analysis (i.e. first k → t͡s, then t͡s → s). This, however, would be a difficult strategy to implement in OT: a given constraint ranking (and hence even a stratal version of OT) is unable to produce intermediate derivational stages. Facing this difficulty, Bolognesi (1998: 464 ff.) gives up on the universal and finite ambition of the constraint set: he allows for language-specific constraints.

Regarding markedness, Bermúdez-Otero (2006b) points out that if the melodic properties of phonological processes are arbitrary, the entire justification of markedness constraints disappears. A reaction parallel to Bolognesi's is explored by Boersma (1998) and Bermúdez-Otero & Börjars (2006) who argue that markedness constraints are acquired/constructed on the basis of available data, rather than innate. Note that this solution also abandons the finite character of the constraint set. Facing the same problem, Green (2003, 2004) takes a different direction: regarding the notorious Celtic mutations, he argues that universal markedness is the yardstick for phonological computation: alternations that cannot be done within the limits of universal markedness are not phonological in kind.

19.6.3 Phonetic or Substantive Reductionists

Finally, it is useful to recall that crazy rules are traditionally used in order to argue against the phonetic determinism of phonological rules, and in favour of the existence of an autonomous phonology, i.e. a computational system that does not care for the phonetic properties of the items that it manipulates (e.g. Anderson 1981, Hyman 2001). Phonology is phonetically arbitrary, as Bermúdez-Otero (2006b: 498) puts it.

That is, crazy rules provide evidence against phonetic (or substantive) reductionists (as Bermúdez-Otero calls them), i.e. voices like John Ohala's (1983, 1992) who deny the existence of a phonological system that is independent from phonetics and claim that *all*

variation in sound that we see is substantive in nature. The functionalist and phonetically oriented 'grounded' strand of OT that was popular in the late 1990s and early 2000s
(cf. 'inductive grounding', Hayes et al. 2004) also comes close to this position.

On a different but related count, Dependency Phonology also faces problems: John
Anderson (2011, vol. 3) holds that 'all aspects of linguistic structure are grounded in
non-linguistic mental 'substance' (first page of the book), and also that '(a) the categories of phonology are phonetically grounded; (b) the categories of syntax are semantically grounded' (p. 10). Finally, we might note that crazy rules certainly do anything but
support Port & Leary's (2005) idea that there is no need for any (formal) phonology in
grammar.

19.6.4 Experimental Evidence: Are Phonetically Plausible Alternations Easier to Learn?

In recent years, artificial language experiments have tested whether natural patterns
are learned more easily than unnatural patterns. Results are inconclusive: while Wilson
(2003), Peperkamp et al. (2006), and Hayes et al. (2009) find that there is a learning
bias in favour of natural alternations, Pycha et al. (2003), Peperkamp & Dupoux (2007),
and Seidl & Buckley (2005) report that phonetically plausible and arbitrary stimuli are
learned with equal ease.

Factors that may stand in the way of converging results are (1) what authors exactly
understand by 'natural' and (2) whether the experiment is conducted with adults or with
infants. Regarding the latter, Seidl & Buckley (2005) take exception to the other experiments by working with nine-month-old infants. Regarding the former, Peperkamp et al.
(2006) use three criteria that make an alternation natural: (1) phonetic proximity (A
and B in A → B / C are phonetically close), (2) contextual relevance (C is 'homogeneous' with respect to the properties of A that are modified), (3) markedness reduction
(the string containing B is less marked than if it contained A). This is certainly one way
to interpret 'natural', but we have seen that the three criteria may or may not be used by
theories (phonetic proximity is used by none that is discussed above, and the purely
surface-based calculus of markedness will make, say, 3 → p natural if p improves the
markedness of the string that it is surrounded by).

Be that as it may, all these tests do not speak to our main issue: how do speakers manage crazy alternations synchronically? As independent lexical entries or by a computational mechanism, and if the latter, by which kind of computation exactly? What
the experimental evidence may be able to show, if a learning bias in favour of 'natural'
alternations turns out to be compelling, is the existence of what Moreton (2008) calls
an analytic bias, i.e. a grammatical (or more broadly cognitive) predisposition to accept
'natural' patterns. This does not mean that speakers are unable to learn and accommodate crazy rules, but it may be held responsible for their typological rarity (Moreton
2008). Bach & Harms's (1972) alternative explanation is that it takes the coincidence

of quite some diachronic events to produce a crazy rule (while non-crazy rules are non-crazy without any diachronic telescoping).

19.7 What is Crazy and What is Not

19.7.1 Crazy Rules Only Concern Melody, Never (Syllable) Structure

The literature on crazy rules is eclectic and there does not appear to be a synoptic collection of cases that are on record. Also, descriptions do not usually provide information regarding the checklist that determines the impact on different theories of synchronic phonology. This being said, a striking convergence of all crazy rules that I have found is that they concern only melody. A, B, and C in a rule A → B / C may change over time in unpredictable and arbitrary ways, but only if they are melodic items: there does not seem to be any equivalent for syllable structure or stress placement. That is, crazy rules which operate compensatory shortening, place stress on light but not on heavy syllables, lengthen vowels in closed syllables, or shorten them in open syllables do not appear to exist (recall note 3). No more than, say, a vowel-zero alternation whereby zero is observed in closed syllables, while the vowel occurs in open syllables. There is only compensatory lengthening, closed syllable shortening, open syllable lengthening, and the regular distribution of vowels (in closed syllables) and zeros (in open syllables) in vowel-zero alternations (see Scheer 2004a: §§16, 416, 470 for an overview).

If this is true, we simply have another diagnostic for the fundamental difference between melody and structure in phonology. Recall that Hale & Reiss (2000a, 2008) propose this division for the split between phonology and substance, the latter escaping grammatical well-formedness restrictions. The same opposition between the areas below and above that skeleton is made by McMahon (2003) for different reasons. Also, I argue (Scheer 2004a: §§215–16, 229) that items below this line of division, i.e. melodic primes, are categories that combine phonetic and phonological properties: they entertain a non-arbitrary relationship with vocal tract anatomy and/or acoustic properties of the signal (which is possibly due to phylogenetic conditioning: had human language used vision/signing for some hundred thousand years, the categories may not look the same today), but are still manipulated by the grammatical system. By contrast, items above the skeleton are not liable to any extra-grammatical constraints. This is where Saussurian *langue* and Chomskyan competence lies: only items and processes above the skeleton have a chance to be universal (also across modalities, i.e. vocal and signed expression of the language faculty) and hence to qualify for UG. Grammatical restrictions can therefore only be expressed at this level.

A list of phenomena that are insensitive to melody or unable to impact it (or both) is established in Scheer (2012): phonology-free syntax (Zwicky & Pullum 1986) is in fact melody-free syntax (syntax can be impacted by properties above the skeleton, but not by melody, Scheer 2011b: §§412, 660), infixation and allomorphy (which may be sensitive to phonological properties, but never to melody), category-sensitive phonology (nouns, verbs, or adjectives produce specific phonological patterns, but never impact melody), stress and syllable structure (which may be sensitive to positional factors, but never to whether a segment is palatal, velar, etc.—note that sonority has been independently identified as not behaving like a melodic prime).

19.7.2 Melodic Arbitrariness Concerns Only Input-Output Relations

The melodic arbitrariness of input-output relations does not mean that nothing needs to be represented below the skeleton, or that all melodic properties and processes are arbitrary. For example, phonological primes have a non-arbitrary identity: some cross-linguistic slack in the melodic representation of segments notwithstanding, an [e] cannot be [–back] in one language (or contain I if privative primes are used), but [+back] (or be made of U alone) in another.

Also, melodic properties play a role in phonological processes beyond the fact that they are subject to input-output transformation: rules may refer to natural classes of segments in either the definition of the input set or the definition of the triggering items. A naturalness requirement for these natural classes can be maintained even if the transformation of segments (or of a natural class of segments) into some other segments is arbitrary. This distinction is suggested by Bermúdez-Otero & Börjars (2006). Consider for instance the ruki-rule: Indo-Iranian and Balto-Slavic develop ʃ (or x in Slavic) from s when this segment is followed by either r, u, k, or i (e.g. Beekes 1995: 134–5). This alternation fails as a case of phonological computation since r, u, k, and i cannot be construed as a natural class. The change from s to ʃ/x is covered by the arbitrariness of melodic transformations, and so is the causal relationship between the triggering environment and the effect observed. However, the fact that the triggering environment is a non-natural disjunction is not.

In sum, the only thing covered by the license for melodic arbitrariness is the transformation of one melodic item into another. All other melodic properties may be argued to be still under grammatical control.

19.8 Conclusion

Our inquiry into regularity and naturalness essentially leads us to the conclusion that the idea that *SPE* was mistaken because it massively overgenerates was wrong. *SPE* was right: phonological computation can transform anything into any other thing in any context. This is what Hale and Reiss have maintained, and it is what the external sandhi evidence from Sardinian suggests.

In other words, there is no synchronic device that enforces naturalness. In its absence, the naturalness that we perceive in a fair number of rules can only have a diachronic origin. 'Diachronic' in this context refers to the shape of rules when they are born, i.e. upon innovation: they are always regular and natural then. Also, they are as synchronic at this point as they are a couple of centuries later when they have aged. It is this aging process of rules (Bach & Harms's 1972 idea) that introduces irregularity, opacity, unnaturalness, and may produce what is called crazy rules.

In this sense, there is no such thing as suspicious rules: all rules are equally well-formed from the point of view of grammar. What is taken to be suspicious ($k \rightarrow s$ for example) always has a diachronic explanation: several independent steps, each plausible and natural, have produced a suspicious or crazy rule that was plausible when it was young.

There is thus no way to understand synchronic patterns in absence of a diachronic analysis. Or, put differently, sometimes there is a whole lot of diachrony in synchronic phonology. In this respect again, *SPE* was right and its critics of the 1970s and 1980s wrong: *SPE* was criticized because it argued that modern English speakers were equipped with Middle English underlying forms and rules that recapitulate historical events of the past millennium. *SPE* did indeed assume that rules such as velar softening, which entered the language in the eleventh century, are still active today. If relevant alternations are not lexicalized, the result of allomorphy or analogy, the eleventh-century rule may indeed still be active today.

SPE may have been wrong, though, in holding that the rule sailed through the centuries without being modified, i.e. without aging. Following the early generative take on innovation that was mentioned in the introduction, *SPE* accounts for the modification of the output by adding an independent rule (context-free $\widehat{ts} \rightarrow s$ that applies after $k \rightarrow \widehat{ts}$). In other words, *SPE* tried to maintain the naturalness requirement of synchronic rules by mimicking their diachronic development. This led to a synchronic grammar that mimics historical events, and critics were right to pinpoint that.

The alternative suggested by Bach and Harms's general scenario, the Sardinian pattern, and the fact that input-output relations do not need to be natural, is that diachronic events are encoded in synchronic grammar not through intermediate stages, but through their flattening: the modification of the output of a rule is not due to the addition of independent rules, but to the modification of the vocabulary of the rule itself: $k \rightarrow \widehat{ts}$ becomes $k \rightarrow s$. Hence synchronic phonology stores quite some diachronic events, but in flattened, or telescoped manner. Sardinian children raised in Genoni have no evidence for any diachronically intermediate stages but still happily build a rule that transforms l into ʁ.

Finally, all that has been said in this conclusion so far only applies to melody, to those items that occur below the skeleton. Grammar is toothless for the transformation of melody, but does control syllable (and other) structure as well as stress assignment. This ties in with independent evidence for an ontological split between the areas below and above the skeleton: only the latter accommodates 'real' phonology, and it is only here that candidates for UG are found.

The perspective of Natural Phonology is entirely different, and the conclusions drawn above do not apply. Like structuralism, NGP, and GP, which oppose phonological and morphophonological computation, NP also builds on the architectural distinction of two distinct computational devices, which are different in kind. One produces alternations that have a plausible causality and enforces naturalness (but not 100 percent regularity or surface truth). This is what NP calls processes, which are the equivalent of true phonology in other frameworks. The other computational system does all the rest: it produces alternations that may have morphological conditioning and does not need to implement a plausible causality. In NP, these alternations are said to be conventionalized, i.e. freed from the naturalness requirement. Crucially, though, this computational system *may* implement morphological conditioning, but does not need to. Hence a purely phonological alternation like Sardinian l-ʁ may fall into its competence. This is not like other theories, where the equivalent computational system, morphophonology, necessarily works with morphological conditions.

We thus face two perspectives: both have two distinct computational systems that manage phonological alternations, but the line of division is not the same: pure phonology *vs* morphophonology on the one hand (structuralism, NGP, GP), natural *vs* conventional on the other (NP). The impact of crazy rules in general and of Sardinian l-ʁ in particular on phonological theory depends on this architectural choice: while NP can claim small-is-beautiful for phonological computation, other theories are forced into big-is-beautiful.

CHAPTER 20

AN I-LANGUAGE APPROACH TO PHONOLOGIZATION AND LEXIFICATION

MARK HALE, MADELYN KISSOCK,
AND CHARLES REISS

20.1 INTRODUCTION

ADOPTING the I-language perspective (e.g. Chomsky 1986) in diachronic linguistics makes it difficult to talk about even the most well-established results and the simplest notions. A statement like 'the English word *knight* began with a *kn* cluster in Middle English' seems innocuous enough, until we realize that there is no scientifically useful or coherent definition of 'English', or 'Middle English', or 'the word *knight*'! There is obviously no direct sense in which a mental representation in Chaucer's mind/brain (or even a sound Chaucer made) that we might refer to as 'Chaucer's word for *knight*' has turned into a representation or sound that we might refer to as 'Chomsky's word for *knight*'.

One strategy for dealing with such difficulties is to ignore them—it is shockingly easy, as we ourselves have done for much of our professional lives, to teach students and write papers as if English, Marshallese, and Vedic Sanskrit were legitimate objects of scientific study. Such work engages our intellect and provides a certain amount of satisfaction, but our acceptance of the correctness of the I-language approach, and the problems and inconsistencies that arise by not adopting that approach, sometimes force us to confront the contradictions that we have helped to perpetuate. There is no question that doing so is difficult and sometimes tedious, but the investment will generate a deeper understanding of what is traditionally called 'language change', and ultimately allow us to reformulate informal statements, like the one about 'the word *knight*', in terms that do not conflict with our basic scientific understanding of languages as properties of individuals.

A tradition among generative linguists interested in diachrony treats 'sound change' or 'phonological change' (or at least the most interesting types of these events) as resulting from direct adult modification of phonological knowledge—sound change is a change in a speaker's phonology (see discussion in Hale 2007, chapters 3 and 6).[1] By explaining sound change as a change in a speaker's grammar, his/her I-language, one can explain the regularity of sound change, the Neogrammarian Hypothesis, thus: since grammars are computational systems, a change in a speaker's grammar will generate regularities in output *vis-à-vis* the output of the pre-change stage. We have argued (Hale 2003, 2007), however, that so-called language 'change' is *not* due to spontaneous adult modification, so we are left without an explanation for regularity. In this chapter, we review arguments against viewing change as occurring in adult phonologies and arguments for localizing 'change' in the imperfect transmission of grammar to learners. In other words, in cases of 'change' there is no entity that changes, no change in the grammar of a speaker or the output of a speaker. Rather, so-called 'change' is a relationship between the grammars or the outputs of the grammars of speakers of different generations. Since this process does not involve phonological computations from underlying forms to surface forms in a single grammar, there is, strictly speaking, no phonology involved in (this kind of) sound change. We thus arrive at the position that phonological change is neither 'phonological' nor 'change'. We offer a partial solution to the puzzle of the regularity of sound change under this view. (Other chapters in this volume have quite different understandings of change, such as the chapters by Bybee and Mailhammer, Restle, & Vennemann, and compare Foulkes & Vihman, this volume, for a different view of the place of acquisition in change.)

The foundation of our approach was laid out most fully in Hale (2007). In this chapter, we review and develop some of those arguments, but our primary purpose is to apply the framework to the study of a particular phenomenon known as *phonologization*, and a putatively related phenomenon called *phonemicization*.

20.2 PHONOLOGIZATION

Phonologization (see also Kiparsky, this volume, and for some relevant discussion also Bermúdez-Otero, this volume) is a label for a variety of diachronic processes in which some observable articulatory or acoustic phenomenon which arises in the course of

---

[1] A reviewer expressed the opinion that this was an inaccurate characterization of the classical generative phonology position. A good summary of the view at the time, published in 1969, is that of George Grace, which says, after noting that the generative approach assumes that adults can make changes in the grammars, that 'these changes define the set of possible linguistic changes (or at least a subset of a particularly significant sort—at least many of the traditional 'sound laws' would typically be members of the subset)' and that 'in some cases the grammatical changes made by adults produce suboptimal grammars, in which case a restructuring is carried out by children so as to produce optimal grammars' and 'that 'linguistic change' (or some important subclass thereof) is most profitably conceptualized in terms of the form of the change in the grammars of adults (primary change), rather than in the grammars of children'. Under this conception, perceptually-driven sound change of the type widely assumed in the contemporary literature, and of the type we will be discussing, is the purview of adults: children simply deal with the fallout (the 'suboptimal' grammar); compare Dresher (this volume) for somewhat different view, however.

Table 20.1 Three stages in the relationship between stop voicing and pitch.

Stage 1	Stage 2	Stage 3
pá[⌐]	pá[⌐]	pá[⌐]
bá[⌐]	bǎ[↗]	pǎ[↗]
pitch lowering as a result of articulatory processes	(exaggerated) lowering of pitch as a result of phonological computation	now redundant voicing eliminated on [b], resulting in phonemic tone contrast
	phonologization	phonemicization

speech without being explicitly represented at the grammatical level (e.g. a coarticulation effect) comes to be represented in the phonology. Though of course by no means
the first work to recognize the concept, the *locus classicus* for modern discussions of the
phenomenon is clearly Hyman (1976). That paper uses the example of the lowering of
pitch on a following vowel intrinsic to the articulation of voiced stops, distinguishing
three stages in the possible diachronic effects of that lowering, shown in Table 20.1.

At Stage 1 there is a lowering of the pitch on the left-edge of a high-tone vowel due to
the articulation of voiced stops.[2] At Stage 2, this lowering has come to be introduced by
phonological rule, rather than being a mechanical by-product of articulation.[3] As such, it
is realized in what Hyman calls an 'exaggerated' fashion (i.e. with greater pitch lowering).
Finally, at Stage 3 the now redundant (because of the induced tonal effects) voicing on
stops is eliminated, leaving an unconditioned (i.e. phonemic) tonal contrast.

Hyman labels the diachronic development from Stage 1 to Stage 2 'phonologization',
reserving the term 'phonemicization' for the development from Stage 2 to Stage 3.[4]
While this usage is still not completely standard,[5] it does seem that most technical discussions of 'phonologization' in the current literature maintain Hyman's distinction,
and we will as well. Sitting as it does at the intersection of both the complex issues surrounding the interface between phonetics, broadly construed, and phonology, and the
equally problematic matters which arise when one seriously considers the relationship
between the synchrony and the diachrony of linguistic systems, it will come as no surprise that 'phonologization' itself is a rich and complex topic for diachronic phonology.

---

[2] See Kingston (2011) and Ratliff (this volume) for treatments of tonogenesis including explorations of
the phonetic motivations of such interactions of voicing and pitch/tone.

[3] Although the term 'rule' is most appropriate when discussing Hyman's analysis, our points are
not tied to a particular theoretical framework beyond one that has, as its fundamental assumption, the
notion of the grammar as a computational system. We therefore use 'rule', 'operation', and 'computation'
indiscriminately in what follows.

[4] Hyman's discussion is compatible with our view that each Stage corresponds to a different grammar
(in different individuals)—there is no reason to think that a person's grammar transitions from one Stage
to another, but see below.

[5] The *Oxford Concise Dictionary of Linguistics* defines 'phonologization' as the '[h]istorical process
by which a phonetic difference becomes a difference between phonemes'—i.e. as being equivalent to
Hyman's 'phonemicization'.

Rather extensive terminological clarification will be required before we turn to a discussion of this concept. The goal is not to advocate one particular terminological system over another, but rather to ensure conceptual transparency. Terminology we will use here will not, or rather would only accidentally, be in agreement with that found in the literature on phonologization, which is itself internally inconsistent, and thus cannot form the basis for coherent discussion.

20.3 TERMINOLOGICAL MATTERS: SYNCHRONIC

If 'phonologization' is to mean anything at all, we must, in order to discover the properties of phonologization events, draw a clear and distinct division between the domain of phonetics (broadly construed) and the domain of phonology—'phonologization' is, after all, *about* crossing that line.[6] As if the difficulties in establishing a meaningful line were not themselves of sufficient complexity, discussion has generally been plagued by an unfortunate ambiguity as to the meaning of 'phonetics', arising at least in part from the use of the symbols of the International Phonetic Alphabet to represent objects of radically different types. A conceptually straightforward division between the physical ('phonetics') and the mental ('phonology'), which is probably the closest approximation to historical conceptions of the place of the division (at least in the early days of the concept of the phoneme) is, in the end, not adequate. Nor would any conception of these matters which fails to consider the physical, limiting itself to the mental, or the mental limiting itself to the physical, be able to provide a meaningful foundation for a theory of 'phonologization'. We need both the mental and the physical, and it seems clear that the physical facts (articulatory, acoustic, or aerodynamic) must fall outside the domain of phonology proper. It is, however, just as clearly inadequate to adopt the position that all mental aspects of speech generation are necessarily 'phonology' in the sense we need.[7]

---

[6] One regularly sees laments about the 'unclarity' of the line between phonetics and phonology, as if this were an ontological problem with the world, instead of reflecting terminological inconsistency and our collective ignorance as scientists. The way to establish the most productive location for a terminological division between phonetics and phonology is to assert some well-defined and coherent division, and explore the implications of that division for the models of the world we are constructing. None of us knows where the most useful line is, and we may never know, but we will never establish the optimal line if we fail to explore the implications of drawing it in some particular place.

[7] We have found it useful (Hale, Kissock, & Reiss 2007) to compare two excellent articles, Keating (1988a) and Hammarberg (1976), which attempt to define a usable phonetics-phonology boundary. For Keating, a phenomenon is 'phonological' if it involves features. For Hammarberg, a phenomenon is 'phonological' if it involves cognition, whether reliant on something like traditional discrete features or non-featural motor planning. Both definitions are coherent, and the cogency of the two positions suggests a need for a three-way contrast in terminology. However, for present purposes, we follow Keating's two-way distinction, collapsing cognitive and non-cognitive 'phonetics' (but distinguishing these from the so-called 'phonetic output' level of phonological computation).

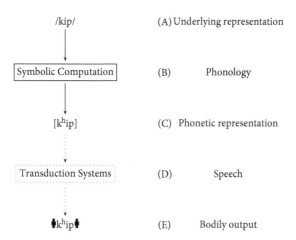

FIG. 20.1 Speech chain: Phonology, Phonetics, and Speech.

A sensible way of dividing things up must recognize that there is a great deal which is mental but not strictly speaking within the computational system which we call 'the grammar' (which system itself houses 'the phonology').[8]

In Figure 20.1, line (A) is the input to the phonological computation. Such an input contains the long-term stored form of a particular morpheme, or a combination of morphemes (say, a root with affixes, all stored in the lexicon). This input to the phonology is sometimes called the 'Phonemic' or 'Phonological' or 'Underlying' Representation, and it is traditionally placed within slash brackets. We assume that these representations are made up of 'features'.[9] Obviously, many different conceptions of the specific features which distinguish underlying representations are consistent with this understanding of things.

We have placed 'phonemic' in scare quotes above because, although this is often glossed over in modern phonology, these representations are not 'classical' phonemes in the, e.g. American structuralist sense. Nor are they 'classical' archiphonemes, in the European structuralist sense. What they really are is a little unclear at present, giving rise to a great deal of difficulty (discussion of which is generally absent) about just how abstract these representations may be, and what empirical facts must be observed to justify some particular degree of abstractness in any specific case. These concerns lie

---

[8] As will become apparent, the IPA characters in Figure 20.1 stand for feature bundles at the 'phonemic' and 'phonetic output' levels, but impressionistic acoustic/articulatory descriptions at the level of bodily output. It is the ambiguous use of IPA symbols in these two very distinct functions that was alluded to earlier.

[9] This would seem to follow by virtual conceptual necessity: the features designate (abstract) properties of these mental objects—how could two representations be distinct without that distinction being due to some difference in properties? The features are the properties that make representations different from one another, and it is these properties which are subjected to modification in the course of phonological computation. Again, since there are no *other* properties of the segments than those designated by their features, phonological computation has nothing else to manipulate.

outside the coverage of this chapter. In *SPE* (Chomsky & Halle 1968:11) the term 'phonemic' is avoided, including 'systematic phonemic' and 'morphophonemic'. Instead, both lexical representations and the phonological representations that are the result of syntactic Surface Structure and readjustment rules are referred to as 'underlying representations', in other words, the input to phonology. We follow this practice here, since the difference between single and multiple morpheme inputs is not relevant.

Line (B) of Figure 20.1 corresponds to the computational system which, in keeping with common practice, we call the 'phonology'. This system is a function mapping phonological properties of the input, (A), to a Phonetic Representation (C). It appears fairly clear that this computational system produces outputs in the same 'representational alphabet' as that provided by UG for the representation of long-term stored forms of the type that constitute (A):[10] feature bundles, syllables, feet, moraic structure, and the like are some possible elements of this representational system. Obviously, the computational system may be any of a wide range of possible types (including both rule-and constraint-based systems)—the question remains open.

Line (C) is referred to variously as the output (of the phonology),[11] the Surface Representation, and the Phonetic Representation—we adopt the latter, following *SPE*. We follow the tradition of placing this type of representation within square brackets. Crucially, it does not seem that the output representation (C) requires anything beyond the representational capacities used for underlying representations; i.e. there is no 'phonetic representation' system (in this sense of 'phonetic') distinct from the phonological one.

This identity in representational systems allows us to classify the phonology as involving *computation*, rather than *transduction*, which involves a conversion of the nature of the objects involved.[12] The conversion of the phonetic representation (C) to actual bodily output (E) (i.e. sound, in the case of speech) is clearly transduction (see below), and the phonology is just as clearly computation. In Figure 20.1 we have contrasted transduction (dotted arrows) with computation (solid arrows).

Thus, as noted, 'the phonetic representation' (C) is a mental object, unaffected by factors like speech rate, muscular fatigue and mucosal lubrication, generated using the same representational system as that provided by UG for the long-term storage of phonological representations. Its status as different from the underlying representation in (A) arises thus not from any particular properties that it has, but rather by virtue of the place in the system at which it comes into existence—it is a short-term computational output in the phonological alphabet. It thus contrasts with the underlying form (A)

[10] Optimality-theoretic notions such as FAITH and other input-output correspondence relations would seem to require such an identity: how could input-output identity ever be satisfied if inputs and outputs consisted of disjoint sets of properties?

[11] Even a term like 'output' is sometimes ambiguous. Within OT the most harmonic candidate is the output of the grammar, but each candidate is referred to as a (potential) output as well, for example, when evaluating Output-Output Identity constraints.

[12] See Hale & Reiss (2008: 109). The air pressure differentials converted to patterns of electron pulses by a microphone would be a good example of transduction, since the elements involved are of radically different types in the two cases.

which contains the representations stored in the lexicon (see note 7); and in its symbolic nature and representational alphabet, it contrasts with the bodily output (E).

A set of poorly understood and relatively complex systems intervene between the phonetic output representation (C) and the actual bodily output (E), which is denoted by placement within 'body' brackets, following Hale (2007). These systems include both factors under some cognitive control (the generation of a 'gestural score', speech planning, rate and loudness considerations, etc.) and more 'chaotic' ones outside of cognitive control (current physical properties of the vocal tract, air pressure, etc.). Some of these systems may be 'computational' in nature, others 'transducers', but when lumped together as space (and competence) limitations compel us to do here on line (D), the entire set of systems taken together act as a transducer, since we get a mapping between phonetic representations and the articulatory gestures that initiate sound waves.

This transduction of the phonetic representation into some bodily realization is, under this conception of things, extra-grammatical, involving both non-grammatical mental computation (e.g. motor planning) and non-grammatical physical modification of the implementation of the motor plan (e.g. salivary interference). For convenience, we call this the 'speech planning and implementation', or, for short, the 'speech' level.

Where in such a figure are we to draw the line which will form the central concern of a theory of 'phonologization'? Here the literature shows some variety of opinion, but, also, rather too frequently, evidence of no opinion at all—i.e. great inexplicitness and confusion. IPA-type transcriptions are used to describe both the output of phonological computation (our 'phonetic representation'—the (C) of Figure 20.1) and the impressionistic rendering by a researcher of the 'phonetic' bodily output of a speaker (E).[13] Claims are then made about 'phonetic' transcriptions, some of which are true of *only* those that correspond to line (C), others that *only* in the latter role correspond to (E): these claims are then conflated, leading to the aforementioned confusion. A cursory examination of the use of the word 'allophone' in almost any introductory textbook on phonology will clearly reveal the confusion at play.[14]

Wherever the line is to be most productively and insightfully drawn, it is clear that the very worst move in trying to discuss technical matters such as 'phonologization' is to fail to draw the line sharply and clearly; from a vague and confused line will come only vague and confused conceptions of 'phonologization'. A very clear place to draw the line, consistent with some past uses of the terms in question, is between (B) and (C) of Figure 20.1. The (combinations of) long-term stored phonological representations, the underlying representations in (A), are the input to the phonology (B), the computational system which modifies those representations. The 'phonetic representation' (C) is the output of the phonology. In our view, a coherent definition of phonetics is the

---

[13] We have continued this confusing use of IPA symbols, but 'body' brackets keep the reader alert to our transgression.

[14] There is a small, mostly ignored literature on the distinction between intrinsic and extrinsic allophones that tries to tease these issues apart (e.g. Tatham 1971).

mapping from (C) to (E), via the many complex systems of (D). We therefore place the phonetics-phonology division just above (C).[15]

20.4 TERMINOLOGICAL MATTERS: DIACHRONIC

Because 'phonologization' is a type of language change, we must also clarify certain diachronic issues. The fundamental matter, from which further clarity can be made to follow, is this: change is not a property of grammars, but rather a relationship between grammars. We refer to G_1, which existed before the change, and G_2, which exists after the change, in an attempt to interpret Hyman's Stages in I-language terms.

Adopting the I-language approach, we see that in spite of the strong superficial similarity between the synchronic and diachronic versions of a statement such as 'k becomes $ʔ$ word-finally', the processes underlying these two kinds of events are radically distinct. A synchronic modification of the feature bundle /k/ to the feature bundle [ʔ] in the phonology represents computation within a human mind, necessarily constrained by the principles of UG which give rise to phonologies in humans. The diachronic version of this modification represents a situation in which one grammar, G_1, manifests ⌈k⌋ -type outputs, while G_2, crucially a 'descendant' of G_1 (to which we will return), manifests ⌈ʔ⌋-type outputs in *corresponding* positions in *corresponding* lexical items.

The crucial concepts in the diachronic domain under this interpretation of change are that of the 'descent' relationship between distinct grammars and that of the 'corresponding' lexical item (and 'corresponding' segments within corresponding lexical items). Neither of these concepts is simple, and neither is particularly clearly articulated in the literature on diachronic phonology. The latter can probably be safely left at the intuitive level (as is the norm in both diachronic and synchronic phonology)—the complications are well-known, if still not fully under our conceptual control.[16]

As to the former matter—the question of when two grammars can be said to stand in a relationship such that it is appropriate to refer to G_2 as having arisen via 'change' from G_1—the only clear answer that has been offered to this question is the following. G_2 arises from G_1 via change only if G_1 provided the primary (or, perhaps more precisely, the relevant) data for the acquirer who has constructed G_2 (compare and contrast 'transmission',

---

[15] Our model of the speech chain in Figure 20.1 contrasts sharply with the widespread advocacy of what is sometimes called 'language-specific phonetics.' The literature on the matter is extensive (e.g. Kingston & Diehl 1994, Kingston 2007, and Hale, Kissock, & Reiss 2007).

[16] The problem is not just one of finding corresponding phonological representations in two grammars; one also must demonstrate that these are linked to corresponding semantic representations. Given normal processes of semantic shift and lexical replacement through borrowing (to use traditional terms) it is hard to imagine how the task can even be defined. For example, is Old English *mete* 'solid food' the 'same word' as Modern English *meat*, which means something like 'edible animal flesh'? Common sense and standard diachronic linguistic practice say 'yes', but it is difficult to make the question coherent under the I-language approach.

discussed in D'Arcy, this volume). Note that this restricts the use of 'phonological change' to chronologically local events—there can be no more question of, e.g. whether the 'sound change' Proto-Indo-European *dw- > Armenian [jerək-] is possible: it is not. The long chain of clearly distinct diachronic events which link PIE *dw to Armenian [jerək-] is not 'a change', but rather a lengthy sequence of changes. This conception of things has the advantage that it may just be possible to develop a systematic and constrained theory of sound change, thus defined, whereas it is difficult to see what kind of coherent restrictions can be placed on sound change if PIE *dw > Arm. [jerək-] must be allowed as an example.

Another significant corollary of this understanding of the nature of sound change is that the great debate in the sound change literature about whether sound changes are 'gradual' or 'abrupt' ceases to be meaningful. If change is a relationship between G_1 and G_2, and the coming into being of G_2 is dependent upon the constructor of G_2 getting his/her data from G_1, then it follows that this relationship—i.e. the 'change' event—only comes into existence the moment the acquirer's grammar G_2 does. All linguistic change is thus abrupt, indeed, instantaneous.[17]

What does this understanding mean for 'phonologization' specifically? For one thing, a great deal of discussion of the process, starting in the late nineteenth century holds that the process of 'phonologization' is a 'gradual' one, transitional effects, for example, becoming steadily 'more pronounced' until such time as they get 'grammaticalized'. There are two clear senses in which this understanding of phonologization is flawed under the assumptions outlined here. First, the phonologization does not take place (by definition) until the moment the process becomes grammatically (as opposed to speech-production) driven. Whatever events precede this, if indeed there can be any, are not part of the phonologization event *per se*. Second, it is hard to see where to locate the 'gradual' developments envisioned in this scenario: we cannot place them in the grammar (or else the process would already be grammaticalized), and the most restrictive theory of the *systematic* transduction systems involved in speech production (as opposed to the more 'chaotic' ones such as amount of saliva in the vocal tract) is that they themselves are constants: as unchanging systems, they can offer no account of a steady increase in coarticulation effects (as an example).

20.5 SYNTHESIS: WHAT IS PHONOLOGIZATION?

Working with these definitions, it is apparent that phonologization cannot be the shifting of responsibility for some property of the acoustic or articulatory output from the

---

[17] Note that contrary to perhaps one's expectation, the acquired grammar under discussion, G_2, comes into being at a single moment, i.e. instantaneously. The acquisition process takes time, but no one has ever considered the child's knowledge state at 20 months, however that might be best characterized, to be an object of *diachronic* linguistic investigation. Historical linguistics enters the picture only once G_2 has come into being, and it becomes relevant the moment that it does.

phonetic representation (C) to the *phonology* (B): the representation in (C) has no properties at all except those provided by the 'phonemic level' in which underlying representations are stored and those provided by the computational system of the phonology—the
phonetic representation is epiphenomenal and fleeting (not stored). 'Phonologization'
must, therefore, concern itself with the shifting of responsibility for properties of the
bodily output in (E) from transduction processes in (D) at one Stage, i.e. in G_1 to the
phonological computation system (B) of G_2 at a later Stage.[18]

Figure 20.1 represents a universal model of the human 'speech chain', instantiated in
each individual—the core of the I-language perspective. When we talk of a shift from the
transduction system to the phonology, we do not mean to imply that this happens 'inside'
the speech chain of an individual. Rather, the difference is between tokens of speech
chains that are in a diachronic relationship of immediate descent—we are referring to
Stages, as in the discussion of Hyman's work above. Thus, phonologization involves no
phonological computation *per se*. Phonologization does involve a relationship between
two different instantiations of level (B), two different phonologies, but this relationship
is not a phonological computation.[19] Typically, as in the tonal case, the later instantiation
B_2 contains a rule which was absent in the earlier instantiation B_1. Understanding phonologization also requires looking at properties of E_1, the bodily output of a grammar at
Stage 1, that are explicable by reference to D_1, and seeing that acoustically similar (but
'exaggerated') properties of E_2 are the result of an aspect of the phonological computation B_2 that was not present in B_1. Table 20.2 sketches the model we intend.[20]

Such phonologization involves the operation of the phonological learning mechanism[21] of the acquirer of G_2 on the bodily outputs produced by the speaker of G_1. The
pitch lowering present in the bodily outputs is noisy, in a technical sense, and thus consistent with more than one possible source (the phonology or the transduction systems).
If the acquirer misattributes responsibility for some property of the bodily output to the
phonology, when, for the speaker of G_1, it was due to the transduction system, phonologization results.

At Stage 1 in Table 20.2, there is a synchronic lowering of the pitch of the vowel following a voiced stop, as compared with a voiceless stop. We identify this as a lowering, only
because we assume that the actual pitch differences are not encoded representationally, as

---

[18] Change may also occur in (A) of G_2 as a result of the analysis of G_1's (E), of course, resulting in a
difference in UR between G_2 and G_1 for the 'same' lexical entry.

[19] It is hard to convince people of this point. Perhaps some analogies would be useful: the relationship
between two people, say, a parent and child, is not a person. The comparison between two cars ('This one
is big and green, whereas that one is small and yellow') is not a car. Similarly, a relationship between two
particular phonologies, yours and that of a parent, is not a phonology, nor is an analyst's comparison of
two particular phonologies a phonology.

[20] The properties of the human transduction systems (which we assume to be universal, thus
constant) that give rise to the phonetic lowering of pitch are, of course, a property of D_2, as well as of D_1.
However, the effect is potentially obscured by the fact that the phonetic representations of C_2 have voiced
stops followed by representational R tones (or LH sequences) in otherwise identical forms of C_1 with
representational H tones. We leave this detail out of D_2 for expository clarity. (Compare and contrast 'rule
scattering' in Bermúdez-Otero, this volume.)

[21] Which is *not* a token of B, but rather a system not shown in our schema.

Table 20.2 Phonologization of pitch lowering effect on vowels after voiced stops. The UR at both stages is /bá/, with a H tone. At Stage 1 pitch lowering is only a transduction effect, arising in the Speech component (D): the phonetic representation has an H tone, whose pitch is realized as slightly lowered at the beginning of the bodily output (compared with output of a UR /pá/), due to the transduction systems. At Stage 2 the (exaggerated) synchronic effect is phonological—the phonetic representation is R, due to a phonological rule. Transducing this phonetic representation leads to a pitch contour that is even more different from that of an output of a UR /pá/ because it is due to explicit 'instruction' (through featural representation) **in addition to** the unavoidable transduction effect.

	Stage 1	Stage 2
Underlying Rep.	A_1: /bá/ (H tone)	A_2: /bá/ (H tone)
Phonology	B_1	B_2: Rule H → R/Voiced Stop __
Phonetic Rep.	C_1: [bá] (H tone)	C_2: [bǎ] (R tone)
Speech	D_1: Phonetic lowering of pitch	D_2
Bodily Output	E_1: ⚇ba⚇ w/ pitch ⌒	E_2: ⚇ba⚇ w/ pitch ⌣

an underlying tonal difference in the lexical entry of the two forms. The synchronic pitch difference between the two forms, /pá/ and /bá/, is due to properties of the transduction system—the realization of any tone in any language will be different after a voiced *vs* voiceless consonant. The difference is thus predictable because of assumed properties of human articulation, but you have to look outside the grammar to see this effect—it is not represented grammatically, either in grammar inputs or grammar outputs.

At Stage 2, the grammar contains a phonological rule that changes the input tone in accordance with the phonological environment. The permanently stored tones in the two lexical items are identical at Stage 2, as they are at Stage 1, but a context sensitive rule changes the representation of the tone, say from H(igh) to R(ising) (perhaps analyzed as a sequence of Low-High) when it follows a voiced stop.

There are three 'lowerings' to note when thinking about Stage 2. First, there remain the effects on pitch following a voiced stop, as compared with a voiceless one—this effect is a constant of human articulation, part of the transducers (D); this effect may be invisible if no sequences of voiced stops followed by high tones are fed to the transduction system, but it exists as a property of D nonetheless, at both stages, D_1 and D_2. Second, there is the synchronic tonal change, a lowering, from an input H to an output R, the effect of a phonological computation (B) encoded in terms of the UG-given representational alphabet for tones and the UG-given phonological computational system.

The third 'lowering' is not actually a property of Stage 2, but a relationship: the relative, diachronic lowering between Stage 1 grammar outputs and Stage 2 grammar outputs, under the assumption that phonological lowering of H to R (due to the rule in Stage 2) effects a more dramatic pitch reduction on an input H than the constant universal effects on articulation of H after a voiced stop would. This 'lowering' is thus the change from pitch lowering to tone lowering from Stage 1 to Stage 2, the difference between E_1 and E_2. The first two lowerings are properties of the Stage 2 speaker. This third lowering is not a property of anything in the world other than the historical linguist's model of change, the result of an analysis.

There is really just one difference between Stage 1 and Stage 2 speakers (with G_1 and G_2, respectively). The only difference that is not epiphenomenal is that seen in B_1 *vs* B_2, the absence *vs* presence of a particular phonological operation.

20.6 IS ALLOPHONY RELEVANT?

We referred above to problems with the term 'phonemic' and associated notions. A possible confusion arises from a failure to adopt the findings of generative phonology. One result, deriving from Halle (1959), is that allophonic rules and neutralizing rules should not be distinguished—there are not two separate rule components of the grammar. In other words, a rule can be labelled allophonic or neutralizing only in the context of a particular lexicon—the difference has no status in the grammar. Now, it is tempting to suppose in discussion of phonologization that added rules are allophonic rules, and this appears to be the case in Table 20.2. At stage two, the R tone appears after the voiced stop, and the H tone appears after a voiceless stop. It looks like the presence of an R is predictable from context. However, nothing in our sketch of the mechanism of change, the misattribution of the pitch lowering to a phonological rule, requires that the change could not take place even if (at both Stage 1 and Stage 2) there are lexical R tones, including some after /b/.

The issue of phonologization is, therefore, orthogonal to the issue of whether a rule is allophonic or not. This is as we expect, since allophony, in generative phonology, has no status. It is perfectly possible that Hyman's Stage 1 has lexical items like /bá/, /pá/, /bǎ/ and /pǎ/, all of which surface distinctly at Stage 1; and that Stage 2 has identical lexical items, but that the contrast between /bá/ and /bǎ/ is neutralized by the computational system (B).[22] The resulting pattern in Stage 2 may be allophonic, predictable from context, since it may be the case that R tones appear only where an input contains a voiced stop followed by a H tone, or the Stage 2 rule may be neutralizing, in case there happen to be underlying R tones after voiced stops. The difference has to do with the content of the lexicon, and has no bearing on the mechanism of phonologization.

---

[22] We need to assume that there is some kind of evidence for underlying /bá/ forms, perhaps a tonal sandhi or other interaction that precedes the tone neutralization in the synchronic grammar of Stage 2.

20.7 IS PHONOLOGIZATION REGULAR?

What would happen if the misattribution we posited as the basis of phonologization were random, rather than consistent? Perhaps phonologization applies irregularly across the lexicon. There are reasons to doubt this happens, and so we need to account for the apparent regularity of phonologization (for a very different view, see Phillips in this volume). First, sound changes are famously quite regular—at least it is easy to find lots of examples of regular ones. Second, when confronted with apparent irregularity one must be certain that diffusion, rather than direct descent, is not at issue (Hale 2007, chapter 3). Third, if the misattribution were truly random, then there would be no consistency in attribution even for tokens of individual lexical items—it would be improbable that all tokens of the word for, say, 'cat' involved a misattribution (*vis-à-vis* the Stage 1 system) whereas all tokens of the word for 'house' did not, assuming no phonological conditioning. So, truly random misattribution appears to be empirically unsupported. Fourth, recall that phonologization involves a learner building G_2, attributing to the phonological computational system of G_1 responsibility for some aspect of the bodily output which, in fact, is due to the transduction system associated with the speaker of G_1. This misattribution has implications for the properties of G_2, the new grammar. Under our conception of phonology as a computation, a *function*, the mapping of input forms to output forms is regular by definition. A grammar cannot have a phonology that says 'lower the tone after voiced stops in certain lexical items'—that is not phonology. If this is a good diachronic description of the stages of a 'language', then we are not dealing with phonologization—some kind of lexical restructuring must have occurred to differentiate some voiced stops from others. (We do not need to decide if this kind of (random, non-conditioned) restructuring is possible—if it is, it is not phonologization.) If a change is restricted to a change in the phonological component—in other words, if phonologization as we have defined it does indeed exist—then it appears that the misattribution process cannot be random. Therefore, the regularity of phonologization follows from the regularity of misattribution (non-regularity would require lexical restructuring—see the discussion of 'phonemicization', below, so not phonologization) combined with the regularity of the computational system that is the phonology.

20.8 IS ALL SOUND CHANGE PHONOLOGIZATION?

It is of some importance to recognize that phonologization does not exhaust the range of phenomena with which diachronic phonology must concern itself. Only some of the phonological learning done by the acquirer is directly based on the parse of input acoustic strings. The morphological analyses that allow learners to posit rules based on alternations require 'batch-learning' over a set of stored lexical items, stored using the phonological representation system provided by UG.[23] Access to such forms is not 'noisy' in the technical sense, since the forms are stored in the speaker's mind and not susceptible to the same type of misparsing as raw acoustic data is. Nevertheless, the precise set of forms to which a learner is sufficiently robustly exposed within the relevant time frame certainly varies from acquirer to acquirer, and thus the batch learning will of necessity be performed on a distinct 'batch' of data for each individual, even those exposed to the output of the same source. Since the data will be different, the generalizations over the data may also differ—to make this concrete, each child of a parent who provides PLD will end up with a distinct I-language. A difference in the productive morphological parses assigned to the data may, in turn, entail a difference in the set of phonological rules which the acquirer must posit in order to synchronically relate allomorphs. This would be phonological change, but it would not be phonologization, as defined here, since the mechanism of change need not involve the elevation of phenomena originally triggered by the transduction systems to the phonological level.

The process of 'dephonologization', to which we turn, is also, strictly speaking, not 'phonologization', obviously. It does, however, bear a close relationship to phonologization.

20.9 DEPHONOLOGIZATION

In Proto-Indo-European an allophone of *t arose before a following syllable-initial *t, of the form *t^s.[24] This presumably resulted from the phonologization of the transition between the two dentals across the syllable juncture[25]—the addition of a rule to the phonological component of the grammar. This rule, or its reflex, survives into many of the daughter languages, including the Iranian branch—the closest relative of the Indic branch to which Sanskrit belongs. However, Sanskrit does not have the rule, i.e. the outcome of late common Indo-European *Vt^{s}tV is *VttV. The allophony-triggering rule was lost from the grammar, and with it the allophony. In the history of Indic, the

---

[23] If the first word a learner hears is *cats* [k^{h}æts], there is no way of knowing whether the initial velar stop is a plural marker, or if the aspiration on that stop is a marker of animacy. An analysis depends on comparison of multiple forms. When the learning extends to additional forms like *cow* [k^{h}aw] and *cows* [k^{h}awz], the learner will be able to identify a distinction between root and plural marker, relating the [z] and [s] plurals as a single underlying form and constructing a phonological rule that generates the alternants from this one form. All this learning requires an initial stage of storage of unanalyzed forms.

[24] Similar developments affected the other dentals in heterosyllabic dental+dental clusters; we consider *t alone simply for expository ease.

[25] Whatever its precise cause, it must have arisen via the reanalysis of the perceived acoustic properties of this juncture, there being no morphological analysis type of explanation available. To be honest, we expect no transition here, just the long closure typically associated with geminates, but our main point is that changes appear to be reversible—misattribution can happen in both directions. Perhaps the development to *t^{s}t* must be taken as evidence that the first stop in the cluster was, in fact, released.

prior phonologization has been lost. There has been dephonologization. Presumably, the stop transitions of *tt* clusters in the pre-phonologization stage and the Sanskrit post-dephonologization stage are identical, since they are due to the universal transduction systems. At some point, in the Sanskrit linguistic tradition, learners misattributed the high frequency noise between the stops to the transducers (D in the chain), instead of to the presence of a feature for stridency in the phonetic representation (C). So, dephonologization is also a kind of sound change.[26]

20.10 RETHINKING PHONEMICIZATION AS LEXIFICATION

Consider the shift from Stage 2 to Stage 3 in Table 20.1, presented in more detail in Table 20.3. Looking at the B step in the chain, it seems obvious that B_3 will not have the rule lowering H to R that is present in B_2—the relevant tones are stored as R (in A_3), so there is no need for a rule to make H into R.

However, there are not one but *two* differences between A_2 and A_3—the tones are different and the consonants are different. This double difference is necessary in the context of a discussion of 'phonemic' changes. It is only because the initial consonant in A_3 is now non-distinct from, for example, the initial consonant of another lexical item, [pá], that the R *vs* H distinction has become phonemic, unpredictable. Since we have already decided to be sceptical of the notion 'phonemic', let's delve deeper.

There is no reason that the H-R contrast could not have been 'phonemic', that is lexically contrastive, even at Stage 1 or Stage 2. Hypothetically, Stage 2 could have had lexical items /bá/, /pá/, /bǎ/ and /pǎ/ with a neutralizing rule that mapped inputs /bá/ and /bǎ/ both to

Table 20.3 'Phonemicization'. This should be broken down in two stages: (1) lexification and loss of the rule; (2) merger of /b/ and/p/.

	Stage 2	Stage 3
Underlying Rep.	A2: /bá/ (H tone)	A3: /pǎ/ (R tone)
Phonology	B2 : Rule H → R /Voiced Stop __	B3
Phonetic Rep.	C2: [bǎ] (R tone)	C3: [pǎ] (R tone)
Speech	D2	D3
Bodily Output	E2: 🧍bǎ🧍 w/ pitch ⤳	E3: 🧍pǎ🧍 w/ pitch ⤳

[26] See Dresher (this volume) for an example of this type ('rule loss') from the history of English as well as for discussion of some of the same issues raised in this chapter.

Table 20.4 'Lexification'. The R tone is derived from H at Stage 2, but stored in the lexicon at Stage 2b. The Stage 2 tone rule is not part of the Stage 2b phonology.

	Stage 2	Stage 2b
Underlying Rep.	A2: /bá/ (H tone)	A2b: /bǎ/ (R tone)
Phonology	B2: Rule H → R / Voiced Stop __	B2b
Phonetic Rep.	C2: [bǎ] (R tone)	C2b: [bǎ] (R tone)
Speech	D2	D2b
Bodily Output	E2: ♟ba♟ w/ pitch ⌒	E2b: ♟ba♟ w/ pitch ⌒

[bǎ] (see note 22). Just the loss of this rule, with its effects transferred into the lexicon, would yield a Stage 2b with lexical entries /pá/, /bǎ/ (occurring with two meanings) and /pǎ/.[27] The voicing contrast remains, as does the (hypothesized) tonal contrast (after /p/), so there is nothing to call 'phonemicization'. Whether this exact change is plausible or not, any case of partial merger provides the same logical structure. This change is sketched in Table 20.4. Since phonemicness is not relevant to the phonology (see discussion of allophonic *vs* neutralization rules above), we don't need to indicate the full range of possible lexical items in Table 20.4. The change, in I-language terms, given our model of the speech chain, is not affected by whether the languages happen to have lexical forms like /pǎ/ or not (compare Kiparsky, this volume).

We conclude from such examples that phonemicization, as illustrated by Hyman's example, is actually a combination of two processes that need to be unpacked in order to understand what is going on. The loss of the phonological rule and the representation of R tones for Stage 2 H tones we will call *lexification*. This parallels our discussion of phonologization in that responsibility for an aspect of speech generation shifts from one component to another between Stages, here from the phonology to the lexicon. The possibility of a subsequent merger of /p/ and /b/ to yield Hyman's Stage 3 is not a logical necessity—it is clear that language change does not have to maintain the number of underlying contrasts from Stage to Stage, although this is perhaps implied by Hyman's example. If such a merger did occur, it would be *just* a difference between the lexical representations of the stages—it might involve a shift in 'phonemic' contrasts, but since these have no status in the modern model of grammar, they deserve no status in a model of the relationships between grammars in the direct descent relation, *a.k.a.* language change.

In old fashioned terms, the lexification of R tones only becomes phonemic through the merger of /p/ and /b/, but this merger is not an inevitable consequence of the

---

[27] For example, whatever provided evidence for an underlying /bá/ might disappear, forcing an analysis of all surface [bǎ]'s as originating exclusively from /bǎ/.

Table 20.5 Merger of /b/ and /p/. The /b/ of earlier Stages corresponds to Stage 3 /p/. The existence of contrast is irrelevant to a characterization of the nature of the changes—earlier Stages may or may not have /p/, as well as /b/.

	Stage 2b	Stage 3
Underlying Rep.	A2b : /bǎ/ (R tone)	A3 : /pǎ/ (R tone)
Phonology	B2b	B3
Phonetic Rep.	C2b : [bǎ] (R tone)	C3: [pǎ] (R tone)
Speech	D2b :see text	D3
Bodily Output	E2b : 👤baꜛ w/ pitch ꜛ	E3: 👤paꜛ w/ pitch ꜛ

occurrence of the change in Table 20.4. Stage 2b is a perfectly reasonable language, with or without lexical /pǎ/.

To get from Stage 2b to Stage 3 we need something like the change in Table 20.5, a merger of /p/ and /b/. As mentioned above, such a change might have the effect of making the H *vs* R distinction phonemic, or it might not—that depends on whether the lexicon already had elements like /pǎ/.[28]

20.11 RELATIONSHIP OF PHONOLOGIZATION AND LEXIFICATION

We have already argued that lexification need not be followed by a merger of the type in Table 20.5: a language tradition can change from Stage 2 to Stage 2b and 'stay there'. There is no mechanism for looking ahead at Stage 2 and only changing to Stage 2b if it is guaranteed that Stage 3 will follow, since each Stage is instantiated in different minds.

We offered a reinterpretation in Table 20.5 of the term phonemicization (now *lexification*) as a relationship between a rule-generated variant at an earlier Stage corresponding to a stored form at the subsequent Stage, a shift of responsibility from the computational system (B) to the lexicon (A). Let's refer to this change as 'Indirect Lexification' for reasons that will immediately become apparent. This contrasted with our discussion of phonologization which involved a shift of responsibility from the Speech step (D) to the Phonology (B), shown in Table 20.2.

There is another possibility that we relied on implicitly in Table 20.5. This corresponds to an unconditioned change from /b/ at Stage 2b to /p/ at Stage 3. It appears to be the

---

[28] That is, at Stage 2b, the lexicon had elements like /pǎ/ that were accurately transmitted to Stage 3.

case, although we are arguing from *lack* of evidence for a relevant rule, so we cannot be certain, that unconditioned changes can, in fact, occur. In other words, lexical representations appear to be able to shift between Stages without an intermediate Stage involving a phonological rule. If there is no such stage involved, then it must be the case that the bodily output (E) at the earlier stage can be misanalyzed directly as a difference in lexical representation. Let's call this 'Direct Lexification'.

We can now express the changes presented in Hyman's example as a sequence of phonologization (call it Output-to-Phonology), followed by Indirect Lexification, followed by Direct Lexification. In this particular case, the effect of the Direct Lexification was to merge a contrast (/b/ *vs* /p/) that had conditioned the Indirect Lexification of R tone. However, the mechanism of change is not logically related to its effects on the system of contrasts present underlyingly or on the surface. This means that Direct Lexification should be able to occur whether or not it results in a merger, and whether or not it is preceded by a 'related' Indirect Lexification.

The unconditioned change of the Indo-European voiceless stops to fricatives in Germanic is an example of an apparent Direct Lexification change, involving no merger.[29] In contrast, the unconditioned change of Indo-European voiced aspirates to plain voiced stops *did* result in a merger with inherited voiced stops in the Balto-Slavic family. So, Direct Lexification changes may or may not result in merger themselves.

How does Direct Lexification occur? We assume that it is quite possible that an initial sample of hits for a given segment with a skewed distribution (predicted, occasionally, if the distribution is stochastic[30]) may lead to a reassignment of the target space for that segment, and thus a direct Direct Lexification 'rephonemicization'—that is G_2 encodes segments in the new lexicon with a different set of features from the 'corresponding' segments in the G_1 lexicon   without a phonological rule ever having been in play. In fact, it is hard to motivate the kind of unconditioned phonological rules that such a scenario would require—why would a learner posit a lexicon full of voiced aspirates along with a rule that changes them *all* into plain voiced stops? Either the learner would perceive the voiced aspirates in the Primary Linguistic Data (PLD), store them and produce them, or not perceive them as such, markedness and repair based models of change notwithstanding (Scheer, this volume).

There is also no reason to suppose that a Direct Lexification needs to be preceded by phonologization (Output-to-Phonology). The unconditioned development of Indo-European *a to Sanskrit /ə/, shows no evidence of a stage involving 'allophony' or the 'exaggeration' of locally conditioned coarticulation effects which are taken to characterize phonologization events.[31]

---

[29] There may have been a stage with aspiration, but the focus here is on the fact that there was no merger and there is no evidence for a rule in any synchronic grammar.

[30] This stochasticness reflects the interaction of all the systems involved in the Speech level—there is no reason to posit a stochastic aspect to the grammar itself.

[31] Indo-European *e and *o also changed to Sanskrit /ə/, without any direct compensation for the loss of contrasts seen in Hyman's illustration—sound changes can't look ahead to evaluate their results.

Table 20.6 Merger without lexification. There is no relevant difference at step B between the Stages. The only difference of any import is at the lexical level A. The differences at C and E are all derivative of the lexical difference. Pitch lowering after voiced stops remains a constant property of the speech level (D), but it is irrelevant once those stops are devoiced. This situation involves a difference in lexical representations, but not the lexification of the effects of a rule.

	Stage 1	Stage 2'
Underlying Rep.	A1 : /bá/ (H tone)	A2' : /pá/ (H tone)
Phonology	B1	B2'
Phonetic Rep.	C1: [bá] (H tone)	C2' : [pá] (H tone)
Speech	D1: Phonetic lowering of pitch	D2' : "Invisible" lowering of pitch
Bodily Output	E1: ⚲ba⚲ w/ pitch ⌒	E2' : ⚲pa⚲ w/ pitch ⁻⁻

We have seen that Hyman's Stage 1 can develop to Stage 3, but it can also remain at Stage 2 indefinitely—Stage 2 is a possible language, showing just phonologization from Stage 1. Stage 2b is a possible language as well, showing phonologization, followed by lexification. Stage 3, in which merger of the stops follows Stage 2b, is also possible, representing what Hyman calls phonemicization. However, the merger of /b/ and /p/ that is necessary for phonemicization could occur without lexification of a new tonal distinction. For completeness we sketch this possibility in Table 20.6. This situation involves a difference in lexical representations, but not the lexification of the effects of an earlier synchronic rule. The development from Stage 1 to Stage 2' in Table 20.6 cannot lead to Hyman's Stage 3 since the distinction between Stage 1 /pá/ and /bá/ has been irrevocably lost. We thus see that lexification and merger which combine in Hyman's phonemicization scenario are logically distinct and completely independent of each other: either can occur without the other.

In addition to illustrating the possibility of dephonologization, the Sanskrit *tt* case bears on the putative relationship of phonologization and phonemicization, and the notion of drift—the idea that sound changes in a 'language' tend in certain directions. Why do we even raise this issue? The relationship between phonologization and phonemicization is sometimes discussed under the general heading of the 'life cycle of phonological rules' (Bermúdez-Otero and Kiparsky, both this volume), the idea being that such rules are 'born' via the mechanism of phonologization, live for some span as phonological rules, and then 'die' via the mechanism of phonemicization. Indeed, Hyman (1976) explicitly ties the two phenomena together, noting that '*the development* [via phonologization—mh,mk&cr] *of a phonological rule carries the seeds of its own destruction*' (emphasis in original). While engagingly phrased, this represents, we fear, an unnecessary oversimplification. While birth provides one of the necessary antecedent conditions (life) for death, phonologization is not necessary for the coming into being of a phonological rule (since these may arise via morphological parsing, as discussed in section 20.8), and thus it is entirely possible that many cases of 'phonemicization' involve the loss of phonological rules which have simply nothing to do with earlier phonologization events. And while birth, unfortunately, entails death as a necessary consequence, phonologization in no way entails phonemicization as a necessary consequence. This is clear from the Sanskrit example discussed above, where the phonologization was just reversed—something like a Stage 1 to Stage 2 shift does not have to be followed by something like a Stage 2 to Stage 3 shift. In the Sanskrit case, we seem to revert back to Stage 1 from Stage 2. Finally, we reiterate that a merger of a distinction can occur between Stages without a concomitant lexicalization of another contrast—losing the voicing contrast, but gaining the tonal contrast. We suspect that the issue only arises due to an abiding crypto-functionalism in the field that expects, in the face of plentiful counter-evidence, that considerations like 'functional load' play some kind of role in either synchronic or diachronic linguistic explanation. (See Hale & Reiss 2000a, 2008 for our views on functionalist reasoning.)

Hyman's discussion of 'life cycles' is part of a long-standing discussion of 'drift' in language change. The notion is discussed by Jespersen, Jakobson, Sapir and more recent scholars, often in a manner that obscures the relationship to earlier work, for example, with claims that language change is a process of optimization or markedness reduction (see also Mailhammer, Restle, & Vennemann, this volume). However, there is no mechanism in the I-language view for the propagation of drift from one generation to another. A learner has no access to previous Stages of his/her linguistic tradition. The learner can only access the outputs of individuals in his/her environment. If there is a difference between the learner's phonology/lexicon and the phonologies/lexicons of those who provided the PLD outputs (a 'change'), then the learner must have misanalyzed that output. Note that discussions of drift and life cycles never make precise claims about the time scales at which these forces work, and this must be for the simple reason that the claims are based on entities, 'languages' like English, Sanskrit or Cree, that are non-existent under the I-language approach. How would the mechanism of drift be encoded in the grammatical knowledge of a speaker? Why did Sanskrit 'drift' back to an earlier Stage while Iranian did not?

The inherited rule affecting Indo-European *tt* clusters was synchronically productive in Proto-Iranian and (with a slightly modified output) in the Old Iranian languages, since its most frequent context of application was across morpheme boundaries, when *t-initial affixes (of which there were many) were added to dental-final roots (ditto). Since those dental stop-final roots also normally appeared before non-dental-initial suffixes, in which context their dental stop was preserved, the rule remained synchronically motivated. This rule, which arose via phonologization, has persisted for these 3,000 years without triggering any phonemicization event into the modern Iranian languages. Maybe someday it will, and the 'life cycle' will find its expression in Iranian (but for how long can one say that a diachronic process is 'in transition'?); but, in any event, it never will, and can't, in Sanskrit (or its descendants).

It seems clear, then, that the two events, phonologization and lexification (the old 'phonemicization'), are simply independent phenomena of diachronic development with merger falling out epiphenomenally depending upon idiosyncratic properties of lexica. As independent phenomena, they may appear to interact, but this 'interaction' has no ontological status—it is an artifact of our point of view as analysts. The 'life cycle' of phonological rules is a mirage—implying causal linkage where none exists. Understanding this allows us to focus our research attention on clarifying the actual factors which give rise to each of these processes, and to turn away from a search for the mystical, pan-generational forces which would need to be in play to enforce a 'life cycle'.

20.12 DESCRIPTION *VS* EXPLANATION OF CHANGE

Finally, we would like to clarify the distinction between the *description* of change and the *explanation* of change. Our model of the speech chain included (A) underlying representations (we didn't treat the thorny issue of how lexical entries are combined into complex forms) which are the input to (B), phonological computation, yielding (C) the output phonetic representation which is fed to a complex system of transducers (D), finally yielding the acoustic output of the body (E). The contents of the lexicon that appears in (A) is subject to variation, but all content is encoded in a single universal alphabet of features. The contents of the computational system (B) is also subject to variation—languages appear to have different computations/processes. None of the other components (C,D,E) are subject to variation: we assume that the transduction systems (D) are constant, and the phonetic output (C) and bodily output (E) are just the fleeting products of the higher steps in the chain. If two languages G_1 and G_2 differ with respect to the respective forms c_1 and c_2 at (C) in the speech chain, then the difference must be due to either a difference in the lexical input for c_1 vs c_2, or a difference in the computation, or both. Different inputs to the phonology can give different outputs; identical inputs (A-level) to the phonology can give different outputs only if the computational system B_1 and B_2 differ appropriately. If the speakers of two I-languages have two different forms at (E), e_1 and e_2, respectively, then the difference is due to one of two sources (or both). One case is that in which there is a difference in what was received by the invariant transduction system, in other words, a difference at step (C). As we have seen, this regresses back to a difference at either (A) or (B) or both. The other case is where a difference is introduced in (D). This is possible, despite the fact that (D) is assumed to be universal, because (D) has other inputs than just (C), a fact alluded to above, but somewhat obscured by Figure 20.1. To give a simple example, the decision to scream a word, rather than whisper it, changes the (non-grammatical) input to the transduction, but does not constitute variation in the transduction system. Intention to scream is not represented at (C), but it does affect (D) by some other (non-linguistic) path.

So, the *description* of a language change (a lack of correspondence between grammars) can only make reference to differences in components (A) and (B)—these are the only components that are subject to change and they are the only components that are linguistic. (C may be considered linguistic, but it is derivative from A and B. E is not linguistic—it includes the effects of shouting or talking with a cigarette dangling from the lips, and it too is derivative.)

However, the *explanation* of a language change must make reference to more than grammar. The batch learning morphological parsing of initially unanalyzed stored forms mentioned briefly above is not part of grammar, but rather part of the learning process that *builds* a grammar by inducing lexical entries and phonological rules (the content of A and B). Similarly, the parse of bodily output by the G_2 acquirer, in which acoustic properties have to be attributed (rightly or wrongly in light of the noise) to C_1 (the phonetic representation output by G_1) is itself not grammar, but transduction, where the acquirer must assign a featural representation to a signal originating in the auditory system.

20.13   CONCLUSION

We have argued that (1) carefully maintaining the I-language perspective and (2) establishing explicit definitions for 'change', 'grammar', 'transduction' and the like, brings clarity to a family of phenomena studied by historical linguists. Most fundamentally, drawing on Hale (2007), we suggest that language 'change' is something of a misnomer, since we assume that languages, that is I-languages, do not change (other than additions to the lexicon) after maturity. We pointed out that language change is by definition punctual under our approach. If G_2 is constructed on the basis of output of G_1, then the change comes into being by virtue of the construction of G_2. We embedded our model of language, that is grammar, inside a model of the speech chain that included the mapping from lexical forms in long-term storage to the sound waves that constitute bodily output. What is traditionally called language change is, under our view, a difference between two stages of a linguistic tradition. Such differences arise via non-convergent grammar construction, giving rise to phonologization, lexification and the related processes we have attempted to sketch in this chapter.

CHAPTER 21

LEXICAL DIFFUSION IN HISTORICAL PHONOLOGY

BETTY S. PHILLIPS

LEXICAL diffusion is, in its essence, a simple concept. Chen & Wang (1975: 256) define it as when 'a phonological rule gradually extends its scope of operation to a larger and larger portion of the lexicon, until all relevant items have been transformed by the process'.[1] This seems straightforward, and the current vowel qualities in *food*, *good*, and *blood*, all traceable to earlier [u], provide a good example. Yet the theory of lexical diffusion is still under construction, as more examples are found and more factors influencing which words are more amenable to change are discovered. Recent theories of the lexicon that attempt to reflect speakers' mental representations and networks of connections recognize the psychological interdependence of words and sounds (Goldrick 2011), rendering moot the question of whether 'the basic unit of change [is] the word or the sound' (Labov 1981: 268). Sounds occur within words, and the phonological system is a psychologically real abstraction derived from speakers' experience of sounds within words (Pierrehumbert 2006, Pisoni & Levi 2007, Goldrick 2011). The impetus for a sound change can begin in either domain. Low-level phonetic changes such as assimilations, for instance, typically start with the effects of articulatory processing in sequences of sounds within or across words (Bybee, this volume). Chain shifts and some vowel mergers, on the other hand, display sensitivity to the system of phonemes of which they are a part (Phillips 1984, Labov 1994, 2010, Gordon, this volume), and phonotactic changes often follow from universal preference laws (Mailhammer et al., this volume). Given the range of sound changes for which lexical diffusion has been documented, the position advocated here is that it is probable that all changes proceed by lexical diffusion, although some spread through the lexicon so quickly that they seem to affect all words fitting the given phonological environment at the same time. This position is controversial, as some maintain that at least some changes are 'neogrammarian'

---

[1] Not to be confused is the use of *lexical diffusion* to describe the areal diffusion through borrowing of lexemes of other languages, as in Bender (2000).

or 'regular' in their implementation (e.g. Labov 1994, 2010, Hale 2003, and also Hale et al. and Bermúdez-Otero, both this volume).

More and more factors are being discovered that affect which words undergo a sound change more readily: Raymond et al. (2006: 76) find for flapping that predictability from the word that follows is significant; Cho (2004) finds that words in stronger prosodic or pragmatic positions may resist coarticulation; Hume & Mailhot (2013) find that the notion of surprisal from information theory helps explain why medium frequency words are less likely to undergo sound change than are low or high frequency words. In turn, studies documenting the different ways that individual sound changes diffuse through the lexicon help inform phonological theory and contribute to our understanding of the structure of the mental lexicon, its relationship to the phonological system of a language, and the process of phonological change. The aim of this chapter is to give an overview of what we have learned thus far about the lexical diffusion of sound change. Each section presents a fundamental feature of lexical diffusion, aiming to dispel misperceptions and to form a clear groundwork for future studies.

21.1 LEXICAL DIFFUSION IS NOT SPORADIC

The first and perhaps most basic misperception about lexical diffusion is that it is 'sporadic'. Hinskens (1998: 169), for example, states, 'Although variable by nature, neogrammarian sound change is pre-eminently 'systematic and recurrent' i.e. regular, as there are no lexical exceptions. Lexically diffuse and lexicalized sound change bring about 'non-systematic but recurrent' facts (Lloret 1997), which are only partially regular, hence 'sporadic'. Labov (2010: 261), in fact, takes arbitrariness and unpredictability as defining characteristics of lexical diffusion: 'Lexical diffusion through the vocabulary cannot be predictable and systematic: if it is, then the basis of that selection is the mechanism of change, not lexical diffusion. To be identified as lexical diffusion, the process of selection must have an arbitrary and unpredictable character'. Yet this stance takes us no nearer to understanding the role of the lexicon in the course of a sound change, and it is not the definition that proponents of lexical diffusion recognize. Rather, lexical diffusion refers to the spread of a sound change via the connections the mind forms between words. And this spread is by no means haphazard. Evidence from frequency effects show that lexical diffusion can be very systematic, affecting both phonetically gradual and abrupt changes, and for each type sometimes spreading to the most frequent words first and sometimes to the least. Even if one cannot predict with complete accuracy which words will undergo a change, the general direction of the change through the lexicon can be traced, with word frequency, reflecting entrenchment, being a strong factor.[2] Such frequency effects fit within a larger framework of probabilistic

[2] With the increasing availability of electronic corpora such as the *Helsinki Corpus of English Texts* (Rissanen et al. 1991) and *The Corpus of Historical American English* [COHA] (Davies 2010), word frequency within a text under study or frequency within certain times and genres has become easier to

phonology. As Jurafsky et al. (2001: 230) explain, in addition to word frequency, 'the probability of a word is conditioned on many aspects of its context, including neighboring words, syntactic and lexical structure, semantic expectations, and discourse factors'.

The awareness of the influence of word frequency on sound change can be traced to Schuchardt's (1885: 58) observation that 'The greater or lesser frequency in the use of individual words that plays such a prominent role in analogical formation is also of great importance for their phonetic transformation, not within rather small differences, but within significant ones. Rarely-used words drag behind; very frequently used ones hurry ahead. Exceptions to the sound laws are formed in both groups'. A good example is Hooper's (1976b) discussion of schwa reduction and deletion in English: words with very high frequency delete the schwa altogether (*every, evening* (noun)); those with medium frequency have syllabic *r* (*memory, salary, summary, nursery*); and those with low frequency retain the schwa (*mammary, artillery, summery, cursory, evening* (verb)). A similar pattern holds for final /t, d/ deletion: frequent *told* deletes final /d/ more often than less frequent *held*; frequent *felt* more often than less frequent *built*; frequent *sent* more often than less frequent *meant* and *lent*, frequent *kept* more often than less frequent *slept* (Bybee 2002a, this volume.) Another, very different change that affects the most frequent words first is the stress shift in two-syllable verbs ending in -*ate* in British English: infrequent verbs such as *filtrate, gestate, palpate,* and *lactate* keep their stress on the initial syllable; moderately frequent verbs like *mandate, truncate, stagnate,* and *pulsate* vary between initial and final stress; whereas frequent verbs such as *dictate, prostrate,* and *frustrate* now have the innovative stress on the final syllable (Phillips 2006: 42).

21.2 LEXICAL DIFFUSION SOMETIMES AFFECTS THE MOST FREQUENT WORDS FIRST AND SOMETIMES THE LEAST FREQUENT

Schuchardt (1885) proposed that the most frequent words are more amenable to change, which Krug (2003) echoes in his statement that 'It has become a linguistic commonplace that high-frequency words and constructions tend to lead phonological change....' Yet lexically diffused changes do not all behave alike in this regard. For instance, early acquired words or words semantically associated with each other such as kinship terms also sometimes behave differently (Yaeger-Dror 1996). In addition, there are clear examples of phonological changes that affect the least frequent words first. For instance, the unrounding of early Middle English /ø:/ > /e:/, as shown in the *Ormulum* manuscript (a poetic homily c.1180 of 10,000 lines), affected, on average, the less frequent words within each grammatical class. For example, *seon* 'see' (frequency 69) has the innovative

---

ascertain. Age of acquisition is more difficult to ascertain, especially for older texts. See Morrison et al. (1997) for modern English.

spelling more often than does the more frequent *beon* 'be' (frequency 355)—52% vs 41%, respectively. Similarly, vowel lengthening before nasal/liquid plus homorganic consonant sequences in the *Ormulum* affected the least frequent words first (Phillips 2006: 87–90), as did loss of /h/ in word-initial /hn, hr, hr, hw/ clusters in Old English, based on spellings in the *Rushworth 1* and *Lindisfarne* manuscripts (Toon 1976: 616–17, Phillips 2006: 82–3).

Two changes currently underway also show the least frequent words changing first. Glide deletion in southern American English affects less frequent words such as *Tudor, tuba, tuber,* and *tunic* before more frequent *tutor* and *tulip,* which are affected more often than the even more frequent *Tuesday, tube,* and *tune* (Phillips 2006: 79–81). The second example is the stress shift affecting noun-verb pairs, whereby infrequent words such as *excise, exploit,* and *extract,* originally stressed on the final syllable for both noun and verb, develop initial stress on the noun, so that the noun *EXcise, EXploit, EXtract* is distinguished from the verb *exCISE, exPLOIT, exTRACT*; frequent words, such as *exCHANGE, exHAUST,* and *exPRESS* in contrast, resist the change. In addition, these frequency effects occur inside prefix categories; that is, within each prefix group (*a-, con-/com-, de-, dis-, es-, ex-, pre-,* and *re-*), the least frequent words have shifted the stress of the noun to the initial syllable—which suggests an organization of the lexicon beyond traditional word class distinctions.[3]

These examples, with those in section 21.1, show how systematic the influence of word frequency is on lexical diffusion. That some changes affect the most frequent words first and others the least frequent apparently has to do with what Bybee (1985: 118) calls 'lexical analysis': '[h]igh frequency words form more distant lexical connections than low-frequency words. In the case of morphologically complex words ... high-frequency words undergo less analysis, and are less dependent on their related base words than low-frequency words'. This observation is linked to psycholinguistic research which finds different activation levels for high- vs low-frequency words, i.e. 'a high-frequency word has a lower activation threshold and hence is quicker to access' (Jurafsky 2003: 88). In an exemplar model, 'because exemplars are strengthened as each new token of use is mapped onto them, high-frequency exemplars will be stronger than low-frequency ones, and high-frequency clusters—words, phrases, constructions—will be stronger than lower frequency ones. The effects of this strength ... are several: first, stronger exemplars are easier to access, thus accounting for the well-known phenomenon by which high-frequency words are easier to access in lexical decision tasks. Second, high-frequency, morphologically complex words show increased morphological stability' (Bybee 2010: 24). The longer it takes for a low-frequency word to be activated

---

[3] The fact that each prefix category behaves independently is a strong argument for an exemplar cum network lexicon. As Gahl and Yu (2006: 213) remark, 'An exemplar-based speech processing system recognizes inputs and generates outputs by analogical evaluation across a lexicon of distinct memory traces of remembered tokens of speech'. Thus, words with the same prefixes may be accessed together, as suggested by Cole et al. (1989). Similarly, Melinger (2003) found that words with the same prefix behaved identically, whether the root were bound (as in *reject*) or free (as in *recharge*).

allows for more associations to be accessed along with it. For instance, the past tense of the more frequent *sleep* historically participated in vowel laxing to become *slept*, ignoring connections to variants with the tense vowel in *sleep, sleeping, sleeper*; but tea is still *steeped*, not *stept. If the information needed to implement a sound change in an individual's speech is relatively shallow—just the phonetic word form—then the most frequent words change first; but if more information is required—word class, syllable structure, phonotactic structure, and so forth—the least frequent words change first (Phillips 1998, 2006: 181). Often the motivation behind the latter types seem rooted in the universal preference laws of the sort discussed in Mailhammer et al. (this volume) or type frequency within a language (Phillips 2006: 38), but it is the implementation of these changes by speakers that the patterns of diffusion through the lexicon reveal.

21.3 LEXICAL INFLUENCES ON SOUND CHANGE OCCUR WITHIN PHONETIC ENVIRONMENTS, NOT INDEPENDENTLY OF THEM

Labov's 'Words Floating on the Surface of Sound Change' (2010: 265) distinguishes between phonetically conditioned changes and lexically diffused ones, disallowing the possibility of lexical influences within phonological constraints: 'If the sound change [the fronting of /uw/] does select words one at a time, the phonological constraints should shrink or disappear, and be replaced by lexical diffusion' (265) and for the raising of /ow/, 'in no case are phonological effects replaced by lexical effects' (272). Yet, as far as I can ascertain, it has never been claimed that lexical diffusion occurs outside of phonological constraints or in competition with them. Phonological constraints do not shrink or disappear; the same constraints affect the last words to change as affect the first words to change. Labov concludes that the phonological environment is stronger than isolated words in predicting the presence of a change, a fact which is undebated.

There are, in fact, numerous examples of phonetically conditioned, lexically diffused changes, in addition to those mentioned above. For such changes the words affected must always first and foremost meet the phonological description of the change. For instance, Bybee (2002a) reveals how the intervocalic shift /d/ to /ð/ proceeds through the lexicon of New Mexican speakers of Spanish, with the more frequent words affected first. Other studies that have found both phonetic conditioning and lexical diffusion for the same sound change include the following: Goeman and van Reenen's (1985) data on deletion of [t] in final [xt] and [st] clusters, when divided into word classes, reveals lexical diffusion by word frequency (Phillips 2006: 64–5). And lexical diffusion affects the most frequent words first in the Middle English diphthongization of vowel + /j, w/ sequences (Phillips 1983); e.g. the more frequent noun *þeoww* 'servant' (55x) shows the diphthongized spelling, but the less frequent *hew* 'form' (2x) does not; the more frequent verb *leȝȝepþ/leȝȝ(d)(e)* 'lay/laid' (16x) contains the diphthongized spelling, but the less frequent *forrleȝenn* 'having committed adultery' (3x) does not.

In a study of the reduction of initial *s-* in Spanish, Raymond and Brown (2012) found that there was 'a correlation between FFC [frequency in a favourable context] and reduction rate for high frequency words (r = .36), but not low frequency words (r = .12).' However, 'an *s*-word's frequency alone did not predict /s-/ reduction'. They write, 'It remains to be tested whether variability in the likelihood that words occur in reducing environments defined by non-phonological variables such as speech rate can also predict reduction and eliminate word frequency effects'. Certainly, the intricate interplay of a variety of influences on each particular change is a research path that should be encouraged.

21.4 LEXICALLY DIFFUSED CHANGES EXHIBIT PRODUCTIVITY

Despite claims such as Bakken's (2001: 67) that 'productivity seems to be incompatible with lexical exceptions, i.e. lexical diffusion', numerous studies have revealed lexical diffusion of ongoing sound changes, a number of which are mentioned in this paper, including /t, d/ deletion in English (Bybee 2002a, Gahl & Garnsey 2004) and Southern American English glide deletion (Phillips 1994). The latter study, using apparent time, shows that for each of the word-frequency groups 0–01, 01–10, 10–100, and 100–1000, teenaged females had more deleted forms than females over 66 years of age: 66.8% *vs* 57.1%, 68.6% *vs* 39.2%, 44.2% *vs* 18.2%, and 42.4% *vs* 5.2%. A similar pattern applied to younger *vs* older males (Phillips 1994: 122). See Table 21.1, where the younger members of each group exhibited a greater percentage of /j/ deletion within each frequency range, indicating a likely change in progress.

Still another example is Hansen's (2001) study of the ongoing vowel shift involving nasal vowels in French, which shows 'significant differences between the percentages' of

Table 21.1 Frequency effects on Southern American English post-alveolar /j/ deletion

Frequency	Percentage with deleted /j/			
	Younger females	Older females	Younger males	Older males
0–01	66.8	57.1	75.6	62.1
01–10	68.6	39.2	84.3	40.0
10–100	44.2	18.2	76.5	22.6
100–1000	42.4	5.2	75.0	20.8

the variants 'from one word to the next, [and that] lexical differences remain when prosodic/phonetic factors are kept constant, and homonyms ... do not behave identically' (p. 248).

Particularly interesting data comes from the Northern Cities Shift, which Labov (1994) presents as a prime example of a regular, neogrammarian sound change, without lexical diffusion. His early work on the shift (Labov, Yaeger, & Steiner 1972) states first that 'We find no strong evidence for lexical diffusion in the (æh) patterns of Detroit and Buffalo and Chicago', adding then, 'Despite some initial oscillations the (æh) word class seems to move upward as a whole, with fine phonetic conditioning in the process. There is some indication that the word *mad* is lower than its phonetic class would justify for several speakers ... It also appears as low and peripheral in the reading passage for Vinney M., an 11-year-old Syracuse boy. Since in other dialects we find that initial *m*- does have a raising effect, the low position of *mad* as compared to *bad, ads*, etc., seems to be lexically determined' (93). This is a clear example of how part of the Northern Cities Shift must be both phonetically conditioned and lexically conditioned. One does not preclude the other, and the Northern Cities Shift is a sound change in progress. It is also an example of how a seemingly sporadic change may be due to lexical frequency. According to the *Corpus of Contemporary American English* (accessed 07/11/2012), the word *mad* has a frequency of 14,594 compared to *bad*, which has a considerably higher frequency of 99,592. And studies of the Great Vowel Shift show that the most frequent words tend to change first (Ogura 1987: 64, 90; 1995), even within fine phonetic environments.

21.5 LEXICAL DIFFUSION AFFECTS BOTH LEXICAL AND POSTLEXICAL RULES

That lexical diffusion affects only lexical rules and not postlexical rules is a position taken by Labov (1994) and Kiparsky (1995). Insofar as lexical and postlexical rules are part of the theory of Lexical Phonology, this is a theory-dependent generalization, but it is related to the previous assumptions in that it assumes that a change is *either* phonetically conditioned and regular or lexically conditioned and irregular (or sporadic). However, even phonetically gradient changes have been shown to be lexically diffused. For example, according to Bybee (2002a: 265), the lexically diffused shift of /d/ to [ð] in New Mexican Spanish discussed above was found by D'Introno and Sosa (1979) to be gradient, ranging in production from [d] to [ð] to Ø along a continuum. Bybee (2002: 265) also reports that her findings on the increased deletion of regular past-tense /t/ and /d/ are matched by Losiewicz's (1992) evidence that such stops are also shorter in high frequency words. Therefore, lexically diffused changes need not involve abrupt substitution of phonemes. Even low-level, gradient changes typical of postlexical rules can vary from word to word.

Perhaps the clearest distinction between lexical and postlexical rules is that postlexical rules also apply after words have been chosen and put into a string, so that palatalization in phrases such as 'Whatchadoin' and 'Didja eat yet' is a postlexical process, as is the reduction across word boundaries in New Mexican Spanish phrases such as *la iglesia* 'the church' and *una hija* 'a daughter', for which Alba (2008) found the stress of the second vowel, the quality of the second vowel, and the ratio frequency combined to influence hiatus resolution, that is, for example, the initial vowel in a noun phrase such as *la escuela* 'the school' becoming either deleted [laskwéla], diphthongized [laiskwéla], or coalesced [liskwéla], [lɛskwéla], [lɪskwéla]. Strings with high ratio frequency underwent hiatus resolution 87 percent of the time, *vs* 48 percent for strings with low ratio frequency. In short, even irrefutable cases of postlexical processes are affected by word and string frequency.

21.6 WORD FREQUENCY EFFECTS ARE MOST NOTICEABLE WITHIN WORD CLASSES

Researchers do not overtly state that word frequency is independent of word class, but they often treat it as if it were, sometimes leading them to the mistaken conclusion that frequency is not involved in the lexical diffusion of a change. For example Goeman et al. (1993) state that, for the diphthongization of West Germanic /i/, they 'do not find a relationship between token frequency and diphthongization. For instance, highly frequent items such as *krijgen, tijd* (>200) do not behave differently as far as diphthongization is concerned from items such as *vijg* (0) and *vijl* (2). And among the items showing diphthongs rather often, such as *vrijdag, vrijen, vrij, fijn* and *vijf*, both low and high frequencies occur'. Yet their examples include several different morphological classes, so Phillips (2006: 99–100) re-organized their data by word class. The results showed that word class did indeed make a difference. The most varied class was the adjectives, with the most frequent, *vrij(e)* 'free', having between 66–77% diphthongs, moderately frequent *blij(de)* and *fijn* between 53–60%, and least frequent *grijs, rijk, rijp(e)/rijpst, stijf*, and *wijd* between 43–51%. (The percentage categories are those given by Goeman et al., so it was not possible to divide the data into finer categories here.) Similarly, Patterson et al. (2003) claimed to find no influence of frequency on vowel deletion in English two- and three-syllable words, saying that such influence was 'not sufficiently robust to hold when the data were analyzed by lexical stress pattern subgroups' (53). Yet, when nouns (for which the most data was available) were separated out from their data set, a clear pattern of word frequency effect was evident. For two-syllable nouns, infrequent ones (*tureen, parole*) deleted the vowel on average 3.35% of the time, medium frequency ones (*balloon, saloon, parade*) 10.37% of the time, and very frequent ones (*career, police*) 15.70% of the time. Three-syllable nouns exhibited the same pattern: 52.70% *vs* 62.24% *vs* 76.35% as the frequency increased (Phillips 2006: 97–8). See Table 21.2.

Table 21.2 Vowel deletion, based on Patterson et al. (2003), from Phillips (2006: 97–8)

Nouns	Frequency Range in Switchboard Corpus	Average % deleted
Two-Syllable:		
tureen, parole	14–20	3.35
balloon, saloon, parade	112–255	10.37
career, police	1187–3694	15.70
Three-Syllable:		
broccoli, gasoline	16–70	52.70
buffalo, surgery, chocolate, envelope, criminal, opera, salary, camera, cabinet	102–835	62.24
memory, history	1584–3414	76.35

Function words constitute a special case. Certain sound changes tend to affect word categories with low sentence stress, such as function words, first, but this does not correlate necessarily with word frequency. For instance, the raising of /a/ before nasals in Old English affected both the most frequent words and function words and adverbs first (Phillips 2006: 104). In contrast, the unrounding of the front mid vowel in the *Ormulum* affected adverbs and function words first but the most frequent words last. So word class and word frequency do act independently in the progress of a sound change. That is, when function words change first, it is not necessarily just a matter of their being frequent.

As for other word classes, not so influenced by stress, word frequency effects are also best seen within each class—if the sound change affects enough words for one to be able to divide them by word class. Sometimes there simply are not enough words affected to be able to find a clear effect. But there seems to be a credible reason why word frequency should appear within word classes—i.e. in production word class is accessed before the word form. Specifically, the retrieval of a word's syntactic information precedes that of phonological information by approximately 40 msec (van Turennout et al. 1998).

21.7 ANALOGY AND BORROWING DO NOT SUFFICE TO ACCOUNT FOR LEXICAL DIFFUSION

A major objection to lexical diffusion as a fundamental factor in sound change has been the assumption that analogy and borrowing suffice to account for lexical diffusion. Janda and Joseph (2003: 115), for example, state that 'diffusionary effects in the spread of phonological change through the lexicons of speakers … are actually epiphenomenal, being the result of already-needed mechanisms of analogical change and dialect borrowing'. But I argue that lexical diffusion is quite different from analogy or borrowing (cf. Fertig, this volume).

One problem with equating lexical diffusion with analogical change, as Kiparsky (1995) does, saying it is no different from 'kine' becoming 'cows' (644), is that such analogical changes typically affect the least frequent words first. The still irregular forms *mice, geese, teeth* are more common, mainly because they also usually occur in the plural. Irregular verbs also tend to be very frequent, such as *be, go*, and *see*. In contrast, irregular (i.e. historically strong) verbs that are not so frequent, especially in the preterite singular, have been more likely to change, both in English (Branchaw 2010), and in German (Carroll et al. 2012). Lexical diffusion thus sometimes affects the least frequent words first, but it also often affects the most frequent words first, as discussed above. (For other arguments against Kiparsky's position, see Hale (2003: 352–4) and Reiss (2003: 150).)

Perhaps the source of this claim is that lexical diffusion does apparently proceed by a path of similarities between word forms. This is because changes do spread word to word via a pattern of spreading activation. Bybee (2001: 21–2) summarizes: 'Experiments on lexical access have shown that subjects can identify a word presented with masking noise more successfully if the preceding word they heard (without masking) is phonetically similar. Moreover, the greater the degree of similarity, the more it aids in recognition of the masked word' (Pisoni et al. 1985). The interpretation of such evidence is that the activation of a word also activates phonetically similar words. One way of accounting for this pattern of spreading activation is to propose that the similarities among words cause them to be organized lexically as spatially proximate. So sound changes travel, if you will, by connections with other words, but it is not the type of analogy that Kiparsky describes, which works 'where memory fails' or only when one phoneme is abruptly substituted for another (as apparently in uvular /ʀ/ for earlier apical /r/ in Western Europe, according to Janson (1983)). Sound change is spread by connections of phonetic analogy as described by Schuchardt (1885: 46), Vennemann (1972a: 185), and de Schryver et al. (2008). Phonetic analogy works in all sound changes, because the mental lexicon is characterized by networks of connections between words. In reductive and assimilatory changes, frequent words are heard and pronounced more often and, because they are produced more often, such changes occur more readily to them. Because of the connected structure of the lexicon, even small, subphonemic change can spread to other, less frequent words. Sometimes that happens so quickly that the change seems neogrammarian, but such changes are more likely just very rapidly diffused across the lexicon, given the number of studies that have found lexical diffusion in even very low-level phonetic changes. Thus Pierrehumbert's (2002: 118) definition of neogrammarian sound change as 'sound changes which get started in the phonetic implementation and eventually sweep through the vocabulary' reflects a common conclusion among certain historical linguists.

As for the confusion of lexical diffusion with borrowing, Campbell (1998: 199) dismisses lexical diffusion as a kind of dialect borrowing, claiming that lexical diffusionists 'see sound change … as change affecting the sound in certain words and then diffusing gradually to other words in the lexicon.... This is like 'dialect borrowing', but with some words borrowing from others in the same dialect'. The rest of the passage suggests that those who point to dialect atlases' data that seems to repudiate the neogrammarian regularity hypothesis are guilty of forgetting 'the long interaction between local dialect forms and the dominant prestige or standard language'. Yet the fact that dialects can and do influence each other does not account for the lexical diffusion of changes within isolated speech communities. For instance, Ogura (1995) demonstrated that locations undergoing different stages of the Great Vowel Shift for particular words often were not contiguous to other locations undergoing the same stage for that word.

One factor in the confusion of lexical diffusion with borrowing is that all change involves borrowing to some extent. As Milroy (1992b: 88) says, 'We have no criteria for determining absolutely that there is an axiomatic distinction between sound change and borrowing (or contact change) because ... all changes must arise from contact between speakers.' Indeed, Wolfram & Schilling-Estes (2003: 717) point out that a change becomes propagated through social groups, through phonological and morphological environments, and through the lexicon, all happening simultaneously, and even within individuals variation is to be expected: 'the notion of variability ... applies to both intra-speaker and inter-speaker variation. In other words, an individual speaker will go through a period of fluctuation between the old and new variant, and speakers within a given speech community will show variation from speaker to speaker with respect to the use of the new and old variant'. In fact, even for changes that clearly imitate an external dialect, there is no difference in the word frequency effect on the lexical diffusion of such 'borrowed' changes and internal changes. The spread of a sound change from one dialect to another apparently follows the same direction of diffusion as the imitated dialect. For example, broad /a:/ (from original /æ/) in such words as *bath, class, laugh*, etc., was borrowed into what Kenyon & Knott (1953) label as the Eastern US as a fashionable import from Britain in the eighteenth or nineteenth century. There were a handful of words whose innovative pronunciations were not borrowed (*haft; aster; rascal; vantage; ranch, stanchion; Alexander, Flanders, slander*), but only one—*alas*—that has the broad /a:/ in the Eastern US but not in England (Phillips 1989). This finding supports Trudgill's (1986: 58) observation that during accommodation people 'modify their pronunciation of *particular words*,... with some words being affected before others', which implies that the spread of a sound change from one group to another must of necessity proceed via lexical diffusion, affecting some words before others. Particularly noteworthy in the broad /a:/ adoption is that not only were the more frequent words more likely to develop the broad /a:/ in British English, but Eastern US English borrowed, on average, the most frequent of those words.

Thus, it appears that since borrowing (i.e. imitation of other speakers) is inherent to the spread of an innovation from speaker to speaker and lexical diffusion is inherent in the spread of an innovation from one word to another, both borrowing and lexical diffusion are inherent to the spread of sound change. And since the spread through the lexicon of all changes depends on the similarities shared by lexical entries, phonetic analogy, too, is endemic to sound change (see De Schryver et al. 2008). Because an exemplar model incorporating connections or 'networks' between similar structures allows such routes of change, as described in Bybee (2010), such a theory is far more amenable to the facts of lexical diffusion than are models which separate phonology from the lexicon.

21.8 AGE OF ACQUISITION AND DISCOURSE FACTORS ALONE CANNOT ACCOUNT FOR ALL PATTERNS OF LEXICAL DIFFUSION

Both age of acquisition and discourse have been advanced as explanations for lexical effects of sound change, but while they may play important roles in the spread of change, including making use of or enhancing frequency effects, neither can account for all of the diffusionary effects that have been attributed to lexical frequency. For the age of acquisition theory, this is because the age of acquisition effect is reliable only for low-frequency words (Gerhand & Berry 1999). In fact, the age of acquisition and word frequency have been found to be separate affects that reinforce each other, as discovered by Gerhand & Berry (1998), who investigated naming latencies in the reading by 33 British college students of 64 words, divided into the following 4 categories: (a) early-acquired, high frequency (*win, cousin*); (b) early-acquired, low-frequency (*elf, rattle*); (c) late-acquired, high-frequency (*sex, union*); and (d) late-acquired, low frequency (*cue, marvel*). They found that the two effects ... were 'entirely additive: Participants were faster to read aloud early-acquired than late-acquired words and were also faster to name high-frequency than low-frequency words' (277). What early-acquired words have in common with frequent words is that they are more entrenched in memory and thus easier and faster to access in the production of a sound change. Therefore early-acquired high-frequency words will be in the forefront of, say, reductive changes, but age of acquisition cannot substitute for word frequency, since early-acquired low-frequency words will not be as entrenched in memory, not as easy to access, and thus should not as readily undergo such a sound change. This conclusion seems to make sense, for there are multiple examples of reduced forms in limited adult groups who use the word more frequently, as in *boatswain* /bosən/, *coxswain* /kaksən/, and *kiln* /kɪl/. An example from a historical study is the patterning with other frequent words of the twelfth-century monk Orm's religious vocabulary, such as *heofenn* 'heaven', *preost* 'priest', and *deofell* 'devil' (Phillips 1984: 330).

Arguments for the influence of discourse on lexical diffusion have been summarized by Wright (2003: 75): 'In these studies talkers have been shown to produce more reduced speech when contextual information within the utterance or in the environment can aid the listener in recognising what is said, and to produce more careful speech when the talker is aware of conditions that may impede the listener's ability to understand what is said'. Lindblom (1990) calls such production of reduced speech *hypospeech* and such production of clearer speech *hyperspeech*. This line of reasoning is also echoed in Berg (1998: 243): 'Frequency speeds up the word-recognition process.... If speakers exploit this principle, they can be more sloppy about the pronunciation of high-frequency words than about that of low-frequency items, while still achieving the same degree of communicative success. In fact, this is precisely what speakers do: the higher the redundancy of a word, the less accurately it is articulated' (Lieberman 1963). (Berg's term 'sloppy' is poorly chosen. See Bybee, this volume, for precise ways in which speech is reduced.) That is, discourse considerations may enhance word frequency effects for some sound changes, in particular reductive ones. In fact, the combination of discourse and word frequency has been a fruitful avenue of inquiry. For example, a study which successfully combines the two is Hay et al. (1999) on Oprah Winfrey's increased monophthongization of /ay/ in introducing African-American guests and in more frequent words.

However, the main shortcoming in depending on discourse explanations of lexial diffusion lies in the fact that discourse cannot account for other changes, such as stress shifts or vowel shifts; for example, the shift of stress in English verbs ending in the -ate suffix (see above) affects the most frequent words first, but does not involve increased articulatory ease. Contrariwise, the shift of stress in diatonic noun-verb pairs like CONvict/conVICT affected the least frequent words first. And vowels don't always change in the same direction, more frequent to less or vice versa, so discourse explanations do not seem to account for the frequency patterns of shifting segments. That is, discourse issues and lexical issues certainly overlap, with Hume & Mailhot (2013) showing how discourse factors can account for why frequent and infrequent words are most likely to undergo change, instead of words of moderate frequency. But discourse considerations alone cannot account for the basic findings in Phillips (2006: 181) that lexical diffusion occurs inside phonological environments and within word classes, and 'changes that affect the most frequent words require no analysis beyond the phonetic encoding' whereas 'changes that affect the least frequent words first require such analysis (word class, syllable structure, phonotactic constraints, etc.)'. Many questions remain about the relationship between lexical frequency, string frequency, neighbourhood density, and discourse in the diachronic development of sounds.

21.9 WORD FREQUENCY EFFECTS ARE FOUND WITHIN INDIVIDUAL SPEAKERS, NOT JUST WITHIN COMMUNITIES OF SPEAKERS

Blevins (2004a: 269) states that 'Labov's (1994) assessment of the "neogrammarian controversy" provides striking confirmation of regular sound change at the level of the individual, and lexical diffusion at the level of speech communities'. Yet even within individuals a sound change does not affect all of the pertinent words at the same time. Even the Northern Cities Shift, as we saw above, can affect words such as *mad* and *bad* differently in the speech of individuals. Similarly, Fidelholz (1975) pointed out that in the pairs *astronomy—gastronomy, mistake—mistook, abstain—abstemious* the first, more frequent word is more likely to reduce the vowel in its initial syllable, and this is at the level of every individual. Work on historical manuscripts is just as convincing. For example, the scribe of the Old English translation of the *Pastoral Care,* the two scribes of the Continuations to the *Peterborough Chronicle,* and the writer of the *Ormulum* not only vary in their spellings of words undergoing a vowel shift, but they do so systematically by word class and word frequency (Phillips 1995, 1997, 2006).

21.10 LEXICAL DIFFUSION IS NOT THE DIFFUSION OF A COMPLETED SOUND CHANGE BUT THE PRIMARY MEANS OF SPREADING A SOUND CHANGE THROUGH THE LEXICON

Labov (2010: 286) defines sound change as 'a shift of targets within the continuous parameters of phonological space. It is opposed to changes in membership of phonological categories at a higher level of abstraction. It is also opposed to fluctuations that respond to frequency and lexical identity'. This view implies that lexical diffusion occurs only after the completion of a sound change. Lass (1997: 141), in direct contrast, suggests that 'all phonological change starts with lexical diffusion and most ends up neogrammarian, given enough time'. These positions are exact opposites of each other. Given the examples above of sound changes in progress that exhibit lexical diffusion, it is not possible to support the position that only a completed sound change is subject to diffusion. Lass's view fits closer to the data, but may be confusing in that it uses the term *neogrammarian* as denoting a stasis rather than a method of implementation. That is, the evidence given above supports Lass's view, if his wording is taken to mean the same as Oliveira's (1991: 103) position that '*all* sound changes are lexically implemented, that is, there are *no* neogrammarian sound changes (although we can have neogrammarian long-term end results)'. In other words, the result may appear to have neogrammarian regularity, if all the eligible words have been affected, but the process of change is always word by word, with all sorts of factors—phonetic, phonological, morphological, semantic, social, pragmatic, and cognitive—influencing which words are affected when, and all influencing the course of change simultaneously (compare Bermúdez-Otero, this volume, for a dissenting view).

A separate view is Janda & Joseph's (2003) 'Big Bang', where phonetic factors alone instigate the onset of a change—indeed they define sound-change narrowly as 'the innovation' (214)—, but 'sound-change rapidly yields to generalization along non-phonetic (phonological or morphological) and social lines that may contribute further regularity

via extension to broader contexts (214). The difficulty with this view is that it narrows
the definition of sound change so as to fit only phonetically induced changes (excluding
stress shifts, reversed changes, changes based on phonotactic structure, etc.) and applies
only to the originator of the change, whom it is impossible to identify, making their
position empirically unverifiable.[4] In addition, even within this narrow scope, I believe
it unlikely that the initiator of even a phonetically conditioned change would have it
apply to all words, when early adopters exhibit lexical influences. For instance, Jurafsky
et al. (2001: 244) find that for '1412 tokens of the final-t/d content words … [o]verall,
high frequency words (at the 95th percentile of frequency) were 18% shorter than low
frequency words (at the 5th percentile)'. This kind of patterning in synchronic phonetic
implementation is mirrored in the phonologization of articulatory processes of the type
discussed in Bybee (this volume).

21.11 CONCLUSION

Our discussion has brought us back to the question posed in Labov (1981: 268): 'In the
evolution of sound systems, is the basic unit of change the word or the sound?' In the
years since this question was first posed, it has become clear that a psychologically plausible model of the lexicon must be able to account for the simultaneous influence of
each. An exemplar cum network lexicon seems the best current model for accounting for the progression of sound change along both phonetic and lexical paths. Labov's
(2006) concerns about such a model's ability to capture the influence of sound structure and what he sees as the 'neogrammarian' regularity of many sound changes (which
others, such as Ogura 1995, see as most likely extremely fast lexically diffused changes)
are answered by Pierrehumbert's (2006: 524) suggestion of a 'hybrid model' with 'multiple levels of representation (like neo-generative models) while also having explicit
mechanisms for statistical learning and situational indexing (like exemplar models)'.
According to Pierrehumbert, 'The existence of changes that are both lexically and phonetically gradual is not surprising, given that phonetic distributions for specific words
can be defined in the model. However, the behavior of the entire perception-production
system is structured by the phonological coding levels' (524). Thus, both the word and
the sound can be seen as basic to sound change. Both function together in the full process of change, from the original innovation through the spread to other speakers and
often to extended environments.

[4] That lexical diffusion is indeed part of the 'transition problem', as defined by Weinreich et al. (1968),
and not part of the 'actuation problem' is reflected in the shift from Phillips's (1984) connection of it
with actuation to her (2006: 26–7) argument that it is instead part of the transition/implementation of a
change, since changes with similar motivations can behave differently regarding word frequency.

CHAPTER 22

....

AMPHICHRONIC EXPLANATION AND THE LIFE CYCLE OF PHONOLOGICAL PROCESSES

....

RICARDO BERMÚDEZ-OTERO

22.1 AMPHICHRONIC EXPLANATION

....

DISAGREEMENT over the appropriate scope of synchronic and diachronic explanation in linguistics is as old as the Saussurean dichotomy itself (Saussure 1916: part one, ch. III). Without Saussure's insight that languages constitute systems amenable to synchronic analysis, much research into linguistic typology and language universals, whether in the Greenbergian or in the Chomskyan tradition, would scarcely be conceivable; yet Saussure himself appears to have simultaneously subscribed to the neogrammarian belief that sound change operates without regard to its effects upon the linguistic system (e.g. 1916: part three, ch. II, §5), and this idea, as noted by Jakobson (1929), renders the very existence of phonological universals problematic (Kiparsky 1995: 641, this volume).

Similarly, current work in phonology offers a wide range of opinion on the relationship between synchrony and diachrony, the issue having become entangled with the debate between rationalist and empiricist approaches to the nature of linguistic knowledge. At one extreme, research in the tradition of classic Optimality Theory (OT; Prince & Smolensky 1993; and see Holt, this volume) commonly treats specific hypotheses about the universal constraint set (CON) as falsified by gaps in factorial typology—a practice which ultimately presupposes that the set of attestable languages can be delimited on purely synchronic grounds. At the opposite extreme, the Evolutionary Phonology programme (Blevins 2004a, this volume) elevates the priority of diachronic over synchronic explanation to the status of an epistemological principle (essentially a special case of Ockham's razor), and, although it attributes a range of domain-general and even possibly domain-specific abilities to learners, these rarely take a prominent role in actual proposals and are rarely elaborated in detail.

Some lines of inquiry seek a more complex and nuanced understanding of the interplay between synchronic and diachronic factors in the genesis of cross-linguistic phonological patterns. This type of work—which, borrowing Kiparsky's term (2006: 222), I call 'amphichronic'—acknowledges that explanation must proceed in both directions. First, certain fundamental observations about the sorts of phonological innovations attested in the empirical record and about recurrent pathways in the historical evolution of phonological systems can be fully explained only by taking into account the cognitive abilities underpinning the transmission of grammars between individuals and the basic design features of those grammars—in particular, their overall architecture. Only such reasoning can make sense, for example, of the existence of neogrammarian sound change (Labov 2010: ch. 13) and of the life cycle of phonological processes (Bermúdez-Otero 2007: 504–5, Bermúdez-Otero & Trousdale 2012: §2, Ramsammy 2015). With such an understanding of phonological change in place, however, many cross-linguistic facts will turn out not to call for enrichments of synchronic theory, but will be seen to emerge from recurrent historical processes. Indeed, we should not be surprised at all if, in many cases, comprehensive accounts of micro- and macro-typological patterns end up cycling repeatedly between synchronic and diachronic explanation.

Needless to say, such an amphichronic outlook is compatible with a broad range of positions on much debated issues such as the nature of phonological markedness (Scheer, this volume). Elaborating Jakobson's (1929) position, for example, Kiparsky (2006) argues that exceptionless universals require the postulation of synchronic cognitive representations of markedness, and that purely emergentist explanations suffice only for typological trends. In contrast, Moreton & Pater (2012a, b) frame the issue in terms of biases: they hypothesize that substantive biases may arise diachronically from properties of the phonetic channel, whereas formal biases, particularly those favouring coarse-grained generalizations, may reflect the cognitive predispositions of the learner (Moreton 2008). Their programme for a Structurally Biased Phonology (Pater & Moreton 2012) differs crucially from that of Evolutionary Phonology in that it incorporates fully formalized and computationally testable proposals concerning the cognitive underpinnings of formal biases. Important though the controversy over markedness is, however, it risks obscuring the need for amphichronic research in other areas of phonology. This chapter illustrates this in two ways.

In section 22.2, I revisit my assertion that the classical modular feedforward architecture of grammar is essential to understanding the modes of implementation of phonological change and the life cycle of phonological processes (Bermúdez-Otero 2007: 501ff, Bermúdez-Otero & Trousdale 2012: 693ff.). The modular feedforward architecture itself has recently been challenged in several ways, and notably by claims that morphological structure can directly affect the application of gradient rules of phonetic implementation (Kawahara 2011: §2.3.3). I show, however, that this appearance often emerges from a side effect of the diachronic life cycle of phonological processes: 'rule scattering' (Bermúdez-Otero 2010, after Robinson 1976). In rule scattering, a process in one component of the grammar gives rise to a new rule at a higher level—fully in line with the life cycle—but without ceasing to apply at the lower level: as a special case, innovative phonological rules do not replace the phonetic rules from which they emerge, but typically coexist with them (Bermúdez-Otero 2007: 506). In this situation, what may pretheoretically be described as a single sound pattern (e.g. English /l/-darkening) turns out in fact to reflect the cumulative effect of several cognate processes simultaneously overlaid within the synchronic grammar, where each individual process impeccably abides by the restrictions of the modular feedforward architecture: only categorical phonological rules apply in morphosyntactically defined domains, and only across-the-board phonetic rules show gradience.

In turn, section 22.3 explores the consequences of the fact that each new process that enters the grammar through a step in a long-term trajectory of change, such as a lenition pathway or a cline of rule generalization, can go through the life cycle of phonological processes on its own. This results in typological trends that may be stated in purely synchronic terms. For example, if two distinct phonological rules within the same grammar perform the same structural change but one subsumes the structural description of the other, then the more general rule is likely to have a wider cyclic domain. Similarly, if two distinct processes of lenition within the same grammar target the same consonant in the same phonological environment but one causes a more drastic weakening of the consonant than the other, then the more aggressive process is likely to have a wider cyclic domain. Although these tendencies can be stated synchronically, they do not require synchronic explanation; they merely reflect that, *ceteris paribus*, processes that embarked on their life cycle earlier in historical time are more likely to have reached higher levels in the grammar.

22.2 THE ARCHITECTURE OF GRAMMAR AND THE LIFE CYCLE OF PHONOLOGICAL PROCESSES

22.2.1 Diachronic Predictions of the Modular Feedforward Architecture

Research has long explored the idea that the synchronic organization of grammars accounts for key facts about phonological change, in particular the existence of neogrammarian regularity and the life cycle of phonological processes. The basic insights date to the dawn of structuralism (Kruszewski 1881). Recent elaborations include works by Kiparsky (1988, 1995), Bermúdez-Otero (2007), and Bermúdez-Otero & Trousdale (2012: §2). The latter argue for a grammatical architecture with three crucial properties.

The first is modularity: the grammar consists of a number of separate components, each characterized by its own proprietary set of representations and communicating with adjacent modules through narrowly constrained interfaces (e.g. Bermúdez-Otero 2012: 45–9). The relevant modules are morphology, phonology, and phonetics:

(1)	Module	Proprietary representations
	morphology	morphs
	phonology	discrete phonological objects (e.g. segmental features, prosodic nodes, association lines)
	phonetics	continuous phonetic dimensions (e.g. formant frequencies, gesture amplitudes and durations)

In this view, the morphology selects and concatenates morphs, but cannot alter their phonological content ('Morph Integrity'); see Bermúdez-Otero (2012: 50ff.).

Second, modules are arranged serially, that is, information flow at the interfaces is feedforward. Thus, morphology precedes phonology within each derivational cycle, and phonology precedes phonetics. By implication, morphology and phonetics do not share an interface. However, the principle of feedforward derivation holds for the computational theory in Marr's (1982) sense, that is, it describes mappings computed by the grammar. Processing implementations may allow varying amounts of cascading activation and feedback (e.g. Rapp & Goldrick 2000, and sections 22.2.2 and 22.2.4).

Finally, the phonological module is cyclic and stratified as in Lexical Phonology (Kiparsky 1982b) and Stratal OT (Bermúdez-Otero 1999, Kiparsky 2000a). In a cyclic derivation, the phonology applies iteratively over a hierarchy of nested domains defined by morphosyntactic structure, starting with the smallest domains and moving outwards. Cyclic domains of different types (stem-level, word-level, phrase-level) are subject to different phonological generalizations. Evidence for this view of the morphosyntax-phonology interface is provided by Bermúdez-Otero (2011). However, it does not particularly matter here whether we conceive of the phonological cycle as operating in an interactionist or non-interactionist fashion (Scheer 2011b: 127ff.). Thus, models (2,a) and (2,b) from the late 1980s are equally possible instantiations—among others—of the modular feedforward architecture assumed here.

(2)

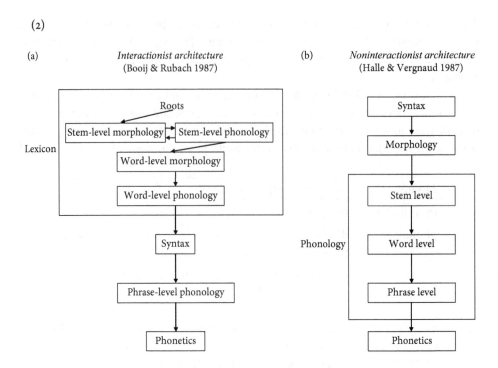

(a)   *Interactionist architecture*
(Booij & Rubach 1987)

(b)   *Noninteractionist architecture*
(Halle & Vergnaud 1987)

In particular, neither model allows direct interactions between morphology and phonetics.

The modular feedforward architecture makes predictions about phonological change in two major ways. First, it defines an inventory of possible types of changes, distinguished from one another by the factors that may or may not affect their implementation (see Bermúdez-Otero 2007: 503 et seq., especially (4)). This follows from the null hypothesis that each component of the grammar may undergo innovations independently of the others. If that is the case, then an innovation in one module will manifest itself as a change conditioned by information available to that module alone; conversely, factors to which the module is blind will not affect the implementation of the change. Notably, innovations in phonetic implementation give rise to neogrammarian changes: these are phonetically gradient because phonetic rules operate over continuous phonetic dimensions, and they are regular because the phonetic module has access to surface phonological representations (including prosodic structure) but not to lexical entries or to morphosyntactic structure. Neogrammarian change is considered in greater detail in section 22.2.2. Its precise mirror image is lexical diffusion in the classic sense of Wang (1969), that is, phonetically abrupt and lexically gradual change (see Kiparsky 1988, 1995; Bermúdez-Otero 2007: 508–12; but cf. Phillips, this volume for a different approach).

Second, the modular feedforward architecture predicts the overall direction in which change will advance through the grammar over time: in other words, the architecture lays down the track for the life cycle of phonological processes (Bermúdez-Otero 2007: 504–5, Bermúdez-Otero & Trousdale 2012: 692–3, 700). This follows from

elementary considerations about the mechanism of grammar transmission, including both the construction of grammars by children and the updating of grammars
by adults—the latter confined, of course, to those areas of linguistic competence
that remain plastic across the individual's lifespan (e.g. Harrington 2006, Sankoff &
Blondeau 2007, and cf. Bowie & Malcah Yaeger-Dror, this volume). In both cases,
individuals lack direct access to the linguistic representations generated by other individuals' mental grammars; rather, they reconstruct those representations from circum-
ambient speech, starting, in the case of phonetic and phonological competence, with
raw acoustic data. As a result, data reanalysis leading to representation restructuring
becomes a primary mechanism for innovation: in neogrammarian change, for example,
raw acoustic data are reanalysed in such a way that the targets assigned by phonetic rules
to surface phonological categories shift in continuous phonetic hyperspace. Because of
the feedforward organization of the grammar, however, representations at lower levels
furnish the data for the construction and updating of representations at higher levels.
During grammar transmission, therefore, information flows predominantly from lower
to higher modules: the grammar is bootstrapped from the bottom up. Mirroring this
process, historical innovations generally propagate from lower to higher modules:

(3)   *phonetics* >

	phonology		
phrase level	>	*word level*	>	*stem level*

> *morphology/lexicon*

The main steps in the life cycle of phonological processes, and their causes in the mechanism of grammar transmission, are described in more detail in section 22.2.3.

Since the balance between synchronic and diachronic explanation has become
a major arena for the innateness controversy (see section 22.1), I emphasize that neither of the predictions just outlined crucially requires that the modular feedforward
architecture be available to the learner prior to all linguistic experience. For example,
Bermúdez-Otero (2012: 31–40, 76) suggests ways in which elements of cyclicity and
stratification may emerge during acquisition from the interaction of factors such as the
schedule of the child's morphosyntactic development, lexical listing, and morphological
blocking. Architectural explanations of properties of phonological change are perfectly
compatible with such epigenetic approaches to the architecture itself, as long as the latter do not presuppose the diachronic facts to be explained.

22.2.2 Neogrammarian Change

In the modular feedforward architecture, innovation in the phonetic component of the
grammar manifests itself as neogrammarian change. Such change is phonetically gradient because it affects the real-valued attributes of the phonetic realizations assigned by
language-specific phonetic rules to surface phonological categories in specific environments.

It is lexically regular in so far as the computation of phonetic targets is exhaustively determined by information present in, or derivable from, the surface phonological representation, and the latter does not contain diacritics of lexical or morphological affiliation: see the 'Phonetic Interpretability Hypothesis' of Bermúdez-Otero (2012: 81), and cf. below for putative counterevidence. By the same token, neogrammarian change is expected to be sensitive to surface prosodification, but not to underlying morphological structure.

Whether changes meeting this description actually exist has long been debated. Few challenge the existence of phonetically gradual innovation—although Wang (1969) did claim that most, if not all, sound changes were classically diffusing, that is, lexically gradual but phonetically abrupt. However, there are contemporary phonological frameworks that cannot accommodate truly gradient change. On the basis of radically rationalist assumptions about language acquisition, Hale et al. (2007, this volume), for example, assert that phonetic implementation is performed by innately specified articulatory and perceptual 'transducers' that refer to surface phonological representations consisting of features drawn from an inventory supplied by Universal Grammar. In this framework, the phonetic target for a particular feature in a particular environment remains fixed through time because it is innately specified by the transducers; only the discrete featural content of surface representations can change. Hale et al.'s theory thus entails that there cannot be continuous phonetic change *stricto sensu*; the illusion of gradience must arise from variation between competing grammars with categorically different outputs.

Fruehwald (2012) argues against this claim, using evidence from the raising of English /aɪ/ before voiceless obstruents in the dialect of Philadelphia during the twentieth century as attested in the Philadelphia Neighbourhood Corpus (PNC). Fruehwald simulated the gradient advance of this change by mixing tokens of two discrete allophones, categorically unraised [aɪ] and categorically raised [ɐi], and gradually increasing the proportion of [ɐi]-tokens over time. In this category-mixing scenario, the overall distribution of prevoiceless tokens of /aɪ/ on the F1 continuum exhibits high kurtosis near the start of the change, when most tokens belong to category [aɪ]; the distribution also displays high kurtosis near the end of the change, when most tokens belong to category [ɐi]; but mid-way through the change kurtosis falls to a minimum because, at this point, /aɪ/ is realized by an even mixture of [aɪ]-tokens and [ɐi]-tokens.[1] The PNC data, however, do not conform to the predicted pattern: the distribution of prevoiceless /aɪ/-realizations shows the most normal-like kurtosis at the mid-point. This failure of kurtosis to fall and then rise again is particularly significant because, of all vowel changes attested in the PNC, /aɪ/-raising covers the longest acoustic distance in the shortest time, and should therefore exhibit the clearest dip in kurtosis. Fruehwald's results indicate that the raising of /aɪ/ before voiceless obstruents in Philadelphia did not involve competition between two categories; it was truly continuous.

The challenge most often levelled against the neogrammarians focuses on regularity rather than on gradience: it is often claimed that no change is fully lexically regular (see Phillips, this volume). Labov (2010: ch. 13), however, shows that /uː/- and /oʊ/-fronting in North American English fit the neogrammarian description admirably.

---

[1] Kurtosis can be thought of as a measure of unimodality (Darlington 1970). Thus, a bimodal mixture of two distributions exhibits low kurtosis.

Allophones of /uː/, in particular, remain categorically back before /l/, but other tokens of the vowel exhibit gradient fronting, forming a unimodal distribution on the F2 dimension. A word's position within this fronting continuum is exquisitely sensitive to the phonetic environment of the vowel, with preceding onsets forming a cline from favouring (e.g. coronals) to disfavouring (e.g. labials). Crucially, the lexical affiliation of /uː/-tokens is not a significant predictor of fronting: in a regression analysis, only affiliation to the words *zoo* and *Vancouver* reached significance at the $p<.01$ level, and even then this effect could not be distinguished from the unique phonological properties of the two items (e.g. the combination of onset /z/ and unchecked /uː/ in *zoo*); revealingly, both lexical effects disappeared when separately tested on two halves of the data. Just as importantly, the token frequency of words was not a significant predicting factor. Thus, the fronting of non-prelateral /uː/ in North American English is a canonical neogrammarian change: phonetically gradient and lexically regular.

Other studies do report continuous phonetic properties to be significantly affected by non-phonological factors such as lexical token frequency and neighbourhood density (see, e.g. Munson & Solomon 2004, among many others). However, the actual scope of such word-specific effects is unclear. Notably, Dinkin (2008) found evidence that high-frequency words do lead in reductive changes such as vowel centralization, but not in non-reductive changes such as the Northern Cities Shift—or indeed /uː/- and /oʊ/-fronting as described by Labov. Moreover, the evidence of lexical effects on phonetic variation often seems compatible with accounts that preserve the essential features of the modular feedforward architecture at Marr's computational level (see section 22.2.1 above): for example, Baese-Berk & Goldrick (2009) propose a speaker-driven model of neighbourhood density effects that relies on cascading activation in production processing (though cf. Goldrick et al. 2011 for limitations).

In contrast, pure exemplar-based models relying on the storage of fine phonetic detail in long-term memory (see, for example, Bybee, Phillips, and Wedel, all this volume) predict the existence of word-specific phonetic effects, but have difficulty accounting for the evidence of neogrammarian change (Pierrehumbert 2002: 120); neogrammarian regularity has been thought to require some dissociation between lexical and phonetic knowledge at least since Bloomfield (1933: 364–5). However, exemplar theories come in many flavours, crucially differing in their ontology for phonological category labels and in the extent to which they acknowledge a role for classical symbolic computation in phonology (Bermúdez-Otero 2007: 512, 515). Exemplar theories in which storage is organized around phonological categories (e.g. Pierrehumbert 2002) enjoy far better prospects than those in which storage is organized around lexical units (e.g. Bybee 2001, this volume): see Sóskuthy (2011) for a comparison of 'category-based' and 'word-based' exemplar storage. Further questions arise if, as argued by Smolensky (2006), a comprehensive framework for understanding human cognition needs to establish lawful relationships between 'computational', 'algorithmic', and 'physical' descriptions (Marr's terms) that are nonetheless radically anisomorphic: in this vein, one wonders if the best category-driven exemplar model might turn out to be a low-level implementation of the best modular symbolic theory, and the best modular symbolic theory might prove to be a high-level approximation to the behaviour of the best category-driven exemplar model.

A third challenge to the existence of neogrammarian change as predicted by the modular feedforward architecture arises from the claim that phonetic implementation is directly sensitive to morphological structure (Kawahara 2011: §2.3.3). This possibility was already explicitly denied by Kruszewski (1881 [1995: 27]), and has since been ruled out in a wide range of theories, including Boersma (2009b), which assert that morphology and phonetics do not share an interface. In section 22.2.4 I demonstrate that phonetic variation may exhibit morphological effects only in appearance, as a result of rule scattering during the life cycle of phonological processes.

22.2.3 The Life Cycle, Input Restructuring, and Rule Scattering

Diagram (4) represents the diachronic pathway along which linguistic sound patterns typically evolve over long periods of time (Bermúdez-Otero 2007: 504–5, Bermúdez-Otero & Trousdale 2012: §2, Ramsammy 2015). In the course of this life cycle, a phonetic phenomenon that is at first exhaustively determined by extragrammatical factors (physics and physiology) becomes ever more deeply embedded in the grammar of a language, first as a language-specific gradient process of phonetic implementation, later as a categorical phonological rule applying in increasingly narrow morphosyntactic domains, until it eventually escapes phonological control altogether. As noted by Bermúdez-Otero & Trousdale (2012: 693 et seq.), the life cycle bears an obvious resemblance to grammaticalization: it is, for example, overwhelmingly unidirectional, allowing at most an occasional retrograde step, always isolated (Kiparsky, this volume: note 12; and see below for an example).

(4) *The life cycle of phonological processes (Bermúdez-Otero and Trousdale 2012: 700)*

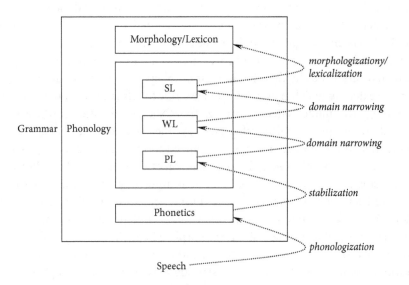

New sound patterns enter the grammar through phonologization (Hyman 1976, Hale et al., and Kiparsky, both this volume). This occurs when a listener/learner misinterprets the effects of a purely physical or physiological phenomenon as being under the control of speakers' grammars, and so adjusts her phonetic implementation rules accordingly (Ohala's 1981 'hypocorrection', see also Yu, this volume). Empirically, phonologization becomes apparent through an increase of the effect beyond the magnitude warranted by extragrammatical causes; feedback and sociolinguistic incrementation (D'Arcy, this volume) may then amplify it further. Boersma (2009a) and Hamann (2009) provide a persuasive formal account of the role of perceptual factors and modular representations in this process, supported with computational simulations. Their model predicts the structure-preserving bias noted by Kiparsky (1995: 656): see Bermúdez-Otero & Trousdale (2012: 694).

Phonologization is conceptually and empirically different from stabilization. The latter takes place when some effect of a gradient process of phonetic implementation is reanalysed as being generated by a categorical phonological rule applying across the board in phrase-level domains; the circumstances that may lead to this development are discussed below. Recognizing stabilization requires empirical tests for distinguishing between gradient and categorical patterns (e.g. Myers 2000): Strycharczuk (2012: 45–7) provides particularly careful discussion. The available criteria have led to the identification of several instances of stabilization in progress within a speech community. Relying on a bimodality criterion, for example, Bermúdez-Otero & Trousdale (2012: 694) show, on the basis of articulatory data from Ellis and Hardcastle (2002), that external sandhi in English /n#k/ clusters involves gradient reduction of the nasal's tongue-tip gesture in some idiolects, but categorical feature delinking and spreading in others. Using a speech-rate test, Strycharczuk (2012: ch. 6) identifies a similar state of affairs in Quito Spanish. In this variety of Spanish, some speakers have a variable phonological rule that categorically voices underlying /s/ in word-final position before sonorant segments (see Bermúdez-Otero 2011: §6 for derivations and their relevance to the architecture of phonology). In the phonetics, categorically voiced tokens of /s/ target a fixed ratio between the duration of the voiced interval and the overall duration of the consonant. Accordingly, speakers with categorically voiced /s/ actively prolong glottal pulsing at slow speech rates as the fricative becomes longer. For other speakers, however, the voicing of word-final /s/ before sonorants is coarticulatory: in these idiolects the ratio of voicing duration to overall consonant duration falls at slow speech rates.

After a sound pattern has become categorical, further changes may reduce its morphosyntactic domain, so that the rule ascends within the phonology from the phrase level to the word level, and from the word level to the stem level. Domain narrowing subsumes many cases of what the neogrammarians called 'analogical change', though by no means all. The evolution of postnasal /g/-loss in Late Modern English provides a particularly beautiful example. This phonological process deletes underlying /g/ in the coda when immediately preceded by homorganic /ŋ/. Thanks to a report from the eighteenth-century orthoepist James Elphinston (Garrett & Blevins 2009: 528), it is possible to reconstruct all the successive changes that the domain of this rule underwent between Early Modern English and the present day (Bermúdez-Otero 2011: 2024–5, Bermúdez-Otero & Trousdale 2012: §2.2).

(5) *Domain narrowing in the history of postnasal /g/-deletion (Bermúdez-Otero 2011: 2024)*

Stage	Realization of underlying /ŋg/				Level reached by the rule	Period or variety
	elongate	*prolong-er*	*prolong it*	*prolong*‖		
0	ŋg	ŋg	ŋg	ŋg	—	Early Modern English
1	ŋg	ŋg	ŋg	ŋ	phrase level	Elphinston (formal)
2	ŋg	ŋg	ŋ	ŋ	word level	Elphinston (casual)
3	ŋg	ŋ	ŋ	ŋ	stem level	present-day RP, GenAm

Below I describe a recent computational study by Lignos (2012) which casts light on the factors that drove this process of domain narrowing and determined its speed.

At the end of their life cycle, sound patterns come under increasing morphological and lexical control. For example, a stem-level phonological process may come to apply as a mere lexical redundancy rule (Jackendoff 1975) subject to blocking; such rules sustain exceptions and exhibit cyclic reapplication effects, which spread and retreat historically by lexical diffusion (see Bermúdez-Otero 2012: 34–9 and 74 for two case studies). Finally, a phonological process may be replaced by a morphological rule of exponence controlling the distribution of a morph (Anderson 1988: 329ff, Fertig, this volume), or it may die altogether, leaving behind no more than inert traces in underlying representations.

Pace Hale et al. (this volume), one need not invoke 'mystical, pan-generational forces' to sustain this life cycle. Rather, as I anticipated in section 22.2.1, the explanation for its predominant unidirectional character lies in the mechanism of phonological innovation. In line with a widespread view, I assume that innovations originate in permanent replication errors during grammar acquisition and grammar updating, that is, replication errors from which the affected individual does not recover—unlike consonant harmony and long word reduction in typically developing children (Foulkes & Vihman, this volume). Crucially, the organization of grammars causes certain permanent replication errors to occur far more frequently than conceivable alternatives. In particular, properties derived in a module or submodule are often misanalysed as being already present in its input, leading to the restructuring of input representations.

The prevalence of this phenomenon reflects the fact that, whereas information flows downwards in production, it propagates generally upwards in grammar acquisition and updating. It is thus recurrent input restructuring, firmly rooted in mechanisms of grammar transmission, that imparts its direction to the life cycle of phonological processes.

Input restructuring can be clearly seen at work in the process of domain narrowing that lifted postnasal /g/-deletion from the phrase level to the word level. Consider an eighteenth-century listener/learner who has acquired a transparent ban on coda [g] after [ŋ]. To replicate Elphinston's phrase-level alternation between [sɪŋl̩] and [ˈsɪŋ.gə.ˈlaʊd], this individual needs to represent the verb *sing* as /sɪŋg/ in the input to the phrase level, so that the final /g/ may be rescued by resyllabification when immediately followed by a vowel in the next word. In turn, this means that this listener/learner must model her word-level representation of *sing* on her experience of prevocalic tokens; but, crucially, the odds are stacked against her: preconsonantal and prepausal tokens outnumber prevocalic ones roughly by three to one. It is therefore not surprising that some individuals should have replaced conservative word-level /sɪŋg/ with innovative /sɪŋ/:

(6) *Input restructuring during postnasal /g/-loss (Bermúdez-Otero and Trousdale 2012: 698)*

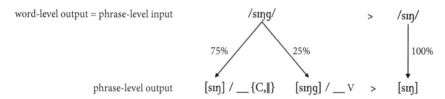

Thus, the likelihood of input restructuring, which sustains the life cycle, does not in the least depend on the ebb and flow of mystical forces, as Hale et al. (this volume) claim, but on quantitative properties of the data available to listeners/learners in particular situations. Indeed, hypotheses about the mechanism of input restructuring can be tested rigorously using computational simulations of learning. Take the striking fact that, in Late Modern English, coda-targeting processes that reach the word level through domain narrowing are never confined to that stratum for long, but continue climbing up into the stem level (Bermúdez-Otero & McMahon 2006: 401–2). This is in stark contrast with Dutch, where, for example, coda devoicing has remained stuck at the word level (Booij 1995: 22, 55–6, 174–5) for centuries, probably since the Old Low Franconian period. A plausible explanation for the divergent evolution of the two languages lies in the relatively impoverished inflectional system of English, which has retained fewer vowel-initial endings than Dutch and uses them less often. In consequence, stem-final consonants surface much more frequently as codas in English inflectional paradigms than in Dutch ones: compare, for example, English *hood* sg [hʊd] ~ pl [hʊdz] with Dutch *hoed* 'hat' sg [hut] ~ pl [hu.dən].

To test this, Lignos (2012) simulated the acquisition of [g]~[Ø] alternations across multiple generations, using Yang's (2005) productivity criterion to estimate the point at which a generation would have enough evidence to posit a rule of postnasal /g/-deletion at a particular level. Lignos found that the deletion process remained confined to the phrase level unless the rate of resyllabification across word boundaries fell below a certain threshold; adding plausible restrictions against /g/-resyllabification before liquids and before stressed vowels allowed domain narrowing to go through. Crucially, once postnasal /g/-deletion became active at the word level, its further ascent to the stem level encountered no resistance. Thus, Lignos's simulation supports the explanation proposed above for the greater vulnerability of word-level phonological rules to domain narrowing in English than in Dutch.

The pace at which phonological processes travel on their life cycle is thus closely dependent on the mechanisms of grammar transmission. As further evidence, consider the fact that unidirectionality has been found to break down in circumstances that favour higher rates of replication error than intergenerational transmission within a speech community: a notable case is the propagation of dialect features across communal groups through contact between adult speakers (Bermúdez-Otero & Trousdale 2012: §2.4). For example, Labov (2007: 369) shows that New York City short-*a* tensing underwent domain broadening—as opposed to the usual domain narrowing—when borrowed into the dialect of New Orleans. Crucially, the vehicle for borrowing was the migration of New York bankers and merchants to New Orleans (Labov 2007: 367–8).

So far I have illustrated the role of input restructuring in the life cycle of phonological processes with examples of domain narrowing. Nonetheless, stabilization as described above also involves input restructuring, for it alters the inventory or distribution of categories in the surface phonological representations that provide the input to phonetic implementation. In this respect, an interesting possibility is that stabilization supervenes when outlying tokens of a surface category are perceived as manifestations of a different, possibly new, category. Consider a hypothetical scenario involving the realization of a surface vowel category in F_1/F_2 space (7). Initially, the tokens of this vowel category are evenly spread around the mean, creating an approximately globular distribution (7,a). However, a subset of the tokens (represented by black circles) occur in a phonetic environment that triggers gradient F_2-lowering: within the overall distribution, therefore, these tokens gravitate towards the back of the vowel space. Suppose now that the magnitude of this conditioned F_2-lowering effect increases historically through phonologization, possibly reinforced by feedback and sociolinguistically driven incrementation: as a result, the distribution becomes skewed, with some affected tokens lying far back of the overall mean (7,b). In (7,c), some outliers have been reanalysed as tokens of a new surface category; speakers for whom this happens develop an innovative phonological rule of conditioned backing that applies variably but categorically.

(7)   (a)   *Initial state*   (b) *Phonologization*   (c)   *Stabilization*

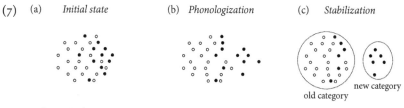

old category   new category

• tokens in F2-lowering environment
○ tokens elsewhere

This scenario implies that the listener/learner's failure to compensate adequately for coarticulatory and reductive effects (Ohalian hypocorrection) plays a key role not only in phonologization (above) but also in stabilization. The idea that distributional skews play an instrumental role in stabilization receives support from experiments on infant perception: Maye et al. (2002) showed that infants familiarized with a continuum of speech sounds learn to discriminate tokens from the endpoints of the continuum if the latter is bimodally distributed, but not if it is unimodal. More generally, the scenario in (7) implies that listeners/learners set up surface phonological categories largely by bottom-up means (Strycharczuk 2012: 15, 164–5, 176), rather than through procedures narrowly constrained by top-down supervision (cf. the contrastivist principle in Dresher & Zhang 2005: 55, Dresher, this volume). Baker et al. (2011) propose a somewhat similar account of stabilization in which outlying tokens also play a key role, but their model additionally emphasizes sociolinguistic heterogeneity within the speech community. Admittedly, these scenarios remain programmatic suggestions: detailed computational simulations are needed to verify the extent to which their predictions actually follow from their premises, and perceptual experiments with children and adults are needed to test the role of both distributional skews and sociolinguistic heterogeneity in phonological category formation. More worryingly, we have at present no good account of how learners assign featural labels to the categories they establish in surface phonological representations (Boersma 2012: §9.3.7).

Nonetheless, an appealing feature of the scenario in (7) is that, without further stipulation, it predicts the fact that stabilization is normally accompanied by rule scattering: in other words, the original gradient process of phonetic implementation remains active in the grammar even after the new categorical rule enters the phonology (Bermúdez-Otero 2007: 506, 2010). Observe that in (7c) vowel tokens in the backing environment are split between the old and the new category. Within the former, it remains the case that tokens in the backing environment exhibit lower than average F2. The overall pattern, therefore, supports the acquisition of two generalizations: an optional rule of categorical backing, overlaid with a gradient process of F2-lowering.

Rule scattering is robustly attested in English phonology (Bermúdez-Otero 2007: 506). For example, Labov (1994) demonstrates that an accurate description of Philadelphia short-*a* tensing requires two separate statements in the grammar: a stem-level phonological rule that applies in lexical redundancy mode and captures the default distribution of lax /æ/ and tense /æ:/, and a gradient phonetic rule that controls the precise location of /æ:/-tokens in F1/F2 space. Two facts confirm that /æ/ and /æ:/ are discrete categories in the dialect of Philadelphia: the two vowels occupy largely non-overlapping regions in acoustic space (Labov 1989b: 8–10), and their occurrence is not fully predictable—as notably shown by the contrast between /æ:/ in *mad, bad, glad* and /æ/ in *sad, fad, lad*. Trends in the distribution of /æ/ and /æ:/ are captured by a default rule that takes the stem as its domain (Labov 2010: 260) and so is rendered opaque by the addition of word-level suffixes (see Bermúdez-Otero 2007: 509–10 for an implementation in Stratal OT); within this stem-level domain, the main generalization is that the vowel is tense before coda /m, n, f, θ, s/. In the phonetics, the precise formant values of /æ:/-tokens are exquisitely sensitive to their environment: salient effects include a sizeable amount of F1-lowering in tokens followed by a nasal, and a smaller amount in tokens preceded by a nasal. Similar effects are found in the Inland North, where short-*a* realizations form a single category subject to neogrammarian raising and fronting. The crucial observation is that, in Philadelphia, the stem-level default rule controlling the distribution of /æ:/ and the gradient process determining its acoustic realization both refer to very similar factors (e.g. coda nasals). This ultimately reflects the fact that both generalizations have similar phonetic grounds; it is just that the stem-level process has distanced itself further from its phonetic origins over centuries of complex history, starting with an allophonic rule that lengthened short /a/ in Early Modern English (Labov 1989b: §2).

22.2.4 Morphology-Free Phonetics: the Case of English /l/-Darkening

Rule scattering can create the appearance of morphologically sensitive phonetics without actually violating the restrictions of the modular feedforward architecture. I illustrate this with one of Kawahara's (2011: 2290–1) putative examples of morphologically conditioned phonetic implementation: English /l/-darkening.

Sproat & Fujimura (1993) show that, articulatorily, darkening causes the gesture of tongue-dorsum retraction for /l/ to increase in magnitude and to reach its peak earlier relative to tongue-tip raising:

(8) *Gestural scores for English /l/ (Sproat and Fujimura 1993: 307)*

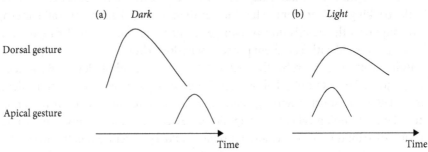

In addition, Sproat and Fujimura observe that, in a sequence of vowel plus [ł], the relative delay of the apical gesture for [ł] increases continuously in proportion to the overall duration of the sequence. They conclude that /l/-darkening is a purely gradient process of phonetic implementation.

At the same time, evidence shows that /l/-darkening is morphologically conditioned. Hayes (2000) asked ten native speakers of American English to rate the well-formedness of light and dark /l/ in various morphologically defined environments; Boersma & Hayes (2001: 76, 82) then used a sigmoid transformation to convert these well-formedness judgements into estimated frequencies of [l] and [ł]. The results show a strong morphological effect: notably, the estimated frequency of light [l] is much lower stem-finally in complex words like *hail-y* than morpheme-medially in simple words like *Hayley*.

(9) *Estimated frequency of light* [l] (*Boersma & Hayes* 2001: 76)

	%
a. light	99.956
b. Louianne	99.923
c. gray-ling, gai-ly, free-ly	94.53
d. Mailer, Hayley, Greeley, Daley	76.69
e. mail-er, hail-y, gale-y, feel-y	16.67
f. mail it	0.49
g. bell, help	0.0011

This morphological effect is not mediated by prosodic structure (Bermúdez-Otero 2011: §4).

The modular feedforward architecture does not allow continuous processes of phonetic implementation to refer directly to morphological structure. If Sproat and Fujimura were right that /l/-darkening is purely gradient, then this phenomenon would disprove the modular feedforward architecture. However, Hayes (2000: 93) and Bermúdez-Otero (2007: 516) reject their claim, and suggest that /l/-darkening involves two separate generalizations coexisting synchronically in the grammar: a morphologically sensitive phonological rule that creates discrete light and dark allophones, and a gradient phonetic process that adjusts the gestural score of [ł] according to duration. In this scenario, only the categorical phonological rule shows morphological conditioning; the constraints of the modular feedforward architecture are therefore satisfied. Bermúdez-Otero (2007: 516) and Bermúdez-Otero & Trousdale (2012: 705) portray this state of affairs as the natural outcome of the diachronic mechanism of rule scattering described in section 22.2.3.

Yuan & Liberman (2009, 2011) provide conclusive evidence against the claim that /l/-darkening is purely gradient. Using forced alignment to analyse a corpus of utterances by the Justices of the United States Supreme Court, they labelled /l/-tokens in canonical onset position (e.g. *like*, *please*) as light, and /l/-tokens in canonical coda position (e.g. *full capacity, felt*) as dark. From this they derived a continuous measure of dark-ness, the 'D score', such that darker tokens of /l/ had larger D scores. As predicted by Sproat and Fujimura, Yuan, & Liberman found that the D score of non-foot-initial /l/ was positively correlated with the duration of the vowel+/l/ string. Contrary to Sproat and Fujimura's claims, however, non-foot-initial tokens of /l/ turned out to have posi-tive D scores even when they belonged to very short vowel+/l/ sequences. Similarly, foot-initial /l/ always had a negative D score, on which duration had no effect. Thus, fully in line with a rule scattering scenario, Yuan and Liberman's findings confirm that English has a categorical distinction between light [l] and dark [ɫ], overlaid with gradi-ent duration-driven adjustments of gestural phasing in the realization of dark [ɫ].

One can detect diachronic rule scattering not only in the synchronic coexistence of a gradient and a categorical version of /l/-darkening, but also in the morphological effects displayed by the latter. Reanalysing Boersma & Hayes's data using Stochastic Stratal OT, Turton (2012) observes that the probability of darkening grows in proportion to the number of cycles in which /l/ is syllabified in coda position:

(10)

form	/l/ not foot-initial?			/l/ in coda?			% of dark [ɫ]
	stem level	word level	phrase level	stem level	word level	phrase level	
Hayley	✓	✓	✓				23.31
mail-er	✓	✓	✓	✓			83.33
mail it	✓	✓	✓	✓	✓		99.51
bell‖	✓	✓	✓	✓	✓	✓	99.9989

In American English, therefore, the phonological process that darkens /l/ in codas applies variably at the stem, word, and phrase levels.[2] Therefore, rule scattering did not stop with stabilization: after splitting into a gradient process of phonetic implementa-tion and a discrete phonological rule, /l/-darkening went on to undergo two rounds of domain narrowing, ascending to the word and stem levels while remaining active in lower strata.

The pattern in (10) provides a striking quantitative illustration of a key prediction of stratified phonological theories: opacity at a stem-suffix boundary, as in the retention of darkened [ɫ] before a vowel-initial suffix in *mail-er*, entails at least the same amount of opacity across word boundaries, as in *mail it*. This follows from the Russian Doll Theorem (Bermúdez-Otero 2011: 2023–4, Ramsammy 2012). The quantitative signa-ture of stratification was first noted in Guy's (1991a, b) Lexical Phonology analysis of English /t,d/-deletion. Turton (2012) develops this in two ways, providing a method for

---

[2] Alongside coda-based darkening, a general process applies variably to /l/ in non-foot-initial positions, including foot-medial onsets, shown by dark [ɫ] in forms like *Hayley* (9,d), where /l/ stays in the onset throughout the derivation. Coda-based and foot-based darkening reflect successive steps in a diachronic trajectory of rule generalization (section 22.3.1).

calculating precise application rates at each phonological level, and showing how these rates emerge from the life cycle of phonological processes. According to (10), for example, the difference in the amount of darkening between *mail-er* and *mail it* corresponds to one application of coda-based darkening at the word level in *mail it*. Extending this line of reasoning to the totality of Boersma & Hayes's data, Turton (2012: 21) deduces the following darkening probabilities for coda /l/:

(11) stem level   0.78
      word level   0.97
      phrase level   0.97

Coda-based darkening turns out to be nearly obligatory at the phrase and word levels, but to apply at a considerably lower rate at the stem level. Turton notes that, given the life cycle of phonological processes, this result is expected: the stem-level rate of /l/-darkening is lower, because the rule reached the stem level by domain narrowing late in its life cycle, only after it had already become active at the phrase and word levels. Thus, diachronic rule scattering in a modular stratified architecture explains not only the synchronic coexistence of phonetic gradience and morphological conditioning, but also the relative size of morphological effects across environments.

More generally, the prevalence of rule scattering leads one to expect that languages will often contain multiple clones of the same process applying simultaneously in different grammatical components, each referring to the type of information and operating on the type of representation determined by its place in the grammar. This expectation is fulfilled. Erker (2012) shows, for example, that the variety of Spanish spoken by New Yorkers of Hispanic origin has two separate processes of reduction applying to /s/ in the coda: one deletes /s/ categorically; the other gradiently reduces the duration of the fricative interval. The morphemic status of /s/, i.e. whether it realizes an inflectional suffix or not, plays a role, but as predicted by the modular architecture it conditions categorical [s]-absence, whilst it has no effect on the continuous dimension of fricative interval duration. Similarly, MacKenzie (2013) demonstrates that variable auxiliary contraction in English has two sources: allomorph selection in the morphology, and segmental reduction in the phonology. Significantly, each auxiliary exhibits a specific rate of insertion of its short allomorph; but the segmental reduction processes applying in the phonology, notably /h/-deletion, are lexically regular. Particularly spectacular instances of rule scattering have been found in popular Brazilian Portuguese: Guy (1996) shows that, in this language, the presence or absence of final sibilant fricatives reflects cognate variable processes in the syntax (variable agreement), the morphology (variable allomorphy), and the phonology (variable sibilant deletion), the latter in turn probably arising from a gradient phonetic process of gestural reduction.

Not all apparent morphological conditioning in phonetics involves rule scattering (cf. Bermúdez-Otero 2010: §9–§21). Many cases submit to standard prosodic analyses. Others may require processing accounts, perhaps involving cascading activation: possible candidates include the effects reported by Cho (2001) and by Sebregts & Strycharczuk

(2012). Time will tell if, after we try these explanations, a recalcitrant residue will remain. In the current state of knowledge, claims that morphology-phonetics interactions falsify the modular feedforward architecture of grammar are decidedly premature.

Finally, it might be objected that rule scattering involves extensive stipulation and rampant redundancy in synchronic grammars. In American English, for example, the conditions on /l/-darkening have to be stated four times: once in the phonetics (referring to duration), and three times in the phonology (referring to suprasegmental structure, and specifying different application rates at the phrase, word, and stem levels). This objection is true, but has no force. There is no good reason to expect that grammars should be individually elegant; they are the contingent products of protracted tinkering by biological and cultural evolution. As in any field, beauty is to be sought only in our global understanding of phenomena, reduced to order by a powerful theory with rich deductive structure. The way the architecture of grammar predicts the life cycle of phonological processes, and in which the life cycle in turn predicts complex synchronic outcomes that might otherwise be thought to challenge the architecture, provides all the elegance that one can legitimately hope for.

22.3 Synchronic Patterns Created by the Life Cycle

In amphichronic phonology, synchronic and diachronic explanation feed each other: in section 22.2, we saw that the synchronic architecture of grammar determines the ways in which change may be implemented and lays down the track for the life cycle of sound patterns, while the diachronic operation of the life cycle accounts for the existence of scattered generalizations in synchronic grammars. In this section I provide two further examples of synchronic phenomena that emerge directly from the life cycle.

Bermúdez-Otero & Trousdale (2012: 699) compare the life cycle with an escalator that continuously lifts sound patterns from lower to higher components of the grammar. This analogy is by no means perfect: ordinary escalators move at a uniform pace, whereas in section 22.2.3 we saw that the speed with which individual phonetic and phonological processes rise through the grammar is contingent on the data available to listeners/learners and on the circumstances of grammar transmission. Nonetheless, the image of the escalator brings out a general prediction of the life cycle: one expects to find a partial but significant correlation between the relative ages of rules and their positions in the grammar. This correlation should manifest itself most clearly in cases where, by successive rounds of phonologization and stabilization, a series of categorical rules enter the phonological module in a recognizable sequence: in such cases, the older phonological rules, which suffer the longest exposure to the factors driving domain narrowing, will tend to apply in smaller cyclic domains than the younger rules.

Below I discuss two types of diachronic pathway that involve sequences of historical innovations following each other in non-random order: rule generalization scenarios and lenition trajectories. As predicted, older phonological rules typically end up applying in higher strata than younger counterparts. The resulting synchronic grammars instantiate certain typological tendencies in the stratal affiliation of phonological processes; however, these are epiphenomena of the life cycle and do not require synchronic explanation.

22.3.1 Rule Generalization and the Life Cycle

Sound change often begins in specific environments where phonetic conditions are highly favourable, and progressively spreads to more general contexts. Schuchardt (1885: 22) described this as the *innere Erweiterung der Lautgesetze* '[the] internal expansion of the sound laws', which he contentiously regarded as caused by 'phonetic analogy', a label still used today. The term I use, 'rule generalization', gained currency in early generative phonology (Vennemann 1972a: 186–7, also Kiparsky 1988: §14.3.1).

The causes of rule generalization are imperfectly understood, but an adequate theory of phonologization and stabilization should account for generalization patterns just as it must predict the existence of rule scattering: see section 22.2.3. Rule generalization is plausibly ultimately rooted in the scalar nature of the physical and physiological effects that initiate sound change. Feedback effects in grammar transmission and sociolinguistic incrementation probably play roles too. Moreover, we have reason to assume the involvement of top-down formal biases favouring relatively simple coarse-grained statements (Hayes 1999, Pater & Moreton 2012), for phonological rules typically distance themselves from their phonetic grounding as their environments become generalized (e.g. Strycharczuk 2012: ch. 5).

The Old High German consonant shift provides a case of rule generalization (also Ramsammy 2015). The Germanic voiceless plosives /p, t, k/ affricate, and subsequently in certain cases spirantize. The change first targeted intervocalic plosives immediately preceded by short stressed vowels, and its environment then went on to expand in several steps, eventually including word-initial positions. For the labial /p/, Davis (2008: 212) reconstructs the progress as follows:

(12)	$'\breve{V}\_V$	$'\breve{V}\_{\omega}]$	$'\breve{V}\_$	$'VC^{[+son]}\_$	$'VC\_V$	$[_{\omega}'\_V$
stage 1	✓					
stage 2	✓	✓				
stage 3	✓	✓	✓			
stage 4	✓	✓	✓	✓		
stage 5	✓	✓	✓	✓	✓	
stage 6	✓	✓	✓	✓	✓	✓
	opfan	*gripf*	*släpfan*	*dorpf*	*scepphen*	*pflëgan*
	'open'	'grasp'	'sleep'	'village'	'create'	'care for'

The synchronic outcomes strikingly illustrate the way in which dialect geography can reflect the historical progress of rule generalization: Schuchardt (1885: 22) referred to this as *die räumliche Projection zeitlicher Unterschiede* 'the spatial projection of temporal differences'. This connection between rule generalization and geographical space arises because sound change originates in a focal area (Hock 1991: 440), from which it propagates outwards in line with Schmidt's (1872) wave theory. A change is therefore active for the longest time in its focal area and there eventually reaches its most general form by rule generalization. In the outermost areas, in contrast, the change may never progress beyond its initial, most narrowly defined environment. In the Old High German shift, the focal area lay south, in the Alemannic region, where the change reached its most advanced instantiation. As one moves northwards away from this focal area, one crosses isoglosses such as the Speyer line: to the south of this line, geminate plosives have undergone affrication (e.g. *Apfel* 'apple'); to the north, they remain unshifted (e.g. *Appel*). The utmost geographical reach of the Old High German shift is marked by the *maken~machen* isogloss, the 'Benrath line'. Not far from this line lies the town of Wermelskirchen, whose Rhenish dialect exhibits consistently spirantized plosives only in the original environment of the shift after short stressed vowels (Iverson & Salmons 2006). Simplifying a great deal, therefore, the geographical signature of rule generalization shown in (12) could be represented graphically as follows:

(13)

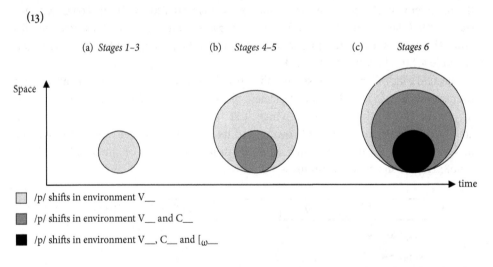

(a) *Stages 1–3*   (b) *Stages 4–5*   (c) *Stages 6*

Space

time

☐ /p/ shifts in environment V__

▨ /p/ shifts in environment V__ and C__

■ /p/ shifts in environment V__, C__ and [$_\omega$__

Late Modern English provides another example of rule generalization whereby the environment of two phonological rules, /ɹ/-deletion in non-rhotic dialects and /l/-darkening, has expanded along parallel prosodic tracks. In conservative dialects, these rules only target weak positions in the syllable, i.e. codas. In more advanced dialects, the processes apply in all weak positions within the foot, everywhere outside foot-initial onsets (Bermúdez-Otero 2011: 2039, and note 2 above). This is an instance of generalization in so far as the set of weak positions in the syllable is a proper subset of the set of weak positions in the foot. In (14) /l/-darkening illustrates the typical implementation of rule generalization in OT: some constraint, here *ł, undergoes stepwise demotion

relative to a markedness scale made up of constraints in a Paninian relationship, here
$*l/Rh \gg *l/[_{Ft} ...\acute{V}...\_\_...]$.

(14) (a) *Rule-based implementation*

$$Rh$$

(1) $1 \rightarrow ł /$ __| (specific)

(2) $1 \rightarrow ł / [_{Ft} ...\acute{V}...\_\_...]$ (general)

(b) *Constraint-based implementation*

(1) $*l/Rh \gg *ł \gg *l/[_{Ft} ...\acute{V}...\_\_...]$ (specific)

(2) $*l/Rh \gg *l/[_{Ft} ...\acute{V}...\_\_...] \gg *ł$ (general)

Now consider how rule generalization interacts with the life cycle of sound patterns. The
key point is that each step in a diachronic trajectory of rule generalization introduces a
new phonological process into the grammar. Characteristically, this new process applies
in a more general environment than its immediate precursor. Through phonologization
and stabilization, the new rule ascends to the phrase level, and there becomes exposed
to the mechanisms of input restructuring that drive domain narrowing (section 22.2.3).
This predicts that, in a trajectory of rule generalization, an older rule subject to relatively
specific phonological conditions can come to apply in a higher stratum than a younger,
more general successor, simply because the older rule became exposed to domain narrowing earlier in historical time.

The history of *o*-lowering in Swiss German provides a clear instance. Robinson (1976)
demonstrated that Swiss German dialects had undergone two waves of innovation
causing *o* to be lowered to ɔ: the first wave introduced a relatively specific rule applying before *r* only; this was later followed by a more general process applying before
all coronal consonants except *n* and *l*. In (15) I provide rewrite-rule statements based
on Robinson's: observe that the structural description of pre-*r o*-lowering is properly
included within that of general *o*-lowering.

(15) (a) *Pre-r o-lowering*

$$\begin{bmatrix} V \\ -high \\ +back \end{bmatrix} \rightarrow [+low] \ / \ \underline{\quad} \overset{\mu}{\underset{|}{\begin{bmatrix} +son \\ +cor \\ -nas \\ -lat \end{bmatrix}}} \qquad \text{i.e.} \qquad \breve{o} \rightarrow \breve{\mathrm{o}} / \underline{\quad} r$$

(b) *General o-lowering*

$$\begin{bmatrix} V \\ -high \\ +back \end{bmatrix} \rightarrow [+low] \ / \ \underline{\quad} \overset{\mu}{\underset{|}{\begin{bmatrix} +cor \\ -nas \\ -lat \end{bmatrix}}} \qquad \text{i.e.} \qquad \breve{o} \rightarrow \breve{\mathrm{o}} / \underline{\quad} \{r, t, d, ...\}$$

Each of the two *o*-lowering rules went through its life cycle separately from the other, and, crucially, we can ascertain its morphosyntactic domain of application in any given dialect by analysing its interactions with regular umlaut (also Ramsammy 2015). Regular umlaut applies at the word level, where it is triggered by certain productive morphological operations such as zero plural inflection, the formation of diminutives in *-li*, etc. (see Kiparsky, this volume): I assume that the relevant suffixes introduce a floating [–back] autosegment that docks onto the stem vowel during the word-level phonological cycle. The key observation is that lowering does not apply to umlauted vowels, since these bear the feature [–back], and umlaut in turn does not alter the height of input vowels, that is, *o* in the input to the word level becomes [ø] when umlauted, whilst ɔ becomes [œ]. Thus, umlauting of underlying /o/ yields surface [œ] only if /o/ is lowered to ɔ already at the stem level. It is thus easy to provide a stratal analysis of the five stages in the history of Swiss German *o*-lowering that Robinson (1976: 151) reconstructed on the basis of dialect geography:

(16)

	'thorn'	'thorns'	'floor'	'floors'
	$[_{WL} [_{SL} \text{torn}]]$	$[_{WL} [_{SL} \text{torn}]^{[-bk]}]$	$[_{WL} [_{SL} \text{bodə}]]$	$[_{WL} [_{SL} \text{bodə}]^{[-bk]}]$
Stage I				
SL	—	—	—	—
WL umlaut	—	tørn	—	bødə
Surface	torn	tørn	bodə	bødə
Stage II				
SL	—	—	—	—
WL umlaut	—	tørn	—	bødə
pre-*r* lowering	tɔrn	—	—	—
Surface	tɔrn	tørn	bodə	bødə
Stage III (St. Galler Rheintal)				
SL pre-*r* lowering	tɔrn	tɔrn	—	—
WL umlaut	—	tœrn	—	bødə
Surface	tɔrn	tœrn	bodə	bødə

Stage IV (Schaffhausen)

SL pre-*r* lowering	tɔrn	tɔrn	—	—
WL umlaut	—	tœrn	—	bødə
general lowering	(vacuous)	—	bɔdə	—
Surface	tɔrn	tœrn	bɔdə	bødə

Stage V (Kesswil)

SL general lowering[1]	tɔrn	tɔrn	bɔdə	bɔdə
WL umlaut	—	tœrn	—	bœdə
Surface	tɔrn	tœrn	bɔdə	bœdə

[1] Subsuming pre-*r* lowering.

As in (16), the older rule of pre-*r* *o*-lowering, which applies in the more restricted environment, was the first to ascend from the word level to the stem level, producing the system attested in the St Galler Rheintal dialect. The younger rule of general *o*-lowering, which applies in the more inclusive environment, undergoes domain narrowing later, producing the grammar of the Kesswil variety. Crucially, the Schaffhausen dialect reflects an intermediate stage in this trajectory, with the older, more specific rule already applying at the stem level, but the younger, more general rule still confined to the word level: in this system, underlying /o/ is lowered to [ɔ] before all coronal consonants other than *n* and *l*, but its umlauted counterpart surfaces as low [œ] only in the more restricted environment before *r*.

The Schaffhausen dialect can thus be regarded as instantiating the following typological generalization:

(17)   If two distinct phonological rules within the same grammar perform the same structural change but one subsumes the structural description of the other, then the more general rule is likely to have a wider cyclic domain.

Formally, this statement bears a certain resemblance to the Elsewhere Condition (Kiparsky 1973a: 94), which also controls the relative ordering of rules by reference to relationships of inclusion between structural descriptions. The Elsewhere Condition is believed by many to be a principle of synchronic grammar. There is no need, however, to endow learners with a bias in favour of systems that obey statement (17): this generalization holds simply by virtue of the diachronic interaction between rule generalization and the life cycle of phonological processes.

22.3.2 Lenition Pathways and the Life Cycle

Like a rule generalization scenario, a lenition trajectory also causes new phonological processes to enter the grammar in a recognizable sequence: in lenition trajectories, mild reductions precede more severe ones. No law dictates that, once a consonant has undergone some sort of weakening, it must stay on the same diachronic path to Ø (cf. Vennemann's famous definition of lenition, recorded in Hyman 1975: 165). But in many cases, it is logically impossible to reorder the steps in a lenition cline. Consider a scenario where [s] is lost through an intermediate stage of debuccalization:

(18) s $>$debuccalization   h $>$deletion   Ø

Clearly, [s] can be lost without previously becoming [h], but it certainly cannot become [h] by disappearing first.

Honeybone (2008) surveys the history of thought about lenition. One question concerns the extent to which diachronic lenition pathways should be mirrored by scales in synchronic theory. Some lenition trajectories bear striking similarities to the sonority hierarchy thought to govern syllabification: e.g. [t] > [d] > [ɾ] > Ø, or [t] > [d] > [ð] > [j] > Ø (see the well-known diagram in Hock 1991: 83). In other cases, lenition correlates fairly directly with segmental complexity as determined by the presence or absence of certain features: e.g. [s] > [h] > Ø, or [t] > [ʔ] > Ø.

For our purposes, the crucial observation is that synchronic grammars often contain separate phonological rules that reflect consecutive steps in a diachronic cline of lenition. When that happens, the older rules, reflecting milder forms of weakening, typically apply in narrower cyclic domains than the younger rules, which effect more drastic reductions. This is precisely the state of affairs predicted by the life cycle. Bermúdez-Otero (2011: 2034–7) discusses the example of /ɹ/ in English non-rhotic dialects: /ɹ/ undergoes reduction to [ɰ] in the coda at the word level, as shown by the opaque over-application of the process in word-final position before a word beginning with a vowel; full deletion, in contrast, operates at the phrase level, and so is transparent. Bermúdez-Otero & Trousdale (2012: 702–4) note that, in many English dialects, /l/ goes through the same type of synchronic derivation: it darkens in the coda at the word level, and vocalizes at the phrase level.

(19)		*see Lynn*	*seal in*	*seal bins*
		[PL [WL siː][WL lɪn]]	[PL [WL siːl][WL ɪn]]	[PL [WL siːl][WL bɪnz]]
WL	(darkening)	.lɪn.	.siːɫ.	.siːɫ.
PL	(vocalization)	.siː.lɪn.	.siː.ɫɪn.	.siːɰ.bɪnz.

This pattern of stratal affiliation for lenition processes is in fact quite pervasive: Broś (2012: ch. 4) reports that, in a dialect of Spanish spoken in northern Chile, coda /s/ debuccalizes to [h] at the word level, and deletes categorically at the phrase level.

In phonological frameworks that endow lenition scales with synchronic status, either directly or indirectly, the examples reviewed could be regarded as instances of the following typological generalization:

(20) If two distinct processes of lenition within the same grammar target the same consonant in the same phonological environment but one causes greater weakening than the other, then the more drastic process is likely to have a wider cyclic domain.

As in the case of (17), however, there is no need to add this statement to our synchronic theory: (20) holds simply by virtue of the diachronic interaction between lenition trajectories and the life cycle of phonological processes.

22.4 THE IRRELEVANCE OF OCKHAM'S RAZOR

There is no simple methodological prescription for balancing synchronic and diachronic explanation. Certainly, one cannot pursue purely synchronic accounts of 'what is out there', trusting that historical change will do no more that shift languages from one permissible state to another within the grammar space defined by synchronic theory. As we saw in section 22.3, 'what is out there' can be non-trivially moulded by diachronic processes in the first place. Conversely, diachronic explanation enjoys no epistemological priority over synchronic explanation: any attempt to justify such priority by appeal to Ockham's razor must fail, for the verdict of Ockham's razor is compelling only when one compares two empirically equivalent theories; but in any reasonably developed field of inquiry substantively different theories are hardly ever empirically equivalent, and so serious questions are settled not by Ockham's razor but by observation and experiment. The evidence in section 22.2 indicates that, in fact, the architecture of grammar provides an indispensable element in the explanation of key properties of sound change, including the existence of neogrammarian regularity and the life cycle of phonological processes. Ultimately, we may expect the best phonological explanations to operate in amphichronic fashion, with synchronic and diachronic inference feeding each other. There are, however, no methodological shortcuts to such explanations: they will be discovered only by the ordinary labour-intensive, unpredictable, intermittently frustrating means of hypothesis formation and testing.

CHAPTER 23

INDIVIDUALS, INNOVATION, AND CHANGE

MARK J. JONES

23.1 INTRODUCTION

THIS chapter is about systematic sources of variation in the speech behaviour of individuals. The focus is on factors in phonetics and phonology which might underlie systematic patterns of stable variation within a given population. These patterns may be useful in distinguishing between individuals but they may not be specific to a single individual, and they may form the source of sound changes which go on to characterize an entire speech community. Extralinguistic factors on variation, like attitude or identity, are not discussed. This is not to say that these are unimportant as sources of variation, but attitude and identity may be unsystematic and fluctuate over time, even during an exchange, and proving them as sources of variation in one instance may be difficult.

The discussion starts by examining the role of the individual in innovation and change, goes on to consider potential sources of individual variation, and finishes with a necessarily brief and speculative discussion of possible causes of individual variation. Several points arise. Firstly, an understanding of variation requires an assessment of sources of variation within speech production and perception. Overall, the prime cause of individual variation can be identified as due to the mapping between surface forms and abstract underlying units rather than indirect transmission between generations, and this mapping can change throughout an individual's lifetime so that diachronic change within a single, even isolated, speaker is possible (see Bowie & Yaeger-Dror, but also compare Hale et al., both this volume). Finally, the need is identified for a greater assessment of systematic behaviour across a range of phenomena in perception and production.

23.2 THE ROLE OF THE INDIVIDUAL IN INNOVATION AND CHANGE

Sound changes must start somewhere, and that starting point is variation. For Ohala (1989: 173), phonetic patterns in everyday speech provide a 'pool of synchronic variation' from which sound changes develop. In this view, phonetic variation has its roots in the architecture of the human vocal tract, physical constraints on sound production using that vocal tract, and perceptual interpretations of the acoustic signal. A great many sound changes parallel processes observed in casual speech and recur across languages and time periods because the indisputably innate endowments of the vocal tract and perceptual mechanisms are shared by all humans. Variation is expected to be remarkably uniform across languages because of the physical-biological nature of speech and its implementation by the shared structure of the human vocal tract. Under the Ohalan view, variation across languages must be relatively uniform in order to account for cross-linguistic patterns, and sound changes of this type can be, and crucially, have been, recreated in the laboratory (see also Yu, this volume; many other chapters in this volume offer similar or complementary approaches to the origins of change). Extralinguistic factors such as historical socioeconomic conditions act as triggers for patterns of variation to be adopted as regularized targets for an entire speech community. Other sound changes are predicted to be rooted in different principles, such as spelling pronunciations which affect specific lexical items, e.g. the orthographic innovation and subsequent inclusion in pronunciation of /l/ in English 'falcon' (Wells 1999). Changes like these are likely to be extremely limited in their application across the lexicon, and infrequent overall.

A complementary view of change is offered by Milroy (1993, 1999, also D'Arcy, this volume), who focuses not on the phonetic explanations for recurring sound changes, but the diffusion or transmission of a change from its point of origin to a whole speech community. Milroy (1993) distinguishes between 'innovations' which are novel realizations present in the speech of certain individuals and 'changes' which are realizations that spread between individuals. Under this view, sociolinguistically significant contact between speakers turns an innovation into a change. The innovations themselves are generally taken to have been learnt from a separate social group where that realization is already established. These innovative realizations—or rather, the role they play in signalling association with a different social group—are desirable for other speakers, and so they are adopted. Adoption is active learning of a feature for a particular sociolinguistic aim (Milroy 1993: 230-1). The ultimate source of this chain of changes, the original innovation, is unclear, though Milroy (1993: 230) does state that language internal and mental factors are important in giving rise to innovations.

These two views of sound change agree that changes become established within a speech community for social reasons. Neither Ohala nor Milroy concern themselves overmuch with the role that variation within individuals could play in sound change.

For Ohala this assumption of uniform variation is justified by his aim of explaining cross-linguistic parallels and appears to have a basis in fact, at least for casual speech (cf. Barry & Andreeva 2001), even if language specific constraints on contrast do appear to exist as well (Manuel 1999, Lavoie 2002, Ortega-Llebaría 2004). For Milroy there is in reality no individual innovation at the phonetic level either, as sociolinguistically diffused changes are adoptions of existing extra-group norms. Individual sociolinguistic variation encompasses changes in the variables present in a speaker's repertoire and changes in the proportional occurrence of those variables in that repertoire. But without individual variation at some level, where do those variables originate?

23.3 SOURCES OF INDIVIDUAL VARIATION

Encoding a message into speech and then decoding it again are complex processes. The encoding process—speech production—is the main focus here, but the input to speech production is derived from a perceptual analysis of the ambient language. The perceptual bases for individual differences are discussed at several points below. Speech production has several stages at which individual variation could potentially arise. The precise nature and relative ordering of each of the following informally identified stages will vary across researchers, but the treatment set out here is thought to be representative of widespread ideas, even if they are not uncontroversial (see Nolan 1983, Pierrehumbert 2001, 2002, Keating 1990). A speaker must select the lexical items to convey the message and apply an appropriate syntactic and morphological structure. The constituent morphemes will be combined into words and phrases, with any phonological adjustments made in terms of lexical and postlexical processes respectively, and the resulting plans will be submitted to the articulators for implementation. When two speakers use the same lexical items and morphosyntactic structures to convey 'the same' message (rather than e.g. stylistic variants), systematic individual variation could creep at any of these stages. Speaker differences may also occur in implementation in terms of the default articulatory setting of the vocal tract, i.e. whether a speaker has a high default pitch or speaks with some degree of nasalization or velarization (Laver 1980), or a fast speech rate (Jacewicz et al. 2009). The focus is on structural segmental differences which may occur between the lexicon and implementation targets, ignoring more global effects such as speech rate and articulatory setting.

The focus is also on systematic differences which would be expected to occur in the vast majority if not all instances of the same units repeated by that speaker within the same task. The effects should also be independent of non-structural considerations such as varying conversational context or the speaker's emotional state. There will of course be differences between speakers in how they indicate emotional states and attitudes, but these patterns, however individual they might be, will not be systematically and arbitrarily present in an individual's speech. Similarly, discourse effects will vary depending on what has gone before, what comes after, who the interlocutor is, etc. While individual differences could undoubtedly occur here, these differences are more transient. One assumption in making this systematic-transient distinction is that only systematic innovations could be used as the basis for sound change. A one-off speech error would not therefore count, e.g. pronouncing initial /t/ as [w] and initial /w/ as [tʰ] in Spooner's infamous 'you have tasted the whole worm' for 'you have wasted the whole term'. Even the most naïve listener with the greatest motivation to signal some kind of affinity with Spooner would refrain from disagreeing with that statement by responding 'I didn't taste (<waste) my wime (<time) completely'.

23.3.1 Lexical Representation

Variation is not usually considered to apply at the level of underlying lexical representation within the same dialect or accent. Underlying lexical representations are taken to be very robust in traditional generative models so that variation, and also change, are located elsewhere (compare Hale et al. and Dresher, both this volume). Even if underlying representations can be restructured eventually, they remain essentially impervious to ongoing revision. In an emergent approach to phonological structure, such as that embodied by exemplar approaches (Pierrehumbert 2001, 2002, and also Bybee, Phillips, and Wedel, all this volume), phonological structures at various levels emerge as categorization labels over auditory transforms of the acoustic signal. Within these models, change over time in the representation of words is expected and is used to explain some lexical frequency effects (e.g. Bybee 2002a,b, this volume, Phillips, this volume). What is perhaps less commonly discussed is the potential for different speakers to compute different categorization labels. These differences arise if speaker-listeners analyse surface effects in different ways.

Ohala (1989) provides one instance. The vowels in 'drink', 'link', 'sink', 'pink', etc. are higher and more fronted than the vowels in the words 'drip', 'lip', 'sip', 'pip', etc. Ohala himself still regards the vowels in these two sets of words as 'the same' underlyingly, so that his representations of 'drink' and 'drip' can be assumed to be /drɪŋk/ and /drɪp/. He has, in effect, perceptually undone any coarticulatory influences on the vowel. Other speakers, according to Ohala, have a more surface-oriented analysis, so that for them 'drink' is /driŋk/, interpreted to have the same vowel as in words like 'dream', while 'drip' is /drɪp/. Unless sound changes intervene to change final /ŋk/ into /n/, at which point presumably Ohala would still have /drɪn/ but others /drin/, the difference in lexical representation would have to be assessed using other methods, e.g. language games, grammaticality judgements on phonotactics and legal word shapes, and psycholinguistic priming experiments. This difference in lexical representation may be scarcely noticeable at the phonetic surface in the vowels themselves but it might have implications for wider effects such as vowel-to-vowel coarticulation or greater frication of /r/ in the speakers who have underlying /i/, and these effects could be implicated in future changes.

Another case is the realization of the onset in words like 'huge' or 'human'. These words are generally analysed as having initial /hj/ for distributional reasons in accents

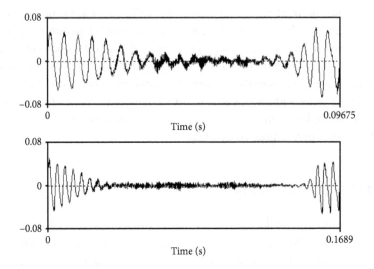

FIG. 23.1 Waveforms showing a portion of the sequence 'two huge' from the sentence 'Sal ate two huge apples' centred on the putative /hj/ sequence for two female speakers of British English. The top waveform shows a periodic signal overlaid with aperiodicity indicating voiced frication, whereas the bottom waveform shows voiceless frication. The top waveform is also just over half the duration of the bottom waveform. See text for interpretation.

which retain /j/ clusters, but surface realizations very often have initial [ç] (Ohala 1983, Cruttenden 2001: 211). The waveforms shown in Figure 23.1 illustrate a possible difference in analysis of the putative /hj/ sequence in the word 'huge' in the phrase 'Sal ate two huge apples' as produced by two speakers.

Speaker 1 tends to have voicing throughout, with only variable frication, suggesting that the frication is a byproduct rather than an intended essential component of the realization. The top panel in Figure 23.1 shows one token with continuous voiced frication. The token of 'huge' from speaker 2 in the bottom panel has persistent voiceless frication, which is around twice the duration of the frication seen for speaker 1, with a rapid offset and onset of voicing. This is typical of the realizations which show sustained voiceless frication with no variation in the occurrence of voicing or manner. Importantly, speaker 2's realizations of intervocalic /h/ in other words are invariably voiced. These observations suggest that speaker 2 intends to produce voiceless frication, and that they may therefore have a different representation of the word, one which includes a fricative onset.

23.3.2 Lexical Processes

Lexical processes apply to morphologically complex words, for example, a plural or past tense form, which can be analysed as having two separately identifiable morphological components. One or both morphemes present in the complex word may differ for systematic phonological reasons. For example, English is taken to have a single plural morpheme which has three variants or allomorphs: a voiceless realization /s/ after most voiceless obstruents (*cats* /kats/, *myths* /mɪθs/), a realization /ɪz/ after voiced and voiceless sibilants (*kisses* /ˈkɪsɪz/, *dishes* /ˈdɪʃɪz/), and a voiced realization /z/ elsewhere (*dogs* /dɒgz/, *bulls* /bʊlz/, *bees* /biːz/). The nature of the representation underlying the allomorphs (i.e. /s/, /z/, /ɪz/, all of these, or none of them) is immaterial here. In some cases, there is a plural form which deviates from expectations, e.g. the plural of *knife* is not the expected /naɪfs/, but /naɪvz/, with its own orthographic form 'knives'. Not much is known about individual variation in allomorphs, though Wells (1999) does show that some forms like *youths* /juːθs/ (for older /juːðz/) are becoming slightly more acceptable in British English.

Past tense allomorphy is very similar to that of plural allomorphy, with a /t/ form after voiceless obstruents except /t, d/, a /ɪd/ form after /t, d/, and a /d/ form elsewhere (Gussmann 2002: 37). The data presented here show voice onset time (VOT) in *lived* /lɪvd/ where the voiced past tense allomorph should have short-lag VOT and *picked* /pɪkt/ where the voiceless past tense allomorph should have long-lag VOT. Figure 23.2 shows average VOT measures (n = 5) for prevocalic realizations of the past tense allomorphs in *lived* and *picked* for five speakers of British English. Three speakers in Figure 23.2 (MS2, MS3, FS4) demonstrate the expected pattern with a long-lag VOT for the allomorph in *picked*, and a short-lag VOT for the allomorph in *lived*. Two subjects show no real difference in VOT between *lived* and *picked*. The short-lag VOT for MS6 could reflect an orthographic effect because the ending contains <d> in both cases, but the long-lag VOT for FS1 is not explicable in these terms. These subjects appear to have encoded morphological unity in their phonetic realizations.

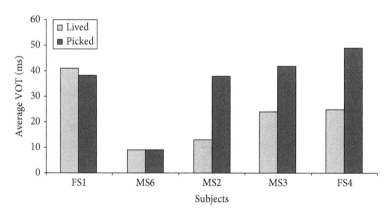

FIG. 23.2 Average VOT (ms) for prevocalic realizations of the past-tense endings in *lived* (left-hand grey bars) and *picked* (right-hand dark bars) elicited from five speakers of British English in the carrier phrase 'Say [word] again'. Subjects FS1 and MS6 show no real separation of VOT in each case, whereas the other subjects illustrate the more prevalent VOT distinction (based on Jones, in progress).

23.3.3 Postlexical Processes

Postlexical processes occur when words are combined into sentences. Ellis & Hardcastle (2002) provide indications of the extent of speaker variation in surface-oriented *vs* sophisticated approaches to the phonetic-phonology mapping in postlexical processes. They used a combination of electropalatography (EPG) and electromagnetic articulography (EMA) to examine the place of articulation of nasals before velars across a word boundary in the phrase 'ban cuts' and to compare it with a velar nasal control in the phrase 'bang comes'. The Ellis & Hardcastle data show that while some British English speakers had fully velar realizations of the word-final nasal in *ban*, supporting a categorical assimilate-by-rule account, others had fully alveolar realizations. Only two speakers showed any kind of gradient pattern.

23.3.4 Implementation Targets

Differences in implementation targets are qualitative subphonemic differences between speakers. English /t/ is generally described as alveolar and French /t/ as dental, but a combined acoustic and palatographic study by Dart (1998) showed that these statements may not be true for a large minority of speakers. Around 40 percent of Dart's English subjects had /t/s which could be described as dental, with a similar percentage of her French subjects showing an 'aberrant' alveolar realization. Other examples of qualitatively different targets come from 'infantilisms', variants associated with child speech which have been retained idiosyncratically by some speakers. An example of this is 'labiodental' /r/, an approximant realization of /r/ which is common in English child speech (Klein 1971, Dalston 1972, Kerswill 1996b) and which differs from adult target /r/ in having a higher third formant (F3, Dalston 1972, Lindsey & Hirson 1999, Nolan & Oh 1996, Docherty & Foulkes 2001). Uvular /r/ realizations are sporadically found among speakers of Russian, Welsh, Italian, Estonian or other languages normally said to exhibit apical trills. These realizations may also be infantilisms, perhaps encouraged by perceptual similarities between apical and uvular trills (Lindau 1985, Engstrand et al. 2007), together with infant vocal tract morphology which may promote uvular trilling (cf. Beck 1997, Widdison 1997).

   In addition to different targets, subtler effects can be revealed with instrumental analysis, showing that the 'same' targets could be achieved in different ways. One example of different implementation targets involves English approximant /r/ realizations in American English. Instrumental analysis such as Magnetic Resonance Imaging (MRI) has confirmed that different speakers use very different parts of the tongue as well as the lips to form different constrictions in different regions of the vocal tract. The articulatory variants form a quasi-continuum from a more traditional retroflex realization through to a 'molar' or bunched /r/, in which the tongue tip is low and retracted into the body of the tongue (Alwan et al. 1997, Westbury et al. 1998). In a similar vein, Johnson et al. (1993) noticed individual differences in tongue and jaw behaviour to achieve certain vowel targets. Bell-Berti et al. (1979: 380) reported that 4 out of 10 subjects showed height effects of EMG activity for the genioglossus muscle, with the remaining six showing tongue tension effects. There may also be differences in coarticulatory behaviour, so that some speakers allow more coarticulation than others, as Nolan (1983) found for British English initial /l/, or differences in the timecourse of acoustic trajectories (cf. McDougall 2005).

23.4 CAUSES OF INDIVIDUAL VARIATION

Discussions of causes for individual differences in the speaker identification literature centre on a distinction between 'learned' and 'organic' effects but as Nolan (1983, 1997) argues, this distinction is oversimplistic as organic effects due to vocal tract shape predict a range of behaviours rather than a particular behaviour because the vocal tract is plastic, and organic predispositions can be overcome. Could the patterns of variation between alveolar and dental /t/ referred to in Dart (1998) be due to the fact that 80 percent of the population is organically predisposed towards either alveolar or dental /t/, with 20 percent of speakers able to opt for either or both? Possible organic effects on speech production patterns are listed in the account of organic variation between individuals in Beck (1997), but on the whole very little is known about the extent to which certain organic differences necessarily entail a certain pattern of speech production. One area that has received quite a lot of attention is male-female differences in the vocal tract (see Henton's 1999: 53–7 overview). However, research on male-female differences across languages seems to show that there is variation which cannot be ascribed entirely to biological differences (Sachs et al. 1973, see Kingston 2005 for a review). Investigations of identical twins' speech have also showed that inherited vocal tract architecture does not result in identical speech patterns (Nolan & Oh 1996, Loakes 2006).

The specific causes of higher-order differences are no less uncertain, but lie within the mapping between lexicon and implementation, which may run both ways. The Ohala *drink-drip* example, the different implementations of *huge*, and the data from Ellis & Hardcastle (2002) all suggest that some speaker-listeners may have very surface-oriented patterns, while others abstract away from patterns they consider to be due to coarticulation. These analytic tendencies have obvious parallels in Ohala's hypo- and hypercorrective changes, respectively (see Yu, this volume). Whether speakers always tend one way or the other, whether they vary in their behaviour across phenomena, and whether there is a straightforward relationship between the production and perception of such effects remains largely unknown. Studies of the production-perception link in the realization of segmental contrasts suggest that more careful speakers are more careful listeners (see Perkell et al. 2004), but it is not clear how these effects apply postlexically. Some speakers may have a more word- or segment-oriented production model, preserving the shape of words like 'ban' in pre-velar contexts and eschewing assimilation, whereas others may have a more sophisticated approach. Individual differences in the production-perception link may drive or inhibit variation. Exposure to high F3 labio-dental /r/ appears to have undermined low F3 as a cue to the /r/-/w/ contrast in British English (Villafaña-Dalcher et al. 2008), but how individual speakers replicate these preferences in their production patterns remains to be seen. Speakers with a close link between perception and production, for whatever reasons, would presumably focus less on F3 in such cases. (See also Yu, this volume, for a discussion of further possible causes of individual variation, related to differences in cognitive processing style.)

Differences in morphological analysis such as those suggested by the data presented here on VOT variation in *picked* and *lived* must have explanations related to the way in which different speakers organize their morphological categories. Guy & Boyd (1990) present an analysis of the realization of word-final plosives in 'semiweak' verbs such as *crept, left, told*, i.e. verbs whose past tense has both a different vowel and a plosive suffix compared with their present tense forms *creep, leave, tell*. Differential rates of /t, d/ realization occurred in these verbs compared with regular past tenses, with three phases distinguished across age groups. Younger speakers had low rates of /t, d/ realization, suggesting they had a holistic analysis of these verbs based on vowel change alone. By adolescence, intermediate levels of /t, d/ realization occurred, and after the age of 30, some speakers seem to produce /t, d/ in semiweak verbs much more consistently. Guy & Boyd interpret these findings as evidence that speakers can spontaneously restructure their grammatical analysis of words during adulthood. If so, whatever their ultimate causes, these differences appear to be emergent within individuals, and the Guy & Boyd data is an example of the way that diachronic changes may take place even in the absence of sociolinguistic transmission. Varied or perceptually weak patterns may also be emergent rather than acquired (cf. Baker et al. 2007, Jones 2007).

There is another possible source of individual innovations. Milroy assumes—as do others—that a sociolinguistic variable is transmitted perfectly from its source. However, the adopters are not native speakers of the 'innovating' variety (L2), and will have a different system of contrasts and different phonetic targets in their native variety (L1; see Evans & Iverson 2004). Whether the varieties concerned are regarded as languages, accents, or sociolects, etc., individuals who acquire more than one system rarely do so perfectly (Eckman & Iverson, this volume). Research on second language acquisition shows that even with considerable exposure and motivation, phonetic transfer effects from the L1 can persist for a long time, even with relatively young speakers (see Flege et al. 1999 and references therein). These effects introduce new innovations into the patterns of variation, perhaps resulting in greater gradience in newly acquired than in native patterns. Interference effects may also arise due to the dispersion of contrasts operating within the existing system. A novel contrast may cause a restructuring of existing contrasts (Hall 1997, Hamann 2004). The 'fudged' STRUT vowel (RP /ʌ/) of Northern English speakers (Chambers & Trudgill 1980: 132-7, Henton 1990) may result from a dispersion effect within the Northern English vowel system with its very centralized /a/. Interference patterns would obviously apply at the individual level in Milroy-type adopters.

23.5 CONCLUSIONS

Variation, the prerequisite for change, is inevitable in any physical-biological process, and speech is no exception. Quantitative analysis of the individual members of an abstract category like 'voiceless unaspirated bilabial plosive' can never produce invariant results, whatever measurable phonetic characteristic is under scrutiny. Such categorization rests on relatively gross parameters, so variation itself is not surprising, but it still needs to be explained. A single instance of a [p] may differ from others on a given occasion because of a speech error, but where consistent and systematic variation is present, something more interesting is afoot.

Individual variation may arise at different levels of the speech implementation process for a variety of reasons involving perception and categorization of the signal, organic and developmental influences on production, and ongoing reanalysis of morphological patterns. None of these sources of individual variation is well understood. Variation may also arise in the acquisition, i.e. adoption, of a non-native sociolinguistic variable, as a kind of second language effect, so that the Milroy innovation-change dichotomy is fatally flawed—both innovation and change may take place at the same point in time. Contact accounts of change must deal with the phonetic complications that arise due to the interaction between pre-existing and adopted variants.

Understanding what patterns of stable variation are possible across speakers is important for assessing how the majority linguistic structures within a speech community may show 'shifts' or non-diffused changes across time. A shift between a surface-oriented analysis (the nasal before a bilabial plosive is intentionally /m/) or a more sophisticated analysis (the nasal before a bilabial plosive is intentionally /n/ assimilated to [m]) may take place without any necessary sociolinguistic conditioning if the balance of speaker-listeners changes in favour of one interpretative extreme or the other. The causes of shifts like these are not entirely extralinguistic in the way that changes in socioeconomic power-bases are, because they may arise in linguistically-relevant areas such as syllable structure, morphological productivity, lexical frequency, or even attentional deficits due to conversational context. Identifying the ultimate causes of variation in one specific case may be so complex as to appear impossible, but the difficulties should not deter researchers from looking for systematic patterns of individual behaviour across phenomena.

The 'acoustic revolution' means that more and more detail is being examined in speech variation studies. As the amount of observed detail increases, the extent of variation becomes clearer, and requires explanations. Fundamental to explaining the true nature of variation is an understanding of its causes, and fundamental to explaining the true nature of change is an understanding of how innovations take place. Individuals are the ultimate sources of these innovations (Baker et al. 2011, even argue that inter-speaker variability is essential for the initiation of change). Speech variation studies have long focused on exploring the wood; it is now time to stop and look at the trees.

CHAPTER 24

....

THE ROLE OF EXPERIMENTAL INVESTIGATION IN UNDERSTANDING SOUND CHANGE

....

ALAN C. L. YU

24.1 INTRODUCTION

....

> When we speak of the systematic effect of sound laws we can only mean that given the same sound change within the same dialect every individual case in which the same phonetic conditions are present will be handled the same. Therefore either wherever earlier the same sound stood, also in the later stages the same sound is found or, where a split into different sounds has taken place, then a specific cause—a cause of a purely phonetic nature like the effects of surrounding sounds, accent, syllabic position, etc.—should be provided to account for why in the one case this sound, in the other that one has come into being.
>
> (Paul 1880: 86; page numbers are from the 2nd edition of 1886)

The neogrammarian position on sound change, as summarized in Hermann Paul's quote above, consists of two assertions: sound change is *regular* and *purely phonetically conditioned*. While there has been widespread recognition that diachronic (and synchronic) phonological phenomena can be attributed to phonetic factors (Whitney 1867, Verner 1877, Paul 1880, Sweet 1888, Jespersen 1922, Hill 1936, Jakobson 1941, Martinet 1952, 1955, Baudouin de Courtenay 1895[1972]), the experimentalist's project on sound change, nonetheless, did not get underway in earnest until relatively recently. As Bloomfield remarked, '[a]lthough many sound-changes shorten linguistic forms, simplify the phonetic system, or in some other way lessen the labor of utterance, yet no student has succeeded in establishing a correlation between sound-change and any antecedent phenomenon: the causes of sound-change are unknown' (Bloomfield 1933: 385). As techniques and methodology in phonetic research become more sophisticated, systematic investigations into variabilities and biases in speech production and, more recently, speech perception offer more resources to investigate the relationship between diachronic sound changes and synchronic variation in speech, even though the impetus to apply experimental methodologies to the investigation of historical events is not always immediately obvious (and the interpretation of the effects of phonetic biases controversial). To be sure, the need to check the validity of any hypothesis concerning the cause of a particular sound change by testing the hypothesis in the laboratory is clear. As Ohala explains, '[i]f particular sound changes are posited to have a phonetic basis then one should be able duplicate the conditions under which they occurred historically and find experimental subjects producing 'mini' sound changes that parallel them. It is because of the posited phonetic character of sound change that a laboratory study is possible: were the initiation caused by grammatical and cultural factors, this would be more difficult or perhaps impossible' (Ohala 1993: 261). The question is what linking theory is needed to connect experimental findings to historical changes that took place in the past and where information regarding the precise conditions that gave rise to the specific changes are no longer available.

One important principle that is assumed, implicitly or explicitly, by all laboratory investigators of sound change is the principle of uniformitarianism (see Murray, this volume). As it applies in linguistics, uniformitarianism asserts that the same processes that operate in language now must have always operated in language in the past. That is, the same laws apply today as in the past. This assumption is crucial for any attempt to link experimental findings to causes of sound change in the past since there is no necessary *a priori* reason to think that observations made in the laboratory would have any bearing on our understanding of the past. While the uniformitarian principle supplies the larger conceptual framework, specific hypotheses about how phonetic conditions shape the emergence of new sounds and sound patterns are also needed. Hypotheses are generated from close examination of explicit theories. To this end, this chapter begins with an overview of theories of the phonetic origins of sound change in Section 24.2, wherein some controversy lies. While theorists differ in terms of their emphasis on which party of the communicative dyads (the speaker *vs* the listener) contributes most to the initiation of change, ultimately, approaches to sound change typically recognize that a major source of variation comes from constraints imposed by the human speech production and perceptual system. As Ohala (1993) argues, common sound changes attested independently in substantially the same form in unrelated languages are generally more likely to be the results of language universal factors such as the physics and physiology of the vocal tract and the nature of the human perceptual system. Thus, Section 24.3 reviews systematic sources of phonetic variation (phonetic biases) that have been associated with common sound changes and the experimental methodologies that uncover them. Section 24.4 discusses recalcitrant problems, including how new variants are registered in the phonetic memory of individuals and how such variants propagate across the speech community, and suggests possible directions for future investigations. Some concluding remarks appear in Section 24.5. The approach taken here fits well with that of several other chapters in this volume, such as Jones (this volume) and Blevins (this volume); other chapters take different approaches, such as Dresher (this volume) and Holt (this volume).

24.2 THEORIES OF THE PHONETIC ORIGINS OF SOUND CHANGE

One of the central questions in sound change is the so-called actuation problem (Weinreich et al. 1968). That is, why does a change occur in a particular manner in a particular time and space? This chapter focuses primarily on how variants come about, although some discussion regarding the diffusion of linguistic variants appears in Section 24.4.4. This section reviews two approaches to the phonetic origins of sound change.

24.2.1 'Ease of Articulation' and Sound Change

Most early theories of sound change appealed to the so-called 'ease of articulation' hypothesis to explain the source of new sounds and sound patterns (see Bybee, this volume). Phonetic precursors to sound change under this view consist of the interplay between the articulatory dynamics of speech production and the functional motivation of 'economy' (e.g. Paul 1880, Sievers 1901). To be sure, a simplistic appeal to 'ease of articulation' offers little insight into the complexity of language variation and change where stability is just as much a reality as change. A more nuanced articulatory view of sound change was most developed in the H & H theory of phonetic variation (Lindblom 1990). From the perspective of this theory, speakers adaptively tune their performance along the H(yper)-H(ypo) continuum according to their estimates of the needs of the listener in that particular situation. These needs include preferences to maximize the distinctiveness of contrasts and to minimize articulatory effort. Speakers hyper-articulate when listeners require maximum acoustic information; they reduce articulatory efforts, hence hypo-articulate, when listeners can supplement the acoustic input with information from other sources. Hyper forms tend to involve increased duration and amplitude of articulatory gestures as well as reduction in gestural overlap while hypo-forms show the opposite characteristics. Speakers and listeners dynamically adjust their production and perception to the communicative demands of the situation. Spectral variation observed in vowel reduction, for example, can be predicted given information about the vowel durations and adjacent consonant loci (Lindblom 1963). Vowel durations in turn are predicated in terms of phonological length, stress, and position within the utterance (Lindblom et al. 1981) and these factors are in turn determined by the morphological and syntactic specification of the utterance. From this perspective, sound change occurs when intelligibility demands are redundantly met or when

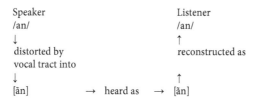

Speaker   Listener
/an/   /an/
↓   ↑
distorted by   reconstructed as
vocal tract into
↓   ↑
[ãn]   → heard as →   [ãn]

FIG. 24.1 Distortion of the speech signal and reconstruction of the intended signal.

the listeners focus their attention on the 'how' (signal-dependent) mode rather than the 'what' (signal-independent) mode of listening (Lindblom et al. 1995). New phonetic variants are accumulated during the 'how' mode of listening.

The listener-turned-speaker may then be free to select new forms from the pool of variants. The selection process is assumed to be governed by a host of different evaluative metrics. A new variant may be evaluated in terms of the economy of gesture (i.e. how much effort is required to produce it?) or it may be judged from the perspective of the listeners (i.e. how confusable is a variant?). The speech community may also evaluate a new variant in terms of its social value.

24.2.2 Listener-oriented Approaches

Unlike the articulatory view of sound change, which affords a large agentive role to the speaker, many have emphasized the important role listeners play as well (Blevins 2004a, Beddor 2009), chief among them the misperception model advocated by John Ohala (1981, 1983, 1989, 1992, 1993, 1995). The basic premise of all listener-oriented views of sound change is the ambiguous nature of the speech signal. Such ambiguities, or 'noise', stem from articulatory, acoustic, auditory, and perceptual constraints inherent to the vocal tract and the auditory and perceptual apparatus. Consider, for example, the case of the development of contrastive nasal vowels from vowel+nasal sequences (VN > Ṽ), a sound change frequently attested in the world's languages. Nasalization is often observed on the preceding vowel due to low-level contextual anticipatory nasalization. When such 'unwanted' coarticulatory nasalization is factored out by the listener[1] via the relevant phonetic 'reconstructive rule' or the general mechanism of perceptual compensation, and an underlying VN sequence is reconstructed. Figure 24.1 provides a schematic representation of the chain of events that is characteristic of canonical transmission of coarticulated speech.

Under the scenario just laid out, listeners are assumed to be able to normalize for whatever contextual influences that distort the speech signal (indicated here in []) and to reconstruct accurately the intended message (forms in //). However, when listeners are unable to factor out 'unwanted' distortions in the speech signal, a mini sound

---

[1] Scarborough (2004) argues coarticulation facilitates speech recognition and may therefore be intended by the speaker.

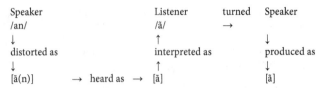

FIG. 24.2 Distortion of the speech signal and absence of reconstruction of the intended signal.

change obtains. Figure 24.2 illustrates what might happen when listeners misperceive. If the listener misattributes the nasalization on the vowel as intended rather than as an artifact of coarticulated speech, a new perceptual norm may be established. Assuming a perception-production feedback loop (Pierrehumbert 2001, Oudeyer 2006, and Wedel, this volume), a mini-sound change is accomplished if the listener-turn-speaker begins to produce that lexical item with the new perceptual and production target.

24.2.3 Points of Convergence and Divergence

The models of sound change reviewed above are not mutually exclusive, especially given that both approaches emphasize the role of the individual in the inception of change (see Jones, this volume).[2] Lindblom's H & H approach to sound change, for example, does not rule out the possibility of misperceptions as a contributor to sound change; misperception is presumably only partial as successful access to the lexical level (i.e. the 'what' mode) is still possible even when the speaker has committed a phonetic 'error'. The main difference between these approaches resides in their treatments of phonetic variability. Variability, from the perspective of the H & H theory, is functional in nature and serves a communicative purpose. For Ohala (1993), on the other hand, variability is viewed as noise to be factored out. Sound change is taken to be phonetically abrupt but lexically gradual since misperception is assumed to lead to an immediate shift from one pronunciation to another; the seeming gradualness of sound change is assumed to be coming from its spread from speaker to speaker, speaking style to speaking style, and word to word. Lindblom, on the other hand, argued that the initiation and spread of sound change rest in the accumulation of new variants and speakers' decision to utilize such variants. Thus, like Ohala, sound change in Lindblom's model also spreads between speakers, speaking styles, and words. However, unlike Ohala, sound change is neither abrupt nor gradual. The addition of new phonetic memories (i.e. the introduction of a new phonetic variant) per se does not lead to change since the new variant is only one of many possible variants of a linguistic form. Linguistic innovations arise through deliberate selection of variants for perceptual, articulatory, or social reasons.

---

[2] Neither approach is designed to address how members of a speech community come to share these new perceptual and production targets. For more discussion on the question of sound change propagation, see Sections 24.4.3 and 24.4.4 as well as D'Arcy, Foulkes, & Vihman, Eckman & Iverson, and Bowie & Yaeger-Dror (all this volume).

Evolutionary Phonology (see Blevins, this volume) can be seen as an attempt to synthesize the strengths of these two perspectives on sound change. Blevins proposes three mechanisms for sound change: CHOICE, CHANCE, and CHANGE. CHOICE refers to innovations grounded in articulatory variation along the H(ypo)-H(yper) continuum, along the same line as that proposed in Lindblom et al. (1995). Variation in the pronunciation of words like *memory* ([mɛməɹi]~[mɛmɹi]) and *camera* ([kæməɹə]~[kæmɹə]) is a case in point. Speakers may choose to hyperarticulate, thus realizing the medial schwa, or they can hypoarticulate, in which case, the schwa is absent. CHANCE refers to innovations based on intrinsic phonological ambiguity. Metathesis (i.e. the re-ordering of sounds; *-rd- > -dr-) is a prime example.[3] When the input signal is consistent with two or more phonological parses, listeners might choose a parse that is incongruent with the parse intended by the speaker. Finally, CHANGE refers to innovations that originate from perceptual bias-induced misperception. Nasal place assimilation in VNTV has been argued to be an instance of CHANGE. Because perceptually-speaking CV transition cues are stronger than VC ones (Fujimura et al. 1978, Repp 1978, Ohala 1990), listeners are biased toward confusing a weak VC transition cue for the place of articulation of a nasal (N) for the strong CV transition cue of the following obstruent (T). Blevins, however, stresses that sound change often involves more than one mechanism. For example, because speakers might show coarticulatory place assimilation in hypo-articulated speech, CHOICE might play a role in the emergence of nasal place assimilation in language.

Because of the differences in emphasis, functional and listener-oriented approaches often utilize different experimental evidence to substantiate their theories and to explain individual instances of sound change. For example, while all approaches to sound change must deal with the question of where phonetic variation comes from, the H & H theorists look for evidence of functional motivations (i.e. issues of articulatory effort and communicative efficiencies) for phonetic variation, while the listener-oriented approach generally seeks to uncover physical and perceptual biases in the speech production and perceptual system that could serve as phonetic precursors to sound change. The next section provides an overview of canonical sources of phonetic biases that give rise to precursors to sound change.

24.3 PHONETIC FACTORS IN SOUND CHANGE

24.3.1 Production Biases

Much variability in speech comes from constraints imposed by the speech production system. Two sources of production constraints are commonly observed: motor planning and coordination and speech aerodynamics.

---

[3] See Section 24.3.2.3 for more discussion.

24.3.1.1 *Motor Planning and Coordination*

One of the most prominent contributing factors to phonetic variation comes from limitations imposed by the motoric aspects of the speech production system. The temporal coordination of the different articulators involved in speech offers a tremendous source of variability and, as a consequence, presents ample opportunities for misanalysis by the listener. Consider the production of nasal+fricative sequences. In order to produce a nasal consonant, the oral passage as controlled by the tongue or the lips must be closed and the nasal passage open. Likewise, for an oral consonant, the reverse condition is required. The production of apical fricatives in particular leaves open the apex as a possible vent. The production of a nasal+apical fricative sequence requires the simultaneous and opposite change of state of the nasal and oral passage. That is, the nasal passage must go from open to closed, while the oral passage must go from closed to open as the articulators transition from a nasal to an apical fricative. If both oral and nasal passages were closed during the transition between these segments, air flowing from the lungs would accumulate in the oral cavity. When the oral constriction is finally released, a burst might become audible as a result of the pressure buildup inside the supraglottal cavity. If the listener misanalysed the audible burst as the presence of an intended obstruent between a nasal and an apical fricative, a new variant with an epenthetic stop will emerge (e.g. English *prince* ~ *prin[t]ce*; Ohala 1997b). A similar explanation applies to stop epenthesis in nasal+lateral sequences (e.g. Latin *templus* < *tem-lo 'a section'; Ohala 1997b).

Another example of potential perceptual ambiguities caused by issues with gestural coordination comes from gestural overlap in connected speech processes. In their examinations of X-ray pellet trajectory data,[4] Browman and Goldstein (1990) demonstrated that perceived assimilation or deletion might arise as a result of subsequent consonantal gestures overlapping to such an extent as to either hide each other when they involve sufficiently independent articulatory gestures or blend their characteristics when they involve the same articulators. Thus in one of the utterances they examined, 'perfect memory', X-ray trajectories revealed, within a fluent phrase, the presence of the /t/ gesture, even though it overlapped with, and is masked by, the following /m/ gesture. The authors further pointed out that not all cases of assimilation include such residual articulations. 'Even deletion, however, can be seen as an extreme reduction, thus as an endpoint in a continuum of gestural reduction, leaving the underlying representation unchanged' (1990: 366).

The inter-dependence of individual components of the speech production apparatus also gives rise to phonetic biases that contribute production variation. An example comes from the production of voicing in stops. In addition to a steady transglottal flow, the production of voicing requires the vocal folds to be adducted to a suitable degree

---

[4] The data came from the AT&T Bell Laboratories archive of X-ray microbeam data (Fujimura et al. 1973). The X-ray microbeam system tracks the position of (up to seven) small lead pellets placed on the lower lip, the jaw, the tongue blade, the tongue dorsum mid, the tongue dorsum rear, and/or the soft palate, in addition to two reference locations.

and the longitudinal tension of the fold must be adjusted within an appropriate range. Voicelessness, on the other hand, requires vocal-fold abduction and a decrease in pressure across the glottis. The coordination of articulatory gestures for these phonation differences often lead to articulatory by-products that may have perceptual consequences. Ewan & Krones (1974) found that the vertical position of the larynx differs for voiced and voiceless stops. Using data obtained by a special photo-electric device called the 'thyroumbrometer' invented by the authors, Ewan & Krones (1974) showed a higher position of the larynx for voiceless as opposed to voiced stops in French, English, and Thai, and f_o was positively correlated with larynx position. The raising of the larynx is accomplished through the contraction of extrinsic muscles attached to the thyroid cartilage and hyoid bone. Such changes probably occur to increase the stiffness while decreasing the mass of the vocal folds, which would make it more difficult for the vocal folds to vibrate. Similarly, cricothyroid muscle activity has been shown to increase for voiceless consonants relative to voiced consonants. An increase in cricothyroid activity tenses the vocal folds longitudinally, which leads to an increase in the frequency of vibration (Löfqvist et al. 1989).

This pitch-perturbation effect has been linked to tonogenesis in many languages (see Ratliff and Hale et al., both this volume). That is, the development of tone splits (e.g. in Chinese, Vietnamese, Khmu) has been attributed to the exaggeration of physiologically-based consonantal voicing-induced pitch perturbations on the neighboring vowel (Hombert 1978, Hombert et al. 1979) to such an extent that the pitch variation cannot be attributed entirely to the physiological properties of the preceding consonant's voicing (*pa > pá and *ba > bà where ´ indicates a high tone and ` indicates a low tone; Hyman 1976). Likewise, many languages show interaction between obstruent voicing and the height of neighbouring vowels.[5] For example, in Madurese, an Austronesian language of Indonesia, vowels are raised following a voiced obstruent (*mɛt̪ɔŋ* 'AV.count' ~ *bit̪ɔŋ* 'count'; *ŋɛpʰi* 'AV.carry' ~ *gipʰi* 'carry'; AV = Agent Voice). No comparable change in vowel height is observed when the vowel is preceded by a sonorant or a voiceless obstruent (*nɔt̪t̪ʰuʔ* 'AV.point' ~ *t̪ʰɔt̪t̪ʰuʔ* 'point').[6] Such an interaction between consonantal voicing and vowel height has been argued to have its origin in the lowering of the larynx that accompanied the production of voicing (Bauer 2009, Moreton 2008), as one important acoustic effect of coarticulatory laryngeal lowering is the lowering of F1 (i.e. raising of vowel height).

24.3.1.2 *Speech Aerodynamics*

Aerodynamic principles govern the movement of air in the vocal tract which, in turn, generates the acoustic output we call sound. The production of speech sounds thus requires not only the movement of the vocal apparatus but also the coordination of the aerodynamic engine that powers sound production. Aerodynamically, the vocal tract

---

[5] Blocking of height harmony in Buchan Scots to be discussed in Section 24.3.2.2 is also an example of this interaction.

[6] Madurese examples are taken from Davies (1999 : 7). See also Stevens (1968), Cohn (1993).

has two relevant air cavities, the lung cavity and the supraglottal cavity. Many acoustic cues, such as voicing, frication, and trills, require a sustained and continuous supply of airflow. In addition to the muscular activities that govern the configuration of the glottis (i.e. the glottis must be adducted), voicing—vibration of the vocal cords—is possible only when a pressure differential exists between the lung and the supraglottal cavities and sufficient air flows past the glottis. Sustained production of voicing is difficult when there is a blockage along the vocal tract downstream from the glottis, as in the case of an oral stop, since the pressure differential across the glottis will eventually equalize at which point airflow will cease and vocal fold vibration will stop. This so-called 'Aerodynamic Voicing Constraint' (AVC; Ohala 1983) has been used to explain why cross-linguistically voiced stops are disfavoured compared to voiceless ones and why voiced stops (b, d, g) tend to give way to voiceless stops (p, t, k) or voiced spirants (β, ð, ɣ). That is, voicing during stop closure might cease as a consequence of the AVC or, if voicing is to be maintained, other aspects of stop production might have to be sacrificed (i.e. spirantization). Even in languages with voiced stops, the velar [g] is often missing (Maddieson 2008b), presumably due to the smaller oral volume for [g] which causes voicing to cease sooner relative to voiced stops of other place of articulation. To be sure, rather than succumbing to the AVC, speakers might employ other compensatory strategies such as larynx lowering and nasal venting to help sustain voicing. Implosives, which are produced in part with the lowering of the larynx, in Sindhi, an Indo-Aryan language, are said to have originated from former voiced geminates (e.g. Prakrit *pabba > paɓuɳi 'lotus plant fruit', bʰagga > bʰaːɠu 'fate'; Ohala 1983). Likewise, voiced stops in many languages are reported to have (spontaneous) prenasalized variants (Iverson & Salmons 1996b, Solé 2009) or have developed into prenasalized stops (Ohala 1983), presumably a result of anticipatory nasal venting.

The production of fricatives and trills is also tightly constrained by aerodynamic factors. The production of fricatives, as well as the fricative release of affricates and the burst of stops, requires the generation of audible turbulence (i.e. noise) in the vocal tract. For the supraglottal fricatives, a delicate balance between subglottal and supralaryngeal pressures is needed to allow airflow through the glottis as well as across the narrow oral constriction downstream from the glottis. That is, subglottal pressure must be higher than supraglottal pressure, which in turn must be higher than atmospheric pressure. Sound change could occur if this delicate balance is disturbed. For example, if supraglottal pressure behind the oral constriction is vented through the nasal cavity, turbulence is endangered. Such a scenario might underlie the development of voiceless nasals in Burmese which has been argued to have come from historical sN sequences where N represents a nasal of any place of articulation (e.g. Written Tibetan sna/Written Burmese hna ~ Modern Burmese /n̥a/ 'nose'; WT smin-po/WB hmaṅ ~ /m̥ɛ̃ʼ/ 'ripe'; Ohala 1975: 295).

Audible frication might also be endangered as a result of variability in articulatory strength in different prosodic positions. Diachronically, syllable-final fricatives often despirantize, which could result in vocalization/gliding (Latin nos, vos, pōst > Italian, Romanian noi, voi, poi 'we'), aspiration (Latin festa, vespa, disjejunare > Lombardian ['fɛhta], ['vɛhpa], [dih'na] 'holidays', 'wasp', 'to dine'), assimilation (Gascon *es lansos* > *el lansos* 'the sheets'), rhotacism (PIE *aus- > English *ear*, German *Ohr*), or elision (Latin *nos*, *vos* > French *nous* [nu], *vous* [vu] 'we', 'you'). Solé (2010) argued that such weakening and loss of final fricative might be the result of audible frication being more difficult for speakers to produce and for listeners to detect on account of a decreased oral gesture in syllable-final position and/or lowered subglottal pressure in utterance-final position. Such modification of the aerodynamic conditions is supported by her findings that compared to onset fricatives, coda fricatives aerodynamically and acoustically exhibit a slower oral pressure build-up, a lower pressure peak, a delayed onset of audible frication as well as lower intensity of frication.

In addition to the patterning of voicing and frication, aerodynamic factors have also been argued to be important for understanding the sound pattern of trills (Solé 1999, 2002a,b). The production of apical trills requires tongue-tip vibration, initiated by muscle contraction of the tongue to be in the appropriate position, shape and elasticity, and a sufficient pressure difference across the lingual constriction. Once trilling is commenced, tongue-tip vibration is maintained as a self-sustaining vibratory system. In an effort to explain the tendency for lingual fricatives to assimilate to the following apical trill (e.g. Iberian Spanish /s (#) r/ *las rojas* [la'roxas] 'the red ones', *Osram* ['oram]), Solé (2002b) showed that lingual trills exhibit highly constrained articulatory and aerodynamic requirements; small variations may result in a lack of tongue-tip vibration. Her investigation showed that, in /s, ʃ + r/ sequences, the generation of audible turbulence of the neighbouring fricative might be imperiled when speakers produce an early onset of the lingual movements for the trill, presumably to attain the tongue configuration and aerodynamic requirements for tongue-tip vibration.

24.3.2 Perceptual Biases

There are three commonly recognized perceptually-motivated sources of phonetic variation: perceptual confusion, hypocorrection, and hypercorrection.

24.3.2.1 *Perceptual Confusion*

Errors in perceptual parsing could be precipitated by the intrinsic perceptual similarity between segments. An intriguing property of similarity-based confusion is that it is not necessarily symmetric. That is, while *a priori*, when segments X and Y are similar to each other, we would expect X to be equally likely to be confused as Y and vice versa. This is, however, not always the case. A prime example comes from asymmetry in consonantal changes. Diachronically, velar palatalization before front vowels is found in many languages, including in the histories of Slavic, Bantu, Indo-Iranian, Mayan, Salish, and Chinese (Guion 1996, 1998). Sound change in the opposite direction, i.e. from an alveo-palatal to a velar before front vowels, are rare, if attested at all. The unidirectionality of this change has been argued to be the result of confusability between velars and alveolars in the context of front vowels (though see Recasens 2011 for an articulatory explanation). Velars before front vowels are similar acoustically to palatal alveolar affricates in the same environment and the acoustic similarity is greater in faster speech than in citation (Guion 1996, 1998). Crucially, velars before front vowels are perceptually more easily confused with alveolars and palatals but not the other way around (Guion 1996, 1998, Chang et al. 2001). The asymmetry in perceptual confusability helps explain the unidirectionality of neutralizing sound changes (see also Kawasaki 1982, Foulkes 1997). Chang et al. (2001) attributes this perceptual asymmetry to the degradation of the compact mid-frequency spectral peak as a cue to differentiate [ki] from [ti]. The otherwise robust F2 formant transition cue for distinguishing consonant place of articulation is neutralized because of the raising F2 of the following high vowel. Thus if the remaining non-robust mid-frequency spectral peak, which indexes the front cavity resonance, was degraded to the point of losing its contrastiveness, listeners are likely to confuse [ki] as [ti]. The confusion of [ti] for [ki] is unlikely since it would entail listeners erroneously inserting a non-existent cue into the speech signal for [ti].

24.3.2.2 *Hypocorrection*

Hypocorrection is characterized by a scenario where fortuitous results of the speech production process are misanalysed as part of the pronunciation norm. The development of Buchan Scots vowel height harmony has been argued to be a case in point. The modern Buchan dialect of north-east Scotland has two high vowels (i, u) and seven non-high vowels (e, ɛ, ɜ, a, ʌ, ɔ, o). Suffixes and clitics that contain an unstressed vowel /i/ or /ɜ/ exhibit height harmony with the vowel of the root (*hair-y* [here], *lassie* [lase], *rocky* [rɔke], but *beanie* [bini], *dearie* [diri] and *housie* [husi]; Paster 2004). Paster (2004) argued that vowel height harmony in Buchan Scots is a consequence of the phonologization of coarticulation in tongue height. Vowel-to-vowel coarticulation, including vowel height, frontness, and rounding, is rampant in natural speech and has been the object of many studies (e.g. Manuel 1990, Beddor & Yavuz 1995, Majors 1998, Beddor et al. 2002). Paster hypothesized that the lowered tongue position used to produce non-high vowels coloured the pronunciation of the following high vowels so much so that they were produced with the tongue body slightly lower than in high vowels in other contexts. When listeners hypocorrected for this coarticulatory effect and misanalysed the height variation as intentional, a phonologized harmony process might develop as a result where high vowels were lowered to non-high after a non-high vowel. Additional evidence in support of this perceptually-driven account comes from blocking in this language. Vowel height harmony in Buchan Scots is blocked when the root-final consonants that intervene between the triggering and target vowels are voiced obstruents (*Eddie* [ɛdi], *lovey* [lʌvi]) or combinations of voiced obstruents with each other and with other sonorants (*bendy* [bɛndi], *hardly* [hardli]). Paster (2004) accounted for the blocking effects in terms of the larynx lowering effect of voicing, which in turn lowers F1. Given that the magnitude of larynx lowering is greater at or near the end of the stops, the F1 lowering effect of voicing should have a more significant effect on the vowel following rather than preceding the consonant in question.

Thus at the stage when suffix vowels are phonetically lowered (i.e. raised F1) when preceded by non-high root vowels, the phonetic effect of vowel lowering (F1 raising) might have been negated when the voiced obstruent intervened because the maintenance of strong, unattenuated voicing in obstruents requires significant laryngeal lowering, which lowers F1. Blocking can thus be explained as the lack of phonologization of vowel height harmony when voiced obstruents intervened between the trigger and target vowels.[7]

Other sound changes that have been argued to be the results of hypocorrection include umlaut (Ohala 1994), vocalic nasalization (Hajek 1997), and /u/-fronting (Harrington et al. 2008). In such hypocorrective changes, listeners are assumed to have failed to perceive or attend to the conditioning, or triggering, environment, thus hypocorrective changes often result in the simultaneous emergence of new segments and loss of the conditioning environment. The emergence of contrastive nasal vowels, for example, often takes place with the simultaneous loss of the conditioning nasal (VN > Ṽ). Of course, cases where the conditioning environment remains are not uncommon as well. Beddor (2009) argued, with experimental support, that the coarticulatory gesture might come to be reinterpreted as distinctive from its source segment as a result of the articulatory covariation between the duration of the coarticulatory source (N in the case of the VN > Ṽ change) and the temporal extent of its effects (Ṽ), and the perceived equivalence between the source and the effects. The loss of the conditioning environment might be attributed to the temporal extent of vowel nasalization overwhelming the duration of the triggering source to such an extent that listeners can no longer recover the presence of the triggering nasal.

24.3.2.3 *Hypercorrection*

A hypercorrective change takes place when listeners misattribute intended cues as superfluous and thus incorrectly factor them out. Dissimilation, which refers to restrictions between similar segments co-occuring adjacent to each other or at a distance, has been argued to be an example of hypercorrective change. For example, in the history of Cantonese, when two labial segments occur in the same syllable, the second consonant lost its labiality (e.g. Ancient Chinese *pjam > Cantonese *pin*). Similarly, in the history of Greek and Sanskrit, aspiration in the first consonant disappeared when two aspirated segments occur within the same form (Grassmann's Law; Proto-Indo-European *bend > Sanskrit *banḍ* 'blind', cf. Cser, this volume). Dissimilation like Grassmann's law takes place on this approach when the listener incorrectly parses the incoming signal and misattributes aspiration on the first consonant as coarticulatory aspiration from another aspirated consonant occurring later in the word. Since dissimilatory changes tend to be long distance, phonetic features that dissimilate tend to have long stretching realization, such as labiality, retroflexion, palatality, laryngealization,

---

[7] The fact that -NT- and -lT- sequences also served as blockers was argued to be the result of analogical extension of the original voiced obstruent blocking pattern to -NT-and -lT- sequences where the T segment is phonetically voiced (Paster 2004).

and pharyngealization (Ohala 1993), presumably because these are precisely the type of phonetic cues that are difficult to localize. Another type of sound change that has been analysed as the result of hypercorrection is metathesis, although recent studies have suggested that there might be multiple contributing factors that give rise to metathesis (Blevins & Garrett 1998, 2004, Hume 2004). Like dissimilation, the so-called perceptual metathesis (Blevins & Garrett 2004) involves features of intrinsically long duration, such as retroflexion. When such features are spread out over a sequence of multisegmental strings, they might be reinterpreted in non-historical positions. For example, in Classical Armenian, the linear order of stop (or affricate) + r clusters was regularly inverted in initial (Armenian *artasu* 'tear(s)' < *brewr < Indo-European bʰrēwr) as well as medial positions (*kʰirtn* 'sweat' < *kʰitrn < *swidros; Blevins & Garrett 2004: 129).

24.3.3 Perceptual Compensation for Coarticulation

The twin notions of hypo- and hyper-correction presuppose that there exists a normative process of perceptual compensation or 'correction' for coarticulation. Much research that appeals to hypo- and hyper-correction as explanatory mechanisms for sound change has focused on establishing a normative compensatory pattern. A classic demonstration of perceptual compensation is Mann & Repp's 1980 study of vocalic effects on sibilant perception (see also Nittrouer & Studdert-Kennedy 1987, Mitterer 2006, Yu 2010a). In this study, listeners were asked to classify sibilants in a series of CV continua where C is a synthesized continuum of /s/ to /ʃ/ and V is either /a/ or /u/. They found that listeners are more likely to report hearing /s/ before /u/ than before /a/, presumably because listeners take into account the lowered noise frequencies of /s/ in a rounded vowel context (see Strand & Johnson 1996, Strand 1999, for a potential role of social awareness in this type of perceptual normalization). Similar methodology has been applied to study perceptual compensation for other coarticulatory processes, such as vowel-to-vowel dependencies (Ohala 1994, Beddor & Yavuz 1995), intrinsic vowel pitches (Hombert 1977), intrinsic vowel duration (Gussenhoven 2004, Yu 2010b), and liquid/rhotic coarticulation (Abrego-Collier 2013). Beddor & Krakow (1999) found evidence of perceptual compensation using a metalinguistic rating task; listeners were accurate in rating acoustically identical nasal vowels as 'equally nasal' when both were in non-nasal contexts (e.g. [CṼC]-[Ṽ]) but were less accurate when only one of the two was in a nasal context ([NṼN]-[Ṽ]). Beddor & Krakow (1999) also found that, while listeners' judgements were least accurate when one vowel was in a nasal context and the other in a non-nasal one, the discrimination of vowels in such pairs as [NṼN]-[V] was consistently above chance, suggesting that listeners attribute some but not all of the context-dependent variation to a coarticulatory source (i.e. the flanking nasal). Partial perceptual compensation of this sort, though not a case of outright misperception, might nonetheless provide seeds for future sound changes.

24.4 POTENTIAL LIMITATIONS
AND FUTURE DIRECTION

Experimental investigations on sound change can offer tremendous insights into the physical, physiological, and perceptual mechanisms that potentiate sound change. These advances have also prompted new questions. In this final section, we discuss some of these new puzzles and, in some cases, offer preliminary answers.

24.4.1 Distinguishing between Phonetic Precursors and Gradient Phonologized Processes

An important development in phonetic research is the discovery of language-specific phonetic realizations of phonetic categories. Consider the case of voicing contrast in language. [+voice] consonants are characterized by the "presence of low-frequency spectral energy or periodicity over a time interval of 20-30 msec in the vicinity of the acoustic discontinuity that precedes or follows the consonantal constriction interval" (Stevens & Blumstein 1981: 29). This low-frequency property, as Kingston and Diehl (1994) call it, has multiple supporting subproperties such as voicing during the consonant constriction interval, a low F1 near the constriction interval, and a low f_0 in the same region, as well as enhancing properties such as the duration ratio between a consonant and its preceding vowel. These properties do not all surface in all positions. The contrastive feature [+voice] in English, for example, shows great variability in its phonetic realization.[8] In word-initial position, [+voice] stops are often realized as voiceless unaspirated, even when the preceding word ends in a vowel (Caisse 1982, Docherty 1989, 1992). Kingston & Diehl (1994) interpret such data as showing that speakers choose between two active articulations in producing initial [+voice] stops in English: delay glottal closure until the stop release, or close the glottis but expand the oral cavity to overcome the difficulty of initiating voicing. Such controlled variation is made possible by the fact that there are typically multiple, auditorily independent correlates that serve as distinct bases for a minimal phonological distinction.

According to Kingston & Diehl's (1994) conception of the phonetics-phonology interface then, elasto-inertial, biomechanical, aerodynamic, psychoacoustic, and perceptual constraints delimit what a speaker (or listener) *can* do, but not what they *must* do. A phonemic contrast is thus taken to be 'any difference in the feature content or arrangement of an utterance's phonological representation which may convey a difference in semantic interpretation' and allophones are 'any phonetic variant of a distinctive feature

---

[8]   Advocates of laryngeal realism (Honeybone 2005, Iverson & Salmons 2007) argue that the contrastive laryngeal feature in English is [spread glottis] rather than [voice].

specification or arrangement of such specification that occurs in a particular context' (p. 420 fn.2). If the phonetic realization of phonological distinctions already admits this wide a range of possibilities, it is only reasonable to assume that the range of possibilities between languages is considerably much bigger. Cho & Ladefoged (1999), for example, found the degree of between-language variation in voice onset time (VOT) realization is tremendous. Crucially, VOT values cannot be predicted from knowledge of the phonological contrasts within a language (Ladefoged & Cho 2001). A language lacking a contrast between /k/ and /kʰ/ does not necessarily have the simplest possible VOT, nor would a language with a /k/ ~ /kʰ/ contrast show the largest VOT for /kʰ/. The mapping between measurable phonetic parameters and phonology is thus largely arbitrary; each language must choose a model VOT value for each voicing category (e.g. [voiced], [voiceless unaspirated], and [voiceless aspirated]) that must be specified in the phonology (Cho & Ladefoged 1999, Ladefoged & Cho 2001).

These differences raise methodological problems on two fronts for experimental investigations on sound change. Recall that an important assumption behind all attempts to employ synchronic evidence to explain sound change is the principle of uniformitarianism. It is the belief that whatever phonetic or linguistic principles that operate today must also have operated in the past. The fact that language-specific phonetic implementation is so pervasive raises concerns about the relevance of findings from laboratory investigations today to changes that have taken place at a different point of human history. Here, it is useful to point out that historical sciences, experimental studies of sound change included, necessarily offer only what Andersen (1989) calls a 'rational explication', rather than to provide actual 'causal explanation'. The problem of actuation can at best be answered probabilistically. All one could hope to do is to provide a rational account of how a particular sound change *could* have happened. While the actual phonetic parameters a language utilizes at a particular instance along the time-space continuum might differ, the principles that govern the physical, physiological, aerodynamic, perceptual, and psychological factors involved in language are presumably unbending, as humans are not likely to have evolved so dramatically within the reconstructible timeframe of linguistic history as to require new principles of speech production and perception.

The other issue raised by the findings of language-specific phonetic implementation concerns the nature of 'change'. That is, how can we distinguish effects of constraints of the speech production and perception system (i.e. the seeds or phonetic precursors of sound change) from language-specific phonetic implementation? One way to discern genuine mechanistic causes of variation in speech from language-specific phonetic realization that entails a change in progress is to investigate the amount of control speakers have over the maintenance of subphonemic phonetic differences. Solé (2007), for example, found that English speakers actively maintain durational differences before voiced and voiceless stops regardless of speaking rates, while speakers of Catalan and Arabic do not. Her findings suggest that English has already partially phonologized the effect of consonant voicing on vowel duration, while Catalan and Arabic have not. Similarly, using aerodynamic evidence, Solé (1992, 1995) showed that Catalan speakers do not have as fine-grained a control as American English speakers have over the degree of vocalic nasalization from a tautosyllabic coda nasal, suggesting that vowel nasalization has been phonologized in American English but not in Catalan.

Evidence of phonologization can be established from a perceptual point of view as well. In an attempt to establish whether /u/-fronting, a sound change that has been in progress for the last 20–30 years in standard southern British (SSB), could be linked synchronically to the fronting effects of a preceding anterior consonant, Harrington et al. (2008) examined the production and perception of /u/ by speakers of two age groups, individuals between the ages of 18–20 and those over 50. They found that, for the younger speakers, of /u/ was phonetically more fronted and that the coarticulatory influence of consonants on /u/ was less. Crucially, they also found that younger listeners compensated perceptually less for the fronting effects of the flanking anterior consonants than older speakers. These findings suggest that younger speakers of SSB not only produce a fronter realization of /u/, they also have a fronter category boundary in perceiving this vowel. Such a change in speech production and perception is consistent with the hypocorrective view of sound change laid out above, assuming that young listeners gave up on compensating perceptually for coarticulation.

24.4.2 Structural Factors in Sound Change

While many experimental investigations have focused on identifying the phonetic precursors to sound change, some scholars have questioned whether non-phonetic factors might have a role in shaping phonetically-conditioned sound change (see, for example, Purnell & Raimy, this volume). One potentially important factor is the role structural constraints have in channelling the directionality of sound change. That is, when the listeners have to resolve ambiguities in the speech signal, the set of possible resolutions might not be equally available. Consider the case of phonotactic influence in speech perception. Listeners' perceptual responses are influenced by their knowledge of what are possible and impossible sound sequences in the language (Massaro & Cohen 1983, Pitt 1998, Hallé et al. 1998, Moreton 2002, Berent et al. 2007). For example, when listeners were asked to classify a synthetic /r/-/l/ continuum embedded in a C_i context where C = {t, p, v, s}, they were most likely to report the ambiguous liquid as [r] when C was either /t/ or /p/ and the least when C was /v/ or /s/ (Massaro & Cohen 1983), presumably because *tl-* and *vr-/sr-* sequences are phonotactically ill-formed in English. Thus, phonotactic knowledge might bias misperception-driven sound changes toward phonotactically licit outcomes.

Structural constraints need not be based on phonotactic information extracted from the lexicon, however. Some scholars have recently argued that there exist phonotactic restrictions that are a prioristic, rather than learned from experience (Berent et al. 2007, 2008, Berent 2009, Berent et al. 2009). In Berent et al. (2007), for example, subjects listened to CCVC and CəCVC words where the first two consonants either have a rising (*bn*), plateau (*bd*), or falling (*lb*) sonority profile and were asked to indicate whether the stimulus has one or two syllables. While all three clusters are illegal word-initially in English, subjects nonetheless showed a tendency for preferring sequences that follow the sonority sequencing principle (i.e. *bn* > *bd* > *lb* where X > Y should be interpreted as X is more preferred than Y). The authors contended that their findings support an interpretation where knowledge of the sonority hierarchy comes from universal constraints on language learning; they argued that their findings cannot be reduced to statistical properties of the English lexicon and also rejected a purely phonetic explanation (cf. Peperkamp 2007).

24.4.3 Systematic Sources of Deviation in Modes of Speech Processing

Both the H & H and the listener-oriented models of sound change presuppose that new variants arise only when individuals deviate from their normative mode of speech perception. In the case of the misperception model, listeners must fail to take the coarticulatory context properly into account by either failing to correct for the coarticulatory influence or overanalysing the potential effects of articulation. In the H & H model, sound change is only possible when individuals focus on the 'how' mode of listening instead of the 'what' mode. A question that must be addressed is why such deviation occurs. Ohala (1993) argued that the listeners who fail to properly take coarticulatory contexts into account presumably do not have the necessary linguistic background. Thus, under his theory, new variants must necessarily be introduced by individuals who are acquiring the language for the first time, i.e. children acquiring their first language, or learners of a second language (compare Foulkes & Vihman and Eckman & Iverson, both this volume). Such an assumption, however, might be too restrictive as recent experimental evidence has suggested that the sound system of individuals might change throughout their life times (see Sancier & Fowler 1997, Harrington et al. 2000, Sankoff 2004, Harrington 2006, Evans & Iverson 2007, and also Bowie & Yaeger-Dror, this volume).

Recent studies, which show that perceptual responses to variation in speech may vary as a function of individual differences in cognitive processing style (Stewart & Ota 2008, Yu 2010a, 2013), offer potential answers to the question of systematic deviation in speech perception. Yu (2010a), for example, found that the magnitude of perceptual compensation for coarticulation, in this case, the effect of vocalic rounding on sibilant perception, is modulated by the level of 'autistic traits' the listener exhibits. Neurotypical individuals exhibiting few 'autistic traits' show the least amount of perceptual compensation for coarticulation. That is, an individual's overall Autism-Spectrum Quotient (AQ; Baron-Cohen et al. 2001) is positively associated with the way linguistic information is processed. Individuals with an imbalanced brain type, defined in terms of the difference in empathising and systemizing abilities (as measured by the normalized Empathy Quotient (EQ; Baron-Cohen & Wheelwright 2004) and the normalized Systemizing Quotient (SQ; Baron-Cohen et al. 2003)), have also been found to not perceptual compensate for coarticulation to the same degree as individuals with a balanced brain type (Yu 2013).

These findings have significant ramifications for theories of sound change, particularly in its potential for reconciling the tension between the H & H emphasis on the speaker and the misperception model's focus on the listener. Recall that the misperception model of sound change maintains that innovation in sound change resides in listeners' failure to properly compensate for contextual variation in speech. The findings reviewed above suggest that variability in perceptual compensation need not be confined to accidental misperception at the level of the individual word or utterance, but might exist pervasively within a speech community as a function of inherent individual differences in cognitive makeup (as measured by individual-difference dimensions such as the AQ, EQ, and SQ). Since variation in cognitive processing style has been shown to covary with differences in the listener's response patterns during speech perception, particularly in the case of perceptual compensation for coarticulation, to the extent that such differences in perceptual response may ultimately lead to individual differences in perceptual and production norms, variability in cognitive processing style stands to be a major contributor to the creation of new linguistic variants in sound change. These findings also suggest an alternative source of new variants from the perspective of the H & H approach to sound change, which see sound change as the result of listeners prioritizing the 'how' mode of listening over the 'what'. If new variants are made possible as a result of individual differences in perceptual compensation, the listeners are presumably deemphasizing the influence of coarticulatory contexts in speech in their listening (i.e. the 'how' mode of listening') and may instead be focusing on the content of the signal (i.e. the 'what' mode). While further research is needed to ascertain the nature of the individual variability in perceptual compensation for coarticulation and in speech perception in general, studies on individual differences highlight the importance of understanding how speech perception and production operate at the level of the individual; much information might be obscured by averaging experimental results across individuals (see Jones, this volume).

24.4.4 Beyond Inception

A crucial aspect of the actuation problem concerns the question of how a speech community comes to adopt a new norm. In recent years, proponents of exemplar-based models of sound change (see Bybee, Phillips, and Wedel, all this volume) have argued that sound change may be modelled in terms of shifts in phonetic memory distributions, or exemplar 'clouds' (de Boer 2001, Pierrehumbert 2001, 2002, Wedel 2006, 2007, Yu 2007, Blevins & Wedel 2009), a view anticipated in Paul 1880 (see Murray, this volume). Such models assume that listeners retain fine phonetic details of particular instances of speech (see also Lindblom et al. 1995), new variants introduced by persistent bias factors would accumulate in such a fashion that eventually moves the distributions of exemplars in the direction of the biased variants, presumably as a consequence of convergence via imitation. That is, speakers' production targets are altered along some phonetic dimensions to become more similar to those of their fellow interlocutors (Goldinger 1998,

Shockley et al. 2004, Pardo 2006, Babel 2009, Nielsen 2011, Yu et al. 2011). One source of evidence for phonetic convergence comes from studies on perceptual learning (Norris et al. 2003, Eisner & McQueen 2005, Kraljic & Samuel 2006). These experiments show that listeners can retune their perceptual categories when exposed to a series of oddly pronounced phonemes embedded somewhere in words in the language (e.g. *ob[ʔsf]ene* or *bro[ʔsf]ure* where [ʔsf] is half way between [s] and [f]). Perceptual learning has been shown to generalize across both speaker and test continua (Kraljic & Samuel 2006).

While the ability to imitate and retune perceptually is assumed to be innate (Dijksterhuis & Bargh 2001), imitation is not likely to be the lone driving force behind the systematic propagation of new variants throughout the speech community, since phonetic imitation is not an entirely automatic or unrestricted process. Kraljic et al. (2008), for example, showed that, while perceptual representations are flexible, such changes are 'pragmatic' in nature. Biological sex difference (Namy et al. 2002, Pardo 2006), speaker attitude toward the interlocutor (Yu et al. 2011, Abrego-Collier et al. 2011), and perceived sexual orientation (Yu et al. 2011) have also been associated with phonetic convergence and divergence, suggesting that social factors are important motivators for imitation (Dijksterhuis & Bargh 2001, Babel 2009). Rather than propagating aimlessly and blindly as implied by a simplistic conception of an exemplar-based model of sound change, these findings suggest that new variants are spread across the speech community when they come to be associated with social significance (Weinreich et al. 1968, Eckert 2000, Labov 2001). The continued engagement between phoneticians, laboratory phonologists and psycholinguists on the one hand, and sociolinguists and historical linguists on the other, should yield fruitful results concerning the nature of sound change propagation as part of the actuation process.

24.5 CONCLUSION

The marriage between historical phonology and experimental investigations in phonetics, laboratory phonology, and psycholinguistics has proven to be fruitful. Over the years, cross-pollination of ideas has pushed both enterprises to new advances and generated numerous useful insights. Students in historical phonology are no longer, and must not be, confined to the archives and libraries. The linguistic laboratory offers a wealth of tools, both conceptual and physical. As historical phonology matures as a science, the need for rigour in establishing sound changes must also rise with the time. Only through empirical confirmations can we be confident that conjectures regarding the nature of sound change stand on firm grounding.

PART V

THEORETICAL HISTORICAL PHONOLOGY

CHAPTER 25

....

NATURAL PHONOLOGY
AND SOUND CHANGE

....

PATRICIA J. DONEGAN AND GEOFFREY S. NATHAN

> If we turn now to the actuating principles that determine the general
> changeability of human speech habits, we shall find that the moving power
> everywhere is an impetus starting from the individual, and that there is a
> curbing power in the mere fact that language exists not for the individual
> alone but for the whole community. The whole history of language is, as
> it were, a tug-of-war between these two principles, each of which gains
> victories in turn.
>
> (Jespersen 1922: 261)

25.1 INTRODUCTORY REMARKS

....

NATURAL Phonology (NP) is a theory of the production and perception of speech
sounds.

In saying this, NP draws a crucial distinction between synchronic phonological processes, which arise from articulatory and perceptual necessity, and morphonological
rules, which are conventional. *Processes* are mental, but based in phonetics and inseparable from it. *Rules* describe alternations that may appear to depend on phonetic classes,
but are, because of their conventional nature and morphological conditioning, part of
a language's morphology. Rules relate lexical forms to each other; processes apply in
speech production and perception.

In order to explain the naturalist view of sound change, we must first outline the NP
understanding of linguistic sounds and their processing. NP views phonology as a system of subconscious mental processes that in real time mediate between intended lexical
representations and pronounceable surface representations. In production, the prosody
maps lexical items in morphological and syntactic structures onto a real-time rhythmic score. The scored sequence is submitted to phonological processes that enhance the

perceptibility of its rhythmic divisions (feet, syllables) and its individual sounds, or that enhance the pronounceability of sequences of sounds within their rhythmic domains. In perception, phonological processes that have applied may be 'undone' by the listener to arrive at the intended forms. Essential works in Natural Phonology include Donegan & Stampe (1978, 1979, 2009), Stampe (1969–72/1979, 1987), Donegan (1978/1985, 1993a, 1995), and Nathan (2008, 2009). We focus firmly on NP here; see Scheer (this volume) for some comparison with other frameworks (and also Mailhammer et al. and Kiparsky, both this volume, for some comment on NP).

The vocal tract and perceptual system impose certain pressures or preferences regarding speech sounds, and the sounds of a particular language are shaped by language-specific limits set on these natural pressures. For example, the vocal tract is configured so that voiced obstruents require complex physiological gymnastics to master (Bell-Berti 1975, Ohala 1983, Westbury & Keating 1986, among others).[1] Polynesian languages, among others, lack voiced obstruents, so their speakers have no need to master them. Speakers of Romance languages, on the other hand, must acquire the ability to perform these feats, so they overcome the inherent pressures against voiced obstruents.

Each pressure brings with it a 'solution'—a substitution that avoids the difficult sound (or class of sounds); this substitution behaviour is known in NP as a *process*. Processes are motivated by our physiology, though they apply in speech planning. They are 'natural' (or 'innate') in the sense that they arise in response to the limitations of the human speech endowment.[2] Processes may emerge as the infant learns to associate articulatory gestures or configurations with their audible results, but unlike the rules of generative phonology, they are not learned by observation and comparison of forms. What is learned, in learning to pronounce a language, is to inhibit processes, or to inhibit them under certain circumstances, and thus to pronounce their potential inputs. In sound change, inhibitions on processes may be relaxed, so that additional processes apply, or processes apply more generally. With such changes, speakers' articulatory and perceptual abilities change. Addition of multiple processes may, over time, require reanalysis or relexicalization by learners; thus we observe splits, mergers, sound shifts, and typological changes.

25.1.1 Phonology and Morphonology

This distinction of 'process' *vs* 'rule' is an old one, related to Baudouin's (1895/1972: 161) distinction between divergence *vs* correlation, Sapir's (1921, 1925) mechanical *vs* grammatical processes, Bloomfield's (1933) and Wells's (1949) automatic *vs* non-automatic alternations, and Bazell's (1954) motivated and unmotivated alternations. In some important respects, this correlates with the traditional neogrammarian contrast of sound law *vs* analogy. Generative phonologists, beginning with Halle (1964) and continuing

---

[1] Also, voiceless obstruents differ more from surrounding sonorants—a perceptual advantage.
[2] This view of 'innateness' differs from Chomsky's, since processes are not directly given in the genetic endowment, but arise as the child learns about its capabilities while interacting with the environment.

through Anderson (1981), rejected such a distinction. Lexical Phonology (Kiparsky 1982, Mohanan 1986) reinstated a similar distinction, but the lexical *vs* postlexical contrast coincides only in part with the rule/process contrast, and lexical phonologists have continued to emphasize the study of morphonological rules over postlexical ones. Early Optimality Theory seems to ignore the distinction. Newer varieties of OT distinguish between constraints that apply at the stem *vs* phrase *vs* word levels (e.g. Bermúdez-Otero and Kiparsky, both this volume), but this distinction in constraint application, unlike the rule–process distinction, is a matter of domains of application. It does not provide a general explanation for the most basic difference between rules and processes, namely that the input of rules is pronounceable (though ungrammatical) and that of processes is not.

Morphonological rules may arise from phonological processes and thus may sometimes resemble them, but we cannot, strictly speaking, say that processes 'become' rules. Phonetically motivated processes represent constraints on speaker abilities, but morphonological rules are conventions, part of the learned grammar of a language. Rules may govern speakers' behaviour, but they do not constrain their abilities. NP does not subscribe to the widespread view of a 'life cycle' of phonological rules (*pace* Bermúdez-Otero, this volume), where 'phonetic regularities' become 'phonologized' and then acquire morphological and lexical limitations. Natural phonological processes do not become rules. *Alternations* become rules.

Processes are not mere physical inaccuracies; they are centrally planned, and they are phonological *right from their beginnings* (in children's substitutions, in connected/casual speech, in exaggerated pronunciations, etc.; see section 25.1.3). The processes mediate between the speaker's phonemic or lexical representation or *intention* e.g. English *can't* /kænt/ (fully specified phonetically), and the speaker's *target* e.g. [kʰæ̃ʔt], the representation after it has been adjusted by the processes—i.e. the phonetic representation. Note that the *target* is the phonetic *representation*—not the actual physical output.

Alternations appear because of processes, but further process applications may obscure the phonetic motivation of older processes. If processes that create an alternation are natural, the input is usually recoverable. English *hint* [hĩt] is recoverable as /hɪnt/; nasalized vowels are absent from the inventory, but sonorants are nasalized before nasals, and nasal consonants are deleted in shortening (pre-fortis) environments.

But opacity may be unrecoverable: in Middle English, processes shortened and laxed vowels in particular prosodic environments (as in the second vowel of *divinity*) and changed long vowels in quality (e.g. diphthongizing the second vowel of *divine*). Later prosodic changes eroded the duration distinction and the difference was reinterpreted as a quality distinction (now [ɪ] *vs* [aɪ]). The phonetic motivation and thus the original intentions are no longer recoverable. The quality alternation has become conventional.

It is this conventionality that pushes the alternation into the grammar (the morphonology), even if it remains 'productive' to some degree. Alternations that become unrecoverably opaque often develop morphological conditions (so the alternation only applies with certain affixes, to certain word classes, at morpheme boundaries, etc.). But neither opacity alone nor morphological conditioning alone is the crucial distinction. Morphological conditioning is an *indicator* that an alternation is rule-governed rather than process-governed. Morphological conditioning does not define conventionality; the loss of synchronic phonetic motivation does this.

25.1.2 The Phonetic Basis of Processes: Fortitions and Lenitions

Processes are *mental* responses either to physiological limitations, such as the voicing/obstruence interaction, or to perceptual limitations, such as the fact that nasalization makes vowel contrasts more difficult to perceive. Some responses to perceptual and articulatory limitations are *fortitions*.[3] These processes enhance or optimize individual sounds: e.g. *Non-sonorants are voiceless. Vowels are non-nasal. Non-sonorant consonants are [–continuant]. Vowels, especially if [–labial], especially if [–low], especially if [+high] are [+palatal]*, and so on. For each language, fortitive (usually context-free) processes limit the universe of sounds to an intendable, perceivable phoneme inventory. This is a set of perceptually idealized (prototypical) sounds (see Nathan 2007, 2008). Fortitions may also result in substitutions, especially in lengthening, accented, or other hyperarticulate environments.

Responses to exclusively articulatory limitations, usually associated with optimization of sound sequences, are *lenitions*; these result in fewer or weaker articulatory gestures, or in relaxation of gestural timing requirements. Lenitions include not only 'weakenings' but also assimilations and deletions: e.g. *Obstruents are voiced between voiced sounds. Consonants are continuant between continuants. Sonorants are nasalized adjacent to nasal sonorants*, etc. While these universal processes represent tendencies for all humans, each linguistic community 'selects' a set of processes to be inhibited. The child's acquisition task becomes one of learning not to apply the locally inappropriate set.

Because processes are based on universals of the articulatory and auditory systems, they appear at the earliest stages of language acquisition, and they recur in child language cross-linguistically (Jakobson 1941/1968, Donegan 1978, MacNeilage 2008, etc.). They also occur in unrelated languages around the world, as documented in the implicational universals of Jakobson (1941/1968) and in more recent catalogues such as Ladefoged & Maddieson (1996). Processes are sensitive to implicational conditions: for example, vowel devoicing preferentially applies to higher, intrinsically shorter vowels; loss of frontness and loss of roundness preferentially apply to lower vowels. (Compare the preference laws considered in Mailhammer et al., this volume.) These implicational conditions indicate the essentially *phonetic* motivation of processes, though their categorical application in terms of classes of sounds reflects their *mental* nature. For example, the

---

[3] The terms *fortition* and *lenition* traditionally applied to consonant 'strengthening' and 'weakening' (see Cser and Mailhammer et al., both this volume), but they were developed by Donegan & Stampe (1979: 142–3, 153 ff.) and extended to apply to all classes of sounds, including vowels (Donegan 1978). Earlier, Stampe used the terms 'paradigmatic *vs* syntagmatic', and subsequently Dressler (1985: 44–5) proposed 'foregrounding *vs* backgrounding'.

fact that high vowels often behave as a class, despite their radically different articulatory requirements (e.g. tongue fronted, lips unrounded *vs* tongue retracted, lips rounded) indicates the cognitive (though unconscious) classification of these sounds, a classification system which underlies the concept of 'features'.

25.1.3 Processes as Mental Operations

Lenitions and fortitions are not implemented autonomously by the vocal tract—they are neither accidental nor unavoidable physical events. Rather, they are implemented by the mind, *on behalf of* the vocal tract and perceptual system. Their mental nature is evident from the fact that they do not apply universally, from their role in variation, from evidence that they alter the targets of the articulators, and from counterfeeding applications ('opacity'). If processes were not (at least potentially) under mental control, we might expect them to apply equally in all languages, given equivalent inputs—but they do not. A language community may require that its speakers not apply a given process (as with obstruent devoicing or voicing—many languages have distinctive voiced obstruents; many do not voice allophonically) or it may allow process application to vary, depending on such social influences as formality, frequency, attention, and emphasis. A specific process—like flapping in *latter*, or [t]-deletion in *last*—can be temporarily suspended (as when dictating over the phone, or when pronouncing an infrequent or misunderstood word); this requires that processes be mental substitutions, not purely physiological inaccuracies.

Each process responds to a specific phonetic difficulty, but a speech community may 'select' from alternative responses to a given difficulty. Stops are devoiced by most children at first, and many languages (Hawaiian, Samoan) accept that, as loan substitutions show. In Vietnamese, on the other hand, voiced stops are canonically implosive (Thompson 1965: 24, Kirby 2011: 382); and Fijian requires them to be pre-nasalized (Schütz 1985: 21). Both options may involve more effort than merely voicing a stop, but both enhance the audibility and articulation of the voiced quality.[4] The processes that devoice, implode, or pre-nasalize voiced stops eliminate their inputs as 'possible sounds' in the phonological inventories of these languages.

25.2 WHAT IS A 'SOUND'?

To understand the NP view of how sounds change, we need to consider both the representation and the realization of phonemes. 'Speech sound' is a term used of a recurring element in speech; sequences of such elements make up words. In NP, phonemes are

---

[4] Compare 'hypervoicing' (with different assumptions) in Henton, Ladefoged, & Maddieson (1992).

speech sounds—recurring units of perception, representation, and intention. Phonemes in structuralist and generative phonology are ordinarily defined by the complementary distribution criterion, combined with a (somewhat ill-defined) notion of phonetic similarity. The structuralist and generativist views of the phoneme differ in important ways from NP's view, particularly in that the NP phoneme is not an abstraction. It is, rather, a perceptible, pronounceable, fully specified combination of features—in Baudouin's terms, it is 'the mental image of a sound' (1895 [1972]: 152).

A 'sound'—a recurring element in speech—can be compared to a 'subroutine' in programming; it is called upon many times during the execution and interpretation of larger units such as words and sentences. An extensive discussion of this issue can be found in Nathan (2009), and similar views are found in MacNeilage (2008) and in Lindblom (1992).[5]

Phonemes are the units of long-term mental storage of lexical forms. They are pronounceable—thus, they are units that morphology can manipulate. And they are perceptible, 'graspable' units, so they can differentiate meaning.[6] And because phonemes are perceivable and intendable as themselves, non-automatic morphophonological substitutions (e.g. English *divine* ~ *divinity* [dɪˈvaɪn] ~ [dɪˈvɪnɪti], French *tenir* ~ *tient* [təniʁ] ~ [tjɛ̃] 'to hold', 'holds'), which depend on morphological information, always involve the substitution of phonemes, not allophones, so that 'structure preservation' is a characteristic of lexical (morphophonological) rules.

Phonemes are fully specified sounds, not underspecified abstractions, but they are interpreted within the (natural) phonology in terms of phonetic features. Phonological substitutions affect (and are conditioned by) features, which are the mental mappings between a physical gesture or configuration and its acoustic effect. Thus, [coronal] is a mapping between a tongue-front gesture and a predictable set of formant effects: the automatic mental equivalent of the thought process underlying this linking could be paraphrased as 'if I move my tongue this way, it sounds that way'.[7] NP phonemes thus imply acoustic/auditory specifications combined with (simultaneous) articulatory specifications.

25.2.1 The Phoneme Inventory

The fortitions that apply in a particular language 'cull' possible representations by eliminating dispreferred feature combinations from the inventory of intendable sounds, so

---

[5] Lindblom's discussion of recurring elements notes the development of connections between articulatory gestures or configurations and their auditory results. He suggests that early representations of speech units are syllables, emphasizing articulatory 'trajectories' associated with sound sequences. NP refers, instead, to the end points of such trajectories—so /ma/ is not just represented as the trajectory /ma/ but as the end points, /m/ and /a/.

[6] This is why analysts use minimal pairs—minimal pairs exist because phonemes are perceived as distinct.

[7] This is not to suggest, of course, that such thought processes are conscious.

processes constrain lexical forms. For example, if obstruent devoicing applies obligatorily and context-freely in a language, the language lacks voiced obstruent phonemes; no voiced obstruents are stored or intended. But in the same language, a lenition-like intersonorant voicing may introduce voiced adaptations of intended voiceless obstruents. Hearers experience the same phonetic pressures that underlie speakers' adaptations and they allow similar substitutions, so they can 'undo' the voicing substitution, and thus they normally perceive only the voiceless intention. This interaction between fortitions and lenitions thus results in an inventory of intendable, memorable, perceivable sounds—the phonemes of the language.

This view contrasts with exemplar theory (e.g. Pierrehumbert 2002, 2003a, and also Bybee, Phillips, and Wedel, all this volume), according to which mental representations consist of large sets of exemplars—exact long-term memories of particular phonetic forms, both words and segments. A more moderate version proposed by Bybee (2001) states 'a given linguistic category (say, /p/) will not have just one prototype, but may have several—one for each frequent context' (p. 37). Because exemplars are apparently based on acoustic form, sets of exemplars are required to allow not only for segmental environments, but also for different speakers, slower or faster speech, varying styles, etc. Although there is no doubt that human mental storage is vast, the possibility that each lexical entry will have perhaps hundreds of variants due not only to the segmental environment (e.g. adjacent voicing, nasalization, etc.) but also to speech rate, speaking style, multiple speakers, and other causes of variation seems unlikely. This would require that a speaker select among a wide variety of stored acoustic variants and interpret them in articulatory terms in the ongoing process of speech construction. NP's causal theory of speech perception, where hearers perceive speakers' intentions in terms of their own limitations and habits, eliminates the need for separate stored representations for each segment for each speaking style for each speaker.

In contrast with usage-based models (Bybee 2001, this volume), the NP phoneme is not merely a set of lexical connections or a repeated element used to construct a schema, where /b/ is the beginning of *bad, book, believe*, etc.[8] Such a conception of the phoneme loses the connection between the syllable-initial [b] of such examples and the medial [b]'s of *rubber, baby, robin*, etc. and the final [b]'s of *rub, babe, rob*, etc. These medial [b]'s may weaken, even to [β], or the final [b]'s could be glottalized or devoiced, but these variations in articulation are governed by regular, shared, phonetically motivated processes, which generate them from a single lexical representation and in perception relate them to that representation. The fact that non-prototypical medial [β]'s surface as [b]'s if we sing, or speak syllable by syllable, or accidentally pronounce them out of place in a Spoonerism compels us to argue that they are true units of mental classification. They are certainly not simply due to spelling: this automatic variation occurs in preliterate children, illiterate adults, and speakers of languages like Chinese which lack phonological orthographies. Further evidence that English speakers are, in general, completely unaware of this variation in /b/'s is the ease with which children learn to spell the

---

[8] '[b] is a possible syllable onset (in effect, [b] is a phoneme)' (Bybee 2001: 22–3).

variants with <b>, as well as the lengthy training required for phoneticians to be able to hear the variation that usage-based models claim we store.

25.3 How Can 'Sounds' Change?

25.3.1 Processes 'Change' Sounds in Speech[9]

In speech processing, lexical representations are altered, fortitively or lenitively, to become representations of the sounds speakers actually produce. What Baudouin called 'divergences' create differences between intention/memory and actual pronunciation (1895[1972]). This is the essential problem of, and fact about, phonology.

Natural substitutions are phonetically motivated but they are mental and thus controllable. It is convenient to distinguish the speaker's *intention*—the lexical representation—from the speaker's *target*[10]—that representation as adapted, within the confines of the language, to the demands of speech. A speaker who intends *can't be* /kænt bi/ may adapt that sequence of phonemes to an altered target, [kʰæ̃ʔpˀbi]. The hearer, sympathetically aware of the processes of the language and their motivations, hears the acoustic effects that result from articulation of the target, and *undoes* these adaptations to arrive at the speaker's intentions. The hearer perceives [kʰæ̃ʔpˀbi] as /kænt bi/ because he would pronounce /kænt bi/ as [kʰæ̃ʔpˀbi] himself. This perception of intention rather than phonetic reality is the core intuition behind the Ohala theory of 'misperception' as a source of sound change (see Yu, this volume). But most of the time sounds don't change, because the 'misperception' is an accurate perception of an intention.

25.3.1.1 *Articulatory Planning*

Phonetic variability in the realization of lexical representations is not just random failure to achieve an articulatory intention, by overshoot, undershoot, mistiming, interpolation, etc. Evidence that substitutions are centrally coordinated comes in part from the fact that, though universally motivated, they are not instantiated in all languages. If speakers have a choice in the matter of articulatory precision or can learn to control it, then undershoot or non-undershoot is not simply the result of an inability of the articulators to reach their target.

The precise timing of speech gestures would be impossible without central planning. Differences in the inertia of different articulators, in conduction speeds of different nerves, etc. require central coordination. Speakers must plan articulations in ways that cope with and anticipate particular phonetic requirements. These phonetic

---

[9] Changes in lexical representations of words due to analogy are not phonological processes and are not addressed here, nor are other morphologically motivated or contact-induced changes that are not strictly speaking 'sound changes'.

[10] The 'intention–target' distinction is clearly drawn in Moosmüller (2007).

requirements are those of the intended sounds—some of which may not even appear in the phonetic representation, or target. The adjustments are independent of each other and occur simultaneously; their coordination cannot simply be left to chance. Experimental results of many kinds (e.g. Whalen 1990, Boyce, Krakow, & Bell-Berti 1991, Kingston & Diehl 1994, Wood 1996, Moosmüller 2007, etc.) argue for central planning of phonetic details.

25.3.2 Diachronic Phonetic Change

Historical sound changes arise when a group of speakers begins to allow a process to apply where it had not applied before. Most, if not all, regular sound changes are motivated by the demands of articulation and audition; that is, they occur for phonetic reasons. The question of why a phonetic change—application of a previously suppressed or latent process—happens at a particular time in a particular place (the 'actuation problem') probably has no answer, but if a process *is* accepted (presumably under certain social conditions), then the pronunciation in the community changes.[11]

Allophonic variants, or 'divergences' from the lexical representation, may be introduced, at first variably, by optional process application. For example, a syllabic consonant may de-syllabify, as in [pʰlis kʰɑr] for *police car*, or may be emphatically syllabified ([pʰl̩'liːz] *pl-lease!*). A vowel may labialize after a labial glide ([wɑʃ] → [wɒʃ] *wash*), or may lose labiality before a labial glide ([ɔu̯nɔu̯] ~ [əu̯nəu̯] *oh, no!*).

In child speech, processes are at first obligatory, and are gradually inhibited—to the limits of the community's tolerance.[12] Within the adult speech community, processes (with the same phonetic motivations as in children[13]) may first appear as optional or occasional substitutions, occurring only in limited contexts (phonological and stylistic), and perhaps only in particular lexical items. Bybee (2001: 40 ff., and see also Bybee, this volume) shows a number of examples[14] where apparently identical phonological environments do not condition identical substitutions: e.g. *every* must have two syllables, but *memory* may have two or three; *summary* may reduce to two syllables, but *summery* does not. The differences appear to be related to word frequency. Phonetic changes, particularly reductive ones, often appear more advanced in higher-frequency words (Bybee claims), and are resisted in less-frequent words, perhaps in aid of disambiguation or for simpler recognition of rarer words.

---

[11] If a processes applies occasionally but is not accepted, the novel pronunciation vanishes.
[12] The gradual inhibition of childhood processes is paralleled by OT's demotion of innate well-formedness constraints below relevant faithfulness constraints. This NP–OT similarity is not obvious in the OT literature.
[13] Most well-studied instances of sociolinguistic variation, e.g. elements of various American vowel shifts, consonant cluster simplification, etc., are well-known processes. Shared phonetic motivation, however, need not imply continuous application from childhood.
[14] Some were observed by Zwicky (1972), who treated them as the result of application of optional fast-speech rules.

Bybee interprets this as evidence that each lexical item has a particular set of lexical representations that depend on the item's use. But such differences in pronunciation need not imply different lexical representations; rather, such variation may instead reflect the sensitivity of process application to pragmatic facts of language use—process application may depend on factors like word frequency, redundancy (or topic familiarity), degree of formality, tempo, etc. Thus, variable process applications may depend on a specific speaking situation (cf. Labov 1994: 157–8).

Within a community, a process that is at first largely inhibited and applies only occasionally may increase its frequency and range of application, generalizing its (phonological and 'usage-based') conditions for application. As the new divergence becomes accepted, learners may allow the process to apply with diminishing inhibitions. If the process becomes uninhibited (obligatory), it ultimately becomes an actual constraint on speaker abilities. For example, unrounding of front vowels became obligatory in Middle English, and English speakers today cannot easily pronounce French, German, or Chinese words with front rounded vowels. More recently, in many varieties of American English, /ɒ/ has unrounded to /ɑ/, and Californian speakers who obligatorily unround low vowels find it hard to pronounce or perceive *caught* [kʰɒt] differently from *cot* [kʰat]. When a process becomes obligatory, speaker abilities have changed.

25.3.3 Variable Process Inhibition

25.3.3.1 *Lenitions*

Lenitions apply first, most frequently, and most generally to frequent items and set phrases (cf. Phillips, this volume); Stampe pointed out long ago (1979: 7–8) that while *I don't know* can reduce to [ãɔ̃nõ̯ũ̯], a similar phrase like *I dent noses* cannot so reduce, and while *I think* in *I think it's raining* can reduce to [aɛ̯ hĩŋk], it cannot in *I think, therefore I am*. Common usages like phatic phrases, anaphorics, clitics, or function words are particularly susceptible. Glide loss is more likely in *I'll* [ɑl] than in *aisle* [ɑi̯l], and the assimilative stopping of /z/ before [n] occurs in *isn't* [ɪdn̩t] or *doesn't* [dʌdn̩t] but not in *pleasant* or *reasoning*. French *je suis* [ʒə sɥi] 'I am' and *je (ne) sais pas* [ʒə se pɑ] 'I don't know' can reduce to [ʃɥi] and [ʃepɑ], but *je saute* [ʒə sot] 'I jump' cannot reduce to *[ʃot]. Bybee (this volume) cites numerous examples of lenitive or reductive changes that diffuse from high-frequency to low-frequency words. Inhibition of lenitions occurs in more self-conscious or careful speech.

25.3.3.2 *Fortitions*

In addition to constraining the phonemic inventory, fortitions apply first, most frequently, and most fully to accented or emphasized forms, in situations that favour enhancement or exaggeration. They apply most often at the edges of phonological constituents,[15] so initial stops may be aspirated or tensed, final stops may be

---

[15] The larger the constituent, the more susceptible to fortitive changes.

glottalized or devoiced, etc. (Donegan & Stampe 1978, cf. Fougeron & Keating 1996, Keating et al. 1999). This does not necessarily mean that fortitions apply more to infrequent forms—fortition application may be orthogonal to frequency. Consider the fronting of /ou/ to [ɛṳ] in some East Coast dialects (Philadelphia, Baltimore): *nose* and *noes* (as in *The noes have it*) seem equally likely to front to [nɛṳz] despite the radical difference in frequency of occurrence.

25.4 REANALYSES: CHANGES IN REPRESENTATIONS

Although the term 'sound change' may refer to the introduction of allophonic differences, it more often refers to changes in lexical representations. This can involve the introduction of new phonemes, loss of phonemes through mergers, sound shifts, or changes in the lexical representations of words without changes in the phoneme inventory (see Salmons & Honeybone, this volume, for an overview of structuralist approaches to such splits, mergers, phonologizations etc.). Phonetic changes do not necessarily change lexical representations, because many changes—especially lenitions—are undoable and transparent, so listeners can subconsciously account for the occurrence of sounds that are eliminated by fortitions from their inventories of intentions.

25.4.1 New Phonemes

Lexical forms are susceptible to changes by fortition. If diphthongization of /e/ and /o/ to [ɛi] and [ou̯] becomes obligatory in stressed syllables, learners may interpret the diphthongal variety as the basic form and consequently, unstressed or short variants like [e, o] will be reinterpreted as allophonic reduced forms. Or if /ɛi/ frequently dissimilates to [ai̯], [ai̯] may become, for learners, the lexical form. Obligatory fortitions can change lexical forms, even if they are context-sensitive. For example, the /əi̯/ which arose from Middle English /i̯/ (the PRICE vowel) remained [əi̯] in some environments in a variety of English dialects (Canada, New England (now limited to Massachusetts Islands), Maryland, Virginia, and some Irish dialects). In these dialects, only the (contextually) lengthened /əi̯/ was lowered to become [ai̯]. But where this lengthened /əi̯/ was lowered obligatorily, some of these dialects now show evidence of a phonemic /əi̯/-/ai̯/ difference, even though the two are nearly in complementary distribution (see Vance 1987b). The phenomenon known as 'Canadian Raising' may be, in some dialects, a result of this lowering.[16]

---

[16] The case for raising in Canadian English is not altogether clear (*pace* Trudgill 1986). In some dialects, [əi̯] ~ [ɑi̯] variation may be raising, but in others, [əi̯] and [ɑi̯] are distinct percepts, and thus

The best understood instances of development of new phonemes from former allophones involve the application of multiple processes. One process results in a conditioned substitution, and the other results in the disappearance of (relevant aspects of) the conditioning environment. Non-low-vowel umlaut in Middle High German (MHG) illustrates such a split. Umlaut fronted vowels before a high front vocalic, /i(ː), j/: *stain > stein* 'stone', *batti > betti* 'bed', *mûsi* [muːs-i] > [myːsi] 'mice'. Twaddell (1938/1963) claimed that umlaut applied generally in Old High German (OHG) but was indicated only for short /ɑ/ (written *e*, e.g. *stein, betti*), which represented a merger with short /ɛ/, also written *e*, as in *weg* 'way', *geba* 'gift'. Other umlauted vowels were generally not written as umlauted until MHG, after loss of unaccented /j/ and reduction or loss of unstressed /i/. Iverson & Salmons (1996a) and Schulze (2010: 40–1) argue that /o(ː)/ and /u(ː)/ did not in fact front as early as /a/, but only later. Twaddell may have erred regarding the timing of non-low-vowel umlaut, but we are concerned here with his groundbreaking observation that umlaut was ordinarily indicated in the orthography only when its conditioning palatal environment was lost—in effect, when the difference became phonemic.[17]

Various authors (e.g. Hooper 1976a, Hyman 1976, Janda 2003, and see also Kiparsky, this volume) find this paradoxical. Janda (2003: 409 ff.) claims that if the phonetic conditions for an allophonic variant are lost, the variant would no longer occur, and he says that 'phonemic split' must occur *before* the loss of the phonetic conditions for the variants—possibly because of phonetic distance between the two allophones.

25.4.1.1 *Phonetic Distance?*

Phonetic distance is problematic, because the phonetic distances that represent distinctions vary widely from language to language. For example, Spanish speakers struggle with English /i/ *vs* /ɪ/, and Japanese speakers have well-known difficulties distinguishing English /r/ and /l/, though these are perceived easily by English speakers.[18] For speakers of English, [ɛj] and [ej] are virtually indistinguishable, but for speakers of the northern dialect of Pohnpeian, they contrast: e.g. /sɛjsɛj/ means 'paddling' and /sejsej/ means 'haircut' (Ken Rehg, p.c. 2009). And if phonetic similarity were an absolute requirement for the interpretation of sounds as the same phoneme, then the allophones of English /oɰ/, which range from [o] in *notation* to [ɛɰ] or, in some British dialects, [ɛy] in *no*, would present a problem. Without something like a phonetic similarity criterion, we might be stumped by cases like English [h] and [ŋ], which are in complementary distribution, but which no one regards as allophones. But as Bazell (1954) noted, it is not lack of phonetic similarity that prevents these two sounds from being perceived as a single phoneme—it is the absence of any phonetically motivated *substitution* of one for the other that requires them to be perceived as distinct.

---

distinct phonemes (Vance 1987b, Donegan 1993a). If obligatory fortitions constrain the inventory, obligatory fortitive lowering of only the lengthened [əi̯] would account for this split.

[17] Kiparsky (this volume) presents an alternative view, which we do not have space to address. See also Hale et al. and Bermúdez-Otero (both this volume) for other perspectives on phonologization.

[18] Although English [ɹ] and [l] are late-acquired and might therefore be viewed as difficult in production, there is no evidence that children confuse them in perception.

25.4.1.2 *Effects of Opacity*

We need not resort to 'phonetic distance'. The claim that split must occur before loss of the conditioning factor ignores the existence of opaque forms. The umlaut split began with assimilative fronting of the stressed vowel before a syllable containing a high palatal. Lexical forms were constrained by the fortitive processes that eliminate labiopalatals, so /yː/, for example, was not a phoneme in OHG or early MHG.

(1) MHG nonlow umlaut forms, no lexical /y(ː), ø(ː)/:

    'mouse'   'mice'

    /muːs/   /muːs-i/   Labial vowels are non-palatal.

    [muːs]   [myːsi]   Umlaut process gives surface labiopalatals.

Later, assimilation was accompanied by depalatalization of the unstressed 'trigger' or conditioning factor, but this loss, like umlaut itself, did not immediately affect phonological representations:

(2) Later MHG intermediate forms:

    /muːs/   /muːs-i/   Labial vowels are non-palatal. Suffix is palatal.

    [muːs]   [myːs-i ~ myːsɛ] Umlaut and optional palatal reduction apply.

The fortitions eliminating labiopalatals continued to apply, and the lexical forms kept their back labial vowels. And since optional palatal reduction did not affect the lexical forms, the umlaut palatalization could continue, creating opaque forms like [myːsɛ].

But when loss of the palatal 'trigger' became general, learners would have heard *only* singulars like [muːs] and plurals like [myːsɛ]. The reduced suffix was insufficient to account for umlaut, so learners had to assume that the labiopalatal [y] was part of the speakers' intentions, and that the fortitions that would eliminate such vowels (e.g. delabialization and/or depalatalization of labiopalatals) could not apply in the language they were learning.

(3) New forms, learned from speakers with general palatal reduction:

    /muːs/   /myːs-ɛ/   Delabialization of palatals inhibited, /y/ is admissible.

    [muːs]   [myːsɛ]   Umlaut is conventional. The alternation becomes a rule.

When the umlaut alternations were no longer phonetically motivated, as lenitions, the new vowels and alternations had to be learned as conventions. With loss of the palatal 'trigger', [y(ː)] and [ø(ː)] could no longer be perceived as assimilatively fronted allophones of /u(ː)/ and /o(ː)/. Learners had to perceive [y(ː)] and [ø(ː)] as /y(ː)/ and /ø(ː)/, and eventually scribes began to spell these now perceptible umlaut vowels. Speakers also began to extend the alternation, now morphological, to cases lacking original phonetic justification.

There are many other examples of split. Having heard a vowel with nasality that cannot be perceived as due even to an elided intended nasal sound, learners perceive the vowel's nasality as basic rather than derived, as happened in French. (If the nasal consonants are restorable, the vowels may remain lexically non-nasal.)[19] In cases like this, more conservative speakers know that the conditioning feature is there, but fail to produce it. The learner does not hear the intention, but only the opaque result, and thus arrives at a different lexical representation from older speakers.

Objections to accounts of re-phonemicization where variants seem to become distinctive just when the conditioning environment is lost seem to assume that allophones are purely mechanical effects. If this were true, then loss of the trigger—the following palatal (in umlaut) or the conditioning nasal consonant (in nasalization)—would imply loss of the assimilation. But both the assimilation and the loss of the trigger apply in speech planning, as argued above. They apply simultaneously,[20] creating opaque phonetic forms in the speech of adults. Examples of such opaque phonetic forms that are clearly synchronic include stops affricated in Japanese before high vowels as in *mat-u, mat-te, mat-imasu*, respectively [matsu, matte, matʃimasu] '(forms of) wait'. When not adjacent to voiced sounds, high short vowels devoice and delete (e.g. [matsu̥] ~ [mats]), but the affricates never revert to stops *[mat] when the vowels that cause affrication are lost (Vance 1987a).

Another 'living' example of opacity is the much-discussed vowel nasalization in Sea Dayak (Kenstowicz & Kisseberth 1979, McCarthy 2003, see Scott 1957 for original data). Rightwards vowel nasalization is entirely allophonic, but a nasal consonant may come to be adjacent to a vowel by optional cluster simplification. For example, /naɲa/ 'straighten' is pronounced [nãɲã?], but /naŋga/ 'set up a ladder' can be either [nãŋga?] or [nãɲa?]. As in many cases of opacity, the lack of nasalization marks the presence of an underlying consonant. To the extent that the oral member of the consonant cluster is still stored by speakers, the nasalization continues to be allophonic, despite the surface 'contrast'.

Mielke et al. (2003) argue that opacity is unnecessary if we assume instead that the nasalization is lexicalized (though they do not mention that such lexicalization would imply additional phonemes). While not impossible, neither is this necessary in a derivational model, even one without 'intermediate levels'.[21] As long as cluster simplification is optional, and [nãŋga?] varies with [nãɲa?], learners can know that the nasality-inhibiting stop is part of the speaker's intention, even if it is not part of the output.

Furthermore, this solution leads to difficulties in other, similar cases: English shortens stressed vowels before tautosyllabic voiceless consonants, *hat* [hæt] *vs had* [hæːd] but

---

[19] One might claim that nasal consonants are restorable in some French words (e.g. determiner–adjective pairs like *un/une* 'one', *fin/fine* 'fine'). But the nasal is not restorable in other words (like *vin* 'wine', *tant* 'such', *dont* 'whose'); this requires that the nasalized vowels must be admitted as phonemes in these words—and therefore can be perceived as phonemes in *un, fin*, etc. Compare the restorable English case in section 25.1.1.

[20] No ordering is required, except that lenitions follow fortitions. The environments for both lenitions—the umlaut assimilation and the unstressed vowel reduction—are present in lexical forms like /muːs-i/, so both processes apply simultaneously, giving [myːsɛ] (cf. Donegan & Stampe 1978).

[21] In Sea Dayak, forms like [nãɲa?] are attested, not theoretical. But [nãɲa?] is *not* intermediate in a derivation. Nasalization and cluster simplification apply simultaneously when /naŋga/ → [nãɲa?].

also frequently devoices final obstruents, yielding what look like minimal pairs: [hæt] *vs* [hæːt]. What is technically surface opacity is almost impossible for native speakers to hear, so beginning phonetics students cannot remember to write the length, but always hear the *phonemic* voicing contrast.

Opacity also accounts for process loss. Final obstruent devoicing in Yiddish was lost because schwa apocope made the voicing alternation opaque: [tɑk]/[tɑgə] 'day/days' became, with apocope, [tɑk]/[tɑg]. Although speakers who applied both processes to lexical forms /tɑg, tɑg-ə/ could maintain final devoicing,[22] learners encountering only the alternation [tɑk]/[tɑg] could not assume that final devoicing was allowed (cf. King 1980). The addition ('phonemicization') of the umlaut vowels to the German inventory implies suppression of the fortitive process(es) that would eliminate them.

25.4.2 Mergers

Languages can 'lose' phonemes by merger (see Gordon, this volume). Allowing unrounding of low vowels in various North American dialects merges the original /ɒ/: /ɑ/ difference distinguishing *caught: cot* and *dawn: Don*. Mergers often arise through fortitive processes. Lenitive processes may neutralize oppositions superficially, but since lenitions are typically context-sensitive, they rarely merge sounds in all occurrences. For example, American English /nd/ and /n/ in words like *bands: bans*, or *tends: tens*, neutralize before /z/. Elsewhere, /nd/ and /n/ often have distinct realizations: *banded: banned*, *banding: banning*, so the underlying representations of *bands* and *bans* remain distinct.[23] When a lenition neutralizes sounds or sequences in certain contexts, but the sounds remain distinct elsewhere, the overall set of oppositions is unaffected.

Fortition processes, on the other hand, are often context-free, at least regarding segmental context. When they apply obligatorily, they merge sounds in all their occurrences. Thus, the surface neutralizations they produce easily become mergers of underlying form, because they leave no surface alternations—as with the /ɒ/-/ɑ/ merger mentioned above. Well-known historical examples include the Sanskrit merger of Indo-European *e and *o with *a (Burrow 1965: 103 ff.), by loss of colour of mid vowels; Sanskrit short /ɑ/ was [ʌ], so *e, *o > [ʌ] (Allen 1953: 58). The Eastern Yiddish mergers of /y/ with /i/ and /ö/ with /e/ (Sapir 1915) were also the result of loss of vowel colour—in this case, the unrounding of palatal vowels. Merger can also result from addition of colour, as when Gutob-Remo *ɨ merged with /u/ in the Mundlipada dialect of Remo, and with /i/ in Gutob (Zide 1965: 44). And the epenthetic or 'enunciative' vowel of Dravidian, elsewhere /ɨ/, becomes [u] in Kannada and Telugu, merging with original or underlying /u/ (Bright 1975: 35–9).

---

[22] By the general (and only) ordering principle 'fortitions first; lenitions last' (Donegan & Stampe 1979), (fortitive) final devoicing would not apply to the result of (lenitive) apocope.

[23] The fact that a frequent surface form may be generalized (paradigm levelling) is a matter of morphology.

The loss of a length distinction can result in mergers, as when Classical Latin short *a* and long *ā* merged as Vulgar Latin *a* (Romeo 1968: 61) (although distinctions between the other long and short Latin vowels were maintained as a tense/lax contrast in Late Latin). A well-known example of wholesale merger—the Greek convergence of six different vocalisms (ι, η, ει, οι, υ, υι) as [i] (Sturtevant 1940: 30)—was the result of a variety of processes (raising, monophthongization, etc.). But mergers may also result from lenitive processes. If the glide of /ae̯/ always assimilates to the nucleus, giving [ɑɑ] = [ɑː], the diphthong may merge with a monophthong /ɑː/ in the system.

Mergers are problematic for theories that view dispersion—maximization of phonological distinctions—as the motivation for context-free changes, because mergers eliminate distinctions. In NP, the motivations for changes are phonetic, not structural. Mergers may result when processes maximize or exaggerate phonetic properties at the expense of phonological distinctiveness. Thus enhancement of palatality by raising merges /e/ with /i/, or by unrounding merges /y/ with /i/, and by both also merges /ø/ with /i/. The mutual independence of processes (each with its *phonetic* causalities) underlies the existence of such mergers.

Mergers occur when a phonetically motivated process is accepted by a community in spite of potential ambiguities. But there seems to be a kind of natural selection that limits such occurrences. We might regard this as 'natural rejection': substitutions which result in mergers are often—though not always—rejected by the speech community. This is not a novel view, as our Jespersen epigraph indicates.

25.4.3 Direction of Change and 'Perceptual Bias'

In the view of Ohala (1981, 1993) or Blevins (2004a) (and see Yu and Blevins, both this volume), perceptual similarity between the phonetic forms of phonologically different segments presumably underlies sound change. But if the problem is simply that hearers cannot easily distinguish possible forms of, say, *input*—like [ĩnpʊt], [ĩm̃pʊt], and [ĩmpʊt], what accounts for the directionality of the change? What accounts for the 'movement' from two distinct phonetic forms to two forms where one is always mistaken for the other, e.g. /i/ and /y/, where /y/ is always heard and reproduced as /i/—but not vice versa? Similarly, while there are numerous cases of /θ/ > /f/, there are virtually no known cases of the reverse, /f/ > /θ/ (Blevins, this volume, cites one case). A simple 'confusion' theory based solely on acoustic similarity would predict an equal number in each direction. Evidence from second language acquisition of English and dialect development (Cockney, for example) confirms the unidirectionality we cite.

Blevins (2004a: 286–8) refers to 'perceptual biases' as a possible factor governing the direction of phonological interpretation. NP attributes such biases to processes with both perceptual and articulatory motivations, thus offering a full theory of 'perceptual bias'. 'Perceptual bias' may be bias toward segments with better perceptual properties ([i] is more clearly palatal than [y]), or less demanding articulations (stops require less precision than fricatives), or toward sequences with less demanding articulations ([np] requires two gestures, while [mp] requires one, Spanish [aɣua] 'water' requires full closure between continuants, while [aɣua] does not).

Processes that optimize segments (e.g. Kannada [i] becomes [u]) limit the phonological inventory, and those that optimize sequences (e.g. *tenth* /tɛn-θ/ becomes [tʰɛ̃n̪θ]) account for phonetic variants that occur in speech. The former constitute learner bias by requiring acquisition of fewer segments; the latter contribute to bias by allowing more-optimal sequences.

25.5 System Changes

If, as NP claims, the motivations for sound changes are phonetic rather than structural, then what are we to make of changes that seem to affect entire systems in languages?

25.5.1 Chain Shifts

Sound shifts—changes in the realization of entire systems of vowels or consonants—may appear to be systematically motivated. Martinet (1955) and other structuralists emphasized the role that the entire system of oppositions might play in sound change, proposing push and drag chains, suggesting that a change in the realization of one phoneme might be the cause of changes in the realization of others. If, for example, voiced stops become voiceless, a single process applies, even though several sounds may be affected. But when voiceless stops become aspirated *and* voiced stops become voiceless, one might suspect that something more systematic is at work. The changes look like a system-wide chain of events.

Two characteristics of chain shifts are definitive (see also Gordon, this volume). First, the processes that underlie the shifts appear to be 'context-free', often involving fortitive rather than lenitive processes. If they show conditioning, the conditioning is prosodic (length, accent, syllable structure), rather than segmental. Second, the changes do not result in the expected merger. In a chain shift, /ɒ/ may become /ɑ/ and /ɑ/ may become /a/, and so on—but the [ɑ]'s from original /ɒ/ do not become /a/, so the oppositions are preserved.

The phonetic motivations of context-free or 'unconditioned' processes are always present; speakers are always under some pressure to enhance the perceptibility of particular phonetic features. But these processes are held in check by the requirements of the community—some enhancements are acceptable, but others are rejected. A phonetic enhancement (for example, vowel raising enhances labiality, or lowering enhances sonority) may be less welcome when it results in confusability—as when the /ɒ/ of words like *caught* becomes /ɑ/, as in *cot*. Such mergers occur, but the unrounding of /ɒ/ would be more acceptable if /ɑ/ has itself undergone a change. The change of /ɒ/ to /ɑ/ does not *cause* the change of /ɑ/ to /a/, nor does the change of /ɑ/ to /a/ *cause* that of /ɒ/ to /ɑ/.

But it may be that /ɒ/ to /ɑ/ is more tolerable when /ɑ/ has become /a/. The structuralist principles of Jakobson & Martinet may play a role in the occurrence of changes—but as constraints rather than as causes. System gaps may seem to 'drag' elements of the system into new realizations, but the gaps themselves are not causal. If maintenance or increase of phonological contrasts were the motivation, mergers would remain inexplicable, but the enhancement of *phonetic* properties (cf. Purnell & Raimy, this volume) can account for occurring changes, whether chains, mergers, or merely isolated variation.

25.5.2 Changes in Type

'Language type' refers to a constellation of phonological, morphological, and syntactic characteristics that seem to pattern together across languages. Vowel reduction, diphthongization, tense–lax vowel distinctions, vowel and consonant shifts, contour tones, consonant clusters, complex syllables, and iambic or monosyllabic word patterns tend to co-occur, while vowel harmony, monophthongal vowels, stable vowel and consonant systems, level tones, geminate consonants, simpler syllable canons, and trochaic or polysyllabic word forms often co-occur (Donegan 1993b). Donegan & Stampe (1983, 2004) examined the case of Austroasiatic, where the western (Munda) and eastern (Mon-Khmer) branches of the family are typologically not merely different, but opposite. They noted the co-occurrence of the former cluster of phonological characteristics (and rising phrase and word accent) with head-first ('VO') ordering, prepositions, proclisis, prefixing, and isolating or fusional morphology, *vs* the latter (and falling phrase and word accent) with head-last ('OV') ordering, postpositions, enclisis, suffixing, and agglutinative morphology. They proposed that the unifying force behind these pervasive tendencies is rhythm, that only a shift in rhythm could explain the wholesale quality of the changes, and that major changes in syllable type, word shape, affixation, etc., which are sometimes viewed as typological indicators, can occur as a result of rhythm change.

Changes in rhythm may include changes between falling and rising accent and changes in patterns of isochrony—shifts among so-called mora, syllable, and stress timing. For example, the Chamic languages changed in type (Thurgood 1999); this branch of Austronesian has become atypically final-accented, and its phonology, morphology, and syntax have changed accordingly. In Old French, vowels diphthongized in stressed open syllables and reduced in unstressed syllables, suggesting a shift from the mora-timing of Latin toward stress-timed rhythm. A subsequent series of changes monophthongized the diphthongs and weakened or deleted syllable-final consonants (e.g. Pope 1934: 103, 190), leading to an open-syllable pattern that became the syllable-timing of modern French. Changes in rhythm can result in wholesale changes in the application of phonological processes because processes are sensitive to prosodic factors such as duration, accent, and syllabication.

It is not clear exactly how such changes occur, or how (or to what degree) language contact is involved. Post (2011) offers evidence that rhythm is particularly susceptible to the influence of contact. Although no consistent pattern seems to predict which aspects of a language change first (word order, word accent, phrase accent, etc.), it seems that rhythmic change is central to typological shifts.

25.6 CONCLUSION

Phonologies are the result of natural processes constrained by speech-community-specific restrictions; they may be limited in feature-specific ways or suppressed entirely. Sound change is change in the restrictions a language community imposes. When Californians merge /ɑ/ and /ɒ/, they have given free rein to a phonetically motivated process unrounding low vowels. As a consequence, they can no longer acquire new words with /ɒ/, nor do they even notice that East-Coast Americans continue to maintain this distinction. Speaker abilities have changed.

The processes that apply in speech production may be undone in perception, so that contextual variants are not necessarily perceived at face value; hearers can interpret speakers' productions and arrive at their intended articulations. Alternative perceptions of the same acoustic configuration are important in sound change, but if an acoustic configuration is truly ambiguous, the directionality of change must be attributed to some articulatory or perceptual advantage.

Where new phonemes develop, they do so because learners are unable to attribute some feature of a sound to an aspect of its environment and must accept as an intention what is, for older speakers, a consequence of an intended but unrealized environment. Alternations fossilize when the motivation of a process is hidden by additional processes, so that learners can no longer attribute the alternants to phonetic adjustments, but instead come to perceive them as associated with morphological patterns. Such changes can require that a process be suppressed.

Chain shifts arise from phonetic motivations. 'Holes' in the phonological pattern may *allow* the context-free changes that typify such shifts, but they do not *cause* the changes. Changes in type are often associated with changes in rhythm, which may affect whole constellations of processes, tilting the phonetic advantage in one way or another.

Our discussion has interpreted 'sound change' narrowly—we have not included the analogical generalization of an alternation to forms where it does not originate phonetically (as umlaut has generalized to new plurals), nor have we included the 'lexical diffusion' that results from gradual relexicalization of individual words. Regular sound changes, like synchronic phonological processing and the reanalyses that sound changes may require, involve the interaction of production and perception. Sound change is motivated by phonetics and constrained by community consensus.

CHAPTER 26

....

PREFERENCE LAWS
IN PHONOLOGICAL CHANGE

....

ROBERT MAILHAMMER, DAVID RESTLE,
AND THEO VENNEMANN

26.1 INTRODUCTION

DURING the 1980s Robert Murray and Theo Vennemann developed an approach to
language change, which, building on theories of markedness and naturalness, aimed to
elucidate the motivations behind sound changes. From the beginning this theory stood
in apparent contrast to traditional approaches, which were largely descriptive. The key
assumptions of this approach are that certain linguistic structures are more preferred
than others and that languages strive towards improvement in line with these preferences. This perspective has provided theoretical underpinnings for more recent phonological theories, most notably Optimality Theory.

We introduce the concept of preference laws, giving an overview of its development,
its most significant features and key applications, as well as discussing critical points
raised in the literature. The chapter is structured as follows. Section 26.2 introduces the
theoretical foundations and basics of preference-law theory. In section 26.3 we apply it
to motivating sound change. In sections 26.4 and 26.5 developments and controversies
involving preference laws are discussed. The main points are summarized in section 26.6.

26.2 PREFERENCE LAWS
AS A THEORETICAL CONCEPT

In a nutshell, preference laws are graded statements about quality. The concept itself
is a generalization of Jakobson's markedness theory (see e.g. Jakobson 1941). Instead
of using a contrasting pair of terms 'marked' *vs* 'unmarked', it works with a gradation

'less marked', 'more preferred' or simply 'better'. In other words, preference laws make a statement about a preferred structure with respect to some parameter, in the sense that 'X is more preferred than Y in terms of Z; Z is a gradable property of X and Y'. The preferences themselves are based on the criteria that Jakobson outlined in his markedness theory (see Scheer, this volume, and see also Holt, this volume, on uses of markedness in change), but essentially they are theorems:

- CROSSLINGUISTIC DISTRIBUTION: The more languages show a certain property, the more preferred it is.
- FIRST LANGUAGE ACQUISITION: The earlier and quicker a certain feature is acquired, the more preferred it is.
- APHASIA: The longer it takes for a certain structure to become lost in aphasia, the more preferred it is.

The qualitative statement implicit in the preference laws comes from the assumption that what is preferred among the languages of the world, i.e. less marked, is somehow closer to being optimal than more marked structures.

Though Jakobson's original markedness theory was applied to sound inventories (phoneme systems), this concept can be applied to all human culture systems and their applications. Related approaches have been used in Natural Phonology, Morphology and Syntax as well as Optimality Theory (see e.g. the chapters by Bybee, Holt, Donegan & Nathan, and Scheer in this volume). The preference laws discussed here apply to syllable structure. The fundamental assumption is that a change in a language's system is always a local improvement with respect to one given parameter. Every parameter permits several configurations, and the tendency towards local meliorization is expressed in the hypothesis that a language will, as a rule, not possess dispreferred structures with respect to a single parameter without possessing more preferred structures at the same time. This can be formulated as the Synchronic Maxim:

(1) Synchronic Maxim (Vennemann 1988: 3)
    A language system will in general not contain a structure on a given parameter without containing those structures constructible with the means of the system that are more preferred in terms of the relevant preference law.

It is necessary to relativize this maxim, because gaps on the graded scale of parameters occur occasionally as a result of more global changes or language contact. In some cases gaps are motivated naturally, i.e. because some sound combinations are phonetically impossible, but in general this hypothesis holds, because it is based on the human natural language endowment and human culture, which form the basis of all language systems.

The corollary to the Synchronic Maxim is the Diachronic Maxim, which makes a statement about how language change proceeds with respect to a certain parameter. Accordingly, language change affects the worst structures first, and then moves up the parametrical scale towards the end of optimal structures.

(2) Diachronic Maxim (Vennemann 1988: 2)
     Linguistic change on a given parameter does not affect a language structure as
     long as there exist structures in the language system that are less preferred in
     terms of the relevant preference law.

It is important to keep in mind the local limitation of the language improvement
assumption. A change in syllable structure naturally takes place on the level of the syllable. Hence, a change that is not an improvement according to a preference law on
the level of the syllable is motivated by a preference on another parameter and not by
a syllabic preference.[1] What is more, as will become evident in section 26.3, preference
laws on a given level can compete with each other. In those cases, the precedence of one
law over the other can be specific to a certain change (this is similar to constraint hierarchies in OT, see also Holt, this volume). For instance, Spanish *escuela* improves the
first-syllable head of ancestral Latin *schola* [sk] in line with the Head Law (cf. (4) below)
by removing the s—from this syllable head.[2] However, in doing so the word becomes
longer by one syllable, against a universal preference for shorter words, and it is also
in disharmony with the Head Law and the Coda Law (see (6) below) with respect to
the newly-created first syllable, which is naked and closed by a fairly strong consonant
(see (3) below). Evidently, breaking up the initial cluster in harmony with a phonotactic
constraint against [sk] in heads has priority over undoing an extra initial syllable with
the stated complexities.

Applying the preference laws diachronically can not only pinpoint the motivation
for a given sound change; it can also explain sound changes that seem to run in opposite directions. Dispreferred syllable structures can usually be improved in more than
one way (see e.g. Vennemann 1988: 50-1 for a catalogue of syllable contact changes),
and a language may use two different strategies at the same time. For instance, 'Pāli
has regularly eliminated cases of word initial clusters by means of cluster reduction or
epenthesis' (Murray 1982: 176), i.e. it simplified heads in accordance with the Head Law
in two different ways: Skrt. *srotas* 'stream' *vs* Pāli *sota* but Skrt. *sneha* 'affection' *vs* Pāli
sineha.

Generally, a language tends towards one solution, but two solutions can appear to
occur with an almost equal distribution (e.g. Labov 2010: ch. 7). The next section illustrates the most important preference laws following Vennemann 1988, and demonstrates their significance for language change.

---

[1] This is also the case with so-called 'crazy changes' (Scheer, this volume).
[2] The terminology on syllable structure used here deviates in parts from the mainstream. *Head* refers
to the *onset* in more mainstream terminology (i.e. [sk] in the example in the main text), whereas *onset*
here only refers to the first sound of a structural position in the syllable, e.g. the head (i.e. in this case
[s]), and conversely *offset* refers only to the last sound of a structural position, e.g. the coda (i.e. [t] in
the English word *ant*). Note, however, that both terms are not restricted to heads or codas respectively.
A *naked* syllable is one with an empty head, e.g. the first syllable of Spanish *escuela*. The *body* comprises
syllable head and nucleus, the *rhyme* nucleus and coda, whereas the *shell* consists of head and coda
without the nucleus. See Vennemann 1988: 5–10 for further details.

26.3 Preference Laws
for Syllable Structure

The concept of consonantal strength as a relational measure of the 'deviation from unimpeded (voiced) airflow' (Vennemann 1988: 8) is pivotal.[3] Inversely related to this measure is the idea of sonority, which orders speech sounds according to how vowel-like they are (see Murray 1988). Several different sonority hierachies have been proposed, see Restle and Vennemann 2001: 1312 for examples. The scale in (3) is simplified but suffices for our purposes.

(3) Scale consonantal strength

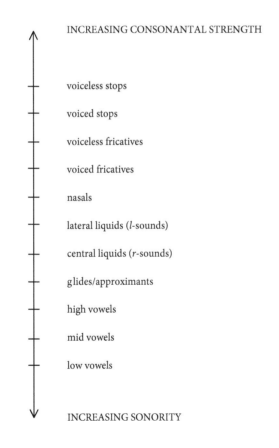

INCREASING CONSONANTAL STRENGTH

voiceless stops

voiced stops

voiceless fricatives

voiced fricatives

nasals

lateral liquids (*l*-sounds)

central liquids (*r*-sounds)

glides/approximants

high vowels

mid vowels

low vowels

INCREASING SONORITY

---

[3] See Restle & Vennemann (2001: 1312) for references discussing the phonetic foundation of sonority concepts.

This categorization aims at explaining the relative position of sounds to the syllable nucleus. Members of sound classes towards the bottom, i.e. more sonorous sounds, tend to be closer to the syllable nucleus than those towards the top, i.e. more consonantal sounds. This has been recognized since Whitney 1865, and is now often discussed as the Sonority Sequencing Generalization (Hooper 1976a, Selkirk 1984, Blevins 1995: 210).

We only discuss selected preference laws for syllable structure in more detail, covering intrasyllabic, intersyllabic and extrasyllabic relations.

26.3.1 Intrasyllabic Relations

The preference laws for syllable structure in Vennemann 1988 reflect empirical studies on syllable structure (e.g. Greenberg 1978). The basic generalization these preferences are based on is that a syllable structure is better the more monotonic it is. Monotonicity is defined as a continuing decrease of consonantal strength in the body and a continuing increase of consonantal strength in the rhyme (see Vennemann 1988: 9-10 for further details). These laws also express that the optimal syllable possesses a head with a single, strong consonant, a nucleus with a low monophthongal vowel and an empty coda, as e.g. *pa, ta,* and *ma.*

26.3.1.1 *The Head Law*

(4) Head Law
A syllable head is the more preferred,
(a) the closer the number of speech sounds is to one,
(b) the greater the consonantal strength value of its onset, and
(c) the more sharply the consonantal strength drops from the onset within a complex syllable head.

(a): Empty syllable heads, i.e. heads with fewer than one speech sound, are dispreferred. This can be seen from the fact that there are no languages allowing only empty heads, but languages banning empty heads are not uncommon. One such example is Tolowa (Athapaskan), which permits the following syllable types, CVV, CCVV, CVC, CCVC, CCVCC, CVCC and—more rarely—CV but not VV, VC and VCC (Collins 1989). Northern Standard German fills empty heads of stressed and of initial syllables with a glottal stop, e.g. *chaotisch* 'chaotic' [kʰɑ.ˈʔo.tʰɪʃ] (but *Chaos* [ˈkʰɑ.ɔs]), *Aorta* 'aorta' [ʔa.ˈʔɔr.tʰa]. But this preference for filled syllable heads is not particularly strong, as there are indeed languages with a considerable number of naked syllables, i.e. syllables with empty heads. For instance, in Basque about half of all words begin with a vowel (see Vennemann 1994b: 255f). Moreover, naked syllables may be treated differently according to syllable position, e.g. a language may have different rules for hiatus (see section 26.3.2.2). Furthermore, in some languages the canonical syllable seems to have an empty head, e.g. the Australian languages Arrernte and Kunjen (Evans 1995: 747).

Conversely, syllable heads with more than one speech sound are not considered optimal either, and this is proportionate to the number of speech sounds above one. This can
be inferred from the fact that a given language (1) will have an upper limit as to the number of speech sounds permitted in the syllable heads; (2) will permit heads with n-1 speech
sounds if it permits heads with n (n > 1) speech sounds, and (3) will have more limitations
as the number of speech sounds in the syllable head increases. For instance, Standard
German permits heads filled with a maximum of three speech sounds, and hence also
with two and one, conforming to the first two postulates. That it is also in line with the
third can be seen once one examines which sequence of two consonants can also occur
with the reverse order (this is not true, for instance, for all possible clusters consisting
of obstruents plus sonorants, e.g. [kr-] but *[rk-], [ʃm-] but *[mʃ-]), and if it is borne in
mind that the roughly 20 permitted speech sounds do not form 20*20*20, i.e. 8000, triple
consonant clusters, but only four, namely [ʃpr-], [ʃpl-], [ʃtr-] and [skr-] (*springen* 'jump',
Splitter 'chip', *streng* 'strict' and *Skrupel* 'scruple'), possibly six if [skl-] and [str-], occurring
in little-integrated loanwords (e.g. *Sklerose* 'sclerosis' and *Strip* 'strip'), are added.[4]

In language change one observable effect of this law is the frequent shortening of
syllable heads. For instance, heads in Vedic and Sanskrit could comprise up to three
speech sounds, whereas in Middle Indic (e.g. Pāli) consonant clusters were no longer
permitted in syllable heads at all. A development in the opposite direction, i.e. a systematic lengthening of syllable heads, does not seem to occur. Lengthening of syllable
heads usually has a specific reason that has nothing to do with syllable structure. The
epenthetic change of *sr* > *str* in Pre-Proto-Germanic is a more global change that eliminates the sequence *sr* generally and not only in syllable heads; the lengthening of syllable heads is just a side-effect: Gmc. ⁺*strauma-* 'river, stream' *vs* OI *srávati* '(3sg) flows',
but also PGmc. ⁺*swester-* < PIE ⁺*swesr-* with epenthentic *t* in the syllable coda or the
syllable contact respectively.[5] Complex syllable heads can also result from syncope, but
this is evidently not aimed at improving syllable structure but at shortening the word.

(b): Many languages do not allow the least consonantal sounds to form syllable
heads, e.g. all vowels in Standard German. This tendency towards maximally consonantal heads is especially apparent in word-initial position, as consonants tend to
weaken by assimilation word-medially. Spanish, for instance, tolerates both /ɾ/ and /r/
as word-medial syllable heads but only /r/ in word-initial heads: *pero* 'but', *perro* 'dog',
but only *rojo* [r-] 'red'. Many languages do not permit voiced fricatives word-initially but
only voiceless ones (e.g. Old English), others aspirate voiceless stops in this position (e.g.
Modern English).

(c): This preference can be illustrated with several well-known cases. Standard
German allows strong consonants (obstruents) before sonorants but not weak consonants (sonorants), not even if they are relatively stronger: *Knie* 'knee', *Platz*, 'place', *blank*

---

[4] Whether [pfr-], [pfl-] and [tsv-] have to be included, depends on whether the affricates [pf] and [ts]
are counted as monophonematic or diphonematic.
[5] To avoid ambiguity, the raised cross '⁺' indicates a reconstructed form, the asterisk '*' marks an
ungrammatical form.

'bare', *groß* 'big', *frei* 'free', *schmal* 'narrow', *Schnee* 'snow', *schlimm* 'bad', *schräg* 'diagonal', but **mn-, *ml-, *mr-, *nl-, *nr-, *lr-*. The history of the Germanic languages shows that [h] too is a weak consonant. It derived from a Proto-Germanic velar fricative [x], which in turn goes back to a PIE velar stop [k]. In all Germanic languages except Icelandic, [h] is then lost in syllable heads before consonants, and in many varieties of English /h/ has already been lost before vowels (e.g. Cockney), whereas it has been preserved before /w/ in others (e.g. in varieties of American English). In Icelandic, /hw/ is threatened by a more general process of strengthening, [w] > [v]; as far as [w] does not resist this development in this cluster, [h] is strengthened instead to maintain a sufficient fall in consonantal strength: /hw/ > /hv-/ > /kv-/, e.g. in *hvítur* /hwitʏr/ or /kvitʏr/ 'white'.

The well-known fate of word-initial *k-* in English is instructive at this point as well. Like Modern German, Old English possessed the clusters *kn-, kl-, kr-, kw-, kV-*, arranged on a scale of increasing head quality from left to right. In Late Middle English the worst of these (*kn-*) became unstable, and [k] was subsequently lost, cf. ModE *knee*. Of the remaining groups *kl-* represents the worst structure according to the theory and is already under attack in certain varieties in England (*kl- > tl-* as a prelude to total loss of the onset, see Lutz 1991: 251f), as predicted by the Diachronic Maxim in (2) above. By contrast, the groups to the right-hand end of the scale—those with the weaker slope consonants—are completely stable in all varieties: *kr-* and *kw-* can only be eliminated after *kl-* has disappeared, and it is predicted that *kr-* will become unstable before *kw-*, unless [w] were to strengthen to [v] like in Icelandic and German (Lutz 1991: ch. IV.B.2 on English and ch. IV.B.3 on other Germanic languages).

However, the Romance languages illustrate another way to improve word-initial consonant clusters, namely by weakening the second consonant rather than strengthening or deleting the first. This can be shown with what happened to inherited clusters consisting of obstruent plus liquid, after obstruent plus nasal had already been eliminated in Latin.

In many Romance languages the worst structures became subsequently unstable, namely those consisting of obstruent plus *l*. In a first step *l* developed into a palatal glide after voiceless obstruents, and then the whole group gradually ended up as a voiceless alveo-palatal fricative ([ʃ], spelt <ch>): Latin *plumbum* 'lead', *clavis* 'key', *flamma* 'flame' > Portugese *chumbo, chave, chama*. In a second step, *l* in new loans changed to *r* following a voiced stop and following a voiceless obstruent in new loans, compare Spanish *blanco* 'white', *obligar* 'pledge', *regla* 'rule', *plancha* 'board', *clavo* 'nail', *flota* 'fleet' with Portugese *branco, obrigar, regra, prancha, cravo, frota*. The aim of these developments was an improved system, which is being undermined by more recent loanwords—sometimes words have been borrowed twice, e.g. *flauta ~ frauta* 'flute'.

(5) Head improvement in Portuguese

      *KN–   *Kl–   Kr–

      ┼────────┼────────┼──────────▶   Increasing quality of syllable head

Heads consisting of obstruent plus *r* have so far been stable everywhere, they even represent partly the target structure in the elimination process of *l*-clusters (cf. Vennemann 1989: 17–21 [1993: 326–30] on head clusters).

26.3.1.2 *The Coda Law*

(6) Coda Law
    A syllable coda is the more preferred,
    (a) the smaller the number of speech sounds,
    (b) the lower the consonantal strength of its offset, and
    (c) the more sharply the consonantal strength rises toward the offset within a complex syllable coda.

(a) and (c): Sanskrit progressively reduces word-final codas from the outside in until maximally the innermost consonant remains: *adan* 'eating', replacing *ad-ant-s* (cf. L *edēns* < *ed-ent-s*, acc. *edentem*). The only exceptions are clusters consisting of /r/ plus stop, i.e. exactly those clusters with the steepest possible drop in consonantal strength: *āvart* '(3sg) turned', *amārṭ* '(3sg.) wiped', *vark* '(3sg.) bent'.

(b): After the implementation of Klingenheben's Law, according to which all lingual coda consonants changed to /r/ and all labial and velar consonants to /w/, Hausa permitted only these two weakest consonants in the coda: ⁺*ma.za.ma.za* 'very fast' > ⁺*maz.ma.za* > *mar.ma.za*; ⁺*ma.kaf.ni.ya* 'a blind female' > *ma.kaw.ni.ya* (~ *ma.kā.fo* 'a blind male'); ⁺*hag.ni* 'left side' > *haw.ni* (~ *ba.ha.go* 'a left-handed person), etc. (cf. Klingenheben 1928).

26.3.1.3 *The Nucleus Law*

(7) Nucleus Law
    A syllable nucleus is the more preferred,
    (a) the closer the number of its speech sounds is to one,
    (b) the lower the consonantal strength of its speech sounds.

(a): If a language has nuclei of a certain length (> 1), then it always has also shorter nuclei (≥ 1), and the upper limit is low in all languages (≤ 3). All languages have monophthongs but not necessarily diphthongs, and triphthongs are rare but do occur, e.g. in Portuguese. Diachronically, this preference surfaces in the shape of crosslinguistically frequent spontaneous monophthongizations. To our knowledge, diphthongizations, by contrast, never occur spontaneously, they are always motivated by some other factors within a given system.

(b): Low vowels may function only as nuclei and as offglides of diphthongs (though they do not make good offglides). The higher a vowel, the more it tends to be marginalized, especially if adjacent to sounds that can also function as nuclei. Consonants generally are poor nuclei, especially if they are strong. This becomes clear from the fact that few languages have consonantal nuclei, and if they do, these tend to occupy continuous sections towards the sonorous end on the scale of consonantal strength, e.g. only *r* (like in Croatian, e.g. *Krk*, an Adriatic island) or *r* and *l* (like in Sanskrit), or these and the nasals (like in English unstressed syllables, e.g. *hammer, saddle, mutton, bottom*).

(8) Corollary to the Nucleus Law
     The shell of a syllable is the more subject to severe restrictions, the higher the consonantal strength of its nucleus.

This corollary is explained by the fact that both the Head and Coda Law cannot easily be completely satisfied if the nucleus is filled with a very consonantal speech sound. If, for instance, a speech gesture in German contains /s/ as its nucleus, this means that, in order to keep it monotonic, its shell is restricted to stops, *pst* 'hush'. This also explains the only exception to the rule for syllable heads in Tolowa (cf. section 26.3.1.1), which is that a syllable with /n/ as nucleus does not permit any speech sound in its shell.

26.3.2 Intersyllabic Relations

Languages can differ not only with respect to their syllable structure, but also with respect to how they string syllables together. This has been a fruitful direction of research. Perhaps the best-known generalization is the principle of Head Maximization (*maximal onset principle, CV-rule, onset-first principle, left-precedence principle,* ONSET, e.g. already Varma 1929, Allen 1953, Bell 1977, Selkirk 1982, Clements 1990, Prince & Smolensky 1993/2004). This principle is, however, inaccurate, at least as a universal. This can easily be seen from the fact that different languages—even one at different chronological stages—can syllabify the same sequence differently.

This has been well-known since antiquity, as clusters of obstruent (K) and sonorant (R) *(muta cum liquida)* in intervocalic position caused problems for Greek and Latin poets if the first vowel was short: the syllabification V.KRV meant that the first syllable was short, and hence light, whereas the syllabification VK.RV meant that the first syllable was long, and thus heavy. In the metric system of a quantity language this is a significant difference. As a result, syllabification was used to manipulate syllable weight. Poets in antiquity even coined a term for making a syllable with short nucleus light by tautosyllabification of a *muta cum liquida* cluster, cf. *correptio Attica* in Classical Greek (von Mess 1903). But varieties of antique languages without *correptio*, in which KR cluster are heterosyllabified, have word-initial KR-clusters too, cf. *kr-* in older Greek *krókos* 'crocus', but *pikrós* 'spicy' with k^sr (Allen 1974: 101-2). The principle of Head Maximization would require the syllabification [pi.krós]. Moreover, the opposite of *correptio*—namely *productio* (lengthening) as in Late Latin, compare Classical Latin *integrum* ['in.te.grum] but Late Latin [in.'teg.ro]—is also well known, which shows that head maximization cannot even be considered a universal tendency.

Since the discussion of this and similar problems it has become clear that syllabification depends strongly on the relative consonantal strength of the speech sounds involved

(Vennemann 1972b, Murray & Vennemann 1982, 1983, Lutz 1985, 1986, Vennemann 1987, 1988: 40-55, Clements 1990). In Faroese, for instance, *muta cum liquida* clusters (except *tl*) always belong to the second syllable, but not in closely related Icelandic, which tautosyllabifies only fortis obstruents and *r* but not *l*. As a matter of fact, Icelandic always syllabifies V$MLV in the case of fortis M and L = *r* (and for L = *v* and = *j*, which, as former glides, are even weaker than *r*), but VM$LV in the case of L = *l* and for all stronger consonants as well as for lenis M (together with all weaker onset consonants). Tautosyllabification can unambiguously be identified from the effect of open syllable lengthening, and conversely, heterosyllabification from shortening. This new allocation of quantity affects all old short and long vowels as well as diphthongs (cf. Vennemann 1972b, 1978).

Languages also differ with respect to the connection between syllabification and prosodic properties, e.g. stress or the position in the word. The next section covers the two main laws applying to intersyllabic relations, the Syllable Contact Law and the Hiatus Law. On the Law of Initials and the Law of Finals, see Vennemann (1988) and Restle & Vennemann (2001).

26.3.2.1 *The Syllable Contact Law*

The term 'syllable contact' is used to refer to the connection between two speech sounds A and B at the syllable boundary A$B.

(9) Syllable Contact Law
     A syllable contact is the better the greater the strength difference between its second and first speech sound.

Tautosyllabifying V$MLV in Icelandic, avoids a contact M$L exactly for the 12 least preferred cases, i.e. for those in which the above-mentioned difference in strength is smallest, in this case even negative. This becomes especially clear if the consonants are arrayed on an arbitrarily numerically interpreted scale of strength, as in (10), cf. Vennemann (1972b: 6).

(10)

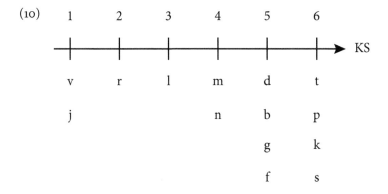

This permits the statement that two consonants only form a syllable contact A$B in Icelandic if the critical difference in consonantal strength, KS(B) – KS(A), is equal to or greater than –3. For instance, this is the case with /pl/: KS(/l/) – KS(/p/) = –3; hence *epli* 'apple' is syllabified /ep.li/, which can be seen from the short stressed vowel and the preaspirated fortis stop ['e^{h}p.li]. But it is not the case with /pr/: KS(/r/) – KS(/p/) = –4; therefore *skopra* 'to roll' is syllabified /sko.pra/, recognizable from the long stressed vowel and the postaspirated fortis stop, [skɔː.p^{h}ra]. Like the other preference laws, the contact law manifests itself in sound changes which improve syllable contacts (see Vennemann 1988: 50-5 for a list of relevant changes).

26.3.2.2 *The Hiatus Law*

(11) Hiatus Law
      A hiatus is dispreferred, in particular, the more properties the two vowels involved share, and also the closer one of them is phonetically to a glide.

From part (a) of the Head Law (see (4)), which disfavours naked syllables, it can be inferred that a hiatus is not a preferred structure. This can also be seen from the fact that many languages do not allow them at all (according to Bell & Hooper 1978: 8 this is valid for about half of the world's languages). To eliminate hiatus structures languages use mechanisms that are similar to those that eliminate empty syllable heads as well as some additional ones, such as the insertion of a glide and others (see Restle & Vennemann 2001: 1318-19 for further details).

26.3.3 Extrasyllabic Relations

Languages also exhibit preferences with respect to the relationship between syllables and stress as well as rhythm. This section highlights some key principles.

26.3.3.1 *Syllabification and Stress*

Although onset maximization as a simple principle is incorrect, it is possible to state conditions for a relatively good syllabification. These are graded and involve multiple factors, which first became apparent from research in historical phonology investigating the way words are separated in handwritten manuscripts and how this is sensitive to syllabification (Lutz 1985, 1986). This section briefly summarizes the results of this work, starting with observations made about certain properties of syllables influencing syllabification and ending with a general preference law of syllabification (see Restle & Vennemann 2001: 1320-1 for further details).

(12) Rhyme Attractiveness
      This is defined as how well a syllable is capable of attracting the onset of the following syllable as part of its rhyme.

(13) Body Attractiveness
This is defined as how well a syllable is capable of attracting the offset of a preceding syllable as part of its body.

(14) Law of Rhyme Attractiveness
The rhyme attractiveness of a syllable (i.e. heterosyllabification into it) is the greater
(a) the more it is stressed in relation to the following syllable,
(b) the shorter its rhyme, and
(c) the lower the consonantal strength of its rhyme, in particular its offset.

(15) Law of Body Attractiveness
The body attractiveness of a syllable (i.e. heterosyllabification into it) is the greater
(a) the more it is stressed in relation to the preceding syllable,
(b) the shorter its body is, and
(c) the lower the consonantal strength of its body, in particular its onset.

(16) Syllable Contact Bed
Let A$B be the syllable contact of a sequence of syllables $S_1.S_2$. The onset syllable of the contact is defined as the rhyme of S_1 minus A, i.e. minus its offset, and the offset syllable as the body of S_2 minus B, i.e. its onset. The sequence of a contact's onset syllable and its offset syllable is called *syllable contact bed*.

(17) Syllable Embedding Law
The bed of a syllable contact is the better the greater the rhyme attractiveness of its onset syllable and the greater the body attractiveness of its offset syllable.

This and what is known about syllable contacts (see section 26.3.2.1 above) permit a more general preference law of syllabification.

(18) General Law of Syllabification (Lutz's Law)
The syllabification of two syllables is the more preferred
(a) the better the resulting syllable contact, and
(b) the better this syllable contact is embedded.

26.3.3.2 *Syllable structure and stress*

Syllable structure and stress are interrelated in multiple ways, but all seem to conform to an overarching preference law (see Vennemann 1988: 58):

(19) Law of Stressed Syllables
Complexities of syllable structure are the less favoured the less rhythmic prominence the syllable possesses.

The clearest illustrations are constraints on syllable structure that are categorically tied to word stress. For instance, unstressed syllables in Icelandic can only have [ɪ], [ʏ] and [a] as nuclei, whereas stressed syllables have a much wider variety of phonologically contrastive nuclei.

26.3.3.3 *Syllable structure and rhythm*

There are also preferences governing the relationship between syllable structure and rhythmical types as well as with syllable weight, which is also relevant to rhythm.

(20) Rhythm Law
Complexities of syllable structure are the less favoured the smaller the rhythmic unit is.

English as a stress timed language possesses a complex syllable structure, whereas a syllable timed language such as Spanish tends to have a less complex structure, and mora timed languages, such as Japanese, seem to prefer fairly simple syllable structures (see Dufter 2003 for a detailed discussion of rhythmical types). There is also a well-known connection between dynamic stress and moraicity, which has also been called Prokosch's Law (see Vennemann 1988: 30):

(21) Weight Law
In stress accent languages an accented syllable is the more preferred the closer its syllable weight is to two moras, and an unaccented syllable is the more preferred the closer its weight is to one mora.

In other words, stressed syllables are preferably bimoraic and unstressed syllables preferably unimoraic. This law has often been used to provide the motivation for quantity changes, e.g. lengthening of open monosyllables in some Germanic dialects, such as Old English (compare OE *bī, nū, swā* vs Goth. *bi, nu, swa*).

26.4 DEVELOPMENTS IN THE CONCEPT OF PREFERENCE LAWS

As mentioned in section 26.2, the theory of linguistic preferences can be seen as a generalization of Jakobson's markedness concept. Historically, the direct forerunners are Natural Generative Grammar and Natural Generative Phonology (Hooper 1976a, also Donegan & Nathan and Scheer, both this volume). Vennemann (1972b) discusses problems of syllabification in Icelandic, considering universal interrelationships between syllable structure and consonantal strength, which also manifest themselves in probabilistic statements about language change. Although Hooper (1976a) is not primarily concerned with diachrony, she discusses implications for principles of diachronic change in connection with her principles of optimal syllable structure, which represent targets in processes of language change.

However, a concrete theory based on linguistic preferences and its application to language change was proposed in Vennemann 1983a and b, as a type of theory that can explain the 'regularities within a certain domain by turning to theories that are not theories for that particular domain' (Vennemann 1983b: 9), as opposed to generative theories that attempt to explain regularities by virtue of deductive inferences within the same domain, in this case, grammar. Consequently, the preferences themselves are motivated by extralinguistic theories, such as 'phonetic theories, theories of learning, semiotic theories, theories of communication, etc.' (Vennemann 1983b: 13). Such a theory makes statements about a space Q in which all real languages are situated and about what is possible and what is impossible for languages in Q. As languages are not evenly distributed within Q, one arrives at a theory operating on the basis of this distribution calling it preference, markedness, naturalness, etc. As Vennemann (1983b: 11) points out, it is exactly this 'concept of rank order' that sets preference theories apart from purely descriptive theories, and that explains linguistic structures, not in a deductive sense, but in a sense that Vennemann (1983b: 13) calls 'elucidation', i.e. by shedding light on a particular structure or development, which can often be taken as an explanation. Discussing the issue of explaining language change, Vennemann (1983b: 18f) also points out that a theory of preferences in connection with a list of possible changes, a 'closed catalogue', can actually be falsified, and permits deductive explanations. Such a catalogue of changes on a macro-level is found in Bartsch & Vennemann (1982: 153), and a nearly 'complete' list of syllable-contact improving sound changes was assembled in Vennemann (1988: 50f).

Further developments took place in subsequent work by Vennemann, Murray, and Lutz in discovering and substantiating preference laws for syllable structure (Murray 1982, 1988, Murray & Vennemann 1982, 1983, Lutz 1985, 1986, Vennemann 1986a, b, 1987, 1988, summarized in Restle & Vennemann 2001). This was meant to be the beginning of a new direction in research in that future energies ought to be directed at assembling catalogues of language change and at discovering new preferences (Vennemann 1983b: 24f).

A further development can be seen in the ways the idea of preference laws was developed from the 1990s onwards. Beginning with Vennemann, (1989 [1993]), which showed the value of this concept for syntactic change, preferences have continued to play a major role in Natural Phonology (see Hurch & Rhodes 1996) and Optimality Theory (Dziubalska-Kołaczyk 2001 and Holt 2003b, this volume). Moreover, a theory of linguistic preferences seems to be an ideal complementation to cases of diffusional and bifurcational sound changes. Beginning with Labov's (1981) seminal paper, it became increasingly apparent that neogrammarian sound laws represent but one end of a continuum of sound changes, namely those with a particularly thorough application (see also Vennemann 2000a). This is underlined by the cases like ModE *cradle* and *saddle* and other bifurcational changes, which cannot be adequately accommodated within the neogrammarian framework (see Murray 2000 for a discussion and Labov 2010: ch.

7 for further details on bifurcational changes).[6] In the description and elucidation of the breakdown of phonological quantity in Germanic a preference-based framework (syllable cut theory) has proven to be useful, because the evaluative character of such a theory can explain why structures change, and also in which direction they change (e.g. Vennemann 2000b, Murray 2000, Mailhammer 2007, 2009, Mailhammer et al., in press). Consequently, the notion that bifurcational changes are the result of an 'unstable structure' which is eliminated in different ways (Labov 2010: 156) can be rendered meaningful by stipulating why a given structure has to be seen as unstable and by predicting the result of the change, even if the change itself cannot be predicted. Vennemann (2000a) provides another especially useful application of a preference-based framework, namely in the area of etymology, connecting words that are deemed unrelated according to the neogrammarian concept. On this approach, words in daughter languages can be the result of differently implemented constraints, similarly to the *cradle/saddle* case in Middle English (see also Mailhammer et al., in press).

As Vennemann ([1989]/1993: 321) points out, preference theory is a way out of the classical argument about whether language change is fashion-like or functional. As language change is seen as language improvement, this is a 'unified principle' to conceptualize language change, which accommodates 'both the conscious and subconscious and both the socially and structurally motivated changes, as well as those motivated by the needs of communication'. It seems that this is the greatest achievement of this theory, which withstands criticism that has been directed at it (see the following section). From the perspective of application, the motivation of bifurcational and diffusional changes is a great strength of preference-based approaches.

26.5 CRITICISM OF PREFERENCE THEORY

Criticism against a theory of linguistic preferences has focused mainly on two issues, namely their empirical foundation and the notion that language change is seen as language improvement (see e.g. Berg 1990 and Hill 2009).

The empirical basis of the stipulated preferences has been repeatedly attacked from two different perspectives. First, authors have questioned their accuracy, saying that positing preferences requires a quantitative investigation of a substantial number of languages and processes of change demonstrating that e.g. CV-syllables are indeed universally more frequent than VC-syllables (e.g. Berg 1990: 570). However, firstly one could simply say that a falsification of an asserted preference is up to those criticizing it. Second, the available

---

[6] OE *cradol* and *sadol* change in different directions towards Middle English despite an identical (relevant) phonological structure. The former is assigned smooth syllable cut on its accented syllable (with so-called Open Syllable Lengthening), the latter abrupt syllable cut (which closes the syllable ambisyllabically and therefore keeps the vowel short), see Murray (2000), Mailhammer (2007, 2009), and Mailhammer et al. (in press) for further details, and also compare Dresher (this volume).

information is probably sufficient to formulate preferences, even though they are not based on an exhaustive database. The felt need for a solid empirical footing stems from the perspective of laws as generalizations based on the data specifying what happens under which circumstances. This is perhaps due to the term *laws* in the title of Vennemann (1988). As Berg (1990: 570) suggests, the term *tendencies* would have maybe been less problematic to some readers. The term *preference laws* simply refers to the qualitative evaluation of linguistic structures. As assumptions they need not be based on quantitative empirical data, they are tested directly by the data, but not in the way generative laws are tested, since we are dealing with statements about better and worse structures and not with simple output rules. For instance, no one would question the preferred nature of open syllables based on crosslinguistic data, even though there is no quantitative study for a sizeable body of the languages of the world and even though there may be languages in which the canonical syllable is closed. Hence, the supposed lack of empirical foundation stems from the view of the preference laws as inductively based, whereas in reality they are hypotheses.

The second angle from which the empirical basis of the preference laws has been criticized is that the observed preference might be an epiphenomenon of a different process and thus no reliable indication of a preferred structure (Hill 2009: 235–42). For instance, Hill (2009: 239–40) notes that an apparent preference for CV-syllables in terms of results of sound changes is in fact a side-effect of sound changes that do not take place on the level of syllable structure. Hill (2009: 242) concludes that the formulation of the preference laws did not take into account that the observed preferences are frequently the result of recent unrelated changes, and that the theory is therefore unreliable, as it offers no method to differentiate between 'real' and 'fake' preferences. However, even though it may be a valid point in principle, in practice it is insignificant. The preference laws discussed here are based on a sufficiently large number of well-researched examples that singular exceptions do not affect their overall validity. It is simply unlikely that such a widely-documented preference for CV-syllables was epiphenomenal in all cases. In addition, it would have to be demonstrated that a concrete preference law was indeed based on such invalid data, which to date has not been done.

The second point of criticism centres on the idea that change is always an improvement with respect to some parameter (Berg 1990: 570, Hill 2009: 244). Again, this is not empirically supported; it is an axiomatic statement founded on the idea that human development is motivated by aiming for improvement. The opposite or the idea that change is completely unmotivated seems difficult to imagine. That there are changes for the worse is obvious but whether it is their motivation to make linguistic structures worse seems doubtful. Rather they always seem to be unfortunate by-products of meliorative changes on other parameters—collateral damage, so to speak, as in the deteriorative creation of a non-empty coda as a by-product of apocope (CV.CV > CVC), itself a meliorating, namely word shortening process.

Consequently, there is no sensible alternative but to assume that a change leading to a dispreferred structure was motivated differently. This is the answer to the point raised in Berg (1990: 570): 'I can see no reason whatsoever why we should follow Vennemann in believing that *ora > gora* is a syllable structure change whereas *la vita > la ita* is not.' If the loss of the head consonant in the second case (representing a decrease in head quality) was not an improvement on some other level it can only have been either a random change or a deliberate move to decrease the quality of the syllable head of *vita*, both of which we find difficult to believe. The example adduced by Berg can be seen as a case of intervocalic assimilatory weakening, which is then obviously not a change motivated by syllable structure.

26.6 SUMMARY

This chapter illustrates and discusses the concept of preference laws and their application in problems of historical phonology. Its key points are the assumptions that language change is always an improvement with respect to a certain parameter and that linguistic structures can be situated on a graded scale of quality. In language change, improvements start with the structure that is worst according to the preference law pertaining to the relevant parameter. But because parameters do not exist in isolation, improvements on one of them can lead to a decrease in quality on another, which explains why change need not be an improvement seen from every perspective. The strength of this concept is in helping elucidate and explain language change as the implementation of preferences, which is especially valuable in accounting for bifurcational changes. Though a concrete sound change may not always be predicted, catalogues of possible changes together with preference laws may at least permit probabilistic predictions. As hypotheses the fundamental tenets of preference theory need not have a quantitative empirical basis, but are assumptions whose value lies in their application (see also Berg 1990: 570).

Preference-like concepts have played a role in various linguistic theories, most notably, Optimality Theory. But in contrast to most of these, they are not one-output models, which is precisely their strength. It seems that a good deal of the controversy that preference laws have caused is due to an imperfect understanding of their nature and their aims. We hope to have succeeded in remedying this to some degree.

CHAPTER 27

···

ARTICULATORY PROCESSING AND FREQUENCY OF USE IN SOUND CHANGE

···

JOAN BYBEE

27.1 INTRODUCTION

···

THIS chapter assumes that an important goal of the study of sound change is the construction of a theory that explains both how and why sound change occurs, while also predicting what is a possible sound change. Here I explore the extent to which current theories of articulatory processing can provide a basis for understanding the factors contributing to sound change, pushing as far as possible the hypothesis that the ongoing automation of repeated behaviours is the primary factor behind sound change. Because automation leads to reduction and streamlining of articulatory effort, I argue that sound change can be viewed as largely consisting of the reduction of the magnitude of articulatory gestures along with their increased overlap. In connection with this, the pattern of lexical diffusion becomes an important diagnostic for the causes of change, as changes that affect high frequency words and phrases earlier than low frequency ones point to the automation of usage as the source of change.

The main focus, then, is on assimilatory sound changes and weakening or lenition, which are taken to be motivated by articulatory tendencies. A much less common type of change, fortition, is also discussed briefly as is the possibility of perceptually-motivated sound change. (Other chapters in this volume present alternative views, for example Yu and Blevins see a role for perception, and Dresher and Purnell & Raimy a role for purely formal factors.)

27.2 SOURCES OF INFORMATION
ABOUT SOUND CHANGE

A typical case of sound change would be one in which a particular sound is attested in particular words in a language at time T_1 while in the same set of words at T_2 a different sound systematically appears. For instance, words spelled in Latin with a geminate consonant, such as *cuppa* 'cup', *gutta* 'drop' and *bucca* 'mouth' are spelled and pronounced in Spanish with a simple consonant, *copa, gota* and *boca,* suggesting degemination sometime between the attestation of Latin and the beginning of writing in Spanish (Menéndez-Pidal 1968). As typical as such cases might be, however, they do not always provide the best evidence for how and why a particular change occurs because the acoustic and articulatory properties of the sounds in question can only be inferred from the written symbols (see Lass, Unger, Minkova, all this volume). Existing alternations are another source of information about sound changes; for instance, the alternations found in the English words *wife, wives; house, hou[z]es* provides evidence (along with other considerations) for a sound change by which fricatives became voiced between vowels (see Fox, this volume, on Internal Reconstruction). Such evidence is subject to the same factors mentioned above—the greater the time depth the greater the difficulty in reconstructing exactly what happened. The comparison of extant dialects, such as varieties of American English, may provide better information, as long as researchers have access to the properties of the sounds involved (see Fox, this volume, on the Comparative Method). The strongest source of evidence about how and why sound change takes place will come from cases where change is ongoing and data on the articulatory and acoustic properties of sounds and their social value is available (see Bowie & Yaeger-Dror and D'Arcy, both this volume). However, for present purposes, we exploit data from a variety of sources, ranging from the 'typical' sound changes described earlier to those that can be studied as they progress. We must, however, remain aware of the differences in the degrees of confidence that we can have in the data.

Another issue concerning sources of data that arises frequently is defining the domain of inquiry. Most everyone would agree that not all changes in sounds are 'sound changes'. It is important to exclude changes that are due to morphological relations, usually designated as 'analogy' (see Fertig, this volume); it is also important to exclude adaptation of loan words and focus on changes that are motivated internal to the language (Mowrey & Pagliuca 1995, Uffmann, this volume). In addition, we exclude sporadic changes that affect only a few words. In general, by 'sound change' we mean changes in sounds that occur in a phonetically-defined environment and that typically end up occurring systematically across the lexicon (though diffusion across the lexicon may be gradual; see section 27.10, and also Bybee 2002a, 2012). Finally there is the question of the point at which a change in pronunciation becomes a change in the grammar. This is also discussed briefly in section 27.10 where the account of sound change in an exemplar model is outlined.

27.3 EASE OF ARTICULATION

Many observers mention trends in sound change; for instance, several current textbooks tell us that assimilation (one sound becoming more like an adjacent sound) is the most common type of sound change (Crowley 1997, Campbell 1998). The other common type of sound change discussed frequently in the literature is lenition or weakening, which can be approached from a variety of perspectives (Foley 1970, Lass & Anderson 1975, Trask 1996, Lass 1997, Kirchner 1998, Bauer 2008, and Brandão de Carvalho, Scheer, & Ségéral 2008). For present purposes, it will be characterized as the decrease in the magnitude of an articulatory gesture (see section 27.7 for details).

Given these two broad categories, which most researchers agree are the most common types, terms such as 'ease of articulation' are unsurprisingly invoked to explain sound change. Hockett (1958) proposes that the directionality of sound change is caused by 'the tendency to speak sloppily' (p. 456) or more specifically the fact that 'the speaker (is) quite sloppy in his aim (at an articulatory target) most of the time' (1958: 440). Hock (1986) also cites 'relaxation' or 'weakening' of articulatory effort, and even 'the lazy tongue phenomenon' as the cause of lenition. Such statements are common in popular textbooks, and indeed reflect the popular conception of phonetic variation as being a degeneration from correct pronunciation.

While it is easy to understand the intuition behind such statements, there are many reasons to be dissatisfied with the characterization of sound change as due to laziness or sloppiness, or even the pursuit of ease. Lehmann (1992: 207) makes the valid observation that what seems easy in one language is difficult in another; indeed, it is practice or the lack of it that makes one articulation seem easier or more difficult than another. Certainly the outcome of a reducing sound change can also be quite complex and difficult on some level, as when Irish lenition produces a bilabial nasal fricative.

Also the proposal that speakers are lazy or sloppy would suggest that speakers of the same dialect might each reduce articulation in an individual way; given an intervocalic /t/, some speakers might voice it, some might make it a fricative and others a glottal stop. However, within a speech community, reduction is quite regular across speakers. There may be differences in the degree of reduction, but the paths that reduction and assimilation follow are conventional within the dialect. In fact, given the extent to which speakers within a dialect produce utterances that are so alike in phonetic detail that one can recognize the dialect of a speaker, it seems implausible to claim that speakers are lazy or sloppy.

Still, one need not totally reject the idea that sound change is largely reductive, but rather than invoking a lack of effort on the part of speakers, it is more reasonable to view speech as just one of many finely-tuned neuromotor activities that can be automated with the effect of becoming more efficient. With repetition, sequences of neuromotor acts become chunked into units and within these units the sequences become more integrated, with transitions between actions becoming smoother, and parts of the actions overlapping.

Thus producing a word or a phrase containing a sequence of articulatory gestures can be seen as analogous to other repeated behaviours, such as stirring pancake batter or tying a bow. Assimilation and lenition can be viewed, then, as a consequence of articulation as a highly practiced neuromotor activity. However, this particular neuromotor activity is embedded in a conventionalized communicative system and as such is constrained by the goal of communicating and made systematic by the fact that the same neuromotor activities (in the form of the gestures that make up the sounds of the language) are repeated across distinct words and phrases. I argue, then, for an articulatory source for many sound changes, with properties of change moulded by articulatory properties.

27.4 REDUCTION AND ASSIMILATION IN ARTICULATORY PROCESSING

Browman & Goldstein's (1990, 1992) theory of articulatory or gestural phonology proposes description in terms of the states and movements of the articulators during production. They argue that choosing gestures as the unit of production rather than segments or features allows for unifying descriptions of seemingly disparate phenomena. In Browman & Goldstein (1990, 1992) they propose that *all* casual speech alternations are (1992: 173):

> due to two gradient modifications to gestural structure during the act of talking—(a) increase in overlap and (b) decrease in magnitude of gestures.

In other words, their examination of casual speech processes, the pool of variation from which sound changes arise according to many researchers (e.g. Ohala 1989), shows a clear directionality. If their hypothesis is correct, then phonological changes that are not of one of the two types described do not come about through language use in casual speech, but possibly by some other mechanism.

A similar proposal is found in Pagliuca & Mowrey (1987) and Mowrey & Pagliuca (1995), where it is hypothesized that sound change is always in the direction of Substantive Reduction (reduction in the magnitude of gestures) or Temporal Reduction (by which gestures are compressed temporally and therefore overlap). Whereas Browman & Goldstein propose casual speech processes as the domain of their hypothesis, Mowrey & Pagliuca choose to deal with diachronic change, so it is necessary for them to make stipulations about the evidence for change (as I have above) and to rule out loanword adaptation and borrowed phonological patterns as sound change. Delimiting the domain of the 'sound change' is a persistent problem; in the present case we might say that all sound change that originates in casual speech processes is reductive in the way described by Browman & Goldstein and Mowrey & Pagliuca.

Lindblom (1990), while not addressing sound change directly, presents a theory of phonetic variation that refers to the competing tendencies operative in the speaker (the tendency of the motor system tends towards economy) and on the needs of the listener (to discriminate stimuli in order to identify lexical items).

Lindblom's view of production efficiency is that the speaker is subject to a general neuromotor principle that balances timing against the degree of displacement of physical movements in such a way as to make actions more economical. Thus co-articulation as well as reduction facilitate production (Lindblom 1990: 425, Yu, this volume). This facilitation is mediated by listener-needs as conceived by the speaker. Speakers can choose to allow co-articulation and reduction or they can choose to suppress these processes depending upon inferences made about the status of the listener's access to information as well as factors associated with the message the speaker intends to convey—such as the expression of emphasis or contrast. Lindblom emphasizes that the listener's system is already activated, both by the categories of the language that are present in the listener's cognitive system and by the properties of the linguistic and non-linguistic context in which the utterance is embedded. The speaker, then, must judge how accessible the lexical items, phrases and constructions being used will be to the listener.

Among the factors that Lindblom mentions as affecting accessibility are word frequency and neighbourhood frequency, based on the well-known effect that high frequency words are recognized faster than low frequency words and the related effect that words with fewer neighbours (neighbours being words that are highly similar phonetically) are recognized faster (Luce & Pisoni 1998). Another factor that could be important is the predictability of the word in context (Gregory et al. 1999, Bell et al. 2009). If the speaker judges the units of the utterance to be highly accessible to the listener, then articulatory reduction and co-articulation are allowed; but if the units are less accessible in the speaker's judgement, then they are articulated more carefully. It is important to note that reduction and co-articulation in Lindblom's theory are not well-described by terms such as 'ease of articulation' or 'least effort'; rather he argues that such online changes are towards a low-cost form of behaviour. There might be rather delicate timing relations (as in phrases such as *didn't you* [dɪʔn̩tʃu]) but what is saved is the amount of muscular displacement or activation.

27.5 SOUND CHANGE
AND THE NATURE OF GESTURES

Fowler & Saltzman (1993) describe gestures as 'smoothly graded waveshapes' (1993: 185). Gestures are activated gradually with the activation increasing to a maximal point and then decreasing gradually. It is normal for successive gestures to overlap: the tongue and lip configuration for a vowel is put into place during the articulation of the consonant. This is necessary for speech to be connected, as Fowler & Saltzman argue; in order for the vowel to have the intended properties, they must be present from the release of the consonant. In fact, for any neuromotor activity to be fluent, overlap of gestures must occur. The timing relations between simultaneous and successive gestures are at once finely tuned and flexible in context.

The hypothesis that casual speech processes and sound changes are attributable to increased overlap or decreased magnitude of gestures receives strong support from a recent crosslinguistic survey of all phonetic processes described in reference grammars of 82 languages chosen to be maximally unrelated (Bybee & Easterday, in preparation). Of the 800+ processes recorded from 82 language descriptions, approximately 49 percent are retiming of gestures and 35 percent are gestural reductions. Thus retiming and reduction make up 84 percent of synchronic phonetic processes, the pool from which sound changes arise.

In a rough correspondence we can say that assimilation is due to the increased overlap of gestures while lenition is due to the decrease in magnitude or duration of gestures. However, the correspondence is not perfect—some changes that appear to be assimilation may actually be due to, or at least involve, the decrease in magnitude of certain gestures. Increased overlap actually has two outcomes, true overlap in which one gesture is retimed to overlap part of another gesture and blending by which two gestures made with the same articulator affect one another. The former may lead to assimilation or deletion (usually classified as lenition) while the latter results in assimilation. For purposes of discussion, the following sections are organized in terms of the traditional categories of assimilation and lenition though the conclusion is that these terms can be misleading.

27.6 ASSIMILATION

A good definition of assimilation is provided by Farnetani 1999:

> Assimilation refers to the contextual variability of speech sounds, by which one or more of their phonetic properties are modified and become similar to those of the adjacent segments (1999: 376).

Thus assimilation is recognized in terms of the outcome—one sound ends up more similar to an adjacent one. A theory of sound change, however, must look more closely at the mechanisms by which such changes occur in order to understand the phenomenon. Taking this perspective we find that assimilation can be caused by different gestural changes, which include increased overlap, blending and decrease in magnitude.

27.6.1 Increased Overlap of Gestures

As gestures are sequenced in connected speech two successive gestures may involve the same articulator, say the tongue dorsum, as when a front vowel precedes a dorsal consonant (such as [k]), or they may involve different articulators, as when a vowel, whose articulation may involve the dorsum and the lips, is followed by a nasal consonant, whose articulation requires opening the velum. First we consider gestures that are made by different articulators.

The common process or sound change by which a vowel preceding a nasal consonant (usually in the same syllable) becomes nasalized is due to the anticipatory opening of the velum during the articulation of the vowel. Thus American English words such as *can, stamp* and *bang* have nasalized vowels. Very often the nasal consonant itself begins to weaken and disappear, e.g. in American English where the nasal consonant occurs before a voiceless consonant, as in *stamp, bank,* and *can't* (Malécot 1960) or in the history of French where final nasal consonants have been lost, leaving only a nasalized vowel. Such cases demonstrate that the retiming of gestures is often accompanied by weakening of other gestures (Mowrey & Pagliuca 1995: 70ff). Thus the timing change leading to assimilation also involves decrease in gestural magnitude.

Consonants acquire secondary articulations from the vowels that follow them through the anticipation of the vowels' gestures: thus labialization and palatalization of consonants takes place through gestural overlap. A classic example is the labialized and palatalized consonant series of Nupe (Kwa, Nigeria) where labialized consonants appear before round vowels and palatalized consonants before front vowels: [ēgʷū] 'mud', [ēgʷó] 'grass', [ēgʲi] 'child' and [ēgʲe] 'beer' *vs* [ēgā] 'stranger' (Hyman 1970b). Consonant-to-consonant assimilation of place of articulation is common in clusters, but may involve different sorts of gestural changes depending upon the place of articulation of the consonants. For instance, the change of Latin clusters of /kt/ and /pt/ to /tt/ in Italian (*nocte* > *notte* 'night', *septe* > *sette* 'seven') is caused by the anticipation of the alveolar gesture and weakening and loss of the dorsal and labial gestures respectively. Nolan (1992) studied the assimilation of alveolars to velars in English phrases such as *late calls* and *boat covered* and found that the variation in the changes in the alveolar closure were quite gradual. The alveolar closure was more often lost in fast speech.

The term 'blending' has been proposed in the gestural model for cases of overlap in which the same articulators are involved in successive gestures (Browman & Goldstein 1990, Fowler & Saltzman 1993). As Browman & Goldstein (1990) put it: 'The blending of gestures shows itself in spatial changes in one or both of the overlapping gestures' (p. 362). When a velar phoneme shows a palatal allophone before or after a high front vowel, we can think of the gesture of raising the back of the tongue for the velar as blending with the gesture that raises the tongue dorsum for the high front vowel. The result is a palatal obstruent rather than a velar. Thus English *key* is produced with a palatal stop, while *car* has a velar one. The German fricative *x* is produced as a velar (or uvular) after a back vowel, as in *Buch* [bux] 'book', *Koch* [kɔx] 'cook' but as a palatal fricative after a front vowel, as in *Pech* [pɛç] 'bad luck' and *siech* [ziːç] 'sickly'. Examples with two consonants are also possible: English *horseshoe* and *this shop* are produced in casual speech with medial [ʃʃ] rather than [sʃ] (Browman & Goldstein 1990).

The case for retiming and blending is supported by the fact that assimilations are usually local, involving adjacent sounds. Distant assimilation is quite irregular (Hock 1986). Only vowels assimilate across consonants. This is not distant assimilation, however, since the coarticulation literature shows that the gestures used in producing vowels, that is, lip rounding, fronting, backing, raising and lowering of the tongue body can be anticipated across consonants (Fowler & Saltzman 1993). Interestingly, Hock notes that all of these features can be assimilated across a consonant, but vowel length (a timing feature and not a gestural one) cannot. Some rather dramatic retimings or anticipations across syllables illustrate this point.

The famous case of West Germanic i-umlaut (see also Kiparsky and Donegan & Nathan, and also other chapters in this volume) involves changes in a vowel when a palatal glide or vowel occurred in the next syllable. In Old English, these involve both the fronting and the raising of vowels, as shown here (Moore & Knott 1955: 63-64):

PreOE *manni	>	OE	menn	'men'
*hāljan	>		hǣlan	'to heal'
*setjanan	>		sittan	'to sit'
*dohtri	>		dehter	'daughter'
*dōmjan	>		dēman	'to judge'
*fulljan	>		fyllan	'to fill'

The forms with back mid vowels that fronted (*dohtri and *dōmjan), later unrounded to merge with existing front mid vowels. In these examples, then, the anticipation of the doming gesture of the tongue affects the vowel of the preceding syllable, without affecting the intervening consonants. This account is consistent with experimental results that show extensive vowel-to-vowel coarticulation, as if vowel production were continuous across the articulation of consonants (see Fowler & Saltzman 1993).

A similar set of anticipatory changes occurred in the Romance languages under the influence of a palatal glide. In some cases, vowels were raised in a syllable preceding a palatal glide (or *yod*), and in some cases consonants were also affected, especially those produced with a tongue tip or dorsum gesture. These changes will be illustrated by comparing Latin and Spanish forms from Menéndez-Pidal (1968), who laid out this complex series of changes and their chronological order. In the earliest set of changes, Latin /t/ and /k/ were palatalized before the *yod*, which disappeared: thus Latin *fŏrtia* > Spanish *fuerza* 'force' and *pĕttia* > *pieza*. The diphthong in Spanish is the normal outcome for the Latin short mid vowel, so these examples show that the consonant was affected but not the vowel. (The extended sequence of developments for the consonant was probably /t/, /k/ > /tʃ/ > /ts/ > Castilian [θ] and American [s]).

A later development involved nasals and liquids; here, the preceding vowel was sometimes raised. Thus Latin *fŏlia* 'leaf' > Spanish *hoja*. The lack of a diphthong in the first syllable in Spanish indicates that the short ŏ [ɔ] in Latin was raised and as a result did not later diphthongize. The lateral plus palatal glide became a palatal lateral which later became the fricative [ʒ] and eventually velar [x]. When the consonant was a nasal, as in Latin *ĭngĕniu*, the vowel was raised and the nasal made a palatal, as in Spanish *engeño* Old Spanish 'ingenuity'. Labial consonants were not affected, though the vowel preceding them might be, as in Latin *nĕrviu* > Spanish *nervio* 'nerve' where a diphthong would have been expected, and Latin *vendēmia* > Spanish *vendimia* (rather than **vendemia*). Stunning testimony to the retiming or anticipation analysis is the case of the *yod* following /r/, /p/ and /s/, where spelling indicates that the *yod* relocated to the preceding syllable without affecting the consonant, as in Latin *caldariu* > *caldairo* > *caldeiro* > Spanish *caldero* 'pot'. Other examples of this metathesis caused by retiming of gestures are *materia* > Portuguese *madeira*; Spanish *madera* 'wood', *sapiat* > Spanish *sepa* 'know, PRES SUBJUNCTIVE' (where the outcome of [aj] was [e]) (Menéndez-Pidal 1968).

The prominence of palatalization in the catalogue of sound changes may be due to the fact that the tongue body, which must be lifted for a palatal vowel or glide, moves more slowly than the more agile tongue tip, and for this reason, its actions are subject both to anticipation and carryover effects (Recasens 1999, Bybee & Easterday in preparation). A raised and fronted tongue body also has a major effect on other gestures involving the tongue.

27.6.2 Directionality: Anticipatory or Perseverative?

In an anticipatory assimilation the first sound becomes more like the following one; while in perseverative change the second becomes more like the preceding one. In terms of gestures, the former occurs when a later gesture is anticipated and thus overlaps with an earlier one; in perseveration, a gesture is extended into a following one. Some sources also mention that anticipatory changes seem more common than perseverative ones (Hock 1986: 63, Crowley 1997: 49–50). It is difficult to test such statements because it is difficult to compile an unbiased sample of sound changes representing the world's languages. However, in the study mentioned earlier of synchronic phonetic processes (Bybee & Easterday in preparation), anticipatory retimings are indeed more common than perseverative (or carryover retimings). Of the 391 retiming processes in this database, 220 or 56 percent are anticipatory, 104 or 27 percent are perseverative and 67 or 17 percent are both. When consonants are affected, the prominence of anticipation is even greater, with 59 percent of consonant assimilation to vowels and 67 percent of consonant assimilation to consonants being anticipatory.

The dominance of anticipatory retimings has a natural explanation in a theory that takes neuromotor production as the source of phonetic processes and change. In both the acquisition of movement sequences and their production after practice, anticipation is observed (Verwey 1995, Miyashita et al. 1996, Rand et al. 1998, Rhodes et al. 2004: 716). Thus overlap of actions and its resultant fluency is in large part a result of anticipation. Racasens's (1999) review of phonetic coarticulation studies concludes that the onset of anticipation effects is more precise than the offset of carryover effects. He suggests that anticipation reflects a gestural formation event while the offset of a gesture reflects mechano-inertial properties such as how quickly the articulator can move. In addition, anticipation is necessary for fluency while carryover is not. Given that these observations would lead us to expect that most overlap of gestures is anticipatory, it is instructive to examine perseverative assimilations to determine their sources. In particular, blending of successive gestures is one source of perseverative assimilation: blending of gestures made by the same articulators may produce a result that is more like the first gesture or the second, or it may be a different compromise articulation that is nonetheless perceived as one of the constituent gestures. Another factor is that some cases of reduction (such as those mentioned just below) appear to produce perseverative assimilation. Finally, in some cases a gesture is carried over into a following gesture, producing perseverative assimilation.

A review of examples of perseverative sound changes mentioned in historical linguistics textbooks reveals that most textbooks mention the same ones. Hock (1986) gives the example of PGmc *wulna > *wull> OE *wull* 'wool' and PGmc *fulnaz > *fullaz > OE *full* 'full'. Campbell (1998) gives PIE *kolnis > Latin *collis* 'hill' and PGmc *hulnis > OE *hyll* 'hill' and OE myln > PDE mill. Campbell also supplies a similar example from alternations in Finnish: *kuul-nut > kuullut* 'heard', *pur-nut > purrut* 'bitten' and *nous-nut > noussut* 'risen'. In these, both consonants are coronal and a notable feature is that nasality is lost. Gesturally, a nasal assimilating to a non-nasal must be viewed as the loss of the gesture that opens the velum. Thus two things are going on here: the two coronal gestures blend, with the [l], [r] and [s], none of which involve closure, affecting the closure of the nasal and the loss of velum opening, perhaps in response to the loss of closure.

Another suggested perseverative assimilation is stop voicing after nasal consonants. For example, in Zoque, this takes place when morphemes are combined and the two consonants are homorganic, as in *k'im-pa* 'rise 3s' which becomes *k'imba* (Herrera Zendejas 1995). Voicing of stops after nasals is also found historically in Kannada, where Proto-Dravidian *onṭu 'one' becomes Kannada *ondu* and PD *kaṇ-ṭV 'warrior' becomes Kannada *gaṇḍu* 'bravery' (Krishnamurti 2003). From a gestural perspective, the voicelessness of the obstruent is created by a gesture which opens the glottis. The voicing is not so much an assimilation as the loss of the glottal-opening gesture. Again, what appears to be a perseverative assimilation is better described as the loss of a gesture.

Such traditional examples do not cover the entire range of possible perseverative assimilations. Some perseverative processes which occur in synchronic processes as the result of sound change are:

(1) Perseverative nasalization of both vowels and consonants after a nasal consonants: in Mwera (Harries 1950) vowels are nasalized after a nasal consonant and in some languages, such as Tucano (West 1980) and Desano (Kaye 1971) nasal harmony extends from a nasal consonant early in the word progressively through the word unless stopped by consonants of certain categories. Ferguson (1973) observes, however, that anticipatory assimilation of nasality is much more common than perseverative assimilation.

(2) Changes in vowels due to contact with a preceding consonant, including raising and fronting of vowels after a palatal vowel, glide or consonant, backing of vowels after velars and uvulars, rounding of vowels after rounded vowels or consonants, lowering of high vowels after uvulars; Bybee & Easterday (in preparation) find such changes are as likely to be perseverative as anticipatory.

(3) The palatalization and labialization of consonants after palatal and labial vowels. For palatalization, Bhat (1978) observes that consonants are more likely to be affected by a following palatal vowel or glide than a preceding one.

These are all changes that can be anticipatory or perseverative and in some cases they are both; however, as noted, anticipation is more common.

Place assimilation in two-consonant sequences leans heavily towards anticipation. Blevins (2004a) reports from her crosslinguistic survey that all such assimilation is anticipatory, except in the case of coronal retroflexion, where a sequence of retroflex consonant plus coronal becomes two retroflex consonants (Steriade 2001b, drawing examples from many Australian languages).

27.7 LENITION OF CONSONANTS: OVERLAP AND DECREASE IN MAGNITUDE OF GESTURES

As mentioned earlier, lenition of consonants has been much discussed in the sound change literature for more than a century (see Honeybone 2008 for an excellent review). The term covers quite a range of types of change (voicing of consonants, spirantization, sonorization, deletion) in a range of contexts (intervocalic, syllable-final) and as might be expected has spawned quite a range of views on how to characterize and explain the phenomenon. Documented changes can be seen as going through several stages, and it is common to talk about paths of change, as below. While some treatments refer to the formal phonological properties of the process of change (Foley 1970, Harris 1990a, Kirchner 1998), I focus here on a treatment grounded in articulation.

The proposal here is that lenition or weakening of consonants is the direct result of the reduction in the magnitude and/or the duration of the articulatory gesture that creates the consonant obstruction. Any gesture used to produce a consonant is subject to weakening—the gestures creating the main obstruction and the glottal opening (if present) are the main gestures to consider. If the main obstruction is weakened or lost, we speak of debuccalization, as when an [s] becomes an [h]. In contrast a weakening of the glottal opening may lead to voicing. Temporal reduction covers cases such as degemination and the case of American English /d/ produced as a flap in intervocalic position (in an unstressed syllable).

Lass & Anderson's (1975) discussion of consonant lenition suggests there are two types—sonorization and opening. Sonorization is reduction towards a glide or vowel; the consonant is voiced and the obstruction is incrementally lessened, as when p > w (e.g. Latin *captive* > Spanish *cautivo*). Opening does not involve voicing, but rather the decrease in the degree of closure, as when p > f > h > zero. Actually, lenition diagrams, such as in Hock (1986) and Lass (1997), seem to indicate that lenition can take various paths, e.g. according to Hock (1986:83), a [t] can become [θ, [h], [d], [ð], [r], [l] or [y].

I suggest that rather than working with only two types of consonant lenition, we consider all the different combinations of gestural weakening or shortening that can occur as well as the degree to which they occur. Consider now the classic examples of consonant lenition and the gestural changes they require.

A chain of consonant lenition occurred in Romance languages in intervocalic position, as follows:

(1) Voiced stops became fricatives or were deleted: Latin *credere* > Spanish *creer* 'to believe', *dubitar* > *dudar* 'to doubt', *frigidu* > *frío* 'cold'. This lenition consists of a reduction in the magnitude of the oral gesture, from full stop closure to fricative and finally loss of the gesture.

(2) Voiceless stops became voiced intervocalically: Latin *vita* > Spanish *vida* 'life', *lupus* > *lobo* 'wolf', *lacus* > *lago* 'lake'. As voicelessness occurring within a stream of voiced sounds is produced by a gesture which opens the glottis, the reduction in duration and magnitude of this gesture will lead to a voiceless obstruent becoming voiced.

(3) Voiceless geminate stops are shortened and remain voiceless: Latin *cŭppa* > Spanish *copa* 'cup', *gutta* > *gota* 'drop', *bucca* > *boca* 'mouth'. As geminates are produced with a single, long gesture, degemination is the temporal reduction of the oral gesture and the glottal one as well.

Perhaps as a continuation of this series of weakenings, voiced stops in Spanish become fricatives intervocalically, as shown in *vida* [biða], *lobo* [loβo] and *lago* [laɣo]. This spirantization is a clear case of the reduction in magnitude of the oral gesture. Additional evidence that such a change should be viewed as a weakening is the fact that some words, especially with *d*, lose the consonant entirely, for instance words such as *lado* 'side' can be pronounced as [lao] (D'Introno & Sosa 1986).

Part of the Second or High German Consonant Shift illustrates a different type of weakening. In word-initial position voiceless stops became affricates: Proto-Germanic **tīde* > High German [tsait] *Zeit* 'time', **pund* > [pfunt] *Pfund* 'pound'. Foley (1970) interprets this as a strengthening since he analyses affricates as stronger than stops. However, this appears to be based on acoustic/perceptual criteria. If we apply articulatory criteria consistently, an affricate should be analysed as a weakened version of a full stop, as part of the closure has been weakened to a fricative (Lass & Anderson 1975, Mowrey & Pagliuca 1995, Honeybone 2001).

Rhotacization is also a kind of lenition by which an [s] or [z] becomes an [r]. Such a change occurred in Latin as exemplified by the alternation *corpus, corpora* 'body, nom./acc. sg. and pl.', and in Germanic where Old English infinitive *cēosan* 'to choose' has the past participle *coren*. This change involves voicing and loss of fricative closure; it takes place intervocalically.

Loss of the oral gesture while the laryngeal state is maintained leads to the reduction of fricatives to [h], as in earlier Spanish, where [f] > [h] (and eventually disappeared entirely) and in current Spanish dialects where syllable-final [s] reduces its tongue tip gesture enough so that the sound is interpreted as [h]. This [h] also tends to be lost. The loss of the oral gesture in voiceless stops tends to result in a glottal stop though an adequate explanation for why the glottal opening gesture changes to a stop gesture has not been proposed (although, see Harris 1990a for one attempt).

While weakening of consonants can occur in any position, many researchers note that intervocalic position is prone to voicing as well as spirantization, and syllable-final position is 'weak' in the sense that consonants in that position tend to undergo reductive changes and can be lost entirely (Lass & Anderson 1975, Vennemann 1988). Some propose hierarchies of positions, with some positions more prone to lenition than others (Honeybone 2001, Ségéral & Scheer 2008).

Finally, it should be mentioned that consonant deletion (a type of lenition) can also be caused by gestural overlap. For instance, Browman & Goldstein (1990) have shown that the perceived deletion of the [t] in the phrase *perfect memory* is due not so much to the weakening of the final [t] as to the fact that the following labial gesture overlaps and obscures the alveolar gesture.

Given the wide variety of opinions about lenition in different frameworks, it seems prudent to work with a phonetic definition that is testable on changes of different types. The articulatory definition of 'reduction in magnitude and/or duration of a gesture' applies well to the disparate phenomena often considered to be lenition. As we will see below, it also allows us to formulate a definition of fortition—the opposite of lenition—that helps sort out which are valid instances of fortition and which are not, as in section 27.9.

27.8 MECHANISMS OF CHANGE AND OUTCOMES

To summarize the previous two sections, we have seen that three types of gestural change—increase in overlap, blending and decrease in magnitude/duration—can provide descriptions of the two most common types of sound change—assimilation and lenition. We have also seen that the classification of a sound change cannot be determined by a description strictly in terms of segments and features, but rather relies on a description in terms of the articulatory gestures involved in the change.

27.9 APPARENT STRENGTHENING AND OTHER TYPES OF CHANGE

Since a large proportion of reported sound changes can be classified according to the gestural mechanisms described above, it is useful from a theoretical point of view to be able to hypothesize that all sound changes are caused by one of these mechanisms.

However, there are several kinds of cases that resist analysis in these terms. Let us first review some apparent problems that turn out to have ready solutions. We have already mentioned that from an articulatory point of view, a stop becoming an affricate is a weakening and not a strengthening. Other changes that superficially appear to be strengthenings can also be dismissed. Consonant 'insertions' such as in OE *brǽmle* > PDE *bramble*, *þunrian* > *thunder* and cases such as Spanish *venirá* > *venrá* > *vendrá* '3s come FUT' are cases of changes in timing (Pagliuca & Mowrey 1987). In each case the anticipation of the non-nasal [r] or [l] leads to the closing of the velum while the stop closure for the nasal is still maintained resulting in an oral stop. Evidence that this is the correct analysis is the fact that the 'inserted' consonant is always at the same place of articulation as the surrounding consonants.

A case that seems more like a true strengthening is the change of a glide, usually a palatal glide, to a fricative or affricate. Such cases are attested in the history of Romance, Slavic, Bantu, and Germanic languages, but at least one ongoing case can also be documented. In Argentinian Spanish, what is a palatal glide in other dialects has become an alveopalatal fricative or in some cases an affricate. A change from glide to fricative indicates that the magnitude of the lingual gesture has increased, counter to the hypothesis offered here. A possible explanation in terms of the size and positioning of the articulator is proposed in Bybee & Easterday (in preparation). As we will see in the next section, a critical factor to examine is the pattern of lexical diffusion for such an apparent strengthening, as lexical diffusion has been shown to be a diagnostic for mechanisms of change (Bybee 2001, Phillips 2006, this volume).

Other changes that need to be investigated in this context are consonant gemination and vowel lengthening, which probably relate to rhythmic and phonotactic patterns, and certain types of metathesis, which are likely caused by the generalization of productive syllabic templates or phonotactic patterns. To the extent that such changes have been studied for their lexical diffusion patterns, it appears that they affect low frequency words first (see Phillips 2006 and Garmann 2008 for vowel lengthening).

The changes discussed above almost all concern consonant changes, but changes in vowels must be considered as well. Vowel reduction processes, which usually occur in unstressed syllables, can be considered a reduction in the magnitude and/or duration of gestures, but vowel shifts—changes in vowel height and backness—occur in stressed syllables and are not always classifiable as reduction. William Labov (1994) has studied vowel shifts extensively, focusing primarily on ongoing vowel shifts in American English. While there seem to be several factors involved, one clear type of conditioning that shows up in many shifts is the influence of the consonants surrounding the vowels. In some cases it appears that a vowel shift may be conditioned by specific surrounding consonants, such as the fronting of a high back vowel conditioned by a preceding palatal consonant. In the cases Labov has studied the shift may be extended to other consonantal environments as well, resulting in a shift of the entire vowel category. For a discussion of other factors involved in vowels shifts, see Gordon (this volume).

27.10 How Sound Change Spreads Through the Lexicon

Recent decades have seen the intense study of factors governing variation occurring when a sound change is in progress (see work by Labov and colleagues, and also Bowie & Yaeger-Dror and D'Arcy, both this volume). Variation in the production of vowels and consonants during a change in progress is affected by social factors such as speech situation, age, gender and social identification. Thus a sound change does not proceed in a uniform manner through a speech community with all speakers keeping completely in sync during the change. Rather the gradual phonetic space of the change allows for numerous variants to be used by speakers given the factors cited above.

Similarly, all words of the language do not change in lock-step. Rather, some variants are more common in some words than in others. The process by which a change spreads through the lexicon affecting individual words is known as 'lexical diffusion' (see Phillips 2006, this volume). Even when a change ends up as completely regular, meaning that all words of the lexicon are affected in the end, the process by which this occurs is gradual (see Bermúdez-Otero and Hale et al., both this volume, for a different view). Given all the factors that affect the progress of a sound change—phonetic as well as social factors—it is often difficult to isolate lexical factors and their influence. However, some recent studies have been able to show that lexical diffusion is gradual, just as phonetic progress is gradual. In particular, words of higher frequency of use undergo some changes before words that are used less often. Examples of studies that have identified this trend are American English t/d deletion (Bybee 2000), Spanish ð-deletion (D'Introno & Sosa 1986, Bybee 2002a), Spanish s-aspiration (Brown 2004), Spanish vowel hiatus resolution (Alba 2008), English vowel reduction (Fidelholtz 1975, Hooper 1976b) and Dutch vowel reduction (Van Bergem 1995) and even some vowel shifts (Moonwomon 1991, Phillips 2006). Other studies have shown that for reduction it is the frequency of the word in the reducing environment that conditions how advanced it will be in the change (Gregory et al. 1999, Bybee 2002, Brown 2004, Bell et al. 2009, Brown & Raymond 2012).

This trend in lexical diffusion supports the view that the automation of production is the factor responsible for many sound changes, particularly those of retiming and reduction of gestures. As practice enhances motor activities and makes them more fluent, the greater practice afforded high frequency words and phrases allows changes to proceed in these contexts earlier than in others. Further evidence for the role of gestural automation due to repetition is the fact that as words and phrases achieve extreme high frequency, they undergo even more reduction, as for instance, when the flap is deleted in the phrase *I don't know* (Bybee & Scheibman 1999; see also Donegan & Nathan, this volume). To explain how such lexical change occurs gradually, Bybee (2000) and Pierrehumbert (2001) have proposed an exemplar model in which each token of experience has an impact on stored cognitive representations, including the phonetic representations of words and phrases. As a reducing or retiming trend occurs in production, the newly produced token cycles back into the stored exemplar cloud for the word experienced and makes a small change in this cloud for both speaker and listener. Thus words that are used more have more exemplars that have undergone a small, gradual change and if these exemplars are chosen for production, they undergo further changes, increasing the pace of change in high frequency words. As more and more words undergo the change, the general production routines are changed, leading finally to the spread of the change to words of lower frequency.

Given the link between changes motivated by the automation of production and the diffusion of the change from high frequency to low frequency words, lexical diffusion can be used as a diagnostic for the causes of change (Hooper 1976b, Phillips 1984, Bybee 2012). Other patterns of lexical diffusion also occur. Phillips (1984, 2006) has shown that some changes affect low frequency words first. Such changes, then, are highly unlikely to have the same motivation as those with the opposite pattern of diffusion. Those that affect low frequency words may be changes based on productive patterns of phonotactics or other aspects of phonological structure. They behave more like morphological regularization, which affects low frequency paradigms before high frequency ones. Thus lexical diffusion patterns provide another view into the causes of sound change.

A related question concerns the point at which we want to recognize that a sound change has occurred. Some theories put coarticulation and phonetic variation outside of the grammar and postulate that a sound change only occurs when such variation and detail become phonologized into the grammar (Ohala 2003, Blevins 2004a, Harrington et al. 2011, and see also Bermúdez-Otero and Hale et al., both this volume). However, the data on lexical diffusion make this seem implausible. These data show that a sound change can be both phonetically gradual and lexically gradual. As pointed out in Bybee (2000, 2001, 2002a) and Pierrehumbert (2001), the fact that lexical items can exhibit individual ranges of variation, based on their frequency and other factors, indicates that language users store clouds of exemplars that reflect the tokens they have actually experienced rather than abstract phonological units. At the moment at which the language user experiences a phonetically distinct token of a word or phrase, this is registered in the exemplar cloud and in effect changes it. In exemplar theory there would be no distinction between phenomena that are 'in' the grammar *vs* those that are not. The potential for a language-wide sound change is registered in the grammar (defined as the cognitive representation of language) from the first instance of experience.

27.11 ARTICULATORY PROCESSING *vs* OTHER SOURCES OF CHANGE

As mentioned above, the pattern of lexical diffusion can tell us something about the mechanism by which sound change occurs. So far we have discussed only the production side of language processing without mentioning the acoustic/perceptual domain. Given the exemplar model just described, it is clear that exemplars are entered in cognitive representation in the form in which they are perceived. Thus any articulatory change can only become part of a speaker's cognitive representation and transmitted from speaker to hearer via perception.

The question to consider briefly now is whether there are changes that originate in a misperception, as argued by Ohala in a number of papers (especially Ohala 2003), as well as Blevins (2004a, this volume), and see also Yu (this volume).

We listed above several changes that are mostly reductive in nature that show diffusion from high to low frequency words and argued that this indicates the change comes about through the automation of production. Consider now whether such changes could originate in misperceptions. Three problems with the claims of faulty perception instigating sound change will be mentioned here (see also Scheer and Yu, both this volume, and also Bybee 2012). First, human language users are exceptionally adept at acquiring the very fine phonetic detail of their native dialect; that makes it implausible that they would misperceive the phonetic shape of words, especially of words they already know. Rather, as change is occurring the perceptual representation keeps pace with the productions experienced (Beddor 2009). Second, the type of change that originates in misperception should not be directional; that is, misperception of X as Y should be as likely as the misperception of Y as X. Changes that move in one direction only are not likely to be due to misperception (Pensado 1996). Third, if misperception were the cause of change, we would expect this to originate in low frequency words, which are less available in the input, rather than in high frequency words. In fact, a change that starts with low frequency words might well be caused by a failure to perceive the correct phonetic shape of a word, e.g. when sounds are first being acquired. This point demonstrates the importance of various patterns of lexical diffusion to determining the causes of sound change.

Unfortunately the lexical diffusion diagnostic has not been applied to the purported cases of misperception. Furthermore, many cases of alleged change by misperception actually are operating on a prior articulatory retiming or reduction, such as vowel nasalization (Ohala 2003) or velar palatalization (Guion 1998). For instance, Guion demonstrates an acoustic and perceptual similarity between a velar before a front vowel and the alveo-palatal affricate [tʃ]. As she notes, a velar in this position is fronted, that is, the velar gesture and the fronted tongue body gesture have already blended before any perceptual change can occur. In this case, as in others, the original innovation was motivated by articulation.

This is not reason, however, to deny that perception may play some role in sound change. Indeed, the results of coarticulation and reduction are often sounds that are gesturally or perceptually complex, and which go on to suffer further changes. Such changes need to be studied in a way that exploits all the potential sources of information about a sound change (see Bybee 2012 for a list, as well as Garrett & Johnson 2013). These sources would include experimental data on both articulation and perception, typological data about possible directions for change, data on gradualness or abruptness of change and data on patterns of lexical diffusion.

27.12 CONCLUSION

The view presented here is that the potential for sound change resides in every utterance produced, as the natural (domain-general) tendency for neuromotor automation of repeated activities is the reduction and overlap of gestures. Supporting this is the fact that assimilation and lenition are the most common types of sound change and that such changes are carried further in casual speech and affect high frequency words and phrases before low frequency ones. Articulatory changes will also be gradual, so there is a set of properties that can be used to identify articulatory changes (Bybee 2012).

Phonological changes that have other motivations or causes will likely turn out to have a different set of characteristics—perhaps being phonetically abrupt, affecting low frequency words before high frequency, failing to achieve lexical generality and showing typological bidirectionality (Bybee 2012). A coherent theory of sound change would require that the phonetic, lexical and typological properties of particular changes be taken into account.

CHAPTER 28

EVOLUTIONARY PHONOLOGY

A Holistic Approach to Sound Change Typology

JULIETTE BLEVINS

28.1 EVOLUTIONARY PHONOLOGY AND SOUND CHANGE TYPOLOGY

A central goal of Evolutionary Phonology (Blevins 2004a, 2006a, 2008a, 2009a, 2009b, 2010b) is to explain why certain sound patterns have the properties and typological distributions they do. Why are sound patterns involving, for example, final obstruent devoicing, extremely common cross-linguistically, while final obstruent voicing is rare? Why is laryngeal epenthesis common but sibilant epenthesis rare? Though such questions relate directly to aspects of synchronic sound patterns, comprehensive answers to them can refer to properties of sound change typology. Common sound patterns often reflect common instances of sound change. Since the most common instances of sound change appear to be those with clear and robust phonetic conditioning, this model offers a direct link between phonetically motivated sound change and common sound patterns. In contrast, rare sound patterns may reflect rare types of sound change, rare historical sequences of change, lack a source in phonetically motivated sound change, reflect language-specific analogical change, or, for other reasons, be the endpoint of a highly unlikely evolutionary pathway.[1]

Sound change typology is a somewhat new area of study, to the extent that clear explanations are sought for properties of sound change (target, structural change, environment), typological distributions of sound change (common, rare, areal properties, structural

---

[1] Assessment of what is common and what is rare is based more and more on attempts to collect sound patterns and instances of sound change in cross-linguistic databases that seek to overcome genetic or areal biases. See Gilman (2012a) for a recent overview of databases of this kind, and Gilman (2012b) on how one can use such databases effectively in applying the comparative method. See also Kümmel (this volume).

associations), and asymmetries in certain types of change (e.g. velar palatalization *vs* palatal velarization, final obstruent devoicing *vs* final obstruent voicing). For common patterns of obstruent devoicing and laryngeal epenthesis, we now have a relatively good grasp of the phonetic origins of both of these processes. Phrase-final obstruent devoicing can have its source in aerodynamic, articulatory, and perceptual properties of the speech stream, while the opposite process of voicing an obstruent in this position has no known phonetic source (Blevins 2006a, 2006b). Phonetic origins for epenthetic laryngeals have also been studied. Laryngeal epenthesis appears to have its origins in laryngeal articulations that mark phrase boundaries in many languages, most notably constriction or spreading of the vocal folds (Blevins 2008a). In contrast, synchronic patterns of sibilant epenthesis do not have direct phonetic sources and are rarer: either a phonetically natural epenthetic glide subsequently undergoes strengthening to a sibilant; or a historical process of sibilant lenition and loss is reanalysed as an inverted rule of sibilant insertion (Blevins 2008a). The prevalence of velar palatalization over palatal (or coronal) velarization appears to be related to perceptual biases (Guion 1998), and supports the common view that perception and misperception play important roles in common types of sound change (see Ohala 1981, 1993, and Yu, this volume, and see also Bybee, this volume, for a different view).

Phonetic explanations for sound patterns not only allow identification of sound patterns with common natural bases in contrast to those lacking the same, but also offer new insights into properties of the sound patterns themselves: final devoicing is more common than initial devoicing because it can be associated with natural decay of intra-oral air pressure and phrase-final lengthening. In contrast, initial and final laryngeal epenthesis are both common due to association of both initial and final phrase boundaries with language-specific laryngeal landmarks. Phonetic explanations for both of these patterns also allow one to better understand the pathway of phonologization (Hyman 1976), the life cycle of sounds (*vs* the life cycle of sound CHANGE, cf. Bermúdez-Otero and Kiparsky, both this volume), from variable phonetic patterns, to statistical regularities, to identifiable sound patterns associated with the phonology of a particular language. Both final-devoicing and laryngeal epenthesis appear to begin as variable phrase boundary phenomena, with phonologization resulting in regularization of the pattern at phrase boundaries, then smaller phrase or word boundaries, and only later to foot and/or syllable boundaries (Blevins 2006a, 2008a, Mielke 2013, and see Bermúdez-Otero, this volume, for a related but more formal view).

As more sound changes have received plausible phonetic explanations grounded in theories of speech production, speech perception, and acoustic and aerodynamic properties of speech,[2] we can ask new questions about sound change typology. Given that a particular sound change is understood to be phonetically natural, grounded in articulatory, perceptual, or aerodynamic properties of speech, can we identify independent phonetic and non-phonetic factors that can encourage or inhibit the particular change?

---

[2] See, for example, Kümmel (this volume) on the Glottalic Theory. A more comprehensive phonetic grounding of laryngeal features, especially voice and breathy voice, and their role in sound change is presented in Miller (2012). Not only sound patterns and sound change but distinctive features themselves are shown to be emergent properties of recurrent sound change (Mielke 2008, 2013).

Are there phonetically natural sound changes that require specific structural phonological preconditions? Are there other structural conditions that can give rise to phonetically unnatural but regular instances of sound change? Are there lexical conditions that can inhibit regular sound change? In this chapter, I briefly summarize recent work on these topics. The general view put forth is that the original neogrammarian dichotomy between phonetic law and analogy (see Murray, this volume) needs to be expanded and elaborated. Phonetic laws may be phonetically natural only in the context of particular phonological systems. Analogy may be word-based, but other types of analogical change must be recognized as well, including those that are based on structural properties of sound patterns (see Fertig, this volume). Further, where relationships between word-forms can form the basis of analogical change, they can also be the nexus of inhibited sound change.

This holistic approach to sound change can be viewed as a natural extension of the integration of analogy and exemplar-based modelling into neogrammarian theories of sound change.[3] As summarized and elaborated on by Karsten (1894: 312):[4]

> The mechanical dissection of individual words could no longer be applied to languages which had inherited these words as ready-made units, but each single word-form *must be judged as a whole* in connection with and in the light of related forms ...

Within this framework, sounds and words are not considered in isolation but form constellations of sounds and words within an exemplar-based model of grammatical knowledge (Goldinger 1996, Johnson 1997, Pierrehumbert 2001, Gahl & Yu 2006, Wedel 2006, and also Bybee, Wedel, and Yu, all this volume). Relationships between exemplars and structural generalizations gleaned from them form the basis of positive and negative forces conditioning sound change.

Three properties of this model are strikingly modern. First, linguistic representations are assumed to contain a great deal of phonetic detail (cf. Pierrehumbert 2002, Jannedy & Hay 2006, Baayen 2007). Second, speakers are thought to store generalizations involving this phonetic detail at multiple intersecting levels, for example, word, syllable, and segment (cf. Bybee 2002, Pierrehumbert 2003b). And third, speakers' mental representations are thought to include a record of previously encountered detail, with this detail influencing subsequent categorization and production (cf. Pierrehumbert 2001, 2006,

---

[3] On exemplar modelling, see chapters by Bybee, Phillips, Wedel and Yu in this volume, as well as Morley (2012, 2014) for specific proposals concerning regular sound change.

[4] Karsten was a student of Hermann Paul. For an overview of Paul's (1880/1920) exemplar-based approach to memories and their role in sound change, see Garrett & Johnson (2013), and for a general history of historical phonology, see Murray (this volume). I focus on Karsten because he explored listener-based innovation, and seemed to have a clear notion of misperception or altered perception and its role in sound change. He, then, is an exception to Garrett & Johnson's (2013: 6) observation that '... in emphasizing the articulatory basis of sound change, neither the neogrammarians nor their successors explored the possible details of listener-based innovation'. Another linguist with early emphasis on the role of listeners in sound change is Kruszewski (e.g. 1881), whose contributions to this area are detailed in Silverman (2012).

Wedel 2007, Blevins & Wedel 2009). This last point results in a grammar which is neither purely synchronic nor diachronic: grammars are constantly changing systems, shifting ever so slightly each time a new linguistic experience of hearing or speaking takes place, and changing in a myriad of ways as memories themselves wax and wane.

This last property is the focus of a lengthy discussion in Karsten's 1894 paper. In recognizing the degree of variation in the signal he questions how categorization occurs, suggesting a merger of exemplars:

> ... it is of extreme importance in speech ... how can repetition take place in such a way that the new impression fits into, and renews or strengthens the memory picture of a previous impression, when in reality, considering the incessant change of subject and object, no two impressions can ever be perfectly equal? They can indeed only be more or less similar to each other, but they are nevertheless connected in our mind and for this reason: similarity means, of course, partial equality, equality of parts, and the apperception of equal impressions into the same memory-picture naturally involves the merging into one another of the corresponding equal parts of two similar impressions.
>
> (Karsten 1894: 318)

His conclusion is that this merger of auditory representations results in shifts or movements, analogous to those posited in modern exemplar models when blended memory traces give rise to what has been termed an aggregate response (e.g. Goldinger 1996, Pierrehumbert 2002):

> It appears that it is not the spoken word that changes, but the acoustic picture in our mind through its transmission from one individual to the other. Treating now first the especially so-called phonetic changes, it is clear that the very act of speaking involves the possibility and the necessity of change ... We at once understand that there must be an infinite number of speech varieties in existence all the time ... All these speech varieties are constantly influencing each other. Even a pronunciation noticeably different from our own and one which we subconsciously feel to be less perfect will affect our own speech as long as the sound-pictures heard promptly call up and join the memory-pictures in our mind, and the result must be a new, composite sound-picture, a compromise between the old and the new.
>
> (Karsten 1894: 325)

Within Evolutionary Phonology also, sound change is a feature of grammars. A synchronic grammar is a useful idealization, but there is no true static grammar.[5] Linguistic experience at every turn alters the memories of an individual, and can thereby minutely

---

[5] It is worth clarifying this, as some criticisms of Evolutionary Phonology and related approaches claim that these models have no role for synchronic grammars. This is not true. Synchronic generalizations can be useful and meaningful in accounting for observed productivity in sound patterns, from observed nonce words and loan phonology, to a range of behaviours exhibited under experimental conditions. However, any formalization of synchronic generalizations of this kind within Evolutionary Phonology (or other models accepting exemplar-based generalization) acknowledges that these generalizations: (i) may differ across speakers; (ii) may differ across periods of a single lifespan of

alter the grammar. The importance of exemplar-based modelling in understanding sound change typology has only recently begun to be appreciated, and I will highlight its role in what follows. (Other chapters in this volume present alternative views, for example Scheer and Bermúdez-Otero argue against phonetic reductionism, and Dresher and Purnell & Raimy see a role for purely formal factors in understanding change.)

A central goal of Evolutionary Phonology is to understand sound patterns, to the extent possible, in terms of their evolutionary history. This requires a clear understanding of the fundamental nature of sound change, and it is this understanding of sound change, and its holistic nature, that provides the focus of the remainder of this chapter.

28.2 THE PHONETIC BASIS OF SOUND CHANGE

The phonetic basis of sound change in neogrammarian models was limited, for the most part, to variable articulation. Evolutionary Phonology follows Karsten (1894), and the extensive research programme of John J. Ohala in the twentieth century in integrating all aspects of phonetic science into a more comprehensive model of sound change and sound change typology. A sound change may have origins in articulatory variation, aspects of speech aerodynamics, perceptual properties of speech, or some combination of these. For example, both articulatory variation in the production of coda nasal consonants and the percepts associated with this variation give rise to common sound change taking VN. (where . = syllable boundary) sequences to nasalized vowels (Beddor 2009). In contrast, the context-free devoicing of voiced obstruents does not seem to be grounded in articulatory variation, but follows, primarily, from the aerodynamics of voicing (Ohala 1997a).[6] Other sound changes, like the shift of θ > f, appear to be based not in articulatory variation or aerodynamics, but in the acoustic/perceptual similarity of the two sounds (Blevins

---

an individual; and (iii) may be formulated in terms of learned or emergent phonological categories as opposed to innate or universally specified ones.

In this way, Evolutionary Phonology differs significantly from generative rule-based approaches and Optimality Theory where rules and their subparts, or constraints and their evaluation, are posited as universally specified components of phonological grammars, and claimed to be uniform across speakers of the same language. See Dresher and Holt (both this volume) for more on these alternative approaches to sound change.

At the same time, Evolutionary Phonology differs centrally from other usage-based models (e.g. Bybee 2001) by acknowledging highly specific synchronic generalizations (constraints on distribution of laryngeal features, anti-gemination, the nature of *TL gaps, etc.) and attempts to understand the extent to which these can be explained by a confluence of external and language-specific factors.

[6] An aerodynamic explanation for context-free devoicing makes predictions regarding the most and least likely stops to passively devoice: [g] is more likely to devoice than [d], which is more likely to devoice than [b]. See Ohala & Riordan (1980), Ohala (1997a), and Pape et al. (2003) for further discussion. Though Blust (1996a) attributes pandemic irregularity of word-initial velar stop reflexes within Austronesian to perceptual confusions of [k] and [g] due to smaller differences in VOT than stops at other points of articulation, the aerodynamics of voicing may also be involved, and may even be primary.

2004a: 134–5, 2006c: 11–12).[7] Within each of these broad categories, finer explanatory models exist. For example, in the articulatory domain, Lindblom (1990) has elaborated the H&H model where articulatory compression and expansion are modelled, giving rise to numerous types of reduction/lenition and strengthening/fortition respectively (see also Yu, this volume). And Articulatory Phonology is refining models of articulatory timing and overlap which can explain many cases of apparent segment deletion and insertion in terms of gestural overlap and non-overlap respectively (e.g. Browman & Goldstein 1992, Byrd 1992, Pouplier & Goldstein 2010, and see also Bybee, this volume, who argues that only articulation and not misperception has any role in change).

An additional feature of new approaches to sound change typology are attempts to classify sound changes in terms of their fundamental phonetic catalyst or source. As phonetic science advances, clearer and more precise explanations for a range of phenomena have emerged, expanding the neogrammarian bipartite scheme of gradual articulatory drift and 'other'. Within Evolutionary Phonology, a primary three-way classification of sound change distinguishes CHANGE, CHANCE, and CHOICE. Of these, the category which includes sound change based on articulatory variation (co-articulation/assimilation, lenition, fortition) is CHOICE. Sound changes with origins in CHOICE differ in several ways from the classical neogrammarian conception of articulatory variability. Variation can be due to compression or expansion along the hyper-to-hypoarticulation continuum, to imprecision, to gestural overlap, or to aerodynamic features of the vocal tract which give rise to variable articulation.[8] It is important to stress that expansion or intensification of articulatory gestures results in fortition or strengthening. While regular sound changes involving strengthening are, overall, less common than weakening, and tend to be associated with strong prosodic positions, they need not be, and require a place in any sound change typology.[9] Consider, for example, the context-free shifts of *w > g^w and *j > dz in the history of Chamorro (Blust 2000). The shift from a glide to an obstruent involves articulatory strengthening, and since these are context-free, they cannot be attributed to retiming of gestures in the context of a strong prosodic position.[10] In addition to glide-strengthening of this kind, strengthenings that are near

---

[7] A reviewer questions whether articulatory difficulty of [θ] may play a role in θ > f sound change. While it could be a factor, one must still explain why [θ] shifts to [f] (which is not an articulatory variant of [θ]), as opposed to [s], [t], etc. For a phonetically based perceptual similarity metric, see Mielke (2012).

[8] This classification differs slightly from that presented in Garrett & Johnson (2013), where variation due to aerodynamic factors is classified separately. Within Evolutionary Phonology, what groups these two types together as CHOICE is the variability of tokens yielding an exemplar space from which speakers 'choose' a norm, or, more accurately, calculate an aggregate based on the distribution of these variants. See Morley (2014) for a precise model of this procedure.

[9] It is striking how often the prevalence of leniting sound changes leads to models where fortition is simply ruled out. Mowrey & Pagliuca (1995), for example, claim that all temporal changes are due to the compression of gestures, while Bybee (2001: 79–81, and see also Bybee, this volume) seems to suggest that temporal and substantive reduction are the main types of articulatory change, but admits that 'one might conclude that strengthening does take place under certain conditions' (Bybee 2001: 81).

[10] It is entirely possible that there was an intermediate stage of voiced fricatives. However, the shift from glides to voiced fricatives is also one of articulatory strengthening. Aerodynamic factors disfavouring voiced fricatives are discussed in the context of sound change in Garrett & Johnson (2013).

mirror images of common weakening processes are also attested. Common debuc-calizations of voiceless fricatives (e.g. s > h, x > h), can be compared with less common context-sensitive strengthening of h to voiceless fricatives, as appears to have occurred in, for example, Singhi, where Pre-Singhi *-i > ih > Singhi /-is/, and Pre-Singhi *-u > -uh > /-ux/, and in the same languages where historical *h yields fricatives. In the same contexts, these final fricatives have been further strengthened to stops, resulting in patterns like Pre-Lom *-i > ih > ic > /-ic/, and *-u > -uh > ux > /-uk/ (Mortensen 2004, cf. Blust 1994).

Under CHANGE, the phonetic signal is misperceived by the listener due to acoustic/perceptual similarities between the utterance and the perceived utterance, and biases in the human perceptual system. The existence of this category has been recently called into question by Garrett & Johnson (2013). For this reason, it is worth listing some of the most convincing cases of perceptual bias in the literature. They include: misperception of palatalized velars as alveopalatals in velar palatalization sound change (Guion 1998);[11] the misperception of heterorganic intervocalic nasal-stop clusters as homorganic nasal-stop clusters based on the place features of the stop, accounting for common regressive place assimilation sound changes $VN_iT_jV > VN_jT_jV$ (Ohala 1990); the misperception of [t] as [k] in languages with /k/-gaps, accounting for common t > k sound changes in Austronesian (Blevins 2004a: 123–5, Blust 2004); the misperception of [kl] as [tl] in languages with /tl/-gaps, accounting for kl > tl sound changes (Blevins & Grawunder 2009); the tendency for listeners to hear long vowels with final devoicing as short vowels, accounting for common final-vowel-shortening sound changes (Myers & Hansen 2007); and the mishearing of [θ] as [f], or [f] as [θ], which accounts for θ > f and f > θ sound changes in a range of unrelated languages (Blevins 2004a: 134–5, 2006c: 11–12).[12] I return to gaps as preconditions for sound change in cases of CHANGE in section 28.4.

The CHANCE classification includes sound changes whose origins lie in the intrinsic phonological ambiguity of the phonetic signal. These typically involve long-domain features which are reanalysed in non-historic positions, and include vowel harmony, compensatory lengthening, dissimilation, and metathesis.

In terms of matching phonetic discoveries in all these areas with sound change typology, there are at least two basic complementary approaches. One can start with unexplained sound changes and search the phonetic literature for potential explanations (e.g. Blevins 2004a), or one can look at phonetic results and attempt to predict types of expected sound changes (Garrett & Johnson 2013). Both approaches appear to be productive, and in many cases, as expected, the methods converge. While many of the most

---

[11] The role of co-articulation in velar palatalization is not questioned; but as in the case of θ > f discussed earlier, a shift in articulator, in this case from dorsal to coronal, still needs to be explained, and can be through perceptual bias.

[12] The existence of f > θ sound change is disputed (e.g. Garrett & Johnson 2013, Donegan & Nathan, this volume); however, there appears to be at least one clear case in Peninsular Spanish, as reported in Fernández (1996: 216).

common sound changes now have well-accepted phonetic explanations (see Blevins 2004a, 2008b, Garrett & Johnson 2013), there remain recalcitrant cases that are not well understood. I turn now to some of these.

28.3 Regular Sound Change without Phonetic Motivation?

28.3.1 Apparent Cases?

In a controversial paper, Blust (2005) has suggested that regular sound change can occur without phonetic motivation. The changes he discusses are not analogical, and have all the hallmarks of regular phonetically based sound change: they target natural classes, they are regular, and they apply in very specific phonetic or phonological environments. Blust classifies ten regular sound changes in Austronesian in this way. Since the majority of these changes involve unlikely single-step changes in the feature composition of segments (e.g. *b > -k- in Berawan), there is always the possibility of intermediate steps which have been erased from the historic record. However, Blust (2005: 264) remarks: 'No amount of speculation about possible intermediate steps is likely to provide a plausible phonetic motivation for more than a few of the changes considered here...'. In light of this, he concludes that they defy phonetic explanation, and, quite radically, that they defy linguistic explanation altogether.[13]

Consider his claim that the sound change of word-final *-b, -d, -g > -m, -n, -ŋ which occurred independently in two Austronesian languages, Northern Batak and Berawan, has no clear phonetic basis. As pointed out by Blevins (2007), if an intermediate stage of pre- or post-nasalized stops can be justified, then a phonetic explanation would be possible, with a final stage involving retiming or loss of oral airflow. Indeed, variation between voiced stops and pre-nasalized voiced stops is common cross-linguistically. Furthermore, in Mwotlap, an Oceanic language, synchronic variation occurs between word-final ^{m}b, ^{n}d, and m, n. In sum, a phonetically natural sequence of changes, *-b/-d/-g > -^{m}b, -^{n}d, -^{ŋ}g > -m/-n/-ŋ or *-b/-d/-g > -b^{m}, -d^{n}, -g^{ŋ} > -m/-n/-ŋ would involve a sequence of changes, each of which is independently evidenced by phonetically based variation or change elsewhere in the world. For a discussion of other cases which lend themselves to reanalysis in terms of intermediate stages or analogical change, see Blevins (2008a, 2008b).

---

[13] This theme, that regular sound change can be phonetically and linguistically unmotivated, is a recurrent one in Blust's recent work. For example, Blust (2001, 2005, 2007) insists that the syncope of stressed vowels in Mussau is a subcase of a regular syncope rule, and therefore, defies phonetic motivation. More recently, Blust (2009) suggests that the Palauan intrusive velar nasal has no plausible historical phonetic or analogical source. See Blevins (2008c) where the Mussau case is reanalysed as a combination of phonetic unstressed vowel syncope and analogical change, and Blevins & Kaufman (2012) on a historical morphological source for the Palauan velar nasal.

28.3.2 Real Cases?

Are there regular sound changes which, to the best of our knowledge, are not the result of analogy, and yet lack a plausible phonetic explanation? There appear to be very few, though Blust's (2005) example of Sundanese w/b > c-, -nc- certainly qualifies. This is a one-of-a-kind change and it is context-free, so, it could involve multiple intermediate stages. Are there other recurrent changes that are context-sensitive and smack of phonetic explanation, though none is apparent?

The ultimate answer to this question should have an important bearing on theories of phonological markedness (e.g. de Lacy 2006) and their relationship to language change. If universal phonological markedness principles can play a role in language change, then phonetically unmotivated regular sound change is expected. For example, if there is a true markedness principle which values open syllables over closed ones, we might expect a phonetically unmotivated sound change of unconditioned coda loss in one or more of the world's languages. Interestingly, the sound changes which come closest to this hypothetical case appear to have interesting structural preconditions which suggest language-specific, as opposed to universal, conditioning. Before looking at these cases, I briefly review two recurrent sound changes that have neither a clear phonetic explanation, nor explanations grounded in phonological markedness.

One sound change that remains in this category is low vowel dissimilation, a recurrent sound change targeting sequences of low vowels in adjacent syllables. Under this sound change, the first of two low vowels becomes non-low: aCa > eCa, aCa > iCa, aCa > əCa. Blust (1996b, 1996c) details at least five seemingly independent cases of low vowel dissimilation sound change in Oceanic, and the discovery of a parallel alternation in Alamblak, a Sepik Hill language of New Guinea suggests that the change is independent of structural pressures unique to Proto-Oceanic (Blevins 2009c). A phonological markedness principle disfavouring *aCa sequences seems ad hoc, and does not explain why the sequence is resolved by vowel raising, nor why it is the first vowel in the sequence which undergoes a change. As with most markedness accounts, a successful analysis in non-phonetic terms will still leave its typology unexplained: why is this sound change common in Oceanic languages but so rare elsewhere in the world?

Another sound change that appears to remain in this category is the wholesale loss of word-initial consonants in a wide range of Australian languages (Blevins 2001).[14] Though weakening of initial consonants in unstressed syllables with subsequent loss is an expected development, some of these languages show no evidence of a lenition phase, with the full range of oral stops, nasals, liquids, and glides seemingly dropping

---

[14] Since direct outputs of this change are vowel-initial words and syllables, which, under most theories, are claimed to be marked sound patterns, the sound change has not, as far as I know, been attributed directly to a phonological markedness account. Again, it could be, but the markedness constraint demanding, for example, that words begin with vowels, would appear to be ad hoc, and again, there would be no explanation for the typological distribution of this change: why is it common in Australian languages and rare elsewhere? See directly below for a re-evaluation of potential phonetic conditioning factors.

off the edge of the word. Until recently, this sound change was limited to Australian languages, suggesting a structural pressure or phonetic property of initial consonants unique to that area or family. However, in a recent study of the historical phonology of the Sogeram languages of Papua New Guinea, Daniels (2010) reports on a strikingly parallel development in the West Sogeram languages Nend and Atemple where 'all word-initial consonants were lost from polysyllabic words' (p. 172). While the polysyllabic condition suggests that stressed monosyllables were exempt, and therefore that, as in Australia, initial C-loss was mostly likely associated with stressless syllables, it is still striking that in West Sogeram voiceless stops, nasals, and the sibilant *s are all lost. At the same time, comparative evidence from other Sogeram languages supports intermediate stages of lenition: in South Central Sogeram, word-initial *p-, *t-, *k- lenited to voiced fricatives. Given that some Australian languages also show evidence of initial lenition as opposed to loss, it seems more likely that what looks like abrupt C-loss in initial unstressed syllables may be the end result of a phonetically natural sequence of changes, with articulatory reduction of the unstressed syllable resulting in lenited consonants, before being lost altogether.

A mirror-image sound change is the regular loss of word-final consonants that has occurred multiple times in the Austronesian family (Blevins 2004b, 2009b). As with the cases just discussed, the phonetically surprising fact about most of these changes is that there is no evidence for intermediate lenition, nor any evidence of a scale of resistance to loss: voiced and voiceless stops, sibilants, and nasals simply fall off the end of the word without a trace. Where they are maintained before suffixes, there is no evidence of lenition.[15] Unlike the two sound changes mentioned above, however, there is a plausible explanation for this change in terms of universal markedness: the loss of a final consonant renders the final syllable open, and can be attributed to a universal preference for open syllables. One central problem with a markedness account is a typological one: if universal markedness is invoked, why is word-final consonant loss relatively common within the Austronesian family, but rare elsewhere in the world's languages?[16]

In this case, a structural phonological account can be proposed, but it is language-specific not universal. As noted in Blevins (2004b), there is a correlation

[15] In a limited number of Southern Melanesian languages only subclasses of consonants are lost (Lynch 2005). For example, in Northern New Caledonia, only final nasals are lost, while in Aneityum, *k, *q, and *R are lost, but nasals and other stops are maintained. Still, in these languages, there is no evidence of gradual loss in the form of lenition.

[16] Final C-loss is limited to a fairly well-defined subgroup within the Austronesian family: it is found only in languages which descend from Proto-Central Eastern Malayo-Polynesian. This means it is not found in any Formosan languages, nor in any Western Malayo-Polynesian languages. The explanation I propose accounts directly for this distribution. Elsewhere, the only sound change I know of which resembles this one is the Middle Indo-Aryan loss of all final consonants but the final velar nasal (or nasal glide) (Masica 1991: 170). However, the retention of the final velar nasal is a significant difference, at least in the context of the explanation below. Preference for open syllables in early stages of first-language acquisition appears to be an unrelated performance effect (Blevins 2004a: 227–32) that quickly disappears. If this developmental stage did play a role in sound change, we would expect far more languages to show the general C-loss pattern.

between final consonant loss, which has occurred independently at least fourteen times within the Austronesian language family, and the elimination of inherited word-medial codas. In Proto-Austronesian, canonical word templates were disyllabic, and many consisted of reduplicated $C_1VC_2 C_1VC_2$ strings. An innovation at the level of Proto-Central Eastern Malayo-Polynesian was a reduction of all medial consonant clusters to single consonants (Blust 1993), resulting in canonical CVCVC words. In every case where abrupt final consonant loss occurred, it resulted in languages which had only open syllables. In other words, in all languages which underwent -C > zero, there were no word-medial codas before the change occurred. The explanation I propose is very simple. In the process of acquiring a language where all non-final syllables are open, there is a strong expectation on the part of the language learner that syllables will be open. It is this expectation or structural analogy that can result in inattention to and subsequent loss of final consonants. Returning to the exemplar-based model introduced at the start, generalizations across sound patterns in the language will result in a dominant CV syllable structure. As new words enter the lexicon in the course of acquisition, this dominant pattern may exert itself in a top-down fashion: where final consonants may be in unstressed syllables and at the end of a phrase, and less prominent than others to begin with, a further structural pressure will lead the listener to assume they are not there at all.[17]

This simple analysis of final C-loss in Central Eastern Malayo-Polynesian languages makes several interesting predictions that can be tested both against new-found typological data and in the laboratory. First, it suggests that in the stage preceding a regular sound change of final consonant loss, there will be no non-final (unambiguous) closed syllables. Second, it suggests that structural priming of the kind necessary to induce the change should be discoverable in properly designed laboratory experiments. Experimental paradigms for testing phonological priming exist, though to date they have been used primarily to explore the nature of phonemic categories. In cases where phonemic category boundaries are shifted, subjects have been shown to have more inclusive phonemic categories depending on the shifts they are exposed to, extending these shifts to new words (e.g. Cutler et al. 2005). Could exposure to open-syllable-only words in the laboratory induce listeners to mishear final VC# sequences as V#, where C is a weak but audible consonant, while others, exposed to only closed syllables, hear the final C more consistently? A positive answer to this question would support the language-specific structural account given above, and the more general thesis that pre-existing phonotactics of a language is important to understanding sound change typology.

In sum, there may be cases of regular sound change that cannot be explained in purely phonetic terms. Although there is some indication that word-final consonants are weaker than word-initial consonants in many Austronesian languages, this relative weakness alone is not enough to result in the regular loss of final consonants. On the

---

[17] See Wedel (this volume) for models of feedback loops in the course of language acquisition with these kinds of effects.

contrary, the majority of Western Malayo-Polynesian languages retain these consonants with little change. However, if this intrinsic weakness is coupled with word phonotactics where all non-final syllables are open, there seems to be a tendency for final consonants to be lost. This hypothesis harks back to Karsten's remarks in section 28.1, that '... each single word-form must be judged as a whole in connection with and in the light of related forms ... ' (p. 2), that 'equality of parts, and the apperception of equal impressions into the same memory-picture naturally involves the merging into one another of the corresponding equal parts of two similar impressions' (p. 3), and that 'a pronunciation ... will affect our own speech ... and join the memory-pictures in our mind, and the result must be a new, composite sound-picture, a compromise between the old and the new' (p. 3).

28.4 WHERE PHONETIC MOTIVATION IS NOT ENOUGH

Sound change typology then is shaped, to a large degree, by phonetic naturalness. However, we have uncovered at least one area where structural properties of a language might encourage a regular sound change that would otherwise not take place. It may also be the case that natural and expected sound changes with solid phonetic motivation are found only when additional structural conditions are met, or that the same changes can be inhibited by other aspects of grammar. I will briefly discuss several cases that may fall into one of these categories.

28.4.1 Pre-existing Contrast as Catalyst

It has long be noted that many sound changes are 'structure-preserving' in the sense that they result in segments or structure types that existed at earlier stages of the language (Kiparsky 1995, this volume). However, as many of these sound changes have been more closely studied, it has become clear that though there is a strong tendency for certain changes to be structure-preserving, the tendency can rarely be stated as an absolute (Blevins 2009b).[18]

One such change is compensatory lengthening. Kavitskaya (2002) argues that compensatory lengthening sound changes result from phonologization of pre-existing differences in phonetic vowel duration. Phonetic factors leading to longer vowel durations include longer V–C transitions, longer vowels before particular consonants, and open-syllable lengthening. In her survey of eighty languages with historical

[18] Within Evolutionary Phonology, the tendency for certain sound changes to be structure-preserving is strongly associated with CHANCE and CHOICE, where perceptual biases are non-primary. In CHANGE, where perceptual bias is primary, this bias can override the ambient effects of pre-existing structures on interpretation of phonetic input.

compensatory lengthening sound changes, 72 or 90 percent occur in languages with pre-existing long/short vowel contrasts, while only 8 or 10 percent are found in languages without a pre-existing vowel length contrast. In other words, in this case, the pre-existence of a vowel length contrast makes it more likely that a compensatory lengthening sound change will occur.

Another sound change that appears to occur more often when there is a pre-existing contrast is the perceptually based context-free shift of θ > f. Though most cases of θ > f known from the literature occur in languages with pre-existing /f/, at least one instance of this sound change has been identified for a language with no historical labiodentals. Northern Athabaskan is reconstructed with *θ and *ð, but with no labiodentals or labial obstruents. In the Dene Tha dialect of South Slave these interdentals persist, but Tulita-Slavey has undergone *θ, *ð > f (Blevins 2011).

Within the exemplar-based model adopted here, the significance of pre-existing contrasts and its role in sound change is expected. In the process of acquiring a language with a clear contrast between long and short vowels, the language learner will begin to form long-vowel and short-vowel categories as clouds of exemplars cluster and resolve themselves. As new words are heard and stored, a word with a vowel whose length is somewhat ambiguous between long and short will be more likely to be categorized as long, for the simple reason that *there is a long vowel category*. In languages where a pre-existing vowel length contrast is absent, the same slightly longer vowel will have no long vowel category to go into. A hypothesis regarding the small percentage of languages that show compensatory lengthening, but lack earlier vowel length contrasts, is that the contrast which evolved was a large and very noticeable one, perhaps combined with other prosodic cues.

28.4.2 Pre-existing Gap as Catalyst

Are there phonetically natural sound changes that occur only when a particular contrast is missing in a language? Gap-filling sound changes are commonly noted, but as far as I am aware, there is no literature on sound changes that require a gap as a precondition, or that are strongly associated with a gap.

Two sound changes of this type have already been noted in passing. One is the misperception of [t] as [k] in languages with /k/-gaps, accounting for common t > k sound changes in Austronesian (Blevins 2004a: 123–5, Blust 2004). The other is the misperception of [kl] as [tl] in languages with /tl/-gaps, accounting for kl- > tl- sound changes (Blevins & Grawunder 2009). In both cases, all languages with regular t > k and regular kl- > tl- show pre-existing /k/ and /tl-/ gaps respectively. In this situation, it appears that the existence of a contrast will inhibit misperception. For the cluster case, the hypothesis is that /tl-/ gaps are structural factors which greatly increase the probability of a kl > tl sound change. Evidence in favour of this position can be found in the experimental phonetics literature and from broader cross-linguistic typological surveys of kl > tl changes, as reported in Blevins & Grawunder (2009).

28.4.3 Pre-existing Structure as Catalyst

Are there phonetically natural sound changes that occur only when a particular structure is present in a language? Structure-preserving sound changes are commonly noted, but as far as I am aware, there is not a large literature on sound changes that require a particular phonotactic pattern as a precondition, or that are strongly associated with a pre-existing foot type or syllable type.

One phonetically natural sound change that may fall into this class is unstressed medial vowel syncope: $VC^VCV > VC.CV$ (where superscript 'V' is a short unstressed vowel). In a typological survey of languages that have undergone this change, Blevins (2009b) observes that in all cases, the unambiguous closed syllables existed prior to the change. As with final C-loss, the analysis of structural factors depends critically on the effect that incoming exemplars have on previously stored auditory representations. If words with closed syllables have been stored again and again, a listener or language learner will be more likely to interpret an incoming VC^VCV string as VC.CV. If only open syllables have been encountered, the medial vowel is more likely to be maintained, and in fact, may even be 'heard' when not present.[19]

As with final C-loss, the holistic approach suggested here shows that phonetic naturalness is just one factor determining sound change typology. A sound change like final C-loss may not have clear or strong phonetic conditioning, and may be a primary consequence of structural factors. On the other hand, unstressed vowel syncope, whose phonetic conditioning is strong and clear, may still require additional structural conditions to shift from an aspect of phonetic variability to a regular sound change.

28.4.4 Predictability as Catalyst for Lenition/Loss

There is growing evidence that in positions where a particular sound or word has a high predictability of occurrence, phonetic reduction is more likely and more extreme than elsewhere (Lindblom 1990, Moon & Lindblom 1994, Bard et al. 2000, Jurafsky et al. 2001, Bell et al. 2003, Scarborough 2010, Bybee, this volume). Lindblom's research programme explores the hypothesis that hypoarticulation correlates with the degree to which speakers or listeners can supplement acoustic information with information from other sources, like knowledge of the world or textual knowledge. Jurafsky and colleagues focus more specifically on transitional probabilities drawn from large corpora, and demonstrate that knowledge of such probabilities plays a role in speech production and processing. When the results of these programmes are pooled, a clear picture emerges: articulatory reduction of words is, in part, a function of contextual predictability and recoverability. The more predictable or recoverable a string is, independent

[19] In fast speech, there is data showing vowel loss in languages like Fijian, despite the fact that the language has maintained a basic CV syllable structure for thousands of years (see Blevins 2009b).

of acoustic information, the more likely the word is to be produced in a phonetically reduced form.

In most domains, predictability is lexically specific, and the reduction expected by models like those mentioned above is also lexically specific. But in at least one domain, predictability is grammatically determined, and that is where reduplication is involved. In regular reduplicated forms, phonological material is predictable from the base. As a consequence, higher rates of reduction are expected in the reduplicated portion of the stem than elsewhere in the word. Can such reduction result in regular sound change? Is there typological support for exclusive associations between leniting sound change and reduplicative morphology? The answer appears to be yes.

One well-studied instance of this is found in the history of Hausa (Newman 2004). Preceding (and bleeding) Klingenheben's Law, three sound changes took place between the coda consonant of a CVC- reduplicative prefix and the following stem-initial consonant: velar and labial (grave) obstruents assimilate totally to the following consonant; coronal obstruents lenite to liquids; and /m/ assimilates in place to a following consonant. The question is why all of these leniting sound changes should occur only at the reduplicative boundary and not elsewhere in the word. The answer requires a holistic approach to sound change typology: since reduplicative prefixes are predictable CVC- strings, phonetic reduction is expected to be more likely and more extreme than elsewhere.

Other well-studied cases involving regular segment loss restricted to reduplicative substrings are found in Oceanic (Blevins 2005). In Bugotu, a South-East Solomonic language, synchronic reduplication of CVCV stems is CVV-, with the medial consonant absent. A more interesting case is the regular historical shift of *CRV > CV in Kokota, another language of the Solomons. In general, the loss of R, a sonorant, in CRV onsets is uncommon cross-linguistically. However, where reduplication is involved, it is found in widely distant unrelated languages: in Kokota; in Klamath-Modoc of south-central Oregon; and Indo-European languages (e.g. Old Irish, Gothic, Attic Greek, and Sanskrit). From a typological perspective, we must ask why the regular sound change *CRV- > CV-, which may look like a phonetically natural process of sonorant lenition, is strongly associated with reduplicative strings.[20] The answer is one grounded in a holistic view of sound patterns: where segmental information is predictable, as in reduplicative affixes, regular leniting sound changes are expected, and unpronounced segments may be interpolated by the hearer, based on their knowledge of the base form. Informal elicitation sessions with Kokota speakers support this view: though CV- reduplicated prefixes were spoken, elders seemed to hear CRV-, and repeated the words with the full copy sequence. While reference to prosodic domains may go some way towards explaining sound changes which are limited to reduplicative prefixes, they cannot account for the skewed distribution of CRV- > CV- sound changes in the world's languages.

---

[20] I say '*may* look like a natural process' deliberately, since in some cases, e.g. Kokota *knusu* 'break', *ku-knusu* 'a broken piece of something', the loss of the nasal stop does not smack of naturalness.

28.4.5 Lexical Competition as an Inhibitor

In section 28.4.3 an inhibiting factor for syncope was hinted at: if a language has only ... CVCV ... syllable structure, it will be less likely to undergo VC^{V}CV > VC.CV medial syncope than a language with pre-existing closed syllables. Are there other non-local features of grammars that can inhibit a phonetically natural sound change?

One non-local feature that may play a role in neutralizing sound changes is the extent to which words 'compete' against each other in running speech. It has often been noted that phonological contrasts with a light functional load are more likely to be neutralized than others. However, functional loads are relative to context. Is it possible that a natural phonetically motivated sound change can apply everywhere except where it is the primary realization of a lexical contrast between two words that engage in a high level of lexical competition? (See also Wedel, this volume.)

A recent investigation of this question by Blevins & Wedel (2009) suggests that lexical competition can inhibit regular sound change. The two examples put forth involve neutralization of a short *vs* long vowel contrast in Banoni, an Oceanic language, and syncope in Dakelh, an Athabaskan language. While exceptions to regular sound change are well known, the locus of exceptionality within paradigms in both of these languages is striking, and requires explanation. The explanation based on lexical competition not only accounts for this locus, but also predicts that in the same contexts of lexical competition, extreme phonetic contrasts may emerge and be maintained. Simulations of lexical competition support the analysis: where similar tokens compete fiercely, categories maintain a healthy distance. Where the level of competition is low, mergers occur. And, where competition is high, aggregates are more likely to shift towards extreme exemplars than to move towards the centre.

28.5 CONCLUDING REMARKS

Our understanding of sound change typology has increased exponentially over the past century, primarily as a result of advances in phonetic science. On this perspective, the majority of regular sound changes are grounded in articulatory, aerodynamic, and perceptual aspects of speech, and technical advances in description and experimentation in these areas continue to deepen our understanding of both the physical underpinnings and cognitive extensions of these components.

At the same time, our understanding of the holistic nature of grammar continues to grow. Exemplar models are easy ways of capturing this holistic nature, since memory traces, independent of their level of decay, are wholes, not parts of wholes. In the study of sound change typology, there is much that remains to be explained. However, by beginning to associate phonetically based regular sound change with structural, morphological, and lexical conditions that inhibit or facilitate change, we are closer to predicting the probability that, from some given pool of variants, sound change will or will not proceed in a given direction. This seems like progress.

CHAPTER 29

RULE-BASED GENERATIVE HISTORICAL PHONOLOGY

B. ELAN DRESHER

29.1 INTRODUCTION

THIS chapter presents an account of historical phonology in terms of classical (rule-based) generative phonology (foundational texts for this include: Chomsky & Halle 1968, Kiparsky 1965, 1982a, King 1969). Generative phonology can contribute to our understanding of diachronic developments because it allows us to view them in richer terms than the traditional two categories of 'sound change' and 'analogy' (for which, see Murray and many other chapters in this volume). In generative phonology, underlying phonological forms that are stored in the lexicon are operated on by a series of ordered rules that derive surface phonetic forms. Any aspect of the phonological grammar is liable to be implicated in a particular change: rules may be added, lost, modified, or reordered, and underlying representations may be restructured. While some phonological changes may originate from outside influences (from other dialects or languages), generative grammar traces many phonological changes to the process of language acquisition. Learners acquire grammars, not just surface forms, and grammars are not transmitted directly from one generation to the next; rather, every learner must construct the grammar anew, based on the available evidence. We might expect that changes in the ambient data available to successive generations of learners will cause them to acquire grammars that differ in some respects from those of previous generations (contrast the position in Foulkes & Vihman, this volume, and compare that in Hale et al., this volume). In this way, diachrony becomes relevant to learnability, and is a source of evidence concerning the cognitive principles that govern language acquisition.

Sections 29.2 to 29.4 relate the change in perspective from the nineteenth-century neogrammarian approach to sound change, understood as applying to surface forms, to a generative approach, in which change affects grammars, not just surface forms. I also show how generative phonology's focus on rules is able to resolve the structuralist

Saussurian problem of the separation between diachronic change and synchronic systems. These points are illustrated with a series of examples from Old and Middle English that show how a generative perspective can shed new light on developments that are otherwise difficult to explain. Section 29.5 presents examples that show how synchronic patterns influence change, and the close relationship between learnability and certain types of phonological change is discussed in section 29.6.

Departing somewhat from the theory of Chomsky & Halle (1968), section 29.7 shows how one could incorporate into generative theory the structuralist notion that sound change can be sensitive to contrastive patterns of the phonological system. Section 29.8 is a brief conclusion. The approach taken here complements other discussion of broadly formal approaches in this volume, such as Bermúdez-Otero, Hale et al., and Kiparsky (all this volume), and contrasts with chapters such as Phillips, Bybee, and Blevins (all this volume).

29.2 NEOGRAMMARIAN DIACHRONIC LINGUISTICS

As is discussed elsewhere in this Handbook, the great achievement of nineteenth-century historical linguistics was arriving at the discovery that sound changes are regular (see in this volume Bermúdez-Otero, Murray, and contrast Phillips). This discovery allowed for the refinement of the comparative method and put historical reconstruction, as well as linguistic theory in general, on a much sounder basis. Nevertheless, nineteenth-century theory, culminating in the work of the neogrammarians, had certain limitations.

The first limitation was caused by the overwhelmingly diachronic orientation of neogrammarian theory. Though nineteenth-century linguists achieved unprecedented levels of precision by following the evolution of each sound in great detail, this approach was unable to capture synchronic relations that might hold between sounds at various stages of their development. The shortcomings of this 'atomistic' approach were revealed by the structuralists, who, following Saussure (1916), put the main emphasis on language as a synchronic system whose parts are interconnected.[1]

A second limitation is the neogrammarian emphasis on surface changes. Their assumption, a natural one in the absence of an articulated notion of a synchronic grammar, is that a sound at a given time is represented the way it sounds; when this sound changes, the older sound is replaced by the newer one, and any further changes relate only to the newer version, not to the older one. For example, the early West Germanic

---

[1] See Murray (this volume) for a more nuanced discussion of nineteenth-century linguistics. Murray shows that Saussure's notion of a synchronic sound system was already being advanced in the nineteenth century, notably by Sievers (1876), and that later linguists sometimes exaggerated the degree to which the neogrammarian approach was focused on individual sound changes viewed in isolation.

stressed *a is believed to have undergone the following changes on its way to Mercian Old English when it stood before a back vowel in the following syllable:

(1) Development of West Germanic stressed *a before a back vowel[2]

a.	Early West Germanic	*a	*habuc	*fatas
b.	Anglo-Frisian Brightening	*æ	*hæbuc	*fætas
c.	*a*-Restoration	a	hafuc	fatas
d.	Second Fronting	æ	*hæfuc	*fætas
e.	Back Mutation	æə	hæəfuc	fæətas
	Mercian *Vespasian Psalter*	<ea>	<heafuc>	<featas>
	Gloss[3]		'hawk N S'	'vats N P'

From the point of view of the phonetics of these sounds (as far as we can reliably reconstruct them), the sequence of changes shown in (1) amount to the successive changes of *a > æ > a > æ > æə*. Apart from the suspicious-looking reversals, this account misses any connections that these changes might have had with other changes taking place in this dialect, as well as any role that the grammar may have played in influencing the changes themselves.

29.3 STRUCTURALISM AND DIACHRONY

Saussure's strict distinction between synchrony and diachrony brought in the notion of (synchronic) grammar as a system whose parts hang together. A basic structuralist notion is the phoneme: determining if two sounds belong to the same or two different phonemes requires a synchronic perspective. Further, a phonemic perspective allows us to distinguish between the contrastive value of a phoneme, conventionally indicated by slash brackets / /, and its phonetic implementation, indicated by square brackets []. Hogg (1992) provides a number of interesting illustrations of instances where his neogrammarian predecessors have been unable to give a satisfactory account of developments in Old English because they lacked a phonemic perspective (see also Salmons & Honeybone, this volume).

One example concerns the prehistory of early Old English long æ:. Since the corresponding vowel in Proto-Germanic is assumed to have also been *æ:, Wright & Wright (1925) had proposed that æ: simply persisted into the Old English period. Against this

---

[2] Forms in angle brackets < > are orthographic. I assume that the spellings <ea> and <eo> represent phonologically short diphthongs pronounced roughly [æə] and [eə], respectively, and that these diphthongs are allophones of the short vowel phonemes /æ/ and /e/, respectively; see Hogg (1992) and Minkova and Lass (both this volume) for discussion of various interpretations of these digraphs.

[3] Abbreviations used in glosses are: s = singular; p = plural; n = nominative; a = accusative; G = genitive; D = dative; M = masculine; F = feminine; N = neuter.

view is historical and comparative evidence which appears to show that it was a back vowel, *aː, in West Germanic. The version of events accepted by most other writers therefore posits, as in (2), that Proto-Germanic *æː retracted to *aː in West Germanic, then fronted again to *æː in Old English when not before a nasal.[4]

(2) Development of Proto-Germanic stressed *æː: pre-phonemic account

Proto-Germanic	*æː
West Germanic	*aː
Anglo-Frisian Brightening	*æː

Hogg (1992: 61–3) considers not just the phonetic value of this vowel, but also its phonemic status at each stage of the language. This approach results in the richer picture shown in (3). He assumes, as in the traditional account, that this phoneme was a contrastively front vowel in early Proto-Germanic (3a).

(3) Development of Proto-Germanic stressed *æː in phonemic perspective

a. Early Proto-Germanic long vowel system

/iː/	/uː/	There is a contrast between /æː/
/eː/	/oː/	and /ɑː/; /æː/ is phonologically and
/æː/ = [æː]	/ɑː/	phonetically front.

b. Later Proto-Germanic long vowel system

/iː/	/uː/	/ɑː/ merged with /oː/; /æː/ shifts
/eː/	/oː/	phonemically to /aː/, but remains
/aː/ = [æː]		phonetically front [æː].

c. Early West Germanic long vowel system

As in (b); the low vowel is contrastively neutral as to front/back status and can develop in some dialects as a central or back vowel.

d. Early Old English

/iː/	/uː/	A new phoneme /ɑː/ develops; [æː]
/eː/	/oː/	is reinterpreted as belonging with
/æː/ = [æː]	/ɑː/	the front vowels.

Due to some changes in Proto-Germanic, notably the merger of /ɑː/ with /oː/, /æː/ was left as the only low vowel phoneme (3b). Hogg proposes that this vowel was contrastively neutral with respect to the front/back dimension; therefore, it can be represented as /aː/, whatever its precise phonetic character. Since it could act neutrally with respect to backness (3c), it appeared to earlier writers as though it were a back vowel in early West Germanic. Hogg suggests that this phoneme may nevertheless have been phonetically front throughout in the dialects that developed into Old English. At a later period (3d),

---

[4] I follow Hogg's account (1992), but see Purnell & Raimy (this volume) for another view.

the development of a contrasting back low vowel (from the monophthongization of older */ai/ which merged with retracted /aː/ before nasals) created a backness contrast which led to a reanalysis of the original low vowel to a contrastively front vowel /æː/. Hence, the alleged shift of Proto-Germanic *æː to West Germanic *aː and then back to æː in Old English and Old Frisian emerges as an artefact of a non-phonemic theory.

Hogg (1992: 77–8) suggests that the short low vowel in (1) developed in parallel to the long low vowel. As with the long vowels, there was only one short low vowel phoneme in early West Germanic; like the long low vowel, */a/ was neutral with respect to the front/ back dimension, though it appears to have had a more back pronunciation than /aː/. In parallel with the long low vowel, it became contrastively front, i.e. */æ/, in early Old English (1b). Thus, a phonemic perspective allows for a simpler sequence of development and allows us to see the relationship between the changes in the long and short low vowel.

Though the introduction of a synchronic structuralist perspective allowed for richer explanations of phonological developments, Kiparsky (1965) demonstrated that, in a classical structuralist theory where phonemes are defined only in terms of contrast, problems arise in the description of dialects and successive diachronic stages. Strictly speaking, the phonemic systems of closely related dialects become incommensurable if they differ in the number of phonemes they have (cf. Moulton 1960). This is because, in an approach that considers only the number of contrasts a phoneme enters into, a /t/ that contrasts with two other coronal stops (say, /d/ and /tʰ/) cannot be compared with a /t/ that contrasts with only one other coronal stop (say, /d/).

Kiparsky's argument draws on developments in the various dialects descending from Proto-Armenian, as shown in (4). He proposed that the current situation can most plausibly be attributed to three sound changes that spread through different geographic regions (5).

(4) Armenian dialects (Kiparsky 1965)

Old Armenian	th	t	d	*Contrasts*	*Sound changes*
East Central	th	t	dh	2	Aspiration
West Central	th	d	dh	2	Voicing, aspiration
Northern	th	t	d	2	——
Eastern	th	t	t	1	Devoicing
Western	th	d	d	1	Voicing
Northwestern	th	d	th	1	Voicing, aspiration
Southern	th	d	t	2	Voicing, devoicing

(5) Armenian sound changes (Kiparsky 1965)

a. Aspiration: /d/ aspirates to [dh] (or [th]) in the Central and Northwestern dialects.

b. Voicing: /t/ voices to [d] in the Western, West Central, Northwestern, and Southern dialects.

c. Devoicing: /d/ devoices to [t] in the Eastern and Southern dialects.

Kiparsky (1965) points out that these sound changes spread from one dialect to another, regardless of how many contrasts they contained. If we were to classify the dialects in terms of oppositions, we would arrive at meaningless groupings for explaining any synchronic or diachronic facts. He writes (1965: 17):

> An incidental feature of the present example is that it highlights the pointlessness of a structural dialectology that ... distinguishes dialects according to points of structural difference rather than according to the innovations through which they diverged ... If in the present example we were to divide the dialects into those with two stop series and those with three, we would be linking together dialects that have nothing to do with each other and separating dialects that are closely related.

This is not to say that the number of contrasts plays no role in diachrony; we saw earlier that attention to the number of contrasts in the low vowels is important in understanding the nature of some of the changes they underwent, and this point will become central in section 29.7. However, Kiparsky showed that attention only to number of contrasts can impede a proper understanding of language change.[5]

29.4 GENERATIVE PHONOLOGY

In the structuralist phonemic theory exemplified above by Hogg's analysis of the development of the low vowels from Proto-Germanic to Old English, a sound has two representations: a phonetic representation that approximates its pronunciation, and a phonemic representation that represents its contrastive value within the phonological system. In the theory of generative phonology (Chomsky & Halle 1968), the phonemic representation is identified with the underlying, or lexical, representation of a sound, and the phonetic representation is its surface realization.[6] Mediating between the underlying and surface representations is a set of partially ordered phonological rules that convert the underlying forms into surface forms.

The notion of a grammar as a set of ordered rules presents a more explicit account of what it means to say that a grammar is a system. At the same time, it allows diachronic changes to interact with the synchronic system because both are expressed in terms of rules. Thus, the Armenian sound changes in (5) can be viewed not just as diachronic events, but as three rules that entered the synchronic grammars of the various Armenian dialects. It does not therefore follow that the synchronic set of rules in a grammar will merely mimic a series of historical sound changes. As Chomsky & Halle (1968: 249–50)

---

[5] See Keyser (1963) for another early discussion of how traditional dialectology could benefit from a generative perspective.

[6] The number and nature of the levels in phonological theory have been the subject of much discussion and a major point of contention between different theories; see Dresher (2005, 2011) for historical overviews, and Bermúdez-Otero, Hale et al., and Kiparsky (all this volume) for a more articulated set of levels.

observed, some rules of grammar may faithfully reflect a sound change that was introduced into the grammar centuries before, but this is the case only if successive generations of learners continue to acquire a grammar containing that rule. Where the data no
longer provide learners with the requisite evidence, a rule will not be preserved intact
in the grammar, but may be acquired in an altered form; or else the underlying representation will be changed and the rule will disappear from the grammar.[7] Moreover, the
grammar may change in other ways, with the result that it will fail to accurately reflect
the history of the language.

Some of these notions can be illustrated by looking at the sequence of Old English
sound changes introduced in (1) above. The change of early West Germanic stressed
*a to early Old English *æ (Anglo-Frisian Brightening) is not easily recoverable in
the synchronic grammar of early Old English, because this rule applied to all or most
stressed *a.[8] That is, once words like *habuc 'hawk' and *fat 'vat' have been changed to
*hæbuc and *fæt, respectively, learners of the new grammar would have no reason to
reconstruct the older /a/ in the lexical representations of these words; rather, these representations would be restructured as in (6), where (6a) represents the stage prior to the
change, (6b) represents the period of the change in which speakers still represent the
underlying form with /a/ and apply a rule to change it to [æ], and (6c) represents a subsequent stage in which learners acquire the [æ] directly as /æ/. The rule from (6b) is no
longer needed, and is not part of this or subsequent grammars.

(6) Restructuring of underlying forms
   a. Before Anglo-Frisian Brightening
       Underlying   /habuc/   /fat/
       Surface   [habuc]   [fat]

   b. During Anglo-Frisian Brightening
       Underlying   /habuc/   /fat/
       A-F Brightening hæbuc   fæt
       Surface   [hæbuc]   [fæt]

   c. After Anglo-Frisian Brightening
       Underlying   /hæbuc/   /fæt/
       Surface   [hæbuc]   [fæt]

The next change listed in (1c), *a*-Restoration, had a different effect on the grammar.
In this change, stressed /æ/ became [a] when preceding a single consonant followed by

---

[7] In the case of Eastern Armenian, we could imagine an initial stage in which speakers would have
acquired lexical items with Old Armenian /d/, and subsequently introduced a rule devoicing this /d/ to
[t]. For these speakers the change of *d* to *t* would exist as a rule of their grammar. But learners in the next
generation who hear this sound as [t] would need synchronic evidence to continue deriving these [t] from
/d/, rather than simply acquiring them with the underlying form /t/, just like [t] from Old Armenian /t/.

[8] See Hogg (1992: 80–2) for discussion of whether this change applied to all stressed *a, or was blocked
in certain environments.

a back vowel. In classical generative grammar, this change can be represented as the rule in (7), where the formalism A → B / C ____ D is read 'A changes to B when preceded by C and followed by D'. For this discussion I assume that sounds are composed of distinctive features, more or less as proposed by Chomsky & Halle (1968).[9]

(7) *a*-Restoration

æ	→	[+back] /	____	C	V
[+stressed]					[+back]

This rule created alternations in many words, such as /fæt/, where the stressed vowel appeared as [æ] in forms where no back vowel followed, and as [a] where a back vowel followed. In such words it is clear that the stressed vowel is [æ] except in the specialized contexts where it is [a], suggesting that the basic vowel remains /æ/. Since surface [a] is easily derivable by rule (7) even in words where it does not alternate with [æ], as in *hafuc*, I assume that such forms also retain underlying /æ/.[10] Thus, sound changes can persist in grammars as synchronic rules if they create conditions whereby learners can still recover the underlying forms of the pre-sound change grammar. The effect of *a*-Restoration on several words in the grammar is shown in (8).

(8) Effect of *a*-Restoration on the grammar

a. Before *a*-Restoration

Underlying	/fæt/	/fæt+um/	/hæfuc/	/hæfuc+e/
Surface	[fæt]	[fætum]	[hæfuc]	[hæfuce]
Gloss	'vat N s'	'vats D P'	'hawk N s'	'hawk D s'

b. After *a*-Restoration

Underlying	/fæt/	/fæt+um/	/hæfuc/	/hæfuc+e/
a-Restoration	—	fatum	hafuc	hafuce
Surface	[fæt]	[fatum]	[hafuc]	[hafuce]

a-Restoration was not the only rule in Mercian Old English that backed /æ/ to [a]: another such rule is Retraction (9), which applies before *w* and back *l* (*l* that is followed by a consonant or a back vowel). Like *a*-Restoration, Retraction sometimes creates alternations, as in *hwæl* ~ *hwalas* 'whale ~ whales'; more usually, however, it does not, as in *ald* 'old', which has inflected forms *aldum, alde, aldra, aldran*, etc., all of which meet the conditions for the rule to apply. Sample forms are shown in (10).

---

[9] See Purnell & Raimy (this volume) for a somewhat different approach to distinctive features; see also section 29.7.

[10] There were, and continue to be, differing views as to how 'abstract' underlying forms could be relative to surface forms (e.g. Donegan & Nathan, this volume, take a different approach; see Scheer, this volume, for discussion). Various constraints on underlying forms have been proposed that would require non-alternating [a] to be derived from /a/. It is an empirical question as to how this issue should be settled. Diachronic change is a valuable source of evidence bearing on this issue, and I have argued (Dresher 1985) that the changes we are considering support the general analysis advanced here.

(9) Retraction

$$\begin{bmatrix} \text{æ} \\ \text{+stressed} \end{bmatrix} \rightarrow [\text{+back}] \ / \ \underline{\hspace{1cm}} \begin{bmatrix} \text{+sonorant} \\ \text{+back} \end{bmatrix}$$

(10) Grammar with Retraction and *a*-Restoration

	/æld/	/hwæl+as/	/fæt+um/	/hæfuc/
Underlying	/æld/	/hwæl+as/	/fæt+um/	/hæfuc/
Retraction	ald	hwalas	—	—
a-Restoration	—	—	fatum	hafuc
Surface	[ald]	[hwalas]	[fatum]	[hafuc]
Gloss	'old'	'whales N P'	'vats D P'	'hawk N s'

Not all sound changes correspond to restructuring of underlying forms or to rules that are added to the grammar. In Mercian Old English there was a change known as Second Fronting (1d) which changed [a] back to [æ] in the *a*-Restoration contexts. That a rule would simply reverse a previous rule is only one of the suspicious characteristics of Second Fronting. The change is a strange sort of dissimilation whereby a back vowel becomes front before a following back vowel. Moreover, Second Fronting does not affect any *a* that is created by Retraction. The confluence of these facts suggests that Second Fronting was not a sound change in the sense of the addition of a new rule, but rather is the result of the loss of the rule of *a*-Restoration (Dresher 1980, 1985), as shown in (11).

(11) Second Fronting as the loss of *a*-Restoration

	/æld/	/hwæl+as/	/fæt+um/	/hæfuc/
Underlying	/æld/	/hwæl+as/	/fæt+um/	/hæfuc/
Retraction	ald	hwalas	—	—
a-Restoration	—	—	L O S T	
Surface	[ald]	[hwalas]	[fætum]	[hæfuc]
Gloss	'old'	'whales N P'	'vats D P'	'hawk N s'

In the *Vespasian Psalter* (*Ps(A)*, Kuhn 1965), the surface forms of the words that had formerly undergone *a*-Restoration are not as shown in (11), however. These forms had undergone a further rule called Back Mutation (12), whereby a schwa-like vowel is added to a stressed short front vowel when it precedes a single consonant followed by a back vowel. With *a*-Restoration gone from the grammar, Back Mutation can apply to /æ/, as shown in (13).

(12) Back Mutation

$$\emptyset \rightarrow \text{ə} \ / \begin{bmatrix} \text{V} \\ \text{--back} \\ \text{--long} \\ \text{+stressed} \end{bmatrix} \underline{\hspace{1cm}} \text{C} \begin{bmatrix} \text{V} \\ \text{+back} \end{bmatrix}$$

(13) Back Mutation as rule addition

Underlying	/fæt+um/	/hæfuc/	/wer+as/	/hefun/
a-Restoration	L O	S T	—	—
Back Mutation	fæətum	hæəfuc	weəras	heəfun
Orthography	\<featum>	\<heafuc>	\<weoras>	\<heofun>
Gloss	'vats D P'	'hawk N S'	'men N P'	'heaven N S'

Although *a*-Restoration is not evident from *Ps(A)*, we know that it had applied in the Mercian dialect because of the evidence of the early *Épinal Glossary* (*EpGl*) and *Corpus Glossary* (*CorpGl*). These glossaries show a variety of spellings that appear to reflect the relative age of the rules that produced them (Toon 1983). For the short low stressed vowel, *EpGl* has spellings in \<a>, \<æ>, and \<ea>, reflecting *a*-Restoration, the loss of that rule, and Back Mutation, respectively. (On the interpretation of English vowel orthography, see Minkova and Lass, both this volume.) Moreover, Back Mutation is more frequently recorded with \<ea> than with \<eo>, suggesting that the rule began with the low vowel and then spread to the other front vowels, illustrating rule generalization – rules are not simply added or lost, but can also change in their patterning. The spellings thus reflect the series of stages in the evolution of *EpGl* shown in (14).

(14) *Épinal Glossary* dialect: historical evolution (Dresher 1985: 241)

    a. *a*-Restoration is added

Underlying	/fæt+u/	/wer+as/
a-Restoration	fatu	—
Orthography	\<fatu>	\<weras>

    b. *a*-Restoration is lost

Underlying	/fæt+u/	/wer+as/
Orthography	\<fætu>	\<weras>

    c. Back Mutation begins in the low vowels

Underlying	/fæt+u/	/wer+as/
Back Mutation of *æ*	fæətu	—
Orthography	\<featu>	\<weras>

    d. Back Mutation generalizes to the non-low vowels

Underlying	/fæt+u/	/wer+as/
Back Mutation	fæətu	weəras
Orthography	\<featu>	\<weoras>

In *CorpGl*, compiled a few years later, the spellings occur in different proportions. Most striking is the absence of spellings representing a stage after the loss of Second Fronting but before the introduction of Back Mutation (corresponding to (14b) in *EpGl*). Rather, it appears that \<a> went directly to \<ea> without passing through \<æ>. On the assumption that Second Fronting was a conventional sound change, this development is problematic, since Back Mutation applies to front vowels, and could not affect [a]. On the rule loss analysis, however, this development is what we would expect if Back Mutation arrived in the *CorpGl* dialect before Second Fronting was lost. In support of this chronology we observe that the Back Mutation of *e* and *i* is relatively advanced in that dialect, being represented two-thirds of the time, next to one-third unmutated spellings. By contrast, the ratio in the low vowels is two-thirds <a> next to one-third <ea>, consistent with the notion that Back Mutation entered the dialect prior to the loss of Second Fronting. The latter would have blocked Back Mutation in the low vowels, as shown in the chronology in (15).

(15) *Corpus Glossary* dialect: historical evolution (Dresher 1985: 242)

    a. *a*-Restoration is added: as in (14a)

    b. Back Mutation is added

Underlying	/fæt+u/	/wer+as/
a-Restoration	fatu	—
Back Mutation	—	weəras
Orthography	<fatu>	<weoras>

    c. *a*-Restoration is lost

Underlying	/fæt+u/	/wer+as/
Back Mutation	fæətu	weəras
Orthography	<featu>	<weoras>

A generative rule-based analysis of the changes in the stressed low vowels of Mercian Old English thus gives us a richer account than the surface-based sequence shown in (1). A crucial ingredient of the generative analysis is the interplay between sound changes and the synchronic grammar. In some cases a change results in reanalysis of underlying forms, in other cases it leaves the underlying forms as they were but persists in the form of a synchronic rule.

The above account does not explain why the changes in question occurred. Traditional neogrammarian theory makes a distinction between sound change and analogy. Whereas analogy is understood as being influenced by the grammar, sound change is assumed to arise from extragrammatical causes, influenced by articulatory, perceptual, and sociolinguistic factors. In generative terms, sound change corresponds either to restructuring of underlying forms (if the change leaves the previous underlying forms unlearnable), or to the addition of a rule to the end of the phonology. Analogy corresponds to other sorts of changes, such as the addition of a rule to the middle of the grammar (rule insertion; King 1969, 1973), or to the loss or reordering of rules.[11] As the example of Second Fronting shows, however, the line between sound change and grammar change (i.e. between rule addition and rule loss) may not be easy to detect. Also,

---

[11] For critiques of traditional notions of analogy and arguments for a generative approach, see Kiparsky (1965, 1982a) and Lahiri (2000a), and Fertig and Kiparsky (both this volume).

we cannot rule out grammatical influences even in the case of apparently simple sound changes. It has been observed, for example, that the rules of *a*-Restoration and Back Mutation appear to be variants of a single process of adding a back element to a stressed vowel under influence of a following back vowel, and that both of these processes appear to be part of a more general pattern whereby features are transferred from an unstressed vowel to the stressed vowel (Colman & Anderson 1983, Dresher 1990, 1993). Such patterns suggest the presence of an overarching grammatical principle that could be influencing these changes.

In the following section I look at another set of changes that at first appear to be sound changes but that turn out to be analogy, broadly speaking. They illustrate other ways in which the grammar influences diachronic change.

29.5 HOW SYNCHRONIC GRAMMAR INFLUENCES DIACHRONIC DEVELOPMENTS

In the light of contemporary approaches that again emphasize surface forms, or seek the explanation of synchronic patterns in diachrony (e.g. Blevins, this volume), it is worth showing the enduring value of the fundamental generative notion that change is something that affects synchronic grammars, and that synchronic patterns in turn can influence change. Language learners acquiring lexical items must do so using the evidence available to them. An exclusively 'vertical' diachronic perspective, focusing on individual sound changes, is liable to miss any 'horizontal' effects caused by the way seemingly unrelated items interact in the course of acquisition. The next example is intended to show the intricate synchronic interaction of different aspects of the grammar in what looks like a simple set of historical changes. It also supports the synchronic analysis presented above in (13).

Early Old English inherited a group of disyllabic noun stems, such as the reconstructed forms shown in (16a) and (16b). In (16a) we know that the *y* in *yfel*, from earlier *ubil, arises from the umlaut of /u/ due to an *i* in the following syllable, which was itself lowered in Old English to *e*. In (16b) the diphthong is caused by Back Mutation (12); the back vowel in the following syllable remains overt in *steaðul* but is reduced to *e* in *heofen* and in inflected forms of both words.

(16) Reconstructed early Mercian Old English

a. yfel	*yfeles	micel	*miceles
'evil N S M'	'evil G S M'	'much N S M'	'much G S M'
b. steaðul	steaðelas	heofen	heofenes
'foundation A S'	'foundations A P'	'heaven N S'	'heaven G S'
c. weter	wetres	fugul	fugles
'water N S'	'water G S'	'bird N S'	'bird G S'

In addition, Old English also inherited a group of noun stems ending in sonorant consonants that were originally monosyllabic, examples of which are shown in (16c). When followed by vowel-initial inflections, such as in *wetres* and *fugles*, the original CVCC form of the stems surfaces; when uninflected, or followed by a consonant-initial inflection, an epenthetic vowel is inserted whose nature is partially determined by the stressed vowel: it is *e* following a front vowel, and *u* following a back vowel. The height asymmetry between the front *e* and back *u* is due to the same rule of *i*-Lowering that must have applied in *yfel*.

The diachronic steps leading to the forms in (16) are summarized in (17):

(17) Diachronic changes from pre-Old English to early Mercian Old English

pre-OE	*ubil	*ubil+es	*stæðul	*stæðul+es	*wætr	*wætr+es
i-Umlaut	*ybil	*ybiles	—	—	—	—
Epenthesis	—	—	—	—	*wætir	—
i-Lowering	*ybel	*ybeles	—	—	*wæter	—
Back Mutation	—	—	stæəðul	*stæəðules	—	—
V-Reduction	—	—	—	stæəðeles	—	—
early OE	<yfel>	<*yfeles>	<steaðul>	steaðeles>	<weter>	<wetres>

What about the synchronic phonology of this stage of early Old English? In the view of generative phonology, we must suppose that learners, in their acquisition of the sound patterns produced by these historical changes, attempt to account for them synchronically. This does not mean, however, that learners simply reconstruct the sequence in (17) as a synchronic grammar. Synchronic sound patterns are not just a record of the past. Though phonologies sometimes display a certain 'inertia' where a series of changes piles up resulting in unnatural-looking synchronic alternations, often we see 'adjustments' of various kinds that give evidence bearing on the grammar. In the Mercian Old English dialect of *Ps(A)*, for example, we find that words of the type (16a) systematically alternate as in (18a), taking on the pattern of (16c).

(18) Vespasian Psalter dialect

a. yfel	yfles	micel	micles
b. steaðul	steaðeles	heofen	heofenes
c. weter	wetres	fugul	fugles

Two questions arise: what does the change consist of, and why does it apply to the words in (a) but not in (b)? As to the nature of the change, one might think that it amounts to the syncope of a medial vowel. But Dresher (1985) shows that there is no general rule syncopating a vowel after a short stressed syllable in this dialect. Rather, the change amounts to a reanalysis of the lexical forms of the morphemes in (a) from disyllables to monosyllables, as in (c).

Next, why did this reanalysis come about? Evidently, learners hearing uninflected forms like *micel* and *weter* had no way to tell, without hearing the inflected forms, whether these would inflect as *miceles, weteres,* or as *micles, wetres.* Put another way, learners hearing the uninflected forms could not be sure if the second vowel is underlying or epenthetic. One might suppose that exposure to thousands of examples would suffice to settle the matter, but evidently this was not the case. As Lahiri & Dresher (1983–4) argue, learners do not always take advantage of the full array of data that may be available to them. In this case, it appears that where the uninflected form was ambiguous, learners erred in favour of monosyllabic forms of type (c).

But why didn't the same reanalysis affect the forms in (b), with short diphthongs? If forms like *steaðul* and *heofen* had been reanalysed to have underlying diphthongs, their status would be the same as the words in (a), and their immunity to reanalysis would be mysterious. Dresher (1985) argues rather that short diphthongs are not underlying in the *Ps(A)* dialect: every occurrence of a short diphthong can be attributed to a synchronic rule accessible to language learners. It follows, then, that the presence of the short diphthongs in words of type (b) serve as evidence to learners that the second vowel is underlying: in these words, there is no other source for the diphthong.

Therefore, this analysis explains why the forms in (b) were not reanalysed like the forms in (a). Note that the synchronic analysis proposed in Dresher (1985) does not simply recapitulate the diachronic sequence in (17): some reanalysis has occurred. The second vowel in *yfel* is reanalysed as epenthetic, despite the presence of the front rounded vowel *y.* I have argued that, though a rule of *i*-mutation persists in the *Ps(A)* dialect, not all cases of *y* can be derived, the rule in some cases having become too opaque to recover. Therefore, /y/ is an underlying phoneme in this dialect, and its presence is not sufficient to show that a following vowel is underlying.[12]

The sort of merger that occurred in Mercian did not happen only once. Moving a few hundred years forward, we have documentary records of the descendant of the Mercian dialect, called the Middle English AB dialect by Tolkien (1929). At some point the short diphthongs merged back with monophthongs. We expect, then, that the descendants of the forms we have been looking at would look as in (19): the old diphthongs (a) should have trisyllabic inflected forms, and the old monophthongs would have disyllabic inflected forms (b).

(19) Reconstructed early Middle English (Old AB dialect)
      a. *stæðel   *stæðeles   *heofen   *heofenes
      b. *weter   *wetres   *muchel   *muchle

Again, this is not what we find. The two classes, now lacking any further distinguishing elements to keep them apart, again merge, this time in the other direction: the second vowel is restored, even to words that never had one, as shown in (20).

---

[12] See Kiparsky (this volume) on the role of *i*-mutation in the creation of new phonemes.

(20) Middle English (AB dialect)
    a. heouene D S   'heaven'   cf. *Ps(A)* heofene
    b. fuheles P   'birds'   cf. *Ps(A)* fuglas
    c. muchel, muchele   'much'   cf. *Ps(A)* micel, micle
    d. water, watere   'water'   cf. *Ps(A)* weter, wetre

It is hard to see how one can account for these developments without a synchronic grammar similar to the one I have argued for. In this case, the diachronic changes give us evidence bearing on the choice of synchronic grammar, and illuminate the sort of principles language learners use to acquire grammars. In turn, the diachronic changes cannot be properly understood in the absence of a synchronic analysis.

29.6 CHANGE AND LEARNABILITY

The above example reveals the close connection between language change and learnability (contrast Foulkes & Vihman, this volume). Children are not directly given the grammars of their parents; rather, they must recreate the grammar given input from the ambient language. If the language children hear is exactly the same as the one their parents heard when they were children, we would expect the children's grammar to be essentially the same as that of their parents. But more usually the language children hear is somewhat different from the one their parents heard. Even without assuming dramatic changes, languages are constantly changing in minor ways, such as, for example, a change in the proportion of certain words or phrases compared to others. In many cases such minor variances do not cause fundamental differences in the grammar acquired, but in some cases the differences may be enough to cause language learners to come to different conclusions about the grammar than their parents, causing a change in the grammar that may itself trigger further changes.

Therefore, without claiming that all language change originates in acquisition, it appears unavoidable that certain types of changes do. In this section I consider a case where a simple sound change appears to have made the grammar unrecoverable to learners. The result was a fundamental change in lexical representations and the loss of quantity alternations in Present-Day English singular ~ plural pairs. Thus, if the phonology had been learnable, the vowel alternation in *staff* ~ *staves* would have been the regular pattern for many English nouns.[13]

In traditional accounts, which I basically follow, with a few elaborations, Middle English had a rule of Open Syllable Lengthening (OSL), which lengthened stressed vowels in open syllables (21) (Prokosch 1939: 140, Luick 1914–40).[14] It interacted with Trisyllabic

---

[13] This section is based on work with Aditi Lahiri, particularly Lahiri & Dresher (1999).
[14] See Scheer (this volume) on open syllable lengthening in various languages.

Shortening (TSS), which shortened a stressed vowel when followed by two unstressed syllables (22) (Wright & Wright 1925, Lahiri & Fikkert 1999).

(21) Open Syllable Lengthening (OSL)
      A short stressed vowel in an open syllable must be long.

(22) Trisyllabic Shortening (TSS)
      A long stressed vowel followed by two unstressed syllables must be short.

As has long been observed, and as underlined particularly by Minkova (1982; see also Mailhammer et al., this volume), there is considerable variation in the Present-Day English length of vowels that should have undergone these rules. Thus, looking only at disyllabic stems, we find outcomes as in (23). The length of the vowel in Old English does not predict the length in Present-Day English.

(23) Old English and Present Day English vowel lengths

	OE	Length	PDE	Length
a.	sadol	short	saddle	short
b.	cradol	short	cradle	long
c.	beofor	short	beaver	long
d.	dēofol	long	devil	short
e.	bēacen	long	beacon	long

Minkova (1982) observes that the only class of nouns in which Open Syllable Lengthening appears to have taken place reliably is in nouns which had once ended in schwa, such as *talə* 'tale'. The coincidence of lengthening with the loss of schwa led her to propose that lengthening was due not to Open Syllable Lengthening, but to Compensatory Lengthening.[15] However, this does not account for the fact that lengthening occurred in many disyllabic nouns which did not lose a schwa, as in (23b,c).

Ritt (1994, 2004) proposes that lengthening occurred in probabilistic fashion, subject to influences as in (24).

(24) Probabilistic vowel lengthening (Ritt 1994)
      The probability of vowel lengthening was proportional to a. the (degree of) stress on it; b. its backness; c. coda sonority;
      and inversely proportional to a. its height; b. syllable weight; c. the overall weight of the weak syllables in the foot.
      The probability of vowel shortening is inversely proportional to the probability of lengthening.

---

[15] Versions of this account have since been presented by Lass (1985), Minkova (1985), Hayes (1989), Kim (1993), and Bermúdez-Otero (1998).

The problem with this sort of analysis is that it does not take account of one simple yet inescapable fact about English singular ~ plural noun pairs: with the exception of *staff* ~ *staves*, and some irregular nouns like *child* ~ *children*, English nouns do not exhibit any length alternations between singular and plural. This despite the fact that many such nouns would have been expected to show such an alternation, because in Old and Middle English plurals typically had one more syllable than their corresponding singular. Thus, according to traditional accounts, the expected outcomes for some common noun classes should have been as in (25).

(25) Predicted effects of OSL and TSS on Old English noun classes

		Stem	OE	Rule	Expected	Gloss
a.	N S	open σ	talu	OSL	taːlu	'tale'
	N P	open σ	tala	OSL	taːla	'tales'
b.	N S	closed σ	hwæl	—	hwæl	'whale'
	N P	open σ	hwalas	OSL	hwaːlas	'whales'
c.	N S	open 2 σ	beofor	OSL	beːofor	'beaver'
	N P	open 3 σ	beoferas	TSS	beoferas	'beavers'
d.	N S	open 2 σ	dēofol	OSL	deːofol	'devil'
	N P	open 3 σ	dēofelas	TSS	deofelas	'devils'

In the forms in (25a) the stressed short vowel occurred consistently in an open syllable: nouns in this class indeed consistently appear in PDE with long vowels, as Minkova (1982) observes. Every other class is expected to have had a length alternation: not only is this not the regular case, it does not happen at all! Therefore, it is futile to consider only whether a short vowel or a long vowel is better adapted for, say, the context of *god* 'god N s': one must also consider the environment of the vowel in *godes* 'god G s', in which the preferences come out differently. Similarly for *beofor* and *beoferas* and *dēofol* and *dēofelas*. No matter how much one context may favour a short vowel and the other one a long vowel, the fact is that we are going to get only one answer for each pair.

Why did this happen? The unstressed inflected vowels in (25) became schwas which were subsequently deleted. Lahiri & Dresher (1999: 698) propose that the loss of schwas in the inflected forms created a hopelessly opaque alternation pattern, as shown in (26).

(26) Expected singular-plural pairs in Middle English

a. Before loss of schwa		b. After loss of vowel	
Singular	Plural	Singular	Plural
stōn	stōnes	stōn	stōns
bōdi	bodies	bōdi	bodis
god	gōdes	god	gōds
bēver	beveres	bēver	bevers

What was a well-behaved and perfectly ordinary length alternation before the loss of the inflectional schwa becomes chaotic and mysterious after: sometimes the addition of plural /s/ leaves the vowel length unchanged; other times it shortens a long vowel; still other times it lengthens a short vowel. In this type of unrecoverable opacity, we expect some sort of major breakdown of the system, which is exactly what we get. Evidently, learners could not make sense of these alternations and gave them up completely. Where all forms of a morpheme had a consistently long or short vowel, that is the vowel that remained. Where there was variation, it appears from the word counts that learners picked one or the other with almost equal odds. It is hard to see any other explanation of the total destruction of what had been a pervasive set of alternations. A further benefit of this account is that we have no reason to suppose that the phonological processes that caused the lengthenings and shortenings were themselves variable or had a statistical character. Variability entered the picture after the breakdown of the old grammar.

Once again, this account crucially relies on a certain model of how language learners react to the language data they are exposed to. It would not have been beyond the cognitive powers of late Middle English speakers to simply commit to memory the pattern of short and long vowels bequeathed to them by the previous generations, no matter how opaque. If synchronic grammars are simply the result of the operation of historical evolutionary processes, then why didn't Middle English speakers simply live with these alternations? We could say it was because they were maladaptive, not user-friendly, evolutionary dead ends, or a dysfunctional meme-complex. But if we ask why this is so, we must find the answers not in history, but in Universal Grammar.

29.7 Change and Contrast

In this section I consider ways that generative grammar can incorporate notions of contrast into phonological change. I deviate somewhat from an 'orthodox' interpretation of generative phonology, because Chomsky & Halle (1968) did not assign a special status to contrastive features as opposed to redundant ones. However, once one makes this distinction it follows naturally that the effects of contrast should turn up in change. Indeed, the insight that phonological change may involve a reorganization of the contrasts of a language goes back to Jakobson (1931): 'Once a phonological change has taken place, the following questions must be asked: what exactly has been modified within the phonological system?... has the structure of individual oppositions [i.e. contrasts/BED] been transformed? Or in other words, has the place of a specific opposition been changed...?' In this section I propose an answer to Jakobson's questions in a generative grammar that assigns a special role to contrastive features.

In some sense, contrast is inherent in a phonemic analysis, as exemplified in section 29.3. Recall that Hogg (1992: 61) proposes that, in the West Germanic dialects from which Old English developed, '*/æː/ is the only low long vowel and there is no front/back contrast in operation. From the structural point of view, therefore, the vowel as it develops in WGmc may be considered to be neutral in this last respect, that is, */aː/.'

In terms of distinctive features, this suggests that */aː/ (and its corresponding short low vowel, */a/) should not be specified as being either [+back] or [−back].

This kind of contrastive underspecification was not incorporated into the theory of Chomsky & Halle (1968), though it was prominent in earlier theories of phonology. To translate Hogg's insight into an explicit theory, we can borrow an idea from Jakobson and his collaborators (Jakobson, Fant, & Halle 1952, Jakobson & Halle 1956), namely: contrastive specifications are assigned by ordering the features into a contrastive hierarchy (Dresher 2009, Purnell & Raimy, this volume), and dividing the inventory by each successive feature in turn until all phonemes have been uniquely distinguished. On the assumption that only contrastive features can be active (the Contrastivist Hypothesis, Hall 2007), phonological activity can serve as a heuristic to ordering the features.

One way of ordering the features so that the low vowels have no specification for the front/back dimension is proposed by Purnell & Raimy (this volume). For the features used in section 29.4, their hierarchy would look as in (27), where the ordering of the features is [low] > [back] > [high] > [long].[16] In addition to the low vowels lacking any contrastive features beyond [low] and [long], the feature [round] does not appear at all in this hierarchy, even though the non-low back vowels are phonetically round; rather, the contrast between the non-low vowels is made by the feature [back] (or possibly [front], as in their account). Purnell & Raimy observe that the omission of [round] is supported by Lass's (1994) observation that rounding is non-distinctive in West Germanic. The fact that the non-low back vowels are nevertheless phonetically round can be attributed to phonetic enhancement (Stevens, Keyser, & Kawasaki 1986, Stevens & Keyser 1989): rounding a non-low back vowel enhances its backness and makes the contrast more salient.[17]

(27)   Contrastive hierarchy for West Germanic vowels

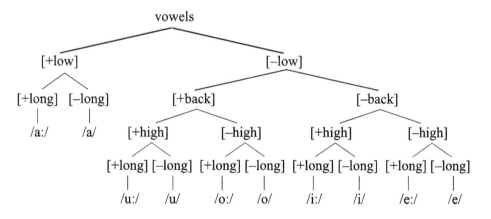

---

[16] The tree in (27) differs from Purnell & Raimy's in several respects. I omit their dimensions and list only terminal features. With respect to the latter, I use [low] instead of [RTR], and [back] instead of [front], and I include a length feature in the tree for completeness. Also, I assume binary features rather than privative ones, though there may well be markedness asymmetries between the positive and negative values.

[17] See Hall (2011) for a lucid discussion of how enhancement operates on contrastive feature specifications.

The contrastive specifications in (27) account for phonological generalizations about West Germanic that would be missed by a theory that requires that every phoneme be specified for every distinctive feature that might apply. As West Germanic evolved into Old English, the grammar changed not just in the rules and underlying representations, but also in the system of contrastive specifications. Even phonemes that do not appear to change overtly may come to have different contrastive features.

In Old English a new contrast developed between front /æ(ː)/ and back /a(ː)/, and, as Purnell & Raimy observe, rounding became phonologically active, hence, by hypothesis, contrastive, as shown by the development of new phonemes /y(ː)/ and /ø(ː)/ from the *i*-mutation of /u(ː)/ and /o(ː)/, respectively. A possible contrastive feature hierarchy for Old English is shown in (28), where the features are ordered [back] > [round] > [high] > [low] > [long] (the contrast between long and short vowels is not shown).[18]

(28)   Contrastive hierarchy for Old English vowels

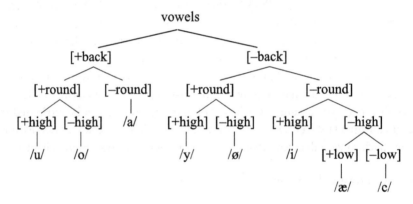

In phonetic terms, the vowels /a/, /u/, /o/, /e/, and /i/ do not appear to change from West Germanic to Old English; however, the representation of each of these vowels has changed, some significantly. These changes in representation correspond to different patterns of phonological activity.

As with every other aspect of the grammar, it is an empirical question whether the feature hierarchy in (28) is correct, in the sense that the assigned feature specifications correspond to observed phonological activity, and sort vowels into the required classes. Though we cannot pursue this analysis here (but see Purnell & Raimy, this volume), there is mounting evidence that contrast shift is an important type of phonological change.[19]

---

[18] The main difference between this feature hierarchy and Purnell & Raimy's, beside those already noted, is that [back] is ordered ahead of [round]. Evidence for this ordering is provided by Mercian Back Mutation, which requires /a/ to be contrastively [+back] (or [−front]).

[19] Other analyses that exploit the contrastive hierarchy in accounting for diachronic change include: Zhang (1996) and Dresher & Zhang (2005) on Manchu, Barrie (2003) on Cantonese, Rohany Rahbar (2008) on Persian, Dresher (2009: 215–25) on East Slavic, Compton & Dresher (2011) on Inuit, Gardner (2012), Roeder & Gardner (2013), and Purnell & Raimy (2013) on North American English vowel shifts, and large-scale studies by Harvey (2012) on Ob-Ugric (Khanty & Mansi), Ko (2010, 2011, 2012) on Korean, Mongolic, and Tungusic, and Oxford (2012, 2015) on Algonquian.

29.8 CONCLUSION

This chapter has sketched how rule-based generative phonology accounts for various types of phonological change. It has also argued for the continuing relevance of a number of fundamental principles. First, it is basic to the generative approach that phonological change, though visible in surface forms, is the result of a change in the grammars of speakers. The relationship between an observed change and the associated changes in grammar is not obvious, however: similar-looking changes may have different consequences for the grammar.

Second, the above analyses support the idea that some typical changes in grammar originate in the course of acquisition, when learners arrive at grammars that are different from that of their parents due to differences in the input data from that which shaped the grammar of their parents. This is not to say that all changes result from acquisition, but an important class of changes do.

It follows that considerations of learnability are central to diachrony as well as to acquisition. Some changes leave lexical representations and previous rules relatively undisturbed, in the sense that they are still learnable by speakers acquiring the new grammar. Other changes, however, make previous representations or rules of grammar difficult or impossible to learn, with sometimes far-reaching consequences to the grammar.

Central to the approach taken here is the notion that synchronic patterns and principles of learnability (aka Universal Grammar) influence the types of changes that language can undergo, and not the other way around; that is, it is not the case that there are universals of change that cause synchronic grammars to be the way they are. To the extent that there are diachronic universals, their source must be sought in properties of learners.

Finally, departing somewhat from classical generative grammar, but incorporating earlier Prague School ideas, I assume that considerations of contrast are important in accounting for synchronic patterns, because only contrastive features can trigger phonological processes. It follows that contrastive features will also affect the outcome of diachronic change, and that contrast may itself be the target of some diachronic changes, in that contrasts may be lost or gained, or old contrasts may be reinterpreted.

CHAPTER 30

....

DISTINCTIVE FEATURES, LEVELS OF REPRESENTATION, AND HISTORICAL PHONOLOGY

....

THOMAS PURNELL AND ERIC RAIMY

30.1 INTRODUCTION

....

OUR goal is to provide insight into the role that phonological (segmental) representations play in sound change. We present a contemporary view of phonological representation, which we view as *modular* and *abstract* in nature. Modular representations are those formal structures resulting from many distinct levels of representation that are required to understand sound patterns. Each level with its unique structure-building operations has distinct characteristics from the operations on other levels, and thus provides different types of explanation of the data. Abstract representations are those where the units present in different levels of representation are related to other levels in a many-to-one fashion. In section 30.2 we outline a brief history of distinctive feature theory. Section 30.3 presents contemporary models of distinctive features and explicates our assumptions about modularity in grammar. We demonstrate in section 30.4 how features are used within a theory of contrasts and applied to a contemporary analysis of the sound change in vowels systems from Proto-Indo-European to Early Old English based on proposals by Lass (1994). Section 30.5 summarizes and concludes the chapter. (Other chapters in this volume present alternative views to those adopted here, for example Bybee and Blevins see less of a role for purely formal factors in understanding change.)

30.2 Distinctive Features

The concept of a subsegmental phonetic distinction between sounds has been known for a very long time, no doubt by Indic linguists and the like. For example, Windfuhr (1971) observed that Avestan orthography was based on what moderns would refer to as distinctive features. Alexander Melville Bell was the first to formulate subsegmental organization of phones in his 1867 book *Visible Speech* (Halle 2009). This line of work was unknown to the majority of linguists (Henry Sweet was an exception), so it was not really until the end of the Prague Circle years that a theory of distinctive features was independently rediscovered and put forth to explain both synchronic phonological distinctions and diachronic changes (see Anderson 1985). The change from the goal of identifying phonemes to considering relationships among them led to the phase of acknowledging that a subconstituent of the phoneme does real work. This can be observed in the adherence to the phoneme by Trubetzkoy (1939/1958; building on Ščerba, Baudouin de Courtenay, and Saussure) as the smallest, indivisible unit that supports an opposition ('Phonological units that ... cannot be analyzed into still smaller successive distinctive units are called phonemes', p. 35), and the development towards Jakobson's description of sounds by distinctive features (Jakobson, Fant, & Halle 1952, Jakobson & Halle 1956).

Because of the parallel research themes pursued by the Geneva, Moscow, and Prague Linguistic Circles, historical linguistics and distinctive features have had a close relationship. One theme was the notion, in modern terms, of contrast; and often a contrast that joins a class of sounds was based on articulatory differences (e.g. Kruszewski's 'colorings', 1881/1978). Sound change, in this context, proceeds from articulatory processes to changes in a distinctive feature-based sound system. Trubetzkoy sketches out how distinctive features fit into a theory of phonemic contrasts in chapter 4 of *Grundzüge*: 'The object of the present chapter is not a classification of the sounds that can be produced by the human vocal apparatus, but a systematic survey of the phonic properties that are in effect utilized for the differentiation of meaning in the various languages of the world' (p. 92). Trubetzkoy recognized that articulatory properties grounded phonologically abstract representations. Moreover, although *Grundzüge* is focused on synchronic distinctions, Trubetzkoy and others were very interested in historical questions and in locating sound change in natural classes.

Distinctive features, as linguists have come to know them, are phonetically grounded building blocks of segments providing a description of a gesture that have contrast-maintaining ability. Three aspects of distinctive features can be traced to the thinking that pervaded participants of the three circles (Geneva, Moscow, and Prague) up to the end of the Second World War and Trubetzkoy's death. Jakobson pushed these claims, and they remain generally agreed upon. The first claim is that phonemes are made of distinctive features that cannot be further decomposed (Jakobson, Fant, & Halle 1952: 3). Or as Jakobson & Halle (1956: 3–4) state:

> Linguistic analysis gradually breaks down complex speech units into MORPHEMES as the ultimate constituents endowed with proper meaning and dissolves these smallest

semantic vehicles into their ultimate components, capable of differentiating morphemes from each other. These components are termed DISTINCTIVE FEATURES.

The second claim is that there is a finite set of features applying to all sounds. Stephen
Anderson (1985: 121) refers to this as the 'one mouth principle', and although there are
variants (e.g. C and V tiers in Clements 1985, 1991, *et seq.*), most phonologists hold to
this position and posit one set of features for all sounds. Where models of distinctive features do not share this assumption, there is a translation function that allows for distinctive features for consonants to influence distinctive features for vowels and vice versa.
Although there is general agreement on the one mouth principle, there is not agreement
on the nature and set of distinctive features and we take this as an indication of active
and fruitful research programmes.

The final claim, and one that has faced various challenges, is that features are essentially binary or oppositional. This binarity claim can be traced back to the three circles,
featured prominently as a possibility in Trubetzkoy's *Grundzüge*, and was adopted and
spelled out in greater detail in Chomsky & Halle (1968) and elsewhere. Since the nature
of feature opposition is binary, distinctive features are specified as being turned on or off.
The adoption of + or − valued distinctive features is implemented as an unordered set in
SPE which implies that there are no dependencies among any distinctive features.

Two revisions to the original 'binary but unrelated features' hypothesis have been generally accepted. The first is that there are dependencies among certain distinctive features.
Clements (1985) recognized that some distinctive features operate together, although
this sentiment is pre-dated in a number of works including *Grundzüge* (chapter 6,
'Phoneme Combinations'), Chomsky's (1957a) review of Jakobson & Halle, and in *SPE*
era writings. Clements's response is the development of *feature geometry* that makes certain distinctive features dependent on other features (e.g. the feature [+/−anterior] only
occurs when the feature [coronal] is positively specified). One way of grounding feature
geometry is to base any dependencies on the articulators in the vocal tract (e.g. Halle
1983, 1995, Sagey 1986, Halle, Vaux, & Wolfe 2000). Thus, [+/−anterior] is a dependent of
[+coronal] because the value of [anterior] is dependent on activation of the front of the
tongue that is associated with [+coronal]. The second revision is closely related to the
articulator-based version of feature geometry in that the organizing articulator nodes
are unary and not binary in value. In other words, the articulator features of LABIAL,
CORONAL, DORSAL, etc. do not have +/− values but instead are interpreted by their presence or absence in the bundle of distinctive features. See Clements & Hume (1995) and
Ní Chiosáin & Padgett (1993) for non-articulator-based feature geometries. An additional aspect of the second revision is the investigation of both scalar and privative
(or unary) distinctive features. Both of these ideas can be found both in Trubetzkoy's
work and in different contemporary approaches. Dependency Phonology (starting with
Anderson & Jones 1974) is one approach which develops privative ideas, and section 30.3
presents a model using privative features.

Chomsky & Halle (1965: 119), defending their position of describing sound alternations only with distinctive features against Householder (1965), say

To repeat once again, if we state rules strictly in terms of features, then we can propose an effective evaluation procedure which distinguishes true generalizations in terms of natural classes (in the sense in which linguists have always intuitively relied on these notions) from linguistically nonsignificant pseudo-generalizations, and which makes the distinction between admissible and inadmissible forms in an interesting class of cases. With a mixed notation, or a purely segmental notation without features, we know of no way to construct an evaluation procedure that will have these properties. For detailed argument, see Halle (1962 & [1964]). Furthermore, the grammar must obviously somewhere contain a specification of elements in terms of features. As has frequently been observed […], all phonology breaks down if we do not assume analysis on the phonetic level in terms of universal phonetic features.

This quotation contains an important claim for diachronic analysis. Until the mid-twentieth century, historical linguistics had been grouping phonemes together. With the advent of features, as Chomsky & Halle say, we have an empirically testable method for describing the natural classes over which sound change occurs. Distinctive features provide a system that can arbitrate whether a group of phonemes that undergo a diachronic change is natural or not. Another aspect of distinctive features is that the way they are mapped between the phonetics and phonology modules provides a restricted context as to how a diachronic change can be interpreted within the grammar. A final note on this quote is that the nature of 'evaluation procedures' in phonology has moved far beyond the purely logical approach espoused by *SPE*. Contemporary evaluation (and vindication) of distinctive features is based on articulatory, typological, computational, and psycholinguistic grounds.

30.3 CONTRAST AND MODULARITY IN DISTINCTIVE FEATURES

For most of this chapter we exemplify issues based on the structure of vowels (acknowledging that similar issues arise for consonants), and we focus on the model of distinctive features proposed by Avery & Idsardi (2001) as in Figure 30.1 (the next subsection considers a few aspects of other subsegmental models). This model adopts articulator-based feature geometry in the spirit of Halle (1995) and Halle, Vaux, & Wolfe (2000) but adds further structure to the organization of distinctive features based on anatomical facts (and thus contrasts with models which have acoustically-based features, such as Jakobson, Fant, & Halle 1952 and Harris 1994). The Avery & Idsardi model has both traditional aspects of feature geometry and some novel ones. There is a root node which has the features [sonorant] and [consonant] that encodes the major classes of vowels/glides, consonant sonorants, and obstruents. While groups of features are based on articulators (i.e. larynx, tongue root, soft palate, tongue body (Dorsal), tongue blade (Coronal), lips (Labial)), there are articulator-free features under the Oral Place node (i.e. [stop], [fricative]). All of these aspects of feature geometry appear in other models.

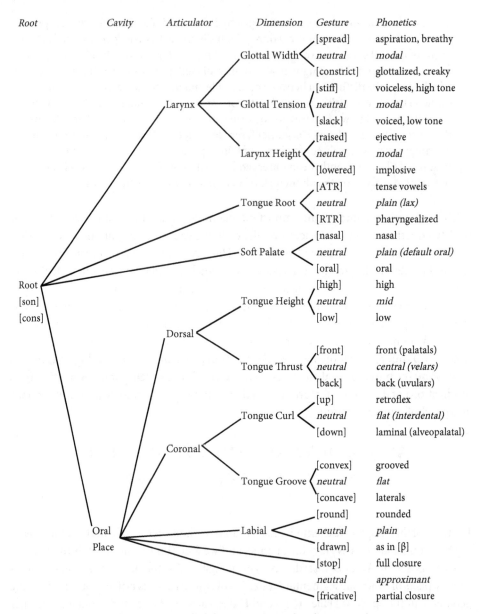

Root	Cavity	Articulator	Dimension	Gesture	Phonetics

FIG. 30.1 Distinctive features (modified from Avery & Idsardi 2001: 66)

30.3.1 Dimensions, Gestures, and Levels of Representation

The truly novel aspect of the Avery & Idsardi model is the *dimension*-organizing node and the dependent *gestures*. The dimension node encodes the observation that muscles for the most part occur in antagonistic pairs (Avery & Idsardi 2001: 44), which means that there are inherent restrictions on articulatory configurations. For example, the muscles of the larynx that control whether the glottis is spread apart to produce aspiration or pulled together to produce glottalization are antagonistic to each other. It is anatomically impossible to both implement constriction of the vocal cords (i.e. to glottalize) and spreading of the vocal cords (i.e. to aspirate) on a phone at the same time. The antagonistic gestures are organized under the dimension nodes and this restricts possible co-occurrences of gestures. A second novel claim of this approach is that phonological contrast is primarily encoded at the dimension level and not at the gesture level. This leads to phonologically sparse representations that must be filled in (*completed* in Avery & Idsardi's terms) through the addition of gestures. The filling of gestures is done by both language-universal and language-specific rules and is part of the work that phonology must do to convert phonologically sparse memorized representations into more fully specified phonetic representations that are the basis for instructions for motor control systems.

Avery & Idsardi (2001) follow an approach known as the Toronto School of Contrast (Dresher, Piggott, & Rice 1994, Avery 1996, Dresher 2009, also Dresher, this volume). The major characteristic of this approach adopted here is that contrast is encoded by marking one member of the contrastive pair through structural specification while leaving the other side of the contrast structurally unspecified. The rightmost column in Figure 30.1 that lists phonetic correlates of different gestures is an attempt to help navigate the ramifications of underspecification in this model. Each gesture has its articulatory or acoustic result and there is also a 'neutral' option, when neither muscle in the pair is innervated. The phonetic 'neutral' option is equivalent to being phonologically unmarked in the structural sense. For the complex relation between structure and markedness, see Rice (2003, 2009).

Each phoneme will have some part of its representation as its 'head' in the Avery & Idsardi model. This is similar in spirit to the designated articulator (see Sagey 1986, Halle 1995, Halle, Vaux, & Wolfe 2000) in that it specifies the part of the representation to be implemented by the articulator-free features (i.e. [stop], [continuant], [sonorant], [consonantal]). Additionally, heads support greater complexity (Dresher & van der Hulst 1999) that allows a gesture to be specified. For example, /h/ lacks any oral specification (Lass 1976, McCarthy 1988) and consists solely of a [spread glottis] gesture as its head. Contrasts are kept to a minimum (consequently, there are no pluses and minuses) in this system, thus representations are phonologically sparse.

We assume throughout that the interaction between the phonological and phonetic components of the speech chain consists of more rather than fewer levels. This means that as distinctive features are implemented, or 'completed', the representations gather other dimensions and gestures for enhancement of the sound (Keyser & Stevens 2006) and become more specified. For the purposes of this chapter, we will posit three distinct levels of phonological representation that we can refer to as *phonological, phonetic-phonological*, and *phonetic*. The phonological level will be defined as consisting solely of the contrastive dimensions within the Avery & Idsardi model. The phonetic-phonology model will be defined as consisting solely of gestures, which means by definition that the phonetic-phonology level will be more specified than the phonology level. Finally, the phonetic level consists of gestures projected to continuous variables on how to implement them (very much in the spirit of Browman & Goldstein 1986). These three levels present a drastically simplified model of phonological levels between lexical access and motor control programmes. In the spirit of our broader assumptions about modularity in cognition

(Carruthers 2008), there are many more levels of representation than presented in this chapter and necessarily specific processes for mapping from one level to another. And we simply adopt a rule-based perspective here—see Scheer (2010) for how issues of modularity play out within Optimality Theory (Prince & Smolensky 1993/2004).

Finally, each level of representation can be underspecified. In fact, the phonological level, since it only traffics in contrast, will necessarily have underspecified representations. The phonetic-phonological level will be more specified since gestures have been inserted, but it is not necessary for each representation to be fully specified. Finally, we follow work by Keating (1988a) and Pierrehumbert & Beckman (1988) showing that even phonetic representations can be underspecified.

30.3.2 Other Models of Features and Segmental Structure

As noted above, many aspects of the Avery & Idsardi model of distinctive features can be found in (or are inherited from) other schools of thought. Dependency Phonology (Anderson & Jones 1974, 1977, Anderson & Ewen 1987), Particle Phonology (Schane 1984), and Government Phonology (Kaye et al. 1985, 1990, Harris 1990a, 1994, Charette 1991) operate within a similar theoretical rubric as Avery & Idsardi and thus provide a similar approach to distinctive features. Common aspects are that features are parametric, non-binary, and provide relative composition of each individual sound. For Dependency phonologists such as Anderson & Ewen (1987), features define basic vocalic elements, of which there are three: |i| representing frontness or palatality, |u| representing roundness or labiality, and |a| representing lowness or sonority (or one can use the vowel elements I, U, and A, respectively—especially in Government Phonology). These basic pure or parametric vowel characteristics (based on work on Lieberman 1976 and Stevens 1972), when alone, define the corner vowels, but when combined provide specification for all vowels (see also Salmons & Honeybone, this volume). A similarly constrained set of primes is typically assumed in this approach for consonantal properties (see, for example, Harris 1990a).

Anderson & Ewen (1987) provide the following set as an example of how vocalic elements (in braces) are combined and correspond to surface values (in parentheses).

(1) Dependency Phonology correspondences (Anderson & Ewen 1987)
    a.   {|i|}   (=/i/)
         {|u|}   (=/u/)
         {|a|}   (=/a/)
    b.   {|i,u|}   (=/y/)
         {|i,a|}   (=/e/)
         {|u,a|}   (=/o/)
    c.   {|i,u,a|}   (=/ø/)

In order to account for all vowels, various notational methods are used to indicate scalar properties. For Schane (1984), this involves repetition of core particles. For example,

[e] is specified by **ai** and [ɛ] is specified by **aai** where the low particle is more prevalent (indicated by the greater number of particles) than the front particle. For Anderson & Ewen (1987), the asymmetry feature, ⇉, is used so that the difference between [e] and [æ] is {|i⇉a|} and {|a⇉i|}, respectively; [ɛ] involves an equal or symmetric relation between the two features, {|i⇄a|}. Jones (1989: 7) informally describes the difference between the pure corner vowels and mixed or complex vowels (read, vowels intermediate between the corners) as combinations where one of the three parameters is more prominent than the other features. For example, while [e, ɛ, æ] join |a|i|, [e] stresses palatality over sonority (son PAL), [ɛ] stresses palatality equally with sonority (SON PAL), and [æ] stresses sonority over palatality (SON pal). We recommend all the works referred to in this section for more information.

Turning to the problem at hand regarding accounting for aspects of language change using distinctive features, the family of theories of distinctive features limits the numbers of processes that can occur. Using Dependency Phonology as an example, two properties of change are intensification (adding a component, lowering [i] to [e] to [a] involves {|i|} > {|i|,|a|} > {|a|}) and reduction (removal of a component, raising from [æ] to [e] involves {|a⇉i|} > {|a⇉i|,|~a|} > {|i⇉a|}) (Anderson & Ewen 1987, parallel to Government Phonology processes of composition and decomposition). Additionally, this family of theories aims at providing accounts of change without the seemingly arbitrary rewrite rules of other generative approaches (*SPE*). Harris (1990a: 256) defines a non-arbitrary account as when an event occurs due to a 'logical connection' with a specific context—that is, referring to a specific phonological environment such that there is a 'local source' for any element added to a segment in composition (see also Scheer, this volume, on the relationship between change and phonological context). In part, this may mean that there is a substantive connection among phonological, phonetic, and acoustic representations where a change at one level may have necessary repercussions at other levels. This approach to features, then, resonates with the Avery & Idsardi model. Other work in commensurable models seeks to directly link patterns observed in change with the possibilities allowed in subsegmental feature theories, as in Iverson & Salmons (1995) and Honeybone (2005); still other work considers the extent to which principles of feature economy might constrain or direct changes, as in Clements (2003, 2009).

30.3.3 The Logic of Contrast

For many theories of distinctive features, feature symmetry is the rule, where phonemic inventories are the product of identical distinctive features operating in the same manner. In contrast, Dresher (1998, 2003, 2004, 2009) proposes the Successive Division Algorithm that posits distinctive features, one at a time, to successively split the sound inventory of a language based on the contrasts in the language. Thus, under a paradigm of feature asymmetry phonological contrast is encoded by marking segments with distinctive features at the system level so not all pairwise contrasts are distinguished through marking. Dresher (2003: 242–3) presents the following logical example of how contrast can be encoded using the Successive Division Algorithm. For this logical example, we have an inventory of three items: a small square, a large square, and a large circle. If we limit ourselves to using only size and shape then there are two ways to encode the minimal contrasts among these three items.

(2)   Two ways of viewing the contrasts

(a) A is the only small member		
small	large	
A.⊡	B.☐	C. ○
	square	round

(b) C is the only round member		
square		round
A.⊡	B.☐	C. ○
small	large	

The contrast depiction in (2a) marks the items by size first and then by shape, producing the marking for each item as 'small', 'large square', and 'large round'. The depiction in (2b) presents the opposite ordering where shape is used first, then size, producing 'square small', 'square large', and 'round'. A key motivation for this approach is that the resultant markings—based on how contrast is viewed—derive different abstract representations for identical surface inventories. Underlying abstract representations drive changes in surface inventories and one way of achieving Harris's goal of non-arbitrary analyses is a strong connection between the abstract representations and the processes that cause changes in the surface inventory. In other words, processes that can be seen at the surface level provide evidence about what abstract representations must be induced as part of the phonology.

A last point to appreciate about Dresher's approach to contrast is the role that unary marking can play in the possible representations for (2). In the example above both size and shape were treated as binary features but this is not necessary. Instead, we could mark the examples in a unary fashion that would produce four different systems if size were marked before shape.

(3)   Unary marking of contrast

	size mark	shape mark	⊡	☐	○
a.	small	square	small	square	Ø
b.	small	round	small	Ø	round
c.	large	square	Ø	large, square	large
d.	large	round	Ø	large	large, round

Depending on which pole of a dimension is marked, a different representation for the three objects can be produced, obtaining the four different systems in (3). Returning to Harris's goal of non-arbitrariness, a lack of specification will make the object inert, thus we can distinguish among the different representational possibilities by determining what the active processes are in the system. A simple hypothetical example from the systems in (3) is that if there is a 'shrinking process' triggered by small items, then systems (3ab) are potential candidates because 'small' is marked in these systems and thus provides a reason behind the 'shrinking'. Systems (3cd) which mark 'large' instead of 'small' have no logical explanation for why small things cause other items to shrink. The ramifications for this approach of unary marking in phonological representations for language change will become more transparent in the following sections.

30.4 Vowels, General and Historical

In this section we present our assumptions about the phonetics of vowels in section 30.4.1. These assumptions provide a background to section 30.4.2 that presents an analysis of the vowel system of ModAmE within the Avery & Idsardi model of distinctive features. Finally, section 30.4.3 consists of an analysis of the changes of the vowel systems of Proto-Indo-European (PIE) through Proto- and West Germanic to Old English.

30.4.1 The Phonetics and Phonology of Vowels

Two assumptions, one phonetic and one phonological, shape how we think about the formal properties of vowels. First, when approaching vowel variation (e.g. Purnell 2008, 2010, Purnell, Raimy, & Salmons 2009), we assume that all vowels are biphthongs, that is, a vowel consists of a head (aka nucleus) and tail (aka offglide). A monophthong is simply a vowel where the difference between the head and tail on horizontal (e.g. F3–F2 in bark) and vertical (e.g. F3–F1 in bark) dimensions is insignificant. A diphthong, on the other hand, has a significant difference in the formant values of its head and tail. The second assumption is that whether a vowel is a monophthong or a diphthong is distinct from whether it is a 'long' or 'short' vowel. Consider Figure 30.2 that presents amount of diphthongization (i.e. spectral difference between head and tail) on the y-axis with duration in ms on the x-axis.

Figure 30.2 presents measurements of vowels in the frame [s__d] from fourteen speakers from the Upper Midwest in the University of Wisconsin Microbeam Database (Westbury 1994). Measurements were taken at 33 percent and 66 percent locations in each vowel to determine the spectral distance between head and tail of the vowel (Assmann & Katz 2000). This figure supports our assumption that diphthongization is independent from length in that we can see that /i/ is longer than /ɪ, ɛ, ʊ/ but shows the least amount of spectral movement. A similar situation holds for /a, ɔ, æ/ in comparison to /e, u, o/, where the longer vowels show less This figure supports spectral movement. In the context of English, monophthongs are traditionally characterized as lax vowels {/ɪ, ɛ, ʊ, ɔ/}. It should be noted that in the Upper Midwest, and in many areas not part of the CAUGHT~COT merger in the US, the BOUGHT vowel, /ɔ/, is perhaps a low back vowel and the COT vowel, /a/, a central vowel. Moreover, /ɔ/ often is longer than the other three traditional lax vowels and may be diphthongal in that its tail trajectory nears the COT position.

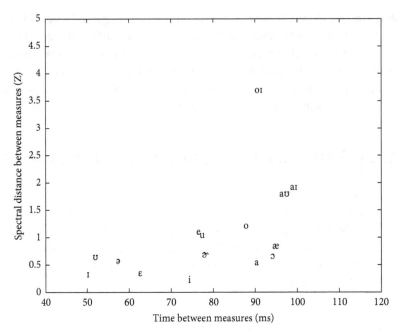

FIG. 30.2 Diphthongization *vs* duration in American English

A final important assumption is that there must be a theory of the phonetics and phonology interface in that the phonetics module must interpret and implement phonetic aspects of phonological representations (Keating 1988a). An example of the mismatch between phonetics and phonology is vowels. The phonetics of vowels in Upper Midwest English require us to have fine-grain control over the head, tail, and duration of a vowel but the phonology of these vowels generally ignores spectral movement (i.e. differences in head *vs* tail) and collapses durational differences to simply be 'long' *vs* 'short'. Our decision to parcel out this interaction between phonetics and phonology into three distinct parts, phonology proper, phonetics proper, and an interface between the two is a direct result of our commitment to hypermodularity.

30.4.2 Modern American English Vowel System

We now present the phonological representation of the vowels of Modern American English (ModAmE), as a prelude to understanding their history. As noted earlier, this system is guided by the ideas of the Toronto School of Contrast, Dresher (2009), and Avery & Idsardi (2001); see also Dresher (this volume). The vowel features for a generic form of ModAmE are presented in (4) and (5). Following Avery & Idsardi (2001), contrast is marked at the *dimension* level with *gestures* being filled in by completion rules. The hierarchy in (4) shows the order of scope for the dimensions using Dresher's Successive Division Algorithm while (5) shows the resulting phonological representations for the vowels of ModAmE. Note that (4) only considers the 'long' vowels of English because we assume that the long *vs* short distinction found in English is encoded via the timing tier with long vowels having two timing slots while short vowels only have one (see Ringen & Vago 2011 on the inadequacy of moras for representing length). The timing tier representation of length thus makes this contrastive dimension non-featural. (We assume this to be the case historically, as well.)

(4) Distinctive features of Modern American English long vowels

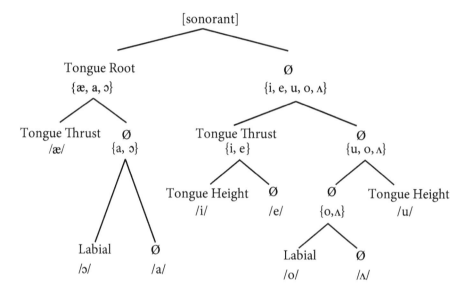

Tongue Root > Tongue Thrust > Tongue Height > Labial

(5) Modern American English Vowels

dimension	completion	i	ɪ	e	ɛ	æ	u	ʊ	o	ɔ	a	ʌ	ə
Tongue Root	[RTR]					✓				✓	✓		
Tongue Thrust	[front]	✓	✓	✓	✓	✓							
Tongue Height	[high]	✓	✓				✓	✓					
Labial	[round]								✓	✓			
Length	N/A	xx	x	xx	x	xx	xx	x	xx	xx	xx	xx	x

The first division of the vowel space in ModAmE is that the vowels /a, ɔ, æ/ are marked for the Tongue Root dimension completed with the gesture [RTR] (retracted tongue root). Stevens (1998: 269) observes that low vowels are made with a lower tongue body due to a lowering mandible (also Perkell 1969). Specifically, the lateral edge of the tongue body is set against the edge of the lower teeth and is articulated with a constricted vocal tract at the tongue root or pharyngeal area. Both /a/ and /æ/ have a narrowed pharynx, where /a/ is lower than /æ/ because of the contraction of the hyoglossus muscle for /a/ (Baer et al. 1988, cited in Stevens 1998: 269). We assume that /ɔ/ is phonologized into this group for three reasons, partially noted above in reference to Figure 30.2. The first is that /ɔ/ is of the approximate length of the vowels /a/ and /æ/ that are traditionally considered to be low. Second, in dialects that have a CAUGHT~COT merger, /ɔ/ is merged with /a/. Finally, for the Northern Cities Chain Shift (Gordon 2001, this volume, Labov et al. 2006), /ɔ/ represents the exit of the lax vowels and the 'start' of the tense portion of the chain shift (although not the start of the shift temporally).

The next two divisions are based on the Tongue Thrust dimension (completed with the gesture [front]) separating the vowel space into the traditional front *vs* non-front distinction and the Tongue Height dimension (completed with the gesture [high]) that creates the contrast between high and mid vowels. Phonetically, Stevens (1998: 263, 272) describes the mid vowels as having the lateral edges of the tongue in the same position as for the high vowels, that is, against the edge of the upper teeth. At the same time, the central plane of the tongue body is flat for mid vowels unlike high vowels. The Labial dimension (completed with [round]) encodes the contrast between the 'low' (actually TR) vowels, non-front vowels /a/ and /ɔ/, and the non-front mid vowels /o/ and /ʌ/. This node distinguishes the non-front, non-high, non-RTR vowels {/o, ʌ/} into the round and non-round variants. Lastly, length contrasts the mid and high vowels into long and non-long sets.

In summary, contrasts for ModAmE vowels are accomplished by the contrastive hierarchy, stated in terms of dimensions (with completion gestures in parentheses): Tongue Root ([RTR]) > Tongue Thrust ([front]) > Tongue Height ([high]) > Labial ([round]). The traditional lax vowels, /ɪ, ɛ, ʊ, ə/, are short variants of their corresponding long vowels, /i, e, u, ʌ/.

30.4.3 Diachrony in Vowel Systems

Distinctive features provide explicit representations for phonological systems. Thus, diachronic change is expressed in phonological systems (on the model considered here) by differences in either the contrastive hierarchy of features or the features that are active. Note that the phonological system provides the contrasts that are available to be expressed in a language and this is different from the phonic inventory of a language (e.g. CAUGHT~COT merged dialects of American English lack the phone [ɔ] but will still have the phonemic system in (4)–(5)). We will now ground the description of ModAmE in section 30.4.2 by expressing Lass's (1994) analysis of the change in vowel systems from PIE through Proto-Germanic to Old English in the same format as (4)–(5).

We start with a 'conservative' (as described by Lass 1994: 18) PIE vowel system in (6) which is encoded in the contrastive hierarchy as Tongue Root > Tongue Thrust > Tongue Height. PIE has both long and short vowels using this same system.

(6)   Contrastive hierarchy for the parent Indo-European vowel system

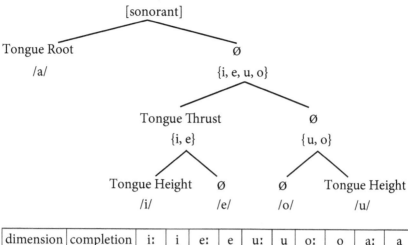

dimension	completion	iː	i	eː	e	uː	u	oː	o	aː	a
Tongue Root	[RTR]									✓	✓
Tongue Thrust	[front]	✓	✓	✓	✓						
Tongue Height	[high]	✓	✓			✓	✓				
Length	N/A	xx	x	xx	x	xx	x	xx	x	xx	x

The contrastive hierarchy in (6) uses the Tongue Thrust dimension to mark the contrast between the front unrounded and back rounded non-low vowels with /a/ being a non-front low vowel (marked by Tongue Root). There are also six diphthongs which are the combination of the vowels not marked for Tongue Height (/e, o, a/) with both front /i/ and back /u/ offglides.

We believe (6) provides a good representation of the distinctive features for PIE because of the ability to express the changes that transform the vowel system of PIE through Proto-Germanic to Old English. The first set of changes from PIE to produce Proto-Germanic that Lass posits is /o/ neutralizing to /a/, /aː/ neutralizing to /oː/, and /ei/ neutralizing to /iː/. The first two changes operating over non-high non-front vowels can be understood as removing the contrasting nature of the Tongue Root dimension. The change of /o/ to /a/ can be understood as a dimension-filling rule which inserts Tongue Root onto any unmarked vowel. In the system in (6), /o/ is the unmarked vowel and the addition of Tongue Root lowers it to /a/. Given this view of /o/ > /a/ we can then understand the mirror change of /aː/ to /oː/ as the reanalysis of the presence of Tongue Root as only being due to the rule that inserts Tongue Root and restricting this rule to only short vowels (possibly as some sort of geminate inalterability effect). The change from /ei/ to /iː/ results from a rule that requires Tongue Height and Tongue Thrust to be aligned in that the Tongue Height dimension will spread from the following /i/ in the diphthong /ei/ to /e/ producing the long /iː/. The effect of these three changes allows Tongue Root to be removed from the contrastive hierarchy to produce the system in (7) for Proto-Germanic.

(7) Proto-Germanic Vowel System

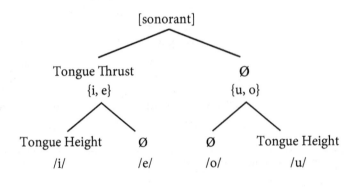

dimension	completion	iː	i	eː	e	uː	u	oː	o (> a)
Tongue Thrust	[front]	✓	✓	✓	✓				
Tongue Height	[high]	✓	✓			✓	✓		
Length	N/A	xx	x	xx	x	xx	x	xx	x
Filling Rule	Tongue Root	--	--	--	--	--	--	--	TR

Lass then claims that two changes characterize Proto-Germanic evolving into Northwest Germanic with respect to the vowel system. Note that both of these changes operate after the rule that inserts Tongue Root on short /o/ to create /a/ has applied. The first change is the lowering and retraction of Proto-Germanic */eː/ to /aː/. This change can be implemented through the addition of Tongue Root to the long vowel /eː/. This will produce a vowel that is specified as both Tongue Root and Tongue Thrust which is /æː/. There is controversy as to whether this particular vowel existed in Northwest Germanic. As Lass says, '[t]he arguments pro and con are extremely complex, but on balance there is probably not enough evidence to suggest a Proto-Germanic */æː/ ...' (p. 26). Under any circumstances in this situation, there must be some process that deletes the Tongue Thrust dimension when it is on the same segment as the Tongue Root dimension. How quickly this constraint removed the Tongue Thrust specification is the question here and whether it is instantaneous (effectively mapping the change from /eː/ to /aː/ directly) or took some time (allowing an intermediate /æː/ to exist for a short period of time) is an open question we will leave for future research.

The second change mentioned by Lass is *a*-umlaut, part of what is often known as 'height harmony'. Here, */u/ lowers when the following vowel is */a/. Using the feature set we argue for in (1) above, we can state this process as the deletion of Tongue Height when the following vowel is specified with Tongue Root. This can be viewed as an instance of a prohibition on the local occurrence of Tongue Height and Tongue Root that we will find active elsewhere over time, especially in Modern English. The reanalysis of these two changes as contrast in the phonological vowel system produces the West Germanic vowel system as in (8) which returns to the symmetrical long/short five-vowel system of PIE.[1]

(8) West Germanic

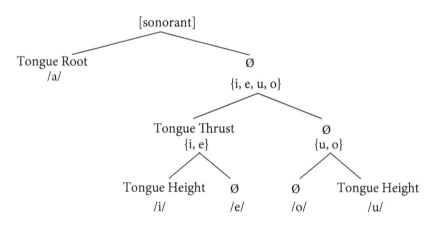

dimension	completion	iː	i	eː	e	uː	u	oː	o	aː	a
Tongue Root	[RTR]									✓	✓
Tongue Thrust	[front]	✓	✓	✓	✓						
Tongue Height	[high]	✓	✓			✓	✓				
Length	N/A	xx	x	xx	x	xx	x	xx	x	xx	x

[1] This is basically the same analysis as found in Dresher's chapter (this volume) example (27). We both agree that the contrastive hierarchy is 'low' > 'backness' > 'high' but have different labels for these dimensions. We have not committed to the scope of vowel length in the hierarchy while Dresher places it at the bottom.

Lass (1994: 28) concludes his description of the changes leading to Early Old English with three characteristics. First, there are no low front vowels in the West Germanic vowel system. We interpret this to mean that the Tongue Thrust dimension is not active contrastively under Tongue Root in the period leading up to Old English. We can see that the contrastive hierarchy for Early Old English (below in (9)) does have a low front vowel, /æ/, marked for both Tongue Thrust and Tongue Root but there is still no strict contrast of Tongue Thrust under Tongue Root in the contrastive hierarchy. Given the changes in and out of the low front position from Old English through the dominant changes in ModAmE (e.g. Northern Cities Chain Shift, Labov et al. 2006, Gordon, this volume), the Tongue Thrust distinction for Tongue Root vowels is a very important innovation.

The second observation Lass makes about the differences between the West Germanic vowel system and Old English is that rounding is 'non-distinctive' in West Germanic. The mid and high back vowels are rounded with all other vowels non-rounded. The feature hierarchy in (8) directly captures this observation because the Labial dimension (which is completed by the gesture [round] as a default in vowels) plays no contrastive role. Rounding of the mid and high back vowels must result from an enhancement (Keyser & Stevens 2006) serving to increase phonetic contrast. Our analysis provides coherence to this rounding enhancement because it is only the non-low vowels (i.e. not marked for Tongue Root) that are contrastive on Tongue Thrust. Inserting Labial (to be completed with [round]) on vowels that are not Tongue Thrust or Tongue Root serves to increase their contrast (see Hall 2011 on the relation between enhancement and contrast). We will see that the reanalysis of this 'rounding enhancement' into a phonological contrast is a key development in Old English.

The last observation that Lass makes is that the second quality in the West Germanic diphthongs is either /i/ or /u/. This restriction is captured by requiring an off-glide of a diphthong to be specified with Tongue Height. With this final point, we can see that the distinctive feature analysis of West Germanic in (8) provides a vocabulary that allows for Lass's observations to be expressed in a very straightforward and easy fashion. This is one of the benefits of distinctive features. The current analysis is also restrictive in that phonology 'proper' can be defined as the operations or restrictions that can be expressed on phonological representations consisting solely of dimensions (i.e. our phonological level). Consequently, Lass's observations about the form of possible diphthongs and no front non-low vowels are phonological in nature because they fall out directly from the dimensions. The observation about rounding being non-distinctive is more complicated because it spans across the phonology–phonetics boundary. /u/ and /o/ are rounded phonetically but not phonologically with at least the phonology side of this captured by distinctive features. A key question of language change is how subtle changes in phonetic representations cause distinct phonological systems (see Bybee, Bermúdez-Otero, and Yu, all this volume).

Early Old English (i.e. prior to the loss of /ø/) provides two excellent examples showing the interaction between phonetics and phonology. The hierarchy in (9) presents the contrastive hierarchy for Early Old English and the most notable feature of this hierarchy is the prominent and contrastive role of the Labial dimension.[2] This dimension is completed with the gesture [round] that causes rounding to be phonologically contrastive in Early Old English as opposed to its non-contrastive nature in West Germanic and ModAmE.

(9) Early Old English

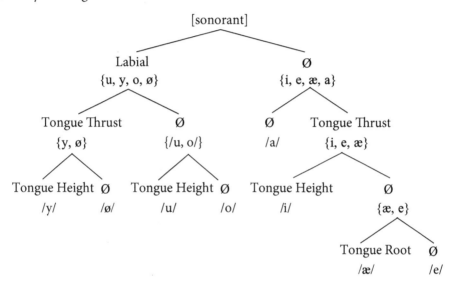

Labial > Tongue Thrust > Tongue Height > Tongue Root

dimension	completion	i	y	e	ø	æ	u	o	a
Labial	[round]		✓		✓		✓	✓	
Tongue Thrust	[front]	✓	✓	✓	✓	✓			
Tongue Height	[high]	✓	✓				✓		
Tongue Root	[RTR]					✓			

² We differ with Dresher's analysis of Early Old English (this volume, example (28)) in one substantial way: how contrastive rounding is added to Old English. We see the addition of a new feature to a contrastive hierarchy as 'more natural' at either the top or the bottom of the hierarchy. Our analysis adds 'labial' to the top of the hierarchy while Dresher adds 'labial' to the middle between 'backness' and 'high'. Dresher does this to have /a/ specified as [+back] to account for Mercian Back Mutation (Dresher 1978). Our analysis prevents us from this particular analysis of Mercian Back Mutation because we have no way to specify [+back] regardless of where we add 'labial' to the contrastive hierarchy. See Purnell & Raimy (in preparation) for an alternative analysis of Mercian Back Mutation.

The key fact about the distinctive feature system in (9) for Old English which meets Harris's goal of non-arbitrariness is *i*-umlaut where suffixes with /i/ caused changes to the preceding vowel. The interesting aspect of this change is that the vowel undergoing the change could front or raise. A first step in understanding this process is to note that /i/ in both Old English and the preceding West Germanic is specified for both Tongue Thrust and Tongue Height which means that there is no surprise that this particular vowel can cause fronting and/or raising. The key question is how to understand the phonologization of roundness as a contrast. This is where the modularity afforded to us through our distinct levels of phonological representation (section 30.3.1) will be very important.

The output of the phonetic level serves as the input to the phonetic-phonology level if we are focusing on perception. We assume that a crucial period in the change from the West Germanic vowel system to the Early Old English system is that this level of representation encodes difference between a vowel based on whether it is followed by an [i] or not. We will use Lass's (1994: 60–1) example of the distinction between the /u/ in *mūs* (< /muːs/) 'mouse nominative singular' and /y/ in *mȳs* (< /muːs-iz/) 'mouse nominative plural' but start at a pre i-umlaut state of affairs. At this point in time, the /u/ in / muːs/ is identical to the /u/ in /muːs-iz/ at both the phonetic-phonology and phonological levels but can be slightly different due to coarticulation effects at the phonetics level, (10). At the phonological level only the contrastive dimensions are listed, thus all vowels are marked as Tongue Height because they are 'high' vowels and only /i/ is marked with Tongue Thrust because this is the contrastive dimension indicating 'front'. The phonetic-phonology level contains predictable content that is the result of enhancement rules and we mark these gestures by enclosing them in curly brackets. The phonetic level indicates whether the gestures involved in the phones are distinct or not. At this first stage the gestures involved in [u] and [y] are distinguishable, but not contrastive.

(10) Pre i-umlaut, coarticulation only

	/u/	[y]	/i/
Phonology	Tongue Height	Tongue Height	Tongue Height Tongue Thrust
Phonetic-Phonology	[high] {[round]}	[high] {[round]}	[high] [front]
Phonetic	/u ≈ y/ ≠ [i]		

The next stage is where i-umlaut has been added to the grammar at the phonetic-phonology level (see also Bermúdez-Otero, Hale et al., and Kiparsky, all this volume, on phonologization). This creates the state where [y] is an allophone of the phoneme /u/. This situation is different because there is now a definitive difference between /u/ and [y] at both the phonetic and the phonetic-phonology levels. The difference at the phonetic-phonology level is indicated by the addition of the [front] gesture to [y]. At the phonetics level, /u/ and [y] are truly distinct with the fronted [y]'s distribution being predictable.

(11) i-umlaut producing allophonic [y]

	/u/	[y]	/i/
Phonology	Tongue Height	Tongue Height	Tongue Height Tongue Thrust
Phonetic-Phonology	[high] {[round]}	[high] {[round]} [front]	[high] [front]
Phonetic	/u/ > [y] ≠ /i/		

The final stage is the full phonologicalization of /y/ as a phoneme. This change in status causes the representation in dimensions at the phonological level (on our model) to be reorganized. The crucial reorganization is to memorize the dimension Labial as a projection of the [round] gesture instead of treating its presence as an enhancement. Another important change is that the [front] gesture in /y/ is no longer predictable and thus also projects the relevant dimension to the phonological level. These two changes are indicated, first, by the dimensions indicated as Labial and Tongue Thrust at the phonology level, and second, by the removal of the curly brackets on [round] at the phonetics-phonology level, indicating that its presence is no longer the product of an enhanced gesture. This produces the system in (12).

(12) Phonemic /y/

	/u/	/y/	/i/
Phonology	Tongue Height Labial	Tongue Height Tongue Thrust Labial	Tongue Height Tongue Thrust
Phonetic-Phonology	[high] [round]	[high] [round] [front]	[high] [front]
Phonetic	/u/ ≠ /y/ ≠ /i/		

The i-umlaut example demonstrates the important role of modularity in a general theory of distinctive features. Distinctive features should only account for the phenomenon they are designed to explain. The phonological level (on our model) has a particular set of distinctive features based on dimensions which encodes lexical contrast and should do nothing more. The phonetics-phonology level consists of distinctive features expressed as gestures which have as one purpose the encoding of more specific information about phonological representations. There is non-contrastive information in this level of representation and this provides direct connection to a gestural score that is at the heart of the phonetic level of representation. The phonetic level of representation uses a much more continuous scale and this provides a source of explanation for partial mergers as opposed to complete mergers.

The process of raising long low vowel /aː/ before a nasal to /oː/, West Germanic 'moon' maːna > moːna (Lass 1994: 38), allows us to demonstrate the differences in explanation at these different levels. If this particular case of raising is phonological in nature then it should be accomplished at the phonological level through a rule that deletes the Tongue Root dimension of /a/ if it precedes a nasal segment. Within the West Germanic vowel system, (8), the only difference between /oː/ and /aː/ is the Tongue Root dimension, thus deleting Tongue Root changes /aː/ to /oː/ in West Germanic. There are two important implications of this analysis. The first is that this process must pre-date and be complete before the innovations of the Old English vowel system because the contrast in Old English between /oː/ and /aː/ is based on the Labial dimension (i.e. rounding). The second is that since this change pre-dates Old English, the contrast between /oː/ and /aː/ before a nasal segment will still be possible because there is no active process at this time.

If this process actually occurs at the phonetic-phonology level then there is more flexibility in what the process actually does and diachronically when it can occur. The reason for the additional flexibility is because the representations are more fully specified at this level. Based on the vowel systems for West Germanic and Old English this process can be understood either as nasal-induced raising (13a) or nasal-induced rounding (13b).

(13) /aː/ raising

	a. West Germanic		b. Old English	
	/oː/	/aː/	/oː/	/aː/
Phonology	Ø	Tongue Root	Labial	Ø
Phonetic-Phonology	{[round]}	[RTR]	[round]	{[RTR]}

The contrast between /oː/ and /aː/ at the phonetic-phonological level is overdifferentiated. /oː/ is a rounded back mid vowel that only needs to be represented by the gesture [round]. /aː/ is a low back unrounded vowel and can be simply represented by the gesture [RTR]. A literal interpretation for the /aː/ to /oː/ before a nasal process is to delete [RTR] and insert [round] before [nasal]. The actual implementation of this change depends on what system it operates in, however.

The West Germanic vowel system supports an analysis at the phonetic-phonology level that is analogous to the one previously proposed at the phonological level. There is simply a rule that deletes [RTR] before a nasal and then the [round] gesture is inserted as part of an enhancement. A possible alternative to this analysis is to insert the [round] gesture before a nasal segment if the vowel is [RTR] and then have a constraint (see Calabrese 2009) which bans a phoneme from being both [RTR] and [round]. Thus, the overall effect of inserting [round] before the nasal is the deletion of [RTR]. This second analysis positing a [round] insertion rule is necessary if the rule is operating in Old English. Because the Labial dimension is contrastive in Old English, a [round] gesture on a vowel is never the result of an enhancement rule, thus it must be inserted by a separate rule. If this rule occurs after enhancements have occurred (which insert [RTR] on /aː/) then the constraint causing the deletion of [RTR] in the presence of [round] is needed too.

A final note about the analysis of /aː/ raising at the phonetic-phonology level is that the core characterization of this level of representation in the Avery & Idsardi system is that gestures can be directly manipulated. This means that there is a question as to the ordering of completion rules which add gestures to contrastive dimensions, enhancement rules that add bare dimensions which can later undergo completion rules, and rules that insert, spread, or delete gestures. One of the open questions both about the specific /aː/ raising process and sound change in general is how to determine exactly where in the overall phonology a change has been grammaticalized.

Having a good handle on /aː/ raising from West Germanic to Old English is important because vowels raising in front of nasals are common in contemporary English (Labov et al. 2006). The contemporary version in certain dialects of American English only affects /æ/ and does not cause neutralization in the contrast between /æ/ and /e/. Because the contrast is maintained we cannot view this process as the deletion of either the gesture [RTR] or the dimension Tongue Root. Instead, this process should be viewed as occurring at the phonetic level where representations are more continuous in nature. The control of continuous type representations is going to be analogous in nature in that the phonetic level will be able to set various aspects of the representations such as amplitude, attack, duration, etc. The pre-nasal /æ/ raising in ModAmE can be understood as the amplitude of the [RTR] gesture of the /æ/ being attenuated. Since the [RTR] gesture is what controls the lowness of /æ/ then by 'turning down' this gesture, the vowel will be slightly raised. The [RTR] gesture is still present, just not as strong, thus creating a vowel that is higher than /æ/ but not as high as /e/. The grammatical control and setting of the continuous nature of the implementation of the gestures is exactly what the phonetic level should account for.

30.5 CONCLUSION

In this chapter we have presented a contemporary view of distinctive features with implications for diachronic analyses. We have focused on vowels but analogous analyses of consonants can be created easily. A specific and updated view of distinctive features is important given the differing contemporary points of view on what distinctive features are and how they operate. One important aspect to recognize is that there is a common core to phonological distinctive features across schools of thought in that they are abstract and have to be actively interpreted to and from phonetic categories. The main change in distinctive features over time is the refinement of their role in different levels of grammatical representation. Many classic points of view can be reinterpreted in modern approaches to distinctive features when the classic point of view is properly matched to a level of grammatical representation. Finally, when details of distinctive features are carefully measured, concrete proposals about how grammars change over time can be identified and mapped to both well-known and novel data. We believe that a crucial tool for the diachronic study of sound patterns is the choice of a distinctive feature system, so proposals about how phonology changes over time can be made explicit and thus evaluated.

CHAPTER 31

HISTORICAL SOUND CHANGE IN OPTIMALITY THEORY

Achievements and Challenges

D. ERIC HOLT

31.1 INTRODUCTION

IN this chapter,[1] I explore the application of classical Optimality Theory to historical sound change, and the development of alternative models of OT that have been advocated to deal with historical phonology, based on systemic, functional, and phonetic motivations, frequently similar to or consistent with models proposed independently for synchronic phonology.[2]

While a thorough introduction to Optimality Theory (Prince & Smolensky 1993 /2004) is beyond my scope,[3] I present a brief summary: OT is a linguistic theory predicated on the interaction of violable constraints that encapsulate cross-linguistic ('universal') patterns of various types. Under OT, Universal Grammar is composed of a set of constraints out of which grammars are constructed (CON), a function that generates for each possible lexical entry, the range of candidate linguistic analyses available (that is, potential outputs) (GEN), and a function that comparatively evaluates sets of forms with respect to a given constraint hierarchy (EVAL); the candidate output that best satisfies ('minimally violates') the grammar's constraint ranking is the 'optimal' candidate (i.e. the actual form of the language). The constraints fall into two broad categories: faithfulness constraints,

---

[1] I have treated similar topics in previous works (Holt 2003b, 2007); see these for fuller discussion. Here I concentrate on works published since those available at the time of submission of the manuscript for the publication of Holt (2003a). Additionally, on multilevel OT—and some other aspects of modelling change in OT in general—see Kiparsky (this volume), where Kiparsky uses the term Stratal OT, and advocates the hierarchy of serially related levels of stem, word, and postlexical phonology.

[2] The reader is also referred to Bermúdez-Otero (2006b, 2007) for an overview from a different perspective and with a different focus.

[3] For a fuller introduction to the basic workings of Optimality Theory, see Kager (1999).

Tableau 31.1 (Sample tableau)

/lexical entry/	Constraint 1	Constraint 2
a. [Candidate output a]	*!	
b. [Candidate output b] ☞		**

which treat the degree of similarity between underlying and surface forms; that is, the degree to which mental representations match physical ones, roughly—e.g. whether there has been deletion, change, or loss of some segment; and markedness constraints, which deal with the relative well-formedness/complexity/difficulty/ease of articulation of surface forms. This is usually illustrated in a *tableau* (such as tableau 31.1), the term for a table in which the input form, constraints, and candidates are presented, with an asterisk ('*') indicating that a candidate violates some constraint, an exclamation mark ('!') signalling that a particular violation is the reason a form is not selected as optimal, and a pointy finger typically showing the 'winning' or optimal output form. Finally, in its classical formulation, constraints are in a relation of strict domination; that is, it is not the total number of violations that determines the optimal output, but minimal violation of the hierarchy, such that in the example presented in tableau 31.1, candidate (a) is ruled out due to its single violation of Constraint 1, leaving candidate (b) as optimal, despite its double violation of Constraint 2.

Almost as early as OT was being established as the dominant paradigm in phonological research, certain researchers saw great promise for its application to issues and data of sound change, starting with Zubritskaya (1995) on Russian segmental changes, Jacobs (1995) on Old French lenition, Gess (1996, 1999) on Old French, Holt (1997) on Hispano-Romance, and the contributions to Holt (2003c).[4] The simplest way to conceptualize historical change within a constraint-based approach to phonology is by constraint reranking, with the scenarios presented by Hutton (1996):[5]

---

[4] For applications to syntactic variation and change, see the contributions to Holt (2003a) by Slade and LaFond.

[5] Bermúdez-Otero & Hogg (2003) present a detailed discussion of the generative notion of phonologization, rule loss, and inversion and how cases attributed to these may be handled in OT. See Dresher (this volume) for a generative approach to several sound changes, which departs somewhat from traditional formulations in acknowledging the involvement of systemic contrast. See also Donegan & Nathan (this volume) on Natural Phonology and various types of sound change (mergers, shifts, splits, etc.) and issues of underlying representation, phonological processes and rules, the role of learners, etc., some of which are akin to assumptions made by practitioners of OT, and see Mailhammer et al. (this volume) for a consideration of preference laws, which also prefigured some of the ideas found in OT. Other chapters in this volume take very different (non-OT) approaches, e.g. Bybee and Blevins. See van Leussen (2008) for a computational model couched in a stochastic version of OT that assumes a bidirectional interaction of phonology and phonetics, and the OT-based model of learning, the Gradual Learning Algorithm (Boersma & Hayes 2001); and, for other OT-based treatments of historical data, see Cho (1998), who treats the linking/intrusive *r* ~ Ø alternation in English and the *n* ~ Ø alternation in Korean, and Oh (2002), who under the Diachronic Reranking Hypothesis Model (p. 134) reanalyses the Korean data from Cho (1998), as well as Green (1998) on the simplification of *kn* > *n* in English.

(1) Alternations to the constraint hierarchy:
   a. Promotion of constraints
   b. Demotion of constraints
   c. Creation of new connections between constraints
       (A, B > A » B)
   d. Dissolution of connections between constraints
       (A » B > A, B)
   e. Alteration of the dominance relationship between two constraints
       (A » B > B » A)

Zubritskaya (1995) treats palatalization assimilation in consonant clusters in Modern Russian and its loss over time, where MAXIMIZE LICENSING (the constraint requiring assimilatory spreading in her account) is reranked below the family of constraints that militate against secondary articulation (that is, palatalization by having a secondary coronal articulation):[6]

(2) MaxLic. >
   *Dor » *Lab   »   *Cor
     | | |
    Cor   Cor   Cor

Thus, there is a gradual reranking over time; assimilation is at first obligatory, but is progressively restricted by the relative unmarkedness of the primary place of articulation (with palatalized coronals remaining the longest), and eventually prohibited in all clusters. For Zubritskaya, this directionality of change not only is natural (from more to less marked) but also the only direction possible; markedness hierarchies, then, allow for explicit predictions about the directionality of sound change.

When taking into consideration that change occurs chiefly between generations of speakers and that transmission implies acquisition by children (see also Hale et al., and Foulkes & Vihman, both this volume, for an alternative viewpoint), a shift in underlying representations is also a likely and logical locus of change as surface structures derived by phonological processes previously are more simply analysed as new input forms ('reanalysis/restructuring' in traditional and previous generative approaches—see Dresher, this volume), characterized as 'lexicon optimization' in OT (Inkelas 1994, and many other authors subsequently).

(3) Lexicon optimization (Prince and Smolensky 1993: 192)
     Suppose that several different inputs $I_1, I_2, ..., I_n$ when parsed by a grammar G lead to corresponding outputs $O_1, O_2, ..., O_n$, all of which are realized as the same phonetic form Φ—these inputs are all *phonetically equivalent* with respect to

---

[6] In Zubritskaya (1997: 127), MAXIMIZE LICENSING is replaced by PAL: 'If F', then it must be maximally associated.' That is, if there is a dependent feature, spread it to neighbouring segments to maximize its perceptibility.

G. Now, one of these outputs must be the most harmonic, by virtue of incurring the least significant violation marks: suppose this optimal one is labelled O_k. Then the learner should choose, as the underlying form for Φ, the input I_k.

This is paraphrased by Inkelas (1994: 6) as follows:[7]

> [O]f all the possible underlying representations that could generate the attested phonetic form of a given morpheme, that particular underlying representation is chosen whose mapping to phonetic form incurs the fewest violations of highly ranked grammatical constraints.

With regard to historical change, Hutton (1996) proposes the Synchronic Base Hypothesis, with obvious ties to lexicon optimization:

(4) Synchronic Base Hypothesis
All input candidates produced by GEN are based on the current output form. Earlier forms of the language are no longer available as underlying representations on which GEN operates.

That is, current speakers do not retain historical forms as underlying representations and apply changes to them, but rather incorporate surface forms back into their lexicon, replacing the outdated ones as input to their current grammar.

In some cases, OT has been argued to provide insights previously impossible to state in theoretically coherent ways under previous models of phonology. For example, I argued (1997, 2003b) for a causal relationship between the loss of vowel length in Latin and the gradual, sonority scale-respecting loss of moraic (both syllable-final and geminate) consonants in the development of Old Spanish.

(5) Reranking of faithfulness vis-à-vis sonority/moraicity hierarchy

MAX		Latin
↓ MAX		Late Spoken Latin, Hispano-Romance
↓	MAX	Modern Spanish, Galician, Portuguese
	↓	
$^*O_\mu \gg {}^*N_\mu \gg {}^*L_\mu \gg {}^*G_\mu \gg {}^*V_\mu$		(Sonority hierarchy)

One stage of this evolution is modelled below:

---

[7] This appears in the 1994 manuscript posted to the Rutgers Optimality Archive, but is absent from the published 1995 version.

(6) The surface moraic status of consonants in early Old Spanish.

/-k, -g/		$*O_\mu$	MAX/IDENT	$*N_\mu, *L_\mu, *G_\mu$
		(Syllable-final obstruents vocalize to bear mora)		
$-k_\mu, -g_\mu$		*!		
☞ $-j_\mu$			* <+cons> * <-son>	*
$/k_\mu, g_\mu/$		(Intervocalic moraic obstruents lose their mora, simplifying)		
k_μ, g_μ		*!		
☞ k, g			* <μ>	
j_μ			* <+cons> *! <-son>	*
$/n_\mu, l_\mu/$		(Sonorant geminates still valid mora-bearers at this stage)		
☞ n_μ, l_μ				*
n, l			*! <μ>	

At this stage, Latin MULTU is realized as Hispano-Romance [mujto], CUPPA as [kopa], and CASTELLUM as [kastillo]. The ranking of MAX/IDENT with respect to the sonority hierarchy encodes the fact that erosion of an offending segment is better than total loss, and relates vocalization to the reduction of geminates.[8] So, while in Latin all segments may bear a mora (permitting both long vowels and geminate consonants), the demotion of MAX leads to degemination of obstruents in later stages of Hispano-Romance (CUPPA > *copa*, GUTTA > *gota*, BUCCA > *boca*), as well as to the weakening and loss of syllable-final consonants (TRUCTA > Moz. *truhta* > Sp. *trucha*, MULTU > *muito* > *mucho*). (The subsequent development of sonorants (ANNUM > *año*, BELLA > *bella*, with palatal [ʎ]) is treated below with Dispersion Theory.) This evolution is schematized below:

(7) Sonority classes from Latin to Old Spanish and Galician/Portuguese

    Latin: μ = unrestricted   all vowels and consonants may bear a mora

    Hispano-Romance: μ = [+sonorant]   vowels and sonorant consonants may bear a mora

    Old Spanish, Galician/Portuguese: μ = [-consonantal]   only vowels may bear a mora

---

[8] An alternative ranking of MAX » IDENT would also encode the fact that erosion of an offending segment is better than total loss, but would not relate the vocalization of *-l* to the reduction of geminates, which I argue both result from the increasing dominance of the constraint against moras being associated with consonantal features.

The change of Proto-Indo-European *dụ to Classical Armenian -rk- is analysed by DeLisi (2013) as an instantiation of sonority-based metathesis, where instead of expected segmental metathesis, the cluster underwent metathesis only of the feature [±continuant], which is motivated by an effect of the emergence of the unmarked ('TETU') due to the markedness of the segment [w] in Classical Armenian (and tentatively based on language contact) in interaction with syllable structure and syllable contact considerations. DeLisi argues that her approach avoids several problematic assumptions about the etymology of words with this cluster, and adopts the notion that diachronic phonology can be modelled as changes in constraint rankings over time.

An example from metrical development comes from Lleó (2003), who analyses the loss of unstressed vowels in Old Spanish and provides an account of why some underwent deletion while others did not (e.g. SĒCŪRU > *seguro* vs OC(U)LU > *ojo* vs SECUNDU > *segund* or *segunt* 'second', later recovered). Increased syncope in Old Spanish is argued to result from Germanic influence, whose stress-timed characteristics impacted the prominence of stressed and unstressed syllables; the later increase of apocope is argued to result from the later French influence. The constraints interacting in determining vocalic/syllabic realization include prosodic concerns (FOOTTROCHEE, STRESS-TO-WEIGHT, PARSE-σ, HEADMAX), as well as phonotactic constraints on complex codas (NOCODA, NOCODACOMPLEX, CODA$_{SON}$>ONSET$_{SON}$) and morphological conditioning that bans deletion of lexical material (MAX-MORPHEME, MAX-SEGMENT, MAX-/a/). Syllable structure constraints are shown to have had a rather variable position in the hierarchy of constraints in different periods of Spanish (going from a rather dominant to a low-ranked position, and back again to a very dominant one) (p. 280), and with regard to constraint reranking as a mechanism of modelling change, Lleó proposes that demotion is the normal means of internal sound change, while constraint promotion may need to be invoked to account for external conditioning.

(8)   Stages in the position of NOCODA and STRESS-TO-WEIGHT
      Stage 1 Late Hispanic Latin: NOCODA dominates STW
          (disfavouring vowel loss that would lead to new codas)
      Stage 2 Early Old Spanish: STW promoted, outranks NOCODA
          (leading to increased vowel deletion and coda formation, under Germanic influence)
      Stage 3 Old Spanish (11th–13th centuries): NOCODA further demoted
          (leading to increase in simple and complex codas and allowing apocope, under French influence)
      Stage 4 Modern Spanish: NOCODA promoted, STW demoted
          (leading to increase in open syllables; closed syllables no longer required to satisfy STW)

Likewise, Crist (2001: 62) argues that various changes from West Germanic to Old English (affrication, lateralization, metathesis, and glide assimilation, all rules whose immediate effect is to eliminate *j in onset position) are due to a rise in the ranking of the single constraint MORAIC[i].

(9) Stage 1: MAX[w], MAX[j] » MORAIC[+high]   (*w and *j are both parsed intact)
     Stage 2: MAX[w] » MORAIC[+high] » MAX[j]   (*j eliminated; *w remains)
     Stage 3: MORAIC[+high], MAX[w], MAX[j]   (*w eliminated)

Similarly, the elimination of voiced fricatives that occurred from Proto-Germanic to Old English corresponds to the gradual rise in the ranking of a constraint prohibiting voiced fricatives (*VOICED-FRIC: A [+voice, −son] segment is not [+cont]). Crist also addresses the questions of why all voiced fricatives are not eliminated simultaneously or in the same way, and the varying prosodic resolution of the resulting stranded mora (gemination or compensatory lengthening, pp. 113–14, 144). And for Slavic, Crist argues that the elimination of codas can be modelled as the reranking of syllable structure constraints; specifically, the language shifted from one ranking of NoCODA to another, with a corresponding change in the set of permissible syllable types (pp. 188–9).

(10) 1. D-CONTIG$_\omega$, MAX-NAS » NoCODA   (no nasals delete)
      2. D-CONTIG$_\omega$ » NoCODA » MAX-NAS   (word-final nasals delete)
      3. NoCODA, D-CONTIG$_\omega$, MAX-NAS   (all coda nasals delete)

Crist, like others, does not disagree that there are phonetic pressures involved with seemingly conspiratorial sets of changes; instead, such pressures are an important factor in determining the probability that a particular conspiracy will occur in a particular language, and the reranking of constraints may be viewed as an orderly response by the phonological grammar to these external pressures (p. 192). Finally, translating the notions of 'sound change in progress' vs 'completed sound change', one might posit that a sound change in progress, which shows variability, is implemented by variability of constraint ranking,[9] and that a completed sound change is modelled by the relevant constraints having become stable (p. 13).

Along these lines, further consider the following (Archangeli 1997: 31):

> Under OT, the formal characterization of language change through time is that constraints are reranked. A prevalent view of diachronic language change is that change occurs when there is imperfect transmission from one generation to the next. Combining these two claims implies that constraints can only be reranked when the evidence for a particular ranking is not very robust. Thus, OT makes clear predictions both about the effects of change and about the type of change that might occur.

---

[9] The modelling of variation has been implemented in a variety of ways, e.g. Anttila (2002) and many others. While intersecting in interesting ways with historical change, a fuller discussion of variation lies beyond my scope; see Cho (1998), Oh (2002), Cutillas Espinosa (2004), Holt (2004), Kostakis (2010), and Coetzee & Pater (2011).

The relevance of these assertions will become especially evident in the discussion of functionally motivated approaches below.

31.2 ADAPTATIONS TO STANDARD OT

Challenges to standard OT spring from consideration of data of many types, including both segmental changes and changes in syllable structure and other aspects of prosody, as well as changes intimately connected with other domains. On the one hand, interactions with functional factors are frequently attested and incorporated into OT analyses; on the other, paradigmatic relations, analogy, and other issues of morphology also challenge the notions of standard OT for modelling historical change.[10]

31.2.1 Functional Considerations

Addressing the first intersection, there is a robust line of research where functional notions like systemic markedness and perceptual- or listener-based factors, which have no easy home in standard OT, are considered and which lead to modifications of the original workings of a standard OT grammar, leading at times to philosophically radical innovations. A significant body of work has emerged that applies Dispersion Theory (building on Liljencrants & Lindblom 1972, Steriade 2001b, Flemming 1995, Padgett 2003b, Boersma & Hamann 2008) to historical phonology (with parallels to the work of Saussure 1916 and Martinet 1964, and see also Jones, Gordon, and Salmons & Honeybone, all this volume). In Dispersion Theory, functional considerations of auditory acoustic space and perceptual distinctiveness and neutralization avoidance are incorporated via constraints like SPACE, MINIMAL DISTANCE, and NoMERGE that reflect a systemic approach to phonology.

(11) (from Itô & Mester 2004)

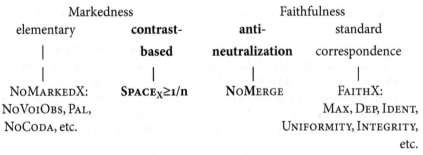

	Markedness			Faithfulness
elementary	**contrast-**	**anti-**	standard
	based	**neutralization**	correspondence
NoMARKEDX:	SPACE$_X$≥1/n	NoMERGE	FAITHX:
NoVOIOBS, PAL,			MAX, DEP, IDENT,
NoCODA, etc.			UNIFORMITY, INTEGRITY,
			etc.

Systemic constraints

[10] See Gordon (this volume) for a variationist approach to chain shifts, mergers, and near-mergers in vowel space like the Northern Cities Shift that likewise relies on the notion of contrast preservation.

(12) Systemic markedness and systemic faithfulness constraints:

Systemic Markedness:	$SPACE_X \geq 1/n$	Potential minimal pairs differing in property X must differ in X by at least $1/n^{th}$ of the available space
Systemic Faithfulness:	NoMERGE	No output word has multiple correspondents

(13) Example of distribution of high vowel space (Padgett 2003b (19))

|....i....|....i....|....u....| Each segment gets 1/3 of the perceptual space
|.......i.......|.......u......| Each segment gets 1/2 of the perceptual space
|..............i................| Each segment gets 1/1 of the perceptual space

Dispersion Theory ('DT') originally was applied diachronically to the analysis of vowel systems (see Minkova & Stockwell 2003 for Old English, and Jones, this volume, §4 for an example from Northern English), and also to consonantal changes (Padgett 2003b for the backing of /i/ to [ɨ] as a consequence of the emerging palatalization contrast in Russian; also Boersma 2003 for a computational simulation that mirrors certain Germanic consonant shifts); more recent work continues these threads and has additionally branched out to include other segment classes as well as consonant clusters.

Returning to the evolution of consonants from Latin to Hispano-Romance (Holt 2003c), eventually even the sonorant consonants lose their license to bear a mora, and further systemic factors having to do with perceptual distinctiveness lead to the simplification-cum-palatalization of /nn, ll/. Whereas Latin /-n-, -l-/ were lost in Galician/Portuguese (*pão, paço*), and the reduction of /nn, ll/ to /n, l/ caused no merger, they were retained in Old Spanish (*cana, pelo*). The further reranking of MAX/ IDENT will cause the loss of the moraic status of /nn, ll/, which ought to yield /n, l/ as well. However, merger avoidance appears to have played a decisive role in Spanish. That is, systemic factors influence the learner/listener to restructure the grammar in a particular way to ensure that former communicative distinctions are maintained, while at the same time continuing to reestablish systemic parity in the distribution of moraic segments according to sonority. That is, because geminates are intervocalic consonants that bear a mora, the added weight yields length; a certain amount of energy is required to manifest this mora, and in production, length, and energy are correlates of this unit of weight (i.e. the mora). Under the assumption that 'palatal' segments are actually doubly articulated corono-dorsal structures (Keating 1988b, Lipski 1989), it turns out that despite the loss of the mora, speakers do maintain some realization of 'doubleness', no longer as duration, but in articulation, with original COR and new DOR, i.e. 'palatal':

(14)   Merger avoidance in Old Spanish of /nn, n/ by palatalization of /nn/

	/nn	n/	NoMoraicSonorant	*Merge	Max/Ident/Dep
a.	n n \\/ COR	n	*!		
b.	n	n		*!	* <μ>
☞ c.	ɲ /\\ COR DOR	n			* <μ> * +DOR

Padgett & Zygis (2004) give a DT account of the historical development of Polish and Russian sibilants, which is of theoretical interest because they show that perceptual distinctiveness may motivate both allophonic rules and so-called unconditioned sound changes to maintain contrast, and show how DT can be extended from vowels to another class of segments, sibilant consonants. Specifically, about 500 years ago, Polish, palatalized palatoalveolars depalatalized, and unexpectedly became retroflexes, similar to a change in Russian two centuries prior.

(15)

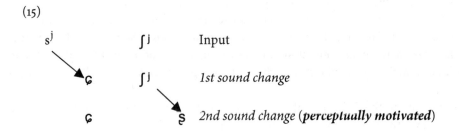

sʲ	ʃʲ	Input
	ʃʲ	1st sound change
ɕ	ʂ	2nd sound change (*perceptually motivated*)

(16)   Spacing of postalveolar sibilants

ɕ		ʃ		ʂ	Each segment gets 1/3 of the perceptual space
	ɕ			ʂ	Each segment gets 1/2 of the perceptual space
		ʃ			Each segment gets 1/1 of the perceptual space

The authors argue that this 'unconditioned' change was in fact motivated by contrast dispersion, with the effect being a more balanced distribution of sibilants in the acoustic-perceptual space (p. 155).

Itô & Mester (2004, 2006) look at systemic markedness broadly, and likewise explore the development of sibilants (as well as front glides) before front vowels in the historical phonology of Japanese. They argue that the historical depalatalization of coronal obstruents in Japanese before the front vowel [e] is not an effect of syntagmatic markedness (i.e. co-occurrence restrictions), but of systemic markedness, since, after all, front

vowels are known to promote and co-occur with palatalization; instead, depalatalization serves to enhance the sibilant system's contrast by polarizing the consonants: overall, [ʃi,se] is a better contrast than [ʃi, ʃe], and this is modelled by the ranking between
PAL and CONTRAST>i/e.

(17)

Input: si ʃi / se ʃe	CONTRAST>i/e	PAL/i	PAL/i,e	NOMERGE	IDENT(ant)	*[−ant]
si ʃi / se ʃe	*!*	*	**			**
ʃi / se ʃe	*!		*	*	*	**
(☞)(old) ʃi / ʃe	*!			**	**	**
si / se	*!	*	**	**	**	
☞(new) ʃi / se			*	**	**	*
ʃi / ʃe		*!	*	**	**	*
ʃi				******	**	*

(18)   Historical reranking for the sibilant system:

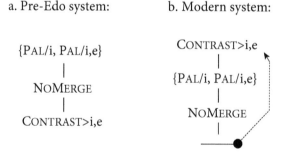

a. Pre-Edo system: b. Modern system:

Also treating consonants (this time lenition from Latin to Spanish) is Baker (2007),
who examines dispersion and duration in stop consonant contrasts. It is well documented that in Latin geminate obstruents simplified, while original singletons voiced
(e.g. CUPPAM 'cup' > copa, vs LUPUM 'wolf' > lobo), but did not end in merger because
the original voiced segments had become spirantized (sometimes further deleted,
e.g. CREDO 'I believe' > creo). This chain shift is analysed in DT terms by Baker via the
interaction of constraints on maintenance and maximization of perceptual contrast
(MAINTAINCONTRAST, MINIMUMDISTANCE), specifically calibrated to the features of

duration, voice, and continuancy (which he collapses as 'ID(DV)' in the chart below), along with a drive to weaken all consonantal articulations (LAZY).[11]

(19)

| Grammar A > |
| Grammar B > |
Grammar C
Classical Latin: loss of voiced geminate stops MINDIST2, *MERGE, ID(DV) » *GEM^DD *MERGE, ID(DV) » « *GEM *MERGE, ID(DV), MINDIST2 » LAZY
Latin to Old Spanish: systemic weakening to [t d ð] *GEM, *MERGE, ID(DV), MINDIST2 » LAZY ID(DV), MINDIST2 » « LAZY *MERGE, ID(DV), MINDIST2 » LAZY
Old Spanish to Modern Spanish: merger and better contrast *MERGE, ID(DV) » LAZY, MINDIST2 *MERGE, ID(DV) » « MINDIST3 MINDIST3, *MERGE, ID(DV) » LAZY

Baker argues that the drag chain (in which simple voiced stops spirantized intervocalically first, which allowed for the voicing of the voiceless ones, followed finally by the degemination of the voiceless geminates) allows meaningful distinctions to be realized at all stages, and ensues from a constraint ranking that requires a three-way stop contrast at all times in Latin and Hispano-Romance, even though the realization of each stop series changes from one period to the next, as LAZY assumes a higher ranking, leading in Modern Spanish to the merger between the voiced stops and approximants. No recourse is needed to other alternations to the classic OT architecture like sympathy theory or local conjunction, which, as Baker notes, undermine key aspects of the original theory (p. 420).

Bradley & Delforge (2006) likewise treat the evolution of Romance, in this case that of the sibilant system from Old to Modern Spanish, applying DT to sibilant voicing (though they also call for a stratal model). The authors examine the well-known development of intervocalic voiced sibilants in medieval Spanish, which devoiced and merged with their voiceless counterparts (e.g. [det^sir] 'to descend' and [ded^zir] 'to

---

[11] The middle column shows the 'toggling' of competing constraints, with the constraint that ends up in dominant position indicated in boldface.

say' both become [desiɾ]), remarkable because of the position in which this occurred, between vowels, and so going against the trend of intervocalic consonant lenition in Western Romance (as discussed above), and involving neutralization in a position favouring contrast preservation, the syllable onset. Bradley & Delforge show that DT allows for an account based on explicit reference to articulatory and perceptual aspects of phonetic detail, yet limits the range of possible phonological contrasts.

Bradley (2006) applies DT to restrictions on onset clusters involving laterals, and proposes that systemic markedness constraints (SPACE) penalize indistinct coronal-velar contrasts in different pre-lateral contexts, with directionality of neutralization (i.e. to coronal, velar, or variably to both) determined by faithfulness constraints (MAX(PLACE)) on input place, whose ranking can vary across languages and dialects. Bradley contends that the proposed analysis encompasses synchronic typological patterns from more than forty languages, with clear applications to historical phenomena like neutralization to velar place in early Romance coronal-lateral clusters (e.g. *vetelus non veclus* from the Appendix Probi). Because his approach does not require reference to continuancy specifications, but to optimal perceptibility between contrasting clusters, it does not face the same problems as an OCP-based account of disallowed Spanish /tl, dl/. Similar patterns of velarization are found in loanword phonology in Mexican Spanish (e.g. *Tlaloc, Tenochtitlan*).

Webb & Bradley (2009) likewise employ a modified version of OT to formalize diachronic rhotic metathesis in dialectal varieties of French (rightward, as in *vendredi, breton*, both with /CVʁ/) and Spanish (leftward, as in *abarcar > abracar, dormir > drumir*) in terms of separate production and perception grammars that are gesturally based. They argue that this framework accounts for both the source of variation and the choice of novel underlying forms (that is, reanalysed/lexicalized ones), respectively. For production, gestural alignment constraints favour complete overlap of adjacent rhotic and vowel gestures, leaving their linear order indeterminate to the listener. This indeterminate and variable output then serves as input to the perception grammar, which maps surface forms to underlying forms in accordance with attested patterns of the language, leading to perceptually induced shifts.

Lief (2006: ch. 6) explores an OT approach to historical phonotactics, in this case syncope in the development of Latin to Hispano-Romance (Spanish and Portuguese), e.g. Lat. COMPUTARE > *contar* 'count, tell', etc. Lief finds need to enrich the types of constraints employed in standard OT to include perceptually or positionally based ones to be able to best model the idea that various phonetic contexts favour the unstressed vowel loss.

Sanders (2003) treats synchronic opacity in a version of OT that does not require intermediate representations (contra a multistratal version of OT), and pursues an analysis under which certain types of opacity are predicted to not occur, instead arising from the interaction of sound change and a strong version of the principle of lexicon optimization whereby the surface results of sound changes are encoded directly into the lexicon as it evolves over time. Sanders adopts a framework that invokes not only the standard features of faithfulness and markedness constraints, but also dispersion,

FDM-OT (for *Faithfulness, Dispersion, and Markedness in OT*), which as noted above integrates functional principles and allows for a unified account of both synchronic and diachronic phonology. He argues that since his model is grounded in cognition, acoustics, and articulation, it explains and predicts phonological patterns with fewer arbitrary or abstract stipulations than are required by competing theories, though there is a trade-off of increased burden on lexical storage (p. 90).

Sanders applies FDM-OT principally to three cases of opacity from Polish (though he also includes treatments of Low German, Turkish, and Tuyuca). He shows that certain alternations, like the raising of ɔ > u, are synchronically non-productive and instead developed over time, with once-contextual realizations adopted into the lexicon, and respecting concerns of vocalic space and distribution, and this invocation of strong lexicon optimization between serially ordered diachronic sound changes (p. 90) allows the monostratal nature of standard OT to be maintained, while the concept of lexical minimality is sacrificed. For nasal vowel alternations, for the fronting of [ɛ̃], Sanders argues (pp. 128–9) that there is a functional motivation, that its colour needs to be more perceptually distinct from that of [ɔ̃w̃]. This is possible because the candidates evaluated are sets of words, and these can influence each other. In this case, the short nasal vowel fronts because the long nasal vowel backs, and the two changes are related in a way that standard OT cannot capture, and so what appears to be an arbitrary sound change is actually predictable in FDM-OT.

31.2.2 Intersection with Issues of Grammaticalization

Phonological issues surrounding grammaticalization have also been treated in OT, e.g. Old Leonese preposition + article contractions (Elsman & Holt 2009). Grammaticalization typically has to do with reanalysis of lexical words into functional ones with concomitant phonological reduction (e.g. *going to > gonna*, Romance auxiliaries > future tense markers). When a short function word undergoes further reduction during the process of grammaticalization, semantic recoverability is threatened; in this case, Elsman & Holt argue, individual features take on a greater importance in indicating contrast and the burden of morphological representation shifts from the segmental to the featural to prevent the complete loss of recoverability of meaning (p. 22) (Figure 31.1).

For Leonese, markedness constraints that favour phonological reduction, if successful, would threaten or compromise the listener's identification of meaning due to the potentially insufficient surface form to interpret (here, of the monosegmental definiteness morpheme /l/ of *la*). So, in palatalizing varieties of Leonese, *con la* 'with the (fem.)' reduces variably to *conna* or *colla* (where *nn* and *ll* represent singleton palatals), a result of blending of the featural and structural content of [n] and [l], and *por la* 'for the (fem.)' becomes *polla*, likewise blending the content of [r] and [l]; in non-palatalizing varieties, the results are *cona* and *pola*. In both, featural content of morphemes is maximized according to the particular constraint hierarchy that holds. Thus, while for free morphemes it is segments that hold the key to contrast, for bound morphemes (like the

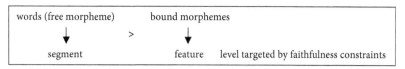

FIG. 31.1 Model of phonological compensation for morphological reduction.

monosegmental definiteness morpheme /l/ of *la*), features themselves may also be targeted by faithfulness constraints to ensure recoverability (in this case, MAX-[C-PLACE] and MAX-F(EATURE)M(ONO)S(EGMENT): the input features of a monosegmental morpheme must be preserved in the output; adapted from Casali 1997), with some content preserved despite the loss of the segment; that is, there is a phonological compensation for the morphological reduction (p. 31).

31.2.3   Intersection with Analogy, Morphology, Lexicon, Acquisition, and Creole Formation

To address the challenges posed to standard OT for modelling historical change by treatments of paradigmatic relations, analogy, and other issues of morphology, a selection of works that treat these is presented below.[12]

Kraska-Szlenk (2007), concentrating on inflectional paradigms in Polish, examines analogy in the context of language use and argues that type and token frequency, along with other language usage criteria (like class size and semantic distance between members), underlie an abstract concept of 'grammar', but are not synonymous with it, instead being interrelated through a system of extended correspondence constraints; the relative ranking of these with markedness constraints represents 'phonologization' of language use. The author argues for an active role for the lexicon in shaping a language's grammar and provides empirical evidence for the role of frequency in analogy using synchronic and diachronic evidence of three vocalic alternations in Polish declensional paradigms (e~o/a, o~u, e~Ø) (Figure 31.2).

According to the author, some historical changes are usage-based and some are grammar-based, and for analogy, most have usage-based motivations, most often frequency-based; 'phonologization' occurs when a given change of this sort is incorporated into the grammar, here modelled by the use of output-output constraints, with their promotion leading to paradigmatic levelling.

Adam (2002) treats the issue of intermediate and variable grammars as evidenced by language acquisition and historical change.[13] In particular, the author considers the acquisition of aspects of Hebrew phonology (prosodic structure like the number of

---

[12]   See Fertig (this volume) for a general review of analogy, including some (critical) discussion of work that adopts OT.

[13]   See Foulkes & Vihman and Dresher (both this volume) on first-language acquisition and phonological change.

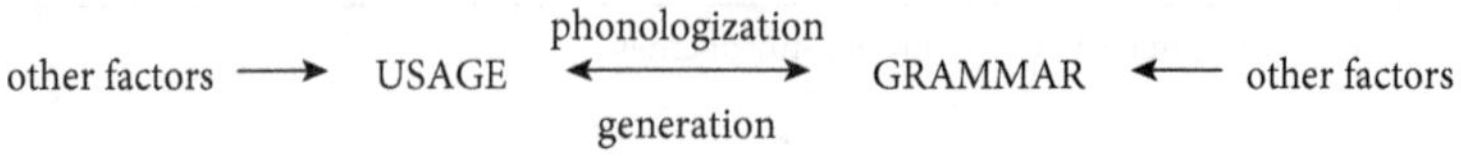

other factors ⟶ USAGE ⟷ GRAMMAR ⟵ other factors

phonologization / generation

FIG. 31.2 Usage and grammar in language.

syllables and variety of stress patterns) and the development of morphological awareness, as well as a case study of a historical change (variation in stop-fricative alternations in Modern Hebrew with historical origins), and proposes a unified formal model
in which the increase in structure and contrast reveals a transition from phonological
dominance to lexical dominance. That is, for acquisition, the path of development of
inflectional endings provides evidence for lexicon optimization—that is, restructuring
of lexical representations by the child, and emergence of knowledge of morphological
alternations. For spirantization, there is a great deal of opacity and free variation, and
Adam argues for multiple paradigms, whose coexistence indicates a change in progress
in the language, with the variable grammar representing an intermediate phase. As with
acquisition, the direction of change in spirantization is towards lexical dominance and
away from phonological generalization.

Drawing on a large corpus, Sano (2009) analyses the morphological realization of voice
in Japanese (causative, honorific, etc.) and the changes of *sa*-insertion, *ra*-deletion, and
re-insertion, and identifies both internal and external factors that govern variation and
change, constructing a probabilistic model of OT that inherently accommodates them.
The author conducts a multivariate analysis and provides a formal account of analogical
levelling via the interaction of a small number of constraints like the Obligatory Contour
Principle (here applied to morphs), PARADIGMCONTRAST (requiring a one-to-one correspondence between form and content), and ALLOMORPHCORRESPONDENCE (morphs
in a relation of allomorphy should be identical) (the latter two from Itô and Mester 2004),
and then explores these in a stochastic and maximum entropy versions of OT.

Sano argues that internal factors have a categorical effect at the onset of a given
change, but become gradient over time, and that conversely, external factors at first have
a gradient effect, but may become categorical as a change progresses. A corollary is that
mutually independent factors may become interrelated, and mutually dependent external factors may become independent over time. This is encapsulated in the Dynamic
Interaction Hypothesis (DIH; Sano 2009: 283 (34)):

(20) Dynamic Interaction Hypothesis
      In language change, internal factors become gradient, showing statistical inter-
      action among themselves, while external factors become statistically independ-
      ent from each other (Figure 31.3).

While Sano's data are more morphological than phonological, it is clear here too
that systemic factors (paradigmatic relations and considerations) play an integral
role is shaping the linguistic competence of the language speaker, and here lead to the

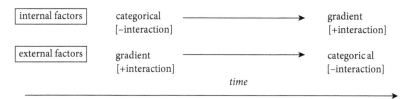

FIG. 31.3 Change of the effects and the relationship of factors.

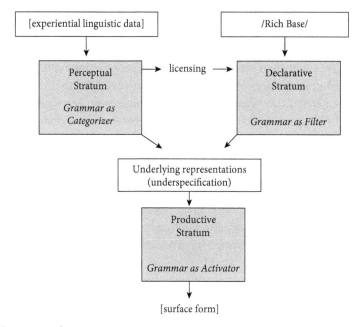

FIG. 31.4 Grammatical stratum.

reduction of the functional load carried by each form in the Japanese voice system, a notion not expressible in standard OT, parallel to the effects of systemic considerations modelled in a dispersion-theoretic analysis of the various phonological phenomena discussed above.

Finally, Webb (2008) treats the formation of French lexifier creoles and the neutralization over time of the feature [round], and describes phonological restructuring in a version of OT that distinguishes perceptual, declarative, and procedural strata, with the OT theorem of richness of the base holding only at the declarative level (the repository of static knowledge), and the perceptual and procedural strata constrained by experience and feature licensing (p. 227). That is, different strata or modules (presented visually in Figure 31.4) accomplish specific functions, with the perception of experiential data, the filtering of a rich base, and the actuation of speech (p. 235).

Under Webb's approach, which relies on the incorporation of phonetic factors in the grammar (in the form of constraints), the explanation of phonological restructuring centres on the perception grammar, where constraints refer to the parsing of experiential input, and reranking at either the declarative or procedural strata is dependent upon learning at the perceptual stratum (p. 227).

31.2.4 Computational Considerations

Finally, considerations of production and perception are likewise incorporated into computational simulations, here of the evolution of linguistic systems. In addition to Boersma (2003), briefly discussed above, van Leussen (2008) treats emergent optimality of simulated inventories and systems, which while not modelling the sound changes of any particular language family, does offer valuable insight into the mechanisms that underlie changes attested in many languages. The insights pursued have to do with the seeming balance between articulatory ease and auditory contrast; van Leussen's work integrates self-organizational, agent-based models of non-teleological vowel dispersion with an existing Optimality Theoretic model of bidirectional phonology and phonetics. Noting both that vowels tend to be at the periphery of the acoustic vowel space and the clear advantage of this for reducing the possibility of one phoneme being perceived as another and its benefit for communicative efficiency (p. 6), he shows that speakers of a language do not consciously strive toward changing the phonological system, but that optimization arises as a side effect of the mechanisms involved in communication and language learning. The model's ability to account for the diachronic process of chain shifts caused by vowel splits or mergers is also explored (p. 3 and §5.4). Van Leussen concludes that innate constraints are not needed to model vowel dispersion and that these types of simulations may be helpful in investigating synchronic and diachronic phonological phenomena.

31.3 CONCLUDING REMARKS

In conclusion, as Zuraw (2003) notes, speaker-hearer interactions can be argued to be the atoms of language change (§4), and linguists are (partly) interested in language change because it can tell us about synchronic language (p. 173). Various practitioners of OT sampled here would agree that treating historical sound change can indeed be illuminating and lead to a better understanding of the organization of the language faculty, and that various modifications to the original workings of OT are required, not only to more adequately model language change over time, but implicitly (and explicitly at times) synchronic phonology as well. The proposals reviewed in later sections draw on diverse theoretical and conceptual foundations, but all converge on the utility and need to incorporate functional, perceptual, and listener-based factors to more adequately describe and explain phonological change. Whether one of the remaining tenets of classical OT, its monostratal architecture, is still appropriate is a matter for another chapter (see Kiparsky, this volume).

....

CHAPTER 32

PHONOLOGIZATION

....

PAUL KIPARSKY

32.1 PHONOLOGIZATION
IN STRUCTURALIST PHONOLOGY

....

IF there is a phonemic level of representation, the question arises how and why phonemes originate and are lost.[1] This is the problem of PHONOLOGIZATION and MERGER. The structuralists held that allophones are phonologized, i.e. become phonemic, when their conditioning environment is eliminated by sound change. The idea was introduced by V. Kiparsky (1932) and Twaddell (1938),[2] who both illustrated it with the phonologization of the front rounded umlaut vowels ö and ü in German. They argued that the umlaut vowels became distinctive when the i or j that conditioned them was reduced or deleted, at which point lexical representations were restructured with the former allophonic variants as phonemes.[3]

(1) a. Old High German (OHG):
   - Nom.Pl. /huot-i/ → *hüeti* 'hats, helmets'
   - Dat.Sg. /huot-e/ → *huote*

   b. Middle High German:
   - Sound change: *hüeti* > *hüete*
   - Restructuring: /huot-i/ > /hüet-e/

---

[1] Some of this material was presented at the San Francisco LSA meeting in January 2002.

[2] Kiparsky's article is an introduction to synchronic and historical structural phonology, written after his stay in Prague where the new theory was just then taking shape. It correctly avoids Twaddell's assumption that OHG orthography was phonemic. Kiparsky's well-meaning academic mentors eventually managed to dissuade the young graduate student from continuing his forays into phonological theory and other such modish nonsense.

[3] The Old High German data cited in this article can be found in Braune & Reiffenstein (2004) or in any standard grammar of the language. In accord with orthography and standard practice in Germanic linguistics I write the front rounded vowels as *ü, ö*.

This mechanism, called SECONDARY SPLIT (Hoenigswald 1960, see also Cser, Fox, and Salmons & Honeybone, all this volume), has been generally assumed to account for phonologization. However, it leaves two questions unanswered. First, when the conditioning environment goes away (as here by reduction of the full vowels to -e or to -ə), why do its effects remain?[4] Secondly, why does the loss of a conditioning environment not *always* cause phonologization? Why do the conditioned allophones sometimes just go away?[5] Let's call them the PHONOLOGIZATION PROBLEM and the NON-PHONOLOGIZATION PROBLEM, respectively.

Both problems are deep ones, and reach the foundations of phonological theory. The phonologization problem has been at the core of phonological theorizing, but has no generally agreed solution. The non-phonologization problem has barely begun to be discussed. I begin by reviewing the two main proposed solutions to the phonologization problem, and suggest a new one based on Lexical Phonology and more particularly its OT version (Stratal OT), which I argue also resolves the non-phonologization problem (phonologization is considered, often along different lines, in many other chapters in this volume: see especially Bermúdez-Otero and Hale et al., and also Blevins, Yu and Cser).

The best-known proposal for resolving the phonologization problem is due to Saussure and Bloomfield. It depends on a paradoxical marriage of synchronic structuralism to diachronic neogrammarianism. The key idea is that a sound change is located outside of the linguistic system that it will transform. A less-known but increasingly popular alternative proposal is to enrich the phonology with phonetic information, abandoning the concept of a phoneme as a contrastive entity, and positing that phonemes-to-be somehow get phonologized *before* they become contrastive through the loss of the conditioning factor.

After reviewing these solutions in turn, I will argue for a version which combines aspects of both, implemented in the Stratal OT framework.

For Saussure, the basic fact about language is the arbitrariness of the sign. Among its consequences are a sharp divide between synchrony and diachrony. This division is not merely a methodological one, still less a practical one or one based on conventional boundaries between academic subdisciplines. It is a conceptually necessary consequence of arbitrariness.

> Linguistics must be separated in two. There is an irreconcilable duality, created by the very nature of things [...] in systems of values.
>
> (Saussure 1993:104, cf. Saussure 1916/1959:79–80)

A historical event such as a sound change qua phonetic mutation, and the restructuring of the phonological system it may cause, are totally different things: a sound

---

[4] "Why did the front vowels not become back again, why did the frontness stay, once the influence of /ij/ was removed?" (Liberman 1991: 126).

[5] "Why do allophones sometimes remain and other times revert?" (King 1971: 4).

change can bring about radical discontinuities, or it could have no effect on the system whatever.

> There is no inner bond between the initial fact [the phonetic change] and the effect that it may subsequently produce on the whole system [phonology or grammar].
>
> (Saussure 1916/1959:87)

The sharp segregation of historical change from synchronic structure—call it SAUSSURE's FIREWALL—implies that, although everything in grammar is interrelated as a system, sound change has no access to that system (see also Bermúdez-Otero, Dresher and Scheer, all this volume). Blindly and structure-independently, it alters merely the material implementation of speech. The abstract synchronic system, characterized by networks of relations and systems of constraints, is affected only indirectly by those alterations. For Saussure, the synchronic constraints in the mind of the speaker and the historical processes that modify the articulation of speech are not only ontologically, but also formally distinct. Constraints are GENERAL (transparent, or inviolable, in current terminology), whereas processes are ACCIDENTAL and PARTICULAR. Constraints are PRECARIOUS (they could be overturned by the next change), while processes are IMPERATIVE (sound change is exceptionless).

Back to the example of umlaut: the phonetic mutations of umlaut and reduction/syncope both altered the physical aspect of speech, but they had very different effects on the system. The structural reflex of umlaut was purely phonetic: it introduced the constraint 'no back vowels before *i*'. This is an allophonic distribution and has no bearing on the phonological system. Vowel reduction and subsequent syncope had no effect on the pronunciation of the umlaut vowels, but an all the more drastic impact on their phonological status: it caused them to be reanalysed as distinct phonemes. The new phonetic givens lead to a restructured phonological system with new phonemes /ü/, /ö/ and a new constraint 'no unstressed full vowels'. The site of phonemic contrast in (1) shifted one syllable to the left.

This is a consistent theory of sound change. But the dualist ontology of Saussure's Firewall is a heavy price to pay. It excludes all structural explanations for sound changes and for constraints on sound change of the sort pioneered by Jakobson and since pursued in different ways by Martinet, Labov and others, and, still differently, in generative and OT work. In particular, it makes inexplicable the fact that sound change never subverts phonological universals.

Another objection to this theory is that it offers no solution to the non-phonologization problem. Why does the predicted secondary split sometimes not happen, and the conditioned allophones just disappear? For example, vowel fronting in various dialects of English (e.g. in *calf, goat, cough*), and vowel backing (*girl*, dialectally in *kit*) usually don't produce contrasts between front and back *k* such as structuralist doctrine predicts should arise (an exception is the Jamaican English contrast *cat* [kʸat] *vs cot* [kat] or [kɒt], Wells 1982: 569).[6] Such cases were discussed under the heading of 'rule insertion' in generative theorizing on sound change (King 1973).

---

[6] Commenting on a proposal that umlaut vowels disappeared in Scandinavian when the triggering front vowels were syncopated, Benediktsson (1982: 9) states: "The principle that phonetic variants, in

Another type of rule insertion, also problematic for the structuralist account of secondary split[7] is that a sound change can interact with, and be constrained by, existing phonological processes and constraints in the language. King notes that Old English syncope of unstressed e in words like *bindest* 'you bind' and *bidest* 'you ask' feeds the previously existing voicing assimilation rule, so that the outcome is *bintst, bitst*. Saussure's Firewall here predicts that syncope should extend the voicing opposition to what was until then a neutralizing assimilation environment, creating a contrast between previously existing assimilated clusters such as *-ts-* and new clusters from syncope such as **-ds-*. This is certainly a conceivable outcome, but it is probably not what happened in Old English; there is no reason to believe that clusters such as **-ds-* ever existed, even immediately after syncope.

The third problem is that sound changes can be *blocked* by existing synchronic constraints. For example, syncope can fail to apply just in those cases where it would create a prohibited stress configuration (e.g. a lapse or clash), or a prohibited syllable structure or foot structure. In English, the variable pre-sonorant syncope in words like *generative* is inapplicable before a stressed syllable, as in *generate (*gen'rate)*, where it would produce back-to-back stresses, which are disfavoured in English. Technically, such conditions on sound changes can be specified as conditioning factors, but only at the cost of a loss of the generalization that the conditioning factors are manifestations of active phonological constraints of the language.

The first two types of problematic cases are the historical analogues of the two types of transparent rule interaction in synchronic phonology: vowel backing in *kit* BLEEDS *k*-fronting, and syncope in *bidest* FEEDS voicing assimilation. The third type of problematic case also involves transparent interaction, in the sense that sound change avoids creating surface exceptions to a constraint that is operative in the language.

In short, sound changes can interact transparently with existing processes. Such transparent interactions can involve feeding or bleeding by the sound change, or blocking of the sound change by a constraint. Alongside such transparent interactions, sound change can also result in opacity, which in terms of change means phonologization and the creation of new contrasts. Structuralist historical phonology has privileged the latter, opacity-creating scenario to the point of all but ignoring the well-documented possibility of transparent interaction.

Post-structuralist theories which relate historical and synchronic phonology have been unable either to replicate Saussure's Firewall without some extrinsic stipulation, or to derive the generalization that it is intended to capture in some other way. Classical generative grammar overcame Saussure's dualism by generalizing the processual approach and modelling sound change as the addition of rules. The question then

consequence of the conditioning factors, may 'revert to the neutral starting-point' […], though perhaps consistent with generative theory, seems hardly compatible with those of structural phonology; at any rate, if it is accepted, the principle of phonemicization is then reduced to an ad-hoc postulate, of little or no explanatory value".

[7] As well as for the theory espoused by Blevins (2004a, this volume), see Kiparsky (2006).

arose: where are they added? Obviously rules cannot be added anywhere, but saying that they are added to the end of the grammar is arbitrary, and in any case fails to do justice to the cases of 'rule insertion'.

King (1971) argued that sound changes interact transparently only with 'phonetic rules'—the 'trivial case' of rule insertion, as he called it. His observation has held up well; the 'non-trivial' cases have been fairly convincingly explained away (on perhaps the most puzzling case see Jasanoff 2004). It is fair to assume that the 'phonetic rules' of King's generalization are a language's postlexical rules. If so, we can rephrase his generalization like this:

(2) a. SECONDARY SPLIT: sound changes render lexical processes opaque.
     b. BLOCKING AND 'RULE INSERTION': sound changes interact transparently with postlexical processes.

The second, less well explored approach to the phonologization problem assumes that prospective phonemes are already phonologized by the time they become contrastive (Ebeling 1960, Korhonen 1969, Liberman 1991). For example, if the umlaut vowels are already phonemes (or QUASI-PHONEMES, as Korhonen calls them) before the -i- that conditions them is lost, then they would naturally remain unaffected by the latter sound change.

There is evidence that non-contrastive allophones can be internalized in the lexical phonology (e.g. Hellberg 1978, 1978), but a theory of phonologization must specify when and why this happens. We must be able to tell that an allophone has become a quasi-phoneme independently of the post hoc information that it is phonologized when another sound change occurs. It has been suggested that features tend to be phonologized if they belong to a feature class which is already distinctive (Kiparsky 1995). Though generally consonant with observations about priming effects in sound change, this idea is not precise enough to make predictions about when phonologization will take place. Another suggestion, made by Janda (2003: 413) in a vigorous plea for early phonologization, is that allophones become quasi-phonemes 'for reasons having to do with phonetic distance', though he does not say how much distance, and on what dimension, or cite evidence that distance matters at all.

A starting point for a more substantive theory of phonologization might be Jakobson's observation that allophonic properties can become perceptually more salient than the phonemic ones that condition them (Jakobson, Fant, & Halle 1952). Russian [ɨ] and [i] are allophones of /i/ after respectively velarized and palatalized consonants, yet the allophonic vowel distinction is a more salient cue to the contrast than the phonemic consonantal one (especially in the case of sibilants because of their high-frequency noise, e.g. /si/ [sɨ] and /s'i/ [s'i]). Related to this perceptual saliency of the vowels, as Jakobson pointed out, is the fact that [ɨ] and [i] are perceived as categorically distinct elements, and even reified in the metalinguistic terms [ɨkat'] 'to pronounce [ɨ]' and [ikat'] 'to pronounce [i]'. The vowels [ɨ] and [i] are like two phonemes in that any unrounded high vowel token is assigned to one or the other type; perceptually they are two distinct categories. Other Russian vowels are also strongly affected by palatalization: e.g. /a/ is fronted towards [æ] to varying degrees before, after, and most of all between palatalized consonants, but the allophones are apparently not categorically perceived as belonging to two types; correspondingly there is no *[ækat'] 'to pronounce [æ]'.

A plausible hypothesis is that allophones become quasi-phonemes when they become governed by categorical rather than gradient constraints (Flemming 2001), and acquire greater perceptual salience than their conditioning environments. How are these two properties related to each other, and how we can build a theory of phonologization on them?

We cannot build on structuralist phonology here because it assigns strict categoriality and saliency only to phonemic representations. Its treats feature specifications at the phonemic level as categorical, though allowing allophonic/postlexical feature specifications to be gradient. On this view, phonemic representations specify exactly the invariant distinctive features of the language. Quasi-phonemes are not allowed at the phonemic level since redundant, predictable feature values are excluded from lexical representations. An approach that does provide a theoretical basis for the quasi-phoneme is Stratal OT.

32.2 PARALLEL OT

Constraint-based theories such as OT eliminate processes in favour of constraints, and model sound change as the promotion of markedness constraints (see Holt, this volume, also for the basics of OT and for some other approaches to change in OT). For present purposes it is important to distinguish parallel and stratal versions of OT. Stratal OT distinguishes levels (strata), and claims that constraints operate transparently within a level, but that the levels themselves interact much as ordered rules did in *SPE* phonology (see also Bermúdez-Otero, this volume). The generalizations in (2) are then predicted. Promotion of a postlexical constraint will lead to non-phonologization (blocking and rule insertion) effects. Blocking arises when the promoted postlexical constraint is dominated within the postlexical phonology by an antagonistic constraint (e.g. syncope by a restriction on syllable structure). 'Rule insertion' (a misnomer in this framework, of course) arises when the promoted postlexical constraint winnows away candidates that would otherwise emerge as winners by the lower-ranking postlexical constraints.

Phonologization (secondary split), on the other hand, takes place because constraints at a given level do not affect the operation of constraints at earlier levels. It arises when the context of a lexical process is made opaque by an innovated postlexical process, that is, by a sound change qua promoted markedness constraint. From the perspective of Stratal OT, then, the reason why the umlaut vowels became phonologized when the triggering context was lost is that they were introduced in the lexical phonology.

Before going into the details, let us emphasize that this solution is not available in parallel OT. As far as I can see, parallel OT actually has no coherent characterization of secondary split, for reasons which are homologous to its failure to deal with opacity. To see why, consider a bare-bones OT constraint system for the pre- and post-phonologization stage of umlaut.

(3) a. IDENT(Hi): the input and output values of [High] are identical.
   b. *ü, *ö: rounded vowels are back.
   c. REDUCE: no full (unreduced) unstressed vowels.
   d. IDENT(Front): the input and output values of [Front] are identical.
   e. AGREE(Front): no back vowels before *i, j* (the constraint that enforces umlaut).

The original grammar has the same ranking in all phonological strata; crucially IDENT(Hi) ≫ REDUCE, and *ü,*ö ≫ IDENT(Front), AGREE(Front).

(4)

Input	Output	\multicolumn{5}{c}{Stage 0: No umlaut}
		IDENT(Hi)	*ü, *ö	REDUCE	IDENT(Front)	AGREE(Front)
uCi	☞ uCi			*		*
	üCi		*	*	*	
	uCe	*				
	üCe	*	*		*	
uCe	uCi	*		*		*
	üCi	*	*	*	*	
	☞ uCe					
	üCe		*		*	
üCe	uCi	*		*	*	*
	üCi	*	*	*		
	☞ uCe				*	
	üCe		*			

The first sound change introduces allophonic umlaut into the language:

(5)

Input	Output	Stage 1: allophonic umlaut				
		AGREE(Front)	IDENT(Hi)	*ü, *ö	REDUCE	IDENT(Front)
uCi	uCi	*			*	
	☞ üCi			*	*	*
	uCe		*			
	üCe		*	*		*
uCe	uCi	*	*		*	
	üCi		*	*	*	*
	☞ uCe					
	üCe			*		*
üCe	uCi	*	*		*	*
	üCi		*	*	*	
	☞ uCe					*
	üCe			*		

Now vowel reduction takes place: an innovating grammar in which REDUCE outranks IDENT(Hi) begins to compete with (5) and eventually supplants it. But the new output üCe cannot be accounted for. No matter how the remaining constraints are ranked, the reduction causes umlaut to be undone. The actual form is HARMONICALLY BOUNDED.

(6)

Input	Output	Stage 2: promotion of Reduce (wrong!)				
		REDUCE	AGREE(Front)	IDENT(Hi)	*ü, ö	IDENT(Front)
uCi	uCi	*	*		*	
	üCi	*			*	*
	☛ uCe			*		
	üCe			*	*	*

The bottom line is that Saussure's Firewall has no place in constraint-based theories such as OT. This is arguably an advantage because, as noted above, it is stipulative, kills structural explanations of sound change, and even on the descriptive side creates more technical problems than it solves.

32.3 STRATAL OT

Stratal OT phonology provides a more articulated theory than parallel OT in that it incorporates Lexical Phonology's stratal organization (level-ordering) to OT's parallelism of constraint interaction (Booij 1996, 1997, Orgun 1996, Kiparsky 2000a; for diachronic phonology, see especially Bermúdez-Otero 1999, 2006, 2007, Bermúdez-Otero & Hogg 2003). Stratal OT does not in principle banish predictable feature values from lexical representations. Rather, it claims that lexical representations are determined by best satisfaction of the lexical phonological constraints. They will include such redundant feature values as those lexical constraints may assign. For this reason they can accommodate quasi-phonemes.

For Stratal OT, the grammar is a hierarchy of serially related modules, each a parallel constraint system of the classical OT type (without Output-Output constraints, Sympathy constraints, Lexical Conservatism constraints, Base-Reduplication constraints, Turbidity, Targeted constraints, or any other added transderivational devices).

(7)
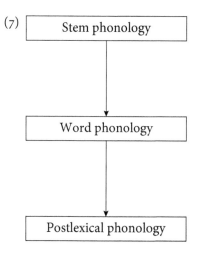

As in Lexical Phonology and Morphology, the Stratal OT levels are morphological as well as phonological subsystems, which form a hierarchy of domains: stems, words, phrases. A constraint system of level $n+1$ may differ in ranking from a constraint system of level n by promotion of constraints to undominated status. Each is governed by a (parallel) constraint system, but they interface serially. The interaction of constraints is determined by the intrinsic relation of the levels. A constraint at level n is visible to a constraint at level m iff $n \leq m$. Opacity reduces to constraint masking, and 'cyclic' effects reduce to ordinary faithfulness: bigger constructions inherit the phonological properties from the smaller constructions they contain, in so far as compatible with the applicable constraints.

Postlexical processes may be restricted to certain prosodic domains, of which the smallest is the CLITIC GROUP, and the larger ones are the PROSODIC PHRASE, the INTONATION GROUP, and perhaps others (Inkelas & Zec 1990). Lexical processes apply to stems (level 1) and prosodic words (level 2).

If we reconstruct quasi-phonemes in Stratal OT as lexically specified but distributionally predictable phonological segment types, we get an interesting additional prediction. In Stratal OT, lexical representations are specified by the word-level constraint system. This entails that quasi-phonemes are elements whose distribution is governed by or relevant to at least one lexical constraint, therefore within the domain of a prosodic word. The same elements may of course also figure in postlexical constraints.[8]

That leads directly to a solution for the secondary split problem. Processes become phonologized when they become applicable to the lexical phonology—formally, when the constraints that drive them are promoted over the antagonistic faithfulness constraints in the lexical constraint system. At that point their outputs become quasi-phonemes, understood as 'lexical allophones'. The effect of this promotion is that they assign categorical feature values, that their distribution is determined by constraints that operate within the word domain, and that in virtue of these very facts they are perceptually salient in the sense stated above. Other than the fact that 'real' phonemes have an at least partly unpredictable distribution, there is no basic difference between quasi-phonemes and ordinary phonemes, on this view.

The promotion of constraint rankings from the postlexical phonology into the lexical phonology does not mean that those rankings necessarily cease to apply postlexically. The process is, in fact, the generalization of new constraint rankings from the postlexical phonology, where they are first introduced as sound changes, into the lexical (word-level and ultimately stem-level) phonology (see Bermúdez-Otero, this volume, for some discussion of related ideas under the heading of 'rule scattering'). The cause of this spread of constraint rankings, I conjecture, is a preference of learners for assigning structure as early as possible. That is, there is a bias in acquisition in favour of locating information in the lexicon.

Although the phonologization of a process in this sense is compatible with its continued postlexical operation, the next step is typically disappearance of its postlexical

---

[8] For example, in Russian [i] and [ɨ] play a role in the lexical phonology, but [i] becomes [ɨ] after a velar consonant across a word boundary within a clitic group or phonological phrase. See Rubach (2000), Blumenfeld (2001), Padgett (2003a) for discussion of this interesting case.

reflexes—formally, by the promotion of antagonistic faithfulness constraints in the postlexical phonology. Once this happens, there is unambiguous evidence for phonologization, in that the process ceases to apply across word boundaries, its output is strictly categorical, and it is perceptually salient.

In the final act of this phonologization scenario, the potential contrasting quasi-phonemes becomes overtly manifested. This can happen either when a sound change (the promotion of a constraint in the postlexical phonology) renders their conditioning environment opaque (this is so-called secondary split), or when new lexical entries from borrowing or other sources exploit them. On this understanding, the rise of phonological contrasts is analogous to the rise of phonological opacity by constraint masking.

Returning to umlaut, we can now offer an analysis of the phonemicization of front rounded vowels. The original grammar has a uniform ranking, with the derivations of (4), in all phonological strata.

As a sound change, umlaut is the acquisition of the constraint ranking (5) in the postlexical phonology. The vowels *ü, ö* (and *æ*, if that is the output of umlaut at this point) are in complementary distribution with *u, o, a*.

In the second phase of the change, the ranking (5) enters the word phonology. At that point, the umlaut vowels become quasi-phonemes, present in lexical representations and constituting inputs to the postlexical phonology. Since lexical umlaut at first applies in a subset of the contexts in which postlexical umlaut applies, this is initially a covert change. It becomes overtly detectable at the latest in the next phase, when back vowels are restored before clitics with *-i-* in clitic configurations (see (9) below), while umlaut continues to apply within the phonological word. Formally, this means that IDENT(Back) is promoted in the postlexical phonology but remains dominated by umlaut in the lexical phonology. The umlaut vowels are not yet overtly contrastive.

In the third phase, another sound change affects the umlaut-triggering *i, j* in such a way as to cause the conditioning of umlaut to become opaque. Let us continue to assume that this happens through the promotion of REDUCE in the postlexical phonology. Lexical umlaut vowels are unaffected, both phonetically and phonologically. The change in the postlexical phonology that masks the context of umlaut does, however, cause them to change from *covertly* contrastive to *overtly* contrastive elements at this point. In principle, they might also become overtly contrastive through the acquisition of any lexical item with an umlaut vowel in a non-umlauting context, whether through borrowing, onomatopoeia, or word-formation, along the lines of the Russian example cited above).

In Old High German, this final phase of the change is reached when postlexical vowel reduction (by promoted REDUCE), *applying to the output of the word-level phonology,* produces minimal contrasts such as *uCe* and *üCe*.

(8)

Input	Output	Reduce	Agree(Front)	Ident(Hi)	Ident(Front)	*ü, *ö
üCi	uCi	*	*		*	
	üCi	*				*
	uCe			*	*	
	☞ üCe			*		*
uCe	uCi	*	*	*		
	üCi	*		*	*	*
	☞ uCe					
	üCe				*	*

Although the postlexical promotion of Reduce renders the conditioning of umlaut opaque, the lexical umlaut vowels themselves are retained. They just become overtly contrastive elements at this point.

Whereas Saussure's Firewall prises apart sound change and phonology and fences them off into separate worlds assigned to distinct fields of inquiry, this alternative explains phonologization through the internal stratification of phonology into a lexical and a postlexical component. And that stratal organization is independently motivated by rich evidence, including cyclic (paradigmatic) effects and phonological opacity. In fact, secondary split is just the historical counterpart of opacity, and Stratal OT provides the same solution to both.

This theory predicts that any phonologization process will proceed in three overt stages. All of them can be documented for umlaut in Old High German. In Otfried's dialect, which we can take here to represent the earliest stage, after the sound change enters the language, umlaut was postlexical, and hence crossed lexical word boundaries, applying within clitic groups:

(9) a. /mag iz/ → *meg iz* 'may it'
    b. /drank ih/ → *drenc ih* 'I drank'
    c. /gab ima/ → *geb ima* 'gave him'
    d. /girah inan/ → *gireh inan* 'avenged them'

In early OHG, umlaut became a lexical process, and ceased to apply across word boundaries, but was still transparently conditioned within the lexical word. The umlaut vowels were now quasi-phonemes. In the third stage, they became overtly contrastive as a result of sound changes that rendered their conditioning environments opaque.

The theory also predicts that our three criteria for quasi-phonemes should be satisfied at the second stage. As far as it is possible to tell, this is the case. The first criterion is certainly satisfied, for umlaut at that stage became restricted to applying inside lexical words. The second criterion is also satisfied: umlaut vowels must have been more salient exponents of vowel frontness than their triggers, at least in the normal cases where the umlaut vowels are stressed and the context is unstressed. The third, categoriality, is hardest to verify. The vowels *ü, ö* began to be written only late, because the Latin alphabet had no letters for them, but the umlaut of *a* was written *e* already at the second stage, that is, well *before* the reduction of *-i* to *-e* that (on the structuralist view) caused it to become phonemic. This could be taken as an indication that they were perceived as categorically distinct from *a* at stage 2, i.e. prior to the point at which the structuralist theory of phonologization claims that they became phonemic.

An attractive facet of the proposed Stratal OT approach to phonologization is that it establishes an inherent causal connection between the loss of the triggering context and the rise of the new phoneme, rather than a merely accidental one. In the case at hand, the progressive reduction of unstressed syllables is a *cause* of the concurrent rise of the umlaut vowels to quasi-phonemic status. Even before the reduction leads to neutralization, it causes the primary cue to shift from the unstressed vowels to the stressed vowels, which is a precondition for the latter to become quasi-phonemes.

We now have a solution to the puzzle why English palatalization of *k-* and *g-* does not become contrastive when vowels that condition it change their backness value. The answer is that the palatalization process is postlexical. We know that because it is gradient rather than categorical, because it is not salient, and because it applies in close contact across word boundaries, e.g. *sock it vs sock us*. Stratal OT predicts that under these circumstances it cannot become phonemic by secondary split. Therefore, vowel fronting and backing does not result in a contrast between front and back *k*.

Crucially, Stratal OT departs from Lexical Phonology by giving up structure-preservation ('Strata, yes, structure-preservation, no', as the slogan of Roca 2005 has it). To put it another way, Stratal OT severs the structuralist link between CONTRASTIVENESS (unpredictable distribution), a *structural* notion, and DISTINCTIVENESS, a *perceptual* notion.[9] Phonemes are contrastive and distinctive, allophones are non-contrastive and non-distinctive. The other two combinations are the surprising ones. Quasi-phonemes are non-contrastive but distinctive—that is, they are predictable but perceptually salient. The fourth logically possible case, contrastive but non-distinctive elements, exists as well. These are near-mergers (Labov 1994, Ch. 12, and see also Gordon, this volume), as when a speaker reliably produces near-merged sounds slightly differently, but cannot distinguish between them, in the speech of other such speakers or in her own speech, e.g. *source* and *sauce* in New York. The four cases are shown in (10).

---

[9] This link was axiomatic at least in post-Bloomfieldian American structuralism. Bloomfield himself allowed distinctive sounds to be non-contrastive, for example if they were morphologically predictable, a practice later condemned as 'mixing levels'. The Prague school distinction between phonetic and allophonic processes might also be seen as implying the separation of distinctiveness from contrastiveness.

(10)

	contrastive	non-contrastive
distinctive	phonemes	quasi-phonemes
non-distinctive	near-mergers	allophones

The upshot is that while delinking contrastiveness and distinctiveness in a sense preserves the phoneme as a theoretical construct, it does so only by negating the founding intuition behind it.[10]

Finally, Stratal OT also offers a solution to the empirical problems for Saussure's Firewall that we identified above. It predicts that sound changes will relate transparently to other postlexical processes. This has the three consequences that we cited above as difficulties for Saussure's Firewall.

First, when conditioned allophones are created in the postlexical constraint system, they will just disappear when their conditioning environments are lost, and no secondary split will occur. In other words, sound changes can bleed existing postlexical processes. That is, they can eliminate some of their former inputs. English velar to palatal assimilation is postlexical, since it is determined by the context across word boundaries (e.g. *sock it vs sock us*). Stratal OT predicts that under these circumstances it cannot become phonemic by secondary split. Therefore, vowel fronting and backing sound changes do not result in a contrast between front and back *k*. While quasi-phonemes survive the loss of their conditioning environment, postlexical allophones disappear.

The second consequence is that a sound change can feed other existing postlexical processes, i.e. add new inputs to them. Consider a language that has obligatory voicing assimilation of obstruents within some postlexical domain, such as the phonological phrase or the phonological word (the clitic group). The prediction is that when sound change creates sequences of obstruents in such a language, voicing assimilation will automatically eliminate them, as in the previously mentioned Old English example *bidest* (> **bidst*) > *bitst*. The parenthesized intermediate form is a 'virtual' stage which is not pronounced but forms part of the sound change itself.

Third, sound changes can be blocked just in case their output does not conform to a constraint that holds at the postlexical level.

In order to account for secondary split and neogrammarian exceptionlessness, we do not have to stipulate that the promotion of constraints is limited to the postlexical stratum. Constraints can be reranked at any stratum. Reranking at the word and stem levels simply

---

[10] It also calls into question Natural Phonology's idea that the phoneme is 'the mental image of a sound' whose perception makes contrast possible ('minimal pairs exist because phonemes are perceived as distinct', Donegan & Nathan, this volume). The point about near mergers is precisely that they give rise to minimal pairs that are not perceived as distinct. Conversely, quasi-phonemes are perceived as distinct even if they do not contrast (Hellberg's 1978 analysis of Swedish [æ] is particularly instructive on this point). Decoupling contrastiveness and distinctiveness in Natural Phonology is not trivial.

amounts to another type of change, namely analogy (including LEXICAL DIFFUSION, the extension of a lexical rule to new items, Kiparsky 1995; compare Phillips, this volume).

This can be illustrated with the more recent development of umlaut in German. It has split into a stem-level and a word-level process. The word-level process applies to word-based formations made with inflectional suffixes and some productive derivational suffixes, illustrated here by the comparative suffix -er. Historically, it is the result of an analogical streamlining of the synchronic umlaut process. It only triggers vowel *fronting*, and only in a syllable *adjacent* to the triggering suffix. Stem-level umlaut, on the other hand, preserves the inherited umlaut process with its historically accreted complexities. It generates, in addition to vowel fronting, the synchronically arbitrary rounding switch of *au* to *oi* (spelled *äu*), as in (11b,c,d,e), and it applies non-locally across a syllabic sonorant, as in (11d,e,f).

(11)			Stem Level	Word Level (Word+Suffix)
	a.	arm 'poor'	ärmlich 'impoverished'	ärmer 'poorer'
	b.	blau 'blue'	bläulich 'bluish'	blauer 'bluer'
	c.	braun 'brown'	bräunen 'to brown'	brauner 'browner'
	d.	sauber 'clean'	säuberlich 'tidy'	sauberer 'cleaner'
	e.	lauter 'pure'	läutern 'to purify'	lauterer 'purer'
	f.	schwanger 'pregnant'	beschwängern 'to impregnate'	schwangerer 'more pregnant'

Level ordering unifies what superficially look like two distinct umlaut processes in the synchronic phonology, and allows the generalization that German umlaut never crosses a syllable. This phonological locality restriction is common to both the word-level and stem-level versions of the process (e.g. *Bubi* → *Bubi-lein*, not *Bübi-lein* 'little Bubi'). Because *r* is not syllabified at the stem level (as can be shown on independent grounds), umlaut in cases like *beschwängern* actually does not cross a syllable. Final *r* after -*C* becomes syllabic at the word level, blocking umlaut in word-based formations such as *schwang[ɻ]-r*.[11]

This later development of umlaut illustrates the next stage of the typical LIFE CYCLE of phonological processes (Hyman 1976, Iverson & Salmons 2009, Roberts 2012, Bermúdez-Otero, this volume). In terms of Stratal OT, the full trajectory begins with gradient variable phonetic implementation processes, which become incorporated into

---

[11] It is also part of the explanation for the contrast between umlaut in common adjectives *vs* lack of umlaut in rarer adjectives, including in particular compounded forms of some of the same adjectives: *klüg-er* 'smarter', *alt-klug-er* 'more precocious', *kält-est-e* 'coldest', *eis-kalt-est-e* 'ice-coldest'. Similarly, the consonantal alternation in *näch-ste* 'nearest' (from *nah* 'near') does not apply in the compound *haut-nah-st-e* 'nearest to the skin'.

the phonology as featurally discrete constraints, first enforced postlexically without any domain restrictions, and then get restricted to increasingly narrow domains, finally retiring as morphologically or lexically conditioned alternations (Bermúdez-Otero & Trousdale 2012). Any phonological theory must account for the robust directionality of the phonological life cycle.[12] One obvious hypothesis would be that the drift reflects learners' bias in favour of precompiling the output and restricting constraints to the narrowest possible lexical domain. Such a bias should be eminently testable in children's language acquisition; in any case it seems more plausible than the 'mystical, pan-generational forces' invoked by Hale et al. (this volume).

32.4 CONCLUSION

Sound change and phonologization pose theoretical problems for structural and generative phonology which are conceptually akin to the ones raised by opacity in synchronic phonological systems. I have argued that Stratal OT provides a parallel solution to both sets of problems, which involves a radical rethinking of the phoneme. A corollary of the move to OT is that the time-honoured formulation of sound changes as context-sensitive replacement processes (A → B / C__D), for all its convenience, is misleading in that it fails to represent the way the process and/or its conditioning environment may be motivated or constrained by the language's existing phonological system.

I conclude by briefly mentioning some further predictions that follow directly from the proposed account of phonologization. Intrinsically lexical processes *must* become opaque if sound change masks their conditioning, for sound changes are by hypothesis postlexical, and therefore cannot affect the operation of lexical processes. For example, consider a language where word stress is assigned in the lexical phonology. A sound change which crucially affects the context that determines the place of stress—let us say an apocope process, or resyllabification—necessarily leaves the stress unchanged. Later analogical changes can of course restore the transparency of stress in various ways, but this cannot happen as part of the original process.

Another consequence is that sound changes cannot be conditioned by word boundaries. That this is the case has been argued by Hock (1991: 239) on the grounds that word boundary restrictions in many cases demonstrably originate as phrasal boundary restrictions. That is, at the first stage word boundaries play a role only insofar as they are phonetically manifested by pauses or other audible effects.

For similar reasons, we predict that secondary split should be controlled by the postlexical phonology, e.g. deletion of C in *V.CV* will result in disyllabic *V.V* just in case hiatus is tolerated in the postlexical phonology (i.e. if *ONSET is dominated by syllabic

---

[12] In rare cases, a single step is reversed, but the whole trajectory never runs backwards: as far as I know no morphological alternation has ever undergone a stepwise domain widening and ended up as a phonetic implementation process.

faithfulness in that component). If the constraint ranking in postlexical phonology favours consonant epenthesis over hiatus, it will yield a disyllabic *V.CV* sequence with an inserted consonant. If the postlexical phonology bars all derivations of a disyllabic output, but permits vowel length, the deletion will yield monosyllabic *VV*.

A constraint-based approach also makes immediate sense of the structure-preserving tendency that has been noted for sound change, that features which fit into the system are more easily lexicalized. For example, the generalization that redundant tones tend to be phonologized in systems which already have tonal contrasts (Kiparsky 1995) follows, since in such languages the constraints of the lexical phonology that admit distinctive tonemes are also likely to admit non-distinctive quasi-tonemes.

Stratal OT was devised as a theory of synchronic phonology. But it makes predictions about sound change that can be subjected to empirical scrutiny. Thus linguistic change gives us a window not only on the grammars of individual languages, but on the principles that underlie all of them.

PART VI

SOCIOLINGUISTIC AND EXOGENOUS FACTORS IN HISTORICAL PHONOLOGY

CHAPTER 33

....

VARIATION, TRANSMISSION, INCREMENTATION

....

ALEXANDRA D'ARCY

33.1 INTRODUCTION

....

'The *fact* of language change is a given; it is too obvious to be recorded or even listed among the assumptions of our research. Yet this fact alone—the existence of language change—is among the most stubborn and difficult to assimilate when we try to come to grips with the nature of language in general as it is reflected in the history of a language'.

(Labov 1994: 9)

THERE are many facets to language change: time, space, linguistic structure, social structure, etc. This chapter is concerned with the way in which a change advances successively in communities through time. It is clear that children must come to speak differently from their parents and that this pattern of parent/child differentiation must not only be recurrent but must also continue in the same direction for a change to both survive and progress. The issue here concerns the mechanism driving intergenerational differentiation. A widely appealed to hypothesis, particularly in the generative framework, is imperfect child language acquisition (Halle 1962; see also Foulkes & Vihman, Hale et al., Scheer, and especially Dresher, all this volume). However, while this premise has been invoked in diachronic perspectives to explain completed changes (e.g. Lightfoot 1997, 1999), the synchronic perspectives provided by sociolinguistic investigations have yielded little support for such a model (Weinreich et al. 1968: 148, Labov 2007: 346, fn.4). At the core of the issue then is the way in which to resolve what is known about historical change with the mounting evidence from the study of change in progress. This latter field of inquiry, spurred by the work of William Labov (e.g. Labov 1963, 1965, 1966, Weinreich et al. 1968, 1972a, etc.), has proved a valuable resource in the investigation of linguistic change in general and of sound change in particular. Of consequence for this discussion are the insights provided by this tradition to the interplay between *transmission*, the unbroken sequence of native-language acquisition, and *incrementation*, the unidirectional progression of a change over time.[1] We can also push the discussion a bit further, implicating language external factors as critical facets of both transmission and incrementation and their historical reflexes.

33.2 LABOVIAN VARIATION AND CHANGE

In the minds of many younger scholars, the name 'William Labov' is synonymous with sociolinguistics and as such, is associated with synchronic linguistics. It is also associated with the descriptive-interpretive mode of linguistic enquiry (Sankoff 1988), which emphasizes quantitative modelling, accountability (all variants must be accounted for), and representative speaker sampling. However, the Labovian paradigm of language variation and change, a programme first detailed in Weinreich et al. (1968), is—as its name suggests—an important branch of the historical enterprise. In his own words, many of Labov's research questions are motivated by the neogrammarian ideas of sound change (1994: 16) and the footprints of Bloomfield, Hockett and Saussure are laced throughout his work (see especially Labov 1994, 2001, 2010, also Salmons & Honeybone, this volume; other chapters in this volume that consider aspects of variation include those by Jones, Gordon, Bermúdez-Otero and Bowie & Yaeger-Dror, and see also Phillips, this volume, for some critical comments on some of Labov's ideas). The historical literature is replete with paradoxes: sound change is at once gradual and abrupt, regular and erratic, phonemic and lexical, etc. (all discussed in many places in this volume). The means through which Labov endeavours to address such issues is the study of change in progress. Before discussing the empirical validity of this approach, it is first necessary to outline some of the basic principles of the Labovian approach to language variation and change.

The Labovian framework begins with the observation that language is inherently heterogeneous. Synchronic (or *static*) variability has long been recognized as a characteristic of speech. This recognition sits at the heart of the Saussurian dichotomy between *langue* and *parole*, a distinction that continues to reverberate in many strands of modern linguistic inquiry. Historical linguistics and dialectology are concerned with patterns of differentiation and similarity across geographic space and the correlations these construe (e.g. as spatial reflexes of diachronic change). But as *parole*, variation within a speech community (loosely defined here as a group of individuals who share a set of norms) has generally been considered something to ignore (e.g. Bloomfield 1933: 42–45, Chomsky 1965: 3). Instead it has been assumed—as a pragmatic principle—that a language system

---

[1] In other words, the focus of this chapter is the temporal continuity of dialects. *Diffusion*, which refers to the geographic continuity of dialects as features transfer from one speech community to another through contact (Labov 2007: 347), is excluded from the discussion (some points that are somewhat relevant to diffusion are considered in Schreier and in Eckman & Iverson, both this volume).

has a consistent and invariant structure (Mathesius 1911: 2, Martinet 1963: vii, Romaine 1982: 10). The Labovian paradigm rejects this view; rather, it assumes that the natural state of language (and hence linguistic structure) is *orderly heterogeneity*. Variable features, whether they be involved in change or not, are systematically constrained by a complex matrix of linguistic and extralinguistic (i.e. social) factors. As summarized by Weinreich et al. (1968: 177), 'interpretation of the data in terms of language change depends upon the entire sociolinguistic structure'. This final point stresses the role of the group in language change, shifting the perspective from the individual lect (cf. Paul 1880, Saussure 1916, Bloch 1948, Chomsky 1965, compare also Hale et al., this volume) to that of the speech community. Thus, Labov maintains 'the language has not in effect changed unless the change is accepted as part of the language by other speakers' (1994: 45, fn.2; also Weinreich et al. 1968: 187).

It is now generally agreed that linguistic change, however it proceeds, can entail a period of oscillation between conservative and innovative forms. *A* does not become *B*; rather, *A* and *B* alternate for a period and the frequency of one (or more) competing variants increases (the focus here is thus not on the origins of the innovative forms—other chapters in the volume consider that, e.g. Bybee, Lahiri, Mailhammer et al., Purnell & Raimy, Ratliff, Yu). In the grammaticalization literature, for example, these phenomena are referred to as *layering* and *specialization* respectively (Hopper 1991). Thus, all change involves variability and heterogeneity. However, the obverse does not hold: not all variability and heterogeneity involves change (Weinreich et al. 1968: 188). While it is certainly true that much heterogeneity in language is not predictable in an absolute sense, it is also true that little of it is random or meaningless.

It is also apparent that, from a synchronic perspective, stable variation such as final /t,d/ deletion in English is the normal case; unstable variation is relatively rare (Labov 1989a: 87). But where sound change was once considered a strictly diachronic phenomenon, perceptible only in retrospect, its observation while in progress is a fundamental tenet of variation studies. To Bloomfield (1933: 347), such surveillance was 'inconceivable'. Sound change occurred too slowly to allow observation. To Hockett (1958: 456–57), who distinguished between sound change (e.g. chain shifts) and phonemic change (e.g. splits, mergers), observation was equally implausible. Sound change progressed too slowly to be observed while phonological change occurred too abruptly. However, Gauchat (1905) had already documented a number of variable features in the Swiss French village of Charmey that appeared to be involved in change: diphthongization of /e/ and /o/, monophthongization of /aw/, and the lenition of /ʎ/. At the time, Gauchat's findings challenged the belief that change is phonetically gradual: all demonstrated that change could entail alternation between incoming and outgoing variants. In the lenition of [ʎ] to [j], for example, the older generation used [ʎ], the younger generation used [j], and the middle generation fluctuated between [ʎ] and [j] rather than using a single, phonetically intermediate, realization.

Resistance to the empirical consequences of Gauchat's findings was strong (e.g. Goidanich 1926), but the replication of his study by Hermann (1929) demonstrated that he had succeeded in locating change in progress. This evidence was significantly bolstered when Fónagy (1956) presented data from more than 60 studies of change in progress in

French, English, German, and Hungarian that supported the position taken by Gauchat. Thus, observing change in progress was not only possible, but could be ascertained within a single 'snap-shot' of the speech community. The theoretical construct that enables this synchronic view is apparent time, an analytical 'surrogate' for real-time (Bailey 2002: 329).

Apparent time is a keystone of variationist methodology. It traces the distribution of forms across the successive age cohorts of a speech community at a single point in time. Should a monotonic relationship between age and use emerge, this correlation is seen to be suggestive of change in progress. The differences between age groups are treated as temporal analogues, reflecting distinct stages in the progression of the change across time. This is precisely the method employed by Gauchat in Charmey: each generation represents a different stage in the lenition of /ʎ/, with the change coming to completion within the youngest cohort. Apparent time cannot be fully diagnostic of change, since a linear correlation between age and frequency may reflect age-grading (i.e. an age-preferential pattern that repeats in every generation), and so observation at a different time is necessary to confirm an interpretation of change rather than stable age-graded variability.

A crucial underpinning of apparent time (and of the model of incrementation explored here) is the assumption that 'individual vernaculars remain stable throughout the course of an adult lifetime' (Bailey 2002: 320). In other words, the linguistic behaviour of any adult cohort can only be interpreted as reflecting a distinct stage of a change if it is assumed that usage has remained essentially fixed or static over the course of the lifetimes of those individuals (on individuals, see Jones, this volume). The empirical validity of this assumption has been subject to much scrutiny in the recent sociolinguistic literature (e.g. Bailey et al. 1991, Bailey 2002, Tillery & Bailey 2003, Boberg 2004, Sankoff 2004, 2006, Sankoff & Blondeau 2007; see also Bowie & Yaeger-Dror, this volume). The general consensus is that while individuals are able to shift the *frequency* of forms well into adulthood, this kind of restricted lability does not undermine the utility of apparent time as heuristic of change in progress (Boberg 2004: 266, Sankoff & Blondeau 2007: 32). If adults participate in change, then apparent time underestimates the rate of change, but does not affect its direction or its social embedding. Generational change (i.e. change in successive generations of speakers) and lifespan change (i.e. change by individuals as they age) function in concert (e.g. Cedergren 1988, Nahkola & Saanilahti 2004). It also remains that speakers are more capable of change earlier in life rather than later: adults do not 'make themselves over' linguistically (Sankoff 2004: 136). Change during this period appears to be the exception rather than the norm (Sankoff et al. 2001, Raumolin-Brunberg 2009). Thus, even allowing for participation in ongoing change across the lifespan (see Harrington et al. 2000a, b and Harrington 2006, for example), apparent time remains a well-grounded and powerful construct for interpreting the (recent) past in synchronic analyses (Sankoff 2004: 137, 2006: 115). Nonetheless, variationists are increasingly drawing on real time, as it provides a broader context in which to interpret synchronic results (see Bowie & Yaeger-Dror, this volume).

Labovian language variation and change is thus predicated on the assumption that language is a differentiated system; that linguistic and social factors are interrelated in the development of a change; and that change is transmitted within the community rather than a product of the individual. These principles enable the view of synchronic variation as a highly structured phenomenon, while apparent time models diachronic stages of ongoing change in living speech communities. Nonetheless, the study of change in progress 'still provides us with some of the greatest intellectual challenges for explanation and understanding' (Labov 1989a: 87).

33.3 LINGUISTIC DESCENT AND THE PROGRESSION OF CHANGE

We can distinguish between two types of change. *Change from above* entails the importation of linguistic features from other systems, and the path of diffusion is often through more formal styles and registers. In the model proposed by Andersen (1973), this kind of change is considered *adaptive*. The normal mode however is *change from below*, which entails system internal innovation (equivalent to Andersen's *evolutive change*). It is this latter mode with which we are concerned here. In focusing on transmission and incrementation, I abstract away from the socioeconomic matrix in which change is embedded in the community. Change from below begins and is most advanced in a central social group, located in the interior of the socioeconomic hierarchy, and subsequently spreads through to the highest and lowest groups (i.e. *the curvilinear principle*; Labov 2001: 188). Labov (2007) argues that whereas change from above derives from language (or dialect) contact and imperfect adult language learning, change from below, as an internal process, preserves linguistic descent.

Linguistic descent states the conditions under which we recognize a language as being a later stage of another. Though the notion is articulated in many places in the literature (e.g. Bloomfield 1933, Hoenigswald 1960), we can define it here as 'an unbroken sequence of instances of native-language acquisition by children' (Ringe et al. 2002: 63; though see Hale et al., this volume, on 'descent' for a contradictory view). Children replicate the structural detail of the older generation's language, but since this replication includes variable elements and the constraints that operate upon them, transmission remains unbroken (see Labov 2007: 345-46; also Labov 1989a, Roberts 1993, Roberts & Labov 1995, Foulkes et al. 1999).[2]

Changes continue in the same direction over several generations. If, however, the adult system is faithfully transmitted to children, we must explain the continuous transitions in the frequencies and modal values of forms involved in change. In 1968, Weinreich et al. wrote (184-85): 'all the empirical evidence gathered to date indicates that children do not preserve the dialect characteristics of their parents'. Since its publication, this claim has been refined. It appears that children first acquire the vernacular of their primary caretaker, usually a woman (e.g. Kerswill 1996b, Foulkes et al. 1999,

---

[2] A different scenario obtains in koinéization (see Schreier, this volume).

Kerswill & Williams 2000). Labov (2001: 415) states: 'The general condition for linguistic change can then be stated in a very simple way: children must learn to talk differently from their mothers'. This changing of the input model is *vernacular reorganization* (Labov 2001: 415). Vernacular reorganization thus underpins incrementation, since it is the process through which successive generations advance a change beyond the level of their caretakers. But for this kind of process to play a meaningful role in a model of language change, it must be more than a theoretical postulate.

The (first) dialect acquisition literature suggests that until the age of about four years, children closely approximate the dialect characteristics of their parents, including most of the social and linguistic constraints on variability (Payne 1980, Kerswill 1994, 1995, 1996a, Kerswill & Williams 2000; for second dialect acquisition, see Chambers 1992 and Kerswill 1996b). By age eight, however, children's variable patterns have veered away from those of their caretakers; they register strong linguistic influence from the speech community and from older peer groups in particular. It seems then that reorganization begins at some point after age four and is well underway by age eight. That it subsequently halts is implicit in the apparent time hypothesis. Although certain individuals may continue to participate in change during adulthood, such participation appears to be restricted to subtle shifts in frequency and to the adoption of lexical features (e.g. Kerswill 1996b: 179, although compare Bowie & Yaeger-Dror, this volume). Both the dialect acquisition literature and the language acquisition literature indicate clear age limitations to acquisition and vernacular reorganization; the converging evidence suggests that during late adolescence the linguistic system stabilizes (see Tagliamonte & D'Arcy 2009: 65). Thus, although age is a critical vector in the advancement of change, full participation in the incrementation process is restricted to an approximate period between the ages of four years and the late teens.

Participation in change, however, does not appear to proceed uniformly through the social matrix. In particular, one of the most consistent findings concerns gender asymmetry. Other things being equal, women lead linguistic change (from above and below). The few exceptions represent isolated cases involving the realization of individual sounds (e.g. the centralization of /ay/ before tautosyllabic voiceless obstruents in Philadelphia; Labov 2001: 315-19),[3] but men do not appear to be at the forefront of more systemic changes, e.g. chain shifts (Labov 1990: 218-19, 2001: 284). But it is not that men simply follow behind women. The gender gap develops early in the progression of a change, and once it becomes associated with women, men either retreat from or resist the incoming variant (Labov 2001: 306). By the mid-point of the change, men are often a full generation behind, displaying levels similar to women of the previous

---

[3] Other examples include the backing and rounding of /a/ in Belfast (Milroy & Milroy 1978), the unrounding of /ɒ/ in Norwich (Trudgill 1972, 1974), and the centralization of /ay/ and /aw/ on Martha's Vineyard (Labov 1963); see Labov (2001: 284). There are other types of communities (i.e. with different social structures) in which it is males who are the implementers of change, such as the well-known example of Kupwar, a town in Maharashtra India (Gumperz & Wilson 1971). In this case, the change was contact-induced and so falls into the category of change from above, entailing diffusion not transmission.

generational cohort (e.g. Gauchat 1905, Wolf & Jiménez 1979, Chae 1995, Chambers & Hardwick 1986). The gap only diminishes when the change nears completion (Labov 2001: 308). As discussed below, males and females also differ in the extent to which they partake in incrementation and the rate at which they advance a change. Indeed, Labov (2001: 452) has suggested that the underlying mechanism of change is distinct between the two sexes (see §5.3).

33.4 TRAJECTORIES OF CHANGE

As summarized by Weinreich et al. (1968: 184): 'All of the changes submitted to careful empirical scrutiny so far have shown continuous distribution through successive age levels of the population'. We are now in a position to theorize that incrementation proceeds through the repeated process of vernacular reorganization in successive generations of children, each group advancing the change further than the last. This accounts for both the directionality and the continuity of change. But it is clear that the rate of change is not constant. Vernacular reorganization does not proceed in a linear fashion from the inception of change through to its completion.[4] Instead it follows an ogive: innovations initially spread slowly and reach a maximum rate at mid-course. The rate then slows again as the change nears completion (Weinreich et al. 1968, Bailey 1973, Altmann, von Buttlar, Rott, & Strauß 1983, Kroch 1989, Labov 1994).

The trajectory I have just described is the S-curve of linguistic change, Figure 33.1, and it is an established template for change when viewed in diachronic perspective (Chambers 2002: 361; though see Denison 2003). But unless a change is moving very quickly, the S-curve does not always appear in apparent time. Even the most comprehensive analysis of change in progress can sample only the members of a living speech community and there are challenges inherent in recording (and analyzing) the speech of both its youngest and most elderly members (e.g. the natural deterioration of the speech organs; see Labov 1994: 46). In the optimum scenario we are dealing with a sample that provides a window on three generations of speakers. For this reason change often appears linear in synchronic perspective, even though we know it does not progress in this fashion.

In fact, in early research it was assumed that this linearity was inherent to the model and that the apparent time trajectory 'would continue in the same direction as the age

---

[4] Change is not deterministic and oscillation between A and B does not always lead to the ousting of A. In referring to the end or the completion of a change I intend only that it has ceased to advance. In this sense I do not differentiate between the /ei/-/ai/ merger in Late Middle English, for example, which in retrospect was regular and exceptionless, or the shift from /ʊ/ to /ʌ/ in Early Modern English, which evidences lexical effects, spatio-temporal effects, and variation across dialects (e.g. *roof* as [ɹʊf] or [ɹʌf] or [ruf]; see, e.g. *Dictionary of American Regional English*). The question of transition (i.e. the route by which a change proceeds through linguistic structure to completion) is a separate issue, dealt with in some detail in chapter 18 of Labov 1994; see also Phillips, this volume, and compare Bermúdez-Otero, this volume).

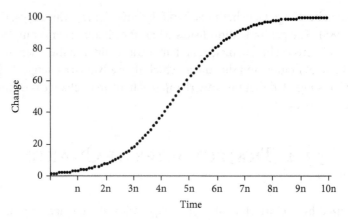

FIG. 33.1 The S-curve of linguistic change.

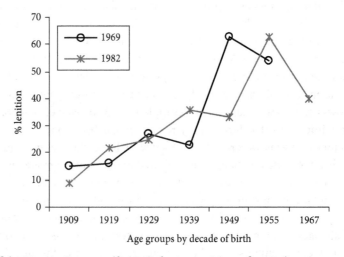

FIG. 33.2 [tʃ] lenition in Panama. (from Cedergren 1988: 54, figure 6)

group became younger and younger' (Labov 2001: 454). This assumption was falsified when, rather than a continued upswing, a crest appeared in the curve (e.g. Cedergren 1973, 1988, Ash 1982). While the locus of the peak depended on the way in which the data were aggregated, it was generally situated among speakers in their late teens and (early) twenties. When preadolescents and cohorts in their early teens were included in apparent time analyses, they consistently used incoming forms less frequently than their immediate elders did.

The most renowned example of the peak in apparent time comes from Cedergren's work on Panamanian Spanish (Cedergren 1973, 1988). Shown in Figure 33.2, analysis of the lenition of [tʃ] revealed a synchronic peak in both the 1969 and the 1982 samples. The existence of a peak in apparent time was 'idiosyncratic' and 'unexpected'

(Chambers 2003: 223), but when it was not only observed for a number of changes but was also similarly situated in the age continuum, a principled explanation was required. It was no longer sufficient, for example, to speculate that a change had reached its limit and was receding (e.g. Ash 1982). Our current understanding suggests that rather than indicating the tailing off or reversal of a change, the peak is in fact a 'general requirement' of change in progress (Labov 2001: 455; see also Tagliamonte & D'Arcy 2009).

33.5 PUTTING THE PIECES TOGETHER

Ultimately, in formulating a model of language change that can account for the facts of both diachronic change and change in progress there are a number of empirical issues to address. With respect to transmission, we must account for linguistic descent and vernacular reorganization. With respect to incrementation, there are the S-shaped curve of historical change, the peak in apparent time, and gender asymmetry with which to contend. Labov (2007: 346) writes: 'Incrementation begins with the faithful transmission of the adult system, including variable elements with their linguistic and social constraints [...]. These variable elements are then advanced further in the direction indicated by the inherited age vectors'. The purpose of this section, based on chapter 14 of Labov (2001), is to unpack this statement.

Because it captures the general trajectory of a change over time, we begin with the S-curve, which is most associated with the logistic function, shown in (1). Initially developed to model population growth (Verhulst 1845), this equation can theoretically model any distribution that initially spreads slowly, speeds up, and subsequently tails off. As implemented by Labov to model language change, K_1 is the maximum possible change in a unit of time, K_2 is the limits of the change, N_0 is the starting point, r is the rate of change, and t is time (Labov 2001: 45).

(1) $I = K_1 / (1 + K_2 / N_0 xe^{-rt})$

The S-curve in Figure 33.1 was generated using the increments produced by this equation with the values set to produce a change that progresses from 1 to 100 over 100 years (see Labov 2001: 450). The full set of increments is listed in Labov's table 14.1 (2001: 452). The crucial point in implementing the logistic function for modelling a linguistic change is that its progress at any point is determined by the sum of the increments for each year the change has been ongoing. At year ten, for example, n in Figure 33.1, the change has a level of 2.65, reached by adding the increments from years two through ten to the initial level in year one.

An increment here can refer to the frequency, extent, scope, or specificity of a variable (Labov 2007: 346). In my own work, where I deal with discrete variants in morphosyntax and discourse-pragmatics, the operand of incrementation is usually frequency. In sound change, however, variants may be discrete or gradient and the relevant unit of change may be subtle shifts along the F1 or F2 dimensions, in voice onset times, in periodicity, etc. But regardless of the kind of change being modelled, the logistic function alone cannot generate the peak that consistently appears in apparent time. To do so, the model must allow for stabilization of the vernacular. Without it, the curves will continue to display monotonicity throughout the age spectrum, a result that does not match the observed facts. If we assume, therefore, that transmission results in acquisition of the adult system; that this system begins to undergo vernacular-reorganization when the child reaches the age of four years; and that this period of lability closes off—for the sake of convenience—at age 17, then we are left with a model that produces the curves of Figure 33.3. In this figure, the hypothetical 100-year change from Figure 33.1 is viewed in apparent time at 25-year intervals.

The most critical observation to be made regarding Figure 33.3 is that, as observed in natural data, a peak occurs in each of the curves. This peak is consistently situated among 17-year-olds. But, it is more pronounced in some curves than it is in others (compare 1950 to 1925 and 1975 respectively). Finally, the curves are linear. Let us address each point in turn.

33.5.1 Creating the Peak in Apparent Time

The peak is created by the cessation of vernacular reorganization combined with the increasingly additive output of the logistic function. For every year a change has been

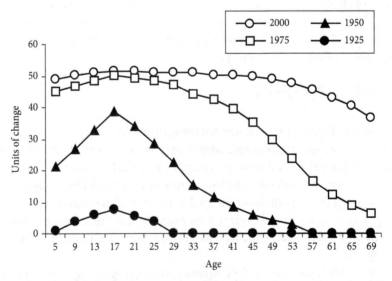

FIG. 33.3 A hypothetical change in progress with logistic incrementation and stabilization at age 17 (from Labov 2001: 453, figure 14.5)

ongoing, its level becomes successively greater; younger children acquire a larger increment than older children did. As a result, each group carries the change further than
the next older one. By the time of stabilization, a cohort will surpass the previous one,
who not only began with a lower increment (because they started sooner) but who also
stopped participating sooner (because they reached the age of stabilization earlier). In
other words, each successive cohort reaches a new 'high' in the progression of a change.
This accounts for the linear curve that is typical of apparent time analyses. In contrast,
younger cohorts, although they too began with a higher increment, have not been active
participants in the incrementation process for as long as the older (pre-stabilized) ones
and so have not yet accrued enough increments to surpass these groups. This situation,
of course, will change by the time they themselves reach the age of stabilization. Until
then, their 'lag' is simply a mathematical consequence of having accrued fewer increments due to a shorter period of participation.

33.5.2 Situating the Peak and Accounting for Its Size

The location of the peak coincides with the age of stabilization. At this point, speakers become 'linguistic adults, with a stabilized phonology' (Labov 2001: 463).
Incrementation halts. The empirical implication is clear: A peak marks the age vector
in which vernacular-reorganization has ceased. The crucial corollary of this, however,
is the rate of change. The upswing of the S-curve indicates the period during which a
change progresses most quickly. Rate is a factor in the logistic equation (r in (1)), and the
greater its value, the greater the increment produced by the formula. This means that
faster moving changes will evidence greater peaks. Slower moving ones will evidence
lesser peaks. And for changes that are moving very slowly, there may be no visible peak
at all.

   In Figure 33.3, the peak for 1950 is the most prominent. This year marks the mid-point
of the change when it is progressing most quickly and the increments are at their maximum value. In 1925 the change was only just gaining speed, while in 1975 it is slowing down again. The rate is slower in both these years than in 1950, resulting in smaller
peaks. In 2000, the change is reaching completion and the rate has slowed considerably. The curve departs little from a straight line among the younger and final cohorts to
participate in the incrementation of this change. The 100-year limit on this hypothetical change was convenient rather than substantive; many changes progress in less time
while others continue over centuries. We can therefore expect an extremely wide range
of variability in the prominence of the peak in apparent time.

33.5.3 Predicting Linearity (and Non-Linearity)

It is not, however, just the rate of change that is predicted to influence the presence and prominence of a peak. Labov's logistic model is intended to account for the

incrementation of a change by women. It is here that we expect to see a linear progression across time. With men, the trajectory tends to be step-wise (see Labov 2001: ch.9 and ch.11), which Labov interprets as reflecting the generational influence of female caretakers. Males inherit their increment but they do not participate in its advancement (Labov 2001:457). This means that vernacular reorganization does not occur, and if there is no period of instability, then there is no point of stabilization. As we have seen, however, stabilization is the underlying cause of the peak in apparent time. The consequence for change in progress is that the peak is a characteristic of the age profile for women only. Among men the curve is expected to culminate in an upward movement to the youngest group.

33.6 DO THE RESULTS MATCH THE PREDICTIONS?

'... it will become apparent that monotonic age functions are in fact impossible, and that every change must show a decline among younger speakers to some extent.

(Labov 2001: 311)

We now have a set of predictions against which we can weigh the evidence gathered from analyses of change in progress. Labov (2001) considers nine sound changes in Philadelphia. All are led by women. As such, the model 'should apply to all of them if it is valid' (Labov 2001: 458). Three of the changes are new and vigorous; they are labelled using symbols explained in Table 33.1: (aw), (eyC) and (æhD). These are changes with the highest age coefficients and which have shifted moderately in phonetic space. Four are middle-range changes: (owC), (owF), (uwC) and (uwF). These have notably lower age coefficients than the changes categorized as new and vigorous, but their degree of phonetic shift is greater (i.e. they have advanced further). Finally, two of the changes are nearly complete: (æhN) and (æhS). These have low age coefficients but the highest degree of shift along the F1 and F2 dimensions.[5] The details of each change are given in Table 33.1; many are part of ongoing chain shifts in the Philadelphian speech community (Labov 1994: ch.6).

The data from these changes, based on the raising of F2, provide a striking corroboration of the predicted patterns of incrementation within the community. Since different patterns are expected among men and women, it is necessary to consider them separately.

First, the women: reproduced from Labov (2001) in Figure 33.4, the curves all peak in apparent time and most are fairly linear in their distribution.[6] For (uwC) the peak

---

[5] For details concerning the calculations involved in categorizing these changes, see Labov (1994: 64–65).

[6] The data in Figures 33.4 and 33.5 were normalized using the logmean method (Neary 1977; see Labov 2001: 157–62). The 'age coefficients' indicate expected F2 values, calculated by adding constants to age regression coefficients.

Table 33.1 Summary of the nine sound changes used by Labov (2001) to test the predictions of his model of logistic incrementation

Variable[9]			Details of change	Stage of change
(aw)	/aw/	*bout, bough*	raising and fronting of the nucleus	new and vigorous
(eyC)	/ey/	*made, raise*	raising and fronting of nucleus in closed syllables	new and vigorous
(æhD)	/æh/[10]	*mad, bad, glad*	raising and fronting (three words only)	new and vigorous
(owC)	/ow/	*boat, robe*	fronting of nucleus, except before liquids	middle-range
(owF)	/ow/	*bow, row*		middle-range
(uwC)	/uw/	*boot, food*	fronting of nucleus, except before liquids	middle-range
(uwF)	/uw/	*do, shoe*		middle-range
(æhN)	/æh/	*can, understand*	fronting and raising before nasals	nearly complete
(æhS)	/æh/	*calf, bath, cast*	fronting and raising before voiceless fricatives	nearly complete

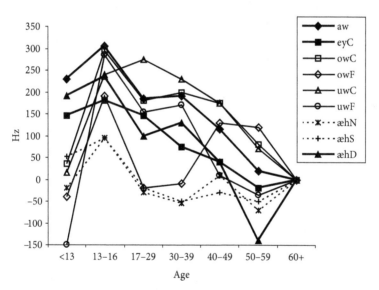

FIG. 33.4 Age coefficients for female speakers in nine linguistic changes in progress led by women in Philadelphia. (Labov 2001: 458, Figure 14.9)

⁹ Sociolinguistic variables are represented (abstractly) in parentheses. In the case of vocalic variables, the convention is to include the phonological context when it is relevant to where variation occurs. In Table 33.1 and all discussion of the Philadelphia data, C indicates a closed (i.e. checked) syllable, D indicates a following /d/, F indicates an open (i.e. free) syllable, N indicates a following nasal, and S indicates a following voiceless fricative.

¹⁰ The short *a* word class has undergone a lexical split in Philadelphia into tense /æh/ (which occurs before nasals and front voiceless fricatives, and in the *mad, bad, glad* set of words) and lax /æ/ (which occurs before palatal and velar consonants). See Labov (1989b) for a full treatment of Philadelphia short *a*.

occurs among the 17–29-year-olds; for the remainder it is situated among the 13–16-year-olds. Finally, the middle-range changes, shown with solid lines and empty symbols, have the most exaggerated peaks. A steep slope demarcates the adolescents from the preadolescents in particular. The new changes are shown with solid figures and heavy lines. These exhibit a clear upward curve. The slowest moving changes are nearly completed (æhN) and (æhS). Shown with dashed lines, these have the most gradient slopes and the peaks are similar to those of the newer changes.

In Figure 33.4 then are a set of results that conform remarkably well to the predictions of Labov's model and it is unlikely that this is accidental. Labov (2001: 459) explains:

> Simply considering the series as a binary choice: a peak present or absent, the probability of getting all nine with a peak is 1/29, or .0019. A more accurate assessment uses the sum of the logarithms of the probabilities derived from the t-test of the regression coefficients.... the probability of such a result being due to chance is .0003.

It seems then that with respect to the role played by women in advancing a linguistic change in the same direction over a number of generations, we are coming to a much better understanding of the mechanical, social, and acquisitional forces underlying the process. But what of the role played by men, if indeed they play a role at all? Labov's results are reproduced here in Figure 33.5.

Stated plainly, the results in Figure 33.5 are 'much less regular' (Labov 2001: 459) than those observed for the women in Figure 33.4. The curves are certainly less linear. But the more crucial prediction concerns monotonic age functions. The expectation was that all nine curves should continue upward to the youngest cohorts; there should

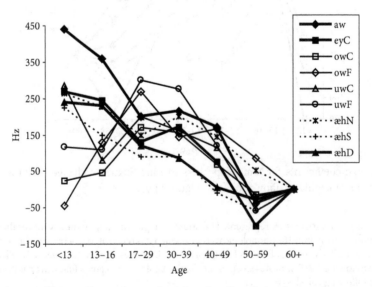

FIG. 33.5 Age coefficients for male speakers in nine linguistic changes in progress led by women in Philadelphia. (Labov 2001: 459, figure 14.10)

be no peaks. This is true for five of the variables: new and vigorous (aw), (eyC), and (æhD), and the nearly completed (æhN) and (æhS). However, contrary to expectation, a peak is evident for middle-range (owC), (owF), and (uwF), located within the 17–29-year-old group.

In sum, the results in Figure 33.5 raise a number of intriguing issues. The first concerns the presence of the peaks when in theory there should be none. The second concerns the prominence of the peaks. The third concerns their location. And finally, there is the nature of the curves, some of which are linear and some of which are step-wise. It is possible, however, that these are all interrelated issues. If such is the case, then in addressing one we can touch on others. Labov's suggestion concerning the meaning of the peaks seems a logical place to begin. In contrast to the peaks in the trajectories for females, which are indicative of change in progress, those that appear among the males may indicate that the changes are receding before they reach completion (Labov 2001: 460). Notably, with respect to (owC) and (owF), Labov had already noted that these changes were 'far less prominent in the sociolinguistic ecology of Philadelphia than the other variables, with only 10-20% of the variation among speakers accounted for by social factors' (2001: 299). He makes a similar kind of observation about (uwF), noting an absence of significant age and social constraints (2001: 312). But what follows is particularly insightful. Separate analysis of the expected values for (uwF) according to age and gender reveals a gradual upward trend as age decreases, with men lagging behind the women as expected. But crucially, the slope is steeper for men. Labov concludes: 'It is now evident that (uwF) is to be ranked among completed changes for women, but among mid-range changes for men' (2001: 312). The same pattern is visible for (owC) and (owF) (2001: 311-12). If the results for these three variables are compared in Figures 33.4 and 33.5, the peaks that appear in the male curves are notably more prominent than are those in the female curves. This, of course, is wholly consistent with women being at a later stage of the change when the rate will have slowed over that of the men.

We are now in a position to hypothesize more concretely about the peaks in Figure 33.5. Rather than indicating recession they likely indicate change, precisely as they do when located in an apparent time curve for females. Prior to Labov's work, the apparent time peak itself had not been subjected to careful analysis; it simply remained an oddity that required explanation (generally in the form of mitigation). But crucially, it was an oddity in aggregate data that compiled the results from men and women alike. We can only conclude that either the female trend (i.e. a peak) was so strong in each of these studies that it 'over-powered' the male one (i.e. continued monotonicity), essentially cancelling it out, or that a peak was in fact a characteristic of both groups.

Labov's discussion centres on sound change, but we can look to other kinds of change for support. Tagliamonte & D'Arcy (2009) test the incrementation model in six ongoing changes in morphosyntax and discourse-pragmatics (see Table 33.2). If we consider first the aggregate results, they report a peak in apparent time for five of the six changes (2009: 86). The exception, modal *have to* (e.g. *I have to be home by six*), exhibits a continued upward swing to the youngest age group. Non-paired Wilcoxan tests between adjacent age groups reveal that for the five changes with peaks, the differences between the

Table 33.2 Summary of regression results for six changes in progress led (historically or synchronically) by women (based on Tagliamonte & D'Arcy 2009: 98, table 7)

Variable	Women		Men	
	Peak (+/–)	Location	Peak (+/–)	Location
Quotative *be like*	+	17–19	+	20–29
Discourse *like*	+	13–16	+	13–16
Intensifier *so*	+	13–16	+	13–16
Possessive *have*	+	13–16	+	13–16
Modal *have to*	–	>13	–	>13
Future *going to*	+	13–16	+	17–29

groups under the age of 40 are significant, most below the .001 level (2009: 87, table 6). In short, the peaks themselves are significant and are highly unlikely to be due to chance. When the males and females are separated, the peaks are retained in both groups, while none appears in either curve for modal *have to* (2009: 91-6). We can conclude, therefore, that the peaks in the aggregate results were not masking an underlying interaction in the social structure of the speech community. But what we cannot conclude is that all these changes have reached their limit and are receding before completion. The associated age vectors, the social embedding, and the historical profiles of the variables in question indicate change in progress.

The consistency of the peak in the male curves suggests that men also participate in the incrementation process. That it should show up in Labov's data among changes with high rates of change in this gender cohort is consistent with the logistic model. Labov's own analyses reveal that at later stages of a change, the group that is farther behind in its advancement begins to accelerate (2001: 308, 311). The presence of the peak can then be accepted as part and parcel of incrementation, in which males participate as well as females. Their prominence is thus a product of rate, as follows from the logistic function. With respect to location, again they can only be created by the stabilization of the vernacular. In Tagliamonte & D'Arcy (2009), the peaks were in general identically situated among males and females, located in the 13-16-year-old group. When the age groups differed, the peaks were consistently situated in adjacent age groups with the males stabilizing later than the females. This is also true of Labov's middle-range sound changes: the male peaks occur in the next older age than the female ones do (females 13-16; males 17-29).

What is particularly striking about the location of the peaks is the clear importance of the 13-16-year-age group. This is where all nine of Labov's female peaks are situated, and four of Tagliamonte & D'Arcy's five female peaks are located in this group as well. This is strongly suggestive that at some point in this window, vernacular reorganization slows markedly among females, and that any residual changes after age 16 are quite minor or are restricted to a limited number of variables. The same is more or less true of males, though the window for stabilization appears to be wider.[7]

The remaining issue is the nature of the male curves. A step-wise pattern must derive from a uniform process of incrementation: each age group would be regularly and abruptly differentiated from the next. This sort of pattern, when it occurs, is associated with male curves (see Labov 2001: 448-9). But the curves in Figure 33.5 cannot be considered step-wise. That for (æhS), for example, is better described as linear. A linear progression does not *ipso facto* entail that males are active participants in incrementation. This same pattern can fall out from acquiring the mother's vernacular and maintaining it, because the mother will have participated in the logistic incrementation of the change and will have stabilized at the appropriate age vector. However, if it were this rather mechanical process of transmission that was responsible for the male patterns then the curves should not have peaks. They should culminate in an upward movement (Labov 2001: 457, figure 14.8). Clearly this is not always the case.

Tagliamonte & D'Arcy (2009: 97) suggest that the explanation 'lies in the observation that for some changes men simply lag behind women in their participation in the incrementation process.' The rate of change is slower, resulting in smaller increments of change, but the operating principle remains the same. Since men have consistently been shown to follow women in the advancement of change from below (see Labov 2001: ch. 8), a gap that extends to a full generation during the upswing of the S-curve, a difference in rate seems obvious. Although Labov hypothesizes that males inherit their increment from their mother in female-dominated changes but do not increase it, the same cannot hold for male-dominated changes. Females would not participate and so would never inherit an increment to maintain or advance (Labov 2001: 460). He therefore proposes a number of ways in which women could follow at a lower level, akin to the pattern observed for men in changes led by women. He suggests (2001: 460-1): '[Women] may have a slower rate of change. Or they may have a lower limit on the amount of change in any given year (the K_1 variable in the logistic formula). Or they may begin to imitate the male change at a later age, at 13, 14, or 15.'[8] Tagliamonte & D'Arcy (2009: 97) argue that the same principle(s) must be at work with respect to the role of males in changes led by females and that Labov's model need only be extended such that, for some changes at least, men may build on the increment inherited from their caregivers.

In fact, all these factors may be relevant in accounting for the role of men in incrementing change from below. A slower rate overall, a lower limit on K_1, and a later start to vernacular reorganization would certainly contribute to many of the empirical observations discussed here. To this we could add a later or more gradual slowing down of

---

[7] The peak for (ay0), a male-led change in Philadelphia, is also located among the 13-16-year-olds (Labov 2001: 172, figure 5.8; 461, figure 14.11).

[8] It seems particularly crucial to the discussion that for (ay0), the male-dominated change, a peak appears for the males while for the females the curve continues to climb upwards (Labov 2001: 461, figure 14.11). Whereas for males this latter pattern is interpreted as falling out from not participating, for females a number of possible explanations are posited.

vernacular reorganization. A further insight comes from the work of Foulkes et al. (2005; see also Foulkes & Vihman, this volume) on child-directed speech (CDS). A number of their findings are relevant to the current discussion. First, mothers used significantly more standard or non-stigmatized variants when speaking to infants (age 2;0 to 4;0) than when speaking to other adults. Second, speech to girls generally contained more standard variants than speech to boys, where vernacular variants were more abundant. Third, despite this last point, in both cases the overall frequency of standard variants remained higher than in speech directed to other adults. Fourth, mothers' patterns in CDS were reflected in their child's performance, where the use of individual variants was correlated between the two. These findings combine to suggest that while mothers may tune their linguistic behaviour in line with the child's developing gender identity, the original vernacular is not the adult model but rather is one in which the frequencies of forms are shifted. If this also holds for features involved in change, then in addition to the points outlined at the start of this paragraph, boys may also begin with an increment that is greater than, not equal to, that which is associated with their mother's age cohort.

33.7 SOME HYPOTHESES

In this section I would simply like to throw out some ideas for further investigation. None of this is substantiated empirically. It is an exploratory exercise, no more.

The logistic model of transmission and incrementation formulated by Labov (2001) receives full support from ongoing, female-led sound changes as they pertain to women and their role in the process. In this latter respect it also receives robust support from ongoing female-led changes in morphosyntax and discourse-pragmatics from Tagliamonte & D'Arcy (2009). From this it can be concluded that the model indeed provides a good approximation of the general principles guiding the unidirectional course of change among women.

The picture that emerges from analysis of the same model with respect to men is less convincing. The evidence from morphosyntactic and discourse-pragmatic change reveals a consistent and similarly situated peak in apparent time. So too do the results for middle-range sound changes. Only the new and vigorous and nearly completed changes pattern as expected, evidencing a continued upward curve. It is possible to reconcile these divergent results if we postulate the following scenarios. Both assume a slower rate of change for men (i.e. a lower value for r in (1)) throughout the progression of the change (see Tagliamonte & D'Arcy 2009: 96–97).

33.7.1 A Male Peak in Apparent Time

This scenario follows straightforwardly from the model if we assume it applies in parallel to what we find among women. The onset and stabilization of vernacular-reorganization, the limit to the degree of possible change in a particular time period, and the starting value will all contribute to the ultimate picture that emerges, but the underlying principles remain the same. Males begin at value X, participate in incrementation, and subsequently stabilize at value Y. The rate of change and the allowable limit must be large enough to create a peak.

33.7.2 Continued Monotonicity

It is hard to imagine that males do not participate in linguistic change. Men as well as women have shown the ability to change elements of their sound system into adulthood (e.g. Sankoff 2004), and yet a linear correlation between age and the unit of change does appear among the males for five of the sound changes considered by Labov (2001). Is it possible that men participate in some changes but not in others? Presumably. But this seems a rather untidy and unprincipled explanation. Let us consider an alternative. Males begin with a higher increment than their mothers (cf. Foulkes et al. 2005). If the rate of change is slow enough, the limit of change small enough, and the waning of vernacular reorganization gradual enough, this could result in a continued upswing. The associated curve could be step-like or more linear depending on the stage of the change (incipient, mid-course, nearing completion) and the consequent relationship to the progress of the change among females. A step-like pattern would result in the following circumstance. If the rate of change were fast among females, they would be pushing it ahead in leaps compared to the males, who would be advancing more slowly due to both an inherently slower rate and being at an earlier stage. This would create large increments among the females, but small ones among the males. This is similar to the new and vigorous changes in Figure 33.5: the curves for (aw) and (eyC) in particular are step-like. A more linear and yet still monotonic progression could appear if the females and the males are progressing at a similar but very slow rate, as occurs when changes are nearly complete. No peak will appear because the increments are too small, but a cumulative advance is possible given the starting point that is higher than the mother's natural (i.e. adult) age vector. This is similar to the nearly completed changes in Figure 33.5, where the curves for (æhN) and (æhS) are quite linear. Nonetheless, it remains for future research to test these hypotheses.

33.8 CONCLUDING REMARKS

Whereas linguistic change, and hence, linguistic variation, has always been at the heart of historical linguistics, a shift has occurred in the way in which it is conceptualized. Once considered generationally discrete and thus regular, change is now recognized as entailing a (sometimes extended) period of variability between new and old forms. The social mechanisms that drive the continued advancement of a change in the same direction over a number of generations are ultimately responsible for its linear progression in apparent time and its S-shaped curve in diachronic perspective. This is not to deny that linguistic change is, in Labov's own words, 'irrational, violent, and unpredictable' (1994: 10). History tells us that change is typically discontinuous (Joseph & Janda 2003a: 20), proceeding chaotically in bursts, fits and starts, and exaggerations (Lass 1997: 304, Janda 1999: 329). The programme outlined by Weinreich et al. (1968) has acknowledged this from the outset, and has argued that the keys to these discontinuities lie within the social fabric of the community. The seeds for Labov's position on vernacular reorganization were already present in the seminal work by Weinreich et al. (1968: 145-6) and they emerge fully formed in his 2001 monograph. We thus have a model of (sound) change in which, as cited above, 'incrementation begins with the faithful transmission of the adult system, including variable elements with their linguistic and social constraints [... which] are then advanced further in the direction indicated by the inherited age vectors' (Labov 2007: 346).

CHAPTER 34

···

PHONOLOGICAL CHANGE IN REAL TIME

···

DAVID BOWIE AND MALCAH YAEGER-DROR

34.1 INTRODUCTION AND OVERVIEW

···

34.1.1 Types of Language Change

THE traditional view of the critical period for language development, going back to Lenneberg (1967), is that it is part of a biological process: a decline in language learning ability reflects a maturational change in brain development. This view makes two strong predictions, namely, that children will be better at acquiring language than adults, and that after a 'critical period' (roughly corresponding to puberty) such linguistic flexibility is lost or, at best, significantly curtailed. This view has been challenged in recent years, and it is clear that individuals change their linguistic behaviour later in life to some extent, but the assumption that the core of one's linguistic system is essentially fixed at some point prior to or during adolescence remains dominant (see Hale et al. and also D'Arcy, both this volume).

This has direct application to studies of linguistic *variation* in speech communities as well as studies of linguistic *change*. Because many studies of linguistic change are now carried out 'in the field' rather than the library, many studies cited here can be found in 'variationist' publications. (See also, e.g. D'Arcy, Schreier, Foulkes & Vihman, Jones, Eckman & Iverson, and Gordon, all this volume.) One strength that such studies lend to the analysis of historical phonology is the ability to track both changes and individual speakers' perception of (and attitudes toward) those changes. Recent historical studies in Scandinavia (Nahkola & Saanilahti 2004, Paunonen 1996, Sundgren 2002, Nevalainen & Fitzmaurice 2011, Nevalainen et al. 2011), and the Western hemisphere (Boyarin 1977, 1978, Kemp & Yaeger-Dror 1991, Fitzmaurice & Minkova 2008, Phillips, this volume) have shown that the methodology and insights gained from field studies discussed in this chapter can be adapted for classical historical analyses.

As Labov (1994) points out, in synchronic studies that plot the distribution of a particular sociolinguistic variable against speaker age, there are four possibilities, shown in Table 34.1. If a study of a feature in, say, 1970 shows no age differentiation among speakers (the 'flat' pattern) that feature may not be undergoing change in the community (interpretation #1). ('Stable' unchanged linguistic behaviour is generally of less interest to historical linguists than the other three possibilities.) However, this is only the case if both the individual speakers and the community as a whole are stable with respect to the feature. Another interpretation of a flat pattern is possible: all the speakers in the community are changing together. In such a case, no age differences appear because older and younger speakers are all at the same stage in a change that is affecting all of them equally (interpretation #4, referred to as 'communal change', and which is of very real interest to historical linguists), reflecting 'diffusion' through a community (Labov 2007).

Another pattern of interest is a monotonic slope with age, which again has two possible interpretations. One is that the community remains stable over time, but that, generation after generation, individuals change in that particular feature as they get older. This interpretation (#2, commonly referred to as 'age grading') means that as individual cohorts of speakers get older, it is typical for them to show a steadily increasing (or decreasing) use of one variant of a studied feature. Examples of age grading include Fisher's (1958) description of (ing) variation, and Van Hofwegen & Wolfram's (2010) description of *ain't* and multiple negation. Alternately, individuals may retain their childhood patterns with each individual age cohort of speakers coming into the speech community increasing (or decreasing) their use of the variant. This is the classic 'apparent time' interpretation (#3), in which a monotonic slope according to age, measured at one point in time, is taken as a reflection of instability in the community, or change in progress, further reflecting 'transmission' of a change from generation to generation (following Labov 2007), with examples provided by much of Labov's work over the last 50 years (Gordon and D'Arcy, both this volume).

Table 34.1 Comparison of five patterns with relation to linguistic change (adapted from Labov 1994: 83, Sankoff 2006: 1004)

	Synchronic Pattern	Individual	Community	Interpretation
1.	Flat	Stable	Stable	No change
2.	Monotonic slope with age	Unstable	Stable	Age grading
3.	Monotonic slope with age	Stable	Unstable	Generational change/ 'apparent time'
4.	Flat	Unstable	Unstable	Communal change
5.	Monotonic slope with age	Unstable	Unstable	Lifespan change

Until recently, the default assumption in sociolinguistics has been that an apparent time analysis is the best way to interpret data showing monotonic age differences, while historical studies have preferred real time analysis. However, in order for either assumption to be valid the critical period hypothesis for language acquisition must apply (Bailey et al. 1991, Bailey 2002, Tillery & Bailey 2003), and so if speakers' ages place their linguistic systems in a temporal relationship with each other, the childhood linguistic system presumably determines adult speech production, and adult linguistic production is stable. Therefore, if speakers actually alter their linguistic systems over the course of their lives, both historical and sociolinguistic research models require modification.

Chambers & Trudgill (1980) noted that many studies have provided evidence of language change, since older and younger speakers very frequently differ in their speech patterns, but they described at least the vast majority of these analyses as evidence of linguistic 'change in apparent time'. They then posited a distinction between that and some hypothetical change that would continue even in the lives of individual speakers who had reached and passed this critical period, referring to the latter as 'change in real time' or 'lifespan change' (interpretation #5, Sankoff 2005: 1011).

While linguists deferred to psycholinguists by accepting the concept of a 'critical period' for language acquisition (Lenneberg 1967) and understood it to preclude dialect change past adolescence, in actuality there was at the time very little, if any, study of speakers 'in real time' as they age. Chambers & Trudgill stated that, therefore, linguists should carry out studies to test for change past adolescence, rather than simply assume that no variation is possible for a mature speaker. In addition, they pointed out that tracking the same speakers for many years would also facilitate distinguishing between change in real time (#5) and age grading (#2, Section 1.3).

Tracking individual speakers permits us to distinguish evidence for each type of linguistic change in Table 34.1. For example, if a study conducted at one point in time demonstrated a difference between older and younger speakers, and a later study shows the same difference with no advancement, this would provide clear evidence of age grading. If there is instability, with each individual's speech stable across the time periods sampled but community speech patterns varying, this would provide evidence of change in apparent time passed on via transmission (Labov 2007). Finally, if speakers change across their lifespan (as evidenced by studies conducted at different points in time) but at all analysis times there appears to be stability within the community, this is understood to be communal change, which can only take place via diffusion through the adult population—and it is claimed that this type of change, since it does occur past the assumed critical period, is more likely to be less complex and to involve lexical or syntactic changes (Labov 1994, 2007).

Nevertheless, the sort of lifespan change proposed by Sankoff & Blondeau (2007) has been supported as more panel studies have been conducted, finding, for example, individual speakers who initially follow conservative linguistic norms but appear to 'catch up' later (Thibault & Daveluy 1989, Yaeger-Dror 1994, 1997, Wagner 2012a,b), or vernacularity peaking in eighth grade for Southern school children before receding (Van Hofwegen & Wolfram 2010, Van Hofwegen 2015b).

This chapter synthesizes work that permits comparison of sound change in real and apparent time to present the current state of the art, considering the evidence in light of Table 34.1 and the theories proposed in relation to it. We begin by briefly mentioning some challenges to the critical period hypothesis from studies of language acquisition. We then discuss the sorts of evidence that can only come from studies of change in real time, and how some of those studies have challenged the concept of a critical period for language acquisition. Sociolinguists are very active in research on real-time change: since this piece was submitted papers on the topic have appeared in several venues (e.g. the *University of Pennsylvania Working Papers in Linguistics*), and new publication venues focusing on real-time change have emerged (e.g. the *Routledge Studies in Language Change* series and the undergraduate journal *Lifespans and Styles*).

34.1.2 Second Language and the Critical Period

Since apparent-time analyses rely so strongly on a rather strict interpretation of the critical period hypothesis (Bailey 2005), it is worth mentioning that even research on second language acquisition, which used to take this critical period as a given, has found that differences between adult and child language acquisition cannot always be ascribed to limitations on plasticity arising from brain maturation. Some of these differences may be the result of differing inputs (Muñoz 2008, Durrant & Schmitt 2009), interference from a speaker's first language (Hopp 2007, Rothman 2008), or even language attitudes (Moyer 2007, Llamas & Watt 2010, Hoffman 2010; see also the review in Horwitz 2010). Further, contrary to conventional wisdom, adult learners have been shown to outperform child learners in some domains (White 1998). Consequently, it seems that the apparent advantage of child (second) language learners over adult language learners may have been over-estimated (Abrahamsson & Hyltenstam 2009). Finally, adult and late childhood learners of language do not show the steep drop-off in acquisition ability that one would expect from critical period constraints (Muñoz & Singleton 2011). All this underscores the fact that speakers have the ability to acquire linguistic features later in life than is often assumed (compare Eckman & Iverson, this volume, for evidence of difference between young children and adults following the exposure to a second language).

34.1.3 Option 2: Age Grading and Language Change

Age grading, with individual variation through time but no resultant linguistic change within the community, can be contrasted with linguistic change where the speech of an entire community is affected and speakers (generally) continue to advance the change until it eventually is completed and everyone uses the newer form. The focus of most sociophonetic research has been on dialect change, with age grading often treated as a sort of afterthought, but both are critical to a thorough understanding of language change.

Studies of age grading have found that communally stable variables can exhibit a curvilinear pattern with age, with adolescents and the elderly using non-standard variants at a higher rate than working-age adults. For example, Fischer (1958) found age grading in a study of (ing), with the [ɪn] realization stable across generations, but favoured by the young (see Wagner 2012a,b for more recent evidence). Age grading is also clearly involved in lexical variation and change (Rickford & Price 2013), including the size of a speaker's vocabulary: Sankoff & Lessard (1975) found that speakers of all classes add to their vocabulary as they age.

It is only possible to fully recognize age grading by conducting studies of communities over real time, since confirming that age grading is occurring requires that a community as a whole is not changing between (at least) two points in time, and that individual age groups show the same distribution at one point in time as people who are the same age at a later point in time. Further, a complete description of linguistic change requires an analysis of changes which allow age grading to be distinguished from other changes, whether the study involves 'apparent' or 'real' time data, and more studies of such a type will result in a better ability to tease apart various forms of change.

34.1.4 Methods of Studying Changes Over Real Time

Soon after Chambers & Trudgill's (1980) challenge to conduct studies of language change in real time, several groups of researchers took it up. To distinguish between a diachronic study based on a new set of interviewees and a study which follows the same set of speakers for several years as Chambers & Trudgill (1980) had suggested, a distinction was drawn between a 'trend' (or cross-sectional) study approach where different speakers are used, and a 'longitudinal' (or panel) approach where the same speakers are compared at two or more points in time (see Labov 1994, Blondeau 2001). Some groups have taken advantage of older recordings to permit comparison of speech at different times (e.g. Kemp & Yaeger-Dror 1991, Van de Velde et al. 1996, Bowie 2005, Harrington 2006, Gordon et al. 2007, Van Hofwegen & Wolfram 2010, Coggshall & Becker 2010); these often took the form of panel studies. Trend studies (such as Cedergren 1988, Trudgill 1988, Van de Velde et al. 1996, Blake & Josey 2003), though, have the advantage that they are less costly and less fraught with complications, but they are much more likely to risk a systematic mismatch between the recording situations in the two corpora, making comparison difficult at best (Thibault & Vincent 1990).

As a result, wherever possible, a corpus records the same speakers some years after the first recordings, and in the same social situation: for example, a Yiddish singer (Prince 1987, 1988); a queen (Harrington et al. 2000a,b, 2005, Harrington 2006, 2007); Americans in the UK (Shockey 1984); the Beatles and Rolling Stones (Trudgill 1983); California teens (Baugh 1996, Rickford & Price 2013); Alabama adults (Feagin 1990, 2003); Philadelphia teens (Wagner 2012a,b); broadcast archives from Montreal (Kemp & Yaeger-Dror 1991), Belgium and the Netherlands (van de Velde et al. 1996), Israel (Yaeger-Dror 1993), and Utah (Bowie 2005, 2010, 2011); political archives (Yaeger-Dror & Hall-Lew 2002, Hall-Lew et al. 2012); and speakers from the UK's *7 Up Series* (Sankoff 2004, Poplack & Leaness 2011, Rhodes 2011).

A panel study can have as few as one or two speakers recorded for particular purposes, but a systematic plan permits comparison of many speakers at two points in time: for example, the Montreal research group, which had already developed an impressive corpus to study change in apparent time (Sankoff & Sankoff 1973), re-interviewed 32 of the speakers from 1971 in 1984 (Thibault & Vincent 1990), forming the basis for many subsequent studies of change in phonology, syntax, lexicon, and discourse particles (Thibault & Daveluy 1989, Yaeger-Dror 1989, 1993, 1994, 1997, Blondeau 2001, 2006, Sankoff & Blondeau 2007, Wagner & Sankoff 2011). Of course, only those speakers who were part of the original study and for whom there are interviews from both 1971 and 1984 could form the panel study of change in real-time (Thibault & Daveluy 1989, Thibault & Vincent 1990, Sankoff & Blondeau 2007). New adolescent speakers who had been too young at the time of the original study were added to provide a trend study of changes in adolescent speech between 1971 and 1984 (Thibault & Vincent 1990). With this, a new benchmark had been set, with a new goal to provide data from panel studies of speech.

Other research has since provided panel studies of change in other locations, some discussed below, with a selection in Table 34.2. Similar in-depth studies of a large group of speakers have been carried out in Québec (Elsig & Poplack 2009), Brazil (Callou et al. 1998, De Paiva & Duarte 2003), Denmark (Brink & Lund 1979, Gregersen 2009, Gregersen & Barner-Rasmussen 2011, Kammacher et al. 2011), Finland (Kurki 2004, Nahkola & Saanilahti 2004, Paunonen 1996), Sweden (Sundgren 2002), and parts of London (e.g. Kerswill 1996b, Cheshire et al. 2011, Sharma 2011).

In each study the goal has been to determine the scope and limitations of speakers' abilities to change their speech, as discussed below. For the most part, we limit our review to longitudinal/panel studies. Section 2 discusses evidence of speech plasticity past adolescence within given dialect areas, including methodological issues. Section 3 treats variation and change for speakers who move from their original dialect area. Section 4 presents conclusions we can draw from these studies, and proposes new directions for future research.

34.2 EVIDENCE OF PLASTICITY PAST ADOLESCENCE

34.2.1 Changing Presentation of Self During the Formative Years Leading to Language Change

Some work on real-time change does not purport to determine change in real time per se, but the changing attitudes and changing self-image of young speakers. Thus, although they do not directly address the issue of change in real time past the critical period, they still address the topic of fluidity of identity management, particularly during the formative years. Van Hofwegen & Wolfram (2010), Renn (2011), and

Table 34.2 A partial list of apparent- and real-time studies (Adapted from Sankoff 2006)

Speech community and variables	Time 1 finding	Time 2 finding
Charmey, 6 phonetic changes (Hermann 1929, Labov 1966: 278, 301, 1994)	apparent time; from below	3 V changes continuing; 3 C changes stable
British letters (Raumolin-Brunberg 1996)		-th>-s as 3rd person-change
British letters (Arnaud 1998)		RT increased ratio of progressives
The queen's English (Harrington et al. 2000a, 2000b, Harrington 2006, 2007)		pattern of vowel shifts toward new norm
Martha's Vineyard, (ay) nucleus raising (Labov 1963, 1994, Blake & Josey 2003, Josey 2004, Pope et al. 2007)	apparent time; from below	possible reversal (Blake & Josey, Josey); possible continuation (Pope)
European Yiddish vowel nuclei; (Prince 1987, 1988)		shift toward 'prestige': open-class lexicon
New York City, (r) (Labov 1966, 1994)	apparent time; from above	age grading > change
Norwich, *beer-bear* merger (Trudgill 1972, 1988)	apparent time; from below	continuing change
Norwich, backing of /ɛl/, [ʔ] for /t/ (Trudgill 1972, 1988)	apparent time; from below	continuing, new style distinction
Norwich, *moan-mown* merger, [eː] (Trudgill 1988)	apparent time; from above	vestigial
Norwich, *r* labialization, (th/dh) 'fronting' (Trudgill 1988)	apparent time	rapid adoption by younger speakers
Panama City, (ch)-lenition (Cedergren 1988)	apparent time; from below	change; age grading (young 'spike')
Glasgow, glottal stop (Macaulay 1977, Chambers 1995, Stuart-Smith 1999, Stuart-Smith et al. 2011)	age grading	age grading; continuing (1990s)
Eskilstuna, Sweden, 7 morphological, morphophonological variables (Sundgren 2002)	apparent time; from above	slower continuing change; age, class and gender effects
Hanhijoki, Finland, [r] > [d] (Kurki 2004)	apparent time; from above	continuing change
Virrat, Finland, 10 changes (Nahkola & Saanilahti 2004)	apparent time; from above	continuing change
Tours, France, *ne*-deletion (Ashby 2001)	apparent time; from below	continuing change
Rio de Janeiro, Brazil, (r)-aspiration (Callou et al. 1998)		age grading (young 'spike')
Rio de Janeiro, Brazil; several morphological and phonological variables (DePaiva & Duarte 2003)	apparent time; from above/ below	continuing change

(continued)

Table 34.2 Continued

Speech community and variables	Time 1 finding	Time 2 finding
Montreal, (Ation)>(a:tion) (Kemp & Yaeger-Dror 1991)	apparent time; social class	continuing; vestigial by WWII
Montreal, (ER) (Yaeger-Dror 1993, Yaeger-Dror & Kemp 1992)	apparent time; social class	continuing change except for retirees, etymological/lexical sets maintained
Montreal, R/aR,oer (Yaeger-Dror 1986, 1994, 1996)	apparent time; social class	continuing change except for retirees, etymological/lexical sets maintained
Montreal, r/R (Sankoff & Blondeau 2007)	apparent time; change from above	continuing change
Montreal, alors (Thibault & Daveluy 1989, 1991)		age graded, but only middle class
Montreal, t'sais (Thibault & Daveluy 1989, 1991)		continuing rapid change
Montreal, t'sais/j'v'dire (Thibault & Daveluy 1989)		continuing rapid change; communal change
Montreal, only (Thibault & Daveluy 1989)		continuing change; age graded
Montreal, we (Laberge 1978, Blondeau 2001)	apparent time	continuing change to nous; age graded
Montreal, periphrastic future (Blondeau 2006, Wagner & Sankoff 2011)	apparent time	age graded, social class.
Montreal, extension particles (Dubois 1992)	apparent time	age graded, social class.
Springville, Texas, Southern Vowel Shift (7 features) (Bailey et al. 1991, 2001, Cukor-Avila 2002)	apparent time	continuation, with ethnic variation
Springville, Texas, double modals, fixin' to (Bailey et al. 1991, 2001)	apparent time	continuation, with ethnic variation
Springville, Texas, verbs of quotation (Cukor-Avila 2002)	apparent time	continuing rapid change; age graded
Danish, possessives (Brink & Lund 1979)	apparent time, from above	continuing change
Helsinki, Finland, possessives (Paunonen 1996)	apparent time, from above	continuing change, except those over 50 on first study

Van Hofwegen (2015a) found no particular linguistic pattern that was consistent for all children across their years of schooling, but found that there was a general tendency to aim toward the standard in the lower grades, and then to shift toward the ethnic vernacular in the teenage years (with a peak in early adolescence), which was followed by 'regression' away from stigmatized forms later in adolescence. One interesting result is the extent to which individual children vary, adopting different socially-marked features at different ages, without showing generalizable patterns of adoption or rejection of stigmatized variables (as is often found among adolescents and adults, as discussed below).

34.2.2 Results from Studies of Teenagers

In studies of preteens and teens, Eckert (1989, 2000, 2008), Moore (2004, 2010), Mendoza-Denton (2008), Rampton (2010), Bigham (2010), Wagner (2012b), and Lawson (2011) have all found a tendency for high school students to shift toward an 'ideal' phonology for their specific social group. Eckert (1989) showed that even before college, high school 'jocks' who are planning to move to larger communities and not return home have begun to shift their vowel phonology toward a more urban(e) pattern, while the 'burnouts' have begun to shift toward a more local pattern. There is often apparent stabilization in adolescence (Tagliamonte & D'Arcy 2009, D'Arcy, this volume, Van Hofwegen 2015b), which recedes as teens move into the 'linguistic market' (Eckert 1996, 2000, Moore 2004, 2010, Mendoza-Denton 2008). Along these lines, Moore (2010) documented how shifts in social practice by two groups of British teens were accompanied by specific linguistic changes, while Mendoza-Denton (2008) demonstrated that even within a short time span, a shift from one high school gang allegiance to another is accompanied by specific phonological (along with sartorial) changes, and similar findings have been found by Drager et al. (2010).

Coupland (2010: 103), in commenting on such findings, points out that 'the emergence of identities and of new linguistic forms' is particularly salient in (transitional) teen identities. Evidence from both apparent and real time studies supports the understanding that there is an emergence of age-relevant identities, and these identities are altered as teenagers transition to other newly age-relevant identities, such as the college-age linguistic market or the adult job-related linguistic market. So, for example, Cukor-Avila & Bailey (2011) studied the production of several variables by individuals in a Texas community and found that teens initially produced similar behaviour, then diverged through the teenage years into early adulthood.

These studies, taken together, present severe difficulties for any claim based on the critical period hypothesis that the core elements of one's linguistic system are frozen in place by the age of twelve or earlier. If anything, they show that there is a great deal of linguistic shifting beyond that point, and that these shifts not only correlate with social networks and allegiances, but can also result in members of any one age cohort becoming more disparate as adolescence progresses (compare D'Arcy, this volume, for an interpretation more compatible with the apparent time approach).

Similarly, while Alim's (2004) and Cutler's (2010) work does not actually track change in teenage speakers' phonology, they do follow teenagers whose role models are socially stigmatized within the linguistic marketplace (and therefore dispreferred in the 'standard' job market) and may not reflect the speaker's own background, and so maximize the chance that a later study might find a shift away from the current phonological preferences as they enter the job market. Cutler's recent study of immigrant youth who identify with the hip-hop community (2010), for example, has shown the degree to which their phonology appears to reflect their choice of role models. Unfortunately, while her teens' phonology does not reflect their ethnic background, and presumably has gravitated toward hip-hop phonology during their teen years, there is evidence neither of their pre-hip hop nor adult phonology. Presumably, following these individuals through their adult years in a study of change in real time would offer a glimpse into their subsequent adult phonology once they have become members of the linguistic marketplace and must earn their living. While Cutler's work does not purport to study change in real time, it does provide a tantalizing glimpse into a research direction which will presumably reveal the extent to which phonological change continues after adolescence, and perhaps the extent to which conflicting motivating factors like communities of practice (Eckert 2000) and the replacement of the 'heterosexual market' (Eckert 1989 *inter alia*) with the job market and the 'linguistic marketplace' as initially formulated (Sankoff & Laberge 1978) are involved in this process.

34.2.3 Moving into the College and Working Years

Other recent studies have found similar changes continuing into the college years: De Decker (2006), Bigham (2010), and Wagner (2012b), for example, found that college students adapt to the larger urban community that they have moved to, at least in places like Ontario and Illinois where the urban variety has more prestige than their more rural home community's variety. In fact, in Bigham's study, the shift toward the 'big city' dialect may have already taken place during high school, as occurred with Eckert's (1989) jocks. While Bigham inferred that the rural speakers had all left high school with a more rural dialect, De Decker compared the panel's high school phonology with that of a year later, and found that the move into college had an effect.

Wagner (2012b) studied teenage girls as they shifted from high school to the college 'market'. She found greater consistency, with preferred ethnic designation and level of aspiration (as defined by choice of university) both influencing the degree to which girls shifted their pronunciation of (ing) between senior year of high school and freshman year in college. She demonstrated that even when all the students are from the same high school community and continue to college within a single dialect area, those who continue to a 'nationally oriented' (read: research university) campus will weaken their local dialect, while those who choose a community college or local parochial campus retain local stigmatized features into their college years. In addition, Rhodes (2011) tracked the vowel system of one *7 Up* interviewee and showed that the greatest change in his vowel system occurred not during his teenage years, but as he settled into the job market.

Baugh (1996) and Rickford & Price (2013), like Cukor-Avila & Bailey (2011), followed African-American English-speaking youth as they exited their teens and entered the workforce. Although the studies take place in three widely dispersed areas, all three support the conclusion that the same interviewee, even with the same interviewer in the same social setting, can adapt radically toward the more 'standard' dialect features as s/he enters the workforce.

Alongside all this, the initial trajectory shown by speakers can echo later in life. So, for example, in research on changes in Montreal French (r), those who had at least a small percentage of the newer (uvular) variant in their youth were likely to continue to change in the direction of the newer norm as they grew older (Sankoff & Blondeau 2007).

34.2.4 Evidence from Adults

There is also work demonstrating that a community of adults can shift their phonology toward a specific phonological model. Much of this work was carried out without the time depth for change in real time suggested by Chambers & Trudgill (1980), but both the Milroys' (Milroy 1980, Milroy & Milroy 1985) work in Belfast and Trudgill's (1988) reanalysis of Norwich permit us a window onto change in real time. In Milroy's corpus, the Catholic women—perhaps motivated by the linguistic marketplace need for 'Protestant' phonology in their workplaces—shifted their vowel system toward the Protestant pattern. Similarly, Trudgill's reanalysis of Norwich is a trend study, but reveals diffusion (Labov 2007) of stigmatized 'estuary' features like theta fronting (e.g. *with* realized as [wɪf]) and *r* labializing into the Norwich area in the late 1970s, with teenagers adopting the London working class innovation. More evidence that older speakers adapt their phonology has been provided by Shapp et al.'s (2014) analysis of US Supreme Court Justice Ruth Bader Ginsburg's speech during her court tenure, and Mackenzie's (2014) analysis of David Attenborough's speech over the last half century. These demonstrate that an extremely nuanced variation occurs over the lifespan of an adult.

34.2.5 After the Working Years Are Over

While the main focus of many studies of change in real time has been speakers who are relatively recently past the claimed critical period, Yaeger-Dror (1994, 1997) included older speakers, who, it was assumed, would not change at all. Her findings demonstrated not only that there was a significant change for these speakers, but that the change was toward an older phonology. Given the small sample size it was difficult to determine whether this could be traced to loss of hearing (as in early studies, where Labov found speakers' accents stronger when they were hearing white noise as they spoke), loss of access to (or interest in) the linguistic marketplace, or merely a shift in community to one no longer including younger speakers.

Of course, a finding that older adults exhibit linguistic changes is not necessarily surprising, given the results of gerontological research. Gerontologists have consistently found that individuals in a given age cohort increasingly differ cognitively as they age. Some of this is the result of illness, injury, or other pathology, but it holds true even absent such factors (e.g. Christensen et al. 1999, Hultsch et al. 2002, Barnes et al. 2007). Thus the linguistic finding that older adults exhibit sociolinguistic change is, perhaps, simply to be expected.

34.2.6 The Use and Importance of Panel-Study Corpora

Panel studies provide clear evidence for linguistic change across the lifespan in real time; Gillian Sankoff and colleagues (Sankoff et al. 2001, Sankoff & Wagner 2006, Sankoff & Blondeau 2007, Wagner & Sankoff 2011, Sankoff 2013) have pointed out that some changes in the Montreal system appear to be categorical over both apparent and real time, while others appear to be more fluid. These studies have generally found that 'most individual speakers … were stable after the critical period, with phonological patterns set by the end of adolescence [while a] sizeable minority … made substantial changes. The window of opportunity for linguistic modification in later life may be expanded with rapid change in progress when linguistic variables take on social significance' (Sankoff & Blondeau 2007: 560).

Panel studies such as the Montreal French 1971–84 study provide clear and simple comparisons of several features for the sampled speakers. So, for example, Sankoff & Blondeau's (2007: figure 3) study of *r* in Montreal found that seven of the ten younger speakers who had not already adopted dorsal (R) by 1971 were those most likely to adopt the newer variant by 1984. Similarly, Wagner & Sankoff (2011) found that 18 of 21 upper-middle- and middle-class speakers increased their use of the inflected future, as did 13 of the 18 mid-range speakers, but only 7 of 20 working-class speakers. In fact, 7 of the 20 working-class speakers actually decreased their use of the inflected future over real time (Suzanne Wagner, p.c., 20 Sept. 2011). Thus, what at first blush appears to be age grading is actually an effect of members of different groups of speakers changing their speech, but in opposite directions.

Because a panel was used for the Montreal study, it is relatively simple to contrast the change in real time for the feature (R) with the age grading noted by Thibault (1991) and Thibault & Daveluy (1989), who demonstrated that the choice of *alors* as a filler is a feature that middle class speakers 'catch' (as it were) as they reach their forties. In a panel study change in real time can be contrasted with age grading, change in apparent time, or stable sex or social status variation; however, in order to do this each speaker must be analysed individually.

Acoustic analysis of diphthongization and shift of the Montreal mid vowels among a different eight-speaker panel from the Montreal French corpus (Yaeger-Dror 1994, 1997, Sankoff & Blondeau 2007: 581), with analysis carried out on each speaker individually, demonstrated that the late adopters of change (like working-class men) were most likely to advance significantly toward the newer local norm well into middle age. The panel study of vowels also revealed that the only middle-class speaker interviewed both before and after retirement had shifted quite radically from the newer norm to a much more conservative Montreal vowel phonology by the later 1984 study.

Nahkola & Saanilahti (2004) carried out a study of Finnish with a panel study of adult speakers (born 1923–72) recorded in both 1986 and 1996, and sufficient older and younger speakers to permit more extensive trend analysis of variables. Mapping several changes, they found that categorical linguistic features generally remain stable, but if a feature is variable the balance shifts toward the newer variant during the speaker's years in the workforce. In fact, even those speakers who were in their sixties when first interviewed appeared to be advancing toward the newer norm during their seventies, despite (presumably) their retirement from the workforce. One might infer from this that the pattern of phonological change in progress is not cross-culturally uniform, but that panel corpora from each culture should be evaluated with no preconceived conclusions concerning expected patterns of change.

Such results demonstrate not only the utility of panel studies, but also the broader fact that one cannot simply analyse group means for these purposes. Rather, the only valid way to definitively analyse change in real time is to interview speakers in the same (or at least a very similar) social situation, and to compare each interview in a sample with the same speaker's own earlier interview (Thibault & Vincent 1990, Gregersen 2009, Gregersen & Barner-Rasmussen 2011). This provides results that cannot be obtained with analysis of change in apparent time, or even with a trend study of different speakers at two points in time.

Many small panel studies have been conducted using performance data, leading to what may feel like a growth industry in panel studies, at least in part because access to the longitudinal data which seems appropriate for panel studies is relatively simple to acquire from archival sources. Along these lines, Trudgill (1983) investigated the linguistic production of the Rolling Stones and Beatles using performance data from the 1960s and 1970s, finding that they altered their native pronunciation (apparently unconsciously) to permit a more US-centric phonology in songs, which, as their own popularity grew, was then jettisoned for a more British style. Yaeger-Dror (1993) found a similar pattern among Israeli Hebrew Mizrahi singers.

Van de Velde et al. (1996) obtained radio sound files for the same news or sports broadcasters in Belgium and the Netherlands over a long stretch of time, and demonstrated that changes take place even in the most careful broadcast media maintaining a fairly consistent style of speech, as well as in apparently less careful settings (like post-game euphoria). Similarly, Bowie (2005, 2010, 2011) has found that individuals show significant phonological variation over the course of their adult lives even in formal settings (in this case, religious sermons). Kemp & Yaeger-Dror (1991) showed that pre-election oratory for national figures also exhibits changing usage, though Yaeger-Dror & Hall-Lew (2002) analysed American political speeches and found considerable variation in syntactic constructions by speaker's region and interactive situation, but none attributable to change in real time. Harrington (2006, 2007, Harrington et al. 2000a,b, 2005) showed that even the short speech segments of the British Queen's Christmas messages from 1952 to 1960 and 1995 to 2002 provided evidence that the Queen's individual phonology has changed over time alongside changes in UK phonology more generally. In addition, Sankoff's (2005), Rhodes's (2011), and Poplack and Lealess's (2011) work on the 7 Up series corpus from the UK has showed that careful use of even small panels sources can be very useful.

Chambers & Trudgill's (1980) suggestion has borne fruit: those studies which compare interactions with speakers several years apart provide evidence of change in real time past adolescence and can clearly distinguish such change from age-grading. Of course, to carry out such studies requires particular forethought, with added permissions provided in forms approved by institutional review boards (or their equivalents), so that the authors can later return to the same speakers, not to mention the added funding needed for reinterviews, even before analysis can take place. *Ad hoc* panel studies can also be carried out using broadcast corpora (which, if they are already publicly available, sometimes require no human subjects review), but researchers have no control over their content. In any such study, though, the 'younger' and 'older' speakers must each be compared with their own speech rather than with that of the entire group, and recording situations should be as nearly identical as possible.

34.3 THE EFFECTS OF SECOND DIALECT EXPOSURE

Even before Chambers & Trudgill (1980) had suggested that more attention needed to be paid to linguistic changes as people age, some linguists had begun to compare the speech of those who move to a new speech community with the speech of more stable members of that community, to determine how speakers can change.

For example, Payne (1980) studied children of domestic immigrants into King of Prussia, an edge city outside Philadelphia, and found that while some changes were only acquired by the youngest children whose local variety was reinforced in the home, other changes were adopted not just by children, but even by teenagers. More recently, Kerswill (1996a) studied children growing up in 'new towns', and Chambers (1992, 1995) and Tagliamonte & Molfenter (2007) studied children who moved to dialect areas even more distinct from their parents', finding parallel results. Feagin (1990) found that an individual with strong motivation could shift toward a more r-ful norm after adolescence, then return to the older, Southern r-less norm when needed. Shockey (1984) carried out a panel study of Americans in the UK workforce, finding that, to varying extents, the speakers also adapted their /r/ to the UK standard. The work of Trudgill (1983) cited earlier can also be understood as adaptation of a speaker to a second dialect.

Similarly, Sankoff (2004, 2006), as mentioned above, took advantage of a British corpus that provided panel-like speech data for several speakers: a film series (the *Up Series*) by British filmmaker Michael Apted, who filmed interviews with 14 7-year-old children in 1963, and has reinterviewed those who were available and willing every seven years (1970, 1977, 1984 ...), with the most recent interviews conducted in 2012, when the participants were 56 years old. These interviews provided not just time depth, but also evidence of individual variation related to the participants' life trajectories. For example, Sankoff (2006) analysed phonological variation in the speech of two of the men as they went from ages 7 to 35; one of them was upwardly mobile, moving from rural youth to Oxford-trained physicist working in the US, while the other began as middle class, but didn't make it into a major university and became downwardly mobile. These are extreme cases, chosen to determine the extent to which people can alter their phonological systems in adolescence and young adulthood. Two vowels were isolated for the men: broad *a* and /ʊ/.

Sankoff found that broad *a* was stable because it was a salient marker of region (matching a prediction from Trudgill 1986), and the speakers were both positive about wanting to retain their local identity. On the other hand, non-split /ʊ/ was adapted to the changing circumstances of the speakers, by either remaining unsplit or splitting into two distinct units. Sankoff's findings can be compared with those of Shockey (1984), Prince (1988), Feagin (1990, 2003), and Yaeger-Dror (1993), who found that their adult speakers altered their phonology (specifically, r-fulness) depending on where they lived, and the degree to which their sense of identity conformed to the region they grew up in or to the region they moved to. None of these studies concluded that the adaptation in r-fulness was purely a product of 'exemplar dynamics', but rather that both the speakers' choice of community and their personal identity were more influential than would be possible if the critical period were operant.

These findings give solid evidence of adaptation past adolescence, especially since such adaptation has been found for both a simple alteration (the loss or reinsertion of *r*) and something more complex (a split into two lexically determined phonological units). This is particularly important given Payne's (1980) finding that lexically determined phonological differences are quite difficult even for young children—clearly, adults are able to adapt their linguistic behaviour in complicated ways, not just simple, straightforward ones.

34.4 CONCLUSIONS

Whether studies of real-time linguistic changes are carried out with data selectively gathered from library resources, from publicly available sound files, or with funding for the gathering of trend or panel corpora to follow up earlier analyses, like Hermann's (1929) follow-up on Gauchat's (1905) findings in Charmey (cf. D'Arcy, this volume), the overall conclusion is clear: it is necessary to consider the possibility of post-adolescent change when evaluating how any linguistic change takes place. The studies discussed in this chapter testify to the fact that historical linguistic analysis should attempt to incorporate a component which permits the comparison of a given speaker at multiple times so that apparent time evidence can be substantiated by real-time comparative data, since the evidence now shows that apparent time results are often ambiguous, since speakers shift linguistically throughout their lifespans (although see D'Arcy, this volume, for claims that there are limits on such change). Work collected in recent volumes (Fitzmaurice & Minkova 2008, Nevalainen & Fitzmaurice 2011) provides ample evidence that such studies can offer new insights.

In fact, even the material from Trudgill's (1988) reanalysis of Norwich, which involved trend rather than panel data, demonstrates how real time analysis reveals a wealth of possibilities which the original study had no inkling of. This is particularly notable given the conclusions of Yaeger-Dror (1994, 1997), Boberg (2004), and Sankoff & Blondeau (2007: 582, emphasis in original): 'to the extent that older speakers change in the direction of change in progress in their adult lives, apparent time UNDERESTIMATES the rate of change'—essentially, while apparent time results give an approximation of linguistic changes in a community, they do not give a complete picture of those changes.

The central question for this chapter was to draw attention to the ways in which historical studies can be enriched by attention to change in real time. The mere fact that research into language change can use changes in usage between two points in time implies that scribal variation by a single writer (within a single genre) can be used to investigate linguistic change. While such evidence has been employed in some earlier studies (Boyarin 1978, Steiner 2007, and see also Lass, this volume), historical linguists could certainly take greater advantage of the data available.

Of course, when obtaining real-time data, researchers must be sure that the method for gathering data does not taint the samples (Thibault & Vincent 1990, Gregersen & Barner-Rasmussen 2011). It is critical to attend to the social situation when gathering data, since it is well-known that social situation strongly influences stylistic variation. Many of the panel studies discussed here took pains to use situations as similar as possible to the initial interaction, but it always bears repeating that the goal in both trend and panel real-time studies must be to match rather than 'improve on' the initial interaction.

Clearly, in historical studies romantic letters cannot be compared with business correspondence or political essays (Nevalainen & Fitzmaurice 2011), just as synchronic studies must isolate political oratory from political debates or news interviews (Kemp & Yaeger-Dror 1991, Yaeger-Dror & Hall-Lew 2002). If there is contamination of the data in an apparent-time study, that contamination could hopefully have affected all of the data gathered equally, but if only one time point is contaminated in a real-time study, the data collected at different times is not actually comparable.

Given that caveat, though, there is certainly a need for study of linguistic changes in real time, using panels of speakers whenever possible. While studies of variation in linguistic behaviour among speakers of different ages have provided insight into the way communal linguistic behaviour shifts over time, changes made by a community are actually the result of a large number of individual linguistic (or scribal) choices. A better understanding of such changes made evident by appropriate comparisons would allow us to improve our study tactics, and would help us refine our methods so that some of the shortcomings of earlier studies could be corrected for, providing a more accurate and nuanced picture of linguistic change over time.

CHAPTER 35

....

HISTORICAL PHONOLOGY
AND KOINÉIZATION

....

DANIEL SCHREIER

35.1 INTRODUCTION

....

THIS chapter deals with the role of dialect contact in phonological change. It complements other chapters in this volume in that it considers change as a contact-induced
phenomenon, not only as an internal process (which many others in this volume focus
on; see for example Bermúdez-Otero, Bybee, Fox, Mailhammer et al., Ratliff, and Yu,
all this volume). The role of new-dialect formation (or koinéization, terms used interchangeably here) has not been prominently dealt with in the literature, at least until very
recently; it has either been discounted overtly (to quote Welmers 1970: 5, 'the established
principles of comparative and historical linguistics, and all we know about language history and language change, demand that ... we seek explanations first on the basis of
recognized processes of internal change'; Thomason & Kaufman 1988: 1) or simply been
ignored (in Lass's standard 1984 book on phonology, for instance, the driving force of
contact is given passing reference in the chapter on phonological change).

 The disregard for contact effects is still evident in modern textbooks on language
change, as for instance when Old English is described as one of the 'classic situations of
language birth in the historical linguistic tradition, dependent primarily on intergenerational, internally motivated change' (Jones & Singh 2005: 64), which presupposes
that there was an ongoing and uninterrupted transmission from continental varieties
upon transplantation to what is now England. Others, such as Baugh & Cable (1993: 49),
mention a possible contact history but downplay its effects ('The English language of
today is the language that has resulted from the history of the dialects spoken by the
Germanic tribes who came to England ... It is impossible to say how much the speech
of the Angles differed from that of the Saxons or that of the Jutes. The differences were
certainly slight'). Such views of phonological change as a predominantly internal process overlook findings by historical linguists, historians and archaeologists alike, who

have left no doubt at all that the contact scenario involved Saxon, Franconian, Jutish, Frankish, Hessian, Frisian and other varieties and have thus offered strong evidence that the genesis of Old English was shaped by extensive contact.

One can speculate at length as to why koinéization has not received the attention it should have; this will not be further explored here, but it is noteworthy that internal factors have been at the forefront of philology (and historical linguistics as well) for a long time and are thus part of the research canon, whereas contact linguistics (fuelled by research on pidgin and creole languages) has made progress only over the last 40 years or so. The goal of this chapter then is to gain some ground in redressing this imbalance, to offer perspectives of contact dialectology with regard to historical phonology and to illustrate its effects in varieties that have undergone extensive dialect contact (see also Eckman & Iverson, this volume, for some other recent results of research on language contact). I emphasize, however, that the aim is by no means to downplay the importance of internal effects, since these are of course inherent in language. Rather, I discuss questions such as: what are the mechanisms of koinéization and how does contact between distinct linguistic systems trigger phonological processes? How do new dialects come into being and in what way do they integrate features of multiple inputs?

By means of an illustration, I concentrate on a few showcase scenarios of dialect contact and new-dialect formation and outline the complex interplay of internal and external factors by drawing on examples from earlier stages of English, German, Veneto Italian and transplanted Dutch. I start with a general discussion of the processes involved and the most common mechanisms of koinéization.

35.2 Koinéization in a Nutshell

Koinéization occurs when several dialects are spoken in a mixed speech community that is in a state of prolonged contact, very often, though not necessarily, under *tabula rasa* conditions (Trudgill 1986). According to Siegel (1985: 375-6),

> Koinéization is the process which leads to the mixing of linguistic subsystems, that is, of language varieties which are either mutually intelligible or share the same genetically related superposed language. It occurs in the context of increased interaction or integration among speakers of these varieties.

Koinéization crucially involves contact between linguistic systems (e.g. dialects or sociolects of a language) with distinct, yet structurally related phonological systems. Children are crucial agents in new-dialect formation (Kerswill 1996a, 2001, Schreier 2012); purely in internal terms, they are facing the task of constructing new grammars in social circumstances of first dialect acquisition, a process characterized by diffuse heterogeneity and different inputs (Trudgill et al. 2000, Trudgill 2004). Crucially, these processes can only operate when the contact scenario is characterized by stability and when it persists for a few generations (though its exact length is disputed; some, e.g. Trudgill (1986), estimate about two generations after initial impact whereas others argue that it takes longer). This is why *nativization* (Thomason & Kaufman 1988, Mufwene 2001, Schneider 2007; further discussion below) is crucial. The crystallization of new phonological norms is a by-product of the stabilization of a new dialect, which in turn is the result of mixing processes by the first generation of native speakers of a developing koiné.

35.2.1 Feature Pool and Mixing

Several stages may operate when the conditions of contact and stabilization are met. First of all, all the coexisting variables feed into a *feature pool*. The total number of variants present in the contact scenario represents a pool out of which the first native speakers select features at an early stage of new-dialect formation (Mufwene 2001). It is crucial to emphasize that none of the input varieties 'wins out' at this stage; were this the case, then all but one variety present in the contact scenario would disappear without a trace and the newly developing variety would represent the equivalent of one of its inputs, as a result of which new-dialect formation simply fails to come into being. Riograndenser Hunsrückisch (RG), spoken in Southeast Brazil (Altenhofen 1996, Auer et al. 2005), would be no more than a transplanted (and systemically unchanged) variety of a Rhineland-Palatinate German dialect, Québec French the equivalent of a regional variety found in France, Australian English exported Cockney (as famously claimed by Hammarström 1980, 1985), etc. It can easily be shown that this is not the case. Dialects mix and interact as speakers accommodate to each other, which is why new-dialect formation is particularly strong when children grow up in a multi-dialectal environment. A first necessary process embryonic koinés have to undergo is *mixing*, which means that the inception phase of a new dialect must display mechanisms of feature selection and retention.

This seems little disputed. Blanc (1968) argues that Hebrew developed from 'a variety of literary dialects, several substrata, and several traditional pronunciations' (p. 238). The formation of modern Hebrew was characterized by extensive feature selection as a consequence of face-to-face accommodation: 'usage [of Israeli Hebrew] had to be established by a gradual and complex process of selection and accommodation which is, in part, still going on, but which now has reached some degree of stabilisation' (p. 239). Similarly, Ferguson (1959) examines the historical development of classical Arabic, arguing that it originated in the interaction of different dialects of Arabic with second language forms of Arabic: 'the [Arabic] koiné came into existence through a complex process of mutual borrowing and leveling among various dialects and not as a result of diffusion from one single source' (p. 619). This is further supported by Samarin (1971), who writes: 'what characterises [koinés] linguistically is the incorporation of features from several regional varieties of a single language' (p. 133).

Newfoundland English (NewfE) provides an excellent case in point. It formed from the seventeenth century onwards with substantial input from Ireland (Counties Wexford and Waterford) and Southwestern England. As Clarke (2004) and Hickey (2002) show, it has inherited features from both these varieties. Old-fashioned NewfE still has initial [v] for /f/ and [z] for /s/: 'a vine zummer' for 'a fine summer', an obvious legacy of Southwestern English English, and it also displays instability with regard to /h/, particularly in initial position (sometimes added before a vowel in stressed syllables ('helbow' for *elbow*), sometimes dropped ('eel' for *heel*)). On the other hand, it has features that can clearly be attributed to Irish English (IrE), to name but: [t, d] for /θ, ð/: 'tree of dem' for *three of them*; dental fricatives are usually replaced with voiced or voiceless dental and alveolar stops ([t] or [d]; Clarke 2004: 376); and clear and dark /l/ are not distinct, the latter being rare or even absent in some speakers (cf. Trudgill 1986: 129). On the other hand, NewfE is mainly rhotic, which may be assigned to both inputs.

Consequently, koinéization can only operate when contact between linguistic systems triggers feature selection processes from several co-existing varieties (Kerswill 2001), a complex process influenced by factors such as total number of features present, salience, stigma and prestige of individual variables, sociodemographic characteristics and social mobility, etc.

35.2.2 Levelling and Focusing

Fully-developed koinés, the end-product of so-called *focusing* (LePage & Tabouret-Keller 1985), thus adopt features from at least two (very often, more) donors. Put differently, a crystallizing contact-based variety combines a mixture of phonological features from several (or even all the) dialects present in the original contact situation. One of the challenges of contact dialectology is to find exactly which of the features are adopted and what criteria enhance their chances at the expense of others, which provides an interesting link with pidgin and creole linguistics (see Mufwene 2001).

This goes hand in hand with a second process involved in koinéization: *levelling*. Levelling has both a regional and a social dimension. We speak of regional dialect levelling when there is reduction in variation in the majority of dialects that coexist in a region (this has been investigated in e.g. southeast British English, Torgersen & Kerswill 2004). To complicate matters, the term levelling is also used in the context of dialect mixing in minorities that are spatially (cf. Milton Keynes in the late twentieth century, Kerswill & Williams 2000), or socially concentrated, for instance when there is a spread of standard forms or vernacular forms among literate minorities (Hernández-Campoy & Conde-Silvestre 2005). Levelling is thus a common process. Tendencies towards regularity and transparency are in some way language-inherent, yet they seem to be particularly common in contact situations. Variants disappear from a diffuse mixture situation as other features are permanently selected, and this is the direct consequence of levelling (Trudgill 1986, Siegel 1987, Britain 1997). The important question here, of course, is which features are most likely to undergo levelling and what reasons we can offer to account for why this should be so. Most would agree that criteria such as status (stigma or prestige of regional/social variants), social networks and sociodemographics as well as the frequency of the competing variants in the contact scenario are all important here. This explains why the surviving feature is usually the one found in the majority of inputs (Siegel 1987, Mesthrie 1993). Variants with the widest social and geographical distribution have the highest chances of surviving the selection process (Trudgill 1986) so that regionally or socially marked features are usually not maintained. This last point is stressed repeatedly:

> As a result of continued contact ... one gathers experience as to which idiosyncrasies of one's own dialect are ill-communicative, mis-communicative, or non-communicative, and accordingly, one starts to shed the hardened localisms in one's speech, allowing one's speech to conform to another's to an ever-growing extent.
>
> (Gambhir 1981: 191)

> The usual result of dialect mixture is the loss of untypical elements, particularly in pronunciation.
>
> (Turner 1994: 283)

The assumption here is that levelling has a communicative function with regard to some alleged 'typicality' of language features; this is not explicitly said but the nature of 'hardened localisms' or 'untypical elements' may in fact be driven by whether or not features are regionally or socially marked or stigmatized. Notwithstanding, all things equal, majority forms usually (but not necessarily) have the highest chances of surviving levelling mechanisms and of being selected when norms crystallize (Siegel 1987, Mesthrie 1993).

The case of New Zealand English (NZE) shows that phonological levelling processes are to a large part shaped by the overall proportions of transplanted dialects in the local input scenario. Schreier et al. (2003) analysed the maintenance of voiceless labiovelar /hw-/ fricatives (minimal pairs *Wales ~ whales, witch ~ which*) in three regions of New Zealand (Otago/Southland, Canterbury, and the North Island) and found considerable regional variation in early twentieth century NZE. Whereas New Zealanders from the North Island and Canterbury were predominantly using /w/ (so that the /hw/ ~ /w/ merger was practically completed by 1950), speakers from the Southland and Otago regions had high levels of /hw-/ well into the second half of the twentieth century (Table 35.1).

The regional distribution of the variable reflects population demographics and ancestral effects, particularly the total input strength of /hw-/ retaining donor dialects. The strong presence of /hw-/ in the Otago/Southland dialect region was explained by high input frequency and the disproportionally high input of Scottish settlers, who made a distinction between /hw-/ and /w-/. In the other regions, however, /hw-/ was not adopted, simply because the social configuration and the local contact and mixture situations were different. The inputs were mainly from the South of England, where /hw-/ was a minority feature, and this enhanced levelling-out in the local forms of NZE. A high overall presence of /hw-/ variants in the Scottish inputs to the Southland/Otago regions

Table 35.1 /hw- ~ w-/ variation in early
20th century New Zealand English

	/hw/	/w/	percent /hw/
Southland	441	666	40.0% (441/1107)
Canterbury	51	596	7.9% (51/647)
North	21	369	5.4% (21/390)

thus had an enhancing effect on the adoption of /hw-/; the impact was so strong that disfavouring factors such as strong regional markedness were overridden (see above).

Levelling may also operate on a nationwide scale. The major Southern Hemisphere English (SHemE) varieties are presently characterized by extreme geographic uniformity (Bernard 1989: 255, Gordon & Deverson 1998: 126), though they developed out of inputs that were regionally diverse and sociolinguistically distinct (Australian English (AusE), for instance, had input from Irish English (IrE) and Southeastern English English (EnglE)). The lack of regional variation in AusE and NZE is unusual and has been commented on frequently:

> [T]he overall picture [of Australia] must remain one of a continent across whose vast reaches there is comparatively little variation.
>
> (Collins & Blair 2001: 9)

> [T]he English of New Zealand is more noted for its uniformity than for its regional dialects. For whatever reason (and this might be grounds for a great deal of speculation) the regional dialects of the immigrants have not obviously given rise to corresponding regional dialects in New Zealand.
>
> (Bauer 2000: 41)

This attests to the scale of levelling; under certain conditions, it can lead to a lack of regional variation on a national level (which, however, may be subject to change and be indicative of the evolutionary path of transplanted varieties; Schneider 2007).

35.2.3 Reallocation

An important point to consider is that the selection chances of features are not necessarily a matter of frequency. Majority features do not necessarily win out, so that a purely deterministic sociodemographically-based approach (as embraced by Trudgill 2004) fails to grasp the complexity of this process. For instance, multiple variants may survive the mixing and levelling stages and (initial) variability is not eliminated at all. In the words of Britain & Trudgill (1999: 247), 'it is not always necessarily the case that the final outcome of the reduction process will be a single victorious variant. In some cases, even after koinéization, a number of competing variants left over from an original mixture may survive'. Though it is debated how often multiple selection occurs, minority forms may under certain conditions be adopted as well, often side by side with majority ones. Following Trudgill (1986), this is usually referred to as *reallocation*, defined as follows: 'Reallocation occurs when two or more variants in the dialect mix survive the leveling process but are refunctionalized, evolving new social or linguistic functions in the new dialect' (Britain & Trudgill 1999: 245).

Domingue (1981) demonstrates multiple selection of variants in her study of Mauritius Bhojpuri (MB), where the total number of coexisting variants had not been reduced at all. In other words, the levelling of regional variants from the input varieties (Indian Bhojpuri is classified into the four subgroups: eastern, western, central and Nagpurian) simply did not take place. Domingue adopted a social explanation for the maintenance of complexity and lack of regularization/levelling (discussion in Trudgill 1986). On Mauritius, more than half of the local population (approximately one million) are native speakers of Bhojpuri/Hindi, but MB differs markedly from Indian varieties of Bhojpuri for several reasons (e.g. contact with other languages, such as a French-based Mauritian Creole). Dialect mixture of the original inputs was so extensive that present-day MB is comparatively homogeneous, with little regional variation (just like the major SHemE varieties, see below). The explanation offered by Domingue was that when MB formed, formerly regional variants were reanalysed as social and stylistic (rather than regional) indicators. If a newly developing colony undergoes social stratification, she argued, then variability from the original mixture situation may be maintained, not as an expression of geographical origins, but of group membership or affiliation to a social class. Reallocation, therefore, refers to the retention and reanalysis of regionally–or socially-marked features from the inputs and to the functional specialization and redistribution of multiple features, either as social or stylistic variants, or as phonological variants in complementary environments. As a consequence, features from different inputs can also undergo a function change and be reanalysed to express regional, social or stylistic variation.

Britain's research on English Fens English (EFE) has provided ample evidence of reallocation. This area, located in the Wash, some 130 kilometers north of London, separates the East Midlands from Norfolk and has an extensive history of dialect contact. Until reclaimed in the mid-seventeenth century, it was largely inaccessible and uninhabitable. As soon as the bogs and marshes had been drained, however, it attracted settlers from rural Norfolk and Suffolk as well as from the Midlands. Dialect contact between Midland and East Anglian English (EAE) gave rise to a distinctive local variety that formed in the seventeenth and eighteenth centuries (Britain 1991). Today, EFE is increasingly influenced by a supra-regionalizing form of London English, a trend that has accelerated due to the concerted planning of New Towns and London 'overspill' developments. With regard to feature selection, Britain (1997) reported that several input features were adopted upon dialect contact in the Fens. Phonological reallocation manifested itself by the fact that EFE has both central and fully open onsets of PRICE diphthongs. The two features were present in roughly similar proportions in the inputs and underwent specialization, so that they are now exclusively conditioned by phonological environment (central onsets adopted for pre-voiceless environments and open onsets elsewhere; in other words, the pattern also known as 'Canadian Raising', Chambers 1973).

Britain & Trudgill (1999) developed this further and suggested a typology of real-location with two subtypes. The first, *socio-stylistic reallocation*, refers to the refunc-tionalization of formerly regional variants into social or stylistic ones, as illustrated by Domingue's work on MB (see above). Another example comes from AusE, where words such as *dance, advantage*, or *chance* take the short TRAP vowel (/æ/) rather than DANCE (/ɑː/). Britain & Trudgill (1999) explain this as simultaneous adoption of southern and northern features of EnglE. At the time Australia was established in the late eighteenth century, the DANCE vowel was more frequent for this set of words in the south whereas TRAP was common in the north. Even though AusE bears a striking resemblance with southern EnglE (in that it is non-rhotic, has six short vowels rather than five, etc.), this is a case where both northern and southern variants survived the leveling process, simply because they were reanalysed into social and stylistic variants, /æ/ having lower social status than /ɑː/. *Phonological reallocation*, on the other hand, refers to the refunction-alization of regional variants into allophonic ones (as illustrated by the adoption of two onsets of PRICE in EFE; see above). Trudgill (1986) offers a similar explanation for the origin of Canadian Raising itself (Chambers 1973), where onsets of PRICE are centralized in pre-voiceless environments (*night, write*, etc.) and open in other contexts. Diphthongs with central onsets were a legacy of Scottish inputs to Canadian English (CanE), whereas [ai] was adopted from southern EngE dialects. The adoption of both allophones is the consequence of specialization and language-internal conditioning, since they were 'real-located a new function as positional allophonic variants' (Britain & Trudgill 1999: 251).

35.2.4 Simplification

Another process involved is what some have called *simplification* (e.g. Trudgill 1986), which may be alternatively considered as a manifestation of *regularization* (or perhaps also as *analogical change*, see Fertig this volume). This term is problematic (Schreier 2008), since it insinuates (misleadingly, in my view) that the outcome of new-dialect formation is necessarily 'simpler' than what is found in the corresponding inputs. From a different point of view, one might claim that a phonological feature X displays less vari-ation in a koiné than in the input varieties, which means one necessarily has to integrate principles of variationist sociolinguistics. As Siegel (1987: 14) points out, simplification is not well understood and should be investigated quantitatively rather than qualita-tively (i.e. we should adopt a variationist perspective to trace a putative decrease in vari-ability). Simplification should be investigated as a diachronic process, i.e. with reference to earlier evolutionary phases of a variety (or, if possible at all, of the input varieties). This problem is also recognized by Britain (1997: 141), who states that simplification represents 'an increase in grammatical regularity and decrease in formal complexity.' Similarly, Mühlhäusler (1997: 236) claims that

> Simplification only refers to the form of the rules in which a language is encoded, indicating optimalisation of existing rules and the development of regularities for formerly irregular aspects, for example, grammaticalisation of the lexicon.

Simplification is a dynamic concept. It expresses the fact that *as one moves along a developmental continuum, more and more regularities appear.* (Emphasis added, DS)

A good example of phonological regularization comes from devoicing of intervocalic alveolar plosives in Afrikaans (Booij 2002b). In Dutch, final voiceless plosives (such as [t]) can alternate with voiced equivalents in intervocalic environments due to final devoicing:

$$/d/ \rightarrow [t] / \_\#$$

Dutch plural formation commonly involves the affixation of an *-en* marker which changes the phonological environment from /-VC#/ to /-VCV#/. If a singular form ends in /t/, or other voiceless obstruent, then the corresponding plural form maintains it. A voiced morpheme-final obstruent such as /d/, however, only surfaces in the plural, and is devoiced in the singular, giving alternations like: *hoed* [hut] 'hat', *hoeden* ['hudə]. Afrikaans, in contrast, has regularized this situation so that the phonological environment has no effect on the alveolar plosive: *hoed* [hut] 'hat', *hoeden* ['hutə], *stad* [stat] 'city', *statten* ['statə] (Table 35.2). Afrikaans is thus more regular than its ancestral variety of Dutch in that it has reduced the number of phonological rules and does not have phonological alternations in this environment (see also Eckman & Iverson, this volume, on L2 phonology and sound change). It is thus phonologically more regular than its ancestor Dutch (or, if one wants to subscribe to simplification, 'simpler'). Of course, it would be simplistic to assume that this is solely explained by dialect contact and koinéization, since language contact was at work as well (see the claim that contact linguistics is inherently 'messy', Schreier 2008; I thank Patrick Honeybone for reminding me of this).

35.2.5 Interdialect Forms

The final process discussed here deals with dialect interaction and the potential for development of 'new' features. The process of new-dialect formation does not only involve picking and mixing, and feature selection and retention are not the only mechanisms to

Table 35.2 Phonological regularization in Afrikaans

		singular	plural
Dutch	/d/ → [t] /__#	hoed [hut] 'hat' stad [stat] 'city' smit [smɪt] 'smith'	hoeden ['hudə] steden ['steːdə] smeden ['smeːdə]
Afrikaans	[no rule]	hoed [hut] 'hat' stad [stat] 'city' smit [smɪt] 'smith'	hoeden ['hutə] statten ['statə] smitten ['smɪtə]

operate in long-term contact situations. New dialects affiliate with their inputs by drawing a vast number of features from them, but it would be simplistic to assume that they are linguistically predetermined by the systemic properties (and the frequency thereof!) of the varieties in contact. Contact-derived dialects are not mixed, levelled and regularized varieties that select *all* their phonological and structural properties from their donors. Furthermore, we must account for the fact that 'contact between two [or more] dialects leads to the development of forms that actually originally occurred in neither dialect' (Trudgill 1986: 62). The role of accommodation is crucial here. Obviously, independent developments are most likely to occur when accommodation has not gone to completion, i.e. when a feature from an original input is not adopted in its original form.

An additional outcome of dialect contact is that variants appear that are absent from any of the input varieties, so-called 'interdialect' variants 'not actually present in any of the dialects contributing to the mixture but [which] arise out of interaction between them' (Trudgill et al. 2003: 106). Whereas semi-rhoticity in JamE can be explained as incomplete accommodation to a feature *present* in the inputs (Schreier 2008), dialect interaction may also give rise to features unattested in the donors. The case of Veneziano or Common Veneto (CoV), the contact dialect that developed in Venice in the late Middle Ages, provides a good example. CoV was formed when Venice urbanized and became an economic and political centre in the fourteenth century; there was massive immigration from the rural hinterlands of the Veneto as well as from northeastern and mid-central Italy. Koinéization that gave rise to CoV is 'best viewed as a more-or-less stable process by which mainland speakers have divested, or are divesting, their speech of its most markedly local, usually rural features in the direction of urban Venetian' (Ferguson 2003: 450). Ferguson (2003) analysed inter–and intra-textual variability in various *scripta* produced between the twelfth and fifteenth centuries, i.e. official, legal, mercantile, epistolary and literary documents, which present the earliest evidence of the variety. He found that the documents 'displayed exceptional levels of variability' (p. 457), which is typical for an early stage of new-dialect formation (prior to focusing). Ferguson analysed a corpus of court proceedings and found strong evidence of dialect mixing ('rather than the reflex of a single mainland type, we seem to be in the presence of a stable koiné with diverse, mainly northern, inputs'; p. 458). Of particular importance is the fact that he found interdialect forms that were not attested in any of the donor dialects. Nouns with an *-arium* suffix in Latin (*herbarium, aquarium*, etc.) took *-er* in northern dialects of the time and *-aro* in central-southern ones.

Several scribes had intermediate writings, combining both forms into a new spelling *-ero*, which was unprecedented and did not occur in any of the inputs (see Table 35.3). This may be interpreted as either a morphosyntactic or a phonological phenomenon (or as both), since two suffixes with distinct roots are combined into an unprecedented morpheme. Crucially, Ferguson found the very same interdialect form in other corpora, which indicates that this interdialect variant made an appearance elsewhere and was by no means idiosyncratic (though it did not survive when CoV formed).

Trudgill (1986), finally, distinguishes between two types of interdialectalisms. First, features that are intermediate between the original dialect forms and thus indicative

Table 35.3 Interdialect forms in fourteenth century Common Veneto

		Interdialect form
Lat. -*arium*	Variant 1: -*er* (northern)	-*ero*
	Variant 2: -*aro* (central-south)	

of incomplete, faulty or simply 'intermediate' accommodation (such as -*ero* suffixes in fourteenth century CoV); and second, forms that originate in *over-generalization* or *hyper-adaptation* (perhaps the most well-known case here is hyper-correction, which occurs when speakers misinterpret and incorrectly generalize rules by applying them to inappropriate contexts, e.g. when a learner of English inappropriately applies the CUP or BATH vowel in words that take TRAP, e.g. *grand* or *cancer*).

35.3 SOME ILLUSTRATIVE CASES

Koinéization has been discussed in a number of varieties around the world, such as transplanted varieties of Hindi (Siegel 1987), Bhojpuri (Domingue 1981), English (particularly in England, Britain 1991, Kerswill 1996a, and New Zealand, Gordon et al. 2004) and Spanish (Tuten 2003). This allows for comparisons and cross-evaluations of dialect contact, which may eventually lead to a more unified and coherent theory of koinéization as a general, language-independent process (Schreier 2008). In the following, I would like to focus on two processes of phonological change via contact between dialects, namely on the Northern Cities Shift (NCS) in North America as well as the formation of Tristan da Cunha English (TdCE) in the early nineteenth century. These are not by any means more representative or more suitable than any of the above-mentioned varieties that have been subject to research.

35.3.1 The Northern Cities Shift

The NCS, researched by Labov and associates since the 1970s (see Labov 1994, Labov et al. 2006, and also Gordon, this volume) involves a more or less clockwise rotation movement of six vowels. It was triggered by the raising and breaking of the TRAP vowel, which must have started in the first half of the twentieth century. TRAP raising was followed by a fronting of LOT and a subsequent lowering of CAUGHT. Moreover, DRESS

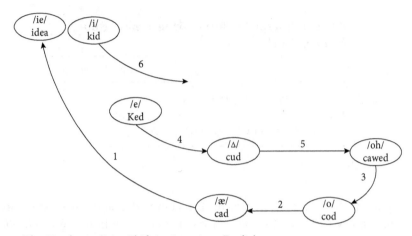

FIG. 35.1 The Northern Cities Shift in American English.

was centralized, STRUT underwent backing and KIT lowered and centralized as well (Figure 35.1).

The NCS is perhaps the best-documented and most widely discussed phonological change in present-day English (see Labov 1994 for its relevance for principles of phonological change or Gordon 2001 on its ramifications for mergers and splits and chain shifts in general; and see also Gordon and D'Arcy, this volume). Whereas the teleology of this pattern, along with its internal conditioning factors, has received much attention in the literature, it is not until recently that the discussion has turned to its possible origins and explanation. Importantly, Labov (2008, 2010; also Gordon 2011) has argued that the motivation of the NCS may in origin be a contact phenomenon and be linked to American dialectology in general, or better: to dialect contact. It is important to bear in mind that regional variation in North America patterns along horizontal dialect boundary lines (Carver 1987), in contrast to Spain, where these are vertical (Tuten 2003). This is explained by population movements, which in North America diffused westward once settlements were established along the Atlantic seaboard (which is a major factor when it comes to explaining why regional variation decreases from east to west, levelling having been more extensive and forceful). As a consequence, American English (AmE) provides a paradigm of dialect mixing and homogenization, since dialect boundaries are more or less clearcut in the east and rather fluid in the west, which goes back to intensified levelling during the colonization phase of the mid-West and West (Trudgill 1986, 2004).

The Great Lakes area received an input stream of settlers from New England and New York (the city and upstate), particularly after the Erie Canal was established in 1825. The so-called New England Stream (Kniffen & Glassie 1966) fanned out into northern Pennsylvania, Ohio, Michigan, Illinois and Wisconsin, the States adjacent to the Great Lakes, and then further into Oklahoma, the Dakotas and beyond. The population effects on the area were immense by any means. With two exceptions (Binghamton and

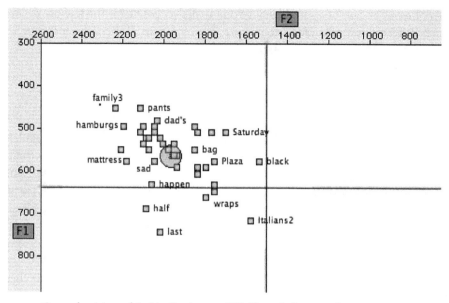

FIG. 35.2 General raising of /æ/ in Rochester, NY. (from Labov 1994)

Elmira), every major city in New York State falls along the trade route established by the Erie Canal, from New York City to Albany, through Schenectady, Utica and Syracuse, to Rochester and Buffalo. Nearly 80% of the present-day population of upstate New York lives within 25 miles of the Erie Canal. The regions of origin of the settlers can be placed to Western and Southwest New England, Boston and Massachusetts, and the Atlantic area of New York State. With focus on raising and breaking of the TRAP vowel (which provided the starting-point for the NCS), Labov (2008, 2010) argues that the settlers had four competing systems, namely:

1. the nasal system from Western New England, in which short-a is raised before nasals and only before nasals;
2. the Boston system, in which an irregular number of broad-a words are realized in low central position;
3. the continuous system found in southwest New England and elsewhere, in which the degree of raising of short-a depends on a wide variety of phonetic conditions;
4. and the split short-a system of New York City, in which tensing and raising is dependent on a complex of phonetic, grammatical and lexical conditions (cf. Figure 35.2).

Today variation in the TRAP vowel is no longer subject to internal constraints (particularly following environment) as it used to be, and dialect contact was a driving force in this development.

Another clear case of a sound change due to dialect contact is the low-back merger, which diffuses westward (see Labov 1994: 95-6), and is now common through the Western United States (Labov et al. 2006).

35.3.2 Koinéization on Tristan da Cunha

Tristan da Cunha English (TdCE) provides a second illustrative case of population movement effects on new-dialect formation and historical phonology. The formation of TdCE in the early to mid-nineteenth century resembles NZE to some extent, namely in that there was predominantly dialect contact (in this case between varieties of British, South African and American English). On the other hand, it shows how complex and intricately interwoven contact-induced change mechanisms are and how little it takes to alter the trajectory path of overseas varieties, particularly when they develop in small, stable and locally confined founding populations.

To start with the socio-historical background: the island of Tristan da Cunha lies in the South Atlantic Ocean, some 2,300 kilometers south of St Helena, 2,800 kilometers west of Cape Town, and about 3,400 kilometers east of Uruguay, with a current population of 285. Originally discovered by the Portuguese admiral Tristão da Cunha (in 1506), it soon attracted the interest of the English and Dutch, the Dutch being the first to effect a landing (in 1643). However, none of the colonial powers developed an interest in establishing a permanent colony on the island. Things changed when, towards the end of the eighteenth century, the American fishing and whaling industry expanded to the South Atlantic Ocean and Tristan da Cunha served as an occasional resort to the sealers and whalers (Brander 1940). The growing economic interest and strategic position along a major sea-route soon attracted discoverers, pirates and adventurers. The island was officially settled in 1816, when the British admiralty formally annexed Ascension Island and Tristan da Cunha, apparently with the intention of blocking a possible escape route for Napoleon, who at the time was exiled on the island of St Helena (Schreier & Lavarello-Schreier 2003). A military garrison was dispatched to the island, withdrawing after only one year. Some army personnel stayed behind with the intention of settling permanently: two stonemasons from Plymouth (Samuel Burnell and John Nankivel), a non-commissioned officer from Kelso, Scotland, named William Glass, his wife, 'the daughter of a Boer Dutchman' (Evans 1994: 245), and their two children.

The population increased when shipwrecked sailors and castaways arrived; some of them stayed behind and added to the permanent population. In 1824, apart from the Glass family, the settlers included Richard 'Old Dick' Riley (from Wapping, East London), Thomas Swain (born in Hastings, Sussex) and Alexander Cotton (from Hull/Yorkshire), who had arrived in the early 1820s (Earle 1966 [1832]). The late 1820s and 1830s saw the arrival of a group of women from St Helena and three settlers from Denmark and the Netherlands. The population grew rapidly and by 1832 there was a total of 34 people on the island, 22 of whom were young children. The 1830s and 1840s saw a renaissance of the whaling industry and numerous ships called at Tristan da

Cunha to barter for fresh water and supplies; this led to the arrival of American whalers, some of whom settled permanently.

The second half of the nineteenth century was a period of growing isolation, for a number of political and economic reasons. The whale trade declined quickly, the increasing use of steam ships made bartering unnecessary, and the opening of the Suez Canal in 1869 drastically reduced the number of ships in the South Atlantic Ocean. This affected the influx of settlers and a weaver from Yorkshire (Crawford 1945) and two Italian sailors were the only new arrivals in the second half of the century (Crabb 1980). The state of self-sufficiency and isolation lasted well into the twentieth century. When visiting the island in 1937, the Norwegian sociologist Peter Munch found that the Tristanians had not partaken in the massive changes that had occurred in the Western world (Munch 1945) and noted that they basically lived in non-industrialized conditions. This situation came to an abrupt end in April 1942, when the British admiralty ordered the installation of a naval station on Tristan da Cunha. The arrival of the navy corps entailed far-reaching economic changes and a South African company obtained exclusive rights to establish a permanent fishing industry on the island, employing practically the entire local workforce. The traditional subsistence economy was replaced by a paid labour force economy, and the traditional way of life was modified as a result of the creation of permanent jobs with regular working hours. Tristan da Cunha was an economic boomtown in the 1950s: the living conditions and housing standards improved and the changes brought about by the development scheme led to a complete transformation of the traditional Tristanian way of life within one generation. These social changes had linguistic consequences as local dialect features eroded due to accommodation to and adoption of outside norms (Schreier 2002, 2003).

In October 1961, unforeseen volcanic activities forced a wholesale evacuation of the entire population. The Tristanians had to leave the island and were transported to England; virtually all of them returned from their exile to the South Atlantic in 1963. The dramatic evacuation and the two 'volcano years' in England affected the islanders more than any other single event in the history of the community and led to quick modernization and adaptation to Western culture. A new fishing company provided all the households with electricity; this improved the living conditions considerably and the 1970s and 1980s were a period of economic prosperity again, which led to an increase in mobility (mostly for secondary education and further job training) and a quick opening-up of the community.

The evolution of TdCE is a showcase scenario of koinéization and historical phonology. There was no contact with indigenous varieties since the island was uninhabited when the garrison arrived. As a result, present-day TdCE formed via contact of the inputs, to which we can hypothetically trace its features, and due to contact of which interdialect forms may have occurred. The following questions are relevant here: how did the settlement history and population dynamics shape the development of a local indigenous variety, and exactly what is the sociolinguistic status of TdCE as an overseas variety of English? As Zettersten (1969) points out, it is absolutely crucial that there was no indigenous population when the island was colonized. Consequently, the community's founders found themselves in *tabula rasa* conditions and did not come into contact with pre-existing language varieties (a major difference to practically all locales in the Caribbean, Africa and Asia). The English input varieties to TdCE were dialects from the British Isles (the founders came from the Scottish Lowlands, East Yorkshire, East London and Hastings), the United States (from the New England area; Captain Andrew Hagan, the most influential American resident, was a native of New London, Massachusetts) and from St Helena. However, TdCE did not form via koinéi-zation alone; we must also take admixture from L2 forms into account since the first languages of the non-British settlers were Afrikaans, Danish, Dutch, and Italian. Several kinds of linguistic contact thus operated during the genesis and formation periods of TdCE, as the following varieties of English were transplanted to the island: British and American English (which led to koinéization), second language (L2) forms of English (as spoken by the settlers from Denmark, the Netherlands and Italy), and St Helenian English (StHE), which emerged in the context of intense language contact involving English, various African and Asian languages and Malagasy (Schreier 2008). Some (e.g. Hancock 1991) have suggested that StHE may have undergone creolization, so that it is structurally similar to English-based creoles in the North Atlantic. This cannot be alto-gether substantiated but there are some parallels indeed (particularly in morphosyntax); these are of high diagnostic value since there were no sociodemographic connections between St Helena and the Caribbean (see Schreier 2008), excluding the possibility of direct transmission.

As for TdCE, this variety primarily derives from varieties of British/late eighteenth century American English and StHE, which served as the most important donors to this variety, and it can be excluded that TdCE emerged in a context of *prima facie* language contact. There is first-hand evidence that all the Tristan settlers had at least some knowl-edge of English (for instance, a visiting Captain described the English of the Dutch set-tler as 'excellent', quoted in Brander 1940: 157, cf. also Earle 1832, Taylor 1856), which excludes pidginization and creolization effects on Tristan da Cunha and reinforces the impact of koinéization. On the other hand, L2 forms had an impact on TdCE and several non-native features were adopted when the local variety nativized (TH sibilization, i.e. dental fricatives realized as [s], as in *think, th*row, etc.).

The existence of Creole-type features in TdCE (such as extremely high rates of con-sonant cluster reduction and absence of *-ed* past tense marking, Schreier 2005: 152; /v/ realised as [b]; lack of word order inversion in questions; copula absence; etc.) can only mean that a creolized form of English was transplanted via (at least some of) the women who cross-migrated in the 1820s. The women had some proficiency in English (Taylor 1856 reports that no other languages were spoken on Tristan in 1851) and they most likely spoke a (perhaps mesolectal) English-based Creole, so that these features were adopted by the first generations of native Tristanians. Zettersten (1969: 134–5) reaches a simi-lar conclusion when stating that 'the speech-habits of the settlers from St. Helena may have contributed towards simplifying the inflectional structures of the Tristan dialect.' Similarly, Cassidy (1974: 176), in his review of Zettersten (1969), states that TdCE 'did not develop its pidgin-creole as Pitcairn did, but appears to have imported many common creole features'. Processes of admixture and creole contact have been documented in other varieties of English around the world, and simplification as a result of extensive contact with a regularized or simplified variety is found in Afrikaans (Roberge 2002; see above) or Singapore English (Platt 1975). Thus, TdCE emerged in a context of dialect contact, yet witnessed admixture with an English derived creole variety and had at the same time some input of ESL and learner varieties of English, which represents a complex development history that is typical of most of the overseas varieties we know of. Table 35.4 lists the origins of features as attested in present-day TdCE, illustrating the complexity of feature selection.

   Of course, the ancestral attestations are by no means exclusive and for some features it is most likely that they appeared in several inputs to TdCE. Multiple origins make it more difficult to pinpoint ancestry but, following Siegel (1987) and Mesthrie (1993), this may well have enhanced their chances of permanent adoption.

35.4 CONCLUSION

Koinéization is a sociolinguistic corollary of populations on the move and has thus a very long history; dialect contact, along with mixing, regularization and levelling, has in all likelihood been a vehicle of external language change for thousands of years. English, for instance, has had an extensive contact history ever since its beginnings in the fifth century (see discussion in Hundt & Schreier 2013), and so dialect contact (and koinéization) has been an important mechanism in externally-induced change here. Similar processes are attested in countless (post-)colonial settings around the world (involving German, Spanish, French, etc.). Though the line between language contact and dialect contact is difficult to draw at times (as witnessed in the much-debated question as to whether Old English and Old Norse were mutually intelligible dialects or not), mechanisms of new-dialect formation have been at work at all stages in the evolution, not only of English but also in German, French, Spanish, etc., both in their home territories

Table 35.4 Origins of present-day features in TdCE

Origin	Feature	Process involved
British Isles/New England	FOOT-STRUT split, slight STRUT fronting, T glottaling, /hw—w/ merger, THOUGHT in the set of *cloth*, diphthonging of GOAT, fronting of nucleus of MOUTH, non-rhoticity, START in *last, dance*, backing of START, TH fronting, glottalization of intervocalic /p, k/	Koinéization
St Helena	/k/ as uvular [q], merger of /v/ with /b/, TH-stopping, highly advanced consonant cluster reduction	Contact with a restructured creole-like variety

(as a result of migration) and perhaps more strongly in overseas offspring varieties. The impact of dialect contact on historical phonology has been studied for languages such as medieval Spanish (Tuten 2003), English (Trudgill 2004) or German (Auer, Arnhold, & Bueno Aniola 2005), and mixing and levelling have been attested for each of these varieties, often also in the context of 'colonial lag' (Görlach 1987, see Schreier 2009 for a discussion of the allegedly conservative character of transplanted varieties). As a consequence, the historical analysis of phonological change can only benefit from including effects of koinéization. These offer vital information on the contact histories of the varieties scrutinized; they allow for detailed cross-comparisons of processes in varieties with distinct sociolinguistic backgrounds and differing contact histories. As a consequence, they throw light on a major mechanism of sound change (contact between structurally related linguistic systems) and at the same time further our understanding of processes such as leveling in different languages, which deserve to be explored in more detail.

CHAPTER 36

....

SECOND LANGUAGE ACQUISITION AND PHONOLOGICAL CHANGE

....

FRED R. ECKMAN AND GREGORY K. IVERSON

36.1 INTRODUCTION

....

THE defining role played by language contact in historical change has long been recognized, particularly in comparative sociolinguistics and in the study of lexical borrowing and of pidginization and the emergence of creoles (Sankoff 2001, Hickey 2010, and see also Schreier, this volume, for the role of contact in new-dialect formation). Other contributions to this volume lay out the influences on historical change that can be attributed to first language acquisition (compare Foulkes & Vihman and Dresher) and synchronic language variation (D'Arcy, Jones), and several address the relationship between phonetics and phonology in historical change (Dresher, Purnell, & Raimy, Hale et al., Kiparsky in the generative paradigm; Bybee, Phillips, Yu more in the exemplar tradition). But in the study of sound systems, it is also appreciated that one language can exert influence on another, as inferred, for example, with respect to the history of Dutch in its shift from a Germanic-type language contrasting voiceless aspirated with weakly voiced stops over to a Romance-type contrasting voiceless unaspirated with prominently voiced stops (Iverson & Salmons 2003, 2008). Modern work in second language (L2) acquisition, with parallels in the phonology of loanword adaptation (Uffmann, this volume), reveals just how close contact with a second language can affect these phonetic changes in a speaker's native language, e.g. shifted voice-onset-time values in Dutch that is influenced by English (Simon 2011), or in English that is influenced by Korean (Chang 2010a,b), French (Flege 2007), Portuguese (Sancier & Fowler 1997) or Spanish (Lord 2008).

At the phonemic level, borrowed pronunciations may induce allophonic splits, as in the often cited (if controversial, see Minkova 2011, and also Salmons & Honeybone, this volume) separation of voiced from voiceless fricatives in the history of French-influenced English, allowing now *veal* (French borrowing) alongside *fox* (native Germanic). In earlier English, voiced fricatives occurred only as allophonic variants (intervocalically, and, at some point, initially in typically unstressed words) of phonemes which were otherwise voiceless, as reflected in modern English relict distributions favouring voiceless initial (*thick*) and final fricatives (*bath*) but voiced medials (*mother, brother*), along with voiced initials in unstressed minor classes (*this, there, thou*). As French all along contrasted voiced (*vin* 'wine') with voiceless fricatives (*fin* 'end'), its status as a prestige L2 in England following the Norman Conquest presumably facilitated the extension of this pattern to native English as well. In other cases, the split of native language allophones into independent phonemes is progressive, leaving subtle traces to be uncovered in analysis of the patterns of second language phonology. We illustrate this patterning with respect to the staged acquisition of the English /s/-/ʃ/ contrast by adult native speakers of Korean *vs* Japanese. Both of these languages deflect [s] in favour of [ʃ] before the high vowel [i], but the L2 contrast between the two fricatives emerges in proportion to the degree that [ʃ] occurs in other contexts in the learner's native language. If we view the acquisition of an L2 as a series of changes in the learner's internalized grammar of the target language, i.e. in the interlanguage (IL) grammar, then the mechanisms of L2 acquisition can be shown to both parallel and inform the process of historical change in phonology.

This chapter is structured as follows. The background section defines the construct 'interlanguage' and motivates the hypothesis that IL grammars obey the same linguistic principles as primary languages. This is followed first by a characterization of L2 phonetic influences on the L1, then of phonological effects as exemplified by the different acquisition patterns of the English /s/-/ʃ/ contrast by native speakers of Korean and Japanese. The chapter concludes with a discussion of implications for historical change in phonology.

36.2 Background

The field of L2 phonology seeks to explain the pronunciation patterns of adult language learners and to understand why these patterns are generally different from those of child learners. One of the most straightforward hypotheses addressing this question, the contrastive analysis hypothesis (Lado 1957), claimed that the divergent L2 phonological patterns could be explained on the basis of the differences between the learner's native language and the target language. Over the decades, empirical tests of this hypothesis have uncovered numerous instances in which the claims were not supported, largely because the L2 pronunciation patterns could not be attributed to differences between the native and the target languages, and, in a number of cases, were independent of both. This kind of data supported the postulation that L2 learners internalized a mental system, their own version of a grammar of the target language, that enabled them to produce and understand utterances in that language. This learner-language system was termed an interlanguage (Selinker 1972). The most compelling kind of evidence for the necessity of hypothesizing an IL is a pattern of L2 utterances that is not attributable to the native language (because it does not exhibit this pattern) nor to input from the target language (which also does not evince the pattern).

In the present context, there are two significant implications of the concept of interlanguage for second language phonology. The first is that the research programme in second language acquisition theory changed from trying to predict L2 learning difficulty to theorizing about the nature of IL grammars. And the second is that second language acquisition can be viewed as the internalization of an interlanguage; specifically, progress in L2 learning is characterized as the acquisition of a series of IL grammars. This naturally raises the question as to whether the learning of IL grammars can affect the native language grammars of L2 learners, leading to historical change. In the next sections, we cite briefly recent findings attesting first to sub-phonemic influences that an L2 may exert on L1 pronunciation (the 'phonetic drift' effect, which may set the stage for subsequent phonological change per se). Second, we exemplify how the progressive imposition of foreign phonemic contrasts onto native allophonic differences prepares a seedbed for classic phonemic (technically, allophonic) split and novel phonemicization. We do not address here, however, the less well studied role played by the phonology of 'heritage' as opposed to second languages per se; but see Polinsky & Kagan (2007) and Rothman (2009) for reviews of some of the issues worth investigating that this rather special type of language contact raises.

36.3 PHONETIC EFFECTS

Grammars learned through second language acquisition, i.e. IL grammars, have the potential to affect the learner's L1 grammar phonetically (with no change in contrasts) as well as phonologically (merging or creating new contrasts). The most widely studied phonetic influences in this direction are the effects of L2 voice onset time values on those of the L1. Thus, in acoustic analysis of American adults learning Korean in Korea, Chang (2010b: abstract) discovered that

> '... experience with Korean stop types is found to influence the production of English stop types in terms of voice onset time (VOT) and/or fundamental frequency (f_o) onset as early as the second week of Korean classes, resulting in the lengthening of VOT in English voiceless stops (in approximation to the longer VOT of the perceptually similar Korean aspirated stops) and the raising of f_o onset following English voiced and voiceless stops (in approximation to the higher f_o levels of Korean).'

Similar influences on English have been reported from other languages, as cited above, and current work by Simon (2011) on Dutch learners of English lends empirical second language acquisition support to the arguments and evidence presented by Iverson &

Salmons (2003, 2008) that the 'voicing language' stops of Modern Dutch (contrasting voiceless unaspirated with voiced) likely emerged out of the typical Germanic 'aspirating language' type (contrasting heavily aspirated with weakly voiced stops) through L2 learning contact with a Romance-type system. Underscoring the synchronic variability of this kind of influence according to the dominant ambient language, Sancier & Fowler (1997: 421) report that

> Acoustic measurements of our speaker's voiceless stops produced in both Brazilian Portuguese [Romance system] and English [Germanic] show that, whereas her VOTs are always shorter for productions in Brazilian Portuguese than in English, VOTs of stops produced in both languages are shorter after a several month stay in Brazil than after a several month stay in the United States.

The common thread running through these findings from second language acquisition research is that an L2 can exert subtle sub-phonemic phonetic influences on the L1, thus laying a foundation for subsequent phonological change. As charted by Iverson & Salmons (2008), for example, a largely non-functional shift such as Grimm's Law likely arose out of such a 'substratum' context, as this effect is traditionally referred to, but the nature of that kind of influence now can be better understood from the findings of synchronic studies on the second language acquisition process. By the same token, modern investigations of the development of simultaneous bilingualism show that the emergence of dual phonetic systems is sharply affected by age of exposure (Bullock, Toribio, González, & Dalola 2006, Abrahamsson & Hyltenstam 2009). For example, Lee & Iverson (2012) found that Korean-English bilingual children at age 10 had established distinct VOT and f_0 values for the two languages, whereas 5-year-olds generally implemented acoustically blended systems. This suggests that language change under L2 influence is more likely to be characteristic of adult learners, or older children, than of very young simultaneous bilinguals, who appear to integrate rather than distinguish the phonological systems they are acquiring.

Finally, the findings of acoustic work among second language learners now can be verified through brain imaging, a research technique that has only recently become available. Thus, in fMRI studies, Park & Iverson (2008) (cf. also Park, Park, & Iverson 2010 and Park, Iverson, & Park 2011) show that there is a significant difference in activation between L1 and L2 speakers with respect to the apprehension of Korean laryngeal contrasts, particularly in areas of the brain associated with pitch perception. These brain imaging results support acoustic findings that the aspiration contrasts of Korean initial stops are increasingly distinguished less by VOT differences between a heavily and a lightly aspirated series than by the differing values of f_0 in the following vowel. This merger of aspiration values, in turn, points toward phonetic influence from English, a pervasive second language (especially for younger Koreans) whose VOT delay properties support only a single, heavily aspirated series of stops.

36.4 Phonological Effects

Efforts by speakers to pronounce foreign words as closely to the source language pronunciation as the rules and constraints of the L1 allow result in predictable adaptations and adjustments (cf. Iverson & Lee 2006), but these constraints may be relaxed as familiarity with the source language increases through its status as an L2. For example, the fricative *f* in Japanese (phonetically [ɸ]) in native vocabulary is restricted to occurrence before *u*, as in the place names *Fuji* or *Fukushima*; elsewhere, the variant is *h*, as in *Hokkaido* or *Hiroshima* (*Fokkaido, *Firoshima). This pattern is imposed on older borrowings as well, as in *hoomu* < '(plat)form', variably in more recent adaptations such as *hooku/fooku* < 'fork', and generally not at all in even more recent loans like *faitto* < 'fight'. The consequence is that the allophonic pairing of *h* and *f* in native vocabulary comes to be split into separate phonemes in words of foreign origin, but only there (compare Uffmann, this volume, on 'lexical strata'). The role played in this process by the widespread learning of English as an L2, with its phonemic /h/ and /f/, seems incontestable.

The phonology of Japanese continues to treat *h* and *f* as allophones of the same phoneme, presumably, but as awareness of the foreign status of words like *fooku* and *faitto* begins to wane, so will the allophonic relationship between *f* and *h*, thus giving rise to phonemic split under the influence of an L2. A similar, but weaker split is also under way in the language with respect to the affricated variant of *t*, which in native vocabulary only occurs before *u*, as in *tatsu* 'to stand' (cf. *tate* 'stand!', *tatanai* 'don't stand'; Kaneko 2004: 52). But now, under English L2 influence, non-affricated renditions occur before *u* in foreign vocabulary, as in *tuba* 'tuba', *tatuu* 'tattoo'. The strength of the allophonic relationship between [t] and [ts] in Japanese native vocabulary remains, but has been weakened in the foreign component by these borrowings and the influence of English as an increasingly prominent L2, setting the stage for ultimate phonemicization of the two segments throughout the language. From a theoretical point of view, moreover, such gradual progression from allophonic to phonemic status within a layered lexicon fits in well with a stratal model of phonological structure and change as laid out by Kiparsky and Bermúdez-Otero (both this volume). In short, the role of foreign pronunciation and L2 influence in the splitting of native language allophones, such as occurred in the history of English voiced and voiceless fricatives alluded to in the introduction above, is a prominent means by which change in phonemic systems takes place.

Depending on the morphological circumstances, however, the path to phonemic split under the effects of L2 learning may be more progressive, and staged, than as just outlined for monomorphemic words. Eckman & Iverson (2013) investigated the learning of the English /s/-/ʃ/ contrast by native speakers of Korean, noting that the sounds [s] and [ʃ] occur in native Korean vocabulary in complementary distribution, with [ʃ] found only before [i] and [j], [s] elsewhere. This pattern is captured by a rule (or equivalent constraint) to the effect that /s/ is realized as [ʃ] before high front vocoids. The task of the

L2 learner, then, is to split these two native allophones into separate phonemes in the IL by suppressing the application of the persisting native rule.

As we have argued in previous work (Eckman, Elreyes, & Iverson 2003, Eckman, Iverson, Fox, Jacewicz, & Lee 2009), L2-conditioned implementation of allophonic split proceeds according to a well-defined, implicational pattern. In early stages, the IL rule applies without limitation, causing learners to err on all target words containing the sequence which violates the phonological constraints of the L1, in this case, [si]. However, once learners acquire the /ʃ/ phoneme in at least some words, the rule applies only in contexts where the [s] plus [i] sequence spans a morpheme boundary, that is, in morphologically derived environments. The final stage emerges with complete suppression of the rule, the IL grammar then evidencing the contrast in the same contexts as found in the L2.

In sum, the first pattern of rule application within the IL is that early learners exhibit no contrast between [s] and [ʃ] in any target words. The second pattern occurs when the learner acquires the /s/-/ʃ/ contrast in at least some words, thus introducing /ʃ/ as a phoneme into the IL lexicon. General principles (structure preservation, the derived environment constraint) then restrict the application of the rule to only morphologically derived contexts. This means that learners show the contrast in morphologically simplex words, as in *mess vs mesh*, but still present [ʃ] in words like *messing*, which remains homophonous with *meshing*. The third pattern is that in which the learner suppresses the NL rule altogether, and has thus acquired the /s/-/ʃ/ contrast in both morphologically simple (*mess ≠ mesh*) and complex environments (*messing ≠ meshing*).

These findings support the claim that the L2 acquisition of an allophonic split may not proceed directly in a single stage from no contrast between the sounds to a final stage in which a complete contrast has been attained. Rather, there is the possibility of an intermediate stage in which the contrast exists in only one class of lexical items.

Taking this work on the acquisition of L2 phonemic contrasts a step further, we tracked the learning of the English /s/-/ʃ/ contrast by native speakers of Japanese as a function of the identical phonological environment considered in the study of Korean learners. Korean parallels Japanese in this respect in that both languages employ the sounds [s] and [ʃ], and both exhibit a pattern whereby [s] is palatalized before high front vocoids. In Japanese, however, the palatalization process arguably is neutralizing because [s] and [ʃ] contrast in the native vocabulary (cf. minimal pairs such as [sakai] 'boundary' *vs* [ʃakai] 'society'); but in Korean, [ʃ] is found other than before [i] only in loanwords (e.g. [ʃawə] 'shower'). A further basis for the claim that these fricatives represent separate phonemes in Japanese, but not in Korean, is the systematic difference between the two languages in the incidence of default epenthetic vowels in the adaptation of loanwords ending in palatoalveolar sibilants (see Iverson & Lee 2006, Heo 2010, Eckman & Iverson 2013 for detailed arguments). In consequence of this difference in phonemic status between otherwise identical L1 segments, native speakers of Japanese acquiring the English /s/-/ʃ/ contrast in our study did not exhibit the same acquisition patterns as the Korean learners, nor did they produce the same kinds of errors.

36.5 IMPLICATIONS

There are several implications that the findings of research on L2 phonology hold for language change. Chief among these is the repeated demonstration that, through phonetic drift, L2 learning may affect L1 pronunciation, modifying the phonetics so as to prime subsequent restructuring of the L1 sound system. Influence from the sounds of one language on the phonological system of another can also be exerted through the adaptation of loanwords, as Uffmann (this volume) exemplifies (and see also Lahiri and Ratliff, both this volume, for some effects of loanwords on a borrowing language at the prosodic level), though the learning of (as opposed to borrowing from) a second language is an even more intimate, and extensive, form of contact. Yet much of interest in this area remains to be explored, including the extent and persistence of phonetic effects on L1, and indeed on L2, that learning another second language (L3) might have, or the variations in phonetic drift that may arise when the phonetic and phonological systems of the L1 and L2 are similar (e.g. English L1 vis-à-vis German L2) or not (English L1 vis-à-vis Korean L2). Another way that analyses in second language acquisition may inform the field of historical linguistics is by attesting stages in the series of IL grammars that occur during L2 acquisition. If we take seriously the claim that interlanguages are, in fact, languages, and that, therefore, IL grammars are subject to the same principles that govern primary languages, then the IL grammars attested in L2 acquisition may well mirror the sequence of grammars that are involved in historical change. With respect to phonological changes involving allophonic splits, specifically, whether in acquisition of the L2 or in historical development of the L1, the possible existence of an intermediate stage is predicted in which the split occurs first in monomorphemic lexical items, then expands to all vocabulary at a later stage. The study of synchronic language contact due to second language learning is thus fertile ground for growing our understanding of historical change in phonology, with many questions yet to be posed, let alone answered.

CHAPTER 37

....

LOANWORD ADAPTATION

....

CHRISTIAN UFFMANN

37.1 INTRODUCTION

....

LOANWORD adaptation has seen renewed interest in the phonological literature, accompanied by a fierce theoretical debate about how words are adapted, whether adaptations are phonological in nature, or based on phonetic and perceptual similarity; this has a number of connections to diachronic phonology and the addition of words to a language is in itself a type of change, although the adaptations of individual words themselves are not canonical cases of diachronic phonological change. This chapter reviews both the empirical facts (section 37.2) and the theoretical debate (section 37.3), proposing a way in which the opposing positions may be unified, suggesting that the two major factors in adaptation are similarity and phonological contrast and arguing that the role of contrast and opposition has received too little attention so far. The relative importance of these two factors also seems to be mediated by sociolinguistic factors, though. I suggest a sociolinguistic turn in section 37.4: we can only understand how words are adapted when we understand the sociolinguistic setting in which they are adapted. Section 37.5 concludes.

37.2 PHONOLOGICAL ADAPTATIONS: AN OVERVIEW

....

When words are borrowed, they are frequently (but see section 37.4) adapted to the phonological system of the borrowing language, both segmentally, identifying native phoneme categories to express the sounds of the original form, and suprasegmentally, making the borrowings conform to native phonotactics and syllable structure constraints, and adapting them to the native stress or tone system. This section looks at what we know about how words are adapted at different levels of phonological description before moving on to theories of loanword adaptation, discussed and compared in section 37.3.

37.2.1 Segmental Adaptations

When we think about how the sounds of an L2 can be expressed in an L1 (see also Eckman & Iverson, this volume, for a general overview of L2 acquisition and phonological change), two possibilities come to mind. First, borrowers may take the incoming raw phonetic signal and find an underlying representation in their L1 whose output is as phonetically similar to the original form as possible. Alternatively, they may analyse the L2 in terms of phonemes and underlying contrasts and map these more abstract categories onto L1 categories. This distinction is at the heart of the difference between perceptual or phonetic and phonological approaches, discussed in detail in section 37.3. It is useful to bear the two approaches in mind when looking at the main patterns of segmental adaptations discussed here. For ease of exposition, let us begin with the hypothesis that adaptations are phonological in nature, mapping an L2 phoneme inventory onto an L1 phoneme inventory, and see if this assumption is sufficient.

We may naively think of adaptation as a process that occurs only when the borrowing language does not have a phoneme which is found in the donor language. However, all borrowings involve adaptations, since the borrower is faced with the non-trivial task of establishing what L1 phoneme should count as equivalent to a specific L2 phoneme. This task is not trivial because sounds, which we may readily class as phonologically equivalent, for example by using the same IPA symbol in transcription, or by assigning them the same distinctive feature values, usually still differ in their exact phonetic realization. For example, both German and Norwegian borrowed English *beat* (as in *beat music, beatnik*), and the word may be transcribed /biːt/ in all three languages, suggesting that no segmental adaptations took place. There are, however, subtle differences in how the three component segments are produced, with variable VOT for initial /b/, somewhat different realizations of long /iː/, which is diphthongized and variably fronted in English (e.g. as [ij, ɪj]), a stable monophthong [iː] in German and realized with a centralized offglide in Norwegian [iˢ]. Final /t/ is often unreleased in English, may be preglottalized, an ejective, or a glottal stop, but can be aspirated in German and Norwegian. Hence, the task of establishing phonological equivalence is not straightforward, even less so where the differences between two potentially equivalent phonemes are phonetically less subtle.

A notorious case of establishing equivalence where a phonetically similar sound is not available is that of English interdental fricatives /θ, ð/ (see e.g. Lombardi 2003 and Blevins 2006c for an overview), which do not exist in many languages. They are adapted as /t, d/ in some languages, as /s, z/ in others. Thus, a phoneme category found in the donor language but not in the borrowing language is mapped onto an existing category in the borrowing language, frequently involving mergers—here mergers with alveolar stops of fricatives. Mergers are unavoidable if the L1 has fewer contrasts than the L2. A well-known rather extreme example is that of Hawaiian, which has only seven consonants, /p, k, ʔ, l, w, n, h/. Many contrasts found in English are therefore obliterated. For instance, all non-labial obstruents (/t, d, k, g, s, z, ... /) map onto /k/ (with qualifications, see, for example, Adler 2006 for detail).

Mergers of L2 distinctions are one way in which differences between L1 and L2 manifest themselves in the adaptation process. Alternatively, there can be a shift in phoneme category, when the borrowing language does not have a category and one perceived as similar is chosen instead (see section 37.3 for a discussion of the notion of similarity). For example, in Burmese and Hindi voiceless aspirated stops are used to adapt an English fricative. In Burmese, /pʰ/ is used for English /f/ (Chang 2012); in Hindi, /tʰ, dʰ/ are used for L2 /θ, ð/ (Hock 1991: 393f.). These realizations do not involve a merger, however; English stops are realized by separate phonemes. In Burmese, English /p/ is realized as /p/ (even though /p/ is aspirated [pʰ] in many positions in English), and /b/ is realized as /b/. In Hindi, English /t, d/ are adapted as retroflexes /ʈ, ɖ/, thus avoiding merger with /θ, ð/. (1) gives an overview of the Burmese adaptations. The three-way phonemic contrast of English is preserved, but there is a case of a phonological non-equivalence when the fricative /f/ maps onto aspirated /pʰ/. The mappings of /b, p/ > /b, p/ could then be seen as mappings between equivalent categories, say between [labial] stops. (This simplifies matters, given the question whether the underlying contrast in English is one of voicing or aspiration, see e.g. Honeybone 2005 on 'laryngeal realism'; see also section 37.3.2.)

(1) English-Burmese mappings for labial obstruents (Chang 2012)

/b/ > /b/	brake	[bəɾeiʔ]	rubber	[ɾàbà]
/p/ > /p/	powder	[pãũda]	plastic	[pɔlaʔsətɪʔ]
/f/ > /pʰ/	four	[pʰóú]	coffee	[kɔpʰì]

(1) illustrates phonological adaptations, matching up phoneme equivalences in the two languages, disregarding phonetic detail in the L2 (here: aspiration). Is it the case, then, that allophonic, non-contrastive information is uniformly disregarded in the adaptation process? One could imagine a situation in which the borrowing language has a phonemic contrast which is only allophonic in the donor language. Will the L2 phoneme then be consistently matched with an L1 phoneme (phonological adaptation), or will the allophonic variation be reflected in the choice of L1 phoneme? The evidence for this is mixed. It seems that in some languages, allophonic information is considered in the adaptation process, while in other languages, segmental adaptations are largely phonemic (see also section 37.3.4).

We saw that in Burmese allophonic aspiration does not influence the adaptation pattern. English /p/ is adapted as /p/ in all positions, keeping it distinct from /f/, which is adapted as /pʰ/. We find a similar pattern in Korean (e.g. Lee 2003, Kenstowicz 2005) where English /b/ is uniformly adapted as lax /p/, and English /p/ is adapted as aspirated /pʰ/, even in contexts where it is never aspirated, as in /sp/ clusters. Thus, spy > [sɨpʰai], with aspiration. As Kenstowicz (2005) points out, it is not the case that Koreans do not pay attention to phonetic detail in laryngeal contrasts in borrowings: French /p/, which is unaspirated, is generally adapted as tense /p'/, as in *Paris* > [p'ari]. However, allophonic variation does play a role in Thai adaptations of English words (Kenstowicz & Suchato 2006). There is aspiration in *pin* > [pʰin] but not in *spare* > [s°pee], unlike in Korean. We will suggest reasons for this variant behaviour later.

In their discussion of French loans in Moroccan Arabic, Kenstowicz & Louriz (2009) show that allophonic information can be taken into account in the adaptation process in a different way as well, not by mapping an allophonic distinction in the L2 onto a phoneme distinction in the L1, but by utilizing an L1 allophonic distinction to capture an L2 phoneme contrast. Like many Arabic dialects, Moroccan has only three vowels /i, a, u/. However, these vowels have lowered/retracted allophones [e, o, ɑ] when in the same syllable as an emphatic consonant. Thus, French words containing mid vowels or /ɑ/ are adapted with emphatic consonants in order to faithfully reproduce the mid vowels. A contrast which is not found in the donor language (emphasis, as pharyngealization or uvularization), is therefore used to preserve a vocalic contrast in the donor language.

Finally, borrowing may aid in the phonemicization of an allophonic contrast. Picard & Nicol (1982) cite an example from Québec French, where a long vowel diphthongizes allophonically in a stressed closed syllable. This process is not found in English loanwords containing a diphthong, however. The diphthong is maintained across phonological contexts, and the allophonic alternation is therefore suspended in loanwords. Consequently, minimal pairs may emerge. (2) provides some examples, from the Québec French alternation (a) and the blocking of this alternation in loans (b). Note the homophonous pair *fête* = *fight* with a derived contrast *fêter* = *fighter*.

(2) Diphthongization and English loans in Québec French (Picard and Nicol 1982)

(a)	beurre	[bawr]	beurrer	[bəːre]	'(to) butter'
	nage	[nawʒ]	nager	[naːʒe]	'(to) swim'
	fête	[fajt]	fêter	[fɛːte]	'(to) party'
(b)	fight	[fajt]	fighter	[fajte]	'(to) fight'
	knockout	[nɑkawt]	knockouter	[nɑkawte]	'(to) knock out'

In sum, we can understand segmental adaptations to a large degree as the mapping of an L2 phoneme system on the categories of the L1. However, allophonic information may interfere in this process. We will discuss the theoretical relevance of this in section 37.3.

37.2.2 Suprasegmental Adaptations

There are two main types of suprasegmental adaptations, syllable structure adaptations (and more generally phonotactic adaptations) and adaptations regarding stress and tone. This section summarizes the main findings.

37.2.2.1 *Syllable Structure and Phonotactics*

Syllable structure adaptations occur when the borrowing language has tighter syllable structure constraints than the donor language, when the donor language allows segment sequences that the borrowing language does not allow. Languages may disallow syllable codas or have restrictions on licit coda segments (Japanese only allows a placeless nasal or the first part of a geminate in coda position, for example). Languages may disallow consonant clusters, especially tautosyllabically, as complex onsets or codas. Languages may have strict sonority sequencing restrictions, disallowing, for example, sonority reversals in onsets and codas, [sC] clusters or imposing a minimal sonority distance on clusters. When languages with some such constraint on possible syllable structures borrow words from languages with laxer constraints, the shape of these words has to be adapted to satisfy the borrowing language's stricter constraints. This can be done in two different ways: by deleting offending segments or by inserting material into disallowed segment sequences.

To be more concrete, assume a language with strict CV syllable structure (as is found in many Niger-Congo or Oceanic languages) borrowing from English, with its tolerance of syllable codas and consonant clusters. When borrowing a word like *bus* or *truck*, the language therefore has two options: to delete the coda consonant and one of the segments in the onset cluster, or to insert vowels to achieve strict alternations between consonants and vowels. Both strategies are attested, as the borrowings from White Hmong (Golston & Yang 2001) and Shona (Uffmann 2007) show in (3).

(3) Loans in White Hmong and Shona (Golston & Yang 2001, Uffmann 2007)

gloss	Hmong	Shona
'bus'	mbă	bhazi
'truck'	c^{h}ùá	tiroko
'cake'	k^{h}ê	keke

Shona inserts a vowel into onset clusters and to avoid codas; White Hmong deletes consonants. Both end up without onsets or coda clusters (though Hmong allows a range of complex segments).[1] While one may expect to find both deletion and insertion as commonly attested strategies, Shona type repairs with epenthetic vowels are much more common than the White Hmong pattern. Paradis & LaCharité (1997) refer to this as the 'Preservation Principle' which they argue is operative as a general principle in loanword phonology. Indeed, vowel epenthesis rather than consonant deletion is attested in many languages, for example Tswana (Batibo 1995), Fijian (Kenstowicz 2007), Samoan (Uffmann 2007), Japanese (Park 1987). Cases of deletion then need to be explained by other overriding principles. In fact, there is a very strong word size restrictor constraint

---

[1] This holds only for full adaptations; in both languages, speakers may decide to leave words partially unadapted, introducing new structures into their L1. See section 37.4 for discussion.

operating in Hmong: words are preferably monosyllabic. The preference for epenthesis over deletion in loanwords is noteworthy, since it has been argued that in regular language change, deletion is a more common process (Vennemann 1988, Singh & Muysken 1995).[2]

37.2.2.2 *Accent and Tone*

Loans are also adapted with regard to accent and tone. L1 and L2 may have different stress systems, or one (or both) may be a tone language, raising the question of how stress in a donor language may map onto the tone system of the borrowing language, or vice versa. The interested reader is also referred to the excellent overview of phenomena in this area of suprasegmental adaptation in Kang (2010), and see also Lahiri (this volume) for a discussion of the effect of borrowing in stress systems, and Ratliff (this volume) for some discussion of borrowing in tone systems.

With respect to stress, a frequently found pattern is that the native stress system is used, overwriting any input stress. See Kang (2010) for a host of examples from different languages. This is the case when stress is entirely predictable in the borrowing language (for example, main stress consistently on the initial or final syllable). Peperkamp & Dupoux (2002) refer to this as stress 'deafness', arguing from psycholinguistic evidence that speakers whose L1 has fully predictable stress lose the ability to accurately perceive stress that deviates from their L1 norm. So speakers of such languages (for example, Hungarian, Finnish, French) ignore L2 stress and simply apply L1 stress assignment principles.

It is not the case that L1 stress is always ignored, however. The claim of 'deafness' is a bit strong, as there are cases in which a word is modified in order to align the L1 and L2 stress patterns. For example, Hungarian speakers can delete an initial unstressed vowel in the loan to bring the loanword in line with the Hungarian pattern of initial main stress (Kang 2010). Kenstowicz (2007) reports that Fijian loanwords follow regular Fijian stress assignment, which builds moraic trochees from the right. However, vowel quantity may change (vowels can lengthen) in order to align the stress in the source word with the stress in the loan. Thus, *tobácco* is borrowed as [ta(váko)], with short vowels, matching loan stress with the original stress, while the initial syllable in *cólony* undergoes lengthening in order to be footed and stressed, even though it only receives secondary stress: [(kòː)(lóni)].

Finally, there are cases in which heavy borrowing modified the original stress system, where loanwords now provide crucial evidence for regular stress assignment in these languages. Crucial cases are Germanic languages that abandoned initial stress as a consequence of borrowing especially from Romance languages and developed innovative stress patterns, as in the analyses of Rice (2006) (Norwegian), Fikkert et al. (2006,

---

[2] Note that the question of what vowel is inserted is also of empirical and theoretical relevance. Many analyses identify a default vowel in a language, typically an unmarked, non-salient vowel. Uffmann (2006, 2007) shows that most languages display a complex interplay of three strategies, default segmentism, vowel harmony, and local assimilation to a consonant (such as inserting [u] after labials); see Uffmann (2007) on how the processes interact in Shona, Sranan, and Samoan, and Kubozono (2002) who identifies all three processes in Japanese.

see also Lahiri, this volume) (English), and Alber (1997), Speyer (2009) (German). This is not restricted to Germanic, of course. Fitzgerald (1999) uses loanword evidence in her discussion of stress in Tohono O'odham. Pitch accent in Japanese loanwords also seems to constitute an innovation with the emergence of a Latin-style accentuation system, although Kubozono (2006) shows how the emergence of such a system can be understood from the interaction of borrowing with the native prosodic system.

When tone languages borrow words from stress languages, they have essentially two options, to map stress onto tones, using the effect stress has on pitch, or to disregard stress and use default tones or let some other factor decide what tone(s) to use in the loan (see also Ratliff, this volume). Languages with a small set of level tones typically equate high (H) tones with stressed syllables and low (L) tones with unstressed syllables (e.g. Hausa, Leben 1996; Yoruba, Kenstowicz 2006). The same pattern, though with a few complications, can hold in languages with contour tones, where level high or falling tones can be associated with stressed syllables in the etymon, as in Cantonese (Silverman 1992) or Mandarin Chinese (Wu 2006). There are, however, cases in which input stress is disregarded for tone assignment. Hsieh & Kenstowicz (2008) find that the choice between H or L tone assignment in English loanwords in Lhasa Tibetan depends on the laryngeal specification of the initial segment of the English word: L if it is a voiced obstruent or sonorant, H if it is voiceless. Golston & Yang (2001) show that a complex mix of segmental and syllabic factors plays a role in tone assignment in English loans in White Hmong, while French loans are realized with default L tones. Kenstowicz and Suchato (2006) find that in Thai, syllable structure decides what tone an English loanword will have: syllables closed by an obstruent will have a high tone, others are mid.[3]

There is comparatively little research on accent languages adopting words from tone languages. Ito & Kenstowicz (2009) is one of the very few studies in this area, looking at how Mandarin tones are adapted in a pitch accent system, Yanbian Korean. The challenge here is how the four contour tones (and combinations of contour tones) can be mapped onto the two pitch accent types, HL and LH. They find that the mapping is largely predictable, though complex, involving the preservation of the most salient tonal properties of the incoming form.

Finally, we can look at how tone languages adapt words from tone languages. Here, the same two options are found as in the adaptation of words from stress languages, either attempting a close match, or disregarding the tonal pattern of the incoming form. The examples discussed in Kang (2010) suggest that languages with similar tone systems can adopt each others' tones (for example, level tones in African languages) but that the mapping is harder the more typologically distinct two systems are. Thus, Lhasa Tibetan speakers disregard tones in Mandarin borrowings but use a strategy similar to the one they use for English loans, assigning L tone to sonorant-initial forms and H to obstruent-initial forms.

---

[3] The high tone can be explained as an effect of the voiceless final obstruent.

In sum, then, one finds a wealth of phenomena when looking at suprasegmental and prosodic adaptations. As with segmental adaptations, the question is what motivates the shape of the borrowings, what exactly happens in the adaptation process, and what this can tell us about language processing or phonological theory. It is to these questions that we turn now.

37.2.3 How are the Adaptations Motivated?

Having established a typology of phonological adaptations, an important question is how the borrower knows what to do with an incoming form to adapt it to the native phonological system. This question was particularly pressing in early generative rule-based theory: where do the adaptation rules originate? How would a speaker set up a rule of, say, /θ, ð/ → /t, d/ when their native grammar does not have /θ, ð/ and there is no existing model for such a rule? The idea of morpheme structure conditions, developed in Stanley (1967) helps motivate why a rule should be set up, but there is no indication of why the rule should be in this specific shape.

It is of no surprise, then, that loanword adaptation received renewed interest with the development of constraint-based models of phonology in which rules are demoted to the status of automatic repairs, as in Paradis (1988), or done away with completely, as in Optimality Theory (OT; Prince & Smolensky 1993/2004, and see also Holt, this volume). For Paradis, rules are replaced with repair strategies that are activated as the result of a constraint violation. These strategies are not arbitrary, but the phonological grammar is strongly constrained with respect to what a possible repair is. The repairs found in loanword adaptation can then emerge from abstract principles of repairs. In OT, there are only constraints on surface forms, no conditions on underlying forms (the principle of Richness of the Base). Thus, any structure not found in a language has to be ruled out by the constraint ranking of that language, which applies to native forms and borrowings alike. To come back to our hypothetical borrower faced with English /θ, ð/, sounds she does not have in her L1, this means that her grammar already has a high-ranked constraint *[θ, ð], and the adaptation should follow from the interaction of this constraint with faithfulness constraints such as IDENT(F). The same argument holds for suprasegmental adaptations. For example, if syllable structure constraints like NoCoda and *ComplexOnset must be satisfied in native forms, their high ranking will also apply to non-native material entering the OT grammar. To scholars working on loanword adaptation, OT was thus a very attractive proposition, offering a principled way of understanding why and how adaptations take place. At the same time, loanword adaptation furnished theorists with a strong argument in favour of OT, or other surface constraint based frameworks: what if no constraints on outputs can motivate loanword adaptation and also give us an understanding of how words are adapted?

One problem remains, though. The constraint ranking that can be deduced from the adaptations may not be directly motivated from the native phonology and thus remain as stipulative as the above-mentioned repair rules. Coming back to the example of adapting English /θ, ð/—why would one language adapt them as /t, d/, not as /s, z/ (while other languages do the opposite)? We could argue that this is due to the relative ranking of different IDENT constraints in each language, but do we always have evidence for these rankings? Worse are cases in which native processes flatly contradict whatever ranking we could stipulate for explaining adaptations. A celebrated example is that of final stops in Korean (Kenstowicz 2005, Boersma & Hamann 2009, among others). In word-final position, Korean only allows plain stops, but not tense or aspirated stops. In the native phonology, an underlying final aspirated stop will neutralize to plain, as in /patʰ/ 'field', realized [pat] (compare locative [patʰɛ], where /tʰ/ is retained faithfully). In loanword adaptation, however, there is no deaspiration, but a word-final aspirated stop, as, for example, in *week*, will usually be repaired by vowel epenthesis, moving the offending consonant into an onset. Hence, *week* > [wikʰi]. Native and loanword phonology treat the same underlying structure differently. One remedy is to invoke output-output faithfulness constraints that hold specifically for relations between the loanword and its source realization, as in Kenstowicz (2005), or to argue for a distinction between perception and production grammars (Boersma & Hamann 2009), assuming that adaptations take part in perception rather than in production, a point we will discuss in greater detail in the next section.

In sum, there is no straightforward way of accounting for all adaptations just by recourse to pre-existing phonological grammars; loanword adaptation contains innovations, and the question is what resources speakers are drawing upon to motivate these innovative processes. This brings us to the more fundamental questions regarding the adaptation process mentioned earlier: what do speakers actually do when they adapt a word?

37.3 How are Loanwords Adapted?

We have seen that there are two main positions regarding how loanwords are adapted: either it is done by choosing an underlying form whose realization is phonetically or perceptually as close to the source phonetic form as possible, or by setting up more abstract phonological correspondences between sounds. Different models have been proposed in either camp, and this section will introduce the different models, outline problems, and make a new proposal that incorporates the findings from both camps, arguing that there are two main principles at work, similarity and contrast.

37.3.1 Perceptual Adaptation

One position in the debate that has gained in popularity in recent years (see e.g. Kenstowicz 2005, 2007, Adler 2006, Shinohara 2006, Peperkamp et al. 2008, Boersma & Hamann 2009 among others) holds that loanword adaptation is a process of primarily phonetic approximation: loanwords are nativized in a phonetically minimal way so that the surface form of the loan deviates as little as possible from the original in perceptual terms. Put more simply, borrowers want the loan to sound as much as possible like the original L2 form. Within this line of thought, there are two opposite camps, however, with respect to where these adaptations take place, in the phonological grammar or already in raw phonetic perception.

The latter point is argued for explicitly in Peperkamp (2005), Peperkamp & Dupoux (2003), Peperkamp et al. (2008), and Silverman (1992), who argue in favour of a perceptual filter that already modifies the incoming acoustic form to match it with native phonological categories (although Silverman proposes an additional phonological level of adaptation). According to Peperkamp, the incoming form is already fully adapted before it reaches the level of phonological computation. She refers to this as perceptual 'deafness': borrowers do not hear that their (adapted) form of the loanword sounds different from the original. Support for this position comes from perception studies indicating that speakers are indeed unable to distinguish between two phonetic stimuli that are non-contrastive in their L1. A particularly striking study is Dupoux et al. (1999) who report that Japanese subjects perceive illusory vowels in certain phonotactic environments. Recall that Japanese does not allow consonant clusters, and that clusters in loanwords are broken up by a vowel, mostly default [u]. Dupoux et al. (1999) found that speakers report hearing medial [u] in stimuli like *ebzo* and fail to distinguish *ebzo* and *ebuzo*. In its focus on (mis-)perception this approach is thus very similar to listener-based approaches to language change (see Ohala 1981, Blevins 2004a, Blevins, this volume, and Yu, this volume), which also rely on speakers not reliably perceiving a distinction and therefore modifying underlying forms.

Alternatively, perceptual adaptation may happen in the phonology. Borrowers are able to perceive the incoming sounds more or less accurately and then match them with the phonetically closest native categories in their phonological grammar, a view espoused in Yip (1993), Shinohara (2006), Kenstowicz (2007), Boersma & Hamann (2009). Perceptual similarity is thus an active choice rather than selective deafness. Shinohara (2006) provides a good example of an adaptation that cannot be purely phonetic because it takes into account prosodic information, the fate of liquids in onset clusters in Cantonese loanwords. /Cl/ clusters are disallowed in Cantonese and have to be repaired. /l/ is deleted if the resulting word is at least disyllabic. If deletion were to result in a monosyllabic form, however, the cluster is broken up by epenthesizing a vowel between the two consonants, creating a disyllabic form. Hence *freezer, place* > *fisa, peysi* (deletion) but *cream, fluke* > *keylim, fuluk* (preservation of the liquid). To Shinohara, this is conclusive evidence that English /l/ is accurately perceived but that additional grammatical factors (here, a word size constraint) decide whether it is also going to be pronounced.

Additional evidence for the phonological view of perceptual adaptation comes from follow-up studies to the illusory vowel perception study of Dupoux et al. (1999), which are more sceptical of Peperkamp's and Dupoux's interpretation of the results. Monahan et al. (2009) look at epenthetic [o] in Japanese, which is inserted after /t, d/, and fail to replicate the effect while confirming illusory perception of [u]: Japanese speakers fail to pick up the difference between *ebzo* and *ebuzo*, but they have no problem with *edma vs edoma* (and *eduma*). Monahan et al. (2009) conclude that phonological knowledge must play a role in the perception task. Speakers parse the signal and know where syllable structure constraints require a vowel. Since /u/ is often devoiced and shortened in Japanese, speakers know that the absence of good cues for [u] in the acoustic signal does not equate the absence of the vowel in the underlying form. This is not the case for Japan-ese /o/, which is never devoiced or shortened. Speakers therefore expect robust perceptual cues for [o] and accurately perceive the difference between *edma* and *edoma*.

Formally, there are two types of proposal for modelling perceptual adaptation in the phonological grammar, both using OT. Kenstowicz (2007) uses the P-map proposal from Steriade (2001a), in which speakers have so-called perceptual maps at their disposal, encoding the perceptual similarity between sounds. Speakers then draw upon this knowledge when the grammar requires an unfaithful parse of the input and choose a candidate form that deviates perceptually the least from the input form.

Boersma & Hamann (2009) take a different approach, analysing loanword adaptation within their bidirectional model of phonology, which unifies production and perception grammars in one constraint ranking. There are, however, different constraints for perception and production, and loanword adaptation occurs in the perception component of the grammar. The approach can thus explain mismatches between loanword adaptations and native processes. They analyse the above-mentioned Korean mismatch by modelling laryngeal neutralization in a traditional OT (production) grammar. Epenthesis in loanwords, however, is perceptually motivated by a high-ranked constraint that prohibits mapping the perception of aspiration to a [–aspirated] segment, and since only [–aspirated] segments can stand in word-final position, epenthesis is necessary to satisfy the constraint on the preservation of perceptual aspiration. The achievement of Boersma & Hamann (2009) is that they do not need to stipulate any loanword-specific rankings or mechanisms. Instead, they can motivate their perception rankings directly from native Korean perception where, indeed, the presence of aspiration in the phonetic signal entails underlying phonological aspiration. The question is, however, if all adaptations are perceptually motivated, especially in the light of the above finding that allophonic information is often not drawn upon in the adaptation process. This brings us to the alternative proposal, that adaptations are based on phonological equivalences.

37.3.2 Phonological Adaptation

The central idea of the phonological approach is that it is not perceptual similarity that counts but phonological equivalence. The approach goes back to Haugen (1950a) and Hyman (1970a), among others, and it is defended and developed in Paradis & LaCharité (1997), LaCharité & Paradis (2002, 2005), Paradis & Tremblay (2009). The core idea is that L2 phonemes are identified and matched with L1 phonemes that are analyzed as equivalent. In many cases, the perceptual approximation account and the phonological equivalence account converge since phonologically equivalent structures should also be phonetically similar, under the relatively uncontroversial assumption that phonological representations are grounded in phonetics (e.g via distinctive features which have consistent phonetic correlates). In some cases, however, they make different predictions, and LaCharité and Paradis support their position by pointing out adaptations that do not go for the closest phonetic match but seem to map phonologically equivalent sounds (see e.g. LaCharité & Paradis 2002, 2005, Paradis & Tremblay 2009). I will now review some of these cases before coming to a critical discussion of their proposal and an attempt to unify the two positions.

A strong case in point is the preservation of laryngeal contrasts such as in /p/ *vs* /b/ in borrowings between languages that have a plain voicing contrast [p] *vs* [b] (such as French, Italian, Dutch, Russian) and languages in which this opposition is expressed primarily as an aspiration contrast [p] *vs* [pʰ] (such as English, German, Korean, Mandarin). Crucially, the 'weaker' member of the aspiration pair corresponds phonetically and perceptually most closely to the stronger member of the voicing pair. One could thus expect French /p/ to be adapted as /b/ in English, or English /b/ to be adapted as /p/ in French, but according to LaCharité & Paradis (2002, 2005) this is never the case. Instead, contrast is preserved, and /p, b/ in one language are borrowed as /p, b/ (or /pʰ, p/) in the other language, irrespective of whether the contrast manifests itself phonetically as voicing or aspiration (see also Iverson & Salmons 2008). Phonetic detail does not seem to play a role: although aspiration on English /p/ is contextual (as is devoicing of English /b/), all English /p/ map onto Mandarin aspirated /pʰ/, irrespective of whether they are aspirated in English (Paradis & Tremblay 2009).

(4) Binary laryngeal contrasts and adaptations

| [pʰ] [p] | Aspiration contrast: English, German … |
| [p] [b] | Voicing contrast: French, Russian … |

This preservation of underlying phonological contrasts despite a potential perceptual pull towards neutralization is not restricted to laryngeal contrasts, as Paradis and LaCharité show. Another case they cite is the cross-linguistic identification of rhotics despite their phonetic variability. So, French /r/, which is a uvular continuant [ʁ ~ ʀ], is adopted in Arabic as [r], although Arabic has uvular fricatives, which are perceptually very close to the French rhotic. A similar perceptual mismatch can be seen in English loans in Japanese, in which the English rhotic, phonetically [ɻ ~ ɹ] is always borrowed as Japanese /r/, a tap or flap, although perception studies show that English /r/ is perceptually more confusable with Japanese /w/. Conversely, intervocalic English /t, d/ which are realized as a flapped [ɾ] in American English, never are adopted as /r/ in languages such as Mexican Spanish where the rhotic is flapped [ɾ]. Vowel adaptations show the same pattern of phonological rather than phonetic equivalence, according to Paradis & LaCharité. A case in point here is seen with the English lax vowels [ɪ, ʊ], which are phonetically closer to /e, o/ than to /i, u/ in languages that do not have a tense-lax contrast. Nevertheless, they are consistently adapted as /i, u/, reflecting their phonological status as [+high] vowels (LaCharité & Paradis 2002).

There has been much recent work on the perception of L2 contrasts, especially associated with Flege's work (e.g. Flege 2003, Flege & MacKay 2004). What is still missing is a systematic survey of the extent to which loanword adaptation patterns match up with findings on perceptual similarity. A casual glance suggests that there may be quite a few mismatches, going far beyond the examples cited by LaCharité & Paradis. For example, Flege & MacKay (2004) show that Italian learners are prone to confusing English /æ/ and /ɛ/ but do not confuse /æ/ and /ʌ/. Yet, in loanwords, both /æ/ and /ʌ/ usually map onto Italian /a/, while /ɛ/ maps onto /ɛ/. Thus, *club, chat, track, hacker* are all realized with /a/ (data from Morandini 2007).[4] From the perceptual viewpoint, such mappings are unexpected.

One final point that is problematic for the perceptual approach concerns variable adaptation. We have seen that English /θ, ð/ are variably adapted as /t, d/ and /s, z/ in different languages. The perceptual approach would have to show that in these languages, the respective choice would, for some reason, be the closer perceptual match. More problematically, the actual closest perceptual match is [f], also witnessed in historical change (Blevins 2006c). In his discussion of vowel epenthesis strategies, Uffmann (2007) points out that different languages use different strategies to establish the quality of the epenthetic segment. Under the perceptual approach, one would have to claim that the different strategies have a different perceptual salience in different languages, for whatever reason. Instead, there seem to be different ways of reducing salience, and that the decision taken in a language, which path to go, is ultimately phonological: very often there is no default perceptual repair, but there is choice.

A necessary condition for adaptations to reflect the phonological rather than the phonetic status of a segment is that borrowers are aware of the phonological status of the borrowed segment. Supporters of the phonological approach therefore argue that loanwords are first introduced by competent bilinguals (Paradis & LaCharité 1997) with a profound knowledge of both phonological systems. The position taken by Dupoux and Peperkamp, on the other hand, requires a relatively low level of competence in the L2 in order for perceptual deafness to play a role. Given that fluent bilinguals have native or native-like perceptual abilities in both languages (see, for example, Flege 2003), their role must be marginal. They may introduce words to a speech community, but it is the monolingual community that adapts them. The phonological-perceptual approach (Kenstowicz 2005, 2007) is comparatively agnostic with respect to this question, although a certain level of perceptual accuracy seems to be required.

All these arguments do not invalidate the perceptual approach, however, since there are phenomena that are hard to capture under an approach that only takes into account phonological equivalence. We have already seen examples of adaptations that are distinct from processes in the native phonology, as in the adaptation of final stops

---

[4] There are some instances of /æ/ > /ɛ/, but these are fewer in number. There is /ɛ/, for example, in *match, sandwich, backup.*

in Korean. The phonological approach has no principled explanation for this, and can only stipulate that different processes apply to loans. Additional support for the relevance of perceptual factors comes from positional asymmetries that can occur in adaptation.

Kenstowicz (2007) reports two such asymmetries from the adaptation of English loanwords in Fijian. The first concerns the adaptation of voiced stops. Fijian does not have a series of voiced stops, but it has prenasalized stops. In word-initial position, voiced stops are adapted as prenasalized stops, thus *desk* > [ⁿdesi]. In non-initial position, however, voiced stops are adapted as voiceless stops, thus *rabbi* > [ra:pai]. Instead, nasal+stop sequences are adapted as prenasalized stops, such as *bank* > [ᵐbaⁿge]. Kenstowicz's explanation is that the nasal portion of prenasalized stops is very weak in initial position, where it lacks support from a preceding vowel and therefore is perceptually similar to a voiced stop, due to its very weak nasal cues, while in non-initial position, the nasal cues are much stronger. The second asymmetry concerns consonant clusters. Onset clusters in Fijian are invariably broken up by an epenthetic vowel, preserving all input consonants. Coda clusters are often adapted by deleting one of the consonants, however. Thus, *east* > [isi] while *steak* > [siteki]; *[seki, teki]. Kenstowicz explains this asymmetry with the weaker perceptual cues that coda consonants have, making them more vulnerable to deletion.

A further point in support of perceptual adaptation is discussed by Hsieh et al. (2009), who find an intriguing contrast shift in Mandarin Chinese. While /n/ and /ŋ/ are two separate phonemes in Mandarin, [æ] and [ɑ] are allophones: front [æ] is used before /n/, back [ɑ] is used before velar /ŋ/. Thus, [æn, ɑŋ] are possible, but *[æŋ, ɑn] are not. Rather than preserving nasal contrast in loanwords (as in *ran vs rang*), however, speakers choose to preserve the vocalic distinction between, for example, *sang vs song*, by selecting the appropriate nasal. Preservation of the accurate vowel thus trumps preservation of the accurate nasal, although the former distinction is allophonic and the latter is phonemic. Hsieh et al. (2009) argue that this reallocation of contrast is perceptually motivated. Nasal place contrast is perceptually weak and therefore lost vis-à-vis the vowel contrast.

There is yet another question that has to be asked about the phonological approach: if it involves the mapping of phonologically corresponding segments, how do speakers, even bilingual speakers, establish this correspondence? If we assume a universal set of distinctive features, we might argue that it is segments with the same feature make-up, but that cannot be right: we have seen above that aspiration contrasts are mapped onto voicing contrasts and vice versa. Equivalence thus has to be calculated at a more abstract level, possibly taking into account feature underspecification (to account for the laryngeal mismatches or the mapping of phonetically distinct rhotics), but—asked polemically—if phonologists cannot agree on a universal set of segment specifications, how can linguistically naive speakers set up correspondence relations between the segments of two languages, if not phonetically? We will come back to this, arguing to replace the idea of phonological equivalence with the idea of contrast and opposition (in the classic sense of Trubetzkoy 1939).

3.3 Intermediate Positions

Recently, more researchers have taken an intermediate position, endorsing the perceptual approach but allowing more abstract phonological principles to play a role as well, as for example the analysis of Korean in Kenstowicz (2005) and the analysis of Sesotho in Rose & Demuth (2006). In his discussion of Korean adaptations, Kenstowicz (2005) distinguishes between perceptually motivated adaptations and adaptations that seem to require a more abstract phonological mapping. Rose & Demuth (2006), while generally taking a phonological approach, also notice a few wrinkles in their analysis of Sesotho borrowings and suggest phonetic approximation in these cases. What is often missing from the mixed approaches, though, is an attempt to explain why certain adaptations are phonological while others are perceptual.

Two studies on Japanese bring us closer to understanding how the two principles interact, Smith (2006) and Dohlus (2010). Smith (2006) looks at doublets in Japanese loanwords and finds that many doublets can be explained by the application of one of the two processes, for example, the adaptation of *jitterbug* as either [dʒittabaggɯ] or [dʒiɾɯba]. The former follows established conventions for Japanese borrowings (see, for example, in Park 1987, Katayama 1998) and also Paradis's Preservation Principle, not deleting underlying material. The latter is odd from that perspective, deleting a final coda and also adapting (flapped) English /t/ as [ɾ], a perceptual assimilation of the kind that Paradis and LaCharité claim does not exist. Smith argues that this is an indication of a purely perceptual borrowing, whereas the longer form is also mediated through orthography. It is unclear, though, how common forms such as [dʒiɾɯba] are, given that it is a non-canonical adaptation. Knowledge about the frequency of such perceptual adaptations could help us understand what the relative role of perception and phonology in a specific contact setting are.

Dohlus (2010) looks at the fate of the front rounded vowels /ø, œ/ in German and French loanwords in Japanese, which lacks these vowels, and finds different strategies in the two languages. German /ø, œ/ are adapted as /e/ (unrounding) while French /ø, œ/ are adapted as /u/. Her perceptual experiments show that Japanese /u/ is indeed the closest perceptual match with /ø, œ/. Dohlus therefore concludes that the French adaptation is perceptual while the German adaptation is phonological (best match in terms of distinctive features, [–back, –high]). The reason for the difference may be that German borrowings are generally older and from the domains of arts and sciences, thus more likely to be introduced via the written form and via educated, possibly bilingual speakers. French borrowings on the other hand are more widely used and found in the oral domain, facilitating perceptual adaptation. She also notices that there used to be variation in the transliteration of German loans, leading to a drive towards standardization in the 20th century, which means that German adaptations are also highly conventionalized.

37.3.4 Unifying the Positions

To summarize the discussion, there is evidence for both perceptual factors in adaptation, borrowers trying to yield a phonetically minimally deviant adaptation, and for more abstract phonological principles. How can we bring the different ideas together?

To begin, the alleged dichotomy between a perceptual and a phonological approach is somewhat misleading. As we have seen, a divide goes right through the proponents of the perceptual approach, dividing those that believe in purely phonetic adaptations (such as Peperkamp & Dupoux) from those who want to integrate perceptual similarity into the phonological grammar (like Kenstowicz). The divide between this position and the 'phonological' approach of Paradis & LaCharité then is less about the fundamentals of adaptation—both camps would agree that adaptations occur in the phonological grammar—but more about what the grammar consists of, whether the phonological grammar can take into account and measure phonetic similarity, or whether it is a fairly abstract symbolic manipulation device. This debate goes beyond loanword adaptation to the heart of many debates in phonological theory today.

We cannot say what the nature of phonological computation is, and will remain agnostic regarding the question of perceptual knowledge in phonology, but we can take a more general look at what kinds of phonological knowledge are utilized in loanword adaptation, without having to commit ourselves to a specific theoretical angle. Two main principles seem to be relevant in loanword adaptation, and these are crucial for the question of what phonologically equivalent or corresponding sounds are: phonetic similarity and phonological contrast. A phoneme system is defined by the segmental contrasts of a language and the oppositions that individual phonemes enter, via distinctive features (see Dresher 2009 for an overview, and also Dresher, this volume, on change and contrast). Identifying two corresponding segments in another language thus consists of two distinct operations: identifying the oppositions that the segment enters in the L2 and finding a phonetically similar segment in the L1 (but not necessarily the most similar segment) that stands in similar oppositions. Thus, voicing contrasts can be mapped onto aspiration contrasts and vice versa, by identifying segment pairs that show some laryngeal contrast and by identifying the stronger and weaker member of the pair. This idea of systemic equivalence may also become clearer by revisiting the vowel adaptations discussed in LaCharité & Paradis (2002). Recall that English /ɪ/ is adapted as /i/ in languages lacking a tense-lax contrast, although it is phonetically closer to /e/. In terms of contrast and opposition, however, /ɪ/ is the highest front lax vowel in English, standing in a three-way height opposition with /ɛ, æ/ and in a backness opposition with /ʊ/. This position within a system of contrasting segments motivates the mapping to /i/, which is in a similar position (highest front vowel).

Contrast can also explain why phonetic detail sometimes seems to matter and sometimes does not. Recall that in Thai, English voiceless stops map on plain voiceless stops or aspirated voiceless stops, in line with English allophony (Kenstowicz & Suchato 2006), but that in other languages with aspirated and unaspirated voiceless stops, English stops map categorically onto the aspirated stop, irrespective of whether it actually is aspirated in that position (for example, in Korean, Burmese and Mandarin Chinese borrowings). The reason for this may lie in the preservation of contrast. Thai has a three-way contrast, and can thus map English /p/ on two distinct categories, /p/ and /p^h/, without obliterating input contrast. In Burmese, however, which also has a three-way contrast, the aspirated stops realize input fricatives. Realizing some English /p/ as [p^h] would therefore cause a partial merger with English /f/. Mandarin has only a two-way contrast, therefore also goes for the mapping that preserves contrast rather than the phonetically closest mapping. Phonetic similarity thus plays a role but is mediated by systemic considerations. When contrast is no longer at stake because a merger is unavoidable, phonetic similarity can come to the fore, whence the Japanese adaptation of French /œ, ø/ as /u/ (Dohlus 2010): when a large vowel system like the French one has to be mapped onto the 5-vowel system of Japanese, loss of contrast is unavoidable. In the absence of clear evidence regarding phonological patterning, the closest perceptual match can then be chosen. How the two factors, similarity and contrast, can exactly be brought together in a formal analysis, is an important question, but has to be outside the scope of this chapter.

Following Paradis and LaCharité, my proposal requires competent bilinguals as agents of change, speakers who are able to assess phonological equivalence between segments as a measure of both phonetic similarity and similar systemic properties, including systems of oppositions and natural class behaviour. Does this mean that perceptual deafness has no role to play? That claim would also be too strong, as the analysis of Japanese doublets by Smith (2006) showed. It is therefore likely that in the process of borrowing there is initially a pool of different variants, with phonological adaptations by competent bilinguals coexisting with some monolinguals' phonetic approximations. This pool of variants then undergoes levelling and conventionalization, and it is possible that the role of conventionalization has also been underestimated in much present research. What this means, though, is that loanwords are not only adapted by individuals, but by speech communities as a whole, suggesting that a sociolinguistic perspective is also necessary. Section 37.4 will look at non-adaptations, variation, and briefly touch upon the role of code-switching, arguing that borrowings can only be understood from the perspective of the speech community, not the individual.

37.4 NON-ADAPTATIONS

While adaptation is the norm, non-adaptations also occur, and a short section on non-adaptations or partial adaptations is important in order to provide a more comprehensive view of the topic. The literature knows many cases of non-adaptation, especially in variationist or explicitly sociolinguistic approaches that look at borrowing embedded in a bilingual or multilingual context, which also involves code-switching. One example of this is Chimhundu (1983), whose account of loanwords in Shona looks at both adaptation patterns and the linguistic situation in Zimbabwe, which is characterized by diglossia and extensive code-switching, with the result that loanwords may be adapted, non-adapted or anything in between. Thus, *train* may be [tireni, treni, tren], under the proviso that the unadapted forms are uttered only by proficient bilinguals—though bilingualism is common in Africa, and therefore unadapted forms are not exceptional (see, for example, also Batibo 1995 for phonotactic adaptations and non-adaptations in Tswana and Swahili).

Unadapted forms have received comparatively little attention in phonological analyses, because the research question typically is how loans are adapted; unadapted forms, then, are little more than 'noise'. A notable exception is LaCharité & Paradis (2005), who provide rates of non-adaptations (which they call 'importations') and discuss some of them, noting in particular the link between rate of adaptation and degree of bilingualism: English loanwords in Québec are more likely to remain unadapted the higher the degree of bilingualism in the speech community is. They never discuss systematically what kinds of non-adaptations are found, however, whether some sounds are less likely to be retained than others, for example. A systematic survey could prove valuable for phonological theory as well, with respect to claims about (universal) markedness, gaps in inventories, and so forth. One of the few surveys I am aware of (without discussing consequences for phonological theory) is the detailed quantitative analysis of Spanish loanwords in Nahuatl in San Giacomo (2009), which gives a tally of non-adaptations per segment, showing that some segments are more likely to remain unadapted than others. More studies of this kind would be interesting for the phonologist and the typologist.

When unadapated forms become established in the borrowing language, this results in phonological change in the language, for example, by introducing new phonemes or by relaxing phonotactic constraints. Investigation into these changes has led to the idea of a stratified lexicon, to which we will turn briefly now.

37.4.1 Lexical Strata

It has long been noted that borrowing can introduce new phonemes into a language (see, e.g. Thomason & Kaufman 1988 and references therein, also Eckman & Iverson, this volume). A common pathway is via the phonemicization of a formerly allophonic distinction. The data from Québec French in Picard & Nicol (1982), shown in (2), are a good example. In the native phonology, the diphthongs [aj, aw] are allophones of long monophthongs. However, when English words containing /aj, aw/ are imported, they fail to alternate, introducing contrast and minimal pairs. Similarly, Eckman & Iverson (this volume) discuss the phonemicization of the allophonic contrast between [h] and [ɸ] in Japanese.

Alternatively, a phoneme may be imported without the previous allophonic conditioning. The likelihood of a successful import seems to depend on how well the existing system accommodates the new arrival: a sound that fills an accidental gap in the borrowing language is more easily integrated into the L1 system. A case in point is the reintroduction of [g] into Dutch via borrowing. Historically, earlier Dutch /g/ under-went spirantization to [χ], leaving a gap in the system: all stops come in voiced-voiceless pairs, except for /k/, which is unpaired. Importing /g/ thus fills a gap that the earlier historical change had created. Besides, the new sound only recombines articulatory ges-tures (or distinctive features) that are already used. Dutch has voiced stops, and it has velar stops. Compare this to the low rate of adaptation of Spanish /r/ in Nahuatl (San Giacomo 2009): Nahuatl does not have a trill; the missing sound is not a combination of familiar gestures, thus /r/ is harder to integrate into the L1 system.

When a new sound is introduced, it is only found in loanwords (although it may subsequently spread to native items). Therefore, different constraints (inventory, phonotactics) may hold for native items and loans in the lexicon of a speaker, a point made already by Fries & Pike (1949), who noted that Spanish loanwords in Mazateco may violate constraints that hold for native items. In particular, they note that a pro-cess of postnasal voicing does not hold for Spanish-origin items, thereby introducing a phonemic voicing distinction on stops. In generative phonology, the idea of a strati-fied or compartmentalized lexicon was developed further. Lightner (1965) notes that native Russian words undergo processes that other, imported forms do not, and that non-Russian Slavic words undergo a subset of these processes. He suggests diacritic fea-tures on lexical items, such as [±Russian] and [±Slavic]. Aronoff (1976) takes up this idea and suggests a feature [±Latinate] for the English lexicon, to account for stem-affix combinatorics, an idea that is extended also into phonology, for example by Plag (1999). The idea of affix classes goes in a similar direction; Siegel (1974) already notices the role of etymology in class membership. Ito and Mester (1995) claim that the relation between such sublexica is not random but argue for a core-periphery structure of the lexicon instead, where constraints that hold on native vocabulary (the core) are increasingly relaxed the more one goes to the periphery, where loanwords first appear. Itô and Mester model this in OT by gradually demoting faithfulness constraints from the core gram-mar to more peripheral grammars. In his careful look at loanwords in Slovenian, Jurgec (2008) argues that faithfulness demotion cannot be the whole story, as he finds instances where there are tighter structural constraints on loans. At the same time, he largely con-firms the core-periphery structure, showing in detail how it works in Slovenian, and what intermediate stages of adaptation are found there, demonstrating once more that adaptation is not an either/or scenario.

37.4.2 The Role of Conventionalization

Now, if full adaptation is not a defining feature of loanwords, if loanwords can stay par-tially or fully unadapted in the lexicon, the question emerges how a loan can be distin-guished from a code-switch, a question that has occupied researchers on code-switching (see e.g. Poplack 1980, and Myers-Scotton 1993, for different positions), since there are one-word switches, while loans can be larger than an individual word (as in *déjà vu, je ne sais quoi*). The only reliable criterion that researchers seem to be able to agree on is listedness (Poplack et al. 1988, Myers-Scotton 1993, Muysken 1995): loanwords are listed in the L1 mental lexicon, and are understood by a large number of speakers.

This finding has important consequences for theories of loanword adaptation, since it is not the individual who borrows an item (an individual may code-switch and idiosyncratically adapt an item) but the speech community. Consequently, psycholinguistic approaches to loanword adaptation, such as studies of online adaptations and L2 perception, which are the main empirical support for the theory of perceptual adaptation, are insufficient, as they only look at the level of the individual speaker. They need to be supported by an explicitly sociolinguistic approach to loanword adaptation, an approach that fully acknowledges the role of conventions and conventionalization in the borrowing process.

I previously alluded to the idea that some segmental correspondences in borrowings may be conventionalized, disregarding actual (synchronic) perceptual similarity or phonological equivalence. I also suggested that there can be initial variation in the adaptation of a word, depending, for example, on the degree of bilingualism, with perceptual approximations, phonological adaptations and non-adaptations competing in a pool of variants, which will then undergo levelling and focusing on one or two variants. If it is the case, though, that adaptation is sociolinguistically mediated, one should also expect the possibility of purely conventionalized mappings, which new words automatically undergo.

A good example of such a conventionalized mapping is the adaptation of /h/ into Russian. Rather than being deleted or mapped onto [x] (a common L2 strategy), it is mapped onto [g], as in *gamburger* 'hamburger' or *galstuk* 'necktie' < German *Halstuch*. The motivation for this surprising mapping lies in the regular correspondence between Russian /g/ and Ukrainian /h/ (and Belarusian [ɣ]). Russian speakers use this knowledge to analyse all instances of [h] as a variant realization of /g/.

Such conventionalized mappings may be more frequent than often assumed. Why is English /ʌ/ borrowed as /a/ in German, but as /œ/ in Norwegian (as e.g. in *muffin*)? Maybe it is convention, each language reflecting different stages in the historical lowering of this vowel in English (from Middle English short /u/) with Norwegian preserving an older approximation—note that some older loanwords in German also have unexpected /œ/, for example *pumps*, *curry*. This conventionalization may be helped by imports via the written medium: orthographical influence may not be restricted to spelling pronunciations but also aid in conventionalizing segmental mappings between L1 and L2. Perhaps conventionalization also is an important factor in the conundrum of the differential adaptation of English interdental fricatives. Anecdotally, I know that German learners of English are told at school that /θ, ð/ are /s, z/ 'spoken with a lisp'. I cannot imagine a similar didactic 'aid' in languages where /θ, ð/ are adapted as /t, d/.

Conventions are, of course, influenced by actual language contact. An increase in L2 proficiency may lead to the modification of conventionalized mappings. In Russian, new borrowings containing /h/ often have the perceptually better motivated mapping to [x], as in *xaker, imxo, xobbi* 'hacker, imho, hobby', or lead to doublets; the Hudson River has [g], while Sherlock Holmes's landlady Mrs Hudson has [x]. The influence of L2 proficiency is also illustrated by the fate of initial /s/ in German loans. Standard German only has /z/, never /s/, in initial position, but English loans like *sex, surfing, singer-songwriter* introduce initial /s/, presumably under the influence of spoken English. Initial /s/ in Japanese loanwords like *samurai, sushi, Suzuki*, however, is conventionally realized as [z].

Further support for the idea of conventionalized mappings comes from what Janda et al. (1994) call 'hyperforeignisms', conventions based on overgeneralizing a perceived regularity. A striking example concerns the fate of final consonants in borrowings from French. American English speakers in particular overgeneralize the observation that final consonants are prone to deletion and consequently realize *coup de grace* as [kudəgrɑ:]. Janda et al. list a host of such examples, demonstrating that loanword adaptation is as much about arbitrary mapping conventions as it is about the desire to faithfully reproduce an input form. Models of loanword adaptation therefore have to take into account the role of the speech community; not every adaptation is phonetically minimal.

37.5 CONCLUSION

It is unlikely that one single strategy determines the loanword adaptation process. Instead, I argue that phonetic similarity and phonological equivalence (via contrast and opposition) both play a role, mediated by the degree of bilingualism found in the contact situation. Raw phonetic approximations should be found in cases of casual contact and contact in the oral medium only. Bilingualism and the introduction of words via the written domain favour phonological adaptations and the emergence of mapping conventions, if contact is sustained and a sufficiently large number of words is borrowed. This also means that we expect variation in the early stages of loanword nativization. I have therefore argued that the phonological and the psycholinguistic perspective, both of which are established in the literature, should be supplemented with a sociolinguistic approach. To my knowledge, there are no studies yet that try to relate the formal properties of the adapted word to the sociolinguistic setting in which it was borrowed. Future research could shed some light on this and potentially resolve the old dispute between 'phonological' and 'perceptual' approaches. Inspiration could be taken from the field of creole studies in which formal and sociolinguistic analyses have been integrated to a larger degree, to a similar end: to establish how the sociodemographic setting during creole formation influenced the outcome, the grammatical properties of the creole. Studies in loanword adaptation may benefit from a similar turn.

So how does loanword adaptation relate to other phonological change? The process of loanword adaptation is, of course, quite different from internally motivated diachronic change. We can see, however, that there are similar theoretical debates, so findings from one domain can potentially yield insight in the other domain as well. Both fields have seen a reorientation toward the listener, in listener-based approaches to diachronic change (Ohala 1981, Blevins 2004a, Yu, this volume) or in the perceptual approach to loanword adaptation, as an alternative to the traditional phonological approach. Central to both fields is the role of markedness, and both were given a fresh angle by Optimality Theory. Historical linguistics has also benefited from developments in quantitative sociolinguistics (see, e.g. Labov 1994, 2001, D'Arcy, this volume); tracing variation and change in real time in a speech community, and loanword adaptation could also benefit from this approach. To conclude, although the linguistic situation is very different, diachronic change and loanword adaptation seem to be subject to the same linguistic forces and principles, with similar debates dividing the scholarly community. Consequently, both fields can probably learn something from inspecting each other's findings, and develop a fresh perspective on the field that goes beyond current divisions.

REFERENCES

Abercrombie, David. 1949. What is a letter? *Lingua* 2: 54–63.

Abrahamsson, Niclas and Kenneth Hyltenstam. 2009. Age of onset and nativelikeness in a second language: listener perception versus linguistic scrutiny. *Language Learning* 59: 249–306.

Abrego-Collier, Carissa. 2013. Liquid dissimilation as listener hypocorrection. In *Proceedings of the 37th Annual Meeting of the Berkeley Linguistics Society*, 3–17.

Abrego-Collier, Carissa, Julian Grove, Morgan Sonderegger, and Alan C. L. Yu. 2011. Effects of speaker evaluation on phonetic convergence. In *Proceedings of the International Congress of the Phonetic Sciences*. Hong Kong: ICPhS.

Adam, Galit. 2002. From variable to optimal grammar: evidence from language acquisition and language change. PhD thesis, Tel-Aviv University.

Adler, Allison N. 2006. Faithfulness and perception in loanword adaptation: a case study from Hawaiian. *Lingua* 116(7): 1024–1045.

Aitchison, Jean. 2003. Psycholinguistic perspectives on language change. In Brian D. Joseph and Richard D. Janda (eds), *Handbook of Historical Linguistics*. Oxford: Blackwell, 736–43.

Aitken, Adam Jack. 1981. The Scottish vowel-length rule. In Michael Benskin and Michael Samuels (eds), *So Meny People, Longages and Tonges: Philological Essays in Scots and Medieval English Presented to Angus McIntosh*. Edinburgh: Edinburgh University Press, 131–157.

Alba, Matthew. 2008. Ratio frequency: insights into usage effects on phonological structure from hiatus resolution in New Mexican Spanish. *Studies in Hispanic and Lusophone Linguistics* 1: 247–86.

Alber, Birgit. 1997. Il sistema metrico dei prestiti del tedesco: aspetti e problemi della teoria prosodica. PhD thesis, University of Padua.

Albright, Adam. 2005. The morphological basis of paradigm leveling. In Laura J. Downing, T. A. Hall, and Renate Raffelsiefen (eds), *Paradigms in Phonological Theory*. New York: Oxford University Press, 17–43.

Albright, Adam. 2008. Explaining universal tendencies and language particulars in analogical change. In Jeff Good (ed.), *Language Universals and Language Change*. New York: Oxford University Press, 144–81.

Albright, Adam. 2009. Modeling analogy as probabilistic grammar. In J. P. Blevins and J. Blevins (eds), *Analogy in Grammar*. New York: Oxford University Press, 185–204.

Albright, Adam and Bruce Hayes. 2002. Modeling English past tense intuitions with minimal generalization. In Michael Maxwell (ed.), *Proceedings of the Sixth Meeting of the ACL Special Interest Group in Computational Phonology*. Cambridge, Mass.: Association for Computational Linguistics, 8–69.

Alim, H. Samy. 2004. *You Know My Steez: an Ethnographic and Sociolinguistic Study of Styleshifting in a Black American Speech Community*. Durham, NC: Duke University Press.

Allen, W. Sidney. 1953. *Phonetics in Ancient India*. London: Oxford University Press.

Allen, W. Sidney. 1965. *Vox Latina*. Cambridge: Cambridge University Press.

Allen, W. Sidney. 1974. *Vox Graeca: a Guide to the Pronunciation of Classical Greek*, 2nd edn. Cambridge: Cambridge University Press. [First edn 1968.]

Allen, Will, Joan Beal, Karen Corrigan, Warren Maguire, and Hermann Moisl. 2006. A linguistic 'time capsule': the Newcastle Electronic Corpus of Tyneside English. In Joan Beal, Karen Corrigan, and Hermann Moisl (eds), *Creating and Digitizing Language Corpora*, vol. 2: *Diachronic Databases*. Basingstoke: Palgrave Macmillan, 16–48.

Altenhofen, Cléo Vilson. 1996. *Hunsrückisch in Rio Grande do Sul: ein Beitrag zur Beschreibung einer deutschbrasilianischen Dialektvarietät im Kontakt mit dem Portugiesischen*. Stuttgart: Steiner.

Altmann, Gabriel, Haro von Buttlar, Walter Rott, and Udo Strauß. 1983. A law of change in language. In B. Brainerd (ed.), *Historical Linguistics*. Bochum: Brockmeyer, 104–15.

Alwan, Abeer, Shrikanth Narayanan, and Katherine Haker. 1997. Toward articulatory-acoustic models for liquid approximants based on MRI and EPG data, Part II: the rhotics. *Journal of the Acoustical Society of America* 101: 1078–89.

Andersen, Henning. 1973. Abductive and deductive change. *Language* 49: 765–93.

Andersen, Henning. 1978. Perceptual and conceptual factors in abductive innovations. In Jacek Fisiak (ed.), *Recent Developments in Historical Phonology*. The Hague: Mouton, 1–22.

Andersen, Henning. 1980. Morphological change: towards a typology. In Jacek Fisiak (ed.), *Historical Morphology*. New York: Mouton, 1–50.

Andersen, Henning. 1982. Bredsdorff: life and work. *Historiographia Linguistica* 9: 24–41.

Andersen, Henning. 1989. Understanding linguistic innovations. In L. E. Breivik and E. H. Jahr (eds), *Language Change: Contributions to the Study of its Causes*. Berlin: Mouton de Gruyter, 5–28.

Andersen, Henning. 2001. Markedness and the theory of linguistic change. In Henning Andersen (ed.), *Actualization Linguistic Change in Progress*. Philadelphia: Benjamins, 21–57.

Andersen, Henning. 2006. Synchrony, diachrony and evolution. In Ole Nedergaard Thomsen (ed.), *Competing Models of Linguistic Change*. Philadelphia: Benjamins, 59–90.

Anderson, John. 2011. *The Substance of Language*, vol. 1: *The Domain of Syntax*; vol. 2: *Morphology, Paradigms, and Periphrases*; vol. 3: *Phonology–Syntax Analogies*. Oxford: Oxford University Press.

Anderson, John and Colin Ewen. 1987. *Principles of Dependency Phonology*. Cambridge: Cambridge University Press.

Anderson, John and Charles Jones. 1974. Three theses concerning phonological representations. *Journal of Linguistics* 10: 1–26.

Anderson, John and Charles Jones. 1977. *Phonological Structure and the History of English*. Amsterdam: North-Holland.

Anderson, Stephen. 1981. Why phonology isn't 'natural'. *Linguistic Inquiry*, 12: 493–539.

Anderson, Stephen R. 1985. *Phonology in the Twentieth Century: Theories of Rules and Theories of Representations*. Chicago: University of Chicago Press.

Anderson, Stephen R. 1988. Morphological change. In Frederick J. Newmeyer (ed.), *Linguistics: The Cambridge Survey*, vol. 1. Cambridge: Cambridge University Press, 324–62.

Andreev, Nikolaj D. 1957. Periodizacija istorii indoevropejskogo prajazyka. *Voprosy Jazykoznanija* 6: 3–18.

Andruski, Jean and Martha Ratliff. 2000. Phonation types in production of phonological tone: the case of Green Mong. *Journal of the International Phonetic Association* 30: 37–61.

Anttila, Arto. 2002. Variation and phonological theory. In J. K. Chambers, Peter Trudgill, and Natalie Schilling-Estes (eds), *The Handbook of Language Variation and Change*. Oxford: Blackwell, 206–43.

Anttila, Raimo. 1977. *Analogy*. New York: Mouton.

Anttila, Raimo. 2003. Analogy: the warp and woof of cognition. In Brian D. Joseph and Richard D. Janda (eds), *Handbook of Historical Linguistics*. Oxford: Blackwell, 425–40.

Apted, Michael. 1964-2012. *Seven Up!, 7 Plus Seven, 21 Up, 28 Up, 35 Up, 42 Up, 49 Up, 56 Up*. Film series.

Archangeli, Diana. 1997. Optimality Theory: an introduction to linguistics in the 1990s. In Diana Archangeli and D. Terence Langendoen (eds), *Optimality Theory: an Overview*. Oxford: Blackwell, 1–32.

Arnaud, René. 1998. The development of the progressive in 19th century English: a quantitative survey. *Language Variation and Change* 10: 123–52.

Aronoff, Mark. 1976. *Word Formation in Generative Grammar*. Cambridge, Mass.: MIT Press,.

Aroui, Jean-Louis. 2009. Proposals for metrical typology. In Jean-Louis Aroui and Andy Arleo (eds), *Towards a Typology of Poetic Forms: From Language to Metrics and Beyond*. Amsterdam: Benjamins, 1–40.

Ash, Sherry. 1982. The vocalization of /l/ in Philadelphia. PhD thesis, University of Pennsylvania.

Ashby, William J. 2001. Un nouveau regard sur la chute du *ne* en français parlé tourangeau: s'agit-il d'un changement en cours? *French Language Studies* 11: 1–22.

Assmann, Peter F. and William F. Katz. 2000. Time-varying spectral change in the vowels of children and adults. *Journal of the Acoustical Society of America* 108: 1856–66.

Auer, Peter, Jacinta Arnhold, and Cintia Bueno Aniola. 2005. Being 'Colono' and being 'Daitsch' in Rio Grande do Sul: language choice and linguistic heterogeneity. *Calidoscópio: Universidade do vale do Rio dos Sinos* 3(3): 170–83.

Avery, Peter. 1996. The representation of voicing contrasts. PhD thesis, University of Toronto.

Avery, Peter and William Idsardi. 2001. Laryngeal dimensions, completion and enhancement. In T. Alan Hall (ed.), *Distinctive Feature Theory*. Berlin: Mouton de Gruyter, 41–70.

Baayen, R. Harald. 2007. Storage and computation in the mental lexicon. In G. Jarema and G. Libben (eds), *The Mental Lexicon: Core Perspectives*. New York: Elsevier, 81–104.

Babel, Molly Elizabeth. 2009. Phonetic and social selectivity in speech accommodation. PhD thesis, University of California, Berkeley.

Babitch, Rose Mary and Eric Lebrun. 1989. Dialectometry as computerized agglomerative hierarchical classification analysis. *Journal of English Linguistics* 22(1): 83–90.

Bach, Emmon and R. T. Harms. 1972. How do languages get crazy rules? In Robert Stockwell and Ronald Macaulay (eds), *Linguistic Change and Generative Theory*. Bloomington: Indiana University Press, 1–21.

Baer, Thomas, Peter J. Alfonso, and Kiyoshi Honda. 1988. Electromyography of the tongue muscles during vowels in /əpVp/ environment. *Annual Bulletin of the Research Institute of Logopedics and Phoniatrics* (University of Tokyo) 22: 7–18.

Baese-Berk, Melissa and Matthew Goldrick. 2009. Mechanisms of interaction in speech production. *Language and Cognitive Processes* 24: 527–54.

Bailey, Charles James. 1973. *Variation and Linguistic Theory*. Washington, DC: Centre for Applied Linguistics.

Bailey, Don Clifford. 1960. Early Japanese Lexicography. *Monumenta Nipponica* 16: 1–52.

Bailey, Guy. 2002. Real and apparent time. In J. K. Chambers, P. Trudgill, and N. Schilling-Estes (eds), *The Handbook of Language Variation and Change*. Malden, Mass.: Blackwell, 312–32. Second edition, 2005.

Bailey, Guy, Tom Wikle, Jan Tillery, and Lori Sand. 1991. The apparent time construct. *Language Variation and Change* 3: 241–64.

Baker, Adam, Diana Archangeli, and Jeff Mielke. 2011. Variability in American English s-retraction suggests a solution to the actuation problem. *Language Variation and Change* 23: 347–74.

Baker, Gary K. 2007. Duration, voice, and dispersion in stop contrasts from Latin to Spanish. In Fernando Martínez-Gil and Sonia Colina (eds), *Optimality-Theoretic Studies in Spanish Phonology*. Amsterdam: Benjamins, 399–423.

Baker, Rachel, Rachel Smith, and Sarah Hawkins. 2007. Phonetic differences between *mis-* and *dis-* in English prefixed and pseudo-prefixed words. In *Proceedings of the XVIth International Congress of the Phonetic Sciences*, Universität des Saarlandes, Saarbrücken, Germany (paper ID: 1507).

Bakken, Kristin. 2001. Patterns of restitution of sound change. In H. Andersen (ed.), *Actualization: Linguistic Change in Progress*. Amsterdam: Benjamins, 59–78.

Ball, Philip. 1999. *The Self-Made Tapestry: Pattern Formation in Nature*. Oxford: Oxford University Press.

Bammesberger, Alfred. 1999. *Die Morphologie des urgermanischen Nomens*. Heidelberg: Winter.

Bard, Ellen Gurman, Anne H. Anderson, Catherine Sotillo, Matthew Aylett, Gwyneth Doherty-Sneddon, and Alison Newlands. 2000. Controlling the intelligibility of referring expressions in dialogue. *Journal of Memory and Language* 42: 1–22.

Barnes, Deborah E., Jane A. Cauley, Li-Yung Lui, H. Fink, Charles McCulloch, Katie L. Stone, and Kristine Yaffe. 2007. Women who maintain optimal cognitive function into old age. *Journal of the American Geriatric Society* 55: 259–64.

Baron, Naomi S. 1977. *Language Acquisition and Historical Change*. Amsterdam: North-Holland.

Baron-Cohen, Simon, Jennifer Richler, Dheraj Bisarya, Nhishanth Gurunathan, and Sally Wheelwright. 2003. The Systemising Quotient (SQ): an investigation of adults with Asperger Syndrome or high functioning autism and normal sex differences. *Philosophical Transactions of the Royal Society*, series B, 358: 361–74.

Baron-Cohen, Simon and Sally Wheelwright. 2004. The Empathy Quotient: an investigation of adults with Asperger Syndrome or high functioning autism and normal sex differences. *Journal of Autism and Developmental Disorders* 34(2): 163–75.

Baron-Cohen, Simon, Sally Wheelwright, Richard Skinner, Joanne Martin, and Emma Clubley. 2001. The autism-spectrum quotient (aq): evidence from Asperger syndrome/ high-functioning autism males, females, scientists and mathematicians. *Journal of Autism and Developmental Disorders* 31: 5–17.

Barrack, Charles M. 2002. The Glottalic Theory revisited: a negative appraisal. *Indogermanische Forschungen* 107: 76–95.

Barrack, Charles M. 2003. The Glottalic Theory revisited, Part II: the typological fallacy underlying the Glottalic Theory. *Indogermanische Forschungen* 108: 1–16.

Barrie, Mike. 2003. Contrast in Cantonese vowels. *Toronto Working Papers in Linguistics* 20: 1–19.

Barry, William J. and Bistra Andreeva. 2001. Cross-language similarities and differences in spontaneous speech patterns. *Journal of the International Phonetic Association* 31: 51–66.

Bartsch, Renate and Theo Vennemann. 1982. *Grundzüge der Sprachtheorie: eine linguistische Einführung*. Tübingen: Niemeyer.

Bat-El, Outi. 1994. Stem modification and cluster transfer in Modern Hebrew. *Natural Language and Linguistic Theory* 12: 571–593.

Bat-El, Outi. 2003. Semitic verb structure within a universal perspective. In J. Shimron (ed.), *Language Processing and Acquisition in Languages of Semitic, Root-Based, Morphology*. Amsterdam: Benjamins, 29–59.

Bat-El, Outi. 2011. Semitic templates. In Marc van Oostendorp, Colin J. Ewen, Elizabeth V. Hume, and Keren Rice (eds), *Blackwell Companion to Phonology*. Malden, Mass.: Wiley-Blackwell, 2586–2608.

Batibo, Herman M. 1995. Loanword clusters nativization rules in Tswana and Swahili. *South African Journal of African Languages* 16: 33–41.

Baudouin de Courtenay, Jan Niecisław. 1895. *Versuch einer Theorie phonetischer Alternationen: ein Capitel aus der Psychophonetik*. Strassburg: Trübner. [Trans. Edward Stankiewicz, An attempt at a theory of phonetic alternations. In E. Stankiewicz (ed.) 1972, *A Baudouin de Courtenay Anthology: the Beginnings of Structural Linguistics*. Bloomington: Indiana University Press, 144–212.]

Baudouin de Courtenay, Jan Niecisław. 1913/17. *Vvedenie v jazykovedenie*, 5th edn. Petrograd: Izd. Kassy vzaimopomoshchi.

Bauer, Laurie. 2000. The dialectal origins of New Zealand English. In Allan Bell and Koenraad Kuiper (eds), *New Zealand English*. Amsterdam: Benjamins, 40–52.

Bauer, Laurie. 2002. Inferring variation and change from public corpora. In J. K. Chambers, Peter Trudgill, and Natalie Schilling-Estes (eds), *The Handbook of Language Variation and Change*. Oxford: Blackwell, 97–114.

Bauer, Laurie. 2008. Lenition revisited. *Journal of Linguistics* 44: 605–24.

Bauer, Matthew. 2009. Sound change and functionalism: the role of laryngeal height. *Proceedings from the Annual Meeting of the Chicago Linguistics Society* 45(1) 29–38.

Baugh, Albert C. and Thomas Cable. 1993. *A History of the English Language*, 4th ed. London: Routledge.

Baugh, John. 1996. Dimensions of the theory of econolinguistics. In G. Guy, C. Feagin, D. Schiffrin, and J. Baugh (eds), *Towards a Social Science of Language: Papers in Honor of William Labov*, vol. 1. Philadelphia: Benjamins, 397–419.

Baxter, William H. and Alexis Manaster Ramer. 1996. Review of Don Ringe, 'On calculating the factor of chance in language comparison'. *Diachronica* 13(2): 371–84.

Baxter, William H. and Alexis Manaster Ramer 2000. Beyond lumping and splitting: probabilistic issues in historical linguistics. In Colin Renfrew, April McMahon, and Larry Trask (eds), *Time Depth in Historical Linguistics*. Cambridge: McDonald Institute for Archaeological Research, 167–88.

Bazell, Charles E. 1954. On the choice of criteria in structural linguistics. *Word* 10: 6–15.

Becanus, Johannes Gropius. 1569. *Origines Antwerpianae*. Antwerp: Ex Officina Christophori Plantinin.

Beck, Janet Mackenzie. 1997. Organic variation of the vocal apparatus. In William J. Hardcastle and John Laver (eds), *The Handbook of Phonetic Sciences*. Oxford: Blackwell, 256–97.

Becker, Thomas. 1990. *Analogie und morphologische Theorie*. Munich: Fink.

Becker, Thomas. 1998. *Das Vokalsystem der deutschen Standardsprache*. Frankfurt am Main: Lang.

Beckner, Clay, Richard Blythe, Joan Bybee, Morten H. Christiansen, William Croft, Nick C. Ellis, John Holland, Jinyun Ke, Diane Larsen-Freeman, and Tom Schoenemann. 2009. Language is a complex adaptive system. *Language Learning* 59: 4S1.

Beckwith, Christopher I. 2007. *Koguryo: Language of Japan's Continental Relatives*, 2nd edn. Leiden: Brill.

Beddor, Patrice. 2009. A coarticulatory path to sound change. *Language* 85: 785–821.

Beddor, Patrice and Handan Yavuz. 1995. The relation between vowel-to-vowel coarticulation and vowel harmony in Turkish. *Proceedings of the International Conference of the Phonetic Sciences 1995*, 2: 44–51.

Beddor, Patrice Speeter and Rena Arens Krakow. 1999. Perception of coarticulatory nasalization by speakers of English and Thai: evidence for partial compensation. *Journal of the Acoustical Society of America* 106(5): 2868–87.

Beddor, Patrice Speeter, James D. Harnsberger, and Stephanie Lindemann. 2002. Language-specific patterns of vowel-to-vowel coarticulation: acoustic structures and their perceptual correlates. *Journal of Phonetics* 30: 591–627.

Beekes, Robert. 1995. *Comparative Indo-European Linguistics: an Introduction*. Amsterdam: Benjamins.

Bell, Alan. 1977. The distributional syllable. In Alphonse Juilland (ed.), *Linguistic Studies Offered to Joseph Greenberg on the Occasion of his Sixtieth Birthday*. Saratoga, Calif.: Anma Libri, 249–62.

Bell, Alan, Jason Brenier, Michelle Gregory, Cynthia Girand, and Dan Jurafsky. 2009. Predictability effects on durations of content and function words in conversational English. *Journal of Memory and Language* 60(1): 92–111.

Bell, Alan and Joan B. Hooper. 1978. Issues and evidence in syllabic phonology. In Alan Bell and Joan B. Hooper (eds), *Syllables and Segments*, Amsterdam: North-Holland, 3–22.

Bell, Alan, Daniel Jurafsky, Eric Folser-Lussier, Cynthia Girand, Michelle Gregory, and Daniel Gildea. 2003. Effect of disfluencies, predictability, and utterance position on word form variation in English conversation. *Journal of the Acoustic Society of America* 113: 1001–24.

Bell-Berti, Fredericka. 1975. Control of pharyngeal cavity size for English voiced and voiceless stops. *Journal of the Acoustical Society of America* 57(2): 456–61.

Bell-Berti, Fredericka, Lawrence J. Raphael, David B. Pisoni, and James R. Sawusch. 1979. Some relationships between speech production and perception. *Phonetica* 36: 373–83.

Bender, Margaret. 2000. Review of *Lexical Acculturation in Native American Languages* by Cecil H. Brown. *American Anthropologist* 102: 643–44.

Benedict, Paul K. 1997. Interphyla flow in Southeast Asia. *Mon-Khmer Studies* 27: 1–11.

Benediktsson, Hreinn. 1972. *The First Grammatical Treatise*. Reykjavik: Institute of Nordic Linguistics.

Benediktsson, Hreinn. 1982. Nordic umlaut and breaking: thirty years of research, 1951–1980. *Nordic Journal of Linguistics* 5: 1–60.

Benjamini, Yoav and Yosef Hochberg. 1995. Controlling the false discovery rate: a practical and powerful approach to multiple testing. *Journal of the Royal Statistical Society*, series B (Methodological) 57(1): 289–300.

Benskin, Michael. 1997. Texts from an English township in late medieval Ireland. *Collegium Mediaevale* 10: 91–173.

Benskin, Michael. 2001. The language of the English texts. In T. Hunt and M. Benskin (eds), *Three Receptaria from Medieval England*. Oxford: Society for the Study of Medieval Languages and Literature, 193–230.

Benskin, Michael and M. Laing. 1981. Translations and *Mischsprachen* in Middle English manuscripts. In M. Benskin and M. L. Samuels (eds), *So Meny People Longages and Tonges: Philological Essays in Scots and Mediaeval English Presented to Angus McIntosh*. Edinburgh: University of Edinburgh, 55–106.

Benson, Erica J., Michael J. Fox, and Jared Balkman. 2011. The bag that Scott bought: the low vowels in northwest Wisconsin. *American Speech* 86(3): 271–311.

Benware, Wilbur A. 1974. *The Study of Indo-European Vocalism in the 19th Century*. Amsterdam: Benjamins.

Benware, Wilbur A. 1996. Processual change and phonetic analogy: Early New High German. *American Journal of Germanic Linguistics and Literatures* 8: 265–87.

Berent, Iris. 2009. Unveiling phonological universals: a linguist who asks 'why' is (inter alia) an experimental psychologist. *Behavioral and Brain Sciences* 32: 450–51.

Berent, Iris, Tracy Lennertz, Jungho Jun, Miguel A. Moreno, and Paul Smolensky. 2008. Language universals in human brains. *Proceedings of the National Academy of Sciences* 105: 5321–5.

Berent, Iris, Tracy Lennertz, and Paul Smolensky. 2009. Listeners' knowledge of phonological universals: evidence from nasal clusters. *Phonology* 26: 75–108.

Berent, Iris, Donca Steriade, Tracy Lennertz, and Vered Vaknin. 2007. What we know about what we have never heard: evidence from perceptual illusions. *Cognition* 104: 591–630.

Berg, Thomas. 1990. Review of Vennemann 1988. *Journal of Linguistics* 26: 569–570.

Berg, Thomas. 1998. *Linguistic Structure and Change: an Explanation from Language Processing*. Oxford: Oxford University Press.

Bermúdez-Otero, Ricardo. 1998. Prosodic optimization: the Middle English length adjustment. *English Language and Linguistics* 2: 169–97.

Bermúdez-Otero, Ricardo. 1999. Constraint interaction in language change: quantity in English and Germanic. PhD thesis, University of Manchester and Universidad de Santiago de Compostela. Available at: <http://www.bermudez-otero.com/Ph.D.pdf>

Bermúdez-Otero, Ricardo. 2005. Review of *Alliteration and Sound Change in Early English* by Donka Minkova. *Diachronica* 22: 438–45.

Bermúdez-Otero, Ricardo. 2006. Phonological change in Optimality Theory. In Keith Brown (ed.), *Encyclopedia of Language and Linguistics*, 2nd edn, vol. 9. Oxford: Elsevier, 497–505.

Bermúdez-Otero, Ricardo. 2007. Diachronic phonology. In Paul de Lacy (ed.), *The Cambridge Handbook of Phonology*. Cambridge: Cambridge University Press, 497–517.

Bermúdez-Otero, Ricardo. 2010. Morphologically conditioned phonetics? Not proven. Paper given at On Linguistic Interfaces II, Belfast, 2 December. Handout available at: <http://www.bermudez-otero.com/Belfast_handout.pdf>

Bermúdez-Otero, Ricardo. 2011. Cyclicity. In Marc van Oostendorp, Colin J. Ewen, Elizabeth Hume and Keren Rice (eds), *The Blackwell Companion to Phonology*, vol. 4. Malden, Mass.: Wiley-Blackwell, 2019–48.

Bermúdez-Otero, Ricardo. 2012. The architecture of grammar and the division of labour in exponence. In Jochen Trommer (ed.), *The Morphology and Phonology of Exponence*. Oxford: Oxford University Press, 8–83.

Bermúdez-Otero, Ricardo. 2013. The Spanish lexicon stores stems with theme vowels, not roots with inflectional class features. *Probus* 25(1): 3–103.

Bermúdez-Otero, Ricardo and Kersti Börjars. 2006. Markedness in phonology and in syntax: the problem of grounding. *Lingua* 116: 710–56.

Bermúdez-Otero, Ricardo and Richard M. Hogg. 2003. The actuation problem in Optimality Theory: phonologization, rule inversion, and rule loss. In D. Eric Holt (ed.), *Optimality Theory and Language Change*. Dordrecht: Kluwer, 91–119.

Bermúdez-Otero, Ricardo and April McMahon. 2006. English phonology and morphology. In Bas Aarts and April McMahon (eds), *The Handbook of English Linguistics*. Oxford: Blackwell, 382–410.

Bermúdez-Otero, Ricardo and Graeme Trousdale. 2012. Cycles and continua: on unidirectionality and gradualness in language change. In Terttu Nevalainen and Elizabeth Closs Traugott (eds), *The Oxford Handbook of the History of English*. New York: Oxford University Press, 691–720.

Bernard, John R. 1989. Quantitative aspects of the sounds of Australian English. In Peter Collins and David Blair (eds), *Australian English: The Language of a New Society*. St Lucia: University of Queensland Press, 187–204.

Bhaskararao, Peri. 1999. Voiced aspiration and tonogenesis in some South-Asian languages. In Shigeki Kaji (ed.), *Proceedings of the Symposium on Cross-Linguistic Studies of Tonal Phenomena: Tonogenesis, Typology, and Related Topics*. Tokyo: Institute for the Study of Languages and Cultures of Asia and Africa, Tokyo University of Foreign Studies, 337–45.

Bhat, D. N. S. 1978. Palatalization. In *Universals of Human Language, 2: Phonology*. Stanford, Calif.: Stanford University Press, 47–92.

Bialystok, Ellen and Kenji Hakuta. 1999. Confounded age: linguistic and cognitive factors in age differences for second language acquisition. In David Birdsong (ed.), *Second Language Acquisition and the Critical Period Hypothesis*. Mahwah, NJ: Erlbaum, 161–81.

Bigham, Douglas S. 2010. Mechanisms of accommodation among emerging adults in a university setting. *Journal of English Linguistics* 38: 193–210.

Birdsong, David. 2005. Interpreting age effects in second language acquisition. In Judith F. Kroll and Annette M. B. De Groot (eds), *Handbook of Bilingualism: Psycholinguistic Approaches*. Oxford: Oxford University Press, 109–27.

Blake, Renée and Meredith Josey. 2003. The /ay/ diphthong in a Martha's Vineyard community: what can we say 40 years after Labov? *Language in Society* 32: 451–85.

Blanc, Haim. 1968. The Israeli Koine as an emergent national standard. In Joshua A. Fishman, Charles A. Ferguson, and Jyotirindra Das Gupta (eds), *Language Problems in Developing Nations*. New York: Wiley, 237–51.

Blevins, James P. 2004. Inflection classes and economy. In Gereon Müller, Lutz Gunkel, and Gisela Zifonun (eds), *Explorations in Nominal Inflection*. New York: de Gruyter, 41–85.

Blevins, James P. and Juliette Blevins. 2009. Introduction: analogy in grammar. In James P. Blevins and Juliette Blevins (eds), *Analogy in Grammar: Form and Acquisition*. New York: Oxford University Press, 1–12.

Blevins, Juliette. 1995. The syllable in phonological theory. In J. A. Goldsmith (ed.), *The Handbook of Phonological Theory*. Cambridge, Mass.: Blackwell, 206–44.

Blevins, Juliette. 2001. Where have all the onsets gone? Initial consonant loss in Australian Aboriginal languages. In Jane Simpson, David Nash, Mary Laughren, Peter Austin, and Barry Alpher (eds), *Forty Years On: Ken Hale and Australian Languages*. Canberra: Australian National University, 481–92.

Blevins, Juliette. 2004a. *Evolutionary Phonology: The Emergence of Sound Patterns*. Cambridge: Cambridge University Press.

Blevins, Juliette. 2004b. The mystery of Austronesian final consonant loss. *Oceanic Linguistics* 43: 179–84.

Blevins, Juliette. 2005. The role of phonological predictability in sound change: privileged reduction in Oceanic reduplicated substrings. *Oceanic Linguistics* 44: 455–64.

Blevins, Juliette. 2006a. A theoretical synopsis of evolutionary phonology. *Theoretical Linguistics* 32: 117–65.

Blevins, Juliette. 2006b. Reply to commentaries. *Theoretical Linguistics* 32: 245–56.

Blevins, Juliette. 2006c. New perspectives on English sound patterns: 'natural' and 'unnatural' in evolutionary phonology. *Journal of English Linguistics* 34: 6–25.

Blevins, Juliette. 2007. The importance of typology in explaining recurrent sound patterns. *Linguistic Typology* 11: 107–13.

Blevins, Juliette. 2008a. Consonant epenthesis: natural and unnatural histories. In Jeff Good (ed.), *Language Universals and Language Change*. Oxford: Oxford University Press, 79–107.

Blevins, Juliette. 2008b. Natural and unnatural sound patterns: a pocket field guide. In Klaas Willems and Ludovic De Cuypere (eds), *Naturalness and Iconicity in Language*. Amsterdam: Benjamins, 121–48.

Blevins, Juliette. 2008c. Phonetic explanation without compromise: the evolution of Mussau syncope. *Diachronica* 25: 1–19.

Blevins, Juliette. 2009a. Phonetic explanations for recurrent sound patterns: diachronic or synchronic? In C. Cairns and E. Raimy (eds), *Contemporary Views on Architecture and Representations in Phonology*. Cambridge, Mass.: MIT Press, 325–36.

Blevins, Juliette. 2009b. Structure-preserving sound change: a look at unstressed vowel syncope in Austronesian. In Alexander Adelaar and Andrew Pawley (eds), *Austronesian Historical Linguistics and Culture History: a Festschrift for Bob Blust*. Canberra: Pacific Linguistics, 33–49.

Blevins, Juliette. 2009c. Low vowel dissimilation outside Oceanic: the case of Alamblak. *Oceanic Linguistics* 48(2): 477–83.

Blevins, Juliette. 2010a. Sound patterns of words across time and space. Handout of talk from CUNY Conference on the Word, January 2010.

Blevins, Juliette. 2010b. Phonetically-based sound patterns: typological tendencies or phonological universals? In C. Fougeron, B. Kühnert, M. D'Imperio, and N. Vallée (eds), *Papers in Laboratory Phonology X: Variation, Phonetic Detail and Phonological Modeling*. Berlin: Mouton de Gruyter, 201–24.

Blevins, Juliette. 2011. Perceptual similarity and sound change typology: notes on θ>f and f>θ. MS, CUNY.

Blevins, Juliette and Andrew Garrett. 1998. The origins of consonant-vowel metathesis. *Language* 74: 508–56.

Blevins, Juliette and Andrew Garrett. 2004. The evolution of metathesis. In Bruce Hayes, Robert Kirchner, and Donca Steriade (eds), *Phonetically Based Phonology*. Cambridge: Cambridge University Press, 117–56.

Blevins, Juliette and Sven Grawunder. 2009. *Kl>Tl sound change in Germanic and elsewhere: descriptions, explanations, and implications. *Linguistic Typology* 13: 267–303.

Blevins, Juliette and Daniel Kaufman. 2012. Origins of Palauan intrusive velar nasals. *Oceanic Linguistics* 51: 18–32.

Blevins, Juliette and Andrew Wedel. 2009. Inhibited sound change: an evolutionary approach to lexical competition. *Diachronica* 26(2): 143–83.

Bloch, Bernard. 1948. A set of postulates for phonemic analysis. *Language* 24: 3–46.

Blondeau, Hélène. 2001. Corpora comparability and changes in real time within the paradigm of the personal pronouns in Montreal French. *Journal of Sociolinguistics* 5: 453–74.

Blondeau, Hélène. 2006. Le trajectoire de l'emploi du futur chez une cohorte de Montréalais francophones entre 1971 et 1995. *Revue canadienne de linguistique appliquée* 9: 73–95.

Bloomfield, Leonard. 1924. Review of F. de Saussure, *Cours de linguistique générale*, 2nd edn. *Modern Language Journal* 8: 317–19.

Bloomfield, Leonard. 1926. A set of postulates for the science of language. *Language* 2: 153–64.

Bloomfield, Leonard. 1933. *Language.* New York: Holt.

Blumenfeld, Lev. 2001. Russian palatalization in Stratal OT. MS, Stanford University.

Blust, Robert A. 1974. A double counter-universal in Kelabit. *Papers in Linguistics* 7(3/4): 309–24.

Blust, Robert. 1993. Central and Central-Eastern Malayo-Polynesian. *Oceanic Linguistics* 32: 241–93.

Blust, Robert. 1994. Obstruent epenthesis and the unity of phonological features. *Lingua* 93: 111–39.

Blust, Robert. 1996a. The neogrammarian hypothesis and pandemic irregularity. In Mark Durie and Malcolm Ross (eds), *The Comparative Method Reviewed: Regularity and Irregularity in Language Change.* Oxford: Oxford University Press, 135–56.

Blust, Robert. 1996b. Low vowel dissimilation in Ere. *Oceanic Linguistics* 35: 96–112.

Blust, Robert. 1996c. Low vowel dissimilation in Oceanic languages: an addendum. *Oceanic Linguistics* 35: 305–9.

Blust, Robert. 2000. Chamorro historical phonology. *Oceanic Linguistics* 39: 83–122.

Blust, Robert. 2001. Some remarks on stress, syncope, and gemination in Mussau. *Oceanic Linguistics* 40: 143–50.

Blust, Robert. 2004. *t to k: an Austronesian sound change revisited. *Oceanic Linguistics* 43: 365–411.

Blust, Robert. 2005. Must sound change be linguistically motivated? *Diachronica* 22: 219–69.

Blust, Robert A. 2006. The origin of the Kelabit voiced aspirates: a historical hypothesis revisited. *Oceanic Linguistics* 45(2): 311–38.

Blust, Robert. 2007. Dyllabic attractors and anti-antigemination in Austronesian sound change. *Phonology* 24: 1–36.

Blust, Robert. 2009. Palauan historical phonology: whence the intrusive velar nasal? *Oceanic Linguistics* 48: 307–36.

Blust, Robert. 2012. Primary split revisited. *Diachronica* 29: 129–38.

Blythe, Richard A. and William Croft. 2012. S-curves and the mechanisms of propagation in language change. *Language* 88: 269–304.

Boberg, Charles. 2001. The phonological status of Western New England. *American Speech* 76: 3–29.

Boberg, Charles. 2004. Real and apparent time in language change: late adoption of changes in Montreal English. *American Speech* 79: 250–69.

Boersma, Paul. 1998. *Functional Phonology: Formalizing the Interactions between Articulatory and Perceptual Drives.* The Hague: Holland Academic Graphics.

Boersma, Paul. 2003. The odds of eternal optimization in Optimality Theory. In D. Eric Holt (ed.), *Optimality Theory and Language Change.* Dordrecht: Kluwer Academic, 31–65.

Boersma, Paul. 2009a. Cue constraints and their interaction in phonological perception and production. In Paul Boersma and Silke Hamann (eds), *Phonology in Perception.* Berlin: Mouton de Gruyter, 55–109.

Boersma, Paul. 2009b. A programme for bidirectional phonology and phonetics and their acquisition and evolution. MS. Amsterdam: Institute of Phonetic Sciences, University of Amsterdam. Available at: <http://www.fon.hum.uva.nl/paul/papers/BiPhon19.pdf>

Boersma, Paul. 2012. Modeling phonological category learning. In Abigail C. Cohn, Cécile Fougeron, and Marie K. Huffman (eds), *The Oxford Handbook of Laboratory Phonology.* Oxford: Oxford University Press, 207–18.

Boersma, Paul and Silke Hamann. 2008. The evolution of auditory dispersion in bidirectional constraint grammars. *Phonology* 25: 217–70.

Boersma, Paul and Silke Hamann. 2009. Loanword adaptation as first-language phonological perception. In A. Calabrese and L. Wetzels (eds), *Loan Phonology*. Amsterdam: Benjamins, 11–58.

Boersma, Paul and Bruce Hayes. 2001. Empirical tests of the gradual learning algorithm. *Linguistic Inquiry* 32: 45–86.

Bolinger, Dwight. 1968. *Aspects of Language*. New York: Harcourt.

Bolognesi, Roberto. 1998. *The Phonology of Campidanian Sardinian*. Dordrecht: HIL.

Booij, Geert. 1995. *The Phonology of Dutch*. Oxford: Clarendon Press.

Booij, Geert. 1996. Lexical Phonology and the derivational residue. In Jacques Durand and Bernard Laks (eds), *Current Trends in Phonology: Models and Methods*. European Studies Research Institute and University of Salford.

Booij, Geert. 1997. Non-derivational phonology meets Lexical Phonology. In Iggy Roca (ed.), *Derivations and Constraints in the Lexicon*. Oxford: Clarendon Press.

Booij, Geert. 1998. Phonological output constraints in morphology. In Wolfgang Kehrein and Richard Wiese (eds), *Phonology and Morphology of the Germanic Languages*. Tübingen: Niemeyer, 143–63.

Booij, Geert. 2002a. *The Morphology of Dutch*. New York: Oxford University Press.

Booij, Geert. 2002b. The balance between storage and computation in the language faculty. Science Prestige Lecture given at the University of Canterbury, Christchurch, 30 July 2002.

Booij, Geert. 2010. *Construction Morphology*. New York: Oxford University Press.

Booij, Geert and Jerzy Rubach. 1987. Postcyclic versus postlexical rules in Lexical Phonology. *Linguistic Inquiry* 18: 1–44.

Bopp, Franz. 1816. *Über das Konjugationssystem der Sanskritsprache in Vergleichung mit jenem der griechischen, lateinischen, persischen und germanischen Sprache*. Frankfurt am Main: Windischmann. Repr. 1975, Hildesheim: Olms.

Botma, Bert. 2004. Phonological aspects of nasality: an element-based dependency approach. PhD thesis, University of Amsterdam.

Bottiglioni, Gino. 1922. *Leggende i tradizioni di Sardegna: texti dialettali in grafia fonetica*. Geneva: Olschki.

Bourciez, Edouard and Jean Bourciez. 1967. *Phonétique française*, 9th edn. Paris: Klincksieck.

Boutkan, Dirk. 1995. *The Germanic 'Auslautgesetze'*. Amsterdam: Rodopi.

Bowie, David. 2005. Language change over the lifespan: a test of the apparent time construct. *University of Pennsylvania Working Papers in Linguistics: Selected Papers from NWAV 33* 11(2): 45–58.

Bowie, David. 2010. The ageing voice: changing identity over time. In C. Llamas and D. Watt (eds), *Language and Identities*. Edinburgh: Edinburgh University Press, 55–66.

Bowie, David. 2011. Aging and sociolinguistic variation. In A. Duszak and U. Okulska (eds), *Language, Culture and the Dynamics of Age*. Berlin: Mouton de Gruyter, 29–51.

Boyarin, Daniel. 1977. Variable rules in philology. Presented at the summer meeting of the Linguistic Society of America, Oswego.

Boyarin, Daniel. 1978. On the history of the Babylonian Jewish Aramaic reading traditions: the reflexes of *a and *ā. *Journal of Near Eastern Studies* 37: 141–60.

Boyce, Suzanne E., Rena A. Krakow, and Fredericka Bell-Berti. 1991. Phonological underspecification and speech motor organization. *Phonology* 8: 219–36.

Boyd, Robert and Peter J. Richerson. 1985. *Culture and the Evolutionary Process*. Chicago: University of Chicago Press.

Bradley, Henry. 1919. *On the Relations between Spoken and Written Language with Special Reference to English*. Oxford: Clarendon Press.

Bradley, Travis G. 2006. Contrast and markedness in complex onset phonotactics. *Southwest Journal of Linguistics* 25: 29–58.

Bradley, Travis G. and Ann Marie Delforge. 2006. Systemic contrast and the diachrony of Spanish sibilant voicing. In Deborah Arteaga and Randall Gess (eds), *Historical Romance Linguistics: Retrospectives and Perspectives*. Amsterdam: Benjamins, 19–53.

Braine, Martin D. S. 1974. On what might constitute learnable phonology. *Language* 50: 270–99.

Branchaw, Sherrylyn. 2010. Survival of the strongest: strong verbs in the history of English. PhD thesis, University of California, Los Angeles.

Brandão de Carvalho, Joaquim, Tobias Scheer, and Philippe Ségéral (eds). 2008. *Lenition and Fortition*. Berlin: Mouton de Gruyter.

Brander, Jan. 1940. *Tristan da Cunha 1506–1902*. London: Allen and Unwin.

Braune, Wilhelm. 2004. *Althochdeutsche Grammatik I: Laut- und Formenlehre*. 15th edn. Ingo Reiffenstein (ed.). Tübingen: Niemeyer.

Bredsdorff, Jakob Hornemann. 1821/1982. On the causes of linguistic change. Trans. Henning Andersen. *Historiographia Linguistica* 9: 1–23.

Bright, William. 1975. The Dravidian enunciative vowel. In Harold F. Schiffman and Carol M. Eastman (eds), *Dravidian Phonological Systems*. Seattle: University of Washington Press, 11–46.

Brink, Lars and Jørn Lund. 1979. Social factors in the sound changes of modern Danish. *Proceedings of the Ninth International Congress of Phonetic Sciences*, vol. 2. Copenhagen: University of Copenhagen, 196–203.

Britain, David. 1991. Dialect and space: a geolinguistic study of speech variables in the Fens. PhD thesis, University of Essex.

Britain, David. 1997. Dialect contact and phonological reallocation: 'Canadian raising' in the English Fens. *Language in Society* 26: 15–46.

Britain, David and Peter Trudgill. 1999. Migration, new dialect formation and sociolinguistic refunctionalisation: reallocation as an outcome of dialect contact. *Transactions of the Philological Society* 97: 245–56.

British Library. Early Spoken Word Recordings archive. Available online at: <http://sounds.bl.uk/Oral-history/Early-spoken-word-recordings>, accessed 26 Oct. 2012.

Bromberger, Sylvain and Morris Halle. 1989. Why phonology is different. *Linguistic Inquiry* 20: 51–70.

Broś, Karolina. 2012. Survival of the fittest: fricative lenition in English and Spanish from the perspective of Optimality Theory. PhD thesis, University of Warsaw.

Broselow, Ellen. 1995. Skeletal positions and moras. In John A. Goldsmith (ed.), *The Handbook of Phonological Theory*. Cambridge, Mass.: Blackwell, 175–205.

Browman, Catherine P. and Louis M. Goldstein. 1986. Towards an articulatory phonology. *Phonology Yearbook*, 3: 219–52.

Browman, Catherine P. and Louis M. Goldstein. 1990. Tiers in articulatory phonology, with some implications for casual speech. In J. Kingston and M. Neckman (eds), *Papers in Laboratory Phonology I: between the Grammar and the Physics of Speech*. Cambridge: Cambridge University Press, 342–76.

Browman, Catharine P. and Louis M. Goldstein. 1992. Articulatory phonology: an overview. *Phonetica* 49: 155–80.

Brown, Cecil H., Eric W. Holman, and Søren Wichmann. 2013. Sound correspondences in the world's languages. *Language* 89: 4–29.

Brown, Cecil H., Eric W. Holman, Søren Wichmann, and Viveka Velupillai. 2008. Automated classification of the world's languages: a description of the method and preliminary results. *STUF: Language Typology and Universals* 61(4): 285–308.

Brown, Esther L. 2004. Reduction of syllable-initial /s/ in the Spanish of New Mexico and southern Colorado: a usage-based approach. PhD thesis, University of New Mexico.

Brown, Esther L. and William D. Raymond. 2012. How discourse context shapes the lexicon: explaining the distribution of Spanish *f-/h-* words. *Diachronica* 92(2): 139–61.

Brown, Gillian. 1977. *Listening to Spoken English*, 2nd edn. London: Longmans.

Brown, Steven. 2000. The 'musilanguage' model of music evolution. In N. L. Wallin, B. Merker, and S. Brown (eds), *The Origins of Music*. Cambridge, Mass.: MIT Press, 271–300.

Brücke, Ernst Wilhelm. 1856. *Grundzüge der Physiologie und Systematik der Sprachlaute für Linguisten und Taubstummenlehrer*. Vienna: Gerold.

Brugmann, Karl. 1876. Nasalis Sonans in der indogermanischen Grundsprache. In Georg Curtius and Karl Brugmann (eds), *Studien zur griechischen und lateinischen Grammatik*, vol. 9. Leipzig: Hirzel, 285–338.

Brugmann, Karl. 1880. Zur Beurtheilung der europäischen Vocale *a, e, o. Morphologische Untersuchungen auf dem Gebiete der indogermanischen Sprachen* 3: 91–130.

Brugmann, Karl. 1885. *Zum heutigen Stand der Sprachwissenschaft*. Strasbourg: Trübner. Repr. in Terence H. Wilbur (ed.), *The Lautgesetz Controversy: a Documentation (1885–1886)*. Amsterdam: Benjamins, 1977.

Brugmann, Karl and Berthold Delbrück. 1886–1900. *Grundriß der vergleichenden Grammatik der indogermanischen Sprachen*. Strasbourg: Trübner.

Buchstaller, Isabelle, Karen Corrigan, Anders Holmberg, Patrick Honeybone, and Warren Maguire. 2013. T-to-R and the Northern Subject Rule: questionnaire-based spatial, social and structural linguistics. *English Language and Linguistics* 17: 85–128.

Buckley, Eugene. 2000. On the naturalness of unnatural rules. *UCSB Working Papers in Linguistics* 9.

Buckley, Eugene. 2003. Children's unnatural phonology. *Proceedings of the Berkeley Linguistics Society* 29: 523–34.

Bullock, Barbara E., Almeida Jacqueline Toribio, Verónica González, and Amanda Dalola. 2006. Language dominance and performance outcomes in bilingual pronunciation. In Mary Grantham O'Brien, Christine Shea, and John Archibald (eds), *Proceedings of the 8th Generative Approaches to Second Language Acquisition Conference*. Somerville, Mass.: Cascadilla Proceedings Project, 9–16.

Burrow, Thomas. 1965. *The Sanskrit Language*. London: Faber and Faber.

Bussmann, Hadumod. 1983. *Lexikon der Sprachwissenschaft*. Stuttgart: Kröner.

Bybee, Joan. 1980. Morphophonemic change from inside and outside the paradigm, *Lingua* 50: 45–89.

Bybee, Joan. 1985. *Morphology: a Study of the Relation between Meaning and Form*. Amsterdam: Benjamins.

Bybee, Joan. 1988. Morphology as lexical organization. In Michael Hammond and Michael Noonan (eds), *Theoretical Morphology*. New York: Academic Press, 119–41.

Bybee, Joan. 2000. The phonology of the lexicon: evidence from lexical diffusion. In Michael Barlow and Suzanne Kemmer (eds), *Usage-based Models of Language*. Stanford, Calif.: CSLI, 65–85.

Bybee, Joan. 2001. *Phonology and Language Use*. Cambridge: Cambridge University Press.

Bybee, Joan 2002a. Word frequency and context of use in the lexical diffusion of phonetically conditioned sound change. *Language Variation and Change* 14: 261–90.

Bybee, Joan 2002b. Lexical diffusion in regular sound change. In David Restle and Dietmar Zaefferer (eds), *Sound and Systems: Studies in Structure and Change. A Festschrift for Theo Vennemann*. Berlin: Mouton de Gruyter, 59–74.

Bybee, Joan. 2006. From usage to grammar: the mind's response to repetition. *Language* 82: 711–33.

Bybee, Joan. 2009. Grammaticization: implications for a theory of language. In Elena Lieven and Jiansheng Guo (eds), *Crosslinguistic Approaches to the Psychology of Language*. New York: Taylor and Francis, 345–55.

Bybee, Joan. 2010. *Language, Usage and Cognition*. Cambridge: Cambridge University Press.

Bybee, Joan. 2012. Patterns of lexical diffusion and articulatory motivation for sound change. In Maria-Josep Solé and Daniel Recasens (eds), *The Initiation of Sound Change: Perception, Production and Social Factors*. Amsterdam: Benjamins, 211–34.

Bybee, Joan and Shelece Easterday. In preparation. The prominence of palatal articulations: a crosslinguistic study of assimilation and strengthening.

Bybee, Joan L. and Carol Lynn Moder. 1983. Morphological classes as natural categories. *Language* 59: 251–70.

Bybee, Joan L. and Jean E. Newman. 1995. Are stem changes as natural as affixes? *Linguistics* 33: 633–54.

Bybee, Joan and Joanne Scheibman. 1999. The effect of usage on degrees of constituency: the reduction of *don't* in English. *Linguistics* 37: 575–96.

Bynon, Theodora. 1986. August Schleicher: Indo-Europeanist and general linguist. In Theodora Bynon and Frank R. Palmer (eds), *Studies in Western Linguistics in Honour of R. H. Robins*. Cambridge: Cambridge University Press, 129–49.

Byrd, Dani. 1992. Perception of assimilation in consonant clusters: a gestural model. *Phonetica* 49: 1–24.

Caha, Pavel and Tobias Scheer. 2008. The syntax and phonology of Czech templatic morphology. In Andrei Antoneko and John Bailyn (eds), *Annual Workshop on Formal Approaches to Slavic Linguistics: The Stony Brook meeting 2007*. Ann Arbor: Michigan Slavic Publications, 68–83.

Caisse, Michelle. 1982. Cross-linguistic differences in fundamental frequency pertubation induced by voiceless unaspirated stops. Master's dissertation, University of California, Berkeley.

Calabrese, Andrea. 2005. *Markedness and Economy in a Derivational Model of Phonology*. Berlin: Mouton de Gruyter.

Calabrese, Andrea. 2009. Markedness Theory versus phonological idiosyncrasies in a realistic model of language. In Eric Raimy and Charles Cairns (eds), *Contemporary Views on Architecture and Representations in Phonology*. Cambridge, Mass.: MIT Press, 261–304.

Callou, Dinah, João Moraes, and Yonne Leite. 1998. Apagamento do *r* final no dialeto carioca: um estudo em tempo aparente e em tempo real. *Revista de documentação de estudos em linguistica teorica e aplicada* 14: 61–72.

Camazine, Scott, Jean-Louis Deneubourg, Nigel R. Franks, James Sneyd, Guy Theraula, and Eric Bonabeau. 2001. *Self-Organization in Biological Systems*. Princeton, NJ: Princeton University Press.

Campbell, Alistair. 1959. *Old English Grammar*. Oxford: Clarendon Press.

Campbell, Lyle. 1988. Review of *Language in the Americas*, by Joseph Greenberg. *Language* 64: 591–615.

Campbell, Lyle. 1998. *Historical Linguistics: an Introduction*. Cambridge, Mass.: MIT Press (also Edinburgh: Edinburgh University Press). [2nd edn, 2004].

Campbell, Lyle. 2002. The history of linguistics. In Mark Aronoff and Janie Rees-Miller (eds), *The Handbook of Linguistics*. Oxford: Wiley-Blackwell, 81–104.

Campbell, Lyle. 2004. *Historical Linguistics: an Introduction*, 2nd edn. Cambridge, Mass.: MIT Press.

Cangelosi, A. and D. Parisi (eds). 2002. *Simulating the Evolution of Language*. Berlin: Springer.

Carr, Philip, Jacques Durand, and Colin Ewen (eds). 2005. *Headhood, Elements, Specification and Contrastivity*. Amsterdam: Benjamins.

Carroll, Julia M. and Margaret Snowling. 2001. The effects of global similarity between stimuli on children's judgment of rime and alliteration. *Applied Psycholinguistics* 22: 327–42.

Carroll, Ryan, Ragnar Svare, and Joseph Salmons. 2012. Quantifying the evolutionary dynamics of German verbs. *Journal of Historical Linguistics* 2: 153–72.

Carruthers, Peter. 2008. *The Architecture of the Mind*. Oxford: Oxford University Press.

Carver, Craig M. 1987. *American Regional Dialects: a Word Geography*. Ann Arbor: University of Michigan Press.

Casali, Roderick F. 1997. Vowel elision in hiatus contexts: which vowel goes? *Language* 73: 493–533.

Case, Theresa. 2000. Kana in the eighth century: an ancient Japanese writing system. PhD thesis, Cornell University.

Cassidy, Fred G. 1974. Review of Arne Zettersten's *The English of Tristan da Cunha*. *Language* 50: 175–77.

Cedergren, Henrietta J. 1973. The interplay of social and linguistic factors in Panama. PhD thesis, Cornell University.

Cedergren, Henrietta J. 1988. The spread of language change: verifying inferences of linguistic diffusion. In P. H. Lowenberg (ed.), *Language Spread and Language Policy: Issues, Implications, and Case Studies*. Washington, DC: Georgetown University Press, 45–60.

Chae, Seo-Yong. 1995. External constraints on sound change: the raising of /o/ in Seoul Korean. PhD thesis, University of Pennsylvania.

Chafe, Wallace L. 1968. The ordering of phonological rules. *International Journal of Applied Linguistics* 34: 115–36.

Chambers, J. K. 1973. Canadian raising. *Canadian Journal of Linguistics* 18: 113–35.

Chambers, J. K. 1992. Dialect acquisition. *Language* 68: 673–705.

Chambers, J. K. 1995. *Sociolinguistic Theory*. Oxford: Blackwell.

Chambers, J. K. 2002. Patterns of variation including change. In J. K. Chambers, P. Trudgill and N. Schilling-Estes (eds), *The Handbook of Language Variation and Change*. Oxford: Blackwell, 349–72.

Chambers, J. K. 2003. *Sociolinguistic Theory: Linguistic Variation and its Social Significance*. Oxford: Blackwell.

Chambers, J. K. and Margaret Hardwick. 1986. Comparative sociolinguistics of a sound change in Canadian English. *English World-Wide* 7: 25–46.

Chambers, J. K., and Peter Trudgill. 1980. *Dialectology*. Cambridge: Cambridge University Press.

Chang, Charles B. 2010a. Tracking second language learning effects on native language production. Paper presented at the Annual Meeting of the Linguistic Society of America, Baltimore.

Chang, Charles B. 2010b. First language phonetic drift during second language acquisition. PhD thesis, University of California, Berkeley.

Chang, Charles B. 2012. Phonetics vs phonology in loanword adaptation: revisiting the role of the bilingual. In: S. Berson, A. Bratkievich, D. Bruhn, A. Campbell, R. Escamilla, A. Giovine, L. Newbold, M. Perez, M. Piqueras-Brunet, and R. Rhomieux (eds.), *Proceedings of the 34th Annual Meeting of the Berkeley Linguistics Society: General Session and Parasession on Information Structure*. Berkeley, CA: Berkeley Linguistics Society, 61–72.

Chang, Steve S., Madelain Plauché, and John J. Ohala. 2001. Markedness and consonant confusion asymmetries. In B. Hume and K. Johnson (eds), *The Role of Speech Perception in Phonology*. San Diego, Calif.: Academic Press, 79–101.

Charette, Monik. 1991. *Conditions on Phonological Government*. Cambridge: Cambridge University Press.

Chen, Matthew and William S.-Y. Wang. 1975. Sound change: actuation and implementation. *Language* 51: 255–81.

Cheshire, Jenny, Paul Kerswill, Sue Fox, and Elvind Torgersen. 2011. Contact, the feature pool and the speech community: the emergence of Multicultural London English. *Journal of Sociolinguistics* 15: 151–96.

Childs, G. Tucker. 1995. Tone and accent in the Atlantic languages: an evolutionary perspective. In A. Traill, R. Vossen, and M. Biesele (eds), *The Complete Linguist: Papers in Memory of Patrick J. Dickens*. Cologne: Köppe, 195–215.

Childs, G. Tucker. 2003. *An Introduction to African Languages*. Amsterdam : Benjamins.

Chimhundu, Herbert 1983. Adoption and adaptation. PhD thesis, University of Zimbabwe.

Chitoran, Ioana and Jose Ignacio Hualde. 2007. From hiatus to diphthong: the evolution of vowel sequences in Romance. *Phonology* 24: 37–75.

Cho, Taehong. 2001. Effects of morpheme boundaries on intergestural timing: evidence from Korean. *Phonetica* 58: 129–62.

Cho, Taehong. 2004. Prosodically conditioned strengthening and vowel-to-vowel coarticulation in English. *Journal of Phonetics* 32: 141–76.

Cho, Taehong and Peter Ladefoged. 1999. Variations and universals in VOT: evidence from 18 languages. *Journal of Phonetics* 27: 207–29.

Cho, Young-mee Yu. 1998. Language change as reranking of constraints. In Richard M. Hogg and Linda van Bergen (eds), *Historical Linguistics 1995*, vol. 2: *Germanic Linguistics*. Amsterdam: Benjamins, 45–62.

Chomsky, Noam. 1957a. Review of *Fundamentals of Language* by Roman Jakobson and Morris Halle. *International Journal of American Linguistics* 23(3): 234–42.

Chomsky, Noam. 1957b. *Syntactic Structures*. Berlin: Mouton de Gruyter.

Chomsky, Noam. 1965. *Aspects of the Theory of Syntax*. Cambridge, Mass.: MIT Press.

Chomsky Noam. 1986. *Knowledge of Language: its Nature, Origin and Use*. New York: Praeger.

Chomsky, Noam and Morris Halle. 1965. Some controversial questions in phonological theory. *Journal of Linguistics* 1(2): 97–138.

Chomsky, Noam and Morris Halle. 1968. *The Sound Pattern of English*. New York: Harper and Row.

Christensen, Helen, A. J. Mackinnon, A. E. Korten, A. F. Jorm, A. S. Henderson, P. Jacomb, and Bryan Rodgers. 1999. An analysis of diversity in the cognitive performance of elderly community dwellers: individual differences in change scores as a function of age. *Psychology and Aging* 14: 365–79.

Clahsen, Harald. 1999. Lexical entries and rules of language: a multidisciplinary study of German inflection. *Behavioral and Brain Sciences* 22(6): 991–1060.

Clarke, Sandra. 2004. Newfoundland English: phonology. In Edgar W. Schneider, Kate Burridge, Bernd Kortmann, Rajend Mesthrie, and Clive Upton (eds), *A Handbook of Varieties of English*, vol. 1. Berlin: Mouton de Gruyter, 366–82.

Clements, George N. 1985. The geometry of phonological features. *Phonology Yearbook* 2: 225–52.

Clements, George N. 1990. The role of the sonority cycle in core syllabification. In M. E. Beckman and J. Kingston (eds), *Papers in Laboratory Phonology I: between the Grammar and Physics of Speech*. Cambridge: Cambridge University Press, 283–333.

Clements, George N. 1991. Place of articulation in consonants and vowels: a unified theory. *Working Papers of the Cornell Phonetics Laboratory* 5. Ithaca, NY: Cornell University, 37–76.

Clements, George N. 2003. Feature economy in sound systems. *Phonology* 20: 287–333.

Clements, George N. 2009. The role of features in speech sound inventories. In Eric Raimy and Charles Cairns (eds), *Contemporary Views on Architecture and Representations in Phonological Theory*. Cambridge, Mass.: MIT Press.

Clements, George N. and John Goldsmith. 1984. Autosegmental studies in Bantu tone: introduction. In George N. Clements and John Goldsmith (eds), *Autosegmental Studies in Bantu Tone*. Dordrecht: Foris, 1–17.

Clements, George N. and Elizabeth Hume. 1995. The internal organization of speech sounds. In John Goldsmith (ed.), *The Handbook of Phonological Theory*. Oxford: Blackwell, 245–306.

Clements, George N. and Sylvester Osu. 2002. Explosives, implosives, and nonexplosives: some linguistic effects of air pressure differences in stops. In C. Gussenhoven and N. Warner (eds), *Laboratory Phonology 7*. Berlin: Mouton de Gruyter, 299–350.

Clements, George N. and Sylvester Osu. 2005. Nasal harmony in Ikwere, a language with no phonemic nasal consonants. *Journal of African Languages and Linguistics* 26: 165–200.

Clements, George N. and Annie Rialland. 2008. Africa as a phonological area. In Bernd Heine and Derek Nurse (eds), *A Linguistic Geography of Africa*. Cambridge: Cambridge University Press, 36–85.

Coetzee, Andries and Joe Pater. 2011. The place of variation in phonological theory. In John Goldsmith, Jason Riggle, and Alan C. L. Yu (eds), *The Handbook of Phonological Theory*, 2nd edn. Oxford: Blackwell, 401–34.

Coggshall, Elizabeth L. and Kara Becker. 2010. A vowel comparison of African American and white New York City residents. In Malcah Yaeger-Dror and Erik R. Thomas (eds), *African American English Speakers and Their Participation in Local Sound Changes: a Comparative Study*. Durham, NC: Duke University Press, 101–28.

Cohn, Abigail. 1993. Consonant–vowel interactions in Madurese: the feature lowered larynx. *Chicago Linguistics Society* 29: 105–19.

Colé, P., C. Beauvillain, and J. Segui. 1989. On the representation and processing of prefixed and suffixed derived words: a differential frequency effect. *Journal of Memory and Language* 28: 1–13.

Collinder, Björn. 1947. *La parenté linguistique et le calcul de probabilités*. Uppsala: Almqvist and Wiksell.

Collinge, Neville E. 1978. Exceptions, their nature and place—and the neogrammarians. *Transactions of the Philological Society* 76(1): 61–86.

Collinge, Neville E. 1985. *The Laws of Indo-European*. Amsterdam: Benjamins.

Collins, James. 1989. Nasalization, lengthening, and phonological rhyme in Tolowa. *International Journal of American Linguistics* 55: 326–40.

Collins, Peter and David Blair. 2001. Language and identity in Australia. In Peter Collins and David Blair (eds), *English in Australia*. Amsterdam: Benjamins, 1–16.

Colman, Fran. 1992. *Money Talks: Reconstructing Old English*. Berlin: Mouton de Gruyter.

Colman, Fran and John Anderson. 1983. Front umlaut: a celebration of 2nd fronting, *i*-umlaut, life, food and sex. In Michael Davenport, Erik Hansen, and Hans Frede Nielsen (eds), *Current Topics in English Historical Linguistics*. Odense: Odense University Press, 165–90.

Compton, Richard and B. Elan Dresher. 2011. Palatalization and 'strong' *i* across Inuit dialects. *Canadian Journal of Linguistics/Revue canadienne de linguistique* 56: 203–28.

Comrie, Bernard. 1993. Typology and reconstruction. In Charles Jones (ed.), *Historical Linguistics: Problems and Perspectives*. London: Longman, 74–97.

Contini, Michel. 1986. Les phénomènes de sandhi dans le domaine sarde. In Henning Andersen (ed.), *Sandhi Phenomena in the Languages of Europe*. Berlin: Mouton de Gruyter, 519–50.

Contini, Michel. 1987. *Étude de géographie phonétique et de phonétique instrumentale du sarde*. 2 vols. Alessandria: dell'Orso.

Contini, Michele 2006. Une frontière oubliée en domaine sarde? *Quaderni del dipartimento di linguistica* 27: 183–98.

Cooper, David L. 1999. *Linguistic Attractors: the Cognitive Dynamics of Language Acquisition and Change*. Amsterdam: Benjamins.

Cossu, Maria G. 2000. Unité et stabilité phonétique dans les parlers sardes méridionaux. PhD thesis, Université Stendhal, Grenoble.

Coulmas, Florian. 1989. *The Writing Systems of the World*. Oxford: Blackwell.

Coulmas, Florian. 2003. *Writing Systems: an Introduction to their Linguistic Analysis*. Cambridge: Cambridge University Press.

Coupland, Nikolas. 2010. The authentic speaker and the speech community. In C. Llamas and D. Watts (eds), *Language and Identities*. Edinburgh: University of Edinburgh Press, 99–112.

Cowan, William. 1971. *Workbook in Comparative Reconstruction*. New York: Holt, Rinehart and Winston.

Crabb, George. 1980. The history and postal history of Tristan da Cunha. MS.

Crawcour, Sydney. 1965. *An Introduction to Kanbun*. Ann Arbor: Center for Japanese Studies.

Crawford, Allan. 1945. *I Went to Tristan*. London: Allen and Unwin.

Crist, Sean Jacob. 2001. Conspiracy in historical phonology. PhD thesis, University of Pennsylvania.

Crowley, Terry. 1997. *An Introduction to Historical Linguistics*, 3rd edn. Oxford: Oxford University Press.

Cruttenden, Alan. 2001. *Gimson's Pronunciation of English*, 6th edn. London: Arnold [7th edn. 2008 London: Hodder Education.]

Cser, András. 2003. *The Typology and Modelling of Obstruent Lenition and Fortition Processes*. Budapest: Akadémiai.

Cukor-Avila, Patricia. 2002. *She say, she go, she be like*: verbs of quotation over time in African American vernacular English. *American Speech* 77: 3–31.

Cukor-Avila, Patricia and Guy Bailey 2011. The interaction of transmission and diffusion in the spread of linguistic forms. In M. Tamminga (ed.), *University of Pennsylvania Working Papers in Linguistics: Selected Papers from NWAV 39* 17(2): article 6.

Curtius, Georg. 1864/1886. *Kleine Schriften*, ed. Ernst Windisch. Leipzig: Hirzel.

Cutillas Espinosa, Juan Antonio. 2004. Meaningful variability: a sociolinguistically-grounded approach to variation in Optimality Theory. In Paul Boersma and Juan Antonio Cutillas

Espinosa (eds), *Advances in Optimality Theory*, a monograph issue of the *International Journal of English Studies*, 4(2): 165–84.

Cutler, Anne, J. M. McQueen, and D. Norris. 2005. The lexical utility of phoneme-category plasticity. In *Proceedings of the ISCA Workshop on Plasticity in Speech Perception*. London: University College London, 103–7.

Cutler, Cecelia. 2010. Hip-hop, white immigrant youth, and African American vernacular English: accommodation as an identity choice. *Journal of English Linguistics* 38: 248–69.

D'Arcy, Alexandra. 2011. Corpora: capturing language in use. In Warren Maguire and April McMahon (eds), *Analysing Variation in English*. Cambridge: Cambridge University Press, 49–72.

D'Introno, Francisco and Juan Manuel Sosa. 1979. *Anuario de la Escuela de letras*. Caracas: Universidad Central de Venezuela, 33–61.

D'Introno, Francisco and Juan Manuel Sosa. 1986. Elisión de la /d/ en el Español de Caracas: aspectos sociolingüísticos e implicaciones teóricas. In Rafael A. Núñez Cedeño, Iraset Páez Urdaneta, and Jorge Guitart (eds), *Estudios sobre la fonología del Español del Caribe*. Caracas: Bello.

Dalbera-Stefanaggi, Marie-José. 2001. *La Corse au regard de la lénition consonantique: aires, strates, systèmes*. Ajaccio: Piazzola.

Dalston, Rodger Millard. 1972. A spectrographic analysis of the spectral and temporal characteristics of English semivowels spoken by three year old children and adults. PhD thesis, Northwestern University.

Damerau, F. J. 1975. Mechanization of cognate recognition in comparative linguistics. *Linguistics* 148: 5–29.

Danchev, Andrei. 1975/1976. On the phonemic and phonetic values of the short *ea* and *eo* diagraphs in Old English. *Annuaire de l'Université de Sofia. Faculté des Lettres, Langues et littératures romanes et germaniques* 70(1): 37–88.

Daniels, Don R. 2010. A preliminary phonological history of the Sogeram languages of Papua New Guinea. *Oceanic Linguistics* 49: 163–93.

Daniels, Peter and William Bright. 1996. *The World's Writing Systems*. Oxford: Oxford University Press.

Danielsson, Bror. 1948. *Studies on Accentuation of Polysyllabic Latin, Greek, and Romance Loan-Words in English*. Stockholm: Almqvist & Wiksells.

Danielsson, Bror. 1955. *John Hart's Works on English Orthography and Pronunciation* [1551–1569–1570], pt 1: *Biographical and Bibliographical Introductions, Texts, and Index Verborum*. Stockholm: Almqvist & Wiksell.

Danielsson, Bror. 1963. *John Hart's Works on English Orthography and Pronunciation* [1551–1569–1570], pt 2: *Phonology*. Stockholm: Almqvist & Wiksell.

Darlington, Richard B. 1970. Is kurtosis really 'peakedness'? *American Statistician* 24: 19–22.

Dart, Sarah N. 1998. Comparing English and French coronal consonant articulation, *Journal of Phonetics* 26: 71–94.

Daunt, Marjorie. 1939. Old English sound changes reconsidered in relation to scribal tradition and practice. *Transactions of the Philological Society* 38: 108–37.

Dauzat, Albert. 1938. Les altérations de l'intervocalique dans le Massif Central. In *Essais de géographie linguistique*, n.s. 3. Paris: Champion, 50–90.

Davies, Mark. 2010–. The Corpus of Historical American English [COHA]. 400+ million words, 1810–2009. <http://corpus.byu.edu/coha>

Davies, William. 1999. *Madurese*. Munich: Lincom Europa.

Davis, Garry W. 2008. Toward a progression theory of the Old High German consonant shift. *Journal of Germanic Linguistics* 20: 197–241.

de Boer, Bart. 2001. *The Origins of Vowel Systems*. Oxford: Oxford University Press.

de Boer, Elisabeth. 2010. *The Historical Development of Japanese Tone: from Proto-Japanese to the Modern Dialects* [and] *The Introduction and Adaptation of the Middle Chinese Tones in Japan*. Wiesbaden: Otto Harrassowitz.

De Decker, Paul. 2006. Real-time investigation of social and phonetic changes in post-adolescence. *University of Pennsylvania Working Papers in Linguistics: Selected Papers from NWAV 34* 12(2): 65–76.

de Groot, A. W. 1931. Phonologie und phonetik als Funktionswissenschaften. *Travaux du Cercle linguistique de Prague* 4: 116–47.

De Paiva, Maria and Maria Eugenia Duarte. 2003. *Mudança lingüística em tempo real*. Rio de Janeiro: Capa.

De Schryver, Johan et al. 2008. Analogy, frequency, and sound change: the case of Dutch devoicing. *Journal of Germanic Linguistics* 20: 159–95.

Dediu, Dan and D. Robert Ladd. 2007. Linguistic tone is related to the population frequency of the adaptive haplogroups of two brain size genes, ASPM and Microcephalin. *Proceedings of the National Academy of Sciences of the USA* 104: 10944–9.

DeFrancis, John. 1977. *Colonialism and Language Policy in Viet Nam*. The Hague: Mouton.

DeFrancis, John. 1984. *The Chinese Language: Fact and Fantasy*. Honolulu: University of Hawai'i Press.

de Lacy, Paul. 2006. *Markedness: Reduction and Preservation in Phonology*. Cambridge: Cambridge University Press.

Delbrück, Berthold. 1885. *Die neueste Sprachforschung: Betrachtungen über Georg Curtius Schrift zur Kritik der neuesten Sprachforschung*. Leipzig: Breitkopf & Härtel.

DeLisi, Jessica. 2013. Feature metathesis and the change of PIE *dụ to Classical Armenian -rk-. *Diachronica* 30(4): 468–91.

Denison, David. 2003. Log(ist)ic and simplistic S-curves. In R. Hickey (ed.), *Motives for Language Change*. Cambridge: Cambridge University Press, 54–70.

Derwing, Bruce L., Terrance M. Nearey, and Maureen L. Dow. 1986. On the phoneme as the unit of the 'second articulation'. *Phonology Yearbook* 3: 45–69.

de Vaan, Michiel. 1999. The PIE root structure *Te(R)Dh-. *Historische Sprachforschung*, 112: 1–25.

Di Paolo, Marianna. 1988. Pronunciation and categorization in sound change. In K. Ferrara et al. (eds), *Linguistic Change and Contact: NWAV XVI*. Austin: Dept. of Linguistics, University of Texas, 84–92.

Di Paolo, Marianna and Alice Faber. 1990. Phonation differences and the phonetic content of the tense-lax contrast in Utah English. *Language Variation and Change* 2: 155–204.

Diderichsen, Paul. 1974. The foundation of comparative linguistics: revolution or continuation? In Dell Hymes (ed.), *Studies in the History of Linguistics: Traditions and Paradigms*. Bloomington: Indiana University Press, 277–306.

Diderichsen, Paul. 1976. *Rasmus Rask und die grammatische Tradition: eine Studie über den Wendepunkt in der Sprachgeschichte*, trans. Monika Wesemann. Munich: Fink. [Translation of *Rasmus Rask og den grammatiske tradition: Studier over vendepunktet i sprogvidenskabens historie*. Copenhagen: Munksgaard, 1960.]

Diem, Werner. 1973. *Skizzen jementischer Dialekte*. Beirut: Steiner.

Diffloth, Gérard. 1982. Registres, dévoisement, timbres vocaliques: leur histoire en katouique. *Mon-Khmer Studies* 11: 47–82.

Diffloth, Gérard. 1984. *The Dvaravati Old Mon Language and Nyah Kur*. Bangkok: Chulalongkorn University Printing House.

Diffloth, Gérard. 1990. Vietnamese tonogenesis and new data on the registers of Thavung. Paper presented at the International Conference on Sino-Tibetan Languages and Linguistics, University of Texas at Arlington.

Dijksterhuis, Ap and John A. Bargh. 2001. The perception-behavior expressway: automatic effects of social perception on social behavior. In M. P. Zanna (ed.), *Advances in Experimental Social Psychology*, vol. 33. San Diego, Calif.: Academic Press, 1–40

Dinkin, Aaron J. 2008. The real effect of word frequency on phonetic variation. In Joshua Tauberer, Aviad Eilam, and Laurel MacKenzie (eds), *Proceedings of the 31st Annual Penn Linguistics Colloquium*. Philadelphia: Penn Linguistics Club, 97–106. Available at: <http://repository.upenn.edu/pwpl/vol14/iss1/8/>

Docherty, Gerard J. 1989. An experimental phonetic study of the timing of voicing in English obstruents. PhD thesis, University of Edinburgh.

Docherty, Gerard J. 1992. *The Timing of Voicing in British English Obstruents*. Berlin: Foris.

Docherty, Gerard J. and Paul Foulkes. 1999. Newcastle upon Tyne and Derby: instrumental phonetics and variationist studies. In Paul Foulkes and Gerard J. Docherty (eds), *Urban Voices: Accent Studies in the British Isles*. London: Arnold, 47–71.

Docherty, Gerard J., and Paul Foulkes. 2001. Variation in (r) production: instrumental perspectives. In H. Van de Velde and R. van Hout (eds), *r-atics: Sociolinguistic, Phonetic, and Phonological Characteristics of /r/*. Brussels: ILVP, 173–84.

Docherty, Gerard J., Paul Foulkes, Barbara Dodd, and Lesley Milroy. 2002. *The Emergence of Structured Variation in the Speech of Tyneside Infants*. Final report to the United Kingdom Economic and Social Research Council, grant R000 237417.

Docherty, Gerard J., Paul Foulkes, James Milroy, Lesley Milroy, and David Walshaw. 1997. Descriptive adequacy in phonology: a variationist perspective. *Journal of Linguistics* 33: 275–310.

Dohlus, Katrin. 2010. *The Role of Phonology and Phonetics in Loanword Adaptation: German and French Rounded Vowels in Japanese*. Frankfurt/Main: Lang.

Dolgopolsky, Aaron B. 1986. A probabilistic hypothesis concerning the oldest relationships among the language families of northern Eurasia. In Vitalij V. Shevoroshkin and Thomas L. Markey (eds), *Typology, Relationship, and Time: a Collection of Papers on Language Change and Relationship by Soviet Linguists*. Ann Arbor, Mich.: Karoma, 27–50.

Domingue, Nicole. 1981. Internal change in a transplanted language. *Studies in the Linguistic Sciences* 4(2): 151–59.

Donegan, Patricia J. 1978. On the natural phonology of vowels. PhD thesis, Ohio State University. [Published 1979 as Ohio State University Working Papers in Linguistics, 23. Also New York: Garland Press, 1985.] Available at: <http://www.ling.hawaii.edu/faculty/donegan/Papers/1978Ph.D.pdf>

Donegan, Patricia J. 1993a. On the phonetic basis of phonological change. In Charles Jones (ed.), *Historical Linguistics: Problems and Perspectives*. London: Longman, 98–130.

Donegan, Patricia J. 1993b. Rhythm and vocalic drift in Munda and Mon-Khmer. *Linguistics of the Tibeto-Burman Area* 16(1): 1–43.

Donegan, Patricia J. 1995. The innateness of phonemic perception. In Vida Samiian (ed.), *WECOL 7: Proceedings of the 24th Western Conference on Linguistics*. Fresno, Calif.: Western Conference on Linguistics, 59–69.

Donegan, Patricia J. and David Stampe. 1978. The syllable in phonological and prosodic structure. In Alan Bell and Joan Bybee Hooper (eds), *Syllables and Segments*. Amsterdam: North-Holland, 25–34.

Donegan, Patricia and David Stampe. 1979. The study of natural phonology. In Daniel Dinnsen (ed.), *Current Approaches to Phonological Theory*. Bloomington: Indiana University Press, 126–73.

Donegan, Patricia J. and David Stampe. 1983. Rhythm and the holistic organization of language structure. In John Richardson et al. (eds), *The Interplay of Phonology, Morphology, and Syntax*. Chicago: Chicago Linguistic Society, 337–53.

Donegan, Patricia and David Stampe. 2002. South-East Asian features in the Munda languages: evidence for the analytic-to-synthetic drift of Munda. In Patrick Chew (ed.), *Proceedings of the Twenty-Eighth Annual Meeting of the Berkeley Linguistic Society*. Berkeley: Berkeley Linguistics Society, 111–20.

Donegan, Patricia J. and David Stampe. 2004. Rhythm and the synthetic drift of Munda. In Rajendra Singh (ed.), *Yearbook of South Asian Languages and Linguistics 2004*. Berlin: Mouton de Gruyter, 3–36.

Donegan, Patricia J. and David Stampe. 2009. Hypotheses of natural phonology. *Poznań Studies in Contemporary Linguistics* 45(1): 3–31.

Dosse, François. 1991. *Histoire du structuralisme*. Paris: La Découverte.

Drachman, Gabarell. 1978. Child language and language change: a conjecture and some refutations. In Jacek Fisiak (ed.), *Recent Developments in Historical Phonology*. The Hague: Mouton, 123–44.

Drager, Katie, Jennifer Hay, and Abby Walker. 2010. Pronounced rivalries: attitudes and speech production. *Te Reo* 53: 28–53.

Dresher, B. Elan. 1978/1985. Old English and the theory of phonology. PhD thesis, University of Massachusetts. [Published 1985, New York: Garland.]

Dresher, B. Elan. 1980. The Mercian Second Fronting: a case of rule loss in Old English. *Linguistic Inquiry* 11: 47–73.

Dresher, B. Elan. 1990. On the unity of the Mercian Second Fronting. In Sylvia M. Adamson, Vivien A. Law, Nigel Vincent, and Susan Wright (eds), *Papers from the 5th International Conference on English Historical Linguistics*. Amsterdam: Benjamins, 141–64.

Dresher, B. Elan. 1993. The chronology and status of Anglian smoothing. In Sharon Hargus and Ellen Kaisse (eds), *Studies in Lexical Phonology*, vol. 4: *Phonetics and Phonology*. New York: Academic Press, 325–41.

Dresher, B. Elan. 1998. Child phonology, learnability and phonological theory. In Tej Bhatias and William C. Ritchie (eds), *Handbook of Language Acquisition*. New York: Academic Press, 299–346.

Dresher, B. Elan. 1999. Ferdinand, we hardly knew you. *Glot International* 4(6): 9. Available at: <https://twpl.library.utoronto.ca/index.php/twpl/article/view/13960>

Dresher, B. Elan. 2000. Analogical levelling of vowel length in West Germanic. In Aditi Lahiri (ed.), *Analogy, Levelling, Markedness*. New York: Mouton de Gruyter, 47–70.

Dresher, B. Elan. 2003. Contrast and asymmetries in inventories. In Anna Maria di Sciullo (ed.), *Asymmetry in Grammar*, vol. 2: *Morphology, Phonology and Acquisition*. Amsterdam: Benjamins, 239–57.

Dresher, B. Elan. 2004. On the acquisition of phonological contrasts. In Willia Sakas (ed.), *Proceedings of the First Workshop on Psycho-computational Models of Human Language*

Acquisition, 41–8. Available at: <http://www.colag.cs.hunter.cuny.edu/psychocomp/PsychoCompProceedings.pdf>

Dresher, B. Elan. 2005. Chomsky and Halle's revolution in phonology. In James McGilvray (ed.), *The Cambridge Companion to Chomsky*. Cambridge: Cambridge University Press, 102–22.

Dresher, B. Elan. 2009. *The Contrastive Hierarchy in Phonology*. Cambridge: Cambridge University Press.

Dresher, B. Elan. 2011. The phoneme. In Marc van Oostendorp, Colin J. Ewen, Elizabeth Hume, and Keren Rice (eds), *The Blackwell Companion to Phonology*, vol. 1: *General Issues and Segmental Phonology*. Oxford: Wiley-Blackwell, 241–66.

Dresher B. Elan and Aditi Lahiri. 1991. The Germanic foot: metrical coherence in Old English. *Linguistic Inquiry* 22: 251–86.

Dresher, B. Elan and Aditi Lahiri. 2005. Main stress left in Early Middle English. In Michael Fortescue, Eva Skafte Jensen, Jens Erik Mogensen, and Lene Schøsler (eds), *Historical Linguistics 2003. Selected Papers from the 16th International Conference on Historical Linguistics*. Amsterdam: Benjamins, 76–85.

Dresher, B. Elan, Glyne Piggott, and Keren Rice. 1994. Contrast in phonology: overview. *Toronto Working Papers in Linguistics* 13: iii–xvii.

Dresher, B. Elan and Harry van der Hulst. 1999. Head-dependent asymmetries in phonology: complexity and visibility. *Phonology* 15: 317–52.

Dresher, B. Elan and Xi Zhang. 2005. Contrast and phonological activity in Manchu vowel systems. *Canadian Journal of Linguistics/Revue canadienne de linguistique* 50: 45–82.

Dressler, Wolfgang U. 1985. *Morphonology: the Dynamics of Derivation*. Ann Arbor: Karoma.

Dubois, Sylvie. 1992. Extension particles, etc. *Language Variation and Change* 4: 179–203.

Dufter, Andreas. 2003. *Typen sprachrhythmischer Konturbildung*. Tübingen: Niemeyer.

Dunkel, George E. 1981. Typology versus reconstruction. In Yoël L. Arbeitman et al. (eds), *Bono Homini Donum: Essays in Historical Linguistics in Memory of J. Alexander Kerns*. Amsterdam: Benjamins, 559–69.

Dunkel, George E. 2001. The sound systems of Proto-Indo-European. In Martin E. Huld et al. (eds), *Proceedings of the Twelfth Annual UCLA Indo-European Conference*. Washington, DC: Institute for the Study of Man, 1–14.

Dunn, Michael, Stephen C. Levinson, Eva Lindstrom, Ger Reesink, and Angela Terrill. 2008. Structural phylogeny in historical linguistics: methodological explorations applied in island Melanesia. *Language* 84: 710–59.

Dupoux, Emmauel, Kazuhiko Kaheki, Yuki Hirose, Christophe Pallier, and Jacques Mehler. 1999. Epenthetic vowels in Japanese: a perceptual illusion? *Journal of Experimental Psychology: Human Perception and Performance* 25: 1568–78.

Durand, Jacques. 2005. Tense/lax, the vowel system of English and phonological theory.' In Philip Carr, Jacques Durand, and Colin Ewen (eds). *Headhood, Elements, Specification and Contrastivity*. Amsterdam: Benjamins.

Durian, David and Brian Joseph. 2011. Making sense of shifty changes: the role of phonetic analogy in vowel shifts. Paper presented at 'New Ways of Analyzing Variation' 40, Washington, DC. Available at: <http://www.ling.ohio-state.edu/~ddurian/NWAV40/Durian_Joseph_NWAV40.pdf>

Durie, Mark and Malcolm Ross (eds). 1996. *The Comparative Method Reviewed: Regularity and Irregularity in Language Change*. New York: Oxford University Press.

Durrant, Philip and Norbert Schmitt. 2009. To what extent do native and non-native writers make use of collocations? *International Review of Applied Linguistics* 47: 157–77.

Dyen, Isidore, A. T. James, and J. W. L. Cole. 1967. Language divergence and estimated word retention rate. *Language* 43: 150–71.

Dyen, Isidore, Joseph B. Kruskal, and Paul Black. 1992. An Indoeuropean classification: a lexicostatistical experiment. *Transactions of the American Philosophical Society* 82(5): 1–132.

Dziubalska-Kołaczyk, Katarzyna. 2001. Phonotactic constraints are preferences. In K. Dziubalska-Kołaczyk (ed.), *Constraints and Preferences*. Berlin: Mouton de Gruyter, 69–100.

Earle, Augustus. 1966 [1832]. *Narrative of a Residence on the Island of Tristan D'Acunha in the South Atlantic Ocean*. Oxford: Clarendon Press.

Eastlack, Charles L. 1977. Iberochange: a program to simulate systematic sound change in Ibero-Romance. *Computers and the Humanities* 11(2): 81–8.

Ebeling, C. L. 1960. *Linguistic Units*. The Hague: Mouton.

Echols, Catharine H. and Elissa L. Newport. 1992. The role of stress and position in determining first words. *Language Acquisition* 2: 189–220.

Eckert, Penelope. 1989. *Jocks and Burnouts: Social Categories and Identity in the High School*. New York: Teachers College Press.

Eckert, Penelope. 1996. Vowels and nail polish: the emergence of linguistic style in fthe preadolescent heterosexual marketplace. In N. Warner, J. Ahlers, L. Bilmes, M. Oliver, S. Wertheim, and M. Chen (eds), *Gender and Belief Systems: Proceedings of the Fourth Berkeley Women and Language Conference*. Berkeley, Calif.: Berkeley Language and Women Group, 183–90.

Eckert, Penelope. 2000. *Linguistic Variation as Social Practice*. Oxford: Blackwell.

Eckert, Penelope. 2008. Where do ethnolects stop? *International Journal of Bilingualism* 12: 25–42.

Eckman, Fred R., Abdulla M. Elreyes and Gregory K. Iverson. 2003. Some principles of second language phonology. *Second Language Research* 19: 169–208.

Eckman, Fred R. and Gregory K. Iverson. 2013. The role of native language phonology in the production of L2 contrasts. *Studies in Second Language Acquisition* 35: 67–92.

Eckman, Fred, Gregory K. Iverson, Robert A. Fox, Ewa Jacewicz, and Sue Ann Lee. 2009. Perception and production in the acquisition of L2 phonemic contrasts. In M. A. Watkins, A. Rauber, and B. O. Baptista (eds), *Recent Research in Second Language Phonetics/ Phonology: Perception and Production*. Newcastle upon Tyne: Cambridge Scholars, 81–96.

Edwards, Jan, Mary E. Beckman, and Ben Munson. 2004. The interaction between vocabulary size and phonotactic probability effects on children's production accuracy and fluency in novel word repetition. *Journal of Speech, Language, and Hearing Research* 47: 421–36.

Eisner, Frank and James M. McQueen. 2005. The specificity of perceptual learning in speech processing. *Perception and Psychophysics* 67(2): 224–38.

Elihay, J. 2005. *The Olive Tree Dictionary: a Transliterated Dictionary of Conversational Eastern Arabic (Palestinian) Arabic–English–Arabic*. Jerusalem: Minerva.

Ellis, Lucy and William J. Hardcastle. 2002. Categorical and gradient properties of assimilation in alveolar to velar sequences: evidence from EPG and EMA data. *Journal of Phonetics* 30: 373–96.

Elsig, Martin and Shana Poplack. 2009. Synchronic variation in diachronic perspective: question formation in Québec French. In Andreas Dufter, Jürg Fleischer, and Guido Seiler (eds), *Describing and Modeling Variation in Grammar*. The Hague: Mouton de Gruyter, 255–69.

Elsman, Minta M. and D. Eric Holt. 2009. When small words collide: morphological reduction and phonological compensation in Old Leonese contractions. In Ronald Leow, Héctor Campos, and Donna Lardiere (eds), *Little Words: their History, Phonology, Syntax, Semantics, Pragmatics, and Acquisition*. Washington, DC: Georgetown University Press, 21–33.

Engstrand, Olle, Johan Frid, and Björn Lindblom. 2007. A perceptual bridge between coronal and dorsal /r/. In Maria-Josep Solé, Patrice Speeter Beddor, and Manjari Ohala (eds), *Experimental Approaches to Phonology*. Oxford: Oxford University Press, 175–91.

Erker, Daniel. 2012. Of categories and continua: relating discrete and gradient properties of sociophonetic variation. *University of Pennsylvania Working Papers in Linguistics 18* (Issue 2, Selected papers from NWAV 40), 11–20. Available at: <http://repository.upenn.edu/pwpl/vol18/iss2/3>

Ernestus, Mirjam and R. Harald Baayen. 2003. Predicting the unpredictable: interpreting neutralized segments in Dutch. *Language 79*: 5–38.

Esper, Erwin A. 1973. *Analogy and Association in Linguistics and Psychology*. Athens: University of Georgia Press.

Evans, Arthur Benoni. 1881. *Leicester Words, Phrases, and Proverbs*, ed. with additions and introduction by Sebastian Evans. London: Trübner for the English Dialect Society.

Evans, Bronwen G., and Paul Iverson. 2004. Vowel normalization for accent: an investigation of best exemplar locations in northern and southern British English sentences. *Journal of the Acoustical Society of America 115*: 352–61.

Evans, Bronwen G. and Paul Iverson. 2007. Plasticity in vowel perception and production: a study of accent change in young adults. *Journal of the Acoustic Society of America 121*: 3814–26.

Evans, Dorothy. 1994. *Schooling in the South Atlantic Islands 1661–1992*. Oswestry: Nelson.

Evans, Nicholas. 1995. Current issues in Australian languages. In J. A Goldsmith (ed.), *The Handbook of Phonological Theory*. Oxford: Blackwell, 723–61.

Ewan, William G. and Robert Krones. 1974. Measuring larynx movement using the thyroumbrometer. *Journal of Phonetics 2*: 327–35.

Fabricius, Anne. 2000. T-glottalling between stigma and prestige: a sociolinguistic study of modern RP. PhD thesis, Copenhagen Business School.

Farnetani, Edda. 1999. Coarticulation and connected speech processes. In W. J. Hardcastle and J. Laver (eds), *A Handbook of Phonetic Science*. Oxford: Blackwell, 371–404.

Feagin, Crawford. 1990. The dynamics of a sound change in southern states English: from r-less to r-ful in three generations. In J. R. Edmondson, C. Feagin, and P. Mühlhäusler (eds), *Development and Diversity: Linguistic Variation Across Time and Space*. Arlington: Summer Institute of Linguistics/University of Texas, 129–46.

Feagin, Crawford. 2003. Vowel shifting in the Southern States. In S. J. Nagle and S. L. Sanders (eds), *English in the Southern United States*. Cambridge: Cambridge University Press, 126–40.

Felsenstein, Joseph. 2008. Distance matrix programs. Available at: <http://evolution.genetics.washington.edu/phylip/doc/distance.html>

Felsenstein, Joseph. 2009. PHYLIP. Available at: <http://evolution.genetics.washington.edu/phylip>

Ferguson, Charles A. 1959. The Arabic koine. *Language 35*(4): 616–30.

Ferguson, Charles A. 1973. Universal tendencies and 'normal' nasality. In Charles A. Ferguson, Larry M. Hyman and John H. Ohala (eds), *Nasalfest*. Language Universals Project. Stanford, Calif.: Department of Linguistics, Stanford University, 47–92.

Ferguson, Charles A. 1990. From esses to aitches: identifying pathways of diachronic change. In William A. Croft, Suzanne Kemmer, and Keith Denning (eds), *Studies in Typology and Diachrony*. Amsterdam: Benjamins, 59–78.

Ferguson, Ronnie. 2003. The formation of the dialect of Venice. *Forum for Modern Language Studies* 39: 450–64.

Fernández, Francisco Moreno. 1996. Castilla la Nueva. In M. Alvar (ed.), *Manual de dialectología hispánica: el español de España*. Barcelona: Ariel Lingüística, 213–32.

Fertig, David. 1999. Analogical 'leveling' from outside the paradigm: stem-vowel changes in the German modals. *Diachronica* 16: 233–60.

Fertig, David. 2000. *Morphological Change Up Close*. Tübingen: Niemeyer.

Fertig, David. 2005. Review of Geert Booij, *The Morphology of Dutch*. *Journal of Germanic Linguistics* 17: 141–8.

Fertig, David. 2013. *Analogy and Morphological Change*. Edinburgh: Edinburgh University Press.

Fidelholtz, James. 1975. Word frequency and vowel reduction in English. *Chicago Linguistics Society* 11: 200–213.

Fikkert, Paula, Elan Dresher, and Aditi Lahiri. 2006. Prosodic preferences: from Old English to Early Modern English. In Ans van Kemenade and Bettelou Los (eds), *Handbook of the History of English*. Oxford: Blackwell, 125–50.

Firth, John Rupert. 1948. Sounds and prosodies. *Transactions of the Philological Society* 7: 127–52.

Fischer, John L. 1958. Social influences on the choice of a linguistic variant. *Word* 14: 47–56.

Fischer-Jørgensen, Eli. 1975. *Trends in Phonological Theory*. Copenhagen: Akademisk Forlag.

Fitzgerald, Colleen M. 1999. Loanwords and stress in Tohono O'odham. *Anthropological Linguistics* 41(2): 193–208.

Fitzmaurice, Susan and Donka Minkova (eds). 2008. *Empirical and Analytical Advances in the Study of English Language Change*. Berlin: Mouton de Gruyter.

Flege, James E. 2003. Assessing constraints on second-language segmental production and perception. In A. Meyer and N. Schiller (eds), *Phonetics and Phonology in Language Comprehension and Production, Differences and Similarities*. Berlin: de Gruyter, 319–55.

Flege, James E. 2007. Language contact in bilingualism: phonetic system interactions. In J. Cole and J. I. Hualde (eds), *Laboratory Phonology 9*. Berlin: de Gruyter, 353–82.

Flege, James E. and Ian R. A. MacKay. 2004. Perceiving vowels in a second language. *Studies in Second Language Acquisition* 26: 1–34.

Flege, James E., Ian R. A. MacKay, and Diane Meador. 1999. Native Italian speakers' production and perception of English vowels. *Journal of the Acoustical Society of America* 106: 2973–87.

Fleischman, Suzanne. 2000. Methodologies and ideologies in historical linguistics: on working with older languages. In S. C. Herring, P. Van Reenen, and L. Schøsler (eds), *Textual Parameters in Older Languages*. Amsterdam: Benjamins, 33–58.

Flemming, Edward. 1995. Auditory representations in phonology. PhD thesis, University of California Los Angeles. [Published 2002, New York: Garland.]

Flemming, Edward. 2001. Scalar and categorical phenomena in a unified model of phonetics and phonology. *Phonology* 18: 7–44.

Flemming, Edward. 2004. Contrast and perceptual distinctiveness. In Bruce Hayes, Robert Kirchner, and Donca Steriade (eds), *Phonetically Based Phonology*. Cambridge: Cambridge University Press, 232–77.

Foley, James. 1970. Phonological distinctive features. *Folia Linguistica* 4(1/2): 87–92.

Foley, James. 1977. *Foundations of Theoretical Phonology*. Cambridge: Cambridge University Press.

Fónagy, Ivan. 1956. Über den Verlauf des Lautwandels. *Acta Linguistica* 6: 173–278.

Fougeron, Cecile and Patricia A. Keating. 1996. Articulatory strengthening in prosodic domain-initial position. *University of California Working Papers in Phonetics* 92: 61–87.

Foulkes, Paul. 1997. Historical laboratory phonology: investigating /p/ > /f/ > /h/ changes. *Language and Speech* 40: 249–76.

Foulkes, Paul and Gerard J. Docherty. 2000. Another chapter in the story of /r/: 'labiodental' variants in British English. *Journal of Sociolinguistics* 4: 30–59.

Foulkes, Paul and Gerard J. Docherty. 2006. The social life of phonetics and phonology. *Journal of Phonetics* 34: 409–38.

Foulkes, Paul, Gerald J. Docherty, and Dominic J. L. Watt. 1999. Tracking the emergence of structured variation: realisations of (t) by Newcastle children. *Leeds Working Papers in Linguistics and Phonetics*, 1–25.

Foulkes, Paul, Gerard J. Docherty, and Dominic J. L. Watt. 2005. Phonological variation in child directed speech. *Language* 81: 177–206.

Fowler, Carol and E. Saltzman. 1993. Coordination and coarticulation in speech production. *Language and Speech* 36: 171–95.

Fox, Anthony T. C. 1995. *Linguistic Reconstruction. An Introduction to Theory and Method*. Oxford: Oxford University Press.

Frantz, Donald G. 1970. A PL/1 program to assist the comparative linguist. *Communications of the ACM* 13: 353–6.

Frellesvig, Bjarke. 2010. *A History of the Japanese Language*. Cambridge: Cambridge University Press.

Fries, Charles C. and Kenneth L. Pike. 1949. Coexistent phonemic systems. *Language* 25: 29–50.

Fromkin, Victoria, Robert Rodman, and Nina Hyams. 2011. *An Introduction to Language*, 9th edn. Boston, Mass.: Wadsworth.

Fruehwald, Josef. 2012. Phonological involvement in phonetic change. MS, University of Pennsylvania. Available at: <http://www.ling.upenn.edu/~joseff/papers/fruehwald_proposal.pdf>

Fujimura, Osamu, S. Kiritani, and H. Ishida. 1973. Computer controlled radiography for observation of movements of articulatory and other human organs. *Computers in Biology and Medicine* 3: 371–84.

Fujimura, Osamu, M. J. Macchi, and L. A. Streeter. 1978. Perception of stop consonants with conflicting transitional cues: a cross-linguistic study. *Language and Speech* 21: 337–46.

Fulk, Robert D. 1992. *A History of Old English Meter*. Philadelphia: University of Pennsylvania Press.

Fulk, Robert D. 1997. Textual criticism. In Robert E. Bjork and John D. Niles (eds), *A Beowulf Handbook*. Lincoln: University of Nebraska Press, 34–53.

Gage, William. 1985. Glottal stops and Vietnamese tonogenesis. In V. Z. Acson and R. L. Leed (eds), *For Gordon H. Fairbanks: Oceanic Linguistics Special Publication 20*. Honolulu: University of Hawai'i Press, 21–36.

Gahl, Susanne and Susan M. Garnsey. 2004. Knowledge of grammar, knowledge of usage: syntactic probabilities affect pronunciation variation. *Language* 80: 707–47.

Gahl, Susanne and Alan Yu. 2006. Introduction to the special issue on exemplar-based models in linguistics. *Linguistic Review* 23: 213–16.

Galambos, Imre. 2006. *Orthography of Early Chinese Writing: Evidence from Newly Excavated Manuscripts*. Budapest: Eötvös Loránd University.

Gambhir, Surendra Kumar. 1981. The East Indian speech community in Guyana: a sociolinguistic study with special reference to koiné formation. PhD thesis, University of Pennsylvania.

Gamkrelidze, T'amaz V. and Vjačeslav V. Ivanov. 1973. Sprachtypologie und die Rekonstruktion der gemeinindogermanischen Verschlüsse: vorläufiger Bericht. *Phonetica* 27: 150–6.

Gamkrelidze, Thomas V. and Vjačeslav V. Ivanov. 1995. *Indo-European and the Indo-Europeans*. Berlin: Mouton de Gruyter.

Ganz, Peter. 1978. Eduard Sievers. *Beiträge zur Geschichte der deutschen Sprache und Literatur* 100: 40–85.

Gardner, Matt Hunt. 2012. Beyond the phonological void: contrast and the Canadian Shift. MS, Department of Linguistics, University of Toronto.

Garmann, Nina Gram. 2008. *The Quantity Shift: a Cognitive Usage-Based Analysis of the Quantity Shift in East Norwegian with Data from Old Norse and North Gudbrandsdal*. Oslo: University of Oslo.

Garrett, Andrew. 1998. Adjarian's Law, the Glottalic Theory, and the position of Armenian. In Benjamin K. Bergen et al. (eds), *Special Session on Indo-European Subgrouping and Internal Relations: Proceedings of the 24th Annual Meeting of the Berkeley Linguistics Society*. Berkeley, Calif.: Berkeley Linguistics Society, 12–23.

Garrett, Andrew. 2008. Paradigmatic uniformity and markedness. In Jeff Good (ed.), *Linguistic Universals and Language Change*. Oxford: Oxford University Press, 125–43.

Garrett, Andrew and Juliette Blevins. 2009. Analogical morphophonology. In Kristin Hanson and Sharon Inkelas (eds), *The Nature of the Word: Essays in Honor of Paul Kiparsky*. Cambridge, Mass.: MIT Press, 527–45.

Garrett, Andrew and Keith Johnson. 2013. Phonetic bias in sound change. In Alan C. L. Yu (ed.), *Origins of Sound Change: Approaches to Phonologization*. Oxford: Oxford University Press, 51–97.

Gauchat, Louis. 1905. L'unité phonétique dans le patois d'une commune. In *Aus Romanischen Sprachen und Literaturen: Festschrift Heinrich Morf*. Halle: Niemeyer, 175–232.

Gedney, William. 1972. A checklist for determining tones in Tai dialects. In M. Estellie Smith (ed.), *Studies in Linguistics in Honor of George L. Trager*. The Hague: Mouton, 423–37.

Gerhand, Simon and Christopher Berry. 1998. Word frequency effects in oral reading are not merely age-of-acquisition effects in disguise. *Journal of Experimental Psychology: Learning, Memory, and Cognition* 24(2): 267–83.

Gerhand, Simon and Christopher Berry. 1999. Age of acquisition, word frequency, and the role of phonology in the lexical decision task. *Memory and Cognition* 27: 592–602.

Gerken, LouAnn, Rachel Wilson, Rebecca Gómez, and Erika Nurmsoo. 2009. The relation between linguistic analogies and lexical categories. In James P. Blevins and Juliette Blevins (eds), *Analogy in Grammar: Form and Acquisition*. New York: Oxford University Press, 101–17.

Gess, Randall. 1996. Optimality Theory in the historical phonology of French. PhD thesis, University of Washington.

Gess, Randall. 1999. Rethinking the dating of Old French syllable-final consonant loss. *Diachronica* 16: 261–96.

Gess, Randall. 2011. Compensatory lengthening. In Marc van Oostendorp et al. (eds), *The Blackwell Companion to Phonology*. Malden, Mass.: Wiley-Blackwell, 1513–36.

Giannelli, Luciano and Leonardo Savoia. 1978. L'indebolimento consonantico in Toscana (I). *Rivista italiana di dialettologia* 2: 25–58.

Gill, Harjeet Singh and Hentry A. Gleason. 1972. The salient features of the Punjabi language, *Pakha Sanjam* 4: 1–3.

Gillies, William. 2009. Scottish Gaelic. In Martin Ball and Nicole Muller (eds), *The Celtic Languages*, 2nd edn. London: Routledge, 230–304.

Gilman, Sophia. 2012a. Comparative Method Algorithm. *Cambridge Occasional Papers in Linguistics* 6: 131–75.

Gilman, Sophia. 2012b. Operationalizing the intuitive aspects of the comparative method. MS, Yale University.

Gnanadesikan, Amalia E. 2009. *The Writing Revolution: Cuneiform to the Internet*. Oxford: Wiley-Blackwell.

Goeman, A. C. M. and P. T. van Reenen. 1985. Word-final T-deletion in Dutch dialects. *VU-Working Papers in Linguistics* 16: 157–208.

Goeman, A. C. M., P. T. van Reenen, and E. Wattel. 1993. The diphthongization of West Germanic î and its relation to West Germanic û in modern Dutch dialects: a quantitative approach. In W. Viereck (ed.), *Verhandlungen des Internationalen Dialektologenkongresses: Bamberg, 29.7-4.8.1990*. Stuttgart: Steiner, 76–97.

Goidanich, Pietro. 1926. Saggio critico sullo studio de L. Gauchat. *Archivio glottologico italiano* 20: 60–71.

Goldinger, Stephen D. 1996. Words and voices, Episodic traces in spoken word identification and recognition memory. *Journal of Experimental Psychology, Learning Memory and Cognition* 22: 1166–82.

Goldinger, Stephen D. 1998. Echoes of echoes? An episodic theory of lexical access. *Psychological Review* 105: 251–79.

Goldrick, Matthew. 2011. Utilizing psychological realism to advance phonological theory. In J. Goldsmith, J. Riggle, and A. Yu (eds), *Handbook of Phonological Theory*, 2nd edn. Oxford: Blackwell, 631–60.

Goldrick, Matthew, H. Ross Baker, Amanda Murphy, and Melissa Baese-Berk. 2011. Interaction and representational integration: evidence from speech errors. *Cognition* 121: 58–72.

Goldsmith, John. 1995. Phonological theory. In J. Goldsmith (ed.), *The Handbook of Phonological Theory*. Oxford: Blackwell, 1–23.

Goldsmith, John 2008. Generative phonology in the late 1940s. *Phonology* 25: 37–59.

Goldsmith, John and Bernard Laks. Forthcoming. Generative phonology: its origins, its principles, and its successors. In Linda Waugh, John E. Joseph, and Monique Monville-Burston (eds), *The Cambridge History of Linguistics*. Cambridge: Cambridge University Press.

Golston, Chris and Phong Yang. 2001. Hmong loanword phonology. In C. Féry, A. D. Green and R. van de Vijver (eds), *Proceedings of HILP 5*. Potsdam: University of Potsdam, 40–57.

Good, Phillip. 1994. *Permutation Tests: a Practical Guide to Resampling Methods for Testing Hypotheses*. New York: Springer.

Gordon, Elizabeth, Lyle Campbell, Jennifer Hay, Margaret Maclagan, Andrea Sudbury, and Peter Trudgill. 2004. *New Zealand English: its Origins and Evolution*. Cambridge: Cambridge University Press.

Gordon, Elizabeth and Tony Deverson. 1998. *New Zealand English and English in New Zealand*. Auckland: New House.

Gordon, Elizabeth and Margaret Maclagan. 2001. Capturing a sound change: a real time study over 15 years of the NEAR/SQUARE diphthong merger in New Zealand English. *Australian Journal of Linguistics* 21: 215–38.

Gordon, Elizabeth, Margaret Maclagan, and Jennifer Hay. 2007. The ONZE corpus. In J. Beal, K. Corrigan, and H. Moisl (eds), *Creating and Digitizing Language Corpora*. Basingstoke: Palgrave Macmillan.

Gordon, Matthew J. 2001. *Small-Town Values and Big-City Vowels: a Study of the Northern Cities Shift in Michigan*. Durham, NC: Duke University Press.

Gordon, Matthew J. 2002. Investigating chain shifts and mergers. In J. K. Chambers, P. Trudgill, and N. Schilling-Estes (eds), *Handbook of Language Variation and Change*. Oxford: Blackwell, 244-66.

Gordon, Matthew J. 2011. Theoretical and methodological issues in the study of chain shifts. *Language and Linguistics Compass* 5(11): 784-94.

Gordon, Matthew J. 2012. Areal features of English in the United States. In Raymond Hickey (ed.), *Areal Features of the Anglophone World*. Berlin: de Gruyter, 109-32.

Gordon, Matthew J. 2013. *Labov: a Guide for the Perplexed*. London: Bloomsbury.

Görlach, Manfred. 1987. Colonial lag? The alleged conservative character of American English and other 'colonial' varieties. *English World-Wide* 8: 41-60.

Grace, George 1969. Speaking of language change. *University of Hawai'i Working Papers in Linguistics* 3: 101-16.

Graff, Eberhard Gottlieb. 1834-42. *Althochdeustcher Sprachschatz oder Wörterbuch der ahd. Sprache*. 6 vols. Berlin: Verfasser und Commission der Nikolaischen Buchhandlung.

Grammont, Maurice. 1902. Observations sur le langage des enfants. In *Mélanges linguistiques offerts à M. Antoine Meillet*. Paris: Klincksieck, 115-31.

Grassmann, Hermann. 1863. Über die Aspiraten und ihr gleichzeitiges Vorhandensein im An- und Auslaute der Wurzeln. *Zeitschrift für vergleichende Sprachforschung auf dem Gebiete des Deutschen, Griechischen und Lateinischen* 12(2): 81-138.

Gray, Russell D., and Quentin D. Atkinson. 2003. Language-tree divergence times support the Anatolian theory of Indo-European origins. *Nature* 426: 435-9.

Green, Antony D. 1998. The promotion of the unmarked: Representing sound change in Optimality Theory. Paper presented at the 10th International Conference on English Historical Linguistics, University of Manchester, August 1998.

Green, Antony D. 2003. The independence of phonology and morphology: the Celtic mutations. *ZAS Papers in Linguistics* 32: 47-86.

Green, Antony D. 2004. Opacity in Tiberian Hebrew: morphology, not phonology. *ZAS Papers in Linguistics* 37: 37-70.

Green, Antony D. 2007. *Phonology Limited*. Potsdam: Universitätsverlag Potsdam.

Greenberg, Joseph. 1966. Some universals of grammar with particular reference to the order of meaningful elements. In Joseph Greenberg (ed.), *Universals of Language*, 2nd edn. Cambridge, Mass.: MIT Press.

Greenberg, Joseph H. 1970. Some generalizations concerning glottalic consonants, especially implosives. *International Journal of American Linguistics* 36: 123-45.

Greenberg, Joseph H. 1971. The Indo-Pacific hypothesis. In Thomas A. Sebeok (ed.), *Linguistics in Oceania*. The Hague: Mouton, 807-71.

Greenberg, Joseph H. 1978. Some generalizations concerning initial and final consonant clusters. In Joseph H. Greenberg (ed.), *Universals of Human Language*, vol. 2. Phonology. Stanford, Calif.: Stanford University Press, 243-79.

Greenberg, Joseph H. 1987. *Language in the Americas*. Stanford, Calif.: Stanford University Press.

Greenberg, Joseph H. 2002. *Indo-European and its Closest Relatives: the Eurasiatic Language Family. Lexicon*. Stanford, Calif: Stanford University Press.

Greenlee, Mel and John J. Ohala 1980. Phonetically motivated parallels between child phonology and historical sound change. *Language Sciences* 2: 283–301.

Gregersen, Frans. 2009. The data and design of the LANCHART study. *Acta Linguistica Hafniensia* 41: 3–29.

Gregersen, Frans and Michael Barner-Rasmussen. 2011. The logic of comparability: on genres and phonetic variation in a project on language change in real time. *Corpus Linguistics and Linguistic Theory* 7: 7–36.

Gregory, Michelle, William D. Raymond, Alan Bell, Eric Fosler-Lussier, and Daniel Jurafsky. 1999. The effects of collocational strength and contextual predictability in lexical production. *Chicago Linguistics Society* 35: 151–66.

Grimes, Joseph E. and Frederick B. Agard. 1959. Linguistic divergence in Romance, *Language* 35: 598–604.

Grimm, Jacob. 1822. *Deutsche Grammatik*, 2nd edn. Göttingen: Dieterichschen Buchhandlung. [1st edn, 1819; 3rd edn, 1840.]

Grotius, Hugo. 1552. *On the Origin of the Native Races of America: a Dissertation by Hugo Grotius*. [Trans. Edmund Goldsmid, 1884. Edinburgh: [n.p.].]

Grunwell, Pamela. 1982. *Clinical Phonology*. London: Croom Helm.

Guion, Susan. 1996. Velar palatalization: coarticulation, perception, and sound change. PhD thesis, University of Texas, Austin.

Guion, Susan. 1998. The role of perception in the sound change of velar palatalization. *Phonetica* 55: 18–52.

Gulya, János. 1974. Some eighteenth-century antecedents of nineteenth-century linguistics: the discovery of Finno-Ugrian. In Dell Hymes (ed.), *Studies in the History of Linguistics: Traditions and Paradigms*. Bloomington: Indiana University Press, 258–76.

Gumperz, John and Robert Wilson. 1971. Convergence and creolization: a case from the Indo-Aryan/Dravidian border. In Dell Hymes (ed.), *Pidginization and Creolization of Languages*. Cambridge: Cambridge University Press, 151–67.

Gussenhoven, Carlos. 1994. English stress in lexical phonology. In W. U. Dressler, M. Prinzhorn, and J. R. Rennison (eds), *Phonologica 1992. Proceedings of the 7th International Phonology Meeting*. Turin: Rosenberg & Sellier, 87–96.

Gussenhoven, Carlos. 2004. Perceived vowel duration. In H. Quené and V. van Heuven (eds), *On Speech and Language: Studies for Sieb G. Nooteboom*. Utrecht: LOT, 65–71.

Gussman, Edmund. 2002. *Phonology: Analysis and Theory*. Cambridge: Cambridge University Press.

Gussmann, Edmund. 2007. *The Phonology of Polish*. Oxford: Oxford University Press.

Guy, Gregory R. 1991a. Contextual conditioning in variable lexical phonology. *Language Variation and Change* 3: 223–39.

Guy, Gregory R. 1991b. Explanation in variable phonology: an exponential model of morphological constraints. *Language Variation and Change* 3: 1–22.

Guy, Gregory R. 1996. Form and function in linguistic variation. In Gregory R. Guy, Crawford Feagin, Deborah Schiffrin, and John Baugh (eds), *Towards a Social Science of Language: Papers in Honor of William Labov*, vol. 1. Amsterdam: Benjamins, 221–52.

Guy, Gregory R. and Sally Boyd. 1990. The development of a morphological class. *Language Variation and Change* 2: 1–18.

Gyarmathi, Sámuel. 1799. *Affinitas linguae Hungaricae cum linguis Fennicae originis grammatice demonstrata*. Göttingen. [Trans. Victor E. Hanzeli, *Sámuel Gyarmathi: Grammatical*

Proof of the Affinity of the Hungarian Language with Languages of Fennic Origin. Amsterdam: Benjamins, 1983.]

Haider, Hubert. 1983. Der Fehlschluß der Typologie. In Wolfgang Meid (ed.), *Philologie und Sprachwissenschaft: Akten der 10. Österreichischen Linguisten-Tagung Innsbruck*. Innsbruck: Institut für Sprachwissenschaft der Universität Innsbruck, 79–92.

Hajek, John. 1997. *Universals of Sound Change in Nasalization*. Oxford: Blackwell.

Hale, Mark. 2003. Neogrammarian sound change. In Brian D. Joseph and Richard D. Janda (eds), *Handbook of Historical Linguistics*. Oxford: Blackwell, 343–68.

Hale, Mark. 2007. *Historical Linguistics: Theory and Method*. Oxford: Wiley-Blackwell.

Hale, Mark, Madelyn Kissock, and Charles Reiss. 2007. Microvariation, variation, and the features of universal grammar. *Lingua* 117: 645–65.

Hale, Mark and Charles Reiss 2000a. Substance abuse and dysfunctionalism: current trends in phonology. *Linguistic Inquiry* 31: 157–69.

Hale, Mark and Charles Reiss. 2000b. Phonology as cognition. In Noel Burton-Roberts, Philip Carr, and Gerard Docherty (eds), *Phonological Knowledge: Conceptual and Empirical Issues*. Oxford: Oxford University Press, 161–84.

Hale, Mark and Charles Reiss. 2008. *The Phonological Enterprise*. Oxford: Oxford University Press.

Hall, Daniel Currie. 2007. The role and representation of contrast in phonological theory. PhD thesis, University of Toronto.

Hall, Daniel Currie. 2011. Phonological contrast and its phonetic enhancement: dispersedness without dispersion. *Phonology* 28: 1–54.

Hall, T. Allan. 1997. The historical development of retroflex consonants in Indo-Aryan. *Lingua* 102: 203–21.

Hall-Lew, Lauren, Rebecca L. Starr, and Elizabeth Coppock. 2012. Style-shifting in the U.S. Congress: the foreign (a) vowel in 'Iraq(i)'. In Juan Manuel Hernández-Campoy and Juan Antonio Cutillas-Espinosa (eds), *Style-Shifting in Public: New Perspectives on Stylistic Variation*. Philadelphia: Benjamins, 45–63.

Halle, Morris. 1959. *The Sound Pattern of Russian*. The Hague: Mouton.

Halle, Morris. 1962. Phonology in generative grammar. *Word* 18: 54–72. [Reprinted 1964 in Jerry A. Fodor and Jerrold J. Katz (eds), *The Structure of Language: Readings in the Philosophy of Language*. Englewood Cliffs, NJ: Prentice-Hall, 334–52.]

Halle, Morris. 1983. On distinctive features and their articulatory implementation. *Natural Language and Linguistic Theory* 8: 149–76.

Halle, Morris. 1995. Feature geometry and feature spreading. *Linguistic Inquiry,* 26(1): 1–46.

Halle, Morris. 2005. Palatalization/velar softening: what it is and what it tells us about the nature of language. *Linguistic Inquiry* 36: 23–41.

Halle, Morris. 2009. Two comments on 'The role of features in phonological inventories'. In Eric Raimy and Charles Cairns (eds), *Contemporary Views on Architecture and Representations in Phonology*. Cambridge, Mass.: MIT Press, 69–73.

Halle, Morris and Samuel Jay Keyser. 1971. *English Stress: its Form, its Growth, and its Role in Verse*. New York: Harper and Row.

Halle, Morris and Jean-Roger Vergnaud. 1987. Stress and the cycle. *Linguistic Inquiry* 18: 45–84.

Halle, Morris, Bert Vaux, and Andrew Wolfe. 2000. On feature spreading and the representation of place of articulation. *Linguistic Inquiry* 31(3): 387–444.

Hallé, Pierre A., Juan Segui, Uli Frauenfelder, and Christine Meunier. 1998. Processing of illegal consonant clusters: a case of perceptual assimilation. *Journal of Experimental Psychology: Human Perception and Performance* 24(2): 592–608.

Hamann, Silke. 2004. Retroflex fricatives in Slavic languages. *Journal of the International Phonetic Association* 34: 53–67.

Hamann, Silke. 2009. The learner of a perception grammar as a source of sound change. In Paul Boersma and Silke Hamann (eds), *Phonology in Perception*. Berlin: Mouton de Gruyter, 111–49.

Hamann, Silke and Susanne Fuchs. 2008. How do retroflex stops evolve? Evidence from typology and an articulatory study. *ZAS Papers in Linguistics* 49: 97–131.

Hammarberg, R. 1976. The metaphysics of coarticulation. *Journal of Phonetics* 4: 353–63.

Hammarström, Göran. 1980. *Australian English: its Origin and Status*. Hamburg: Buske.

Hammarström, Göran. 1985. On the origin of Australian English. *Beiträge zur Phonetik und Linguistik* 48: 369–72.

Hancock, Ian F. 1991. St. Helena English. In Francis Byrne and Thom Huebner (eds), *Development and Structures of Creole Languages: Essays in Honor of Derek Bickerton*. Amsterdam: Benjamins, 17–28.

Hansen, Anita Berit. 2001. Lexical diffusion as a factor of phonetic change: the case of modern French nasal vowels. *Language Variation and Change* 13: 209–52.

Hansson, Gunnar Ólafur. 2008. Diachronic explanations of sound patterns. *Language and Linguistics Compass* 2(5): 859–93.

Hanzeli, Victor E. 1983. *Sámuel Gyarmathi: Grammatical Proof of the Affinity of the Hungarian Language with Languages of Fennic Origin*. Amsterdam: Benjamins.

Hare, Mary and Jeffrey L. Elman. 1995. Learning and morphological change. *Cognition* 56: 61–98.

Harries, Lyndon. 1950. *A Grammar of Mwera*. Johannesburg: Witwatersrand University.

Harrington, Jonathan. 2006. An acoustic analysis of 'happy-tensing' in the Queen's annual Christmas broadcasts. *Journal of Phonetics* 34: 439–57.

Harrington, Jonathan. 2007. Evidence for the relationship between synchronic variability and diachronic change in the Queen's annual Christmas broadcasts. In J. Cole, and J. Hualde (eds), *Laboratory Phonology 9: Phonetics and Phonology*. Berlin: de Gruyter, 125–44.

Harrington, Jonathan, Phil Hoole, Felicitas Kleber, and Ulrich Reubold. 2011. The physiological, acoustic and perceptual basis of high back vowel fronting: evidence from German tense and lax vowels. *Journal of Phonetics* 39: 121–31.

Harrington, Jonathan, Felicitas Kleber, and Ulrich Reubold. 2008. Compensation for coarticulation, /u/-fronting, and sound change in standard southern British: an acoustic and perceptual study. *Journal of the Acoustical Society of America* 123(5): 2825–35.

Harrington, Jonathan, Sallyanne Palethorpe, and Catherine I. Watson. 2000a. Does the Queen speak the Queen's English? *Nature* 408: 927–28.

Harrington, Jonathan, Sallyanne Palethorpe, and Catherine I. Watson. 2000b. Monophthongal vowel changes in received pronunciation: an acoustic analysis of the Queen's Christmas broadcasts. *Journal of the International Phonetic Association* 30: 63–78.

Harrington, Jonathan, Sallyanne Palethorpe, and Catherine I. Watson. 2005. Deepening or lessening the divide between diphthongs? An analysis of the Queen's annual Christmas broadcasts. In W. Hardcastle, and J. Beck (eds), *A Figure of Speech*. Mahwah, NJ: Erlbaum, 227–63.

Harris, John. 1990a. Segmental complexity and phonological government. *Phonology* 7: 255–300.

Harris, John. 1990b. Derived phonological contrasts. In Susan Ramsaran (ed.), *Studies in the Pronunciation of English: a Commemorative Volume in Honour of A. C. Gimson*. London: Routledge, 87–105.

Harris, John. 1994. *English Sound Structure*. Oxford: Blackwell.

Harris, John. 2004. Release the captive coda: the foot as a domain of phonetic interpretation. In J. Local, R. Ogden, and R. Temple (eds), *Phonetic Interpretation*. Cambridge: Cambridge University Press, 103–129.

Harris-Northall, Ray. 1990. *Weakening Processes in the History of Spanish Consonants*. London: Routledge.

Hart, John. 1569. *An orthographie, conteyning the due order, and reason, howe to write or paint thimage of mannes voice, most like to the life or nature*. N.p.

Hartman, Steven Lee. 1993. Writing rules for a computer model of sound change, *Southern Illinois Working Papers in Linguistics and Language Teaching* 2: 31–9. Rule sets available at: <http://mypage.siu.edu/lhartman/phono.html>

Harvey, Christopher. 2012. Contrastive shift in Ob-Ugric vowel systems. MS, Department of Linguistics, University of Toronto.

Hashimoto, Mantaro J. 1978. *Phonology of Ancient Chinese*. Tokyo: Institute for the Study of Languages and Cultures of Asia and Africa.

Haspelmath, Martin. 1998. Does grammaticalization need reanalysis? *Studies in Language* 22: 315–51.

Haudricourt, André-Georges. 1954. De l'origine des tons du vietnamien. *Journal asiatique* 242: 69–82.

Haugen, Einar. 1950a. The analysis of linguistic borrowing. *Language* 26: 210–31.

Haugen, Einar. 1950b. *First Grammatical Treatise. The Earliest Germanic Phonology: an Edition, Translation, and Commentary*. Baltimore, Md.: Waverly Press.

Hay, Jennifer, Stefanie Jannedy, and Norma Mendoza-Denton. 1999. Oprah and /ay/: lexical frequency, referee design and style. In J. Ohala (ed.), *Proceedings of the 14th International Congress of Phonetic Sciences*, . Amsterdam: Benjamins, 1389–92.

Hay, Jennifer and Margaret Maclagan. 2012. /r/-sandhi in early 20th-century New Zealand English. *Linguistics* 50(4): 745–63.

Hay, Jennifer, Paul Warren, and Katie Drager. 2006. Factors influencing speech perception in the context of a merger-in-progress. *Journal of Phonetics* 34: 458–84.

Hayes, Bruce. 1981. A metrical theory of stress rules. PhD thesis, MIT. [Distributed by Indiana University Linguistics club and published by Garland Press in 1985.]

Hayes, Bruce. 1988. Metrics and phonological theory. In Frederick Newmeyer (ed.), *Linguistics: The Cambridge Survey*, vol. 2: *Linguistic Theory: Extensions and Implications*. Cambridge: Cambridge University Press, 220–49.

Hayes, Bruce. 1989. Compensatory lengthening in moraic phonology. *Linguistic Inquiry* 20: 253–306.

Hayes, Bruce. 1995. *Metrical Stress Theory: Principles and Case Studies*. Chicago: University of Chicago Press.

Hayes, Bruce. 1999. Phonetically-driven phonology: the role of Optimality Theory and inductive grounding. In Michael Darnell et al. (eds), *Functionalism and Formalism in Linguistics*, vol. 1. Amsterdam: Benjamins, 243–85.

Hayes, Bruce. 2000. Gradient well-formedness in Optimality Theory. In Joost Dekkers, Frank van der Leeuw and Jeroen van de Weijer (eds), *Optimality Theory: Phonology, Syntax, and Acquisition*. Oxford: Oxford University Press, 88–120.

Hayes, Bruce. 2009. *Introductory Phonology*. Oxford: Wiley-Blackwell.

Hayes, Bruce, Robert Kirchner, and Donca Steriade (eds). 2004. *Phonetically Based Phonology*. Cambridge: Cambridge University Press.

Hayes, Bruce, Kie Zuraw, Péter Siptár, and Zsuzsa Londe. 2009. Natural and unnatural constraints in Hungarian vowel harmony. *Language* 85: 822–63.

Hazen, Kirk. 2002. The family. In Jack K. Chambers, Peter Trudgill, and Natalie Schilling-Estes
(eds), *The Handbook of Language Variation and Change*. Oxford: Blackwell, 500–525.

Heeringa, Wilbert J. 2004. Measuring dialect pronunciation differences using Levenshtein
distance. PhD thesis, Rijksuniversiteit Groningen.

Heeringa, Wilbert, Peter Kleiweg, Charlotte Gooskens, and John Nerbonne. 2006. Evaluation
of string distance algorithms for dialectology. In John Nerbonne, and Erhard Hinrichs
(eds), *Linguistic Distances: Proceedings of the Workshop, 23 July 2006, Sydney, Australia
(COLING/ACL)*. Stroudsburg, Penn.: Association for Computational Linguistics, 51–62.
Available at: <http://www.aclweb.org/anthology/W/W06/W06-1108.pdf>

Hellberg, Staffan. 1978. Unnatural phonology. *Journal of Linguistics* 14: 157–77.

Henton, Caroline. 1990. One vowel's life (and death?) across languages: the moribundity and
prestige of /ʌ/. *Journal of Phonetics* 18: 203–27.

Henton, Caroline. 1999. Where is female synthetic speech? *Journal of the International Phonetic
Association* 34: 51–61.

Henton, Leanne, Peter Ladefoged, and Ian Maddieson. 1992. Stops in the world's languages.
Phonetica 49: 65–101.

Heo, Younghyon. 2010. Vowel insertion as perceptual intrusion in loanword adaptation. PhD
thesis, University of Wisconsin-Milwaukee.

Hermann, Eduard. 1929. Lautveränderungen in der Individualsprache einer Mundart.
Nachrichten der Gesellsch. der Wissenschaften zu Göttingen. *Philosophisch-Historische
Klasse* 11: 195–214.

Hermann, Eduard. 1931. *Lautgesetz und Analogie*. Berlin: Weidmannsche Buchhandlung.

Hernández-Campoy, Juan Manuel, and Juan Camilo Conde-Silvestre. 2005. Sociolinguistic
and geolinguistic approaches to the historical diffusion of linguistic innovations: incipient
standardisation in Late Middle English. *International Journal of English Studies* 5(1): 101–34.

Herold, Ruth. 1990. Mechanisms of merger: the implementation and distribution of the low
back merger in Eastern Pennsylvania. PhD thesis, University of Pennsylvania.

Herrera Zendejas, Esther. 1995. *Palabras, estratos y representaciones: temas de fonología lexica
en zoque*. Mexico City: Colegio de México.

Hewson, John. 1974. Comparative reconstruction on the computer. In John M. Anderson and
Charles Jones (eds), *Historical Linguistics* I: *Syntax, Morphology, Internal and Comparative
Reconstruction*. Amsterdam: North-Holland, 191–7.

Hewson, John. 1993. *A Computer-Generated Dictionary of Proto-Algonquian*. Hull, Québec:
Canadian Museum of Civilization.

Hickey, Raymond. 2002. The Atlantic edge: the relationship between Irish English and
Newfoundland English. *English World-Wide* 23: 283–316.

Hickey, Raymond (ed.). 2010. *Handbook of Language Contact*. Oxford: Blackwell.

Hill, Archibald A. 1936. Phonetic and phonemic change. *Language* 12: 15–22.

Hill, Eugen. 2007. Proportionale Analogie, paradigmatischer Ausgleich und Formerweiterung:
ein Beitrag zur Typologie des morphologischen Wandels. *Diachronica* 24: 81–118.

Hill, Eugen. 2009. Die Präferenztheorie in der historischen Phonologie aus junggramma-
tischer Perspektive. *Zeitschrift für Sprachwissenschaft* 28: 231–63.

Hill, Eugen. 2010. A case study in grammaticalized inflectional morphology: origin and development of the Germanic weak preterite. *Diachronica* 27: 411–458.

Hinskens, Frans. 1998. Variation studies in dialectology and three types of sound change. *Sociolinguistica* 12: 155–93.

Hirt, Hermann. 1939. *Die Hauptprobleme der indogermanischen Sprachwissenschaft*. Halle: Niemeyer.

Hock, Hans H. 1986. *Principles of Historical Linguistics*. Berlin: Mouton de Gruyter [2nd edn. 1991.].

Hock, Hans H. 2003. Analogical change. In Brian Joseph and Richard Janda (eds), *The Handbook of Historical Linguistics*. Oxford: Blackwell, 441–80.

Hock, Hans H. and Brian D. Joseph. 2009. *Language History, Language Change, and Language Relationship*, 2nd edn. New York: Mouton de Gruyter.

Hockett, Charles F. 1955. *A Manual of Phonology*. Baltimore, Md.: Waverly Press.

Hockett, Charles. 1958. *A Course in Modern Linguistics*. New York: Macmillan.

Hockett, Charles. 1965. Sound change. *Language* 41: 185–204.

Hockett, Charles. 1967. The quantification of functional load. *Word* 23: 320–39.

Hoenigswald, Henry M. 1960. *Language Change and Linguistic Reconstruction*. Chicago: University of Chicago Press.

Hoenigswald, Henry M. 1974. Fallacies in the history of linguistics: notes on the appraisal of the nineteenth century. In Dell Hymes (ed.), *Studies in the History of Linguistics: Traditions and Paradigms*. Bloomington: Indiana University Press, 346–58.

Hoenigswald, Henry M. 1978. The annus mirabilis 1876 and posterity. *Transactions of the Philological Society* 76(1): 17–35.

Hoffman, Michol. 2010. The role of social factors in the Canadian vowel shift. *American Speech* 85: 121–40.

Hogg, Richard M. 1992. *A Grammar of Old English*, vol. 1: *Phonology*. Oxford: Blackwell.

Holman, Eric W., Cecil H. Brown, Søren Wichmann, André Müller, Viveka Velupillai, . . . and Dmitry Egorov. 2011. Automated dating of the world's language families based on lexical similarity. *Current Anthropology* 52(6): 841–75.

Holman, Eric W., Søren Wichmann, Cecil H. Brown, Viveka Velupillai, André Müller, and Dik Bakker. 2008. Explorations in automated language classification, *Folia Linguistica* 42(2): 331–54.

Holsinger, David J. 2000. Lenition in Germanic: prosodic templates in sound change. PhD thesis, University of Wisconsin-Madison.

Holsinger, David J. 2009. Germanic prosody and consonantal strength. In Joaquim Brandão de Carvalho, Tobias Scheer, and Philippe Ségéral (eds), *Lenition and Fortition*. Berlin: Mouton de Gruyter, 273–300.

Holt, D. Eric. 1997. The role of the listener in the historical phonology of Spanish and Portuguese: an Optimality-Theoretic account. PhD thesis, Georgetown University.

Holt, D. Eric (ed.). 2003a. *Optimality Theory and Language Change*. Dordrecht: Kluwer Academic.

Holt, D. Eric. 2003b. Remarks on optimality theory and language change. In D. Eric Holt (ed.), *Optimality Theory and Language Change*. Dordrecht: Kluwer Academic, 1–30.

Holt, D. Eric. 2003c. The emergence of palatal sonorants and alternating diphthongs in Hispano-Romance. In D. Eric Holt (ed.), *Optimality Theory and Language Change*. Dordrecht: Kluwer, 285–305.

Holt, D. Eric. 2004. Optimization of syllable contact in Old Spanish via the sporadic sound change metathesis. *Probus* 16: 43–61.

Holt, D. Eric. 2007. Optimality Theory and language change in Spanish. In Fernando Martínez-Gil and Sonia Colina (eds), *Optimality-Theoretic Advances in Spanish Phonology*. Amsterdam: Benjamins, 378–98.

Hombert, Jean-Marie. 1977. Development of tones from vowel height? *Journal of Phonetics* 5: 9–16.

Hombert, Jean-Marie. 1978. Consonant types, vowel quality, and tone. In Victoria A. Fromkin (ed.), *Tone: a Linguistic Survey*. New York: Academic Press, 77–111.

Hombert, Jean-Marie. 1984. Tonogenesis revisited. *Pholia* (Laboratoire de phonétique et linguistique africaine) 1: 77–86.

Hombert, Jean-Marie, John J. Ohala, and William G. Ewan. 1979. Phonetic explanations for the development of tones. *Language* 55(1): 37–58.

Honeybone, Patrick. 2001. Lenition inhibition in Liverpool English. *English Language and Linguistics* 5(2): 213–249.

Honeybone, Patrick. 2005. Diachronic evidence in segmental phonology: the case of laryngeal specifications. In M. van Oostendorp and J. van de Weijer (eds), *The Internal Organization of Phonological Segments*. Berlin: Mouton de Gruyter, 319–54.

Honeybone, Patrick. 2008. Lenition, weakening and consonantal strength: tracing concepts through the history of phonology. In Joaquim Brandão de Carvalho, Tobias Scheer, and Philippe Ségéral (eds), *Lenition and Fortition*. Berlin: Mouton de Gruyter, 9–92.

Honeybone, Patrick. 2010. How symmetrical are English vowels? *Yazyk i rechevaya deyatel'nost'* [Language and language behavior]. *Journal of the Linguistic Society of St. Petersburg* 9 [issue dated 2006]: 33–63.

Hooper, Joan B. 1976a. *An Introduction to Natural Generative Phonology*. New York: Academic Press.

Hooper, Joan B. 1976b. Word frequency in lexical diffusion and the source of morphophonological change. In William Christie (ed.), *Current Progress in Historical Linguistics*. Amsterdam: North-Holland, 96–105.

Hooper, Joan B. 1980. Child morphology and morphophonemic change. In Jacek Fisiak (ed.), *Historical Morphology*. The Hague: Mouton, 157–87.

Hopp, Holger. 2007. Ultimate attainment at the interfaces in second language acquisition: grammar and processing. PhD thesis, University of Groningen.

Hopper, Paul J. 1973. Glottalized and murmured occlusives in Indo-European. *Glossa* 7: 141–66.

Hopper, Paul J. 1977. The typology of the Proto-Indo-European segmental inventory. *Journal of Indo-European Studies* 5: 41–53.

Hopper, Paul. 1991. On some principles of grammaticalization. In Elizabeth Closs Traugott and Bernd Heine (eds), *Approaches to Grammaticalization*. Amsterdam: Benjamins, 17–35.

Hopper, Paul. 2009. Plus ça change.: Hermann Paul and recent theories of language. Paper presented at the Colloquy on Hermann Paul, Freiburg Institute for Advanced Studies/ Hermann Paul Centre for Linguistics, Freiburg im Breisgau, 15 May 2009.

Hopper, Paul J. and Elizabeth Closs Traugott. 2003. *Grammaticalization*, 2nd edn. New York: Cambridge University Press.

Horwitz, Elaine K. 2010. Foreign and second language anxiety. *Language Teaching* 43: 154–67.

Householder, Fred W. 1965. On some recent claims in phonological theory. *Journal of Linguistics* 1(1): 13–34.

Hsieh, Feng-fan and Michael Kenstowicz. 2008. Phonetic knowledge in tonal adaptation: Mandarin and English loanwords in Lhasa Tibetan. *Journal of East Asian Linguistics* 17(4): 279–97.

Hsieh, Feng-fan, Michael Kenstowicz, and Xiaomin Mou. 2009. Mandarin adaptations of coda nasals in English loanwords. In A. Calabrese and L. Wetzels (eds), *Loan Phonology*. Amsterdam: Benjamins, 131–54.

Hua, Zhu and Barbara Dodd. 2000. The phonological acquisition of Putonghua (Modern Standard Chinese). *Journal of Child Language* 27: 3–42.

Hudak, Thomas John. 2004. William J. Gedney's elicitation questionnaire. *Journal of the American Oriental Society* 124(3): 549–59.

Hulst, Harry van der, ed. 1999. *Word Prosodic Systems in the Languages of Europe*. Berlin: Moulton de Gruyter.

Hultsch, David F., Stuart W. S. MacDonald, and Roger A. Dixon. 2002. Variability in reaction time performance of younger and older adults. *Journal of Gerontology* 57B: 101–15.

Hume, Elizabeth. 2001. Metathesis: formal and functional considerations. In Elizabeth Hume, Norval Smith, and Jeroen van de Weijer (eds), *Surface Syllable Structure and Segment Sequencing*. Leiden: HIL, 1–25.

Hume, Elizabeth. 2004. The indeterminacy/attestation model of metathesis. *Language* 80: 203–37.

Hume, Elizabeth and Frédéric Mailhot. 2013. The role of entropy and surprisal in phonologization and language change. In Alan C.L. Yu (ed.), *Origins of Sound Patterns: Approaches to Phonologization*. Oxford: Oxford University Press.

Hurch, Bernhard and Richard A. Rhodes (eds). 1996. *Natural Phonology: The State of the Art*. Berlin: Mouton de Gruyter.

Huson, Daniel H. 1998. SplitsTree: analyzing and visualizing evolutionary data. *Bioinformatics* 14(1): 68–73.

Huson, Daniel H. and David Bryant. 2006. Application of phylogenetic networks in evolutionary studies. *Molecular Biology and Evolution* 23(2): 254–67. Software available at: <http://www.splitstree.org>

Hutcheson, Rand. 1995. *Old English Poetic Metre*. Woodbridge: Boydell and Brewer.

Hutton, John. 1996. Optimality Theory and historical language change. Paper presented at the 4th Phonology Meeting, University of Manchester.

Hyman, Larry. 1970a. The role of borrowings in the justification of phonological grammars. *Studies in African Linguistics* 1: 1–48.

Hyman, Larry. 1970b. How concrete is phonology? *Language* 46: 58–76.

Hyman, Larry. 1975. *Phonology: Theory and Analysis*. New York: Holt, Rinehart and Winston.

Hyman, Larry. 1976. Phonologization. In Alphonse Juilland, A. M. Devine, and Laurence D. Stephens (eds), *Linguistic Studies Offered to Joseph Greenberg*. Anma Libri: Saratoga, Calif.: Anma Libri, 407–18.

Hyman, Larry. 2001. The limits of phonetic determinism in phonology: *NC revisited. In Elizabeth Hume and Keith Johnson (eds), *The Role of Speech Perception in Phonology*. New York: Academic Press, 141–85.

Hyman, Larry. 2006. Word-prosodic typology. *Phonology* 23: 225–57.

Hymes, Dell H. 1956. Na-Dene and positional analysis of categories. *American Anthropologist* 58: 624–38.

Idsardi, William. 1994. Open and closed feet in Old English. *Linguistic Inquiry* 25: 522–33.

Igarashi Jin'ichi. 1969. *Jōdai kanazukai jiten* [Dictionary of ancient kana usage]. Tokyo: Shōgakukan.

Inkelas, Sharon. 1994. Consequences of optimization for underspecification. Available at: <http://roa.rutgers.edu/files/40-1294/40-1294-INKELAS-0-0.pdf> [Subsequently published in 1995 in Jill Beckman (ed.), *Proceedings of the North-Eastern Linguistic Society* 25. Amherst, Mass.: GLSA, 289–302.]

Inkelas, Sharon and Draga Zec. 1990. *The Phonology–Syntax Connection*. Chicago: University of Chicago Press.

Irons, Terry Lynn. 2007. On the status of the low back vowels in Kentucky English: more evidence of merger. *Language Variation and Change* 19: 137–80.

Itkonen, Esa. 2005. *Analogy as Structure and Process Approaches in Linguistics, Cognitive Psychology and Philosophy of Science*. Philadelphia: Benjamins.

Ito, Chiyuki and Michael Kenstowicz. 2009. Mandarin loanwords in Yanbian Korean II: tones. *Language Research* 45(1): 85–109.

Ito, Junko and Armin Mester. 1995. The core–periphery structure of the lexicon and constraints on reranking. In J. Beckman, L. Walsh Dickey, and S. Urbanczyk (eds), *Papers in Optimality Theory*. Amherst, Mass.: GLSA, 181–209.

Itô, Junko and Armin Mester. 2004. Morphological contrast and merger: ranuki in Japanese. *Journal of Japanese Linguistics* 20: 1–18.

Itô, Junko and Armin Mester. 2006. Systemic markedness and faithfulness. In J. Cihlar, A. Franklin, D. Kaiser, and I. Kimbara (eds), *Proceedings of the 39th Meeting of the Chicago Linguistics Society*. Chicago: University of Chicago, 665–89.

Iverson, Gregory K. and Ahrong Lee. 2006. Perception of contrast in Korean loanword adaptation. *Korean Linguistics* 13: 49–87.

Iverson, Gregory K. and Joseph C. Salmons. 1995. Aspiration and laryngeal representation in Germanic. *Phonology* 12: 369–96.

Iverson, Gregory K. and Joseph C. Salmons. 1996a. The primacy of primary umlaut. *Beiträge zur Geschichte der deutschen Sprache und Literatur* 118: 69–86.

Iverson, Gregory K. and Joseph C. Salmons. 1996b. Mixtec prenasalization as hypervoicing. *International Journal of American Linguistics* 62(2): 165–75.

Iverson, Gregory K. and Joseph C. Salmons. 2003. Legacy specification in the laryngeal phonology of Dutch. *Journal of Germanic Linguistics* 15: 1–26.

Iverson, Gregory and Joseph Salmons. 2005. Filling the gap: English tense vowel plus final /š/. *Journal of English Linguistics* 33: 207–21.

Iverson, Gregory K. and Joseph C. Salmons. 2006. Fundamental regularities in the Second Consonant Shift. *Journal of Germanic Linguistics* 18: 45–70.

Iverson, Gregory K. and Joseph Salmons. 2007. Domains and directionality in the evolution of German final fortition. *Phonology* 24: 121–45.

Iverson, Gregory K. and Joseph Salmons. 2008. Germanic aspiration: phonetic enhancement and language contact. *Sprachwissenschaft* 33: 257–78.

Iverson, Gregory K. and Joseph C. Salmons. 2009. Naturalness and the lifecycle of sound change. In Patrick Steinkrüger and Manfred Krifka (eds), *On Inflection: In Memory of Wolfgang U. Wurzel*. Berlin: Mouton de Gruyter, 89–105.

Iverson, Gregory K. and Joseph C. Salmons. 2011. Final devoicing and final laryngeal neutralization. In Marc van Oostendorp, Colin J. Ewen, Elizabeth Hume, and Keren Rice (eds), *The Blackwell Companion to Phonology*. Oxford: Blackwell.

Iverson, Gregory K. and Joseph Salmons. 2012. Parasitic rule loss in Norse umlaut. *Journal of Germanic Linguistics* 24: 101–31.

Jacewicz, Ewa, Robert A. Fox, Caitlin O'Neill, and Joseph Salmons. 2009. Articulation rate across dialect, age, and gender. *Language Variation and Change* 21: 233–56.

Jacewicz, Ewa, Robert A. Fox, and Joseph Salmons. 2006. Prosodic prominence effects on vowels in chain shifts. *Language Variation and Change* 18: 285–316.

Jackendoff, Ray. 1975. Morphological and semantic regularities in the lexicon. *Language* 51: 639–71.

Jackson, Leonard. 1991. *The Poverty of Structuralism: Literature and Structuralist Theory*. London: Longman.

Jacobs, Haike. 1995. Optimality Theory and sound change. In J. Beckman (ed.), *Proceedings of the North-Eastern Linguistic Society 25*. Amherst, Mass.: GLSA, 219–32.

Jacobs, Haike. 2000. The revenge of the uneven trochee: Latin main stress, metrical constituency, stress-related phenomena and OT. In Aditi Lahiri (ed.), *Analogy, Levelling, Markedness: Principles of Change in Phonology and Morphology*. Berlin: Mouton de Gruyter, 333–52.

Jaeger, Jeri J. 2005. *Kids' Slips: What Young Children's Slips of the Tongue Reveal about Language Development*. Mahwah, NJ: Erlbaum.

Jäger, Andreas. 1686. *De lingua vetustissima Europae, Scytho-Celtica et Gothica*. Wittenberg: Schrödter.

Jakobson, Roman. 1929. Remarques sur l'évolution phonologique du russe comparée à celle des autres langues slaves. *Travaux du Cercle linguistique de Prague* 2.

Jakobson, Roman. 1931. Prinzipien der historischen Phonologie. *Travaux du cercle linguistique de Prague* 4: 247–67. [English translation: 'Principles of historical phonology', in Allan R. Keiler (ed.), *A Reader in Historical and Comparative Linguistics*, 121–38. New York: Holt, Rinehart and Winston, 1972. Also in Linda R. Waugh and Monique Monville-Burston (eds), *Roman Jakobson: On Language*, 184–201. Cambridge, Mass.: Harvard University Press, 1990.]

Jakobson, Roman. 1941. *Kindersprache, Aphasie und allgemeine Lautgesetze*. Uppsala: Uppsala Universitets Arsskrift. [Trans. Allan R. Keiler, *Child Language, Aphasia, and Phonological Universals*. The Hague: Mouton de Gruyter, 1968.]

Jakobson, Roman. 1958. Typological studies and their contribution to historical and comparative linguistics. In Eva Sivertsen (ed), *Proceedings of the Eighth International Congress of Linguists*. Oslo: Oslo University Press, 17–25.

Jakobson, Roman. 1966. Grammatical parallelism and its Russian facet. *Language* 42(2): 399–429.

Jakobson, Roman, C. Gunnar M. Fant, and Morris Halle. 1952. *Preliminaries to Speech Analysis*. MIT Acoustics Laboratory, Technical Report No. 13. [Reissued by MIT Press, 1976.]

Jakobson, Roman and Morris Halle. 1956. *Fundamentals of Language*. The Hague: Mouton.

Janda, Richard D. 1999. Accounts of phonemic split have been greatly exaggerated—but not enough. *Proceedings of the International Congress of Phonetic Sciences* 14: 329–32.

Janda, Richard D. 2003. Phonologization as the start of dephoneticization—or, on sound change and its aftermath: of extension, lexicalization, and morphologization. In Brian D. Joseph and Richard D. Janda (eds), *The Handbook of Historical Linguistics*. Oxford: Blackwell, 401–22.

Janda, Richard D. and Brian D. Joseph. 2003. On language, change, and language change—or, of history, linguistics, and historical linguistics. In Brian D. Joseph and Richard D. Janda (eds), *A Handbook of Historical Linguistics*. Oxford: Blackwell, 3–180.

Janda, Richard D., Brian D. Joseph, and Neil G. Jacobs. 1994. Systematic hyperforeignisms as maximally external evidence for linguistic rules. In S. Lima, R. Corrigan, and G. K. Iverson (eds), *The Reality of Linguistic Rules*. Amsterdam: Benjamins, 67–92.

Janhunen, Juha, Marja Peltomaa, Erika Sandman, and Xiawu Dongzhou. 2008. *Wutun*. Munich: Lincom.

Jankowsky, Kurt R. 1999a. The works of Ernst Wilhelm Brücke (1819–1892) and Johann N. Czermak (1828–1873): landmarks in the history of phonetics. In David Cram, Andrew R. Linn, and Elke Nowak (eds), *History of Linguistics*, vol. 2: *From Classical to Contemporary Linguistics*. Amsterdam: Benjamins, 241–55.

Jankowsky, Kurt R. 1999b. Sound physiology in the making: on the role of Henry Sweet (1845–1912) and Eduard Sievers (1850–1932) in the development of linguistic science. In Sheila Embleton, John E. Joseph, and Hans-Josef Niederehe (eds), *Emergence of the Modern Language Sciences*, vol. 1. Amsterdam: Benjamins, 77–87.

Jannedy, Stefanie and Jennifer Hay. 2006. Modelling sociophonetic variation. *Journal of Phonetics* 34: 405–8.

Janson, Tore. 1983. Sound change in perception and production. *Language* 59: 18–34.

Jasanoff, Jay. 2004. Plus ça change … : Lachmann's Law in Latin. In J. H. W. Penney (ed.), *Indo-European Perspectives: Studies in Honour of Anna Morpurgo Davies*. Oxford: Oxford University Press, 405–16.

Jeffers, Robert J. and Ilse Lehiste. 1979. *Principles and Methods for Historical Linguistics*. Cambridge, Mass.: MIT Press.

Jespersen, Otto. 1922. *Language: Its Nature, Development and Origin*. London: Allen and Unwin.

Jespersen, Otto. 1933/1970. *Linguistica: Selected Papers in English, French, and German*. College Park, Md.: McGrath.

Job, Michael. 1989. Sound change typology and the 'Ejective Model'. In Theo Venneman (ed.), *The New Sound of Indo-European: Essays in Phonological Reconstruction*. Berlin: Mouton de Gruyter, 123–36.

Johnson, Daniel Ezra. 2010. *Stability and Change along a Dialect Boundary: The Low Vowels of Southeastern New England*. Durham, NC: Duke University Press.

Johnson, Jacqueline S. and Elissa L. Newport. 1989. Critical period effects in second language learning: the influence of maturational state on the acquisition of English as a second language. *Cognitive Psychology* 21: 60–99.

Johnson, Keith. 2000. Adaptive dispersion in vowel perception. *Phonetica* 57: 181–8.

Johnson, Keith, Peter Ladefoged, and Mona Lindau. 1993. Individual differences in vowel production. *Journal of the Acoustical Society of America* 94: 701–14.

Johnson, Keith. 1997. The auditory/perceptual basis for speech segmentation. *Ohio State University Working Papers in Linguistics* 50: 101–13.

Jones, Charles. 1989. *A History of English Phonology*. London: Longman.

Jones, Mari C. and Ishtla Singh. 2005. *Exploring Language Change*. London: Routledge.

Jones, Mark J. 2007. Glottals and grammar: definite article reduction and morpheme boundaries. *Leeds Working Papers in Linguistics* 12. Available at: <http://www.leeds.ac.uk/linguistics/WPL/WP2007/4.pdf>

Jones, Mark J. (in progress). VOT in English /s/-stop clusters: the voicing paradox that isn't.

Joseph, Brian D. and Richard D. Janda. 1988. The how and why of diachronic morphologization and demorphologization. In Michael Hammond and Michael Noonan (eds), *Theoretical Morphology*. New York: Academic Press, 193–210.

Joseph, Brian D. and Richard D. Janda. 2003a. On language, change, and language change—or, of history, linguistics, and historical linguistics. In Brian D. Joseph and Richard D. Janda (eds), *The Handbook of Historical Linguistics*. Oxford: Blackwell, 3–180.

Joseph, Brian D. and Richard D. Janda (eds). 2003b. *The Handbook of Historical Linguistics*. Oxford: Blackwell.

Josey, Meredith P. 2004. A sociolinguistic study of phonetic variation and change on the island of Martha's Vineyard. PhD thesis, New York University.

Juola, Patrick. 1996. Isolated-word confusion metrics and the PGPfone alphabet. In Kemal Oflazer, and Harold Somers (eds), *NeMLaP-2: Proceedings of the Second International Conference on New Methods in Language Processing*. Ankara: Bilkent University.

Jurafsky, Dan. 2003. Probabilistic modeling in psycholinguistics: linguistic comprehension and production. In R. Bod, J. Hay, and S. Jannedy (eds), *Probabilistic Linguistics*. Cambridge, Mass.: MIT Press, 39–95.

Jurafsky, Daniel, Alan Bell, Michelle Gregory, and William D. Raymond. 2001. Probabilistic relations between words: evidence from reduction in lexical production. In J. Bybee and P. Hopper (eds), *Frequency and the Emergence of Linguistic Structure*. Amsterdam: Benjamins, 229–54.

Jurgec, Peter. 2008. Novejše besedje s stališča fonologije: Primer slovenščine. PhD thesis, University of Ljubljana.

Jusczyk, Peter W., Derek M. Houston, and Mary Newsome.1999. The beginnings of word segmentation in English-learning infants. *Cognitive Psychology* 39: 159–207.

Kager, René. 1989. *A Metrical Theory of Stress and Destressing in English and Dutch*. Dordrecht: Foris.

Kager, René. 1999. *Introduction to Optimality Theory*. Cambridge: Cambridge University Press.

Kammacher, Louise, Andreas Stæer, and J. Normann Jørgensen. 2011. Attitudinal and sociostructural factors and their role in dialect change: testing a model of subjective factors. *Language Variation and Change* 23: 87–104.

Kaneko, Emiko. 2004. Vowel selection in Japanese loanwords from English. *LSO Working Papers in Linguistics* 4: 49–62. Linguistics Student Organization, University of Wisconsin-Madison.

Kang, Yoonjung. 2010. Tutorial overview: suprasegmental adaptation in loanwords. *Lingua* 120(9): 2295–2310.

Kaplan, Abby. 2011. How much homophony is normal? *Journal of Linguistics* 47(3): 631–71.

Karsten, Gustaf E. 1894. The psychological basis of phonetic law and analogy. *PMLA* 9(2): 312–41.

Katayama, Motoko 1998. Optimality Theory and Japanese loanword phonology. PhD thesis, University of California at Santa Cruz.

Kauffman, Stuart 1995. *At Home in the Universe: The Search for the Laws of Self-Organization and Complexity*. Oxford: Oxford University Press.

Kavitskaya, Darya. 2002. *Compensatory Lengthening: Phonetics, Phonology, Diachrony*. New York: Garland.

Kawahara, Shigeto. 2011. Experimental approaches in theoretical phonology. In Marc van Oostendorp, Colin J. Ewen, Elizabeth Hume, and Keren Rice (eds), *The Blackwell Companion to Phonology*, vol. 4. Malden, Mass.: Wiley-Blackwell.

Kawasaki, Haruko. 1982. An acoustical basis for universal constraints on sound sequences. PhD thesis, University of California, Berkeley.

Kay, Martin. 1964. *The Logic of Cognate Recognition in Historical Linguistics*. Santa Monica, Calif.: RAND.

Kaye, Jonathan D. 1971. Nasal harmony in Desano. *Linguistic Inquiry* 2: 37–56.

Kaye, Jonathan D., Jean Lowenstamm, and Jean-Roger Vergnaud. 1985. The internal structure of phonological representations: a theory of charm and government. *Phonology Yearbook* 2: 305–28.

Kaye, Jonathan, Jean Lowenstamm, and Jean-Roger Vergnaud. 1990. Constituent structure and government in phonology. *Phonology* 7: 193–231.

Keating, Patricia 1988a. Underspecification in phonetics. *Phonology* 5: 275–92.

Keating, Patricia. 1988b. Palatals as complex segments: X-ray evidence. *UCLA Working Papers in Phonetics* 69: 77–91.

Keating, Patricia. 1990. Phonological representations in a generative grammar, *Journal of Phonetics* 18: 321–34.

Keating, Patricia, Taehong Cho, Cecile Fougeron, and Chai-Shune Hsu. 1999. Domain-initial articulatory strengthening in four languages. *University of California Working Papers in Phonetics* 97: 139–51.

Keller, Rudi 1994. *On Language Change: the Invisible Hand in Language*. London: Routledge.

Kemp, William, and Malcah Yaeger-Dror. 1991. Changing realizations of *a* in *-(a)tion* in relation to the front *a*-back *a* opposition in Quebec French. In P. Eckert (ed.), *New Ways of Analyzing Sound Change*. New York: Academic Press, 127–84.

Kenstowicz, Michael. 2005. The phonetics and phonology of Korean loanword adaptation. MS, MIT. [To appear in *Proceedings of First European Conference on Korean Linguistics*, ed. S.-J. Rhee.]

Kenstowicz, Michael. 2006. Tone loans: the adaptation of English loanwords into Yoruba. In J. Mugane, J. P. Hutchison, and D. A. Worman (eds), *Selected Proceedings of the 35th Annual Conference on African Linguistics*. Somerville, Mass.: Cascadilla Proceedings Project, 136–46.

Kenstowicz, Michael. 2007. Salience and similarity in loanword adaptation: a case study from Fijian. *Language Sciences* 29: 316–40.

Kenstowicz, Michael and Charles Kisseberth. 1979. *Generative Phonology: Description and Theory*. New York: Academic Press.

Kenstowicz, Michael and Nabila Louriz. 2009. Reverse engineering: emphatic consonants and the adaptation of vowels in French loanwords into Moroccan Arabic. *Brill's Annual of Afroasiatic Languages and Linguistics* 1: 41–74.

Kenstowicz, Michael and A. Suchato. 2006. Issues in loanword adaptation: a case study from Thai. *Lingua* 116(7): 921–49.

Kent, Raymond D. 1981. Articulatory-acoustic perspectives on speech development. In Rachel E. Stark (ed.), *Language Behavior in Infancy and Early Childhood*. New York: Elsevier/North-Holland, 105–26.

Kenyon, John, and Thomas Knott. 1953. *A Pronouncing Dictionary of American English*. Springfield, Mass.: Merriam.

Kerswill, Paul. 1994. *Dialects Converging: Rural Speech in Urban Norway*. Oxford: Clarendon Press.

Kerswill, Paul. 1995. Children, adolescents and language change. *Working Papers in Linguistics* 2, Department of Linguistic Science, University of Reading, 201–22.

Kerswill, Paul. 1996a. Milton Keynes and dialect levelling in South-Eastern British English. In D. Graddol, D. Leith and J. Swann (eds), *English: History, Diversity and Change*. London: Routledge, 292–300.

Kerswill, Paul. 1996b. Children, adolescents and language change. *Language Variation and Change* 8: 177–202.

Kerswill, Paul. 2001. Koineization and accommodation. In J. K. Chambers, Peter Trudgill, and Natalie Schiling-Estes (eds), *The Handbook of Language Variation and Change*. Oxford: Blackwell, 669–702.

Kerswill, Paul and Ann Williams. 2000. Creating a new town koiné: children and language change in Milton Keynes. *Language in Society* 29: 65–115.

Kerswill, Paul and Ann Williams. 2005. New towns and koineization: linguistic and social correlates. *Linguistics* 43: 1023–48.

Kessler, Brett. 1995. Computational dialectology in Irish Gaelic. *Proceedings of the Seventh Conference of the European Chapter of the Association for Computational Linguistics*. San Francisco, Calif.: Morgan Kaufmann, 60–66.

Kessler, Brett. 2001. *The Significance of Word Lists*. Stanford, Calif.: CSLI.

Kessler, Brett. 2005. Phonetic comparison algorithms. *Transactions of the Philological Society* 103(2): 243–60.

Kessler, Brett. 2007. Word similarity metrics and multilateral comparison. In John Nerbonne, Mark T. Ellison, and Grzegorz Kondrak (eds), *Proceedings of the Ninth Meeting of the ACL Special Interest Group on Computational Morphology and Phonology*. Stroudsburg, Penn.: Association for Computational Linguistics, 6–14.

Kessler, Brett and Annukka Lehtonen. 2006. Multilateral comparison and significance testing of the Indo-Uralic question. In Peter Forster and Colin Renfrew (eds), *Phylogenetic Methods and the Prehistory of Languages*. Cambridge: McDonald Institute for Archaeological Research, 33–42.

Keyser, Samuel Jay. 1963. Review of *The Pronunciation of English in the Atlantic States*. *Language* 39: 303–16.

Keyser, Samuel Jay and Kenneth Stevens. 2006. Enhancement and overlap in the speech chain. *Language* 82(1): 33–63.

Kharlamov, Viktor. 2012. Incomplete neutralization and task effects in experimentally-elicited speech: evidence from the production and perception of word-final devoicing in Russian. PhD thesis, University of Ottawa.

Kim, Myungsook. 1993. On lengthening in the open syllables of Middle English. *Lingua* 91: 261–77.

King, Anne. 1992. You say [ajðər] and I say [æjhwæðər]? Interpreting Old English written data. In Fran Colman (ed.), *Evidence for Old English: Material and Theoretical Bases for Reconstruction*. Edinburgh: Donald, 20–44.

King, Robert D. 1969. *Historical Linguistics and Generative Grammar*. Englewood Cliffs, NJ: Prentice-Hall.

King, Robert D. 1971. Syncope and Old Icelandic i-umlaut. *Arkiv för Nordisk Filologi* 86: 1–18.

King, Robert D. 1973. Rule insertion. *Language* 49: 551–78.

King, Robert D. 1980. The history of final devoicing in Yiddish. In M. I. Herzog, B. Kirshenblatt-Gimblett, D. Miron, and R. Wisse (eds), *The Field of Yiddish: Studies in Language, Folklore, and Literature, Fourth Collection*. Philadelphia: Institute for the Study of Human Issues, 371–430.

Kingston, John. 2003. Mechanisms of tone reversal. In Shigeki Kaji (ed.), *Cross-Linguistic Studies of Tonal Phenomena: Historical Development, Phonetics of Tone, and Descriptive Studies*. Tokyo: Research Institute for Languages and Cultures of Asia and Africa, 57–120.

Kingston, John. 2005. The phonetics of Athabaskan tonogenesis. In Sharon Hargus and Keren Rice (eds), *Athabaskan Prosody*. Amsterdam: Benjamins, 137–84.

Kingston, John 2007. The phonetics–phonology interface. In Paul de Lacy (ed.), *The Cambridge Handbook of Phonology*. Cambridge: Cambridge University Press, 401–34.

Kingston, John. 2011. Tonogenesis. In Marc van Oostendorp, Colin Ewan, Elizabeth Hume, and Keren Rice (eds), *Blackwell Companion to Phonology*. Oxford: Blackwell, 2304–33.

Kingston, John and Randy L. Diehl. 1994. Phonetic knowledge. *Language* 70(3): 419–54.

Kiparsky, Paul. 1965. Phonological change. PhD thesis, MIT. [Repr. by the Indiana University Linguistics Club 1971.]

Kiparsky, Paul. 1968. Linguistic universals and linguistic change. In Emmon W. Bach and Robert T. Harms (eds), *Universals in Linguistic Theory*. New York: Holt, Rinehart and Winston, 171–202.

Kiparsky, Paul. 1968/1973. How abstract is phonology? MS. [Published 1973 in Osamu Fujimura (ed.), *Three Dimensions of Linguistic Theory*. Tokyo: TEC, 5–56.]

Kiparsky, Paul. 1971. Historical linguistics. In William O. Dingwall (ed.), *A Survey of Linguistic Science*. College Park: University of Maryland Linguistics Program.

Kiparsky, Paul. 1973a. 'Elsewhere' in phonology. In Stephen R. Anderson and Paul Kiparsky (eds), *A Festschrift for Morris Halle*. New York: Holt, Rinehart and Winston, 93–106.

Kiparsky, Paul. 1973b. Phonological representations. In O. Fujimura (ed.), *Three Dimensions of Linguistic Theory*. Tokyo: TEC Co., 1–136.

Kiparsky, Paul. 1974a. Remarks on analogical change. In J. M. Anderson and C. Jones (eds), *Historical Linguistics II*. New York: American Elsevier, 257–75.

Kiparsky, Paul. 1974b. On the evaluation measure. In A. Bruck, R. Fox, and M. La Galy (eds), *Papers from the Parasession on Natural Phonology*. Chicago: Chicago Linguistic Society, 328–37.

Kiparsky, Paul. 1974c. From paleogrammarians to neogrammarians. In Dell Hymes (ed.), *Studies in the History of Linguistics: Traditions and Paradigms*. Bloomington: Indiana University Press, 331–45.

Kiparsky, Paul. 1979. Metrical structure assignment is cyclic. *Linguistic Inquiry* 10: 421–41.

Kiparsky, Paul. 1982a. *Explanation in Phonology*. Dordrecht: Foris.

Kiparsky, Paul. 1982b. Lexical morphology and phonology. In In-Seok Yang (ed.), *Linguistics in the Morning Calm: Selected Papers from SICOL–1981*, vol. 1. Seoul: Hanshin, 3–91.

Kiparsky, Paul. 1998a. Sievers' Law as prosodic optimization. In Jay Jasanoff, H. Craig Melchert, and Lisi Olivier (eds), *Mir Curad: Studies in Honor of Calvert Watkins*. Innsbruck.

Kiparsky, Paul. 1988b. Phonological change. In Frederick J. Newmeyer (ed.), *Linguistics: the Cambridge Survey*, vol. 1. Cambridge: Cambridge University Press, 363–415.

Kiparsky, Paul. 1992. Analogy. In William Bright (ed.), *International Encyclopedia of Linguistics*, vol. 1. New York: Oxford University Press, 56–61.

Kiparsky, Paul. 1995. The phonological basis of sound change. In John A. Goldsmith (ed.), *The Handbook of Phonological Theory*. Oxford: Blackwell, 640–70.

Kiparsky, Paul. 2000a. Opacity and cyclicity. In Nancy A. Ritter (ed.), *A Review of Optimality Theory*. Special issue, *Linguistic Review* 17: 351–67.

Kiparsky, Paul. 2000b. Analogy as optimization: 'exceptions' to Sievers' Law in Gothic. In Aditi Lahiri (ed.), *Analogy, Levelling and Markedness*. Berlin: Mouton, 15–47.

Kiparsky, Paul. 2006. The amphichronic program vs. evolutionary phonology. *Theoretical Linguistics* 32: 217–36.

Kiparsky, Paul. 2011. Compensatory lengthening. In Charles E. Cairns and Eric Raimy (eds), *Handbook of the Syllable*. Leiden: Brill, 33–69.

Kiparsky, Paul. 2014. New perspectives in historical linguistics. In Claire Bowern and Bethwyn Evans (eds), *The Routledge Handbook of Historical Linguistics*. London: Routledge, 64–102.

Kiparsky, Valentin. 1932. Johdatusta fonologiaan. *Virittäjä* 36: 230–50.

Kirby, James P. 2011. Vietnamese (Hanoi Vietnamese). *Journal of the International Phonetic Association* 41(3): 381–92.

Kirby, Simon 1999. *Function, Selection and Innateness: the Emergence of Language Universals*. Oxford: Oxford University Press.

Kirby, Simon 2000. Syntax without natural selection: how compositionality emerges from vocabulary in a population of learners. In C. Knight, J. Hurford, and M. Studdert-Kennedy (eds), *The Emergence of Language*. Cambridge: Cambridge University Press, 303–323.

Kirby, Simon and James Hurford. 2002. The emergence of linguistic structure: an overview of the iterated learning model. In A. Cangelosi and D. Parisi (eds), *Simulating the Evolution of Language*. London: Springer, 121–147.

Kirchner, Robert. 1998. An effort-based approach to consonant lenition. PhD thesis, University of California Los Angeles.

Klein, Robert P. 1971. Acoustic analysis of the acquisition of acceptable *r* in American English. *Child Development* 42: 543–50.

Klingenheben, August. 1928. Die Silbenauslautgesetze des Hausa. *Zeitschrift für Eingeborenensprachen* 18: 272–97.

Kniffen, Fred and Henry Glassie. 1966. Building in wood in the Eastern United States: a time–place perspective. *Geographical Review* 56(1): 40–66.

Ko, Seongyeon. 2010. A contrastivist view on the evolution of the Korean vowel system. In Hiroki Maezawa and Azusa Yokogoshi (eds), *MIT Working Papers in Linguistics (MITWPL) 61*. Cambridge, Mass.: MIT Department of Linguistics and Philosophy, 181–96.

Ko, Seongyeon. 2011. Vowel contrast and vowel harmony shift in the Mongolic languages. In Andrew Simpson (ed.), *MIT Working Papers in Linguistics (MITWPL) 62*. Cambridge, Mass.: MIT Department of Linguistics and Philosophy, 187–202.

Ko, Seongyeon. 2012. Tongue root harmony and vowel contrast in Northeast Asian languages. PhD thesis, Cornell University.

Kobayashi, Yoshinori. 1987. *Kakuhitsu bunken no kokugogakuteki kenkyū* [Japanese philological studies of kakuhitsu texts]. 2 vols. Tokyo: Kyūko shoin.

Kobayashi, Yoshinori. 2003. Kore kara no kakuhitsu no kenkyū: higashi Ajia o shiya ni [Future studies of kakuhitsu encompassing all of East Asia]. *Liaison (Hiroshima Daigaku fuzoku toshokan kanpō)* [Bulletin of the libraries affiliated with Hiroshima University] 28: 5–22.

Koerner, E. F. Konrad. 1981. The Neogrammarian doctrine: breakthrough or extension of the Schleicherian paradigm. A problem in linguistic historiography. *Folia Linguistica Historica* 2: 157–78. [Repr. in E. F. Konrad Koerner, *Practicing Linguistic Historiography*. Amsterdam: Benjamins, 1989, 79–100.]

Koerner, E. F. Konrad. 1989a. Jacob Grimm's place in the foundation of linguistics as a science. In E. F. Konrad Koerner (ed), *Practicing Linguistic Historiography*. Amsterdam: Benjamins, 303–23.

Koerner, E. F. Konrad. 1989b. *Practicing Linguistic Historiography*. Amsterdam: Benjamins.

Koerner, E. F. Konrad (ed.). 1995. *Mikołaj Kruszewski: Writings in General Linguistics*. Amsterdam: Benjamins.

Kohler, Klaus. 1981. Three trends in phonetics: the development of phonetics as a discipline in Germany since the nineteenth century. In R. E. Asher and Eugénie J. A. Henderson (eds), *Towards a History of Phonetics*. Edinburgh: Edinburgh University Press, 161–78.

Kohrt, Manfred. 1985. *Problemgeschichte des Graphembegriffs und des frühen Phonembegriffs*. Tübingen: Niemeyer.

Kohrt, Manfred. 1990. 'Sound inventory' and 'sound system' in 19th-century linguistics. In Hans-Josef Niederehe and Konrad Koerner (eds), *History and Historiography of Linguistics*, vol. 2. Amsterdam: Benjamins, 589–603.

Komai Akira and Thomas H. Rohlich. 1988. *An Introduction to Japanese Kanbun*. Nagoya: University of Nagoya Press.

Kondrak, Grzegorz. 2000. A new algorithm for the alignment of phonetic sequences. In *Proceedings of the 1st North American Chapter of the Association for Computational Linguistics Conference*. San Francisco, Calif.: Morgan Kaufmann, 288–95.

Kondrak, Grzegorz. 2002. Algorithms for language reconstruction. PhD thesis, University of Toronto.

Kondrak, Grzegorz. 2005. N-gram similarity and distance. In Mariano Consens and Gonzalo Navarro (eds), *String Processing and Information Retrieval: 12th International Conference, SPIRE 2005*. Berlin: Springer, 115–26.

Korhonen, Mikko. 1969. Die Entwicklung der morphologischen Methode im Lappischen. *Finnisch-Ugrische Forschungen* 37: 203–62.

Kortlandt, Frederik H. H. 1978. Proto-Indo-European Obstruents. *Indogermanische Forschungen* 83: 107–18.

Kortlandt, Frederik H. H. 1981. Glottalic consonants in Sindhi and Proto-Indo-European. *Indo-Iranian Journal* 23: 15–19.

Kortlandt, Frederik H. H. 1985. Proto-Indo-European glottalic stops: the comparative evidence. *Folia Linguistica Historica* 6(2): 183–201.

Kortlandt, Frederik H. H. 1988. *Vestjysk stød*, Icelandic preaspiration, and Proto-Indo-European glottalic stops. In Mohamad Ali Jazayery and Werner Winter (eds), *Languages and Cultures: Studies in Honor of Edgar C. Polomé*. Berlin: Mouton de Gruyter, 353–6.

Kortlandt, Frederik H. H. 1997. How old is the English glottal stop? In *North-Western European Language Evolution (NOWELE)* 31–2 (*Germanic Studies in Honor of Anatoly Liberman*): 175–9.

Kostakis, Andrew. 2010. Vestige Theory: sociolinguistic evidence for output–output constraints. *Lingua* 120: 2476–96.

Kraljic, Tanya, and Arthur G. Samuel. 2005. Perceptual learning for speech: is there a return to normal? *Cognitive Psychology* 51: 141–78.

Kraljic, Tanya and Arthur G. Samuel. 2006. Generalization in perceptual learning for speech. *Psychonomic Bulletin and Review* 13(2): 262–8.

Kraljic, Tanya, Arthur G. Samuel, and Susan E. Brennan. 2008. First impressions and last resorts: how listeners adjust to speaker variability. *Psychological Science* 19(4): 332–8.

Kraska-Szlenk, Iwona. 2007. Analogy: the relation between lexicon and grammar. PhD thesis, Warsaw University.

Krishnamurti, Bhadriraju. 2003. *The Dravidian Languages*. Cambridge: Cambridge University Press.

Kroch, Anthony S. 1989. Reflexes of grammar in patterns of language change. *Language Variation and Change* 1: 199–244.

Krug, Manfred. 2003. (Great) vowel shifts present and past: meeting ground for structural and natural phonologists. In *University of Pennsylvania Working Papers in Linguistics: Selected papers from 11 NWAV* 9(2): 107–22.

Kruskal, Joseph B. 1999. An overview of sequence comparison. In David Sankoff and Joseph Kruskal (eds), *Time Warps, String Edits, and Macromolecules*. Stanford, Calif.: CSLI, 1–44.

Kruskal, Joseph B. and Myron Wish. 1978. *Multidimensional Scaling*. Beverly Hills, Calif.: Sage.

Kruskal, Joseph B., Isidore Dyen, and Paul Black. 1973. Some results from the vocabulary method of reconstructing language trees. In Isidore Dyen (ed.), *Lexicostatistics in Genetic Linguistics: Proceedings of the Yale Conference, 1971*. The Hague: Mouton, 30–55.

Kruszewski, Mikołaj. 1881. *Ueber die Lautabwechslung*. Kazan: Universitätsbuchdruckerei. [Also published 1978 as 'On sound alternation', in Philip Baldi and Ronald and Werth (eds), *Readings in Historical Phonology: Chapters in the Theory of Sound Change*. University Park: Pennsylvania State University Press, 64–91; and also trans. by Robert Austerlitz, 'On sound alternation', in Konrad Koerner (ed.), *Writings in General Linguistics*. Amsterdam: Benjamins, 1995, 3–34.]

Kruszewski, Mikołaj. 1885. Prinzipien der Sprachentwickelung [continuation]. *(Techmer's) Internationale Zeitschrift für allgemeine Sprachwissenschaft* 2: 258–68.

Kruszewski, Mikołaj. 1887. Prinzipien der Sprachentwickelung [continuation]. *(Techmer's) Internationale Zeitschrift für allgemeine Sprachwissenschaft* 3: 145–87.

Kubozono, Haruo. 2002. Prosodic structure of loanwords in Japanese: syllable structure, accent and morphology. *Journal of the Phonetic Society of Japan* 6: 79–97.

Kubozono, Haruo. 2006. Where does loanword prosody come from? A case study of Japanese loanword accent. *Lingua* 116(7): 1140–70.

Kuhn, Sherman M. 1965. *The Vespasian Psalter*. Ann Arbor: University of Michigan Press.

Kümmel, Martin Joachim. 2007. *Konsonantenwandel: Bausteine zu einer Typologie des Lautwandels und ihre Konsequenzen für die vergleichende Rekonstruktion*. Wiesbaden: Reichert.

Kümmel, Martin Joachim. 2012. Typology and reconstruction: the consonants and vowels of Proto-Indo-European. In Benedicte Nielsen Whitehead, Thomas Olander, Birgit Anette Olsen, and Jens Elmegård Rasmussen (eds), *The Sound of Indo-European: Phonetics, Phonemics and Morphophonemics*. Copenhagen: Museum Tusculanum, 291–329.

Kurki, Tommi. 2004. Applying the apparent-time method and the real-time method on Finnish. In B. Gunnarsson (ed.), *Language Variation in Europe: Papers from the Second International Conference on Language Variation in Europe*. Uppsala: Department of Scandinavian Languages, 241–52.

Kürsten, Otto, and Otto Bremer. 1910. *Lautlehre der Mundart von Buttelstedt bei Weimar*. Leipzig: Breitkopf & Härtel.

Kuryłowicz, Jerzy. 1964. *The Inflectional Categories of Indo-European*. Heidelberg: Winter.

Kuryłowicz, Jerzy. 1966. La nature des procès dits 'analogiques'. In Eric P. Hamp, Fred W. Householder, and Robert Austerlitz (eds), *Readings in Linguistics II*. Chicago: Chicago University Press, 158–74. [Repr. from *Acta Linguistica* 5(1945–9), 121–38.]

Labov, William. 1963. The social motivation of a sound change. *Word* 19: 273–309.

Labov, William. 1965. On the mechanism of linguistic change. *Georgetown Monographs on Language and Linguistics* 18: 91–114.

Labov, William. 1966. *The Social Stratification of English in New York City*. Washington, DC: Center for Applied Linguistics.

Labov, William. 1972a. *Sociolinguistic Patterns*. Philadelphia: University of Pennsylvania Press.

Labov, William. 1972b. Some principles of linguistic methodology. *Language in Society* 1: 97–120.

Labov, William. 1981. Resolving the Neogrammarian controversy. *Language* 57: 267–308.

Labov, William. 1989a. The child as linguistic historian. *Language Variation and Change* 1: 85–94.

Labov, William. 1989b. The exact description of the speech community: short *a* in Philadelphia. In Ralph W. Fasold and Deborah Schiffrin (eds), *Language Change and Variation*. Washington, DC: Georgetown University Press, 1–57.

Labov, William. 1990. The intersection of sex and social class in the course of linguistic change. *Language Variation and Change* 2: 205–54.

Labov, William. 1991. The three dialects of English. In Penelope Eckert (ed.), *Quantitative Analyses of Sound Change*. New York: Academic Press, 1–44.

Labov, William 1994. *Principles of Linguistic Change*, vol. 1: *Internal Factors*. Oxford: Blackwell.

Labov, William 2001. *Principles of Linguistic Change*, vol. 2: *Social Factors*. Oxford: Blackwell.

Labov, William. 2006. A sociolinguistic perspective on sociophonetic research. *Journal of Phonetics* 34: 500–515.

Labov, William. 2007. Transmission and diffusion. *Language* 83: 344–87.

Labov, William. 2008. Triggering events. In Susan Fitzmaurice and Donka Minkova (eds), *Studies in the History of the English Language IV: Empirical and Analytical Advances in the Study of English Language Change*. Berlin: Mouton de Gruyter, 11–54.

Labov, William. 2010. *Principles of Linguistic Change*, vol. 3: *Cognitive and Cultural Factors*. Oxford: Blackwell.

Labov, William, Sharon Ash, and Charles Boberg. 2006. *Atlas of North American English: Phonetics, Phonology and Sound*. Berlin: Mouton de Gruyter.

Labov, William, and Maciej Baranowski. 2006. 50 msec. *Language Variation and Change* 18: 1–18.

Labov, William, Malcah Yaeger, and Richard Steiner. 1972. *A Quantitative Study of Sound Change in Progress*, vol. 1. Philadelphia: US Regional Survey.

LaCharité, Darlene and Carole Paradis. 2002. Addressing and disconfirming some predictions of phonetic approximation for loanword adaptation. *Langues et linguistique* 28: 73–91.

LaCharité, Darlene and Carole Paradis. 2005. Category preservation and proximity versus phonetic approximation in loanword adaptation. *Linguistic Inquiry* 36(2): 223–58.

Lachs, Lorin, Kipp McMichael, and David B. Pisoni. 2003. Speech perception and implicit memory: evidence for detailed episodic encoding. In J. Bowes and C. Marsolek (eds), *Rethinking Implicit Memory*. Oxford: Oxford University Press, 215–35.

Ladd, D. Robert, Dan Dediu, and Anna R. Kinsella. 2008. Languages and genes: reflections on biolinguistics and the nature–nurture question. *Biolinguistics* 2(1): 114–26.

Ladefoged, Peter and Taehong Cho. 2001. Linking linguistic contrasts to reality: the case of VOT. In N. Gronnum and J. Rischel (eds), *Travaux du Cercle linguistique de Copenhague*, vol. 31. Copenhagen: Reitzel, 212–25.

Ladefoged, Peter and Ian Maddieson. 1996. *The Sounds of the World's Languages*. Oxford: Blackwell.

Lado, Robert. 1957. *Linguistics Across Cultures: Applied Linguistics for Language Teachers*. Ann Arbor: University of Michigan Press.

LAEME = A Linguistic Atlas of Early Middle English 1150–1325. 2008–. Electronic text corpus with accompanying software (Keith Williamson) index of sources and theoretical introduction. <http://www.lel.ed.ac.uk/ihd/laeme1/laeme1.html>. Compiled by Margaret Laing and Roger Lass. Edinburgh: University of Edinburgh.

LaFond, Larry L. 2003. Historical changes in verb-second and null subjects from Old to Modern French. In D. Eric Holt (ed.), *Optimality Theory and Language Change*. Dordrecht: Kluwer Academic, 387–412.

Lahiri, Aditi (ed.). 2000a. *Analogy, Levelling, Markedness: Principles of Change in Phonology and Morphology*. Berlin: Mouton de Gruyter.

Lahiri, Aditi. 2000b. Introduction. In Aditi Lahiri (ed.), *Analogy, Levelling, Markedness*. New York: Mouton de Gruyter, 1–14.

Lahiri, Aditi. 2002. Pertinacity in representation and change. Paper presented at the Workshop on Pertinacity, Schloss Freudental, July 10–14, 2002.

Lahiri, Aditi. 2009. The dental preterites in the history of English. In K. Hanson and S. Inkelas (eds), *The Nature of the Word: Essays in Honour of Paul Kiparsky*. Cambridge, Mass.: MIT Press, 507–529.

Lahiri, Aditi and B. Elan Dresher. 1983–4. Diachronic and synchronic implications of declension shifts. *Linguistic Review* 3: 141–63.

Lahiri, Aditi and B. Elan Dresher. 1999. Open syllable lengthening in West Germanic. *Language* 75: 678–719.

Lahiri, Aditi and Paula Fikkert. 1999. Trisyllabic shortening in English: past and present. *English Language and Linguistics* 3(2): 229–67.

Lahiri, Aditi, Tomas Riad, and Haike Jacobs. 1999. Diachrony. In Harry van der Hulst (ed.), *Word Prosodic Systems in the Languages of Europe*. Berlin: Mouton de Gruyter, 335–422.

Lai, Rosangela. 2014. Positional factors in the evolution of Sardinian Muta cum Liquida: a case study. MS, University of Florence.

Laing, Margaret. 1999. Confusion wrs confounded: litteral substitution sets in early Middle English writing systems. *Neuphilologische Mitteilungen* 100: 251–70.

Laing, Margaret and Roger Lass. 2003. Tales of the 1001 nists: the phonological implications of litteral substitution sets in 13th-century South-West Midland texts. *English Language and Linguistics* 7: 257–78.

Laker, Stephen. 2009. An explanation for the early phonemicisation of a voice contrast in English fricatives. *English Language and Linguistics* 13: 213–26.

Laks, Lior. 2008. Verb innovation in Palestinian Arabic. Paper presented at the Twenty-Second Annual Symposium on Arabic Linguistics, University of Maryland, College Park.

Laks, Lior. 2010. The formation of Arabic passive verbs: lexical or syntactic? *Proceedings of IATL* 25.

Laks, Lior. 2011. Morphological restrictions on verb formation: evidence from Palestinian Arabic. Paper presented at The Twenty-Fifth Annual Symposium on Arabic Linguistics, University of Arizona, Tucson.

Laks, Lior (to appear). Verb innovation in Hebrew and Palestinian Arabic: The interaction of morpho-phonological and thematic-semantic criteria. *Brill's Annual Afroasiatic Languages and Linguistics*.

Lange, Roland A. 1973. *The Phonology of Eighth-Century Japanese*. Tokyo: Sophia University Press.

Langstrof, Christian. 2006. Acoustic evidence for a push-chain shift in the intermediate period of New Zealand English. *Language Variation and Change* 18: 141–64.

Lapidge, Michael (ed.). 2002. *Interpreters of Early Medieval Britain*. Oxford: Oxford University Press.

Lass, Roger. 1975. Internal reconstruction and generative phonology. *Transactions of the Philological Society* 74(1): 1–26.

Lass, Roger. 1976. *English Phonology and Phonological Theory*. Cambridge: Cambridge University Press.

Lass, Roger. 1981. John Hart vindicatus? A study in the interpretations of early phoneticians. *Folia Linguistica Historica* 1: 75–96.

Lass, Roger. 1984. *Phonology: an Introduction to Basic Concepts*. Cambridge: Cambridge University Press.

Lass, Roger. 1985. Minkova noch einmal: MEOSL and the resolved foot. *Folia Linguistica Historica* 6(2): 245–65.

Lass, Roger 1987. How reliable is Goldswain? On the credibility of an early South African English source. *African Studies* 46(2): 155–62.

Lass, Roger 1989. How early does English get modern? Or what happens if you listen to orthoepists and not to historians? *Diachronica* 6: 75–110.

Lass, Roger. 1990. How to do things with junk: exaptation in language evolution. *Journal of Linguistics* 26: 79–102.

Lass, Roger. 1994. *Old English: a Historical Linguistic Companion*. Cambridge: Cambridge University Press.

Lass, Roger. 1997. *Historical Linguistics and Language Change*. Cambridge: Cambridge University Press.

Lass, Roger. 1999. Phonology. In R. Lass (ed.), *The Cambridge History of the English Language*, vol. 3: *1476–1776*. Cambridge: Cambridge University Press, 56–186.

Lass, Roger. 2004. Ut custodiant litteras: editions, corpora and witnesshood. In M. Dossena and R. Lass (eds), *Methods and Data in Historical Dialectology*. Bern: Lang, 21–48.

Lass, Roger. 2006. Phonology and morphology. In R. M. Hogg and D. Denison (eds), *A History of the English Language*. Cambridge: Cambridge University Press, 43–108.

Lass, Roger and J. M. Anderson. 1975. *Old English Phonology*. Cambridge: Cambridge University Press.

Lass, Roger and Margaret Laing. 2005. Did front rounded vowels remain in the Southwest Midlands? In N. Ritt and H. Schendl (eds), *Rethinking Middle English: Linguistic and Literary Approaches*. Berlin: Lang, 280–90.

Lass, Roger and Margaret Laing. 2009. Databases, dictionaries and dialectology: dental instability in Early Middle English. A case study. In M. Dossena and R. Lass (eds), *Studies in English and European Historical Dialectology*. Bern: Lang, 91–131.

Lass, Roger and Margaret Laing. 2012. 'ea' in Early Middle English: from diphthong to digraph. In D. Denison, R. Bermúdez-Otero, C. McCully, and E. Moore with the assistance of A. Miura (eds), *Analysing Older English*. Cambridge: Cambridge University Press, 75–117.

Latane, Bibb. 1981. The psychology of social impact. *American Psychologist* 36: 343–65.

Laver, John. 1980. *Voice Quality*. Cambridge: Cambridge University Press.

Lavoie, Lisa M. 2001. *Consonant Strength: Phonological Patterns and Phonetic Manifestations*. New York: Garland.

Lavoie, Lisa M. 2002. Subphonemic and suballophonic consonant variation. *ZAS Papers in Linguistics* 28: 39–54.

Lawson, Robert. 2011. Patterns of linguistic variation among Glaswegian adolescent males. *Journal of Sociolinguistics* 15: 226–55.

Leben, William R. 1996. Tonal feet and the adaptation of English borrowings into Hausa. *Studies in African Linguistics* 25: 139–54.

Lee, Iksop and S. Robert Ramsey. 2000. *The Korean Language*. Albany: State University of New York Press.

Lee, Juhee. 2003. The phonology of loanwords and lexical stratification in Korean. PhD thesis, University of Essex.

Lee, Sue Ann and Gregory K. Iverson. 2012. Stop consonant productions of Korean-English bilingual children. *Bilingualism: Language and Cognition* 15: 275–87.

Lehiste, Ilse. 1978. Polytonicity in the area surrounding the Baltic Sea. In Eva Gårding, Gösta Bruce, and Robert Bannert (eds), *Nordic Prosody: Papers from a Symposium*. Lund: Department of Linguistics, Lund University, 237–47.

Lehiste, Ilse. 2004. Bisyllabicity and tone. Paper presented at the International Symposium on Tonal Aspects of Languages: with emphasis on tone languages. Beijing: Chinese Academy of Social Sciences.

Lehmann, Winfred P. 1967. *A Reader in Nineteenth-Century Historical Indo-European Linguistics*. Bloomington: Indiana University. Available at: <http://www.utexas.edu/cola/centers/lrc/books/readT.html>

Lehmann, Winfred P. 1986. *A Gothic Etymological Dictionary*. Leiden: Brill.

Lehmann, Winfred P. 1992. *Historical Linguistics*, 3rd edn. London: Routledge.

Lehmann, Winfred P. 1999. The structural approach of Jacob Grimm and his contemporaries. *Journal of Indo-European Studies* 27: 1–13.

Lenneberg, Eric H. 1967. *Biological Foundations of Language*. New York: Wiley.

LePage, Robert and Andrée Tabouret-Keller. 1985. *Acts of Identity*. Cambridge: Cambridge University Press.

Levenshtein, Vladimir Iosifovich. 1965. Двоичные коды с исправлением выпадений, вставок и замещений символов [Binary codes for correcting deletions, insertions, and substitutions of symbols], Доклады Академий Наук СССР [Reports of the Academy of Sciences of the USSR] 163(4): 845–8.

Levins, Peter 1570. *Manipulus Vocabulorum: a Rhyming Dictionary of the English language.* [Edited with an alphabetical index by Henry Wheatley, London, Trübner, 1867.]

Lhuyd, Eduard. 1707. *Archaeologia Britannica.* Oxford: Printed at the Theater.

Li, Fang Kuei. 1977. *A Handbook of Comparative Tai.* Honolulu: University of Hawai'i Press.

Liberman, Anatoly. 1991. Phonologization in Germanic: umlaut and vowel shifts. In Elmer H. Antonsen and Hans Hock (eds), *Stæfcræft: Studies in Germanic Linguistics.* Amsterdam: Benjamins.

Liberman, Mark and Alan Prince. 1977. On stress and linguistic rhythm. *Linguistic Inquiry* 8: 249–336.

Lieberman, Philip. 1963. Some effects of semantic and grammatical context on the production and perception of speech. *Language and Speech* 6: 172–87.

Lieberman, Philip. 1976. Phonetic features and physiology: a reappraisal. *Journal of Phonetics* 4: 91–112.

Lieberman, Philip, Edmund S. Crelin, and Dennis H. Klatt 1972. Phonetic ability and related anatomy of the newborn and adult human, Neanderthal man, and the chimpanzee. *American Anthropologist* 84: 287–307.

Lief, Eric. 2006. Syncope in Spanish and Portuguese: the diachrony of Hispano-Romance phonotactics. PhD thesis, Cornell University.

Lightfoot, David W. 1979. *Principles of Diachronic Syntax.* New York: Cambridge University Press.

Lightfoot, David. 1997. Catastrophic change and learning theory. *Lingua* 100: 171–92.

Lightfoot, David. 1999. *The Development of Language: Acquisition, Change and Evolution.* Oxford: Blackwell.

Lightner, Theodore. 1965. Segmental Phonology of Contemporary Standard Russian. PhD thesis, MIT.

Lignos, Constantine. 2012. Productivity in analogical change. Paper given at the Manchester and Salford New Researchers Forum in Linguistics, Manchester. Slides available at: <http://www.seas.upenn.edu/~lignos/talks/MancSalFiL_Postnasal_Deletion_Lignos_web.pdf>

Liljencrants, Johan and Björn Lindblom. 1972. Numerical simulation of vowel quality systems: the role of perceptual contrast. *Language* 48: 839–62.

Lindau, Mona. 1985. The story of /r/. In Victoria A. Fromkin (ed.), *Phonetic Linguistics.* New York: Academic Press, 157–68.

Lindblom, Björn. 1963. Spectrographic study of vowel reduction. *Journal of the Acoustical Society of America* 35: 1773–81.

Lindblom, Björn. 1986. Phonetic universals in vowel systems. In J. J. Ohala and J. J. Jaeger (eds), *Experimental Phonology.* Orlando, Fla.: Academic Press, 13–44.

Lindblom, Björn. 1990. Explaining phonetic variation: a sketch of the H and H theory. In W. J. Hardcastle and A. Marchal (eds), *Speech Production and Speech Modelling.* Dordercht: Kluwer, 403–39.

Lindblom, Björn. 1992. Phonological units as adaptive emergents of lexical development. In Charles Ferguson, Lisa Menn, and Carol Stoel-Gammon (eds), *Phonological Development: Models, Research, Implications.* Timonium, Md.: York Press, 131–63.

Lindblom, Björn. 2000. Developmental origins of adult phonology: the interplay between phonetic emergents and the evolutionary adaptations of sound patterns. *Phonetica* 57: 297–314.

Lindblom, Björn, Susan Guion, Susan Hura, Seung-Jae Moon, and Raquel Willerman. 1995. Is sound change adaptive? *Rivista di linguistica* 7: 5–36.

Lindblom, Björn, B. Lyberg, and K. Holmgren. 1981. *Durational Patterns of Swedish Phonology: do They Reflect Short-Term Memory Processes?* Bloomington: Indiana University Linguistic Club.

Lindblom, Björn, P. MacNeilage, and M. Studdert-Kennedy. 1984. Self-organizing processes and the explanation of language universals. In B. Butterworth, B. Comrie, and Ö. Dahl (eds), *Explanations for Language Universals*. Berlin: de Gruyter, 181–203.

Lindblom, Bjorn and Ian Maddieson. 1988. Phonetic universals in consonant systems. In Larry Hman and Charles Li (eds), *Language, Speech, and Mind*. London: Routledge & Kegan Paul.

Lindsey, Geoffrey and Allen Hirson. 1999. Variable robustness of non-standard /r/ in English: evidence from accent disguise. *International Journal of Speech, Language and the Law* 6: 278–88.

Linell, Per. 2005. *The Written Bias in Linguistics and its Origins*. New York: Routledge.

Lipski, John. 1989. Spanish *yeísmo* and the palatal resonants: toward a unified account. *Probus* 1: 211–23.

Llamas, Carmen and Dominic Watt (eds). 2010. *Language and Identities*. Edinburgh: University of Edinburgh Press.

Lleó, Conxita. 2003. Some interactions between word, foot, and syllable structure in the history of Spanish. In D. Eric Holt (ed.), *Optimality Theory and Language Change*. Dordrecht: Kluwer Academic, 249–83.

Lloret, Maria-Rosa. 1997. When does variability become relevant to formal linguistic theory? In Frans Hinskens, Roeland van Hout, and W. Leo Wetzels (eds), *Variation, Change, and Phonological Theory*. Amsterdam: Benjamins, 183–210.

Loakes, Deborah. 2006. A forensic phonetic investigation into the speech patterns of identical and non-identical twins. PhD thesis, University of Melbourne.

Local, John. 1982. Modelling intonational variability in children's speech. In Suzanne Romaine (ed.), *Sociolinguistic Variation in Speech Communities*. London: Arnold, 85–103.

Locke, John L. 1983. *Phonological Acquisition and Change*. New York: Academic Press.

Löfqvist, Anders, Thomas Baer, Nancy S. McGarr, and Robin Seider Story. 1989. The cricothyroid muscle in voicing control. *Journal of the Acoustical Society of America* 85: 1314–21.

Lohr, Marisa. 1999. Methods for the genetic classification of languages. PhD thesis, University of Cambridge.

Lombardi, Linda 2003. Second language data and constraints on manner: explaining substitutions for the English interdentals. *Second Language Research* 19: 225–50.

Long, Christopher and Amit Almor. 2000. Irregularization: the interaction of item frequency and phonological interference in regular past tense production. In L. R. Gleitman and A. K. Joshi (eds), *Proceedings of the Twenty-Second Annual Conference of the Cognitive Science Society*. Hillsdale, NJ: Erlbaum, 310–15.

Lord, Gillian. 2008. Second language acquisition and first language phonological modification. In Joyce Bruhn de Garavito and Elena Valenzuela (eds), *Selected Proceedings of the 10th Hispanic Linguistics Symposium*. Somerville, Mass.: Cascadilla Proceedings Project, 184–93.

Losiewicz, Beth L. 1992. The effect of frequency on linguistic morphology. PhD thesis, University of Texas at Austin.

Lottner, Carl. 1862. Ausnahmen der ersten Lautverschiebung. *Zeitschrift für vergleichende Sprachforschung auf dem Gebiete des Deutschen, Griechischen und Lateinischen* 11: 161–205.

Lotto, Andrew J. and Lori L. Holt. 2000. The illusion of the phoneme. In S. J. Billings, J. P. Boyle, and A. M. Griffith (eds), *Chicago Linguistic Society*, vol. 35: *The Panels*. Chicago: Chicago Linguistic Society, 191–204.

Lowe, John B., and Martine Mazaudon. 1994. The Reconstruction Engine: a computer implementation of the comparative method. *Computational Linguistics* 20(3): 381–417.

Luang-Thongkum, Theraphan. 1990. The interaction between pitch and phonation type in Mon: phonetic implications for a theory of tonogenesis. *Mon-Khmer Studies* 16–17: 11–24.

Luang-Thongkum, Theraphan. 1991. An instrumental study of Chong registers. In J. H. C. S. Davidson (ed.), *Austroasiatic Languages: Essays in Honour of H. L. Shorto*. London: School of Oriental and African Studies, 141–60.

Luang-Thongkum, Theraphan. 1997. Tone change and language contact: a case study of Mien-Yao and Thai. In Arthur S. Abramson (ed.), *Southeast Asian Linguistic Studies in Honour of Vichin Panupong*. Bangkok: Chulalongkorn University Press, 153–60.

Luce, Paul A. and David B. Pisoni. 1998. Recognizing spoken words: the neighborhood activation model. *Ear and Hearing* 19: 1–36.

Luick, Karl. 1914–40/1964. *Historische Grammatik der englischen Sprache*. Stuttgart/Oxford: Tauchnitz/Blackwell.

Luraghi, Silvia. 2010. Causes of language change. In Vit Bubenik and Silvia Luraghi (eds), *The Continuum Companion to Historical Linguistics*. London: Continuum, 358–69.

Lutz, Angelika. 1985. Die Worttrennung am Zeilenende in altenglischen Handschriften: phonologische Betrachtungen zu Dieter Wetzels gleichnamigem Buch. *Indogermanische Forschungen* 90: 227–38.

Lutz, Angelika. 1986. The syllabic basis of word division in Old English manuscripts. *English Studies* 6: 193–210.

Lutz, Angelika. 1991. *Phonotaktisch gesteuerte Konsonantenentwicklungen in der Geschichte des Englischen*. Tübingen: Niemeyer.

Lynch, John. 2005. Final consonants in remote Oceanic. *Oceanic Linguistics* 44: 90–112.

Macaulay, Ronald K.S. 1977. *Language, Social Class, and Education: a Glasgow Study*. Edinburgh: Edinburgh University Press.

Mackay, Wesley, and Grzegorz Kondrak. 2005. Computing word similarity and identifying cognates with pair hidden Markov models. In Ido Dagan and Daniel Gildea (eds), *Proceedings of the Ninth Conference on Computational Natural Language Learning*. New Brunswick, NJ: Association for Computational Linguistics, 40–47. <http://www.aclweb.org/anthology/W/W05/W05-0606.pdf>

Macken, Marlys, and Joseph Salmons. 1997. Prosodic templates in sound change. *Diachronica* 14: 33–66.

MacKenzie, Laurel. 2013. Variation in English auxiliary realization: a new take on contraction. *Language Variation and Change* 25: 17–41.

MacKenzie, Laurel. 2014. Testing the predictions of usage-based models on language change across the lifespan. Paper presented at New Ways of Analyzing Variation 43, Chicago, Illinois, 26 October.

Maclagan, Margaret and Jennifer Hay. 2007. Getting fed up with our feet: contrast maintenance and the New Zealand English 'short' front vowel shift. *Language Variation and Change* 19: 1–25.

MacNeilage, Peter F. 2008. *The Origin of Speech*. Oxford: Oxford University Press.

MacWhinney, Brian. 1975. Rules, rote, and analogy in morphological formations by Hungarian children. *Journal of Child Language* 2: 65–77.

MacWhinney, Brian. 2006. The emergence of linguistic form in time. *Connection Science* 17: 191–211.

Maddieson, Ian. 1984. *Patterns of Sounds*. Cambridge: Cambridge University Press.

Maddieson, Ian. 2008a. Tone. In Martin Haspelmath, Matthew S. Dryer, David Gil, and Bernard Comrie (eds), *The World Atlas of Language Structures Online*. Munich: Max Planck Digital Library, ch. 13. Available at: <http://wals.info/feature/13>

Maddieson, Ian. 2008b. Voicing and gaps in plosive systems. In Martin Haspelmath, Matthew S. Dryer, David Gil, and Bernard Comrie (eds), *The World Atlas of Language Structures Online*. Munich: Max Planck Digital Library, ch. 5. Munich: Max Planck Digital Library.

Maddieson, Ian and Kristin Precoda. 1989. Updating UPSID. *UCLA Working Papers in Phonetics* 74: 104–11. See also: <http://web.phonetik.uni-frankfurt.de/upsid_info.html>

Maguire, Warren. 2008. What is a merger, and can it be reversed? The origin, status and reversal of the 'NURSE–NORTH Merger' in Tyneside English. PhD thesis, Newcastle University.

Maguire, Warren, April McMahon, Paul Heggarty, and Dan Dediu. 2010. The past, present and future of English dialects: quantifying convergence, divergence and dynamic equilibrium. *Language Variation and Change* 22(1): 1–36.

Mailhammer, Robert. 2007. On syllable cut in the *Orrmulum*. In C. M. Cain and G. Russom (eds), *Studies in the History of the English Language*, vol. 3: *Managing Chaos: Strategies for Identifying Change in English*. Berlin: de Gruyter, 37–61.

Mailhammer, Robert. 2009. Thoughts on the genesis and the development of syllable cut in English. *Anglia* 127: 261–82.

Mailhammer, Robert, William Kruger and Alexander Makiyama (in press). Type frequency influences phonological generalizations: eliminating stressed open syllables with short vowels in West-Germanic. *Journal of Germanic Linguistics* 27.

Majors, Tivoli. 1998. Stress-dependent harmony: phonetic origins and phonological analysis. PhD thesis, University of Texas, Austin.

Majors, Tivoli. 2005. Low back vowel merger in Missouri speech: acoustic description and explanation, *American Speech* 80: 165–79.

Malécot, André. 1960. Vowel nasality as a distinctive feature in American English. *Language* 36: 222–29.

Malkiel, Yakov. 1993. *Etymology*. Cambridge: Cambridge University Press.

Manaster Ramer, Alexis. 1986. Genesis of Hopi tones. *International Journal of American Linguistics* 52(2): 154–60.

Manaster Ramer, Alexis. 1994. Stefan George and phonological theory. *Phonology* 11: 317–23.

Manly, J. M. 1930. From generation to generation. In Niels Børgholm, Aage Brusendorff and Carl A. Bodelsen (eds), *A Grammatical Miscellany Offered to Otto Jespersen on his 70th Birthday*. London: Allen and Unwin, 287–9.

Mann, Virginia A. and Bruno H. Repp. 1980. Influence of vocalic context on perception of the [sh]–[s] distinction. *Perception and Psychophysics* 28: 213–28.

Mansuroğlu, Mecdut. 1959. Das Karakhandische. In Jean Deny et al. (eds), *Philologiae Turcicae Fundamenta*. Wiesbaden: Steiner, 87–112.

Manuel, Sharon Y. 1990. The role of contrast in limiting vowel-to-vowel coarticulation in different languages. *Journal of the Acoustic Society of America* 88: 1286–98.

Manuel, Sharon Y. 1999. Cross-language studies: relating language-particular coarticulation patterns to other language-particular facts. In William J. Hardcastle and Nigel Hewlett (eds), *Coarticulation: Theory, Data, and Techniques*. Cambridge: Cambridge University Press, 179–98.

Marcus, Gary F., Ursula Brinkmann, Harald Clahsen, Richard Wiese, and Steven Pinker. 1995. German inflection: the exception that proves the rule. *Cognitive Psychology* 29: 189–256.

Marotta, Giovanna. 2008. Lenition in Tuscan Italian (Gorgia Toscana). In Joaquim Brandão de Carvalho, Tobias Scheer, and Philippe Ségéral (eds), *Lenition and Fortition*, 235–71. Berlin: Mouton de Gruyter.

Marr, David. 1982. *Vision: a Computational Investigation into the Human Representation and Processing of Visual Information*. San Francisco, Calif.: Freeman.

Martin, Samuel E. 1953. *The Phonemes of Ancient Chinese*. Supplement to the *Journal of the American Oriental Society*, 16. Baltimore, Md.: American Oriental Society.

Martin, Samuel E. 1987. *The Japanese Language Through Time*. New Haven, Conn.: Yale University Press.

Martinet, André. 1952. Function, structure and sound change. *Word* 8: 1–32. [Repr. in P. Baldi and R. Werth (eds), 1978. *Readings in Historical Phonology*, University Park: Pennsylvania State University Press, 1978, 121–59.]

Martinet, André. 1955. *Économie des changements phonétiques: traité de phonologie diachronique*. Berne: Francke.

Martinet, André. 1963. Preface. In U. Weinreich (ed.), *Languages in Contact: Findings and Problems*. The Hague: Mouton.

Martinet, André. 1964. *Elements of General Linguistics*. Chicago: University of Chicago Press.

Masel, Joanna. 2011. Genetic drift. *Current Biology* 21: R837–8.

Masica, Colin P. 1991. *The Indo-Aryan Languages*. Cambridge: Cambridge University Press.

Massaro, Dominic W. and Michael M. Cohen. 1983. Phonological constraints in speech perception. *Perception and Psychophysics* 34: 338–48.

Mathesius, Vilém. 1911. O potenciálnosti jevu jazykových. [English translation in Josef Vachek (ed.), *A Prague School Reader in Linguistics*. Bloomington: Indiana University Press, 1964, 1–32.]

Matisoff, James A. 1970. Glottal dissimilation and the Lahu high-rising tone: a tonogenetic case-study. *Journal of the American Oriental Society* 90(1): 13–44.

Matisoff, James A. 1973. Tonogenesis in Southeast Asia. In Larry M. Hyman (ed.), *Consonant Types and Tone*. Los Angeles: University of Southern California, 71–95.

Matisoff, James A. 1990. On megalocomparison. *Language* 66: 106–20.

Matisoff, James A. 1999. Tibeto-Burman tonology in an areal context. In Shigeki Kaji (ed.), *Proceedings of the Symposium Cross-Linguistic Studies of Tonal Phenomena: Tonogenesis, Typology, and Related Topics*. Tokyo: Institute for the Study of Languages and Cultures of Asia and Africa, Tokyo University of Foreign Studies, 3–32.

Matisoff, James A. 2006. Genetic versus contact relationship: prosodic diffusibility in South-East Asian languages. In Alexandra Y. Aikhenvald and R. M. W. Dixon (eds), *Areal Diffusion and Genetic Inheritance: Problems in Comparative Linguistics*. Oxford: Oxford University Press, 291–327.

Mayans y Siscar, D. Gregorio. 1737. *Orígenes de la lengua española*. Madrid: [n.p.].

Maye, Jessica, Janet F. Werker, and LouAnn Gerken. 2002. Infant sensitivity to distributional information can affect phonetic discrimination. *Cognition* 82: B101–B111.

Mayerthaler, Willi. 1981. *Morphologische Natürlichkeit*. Wiesbaden: Athenaion.

Mayrhofer, Manfred. 1986. *Indogermanische Grammatik, Halbband I/2: Lautlehre (Segmentale Phonologie des Indogermanischen)*. Heidelberg: Winter.

McAllister, Tara K. 2009. The articulatory basis of positional asymmetries in phonological acquisition. PhD thesis, MIT.

McCarthy, John. 1979. Formal problems in Semitic phonology and morphology. PhD thesis, MIT. [Published 1985, Garland.]

McCarthy, John. 1981. A prosodic theory of nonconcatenative morphology. *Linguistic Inquiry* 12: 373–418.

McCarthy, John. 1986. OCP effects: gemination and antigemination. *Linguistic Inquiry* 17: 207–63.

McCarthy, John. 1988. Feature geometry and dependency: a review. *Phonetica* 45: 84–108.

McCarthy, John 2003. What does comparative markedness explain, what should it explain, and how? *Theoretical Linguistics* 29(1–2): 141–55.

McCarthy, John 2005. Optimal paradigms. In Laura J. Downing, T. A. Hall and Renate Raffelsiefen (eds), *Paradigms in Phonological Theory*. New York: Oxford University Press, 170–210.

McCarthy, John and Alan Prince. 1986. Prosodic morphology. MS.

McCarthy, John and Alan Prince. 1990. Foot and word in prosodic morphology: the Arabic broken plural. *Natural Language and Linguistic Theory* 8: 209–282.

McCarthy, John and Alan Prince. 1995. Faithfulness and reduplicative identity. In Jill Beckman, Suzanne Urbanczyk, and Laura Walsh (eds) *University of Massachusetts Occasional Papers in Linguistics 18: Papers in Optimality Theory*, 249–384. Amherst: University of Massachusetts.

McDougall, Kirsty M. 2005. The role of formant dynamics in determining speaker identity. PhD thesis, University of Cambridge.

McIntosh, Angus 1956. The analysis of written Middle English. *Transactions of the Philological Society* 55(1): 26–55.

McMahon, April 1994. *Understanding Language Change*. Cambridge: Cambridge University Press.

McMahon, April. 2003. Phonology and the Holy Grail. *Lingua* 113: 103–15.

McMahon, April. 2007. Who's afraid of the vowel shift rule? *Language Sciences* 29: 341–59.

McMahon, April, Paul Heggarty, Robert McMahon, and Warren Maguire. 2007. The sound patterns of Englishes: representing phonetic similarity. *English Language and Linguistics* 11(1): 113–42.

McMahon, April and Robert McMahon. 2003. Finding families: quantitative methods in language classification. *Transactions of the Philological Society* 101(1): 7–55.

McMahon, April and Robert McMahon. 2005. *Language Classification by Numbers*. Oxford: Oxford University Press.

Meillet, Antoine. 1925. *La méthode comparative en linguistique historique*. Oslo: Aschehaug.

Meillet, Antoine. 1934. *Introduction à l'étude comparative des langues indo-européennes*, 7th edn. Paris: Hachette.

Meillet, Antoine. 1951. *Linguistique historique et linguistique générale*, vol. 2. Paris: Klincksieck.

Melinger, Alissa. 2003. Morphological structure in the lexical representation of prefixed words: evidence from speech errors. *Language and Cognitive Processes* 18(3): 335–62.

Mendoza-Denton, Norma. 2008. *Homegirls: Language and Cultural Practice among Latina Youth Gangs*. Oxford: Blackwell.

Menéndez-Pidal, Ramón. 1949. *Manual de grámatica histórica española*, 8th edn. Madrid: Espasa-Calpe. [First published 1904, new edition 1968.]

Menn, Lise. 1983. Development of articulatory, phonetic, and phonological capabilities. In Brian Butterworth (ed.), *Language Production*, vol. 2. London: Academic Press, 3–50.

Menn, Lise and Marilyn M. Vihman. 2011. Features in child phonology: inherent, emergent, or artefacts of analysis? In G. Nick Clements and Rachid Ridouane (eds), *Where Do Phonological Features Come From? The Nature and Sources of Phonological Primitives*. Amsterdam: Benjamins, 261–301.

Mesthrie, Rajend. 1993. Koineization in the Bhojpuri–Hindi diaspora—with special reference to South Africa. *International Journal of the Sociology of Language* 99: 25–44.

Metcalf, George J. 1974. The Indo-European hypothesis in the sixteenth and seventeenth centuries. In Dell Hymes (ed.), *Studies in the History of Linguistics: Traditions and Paradigms*. Bloomington: Indiana University Press, 233–57.

Michener, C. D. and Robert R. Sokal. 1957. A quantitative approach to a problem in classification. *Evolution* 11: 130–62.

Mielke, Jeff. 2008. *The Emergence of Distinctive Features*. Oxford: Oxford University Press. See also: <http://phon.chass.ncsu.edu/pbase-app/query>

Mielke, Jeff. 2009. Segment inventories. *Language and Linguistics Compass* 3: 700–718.

Mielke, Jeff. 2012. A phonetically-based metric of sound similarity. *Lingua*, 122: 145–63.

Mielke, Jeff. 2013. Phonologization and the typology of feature behavior. In Alan C. Yu (eds), *Origins of Sound Change: Approaches to Phonologization*. Oxford: Oxford University Press, 165–80.

Mielke, Jeff, Mike Armstrong, and Elisabeth Hume. 2003. Looking through opacity. *Theoretical Linguistics* 29: 123–39.

Mifsud, Manwel. 1995. *Loan Verbs in Maltese: a Descriptive and Comparative Study*. Leiden: Brill.

Miller, Brett. 2012. Feature patterns: their source and status in grammar and reconstruction. PhD thesis, University of Cambridge.

Miller, D. Gary. 1977a. Some theoretical and typological implications of an Indo-European root structure constraint. *Journal of Indo-European Studies* 5: 31–130.

Miller, D. Gary. 1977b. Bartholomae's Law and an IE root constraint. In Paul J. Hopper (ed.), *Studies in Descriptive and Historical Linguistics: Festschrift for W. P. Lehmann*. Amsterdam: Benjamins, 365–92.

Miller, Joanne. 1994. On the internal structure of phonetic categories: a progress report. *Cognition* 50: 271–85.

Milroy, James. 1992a. A social model for the interpretation of language change. In Matti Rissanen et al. (eds), *New Methods and Interpretations in Historical Linguistics*. Berlin: Mouton de Gruyter, 72–91.

Milroy, James. 1992b. *Linguistic Variation and Change*. Oxford: Blackwell.

Milroy, James. 1993. On the social origins of language change. In Charles Jones (ed.), *Historical Linguistics: Problems and Perspectives*. London: Longman, 215–36.

Milroy, James. 1995. Investigating the Scottish vowel length rule in a Northumbrian dialect. *Newcastle and Durham Working Papers in Linguistics* 4: 187–96.

Milroy, James. 1999. Towards a speaker-based account of language change. In Ernst Håkon Jahr (ed.), *Language Change: Advances in Historical Sociolinguistics*. Berlin: Mouton de Gruyter, 21–36.

Milroy, James and John Harris. 1980. When is a merger not a merger? The *meat/mate* problem in a present-day English vernacular. *English World-Wide* 1: 199–210.

Milroy, James and Lesley Milroy. 1978. Belfast: change and variation in an urban vernacular. In P. Trudgill (ed.), *Sociolinguistic Patterns in British English*. London: Arnold, 19–36.

Milroy, James and Lesley Milroy. 1985. Linguistic change: social network and innovation. *Journal of Linguistics* 2: 339–84.

Milroy, James, Lesley Milroy, Sue Hartley, and David Walshaw. 1994. Glottal stops and Tyneside glottalization: competing patterns of variation and change in British English. *Language Variation and Change* 6: 327–57.

Milroy, Lesley. 1980. *Language and Social Networks*. Oxford: Blackwell. [2nd end. 1987.]

Milroy, Lesley. 2007. Off the shelf or under the counter? On the social dynamics of sound changes. In Christopher Cain and Geoffrey Russom (eds), *Managing Chaos: Strategies for Identifying Change in English*. Berlin: Mouton de Gruyter, 149–71.

Minkova, Donka. 1982. The environment for open syllable lengthening in Middle English. *Folia Linguistica Historica* 3(2): 29–58.

Minkova, Donka. 1985. Of rhyme and reason: some foot-governed quantity changes in English. In Roger Eaton, Olga Fischer, Willem Koopman, and Frederike van der Leek et al. (eds), *Papers from the 4th International Conference on English Historical Linguistics*. Amsterdam: Benjamins, 163–78.

Minkova, Donka. 1997. Constraint ranking in Middle English stress-shifting. *English Language and Linguistics* 1: 135–75.

Minkova, Donka. 2003. *Alliteration and Sound Change in Early English*. Cambridge: Cambridge University Press.

Minkova, Donka. 2011. Phonemically contrastive fricatives in Old English? *English Language and Linguistics* 15: 31–59.

Minkova, Donka. 2014. *A Historical Phonology of English*. Edinburgh: Edinburgh University Press.

Minkova, Donka and Robert P. Stockwell. 1996. The origins of long-short allomorphy in English. In Jacek Fisiak and Marcin Krygier (eds), *Advances in English Historical Linguistics 1996*. Berlin: Mouton de Gruyter, 211–39.

Minkova, Donka and Robert P. Stockwell. 2003. English vowel shifts and 'optimal' diphthongs: is there a logical link? In D. Eric Holt (ed.), *Optimality Theory and Language Change*. Dordrecht: Kluwer Academic, 169–90.

Mithen, Steven. 2005. *The Singing Neanderthals: the Origins of Music, Language, Mind and Body*. London: Weidenfeld and Nicholson.

Mitterer, Holger. 2006. On the causes of compensation for coarticulation: evidence for phonological mediation. *Perception and Psychophysics* 68(7): 1227–40.

Miyashita, Kae, Miya Kato Rand, Shigehiro Miyachi, and Okihide Hikosaka. 1996. Anticipatory saccades in sequential procedural learning in monkeys. *Journal of Neurophysiology* 76: 1361–66.

Moder, Carol Lynn. 1992. Rules and analogy. In Garry W. Davis and Gregory K. Iverson (eds), *Explanation in Historical Linguistics*. Philadelphia: Benjamins, 179–91.

Mohanan, K. P. 1986. *The Theory of Lexical Phonology*. Dordrecht: Reidel.

Mohanan, K. P. and Tara Mohanan. 1984. Lexical phonology of the consonant system in Malayalam. *Linguistic Inquiry* 15: 575–602.

Mohanan, Karuvannur. 1982. Lexical phonology. PhD thesis, MIT.

Molinu, Lucia. 1998. La syllabe en sarde. PhD thesis, Université Stendhal de Grenoble.

Molinu, Lucia. 2009. La latérale intervocalique non géminée en sarde méridional. *Vox Romanica* 68: 129–55.

Monahan, Philip J., Eri Takahashi, Chizuru Nakao, and William Idsardi 2009. Not all epenthetic contexts are equal: differential effects in Japanese illusory vowel perception. In S. Iwasaki, H. Hoji, P. M. Clancy and S.-O. Sohn (eds), *Japanese/Korean Linguistics*, vol. 17. Stanford, Calif.: CSLI, 391–405.

Moon, Seung-Jae and Björn Lindblom. 1994. Interaction between duration, context, and speaking style in English stressed vowels. *Journal of the Acoustical Society of America*, 96: 40–55.

Moonwomon, Birch. 1991. Sound change in San Francisco English. PhD thesis, University of California.

Moore, Emma. 2004. Sociolinguistic style: a multidimensional resource for shared identity creation. *Canadian Journal of Linguistics* 49: 375–96.

Moore, Emma. 2010. Communities of practice and peripherality. In C. Llamas and D. Watt (eds), *Language and Identities*. Edinburgh: Edinburgh University Press, 123–33.

Moore, Samuel and Thomas A. Knott. 1955. *The Elements of Old English*. Ann Arbor, Mich.: Wahr.

Moosmüller, Sylvia. 2007. Phonetics needs phonology. In Vsevolod A. Vinogradov (ed.), *Lingvisticeskaja polifonija: Sbornik v cest' jubileja professora R. K. Potapovoj*. Moscow: Jazyki Slavjanskich Kul'tur, 488–503.

Morandini, Diego. 2007. The phonology of loanwords into Italian. Master's dissertation, University College London.

Moreton, Elliott. 2002. Structural constraints in the perception of English stop-sonorant clusters. *Cognition* 84(1): 55–71.

Moreton, Elliot. 2008. Analytic bias and phonological typology. *Phonology* 25(1): 83–127.

Moreton, Elliott and Joe Pater. 2012a. Structure and substance in artificial-phonology learning, part 1: Structure. *Language and Linguistics Compass* 6(11): 686–701.

Moreton, Elliott and Joe Pater. 2012b. Structure and substance in artificial-phonology learning, part 2: Substance. *Language and Linguistics Compass* 6(11): 702–18.

Morley, Rebecca. 2012. The emergence of epenthesis: an incremental model of grammar change. *Language Dynamics and Change* 2: 59–97.

Morley, Rebecca. 2014. Implications of an exemplar-theoretic model of phoneme genesis: a velar palatalization case study. *Language and Speech* 57(1): 3–41.

Morpurgo Davies, Anna. 1998. *History of Linguistics*, vol. 4: *Nineteenth-Century Linguistics*. London: Longman.

Morrison, Catriona, Andrew Chappell, and Andrew W. Ellis 1997. Age of acquisition norms for a large set of object names and their relation to adult estimates and other variables. *Quarterly Journal of Experimental Psychology* 50A: 528–59.

Mortensen, David. 2004. The emergence of dorsal stops after high vowels in Huishu. In *Proceedings of the Thirtieth Annual Meeting of the Berkeley Linguistics Society*. Berkeley, Calif.: Berkeley Linguistics Society, 292–303.

Morton, David. 2004. *Sound Recording: the Life Story of a Technology*. Westport, Conn.: Greenwood Press.

Moscati, Sabatino (ed.). 1980. *An Introduction to the Comparative Grammar of the Semitic Languages: Phonology and Morphology*. Wiesbaden: Harassowitz.

Moulton, William G. 1960. The short vowel systems of northern Switzerland: a study in structural dialectology. *Word* 16: 155–82.

Moulton, William G. 1967. The mapping of phonemic systems. In Ludwig Erich Schmitt (ed.), *Verhandlungen des 2. Internationalen Dialektologenkongresses*, vol. 2. Wiesbaden: Steiner, 574–91.

Moulton, William G. 1972. Review of *Phonetisch-phonologische Untersuchungen zur Vokalentwicklung in den deutschen Dialekten*, 1: *Die Langvokale im Hochdeutschen* by Peter Wiesinger. *German Quarterly* 45(2): 377–80.

Mowrey, Richard and William Pagliuca. 1995. The reductive character of articulatory evolution. *Rivista di linguistica* 7(1): 37–124.

Moyer, Alene. 2007. Do language attitudes determine accent? A study of bilinguals in the USA. *Journal of Multilingual and Multicultural Development* 28: 502–18.

Mufwene, Salikoko. 2001. *The Ecology of Language Evolution*. Cambridge: Cambridge University Press.

Mühlhäusler, Peter. 1997. *Pidgin and Creole Linguistics*. London: Battlebridge.

Müller, André, Søren Wichmann, Viveka Velupillai, Cecil H. Brown, Pamela Brown, and Anthony Grant. 2010. ASJP world language tree of lexical similarity. Version 3. Available at: <http://email.eva.mpg.de/~wichmann/WorldLanguageTree-003.pdf>

Müller, Max. 1890. *The Science of Language*. New York: Scribner.

Munch, Peter A. 1945. *Sociology of Tristan da Cunha*. Oslo: Det Norske Videnskaps–Akademi.

Muñoz, Carmen. 2008. Symmetries and asymmetries of age effects in naturalistic and instructed L2 learning. *Applied Linguistics* 29: 578–96.

Muñoz, Carmen and David Singleton. 2011. A critical review of age-related research on L2 ultimate attainment. *Language Teaching* 44: 1–35.

Munson, Benjamin and Nancy Pearl Solomon. 2004. The influence of phonological neighborhood density on vowel articulation. *Journal of Speech, Language, and Hearing Research* 47: 1048–58.

Murray, Robert. 1982. Consonant cluster development in Pāli. *Folia Linguistica Historica* 111: 163–84.

Murray, Robert. 1988. *Phonological Strength and Early Germanic Syllable Structure*. Munich: Fink.

Murray, Robert W. 2000. Syllable cut prosody in Early Middle English. *Language* 76: 617–54.

Murray, Robert W. 2002. Syllable cut prosody in Early Modern English: John Hart's testimony. In Peter Auer, Peter Gilles, and Helmut Spiekermann (eds), *Silbenschnitt und Tonakzente*. Tübingen: Niemeyer, 103–27.

Murray, Robert W. 2010. Language and space: the neogrammarian tradition. In Peter Auer and Jürgen Erich Schmidt (eds), *Language and Space. An International Handbook of Linguistic Variation*. Berlin: Mouton de Gruyter, 70–87.

Murray, Robert W. and Theo Vennemann. 1982. Syllable contact change in Germanic, Greek and Sidamo. *Klagenfurter Beiträge zur Sprachwissenschaft* 8: 321–49.

Murray, Robert W. and Theo Vennemann. 1983. Sound change and syllable structure in Germanic phonology. *Language* 59: 514–28.

Muysken, Pieter. 1995. Code-switching and grammatical theory. In L. Milroy and P. Muysken (eds), *One Speaker, Two Languages: Cross-Disciplinary Perspectives on Code-Switching*. Cambridge: Cambridge University Press, 177–98.

Myers, Scott. 1987. Vowel shortening in English. *Natural Language and Linguistic Theory* 5: 485–518.

Myers, Scott. 1991. Persistent rules. *Linguistic Inquiry* 22: 315–44.

Myers, Scott. 2000. Boundary disputes: the distinction between phonetic and phonological sound patterns. In Noel Burton-Roberts, Philip Carr, and Gerard Docherty (eds), *Phonological Knowledge: Conceptual and Empirical Issues*. Oxford: Oxford University Press, 245–72.

Myers, Scott and Benjamin B. Hansen. 2007. The origin of vowel length neutralization in final position: evidence from Finnish speakers. *Natural Language and Linguistic Theory* 25: 157–93.

Myers-Scotton, Carol 1993. *Duelling Languages: Grammatical Structure in Codeswitching*. Oxford: Clarendon.

Nahkola, Kari and Marja Saanilahti. 2004. Mapping language changes in real time: a panel study on Finnish. *Language Variation and Change* 16: 75–92.

Nakhleh, Luay, Tandy Warnow, Donald A. Ringe, and Steven N. Evans. 2005. A comparison of phylogenetic reconstruction methods on an IE dataset, *Transactions of the Philological Society* 3(2): 171–92.

Namy, Laura L., Lynne C. Nygaard, and Denise Sauerteig. 2002. Gender differences in vocal accommodation: the role of perception. *Journal of Language and Social Psychology* 21(4): 422–32.

Nathan, Geoffrey S. 2007. Phonology. In Dirk Geeraerts and Hubert Cuykens (eds), *The Oxford Handbook of Cognitive Linguistics*. Oxford: Oxford University Press, 611–31.

Nathan, Geoffrey S. 2008. *Phonology: a Cognitive Grammar Introduction*. Amsterdam: Benjamins.

Nathan, Geoffrey S. 2009. Where is the Natural Phonology phoneme in 2009? *Poznań Studies in Contemporary Linguistics* 45(1): 141–8. Available at: <http://versita.metapress.com/content/9u12gl5248503876/fulltext.pdf>

Neary, Terence. 1977. Phonetic feature system for vowels. PhD thesis, University of Connecticut, Storrs.

Nerbonne, John and Wilbert Heeringa. 1997. Measuring dialect distance phonetically. In John Coleman (ed.), *Third Meeting of the ACL Special Interest Group in Computational Phonology*. Somerset, NJ: Association for Computational Linguistics.

Nettle, Daniel. 1999. Using Social Impact Theory to simulate language change. *Lingua* 108: 95–117.

Nevalainen, Terttu and Susan M. Fitzmaurice (eds). 2011. *Problems and Approaches to the Investigation of the English Language over Time and Space*, vol. 7. Helsinki: Research Unit for Variation, Contacts and Change in English.

Nevalainen, Terttu, Helena Raumolin-Bromberg, and Heiki Mannila. 2011. The diffusion of language change in real time: progressive and conservative individuals and the time depth of change. *Language Variation and Change* 23: 1–43.

Newman, Paul. 1974. *The Kanakuru Language*. Leeds: University of Leeds Institute of English Language Studies in association with the West African Linguistic Society.

Newman, Paul. 2004. *Klingenheben's Law in Hausa*. Cologne: Köppe.

Newport, Elissa and Robert Aslin. 2004. Learning at a distance I: Statistical learning of non-adjacent dependencies. *Cognitive Psychology* 48: 127–62.

Ní Chiosáin, Máire and Jaye Padgett. 1993. Inherent V-Place. *UC Santa Cruz Working Papers*. Linguistics Research Center, University of California, Santa Cruz.

Ní Chiosáin, Máire and Jaye Padgett. 2010. Contrast, comparison sets, and the perceptual space. In Steve Parker (ed.), *Phonological Argumentation: Essays of Evidence and Motivation*. London: Equinox.

Nichols, Johanna. 1996. The comparative method as heuristic. In Mark Durie and Malcolm Ross (eds), *The Comparative Method Reviewed*. New York: Oxford University Press, 39–71.

Nichols, Johanna and Tandy Warnow. 2008. Tutorial on computational linguistic phylogeny. *Language and Linguistics Compass* 2(5): 760–820.

Nicolas Gregoire and Ilya Prigogine 1977. *Self-organization in Non-equilibrium Systems: From Dissipative Structures to Order through Fluctuations*. New York: Wiley.

Nielsen, Hans F. 1981. *Old English and the Continental Germanic Languages: a Survey of Morphological and Phonological Interrelations*. Innsbruck: Innsbrucker Beiträge zur Sprachwissenschaft.

Nielsen, Kuniko. 2011. Specificity and abstractness of VOT imitation. *Journal of Phonetics* 39(2): 132–42.

Nittrouer, Susan and Michael Studdert-Kennedy. 1987. The role of coarticulatory effects on the perception of fricatives by children and adults. *Journal of Speech and Hearing Research* 30: 319–29.

Nolan, Francis. 1983. *The Phonetic Bases of Speaker Recognition*. Cambridge: Cambridge University Press.

Nolan, Francis. 1992. The descriptive role of segments: evidence from assimilation. In Gerald Docherty and Robert Ladd (eds), *Papers in Laboratory Phonology*, 2: *Gesture, Segment, Prosody*. Cambridge: Cambridge University Press, 261–80.

Nolan, Francis. 1997. Speaker recognition and forensic phonetics. In William J. Hardcastle and John Laver (eds), *The Handbook of Phonetic Sciences*. Oxford: Blackwell, 744–67.

Nolan, Francis, and Tomasina Oh. 1996. Identical twins, different voices. *Forensic Linguistics* 3: 39–49.

Normier, Rudolf. 1977. Idg. Konsonantismus, germ. 'Lautverschiebung' und Vernersches Gesetz. *Zeitschrift für Vergleichende Sprachforschung* 91: 171–218.

Norris, Dennis, James M. McQueen, and Anne Cutler. 2003. Perceptual learning in speech. *Cognitive Psychology* 47: 204–38.

Oakes, Michael P. 2000. Computer estimation of vocabulary in a protolanguage from word lists in four daughter languages. *Journal of Quantitative Linguistics* 7(3): 233–43.

Oertel, Hanns. 1901. *Lectures on the Study of Language*. New York: Scribner's.

Ogura, Mieko. 1987. *Historical English Phonology: a Lexical Perspective*. Tokyo: Kenkyusha.

Ogura, Mieko. 1995. The development of Middle English ī and ū: a reply to Labov. *Diachronica* 12: 31–53.

Oh, Young-Il. 2002. Historical sound change in Optimality Theory. *SNU Working Papers in English Language and Linguistics* 1: 127–41.

Ohala, John J. 1973. The physiology of tone. In Larry M. Hyman (ed.), *Consonant Types and Tone*. Los Angeles: University of Southern California, 2–14.

Ohala, John J. 1975. Phonetic explanations for nasal sound patterns. In C. A. Ferguson, L. M. Hyman, and J. J. Ohala (eds), *Nasalfest: Papers From a Symposium on Nasals and Nasalization*. Stanford, Calif.: Language Universals Project, 289–316.

Ohala, John J. 1980. Introduction to the symposium on phonetic universals in phonological systems and their explanation. In *Proceedings of the 9th International Congress of Phonetic Sciences*, vol. 3. Copenhagen: University of Copenhagen, Institute of Phonetics, 180–85.

Ohala, John J. 1981. The listener as a source of sound change. In C. S. Masek, R. A. Hendrick, and M. F. Miller (eds), *Papers from the Parasession on Language and Behavior*. Chicago: Chicago Linguistic Society, 178–203.

Ohala, John J. 1983. The origin of sound patterns in vocal tract constraints. In P. MacNeilage (ed.), *The Production of Speech*. New York: Springer, 189–216.

Ohala, John J. 1989. Sound change is drawn from a pool of synchronic variation. In L. E. Breivik and E. H. Jahr (eds), *Language Change: Contributions to the Study of its Causes*. Berlin: Mouton de Gruyter, 173–98.

Ohala, John J. 1990. The phonetics and phonology of aspects of assimilation. In J. Kingston and M. Beckman (eds), *Papers in Laboratory Phonology*, vol 1. Cambridge: Cambridge University Press, 258–75.

Ohala, John J. 1992. What's cognitive, what's not. In sound change. In G. Kellerman and M. D. Morrissey (eds), *Diachrony Within Synchrony: Language History and Cognition*. Frankfurt: Lang, 309–55. [Repr. in *Lingua e stile* 27 (1992): 321–62.]

Ohala, John J. 1993. The phonetics of sound change. In Charles Jones (ed.), *Historical Linguistics: Problems and Perspectives*. London: Longman, 237–78.

Ohala, John J. 1994. Towards a universal, phonetically-based, theory of vowel harmony. In ICSLP 3, Yokohama, 491–4.

Ohala, John J. 1995. Experimental phonology. In J. A. Goldsmith (ed.), *A Handbook of Phonological Theory*. Oxford: Blackwell, 713–22.

Ohala, John J. 1997a. Aerodynamics of phonology. In *Proceedings of the 4th Seoul International Conference on Linguistics*. Seoul: Hankuk, 92–7.

Ohala, John J. 1997b. Emergent stops. In *Proceedings of the 4th Seoul International Conference on Linguistics*, 84–91.

Ohala, John J. 2003. Phonetics and historical phonology. In Brian D. Joseph and Richard D. Janda (eds), *The Handbook of Historical Linguistics*. Oxford: Blackwell, 669–86.

Ohala, John J. 2005. Phonetic explanations for sound patterns: implications for grammars of competence. In William J. Hardcastle and Janet M. Beck (eds), *A Figure of Speech: a Festschrift for John Laver*. London: Erlbaum, 23–38.

Ohala, John J. and C. Riordan. 1980. Passive vocal tract enlargement during voiced speech. Report of the Phonological Laboratory, University of California Berkeley.

Oliveira, Marco Antonio de. 1991. The neogrammarian controversy revisited, *International Journal of the Sociology of Language* 89: 93–105.

Orgun, Orhan. 1996. Sign-based phonology and morphology, with special attention to optimality. PhD thesis. University of California, Berkeley.

Ortega-Llebaría, Marta. 2004. Interplay between phonetic and inventory constraints in the degree of spirantization of voiced stops, comparing intervocalic /b/ and intervocalic /g/ in Spanish and English. In Timothy L. Face (ed.), *Laboratory Approaches to Spanish Phonology*. Berlin: Mouton de Gruyter, 237–53.

Orton, Harold and Eugen Dieth et al. 1962–71. *Survey of English Dialects: Basic Material*. Leeds: E. J. Arnold.

Osthoff, Hermann. 1878a. *Das Verbum in der Nominalkomposition*. Jena: Costenoble.

Osthoff, Hermann. 1878b. Formassociation bei Zahlwörtern. In Hermann Osthoff and Karl Brugmann, *Morphologische Untersuchungen auf dem Gebiete der Indogermanischen Sprachen*, vol. 1. Leipzig: Hirzel, 92–132.

Osthoff, Hermann. 1879. *Das physiologische und psychologische Moment in der sprachlichen Formenbildung*. Berlin: Habel.

Osthoff, Hermann and Karl Brugmann. 1878. Vorwort. In Hermann Osthoff and Karl Brugmann, *Morphologische Untersuchungen auf dem Gebiete der indogermanischen Sprachen*, vol. 1. Leipzig: Hirzel, iii–xx. ;

Ostler, Nicholas. 2005. *Empires of the Word: a Language History of the World*. New York: HarperCollins.

Oswalt, Robert L. 1970. The detection of remote linguistic relationships. *Computer Studies in the Humanities and Verbal Behavior* 3: 117–29.

Oswalt, Robert L. 1975. The relative stability of some syntactic and semantic categories. *Working Papers on Language Universals* 19: 1–19.

Oudeyer, Pierre-Yves. 2006. *Self-Organization in the Evolution of Speech*. Oxford: Oxford University Press.

Oxford, Will. 2012. 'Contrast shift' in the Algonquian languages. In A. McKillen and J. Loughren (eds), *Proceedings from the Montreal-Ottawa-Toronto (MOT) Phonology Workshop 2011: Phonology in the 21st Century*. Montreal: McGill University.

Oxford, Will. 2015. Patterns of contrast in phonological change: evidence from Algonquian vowel systems. *Language* 91(2).

Padgett, Jaye. 2003a. Contrast and post-velar fronting in Russian. *Natural Language and Linguistic Theory* 21: 39–87.

Padgett, Jaye. 2003b. The emergence of contrastive palatalization in Russian. In D. Eric Holt (ed.), *Optimality Theory and Language Change*. Dordrecht: Kluwer Academic, 307–35.

Padgett, Jaye and Marzena Zygis. 2004. The evolution of sibilants in Polish and Russian. In T. A. Hall and Silke Hamann (eds), *ZAS Papers in Linguistics*, vol. 32. Berlin: ZAS, 155–74.

Page, Richard I. 1973. *An Introduction to English Runes*. London: Methuen.

Pagliuca, William and Richard Mowrey. 1987. Articulatory evolution. In A. G. Ramat, O. Carruba, and G. Bernini (eds), *Papers from the 7th International Conference on Historical Linguistics*. Amsterdam: Benjamins, 459–72.

Pape, Daniel, Christine Mooshammer, Phil Hoole, and Susanne Fuchs. 2003. Devoicing of word-initial stops: a consequence of the following vowel? *Proceedings of the 6th International Seminar on Speech Production*, 207–12.

Paradis, Carole. 1988. On constraints and repair strategies. *Linguistic Review* 6: 71–97.

Paradis, Carole and Darlene LaCharité. 1997. Preservation and minimality in loanword adaptation. *Journal of Linguistics* 33: 379–430.

Paradis, Carole and Antoine Tremblay. 2009. Nondistinctive features in loanword adaptation: the unimportance of English aspiration in Mandarin Chinese phoneme categorization. In A. Calabrese and L. Wetzels (eds), *Loan Phonology*. Amsterdam: Benjamins, 211–24.

Pardo, Jennifer S. 2006. On phonetic convergence during conversational interaction. *Journal of the Acoustical Society of America* 119(4): 2382–93.

Park, Haeil and Gregory K. Iverson. 2008. First and second language patterns of brain activation in Korean laryngeal contrasts. *Korean Linguistics* 14: 1–19.

Park, Haeil, Gregory K. Iverson, and Hae-Jeong Park. 2011. Neural correlates in the processing of phoneme-level complexity in vowel production. *Brain and Language* 119: 158–66.

Park, Haeil, Hae-Jeong Park, and Gregory K. Iverson. 2010. The frontal and temporal lobe in the identification of laryngeal contrasts. *NeuroReport* 21: 474–78.

Park, Whaja. 1987. *Western Loan-Words in Japanese*. Stockholm: Stockholm Universitet.

Paster, Mary. 2004. Vowel height harmony and blocking in Buchan Scots. *Phonology* 21(3): 359–407.

Pater, Joe and Elliott Moreton. 2012. Structurally biased phonology: complexity and learning in typology. *EFL Journal (Journal of the English and Foreign Languages University, Hyderabad)* 3: 1–44.

Patterson, David, Paul C. LoCasto, and Cyntia M. Connine. 2003. Corpora analyses of frequency of schwa deletion in conversational American English. *Phonetica* 60: 45–69.

Paul, Hermann. 1877. Die Vocale der Flexions- und Ableitungs-Silben in den aeltesten germanischen Dialecten. *Beiträge zur Geschichte der deutschen Sprache und Literatur* 4: 315–475.

Paul, Hermann 1880. *Prinzipien der Sprachgeschichte*. Halle: Niemeyer. [2nd edn, 1886; 5th edn, 1920; also reprinted 1995. Selected chapters translated in P. Auer and R. W. Murray (eds), 2015, *Hermann Paul's 'Principles of Language History': Translations and Reflections*. Berlin: Mouton de Gruyter.]

Paul, Hermann. 1886. Review of Hugo Schuchardt, *Über die Lautgesetze: Gegen die Junggrammatiker*. *Literaturblatt für die germanische und romanische Philologie* 7: 1–6.

Paunonen, Heikki. 1996. Language change in apparent time and in real time: possessive constructions in Helsinki colloquial Finnish. In M. Thelander, L. Elmevik, B. Gunnarsson, and

B. Melander (eds), *Samspel och variation: Språkliga studier tillägnade Bengt Nordberg på 60-årsdagen*. Uppsala: Institutionen för nordiska språk, 375–86.

Payne, Arvilla C. 1980. Factors controlling the acquisition of the Philadelphia dialect by out-of-state children. In W. Labov (ed.), *Locating Language in Time and Space*. New York: Academic Press, 143–78.

Peck, Steven L. 2004. Simulation as experiment: a philosophical reassessment for biological modeling. *Trends in Ecology and Evolution* 19: 530–4.

Pedersen, Holger. 1916/1983. *A Glance at the History of Linguistics with Particular Regard to the Historical Study of Phonology*. Amsterdam: Benjamins.

Pedersen, Holger. 1924/1931. *The Discovery of Language*. Bloomington: Indiana University Press.

Pedersen, Holger. 1951. *Die gemeinindoeuropäischen und die vorindoeuropäischen Verschlußlaute*. Copenhagen: Munksgaard.

Pellis, Ugo. 1934. Cinquanta inchieste linguistiche in Sardegna. *Bollettino dell'Atlante linguistico italiano*, 1: 49–76.

Pellowe, John, Barbara Strang, Graham Nixon, and Vincent McNeany. 1972. A dynamic modelling of linguistic variation: the urban (Tyneside) linguistic survey. *Lingua* 30: 1–30.

Penny, Ralph. 2002. *A History of the Spanish Language*. Cambridge: Cambridge University Press.

Pensado, Carmen 1996. La velarización Castellana /ʃ/ > /x/ y sus paralelos romances. In Alegría Alonso González et al. (eds), *Actas del III Congreso Internacional de Historia de la Lengua Española* vol. 1. Madrid: Arco/Libros, 153–70..

Penzl, Herbert. 1957. The evidence for phonemic change. In Ernst Pulgram (ed.), *Studies Presented to Joshua Whatmough on his Sixtieth Birthday*. The Hague: Mouton de Gruyter, 193–208. [Repr. in Roger Lass (ed.), *Approaches to English Historical Linguistics*. New York: Holt, Rinehart and Winston, 1969, 10–25.]

Peperkamp, Sharon. 2005. A psycholinguistic theory of loanword adaptation. *BLS* 30: 341–52.

Peperkamp, Sharon. 2007. Do we have innate knowledge about phonological markedness? *Cognition* 104: 631–7.

Peperkamp, Sharon and Emmanuel Dupoux. 2002. A typological study of stress 'deafness'. In C. Gussenhoven and N. Warner (eds), *Laboratory Phonology 7*. Berlin: de Gruyter, 203–40.

Peperkamp, Sharon and Emmanuel Dupoux. 2003. Reinterpreting loanword adaptations: the role of perception. In M. Solé, D. Recasens, and J. Romero (eds), *Proceedings of the 15th International Congress of Phonetic Sciences*. Adelaide: Causal Productions, 367–70.

Peperkamp, Sharon and Emmanuel Dupoux. 2007. Learning the mapping from surface to underlying representations in an artificial language. In Jennifer Cole and José Hualde (eds), *Laboratory Phonology*, vol. 9. Berlin: Mouton de Gruyter, 315–38.

Peperkamp, Sharon, Karin Skoruppa, and Emmanuel Dupoux. 2006. The role of phonetic naturalness in phonological rule acquisition. In David Bamman, Tatiana Magnitskaia, and Colleen Zaller (eds), *Proceedings of the 30th Boston University Conference on Language Development*. Somerville, Mass.: Cascadilla Press, 464–75.

Peperkamp, Sharon, Inga Vendelin, and Kimihiro Nakamura. 2008. On the perceptual origin of loanword adaptations: experimental evidence from Japanese. *Phonology* 25(1): 129–64.

Peramunage, D., S. E. Blumstein, E. Myers, M. Goldrick, and M. Baese-Berk. 2011. Phonological neighborhood effects in spoken word production: an fMRI study. *Journal of Cognitive Neuroscience* 23: 593–603.

Percival, W. Keith. 1974. Rask's view of linguistic development and phonetic correspondences. In Dell Hymes (ed.), *Studies in the History of Linguistics: Traditions and Paradigms.* Bloomington: Indiana University Press, 307–14.

Percival, W. Keith. 2011. Roman Jakobson and the birth of linguistic structuralism. *Sign Systems Studies* 39: 236–62.

Perin, Dolores. 1983. Phonemic segmentation and spelling. *British Journal of Psychology* 74: 129–44.

Perkell, Joseph S., Frank H. Guenther, Harlan Lane, Melanie L. Mathies, Ellen Stockmann, Mark Tiede, and Majod Zandipour. 2004. The distinctness of speakers' productions of vowel contrasts is related to their discrimination of the contrasts. *Journal of the Acoustical Society of America* 116: 2338–44.

Perkell, Joseph. 1969. *Physiology of Speech: Results and Implications of a Quantitative Cineradiographic Study.* Cambridge, Mass.: MIT Press.

Petersen, Uwe. 1992. *Rasmus Kristian Rask. Von der Etymologie überhaupt: eine Einleitung in die Sprachvergleichung.* Tübingen: Narr.

Pham, Andrea. 2005. Vietnamese tonal system in Nghi Loc dialect: a preliminary report. *Toronto Working Papers in Linguistics*: special issue on similarity in phonology 24: 183–201.

Philadelphia Neighborhood Corpus (PNC) of LING560 Studies, 1971–2010. With the support of NSF contract 921643 to William Labov. Available at: <http://fave.ling.upenn.edu/pnc.html>

Phillips, Betty. 1983. ME diphthongization, phonetic analogy, and lexical diffusion. *Word* 34: 11–23.

Phillips, Betty. 1984. Word frequency and the actuation of sound change. *Language* 60: 320–42.

Phillips, Betty. 1989. The diffusion of a borrowed sound change. *Journal of English Linguistics* 22: 197–204.

Phillips, Betty. 1994. Southern English glide deletion revisited. *American Speech* 69: 115–27.

Phillips, Betty. 1995. Lexical diffusion as a guide to scribal intent: a comparison of ME <eo> vs. <e> spellings in the Peterborough Chronicle and the Ormulum. In Henning Andersen (ed.), *Historical Linguistics 1993: Selected Papers from the 11th International Conference on Historical Linguistics.* Amsterdam: Benjamins, 379–86.

Phillips, Betty. 1997. The Peterborough Chronicle diphthongs. In J. Fisiak (ed.), *Studies in Middle English Linguistics.* Berlin: Mouton de Gruyter, 429–38.

Phillips, Betty. 1998. Word frequency and lexical diffusion in English stress shifts. In Richard Hogg and Linda van Bergen (eds), *Historical Linguistics 1995*, vol. 2: *Germanic Linguistics.* Amsterdam: Benjamins, 223–32.

Phillips, Betty. 2006. *Word Frequency and Lexical Diffusion.* New York: Palgrave Macmillan.

Pian, Rulan Chao. 1967. *Sonq Dynasty Musical Sources and their Interpretation.* Cambridge, Mass.: Harvard University Press.

Picard, M. and J. Nicol. 1982. Vers un modèle concret de la phonologie des emprunts. *Canadian Journal of Linguistics* 27: 156–69.

Pierrehumbert, Janet. 2001. Exemplar dynamics: word frequency, lenition and contrast. In Joan Bybee and Paul Hopper (eds), *Frequency and the Emergence of Linguistic Structure.* Amsterdam: Benjamins, 137–57.

Pierrehumbert, Janet. 2002. Word-specific phonetics. In Carlos Gussenhoven, Tanya Rietvelt, and Natasha Warner (eds), *Laboratory Phonology 7.* Berlin: Mouton de Gruyter, 101–39.

Pierrehumbert, Janet. 2003a. Phonetic diversity, statistical learning, and acquisition of phonology. *Language and Speech* 46(2–3): 115–54.

Pierrehumbert, Janet. 2003b. Probabilistic phonology: discrimination and robustness. In R. Bod, J. Hay, and S. Jannedy (eds), *Probabilistic Linguistics*. Cambridge, Mass.: MIT Press, 177–228.

Pierrehumbert, Janet. 2006. The next toolkit. *Journal of Phonetics* 34: 516–30.

Pierrehumbert, Janet and Mary Beckman. 1988. *Japanese Tone Structure*. Cambridge, Mass.: MIT Press.

Pike, Kenneth L. 1947. *Phonemics: a Technique for Reducing Languages to Writing*. Ann Arbor: University of Michigan.

Pinker, Steven and Alan Prince. 1988. On language and connectionism: analysis of a parallel distributed processing model of language acquisition. *Cognition* 28: 73–194.

Pisoni, David et al. 1985. Speech perception, word recognition and the structure of the lexicon. *Speech Communication* 4: 75–95.

Pisoni, David, and Susannah Levi 2007. Representations and representational specificity in speech perception and spoken word recognition. In M. Gareth Gaskell (ed.), *Oxford Handbook of Psycholinguistics*. Oxford: Oxford University Press, 3–18.

Pisowicz, Andrzej. 1976. *Le développement du consonantisme arménien*. Wrocław: Zakład Narodowy im Ossolińskich.

Pitt, Mark. 1998. Phonological processes and the perception of phonotactically illegal consonant clusters. *Perception and Psychophysics* 60(6): 941–51.

Pittayawat, Pittayaporn. 2009. The phonology of Proto-Tai. PhD thesis, Cornell University.

Plag, Ingo 1999. *Morphological Productivity: Structural Constraints in English Derivation*. Berlin: Mouton de Gruyter.

Platt, John T. 1975. The Singapore English speech continuum and its basilect 'Singlish' as a 'creoloid'. *Anthropological Linguistics* 17: 363–74.

Pöchtrager, Markus. 2006. The structure of length. PhD thesis, University of Vienna.

Poldauf, Ivan. 1981. The genesis of terminational stress in English. *Lingua* 54: 335–59.

Polinsky, Maria and Olga Kagan. 2007. Heritage languages in the 'wild' and in the classroom. *Language and Linguistics Compass* 1: 368–95.

Pollock, Sheldon. 2006. *The Language of the Gods in the World of Men: Sanskrit, Culture, and Power in Premodern India*. Berkeley: University of California Press.

Pope, Jennifer, Miriam Meyerhoff, and D. Robert Ladd. 2007. Forty years of language change on Martha's Vineyard. *Language* 83: 615–27.

Pope, Mildred K. 1934. *From Latin to Modern French*. Manchester: Manchester University Press.

Pope, Mildred K. 1952. *From Latin to Modern French with Especial Consideration of Anglo-Norman*, 2nd edn. Manchester: Manchester University Press.

Poplack, Shana 1980. Sometimes I'll start a sentence in Spanish y termino en español: toward a typology of code-switching. *Linguistics* 18: 581–618.

Poplack, Shana and Allison V. Lealess. 2011. Methods in the study of lifespan change: revisiting the 'Up' series. Paper presented at 'Methods in Dialectology' 14, London, Ontario, 4 August.

Poplack, Shana, David Sankoff, and Christopher Miller. 1988. The social correlates and linguistic processes of lexical borrowing and assimilation. *Linguistics* 26: 47–104.

Port, Robert and Adam Leary. 2005. Against formal phonology. *Language* 81: 927–64.

Post, Mark. 2011. Prosody and typological drift in Austroasiatic and Tibeto-Burman. In Sophana Srichampa, Paul Sidwell, and Kenneth Gregerson (eds), *Austroasiatic Studies: Papers from the Fourth International Conference on Austroasiatic Linguistics* (*Mon-Khmer Studies Journal*, Special Issue no. 3), 198–221.

Postal, Paul. 1968. *Aspects of Phonological Theory*. New York: Harper and Row.

Pott, August Friedrich. 1833–6. *Etymologische Forschungen auf dem Gebiete der Indo-Germanischen Sprachen mit besonderem Bezug auf die Lautumwandlung im Sanskrit, Griechischen, Lateinischen, Littauischen und Gothischen*. Lemgo: Meyer.

Pouplier, Marianne and Louis Goldstein. 2010. Intention in articulation: articulatory timing of coproduced gestures and its implications for models of speech production. *Language and Cognitive Processes* 25: 616–49.

Premsrirat, Suwilai. 1999. Tonogenesis in Khmu Dialects of SEA. In Graham W. Thurgood (ed.), *Papers from the Ninth Annual Meeting of the Southeast Asian Linguistics Society*. Tempe: Program for Southeast Asia Studies, Arizona State University, 121–34.

Prince, Alan and Paul Smolensky. 1993. *Optimality Theory: Constraint Interaction in Generative Grammar* (Technical Reports of the Rutgers University Center for Cognitive Science, RuCCS-TR-2). New Brunswick, NJ: Rutgers University Center for Cognitive Science. [Also available at: <http://roa.rutgers.edu/files/537-0802/537-0802-PRINCE-0-0.PDF>; published 2004, Oxford: Blackwell.]

Prince, Ellen. 1987. Sara Gorby, Yiddish folksinger: a case study of dialect shift. *International Journal of the Sociology of Language* 61: 83–116.

Prince, Ellen. 1988. Accommodation theory and dialect shift. *Language and Communication* 8: 307–20.

Prokosch, Eduard. 1939. *A Comparative Germanic Grammar*. Baltimore, Md.: Linguistic Society of America.

Przyluski, Jean. 1924. Vietnamien. In Antoine Meillet and Marcel Cohen (eds), *Les langues du monde*. Paris: Champion, 395–96.

Pulleyblank, Edwin G. 1991. *Lexicon of Reconstructed Pronunciation in Early Middle Chinese, Late Middle Chinese, and Early Mandarin*. Vancouver: University of British Columbia Press.

Purcell, E. T., G. Villegas, and S. P. Young. 1978. A before and after for tonogenesis. *Phonetica* 35: 284–93.

Purnell, Thomas. 2008. Pre-velar raising and phonetic conditioning: role of labial and anterior tongue gestures. *American Speech* 83: 373–402.

Purnell, Thomas. 2010. The vowel phonology of urban Southeastern Wisconsin. In Malcah Yaeger-Dror and Erik Thomas (eds), *AAE Speakers and their Participation in Local Sound Changes: a Comparative*. Durham, NC: Duke University Press.

Purnell, Thomas and Eric Raimy. 2013. Contrastive features in phonetic implementation: the English vowel system. Paper presented at the CUNY Phonology Forum Conference on the Feature, CUNY Graduate Center, New York, 16–18 January.

Purnell, Thomas and Eric Raimy. In preparation. Mercian backing without [+back]. MS, University of Wisconsin-Madison.

Purnell, Thomas, Eric Raimy, and Joseph Salmons. 2009. Defining dialect, perceiving dialect and new dialect formation: Sarah Palin's speech. *Journal of English Linguistics,* 37(4): 331–55.

Purnell, Thomas, Eric Raimy, and Joseph Salmons. Forthcoming. *Modularity in Phonology*. Cambridge: Cambridge University Press.

Purnell, Thomas, Joseph Salmons, and Dilara Tepeli. 2005a. German substrate effects in Wisconsin English: evidence for final fortition. *American Speech* 80(2): 135–64.

Purnell, Thomas, Joseph Salmons, Dilara Tepeli, and Jennifer Mercer. 2005b. Structured heterogeneity and change in laryngeal phonetics: upper Midwestern final obstruents. *Journal of English Linguistics* 33(4): 307–38.

Putschke, Wolfgang. 1969. Zur forschungsgeschichtlichen Stellung der junggrammatischen Schule. *Zeitschrift für Dialektologie und Linguistik* 36: 19–48.

Pycha, Anne, Pawel Nowak, Eurie Shin, and Ryan Shosted. 2003. Phonological rule-learning and its implications for a theory of vowel harmony. *Proceedings of the West Coast Conference on Formal Linguistics* 22: 423–35.

Rampton, Ben. 2010. Crossing into class: language ethnicities and class sensibility in England. In C. Llamas and D. Watt (eds), *Language and Identities*. Edinburgh: Edinburgh University Press, 134–43.

Ramsammy, Michael. 2012. Word-final nasal velarisation in Spanish. *Journal of Linguistics* 49(1): 215–55.

Ramsammy, Michael. 2015. The life cycle of phonological processes: accounting for dialectal microtypologies. *Linguistics and Language Compass* 9(1): 33–54.

Rand, M. K., O. Hikosaka, S. Miyachi, X. Lu, and K. Miyashita. 1998. Characteristics of a long-term procedural skill in the monkey. *Experimental Brain Research* 118: 293–97.

Rankin, Robert L. 2005. The comparative method. In Brian D. Joseph, and Richard D. Janda (eds), *The Handbook of Historical Linguistics*. Malden, Mass.: Blackwell, 183–212.

Rapp, Brenda and Matthew Goldrick. 2000. Discreteness and interactivity in spoken word production. *Psychological Review* 107: 460–99.

Rapp, Moriz. 1836–41. *Versuch einer Physiologie der Sprache*. Stuttgart: Cotta.

Rask, Rasmus. 1811. *Vejledning til det Islandske eller gamle Nordiske Sprog*. Copenhagen: Schubothe.

Rask, Rasmus. 1818/1992. *Undersøgelse om det gamle Nordiske eller Islandske Sprogs Oprindelse*. Copenhagen: Gyldendalske Boghandlings Forlag. [Partial translation into German in Uwe Petersen, *Rasmus Kristian Rask. Von der Etymologie überhaupt: eine Einleitung in die Sprachvergleichung*. Tübingen: Narr 1992, 31–80. Excerpt in Winfred P. Lehmann (ed.), *A Reader in Nineteenth-Century Historical Indo-European Linguistics*. Bloomington: Indiana University, 1967: <http://www.utexas.edu/cola/centers/lrc/books/readT.html>.]

Rask, Rasmus. 1830. Review of Jacob Grimm, *Deutsche Grammatik*. *Foreign Review and Continental Miscellany* 5: 493–500.

Rasmussen, Jens Elmegård. 1987. On the status of the aspirated tenues and the Indo-European phonation series. *Acta Linguistica Hafnensia* 20: 81–109. [= *Selected Papers on Indo-European Linguistics* (1999), vol. 1: 216–43.]

Rasmussen, Jens Elmegård. 1999. *Selected Papers on Indo-European Linguistics. With a Section on Comparative Eskimo Linguistics*. 2 vols. Copenhagen: Museum Tusculanum Press.

Ratliff, Martha. 1992. Tone language type change in Africa and Asia: !Xu, Gokana and Mpi. *Diachronica* 9(2): 239–57.

Ratliff, Martha. 2005. Timing tonogenesis: evidence from borrowing. In Patrick Chew (ed.), *Special Session on Tibeto-Burman and Southeast Asian Linguistics, Berkeley Linguistics Society* 28. Berkeley, Calif.: BLS, 29–41.

Ratliff, Martha. 2007. Contrastive vowel length in Mienic: inheritance or diffusion? In Shoichi Iwasaki, Andrew Simpson, Paul Sidwell, and Karen Adams (eds), *Papers from the Thirteenth Annual Meeting of the Southeast Asian Linguistics Society*. Canberra: Pacific Linguistics, 225–31.

Ratliff, Martha. 2010. *Hmong-Mien Language History*. Canberra: Pacific Linguistics.

Raumer, Rudolf von. 1837. *Die Aspiration und die Lautverschiebung: Eine sprachgeschichtliche Untersuchung*. Leipzig: Brockhaus.

Raumer, Rudolf von. 1856. Die sprachgeschichtliche Umwandlung und die naturgeschichtliche Bestimmung der Laute. *Zeitschrift für die Österreichischen Gymnasien* 5: 353–73. [Excerpt in Winfred P. Lehmann (ed.), *A Reader in Nineteenth-Century Historical Indo-European*

Linguistics. Bloomington: Indiana University, 1967. Available at: <http://www.utexas.edu/cola/centers/lrc/books/readT.html>.]

Raumer, Rudolf von. 1870. *Geschichte der germanischen Philologie vorzugsweise in Deutschland*. Munich: Oldenbourg.

Raumolin-Brunberg, Helena. 1996. Apparent time. In T. Nevalainen and H. Raumolin-Brunberg (eds), *Sociolinguistics and Language History: Studies Based on the Corpus of Early English Correspondence*. Amsterdam: Rodopi, 93–109.

Raumolin-Brunberg, Helena. 2009. Lifespan changes in the language of three early modern gentlemen. In A. Nurmi, M. Nevala, and M. Palander-Collin (eds), *The Language of Daily Life in England (1450–1800)*. Amsterdam: Benjamins, 165–96.

Raymond, William, and Esther L. Brown. 2012. Are effects of word frequency effects of context of use? An analysis of initial fricative reduction in Spanish. In S. T. Gries and D. Divjak (eds), *Frequency Effects in Language: Learning and Processing*. Berlin: Mouton de Gruyter, 35–52.

Raymond, William, Robin Dautricourt, and Elizabeth Hume. 2006. Word-internal /t, d/ deletion in spontaneous speech: modeling the effects of extra-linguistic, lexical, and phonological factors. *Language Variation and Change* 18: 55–97.

Recasens, Daniel. 1999. Lingual coarticulation. In W. J. Hardcastle and N. Hewlett (eds), *Coarticulation: Theory, Data and Techniques*. Cambridge: Cambridge University Press, 80–104.

Recasens, Daniel. 2011. Velar and dental stop consonant softening in romance. *Diachronica* 28: 186–224.

Redford, Michael. 2003. Chaucer and Middle English stress. MS, Leiden University.

Reiss, Charles. 2003. Language change without constraint reranking. In D. E. Holt (ed.), *Optimality Theory and Language Change*. Dordrecht: Kluwer Academic, 143–68.

Reiss, Charles. 2006. Morphological change, paradigm leveling, and analogy. In Keith Brown (ed.), *Encyclopedia of Language & Linguistics*, 2nd edn. Amsterdam: Elsevier, 277–8.

Renn, Jennifer. 2011. Patterns of style in the language of African American children and adolescents. In N. Danis, K. Mesh, and H. Sung (eds), *Proceedings of the Boston University Conference on Language Development*. Somerville, Mass.: Cascadilla Press, 513–25.

Repp, Bruno. 1978. Perceptual integration and differentiation of spectral cues for intervocalic stop consonants. *Perception and Psychophysics* 24: 471–85.

Restle, David and Theo Vennemann. 2001. Silbenstruktur. In M. Haspelmath, E. König, W. Oesterreicher, and W. Raible (eds), *Language Typology and Language Universals*, vol. 2. Berlin: Mouton de Gruyter, 1310–36.

Rhodes, Bradley J., Daniel Bullock, Willem B. Verwey, Bruno B. Averbeck, and Michael P. A. Page. 2004. Learning and production of movement sequences: behavioral, neurophysiological, and modeling perspectives. *Human Movement Science* 23: 699–746.

Rhodes, Richard. 2011. Changes in the voice across early adulthood. Paper presented at the International Association for Forensic Phonetics and Acoustics.

Rice, Curt 2006. Norwegian stress and quantity: the implications of loanwords. *Lingua* 116(7): 1171–194.

Rice, Keren. 2003. Featural markedness in phonology: variation. In Lisa Cheng and Rint Sybesma (eds), *The Second GLOT International State-of-the-Article Book*. Berlin: Mouton de Gruyter, 389–430.

Rice, Keren. 2009. Nuancing markedness: a place for contrast. In Eric Raimy and Charles Cairns (eds), *Contemporary Views on Architecture and Representations in Phonology*. Cambridge, Mass.: MIT Press, 311–21.

Rickford, John and Mackenzie Price. 2013. Girlz II women: age-grading, language change, and stylistic variation. *Journal of Sociolinguistics* 17(2): 143–79.

Ringe, Donald A., Jr. 1992. *On Calculating the Factor of Chance in Language Comparison*. Philadelphia: American Philosophical Society.

Ringe, Donald A., Jr. 1993. A reply to Professor Greenberg. *Proceedings of the American Philosophical Society* 137: 91–109.

Ringe, Donald A., Jr. 1996a. The mathematics of 'Amerind'. *Diachronica* 13: 135–54.

Ringe, Donald A., Jr. 1996b. *On the Chronology of Sound Changes in Tocharian*, vol. 1: *From Proto-Indo-European to Proto-Tocharian*. New Haven, Conn.: American Oriental Society.

Ringe, Donald A., Jr, Tandy Warnow, and Ann Taylor. 2002. Indo-European and computational cladistics. *Transactions of the Philological Society* 100: 59–129.

Ringen, Catherine O. and Robert M. Vago. 2011. Geminates: heavy or long? In Charles Cairns and Eric Raimy (eds), *Handbook of the Syllable*. Leiden: Brill, 155–72.

Rissanen, Matti et al. 1991. *The Helsinki Corpus of English Texts*. Department of English, University of Helsinki.

Ritt, Nikolaus. 1994. *Quantity Adjustment: Vowel Lengthening and Shortening in Early Middle English*. Cambridge: Cambridge University Press.

Ritt, Nikolaus. 2004. *Selfish Sounds and Linguistic Evolution: a Darwinian Approach to Language Change*. Cambridge: Cambridge University Press.

Rivierre, Jean-Claude. 1993. Tonogenesis in New Caledonia. In Jerry Edmondson and Kenneth Gregerson (eds), *Tonality in Austronesian Languages*. Honolulu: University of Hawai'i Press, 155–73.

Rivierre, Jean-Claude. 2001. Tonogenesis and evolution of the tonal systems in New Caledonia: the example of Cèmuhî. In Shigeki Kaji (ed.), *Proceedings of the Symposium Cross-Linguistic Studies of Tonal Phenomena: Tonogenesis, Japanese Accentology, and Other Topics*. Tokyo: Institute for the Study of Languages and Cultures of Asia and Africa, Tokyo University of Foreign Studies, 23–42.

Roberge, Paul T. 2002. Afrikaans: considering origins. In Rajend Mesthrie (ed.), *Language in South Africa*. Cambridge: Cambridge University Press, 79–103.

Robert, Gruffyd. 1567. *A Welsh Grammar and Other Tracts*. Facsimile reprint published as supplement to the *Revue celtique*, 1870–1883. Paris: Vieweg.

Roberts, Jane. 2005. *Guide to Scripts Used in English Writings up to 1500*. London: British Library.

Roberts, Julie. 1993. The acquisition of variable rules: *t, d* deletion and *-ing* production in preschool children. PhD thesis, University of Pennsylvania.

Roberts, Julie and William Labov. 1995. Learning to talk Philadelphian: acquisition of short *a* by preschool children. *Language Variation and Change* 7: 101–12.

Roberts, Julie. 2002. Child language variation. In Jack K. Chambers, Peter Trudgill, and Natalie Schilling-Estes (eds), *The Handbook of Language Variation and Change*. Oxford: Blackwell, 333–48.

Roberts, Philip. 2012. Towards a computer model of the historical phonology and morphology of Latin. PhD thesis, Oxford University.

Robins, Robert H. 1978. The neogrammarians and their nineteenth-century predecessors. *Transactions of the Philological Society* 76(1): 1–16.

Robinson, Orrin Warner. 1976. A 'scattered' rule in Swiss German. *Language* 52: 148–62.

Roca, Iggy. 2005. Strata, yes, structure-preservation, no. In Twan Geerts, Ivo van Ginneken, and Haike Jacobs (eds), *Romance Languages and Linguistic Theory*. Amsterdam: Benjamins.

Roeder, Rebecca and Matt Hunt Gardner. 2013. The phonology of the Canadian Shift revisited: Thunder Bay and Cape Breton. *University of Pennsylvania Working Papers in Linguistics (Selected Papers from NWAV 41)* 19(2): 161–70.

Rohany Rahbar, Elham. 2008. A historical study of the Persian vowel system. *Kansas Working Papers in Linguistics* 30: 233–45.

Romaine, Suzanne. 1982. *Socio-historical Linguistics: its Status and Methodology*. Cambridge: Cambridge University Press.

Romeo, Luigi. 1968. *The Economy of Diphthongization in Early Romance*. The Hague: Mouton de Gruyter.

Ronquist, Fredrik, John P. Huelsenbeck, and Paul van der Mark, Paul. 2005. MrBayes 3.1 manual. Available at: <http://mrbayes.sourceforge.net>

Rose, Y. and K. Demuth. 2006. Vowel epenthesis in loanword adaptation: representational and phonetic considerations. *Lingua* 116(7): 1112–39.

Ross, Alan S. C. 1950. Philological probability problems. *Journal of the Royal Statistical Society, series B (Methodological)* 12(1).

Rothman, Jason. 2008. Why all counter-evidence to the critical period hypothesis in second language acquisition is not equal or problematic. *Language and Linguistics Compass* 2: 1063–88.

Rothman, Jason. 2009. Understanding the nature and outcomes of early bilingualism: Romance languages as heritage languages. *International Journal of Bilingualism* 13: 155–63.

Rubach, Jerzy. 2000. Backness switch in Russian. *Phonology* 17, 39–64.

Rumelhart, David E. and James L. McClelland. 1986. On learning the past tenses of English verbs. In David E. Rumelhart and James L. McClelland (eds), *Parallel Distributed Processing: Explorations in the Microstructure of Cognition*, vol. 1. Cambridge, Mass.: Bradford, 216–71.

Rumpelt, Hermann B. 1869. *Das natürliche System der Sprachlaute*. Halle: Waisenhaus.

Russell, Paul. 1995. *An Introduction to the Celtic Languages*. New York: Longman.

Sachs, Jacqueline, Philip Lieberman, and Donna Erickson. 1973. Anatomical and cultural determinants of male and female speech. In Roger Shuy and Ralph W. Fasold (eds), *Language Attitudes: Current Trends and Prospects*. Washington DC: Georgetown University Press, 74–84.

Sagey, Elizabeth. 1986. The representation of features and relations in nonlinear phonology. PhD thesis, Massachusetts Institute of Technology.

Saitou, Naruya, and Masastoshi Nei. 1987. The neighbor-joining method: a new method for reconstructing phylogenetic trees. *Molecular Biology and Evolution* 4(4): 406–25.

Sajnovics, János. 1770. *Demonstratio: Idioma ungarorum et lapponum idem esse*. Copenhagen: Typis Orphanotropii Regii. [Repr. 1968, Bloomington: Indiana University.]

Salmons, Joe. 1992a. *Accentual Change and Language Contact: Comparative Survey and a Case Study of Early Northern Europe*. Stanford, Calif.: Stanford University Press.

Salmons, Joe. 1992b. Diachronic typology and tone-to-stress shift. *Journal of Indo-European Studies* 20(3–4): 269–81.

Salmons, Joseph C. 1992c. A look at the data for a global etymology: *tik 'finger'. In Gary W. Davis, and Gregory K. Iverson (eds), *Explanation in Historical Linguistics*. Amsterdam: Benjamins, 207–28.

Salmons, Joseph C. 1993. *The Glottalic Theory: Survey and Synthesis*. McLean, VAa.: Institute for the Study of Man.

Salmons, Joseph. 2010. Segmental phonological change. In Vit Bubenik and Silvia Luraghi (eds), *The Continuum Companion to Historical Linguistics*. London: Continuum, 89–105.

Salmons, Joseph, Robert Fox, and Ewa Jacewicz. 2012. Prosodic skewing of input and the initiation of cross-generational sound change. In Maria-Josep Solé and Daniel Recasens (eds), *The Initiation of Sound Change: Perception, Production, and Social Factors*. Amsterdam: Benjamins, 167–84.

Samarin, William J. 1971. Salient and substantive pidginization. In Dell Hymes (ed). *Pidginization and Creolization of Languages*. Cambridge: Cambridge University Press, 117–40.

Sammallahti, Pekka. 1988. Historical phonology of the Uralic languages. In Denis Sinor (ed.), *The Uralic Languages*. Leiden: Brill, 478–554.

Sampson, Geoffrey. 1985. *Writing Systems: a Linguistic Introduction*. London: Hutchinson.

San Giacomo, Marcela 2009. La présence de l'espagnol en Nahuatl: une étude sociolinguistique des adaptations et non-adaptations des emprunts. PhD thesis, Université Paris VIII, Saint-Denis.

Sancier, Michele L. and Carol A. Fowler. 1997. Gestural drift in a bilingual speaker of Brazilian Portuguese and English. *Journal of Phonetics* 25: 421–36.

Sanders, Robert Nathaniel. 2003. Opacity and sound change in the Polish lexicon. PhD thesis, University of California Santa Cruz.

Sankoff, David. 1988. Sociolinguistics and syntactic variation. In F. J. Newmeyer (ed.), *Linguistics: the Cambridge Survey*. Cambridge: Cambridge University Press, 140–61.

Sankoff, David and Suzanne Laberge. 1978. The linguistic market and the statistical explanation of variability. In David Sankoff (ed.), *Linguistic Variation: Models and Methods*. New York: Academic Press, 239–50.

Sankoff, David and Réjean Lessard. 1975. Vocabulary richness: a sociolinguistic analysis. *Science* 190: 689–90.

Sankoff, David and Gillian Sankoff. 1973. Sample survey methods and computer assisted analysis in the study of grammatical variation. In R. Darnell (ed.), *Canadian Languages in Their Social Context*, Edmonton: Linguistic Research, 7–64.

Sankoff, Gillian. 2001. Linguistic outcomes of language contact. In J. K. Chambers, Peter Trudgill, and Natalie Schilling-Estes (eds), *Handbook of Sociolinguistics*. Oxford: Blackwell, 638–68.

Sankoff, Gillian. 2004. Adolescents, young adults and the critical period: two case studies from 'Seven Up'. In C. Fought (ed.), *Sociolinguistic Variation: Critical Reflections*. Oxford: Oxford University Press, 121–39.

Sankoff, Gillian. 2005. Cross-sectional and longitudinal studies in sociolinguistics. In U. Ammon, N. Dittmar, K. J. Mattheier, and P. Trudgill (eds), *An International Handbook of the Science of Language and Society*, vol. 2. Berlin: Mouton de Gruyter, 1003–13.

Sankoff, Gillian. 2006. Age: apparent time and real time. In Keith Brown (ed.), *Elsevier Encyclopedia of Language and Linguistics*, 2nd edn. Amsterdam: Elsevier, 110–16.

Sankoff, Gillian. 2013. Linguistic outcomes of bilingualism. In J.K. Chambers and Natalie Schilling-Estes (eds), *The Handbook of Language Variation and Change*. Malden, Mass.: John Wiley & Sons, 501–18.

Sankoff, Gillian and Hélène Blondeau. 2007. Language change across the lifespan: /r/ in Montreal French. *Language* 83: 560–88.

Sankoff, Gillian, Hélène Blondeau, and Anne Charity. 2001. Individual roles in a real-time change: Montreal (r > R) 1947–1995. *Etudes et travaux* 4: 141–57.

Sankoff, Gillian, and Suzanne Evans Wagner. 2006. Age grading in retrograde movement: the inflected future in Montréal French. In M. L. Friesner and M. Ravindranath (eds), *University of Pennsylvania Working Papers in Linguistics* 12(2): 1–14.

Sano, Shin-ichiro. 2009. The roles of internal and external factors and the mechanism of analogical leveling: variationist and probabilistic OT approach to ongoing language change in Japanese voice system. PhD thesis, Sophia University.

Sapir, Edward. 1915. Notes on Judeo-German phonology. *Jewish Quarterly Review* 6: 231–66.

Sapir, Edward. 1921. *Language*. New York: Harcourt Brace.

Sapir, Edward. 1925. Sound patterns in language. *Language* 1: 37–51.

Saussure, Ferdinand de. 1879. *Mémoire sur le système primitif des voyelles dans les langues indo-européennes*. Leipzig: Teubner. [Repr. 1968, Hildesheim: Olms.]

Saussure, Ferdinand de. 1916. *Cours de linguistique générale*, ed. Charles Bally and Albert Sechehaye. Lausanne: Payot. [Trans. Wade Baskin, *Course in General Linguistics*. New York: Philosophical Library, 1959, and republished in 1974, London: Fontana, and also reprinted 1995.]

Saussure, Ferdinand de. 1993. *Saussure's Third Course of Lectures on General Linguistics, 1910–1911*, ed. and trans. E. Kimatsu and Roy Harris. Oxford: Pergamon.

Scarborough, Rebecca Anne. 2004. Coarticulation and the structure of the lexicon. PhD thesis, University of California, Los Angeles.

Scarborough, Rebecca. 2010. Lexical and contextual predictability: confluent effects on the production of vowels. In Cécile Fougeron, Barbara Kuehner, Mariapaola Imperio, and Nathalie Vallée (eds), *Laboratory Phonology* 10. Berlin: Mouton de Gruyter, 557–86.

Schabert, Peter. 1976. *Laut- und Formenlehre des Maltesischen anhand zweier Mundarten*. Erlangen: Palm & Enke.

Schadeberg, Thilo C. 2009. Loanwords in Swahili. In Martin Haspelmath and Uri Tadmor (eds), *Loanwords in the World's Languages: a Comparative Handbook*. Berlin: Mouton de Gruyter, 76–102.

Schane, Sanford. 1984. The fundamentals of Particle Phonology. *Phonology Yearbook* 1: 129–55.

Schane, Sanford. 2005. The aperture particle /a/: its role and functions. In Philip Carr, Jacques Durand, and Colin Ewen (eds). *Headhood, Elements, Specification and Contrastivity*. Amsterdam: Benjamins.

Scheer, Tobias. 2004a. *A Lateral Theory of Phonology*, vol. 1: *What is CVCV, and Why Should It Be?* Berlin: Mouton de Gruyter.

Scheer, Tobias. 2004b. En quoi la phonologie est vraiment différente. *Corpus* 3: 5–84.

Scheer, Tobias. 2010. What OT is, and what it is not: review of Paul de Lacy (ed.), *The Cambridge Handbook of Phonology. Journal of Linguistics* 46(1): 193–218.

Scheer, Tobias. 2011a. Aspects of the development of generative phonology. In Bert Botma, Nancy C. Kula, and Kuniya Nasukawa (eds), *The Continuum Companion to Phonology*. New York: Continuum, 397–446.

Scheer, Tobias. 2011b. *A Guide to Morphosyntax-Phonology Interface Theories: How Extra-Phonological Information is Treated in Phonology since Trubetzkoy's Grenzsignale.* Berlin: Mouton de Gruyter.

Scheer, Tobias 2012. Melody-free syntax and two phonologies. Paper presented at the annual conference of the Réseau Français de Phonologie (RFP), Paris, 25–7 June.

Schenker, Alexander M. 2002. Proto-Slavonic. In Bernard Cmrie and Greville G. Corbett (eds), *The Slavonic Languages.* London: Routledge, 60–121.

Scherer, Wilhelm. 1868. *Zur Geschichte der deutschen Sprache.* Berlin: Duncker.

Schleicher, August. 1861–2. *Compendium der vergleichenden Grammatik der indogermanis-chen Sprachen: kurzer Abriss einer Laut- und Formenlehre der indogermanischen Ursprache, des Altindischen, Alteranischen, Altgriechischen, Altitalischen, Altkeltischen, Altslawischen, Litauischen und Altdeutschen.* Weimar: Böhlau.

Schleicher, August. 1868. Eine Fabel in der indogermanischen Ursprache. *Beiträge zur ver-gleichenden Sprachforschung* 5: 206–8.

Schleicher, August. 1971 [1861]. Some observations made on children. In Aaron Bar-Adon and Werner F. Leopold (eds), *Child Language: a Book of Readings.* Englewood Cliffs: Prentice-Hall, 19–20.

Schmidt, Johannes 1872. *Die Verwandtschaftsverhältnisse der indogermanischen Sprachen.* Weimar: Böhlau.

Schneider, Edgar W. 2007. *Postcolonial English: Varieties Around the World.* Cambridge: Cambridge University Press.

Schreier, Daniel. 2002. *Terra incognita* in the Anglophone world: Tristan da Cunha, South Atlantic Ocean. *English World-Wide* 23: 1–29.

Schreier, Daniel. 2003. *Isolation and Language Change: Sociohistorical and Contemporary Evidence from Tristan da Cunha English.* Basingstoke: Palgrave Macmillan.

Schreier, Daniel. 2005. *Consonant Change in English Worldwide: Synchrony Meets Diachrony.* Basingstoke: Palgrave Macmillan.

Schreier, Daniel. 2008. *St Helenian English: Origins, Evolution and Variation.* Amsterdam: Benjamins.

Schreier, Daniel. 2009. Language in isolation, and its implications for variation and change. *Blackwell Language and Linguistics Compass* 3.

Schreier, Daniel. 2012. The impact of migratory movements on linguistic systems: trans-planted speech communities and varieties from a historical sociolinguistic perspective. In J. M. Hernández-Campoy and J. Camilo Conde-Sylvestre (eds), *The Handbook of Historical Sociolinguistics.* Oxford: Wiley-Blackwell, 534–51.

Schreier, Daniel, Elizabeth Gordon, Jennifer Hay, and Margaret Maclagan. 2003. The regional and sociolinguistic dimension of /hw-/ maintenance and loss in early 20th century New Zealand English. *English World-Wide* 24: 245–69.

Schreier, Daniel and Marianne Hundt, eds. 2013. *English as a Contact Language.* Cambridge: Cambridge University Press.

Schreier, Daniel and Karen Lavarello-Schreier. 2003. *Tristan da Cunha: History, People, Language.* London: Battlebridge.

Schrijver, Peter. 2009. Celtic influence on Old English: phonological and phonetic evidence. *English Language and Linguistics* 13(2): 193–211.

Schuchardt, Hugo. 1885. [repr. and trans. 1972]. On sound laws: against the neogrammarians. In Theo Vennemann and Terence H. Wilbur (eds), *Schuchardt, the Neogrammarians, and the Transformational Theory of Phonological Change: Four Essays.* Frankfurt: Athenäum, 39–72.

Schuessler, Axel. 2009. *Minimal Old Chinese and Later Han Chinese: a Companion to [Karlgren's] 'Grammata serica recensa'.* Honolulu: University of Hawai'i Press.

Schuh, Russell G. 2003. Chadic overview. In M. Lionel Bender, Gábor Takàcs, and David L. Appleyard (eds), *Selected Historical-Comparative Afrasian Linguistic Studies: in Memory of Igor M. Diakonoff*. Munich: Lincom, 55–60.

Schulze, Jan Henning. 2010. *Der i-Umlaut im Althochdeutschen: Theorie, Phonetik und Typologie sowie eine Optimalitätstheoretische Analyse*. Bamberg: University of Bamberg Press.

Schütz, Albert J. 1985. *The Fijian Language*. Honolulu: University of Hawai'i Press.

Scott, N. C. 1957. Notes on the pronunciation of Sea Dayak. *Bulletin of the School of Oriental and African Studies* 20: 509–12.

Sebregts, Koen and Patrycja Strycharczuk. 2012. Phonetically gradient allomorphy: the case of the Dutch past tense. Paper given at the 20th Manchester Phonology Meeting, 24 May. Available at: <http://personalpages.manchester.ac.uk/staff/patrycja.strycharczuk/CV_files/20mfmslides.pdf>

Ségéral, Phillippe and Tobias Scheer. 2008. Positional factors in lenition and fortition. In Joaquim Brandão de Carvalho, Tobias Scheer, Philippe Ségéral (eds) *Lenition and Fortition*. Berlin: Mouton de Gruyter, 131–72.

Séguy, Jean. 1971. La relation entre la distance spatiale et la distance lexicale. *Revue de linguistique romane* 35: 335–57.

Seidl, Amanda and Eugene Buckley. 2005. On the learning of arbitrary phonological rules. *Language Learning and Development* 1: 289–316.

Selinker, Larry. 1972. Interlanguage. *International Review of Applied Linguistics* 10: 209–31.

Selkirk, Elisabeth. 1980a. Prosodic domains in phonology: Sanskrit revisited. In Mark Aronoff and Mary-Louise Kean (eds), *Juncture*. Saratoga, Calif.: Anma Libri, 107–129.

Selkirk, Elisabeth. 1980b. The role of prosodic categories in English word stress. *Linguistic Inquiry* 11: 563–605.

Selkirk, Elisabeth 1982. Syllables. In H. van der Hulst and N. Smith (eds), *The Structure of Phonological Representations*, vol. 2. Dordrecht: Foris, 337–83.

Selkirk, Elisabeth. 1984. On the major class features and syllable theory. In Mark Aronoff and R. T. Oehrle (eds), *Language Sound Structure*. Cambridge, Mass.: MIT Press, 107–36.

Shapp, Allison, Nathan LaFave, and John Victor Singler. 2014. Ginsburg v. Ginsburg: a longitudinal study of regional features in a Supreme Court justice's speech. *University of Pennsylvania Working Papers in Linguistics* 20(2): 149–58.

Shevelov, George Y. 1964. *A Prehistory of Slavic: the Historical Phonology of Common Slavic*. Heidelberg: Winter.

Sharma, Devyani. 2011. Style repertoire and social change in British Asian English. *Journal of Sociolinguistics* 15: 464–92.

Shih, Chi-lin. 1985. From tonal to accentual: Fuzhou tone sandhi revisited. In *Proceedings of the Eleventh Annual Meeting of the Berkeley Linguistics Society*, 316–26.

Shinohara, Shigeko 2006. Perceptual effects in final cluster reduction patterns. *Lingua* 116(7): 1046–78.

Shockey, Linda. 1984. All in a flap: long-term accommodation in phonology. *International Journal of the Sociology of Language* 46: 87–96.

Shockley, Kevin, Laura Sabadini, and Carol Fowler. 2004. Imitation in shadowing words. *Perception and Psychophysics* 66(3): 422–9.

Short, David. 2002. Czech. In Bernard Comrie and Greville G. Corbett (eds), *The Slavonic Languages*. London: Routledge, 455–532.

Siegel, Dorothy C. 1974. Topics in English morphology. PhD thesis, MIT.

Siegel, Jeff. 1985. Koines and koineisation. *Language in Society* 14: 357–78.

Siegel, Jeff. 1987. *Language Contact in a Plantation Environment*. Cambridge: Cambridge University Press.

Sievers, Eduard. 1876. *Grundzüge der Lautphysiologie zur Einführung in das Studium der Lautlehre der indogermanischen Sprachen*. Leipzig: Breitkopf & Härtel. [2nd edn, 1881 *Grundzüge der Phonetik zur Einführung in das Studium der Lautlehre der indogermanischen Sprachen*; 3rd edn, 1885; 4th edn, 1893; 5th edn, 1901.]

Sievers, Eduard. 1901/1967. Foundations of phonetics. In W. Lehmann (ed.), *A Reader in Nineteenth Century Historical Indo-European Linguistics*. Bloomington: Indiana University Press, 258–66 [translated excerpt from 5th edn of Sievers 1876.].

Sihler, Andrew L. 1995. *New Comparative Grammar of Greek and Latin*. Oxford: Oxford University Press.

Silverman, Daniel. 1992. Multiple scansions in loanword phonology. *Phonology* 9: 289–328.

Silverman, Daniel. 2003. On the rarity of pre-aspirated stops. *Journal of Linguistics* 39: 575–98.

Silverman, Daniel. 2010. Neutralization and anti-homophony in Korean. *Journal of Linguistics* 46(2): 453–82.

Silverman, Daniel. 2012. Mikołaj Kruszewski: theory and vision. *Language and Linguistics Compass* 6(6): pt 1: 6(6): 330–42; pt 2: 6(5): 296–309.

Simon, Ellen. 2011. Laryngeal stop systems in contact: connecting present-day acquisition findings and historical contact hypotheses. *Diachronica* 28: 225–54.

Simpson, Andrew. 2009. The origin and development of nonconcatenative morphology. PhD thesis, University of California, Berkeley.

Singh, Rajendra (ed.). 1994. *Trubetzkoy's Orphan: Proceedings of the Montréal Roundtable 'Morphonology: Contemporary Responses'*. Amsterdam: Benjamins.

Singh, R. and P. Muysken. 1995. Wanted: a debate in pidgin/creole phonology. *Journal of Pidgin and Creole Languages* 10: 157–69.

Skousen, Royal. 1989. *Analogical Modeling of Language*. Boston: Kluwer.

Slade, Benjamin. 2003. How to rank constraints: constraint conflict, grammatical competition, and the rise of periphrastic do. In D. Eric Holt (ed.), *Optimality Theory and Language Change*. Dordrecht: Kluwer Academic, 337–85.

Smith, Jennifer L. 2006. Loan phonology is not all perception: evidence from Japanese loan doublets. In T. J. Vance (ed.), *Japanese/Korean Linguistics*, vol. 14. Stanford, Calif.: CSLI, 63–74.

Smith, Jennifer, Mercedes Durham, and Liane Fortune. 2007. Community, caregiver and child in the acquisition of variation in a Scottish dialect. *Language Variation and Change* 19: 63–99.

Smith, Jeremy J. 2009. *Old English: a Linguistic Introduction*. Cambridge: Cambridge University Press.

Smith, Kenny, Simon Kirby, and Henry Brighton. 2003. Iterative learning: a framework for the emergence of language. *Artificial Life* 9: 371–86.

Smith, Laura Catharine. 2004. Cross-level interactions in West Germanic phonology and morphology. PhD thesis, University of Wisconsin-Madison.

Smith, Laura Catharine. 2007a. Old Frisian vowel balance and its relationship to West Germanic apocope and syncope. In Rolf H. Bremmer, Jr, Stephen Laker, and Oebele Vries (eds), *Advances in Old Frisian Philology*. Amsterdam: Rodopi, 379–410.

Smith, Laura Catharine. 2007b. The resilience of prosodic templates in the history of West Germanic. In Joseph C. Salmons and Shannon Dubenion-Smith (eds), *Historical Linguistics*

2005: Selected papers from the 17th International Conference on Historical Linguistics. Amsterdam: Benjamins, 351–65.

Smith, Laura Catharine. 2009. Dialect variation and the Dutch diminutive: loss, maintenance and extension of prosodic templates. In Monique Dufresne, Fernande Dupuis, and Etleva Vocaj (eds), *Historical Linguistics 2007.* Amsterdam: Benjamins, 37–46.

Smith, Laura Catharine and Bryant Pulsipher. 2008. Gemination and the reinterpretation of light stems as heavy in Old High German *jan*-verbs. Paper presented at Germanic Linguistics Annual Conference, University of Wisconsin-Madison, April.

Smith, Neil V. 1973. *The Acquisition of Phonology: a Case Study.* Cambridge: Cambridge University Press.

Smith, Raoul N. 1969. Automatic simulation of historical change. In *Proceedings of the 1969 Conference on Computational Linguistics, Sång-Säby, Sweden.* Morristown, NJ: Association for Computational Linguistics, 1–14.

Smolensky, Paul. 2006. Computational levels and integrated connectionist/symbolic explanation. In Paul Smolensky and Géraldine Legendre (eds), *The Harmonic Mind: From Neural Computation to Optimality-Theoretic Grammar,* vol. 2. Cambridge, Mass.: MIT Press, 503–92.

Snow, David. 1998. A prominence account of syllable reduction in early speech development: the child's prosodic phonology of tiger and giraffe. *Journal of Speech, Language, and Hearing Research* 41: 1171–84.

Solé, Maria-Josep. 1992. Phonetic and phonological processes: the case of nasalization. *Language and Speech* 35(1-2): 29–43.

Solé, Maria-Josep. 1995. Spatio-temporal patterns of velo-pharyngeal action in phonetic and phonological nasalization. *Language and Speech* 38(1): 1–23.

Solé, Maria-Josep. 1999. The phonetic basis of phonological structure: the role of aerodynamic factors. In *Proceedings of the Congress of Experimental Phonetics.* Tarragona, 77–94.

Solé, Maria-Josep. 2002a. Aerodynamic characteristics of trills and phonological patterning. *Journal of Phonetics* 30: 655–88.

Solé, Maria-Josep. 2002b. Assimilatory processes and aerodynamic factors. In C. Gussenhoven and N. Warner (eds), *Papers in Laboratory Phonology 7.* Berlin: Mouton de Gruyter, 351–86.

Solé, Maria-Josep. 2007. Controlled and mechanical properties in speech: a review of the literature. In M.-J. Solé, P. Beddor, and M. Ohala (eds), *Experimental Approaches to Phonology.* Oxford: Oxford University Press, 302–21.

Solé, Maria-Josep. 2009. Acoustic and aerodynamic factors in the interaction of features: the case of nasality and voicing. In M. J. F. Marina, Cláudia Vigário, and Sónia Frota (eds), *Phonetics and Phonology: Interactions and Interrelations.* Amsterdam: Benjamins, 205–34.

Solé, Maria-Joseph. 2010. Effects of syllable position on sound change: an aerodynamic study of final fricative weakening. *Journal of Phonetics* 38: 289–305.

Sóskuthy, Márton. 2011. Why phonologists should care about exemplar theory. Paper given at the 19th Manchester Phonology Meeting, 19 May. Available at: <http://www.lel.ed.ac.uk/~so954634/soskuthy11_mfm19.zip>

Sóskuthy, Marton. 2013. Phonetic biases and systemic effects in the actuation of sound change. PhD thesis, University of Edinburgh.

Speyer, Augustin. 2009. On the change of word stress in the history of German. *Beiträge zur Geschichte der deutschen Sprache und Literatur* 133: 413–41.

Sproat, Richard and Osamu Fujimura. 1993. Allophonic variation in English /l/ and its implications for phonetic implementation. *Journal of Phonetics* 21: 291–311.

746 REFERENCES

Stampe, David. 1969. The acquisition of phonetic representation. In Robert I. Binnick, Alice Davison, Georgia M. Green, and Jerry L. Morgan (eds), *Papers from the Fifth Regional Meeting of the Chicago Linguistic Society*, 443–54. Chicago: University of Chicago, Chicago Linguistic Society. [Repr. in *A Dissertation on Natural Phonology*. New York: Garland/ Bloomington: Indiana University Linguistics Club.]

Stampe, David. 1969–72/1979. How I spent my summer vacation: a dissertation on natural phonology. PhD thesis, University of Chicago. [Repr. 1979 with 'The acquisition of phonetic representation' and 'Afterthoughts' as *A Dissertation on Natural Phonology*. New York: Garland/Bloomington: Indiana University Linguistics Club.]

Stampe, David. 1987. On phonological representation. In Wolfgang U. Dressler, Hans C. Luschützky, Oskar E. Pfeiffer, and John Rennison (eds), *Phonologica 1984*. Cambridge: Cambridge University Press, 287–300.

Stanley, Richard. 1967. Redundancy rules in phonology. *Language* 43(2): 393–436.

Stark, Rachel E. 1980. Stages of speech development in the first year of life. In Grace Yeni-Komshian, James F. Kavanagh, and Charles A. Ferguson (eds), *Child Phonology*, vol. 1: *Production*. New York: Academic Press, 73–92.

Starostin, Sergei. 1991. *Алтайская проблема и происхождение японского языка* [The Altaic problem and the origin of Japanese]. Moscow: Nauka.

Steels, Luc. 2000. Language as a complex adaptive system. In M. Shoenauer (ed.), *Proceedings of PPSN VI*. Berlin: Springer, 17–26.

Steiner, Richard. 2007. Variation, simplifying assumptions and the history of spirantization in Aramaic and Hebrew. In Aharon Maman, Shemu'el Fasberg, and Yoḥanan Broyar (eds), *Sha'are Lashon: Festschrift for Moshe Bar Asher*. Jerusalem: Mossad Bialik, 52–65.

Steiner, Richard C. 1998. Ancient Hebrew. In Robert Hetzron (ed.), *The Semitic Languages*. London: Routledge, 145–73.

Stemberger, Joseph Paul and Brian MacWhinney. 1988. Are inflected forms stored in the lexicon? In M. Hammond and M. Noonan (eds), *Theoretical Morphology*. New York: Academic Press, 101–16.

Steriade, Donca. 2000. Paradigm uniformity and the phonetics–phonology boundary. In Michael Broe and Janet Pierrehumbert (eds), *Papers in Laboratory Phonology 5*. Cambridge: Cambridge University Press, 313–34.

Steriade, Donca. 2001a. The phonology of perceptibility effects: the P-map and its consequences for constraint organization. MS, University of California at Los Angeles.

Steriade, Donca. 2001b. Directional asymmetries in place assimilation. In E. Hume and K. Johnson (eds), *The Role of Speech Perception in Phonology*. San Diego, Calif.: Academic Press, 219–50.

Stevens, Alan M. 1966. The Madurese reflexes of Proto-Malayopolynesian. *Journal of the American Oriental Society* 86: 147–56.

Stevens, Alan M. 1968. *Madurese Phonology and Morphology*. New Haven, Conn.: American Oriental Series.

Stevens, Kenneth. 1972. The quantal nature of speech: evidence from articulatory-acoustic data. In P. B. Denes and E. E. Davids (eds), *Human Communication: a Unified View*. New York: McGraw-Hill, 51–6.

Stevens, Kenneth. 1998. *Acoustic Phonetics*. Cambridge, Mass.: MIT Press.

Stevens, Kenneth N. and Sheila Blumstein. 1981. The search for invariant acoustic correlates of phonetic features. In P. D. Eimas and J. L. Miller (eds), *Perspectives on the Study of Speech*. Hillsdale, NJ: Erlbaum, 1–38.

Stevens, Kenneth N. and Samuel Jay Keyser. 1989. Primary features and their enhancement in consonants. *Language* 65: 81–106.

Stevens, Kenneth N., Samuel Jay Keyser, and Haruko Kawasaki. 1986. Toward a phonetic and phonological theory of redundant features. In Joseph S. Perkell and Dennis H. Klatt (eds), *Symposium on Invariance and Variability of Speech Processes*. Hillsdale, NJ: Erlbaum, 432–69.

Stewart, John M. 1989. Kwa. In John Bendor-Samuel (ed.), *The Niger-Congo Languages: a Classification and Description of Africa's Largest Language Family*. Lanham, Md.: University Press of America, 216–45.

Stewart, John M. 1993. The second Tano consonant shift and its likeness to Grimm's Law. *Journal of West African Languages* 23: 3–39.

Stewart, Mary E. and Mitsuhiko Ota. 2008. Lexical effects on speech perception in individuals with 'autistic' traits. *Cognition* 109: 157–62.

Stockwell, Robert P. 1968. Mirrors in the history of English pronunciation. In E. Bagby Atwood and Archibald A. Hill (eds), *Studies in Language, Literature, and Culture of the Middle Ages and Later*. Austin: University of Texas Press, 20–37.

Stockwell, Robert. 1978. Perseverance in the English vowel shift. In Jacek Fisiak (ed.), *Recent Developments in Historical Phonology*. The Hague: Mouton, 337–48.

Stockwell, Robert P. and C. Westbrook Barritt. 1955. The Old English short di-graphs: some considerations. *Language* 31: 372–89.

Stockwell, Robert P. and C. Westbrook Barritt. 1961. Scribal practice: some assumptions. *Language* 37(1): 75–82. [Repr. in Roger Lass (ed.), *Approaches to English Historical Linguistics*, New York: Holt, Rinehart and Winston, 1969, 133–42.]

Stockwell, Robert and Donka Minkova. 1997. On drifts and shifts. *Studia Anglica Posnaniensia* 31: 283–303.

Stoel-Gammon, Carol. 1992. Prelinguistic vocal development: measurement and predictions. In Charles A. Ferguson, Lise Menn, and Carol Stoel-Gammon (eds), *Phonological Development: Models, Research, Implications*. Timonium, Md.: York Press, 439–56.

Storkel, Holly L. 2001. Learning new words: phonotactic probability in language development. *Journal of Speech, Language, and Hearing Research* 44: 1321–37.

Strand, Elizabeth A. 1999. Uncovering the role of gender stereotypes in speech perception. *Journal of Language and Psychology* 18: 86–99.

Strand, Elizabeth A. and Keith Johnson. 1996. Gradient and visual speaker normalization in the perception of fricatives. In D. Gibbon (ed.), *Natural Language Processing and Speech Technology*. Berlin: Mouton, 14–26.

Strycharczuk, Patrycja. 2012. Phonetics–phonology interactions in pre-sonorant voicing. PhD thesis, University of Manchester. Available at: <http://ling.auf.net/lingbuzz/001645>

Stuart-Smith, Jane. 1999. Glottals past and present: a study of t-glottaling in Glaswegian. In C. Upton and K. Wales (eds), *Leeds Studies in English*. Leeds: University of Leeds, 181–204.

Stuart-Smith, Jane. 2004. *Phonetics and Philology: Sound Change in Italic*. Oxford: Oxford University Press.

Stuart-Smith, Jane, Claire Timmins, and Farhana Alam. 2011. Hybridity and ethnic accents: a sociophonetic analysis of 'Glaswegian'. In F. Gregersen, J. Parrott, and P. Quist (eds), *Language Variation: European Perspectives III*. Amsterdam: Benjamins, 43–58.

Sturtevant, Edgar H. 1917. *Linguistic Change*. Chicago: University of Chicago Press.

Sturtevant, Edgar H. 1940. *The Pronunciation of Greek and Latin*. Philadelphia: Linguistic Society of America.

Sully, James. 1896. *Studies of Childhood*. New York: Appleton.

Sundgren, Eva. 2002. Aterbesok i eskilstuna: en undersokning av morfologisk variation och forandring i nutida talsprak. PhD thesis, Uppsala University.

Surendran, Dinoj and Partha Niyogi. 2006. Quantifying the functional load of phonemic oppositions, distinctive features, and suprasegmentals. In O. Nedergaard Thomsen (ed.), *Competing Models of Language Change: Evolution and Beyond*. Amsterdam: Benjamins, 43–58.

Svantesson, Jan-Olof. 1991. Hu: a language with unorthodox tonogenesis. In Jeremy Davidson (ed.), *Austroasiatic Languages: Essays in Honour of H. L. Shorto*. London: SOAS, 67–79.

Svensson, Ann-Marie and Jürgen Hering. 2003. Germanic prosody and French loanwords. Paper presented at NWAVE 32, University of Pennsylvania, Philadelphia, October.

Swadesh, Morris. 1950. Salish internal relationships. *International Journal of American Linguistics* 16: 157–67.

Swadesh, Morris. 1955. Towards greater accuracy in lexicostatistic dating. *International Journal of American Linguistics* 21: 121–37.

Sweet, Henry. 1877. *A Handbook of Phonetics*. Oxford: Clarendon Press.

Sweet, Henry. 1888. *A History of English Sounds from the Earliest Period*. Oxford: Clarendon Press.

Swofford, David L. 2007. PAUP*. <http://paup.csit.fsu.edu>

Szigetvári, Péter. 2008. What and where. In Joaquim Brandão de Carvalho, Tobias Scheer, and Philippe Ségéral (eds). 2008. *Lenition and Fortition*. Berlin: Mouton de Gruyter, 93–129.

Tadmor, Uri, Martin Haspelmath, and Bradley Taylor. 2010. Borrowability and the notion of basic vocabulary. *Diachronica* 27(2): 226–46.

Tagliamonte, Sali and Alex D'Arcy. 2009. Peaks beyond phonology: adolescence, incrementation, and language change. *Language* 85: 58–108.

Tagliamonte, Sali and Sonja Molfenter. 2007. How'd you get that accent? Acquiring a second dialect of the same language. *Language in Society* 36: 649–75.

Tatham, Marcel A. A. 1971. Classifying allophones. *Language and Speech* 14: 140–5.

Taylor, William F. 1856. *Some Account of the Settlement of Tristan d'Acunha in the South Atlantic Ocean*. London: Cassell.

Tesfaye, Ashenafe and Klaus Wedekind. 1994. Aspects of omotic tonogenesis: Shinasha. *Journal of Ethiopian Studies* 25(2): 1–19.

Thibault, Pierrette. 1991. La langue en mouvement: simplification, régularisation, restructuration. *LINX (Linguistique—Paris X, Nanterre)* 25: 79–92.

Thibault, Pierrette and Michelle Daveluy. 1989. Quelques traces du passage du temps dans le parler des Montréalais 1971–1984. *Language Variation and Change* 1: 19–46.

Thibault, Pierrette and Diane Vincent. 1990. *Un corpus de francais parlé*. Montréal: Recherches Sociolinguistiques.

Thomas, Erik R. 2001. *An Acoustic Analysis of Vowel Variation in New World English*. Durham, NC: Duke University Press.

Thomas, Erik R. 2011. *Sociophonetics: an Introduction*. Basingstoke: Palgrave Macmillan.

Thomason, Sarah G. and Terrence Kaufman. 1988. *Language Contact, Creolization, and Genetic Linguistics*. Los Angeles: University of California Press.

Thompson, Laurence C. 1965. *A Vietnamese Grammar*. Seattle: University of Washington Press.

Thomsen, Vilhelm. 1919/1927. *Geschichte der Sprachwissenschaft bis zum Ausgang des 19. Jahrhunderts*. Halle: Niemeyer.

Thurgood, Graham. 1999. *From Ancient Cham to Modern Dialects: Two Thousand Years of Language Contact and Change*. Honolulu: University of Hawai'i Press.

Thurgood, Graham. 2002. Vietnamese and tonogenesis: revising the model and the analysis. *Diachronica* 19(2): 333–63.

Tillery, Jan and Guy Bailey. 2003. Approaches to real time in dialectology and sociolinguistics. *World Englishes* 22: 351–65.

Timberlake, Alan. 1977. Reanalysis and actualization in syntactic change. In Charles N. Li (ed.), *Mechanisms of Syntactic Change*. Austin: University of Texas Press, 141–80.

Tolkien, J. R. R. 1929. *Ancrene Wisse* and *Hali Meiðhad. Essays and Studies by Members of the English Association* 14: 104–26.

Toon, Thomas. 1976. The actuation and implementation of an Old English sound change. *Proceedings of the Linguistic Association of Canada and the United States* 3: 614–22.

Toon, Thomas E. 1983. *The Politics of Early Old English Sound Change*. New York: Academic Press.

Torgersen, Eivind and Paul Kerswill. 2004. Internal and external motivation in phonetic change: dialect levelling outcomes for an English vowel shift. *Journal of Sociolinguistics* 8: 24–53.

Trask, Robert Lawrence. 1996. *Historical Linguistics*. London: Arnold.

Trask, Robert Lawrence. 1997. *The History of Basque*. London: Routledge.

Trask, Robert Lawrence. 2000. *Dictionary of Historical and Comparative Linguistics*. Edinburgh: Edinburgh University Press.

Trommelen, Mieke and Wim Zonneveld. 1999. Dutch. In Harry van der Hulst (ed.), *Word Prosodic Systems in the Languages of Europe*. Berlin: Mouton de Gruyter, 492–515.

Trubetzkoy, Nikolai S. 1939. *Grundzüge der Phonologie*. Göttingen: Vandenhoek & Ruprecht. Trans. Christiane A. M. Baltaxe, *Principles of Phonology*. Berkeley: University of California Press, 1969.

Trudgill, Peter. 1972. Sex, covert prestige and linguistic change in the urban British English of Norwich. *Language in Society* 1: 179–95.

Trudgill, Peter. 1974. *The Social Differentiation of English in Norwich*. Cambridge: Cambridge University Press.

Trudgill, Peter. 1983. *On Dialect: Social and Geographical Perspectives*. Oxford: Blackwell.

Trudgill, Peter. 1986. *Dialects in Contact*. Oxford: Blackwell.

Trudgill, Peter. 1988. Norwich revisited: recent linguistic changes in an English urban dialect. *English World-Wide* 9: 33–49.

Trudgill, Peter. 2004. *New-dialect Formation: The Inevitability of Colonial Englishes*. Edinburgh: Edinburgh University Press.

Trudgill, Peter and Nina Foxcroft. 1978. On the sociolinguistics of vocalic mergers: transfer and approximation in East Anglia. In Peter Trudgill (ed.), *Sociolinguistic Patterns in British English*. London: Arnold, 69–79.

Trudgill, Peter, Elizabeth Gordon, Gillian Lewis, and Margaret Maclagan. 2000. Determinism in new-dialect formation and the genesis of New Zealand English. *Journal of Linguistics* 36: 299–318.

Trudgill, Peter, Gillian Lewis, and Margaret Maclagan. 2003. Linguistic archaeology: the Scottish input to New Zealand English phonology. *Journal of English Linguistics* 31: 103–24.

Turchin, Peter, Ilia Peiros, and Muray Gell-Mann. 2010. Analyzing genetic connections between languages by matching consonant classes. *Journal of Language Relationship* 3: 117–26.

Turgot, Anne Robert Jacques. 1756. Etymologie. In *L'Encyclopédie de Diderot et d'Alembert*. [*Etymologie*, ed. Maurice Piron. Brugge: De Tempel, 1961.]

Turner, George W. 1994. English in Australia. In Robert Burchfield (ed.), *The Cambridge History of the English Language*, vol. 5: *English in Britain and Overseas: Origins and Development*. Cambridge: Cambridge University Press, 277–327.

Turton, Danielle. 2012. The darkening of English /l/: a stochastic stratal OT analysis. MS, University of Manchester. Available at: <http://ling.auf.net/lingbuzz/001524>

Tuten, Donald N. 2003. *Koineization in Medieval Spanish*. Berlin: Mouton de Gruyter.

Twaddell, W. Freeman. 1938. A note on OHG umlaut. *Monatshefte für deutschen Unterricht* 30: 177–81. [Repr. in Martin Joos (ed.), *Readings in Linguistics*, New York: American Council of Learned Societies, 1963, 85–7.]

Uffmann, Christian 2006. Epenthetic vowel quality in loanwords: empirical and formal issues. *Lingua* 116: 1079–111.

Uffmann, Christian 2007. *Vowel Epenthesis in Loanword Adaptation*. Tübingen: Niemeyer.

Unger, J. Marshall. 2005a. *Ideogram: Chinese Characters and the Myth of Disembodied Meaning*. Honolulu: University of Hawai'i Press.

Unger, J. Marshall. 2005b. Japan: writing system. In Keith Brown (ed.), *Encyclopedia of Language and Linguistics*, 2nd edn. Amsterdam: Elsevier, 95–102.

Unger, J. Marshall. 2009. *The Role of Contact in the Origins of the Japanese and Korean Languages*. Honolulu: University of Hawai'i Press.

Unger, J. Marshall. 2012. Describing Old Japanese *kanji* usage: the inadequacy of traditional terminology. *Scripta* 4: 93–105.

Unger, J. Marshall. 2014. No rush to judgment: the case against Japanese as an isolate. *NINJAL Project Review*, 4(3): 211–30.

Ussishkin, Adam. 2000. The emergence of fixed prosody. PhD thesis, University of California Santa Cruz.

Ussishkin, Adam. 2005. A fixed prosodic theory of nonconcatenative templatic morphology. *Natural Language and Linguistic Inquiry* 23: 169–218.

Vajda, Edward. 2010. A Siberian link with Na-Dene languages. In J. Kari and B. Potter (eds), *The Dene–Yeniseian Connection*. Fairbanks: University of Alaska, Department of Anthropology, 33–99.

Van Bergem, Dick. 1995. *Acoustic and Lexical Vowel Reduction*. Amsterdam: IFOTT.

Vance, Timothy J. 1987a. *Introduction to Japanese Phonology*. Albany, NY: State University of New York Press.

Vance, Timothy J. 1987b. 'Canadian raising' in some dialects of the northern United States. *American Speech* 62(3): 195–210.

van de Velde, Hans, Marinel Gerritsen, and Roeland van Hout. 1996. The devoicing of fricatives in standard Dutch: a real-time study based on radio recordings. *Language Variation and Change* 8: 149–75.

Van Hofwegen, Janneke. 2015a. Dyadic analysis: factors affecting African American English usage and accommodation in adolescent peer dyads. *Language & Communication* 41: 28–45.

Van Hofwegen, Janneke. 2015b. The development of African American English through childhood and adolescence. In Sonja Lanehart, Lisa Green, and Jennifer Bloomquist (eds), *Oxford Handbook of African American Language*. Oxford: Oxford University Press, 454–74.

Van Hofwegen, Janneke and Walt Wolfram. 2010. Coming of age in African American English: a longitudinal study. *Journal of Sociolinguistics* 14: 427–55.

van Leussen, Jan-Willem. 2008. Emergent optimal vowel systems. Master's dissertation, University of Amsterdam. Available at: <http://roa.rutgers.edu/files/1006-1208/1006-VAN_LEUSSEN-0-0.PDF>

van Oostendorp, Marc. 2002. The phonological and morphological status of the prosodic word adjunct. In Gisbert Fanselow and Caroline Féry (eds), *Resolving Conflicts in Grammars: Optimality Theory in Syntax, Morphology, and Phonology.* Hamburg: Buske, 209–235.

Van Turennout, Miranda, Peter Hagoort, and Colin M. Brown. 1998. Brain activity during speaking: from syntax to phonology in 40 milliseconds. *Science* 280: 572–74.

Varma, Siddheswar. 1929. *Critical Studies in the Phonetic Observations of Indian Grammarians.* London: Royal Asiatic Society. [Repr. 1961, New Delhi: Munshiram Manoharlal, 1961.]

Vater, Johann Severin (ed.). 1822. *R. K. Rask über die Thrakische Sprachclasse, aus dem Dänischen.* Halle: Rengersche Verlagsbuchhandlung.

Vaux, Bert. 1998. *The Phonology of Armenian.* Oxford: Clarendon Press.

Vaux, Bert and Bridget Samuels. 2015. Explaining vowel systems: Dispersion Theory vs. natural selection. *The Linguistic Review* 32: 573–99.

Vennemann, Theo. 1972a. Phonetic analogy and conceptual analogy. In Theo Vennemann and Terence H. Wilbur (eds), *Schuchardt, the Neogrammarians, and the Transformational Theory of Phonological Change: Four Essays.* Frankfurt am Main: Athenäum, 181–204.

Vennemann, Theo. 1972b. On the theory of syllabic phonology. *Linguistische Berichte* 18: 1–18.

Vennemann, Theo. 1972c. Rule inversion. *Lingua* 29: 209–42.

Vennemann, Theo. 1972d. Sound change and markedness theory: on the history of the German consonant system. In R. P. Stockwell and R. K. S. Macaulay (eds), *Linguistic Change and Generative Theory: Essays from the UCLA Conference on Historical Linguistics in the Perspective of Transformational Theory.* Bloomington: Indiana University Press, 230–74.

Vennemann, Theo. 1972e. Hugo Schuchhardt's theory of phonological change. In Theo Vennemann and Terence Wilbur (eds), *Schuchardt, the Neogrammarians, and the Transformational Theory of Phonological Change.* Frankfurt: Athenäum, 115–79.

Vennemann, Theo. 1974a. Phonological concreteness in natural generative grammar. In Roger Shuy and Charles Bailey (eds), *Toward Tomorrow's Linguistics.* Washington, DC: Georgetown University Press, 202–19.

Vennemann, Theo. 1974b. Words and syllables in natural generative grammar. In *Papers from the Regional Meetings.* Chicago: Chicago Linguistic Society, 346–74.

Vennemann, Theo. 1978. Universal Syllabic Phonology. *Theoretical Linguistics* 5(2–3): 175–215.

Vennemann, Theo. 1983a. Überlegungen zu einer Theorie der linguistischen Präferenzen. *Klagenfurter Beiträge zur Sprachwissenschaft* 9: 262–92.

Vennemann, Theo. 1983b. Causality in language change: theories of linguistic preferences as a basis for linguistic explanations. *Folia Liguistica Historica* 4: 5–26.

Vennemann, Theo. 1984. Hochgermanisch und Niedergermanisch: die Verzweigungstheorie der germanisch-deutschen Lautverschiebung. *Beiträge zur Geschichte der deutschen Sprache und Literatur* (Tübingen) 106: 1–45.

Vennemann, Theo. 1986a. *Neuere Entwicklungen in der Phonologie.* Berlin: Mouton de Gruyter.

Vennemann, Theo. 1986b. Syllable based sound changes in Early Armenian. *Annual of Armenian Linguistics* 7: 27–43.

Vennemann, Theo. 1987. Muta cum Liquida: Worttrennung und Syllabierung im Gotischen. *Zeitschrift für deutsches Altertum und deutsche Literatur* 116: 165–204.

Vennemann, Theo. 1988. *Preference Laws for Syllable Structure and the Explanation of Sound Change.* Berlin: Mouton de Gryuter.

Vennemann, Theo. 1989. Language change as language improvement. In V. Orioles (ed.), *Modelli esplicativi della diacronica linguistica: atti del convegno della Società italiana de glottologica, Pavia*, 11–35. [Repr. in C. Jones (ed.), *Historical Linguistics: Problems and Perspectives*. London: Longman, 1993, 310–44.]

Vennemann, Theo. 1994a. Universelle Nuklearphonologie mit epiphänomenaler Silbenstruktur. In Karl Heinz Ramers, Heinz Vater, and Henning Wode (eds), *Universale phonologische Prozesse und Strukturen*. Tübingen: Niemeyer, 7–54.

Vennemann, Theo. 1994b. Linguistic reconstruction in the context of European prehistory. *Transactions of the Philological Society* 92: 215–84.

Vennemann, Theo. 1995. Der Zusammenbruch der Quantität im Spätmittelalter und sein Einfluß auf die Metrik. In Hans Fix (ed.), *Quantätsproblematik und Metrik: Greifswalder Symposion zur germanischen Grammatik*. Amsterdam: Rodopi, 195–223.

Vennemann, Theo. 2000a. Triple-cluster reduction in Germanic: etymology without sound laws? *Historische Sprachforschung* 113: 239–58.

Vennemann, Theo. 2000b. From quantity to syllable cuts: on so-called lengthening in the Germanic languages. *Italian Journal of Linguistics* 12: 251–82.

Verhulst, Pierre-François. 1845. Recherches mathématiques sur la loi d'accroissement de la population. *Nouvelles mémoires de l'Academie royale des sciences et belles-lettres de Bruxelles* 18.

Verner, Carl. 1877. Eine Ausnahme der Ersten Lautvershiebung. *Zeitschrift für Vergleichende Sprachforschung* 23: 97–130 (Also cited in the literature as written in 1875 and published in 1876.). [Excerpt in Winfred P. Lehmann (ed.), *A Reader in Nineteenth-Century Historical Indo-European Linguistics*. Bloomington: Indiana University, 1967. Available at: <http://www.utexas.edu/cola/centers/lrc/books/readT.html>]

Verwey, Willem B. 1995. A forthcoming keypress can be selected while earlier ones are executed. *Journal of Motor Behavior* 27: 275–84.

Vihman, Marilyn M. 1978. Consonant harmony: its scope and function in child language. In Joseph H. Greenberg, Charles A. Ferguson, and Edith A. Moravcsik (eds), *Universals of Human Language*. Stanford, Calif.: Stanford University Press, 281–334.

Vihman, Marilyn M. 1980. Sound change and child language. In Elizabeth C. Traugott, Rebecca La Brum, and Susan Shepherd (eds), *Papers from the 4th International Conference on Historical Linguistics*. Amsterdam: Benjamins, 303–20.

Vihman, Marilyn M. 1981. Phonology and the development of the lexicon: evidence from children's errors. *Journal of Child Language* 8: 239–64.

Vihman, Marilyn M. 1996. *Phonological Development*. Oxford: Blackwell.

Vihman, Marilyn M., Rory A. DePaolis, and Barbara L. Davis. 1998. Is there a 'trochaic bias' in early word learning? Evidence from English and French. *Child Development* 69: 933–47.

Vihman, Marilyn M., Edwin Kay, Bénédicte de Boysson-Bardies, Catherine Durand, and Ulla Sundberg. 1994. External sources of individual differences? A cross-linguistic analysis of the phonetics of mothers' speech to one-year-old children. *Developmental Psychology* 30: 652–63.

Vihman, Marilyn M., Tamar Keren-Portnoy, Chris Whitaker, Amy Bidgood, and Michelle McGillion. Submitted. Late-talking toddlers: relating early phonological development to later language advance.

Villafaña Dalcher, Christina, Rachael-Anne Knight, and Mark J. Jones. 2008. Cue switching in the perception of approximants: evidence from two English dialects. In *Penn Working Papers in Linguistics*, 14(2): *Selected Papers from NWAV 36*.

Villemin, François. 1983. Un essai de détection des origines du japonais à partir de deux méthodes statistiques. In B. Brainerd (ed.), *Historical Linguistics*. Bochum: Brockmeyer, 116–35.

Virdis, Maurizio. 1978. *Fonologia del dialetto campidanese*. Cagliari: Edizioni della Torre.

von Mess, Adolf. 1903. Zur Positionsdehnung vor Muta cum Liquida bei den attischen Dichtern. *Rheinisches Museum für Philologie* (n.s.) 58: 270–93.

Vossius, Gerardus Johannes. 1664. *Etymologicon linguae latinae*, ed. Isaac Vossius. Lyon: P. Guillimin.

Wagener, Peter. 1997. Nach 40 Jahren: Zu individuellen Veränderungen der gesprochenen Sprache. In Gerhard Stickel (ed.), *Varietäten des Deutschen: Regional- und Umgangssprachen*. Berlin: Mouton de Gruyter, 291–307.

Wagner, Heinrich. 1958. *Linguistic Atlas and Survey of Irish Dialects*. Dublin: Dublin Institute for Advanced Studies.

Wagner, Max L. 1941. *Historische Lautlehre des Sardischen*. Halle: Niemeyer.

Wagner, Suzanne Evans. 2012a. Age grading in sociolinguistic theory. *Language and Linguistic Compass* 6: 371–82.

Wagner, Suzanne Evans. 2012b. Real-time evidence for age grad(ing) in late adolescence. *Language Variation and Change* 24: 179–202.

Wagner, Suzanne Evans and Gillian Sankoff. 2011. Age grading in the Montréal French inflected future. *Language Variation and Change* 23: 1–39.

Walker, John. 1791. *A Critical Pronouncing Dictionary and Expositor of the English Language*. London: Robinson.

Wallis, John. 1653. *Joannis Wallisii Grammatica linguae Anglicanae*, 6th edn. London: William Bowyer.

Walsh, Michael, Bernd Möbius, Travis Wade, and Hinrich Schütze. 2010. Multilevel Exemplar Theory. *Cognitive Science* 34: 537–82.

Wang, Fushi and Zongwu Mao. 1995. *Miáoyáoyǔ Gǔyīn Gòunǐ* [Reconstruction of the sound system of proto-Miao-Yao]. Beijing: Zhōngguó shèhuì kēxué chūbǎnshè [China Social Sciences Press].

Wang, William S-Y. 1969. Competing changes as a cause of residue. *Language* 45: 9–25.

Wanner, Dieter. 2006. *The Power of Analogy: an Essay on Historical Linguistics*. New York: Mouton de Gruyter.

Watson, Janet C. E. 2002. *The Phonology and Morphology of Arabic*. Oxford: Oxford University Press.

Watt, Dominic. 1998a. Variation and change in the vowel system of Tyneside English. PhD thesis, University of Newcastle upon Tyne.

Watt, Dominic. 1998b. One vowel short: the (reported) merger of NURSE and NORTH in Tyneside English. In Claude Paradis, Diane Vincent, Denis Deshaies, and Marty Laforest (eds), *Papers in Sociolinguistics: NWAVE-26 à l'Université Laval*. Québec: Éditions Nota bene, 149–58.

Watt, Dominic and Lesley Milroy. 1999. Patterns of variation and change in three Newcastle vowels: is this dialect levelling? In Paul Foulkes and Gerard J. Docherty (eds), *Urban Voices: Accent Studies in the British Isles*. London: Arnold, 25–47.

Webb, Eric Russell. 2008. Formalizing creole sound change: an Optimality Theoretic account. *Journal of Pidgin and Creole Languages* 23(2): 227–63.

Webb, Eric Russell and Travis Bradley. 2009. Rhotic metathesis asymmetries in Romance: formalizing the effects of articulation and perception on sound change. In Pascual J. Masullo,

Erin O'Rourke, and Chia-Hui Huang (eds), *Romance Linguistics 2007: Structures, Interfaces, and Microparametric Variation*. Amsterdam: Benjamins, 321–7.

Wedekind, Klaus. 1985. Thoughts when drawing a tone map of Africa. *Afrikanistische Arbeitspapiere* 1: 105–24.

Wedel, Andy. 2004. Category competition drives contrast maintenance within an exemplar-based production/perception loop. In J. Goldsmith and R. Wicentowski (eds), *Proceedings of the Seventh Meeting of the ACL Special Interest Group in Computational Phonology* 7: 1–10.

Wedel, Andrew. 2006. Exemplar models, evolution and language change. *Linguistic Review* 23: 247–74.

Wedel, Andrew. 2007. Feedback and regularity in the lexicon. *Phonology* 24: 147–85.

Wedel, Andrew. 2009. Variation, multi-level selection and conflicts between phonological and morphological regularities. In James P. Blevins and Juliette Blevins (eds), *Analogy in Grammar: Form and Acquisition*. Oxford: Oxford University Press, 83–100.

Wedel, Andrew. 2012. Lexical contrast maintenance and the organization of sublexical contrast systems. *Language and Cognition* 4: 319–55.

Wedel, Andrew, Abby Kaplan, and Scott Jackson. 2013. Lexical contrast constrains phoneme merger: a corpus study. *Cognition* 128: 179–86.

Weinreich, Uriel, William Labov, and Marvin I. Herzog. 1968. Empirical foundations for a theory of language change. In Winfred P. Lehmann and Yakov Malkiel (eds), *Directions for Historical Linguistics: a Symposium*. Austin: University of Texas Press, 95–195.

Weiss, Michael. 2009. *The Cao Bang Theory*. Available at: <http://conf.ling.cornell.edu/weiss/Cao_Bang_Theory.pptx>, accessed 6 June 2014.

Wells, John C. 1982. Accents of English. 3 vols. Cambridge: Cambridge University Press.

Wells, John C. 1999. British English pronunciation preferences: a changing scene. *Journal of the International Phonetic Association* 29: 33–50.

Wells, Rulon S. 1949. Automatic alternation. *Language* 25: 99–116.

Wells, Rulon S. 1974. Phonemics in the nineteenth century, 1876–1900. In Dell Hymes (ed.), *Studies in the History of Linguistics: Traditions and Paradigms*. Bloomington: Indiana University Press, 434–53.

Welmers, William E. 1970. Language change and language relationships in Africa. *Language Sciences* 12: 1–8.

West, Birdie. 1980. *Gramática popular de Tucano*. Bogotá: Ministerio de Gobierno, Instituto lingüística de Verano.

Westbury, John R. 1994. *X-ray Microbeam Speech Production Database User's Handbook, version 1. Software Manual*. Madison: Waisman Research Center, University of Wisconsin-Madison.

Westbury, John R. and Patricia A. Keating. 1986. On the naturalness of stop consonant voicing. *Journal of Linguistics* 22: 145–66.

Westbury, John R., Michiko Hashi, and Mary J. Lindstrom. 1998. Differences among speakers in lingual articulation for American English /ɹ/. *Speech Communication* 26: 203–26.

Wetzels, Leo and Engin Sezer (eds). 1985. *Studies in Compensatory Lengthening*. Dordrecht: Foris.

Whalen, Douglas H. 1990. Coarticulation is largely planned. *Journal of Phonetics* 18: 3–35.

White, David. 2004. Why we should not believe in short diphthongs. In Anne Curzan and Kim Emmons (eds), *Studies in the History of the English Language, 2: Unfolding Conversations*. Berlin: Mouton de Gruyter, 57–84.

White, Lydia. 1998. Second language acquisition and binding principle b: child/adult differences. *Second Language Research* 14: 425–39.

Whitney, William Dwight. 1865. On the relation of vowels and consonants. *Journal of the American Oriental Society* 8: 357–73.

Whitney, William Dwight. 1867. *Language and the Study of Language: Twelve Lectures on the Principles of Linguistic Science.* New York: Scribner's.

Wichmann, Søren and Arpiar Saunders. 2007. How to use typological databases in historical linguistic research. *Diachronica* 24: 373–404.

Widdison, Kirk A. 1997. Variability in lingual vibrants: changes in the story of /r/. *Language and Communication* 17: 187–93.

Wieling, Martijn, Jelena Prokić, and John Nerbonne. 2009. Evaluating the pairwise string alignment of pronunciations. In Lars Borin and Piroska Lendvai (eds), *Proceedings of the EACL 2009 Workshop on Language Technology and Resources for Cultural Heritage, Social Sciences, Humanities, and Education*, 26–34. Available at: <http://www.aclweb.org/anthology/W/W09/W09-0304.pdf>

Wiese, Richard. 1996. *The Phonology of German.* Oxford: Oxford University Press.

Wiese, Richard. 2001. How prosody shapes German words and morphemes. *Interdisciplinary Journal for Germanic Linguistics and Semiotic Analysis* 6: 155–84.

Wiesinger, Peter. 1976. Die Wiener dialektologische Schule. In Helmut Birkhan (ed.), *Festgabe für Otto Höfler.* Vienna: Braumüller, 661–703.

Wilbur, Terence H. 1972. Hugo Schuchardt and the neogrammarians. In Theo Vennemann and Terence Wilbur (eds), *Schuchardt, the Neogrammarians, and the Transformational Theory of Phonological Change.* Frankfurt: Athenäum, 73–113.

Wilbur, Terence H. (ed.). 1977. *The Lautgesetz Controversy: a Documentation (1885–1886).* Amsterdam: Benjamins.

Wilson, Colin. 2003. Experimental investigation of phonological naturalness. *Proceedings of the West Coast Conference on Formal Linguistics* 22: 533–46.

Windfuhr, Gernot L. 1971. Diacritic and distinctive features in Avestan. *Journal of the American Oriental Society* 91(1): 104–24.

Winteler, Jost. 1876. *Die Kerenzer Mundart in ihren Grundzügen dargestellt.* Leipzig: Winter.

Wolf, Clara and Elena Jiménez. 1979. El ensordecimiento del yeísmo porteño [Devoicing of Buenos Aires /z/]. In A. M. Barrenechea (ed.), *Estudios lingüísticos y dialectológicos.* Buenos Aires: Hachette, 115–45.

Wolff, Ekkehard. 1987. Consonant-tone interference in Chadic and its implications for a theory of tonogenesis in Afroasiatic. In Daniel Barreteau (ed.), *Langues et cultures dans le bassin du Lac Tchad.* Paris: ORSTOM, 193–216.

Wolfram, Walt and Natalie Schilling-Estes. 2003. Dialectology and linguistic diffusion. In B. D. Joseph and R. D. Janda (eds), *The Handbook of Historical Linguistics.* Oxford: Blackwell, 713–35.

Wood, Sidney. 1996. Assimilation or coarticulation? Evidence from the temporal co-ordination of tongue gestures for the palatalization of Bulgarian alveolar stops. *Journal of Phonetics* 24: 139–64.

Wright, Joseph and Elizabeth Mary Wright. 1925. *Old English Grammar*, 3rd edn. London: Oxford University Press.

Wright, Richard. 2003. Factors of lexical competition in vowel articulation. In J. Local, R. Ogden, and R. Temple (eds), *Phonetic Interpretation: Papers in Laboratory Phonology VI.* Cambridge: Cambridge University Press, 75–87.

Wu, Hsiao-hung Iris. 2006. Stress to tone: a study of tone loans in Mandarin Chinese. *MIT Working Papers in Linguistics* 52: 227–53.

Wu, Trong. 1993. An accurate computation of the hypergeometric distribution function. *ACM Transactions on Mathematical Software* 19(1): 33–43.

Wurzel, Wolfgang Ullrich. 1984. *Flexionsmorphologie und Natürlichkeit*. Berlin: Akademie.

Yaeger-Dror, Malcah. 1989. Real time vs. apparent time change in Montreal French. *York Papers in Linguistics* 13: 141–53.

Yaeger-Dror, Malcah. 1993. Linguistic analysis of dialect correction and its interaction with dialect salience. *Language Variation and Change* 5: 189–224.

Yaeger-Dror, Malcah. 1994. Sound change in Montreal French. In P. Keating (ed.), *Phonological Structure and Phonetic Form*. Cambridge: Cambridge University Press, 267–92.

Yaeger-Dror, Malcah. 1996. Phonetic evidence for the evolution of lexical classes: the case of a Montreal French vowel shift. In Gregory Guy et al. (eds), *Towards a Social Science of Language*, vol. 1: *Variation and Change in Language and Society*. Amsterdam: Benjamins, 263–87.

Yaeger-Dror, Malcah. 1997. Phonetic evidence for the evolution of lexical classes: the case of a Montreal French vowel shift. In G. R. Guy, C. Feagin, D. Schiffrin, and J. Baugh (eds), *Towards a Social Science of Language: Papers in Honor of William Labov*, vol. 2. Amsterdam: Benjamins, 263–87.

Yaeger-Dror, Malcah and Lauren Hall-Lew. 2002. Presidential use of negation. *Texas Linguistic Forum* 45: 187–94.

Yaeger-Dror, Malcah and William Kemp. 1992. Lexical classes in Montreal French: the case of (ɛː). *Language and Speech* 35: 251–93.

Yang, Charles. 2005. On productivity. *Linguistic Variation Yearbook* 5: 265–302.

Yeni-Komshian, Grace H., J. F. Kavanagh, and Charles A. Ferguson (eds). 1980. *Child Phonology*, vol. 1: *Production*. New York: Academic Press.

Ying, Lin. 1972. Chinese loanwords in Miao. In Herbert C. Purnell, Jr. (ed.), *Miao and Yao Linguistic Studies: Selected Articles in Chinese*. Ithaca, NY: Cornell University Southeast Asia Program, Department of Asian Studies, 55–81.

Yip, Moira 1993. Cantonese loanword phonology and Optimality Theory. *Journal of East Asian Linguistics* 2: 261–91.

Yip, Moira. 2002. *Tone*. Cambridge: Cambridge University Press.

Yu, Alan C. L. 2007. Understanding near mergers: the case of morphological tone in Cantonese. *Phonology* 24(1): 187–214.

Yu, Alan C. L. 2010a. Perceptual compensation is correlated with individuals' 'autistic' traits: implications for models of sound change. *PLoS One* 5(8): e11950.

Yu, Alan C. L. 2010b. Tonal effects on perceived vowel duration. In C. Fougeron, B. Kühnert, M. D'Imperio, and N. Vallée (eds), *Laboratory Phonology 10*. Berlin: Mouton de Gruyter, 151–68.

Yu, Alan C. L. 2013. Individual differences in socio-cognitive processing and the actuation of sound change. In Alan C. L. Yu (ed.), *Origins of Sound Change: Approaches to Phonologization*. Oxford: Oxford University Press.

Yu, Alan C. L., Carissa Abrego-Collier, Rebekah Baglini, Tommy Grano, Martina Martinovic, Charles Ohtte III, Julia Thomas, and Jasmin Urban. 2011. Speaker attitude and sexual orientation affect phonetic imitation. *Penn Working Papers in Linguistics* 17(1): 235–42.

Yuan, Jiahong and Mark Liberman. 2009. Investigating /l/ variation in English through forced alignment. *INTERSPEECH 2009: 10th Annual Conference of the International Speech Communication Association*. Brighton: International Speech Communication Association, 2215–18.

Yuan, Jiahong and Mark Liberman. 2011. /l/ variation in American English: a corpus approach. *Journal of Speech Sciences* 1: 35–46.

Zettersten, Arne. 1969. *The English of Tristan da Cunha*. Lund: Gleerup.

Zhang, Xi. 1996. Vowel systems of the Manchu-Tungus languages of China. PhD thesis, University of Toronto.

Zide, Norman H. 1965. Gutob-Remo vocalism and glottalized vowels in Proto-Munda. In George B. Milner and Eugénie A. Henderson (eds), *Indo-Pacific Linguistic Studies I*. Amsterdam: North-Holland, 43–53.

Zubritskaya, Katya. 1995. Markedness and sound change in OT. In J. Beckman (ed.), *Proceedings of the North-Eastern Linguistic Society* 25. Amherst, Mass.: GLSA, 249–64.

Zubritskaya, Katya. 1997. Mechanism of sound change in Optimality Theory. *Language Variation and Change* 9: 121–48.

Zuraw, Kie. 2003. Probability in language change. In Rens Bod, Jennifer Hay, and Stefanie Jannedy (eds), *Probabilistic Linguistics*. Cambridge, Mass.: MIT Press, 139–76.

Zwicky, Arnold M. 1972. Note on a phonological hierarchy in English. In Robert P. Stockwell and Ronald K. S. Macaulay (eds), *Linguistic Change and Generative Theory*. Bloomington: Indiana University Press, 275–301.

Zwicky, Arnold and Geoffrey Pullum. 1986. The principle of phonology-free syntax: introductory remarks. *Ohio State University Working Papers in Linguistics* 32: 63–91.

INDEXES

LANGUAGES, FAMILIES, AND DIALECTS

AUTHORS

Subjects

near merger, *see* merger (vowel, consonant)
neogrammarians, neogrammarian 9, 11–31,
    34, 35, 188, 195, 201, 206–18, 289, 316, 318,
    338, 359, 360, 365, 368, 369, 371–3, 374–6,
    378, 379–82, 383, 388, 399, 410, 432, 463,
    464, 487, 489–90, 501–3, 511, 564, 576, 584
Northern Cities Shift 44, 166, 175–81, 365, 371,
    381, 534, 538, 552, 629–30

Observer's Paradox 171
Ockham's Razor 375, 399
ogham 73
opacity 43, 225, 230–1, 335, 390, 433, 435,
    443–5, 518, 557–8, 560, 566, 569,
    572–4, 578
Optimality Theory 7, 38, 39, 293, 319, 331–2,
    342, 374, 433, 450, 451, 463, 466, 489, 528,
    545–62, 651, 655; *see also* Stratal OT
orthography, *see* writing systems

palatalization, palatality 68, 81, 83, 105, 119,
    195, 198, 202, 298, 303–5, 315, 317–18, 322,
    366, 419, 443, 446, 473–7, 483, 486, 491,
    528–9, 547, 553–5, 558, 567–8, 575, 642
panel studies 165, 605–8, 613–16, 617–18
parameters (grammatical, phonological) 79,
    451–2, 465–6, 528–9
    stress 221–6, 230, 232, 237–44
    social 166, 182
past tense allomorphy (English) 152–5,
    162, 170, 207–9, 212, 229, 363, 365, 405,
    408, 634
pathways of change 7, 23, 149, 151–2, 477,
    485, 661
peak (in apparent time) 308, 590–4,
    597–601, 610
perception 6, 28, 38, 43, 75, 77–80, 136, 156,
    158–9, 171–2, 175–7, 178, 182, 184–6,
    188–90, 206, 211, 213, 218, 248, 257, 294–6,
    298, 311, 338, 373, 380, 383, 387, 400–3,
    406–9, 411–17, 423–8, 431–2, 434–8, 441–3,
    449, 467, 478, 482–4, 486, 489–91, 497,
    500, 511, 540, 547, 552–5, 557–8, 561–2,
    567–8, 572–3, 575–6, 603, 640, 644, 645,
    652, 655–60, 663–5
    imperceptibility hypothesis 30
    perceptual adaptation 652–4

perceptual bias 419–22, 436–7, 496
perceptual compensation 422
perceptual markedness 83
see also misperception
phenetics 144–6
phonation 43, 139, 186, 189, 248–52, 254–5, 257,
    417; *see also* register
phoneme 15, 19, 26, 28, 42, 45–6, 72–85, 87–8,
    90, 93–5, 101–3, 108–16, 119, 159–60,
    165–6, 171, 173, 175–6, 178–81, 183–8, 195,
    215, 221, 273, 293, 340–2, 346, 348, 359,
    365, 368, 423, 428, 433, 440–5, 447, 449,
    495, 503–6, 514, 518–20, 523–5, 527, 584–5,
    637–42, 644–7, 654, 657, 659
    inventory, system 27, 33, 34–6, 122, 135, 141,
    143, 163, 301, 434–8, 451, 529, 534, 541, 543,
    562, 563–8, 572, 575–6
    proto-phoneme 54–61, 63–8
    see also contrast
phonemicization 338–9, 349, 351–3, 355–7,
    573, 661
phonetic change 6, 13, 27–8, 55, 60, 254–5, 359,
    368, 380, 439–41, 488, 565, 609, 637
    phonetic implementation 196, 343, 368, 373,
    375, 378, 380–3, 386–90, 402, 406–7, 409,
    424, 503, 543, 565, 577–8
    language specific phonetics 344,
    379–80, 423–4
    phonetic precursors 412, 415, 423–5
phonography 87–9, 95, 97
phonologization 6–7, 25, 42–3, 55, 196–7, 248,
    257, 294, 337–58, 373, 382–3, 386–7, 392,
    395, 420–1, 423–5, 441, 482, 486, 496, 534,
    540, 559–60, 563–79
pitch 97, 245, 248–57, 339, 346–8, 351–3, 355,
    402, 417, 422, 640, 650
    pitch accent 245, 650
place assimilation 415, 477, 491
plasticity 606, 608–10
postlexical (process, rule) 36, 365–6, 402,
    406–7, 433, 545, 567–8, 571–6, 578–9
pre-language 63, 65, 66, 69, 70
predictability 82, 214, 221, 333, 348, 351,
    360, 471, 498–9, 541, 568, 571, 575, 585,
    602, 649–50
Preference Laws (preference theory) 6, 263,
    359, 363, 434, 450–69

OXFORD HANDBOOKS IN LINGUISTICS

THE OXFORD HANDBOOK OF APPLIED LINGUISTICS
Second Edition
Edited by Robert B. Kaplan

THE OXFORD HANDBOOK OF ARABIC LINGUISTICS
Edited by Jonathan Owens

THE OXFORD HANDBOOK OF CASE
Edited by Andrej Malchukov and Andrew Spencer

THE OXFORD HANDBOOK OF COGNITIVE LINGUISTICS
Edited by Dirk Geeraerts and Hubert Cuyckens

THE OXFORD HANDBOOK OF COMPARATIVE SYNTAX
Edited by Gugliemo Cinque and Richard S. Kayne

THE OXFORD HANDBOOK OF COMPOSITIONALITY
Edited by Markus Werning, Wolfram Hinzen, and Edouard Machery

THE OXFORD HANDBOOK OF COMPOUNDING
Edited by Rochelle Lieber and Pavol Štekauer

THE OXFORD HANDBOOK OF COMPUTATIONAL LINGUISTICS
Edited by Ruslan Mitkov

THE OXFORD HANDBOOK OF CONSTRUCTION GRAMMAR
Edited by Thomas Hoffman and Graeme Trousdale

THE OXFORD HANDBOOK OF CORPUS PHONOLOGY
Edited by Jacques Durand, Ulrike Gut, and Gjert Kristoffersen

THE OXFORD HANDBOOK OF DERIVATIONAL MORPHOLOGY
Rochelle Lieber and Pavol Štekauer

THE OXFORD HANDBOOK OF DEVELOPMENTAL LINGUISTICS
Edited by Jeffrey Lidz, William Snyder, and Joe Pater

THE OXFORD HANDBOOK OF GRAMMATICALIZATION
Edited by Heiko Narrog and Bernd Heine

THE OXFORD HANDBOOK OF HISTORICAL PHONOLOGY
Edited by Patrick Honeybone and Joseph Salmons

THE OXFORD HANDBOOK OF THE HISTORY OF ENGLISH
Edited by Terttu Nevalainen and Elizabeth Closs Traugott